Rick Steves'

ITALY

2012

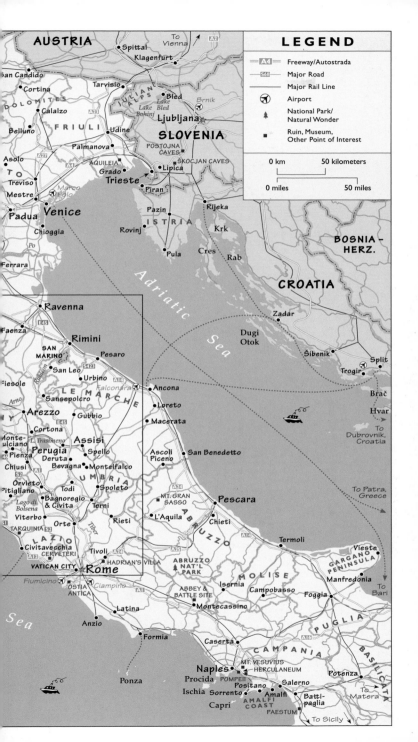

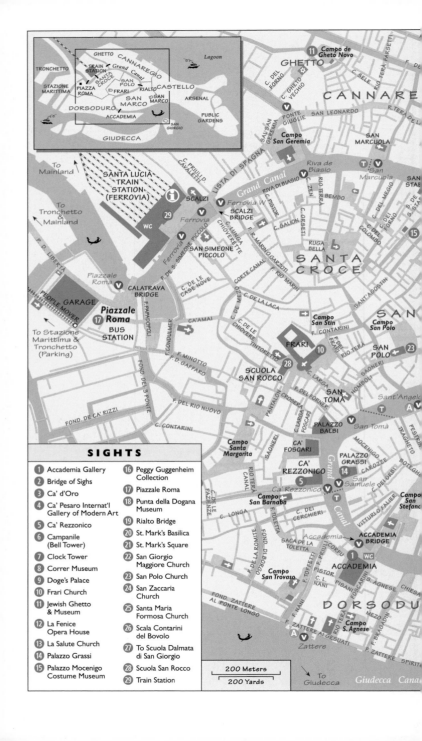

SIGHTS

1. Accademia Gallery
2. Bridge of Sighs
3. Ca' d'Oro
4. Ca' Pesaro Internat'l Gallery of Modern Art
5. Ca' Rezzonico
6. Campanile (Bell Tower)
7. Clock Tower
8. Correr Museum
9. Doge's Palace
10. Frari Church
11. Jewish Ghetto & Museum
12. La Fenice Opera House
13. La Salute Church
14. Palazzo Grassi
15. Palazzo Mocenigo Costume Museum
16. Peggy Guggenheim Collection
17. Piazzale Roma
18. Punta della Dogana Museum
19. Rialto Bridge
20. St. Mark's Basilica
21. St. Mark's Square
22. San Giorgio Maggiore Church
23. San Polo Church
24. San Zaccaria Church
25. Santa Maria Formosa Church
26. Scala Contarini del Bovolo
27. To Scuola Dalmata di San Giorgio
28. Scuola San Rocco
29. Train Station

200 Meters
200 Yards

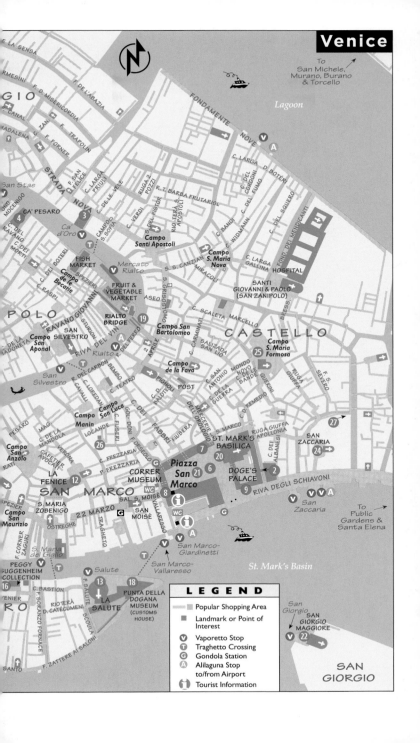

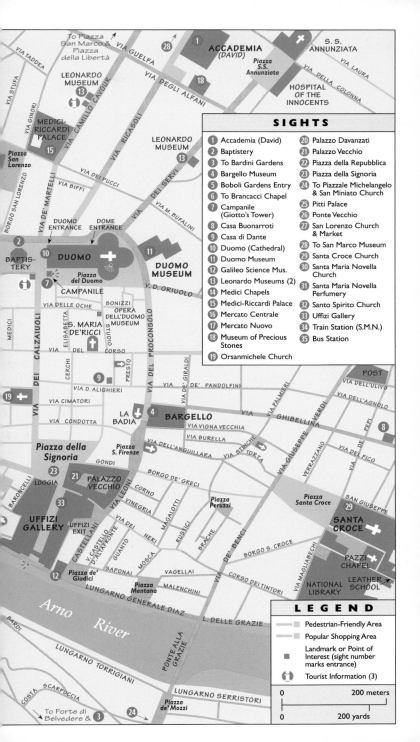

SIGHTS

1 Accademia (David)
2 Baptistery
3 To Bardini Gardens
4 Bargello Museum
5 Boboli Gardens Entry
6 To Brancacci Chapel
7 Campanile (Giotto's Tower)
8 Casa Buonarroti
9 Casa di Dante
10 Duomo (Cathedral)
11 Duomo Museum
12 Galileo Science Mus.
13 Leonardo Museums (2)
14 Medici Chapels
15 Medici-Riccardi Palace
16 Mercato Centrale
17 Mercato Nuovo
18 Museum of Precious Stones
19 Orsanmichele Church
20 Palazzo Davanzati
21 Palazzo Vecchio
22 Piazza della Repubblica
23 Piazza della Signoria
24 To Piazzale Michelangelo & San Miniato Church
25 Pitti Palace
26 Ponte Vecchio
27 San Lorenzo Church & Market
28 To San Marco Museum
29 Santa Croce Church
30 Santa Maria Novella Church
31 Santa Maria Novella Perfumery
32 Santo Spirito Church
33 Uffizi Gallery
34 Train Station (S.M.N.)
35 Bus Station

LEGEND

Pedestrian-Friendly Area

Popular Shopping Area

Landmark or Point of Interest (sight number marks entrance)

Tourist Information (3)

0 ——— 200 meters

0 ——— 200 yards

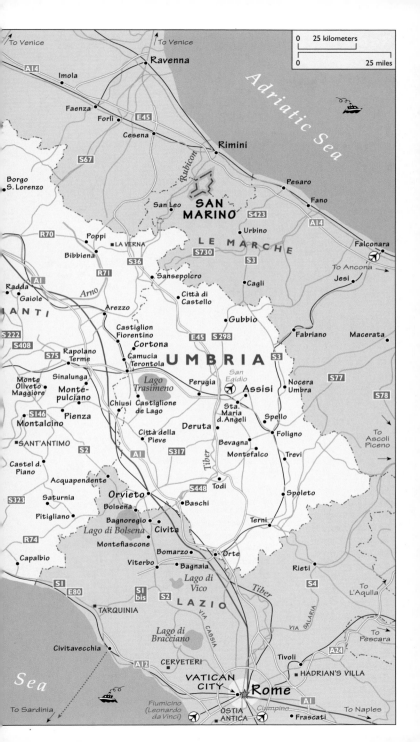

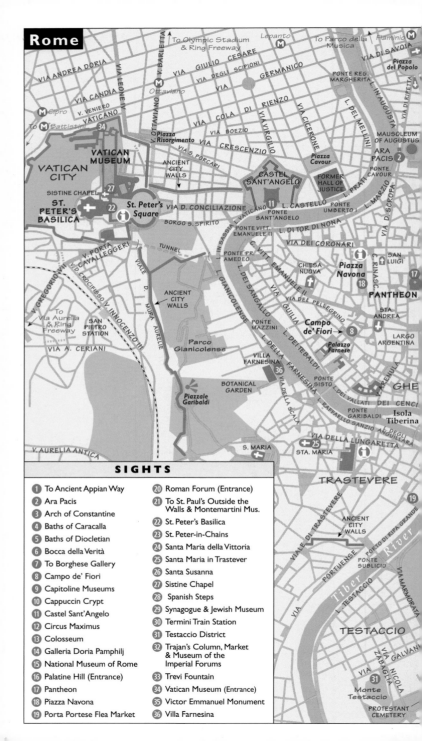

Rome

SIGHTS

1. To Ancient Appian Way
2. Ara Pacis
3. Arch of Constantine
4. Baths of Caracalla
5. Baths of Diocletian
6. Bocca della Verità
7. To Borghese Gallery
8. Campo de' Fiori
9. Capitoline Museums
10. Cappuccin Crypt
11. Castel Sant'Angelo
12. Circus Maximus
13. Colosseum
14. Galleria Doria Pamphilj
15. National Museum of Rome
16. Palatine Hill (Entrance)
17. Pantheon
18. Piazza Navona
19. Porta Portese Flea Market
20. Roman Forum (Entrance)
21. To St. Paul's Outside the Walls & Montemartini Mus.
22. St. Peter's Basilica
23. St. Peter-in-Chains
24. Santa Maria della Vittoria
25. Santa Maria in Trastever
26. Santa Susanna
27. Sistine Chapel
28. Spanish Steps
29. Synagogue & Jewish Museum
30. Termini Train Station
31. Testaccio District
32. Trajan's Column, Market & Museum of the Imperial Forums
33. Trevi Fountain
34. Vatican Museum (Entrance)
35. Victor Emmanuel Monument
36. Villa Farnesina

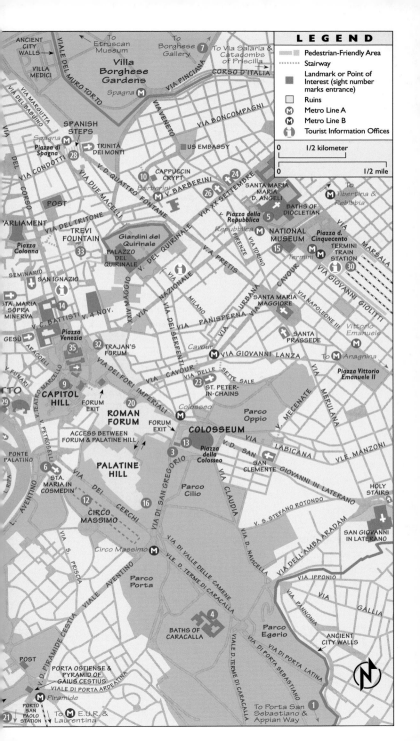

CONTENTS

Italy
Italia

Bella Italia! Italy has Europe's richest, craziest culture. If you take Italy on its own terms, you'll experience a cultural keelhauling that actually feels good.

Some people, often with considerable effort, manage to hate this country. Italy bubbles with emotion, corruption, stray hairs, inflation, traffic jams, strikes, rallies, holidays, crowded squalor, and irate ranters shaking their fists at each other one minute and walking arm-in-arm the next. Have a talk with yourself before you cross the border. Promise yourself to relax and accept it all as a package deal.

After all, Italy is the cradle of European civilization—established by the Roman Empire and carried on by the Roman Catholic Church. As you explore Italy, you'll stand face-to-face with some of the world's most iconic images from this 2,000-year history: the Colosseum of Ancient Rome, the medieval Leaning Tower of Pisa, Michelangelo's *David* and Botticelli's *Venus*, the playful Baroque exuberance of the Trevi Fountain...and the Italian city that preserves this legacy in a state of elegant decay: Venice.

Beyond these famous sights, though, Italy offers Europe's richest culture. Traditions still live within a country that is vibrant and fully modern. Go with an eye open to both the Italy of the past and of the present.

Italy is diverse, encompassing German-flavored Alps, Mediterranean beaches, sun-baked Sicily, romantic hill towns, the urban jungle of Naples, the business center of

Milan, and the art-drenched cities of Venice, Florence, and Rome. The country is reasonably small and laced with freeways and train lines, so you're never more than a day's journey away from any of these places. Each of Italy's 20 regions has its own distinct character, whether it's scenic Tuscany, busy Lombardy, or the place where it all mixes together—Lazio, home of the capital, Rome.

Many travelers discover that there are two Italys: The North is industrial, aggressive, and "time is money" in its outlook. The weather is temperate, and the people are more like Northern Europeans. The South is hot and sunny, crowded, poor, relaxed, farm-oriented, and traditional. Families here are very close-knit and usually live in the same house for many generations. Loyalties are to family, city, region, soccer team, and country—in that order. (For more on the two Italys, see "Rome vs. Milan: A Classic Squabble" on page 292).

Economically, Italy has had its problems, but somehow

things have always worked out. Today, Italy is the world's eighth-largest industrial power, and the fourth-largest in Europe. Ferraris, Fiats, Maseratis, and Lamborghinis are world-renowned (though they're not really major exports). Tourism is big business—Italy is considered the world's fifth most-visited tourist destination.

Cronyism, which complicates my work, is an integral part of the economy. Much of Italy's business is hidden in a large "black market" unreported to government officials. Labor unions are strong, strikes are frequent, and the country today is faced with pressure to compete globally.

While most Italians are nominally Catholic, the true dominant religion is life—motor scooters, soccer, fashion, girl-watching, boy-watching, good coffee, good wine, and *il dolce far niente* (the sweetness of doing nothing). The Italian character shows itself on the streets, in the maniacal yet skilled drivers and the classy dressers who star in the ritual evening stroll, or *passeggiata*.

Italians are more social and communal than most other Europeans. In small towns, everyone knows everyone. People get out of their apartments to socialize on the main square. Young women walk hand in hand, and young teenagers shove or punch each other playfully or hang all over

each other.

Because they're so outgoing and their language is so fun, Italians are a pleasure to communicate with. Be melodramatic and talk with your hands. Hear the melody; get into the flow. Italians want to connect, and they try harder than any other Europeans. Play with them. Even in non-touristy towns, where English is rare and Italian

Italy Almanac

Official Name: Repubblica Italiana (Italian Republic), or Italia for short.

Population: 60 million, comprised almost entirely of indigenous Italians who speak Italian (German and French are spoken in some Alpine regions) and are nominally Roman Catholic (90 percent).

Latitude and Longitude: 43°N and 12°E (similar to Oregon and Maine).

Area: 116,000 square miles, including the islands of Sicily, Sardinia, and others.

Geography: Italy is shaped like a boot, 850 miles long and 150 miles wide, jutting into the central Mediterranean. (By comparison, Florida is 500 miles long.) The terrain is generally mountainous or hilly, with the Alps in the north and a north-south "spine" of the Apennine Mountains. The highest point is Mont Blanc (15,771 feet), on the border with France. Outside the Alps, the highest point is Monte Cimone (7,100 feet). Italy has 5,000 miles of coastline. Major rivers include the Po (the longest at 400 miles), Arno, Adige, and Tiber. Italy has three active volcanoes: Vesuvius, Etna, and Stromboli.

Regions: Italy is divided into 20 regions (including Tuscany, Umbria, Veneto, and Lazio). Locally, there are some 8,000 "communes," each with a community council and mayor.

Major Cities: Rome (the capital, 2.7 million), Milan (1.3 million), and Naples (1 million).

Economy: The Gross Domestic Product is $1.8 trillion; the GDP per capita is $30,000. About 73 percent of the economy consists of service jobs (especially tourism), 25 percent is industry (textiles, chemicals), and 2 percent is agriculture (fruit, vegetables, olives, wine, plus fishing). There are 10,000 miles of train lines (mostly government-run) and 4,300 miles of expressway (autostrada).

Government: Italy is a republic, with three branches of government. The chief executive is three-term Prime Minister Silvio Berlusconi. The bicameral legislature is elected by (mostly) direct voting. Since World War II, the fragmented country has had 61 national governments.

Flag: Three vertical bands of green, white, and red.

Italian Inventions: Opera, cologne, thermometer, barometer, pizza, wireless telegraph, espresso machine, typewriter, batteries, nitroglycerin, yo-yos...and the ice-cream cone.

Museums: 3,000.

Average "Gio": The average Italian is 43 years old, has 1.3 kids, and will live to the ripe old age of 80 (one in five Italians is older than 65). Every day, he or she consumes two servings of pasta, a half-pound of bread, and two glasses of wine. Nearly half of all Italians use the Internet.

is the norm, showing a little warmth lets you hop right over the language barrier.

Like most Europeans (and Americans), Italians enjoy watching TV (game shows, sitcoms, etc.), going to movies (American films are almost always dubbed, not subtitled), and listening to their homegrown pop music. Though Italy is the birthplace of opera and much classical music, it's not much more "cultured" today than America is.

Italian food, however, is a cut above. If America's specialty is fast food, Italy's is slow food: locally grown ingredients, in season, bought daily, prepared with love, and

enjoyed in social circumstances with friends and family. Even in modern cities, big supermarkets are rare. Instead, people buy their bread from the baker and their meats from the butcher, enjoying a chance to catch up on gossip with the shopkeeper. Italians buy foods in season, celebrating the arrival of fresh artichokes in the spring and porcini mushrooms in the fall.

The three-hour meal is common. For many Italians, dinner is the evening's entertainment. They eat in courses, lingering over each one. A typical meal might start with an antipasto plate of cold cuts and veggies. Next comes the pasta, then the meat dish, then a salad. No meal is complete without dessert (Italian gelato is considered the best ice cream in the world), accompanied by coffee or a digestif.

Wine complements each course. Italy is the world's number-one wine producer (just ahead of France). It'd be a shame to visit Italy without sampling the specialties from each region, whether it's the famous Chianti from central Italy, a white Soave from the Veneto, Bardolinos from the North, or a Lacryma Christi from the South.

Italian "bars" are not taverns, but cafés...and social watering holes. In the morning, they serve coffee, orange juice, and croissants to workers on the go. At lunch, it's sandwiches *(panini)* and mini-pizzas for university students. In the afternoon, housewives might drop in for an ice-cream bar. At night, men and women enjoy a glass of wine and watch TV while the kids play a video game in the corner.

Besides food, travelers enjoy sampling Italy's other wares. While no longer a cheap country, Italy is still a hit with shoppers. Find glassware in Venice; gold, silver, leather, and prints in Florence; and high fashion in Rome and Milan.

Italians are obsessed with sports—though not American sports. Italian sports idols are soccer players (Francesco Totti, Antonio Cassano), skiers (Giorgio Rocca), and cyclists (Paolo Savodelli). Motor racing—Formula 1/Grand Prix—is huge. And since many Italians grow up zipping through narrow streets on small Vespas, it's little wonder that motorcycle racing *(moto,* led by Valentino Rossi) is a major sport here. A favorite participant sport is bocce, played casually at parks throughout Italy. The players take turns tossing small metal balls on a dirt court, aiming at a small wooden ball.

Italy's undisputed number-one sport is soccer (called *il calcio*). Soccer fans *(tifosi)* are passionate. Star players are paid millions and treated like movie stars. Little kids everywhere grow up pretending to score the winning goal just like them. On big game nights, bars are packed with men crowded around TV sets. After a loss, they drown their sorrows. After a victory, fans celebrate by driving through the city streets honking horns and waving team flags. Many Italians place their national, regional, and personal pride on the backs of their athletes. It's a cliché that remains true: In a Europe at peace, the soccer field is the battleground.

But even as Europe evolves, Italy remains a mix of old and new. Appreciate the extreme changes Italian society has gone through in just 50 years: the "economic miracle" of the 1950s, the liberal reforms of the 1960s, a wave of domestic terrorism (from the left and the right) in the 1970s and 1980s, the entry into the European Union in the 1990s, and several years ago, the Berlusconi government's unpopular support of the Iraq war. Italian politics are a reckless pendulum that swings between right- and left-wing extremes. It seems that nobody holds office for very long. But, as Berlusconi demonstrated in the 2008 elections, it's always possible to bounce back.

Italy, home of the Vatican, is still 90 percent Catholic...but not particularly devout. Most people would never think of renouncing their faith, but they don't attend church regularly. They baptize their kids at the local church (there's one every few blocks), but they hold modern opinions on social issues, often in conflict

with strict Catholic dogma. Italy is now the land of legalized abortion, the lowest birth rate in Europe, nudity on TV, socialist politics, and a society whose common language is decidedly secular.

Some traditions thrive. Italian families and communities are still more close-knit than many others in the modern world. Many Italians, especially in rural regions, still follow the traditional siesta schedule (called *reposo* in Italy). At about 1:00 p.m., shops close and people go home for a three-hour break to have lunch, socialize with friends and family, and maybe take a short nap in front of the TV. And on festival days, locals still dress up in medieval garb to paddle gondolas (Venice), race horses (Siena), battle over a bridge (Pisa), or play rugby or soccer (Florence). But these days, the traditional ways are carried on by choice. Italians are wary of the dangers of a fast-paced global lifestyle. Their history is long, and they're secure in their place in the world.

Accept Italy as Italy. Zero in on the fine points. Don't dwell on the problems. Savor your cappuccino, dangle your feet over a canal (if it smells, breathe through your mouth), and imagine what it was like centuries ago. Ramble through the rabble and rubble of Rome and mentally resurrect those ancient stones. Look into the famous sculpted eyes of Michelangelo's *David* and understand Renaissance Man's assertion of himself. Sit silently on a hilltop rooftop. Get chummy with the winds of the past. Write a poem over a glass of local wine in a sun-splashed, wave-dashed Riviera village. If you fall off your moral horse, call it a cultural experience. Italy is for romantics.

INTRODUCTION

This book will help you make the most of your trip. It breaks Italy into its top destinations—offering a balanced, comfortable mix of exciting cities and cozy towns, from brutal but *bella* Rome to *tranquillo,* traffic-free Riviera villages. It covers the predictable biggies and stirs in a healthy dose of "Back Door" intimacy. Along with marveling at Michelangelo's masterpieces, you'll enjoy a snack of *bruschetta* (fresh garlic rubbed on toast) prepared by a village boy. I've been selective, including only the most exciting sights and experiences. For example, after visiting many hill towns, I recommend just my favorites.

You'll get all the specifics and opinions necessary to wring the maximum value out of your limited time and money. If you plan a month or less in Italy, and you have a normal appetite for information, this book is all you need. If you're a travel-info fiend like me, you'll find that this book sorts through all the superlatives and provides a handy rack upon which to hang your supplemental information.

Italy is my favorite European country. Experiencing its culture, people, and natural wonders economically and hassle-free has

been my goal for three decades of traveling, tour guiding, and writing. With this book, I pass on to you the lessons I've learned, updated for 2012.

The best of Italy is, of course, only my opinion. But after spending half my adult life researching Europe, I've developed a sixth sense for what travelers enjoy.

Map Legend

⅍	Viewpoint	✈	Airport	) (	Tunnel
↑	Entry Arrow	⊤	Taxi Stand		Pedestrian Zone
✆	Tourist Info	⊤	Tram Stop		Railway
WC	Restroom	Ⓑ	Bus Stop		Ferry/Boat Route
⚏	Castle	Ⓟ	Parking	⊢—⊢	Tram
⌂	Church	)(	Mtn. Pass		Stairs
V	Vaporetto Stop		Park		Walk/Tour Route
T	Traghetto Crossing	▪	Statue/Point of Interest		Trail
G	Gondola Station				
A	Alilaguana Stop				

Use this legend to help you navigate the maps in this book.

About This Book

Rick Steves' Italy 2012 is a personal tour guide in your pocket. This book is organized by destinations. Each destination is a mini-vacation on its own, filled with exciting sights, strollable neighborhoods, affordable places to stay, and memorable places to eat. In the following chapters, you'll find these sections:

Planning Your Time suggests a schedule for how to best use your limited time.

Orientation includes specifics on public transportation, helpful hints, local tour options, easy-to-read maps, and tourist information.

Sights describes the top attractions and includes their cost and hours.

Self-Guided Walks take you through interesting neighborhoods, with a personal tour guide in hand.

Sleeping describes my favorite hotels, from good-value deals to cushy splurges.

Eating serves up a range of options, from inexpensive cafés to fancy restaurants.

Connections outlines your options for traveling to destinations by train, bus, plane, and cruise ship. In car-friendly regions, I've included route tips for drivers.

Italian History gives you a helpful overview of Italy's history, art, and architecture.

The **appendix** is a traveler's tool kit, with telephone tips, useful phone numbers, the basics on transportation in Italy, recommended books and films, a festival list, a climate chart, a handy packing checklist, a hotel reservation form, and Italian survival phrases.

Browse through this book, choose your favorite destinations, and link them up. Then have a *buono* trip! Traveling like a temporary local, you'll get the absolute most out of every mile, minute,

Key to This Book

Updates

This book is updated every year—but as soon as you pin down Italy, it wiggles. For the latest, visit www.ricksteves.com/update. For a valuable list of reports and experiences—good and bad—from fellow travelers, check www.ricksteves.com/feedback.

Abbreviations and Times

I use the following symbols and abbreviations in this book:

Sights are rated:

▲▲▲	**Don't miss**
▲▲	**Try hard to see**
▲	**Worthwhile if you can make it**
No rating	**Worth knowing about**

Tourist information offices are abbreviated as **TI,** and bathrooms are **WCs.** To categorize accommodations, I use a **Sleep Code** (described on page 22).

Like Europe, this book uses the **24-hour clock.** It's the same through 12:00 noon, then keep going: 13:00, 14:00, and so on. For anything over 12, subtract 12 and add p.m. (14:00 is 2:00 p.m.).

When giving **opening times,** I include both peak season and off-season hours if they differ. So, if a museum is listed as "May-Oct daily 9:00-16:00," it should be open from 9 a.m. until 4 p.m. from the first day of May until the last day of October (but expect exceptions).

For **transit** or **tour departures,** I first list the frequency, then the duration. So, a train connection listed as "2/hour, 1.5 hours" departs twice each hour and the journey lasts an hour and a half.

and dollar. As you visit places I know and love, I'm happy that you'll be meeting some of my favorite Italian people.

Planning

This section will help you get started planning your trip—with advice on trip costs, when to go, and what you should know before you take off.

Travel Smart

Many people travel through Italy thinking it's a chaotic mess. They feel that any attempt at efficient travel is futile. This is dead wrong—and expensive. Italy, which seems as orderly as spilled spaghetti, actually functions quite well. Only those who understand this and travel smart can enjoy Italy on a budget.

This book can save you lots of time and money. But to have an "A" trip, you need to be an "A" student. Read it all before your trip, noting holidays, specific advice on sights, and days when sights are closed. A smart trip is a puzzle—a fun, doable, and worthwhile challenge.

Be sure to mix intense and relaxed periods in your itinerary. To maximize rootedness, minimize one-night stands. It's worth a long drive after dinner to be settled into a town for two nights. Hotels are more likely to give a better price to someone staying more than one night. Every trip—and every traveler—needs slack time (laundry, picnics, people-watching, and so on). Pace yourself. Assume you will return.

Reread this book as you travel, and visit local TIs. Upon arrival in a new town, lay the groundwork for a smooth departure; write down (or print out from an online source) the schedule for the train or bus that you'll take when you depart. Drivers can study the best route to their next destination.

Get online at Internet cafés or your hotel, and buy a phone card or carry a mobile phone: You can find tourist information, learn the latest on sights (special events, English tour schedule, etc.), book tickets and tours, make reservations, reconfirm hotels, research transportation connections, and keep in touch with your loved ones.

Enjoy the friendliness of the Italian people. Connect with the culture. Set up your own quest for the best piazza, bell tower, or gelato. Slow down and be open to unexpected experiences. Ask questions—most locals are eager to point you in their idea of the right direction. Keep a notepad in your pocket for organizing your thoughts. Wear your money belt, learn the currency, and figure out how to estimate prices in dollars. Those who expect to travel smart, do.

Trip Costs

Six components make up your trip costs: airfare, surface transportation, room and board, sightseeing and entertainment, shopping and miscellany, and gelato.

Airfare: A basic round-trip flight from the US to Milan or Rome can cost from $950 to $1,600, depending on where you fly from and when (cheaper in winter). Smaller budget airlines provide bargain service from several European capitals to many cities in Italy. If your trip covers a wide area, consider saving time and money in Europe by flying into one city and out of another; for instance, into Milan and out of Rome.

Surface Transportation: For a three-week whirlwind trip of all of my recommended destinations, allow $550 per person for buses and second-class trains ($750 for first-class trains). For a three-week car rental, tolls, gas, and insurance, allow $900 per person (based on two people sharing). Leasing is worth considering for trips of two-and-a-half weeks or more. Car rentals and leases are cheapest if arranged from the US. Train passes are normally available only outside of Europe. You may save money by simply buying tickets as you go. For more on public transportation and car rental, see "Transportation" in the appendix.

Room and Board: You can thrive in Italy in 2012 on $120 a day per person for room and board (more in big cities). This allows $15 for lunch, $25 for dinner, and $80 for lodging (based on two people splitting the cost of a $160 double room that includes breakfast). Students and tightwads can enjoy Italy for as little as $60 a day ($30 for a bed, $30 for meals and snacks).

Sightseeing and Entertainment: In big cities, figure about

Italy's Best Three-Week Trip
(by Train and Bus)

Day	Plan	Sleep in
1	Arrive in Milan	Milan
2	Milan to Lake Como	Varenna
3	Lake Como	Varenna
4	To Dolomites via Verona	Bolzano/Castelrotto
5	Dolomites	Bolzano/Castelrotto
6	To Venice	Venice
7	Venice	Venice
8	To Cinque Terre	Vernazza
9	Cinque Terre	Vernazza
10	Pisa, then to Florence	Florence
11	Florence	Florence
12	Florence, late to Siena	Siena
13	Siena	Siena
14	To Assisi (by bus)	Assisi
15	To Orvieto and Civita	Orvieto
16	To Sorrento	Sorrento
17	Naples and Pompeii	Sorrento
18	Capri or Amalfi Coast	Sorrento
19	Morning to Rome	Rome
20	Rome	Rome
21	Rome	Rome
22	Fly home	

Itinerary options: Save time by skipping the Dolomites. You could save Venice for last by starting in Milan and seeing everything but Venice on the way south, then sleep through everything you've already seen by catching the night train from Naples to Venice. This saves you a day and gives you an early arrival in Venice. (Or consider taking a cheap flight to connect Rome and

$15-20 per major sight (museums, Colosseum), $5-10 for minor ones (climbing church towers), and $25-30 for splurge experiences (e.g., walking tours and concerts). An overall average of $35 a day works for most people. Don't skimp here. After all, this category is the driving force behind your trip—you came to sightsee, enjoy, and experience Italy.

Shopping and Miscellany: Figure $3 per postcard, coffee, soft drink, or gelato. Shopping can vary in cost from nearly nothing to a small fortune. Good budget travelers find that this category has little to do with assembling a trip full of lifelong and wonderful memories.

Italy's Best Three-Week Trip

* Overnights
• Other Stops

Venice—see page 1030.)

To modify for drivers: The big sights of Italy (Rome, Florence, Venice, Sorrento/Naples/Capri/Amalfi, and Cinque Terre) are inconvenient by car and easy by public transportation. Those wanting to drive in Italy will find a car most helpful for the hill towns of Tuscany and Umbria and the Dolomites. I'd start by touring most of the country by train, then use a car to explore a region or two (even if it means backtracking a few extra hours by train or car).

Sightseeing Priorities

Depending on the length of your trip, and taking geographic proximity into account, here are my recommended priorities:

4 days:	Florence, Venice
6 days, add:	Rome
8 days, add:	Cinque Terre
10 days, add:	Civita and Siena
14 days, add:	Sorrento, Naples, Pompeii, Amalfi Coast, Paestum
18 days, add:	Milan, Lake Como, Varenna, Assisi
21 days, add:	Dolomites, Verona, Padua

This includes nearly everything on the above map.

Italy at a Glance

These attractions are listed (as in this book) roughly from north to south.

▲▲▲**Venice** Romantic island city, powerful in medieval times; famous for St. Mark's Basilica, the Grand Canal, and singing gondoliers.

▲**Near Venice** Several interesting towns: Padua (with Giotto's gloriously frescoed Scrovegni Chapel), Verona (Roman amphi-theater plus Romeo and Juliet sights), and Ravenna (top Byzantine mosaics).

▲**The Dolomites** Italy's rugged rooftop with a Germanic flair, fea-turing Bolzano (home of Ötzi the Ice Man), Castelrotto (charming village), and Alpe di Siusi (alpine meadows laced with lifts and hiking trails).

▲**The Lakes** Two relaxing lakes, each with low-key resort towns and a mountainous backdrop: Lake Como, with quaint Varenna and upscale Bellagio; and Lake Maggiore, with straightforward Stresa, manicured islands, and elegant villas.

▲▲**Milan** Powerhouse city of commerce and fashion, with the prestigious La Scala opera house, Leonardo's *The Last Supper,* and two airports.

▲▲▲**The Cinque Terre** Five idyllic Riviera hamlets along a rug-ged coastline (and part of a national park), connected by scenic hiking trails and dotted with beaches.

Riviera Towns near the Cinque Terre More Italian Riviera fun, including the beach towns of Levanto, Sestri Levante, the larger Santa Margherita Ligure, and trendier Portofino nearby, and to the south, resorty Portovenere and workaday La Spezia (trans-portation hub).

▲▲▲**Florence** The cradle of the Renaissance, with the world-class Uffizi Gallery, Brunelleschi's dome-topped Duomo,

When to Go

Italy's best travel months (also its busiest and most expensive) are May, June, September, and October. These months combine the convenience of peak season with pleasant weather.

The most grueling thing about travel in Italy is the summer heat in July and August, when temperatures hit the high 80s and 90s. Most mid-range hotels come with air-conditioning—a worth-

Michelangelo's *David,* and Italy's best gelato.

▲**Pisa and Lucca** Two classic towns: Pisa, with its famous Leaning Tower and surrounding Field of Miracles, and Lucca, with a charming walled old center.

▲▲▲**Siena** Florence's smaller and (some say) more appealing rival, with its grand Il Campo square and striking striped cathedral.

▲▲**Assisi** St. Francis' hometown, perched on a hillside, with a divinely Giotto-decorated basilica.

▲▲**Hill Towns of Central Italy** Picturesque, wine-soaked villages of Italy's heartland, including San Gimignano, Volterra, Montalcino, Pienza, Montepulciano, Cortona, Orvieto, and the adorable pocket-sized Civita di Bagnoregio.

▲▲▲**Rome** Italy's capital, the Eternal City, studded with Roman remnants (Forum, Colosseum, Pantheon), romantic floodlit-fountain squares, and the Vatican—home to one of Italy's top museums and the Sistine Chapel.

▲▲**Naples** Gritty, in-love-with-life port city featuring vibrant street life and a top archaeological museum, with the famous Pompeii ruins a day-trip away.

▲**Sorrento and Capri** The seaside resort port of Sorrento, and a short cruise away, the jet-set island getaway of Capri, with its Blue Grotto.

▲**Amalfi Coast and Paestum** String of seafront villages—including hilly Positano and Amalfi—tied together by a scenic mountainous coastal road, plus nearby Paestum, with its well-preserved ancient Greek temples.

while splurge in the summer—but it's usually available only from June through September.

Peak season (roughly May-Sept) offers the longest hours and the most exciting slate of activities—but terrible crowds. During peak times, many resort-area hotels maximize business by requiring that guests take half-pension, which means buying a meal per day (usually dinner) in their restaurants. August, the local holiday month, isn't as bad as many make it out to be, but big cities tend to be quiet (with discounted hotel prices), and beach and mountain resorts are jammed (with higher hotel prices). Note that Italians generally wear shorts only at beach resort towns. If you want to blend in, wear lightweight long (or Capri) pants in Italy, even in summer, except at the beach.

Between November and April, you can usually expect pleasant weather, and you'll miss most of the sweat and stress of the tourist season. Off-season, expect shorter hours, more lunchtime breaks, and fewer activities. However, spring and fall can be cool (and most hotels don't turn the heat on until winter). In the winter, it often drops to the 40s in Milan and the 50s in Rome (see the climate chart in the appendix).

Know Before You Go

Your trip is more likely to go smoothly if you plan ahead. Check this list of things to arrange while you're still at home.

You need a **passport**—but no visa or shots—to travel in Italy. You may be denied entry into certain European countries if your passport is due to expire within three to six months of your ticketed date of return. Get it renewed if you'll be cutting it close. It can take up to six weeks to get or renew a passport (for more on passports, see www.travel.state.gov). Pack a photocopy of your passport in your luggage in case the original is lost or stolen.

Book rooms well in advance if you'll be traveling during peak season (spring and fall) and any major holidays (see page 1037).

Make reservations ahead of time for major sights. Book at least a month in advance for **Florence's** Uffizi Gallery (Renaissance paintings) and a few days ahead for the Accademia (Michelangelo's *David*); or for an easy but pricey way to avoid making reservations, you can buy a Florence Card when you arrive (see page 457). While reservations are mandatory and free for Florence's Brancacci Chapel, you only need to call a day in advance (see page 482). For **Milan,** book several months ahead for da Vinci's *Last Supper* (see page 317); for **Padua,** at least 72 hours in advance for Giotto's Scrovegni Chapel (see page 153); and for **Rome,** a week ahead for the Borghese Gallery (Bernini sculptures; see page 806). The Vatican Museum now takes online reservations, and while not mandatory, these can save you substantial time in line (see page 796).

Call your **debit- and credit-card companies** to let them know the countries you'll be visiting, to ask about fees, and more (see page 14).

Do your homework if you want to buy **travel insurance.** Compare the cost of the insurance to the likelihood of your using it and your potential loss if something goes wrong. For more tips, see www.ricksteves.com/insurance.

If you're bringing a mobile device, you can download free information from **Rick Steves Audio Europe,** featuring audio tours of major sights, hours of travel interviews on Italy, and more (via www.ricksteves.com/audioeurope, iTunes, or the Rick Steves Audio Europe smartphone app; for details, see page 1032).

If you're planning on **renting a car** in Italy, you'll need your driver's license. You're also required to have an International Driving Permit (see page 1025). Driving is prohibited in some city centers; obey the signage or risk getting a huge fine (see page 1028).

If you're taking an **overnight train** and need a couchette *(cuccetta)* or sleeper—and you must leave on a certain day—consider booking it in advance through a US travel agent (such as www.raileurope.com), even though it may cost more than buying it in Italy. Other Italian trains, such as the high-speed ES trains, require a seat reservation, but for these it's usually possible to make arrangements in Italy just a few days ahead. (For more on train travel, see the appendix.)

Because **airline carry-on restrictions** are always changing, visit the Transportation Security Administration's website (www.tsa.gov/travelers) for an up-to-date list of what you can bring on the plane with you...and what you have to check.

Practicalities

Emergency and Medical Help: In Italy, dial 113 for English-speaking police help. To summon an ambulance, call 118. If you get sick, do as the Italians do and go to a pharmacist for advice. Or ask at your hotel for help; they know of the nearest medical and emergency services.

Theft or Loss: To replace a passport, you'll need to go in person to your embassy (see page 1013). If your credit and debit cards disappear, cancel and replace them (see "Damage Control for Lost Cards" on page 15). File a police report, either on the spot or within a day or two; it's required to submit an insurance claim for lost or stolen railpasses or travel gear, and can help with replacing your passport or credit and debit cards. For more information, see www.ricksteves.com/help.

More Help: A service of the Italian government, **EasyItalia,** offers English-language tourist information, emergency assistance, and help with everything from flight cancellations to car-rental trouble (call toll-free 800-000-039 from a land line or pay phone, otherwise call 039-039-039, phone answered daily 9:00-22:00; or use their online form at www.easy-italia.com for a response within 48 hours).

Time Zones: Italy, like most of continental Europe, is generally six/nine hours ahead of the East/West Coasts of the US. The exceptions are the beginning and end of Daylight Saving Time: Europe "springs forward" the last Sunday in March (two weeks after most of North America), and "falls back" the last Sunday in October (one week before North America). For a handy online time converter, see www.timeanddate.com/worldclock.

Business Hours: Traditionally, Italy uses the siesta plan, where people usually work from about 9:00 to 13:00 and from 15:30 to 19:00, Monday through Saturday. However, many businesses have adopted the government's recommended 8:00 to 14:00 workday. In tourist areas, shops are open longer. Stores are usually closed on Sunday, and often on Monday, as well as for a couple of weeks around August 15. Banking hours are generally Monday through Friday from 8:30 to 13:30 and 15:30 to 16:30, but can vary wildly.

Saturdays are virtually weekdays, with earlier closing hours. Sundays have the same pros and cons as they do for travelers in the US: Sightseeing attractions are generally open but public transportation options are fewer (e.g., no bus service to or from the smaller hill towns), and there's no rush hour. Rowdy evenings are rare on Sundays.

Watt's Up? Europe's electrical system is 220 volts, instead of North America's 110 volts. Most newer electronics (such as laptops, battery chargers, and hair dryers) convert automatically, so you won't need a converter plug, but you will need an adapter plug with two round prongs, sold inexpensively at travel stores in the US. Avoid bringing older appliances that don't automatically convert voltage; instead, buy a cheap replacement in Europe.

Discounts: Discounts are not listed in this book. However, many sights offer discounts for youths (up to age 18), students (with proper identification cards, www.isic.org), families, seniors (loosely defined as retirees or those willing to call themselves a senior), and groups of 10 or more. Always ask. Some discounts are available only for EU citizens.

News: Americans keep in touch via the *International Herald Tribune* (published almost daily throughout Europe and online at www.iht.com). Another informative site is http://news.bbc.co.uk. Every Tuesday, the European editions of *Time* and *Newsweek* hit the stands with articles of particular interest to travelers in Europe. Sports addicts can get their daily fix online or from *USA Today*. Many hotels have CNN and BBC News television channels.

Tobacco Shops: Tobacco shops (known as *tabacchi,* often indicated with a big *T* sign) are ubiquitous across Italy as handy places to pay for street parking, and to buy postage or tickets for city buses or subways.

Money

This section offers advice on how to pay for purchases on your trip (including getting cash from ATMs and paying with plastic), dealing with lost or stolen cards, VAT (sales tax) refunds, and tipping.

What to Bring

Bring both a credit card and a debit card. You'll use the debit card at cash machines (ATMs) to withdraw local cash for most purchases, and the credit card to pay for larger items. Some travelers carry a third card as a backup, in case one gets demagnetized or eaten by a temperamental machine.

For an emergency reserve, bring several hundred dollars in hard cash in easy-to-exchange $20 bills. Avoid using currency exchange booths (lousy rates and/or outrageous fees); if you have foreign currency to exchange, take it to a bank. Don't use traveler's checks—they're not worth the fees or long waits at slow banks.

Cash

Cash is just as desirable in Europe as it is at home. Small businesses (hotels, restaurants, shops, etc.) prefer that you pay in cash. Some vendors will charge you extra for using a credit card, and some won't take credit cards at all. Cash is the best—and sometimes only—way to pay for bus fare, taxis, and local guides.

Throughout Europe, ATMs are the standard way for travelers to get cash. Most ATMs in Italy are located outside of a bank. Try to use the ATM when the branch is open; if your card is munched by a machine, you can immediately go inside for help.

To withdraw money from an ATM (known as a *bancomat*), you'll need a debit card (ideally with a Visa or MasterCard logo for maximum usability), plus a PIN code. Know your PIN code in numbers; there are only numbers—no letters—on European keypads. For security, it's best to shield the keypad when entering your PIN at an ATM. Although you can use a credit card for ATM transactions, it's generally more expensive because it's considered a "cash advance" rather than a withdrawal.

When using an ATM, try to withdraw large sums of money to reduce the number of per-transaction bank fees you'll pay. If the machine refuses your request, try again and select a smaller amount (some cash machines limit the amount you can withdraw—don't take it personally). If that doesn't work, try a different machine. Be aware that some ATMS will tell you to take your cash within 30 seconds, and if you aren't fast enough, your cash may be sucked back into the machine...and you'll have a hassle trying to get it from the bank.

It's easier to pay for purchases with smaller bills; if the ATM

Exchange Rate

1 euro (€) = about $1.40

To convert prices in euros to dollars, add about 40 percent: €20 = about $28, €50 = about $70. (Check www.oanda.com for the latest exchange rates.) Just like the dollar, one euro is broken down into 100 cents. You'll find coins ranging from €0.01 to €2, and bills ranging from €5 to €500.

Look carefully at any €2 coin you get in change. Some unscrupulous merchants are giving out similar-looking gold-rimmed old 500-lire coins (worth $0) instead of €2 coins (worth $2.80). You are now warned!

gives you big bills, try to break them at a bank or larger store.

To keep your cash safe, use a money belt—a pouch with a strap that you buckle around your waist like a belt, and wear under your clothes. Pickpockets target tourists. A money belt provides peace of mind, allowing you to carry lots of cash safely. Don't waste time every few days tracking down a cash machine—withdraw a week's worth of money, stuff it in your money belt, and travel!

Credit and Debit Cards

For purchases, Visa and MasterCard are more commonly accepted than American Express. Just like at home, credit or debit cards work easily at larger hotels, restaurants, and shops. I typically use my debit card to withdraw cash to pay for most purchases. I use my credit card only in a few specific situations: to book hotel reservations by phone, to make major purchases (such as car rentals, plane tickets, and long hotel stays), and to pay for things near the end of my trip (to avoid another visit to the ATM). While you could use a debit card to make most large purchases, using a credit card offers a greater degree of fraud protection (because debit cards draw funds directly from your account).

Ask Your Credit- or Debit-Card Company: Before your trip, contact the company that issued your debit or credit cards.

• Confirm your card will work overseas, and alert them that you'll be using it in Europe; otherwise, they may deny transactions if they perceive unusual spending patterns.

• Ask for the specifics on transaction **fees.** When you use your credit or debit card—either for purchases or ATM withdrawals—you'll often be charged additional "international transaction" fees of up to 3 percent (1 percent is normal) plus $5 per transaction. If your card's fees are too high, consider getting a card just for your trip: Capital One (credit cards only, www.capitalone.com) and most credit unions have low-to-no international fees.

• If you plan to withdraw cash from ATMs, confirm your daily **withdrawal limit** ($300 is usually the maximum). Some travelers prefer a high limit that allows them to take out more cash at each ATM stop, while others prefer to set a lower limit in case their card is stolen.

• Ask for your credit card's **PIN** in case you encounter Europe's "chip-and-PIN" system; since they're unlikely to tell you your PIN over the phone, allow time for the bank to mail it to you.

Chip and PIN: If your card is declined for a purchase in Europe, it may be because of chip and PIN, which requires card-holders to punch in a PIN instead of signing a receipt. While chip and PIN is not yet common in Italy, much of Europe, including Great Britain, Ireland, France, Belgium, the Netherlands, and Scandinavia, is adopting it. Some merchants rely on it exclusively. If, when you're using your card, you're prompted to enter your PIN but don't know it, ask if the cashier can swipe your card and print a receipt for you to sign instead; if not, just pay cash. You're most likely to encounter chip and PIN at automated payment machines, such as those at train and subway stations, toll roads, parking garages, luggage lockers, bike-rental kiosks, and self-serve pumps at gas stations. If a machine won't take your card, look for a cashier nearby who can make your card work, or see if one of the machines takes cash.

You can avoid potential hassles by getting your own chip-and-PIN card just for your trip, but so far your options are limited. Chase offers a Visa credit card with a chip called J. P. Morgan Select, but it comes with a hefty annual fee and requires a stellar credit rating. Travelex has a chip-and-PIN cash card called "Cash Passport" that's preloaded with euros or British pounds and sold at many airports; it comes with exorbitant exchange rates and only works at places that accept MasterCard. While handy, these cards are probably not worth it unless you're staying for several weeks in a country that's converted to chip-and-PIN cards, and you're willing to pay for the convenience.

Dynamic Currency Conversion: If merchants offer to convert your purchase price into dollars (called dynamic currency conversion, or DCC), refuse this "service." You'll pay even more in fees for the expensive convenience of seeing your charge in dollars.

Damage Control for Lost Cards

If you lose your credit, debit, or ATM card, you can stop people from using your card by reporting the loss immediately to the respective global customer-assistance centers. Call these 24-hour US numbers collect: Visa (410/581-9994), MasterCard (636/722-7111), and American Express (623/492-8427).

At a minimum, you'll need to know the name of the financial

institution that issued you the card, along with the type of card (classic, platinum, or whatever). Providing the following information will allow for a quicker cancellation of your missing card: full card number, whether you are the primary or secondary cardholder, the cardholder's name exactly as printed on the card, billing address, home phone number, circumstances of the loss or theft, and identification verification (your birth date, your mother's maiden name, or your Social Security number—memorize this, don't carry a copy). If you are the secondary cardholder, you'll also need to provide the primary cardholder's identification-verification details. You can generally receive a temporary card within two or three business days in Europe (see www.ricksteves.com/help for more).

If you promptly report your card lost or stolen, you typically won't be responsible for any unauthorized transactions on your account, although many banks charge a liability fee of $50.

Tipping

Tipping in Italy isn't as automatic and generous as it is in the US, but for special service, tips are appreciated, if not expected. As in the US, the proper amount depends on your resources, tipping philosophy, and the circumstances, but some general guidelines apply.

Restaurants: In Italy, the service charge *(servizio)* is usually built into your bill's grand total in one of two ways. If the menu states *servizio incluso* (or nothing at all), the listed prices already include service. If the menu states *servizio non incluso,* or *servizio* with a specific percentage, a fixed percentage (usually 10-15 percent of the total) will be added as a line item to the bottom of the bill. In either case, the total you pay already includes a basic tip. Most Italians don't tip beyond this, but if you're happy with the service, you can round up a euro or two. If you pay your bill with a credit card, it's best to tip in cash—leave it on the table or hand it directly to your server. If you order at a counter rather than from waitstaff, there's no need to tip.

Taxis: To tip the cabbie, round up. For a typical ride, round up your fare a bit (to pay a €4.50 fare, give €5). If the cabbie hauls your bags and zips you to the airport to help you catch your flight, you might want to toss in a little more. But if you feel like you're being driven in circles or otherwise ripped off, skip the tip.

Special Services: Tour guides at public sights sometimes hold out their hands for tips after they give their spiel. If I've already paid for the tour, I don't tip extra, unless they've really impressed me. At hotels, if you let the porter carry your luggage, it's polite to give them a euro for each bag (another reason to pack light). If you like to tip maids, leave a euro per overnight at the end of your stay.

In general, if someone in the service industry does a super job for you, a small tip (the equivalent of a euro or two) is appropriate...but not required.

When in doubt, ask. If you're not sure whether (or how much) to tip for a service, ask your hotelier or the TI; they'll fill you in on how it's done on their turf.

Getting a VAT Refund

Wrapped into the purchase price of your Italian souvenirs is a Value-Added Tax (VAT) of about 20 percent. You're entitled to get most of that tax back if you purchase more than €155 (about $220) worth of goods at a store that participates in the VAT-refund scheme. Typically, you must ring up the minimum at a single retailer—you can't add up your purchases from various shops to reach the required amount.

Getting your refund is usually straightforward and, if you buy a substantial amount of souvenirs, well worth the hassle. If you're lucky, the merchant will subtract the tax when you make your purchase. (This is more likely to occur if the store ships the goods to your home.) Otherwise, you'll need to:

Get the paperwork. Have the merchant completely fill out the necessary refund document, called a "cheque." You'll have to present your passport. Be sure to retain your original sales receipt.

Get your stamp at the border or airport. Process your VAT document at your last stop in the EU (for instance, at the airport) with the customs agent who deals with VAT refunds. Before checking in for your flight, find the local customs office, and be prepared to stand in line. It's best to keep your purchases in your carry-on for viewing, but if they're too large or dangerous to carry on (such as knives), have your purchases easily accessible in the bag you're about to check, ready to show the customs agent. You're not supposed to use your purchased goods before you leave. If you show up at customs wearing your new leather shoes, officials might look the other way—or deny you a refund.

Collect your refund. You'll need to return your stamped document to the retailer or its representative. Many merchants work with a service, such as Global Blue (www.global-blue.com) or Premier Tax Free (www.premiertaxfree.com), which have offices at major airports, ports, or border crossings (after check-in and security, probably strategically located near a duty-free shop). These services, which extract a 4 percent fee, can refund your money immediately in cash or credit your card (within two billing cycles). If the retailer handles VAT refunds directly, it's up to you to contact the merchant for your refund. You can mail the documents from home, or more quickly, from your point of departure (using a stamped, self-addressed envelope you've prepared or one that's been provided by the merchant). You'll then have to wait—it can take months.

Customs for American Shoppers

You are allowed to take home $800 worth of items per person duty-free, once every 30 days. You can also bring in a liter of alcohol duty-free. As for food, you can take home many processed and packaged foods: vacuum-packed cheeses, dried herbs, jams, chocolate, oil, vinegar, and honey. However, fresh fruits and vegetables and most meats are not allowed. Any liquid-containing foods must be packed in checked luggage, a potential recipe for disaster. To check customs rules and duty rates, visit www.cbp.gov.

Sightseeing

Sightseeing can be hard work. Use these tips to make your visits to Italy's finest museums meaningful, fun, efficient, and painless.

Plan Ahead

Set up an itinerary that allows you to fit in all your must-see sights. For a one-stop look at opening hours, see the "At a Glance" sidebars for each major city (Venice, Milan, Florence, Siena, and Rome). Most sights keep stable hours, but you can easily confirm the latest by checking with the TI or visiting museums' websites. Or call sights in the morning and ask: "Are you open today?" (*"Aperto oggi?"*; ah-PER-toh OH-jee) and "What time do you close?" (*"A che ora chiuso?"*; ah kay OH-rah kee-OO-zoh). I've included telephone numbers for this purpose.

Sometimes you can make reservations for an entry time (for example, at Florence's Uffizi Gallery or Rome's Vatican Museum). Some cities offer museum passes for admission to several museums (e.g., Roma Pass and Florence Pass) that let you skip ticket-buying lines. At some popular places (such as Rome's Colosseum or Venice's Doge's Palace), you can get in more quickly by buying your ticket or pass at a less-crowded sight. Booking a guided tour can help you avoid lines at many sights.

Don't put off visiting a must-see sight—you never know when a place will close unexpectedly for a holiday, strike, or restoration. On holidays (see list on page 1037), expect reduced hours or closures—find out if a particular sight will be open by phoning ahead or checking its website. In summer, some sights may stay open late. Off-season, many museums have shorter hours.

When possible, visit the major sights in the morning (when your energy is best) and save other activities for the afternoon. Hit the highlights first, then go back to other things if you have the stamina and time.

Rick Steves' Free Audio Tours

I've produced free, self-guided audio versions of my tours of the major sights in Venice, Florence, and Rome (download them via www.ricksteves.com/audioeurope, iTunes, or my Rick Steves Audio Europe smartphone app). These user-friendly, easy-to-follow, fun, and informative audio tours are available for **Venice**'s Grand Canal, St. Mark's Square, St. Mark's Basilica, and Frari Church; **Florence**'s Renaissance Walk, Accademia, and Uffizi Gallery; and **Rome**'s Colosseum, Roman Forum, Pantheon, St. Peter's Basilica, Sistine Chapel, Trastevere neighborhood, and Jewish Ghetto, plus nearby Ostia Antica and Pompeii. Compared to live tours, these audio tours are hard to beat: Nobody will stand you up, the quality is reliable, you can take the tour exactly when you like, and they're free.

Going at the right time helps avoid crowds. This book offers tips on specific sights. Try visiting popular sights very early, at lunch, or very late. Evening visits are usually peaceful, with fewer crowds.

Study up. To get the most out of the sight descriptions in this book, read them before you visit.

At Sights

Here's what you can typically expect:

Some important sights have metal detectors or conduct bag searches that will slow your entry, while others require you to check daypacks and coats. They'll be kept safely. If you have something you can't bear to part with, stash it in a pocket or purse. To avoid checking a small backpack, carry it under your arm like a purse as you enter. From a guard's point of view, a backpack is generally a problem while a purse is not.

Flash photography is often banned, but taking photos without a flash is usually allowed. Look for signs or ask. Flashes damage oil paintings and distract others in the room. Even without a flash, a handheld camera will take a decent picture (or buy postcards or posters at the museum bookstore). If photos are permitted, video cameras generally are OK, too.

You'll likely have to pay cash for the admission fee; few sights take credit cards. Some sights have found a clever way to squeeze more money out of visitors by hosting special exhibits in addition to their permanent collection. Most of these come at an extra cost (which you'll likely have to pay even if you don't want to see the special exhibit). The prices I've listed in this book generally include these obligatory temporary exhibits. Come expecting this higher price...and consider yourself lucky if you happen to visit on the rare occasion when you can get in for less.

Expect changes—artwork can be on tour, on loan, out sick, or shifted at the whim of the curator. To adapt, pick up any available free floor plans as you enter, and ask museum staff if you can't find a particular item. Say the title or artist's name, or point to the photograph in this book and ask, *"Dov'è?"* (doh-VEH; meaning "Where is?").

Many sights rent audioguides, which generally offer dry-but-useful recorded descriptions in English (about $4). If you bring along your own pair of headphones and a Y-jack, you can sometimes share one audioguide with your travel partner and save money. I've produced free downloadable audio tours of some of Italy's major sights; see the sidebar on the previous page.

Guided tours in English are most likely to be available during peak season (usually €5-15 and widely ranging in quality). Some sights also run short films featuring their highlights and history. These are generally well worth your time. I make it standard operating procedure to ask when I arrive at a sight if there is a film in English.

It helps to know the terms. Art historians and Italians refer to the great Florentine centuries by dropping a thousand years. The Trecento (300s), Quattrocento (400s), and Cinquecento (500s) were the 1300s, 1400s, and 1500s. Also, in Italian museums, art is dated with *sec* for *secolo* (century, often indicated with Roman numerals), A.C. (for *Avanti Cristo*, or B.C.), and D.C. (for *Dopo Cristo*, or A.D.). O.K.?

Important sights may have an on-site café or cafeteria (usually a good place to rest and have a snack or light meal). The WCs at sights are free and generally clean (it's smart to carry tissues in case a WC runs out of TP).

Many places sell postcards that highlight their attractions. Before you leave, scan the postcards and thumb through the biggest guidebook (or skim its index) to be sure that you haven't overlooked something that you'd like to see.

Most sights stop admitting people 30-60 minutes before closing time, and some rooms close early (often about 45 minutes before the actual closing time). Guards usher people out, so don't save the best for last.

Every sight or museum offers more than what is covered in this book. Use the information in this book as an introduction—not the final word.

Find Religion

Churches offer some amazing art (usually free), a cool respite from heat, and a welcome seat.

A modest dress code (no bare shoulders or shorts for anyone, even kids) is enforced at larger churches, such as Venice's St. Mark's and the Vatican's St. Peter's, but is often overlooked elsewhere. If you are caught by surprise, you can improvise, using maps to cover your shoulders and a jacket for your knees. (I wear a super-lightweight pair of long pants rather than shorts for my hot and muggy big-city Italian sightseeing.)

Some churches have coin-operated audioboxes that describe the art and history; just set the dial on English, put in your coins, and listen. Coin boxes near a piece of art illuminate the art (and present a better photo opportunity). I pop in a coin whenever I can. It improves my experience, is a favor to other visitors trying to appreciate a great piece of art in the dark, and is a little contribution to that church and its work. Whenever possible, let there be light.

Sleeping

For hassle-free efficiency, I favor hotels and restaurants that are handy to your sightseeing activities. Rather than list hotels scattered throughout a city, I describe two or three favorite neighborhoods and recommend the best accommodations values in each, from $30 bunk beds to fancy-for-my-book $300 doubles with all the comforts.

Sleeping in Italy is expensive. Cheap big-city hotels can be depressing. Tourist information services cannot give opinions on quality of hotels. A major feature of this book is its extensive listing of good-value accommodations. I like places that are clean, central, relatively quiet at night, reasonably priced, friendly, small enough to have a hands-on owner and stable staff, run with a respect for Italian traditions, and not listed in other guidebooks. (In Italy, for me, satisfying six out of eight of these criteria means it's a keeper.) Some places listed are old and rickety, and I've described them as such. I'm more impressed by a handy location and a fun-loving philosophy than flat-screen TVs and shoeshine machines.

Book your accommodations well in advance if you'll be traveling during busy times. See page 1037 for a list of major holidays and festivals in Italy; for tips on making reservations, see page 26.

Rates, Deals, and Tips

I've described my recommended accommodations using a Sleep Code (see the sidebar on the next page). Prices listed are for one-night stays in peak season and assume you're booking directly (not through a TI or online hotel-booking engine). Using an online booking service costs the hotel about 20 percent and logically closes the door on special deals. Book direct.

Sleep Code

(€1 = about $1.40, country code: 39)

Price Rankings

To help you easily sort through my hotel listings, I've divided the accommodations into three categories based on the price for a double room with bath during high season:

$$$	**Higher Priced**
$$	**Moderately Priced**
$	**Lower Priced**

I always rate hostels as $, whether or not they have double rooms, because they have the cheapest beds in town. Prices can change without notice; verify the hotel's current rates online or by email. For other updates, see www.ricksteves.com/update.

Abbreviations

To pack maximum information into minimum space, I use the following code to describe accommodations in this book. Prices listed are per room, not per person. When a price range is given for a type of room (such as double rooms listing for €100-150), it means the price fluctuates with the season, size of room, or length of stay; expect to pay the upper end for peak-season stays.

S = Single room (or price for one person in a double).

D = Double or Twin room. "Double beds" are often two twins sheeted together and are usually big enough for nonromantic couples.

T = Triple (generally a double bed with a single).

Q = Quad (usually two double beds; adding an extra child's bed to a T is usually cheaper).

b = Private bathroom with toilet and shower or tub.

s = Private shower or tub only (the toilet is down the hall).

According to this code, a couple staying at a "Db-€140" hotel would pay a total of €140 (about $195) for a double room with a private bathroom. Unless otherwise noted, breakfast is included, hotel staff speak basic English, and credit cards are accepted.

If I mention "Internet access" in a listing, there's a public terminal in the lobby for guests to use. If I use the terms "Wi-Fi" or "cable Internet," you can access it in your room, but only if you have your own laptop or other wireless device.

Given the economic downturn, hoteliers are willing and eager to make a deal. I'd suggest emailing several hotels to ask for their best price. Comparison-shop and make your choice. In general, prices can soften if you do any of the following: offer to pay cash, stay at least three nights, or mention this book. You can also try asking for a cheaper room or a discount, or offer to skip breakfast.

As you look over the listings, you'll notice that some accommodations promise special prices to my readers who book direct (without using a room-finding service or hotel-booking website, which take a commission). To get these rates, you must mention this book when you reserve, and then show the book upon arrival. Some readers with ebooks have reported difficulty getting a Rick Steves discount. If this happens to you, please show this to the hotelier: Rick Steves discounts apply to readers with ebooks as well as printed books.

Travel Review Websites: TripAdvisor (www.tripadvisor.com) and similar review websites are popular tools for finding hotels, but have drawbacks. To write a review, people need only an email address—making it easy to hide their true identity. If a hotel is well reviewed in a guidebook or two, and also gets good ratings on TripAdvisor, it's probably a safe bet—but I wouldn't stay at a hotel based solely on a TripAdvisor recommendation.

Types of Accommodations
Hotels
Double rooms listed in this book will range from about €50 (very simple, toilet and shower down the hall) to €300 (maximum plumbing and more), with most clustered around €130 (with private bathrooms). Prices are higher in big cities and heavily touristed cities, and lower off the beaten path.

Solo travelers find that the cost of a *camera singola* is often only 25 percent less than a *camera doppia*. Three or four people can economize by requesting larger rooms. (If a double room is €110, a quad would be about €150.) Most listed hotels have a variety of rooms that can accommodate from one to five people. If there's space for an extra cot, they'll cram it in for you (charging you around €25).

The Italian word for "hotel" is *hotel*, and in smaller, non-touristy towns, *albergo*. A few places have kept the old titles *locanda* or *pensione*, indicating that they offer budget beds. English works in all but the cheapest places.

You'll save €30 if you request a room without a shower and just use the shower down the hall. Generally rooms with a bath or shower also have a toilet and a bidet (which Italians use for quick sponge baths). The cord that dangles over the tub or shower is not a clothesline. You pull it when you've fallen and can't get up.

Chill Out

Nearly all hotels, except for the rock-bottom basic ones, have air-conditioning. Because Europeans are generally careful with energy use, you'll find government-enforced limits on air-conditioning and heating. There's a one-month period each spring and fall when neither is allowed. Air-conditioning sometimes costs an extra per-day charge, is worth seeking out in summer (though it may be on only at certain times of the day), and is rarely available from fall through spring. Fancier hotel rooms usually include air-conditioning in the price. Conveniently, many business-class hotels drop their prices in July and August, just when the air-conditioned comfort they offer is most important.

Most hotel rooms with air conditioners come with a control stick (like a TV remote) that generally has the same symbols and features: fan icon (click to toggle through wind power, from light to gale); louver icon (choose steady airflow or waves); snowflake and sunshine icons (cold air or heat, depending on season); clock ("O" setting: run x hours before turning off; "I" setting: wait x hours to start); and the temperature control (20 or 21 degrees Celsius is comfortable).

Double beds are called *matrimoniale*, even though hotels aren't interested in your marital status. Twins are *due letti singoli*. Convents offer cheap accommodation but only *letti singoli*.

When you check in, the receptionist will normally ask for your passport and keep it for a couple of hours. Hotels are legally required to register each guest with the local police. Relax. Americans are notorious for making this chore more difficult than it needs to be.

Assume that breakfast is included in the prices I've listed, unless otherwise noted. If breakfast is optional, you may want to skip it. While convenient, it's usually expensive—€5-6 per person for a simple continental buffet with (at its most generous) ham, cheese, yogurt, cereal, and unlimited *caffè latte*. A picnic in your room followed by a coffee at the corner café can be a lot cheaper.

More pillows and blankets are usually in the closet or available on request. In Italy, towels and linen aren't always replaced every day. Hang your towel up to dry. Budget hotels often use "waffle" or very thin tablecloth-type towels, which use less water and electricity to launder.

Most hotel rooms have a TV and phone, and Internet access (usually Wi-Fi) is increasingly common. Simpler places rarely have a phone. Pricier hotels usually come with a small stocked fridge called a *frigo bar* (FREE-goh bar; pay for what you use).

Hotels in resort areas will often charge you for half-pension, called *mezza pensione*, during peak season (which can run from May through mid-October for resorts). Half-pension means that you pay for one meal per day per person (lunch or dinner, though usually dinner), whether you want to or not. Wine is rarely included. If half-pension is required, you can't opt out and pay less. Some places offer half-pension as an option; it can be worth considering. If they charge you less per meal than you've been paying for an average restaurant meal on your trip, half-pension is a fine value—if the chef is good. Ask other guests about the quality or check out their restaurant yourself.

If you arrive at your hotel very early in the morning after an overnight flight or train ride, your room probably won't be ready; you should be able to safely check your bag at the hotel and dive right into sightseeing.

Hoteliers can be a great help and source of advice. Most know their city well, and can assist you with everything from public transit and airport connections to finding a good restaurant, the nearest launderette, or an Internet café. But even at the best places, mechanical breakdowns occur: Air-conditioning malfunctions, sinks leak, hot water turns cold, and toilets gurgle and smell. Report your concerns clearly and calmly at the front desk. For more complicated problems, don't expect instant results.

If you suspect night noise will be a problem, ask for a quiet room in the back or on an upper floor. To guard against theft in your room, keep valuables out of sight. Some rooms come with a safe, and other hotels have safes at the front desk. Use them if you're concerned.

Checkout can pose problems if surprise charges pop up on your bill. If you settle up your bill the night before you leave, you'll have time to discuss and address any points of contention (before 19:00, when the night shift usually arrives).

Above all, keep a positive attitude. Remember, you're on vacation. If your hotel is a disappointment, spend more time out enjoying the city you came to see.

Hotels Beyond this Book: If you're traveling beyond my recommended destinations, you'll find accommodations where you need them. Any town with tourists has a TI that books rooms or can give you a list and point you in the right direction. In the absence of a TI, ask people on the street or in restaurants for help.

Hostels

You'll pay about €25 per bed to stay at a hostel. Travelers of any age are welcome if they don't mind dorm-style accommodations and meeting other travelers. Most hostels offer kitchen facilities, Internet access, Wi-Fi, and laundry (generally self-service). **Independent hostels** tend to be easygoing, colorful, and informal

Making Reservations

Given the good value of the accommodations I've found for this book, I'd recommend that you reserve your rooms in advance, particularly if you'll be traveling during peak season. Book several weeks ahead, or as soon as you've pinned down your travel dates. Note that some national holidays jam things up and merit your making reservations far in advance (see "Holidays and Festivals" on page 1037).

Phoning: To call Italy from the US or Canada, dial 011-39 and then the local number. (The 011 is our international access code, and 39 is Italy's country code.) If you're calling Italy from another European country, dial 00-39-local number. (The 00 is Europe's international access code.) To make calls within Italy, simply dial the local number. Land lines start with 0; mobile lines start with 3. For more tips on calling, see the appendix.

Requesting a Reservation: To make a reservation, contact hotels directly by email, phone, or fax. Email is the clearest and most economical way to make a reservation. Or you can go straight to the hotel website; many have secure online reservation forms and you can instantly check availability and any special deals. But be sure you use the hotel's official site and not a booking agency's site—otherwise you may pay higher rates than you should. Most recommended hotels are accustomed to guests who speak only English.

The hotelier wants to know these key pieces of information about your stay (also included in the sample request form in the appendix):

- number and type of rooms
- number of nights
- date of arrival
- date of departure
- any special needs (e.g., bathroom in the room or down the hall, twin beds vs. double bed, air-conditioning, quiet, view, ground floor, etc.)

When you request a room, use the European style for writing dates: day/month/year. For example, for a two-night stay in July, I would request "1 double room for 2 nights, arrive 16/07/12, depart 18/07/12." Consider carefully how long you'll stay; don't just assume you can tack on extra days once you arrive. Make sure you mention any discounts—for Rick Steves readers or otherwise—when you make the reservation.

INTRODUCTION

Confirming a Reservation: If the hotel's response tells you its room availability and rates, it's not a confirmation. You must tell them that you want that room at the given rate. Most hoteliers will request your credit-card number to hold the room. While you can email your credit-card information (I do), it's safer to share that confidential info via phone call, fax, split between two emails, or via a secure online reservation form (if the hotel has one on its website).

Canceling a Reservation: If you must cancel your reservation, it's courteous to do so with as much advance notice as possible. Simply make a quick phone call or send an email. Family-run hotels lose money if they turn away customers while holding a room for someone who doesn't show up. Understandably, many hoteliers bill no-shows for one night.

Cancellation policies can be strict: For example, you might lose a deposit if you cancel within two weeks of your reserved stay, or you might be billed for the entire visit if you leave early. Internet deals may require prepayment, with no refunds for cancellations. Ask about cancellation policies before you book.

If canceling via email, request confirmation that your cancellation was received to avoid being accidentally billed.

Reconfirming Your Reservation: Always call to reconfirm your room reservation a few days in advance from the road. (Don't have a TI call for you; they may take a commission.) Smaller hotels and B&Bs appreciate knowing your estimated time of arrival, especially if you'll be arriving late (after 17:00). On the small chance that a hotel loses track of your reservation, bring along a hard copy of their emailed or faxed confirmation.

Reserving Rooms as You Travel: You can make reservations as you travel, calling hotels a few days to a week before your arrival. If everything's full, don't despair. Call a day or two in advance and fill in a cancellation. If you'd rather travel without any reservations at all, you'll have greater success snaring rooms if you arrive at your destination early in the day. When you anticipate crowds (weekends are worst), call hotels at about 9:00 or 10:00 on the day you plan to arrive, when the hotel clerk knows who'll be checking out and just which rooms will be available. If you encounter a language barrier, ask the fluent receptionist at your current hotel to call for you.

(no membership required); see www.hostelz.com, www.hostels europe.com, www.hostels.com, and www.hostelworld.com. **Official hostels** are part of Hostelling International and adhere to various rules (such as a 17:00 check-in, lockout during the day, a curfew at night); they require that you either have a membership card or pay extra per night (www.hihostels.com).

Private Rooms and Apartments

In small towns, there are often few hotels to choose from, but an abundance of *affitta camere,* or rental rooms. This can be anything from a set of keys and a basic bed to a cozy B&B with your own Tuscan grandmother. Local TIs can give you a list of possibilities (or try the free Ciao Italia Bed & Breakfast, which books B&Bs and hostels in Rome, Florence, and Venice at www .ciaoitalia-bb.com). These rooms are usually a good budget option, but since they vary in quality, shop around to find the best value. It's always OK to ask to see the room before you commit.

Apartment rentals, a great value for families or multiple couples traveling together, are also listed at TIs and are common in small towns. Rentals are generally by the week, with prices starting around €100 per day. A bigger place for a group of four to five rents for around €200. Apartments generally offer a couple of bedrooms, a sitting area, and a teensy *cucinetta* (kitchenette), usually stocked with dishes and flatware. After you check in, you're basically on your own. While you won't have a doorman to carry your bags or a maid to clean your room each day, you will get an inside peek at an Italian home, and you can save lots of money—especially if you take advantage of the cooking facilities—with no loss of comfort.

Agritourism

Agriturismo (agricultural tourism), or rural B&Bs, began in the 1980s as a way to encourage small farmers in the countryside to survive in a modern economy where, like in the US, so many have been run out of business by giant agricultural corporations. By renting rooms to travelers, farmers can remain on their land and continue to produce food. A peaceful home base for exploring the region, these rural Italian B&Bs are ideal for those traveling by car—especially families.

It's wise to book several months in advance for high season (May-Sept). Weeklong stays are preferred in July and August, but shorter stays are possible off-season. To sleep cheaper, avoid peak season. A farmhouse that rents for as much as $2,000 a week at peak times can go for as little as $700 in late September or October. In the winter, you might be charged extra for heat, so confirm the price ahead of time. Payment policies vary, but generally a 25 percent deposit is required (lost if you cancel), and the balance is due one month before arrival.

As the name implies, *agriturismi* are in the countryside, although some are located within a mile of town. Most are family-run. *Agriturismi* vary wildly in quality—some properties are rustic, while others are downright luxurious, offering amenities such as swimming pools and riding stables. The rooms are usually clean and comfortable. Breakfast is often included, and *mezza pensione* (half-pension, which in this case means a home-cooked dinner) might be built into the price whether you want it or not. Most places serve tasty homegrown food; some are vegetarian or organic, others are gourmet. Kitchenettes are often available to cook up your own feast. Make sure you know how to operate the appliances. To maximize your time, ask the owner for suggestions on local restaurants, sights, and activities.

To qualify officially as an *agriturismo*, the farm must still generate more money from its farm activities, thereby insuring that the land is worked and preserved. Some farmhouse B&Bs aren't actual farms, though are fine places to stay. But if you want the real thing, make sure the owners call their place an *agriturismo*.

In this book, I've listed some *agriturismi* and farmhouses under the towns that they're nearest to, but there are many, many more. Local TIs can give you a list of farms in their area, and many *agriturismi* now have their own websites. For a sampling, visit www.agriturismoitaly.it or do a Web search for *agriturismo*. One booking agency among many is Farm Holidays in Tuscany (closed Sat-Sun, tel. 0564-417-418, www.byfarmholidays.com, info@byfarmholidays.com).

Eating

The Italians are masters of the art of fine living. That means eating...long and well. Lengthy, multicourse lunches and dinners and

endless hours sitting in outdoor cafés are the norm. Americans eat on their way to an evening event and complain if the check is slow in coming. For Italians, the meal is an end in itself, and only rude waiters rush you. When you want the bill, mime-scribble on your raised palm or

Eating with the Seasons

Italian cooks love to serve you fresh produce and seafood at its tastiest. If you must have porcini mushrooms outside of fall, they'll be frozen. Each region in Italy has its specialties, which you'll see displayed in open-air markets. To get a plate of the freshest veggies at a fine restaurant, request *"Un piatto di verdure della stagioni, per favore."*

Here are a few examples of what's fresh when:

April-May:	Calamari, squid, green beans, asparagus, artichokes, and zucchini flowers
April-May and Sept-Oct:	Black truffles
May-June:	Mussels, asparagus, zucchini, cantaloupe, and strawberries
May-Aug:	Eggplant
Oct-Nov:	Mushrooms, white truffles, and chestnuts
Nov-Feb:	Radicchio
Fresh year-round:	Clams, meats, and cheese

ask for it: *"Il conto?"* You may have to ask for it more than once. To save time, ask for the check when you receive the last item you order.

Even those of us who liked dorm food will find that the local cafés, cuisine, and wines become a highlight of our Italian adventure. Trust me: This is sightseeing for your palate, and even if the rest of you is sleeping in cheap hotels, your taste buds will relish an occasional first-class splurge. You can eat well without going broke. But be careful: You're just as likely to blow a small fortune on a disappointing meal as you are to dine wonderfully for €25.

Restaurants

When restaurant-hunting, choose places filled with locals, not the place with the big neon signs boasting, "We Speak English and Accept Credit Cards." Venturing even a block or two off the main drag leads to higher-quality food for less than half the price of the tourist-oriented places. Locals eat better at lower-rent locales. Family-run places operate without hired help and can offer cheaper meals. Good restaurants don't open for dinner before 19:00.

Before you sit down, look at a

MENU € 19,00
TURISTICO

ANTIPASTO di MARE

PRIMI PIATTI
RISOTTO alla PESCATORA
SPAGHETTI alla MARINARA
SPAGHETTI allo SCOGLIO
TRENETTE al PESTO

SECONDI PIATTI
PESCE ai FERRI
FRITTO MISTO
GRIGLIATA di CARNE

CONTORNI
PATATE FRITTE o INSALATA

menu to see what extra charges a restaurant tacks on. Many (but not all) restaurants in Italy add a cover charge *(coperto)* of €1.50-3.50 per person to your bill. Sometimes this is phrased as "bread and cover" *(pane e coperto)*. It's not negotiable, even if you don't eat the bread. Restaurants with a service charge (usually around 10-15 percent) are in the minority. Places with both a cover *and* a service charge are best avoided—that's a clue that a restaurant could be overpriced and touristy.

Because the tip is generally built into the bill, most Italians never tip, but if you liked the service, you can round up a euro or two; see "Tipping" on page 16.

You can save a lot by getting fixed-priced meals, which are frequently exempt from cover and service charges. However, the cheapest ones tend to be bland and heavy, pairing a very basic pasta with reheated schnitzel and roast meats (usually around €15-20, often called *menù turistico,* or sometimes, usually falsely, *menù del giorno*—menu of the day). It's worth paying more for an inventive fixed-price meal that shows off the chef's creativity. While fixed-price meals can be easy and convenient, galloping gourmets order à la carte with the help of a menu translator. (The *Rick Steves' Italian Phrase Book & Dictionary* has a menu decoder with enough phrases for intermediate eaters.) When going to an especially good restaurant with an approachable staff, I like to find out what they're eager to serve, or I'll simply say, "Make me happy" (in this case, it's just fine to set a price limit).

A full meal consists of an appetizer (antipasto, €4-6), a first course *(primo piatto,* pasta or soup, €5-12), and a second course *(secondo piatto,* expensive meat and fish dishes, €10-20). Vegetables *(contorni, verdure)* may come with the *secondo* or cost extra (€4-6) as a side dish.

The euros can add up in a hurry. Light and budget eaters get a *primo piatto* each and share an antipasto. (Italians admit the *secondo* is the least interesting part of their cuisine.) Another good option is sharing an array of *antipasti*—either by ordering several specific dishes or, at restaurants that offer self-serve buffets, by choosing a variety of cold and cooked appetizers from an *antipasti* buffet spread out like a salad bar. At buffets, you pay per plate, not by weight; a typical serving costs about €8 (generally Italians don't treat buffets as all-you-can-eat, but take a one-time moderate serving; watch others and imitate).

To maximize the experience and flavors, small groups can

Wine Labels and Lingo

The ancient Greeks who colonized Italy more than 2,000 years ago called it *"Oenotria"*—land of the grape. Little has changed over the centuries. Ideal conditions for grapes (warm climate, well-draining soil, and an abundance of hillsides) make the Italian peninsula a paradise for grape-growers, winemakers, and wine drinkers. Italy makes and consumes more wine per capita than any other country.

In almost every part of Italy you'll find wine varieties designed to go with the regional cuisine. Choosing a wine can be intimidating, but the Italian government tries to help you choose something decent, even if you're clueless. In general, wines are designated by one of four categories:

Vino da Tavola (table wine) is the lowest grade. It's inexpensive, but Italy's wines are so good that, for many people, a basic *vino da tavola* is just fine with a meal. Many restaurants, even modest ones, take pride in their house wine *("vino della casa")*, bottling their own or working with wineries.

Denominazione di Origine Controllata (DOC), a cut above table wine, is usually cheap, but can be surprisingly good. Hundreds of wines have earned the DOC designation. In Tuscany, for example, many such wines come from the Chianti region, located between Florence and Siena.

Denominazione di Origine Controllata e Guarantita (DOCG) is the highest grade, and can be identified by the pink or green label on the neck and the scary price tag on the shelf. Only a limited number of wines in Italy can be called DOCG. They're generally a good bet if you want a quality wine, but you don't know anything else about the winemaker. (**Riserva** is a DOC or

---

mix *antipasti* and *primi piatti* family-style (skipping *secondi*). If you do this right (e.g., under-ordering because courses are often bigger than necessary), you can eat well in better places for less than the cost of a tourist *menù* in a cheap place.

Some special dishes come in large quantities meant for two people; the shorthand way of showing this on a menu is "X2" (meaning "for two people"). The price listed generally indicates the cost per person.

Seafood and steak may be sold by weight (priced by the kilo—1,000 grams, or just over two pounds; or by the *etto*—100 grams). The letters *s.q.* mean "according to quantity." Fish is usually served whole with the head and tail; you can't just get half a fish or a

DOCG wine matured for a longer, more specific time.)
   Indicazione Geographica Tipica (IGT) is a broad group of wines that range from basic to some of Italy's best. It includes the "Super Tuscans"—wines that don't follow the strict "recipe" required for DOC or DOCG status, but that give local vintners more opportunity to be creative. Super Tuscans are made from a mix of international grapes (such as cabernet sauvignon) grown in Tuscany and aged in small oak barrels for only two years. The result is a lively full-bodied wine that dances all over your head... and is worth the steep price for aficionados.
   Visit an *enoteca* (wine bar) and sample these wines side-by-side to figure out what you like—and what suits your pocketbook.

Words to Live By, or...
How to Describe Wine in Italian

As you can see from many of the words listed below, adding a vowel to the English word often gets you close to the Italian one. Have some fun, gesture like a local, and you'll have no problems speaking the language of the *enoteca. Salute!*

dry	*secco*	SAY-koh
sweet	*dolce*	DOHL-chay
earthy	*terroso*	tay-ROH-zoh
tannic	*tannico*	TAH-nee-koh
young	*giovane*	JOH-vah-nay
mature	*maturo*	mah-TOO-roh
sparkling	*spumante*	spoo-MAHN-tay
fruity	*fruttoso*	froo-TOH-zoh
full-bodied	*corposo*	kor-POH-zoh
elegant	*elegante*	ay-lay-GAHN-tay

fillet unless it already comes prepared as just a fillet (*filetto*, sometimes *trancio*—slice, as in tuna or swordfish). However, you can ask your waiter to select a smaller fish for you. Sometimes, especially for steak, restaurants require a minimum order of four or five *etti*. Beware, or be shell-shocked by €50 entrées. Make sure you're really clear on the price before ordering.

Wine Bars *(Enoteche)*

An *enoteca* (wine bar) is a popular, fast, and inexpensive option for lunch. Surrounded by the local office crowd, you can get a fancy salad, plate of meats and cheeses, and a glass of fine wine (see blackboards for the day's selection and price per glass—and go for the top end). A good *enoteca* aims to impress visitors with its wines and will generally choose excellent-quality ingredients for the simple dishes it offers with the wine. Some of my favorite Italian eating experiences have been at *enoteche*.

Bars/Cafés

Italian "bars" are not taverns, but cafés. These neighborhood hang-outs serve coffee, mini-pizzas, sandwiches, and drinks from the cooler. Many dish up plates of fried cheese and vegetables from under the glass counter, ready to reheat. This budget choice is the Italian equivalent of English pub grub.

For quick meals, bars usually have trays of cheap, pre-made sandwiches (*panini* or *tramezzini*)—some are delightful grilled. Others have lots of mayo between crustless slices of Wonder Bread. To save time for sightseeing and room for dinner, consider a ham-and-cheese *panino* (called *toast*) at a bar for lunch; have it grilled twice if you want it really hot. Many bars are small—if you can't find a table, you'll need to stand up to eat. To get food to go, say, "*Da portar via*" (for the road). All bars have a WC *(toilette, bagno)* in the back, and customers—and the discreet public—can use it.

Bars serve great drinks—hot, cold, sweet, caffeinated, or alcoholic. Chilled bottled water, still *(naturale)* or carbonated *(frizzante)*, is sold cheap to go.

Coffee: If you ask for "*un caffè,*" you'll get espresso. Cappuccino is served to locals before noon and to tourists any time of day. (To an Italian, cappuccino is a breakfast drink and a travesty after eating anything with tomatoes.) Italians like their coffee only warm—to get it hot, request "*Molto caldo*" (MOHL-toh KAHL-doh; very hot) or "*Più caldo, per favore*" (pew KAHL-doh pehr fah-VOH-ray; hotter, please).

Experiment with a few of the options:
- cappuccino: Espresso with foamed milk on top
- *caffè latte:* Tall glass with espresso mixed with hot milk, no foam (ordering just a "latte" gets you only milk)
- *caffè hag:* instant decaf (any coffee drink is available decaffeinated—ask for it *decaffeinato:* day-kah-fey-een-AH-toh)
- *macchiato* (mah-kee-AH-toh): Espresso with only a little milk (*macchiato* means "marked" or "stained")
- *latte macchiato:* Hot milk with a shot of espresso
- *caffè americano:* Espresso diluted with water
- *caffè freddo:* Sweet and iced espresso
- *cappuccino freddo:* Iced cappuccino
- *caffè corretto:* Espresso with a shot of liqueur, usually grappa or Sambuca, but amaretto is also good.

More Hot Drinks: *Cioccolato* is hot chocolate. *Tè* is hot tea. *Tè freddo* (iced tea) is usually from a can—sweetened and flavored with lemon or peach.

Juice: *Spremuta* means freshly squeezed as far as *succo* (fruit juice) is concerned (order *una spremuta*); it's usually orange juice, and February through April it's almost always made from blood oranges. (Note: *Spumante* is sparkling wine.)

Beer: Beer on tap is *alla spina*. Get it *piccola* (33 cl, 11 oz), *media* (50 cl, about a pint), or *grande* (a liter, about two pints). Italians drink mainly lager beers. You'll find local brews (Peroni or Moretti) and imports such as Heineken as well. A *lattina* is a can and a *bottiglia* (boh-TEEL-yah) is a bottle.

Wine: To order a glass (*bicchiere;* bee-kee-AY-ree) of red *(rosso)* or white *(bianco)* wine, say, "*Un bicchiere di vino rosso/bianco.*" *Secco* is dry, *corposo* means full-bodied, and *frizzante* is fizzy. House wine *(vino della casa)* comes in a carafe: quarter-liter (8.5 oz, *un quarto*), half-liter pitcher (17 oz, *un mezzo*), or one-liter pitcher (34 oz, *un litro*). An *ombra* is the smallest glass. Trendy wines with small production (such as Brunello di Montalcino) are good but overpriced.

Other Drinks: Some restaurants make their own after-dinner alcoholic brew (called a *digestivo*), using a secret combination of herbs to aid digestion. Popular commercial brands are Fernet Branca and Montenegro. If your tastes run sweeter, try an anise-flavored liqueur called Sambuca, served *con moscha* (with three "flies"—coffee beans).

Prices: You'll notice a two-tiered pricing system. Drinking a cup of coffee while standing at the bar is cheaper than drinking it at a table. Many places have a *listino prezzi* (price list) with two columns—*al bar* and *al tavolo* (table)—posted somewhere by the bar or cash register. If you're on a budget, don't sit down without first checking out the financial consequences. Ask, "Same price if I sit or stand?" by saying, *"Costa uguale al tavolo o al banco?"* (KOH-stah oo-GWAH-lay ahl TAH-voh-loh oh ahl BAHN-koh). A cup of coffee at any bar generally costs only a euro if you stand. While coffee may cost €5 at a table, you can stand at the fanciest place in town and sip your coffee at the bar for the same price as at a basic café.

If the bar isn't busy, you can probably just order and pay when you leave. Otherwise: 1) Decide what you want; 2) find out the price by checking the price list on the wall, the prices posted near the food, or by asking the barista; 3) pay the cashier; and 4) give the receipt to the barista (whose clean fingers handle no dirty euros) and tell him or her what you want.

Budget Eating

Italy offers many budget options for hungry travelers, but beware of cheap eateries that sport big color photos of pizza and piles of different pastas. They have no kitchens and simply microwave disgusting prepackaged food.

Stop by a *rosticcería* for great cooked deli food. Self-service cafeterias (called "free flow" in Italian) offer the basics without add-on charges. *Döner kebab* places sell veal, chicken, or falafel and salad fixings wrapped in pita bread, offering a budget break from Italian food.

Pizzerias

Pizza is cheap and readily available. Stop by a pizza shop for stand-up or take-out pizza. *Pizza a taglio* ("by the slice") is usually round, Naples-style pizza. *Pizza rustica* is thick, rustic, baked in a square pan, and sold by the weight (clearly explain how much you want—100 grams, or *un etto*, is a hot and cheap snack; 200 grams, or *due etti*, makes a light meal).

Key pizza vocabulary: *capricciosa* (generally ham, mushrooms, olives, and artichokes), *funghi* (mushrooms), *marinara* (tomato sauce, oregano, garlic, no cheese), *quattro formaggi* (four different cheeses), and *quattro stagioni* (different toppings on each of the four quarters, for those who can't choose just one menu item). If you ask for pepperoni on your pizza, you'll get *peperoni* (green or red peppers, not sausage); request *diavola* instead (the closest thing in Italy to American pepperoni). Kids like the bland *margherita* (cheese with tomato sauce).

Tavola Caldas ("Hot Tables")

For a fast, cheap, and healthy lunch, find a *tavola calda* bar with a buffet spread of meat and vegetables, and ask for a mixed plate of vegetables with a hunk of mozzarella *(piatto misto di verdure con mozzarella)*. Don't be limited by what's displayed. If you'd like a salad with a slice of cantaloupe and a hunk of cheese, they'll whip that up for you in a snap. Belly up to the bar and, with a pointing finger and key words in the chart in this chapter, you can get a fine mixed plate of vegetables. If something's a mystery, ask for *un assaggio* (oon ah-SAH-joh) to get a little taste.

Picnics

Picnicking saves lots of euros and is a great way to sample regional specialties. In the process of assembling your meal, you get to deal with the Italians in the market scene. For a colorful experience, gather your ingredients in the morning at the produce market; you'll probably visit several small stores or market stalls to put together a complete meal (note that many close around noon). While it's fun to visit the small specialty shops, an *alimentari* is

Ordering Food at *Tavola Caldas*

plate of mixed veggies	*piatto misto di verdure*	pee-AH-toh MEES-toh dee vehr-DOO-ray
"Heated, please."	*"Scaldare, per favore."*	skahl-DAH-ray, pehr fah-VOH-ray
"A taste, please."	*"Un assaggio, per favore."*	oon ah-SAH-joh, pehr fah-VOH-ray
artichoke	*carciofi*	kar-CHOH-fee
asparagus	*asparagi*	ah-spah-RAH-jee
beans	*fagioli*	fah-JOH-lee
breadsticks	*grissini*	gree-SEE-nee
broccoli	*broccoli*	BROH-koh-lee
cantaloupe	*melone*	may-LOH-nay
carrots	*carote*	kah-ROT-ay
green beans	*fagiolini*	fah-joh-LEE-nee
ham	*prosciutto*	proh-SHOO-toh
mushrooms	*funghi*	FOONG-ghee
potatoes	*patate*	pah-TAH-tay
rice	*riso*	REE-zoh
spinach	*spinaci*	speen-AH-chee
tomatoes	*pomodori*	poh-moh-DOH-ree
zucchini	*zucchine*	zoo-KEE-nay

(Excerpted from *Rick Steves' Italian Phrase Book & Dictionary*)

your one-stop corner grocery store (most will slice and stuff your sandwich for you if you buy the ingredients there). The rare *super-mercato* gives you more efficiency with less color for less cost. At busier supermarkets you'll need to take a number for deli service.

Juice-lovers can get a liter of O.J. for the price of a Coke or coffee. Look for "100% *succo*" (juice) on the label. Hang on to the half-liter mineral-water bottles (sold everywhere for about €1). Buy juice in cheap liter boxes, then drink some and store the extra in your water bottle. (Like locals, I refill my water bottle with tap water—*acqua del rubinetto*.)

Picnics can be an adventure in high cuisine. Be daring. Try the fresh mozzarella, *presto* pesto, shriveled olives, and any UFOs the locals are excited about. Shopkeepers are happy to sell small quantities of produce. They seem to enjoy giving you a taste *(un assaggio)*. It's customary to let the merchant choose the produce for you. Say *"Per oggi"* (pehr OH-jee; "For today") and he or she will grab you something ready to eat, weigh it, and make the sale.

A typical picnic for two might be fresh rolls, 100 grams (*un etto*, about a quarter pound) of cheese, 100 grams of meat, two tomatoes, three carrots, two apples, yogurt, and a liter box of juice. Total cost: about €10.

Traveling as a Temporary Local

We travel all the way to Italy to enjoy differences—to become temporary locals. You'll experience frustrations. Certain truths that we find "God-given" or "self-evident," such as cold beer, ice in drinks, bottomless cups of coffee, hot showers, and bigger being better, are suddenly not so true. One of the benefits of travel is the eye-opening realization that there are logical, civil, and even better alternatives. A willingness to go local ensures that you'll enjoy a full dose of Italian hospitality.

Europeans generally like Americans. But if there is a negative aspect to Italians' image of Americans, it's that we are big, loud, aggressive, impolite, rich, and a bit naive. Think about the rationale behind "crazy" Italian decisions. For instance, many hoteliers turn off the heat in early April and can't turn on air-conditioning until summer. The point is to conserve energy, and it's mandated by the Italian government. You could complain about being cold or hot...or bring a sweater in winter, and in summer, be prepared to sweat a little like everyone else.

While Italians, flabbergasted by our Yankee excesses, say in disbelief, *"Mi sono cadute le braccia!"* ("I throw my arms down!"), they nearly always afford us individual travelers all the warmth that we deserve. Judging from all the happy feedback I receive from travelers who have used this book, it's safe to assume you'll enjoy a great, affordable vacation—with the finesse of an independent, experienced traveler.

Thanks, and *buon viaggio!*

Back Door Travel Philosophy
From *Rick Steves' Europe Through the Back Door*

Travel is intensified living—maximum thrills per minute and one of the last great sources of legal adventure. Travel is freedom. It's recess, and we need it.

Experiencing the real Europe requires catching it by surprise, going casual..."Through the Back Door."

Affording travel is a matter of priorities. (Make do with the old car.) You can travel—simply, safely, and comfortably—anywhere in Europe for $120 a day plus transportation costs (allow more for bigger cities). In many ways, spending more money only builds a thicker wall between you and what you came to see. Europe is a cultural carnival, and time after time, you'll find that its best acts are free and the best seats are the cheap ones.

A tight budget forces you to travel close to the ground, meeting and communicating with the people. Never sacrifice sleep, nutrition, safety, or cleanliness to save money. Simply enjoy the local-style alternatives to expensive hotels and restaurants.

Connecting with people carbonates your experience. Extroverts have more fun. If your trip is low on magic moments, kick yourself and make things happen. If you don't enjoy a place, maybe you don't know enough about it. Seek the truth. Recognize tourist traps. Give a culture the benefit of your open mind. See things as different but not better or worse. Any culture has plenty to share.

Of course, travel, like the world, is a series of hills and valleys. Be fanatically positive and militantly optimistic. If something's not to your liking, change your liking.

Travel can make you a happier American, as well as a citizen of the world. Our earth is home to nearly seven billion equally precious people. It's humbling to travel and find that other people don't have the "American Dream"—they have their own dreams. Europeans like us, but, with all due respect, they wouldn't trade passports.

Thoughtful travel engages us with the world. In tough economic times, it reminds us what is truly important. By broadening perspectives, travel teaches new ways to measure quality of life.

Globetrotting destroys ethnocentricity, helping us understand and appreciate other cultures. Rather than fear the diversity on this planet, celebrate it. Among your most prized souvenirs will be the strands of different cultures you choose to knit into your own character. The world is a cultural yarn shop, and Back Door travelers are weaving the ultimate tapestry. Join in!

VENICE

Venezia

Soak all day in this puddle of elegant decay. Venice is Europe's best-preserved big city. This car-free urban wonderland of a hundred islands—laced together by 400 bridges and 2,000 alleys—survives on the artificial respirator of tourism.

Born in a lagoon 1,500 years ago as a refuge from barbarians, Venice is overloaded with tourists and is slowly sinking (not because of the tourists). In the Middle Ages, the Venetians became Europe's clever middlemen for East-West trade and created a great trading empire. By smuggling in the bones of St. Mark (San Marco) in A.D. 828, Venice gained religious importance as well. With the discovery of America and new trading routes to the Orient, Venetian power ebbed. But as Venice fell, her appetite for decadence grew. Through the 17th and 18th centuries, Venice partied on the wealth accumulated through earlier centuries as a trading power.

Today, Venice is home to just over 60,000 people in its old city, down from about twice that number just three decades ago. While there are about 270,000 people in greater Venice (counting the mainland, not counting tourists), the old town has a small-town feel. Locals seem to know everyone. To see small-town Venice away from the touristic flak, escape the Rialto-San Marco tourist zone and savor the town early and late, without the hordes of vacationers day-tripping in from cruise ships and nearby beach resorts. A 10-minute walk from the madness puts you in an idyllic Venice that few tourists see.

VENICE

Venice Overview

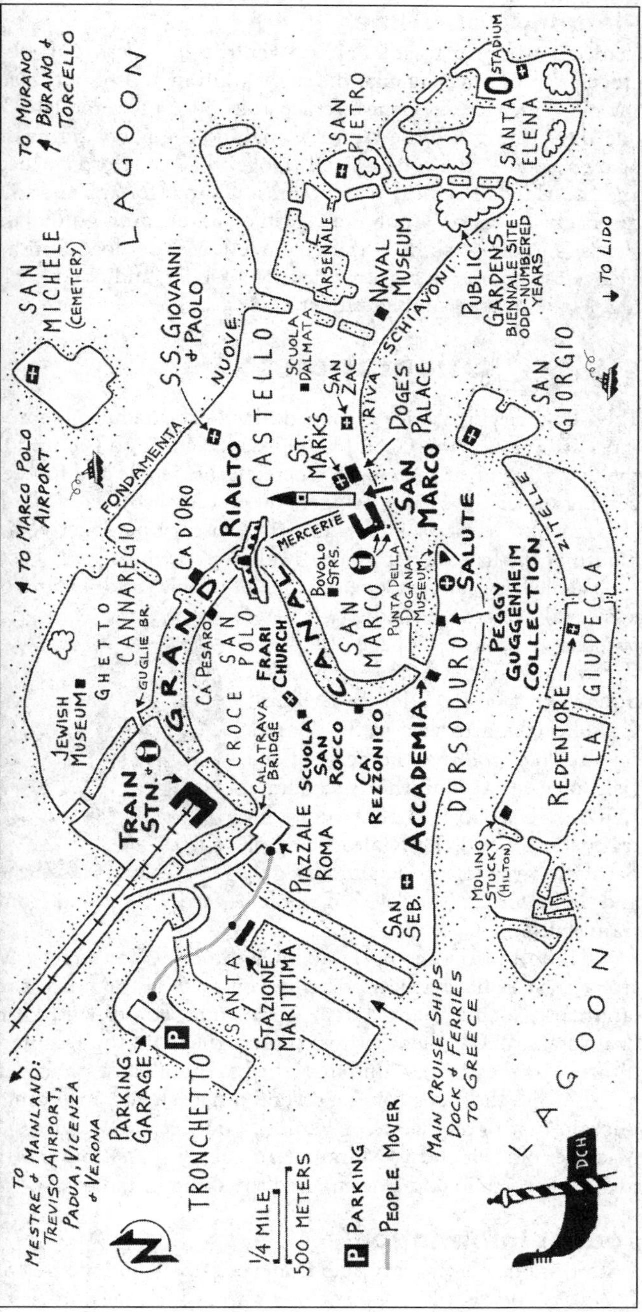

To Murano & Burano & Torcello

LAGOON

SAN MICHELE (CEMETERY)

To Marco Polo Airport

SAN PIETRO

STADIUM

SANTA ELENA

S.S. GIOVANNI & PAOLO

NUOVE

ARSENALE

CASTELLO

NAVAL MUSEUM

SCUOLA DALMATA

SAN ZAC.

RIVA

SCHIAVONI

PUBLIC GARDENS BIENNALE SITE ODD-NUMBERED YEARS

To Lido

FONDAMENTA

CA' D'ORO

RIALTO

ST. MARK'S

MERCERIE

Bovolo STRS.

DOGE'S PALACE

SAN MARCO

SAN GIORGIO

GHETTO

CANNAREGIO

GUGLIE BR.

GRAND

CA' PESARO

SANTA CROCE

SAN POLO

FRARI CHURCH

CALATRAVA BRIDGE

SCUOLA SAN ROCCO

CA' REZZONICO

CANAL

SAN MARCO

Punta Della Dogana

SALUTE

PEGGY GUGGENHEIM COLLECTION

ACCADEMIA

DORSODURO

ZITELLE

REDENTORE

LA GIUDECCA

To Marco Polo Airport

JEWISH MUSEUM

TRAIN STN.

PIAZZALE ROMA

SAN SEB.

MOLINO STUCKY (HILTON)

To Mainland: Treviso Airport, Padua, Vicenza & Verona

Mestre & Mainland:

PARKING GARAGE

TRONCHETTO

SANTA

STAZIONE MARITTIMA

MAIN CRUISE SHIPS DOCK & FERRIES TO GREECE

LAGOON

DCH

1/4 MILE

500 METERS

P PARKING

PEOPLE MOVER

LAGOON

Planning Your Time

Venice is worth at least a day on even the speediest tour. Hyper-efficient train travelers take the night train in and/or out. Sleep in the old center to experience Venice at its best: early and late. For a one-day visit, cruise the Grand Canal, do the major sights on St. Mark's Square (the square itself, Doge's Palace, Correr Museum, and St. Mark's Basilica), see the Frari Church for art, and wander the back streets on a pub crawl. Enjoy an evening gondola ride. Venice's greatest sight is the city itself. While doable in a day, Venice is worth two. It's a medieval cookie jar, and nobody's looking. Make time to simply wander.

Orientation to Venice

The island city of Venice is shaped like a fish. Its major thorough-fares are canals. The Grand Canal winds through the middle of the fish, starting at the mouth where all the people and food enter, passing under the Rialto Bridge, and ending at St. Mark's Square (Piazza San Marco). Park your 21st-century perspective at the mouth of the fish and let Venice swallow you whole.

Venice is a car-free kaleidoscope of people, bridges, and odor-less canals. There are six districts (*sest-ieri*, shown on map on page 41):

San Marco (from St. Mark's Square to the Accademia Bridge), Castello (the area east of St. Mark's Square), Dorsoduro (the belly of the fish, on the far side the Accademia Bridge), Cannaregio (between the train station and the Rialto Bridge), San Polo (west of the Rialto Bridge), and Santa Croce (the "eye" of the fish, across the canal from the train station).

To find your way, navigate by landmarks, not streets. Many street corners have a sign pointing you to *(per)* the nearest major landmark, such as San Marco, Accademia, Rialto, and Ferrovia (train station). Obedient visitors stick to the main thoroughfares as directed by these signs...and miss the charm of back-street Venice.

Beyond the city's core lie several other islands, including San Giorgio (with great views of Venice), Giudecca (more views), San Michele (old cemetery), Murano (famous for glass), Burano (lace-making), Torcello (old church), and the skinny Lido beach.

Tourist Information

With this book, a free city map from your hotel, and the free *Shows & Events* booklet (described below), there's little need to visit a TI in Venice. That's fortunate, because the city's TIs are crowded and clunky. If you need to check or confirm something, TIs are located at the **train station** (daily 8:00-18:30), on **St. Mark's Square** (daily 9:00-15:30, in far-left corner with your back to the basilica), nearby at the **San Marco-Vallaresso vaporetto stop** (daily 11:00-18:00), and at the **airport** (daily 9:00-21:00). You can save time by phoning the TI at 041-529-8711 or visiting www.turismovenezia.it.

The TI publishes a useful, free booklet called *Shows & Events,* available at hotels and on the TI website (click on "Venezia"). It lists upcoming events and nightlife, museum hours, and emergency telephone numbers, and includes a vaporetto route map.

For a creative travel guide written by young Venetians, consider *My Local Guide Venice,* for its neighborhood histories, self-guided walking tours, and recommendations on sights and activities (sold at TIs for €13).

Maps: Of all places, you need a good map in Venice. Hotels give away freebies (which are no better than the small color one at the front of this book). The TI sells a decent €2.50 map and mini-guide—but you can find a wider range at bookshops, newsstands, and postcard stands. The cheap maps are pretty bad, but if you spend €5, you'll get a map that shows you everything. Investing in a good map can be the best €5 you'll spend in Venice. Map lovers should look for the book *Calli, Campielli e Canali,* sold at bookstores for €22.50, with 1:2000 maps of the whole city.

Arrival in Venice

A two-mile-long causeway (with highway and train lines) connects Venice to the mainland. Mestre, the sprawling mainland section of Venice, has fewer crowds, cheaper hotels, and plenty of inexpensive parking lots, but zero charm. Don't stop in Mestre unless you're parking your car or transferring trains.

By Train

All trains to "Venice" stop at Venezia Mestre (on the mainland). Most continue on to Santa Lucia Station on the island of Venice itself. If your train only stops at Mestre, worry not. Shuttle trains regularly connect Mestre with Venice's Santa Lucia Station (6/hour, 10 minutes, €1, buy tickets with coins from machines marked *Rete Regionale* and validate before boarding).

Venice's **Santa Lucia train station** (Ferrovia) plops you right into the old town on the Grand Canal, an easy vaporetto ride or fascinating 40-minute walk to St. Mark's Square. If the station's TI is crowded when you arrive, consider visiting one of the two TIs at St. Mark's Square instead. It's not worth a long wait for a minimal TI map (buy a good one from a newsstand or pick up a free one at your hotel). Confirm your departure plan

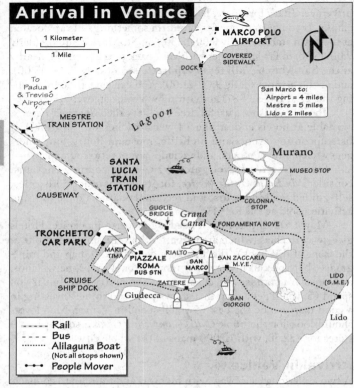

Arrival in Venice

MARCO POLO AIRPORT

1 Kilometer

1 Mile

To Padua & Treviso Airport

COVERED SIDEWALK

DOCK

San Marco to:
Airport = 4 miles
Mestre = 5 miles
Lido = 2 miles

MESTRE TRAIN STATION

Lagoon

Murano

SANTA LUCIA TRAIN STATION

MUSEO STOP

CAUSEWAY

COLONNA STOP

GUGLIE BRIDGE   *Grand Canal*

FONDAMENTA NOVE

TRONCHETTO CAR PARK

MARIT-TIMA   RIALTO

PIAZZALE ROMA BUS STN   SAN MARCO   SAN ZACCARIA M.V.E.

LIDO (S.M.E.)

CRUISE SHIP DOCK   ZATTERE

Giudecca   SAN GIORGIO   SAN GIORGIO

Lido

------ Rail
- - - - Bus
········· Alilaguna Boat
           (Not all stops shown)
•—•—• People Mover

(use the machines or just study the *partenze*/departures posters on walls).

Consider storing unnecessary heavy bags, although lines for **baggage check** may be very long (at track 1, €4/5 hours, €11/24 hours, daily 6:00-23:50, no lockers, 44-pound weight limit on bags). **WCs** (€0.80) are at track 1 and in the back of the big bar/cafeteria area inside the station.

Minimize your time in the station—the banks of user-friendly automated ticket machines (marked *Biglietto Veloce/Fast Ticket*) are handy but cover Italian destinations only. They take euros and credit cards, display schedules, issue tickets, and even make reservations for railpass-holders. The gray-and-blue *Rete Regionale* machines are another option for tickets to nearby destinations such as Padua (coins only, push button for English). If you need international tickets or live help, the ticket windows are open from 6:00 to 20:30. Or you could take care of these tasks for a fee at downtown travel agencies (see page 50).

To get from the train station to downtown Venice, walk

straight out of the station to the canal. You'll see vaporetto docks and ticket booths on both sides. For vaporetto #2 (fast boat down Grand Canal), go left. For vaporetto #1 (slow boat down Grand Canal), go right. See "Getting Around Venice—By Vaporetto," on page 54, for details on vaporetto tickets and passes.

By Bus

If you arrive in Venice at the Piazzale Roma bus station, find the vaporetto docks (by the six-story white building) and take #1 or the faster #2 down the Grand Canal to reach the Rialto, Accademia, or San Marco (St. Mark's Square) stops. If your hotel is near the train station, you can walk there from Piazzale Roma across the Calatrava Bridge.

Arriving by bus at Piazzale Roma is easy, but it can be difficult to figure out how to leave Venice from here. The square is a confusing jumble of different operators, platforms, and crosswalks over busy lanes of traffic. The ticket windows for ACTV (local public buses, including #5 to Marco Polo Airport) are by the vaporetto stop. The ATVO ticket office is on the right side of the square as you face away from the canal (for express buses to Marco Polo and Treviso Airports; office open daily 7:15-19:30). The ATVO office also sells tickets for the SITA bus to Padua, though it's more convenient to go to Padua by train. At odd hours, you may be able to buy tickets from bus drivers.

At Piazzale Roma, you'll also see the parking garages and the People Mover monorail to the parking-lot island of Tronchetto. A baggage-storage office is next to the monorail at #497m (€5/24 hours, daily 6:00-21:00).

By Car

The freeway dead-ends after crossing the causeway to Venice. The best balance of cost and convenience is the parking-lot island of **Tronchetto,** well-signed as you approach Venice. The rates for the multi-story Tronchetto parking garage are affordable (€3-4/hour, €21/24 hours, discounts for longer stays, tel. 041-520-7555, www .veniceparking.it). From the garage, head directly to the yellow-and-white vaporetto docks and take line #2, the express boat which stops at the Rialto, San Marco, Zattere, and other main points in the center. I like the approach from Tronchetto into town by sea. Don't let water taxi boatmen con you out of the relatively inexpensive €6.50 vaporetto ride. Also avoid the travel agencies masquerading as TIs; deal only with the ticket booth at the vaporetto dock or the HelloVenezia public transport office. Consider whether a local transport pass will pay off (see page 55); you can buy it here.

If you're parking at Tronchetto and staying near the train station, you can take the €1 People Mover monorail instead of paying

€6.50 for the two-stop vaporetto ride. The monorail brings you from Tronchetto to the bus station at Piazzale Roma, then it's a five-minute walk across the Calatrava Bridge to the train station (buy monorail tickets with coins from machine, 3-minute trip, runs Mon-Sat 7:00-23:00, Sun 8:30-21:00).

You can also park at **Piazzale Roma,** the busy square where the expressway dead-ends and which doubles as Venice's bus station. The big white building on your right is a 2,200-space public parking garage, the Autorimessa Communale (€25/24 hours, tel. 041-272-7211, www.asmvenezia.it) and in a back corner of the square is the private San Marco garage (€30/24 hours, tel. 041-523-2213, www.garagesanmarco.it). At either of these, you'll have to give up your keys. You can reserve ahead at both garages and at Tronchetto, but it's rarely necessary.

Parking in the garage across from the train station in **Mestre** (on the mainland) only makes sense if you have light bags and are staying within walking distance of the Santa Lucia train station (€8/day Mon-Fri, €12-16/day Sat-Sun; www.sabait.it).

Ask your hotel for parking advice—some can get you a small discount.

By Plane or Cruise Ship

For information on Venice's airport and cruise ship terminal, see the end of this chapter.

Helpful Hints

Theft Alert: The dark, late-night streets of Venice are safe. Even so, pickpockets (often elegantly dressed) work the crowded main streets, docks, and *vaporetti* (wear your money belt, zip up your valuables, and watch your purse or day bag). Your biggest risk of pickpockets is inside St. Mark's Basilica.

A handy Polizia station is on the right side of St. Mark's Square (near Caffè Florian). To call the police, dial 113. The Venice TI handles complaints—which must be submitted in writing—about local crooks, including gondola, restaurant, or hotel rip-offs (fax 041-523-0399, complaint.apt@turismovenezia.it).

It's illegal for street vendors to sell knock-off handbags and it's also illegal for you to buy them; both you and the vendor can get big fines.

Be Prepared to Splurge: Venice is expensive for residents as well as tourists, as everything must be shipped in and hand-trucked

Daily Reminder

Sunday: While anyone is welcome to worship, sightseers are asked to avoid Mass—which means that today, many churches are open to visitors only in the afternoon, including St. Mark's Basilica (14:00-17:00, until 16:00 Nov-March), Frari Church (13:00-18:00), and the Church of San Zaccaria (16:00-18:00). The Church of San Polo is closed all day. Today, the Rialto open-air market consists mainly of souvenir stalls (fish and produce sections closed). It's a bad day for a pub crawl, as most pubs are closed.

Monday: All sights are open except the Rialto produce market, Ca' Pesaro, the Lace Museum (on the island of Burano), and Torcello Museum (on the island of Torcello). The Accademia and Ca' d'Oro close at 14:00. Don't side-trip to Verona today, as most sights there are closed in the morning, if not all day.

Tuesday: All sights are open except the Peggy Guggenheim Collection, Ca' Rezzonico (Museum of 18th-Century Venice), and Punta della Dogana.

Wednesday/Thursday/Friday: All sights are open.

Saturday: All sights are open except the Jewish Museum.

Notes: The Accademia is open earlier (daily at 8:15) and closes later (19:15 Tue-Sun) than most sights in Venice. Some sights close earlier off-season (such as the Correr Museum, Campanile bell tower, St. Mark's Basilica, and the Church of San Giorgio Maggiore). Modest dress is recommended at churches and required at St. Mark's Basilica—no bare shoulders, shorts, or short skirts.

Crowd Control: The city is inundated with cruise-ship crowds and tours from mainland hotels daily from 10:00 to about 17:00. Crowds can be a serious problem at **St. Mark's Basilica.** Try going early or late, or even better, you can bypass the line if you have a bag to check (see page 78).

At the **Doge's Palace,** avoid the long line by purchasing your ticket at the less-crowded Correr Museum. You can also visit late in the day, buy your ticket online, or book a tour.

For the **Campanile,** ascend late (it's open until 21:00 July-Sept), or skip it entirely if you're going to the similar San Giorgio Maggiore bell tower.

For the **Accademia,** go early or late—or you can reserve a ticket at least a day in advance by phone or online.

The sights that have crowd problems get even more crowded when it rains.

to its destination. Perhaps the best way to enjoy Venice is just to succumb to its charms and blow a little money.

Medical Help: Venice's Santi Giovanni e Paolo hospital (tel. 118) is a 10-minute walk from both the Rialto and San Marco neighborhoods, located on Fondamenta dei Mendicanti toward Fondamente Nove. You can take vaporetto #41 from San Zaccaria-Jolanda, or #52 from the train station or Piazzale Roma, to the Ospedale stop.

Take Breaks: Venice's endless pavement, crowds, and tight spaces are hard on tourists, especially in hot weather. Schedule breaks in your sightseeing. Grab a cool place to sit down, relax, and recoup—meditate on a pew in an uncrowded church, or stop in a café.

Etiquette: Walk on the right and don't loiter on bridges. On St. Mark's Square, a "decorum patrol" admonishes snackers and sunbathers. Picnicking is forbidden (keep a low profile). The only place for a legal picnic is in Giardinetti Reali, the small park along the waterfront west of the Piazzetta near St. Mark's Square.

Dress Modestly: Men should keep their shirts on. When visiting St. Mark's Basilica or other major churches, men, women, and even children must cover their shoulders and knees (or risk being turned away). Remove hats when entering a church.

Public Toilets: Handy public WCs (€1.50) are near major landmarks, including: St. Mark's Square (one is behind the Correr Museum, to the left of the post office; another is at the waterfront park, Giardinetti Reali), Rialto, and at the Accademia Bridge. Use free toilets whenever you can—in a museum you're visiting or a café you're eating in. Like Mom always said, "Just try."

Best Views: While the best views of Venice may be from water level, several upper-altitude viewing spots are also worth the ascent: On St. Mark's Square, try the soaring Campanile or St. Mark's Basilica (specifically the balcony of the San Marco Museum, requires admission). The Rialto and Accademia bridges provide free, expansive views of the Grand Canal, along with a cooling breeze. Or get off the main island for a view of the Venetian skyline: Ascend the Church of San Giorgio Maggiore's bell tower, or venture to La Giudecca island to visit the swanky bar of the Molino Stucky Hilton Hotel (free shuttle boat from San Zaccaria-M.V.E. vaporetto stop).

Pigeon Poop: If your head is bombed by a pigeon, resist the initial response to wipe it off immediately—it'll just smear into your hair. Wait until it dries, and it should flake off cleanly. But if the poop splatters on your clothes, wipe it off immediately to avoid a stain.

Water: I carry a water bottle to refill at public fountains. Venetians pride themselves on having pure, safe, and tasty tap water piped in from the foothills of the Alps. You can actually see the mountains from Venice's bell towers on crisp, clear winter days.

Services

Internet Access: Almost all hotels have Wi-Fi, many have a computer that guests can use, and most provide these services for free. If Internet access is important to you, choose a hotel that doesn't charge for it. Otherwise, look for one of the handy, if pricey, little Internet places scattered around town, usually on back streets and marked with an @ sign. The going rate is €5/ hour—more expensive than in other Italian cities. Ask your hotelier for the nearest place.

Post Office: The main post office is on Marzaria San Salvador, a few blocks towards St. Mark's Square from the Rialto, just beyond the Bata shoe store at #5016 (Mon-Fri 8:30-18:30, Sat 8:30-13:00, closed Sun). Branch offices (open shorter hours) are at Piazzale Roma, behind the Correr Museum, and elsewhere. Use post offices only as a last resort, as simple transactions can take 45 minutes if you get in the wrong line. You can buy stamps from tobacco shops and mail postcards at any of the red postboxes around town.

Bookstores: In keeping with its literary heritage, Venice has classy and inviting bookstores. The small **Libreria Studium,** a block behind St. Mark's Basilica, has a carefully chosen selection of new English books, including my guidebooks (Mon-Sat 9:00-19:30, Sun 9:30-13:30 & 14:00-18:00, on Calle de la Canonica at #337, tel. 041-522-2382). Used-bookstore lovers shouldn't miss the funky **Acqua Alta** ("high water") bookstore, whose

quirky owner Luigi has prepared for the next flood by displaying his wares in a selection of vessels, including bathtubs and a gondola (daily 9:00-21:00, large and classically disorganized selection includes prints of Venice, just beyond Campo Santa Maria Formosa on Calle Longa Santa Maria Formosa at #5176, tel. 041-296-0841, mobile 340-680-0704). For a solid selection of used books in English, visit **Marco Polo,** on Calle del Teatro Malibran at #5886a, close to the St. Mark's side of the Rialto Bridge on the way to Corte del Milion (Mon-Sat 10:00-19:00, closed Sun, mobile 348-569-1125, www.booksmarcopolo.com).

Laundry: You'll find coin-operated launderettes near the train station and off Campo Santa Maria Formosa. I've listed details for a self-service *lavanderia* and a competitively-priced full-service laundry near St. Mark's Square (see page 106), and for a self-serve laundry near the train station (page 120). Or ask your hotelier for the nearest launderette.

Travel Agencies: If you need to get train tickets, make seat reservations, or arrange a *cuccetta* (koo-CHET-tah—a berth on a night train), save a time-consuming trip to Venice's crowded train station by using a downtown travel agency. Most trains between Venice, Florence, and Rome require reservations, even for railpass-holders. A travel agency can also give advice on cheap flights (book at least a week in advance for the best fares).

Near St. Mark's Square, **Oltrex Change and Travel** sells train and plane tickets and books train reservations for a €4 fee (tickets sold daily May-Oct 9:00-18:00, Nov-April 9:00-16:30; on Riva degli Schiavoni, one bridge past the Bridge of Sighs, at #4192; tel. 041-524-2828, Luca and Beatrice).

Near Rialto, **Kele & Teo Travel** sells train tickets for a €4 per-person service charge (Mon-Fri 9:00-18:00, Sat 9:00-12:00, closed Sun; leaving the Rialto Bridge heading for St. Mark's, it's half a block away, tucked down a side street on the right at #5097; tel. 041-520-8722).

English Church Services: The **San Zulian Church**—the only church in Venice that you can actually walk around—offers a Mass in English (generally May-Sept Mon-Fri at 9:30 and Sun at 11:30, Sun only Oct-April, 2 blocks toward Rialto off St. Mark's Square, tel. 041-523-5383). **St. George's Anglican Church** welcomes all Christians to its English-language Eucharist (Sun at 10:30, located on Campo San Zio in Dorsoduro, midway between Accademia and Peggy Guggenheim Collection, www.stgeorgesvenice.com).

Haircuts: I've been getting my hair cut at **Coiffeur Benito** for nearly two decades. Benito has been keeping men and women trim for 28 years. He's an artist—actually a "hair sculptor"—and a cut here is a fun diversion from the tourist grind (about €20 for women or men, Tue-Fri 8:30-13:00 & 15:30-19:30, Sat 8:30-13:00 only, closed Sun-Mon; between St. Mark's Square and

Rialto, on Calle San Zulian Già del Strazzariol, by back corner of San Zulian Church at #592a; tel. 041-528-6221).

Getting Around Venice

On Foot

The city's "streets" are narrow pedestrian walkways connecting its docks, squares, bridges, and courtyards. To navigate, look for yellow signs on street corners pointing you to *(per)* the nearest major landmark. The first landmarks you'll get to know are San Marco (St. Mark's Square), Rialto (the bridge), Accademia (another bridge), Ferrovia (the train station), and Piazzale Roma (the bus station). Determine whether your destination is in the direction of a major signposted landmark, then follow the signs through the maze.

Dare to turn off the posted routes and make your own discoveries. While 80 percent of Venice is, in fact, not touristy, 80 percent of the tourists never notice. Escape the crowds and explore on foot. Walk and walk to the far reaches of the town. Don't worry about getting lost—in fact, get as lost as possible. Keep reminding yourself, "I'm on an island, and I can't get off." When it comes time to find your way, just follow the arrows on building corners or simply ask a local, *"Dov'è San Marco?"* ("Where is St. Mark's?") People in the tourist business (that's most Venetians) speak some English. If they don't, listen politely, watch where their hands point, say *"Grazie,"* and head off in that direction. If you're lost, refer to your map, or pop into a hotel and ask for their business card—it probably comes with a map and a prominent "You are here."

If you need to find a specific address, it helps to know its district, street, house number, street, and nearby landmarks. Every building in Venice has a house number, which is usually stenciled in red letters surrounded by a black oval above the doorway. The numbers relate to the district (each with about 6,000 address numbers), not the street. For example, say you wanted to find the recommended Acqua Alta bookstore at Castello 5176 (that is, in the Castello district, at house number 5176). It's on a street called Calle Longa Santa Maria Formosa, near the square called Campo Santa Maria Formosa, which in turn is near two major landmarks: the Rialto Bridge and St. Mark's Square. Once you've found Campo Santa Maria Formosa, you can look for a painted sign on one corner (like the one in this photo) which marks where the street begins. If you can find the Rialto Bridge and then the square—you can find the bookstore.

CALLE DE LA VERONA

Some helpful street lingo: *Campo* means square, *campiello* is a small square, *calle* is a street, *fondamenta* is the embankment along

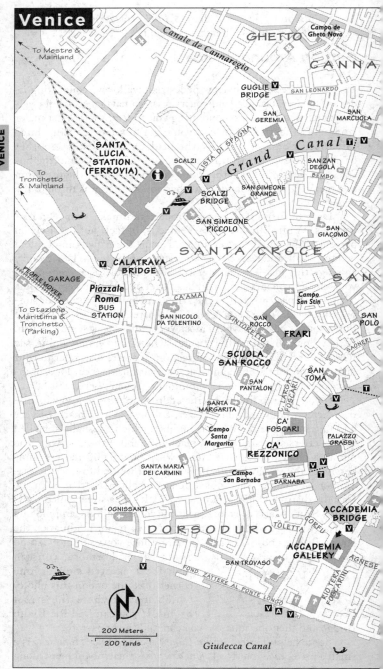

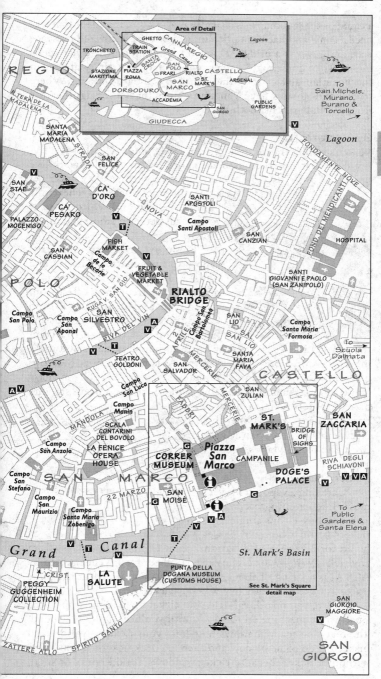

VENICE

a canal or the lagoon, *rio* is a small canal, *rio terà* is a street that was once a canal and has been filled in, *sotoportego* is a covered passageway, and *ponte* is a bridge. Don't get hung up on the exact spelling of street and square names, which may sometimes appear in the Venetian dialect and other times in standard Italian. (Where streets and squares have Venetian names that differ significantly from the Italian, I list both.)

By Vaporetto

Venice's public transit system, run by a company called ACTV, is a fleet of motorized bus-boats called *vaporetti*. They work like

city buses except that they never get a flat, the stops are docks (cheerfully painted yellow and white), and if you get off between stops, you might drown.

For most travelers, only two vaporetto lines matter: Line #1 and line #2. These lines leave every 10 minutes (less frequently off-season) and go up and down the Grand Canal, between the "mouth of the fish" at one end and San Marco at the other. Line #1 is the slow boat, taking 45 minutes and making every stop along the way. Line #2 is the fast boat that zips down the Grand Canal in 25 minutes, stopping only at Tronchetto (parking lot), Piazzale Roma (bus station), Ferrovia (train station), San Marcuola, Rialto Bridge, San Tomà (Frari Church), Accademia Bridge, San Marco (west end of St. Mark's Square), and San Zaccaria (east end of St. Mark's Square).

Catching a vaporetto is very much like catching a city bus. You can buy either single-ride tickets (valid 1 hour) or passes (valid for a variety of durations, from 12 hours to 7 days) from any ticket window or HelloVenezia office. HelloVenezia, run by ACTV, is a string of shops selling tickets and passes at the same prices as ticket windows (www.hellovenezia.com).

Before you board, validate your ticket by holding it up to the small white machine on the dock until you hear a pinging sound. The machine readout shows how long your ticket is valid—and inspectors do come by now and then to check tickets. If you board without a ticket (because ticket windows at odd hours or small stops may be closed), seek out the conductor immediately to buy a single ticket on board (or risk a €50 fine). Large stops—such as San Marco, San Zaccaria, and Piazzale Roma—have multiple docks, and each dock has its own name, such as San Marco-Vallaresso, San Zaccaria-Jolanda, and Piazzale Roma-Parisi. Helpful electronic boards at larger stops display which boats are coming next and when, and give information for all docks at that stop.

At smaller stops, check the charts and signs to figure out which dock your boat will use. Signs on each dock show the vaporetto lines that stop there and the direction they are headed: Along the Grand Canal, a #1 or #2 boat might be headed toward St. Mark's Square (signposted *San Marco*), or back toward the mainland (signposted *Ferrovia, Piazzale Roma,* or *Tronchetto*). Sorting out the different directions of travel can be confusing, especially as boats on some circular routes travel in one direction (true for lines #51 and #52, plus the non-Murano sections of lines #41 and #42).

To clear up any confusion, ask a ticket-seller or conductor for help (sometimes they're stationed on the dock to help confused tourists), or look at the most current ACTV timetable (in English and Italian, free at ticket booths but often unavailable—can be downloaded from the ACTV website, tel. 041-2424, www.actv.it).

These are your ticket and pass options:

Individual Vaporetto Tickets: A single ticket costs a whopping €6.50. (Don't worry—cheaper passes are described below.) Tickets are good for one hour in one direction; you can hop on and off at stops and change boats during that time. Technically, you're not allowed a round-trip (though in practice, a round-trip is allowed if you can complete it within a one-hour span). Tickets are electronic and refillable. The fare is reduced to €3 for a few one-stop runs that are hard to do by foot, including the route from San Marco to La Salute, from Fondamente Nove to Murano-Colonna, and from San Zaccaria-M.V.E. to San Giorgio Maggiore.

Vaporetto Passes: You can buy a pass for unlimited use of *vaporetti* and ACTV buses: €16/12 hours, €18/24 hours, €23/36 hours, €28/48 hours, €33/72 hours, €50/7-day pass; pass must be validated once, before use). Because single tickets cost a hefty €6.50 a pop, these passes can pay for themselves in a hurry. Think through your Venice itinerary before you step up to the ticket booth to pay for your first vaporetto trip. The 48-hour pass pays for itself with five rides (e.g., to your hotel, on a Grand Canal joyride, into the lagoon and back, to the train station). And it's fun to be able to hop on and off spontaneously, and avoid long ticket lines. On the other hand, many tourists just walk and rarely use a boat.

Anyone under 30 years old can get a 72-hour pass for €18 if they also buy a **Rolling Venice** discount card for €4 (available from TIs, larger ticket windows, and HelloVenezia shops). Those

Handy *Vaporetti* from San Zaccaria, near St. Mark's Square

Several *vaporetti* leave from the San Zaccaria docks, located 150 yards east of St. Mark's Square. There are four separate San Zaccaria docks spaced about 70 yards apart: Danieli, Jolanda, M.V.E., and Pietà. Although I list which specific dock these lines leave from, they often change from season to season—confirm before boarding.

- Line #1 goes up the Grand Canal, making all the stops, including San Marco-Vallaresso, Rialto, Ferrovia (train station), and Piazzale Roma (but it does not go as far as Tronchetto). In the other direction, it goes to the Lido. Line #1 departs from the San Zaccaria stop (usually from the Danieli dock).
- Line #2 zips over to San Giorgio Maggiore, the island church across from St. Mark's Square (5 minutes, €3 ride). From there, it continues on to the parking lot at Tronchetto (departs from the San Zaccaria stop, generally from the M.V.E. dock).
- Line #41 goes to San Michele and Murano in 45 minutes (departs from San Zaccaria stop, usually from the Jolanda dock).
- The "LN" heads to Burano (70 minutes, from San Zaccaria stop, usually from the Pietà dock).
- The Molino Stucky shuttle boat takes even non-guests to the Hilton Hotel, with its popular view bar (free, 20-minute ride, leaves at 0:20 past the hour from near the San Zaccaria-M.V.E. dock).
- Lines #51 and #52 are the *circulare* (cheer-koo-LAH-ray), making a loop around the perimeter of the island, with a stop at the Lido—perfect if you just like riding boats. Line

settling in for a longer stay can ride like a local by buying the **CartaVenezia** ID card (€40/year, which lets you ride for about €1 per trip). See www.actv.it for details.

Passes are also valid on ACTV's mainland buses, including bus #5 to the airport (but not the airport buses run by ATVO, a separate company).

Vaporetto Tips: For fun, take my Grand Canal Cruise. Boats can be literally packed during the tourist rush hour. Morning rush hour (8:00-10:00) is headed in the direction of St. Mark's Square, as tourists and commuters arrive. Afternoon rush hour (about 17:00) is when they're headed in the other direction for the train station. Riding at night, with nearly empty boats and chandelier-lit palace interiors viewable from the Grand Canal, is an entirely different experience.

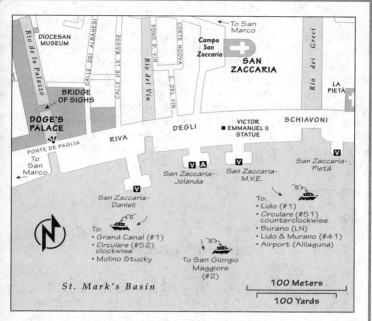

#51 goes counterclockwise (departs from San Zaccaria stop, generally from the Danieli dock), and #52 goes clockwise (also departs from San Zaccaria, but usually from the Jolanda dock).
- The Alilaguna airport shuttle to and from the airport stops at the San Zaccaria stop (generally at the Jolanda dock).

By Traghetto

Only four bridges cross the Grand Canal, but *traghetti* (gondola-like row-boats) shuttle locals and in-the-know tourists across the Grand Canal at eight handy locations (marked on the color map of Venice at the front of this book). Venetians stand while riding, but you shouldn't (€0.50, don't tip—

literally). Note that some *traghetti* stop running as early as 13:00 and all stop by 18:00.

By Water Taxi

Venetian taxis, like speedboat limos, hang out at busy points along the Grand Canal. Prices are regulated and listed in the TI's *Shows*

& Events brochure: €13 for the first seven minutes plus €1.80 per minute thereafter; €5 per person for more than two passengers; and €8 between 22:00 and 6:00. Large bags cost €3 apiece. To the airport, a flat fee of about €100 for up to five people is common (for more information see "Venice Connections," at the end of this chapter). Despite regulation, prices can be soft; negotiate and settle on the price or rate before stepping in. For travelers with lots of luggage or small groups who can split the cost, taxi boat rides can be a worthwhile and time-saving convenience—and skipping across the lagoon in a classic wooden motorboat is a cool indulgence. For a little more than €100 an hour, you can have a private, unguided taxi-boat tour.

By Gondola

If you're interested in hiring a gondolier for your own private cruise, see page 97.

Tours in Venice

Tours of Venice on foot and afloat abound. If you'd rather sight-see on your own, you can download my series of free audio tours that illuminate St. Mark's Square, St. Mark's Basilica, the Frari Church, and sights along the Grand Canal, covered the way my readers appreciate (see sidebar on page 19 for details).

Avventure Bellissime Venice Tours—This company offers several two-hour walks, including a basic St. Mark's Square introduction called the "Original Venice Walking Tour" (€21.50, includes church entry, most days at 11:00, Sun at 14:00; 45 minutes on the square, 15 minutes in the church, one hour along back streets). Other walks include Cannaregio/Jewish Ghetto, "Hidden Venice," ghost stories and legends, and a Doge's Palace tour (€20, group size 8-22, English-

language only, tel. 041-970-499, www.tours-italy.com, info@tours-italy.com, Monica or Jonathan). Their 70-minute Grand Canal boat tour is timed for good late-afternoon light (€40, daily at 16:30, 8 people maximum). They also offer small-group excursions to the Dolomites and Veneto hill towns. For a 10 percent discount on certain tours, say "Rick sent me."

Classic Venice Bars Tour—Debonair guide Alessandro Schezzini is a connoisseur of Venetian *bacari*—classic old bars serving wine and traditional *cicchetti* snacks. He organizes two-hour Venetian pub tours (€30, any night on request at 18:00, depart from the top of the Rialto Bridge, better to book by email—alessandro @schezzini.it—than by phone, mobile 335-530-9024, www .schezzini.it). Alessandro's tours include sampling *cicchetti* with wines at three different *bacari*, plus he'll answer all of your questions about Venice. (If you think of this tour as a light dinner with a local friend, you can consider it part of your eating budget.)

Artviva: The Original and Best Walking Tours—This company offers a number of group and private tours, including a Venice in One Glorious Day Special and four themed tours (Grand Canal, Venice Walk, Doge's Palace, Gondola Tour). The 1.25-hour Gondola Tour (€60) includes a 35-minute gondola ride, followed by a 40-minute walk culminating at St. Mark's Square, while the two-hour "Learn to Be a Gondolier" tour teaches the ancient craft of rowing Venetian-style (€80, 4 people maximum). See the tour details and Rick Steves readers' discounts on their website (book in advance, tours run March-Nov, tel. 055-264-5033, www.italy .artviva.com, staff@artviva.com).

Venicescapes—Michael Broderick's private theme tours of Venice are intellectually demanding and beyond the attention span of most mortal tourists. But those with a keen interest and a desire to gain a solid understanding of Venice find him passionate and engaging. Rather than a "sightseeing tour," your time with Michael is more like a rolling, graduate-level lecture. See his website for descriptions of his various itineraries (book well in advance, tours last 4-6 hours: $250-290 for 2 people, $60/person after that, pay in dollars or the current euro equivalent, price includes maps and printed info but not admissions or transportation, tel. 041-520-6361, www.venicescapes.org, info@venicescapes.org).

Local Guides—Plenty of licensed, trained guides are available. If you organize a small group from your hotel at breakfast to split the cost (figure on roughly €70/hour with a 2-hour minimum), the fee becomes more reasonable. The following companies and guides give tours to individuals, families, and small groups.

Elisabetta Morelli guides many of my tour groups around Venice (€65/hour with this book in 2012, 2-hour minimum, tel. 041-526-7816, mobile 328-753-5220, www.elisabettamorelli.it, betta morelli@inwind.it).

Walks Inside Venice is a group of three women enthusiastic about teaching (€70/hour per group with this book, 3-hour minimum; Roberta: mobile 347-253-0560; Cristina: mobile 348-341-5421; Sara: mobile 335-522-9714; www.walksinsidevenice.com, info@walksinsidevenice.com). They also do regularly scheduled small-group walking tours (see details on their site).

Venice with a Guide is a co-op of 10 equally good guides (www.venicewithaguide.com).

Alessandro Schezzini, mentioned earlier for his Classic

Is Venice Sinking?

Venice has battled rising water levels since the fifth century. But today, the water seems to be winning. Several factors, both natural and man-made, cause Venice to flood about 100 times a year—usually from October until late winter—a phenomenon called the *acqua alta*.

Simply put, Venice is sinking and the water is rising. Venice sits atop sediments deposited at the ancient mouth of the Po River, which are still compacting and settling. Early industrial projects, such as offshore piers and the railroad bridge to the mainland, affected the sea floor and tidal cycles in ways that made the city more vulnerable to flooding. Twentieth-century industry worsened things by pumping out massive amounts of groundwater from the aquifer beneath the lagoon for nearly 50 years, before the government stopped the practice in the 1970s. In the last century, Venice has sunk by about nine inches.

Meanwhile, the waters around Venice are rising, a phenomenon that's especially apparent in winter. The highest so far was in November 1966, when a huge storm (the same one that famously flooded Florence) raised Venice's water level to more than six feet above the norm. The notorious *acqua alta* happens when an unusually high tide combines with strong sirocco winds and a storm. Although tides are miniscule in the Mediterranean, the narrow, shallow Adriatic Sea has about a three-foot tidal range. When a storm—an area of low pressure—travels over a body of water, it pulls the surface of the water up into a dome. As strong sirocco winds from Africa blow storms north up the Adriatic, they push this high water ahead of the front, causing a surging storm tide. Add to that the world-wide sea-level rise that's resulted from recent climate change (melting ice caps, thermal expansion of the water, more frequent and more powerful storms) and it makes a high sea that much higher.

If the *acqua alta* appears during your visit, you'll see the first

Venice Bars Tour, isn't a licensed Italian guide and therefore can't take you into sights. But his relaxed, two-hour, back-streets "Rick Steves" tour does a great job of getting you beyond the clichés and into offbeat Venice (€15/person, see page 59 for contact info).

Tour Leader Venice, a.k.a. **Treviso Car Service,** offers small-group tours beyond Venice to 16th-century villas, wine-and-cheese tastings, and the Dolomites. Within Venice, their guided excursions include visits to the Rialto produce market, the lagoon, artisan shops, and a one-hour gondola tour (also provides airport puddles farthest from the sea—not near overflowing canals but in the center of paved squares, pooling around the limestone grates at the square's lowest point. These grates cover cisterns that long held Venice's only source of drinking water. That's right: Surrounded by the lagoon and beset by constant flooding, this city had no natural source of fresh water. For centuries, residents

carried water from the mainland with much effort and risk. In the ninth century, they devised a way to collect rainwater by using paved, cleverly sloped squares as catchment systems, with limestone filters covering underground clay tubs. Venice's population grew markedly once citizens were able to access fresh water by simply dropping buckets down into these "wells."

Several thousand cisterns provided the city with drinking water up until 1886, when an aqueduct was built (paralleling the railroad bridge) to bring in water from nearby mountains. Now the wells are capped, the clay tubs are rotted out, and rain drains from squares into the lagoon—or up from it, as the case may be.

So what is Venice doing about the flooding? Since the 1966 flood, officials knew something had to be done, but it took about four decades to come up with a solution that some are still unhappy about. In 2003, a consortium of engineering firms began construction on the MOSE Project, which is expected to be operational by 2014. Named for the acronym of its Italian name, *Modulo Sperimentale Elettromeccanico*, it's also a nod to Moses and his (albeit temporary) mastery over the sea.

Underwater "mobile" gates are being built on the floor of the sea that will lie flat at the entrances of the three inlets that lead into Venice's lagoon. When the seawater rises above a certain level, air will be pumped into the gates, causing them to rise, and shutting out the Adriatic.

Will it work? Time...and tides...will tell.

transfers—see page 140, mobile 348-900-0700 or 333-411-2840; in Venice: www.tourleadervenice.com, info@tourleadervenice.com; beyond Venice: www.trevisocarservice.com, tvcarservice@gmail.com; Igor, Andrea, and Marta).

Weekend Tour Packages for Students in Venice—Andy Steves (my son) runs Weekend Student Adventures, offering experiential three-day weekend tours for €250, designed for American students studying abroad (www.wsaeurope.com for details on tours of Venice and other great cities).

VENICE

Self-Guided Cruise

▲▲▲Welcome to Venice's Grand Canal Cruise

Take a joyride and introduce yourself to Venice by boat. Cruise the Canal Grande all the way to San Marco, starting at the train station (Ferrovia) or the bus station (Piazzale Roma).

If it's your first trip down the Grand Canal, you might want to stow this book and just take it all in—Venice is a barrage on the senses that hardly needs narration. But these notes give the cruise a little meaning and help orient you to this great city.

This tour is designed to be done on the slow boat #1 (which takes about 45 minutes). The express boat #2 travels the same route, but it skips many stops and takes only 25 minutes, making it hard to sightsee. Also, some #2 boats terminate at Rialto; confirm that you're on a boat that goes all the way to San Marco.

To help you enjoy the visual parade of canal wonders, I've organized this tour by boat stop. I'll point out both what you can see from the current stop, and what to look forward to as you cruise to the next stop. You can download a free Rick Steves **audio version** of this Grand Canal cruise to your mobile device; see page 19.

A Few Tips: You're more likely to find an empty seat if you catch the vaporetto at Piazzale Roma. You can break up the tour by hopping on and off at various sights described in greater depth elsewhere in this chapter (but remember, a single-fare vaporetto ticket is good for just 60 minutes; passes let you hop on and off all day). As you board the vaporetto, make a beeline for an open-air seat in the front of the boat, which has the best seats for this tour. From the front, you can easily look left, right, and forward. If you find yourself stuck on the side or in the cabin, do your best. Avoid sitting in the back, only because you'll miss the wonderful forward views.

Overview

The Grand Canal is Venice's "Main Street." At more than two miles long, nearly 150 feet wide, and nearly 15 feet deep, the Grand Canal is the city's largest, lined with its most impressive palaces. It's the remnant of a river that once spilled from the mainland into the Adriatic. The sediment it carried formed barrier islands that cut Venice off from the sea, forming a lagoon.

Venice was built on the marshy islands of the former delta, sitting on wood pilings driven nearly 15 feet into the clay (alder was the preferred wood). About 25 miles of canals drain the city, dumping like streams into the Grand Canal. Technically, Venice has only three canals: Grand, Giudecca, and Cannaregio. The 45 small waterways that dump into the Grand Canal are referred to as rivers (e.g., Rio Novo).

Venice is a city of palaces, dating from the days when the city was the world's richest. The most lavish palaces formed a grand chorus line along the Grand Canal. Once frescoed in reds and blues, with black-and-white borders and gold-leaf trim, they made Venice a city of dazzling color. This cruise is the only way to truly appreciate the palaces, approaching them at water level, where their main entrances were located. Today, strict laws prohibit any changes in these buildings, so while landowners gnash their teeth, we can enjoy Europe's best-preserved medieval city—slowly rotting. Many of the grand buildings are now vacant. Others harbor chandeliered elegance above mossy, empty (often flooded) ground floors.

The Grand Canal Cruise Begins

This tour starts at the Ferrovia vaporetto stop (at Santa Lucia train station). It also works if you board upstream from Ferrovia at Piazzale Roma (where airport buses and the People Mover monorail from Tronchetto arrive), a short walk from Ferrovia over the Calatrava Bridge. Just start the tour when your vaporetto reaches Ferrovia.

Ferrovia: The **Santa Lucia train station,** one of the few modern buildings in town, was built in 1954. It's been the gateway into Venice since 1860, when the first station was built. "F.S." stands for "Ferrovie dello Stato," the Italian state railway system.

More than 20,000 people a day commute in from the mainland, making this the busiest part of Venice during rush hour. The **Calatrava Bridge,** spanning the Grand Canal between the train station and Piazzale Roma upstream, was built in 2008 to alleviate some of the congestion and make the commute easier (see page 94).

Opposite the train station, atop the green dome of **San Simeone Piccolo** church, St. Simeon waves *ciao* to whoever enters or leaves the "old" city. The pink church with the white Carrara-marble facade, just beyond the train station, is the **Church of the Scalzi** (Church of the Barefoot, named after the shoeless Carmelite monks), where the last doge (Venetian ruler) rests. It looks relatively new because it was partially rebuilt after being bombed in

VENICE

Grand Canal

To Jewish Ghetto
To Jewish Ghetto

STRADA
Canale de Cannaregio
GUGLIE BRIDGE
SAN MARCUOLA
PALAZZO CORRER CONTARINI
SAN GEREMIA
PALAZZO GRITTI
CASINÒ
PALAZZO VENDRAMIN CALERGI
LISTA DI SPAGNA
PALAZZO FLANGINI
Grand
Canal
2
3
SCALZI
SANTA LUCIA TRAIN STATION (FERROVIA)
PALAZZO CALBO-CROTTA
PALAZZO GIOVANELLI
TURKISH "FONDACO" EXCHANGE
PALAZZO MARCELLO
SCALZI BRIDGE
PAL GRITTI
PALAZZO DONA BALBI
SAN ZAN DEGOLA
PALAZZO CA'TRON
1
SAN SIMEONE PICCOLO
SANTA CROCE
SAN
CALATRAVA BRIDGE
PIAZZALE ROMA
& PEOPLE MOVER TO STAZIONE MARITTIMA & TRONCHETTO
FRARI
PALAZZO CAPPELLO-LAYARD
PALAZZO BARBARIGO
SAN TOMÀ
9
A
PALAZZO GIUSTINIANI
PALAZZO MOCENIGO
10
PALAZZO BALBI
FIRE STATION
CA' FOSCARI
PALAZZO VECCHIA
PALAZZO MORO LIN
PALAZZO GRASSI
PALAZZO GIUSTINIAN
CA' REZZONICO
11
PALAZZO MALIPIERO-CAPPELLO
PALAZZO FALIER
PALAZZO LOREDAN
PALAZZO GIUSTINIAN LOLIN
PALAZZO CONTARINI DEGLI SCRIGNI
PALAZZO QUERINI
12
PALAZZO BARBARO
ACCADEMIA BRIDGE & GALLERY
PALAZZO BARBARIGO
FONDAMENTA ZATTERE AL PONTE LONGO
Giudecca Canal
DORSODURO
To Zattere

Vaporetto Stops
1. Ferrovia
2. Riva de Biasio
3. San Marcuola
4. San Stae
5. Ca' d'Oro
6. Mercato Rialto
7. Rialto
8. San Silvestro
9. Sant'Angelo
10. San Tomà
11. Ca' Rezzonico
12. Accademia
13. Santa Maria del Giglio
14. Salute
15. San Marco
16. San Zaccaria

VENICE

Lagoon

FONDAMENTE NOVE

200 Meters
200 Yards

CANNAREGIO

NOVA

PALAZZO MARCELLO

PALAZZO MOLIN

PALAZZO ZULLAN

4

SAN STAE

PALAZZO BARBARIGO

PALAZZO FONTANA

PALAZZO GIUSTI

PALAZZO SAGREDO

PALAZZO MICHIEL COLONNE

CA' PESARO

PALAZZO DONÀ

PALAZZO FAVRETTO

CA' D'ORO

STRADA NOVA

PALAZZO CORNER DELLA REGINA

PALAZZO BRANDOLIN

5

PALAZZO VALMARANA

FISH MARKET

PALAZZO CA' DA MOSTO

6

FRUIT & VEGETABLE MARKET

PALAZZO CIVRAN

POLO

GERMAN EXCHANGE (FORMER POST)

RIALTO BRIDGE

SAL S. LIO

S. MARIA FORMOSA

7

PALAZZO DOLFIN-MANIN

PALAZZO PAPADOPOLI

PALAZZO BARZIZZA

MERCERIE

PALAZZO BEMBO

PALAZZO DONÀ

PALAZZO CORNER-CONTARINI

8

PALAZZO FARSETTI-DANDOLO

CASTELLO

PALAZZO BERNARDO

PALAZZO BENZON

PALAZZO MARTINENGO

PALAZZO GRIMANI

PALAZZO CORNER-SPINELLI

FABBRI

MERCERIE

CAMPANILE

ST. MARK'S BASILICA

BRIDGE OF SIGHS

SAN MARCO

SAN MARCO

DOGE'S PALACE

CALLE LARGA XXII MARZO

16

HARRY'S AMERICAN BAR

15

To Lido

CA' GRANDE

GRITTI PALACE HOTEL

PALAZZO FLANGINI

13

Canal

14

LA SALUTE CHURCH

St. Mark's Basin

Grand

PALAZZO GENOVESE

PEGGY GUGGENHEIM COLLECTION

PUNTA DELLA DOGANA MUSEUM (CUSTOMS HOUSE)

To San Giorgio Maggiore & Guidecca

1915 by Austrians aiming (poorly) at the train station.

Riva de Biasio: Venice's main thoroughfare is busy with all kinds of **boats:** taxis, police boats, garbage boats, ambulances, construction cranes, and even brown-and-white UPS boats. Somehow they all manage to share the canal in relative peace.

About 25 yards past the Riva de Biasio stop, you'll look left down the broad **Cannaregio Canal** to see what was the **Jewish Ghetto** (see page 93). The twin, pale-pink, six-story "skyscrapers"—the tallest buildings you'll see at this end of the canal—are reminders of how densely populated the world's original ghetto was. Set aside as the local Jewish quarter in 1516, this area became extremely crowded. This urban island developed into one of the most closely knit business and cultural quarters of all the Jewish communities in Italy, and gave us our word "ghetto" (from *geto,* the copper foundry located here).

San Marcuola: At this stop, facing a tiny square just ahead, stands the unfinished church of San Marcuola, one of only five churches fronting the Grand Canal. Centuries ago, this canal was a commercial drag of expensive real estate in high demand by wealthy merchants. About 20 yards ahead on the right stands the stately gray **Turkish "Fondaco" Exchange,** one of the oldest houses in Venice. Its horseshoe arches and roofline of triangles and dingle-balls are reminders of its Byzantine heritage. Turkish traders in turbans docked here, unloaded their goods into the warehouse on the  bottom story, then went upstairs for a home-style meal and a place to sleep. Venice in the 1500s was very cosmopolitan, welcoming every religion and ethnicity, so long as they carried cash. (Today the building contains the city's Museum of Natural History—and Venice's only dinosaur skeleton.)

Just 100 yards ahead on the left, Venice's **Casinò** is housed in the palace where German composer Richard *(The Ring)* Wagner died in 1883. See his distinct, strong-jawed profile in the white plaque on the brick wall. In the 1700s, Venice was Europe's Vegas, with casinos and prostitutes everywhere. Casinòs ("little houses") have long provided Italians with a handy escape from daily life. Today they're run by the state to keep Mafia influence at bay. Notice the fancy front porch, rolling out the red carpet for high rollers arriving by taxi or hotel boat.

San Stae: The San Stae Church sports a delightful Baroque facade. Opposite the San Stae stop, look for the peeling plaster that once made up **frescoes** (scant remains on the lower floors).

Imagine the facades of the Grand Canal at their finest. As colorful as the city is today, it's still only a faded, sepia-toned remnant of a long-gone era, a time of lavishly decorated, brilliantly colored palaces.

Just ahead, jutting out a bit on the right, is the ornate white facade of **Ca' Pesaro.** *"Ca'"* is short for *casa* (house). Because only the house of the doge (Venetian ruler) could be called a palace *(palazzo),* all other Venetian palaces are technically *"Ca'."*

In this city of masks, notice how the rich marble facades along the Grand Canal mask what are generally just simple, no-nonsense brick buildings. Most merchants enjoyed showing off. However, being smart businessmen, they only decorated the side of the buildings that would be seen and appreciated. But look back as you pass Ca' Pesaro (which houses the International Gallery of Modern Art—see page 90). It's the only building you'll see with a fine side facade. Ahead, on the left, with its glorious triple-decker medieval arcade (just before the next stop) is Ca' d'Oro.

Ca' d'Oro: The lacy **Ca' d'Oro** (House of Gold) is the best example of Venetian Gothic architecture on the canal. Its three

stories offer different variations on balcony design, topped with a spiny white roofline. Venetian Gothic mixes traditional Gothic (pointed arches and round medallions stamped with a four-leaf clover) with Byzantine styles (tall, narrow arches atop thin columns), filled in with Islamic frills. Like all the palaces, this was originally painted and gilded to make it even more glorious than it is now. Today the Ca' d'Oro is an art gallery (see page 95).

Look at the Venetian chorus line of palaces in front of the boat doing an architectural cancan. On the right is the arcade of the covered **fish market,** with the open-air **produce market** just beyond. It bustles in the morning but is quiet the rest of the day. This is a great scene to wander through—even though European Union hygiene standards have made it cleaner, but less colorful than it once was. Find the *traghetto* gondola ferrying shoppers—standing like Washington crossing the Delaware—back and forth. There are eight *traghetto* crossings along the Grand Canal, each one marked by a classy low-key green-and-black sign. Make a point to use them. At €0.50 a ride, they are one of the best deals in Venice.

Mercato Rialto: This stop was opened in 2007 to serve the busy market (boats only stop here between 8:00 and 20:00). The long and officious-looking building at this stop is the Venice court-house. Straight ahead in the distance, rising above the huge post office, is the tip of the Campanile (bell tower) crowned by its golden angel at St. Mark's Square, where this tour will end. The former post office (100 yards directly ahead, on left side, soon to be a shopping center) was once the German Exchange, the trading center for German metal merchants in the early 1500s.

You'll cruise by some trendy and beautifully situated wine bars on the right, but look ahead as you round the corner and see the impressive Rialto Bridge come into view.

A major landmark of Venice, the **Rialto Bridge** is lined with shops and tourists. Constructed in 1588, it's the third bridge built

on this spot. Until the 1850s, this was the only bridge crossing the Grand Canal. With a span of 160 feet and foundations stretching 650 feet on either side, the Rialto was an impressive engineering feat in its day. Earlier Rialto Bridges could open to let big ships in, but not this one. When this new bridge was completed, much of the Grand Canal was closed to shipping and became a canal of palaces.

When gondoliers pass under the fat arch of the Rialto Bridge, they take full advantage of its acoustics: *"Volare, oh, oh..."*

Rialto: Rialto, a separate town in the early days of Venice, has always been the commercial district, while San Marco was the religious and governmental center. Today, a winding street called the Mercerie connects the two, providing travelers with human traffic jams and a mesmerizing gauntlet of shopping temptations. This is the only stretch of the historic Grand Canal with landings upon which you can walk. They unloaded the city's basic necessities here: oil, wine, charcoal, iron. Today, the quay is lined with tourist-trap restaurants.

Venice's sleek, black, graceful **gondolas** are a symbol of the city (for more on gondolas, see page 97). With about 500 gondoliers joyriding amid the churning *vaporetti*, there's a lot of congestion on the Grand Canal. Pay attention—this is where most of the gondola and vaporetto accidents take place. While the Rialto is the highlight of many gondola rides, gondoliers understandably prefer the smaller, quieter canals. Watch your vaporetto driver curse the better-paid gondoliers.

Ahead 100 yards on the left, two gray-colored **palaces** stand side by side (the City Hall and the mayor's office). Their horseshoe-shaped, arched windows are similar and their stories are the same height, lining up to create the effect of one long balcony.

San Silvestro: We now enter a long stretch of important **merchants' palaces,** each with proud and different facades. Because ships couldn't navigate beyond the Rialto Bridge, the biggest palaces—with the major shipping needs—line this last stretch of the navigable Grand Canal.

Palaces like these were multi-functional: ground floor for the warehouse, offices and showrooms upstairs, and the living quarters above the offices on the "noble floors" (with big windows designed to allow in maximum light). Servants lived and worked on the top floors (with the smallest windows). For fire-safety reasons, the kitchens were also located on the top floors. Peek into the noble floors to catch a glimpse of their still-glorious chandeliers of Murano glass.

Sant'Angelo: Notice how many buildings have a foundation of waterproof white stone *(pietra d'Istria)* upon which the bricks sit high and dry. Many canal-level floors are abandoned as the rising water level takes its toll. The **posts**—historically painted gaily with the equivalent of family coats of arms—don't rot underwater. But the wood at the waterline, where it's exposed to oxygen, does. On the smallest canals, little blue gondola signs indicate that these docks are for gondolas only (no taxis or motor boats).

San Tomà: Fifty yards ahead, on the right side (with twin obelisks on the rooftop) stands **Palazzo Balbi,** the palace of an early-17th-century captain general of the sea. These Venetian equivalents of five-star admirals were honored with twin obelisks decorating their palaces. This palace, like so many in the city, flies three flags: Italy (green-white-red), the European Union (blue with ring of stars), and Venice (a lion on a field of red and gold). Today it houses the administrative headquarters of the regional government.

Just past the admiral's palace, look immediately to the right, down a side canal. On the right side of that canal, before the bridge, see the traffic light and the **fire station** (with four arches hiding fireboats parked and ready to go).

The impressive **Ca' Foscari,** with a classic Venetian facade (on

the corner, across from the fire station), dominates the bend in the canal. This is the main building of the University of Venice, which has about 25,000 students. Notice the elegant lamp on the corner.

The grand, heavy, white **Ca' Rezzonico,** just before the Ca' Rezzonico stop, houses the Museum of 18th-Century Venice (see page 89). Across the canal is the cleaner and leaner **Palazzo Grassi,** the last major palace built on the canal, erected in the late 1700s. It was purchased by a French tycoon and now displays a contemporary art collection.

Ca' Rezzonico: Up ahead, the Accademia Bridge leads over the Grand Canal to the **Accademia Gallery** (right side), filled with the best Venetian paintings (see page 86). The bridge was put up in 1934 as a temporary structure. Locals liked it, so it stayed.

Accademia: From here, look through the graceful bridge and way ahead to enjoy a classic view of **La Salute Church,** topped by a crown-shaped dome supported by scrolls (see page 89). This Church of St. Mary of Good Health was built to thank God for delivering Venetians from the devastating plague of 1630 (which had killed about a third of the city's population).

The low, white building among greenery (100 yards ahead, on the right, between the Accademia Bridge and the church) is the **Peggy Guggenheim Collection.** The American heiress "retired" here, sprucing up a palace that had been abandoned in mid-construction. Peggy willed the city her fine collection of modern art (described on page 88).

As you approach the next stop, notice on the right how the fine line of higgledy-piggledy palaces evokes old-time Venice. Two doors past the Guggenheim, Palazzo Dario has a great set of characteristic **funnel-shaped chimneys.** These forced embers through a loop-the-loop channel until they were dead—required

in the days when stone palaces were surrounded by humble, wooden buildings, and a live spark could make a merchant's workforce homeless. Notice this early Renaissance building's flat-feeling facade with "pasted-on" Renaissance motifs. Three doors later is the **Salviati building** (with the fine mosaics), which was once a glassworks.

Santa Maria del Giglio: Back on the left stands the fancy Gritti Palace hotel. Hemingway and Woody Allen both stayed here (but not together).

Take a deep whiff of Venice. What's all this nonsense about stinky canals? All I smell is my shirt. By the way, how's your captain? Smooth dockings? To get to know him, stand up in the bow and block his view.

Salute: The huge **La Salute Church** towers overhead as if squirted from a can of Catholic Reddi-wip. Like Venice itself, the church rests upon pilings.

To build the foundation for the city, more than a million trees were piled together, reaching beneath the mud to the solid clay. Much of the surrounding countryside was deforested by Venice. Trees were exported and consumed locally to fuel the furnaces of Venice's booming glass industry, to build Europe's biggest merchant marine, and to prop up this city in the mud.

As the Grand Canal opens up into the lagoon, the last building on the right with the golden ball is the 17th-century **Customs House,** which now houses the Punta della Dogana Museum of Contemporary Art (see page 89). Its two bronze Atlases hold a statue of Fortune riding the ball. Arriving ships stopped here to pay their tolls.

San Marco: Up ahead on the left, the green pointed tip of the Campanile marks **St. Mark's Square,** the political and religious center of Venice...and the final destination of this tour. You could get off at the San Marco stop and go straight to St. Mark's Square. But I'm staying on the boat for one more

Venice at a Glance

▲▲▲**St. Mark's Square** Venice's grand main square. **Hours:** Always open. See page 76.

▲▲▲**St. Mark's Basilica** Cathedral with mosaics, saint's bones, treasury, museum, and viewpoint of square. **Hours:** Basilica—Mon-Sat 9:45-17:00, Sun 14:00-17:00 (until 16:00 Nov-March); Treasury and Golden Altarpiece close 15 minutes before church; San Marco Museum—daily 9:45-16:45. See page 77.

▲▲▲**Doge's Palace** Art-splashed palace of former rulers, with prison accessible through Bridge of Sighs. **Hours:** Daily April-Oct 8:30-18:30, Nov-March 8:00-17:30. See page 82.

▲▲▲**Rialto Bridge** Distinctive bridge spanning the Grand Canal, with a market nearby. **Hours:** Bridge—always open; market—souvenir stalls open daily, produce market closed Sun-Mon, fish market closed Sun. See page 90.

▲▲**Correr Museum** Venetian history and art. **Hours:** Daily April-Oct 10:00-19:00, Nov-March 10:00-17:00. See page 84.

▲▲**Accademia** Venice's top art museum. **Hours:** Mon 8:15-14:00, Tue-Sun 8:15-19:15. See page 86.

▲▲**Peggy Guggenheim Collection** Popular display of 20th-century art. **Hours:** Wed-Mon 10:00-18:00, closed Tue. See page 88.

▲▲**Frari Church** Franciscan church featuring Renaissance masters. **Hours:** Mon-Sat 9:00-18:00, Sun 13:00-18:00. See page 90.

▲▲**Scuola San Rocco** "Tintoretto's Sistine Chapel." **Hours:** Daily 9:30-17:30. See page 92.

▲**Campanile** Dramatic bell tower on St. Mark's Square with elevator to the top. **Hours:** Daily Easter-June and Oct 9:00-19:00, July-Sept 9:00-21:00; Nov-Easter 9:30-15:45 except closed from Christmas to mid-Jan. See page 85.

▲**Bridge of Sighs** Famous enclosed bridge, part of Doge's Palace, near St. Mark's Square. **Hours:** Generally viewable, but covered with scaffolding during renovation. See page 85.

▲**La Salute Church** Striking church dedicated to the Virgin Mary. **Hours:** Daily 9:00-12:00 & 15:00-17:30. See page 89.

▲**Ca' Rezzonico** Posh Grand Canal palazzo with 18th-century Venetian art. **Hours:** April-Oct Wed-Mon 10:00-18:00, Nov-March Wed-Mon 10:00-17:00; closed Tue year-round. See page 89.

▲**Punta della Dogana** Museum of contemporary art. **Hours:** Wed-Mon 10:00-19:00, closed Tue. See page 89.

▲**Ca' Pesaro International Gallery of Modern Art** in a canalside palazzo. **Hours:** Tue-Sun 10:00-18:00, closed Mon. See page 90.

▲**Scuola Dalmata di San Giorgio** Exquisite Renaissance meeting house. **Hours:** Mon 14:45-18:00, Tue-Sat 9:15-13:00 & 14:45-18:00, Sun 9:15-13:00. See page 95.

Church of San Zaccaria Final resting place of St. Zachariah, plus a Bellini altarpiece and an eerie crypt. **Hours:** Mon-Sat 10:00-12:00 & 16:00-18:00, Sun 16:00-18:00. See page 86.

Church of San Polo Ninth-century church with works by Tintoretto, Veronese, and Tiepolo. **Hours:** Mon-Sat 10:00-17:00, closed Sun. See page 92.

Nearby Islands

▲**San Giorgio Maggiore** Island across the lagoon featuring church with Palladio architecture, Tintoretto paintings, and fine views back on Venice. **Hours:** May-Sept Mon-Sat 9:30-12:30 & 14:30-18:00, Sun 8:30-11:00 & 14:30-18:00; Oct-April until 16:30. See page 86.

San Michele Cemetery island on the lagoon. **Hours:** Daily April-Sept 7:30-18:00, Oct-March 7:30-16:30. See page 96.

Murano Island famous for glass factories and glassmaking museum. **Hours:** Glass Museum open daily April-Oct 10:00-18:00, Nov-March 10:00-17:00. See page 96.

Burano Sleepy island known for lacemaking and a Lace Museum. **Hours:** Lace Museum open April-Oct Tue-Sun 10:00-18:00, Nov-March Tue-Sun 10:00-17:00, closed Mon, year-round. See page 96.

Torcello Near-deserted island with old church, bell tower, and museum. **Hours:** Most sights open daily March-Oct 10:30-18:00, Nov-Feb 10:00-16:30, museum closed Mon. See page 97.

stop, just past St. Mark's Square (it's a quick walk back).

Survey the lagoon. Opposite St. Mark's Square, across the water, the ghostly white church with the pointy bell tower is **San Giorgio Maggiore,** with great views of Venice (see page 86). Next to it is the residential island Giudecca, stretching from close to San Giorgio Maggiore past the Venice youth hostel (with a nice view, directly across) to the Hilton Hotel (good nighttime view, far right end of island).

Still on board? If you are, as we leave the San Marco stop, prepare for a drive-by view of St. Mark's Square. First comes the bold white facade of the old mint (where Venice's golden ducat, the "dollar" of the Venetian Republic, was made) and the library facade. Then the twin columns, topped by St. Theodore and St. Mark, who've welcomed visitors since the 15th century. Between the columns, catch a glimpse of two giant figures atop the **Clock Tower**—they've been whacking their clappers every hour since 1499. The domes of **St. Mark's Basilica** are soon eclipsed by the lacy facade of the **Doge's Palace.** Next you'll see the **Bridge of Sighs** (currently under scaffolding), and then the grand harborside promenade—the **Riva.**

Follow the Riva with your eye, past elegant hotels to the green area in the distance. This is the largest of Venice's few **parks,** which hosts the Biennale art show every odd year (next in 2013). Much farther in the distance is the **Lido,** the island with Venice's beach. Its sand and casinos are tempting, but its car traffic disrupts the medieval charm of Venice.

San Zaccaria: OK, you're at your last stop. Quick—muscle your way off this boat! (If you don't, you'll eventually end up at the Lido.)

At San Zaccaria, you're right in the thick of the action. A number of other *vaporetti* depart from here (see page 56). Otherwise, it's a short walk back along the Riva to St. Mark's Square. Ahoy!

Sights in Venice

For information on sightseeing passes, see below. Venice's city museums offer youth and senior discounts to Americans and other non-EU citizens.

Sightseeing Passes for Venice

Venice offers an array of passes. For most people, the best choice is the combo-ticket, which covers entry into the Doge's Palace and more. Note that some major sights (Accademia, Peggy Guggenheim Collection, Scuola San Rocco, Campanile, and the three sights within St. Mark's Basilica that charge admission) are not covered on any pass.

Combo-Ticket: The combo-ticket for the Doge's Palace or Correr Museum, which are at opposite ends of St. Mark's Square, always gets you into the other museum as well (and includes two other museums within the Correr: the National Archaeological Museum and the Monumental Rooms of Marciana National Library). From April through October, this ticket costs €14 and gives you a single bonus entry into your choice of one of these other city-run museums: Ca' Rezzonico (Museum of 18th-Century Venice); Palazzo Mocenigo Costume Museum; Casa Goldoni (home of the Italian playwright); Ca' Pesaro (modern art); Museum of Natural History in the Santa Croce district; the Glass Museum on the island of Murano; and the Lace Museum on the island of Burano (full details at www.museicivicivenezieni.it; this €14 version is technically called the San Marco Museum Plus ticket). In winter (Nov-March), this ticket costs €13 and covers only the Doge's Palace and Correr Museum. To bypass the long line at the Doge's Palace, buy your combo-ticket at the Correr Museum or at any other included museum. Note that you can't buy an individual ticket for just the Doge's Palace or solely for the Correr.

Museum Pass: Busy sightseers may prefer this more expensive pass, which covers all 11 museums listed in the preceding paragraph, including the Doge's Palace and Correr Museum (€18, available all year). In general, this pass saves you money only if you visit five or more sights; before you buy, make sure they're sights you really want to see.

Chorus Pass: This pass gives church-lovers admission to 16 of Venice's churches and their art (generally €3 each)—including the Frari Church—for €10 (€20 family pass, www.chorusvenezia.org).

Venice Card: This pass combines the 11 city-run museums and the 16 churches covered by the Chorus Pass, plus a few minor discounts, for €40, but it's hard to make it pay off if you're over 29 (€30 for anyone under 30, valid 7 days, info at www.hellovenezia .com). Don't confuse this pass with CartaVenezia, a discount transit card used mainly by locals.

Rolling Venice: This youth pass offers discounts at dozens of sights and shops, but its best deal is for transit. If you're under 30 and want to buy a three-day transit pass, it'll cost you just €18—rather than €33—with the Rolling Venice pass (€4 for anyone 14-29, sold at TIs and HelloVenezia shops).

Venice Connected: This confusing web-based system allows you to buy vouchers exchangeable for sightseeing and transport tickets; it's generally not worth the trouble (www.veniceconnected .com).

Transportation Passes: Venice sells transit-only passes that cover *vaporetti* and mainland buses. For a rundown on these, see "Vaporetto Passes" on page 55.

San Marco District

▲▲▲**St. Mark's Square (Piazza San Marco)**—This grand square is surrounded by splashy, historic buildings and sights: St. Mark's Basilica, the Doge's Palace, the Campanile bell tower, and the Correr Museum. The square is filled with music, lovers, pigeons, and tourists by day, and is your private rendezvous with the Venetian past late at night, when Europe's most magnificent dance floor is *the* romantic place to be.

With your back to the church, survey one of Europe's great urban spaces, and the only square in Venice to merit the title "Piazza." Nearly two football fields long, it's surrounded by the offices of the republic. On the right are the "old offices" (16th-century Renaissance). At left are the "new offices" (17th-century High Renaissance). Napoleon called the piazza "the most beautiful drawing room in Europe," and added to the intimacy by building the final wing, opposite the basilica, that encloses the square.

For a slow and pricey evening thrill, invest about €12-20 (including the cover charge for the music) for a drink at one of the elegant cafés with the dueling orchestras (see the "Cafés on St. Mark's Square" sidebar, page 81). For an unmatched experience that offers the best people-watching in Venice, it's worth the small splurge.

The **Clock Tower** (Torre dell'Orologio), built during the Renaissance in 1496, marks the entry to the main shopping drag,

called the Mercerie (or "Marzarie," in Venetian dialect), which connects St. Mark's Square with the Rialto. From the piazza, you can see the bronze men (Moors) swing their huge clappers at the top of each hour. In the 17th century, one of them knocked an unsuspecting worker off the top and to his death—probably the first-ever killing by a robot. Notice one of the world's first "digital" clocks on the tower facing the square (with dramatic flips every five minutes). You can go inside the Clock Tower with a pre-booked guided tour that takes you close to the clock's innards and out to a terrace with good views over the square and city rooftops. Reserve by calling 848-082-000, booking online at www.museicivicivenziani.it, going in person to the Correr Museum a day in advance, or even just showing up at the Correr prior to a scheduled tour to see if space is available (€12 combo-ticket includes Correr Museum, where tour starts; tours in English Mon-Wed at 10:00 and 11:00, Thu-Sun at 14:00 and 15:00; no kids under age 6).

A good **TI** is on the square (with your back to the basilica, it's in the far-left, southwest corner; daily 9:00-15:30), and a €1.50

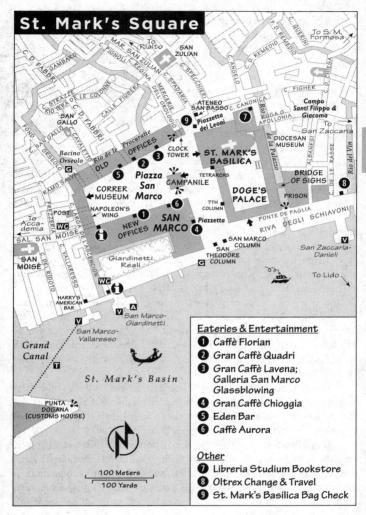

St. Mark's Square

To S. M.
Formosa
To Rialto
SAN ZULIAN
C. D. QUERINI
F. D. REMEDIO
C. D. REMEDIO
C. D. FABBRI
MAR SAN ZULIAN
C. PIGNOLI REGINA
C. SPECHIERI
C. D. CHIESA
FIGHER
C. ANGELO
C. D. FABBRI
MERCERIE DELL'OROLOGIO
ATENEO SAN BASSO
CANONICA
Campo Santi Filippo & Giacomo
SAN GALLO
CALLE FIUBERA
Piazzetta dei Leoni
RUGA G. APOLLONIA
To San Zaccaria
FOND. ORSEOLO
C. D. ANGELO
Bacino Orseolo
Procuratie
OLD OFFICES
CLOCK TOWER
ST. MARK'S BASILICA
DIOCESAN MUSEUM
RAMO SALVA
Rio de Te
Piazza San Marco
TETRARCHS
CAMPANILE
de la Palazzo
ALBANESI
C. DE LE RASSE
BRIDGE OF SIGHS
Rio del Vin
To Accademia
CORRER MUSEUM
NAPOLEON'S WING
7TH COLUMN
DOGE'S PALACE
PRISON
POST
FREZZERIA
NEW OFFICES
SAN MARCO
Piazzetta
PONTE DE PAGLIA
RIVA DEGLI SCHIAVONI
SAL. SAN MOISÈ
SAN MOISÈ
C. DEL RIDOTO
VALLARESSO
WC
Giardinetti Reali
SAN MARCO COLUMN
SAN THEODORE COLUMN
San Zaccaria-Danieli
WC
To Lido
HARRY'S AMERICAN BAR
San Marco-Giardinetti
A
V
Grand Canal
San Marco-Vallaresso
T
St. Mark's Basin
PUNTA DOGANA (CUSTOMS HOUSE)

N

100 Meters
100 Yards

Eateries & Entertainment
1. Caffè Florian
2. Gran Caffè Quadri
3. Gran Caffè Lavena; Galleria San Marco Glassblowing
4. Gran Caffè Chioggia
5. Eden Bar
6. Caffè Aurora

Other
7. Libreria Studium Bookstore
8. Oltrex Change & Travel
9. St. Mark's Basilica Bag Check

WC is 30 yards beyond the square (see *Albergo Diorno* sign marked on pavement, WC open daily 9:00-17:30). Another TI is on the lagoon near the San Marco-Vallaresso vaporetto stop (daily 10:00-18:00, walk toward the water by the Doge's Palace and go right, €1.50 WCs nearby).

You can download a free Rick Steves **audio tour** of St. Mark's Square to your mobile device; see page 19.

▲▲▲**St. Mark's Basilica (Basilica di San Marco)**—Built in the 11th century to replace an earlier church, this basilica's distinctly Eastern-style architecture underlines Venice's connection with Byzantium (which protected it from the ambition of Charlemagne and his Holy Roman Empire). It's decorated with booty from returning sea captains—a kind of architectural Venetian trophy chest. The interior glows mysteriously with gold mosaics and colored marble. Since about A.D. 830, the saint's bones have been housed on this site.

Cost and Hours: Basilica entry is free, three interior sights charge admission, open Mon-Sat 9:45-17:00, Sun 14:00-17:00 (Sun until 16:00 Nov-March), St. Mark's Square, vaporetto stops: San Marco or San Zaccaria, tel. 041-270-8311, www.basilicasanmarco .it. The dress code is strictly enforced for everyone (no bare shoulders or bare knees). Lines can be long, and bag check is mandatory, free, and can save you time in line. No photos are allowed inside.

Three separate exhibits within the church charge admission: the **Treasury** (€3, includes audioguide free for the asking), **Golden Altarpiece** (€2), and **San Marco Museum** (€4). The San Marco Museum—the sight most worth its entry fee—has the original bronze horses (copies of these overlook the square), a balcony offering a remarkable view over St. Mark's Square, and various works related to the church. The Treasury and Golden Altarpiece close 15 minutes before the church, while the San Marco Museum is open daily 9:45-16:45.

Dress Code: Modest dress (no bare knees or bare shoulders) is strictly enforced, even for kids. Shorts are OK if they cover the knees. To cover bare shoulders, women may be able to buy a shawl *(coprispale)* at the atrium gift shop.

Bag Check (and Skipping the Line): Small purses and shoulder-slung bags may be allowed inside the church, but larger bags and backpacks are not. Check them for free for up to one hour at the nearby Ateneo San Basso, 30 yards to the left of the basilica, down narrow Calle San Basso (see map on page 79 for location; open daily 9:30-17:00).

Those with a bag to check actually get to skip the line, along with their companions (up to three or so). Leave your bag at Ateneo San Basso and pick up your claim tag. Take your tag to the basilica's tourist entrance. Keep to the left of the railing where the line forms and show your tag to the gatekeeper. He'll let you in, ahead of the line. After touring the church, come back and pick up your bag. (Note: Ateneo San Basso will not let you check small bags that would be allowed inside.)

Theft Alert: St. Mark's Basilica is the most dangerous place in Venice for pickpocketing—inside, it's always a crowded jostle.

St. Mark's Basilica

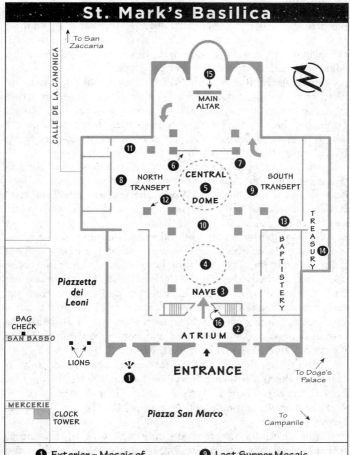

To San Zaccaria

CALLE DE LA CANONICA

⑮
MAIN ALTAR

⑪

⑥ ⑦

⑧ NORTH TRANSEPT   CENTRAL ⑤ DOME   SOUTH TRANSEPT ⑨

⑫

⑬

⑩

BAPTISTERY

TREASURY ⑭

④

Piazzetta dei Leoni

NAVE ③

⑯
②

ATRIUM

BAG CHECK
SAN BASSO

LIONS

① ENTRANCE

To Doge's Palace

MERCERIE

CLOCK TOWER

Piazza San Marco

To Campanile

① **Exterior – Mosaic of Mark's Relics**

② **Atrium – Mosaic of Noah's Ark & the Great Flood**

③ **Nave – Mosaics & Greek-Cross Floor Plan**

④ **Pentecost Mosaic**

⑤ **Central Dome – Ascension Mosaic**

⑥ **Rood Screen**

⑦ **Doge's Pulpit**

⑧ **Tree of Jesse Mosaic**

⑨ **Last Supper Mosaic**

⑩ **Crucifixion Mosaic**

⑪ **Nicopeia Icon**

⑫ **Rifle on Pillar**

⑬ **Discovery of Mark Mosaic**

⑭ **Treasury**

⑮ **Golden Altarpiece**

⑯ **Stairs up to Loggia: San Marco Museum & Bronze Horses**

Tours: Free, hour-long English tours (heavy on the mosaics' religious symbolism) are generally offered Mon-Sat at 11:00; meet in the atrium. But the schedule varies, so see the schedule board in the atrium. You can download a free Rick Steves audio tour of St. Mark's Basilica to your mobile device; see page 19.

Visiting the Basilica: St. Mark's Basilica has 4,750 square yards of Byzantine mosaics, though many were designed by artists from the Italian Renaissance and later. Start outside in the square, far enough back to take in the whole facade. Then zero in on the details. The mosaic over the far left door shows the theft of ❶ **St. Mark's relics** that put Venice on the pilgrimage map.

The best and oldest mosaics are in the atrium (turn right as you enter and stop under the last dome). Facing the piazza, look domeward for the story of ❷ **Noah, the ark, and the flood** (two by two, the wicked being drowned, Noah sending out the dove, a happy rainbow, and a sacrifice of thanks).

Step inside the church and follow the one-way tourist route. Notice how the marble floor is richly decorated in mosaics. As in many Venetian buildings, because the best foundation pilings were made around the perimeter, the floor rolls. The church is laid out with four equal arms, topped with domes, radiating out from the center to form a ❸ **Greek cross** (+). Those familiar with Eastern Orthodox churches will find common elements in St. Mark's: a central floor plan, domes, mosaics, and iconic images of Mary and Christ as Pantocrator—ruler of all things.

Find the chandelier near the entrance doorway, and run your eyes up to the ❹ **Pentecost** mosaic in the dome above. In a golden heaven, the dove of the Holy Spirit shoots out a pinwheel of spiritual lasers, igniting tongues of fire on the heads of the 12 apostles below.

Shuffle under the central dome, and look up for the ❺ **Ascension** mosaic. Christ—having lived his miraculous life and having been crucified for man's sins—ascends into the starry sky on a rainbow.

Look around at the church's furniture: the ❻ **rood screen**, topped with 14 saints, separates the congregation from the high altar. The ❼ **pulpit** on the right was reserved for the doge, who led prayers and made important announcements. Mosaics told the story of Jesus, starting with his ancestors perched in the ❽ **Tree of Jesse** (in the north transept, to the left as you face the altar), and continuing through to the ❾ **Last Supper** (in the arch leading to the south transept), and culminating in the ❿ **Crucifixion** (in the west arch).

In the north transept, today's Venetians pray to a painted wooden icon of Mary and baby Jesus known as ⓫ **Nicopeia,** or "Our Lady of Victory." This Madonna has helped Venice persevere

Cafés on St. Mark's Square

Cafés line the square. Those with live music feature similar food, prices, and a three- to five-piece combo playing a selection of classical and pop hits, from Brahms to "Bésame Mucho." If you sit outside and get just a drink, expect to pay €12-20, including a €6 cover charge when the orchestra is playing (no cover charge otherwise). A coffee—your cheapest option—costs about €6 if you sit at an outside table, plus the €6 cover charge when the music plays, bringing it to €12 total (even at the venerable Caffè Florian). It's perfectly acceptable to nurse a cappuccino for an hour—you're paying for the music with the cover charge. For locations of the following cafés, see the map on page 77.

Caffè Florian (on the right as you face the church) is the most famous Venetian café and one of the first places in Europe to serve coffee (daily April-Oct 10:00-24:00, Nov-March 10:00-21:00). It's been a popular spot for a discreet rendezvous in Venice since 1720. The orchestra here plays a more classical repertoire than at the other cafés. The outside tables are the main action, but do walk inside through the richly decorated, old-time rooms where Casanova, Lord Byron, Charles Dickens, and Woody Allen have all paid too much for a drink (reasonable prices at bar in back).

Gran Caffè Quadri, opposite the Florian, has an equally illustrious history of famous clientele, including the writers Stendhal and Dumas, and composer Richard Wagner. **Gran Caffè Lavena,** near the Clock Tower, is newer and less storied.

Gran Caffè Chioggia, on the Piazzetta facing the Doge's Palace, charges slightly less, with one or two musicians, usually a pianist, playing cocktail jazz.

The following less-expensive options don't have live music, but you can enjoy overhearing music from nearby cafés: **Eden Bar,** next to Gran Caffè Quadri, is touristy, but that doesn't matter when you're enjoying your hot dog and Coke while sitting out on the piazza. **Caffè Aurora,** in the shadow of the Campanile, features nearly all the ambience of the orchestra cafés at half the price.

through plagues, wars, and crucial soccer games. When Mary answers a prayer, grateful Venetians leave offerings, like the old ⓬ **rifle** that hangs next to a Madonna-and-child on a pillar (as you approach the north transept).

In the south transept (to right of main altar), find the dim ⓭ **Discovery of Mark** mosaic high up on the west wall. This mosaic recreates the happy scene in 1094 when Mark's misplaced relics were found within a hollow column.

Additional Sights: The ⓮ **Treasury** (ask for the included and informative audioguide when you buy your ticket) and ⓯ **Golden Altarpiece** give you the best chance outside of Istanbul or Ravenna to see the glories of the Byzantine Empire. Venetian crusaders looted the Christian city of Constantinople and brought home piles of lavish loot (perhaps the lowest point in Christian history until the advent of TV evangelism). Much of this plunder is stored in the Treasury (Tesoro) of San Marco. As you view these treasures, remember that most were made in about A.D. 500, while Western Europe was stuck in the Dark Ages. Beneath the high altar lies the body of St. Mark ("Marce") and the Golden Altarpiece (Pala d'Oro), made of 250 blue-backed enamels with religious scenes, all set in a gold frame and studded with 15 hefty rubies, 300 emeralds, 1,500 pearls, and assorted sapphires, amethysts, and topaz (c. 1100).

In the ⓰ **San Marco Museum** (Museo di San Marco) upstairs you can see an up-close mosaic exhibition, a fine view of the church interior, a view of the square from the balcony with bronze horses, and (inside, in their own room) the original horses. These well-traveled horses, made during the days of Alexander the Great (fourth century B.C.), were taken to Rome by Nero, to Constantinople/Istanbul by Constantine, to Venice by crusaders, to Paris by Napoleon, back "home" to Venice when Napoleon fell, and finally indoors and out of the acidic air. The staircase up to the museum is in the atrium, near the basilica's main entrance, marked by a sign that says *Loggia dei Cavalli, Museo.*

▲▲▲**Doge's Palace (Palazzo Ducale)**—The seat of the Venetian government and home of its ruling duke, or doge, this was the most powerful half-acre in Europe for 400 years. The Doge's Palace was built to show off the power and wealth of the Republic. The doge lived with his family on the first floor, near the halls of power. From his once-lavish (now sparse) quarters, you'll follow the one-way tour through the public rooms of the top floor, finishing with the Bridge of Sighs and the prison. The place is

wallpapered with masterpieces by Veronese and Tintoretto. Don't worry much about the great art. Enjoy the building.

You'll see the restored facades from the **courtyard.** Notice a grand staircase (with nearly naked Moses and Paul Newman at the top). Even the most powerful visitors climbed this to meet the doge. This was the beginning of an architectural power trip.

In the **Senate Hall,** the 120 senators met, debated, and passed laws. Tintoretto's large *Triumph of Venice* on the ceiling (central painting, best viewed from the top) shows the city in all its glory. Lady Venice is up in heaven with the Greek gods, while barbaric lesser nations swirl up to give her gifts and tribute.

The **Armory**—a dazzling display originally assembled to intimidate potential adversaries—shows remnants of the military might that the empire employed to keep the East-West trade lines open (and the local economy booming).

The giant **Hall of the Grand Council** (175 feet by 80 feet, capacity 2,600) is where the entire nobility met to elect the senate and doge. It took a room this size to contain the grandeur of the Most Serene Republic. Ringing the room are portraits of the first 76 doges (in chronological order). The one at the far end that's blacked out is the notorious Doge Marin Falier, who opposed the will of the Grand Council in 1355. He was tried for treason, beheaded, and airbrushed from history.

On the wall over the doge's throne is Tintoretto's monster-piece, *Paradise,* the largest oil painting in the world. Christ and Mary are surrounded by a heavenly host of 500 saints. The painting leaves you feeling that you get to heaven not by being a good Christian, but by being a good Venetian.

Cross the covered **Bridge of Sighs** over the canal to the **prisons.** Circle the cells. Notice the carvings made by prisoners—from olden days up until 1930—on some of the stone windowsills of the cells, especially in the far corner of the building.

Cross back over the Bridge of Sighs, pausing to look through the marble-trellised windows at all of the tourists.

Cost and Hours: €14 combo-ticket (€13 Nov-March) includes admission to the Correr Museum; from April through October the combo-ticket includes your choice of a third city-run museum. The palace is also covered by the €18 Museum Pass—see page 75. If the line is long at the Doge's Palace, buy your ticket or pass at the Correr Museum across the square; then you can go straight to the Doge's turnstile, skirting along to the right of the long ticket-buying line and entering at the "prepaid tickets" entrance. Open daily April-Oct 8:30-18:30, Nov-March 8:00-17:30, last entry one hour before closing, tel. 041-271-5911, possible to book online at www.museicivicivineziani.it at least 48 hours in advance. It's next to St. Mark's Basilica, just off St. Mark's Square. Vaporetto stops:

San Marco or San Zaccaria.

Tours: The dry but informative audioguide costs €5 (€8/2 people, 1.5 hours, need ID or credit card for deposit). For a 1.25-hour live guided tour, consider the Secret Itineraries Tour, which takes you into palace rooms not otherwise open to the public (€18 includes Doge's Palace admission but not Correr Museum; €12 with combo-ticket or Museum Pass; 2-3 English-language tours each morning). Though the tour skips the palace's main hall, you're welcome to visit the hall afterward on your own. Reserve ahead for this tour in peak season—it can fill up as much as a month in advance. Book online at www.museicivicivenaziani.it or reserve by phone (tel. 848-082-000, from the US dial 011-39-041-4273-0892), or you can try just showing up at the info desk.

▲▲**Correr Museum (Museo Correr)**—This uncrowded museum gives you a good overview of Venetian history and art. The doge memorabilia, armor, banners, statues (by Canova), and paintings (by the Bellini family and others) re-create the festive days of the Venetian Republic. There are English descriptions and breathtaking views of St. Mark's Square throughout the museum.

Cost and Hours: €14 combo-ticket (€13 Nov-March) includes the Doge's Palace; from April through October the combo-ticket includes your choice of a third city-run museum. The combo-ticket always includes two other museums within the Correr: the National Archaeological Museum and the Monumental Rooms of Marciana National Library. The Correr is also covered by the €18 Museum Pass—see page 75. Open daily April-Oct 10:00-19:00, Nov-March 10:00-17:00, last entry one hour before closing, free and mandatory baggage check for bags bigger than a large purse, no photos, enter at far end of square directly opposite basilica, tel. 041-240-5211, www.museicivicivenaziani.it.

Avoid long lines at the crowded Doge's Palace by buying either of the museum passes listed above at the Correr Museum. For €12 you can see the Correr Museum and tour the Clock Tower on St. Mark's Square, but your ticket won't include the Doge's Palace. For more on reserving a Clock Tower tour, see page 76.

▲**Campanile (Campanile di San Marco)**—This dramatic bell tower replaced a shorter lighthouse, part of the original fortress that guarded the entry of the Grand Canal. The lighthouse crumbled into a pile of bricks in 1902, a thousand years after it was built. Today you'll see construction work being done to strengthen the base of the rebuilt tower. Ride the elevator 300 feet to the top of the bell tower for the best view in Venice (especially at sunset). For an ear-shattering experience, be on

top when the bells ring. The golden archangel Gabriel at the top always faces into the wind. Lines are longest at midday; beat the crowds and enjoy the crisp morning air at 9:00 or the cool evening breeze at 18:00.

Cost and Hours: €8, daily Easter-June and Oct 9:00-19:00, July-Sept 9:00-21:00, Nov-Easter 9:30-15:45, closed from Christmas to mid-Jan, tel. 041-522-4064, www.basilicosanmarco.it.

La Fenice Opera House (Gran Teatro alla Fenice)—During Venice's glorious decline in the 18th century, this was one of seven

opera houses in the city, and one of the most famous in Europe. For 200 years, great operas and famous divas debuted here, applauded by ladies and gentlemen in their finery. Then in 1996, an arson fire completely gutted the theater. But La Fenice ("The Phoenix") has risen from the ashes, thanks to an eight-year effort to rebuild the historic landmark according to photographic archives of the interior. To see the results at their most glorious, attend an evening **performance** (theater box office open daily 9:30-18:30, tel. 041-2424 answered daily 9:00-18:00, www.teatrolafenice.it).

You can also **tour the opera house** during the day. All you really see is the theater itself; there's no "backstage" tour of dressing rooms, or an opera museum. The auditorium, ringed with box seats, is impressive: pastel blue with sparkling gold filigree, muses depicted on the ceiling, and a starburst chandelier. It's also a bit saccharine and brings sadness to Venetians who remember the place before the fire. Other than a minor exhibit of opera scores and Maria Callas memorabilia, there's little to see from the world of opera. A dry 45-minute audioguide recounts two centuries of construction.

Cost and Hours: €8 tours, generally open daily 9:30-13:30, but can vary wildly, depending on the performance schedule—from being closed, open only an hour or two, or being open all day—so confirm in advance (call box office number listed above, schedule not posted on web). La Fenice is on Campo San Fantin, between St. Mark's Square and the Accademia Bridge. Nearest vaporetto stops: Santa Maria del Giglio and San Marco.

Behind St. Mark's Basilica

▲**Bridge of Sighs**—Connecting two wings of the Doge's Palace high over a canal, this enclosed bridge is currently being restored, so it's surrounded by scaffolding. Travelers popularized this bridge in the Romantic 19th century. Supposedly, a condemned man would be led over this bridge on his way to the prison, take one last

VENICE

look at the glory of Venice, and sigh. Though overhyped, when it's uncovered the Bridge of Sighs is undeniably tingle-worthy—especially after dark, when the crowds have dispersed and it's just you and floodlit Venice. A local legend says that lovers will be assured eternal love if they kiss on a gondola at sunset under the bridge.

The Bridge of Sighs is around the corner from the Doge's Palace: Walk toward the waterfront, turn left along the water, and look up the first canal on your left. You can walk across the bridge (from the inside) by visiting the Doge's Palace.

Church of San Zaccaria—This historic church is home to a sometimes-waterlogged crypt, a Bellini altarpiece, a Tintoretto painting, and the final resting place of St. Zachariah, the father of John the Baptist.

Cost and Hours: Free, €1 to enter crypt, €0.50 coin to light up Bellini's altarpiece, Mon-Sat 10:00-12:00 & 16:00-18:00, Sun 16:00-18:00 only, 2 canals behind St. Mark's Basilica.

Across the Lagoon from St. Mark's Square

▲**San Giorgio Maggiore**—This is the dreamy church-topped island you can see from the waterfront by St. Mark's Square. The striking church, designed by Palladio, features art by Tintoretto, a bell tower, and good views of Venice.

Cost and Hours: Free entry to church; May-Sept Mon-Sat 9:30-12:30 & 14:30-18:00, Sun 8:30-11:00 & 14:30-18:00; Oct-April until 16:30. The bell tower costs €3 and is accessible by elevator (runs from 30 minutes after the church opens until 30 minutes before the church closes).

Getting There: To reach the island from St. Mark's Square, take the five-minute ride on vaporetto #2 (€3, 6/hour, ticket valid for one hour; leaves from San Zaccaria-M.V.E. stop located east of Bridge of Sighs by equestrian statue, direction: Tronchetto). To get back to St. Mark's Square, take the #2 headed the opposite way (direction: San Marco).

Dorsoduro District

▲▲**Accademia (Galleria dell'Accademia)**—Venice's top art museum, packed with highlights of the Venetian Renaissance, fea-

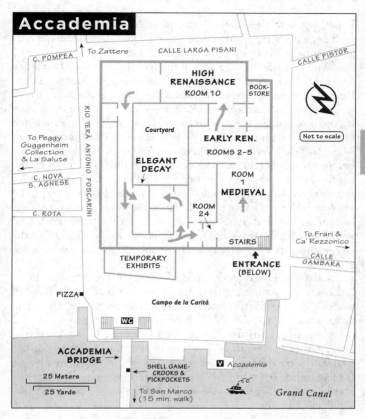

Accademia

To Zattere — CALLE LARGA PISANI — CALLE PISTOR

C. POMPEA

RIO TERÀ ANTONIO FOSCARINI

To Peggy Guggenheim Collection & La Salute

C. NOVA S. AGNESE

C. ROTA

HIGH RENAISSANCE
ROOM 10

BOOK-STORE

Courtyard

EARLY REN.
ROOMS 2–5

ELEGANT DECAY

ROOM 1
MEDIEVAL

ROOM 24

STAIRS

TEMPORARY EXHIBITS

ENTRANCE
(BELOW)

Not to scale

VENICE

To Frari & Ca' Rezzonico

CALLE GAMBARA

PIZZA

Campo de la Carità

WC

ACCADEMIA BRIDGE

25 Meters
25 Yards

SHELL GAME–CROOKS & PICKPOCKETS

To San Marco
(15 min. walk)

V *Accademia*

Grand Canal

tures paintings by the Bellini family, Titian, Tintoretto, Veronese, Tiepolo, Giorgione, Canaletto, and Testosterone. It's just over the wooden Accademia Bridge from the San Marco action.

The Accademia is the greatest museum anywhere for Venetian Renaissance art and a good overview of painters whose works you'll see all over town. Venetian art is underrated and, I think, misunderstood. It's nowhere near as famous today as the work of the florescent Florentines, but—with historical slices of Venice, ravishing nudes, and very human Madonnas—it's livelier, more colorful, and simply more fun. The Venetian love of luxury shines through in this collection, which starts in the Middle Ages and runs to the 1700s. Look for grand canvases of colorful, spacious settings, peopled with happy locals in extravagant clothes having a great time.

Medieval highlights include elaborate altarpieces and golden-haloed Madonnas, all painted at a time when realism, depth of field, and emotion were considered beside the point. Medieval

Venetians, with their close ties to the East, borrowed techniques such as gold-leafing, frontal poses, and "iconic" faces from the religious icons of Byzantium (modern-day Istanbul).

Among early masterpieces of the Renaissance are Mantegna's studly *St. George* and Giorgione's mysterious *The Tempest*. As the Renaissance reaches its heights, so do the paintings, such as Titian's magnificent *Presentation of the Virgin*. It's a religious scene, yes, but it's really just an excuse to display secular splendor (Titian was the most famous painter of his day—perhaps even more famous than Michelangelo). Veronese's sumptuous *Feast of the House of Levi* also has an ostensibly religious theme (in the middle, find Jesus eating his final meal)—but it's outdone by the luxury and optimism of Renaissance Venice. Life was a good thing and beauty was to be enjoyed. (Veronese was hauled before the Inquisition for painting such a bawdy Last Supper...so he fine-tuned the title). End your tour with Guardi's and Canaletto's painted "postcards" of the city—landscapes for visitors who lost their hearts to the romance of Venice.

Cost and Hours: €6.50, Mon 8:15-14:00, Tue-Sun 8:15-19:15, last entry 45 minutes before closing, no photos allowed. The dull audioguide costs €5 (€7/2 people). At Accademia Bridge, vaporetto: Accademia, tel. 041-522-2247, www.gallerieaccademia.org.

Avoiding Crowds: Expect long lines in the late morning, because they allow only 300 visitors in at a time; visit early or late to miss the crowds, or make a reservation at least a day in advance (€1 fee; calling 041-520-0345 is easier than reserving online at their clunky website; calls answered Mon-Fri 9:00-18:00, Sat 9:00-14:00, closed Sun).

Renovation: The museum is nearing the end of a years-long expansion, which will open up the ground floor to visitors. In 2012, some rooms may still be closed for construction, traffic may be rerouted, and some paintings may reside temporarily in other rooms. A few key works may not be on view at all.

▲▲**Peggy Guggenheim Collection**—The popular museum of far-out art, housed in the American heiress' former retirement palazzo, offers one of Europe's best reviews of the art of the first half of the 20th century. Stroll through styles represented by artists whom Peggy knew personally—Cubism (Picasso, Braque), Surrealism (Dalí, Ernst), Futurism (Boccioni), American Abstract Expressionism (Pollock), and a sprinkling of Klee, Calder, and Chagall.

Cost and Hours: €12, usually includes temporary exhibits, Wed-Mon 10:00-18:00, closed Tue, last entry 15 minutes before closing, audioguide-€7, 1- to 1.5-hour guided tour-€60, free and mandatory baggage check, no photos inside, a five-minute walk from the Accademia Bridge at Dorsoduro 704, vaporetto: Accademia or Salute, tel. 041-240-5411, www.guggenheim-venice.it.

▲**La Salute Church (Santa Maria della Salute)**—This impressive church with a crown-shaped dome was built and dedicated to the Virgin Mary by grateful survivors of the 1630 plague.

Cost and Hours: Free entry to church, daily 9:00-12:00 & 15:00-17:30. Sacristy—€2, may have shorter hours than church. It's a 10-minute walk from the Accademia Bridge; the Salute vaporetto stop is at its doorstep, tel. 041-241-1018, www.seminariovenezia.it.

▲**Ca' Rezzonico (Museum of 18th-Century Venice)**—This grand Grand Canal palazzo offers the best look in town at the life of Venice's rich and famous in the 1700s. Wander under ceilings by Tiepolo, among furnishings from that most decadent century, enjoying views of the canal and paintings by Guardi, Canaletto, and Longhi.

Cost and Hours: €8, covered by Museum Pass—see page 75; April-Oct Wed-Mon 10:00-18:00, Nov-March Wed-Mon 10:00-17:00; closed Tue year-round; last entry one hour before closing, 1.5-hour audioguide-€4 (€6/2 people), free and mandatory baggage check, at Ca' Rezzonico vaporetto stop, tel. 041-241-0100, www.museiciviciveneziani.it.

▲**Punta della Dogana**—This new museum of contemporary art makes the Dorsoduro a major destination for art-lovers. Housed in the former Customs House at the end of the Grand Canal, it features cutting-edge 21st-century art in spacious rooms. This isn't Picasso and Matisse, or even Pollock and Warhol— those guys are ancient history. But if you're into the likes of Jeff Koons, Cy Twombly, Rachel Whiteread, and a host of newer artists, the museum  is world-class. The displays change completely about every year, drawn from the museum's large collection. In fact, the art spreads over two locations—the triangular Customs House and Palazzo Grassi.

Cost and Hours: €15 for one locale, €20 for both; Wed-Mon 10:00-19:00, closed Tue, last entry one hour before closing; audioguide-€5 (€8/2 people), small café; in Italy call 199-139-139, otherwise use tel. 041-523-0313; www.palazzograssi.it. Punta della Dogana is near La Salute Church (Dogana *traghetto* or vaporetto: Salute). Palazzo Grassi is a bit upstream, on the east side of the Grand Canal (vaporetto: San Samuele).

Santa Croce District

▲▲▲Rialto Bridge—One of the world's most famous bridges, this distinctive and dramatic stone structure crosses the Grand Canal with a single confident span. The arcades along the top of the bridge help reinforce the structure...and offer some enjoyable shopping diversions, as does the **market** east of the bridge (souvenir stalls open daily, produce market closed Sun-Mon, fish market closed Sun).

▲Ca' Pesaro International Gallery of Modern Art—This museum features 19th- and early 20th-century art in a 17th-century canalside palazzo. The collection is strongest on Italian (especially Venetian) artists, but also presents a broad array of other well-known artists. The highlights are in one large room: Klimt's beautiful/creepy *Judith II,* with eagle-talon fingers; Kandinsky's *White Zig Zags* (plus other recognizable shapes); the colorful *Nude in the Mirror* by Bonnard that flattens the 3-D scene into a 2-D pattern of rectangles; and Chagall's surprisingly realistic portrait of his hometown rabbi, *The Rabbi of Vitebsk.* The adjoining Room VII features small-scale works by Matisse, Max Ernst, Mark Tobey, and a Calder mobile. Admission also includes an Oriental Art wing.

Cost and Hours: €8, covered by Museum Pass—see page 75, Tue-Sun 10:00-18:00, closed Mon, last entry one hour before closing, 2-minute walk from San Stae vaporetto stop, tel. 041-524-0662, www.museicivicieneziani.it.

Palazzo Mocenigo Costume Museum—The Museo di Palazzo Mocenigo offers a walk through six rooms of a fine 17th-century mansion with period furnishings, family portraits, ceilings painted (c. 1790) with family triumphs (the Mocenigos produced seven doges), Murano glass chandeliers in situ, and a paltry collection of costumes with sparse descriptions.

Cost and Hours: €5, covered by Museum Pass—see page 75, Tue-Sun 10:00-17:00, closed Mon, last entry one hour before closing, a block in from San Stae vaporetto stop, tel. 041-721-798, www.museicivicieneziani.it.

San Polo District

▲▲Frari Church (Basilica di Santa Maria Gloriosa dei Frari)—My favorite art experience in Venice is seeing art in the setting for which it was designed—as it is at the Frari Church. The Franciscan "Church of the Brothers" and the art that decorates it are warmed by the spirit of St. Francis. It features the work

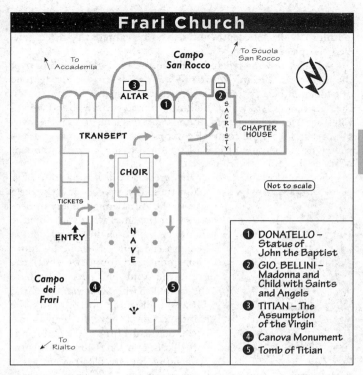

Frari Church

To Accademia

Campo San Rocco

To Scuola San Rocco

3 ALTAR

1

2 SACRISTY

CHAPTER HOUSE

TRANSEPT

CHOIR

Not to scale

TICKETS

ENTRY

NAVE

Campo dei Frari

4

5

To Rialto

1 DONATELLO – Statue of John the Baptist

2 GIO. BELLINI – Madonna and Child with Saints and Angels

3 TITIAN – The Assumption of the Virgin

4 Canova Monument

5 Tomb of Titian

of three great Renaissance masters: Donatello, Giovanni Bellini, and Titian—each showing worshippers the glory of God in human terms.

In **Donatello's wood statue of St. John the Baptist** (just to the right of the high altar), the prophet of the desert—dressed in animal skins and nearly starving from his diet of bugs 'n' honey—announces the coming of the Messiah. Donatello was a Florentine working at the dawn of the Renaissance.

Bellini's *Madonna and Child with Saints and Angels* painting (in the sacristy farther to the right) came later, done by a Venetian in a more Venetian style—soft focus without Donatello's harsh realism. While Renaissance humanism demanded Madonnas and saints that were accessible and human, Bellini places them in a physical setting so beautiful that it creates its own mood of serene holiness. The genius of Bellini, perhaps the greatest Venetian painter, is obvious in the pristine clarity, rich colors (notice Mary's clothing), believable depth, and reassuring calm of this three-paneled altarpiece.

Finally, glowing red and gold like a stained-glass window over the high altar, **Titian's** *The Assumption of the Virgin* sets the tone of exuberant beauty found in the otherwise sparse church. Titian the Venetian—a student of Bellini—painted steadily for 60 years... you'll see a lot of his art. As stunned apostles look up past the swirl of arms and legs, the complex composition of this painting draws you right to the radiant face of the once-dying, now-triumphant Mary as she joins God in heaven.

Feel comfortable to discreetly freeload off passing tours. For

many, these three pieces of art make a visit to the Accademia Gallery unnecessary (or they may whet your appetite for more). Before leaving, check out the Neoclassical pyramid-shaped Canova monument and (opposite that) the grandiose tomb of Titian. Compare the carved marble *Assumption* behind Titian's tombstone portrait with the painted original above the high altar.

Cost and Hours: €3, Mon-Sat 9:00-18:00, Sun 13:00-18:00, last entry 30 minutes before closing, no visits during services, modest dress recommended. On Campo dei Frari, near San Tomà vaporetto and *traghetto* stops.

Audioguides: You can rent an audioguide for €2 (€3/2 people). Or download a free Rick Steves audio tour of the Frari Church to your mobile device; see page 19.

Concerts: The church occasionally hosts evening concerts (€20, buy ticket at church, no concerts in winter). For concert details, look for fliers, check www.basilicadeifrari.it, or call the church at 041-272-8611.

▲▲Scuola San Rocco—Sometimes called "Tintoretto's Sistine Chapel," this lavish meeting hall (next to the Frari Church) has some 50 large, colorful Tintoretto paintings plastered to the walls and ceilings. The best paintings are upstairs, especially the *Crucifixion* in the smaller room. View the neck-breaking splendor with one of the mirrors available at the entrance.

Cost and Hours: €7, audioguide-€1, daily 9:30-17:30, last entry 30 minutes before closing, tel. 041-523-4864, www.scuola grandesanrocco.it.

Church of San Polo—This nearby church, which pales in comparison to the two sights just listed, is only worth a visit for art-lovers. One of Venice's oldest churches (from the ninth century),

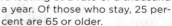

A Dying City?

Venice's population (about 60,000) is half what it was just 30 years ago, and people are leaving at a rate of a thousand a year. Of those who stay, 25 percent are 65 or older.

Sad, yes, but imagine raising a family here: Apartments are small, high up, and expensive. Humidity and occasional flooding make basic maintenance a pain. Home-improvement projects require navigating miles of bureaucratic red tape, and you must follow regulations intended to preserve the historical ambience. Everything is expensive because it has to be shipped in from the mainland. You can easily get glass and tourist trinkets, but it's hard to find groceries or get your shoes fixed. Running basic errands involves lots of walking and stairs—imagine crossing over arched bridges while pushing a child in a stroller and carrying a day's worth of groceries.

With millions of visitors a year (150,000 a day at peak times), on any given day Venetians are likely outnumbered by tourists. Despite government efforts to subsidize rents and build cheap housing, the city is losing its residents. The economy itself is thriving, thanks to tourist dollars and rich foreigners buying second homes. But the culture is dying. Even the most hopeful city planners worry that in a few decades, Venice will not be a city at all, but a museum, a cultural theme park, a decaying Disneyland for adults.

San Polo features works by Tintoretto, Veronese, and Tiepolo and son.

Cost and Hours: €3, Mon-Sat 10:00-17:00, closed Sun, last entry 15 minutes before closing.

Cannaregio District
Jewish Ghetto—Tucked away in the Cannaregio District is the ghetto where Venice's Jewish population once lived segregated from their non-Jewish neighbors. While today's Jewish population is dwindling, the neighborhood still has centuries of history, not to mention Jewish-themed sights and eateries.

In medieval times, Jews were grudgingly allowed to do business in Venice, but they weren't permitted to live there until 1385 (subject to strict laws and special taxes). Anti-Semitic forces tried to oust them from the city, but in 1516, the doge compromised by restricting Jews to a special (undesirable) neighborhood. It was located on an easy-to-isolate island near the former foundry *(geto)*—in time the word "ghetto" caught on across Europe as a term for any segregated neighborhood.

The population swelled with immigrants from elsewhere in Europe, reaching 5,000 in the 1600s, the Golden Age of Venice's Jews. Restricted within their tiny neighborhood (the Gheto Novo, or "New Ghetto"), they expanded upward, building six-story "sky-scrapers" that still stand today. The community's five synagogues were built atop the high-rise tenements. (As space was very tight and you couldn't live above a house of worship, this was the most practical use of precious land.) Only two synagogues are still active. You can spot them (with their five windows) from the square, but to visit them you have to book a tour through the Jewish Museum.

This original ghetto becomes most interesting after touring the **Jewish Museum** (Museo Ebraico) at #2902b. Exhibits include silver menorahs, cloth covers for Torah scrolls, and a concise bilin-gual exhibit on the Venetian Jewish community up through 1797 (€3, June-Sept Sun-Fri 10:00-19:00, Oct-May Sun-Fri 10:00-17:30, closed Sat and Jewish holidays, bookstore, small café, Campo de Gheto Novo, tel. 041-715-359, www.museoebraico.it). You can see three of the ghetto's five **synagogues** with the 45-minute English tour (€8.50, tours run hourly on the half-hour June-Sept Sun-Fri 10:30-17:30, Oct-May Sun-Fri 10:30-16:30, no tours Sat and Jewish holidays). Group sizes are limited (the 11:30 and 12:30 tours are the most popular), so show up 20 minutes early to be sure you get in.

Getting There: From either the San Marcuola vaporetto stop or the train station, walk five minutes to the Ponte de Guglie bridge that crosses the Cannaregio Canal. About 50 yards north of the bridge, a small covered alleyway (Sotoportego del Gheto Novo) leads between the *farmacia* and the Gam-Gam Kosher Restaurant, through a newer Jewish section, across a bridge, and into the his-toric core of the ghetto at Campo de Gheto Novo.

Calatrava Bridge (a.k.a. Ponte della Costituzione)—This controversial bridge, officially called "Constitution Bridge," is just upstream and around the bend from the train station. Only the fourth bridge to cross the Grand Canal, it carries foot traf-fic between the train station and Piazzale Roma. A modern struc-ture of glass, steel, and stone, the bridge finally opened in 2008 after delays, cost overruns, and questions about its stability.

The bridge was designed by Spanish architect Santiago Calatrava, whose other projects include a museum in his hometown of Valencia, Spain; the twisting torso skyscraper in Malmö, Sweden; and the Olympic Sports complex in Athens, Greece.

Interestingly, Calatrava's modern structure harkens back to the past, employing the same low-arch design of many older Venetian bridges. Pedestrians walk over similar shallow stair steps, and the bridge uses local Istrian stone.

Ca' d'Oro—This "House of Gold" palace, fronting the Grand Canal, is quintessential Venetian Gothic (Gothic seasoned with Byzantine and Islamic accents—see "Ca' d'Oro" on page 67). Inside, the permanent collection includes a few big names in Renaissance painting—Ghirlandaio, Signorelli, and Mantegna; a glimpse at a lush courtyard; and a grand view of the Grand Canal.

Cost and Hours: €6, slow and dry audioguide-€4, Mon 8:15-14:00, Tue-Sun 8:15-19:15, last entry 30 minutes before closing, free peek through hole in door of courtyard, vaporetto: Ca' d'Oro, on Calle Ca' d'Oro at #3932, tel. 041-520-0345, www.cadoro.org.

Castello District

▲Scuola Dalmata di San Giorgio—This little-visited "school" (which means "meeting place") features an exquisite wood-paneled chapel decorated with the world's best collection of paintings by Vittorio Carpaccio (1465-1526).

The Scuola, a reminder that cosmopolitan Venice was once Europe's melting-pot, was one of a hundred such community centers for various ethnic, religious, and economic groups, supported by the government partly to keep an eye on foreigners. It was here that the Dalmatians (from the southern coast of present-day Croatia) worshipped in their own way, held neighborhood meetings, and preserved their culture.

Cost and Hours: €4, Mon 14:45-18:00, Tue-Sat 9:15-13:00 & 14:45-18:00, Sun 9:15-13:00, midway between St. Mark's Square and the Arsenale, on Calle dei Furlani at #3259a, tel. 041-522-8828.

Santa Elena—For a pleasant peek into a completely non-touristy, residential side of Venice, walk or catch vaporetto #1 from St. Mark's Square to the neighborhood of Santa Elena (at the fish's tail). This 100-year-old suburb lives as if there were no tourism. You'll find a kid-friendly park, a few lazy restaurants, and beautiful sunsets over San Marco.

La Biennale—Every odd year (next in 2013), Venice hosts a world's fair of contemporary art in buildings and pavilions scattered over the Giardini park and the Arsenale. The festival is an excuse for temporary art exhibitions, concerts, and other cultural events around the city (roughly Feb-Nov, take vaporetto #1 or #2 to Giardini-Biennale stop, www.labiennale.org).

Venice's Lagoon

The island of Venice sits in a lagoon—a calm section of the Adriatic protected from wind and waves by the natural breakwater of the Lido. Beyond the church-topped island of San Giorgio Maggiore (directly in front of St. Mark's Square—see page 86), four interesting islands hide out in the lagoon: Cimitero, Murano, Burano, and Torcello.

San Michele (a.k.a. Cimitero) is the cemetery island—the final resting place of Venetians and a few foreign VIPs, from poet Ezra Pound to composer Igor Stravinsky. The stopover is easy, since boats come every 10 minutes. If you even half-enjoy wandering through old cemeteries, you'll dig this one—it's full of flowers, trees, and birdsong, and has an intriguing chapel. Many visitors find this island (expectedly) pretty dead (cemetery open daily April-Sept 7:30-18:00, Oct-March 7:30-16:30; reception to the left as you enter, free WC to the right, no picnicking).

Murano is famous for its glassmaking. From the Colonna vaporetto stop, skip the glass shops in front of you, walk to the right, and wander up the street along the canal, **Fondamenta dei Vetrai** (Glassmakers' Embankment). The Faro district of Murano, on the other side of the canal, is packed with factories *(fabriche)* and their furnaces *(fornaci)*. They each offer a similar, usually free, 20-minute glassblowing demonstration of an  artisan in action firing up something in a furnace, followed by an almost comically high-pressure sales pitch. (The spiel is brief, and there's absolutely no obligation to buy anything.)

Murano's **Glass Museum** (Museo Vetrario) traces the history of this delicate art (€6.50, covered by Museum Pass—see page 75, daily April-Oct 10:00-18:00, Nov-March 10:00-17:00, last entry 30 minutes before closing, Fondamenta Giustinian 8, tel. 041-739-586, www.museiciviciveneziani.it).

Burano, known for its lacemaking and countless lace shops, offers a delightful pastel village alternative to big, bustling Venice. The main drag from the vaporetto stop into town is packed with tourists and lined with shops, some of which sell Burano's locally produced white wine. Wander to the far side of the island, and the mood shifts. Explore to the right of the leaning tower for a peaceful yet intensely pastel, small-town lagoon world. Benches lining a little promenade at the water's edge make another pretty picnic spot.

Burano's **Lace Museum** (Museo del Merletto di Burano) is newly renovated (€5, covered by Museum Pass—see page 75;

April-Oct Tue-Sun 10:00-18:00, Nov-March Tue-Sun 10:00-17:00, closed Mon year-round, last entry 30 minutes before closing, tel. 041-730-034, www.museicivicivenezia.it).

Torcello is the birthplace of Venice, where the first mainland refugees settled, escaping the barbarian hordes. Yet today, it's the least-developed island (pop. 20) and is mostly in its natural state, marshy and shrub-covered. There's little for tourists to see except the church (a 10-minute walk from the dock), which claims to be the oldest in Venice and has impressive mosaics, a climbable bell tower, and a modest museum containing Roman and medieval sculpture, and medieval manuscripts (€3 for any one sight or €10 for all sights plus an audioguide; most sights open daily March-Oct 10:30-18:00, Nov-Feb 10:00-16:30, museum closed Mon; museum tel. 041-730-761, church/bell tower tel. 041-730-119).

Getting There: You can travel to any of the four islands by vaporetto. Since single vaporetto tickets (€6.50) expire after one hour, using a vaporetto pass for a lagoon excursion makes more sense (e.g., a 12-hour pass for €16; see page 55 for more on vaporetto tickets).

The Route from the Rialto and Campo Santa Maria Formosa: Walk 15 minutes to the Fondamente Nove vaporetto stop on the north shore of Venice (the "back" of the fish). Lines #41 and #42 converge here before heading out to Murano. Catch either one (every 10 minutes).

From Fondamente Nove the boats cross to San Michele (whose stop is called Cimitero) in six minutes, then continue another three minutes to Murano-Colonna.

On the way to Murano, we'll make a quick visit to the cemetery (Cimitero stop). We'll arrive at Murano-Colonna, but leave Murano from a different stop (Murano-Faro). At Murano-Faro, we'll board vaporetto LN for the 30-minute trip to Burano. From Burano, we'll side-trip to Torcello on vaporetto T (5-minute trip each way). From Burano, we'll return to Venice on vaporetto LN, arriving either at Fondamente Nove (quicker, 40 minutes) or the San Zaccaria-Pietà stop near St. Mark's Square (more scenic, 70 minutes).

Experiences in Venice

Gondola Rides

Gondolas cost lots more after 19:00 but are also more romantic and relaxing under the moon. A rip-off for some, this is a traditional must for romantics. Gondoliers charge €80 for a 40-minute ride during the day; €100 from 19:00 on. These prices are standard, and listed in the TI's *Shows & Events* brochure, as well as on the gondoliers' association website (www.gondolavenezia.it).

VENICE

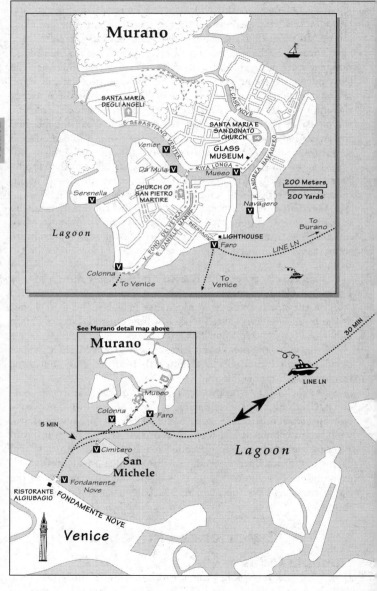

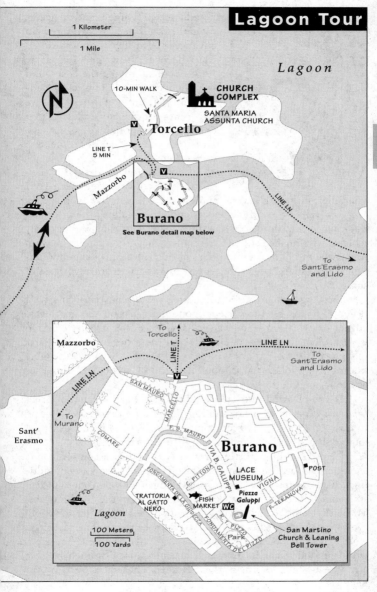

Lagoon Tour

1 Kilometer

1 Mile

Lagoon

10-MIN WALK

CHURCH COMPLEX

SANTA MARIA ASSUNTA CHURCH

Torcello

LINE T 5 MIN

Mazzorbo

Burano

See Burano detail map below

LINE LN

To Sant'Erasmo and Lido

VENICE

Burano detail map

To Torcello

LINE T

LINE LN

Mazzorbo

LINE LN

To Sant'Erasmo and Lido

SAN MAURO

To Murano

COMARE

F. B. MAURO

C. PITTONA

FONDAMENTA DELLA GIUDECCA

Sant' Erasmo

Lagoon

100 Meters

100 Yards

MARCELLO

VIA B. GALUPPI

FISH MARKET

TRATTORIA AL GATTO NERO

WC

FONDAMENTA DEL PIZZO

Pizzo Park

Burano

LACE MUSEUM

VIGNA

Piazza Galuppi

F. TERRANOVA

POST

San Martino Church & Leaning Bell Tower

To add *musica* (a singer and an accordionist), you'll need to arrange it in advance, and it'll cost an additional €110 before 19:00, or €130 after 19:00. You can divide the cost—and the romance—among up to six people per boat, but you'll need to save two seats for the musicians if you choose to be serenaded. Only two seats (the ones in back) are next to each other.

Because you might get a narration plus conversation with your gondolier, talk with several and choose one you like who speaks English well. To avoid misunderstandings, establish the price and duration of the trip before boarding, enjoy your ride, and pay only when you're finished. I don't recommend haggling, but if you want to try, you might find softer prices during the day. Most gondoliers honor the official prices, but a few might try to scam you out of some extra euros.

Pick a gondola station in an area you'd enjoy paddling in. I often go to the Bacino Orseolo gondoliers just off the northwest corner of St. Mark's Square (go through Sotoportego de l'Arco Celeste), but there are stations all over the more frequented parts of Venice. On cold, dark winter evenings, you will have trouble finding a gondolier; try at Hotel Bauer, on Campo San Moisè, or ask your hotelier for help.

If you've hired musicians and want to hear a Venetian song *(un canto Veneziano),* try requesting *"Venezia La Luna e Tu."* Asking to hear *"O Sole Mio"* (which comes from Naples) is like asking a lounge singer in Cleveland to sing "The Eyes of Texas."

Glide through nighttime Venice with your head on someone's shoulder. Follow the moon as it sails past otherwise unseen buildings. Silhouettes gaze down from bridges while window glitter spills onto the black water. You're anonymous in the city of masks, as the rhythmic thrust of your striped-shirted gondolier turns old crows into songbirds. This is extremely relaxing (and, I think, worth the extra cost to experience at night). Women, beware... while gondoliers can be extremely charming, local women say that anyone who falls for one of these Romeos "has slices of ham over her eyes."

For cheap gondola thrills during the day, stick to the €0.50 one-minute ferry ride on a Grand Canal *traghetto.* At night, *vaporetti* are nearly empty, and it's a great time to cruise the Grand Canal on the slow boat #1. Or hang out on a bridge along the gondola route and wave at romantics.

Festivals

Venice's most famous festival is **Carnevale,** the celebration Americans call Mardi Gras (Feb 11-21 in 2012, www.carnevale

.venezia.it). Carnevale, which means "farewell to meat," originated centuries ago as a wild two-month-long party leading up to the austerity of Lent. In Carnevale's heyday—the 1600s and 1700s—you could do pretty much anything with anybody from any social class if you were wearing a mask. These days it's a tamer 10-day celebration, culminating in a huge dance lit with fireworks on St. Mark's Square. Sporting masks and costumes, Venetians from kids to businessmen join in the fun. Drawing the biggest crowds of the year, Carnevale has nearly been a victim of its own success, driving away many Venetians (who skip out on the craziness to go skiing in the Dolomites).

VENICE

Every odd year (next in 2013), the city hosts the **Venice Biennale International Art Exhibition,** a world-class contemporary art fair spread over the Arsenale and sprawling Castello Gardens. Artists representing 70 nations from around the world offer the latest in contemporary art forms: video, computer art, performance art, and digital photography, along with painting and sculpture (take vaporetto #1 or #2 to Giardini-Biennale; for details and an events calendar, see www.labiennale.org). The actual exhibition usually runs from June through November, but other events—film, dance, theater—loosely connected with the Biennale are held throughout the year (starting as early as Feb) in various venues on the island.

Other typically Venetian festival days filling the city's hotels with visitors and its canals with decked-out boats are **Feast of the Ascension Day** (May 17 in 2012), **Feast and Regatta of the Redeemer** (third Sun in July and the preceding Sat evening, June 20-21 in 2012), and the **Historical Regatta** (old-time boats and pageantry, first Sat and Sun in Sept, Sept 1-2 in 2012). **Vogalonga** is a colorful regatta that attracts more than 1,500 human-powered watercraft; teams of often costumed participants follow a 20-mile course through the canals and lagoon (late May-early June, www.vogalonga.it). Smaller regattas include the **Murano Regatta** (early July) and the **Burano Regatta** (mid-Sept).

Venice's patron saint, **St. Mark,** is commemorated every April 25. Venetian men celebrate the day by presenting roses to the women in their lives (mothers, wives, and lovers).

Every November 21 is the **Feast of Our Lady of Good Health.** On this local "Thanksgiving," a bridge is built over the Grand Canal so that the city can pile into La Salute Church and remember how Venice survived the gruesome plague of 1630. On this day, Venetians eat smoked lamb from Dalmatia (which was the cargo of the first ship admitted when the plague lifted).

Shopping in Venice

Shoppers like Murano glass (described earlier), Burano lace (fun lace umbrellas for little girls), Carnevale masks (fine shops and artisans all over town), art repro-  ductions (posters, postcards, and books), prints of Venetian scenes, traditional stationery (pens and marbled paper prod- ucts of all kinds), calendars with Venetian scenes, silk ties, scarves, and plenty of goofy knickknacks (Titian mousepads, gondolier T-shirts, and little plastic gondola condom holders).

Shops are generally open from 9:00 to 13:00 and from 15:00 to 19:30. In touristy Venice, more shops are open on Sunday than in the rest of the country. If you're  buying a substantial amount from nearly any shop, bar- gain—it's accepted and almost expected. Offer less and offer to pay cash; merchants are very conscious of the bite taken by credit-card companies.

Popular **Venetian glass** is available in many forms: vases, tea sets, decanters, glasses, jewelry, lamps, mod sculptures (such as solid-glass aquariums), and on and on. Shops will ship it home for you, but you're likely to pay as much or more for the shipping as you are for the item(s), and you may have to pay duty on larger pur- chases. Make sure the shop insures their merchandise *(assicurazi- one)*, or you're out of luck if it breaks. If your item arrives broken and it has been insured, take a photo of the pieces, send it to the shop, and they'll replace it for free. For a cheap, packable souvenir, consider the glass-bead necklaces sold at vendors' stalls throughout Venice.

If you'd like to watch a quick glassblowing demonstration, try **Galleria San Marco**, a tour-group staple on St. Mark's Square at #139, which offers great demos every few minutes. They let indi- vidual travelers flashing this book sneak in with tour groups to see the show (and sales pitch). And, if you buy anything, show this book and they'll take 20 percent off the listed price. The gallery faces the square behind the orchestra nearest the church; come to the door at #139, go through the shop and climb the stairs (daily 9:00-18:00, tel. 041-271-8671, fax 041-271-8679, info@galleriasanmarco.it, manager Marino Busetto, see map on page 77).

If you're serious about glass, visit the island of **Murano,** its Glass Museum, and many shops. Their glassblowing demonstrations are fun; you'll usually see a vase and a "leetle 'orse" made from molten glass. You'll find greater variety on Murano, but prices are usually the same as in Venice.

Along Venice's many shopping streets, you'll notice fly-by-night street vendors selling knockoffs of famous-maker handbags (Louis Vuitton, Gucci, etc.). These vendors are willing to bargain. But buyer beware: If you're caught purchasing fakes, you could get hit with a fine. Legitimate manufacturers are raising a stink about these street merchants, and the government is trying to rid the city of them. Authorities frustrated in their attempts to actually arrest the merchants have made it illegal to buy counterfeit items. Their hope: The threat of a huge fine will scare potential customers away—so unlicensed merchants will be driven out of business and off the streets.

Nightlife in Venice

You must experience Venice after dark. The city is quiet at night, as tour groups stay in the cheaper hotels of Mestre on the mainland, and the masses of day-trippers return to their beach resorts and cruise ships. Gondolas cost more, but are worth the extra expense (see page 97). At night, *vaporetti* are nearly empty, and it's a great time to cruise the Grand Canal on the slow boat #1.

Venice has a busy schedule of events, festivals, and entertainment. Check at the TI for listings, and keep an eye out for publications such as *Shows & Events* (bilingual, available at some hotels and online at www.turismovenezia.it, click on "Venezia").

Baroque Concerts—Venice is a city of the powdered-wig Baroque era. For about €25 (prices vary), you can take your pick of traditional Vivaldi concerts in churches throughout town. Homegrown Vivaldi is as ubiquitous here as Strauss is in Vienna and Mozart is in Salzburg. In fact, you'll find frilly young Vivaldis hawking concert tickets on many corners. The TI has a list of this week's Baroque concerts. Most shows start at 20:30 and generally last 1.5 hours. You'll see posters in hotels all over town (hotels sell tickets at face-value). A one-stop shop for concerts is the Vivaldi Store, at the east end of Rialto Bridge (on Salizada del Fontego dei Tedeschi at #5537, tel. 041-522-1343). Tickets for Baroque concerts in Venice can usually be bought the same day as the concert, so don't bother with websites that sell tickets with a surcharge.

Consider the venue carefully. The general rule of thumb: Musicians in wigs and tights offer better spectacle; musicians in black-and-white suits are better performers. **San Vidal Church** (at the north end of Accademia Bridge) and the **Interpreti Veneziani orchestra** (which often plays there) are reliably top-notch (tel. 041-277-0561, www.interpretiveneziani.com). For the latest on church concerts, check any TI or visit www.turismovenezia.it. If you're attending a concert at **Scuola San Rocco** (tickets €15-30), arrive 30 minutes early to enjoy the art (which you'd have to pay €7 to see during the day).

Other Performances—Venice's most famous theaters are **La Fenice** (grand old opera house, box office tel. 041-2424, see page 85), **Teatro Goldoni** (mostly Italian live theater), and **Teatro della Fondamenta Nuove** (theater, music, and dance).

Musica a Palazzo is a unique evening of opera at the Doge's Palace. You'll spend about 45 minutes in three sumptuous rooms as eight musicians (generally four instruments and four singers) perform. With these kinds of surroundings, under Tiepolo frescoes, you'll be glad you dressed up. As there are only 70 seats, you must book by phone or online in advance. Opera-lovers find this to be a wonderful evening (€50, nightly shows at 20:30, Palazzo Barbarigo-Minotto, Fondamenta Duodo o Barbarigo—on the Grand Canal next to the Santa Maria del Giglio vaporetto stop, mobile 340-971-7272, www.musicapalazzo.com).

Venezia is advertised as "the show that tells the great story of Venice" and "simply the best show in town." I found the performance to be slow-moving and a bit cheesy, and the venue to be disappointing (€39, nightly May-Oct at 20:00, Nov-April at 19:00; 80 minutes, Teatro San Gallo, just off St. Mark's Square on Campo San Gallo, tel. 041-241-2002, www.teatrosangallo.net).

St. Mark's Square—For tourists, St. Mark's Square is the highlight, with lantern light and live music echoing from the cafés. Just being here after dark is a thrill, as **dueling café orchestras** entertain (see sidebar on page 81). Every night, enthusiastic musicians play the same songs, creating the same irresistible magic. Hang out for free behind the tables (allowing you to move easily on to the next orchestra when the musicians take a break), or spring for a seat and enjoy a fun and gorgeously set concert. If you sit a while, it can be €12-20 well spent (for a drink and the cover charge for music). Dancing on the square is free (and encouraged). Streetlamp halos, live music, floodlit history, and a ceiling of stars make St. Mark's magic at midnight. You're not a tourist, you're a living part of a soft Venetian night...an alley cat with money. In the misty light, the moon has a golden hue. Shine with the old lanterns on the gondola piers, where the sloppy lagoon splashes at the Doge's Palace...reminiscing.

Sleeping in Venice

For hassle-free efficiency and the sheer magic of being close to the action, I favor hotels that are handy to sightseeing activities. I've listed rooms in four neighborhoods: St. Mark's bustle, the Rialto action, the quiet Dorsoduro area behind the Accademia art museum, and near the train station (handy for train travelers, but far from the action). I also mention several apartment rentals, big fancy hotels, cheap dorms, and places on the mainland.

Outside of holidays and weekends, it's possible to visit Venice without booking ahead, but it's smart, simple, and less stressful to have a reservation in place. Book a room as soon as you know when you'll be in town. Contact the hotel directly, not through any tourist information room-finding service (they can't give opinions on quality).

Note that hotel websites are particularly valuable for Venice, because they often include detailed directions that can help you (and your bags) get to your rooms with a minimum of wrong turns in this navigationally challenging city.

Over the past decade, Venice has seen the opening of several big new hotels, countless little boutique hotels, and the conversion of many private homes to short-term rental apartments. This glut of hotels means that demand is soft and, therefore, so are prices. Most hotels have tossed straight pricing out the window. Many hoteliers are happy to make a deal. Email several hotels to ask for their best price, then compare and make your choice.

Prices listed are for one-night stays in peak season (April, May, June, Sept, and Oct), include breakfast, and assume you're

Sleep Code

(€1 = about $1.40, country code: 39)
S = Single, **D** = Double/Twin, **T** = Triple, **Q** = Quad, **b** = bathroom, **s** = shower only. Unless otherwise noted, credit cards are accepted, breakfast is included, and English is generally spoken.

To help you easily sort through these listings, I've divided the accommodations into three categories based on the price for a standard double room with bath:

$$$ **Higher Priced**—Most rooms €180 or more.
$$ **Moderately Priced**—Most rooms between €130-180.
$ **Lower Priced**—Most rooms €130 or less.

Prices can change without notice; verify the hotel's current rates online or by email. For other updates, see www.ricksteves.com/update.

booking directly (not through a TI or online hotel-booking engine). Prices can climb even higher during a few festivals. Almost all places drop prices from November through March (except during Carnevale—Feb 11-March 21 in 2012—and Christmas) and in July and August. A €180 double can cost €80-90 in winter. Off-season, don't pay the rates I list.

Many hotels in Venice list rooms on www.venere.com, especially for last-minute vacancies (two to three weeks before the date). Before you bite, check to see if rates are lower than the prices in this book.

For tips on making reservations, see page 26.

Near St. Mark's Square

To get here from the train station or Piazzale Roma bus station, ride the vaporetto to San Zaccaria—either the slow #1 or the fast #2 (from the Tronchetto parking lot, it's #2 only). Consider using your ride to follow my tour of the Grand Canal (see page 62); to make sure you arrive via the Grand Canal, confirm that your boat goes "*via Rialto*."

Nearby Laundries: Lavanderia Gabriella offers full service a few streets north of St. Mark's Square (€15/load includes wash, dry, and fold; drop off Mon-Fri 8:00-12:30, closed Sat-Sun; pick up 2 hours later or next working day; with your back to the door of San Zulian Church, go over Ponte dei Ferali, take first right down Calle dei Armeni, then first left on Rio Terà de le Colonne to #985; tel. 041-522-1758, Elisabetta).

Effe Erre, a modern self-service *lavanderia*, is near recommended Hotel al Piave on Ruga Giuffa at #4826 (daily 6:30-23:00, €14/load, mobile 349-058-3881, Massimo).

East of St. Mark's Square

Located near the Bridge of Sighs, just off the Riva degli Schiavoni waterfront promenade, these places rub drainpipes with Venice's most palatial five-star hotels.

$$$ Hotel Campiello, lacy and bright, was once part of a 19th-century convent. Ideally located 50 yards off the waterfront, on a tiny square, its 16 rooms offer a tranquil, friendly refuge for travelers who appreciate comfort and professional service (Sb-€130, Db-€180, 10 percent discount with cash and this book if you reserve direct and pay on arrival, air-con, elevator, free Wi-Fi; from the San Zaccaria vaporetto stop, take Calle del Vin, between pink Hotel Danieli and Hotel Savoia e Jolanda, to Castello 4647; tel. 041-520-5764, fax 041-520-5798, www.hcampiello .it, campiello@hcampiello.it; family-run for four generations, currently by Thomas, Monica, Nicoletta, and Marco). They also rent three modern family apartments, under rustic timbers just steps away (up to €380/night).

$$$ Hotel Fontana is a nice family-run place with 15 rooms near a school, two bridges behind St. Mark's Square. Their annex across the street has much lower ceilings and slightly lower prices (Sb-€120, Db-€180, family rooms, 10 percent cash discount, quieter rooms on garden side, 2 rooms have terraces for €20 extra, air-con, elevator, free Internet access, pay Wi-Fi by reception, on Campo San Provolo at Castello 4701, tel. 041-522-0579, fax 041-523-1040, www.hotelfontana.it, info@hotelfontana.it, cousins Diego and Gabriele). From the San Zaccaria vaporetto dock, take Calle de le Rasse—to the left of pink Hotel Danieli —then turn right at the end, and continue to the first square.

$$ Locanda al Leon rents 14 decent, reasonably priced rooms just off Campo Santi Filippo e Giacomo (Db-€145-155, Tb-€180, Qb-€230, these prices with cash and this book, air-con, free Internet access and Wi-Fi, Campo Santi Filippo e Giacomo, Castello 4270, tel. 041-277-0393, fax 041-521-0348, www.hotelal leon.com, leon@hotelalleon.com, Giuliano and Marcella). From the San Zaccaria vaporetto stop, take Calle dei Albanesi (two streets left of pink Hotel Danieli) to its far end.

$$ Hotel la Residenza is a grand old palace facing a peaceful square. It has 15 great rooms on three levels and a huge, luxurious lounge with a piano. This is a great value for romantics—you'll feel like you're in the Doge's Palace after hours. Hang out in the living room and you become royalty (Sb-€100, Db-€165-200, air-con, free Wi-Fi, on Campo Bandiera e Moro at Castello 3608, tel. 041-528-5315, fax 041-523-8859, www.venicelaresidenza.com, info @venicelaresidenza.com, Giovanni). From the Bridge of Sighs, walk east along Riva degli Schiavoni, cross three bridges, and take the first left up Calle del Dose to Campo Bandiera e Moro.

$ Albergo Doni is dark and quiet—a bit of a time-warp— with 13 well-worn, once-classy rooms up a creaky stairway. It's run by a likable smart aleck named Gina, her niece Tessa, and her nephew, an Italian stallion named Nikos (D-€95, Db-€120, T-€125, Tb-€160, reserve with credit card but pay in cash, ceiling fans, three Db rooms have air-con, free Wi-Fi by reception, avoid their overflow apartment, on Fondamenta del Vin at Castello 4656, tel. & fax 041-522-4267, www.albergodoni.it, albergodoni @hotmail.it). From the San Zaccaria vaporetto stop, cross one bridge to the right and take the first left (marked Calle del Vin), then turn left at the little square named Ramo del Vin, jog left, and find the hotel ahead on Fondamenta del Vin.

North of St. Mark's Square

$$ Hotel al Piave, with 28 fine, air-conditioned rooms above a bright and classy lobby, is fresh, modern, and comfortable. You'll

VENICE

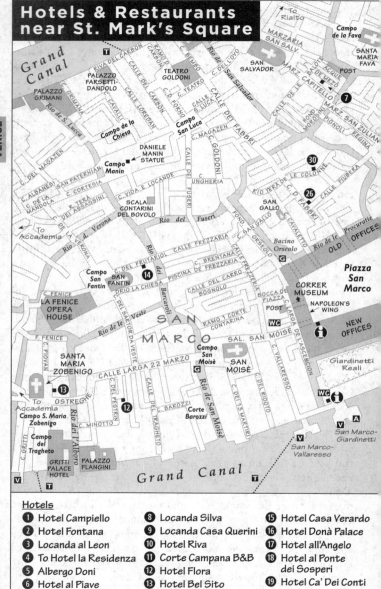

Hotels & Restaurants near St. Mark's Square

Hotels

1. Hotel Campiello
2. Hotel Fontana
3. Locanda al Leon
4. To Hotel la Residenza
5. Albergo Doni
6. Hotel al Piave
7. Casa Cosmo
8. Locanda Silva
9. Locanda Casa Querini
10. Hotel Riva
11. Corte Campana B&B
12. Hotel Flora
13. Hotel Bel Sito
14. Hotel Mercurio
15. Hotel Casa Verardo
16. Hotel Donà Palace
17. Hotel all'Angelo
18. Hotel al Ponte dei Sosperi
19. Hotel Ca' Dei Conti

VENICE

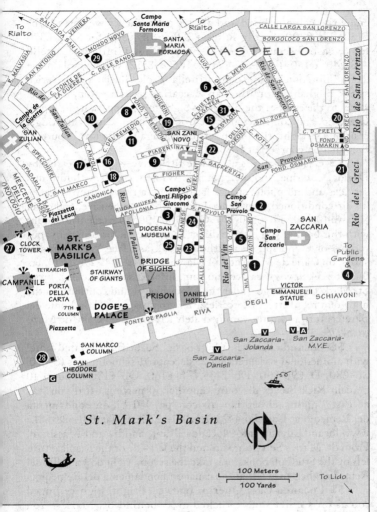

Eateries & Services

- ⑳ Ristorante alla Conchiglia
- ㉑ Trattoria da Giorgio ai Greci
- ㉒ Ristorante Antica Sacrestia
- ㉓ Birreria Forst Café
- ㉔ Bar Verde
- ㉕ Ristorante alla Basilica
- ㉖ Rizzo Café
- ㉗ Gran Caffè Lavena (Gelato)
- ㉘ Todaro Gelateria
- ㉙ Coop Supermarket
- ㉚ Lavanderia Gabriella
- ㉛ Lavanderia Effe Erre

enjoy the neighborhood and always get a cheery welcome (Db-
€150, Tb-€200; family suites-€280 for 4, €300 for 5, or €320
for 6; cash discount, free Wi-Fi, on Ruga Giuffa at Castello
4838/40, tel. 041-528-5174, fax 041-523-8512, www.hotelalpiave
.com, info@hotelalpiave.com, Mirella, Paolo, Ilaria, and Federico
speak English). From the San Zaccaria vaporetto stop, take the
street to the right of the Bridge of Sighs to Campo Santi Filippo e
Giacomo, and continue on Calle drio la Chiesa. Cross the bridge,
continue straight, then turn left onto Ruga Giuffa until you find
the hotel on your left at #4838.

$$ Casa Cosmo is a humble little five-room place run by
Davide, Caterina, and their parents. While it comes with minimal
services and no public spaces (aside from a tiny rooftop terrace),
it's air-conditioned, very central, somewhat inexpensive, and quiet
(Db-€140-150, Tb-€160-170, Qb-€180-190, 10 percent discount
with this book if you reserve direct and pay cash, breakfast in your
room—or €5/person less without breakfast, free Wi-Fi, lots of
stairs, on Calle de Mezo at San Marco 4976, tel. 041-296-0710, fax
041-862-3439, www.casacosmo.com, info@casacosmo.com). From
St. Mark's Square, go under the Clock Tower and continue on the
high-rent retail street Mercerie, after crossing a canal on Ponte dei
Bareteri turn right, then immediately left onto tiny Calle de Mezo
to #4976.

$$ Locanda Silva is a big, basic, beautifully located hotel
with a functional style, renting 23 decent old-school rooms (S-€70,
Sb-€80, D-€90-100, Db-€135, Tb-€160, Qb-€180, request 10
percent Rick Steves discount, another 10 percent off if you stay
at least 2 nights, closed Jan, air-con, pay Wi-Fi, on Fondamenta
del Remedio at Castello 4423, tel. 041-522-7643, fax 041-528-6817,
www.locandasilva.it, info@locandasilva.it, Sandra and Massimo).
From St. Mark's Square, go around the left side of the basilica, turn
left by the Studium bookstore, take the second right down Calle del
Remedio, then turn left at the canal on Fondamenta del Remedio.

$$ Locanda Casa Querini rents six bright, high-ceilinged
rooms on a quiet square tucked away behind St. Mark's. You
can enjoy your breakfast or a sunny picnic/happy hour sitting at
their tables right on the sleepy little square (Db-€150, third per-
son-€20-25, one cheaper small double, ask for cash discount, air-
con, pay Wi-Fi, halfway between San Zaccaria vaporetto stop and
Campo Santa Maria Formosa at Castello 4388 on Campo San
Zaninovo/Giovanni Novo, tel. 041-241-1294, fax 041-523-6188,
www.locandaquerini.com, casaquerini@hotmail.com, Patrizia
and Silvia). From the San Zaccaria vaporetto stop, take the street
to the right of the Bridge of Sighs to Campo Santi Filippo e
Giacomo, continue on Calle drio la Chiesa, take the second left,
and curl around to the left into the little square, Campo San

Zaninovo/Giovanni Novo.

$ Hotel Riva, with gleaming marble hallways, big exposed beams, fine antique furnishings, and lots of stairs, is romantically situated on a canal along the gondola serenade route. You could actually dunk your breakfast rolls in the canal (but don't). Ten of the 30 rooms come with air-conditioning for no extra charge—request one when you reserve. Or, if you prefer a view and lots of light but no air-conditioning, you can ask Sandro to hold a corner *(angolo)* room for you (Sb-€90, D-€100, Db-€120-140, Tb-€170-190, higher prices are for corner rooms, reserve with credit card but pay with cash only, on Ponte de l'Anzolo at Castello 5310, tel. 041-522-7034, fax 041-528-5551, www.hotelriva.it, info@hotelriva .it, Daniella). Facing St. Mark's Basilica, walk behind it on the left along Calle de la Canonica, take the first left (at blue *Pauly & C* mosaic in street), continue straight, go over the bridge, and angle right to the hotel at Ponte de l'Anzolo.

$ Corte Campana B&B, run by enthusiastic and helpful Riccardo, rents three quiet and characteristic rooms just behind St. Mark's Square. One room has a private bath down the hall (Db-€125, Qb-€190, prices are soft, cash only, 2-night minimum, at least €10/night less for stays of 4 nights, air-con, free Internet access, pay Wi-Fi, on Calle del Remedio at Castello 4410, 4th floor, tel. & fax 041-523-3603, mobile 389-272-6500, www.cortecampana.com, info@cortecampana.com). Print out complete directions, including photos of all the street signs, from Riccardo's website.

West of St. Mark's Square

$$$ Hotel Flora sits buried in a sea of fancy designer boutiques and elegant hotels almost on the Grand Canal. It's formal, with uniformed staff and grand public spaces, yet the 43 rooms have a homey warmth and the garden oasis is a sanctuary for foot-weary guests (generally Db-€260, check website for special discounts or email Sr. Romanelli for 10 percent Rick Steves discount off standard prices, air-con, elevator, free Wi-Fi and Internet access, San Marco 2283a, tel. 041-520-5844, fax 041-522-8217, www.hotelflora .it, info@hotelflora.it). It's at the end of Calle dei Bergamaschi, one of several skinny lanes just off Calle Larga XXII Marzo.

$$$ Hotel Bel Sito offers pleasing yet well-worn Old World character, 34 rooms, generous public spaces, a peaceful courtyard, and a picturesque location—facing a church on a small square between St. Mark's Square and the Accademia (Sb-€110, Db-€185, air-con, free Wi-Fi, elevator; catch vaporetto #1 to Santa Maria del Giglio stop, take street inland to square, hotel is at far end to your right on Campo Santa Maria Zobenigo/del Giglio at San Marco 2517; tel. 041-522-3365, fax 041-520-4083, www.hotelbelsito venezia.it, info@hotelbelsito.info, manager Rossella).

$$ Hotel Mercurio offers 25 peaceful, comfortable, and recently renovated rooms near La Fenice Opera House. Some rooms offer canal views (Sb-€130, Db-€170, Tb-€200, Qb-€230-250, €10 less with cash, air-con, pay Wi-Fi, on Calle del Fruttariol at San Marco 1848, tel. 041-522-0947, fax 041-241-1079, www.hotelmercurio.com, info@hotelmercurio.com, Monica, Vittorio, and Natale). From the San Marco-Vallaresso vaporetto stop, follow Calle Vallaresso to Calle Frezzaria, turn right, and follow it over a bridge as it becomes Calle del Frutariol. The hotel is on the left just before La Fenice Opera House.

Near the Rialto Bridge

Vaporetto #2 brings you to the Rialto quickly from the train station, the Piazzale Roma bus station, and the parking-lot island of Tronchetto. You can also take the slower vaporetto #1 (but not from Tronchetto).

West of the Rialto Bridge

$ Pensione Guerrato, above the colorful Rialto produce market and just two minutes from the Rialto Bridge, is run by friendly, creative, and hardworking Roberto and Piero. Their 800-year-old building—with 24 spacious, air-conditioned, and charming rooms—is simple, airy, and wonderfully characteristic (D-€90, Db-€130, Tb-€150, Qb-€170, Quint/b-€185, these prices with this book and cash, check website for special discounts, Rick Steves readers can ask for €5/night discount below Web specials, free Wi-Fi, on Calle drio la Scimia at San Polo 240a, tel. & fax 041-528-5927, www.pensioneguerrato.it, pensione.guerrato@gmail.com, Monica and Rosanna). From the train station, take vaporetto #1 to the Mercato Rialto stop (comes before the "Rialto" stop), exit the boat to your right, and follow the waterfront. Calle drio la Scimia (not simply Scimia, the block before), is on the left—you'll see the hotel sign. My tour groups book this place for 50 nights each year. Sorry. The Guerrato also rents family apartments in the old center (great for groups of 4-8) for around €55 per person.

East of the Rialto Bridge

$$$ Hotel al Ponte Antico is exquisite, professional, and small. With nine plush rooms, a velvety royal living/breakfast room, and its own dock for water taxi arrivals, it's perfect for a romantic anniversary. Because its wonderful terrace overlooks the Grand Canal, Rialto Bridge, and market action, its non-canal-view rooms may be a better value (Db-€310, superior Db-€390, deluxe canal-front Db-€470, air-con, free Wi-Fi and Internet access; 100 yards from Rialto Bridge, find Campo San Bartolomeo, exit square on the statue's back side, cross bridge, pass Coin department store on right, then turn left down the dark and empty Calle del Aseo to Cannaregio 5768; tel. 041-241-1944, fax 041-241-1828, www.al ponteantico.com, info@alponteantico.com).

$ Locanda la Corte is perfumed with elegance without being snooty. Its 19 attractive, high-ceilinged, wood-beamed rooms— Venetian-style, done in earthy pastels—circle a small, quiet court-yard (Sb-€100, standard Db-€120, superior Db-€150, 10 percent discount with cash, ask for Rick Steves discount, suites and family rooms available, air-con, free Wi-Fi and Internet access, on Calle Bressana at Castello 6317, tel. 041-241-1300, fax 041-241-5982, www.locandalacorte.it, info@locandalacorte.it, Marco, Raffaela, and Tommy the cat). Take vaporetto #52 from the train station to Fondamente Nove, exit the boat to your left, follow the waterfront, and turn right after the second bridge to reach Santi Giovanni e Paolo. Facing the Rosa Salva bar, take the street to the left (Calle Bressana); the hotel is a short block away at #6317, before the bridge.

$ Casa Pisani Canal Hotel is a sweet little place rent-ing five rooms (Db-€110-130, huge Db suite overlooking canal-€240, air-con, free Wi-Fi and Internet access, on Calle de le Erbe at Cannaregio 6105, tel. 041-724-1030, fax 041-724-1039, www .casapisanicanal.it, info@casapisanicanal.it, Tortorella family). It's close to Campo Santi Giovanni e Paolo, and reachable either from Fondamente Nove or Rialto; see their website for directions.

$ Alloggi Barbaria rents eight backpacker-type rooms on one floor around a bright but institutional-feeling common area. Beyond Campo Santi Giovanni e Paolo, this Ikea-style place is a long walk from the action, in a residential neighborhood, and only a step above a youth hostel (Db-€90-100, third or fourth per-son-€25 each, pay cash for best price, family deals, limited break-fast, air-con, free Wi-Fi, on Calle de le Capucine at Castello 6573, tel. 041-522-2750, fax 041-277-5540, www.alloggibarbaria.it, info @alloggibarbaria.it, Giorgio and Fausto). Take vaporetto #52 from the train or bus stations to Ospedale stop, turn left as you get off the boat, then right down Calle de le Capucine.

Near the Accademia Bridge

When you step over the Accademia Bridge, the commotion of touristy Venice is replaced by a sleepy village laced with canals. This quiet area, next to the best painting gallery in town, is a 15-minute walk from the Rialto or St. Mark's Square.

The fast vaporetto #2 connects the Accademia Bridge with the train station (15 minutes), Piazzale Roma bus stop (20 min-utes), Tronchetto parking lot (25 minutes), and St. Mark's Square (5 minutes). For hotels south of the Accademia Bridge, vaporetto #51 to Zattere (or the Alilaguna speedboat from the airport to Zattere) are good options.

VENICE

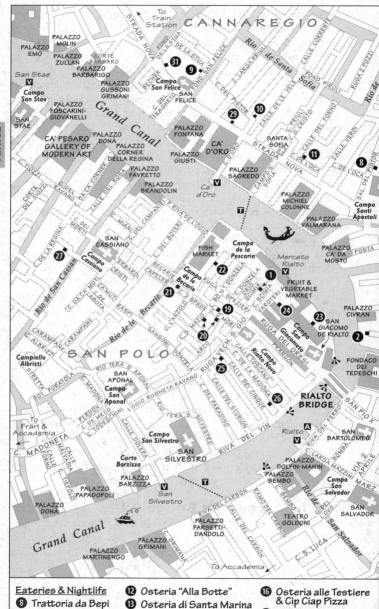

Eateries & Nightlife

8 Trattoria da Bepi
9 Vini da Gigio
10 Trattoria Ca' d'Oro
11 Osteria al Bomba
12 Osteria "Alla Botte"
13 Osteria di Santa Marina
14 Rosticceria San Bartolomeo
15 Osteria al Portego
16 Osteria alle Testiere & Cip Ciap Pizza
17 Osteria al Mascaron
18 Peter Pan Kebabs
19 Cantina Do Mori

VENICE

Hotels & Restaurants near the Rialto Bridge

Hotels

1. Pensione Guerrato
2. Hotel al Ponte Antico
3. Locanda la Corte
4. Casa Pisani Canal Hotel
5. To Alloggi Barbaria
6. Hotel Giorgione
7. Foresteria della Chiesa Valdese

100 Meters
100 Yards

To Vaporetto Dock

Lagoon

FONDAMENTE NOVE

CANNAREGIO

L'Acqua Dolce

C. VENIER

C. DEL FORNO

C. PROVERBI

PRETI

SANTI APOSTOLI

Campo de la Cason

C. MAL.

SAN CANZIAN

Campo San Canzian

C. WIDMANN

Rio dei Santi Apostoli

Campo Corner

MAGAZEN

RIO TERA

SALIZADA SAN CANZIAN

BOLDU

Rio de San Gio Grisostomo

BAGARAN

MIRACOLI

SAN GRISOSTOMO

SAN GIOVANNI GRISOSTOMO

SEOSTOMO

COIN DEP'T STORE

Campo Santa Maria Nova

SANTA MARIA DEI MIRACOLI

C. CASTELI

CALLE DE LA TESTA

Rio de la Panada

CALLE LARGA GALLINA

Campo Santi Giovanni & Paolo

COLLEONI STATUE

C. DE LA ERBE

Rio dei Mendicanti

FONDAMENTA DEI MENDICANTI

HOSPITAL

SANTI GIOVANNI & PAOLO (SAN ZANIPOLO)

SALIZADA S. ZANIPOLO

MADONA S. ZANIPOLO

C. BRESSANA

To 5

C. FELZI

Rio de Santa Marina

CASTELLO

C. SCALETA

Campo Santa Marina

FRUTARIOL

C. PIOMBO

MARGA

MARCELLO

Rio del Piombo

Rio del DOSE

Campo S. Bartolomeo

BISSA

C. CARMINATI

C. DE LA NAVE

SAN LIO

Rio de la Fava

PONTE S. ANTONIO

C. FAVA

C. DE L'AQUILA NERA

SALIZADA SAN LIO

DEL PARADISO

VENIERA

C. SAN ANTONIO

FOND. DEI PRETI

Rio d. Pestrin

Campo Santa Maria Formosa

C. LONGA S. MARIA FORMOSA

SANTA MARIA FORMOSA

C. DEI ORDI

C. DE MEZO

DEI STAGNERI

C. DEL STAGNER

Campo de la Fava

SANTA MARIA FAVA

C. NAVASIA

MONDO NOVO

C. DE LE BANDE

Rio de S. M. Formosa

RUGA GIUFFA

C. MEZO

C. DETRIO MAGAZEN

SALV.

C. DE ACQUA

C. DE MEZO

MARZ.

CAPITELLO

S. ZUL.

DE LE

S. CAPITELLO

POST

SAN MARCO

F. D. REMEDIO

CALLE QUEREN

To San Marco

To San Marco

To San Marco

OSPEDALETO

20. Bar all'Arco & Ostaria ai Storti
21. Cantina Do Spade
22. Pesce Pronto
23. Bancogiro Bar
24. Al Mercà
25. Antica Ostaria Ruga Rialto
26. Osteria al Diavolo e l'Acquasanta
27. Trattoria Pizzeria al Nono Risorto
28. Osteria da Alberto
29. Grom Gelateria
30. Coop Supermarket
31. Billa Supermarket

South of the Accademia Bridge

$$$ Pensione Accademia fills the 17th-century Villa Maravege like a Bellini painting. Its 27 rooms are comfortable, elegant, and air-conditioned. You'll feel aristocratic gliding through its grand public spaces and lounging in its wistful, breezy gardens (Sb-€140, standard Db-€239, bigger "superior" Db-€289, Qb-€335, ask for discount when you book, pay Wi-Fi; on Fondamenta Bollani at Dorsoduro 1058; facing Accademia art museum, go right, cross the bridge, go right to where the small canal hits the big one; tel. 041-521-0188, fax 041-523-9152, www.pensioneaccademia.it, info @pensioneaccademia.it).

$$$ Hotel Agli Alboretti is a cozy, family-run, 23-room place in a quiet neighborhood a block behind the Accademia art museum. With red carpeting and wood-beamed ceilings, it feels classy (Sb-€120, Db-€210, Tb-€240, Qb-€260, air-con, elevator, free Wi-Fi, 100 yards from the Accademia vaporetto stop on Rio Terà A. Foscarini at Dorsoduro 884, tel. 041-523-0058, fax 041-521-0158, www.aglialboretti.com, info@aglialboretti.com, Anna).

$$$ Hotel Belle Arti has a grand entry and a formal, stern staff. With the ambience of a modern American hotel, its 64 rooms feel out of place in musty Old World Venice (Sb-€150, Db-€240, Tb-€270, air-con, elevator, pay Wi-Fi in lobby; 100 yards behind Accademia art museum: facing museum, jog left, then right, down Rio Terà A. Foscarini to Dorsoduro 912a; tel. 041-522-6230, fax 041-528-0043, www.hotelbellearti.com, info@hotelbellearti.com).

$$ Pensione la Calcina, the home of English writer John Ruskin in 1876, maintains a 19th-century formality. It comes with all the three-star comforts in a professional yet intimate package. Its 32 rosy, perfumed rooms are squeaky clean, with nice wood furniture, hardwood floors, and a peaceful canalside setting facing Giudecca Island (Sb-€140, Sb with view-€150, Db-€150-240, Db with view-€290-310, Qb-€280, air-con, free Wi-Fi and Internet access, rooftop terrace, buffet breakfast outdoors on platform over lagoon, near Zattere vaporetto stop at south end of Rio de San Vio at Dorsoduro 780, tel. 041-520-6466, fax 041-522-7045, www .lacalcina.com, info@lacalcina.com). Guests get discounted meals at their La Piscina restaurant.

$$ Casa Rezzonico is a silent getaway far from the madding crowds. Its private garden terrace has perhaps the lushest grass in Italy, and its seven spacious, very Venetian rooms have garden/ canal views (Sb-€130, Db-€160, Tb-€190, Qb-€220, ask for discount when you book, air-con, free Wi-Fi, on Fondamenta Gherardini at Dorsoduro 2813, tel. 041-277-0653, fax 041-277-5435, www .casarezzonico.it, info@casarezzonico.it). Take vaporetto #1 to Ca' Rezzonico, head up Calle del Traghetto, cross Campo San Barnaba to the canal, and continue on Fondamenta Gherardini to #2813.

$$ Hotel Galleria has nine tight, velvety rooms, most with views of the Grand Canal. Some rooms are quite narrow. It's run with a family feel by Luciano and Stefano (S-€85, D-€125, skinny Grand Canal view Db-€155, palatial Grand Canal view Db-€185, includes breakfast in room, ceiling fans, free Wi-Fi, 30 yards from Accademia art museum, next to recommended Foscarini pizzeria at Dorsoduro 878a, tel. 041-523-2489, fax 041-520-4172, www .hotelgalleria.it, info@hotelgalleria.it).

$$ Don Orione Religious Guest House is a big cultural center dedicated to the work of a local man who became a saint in modern times. Filling an old monastery, it feels institutional, like a modern retreat center—clean, peaceful, and strictly run, with 74 rooms. It's beautifully located, comfortable, and a fine value (Sb-€88, Db-€144, Tb-€187, Qb-€224, profits go to mission work in the developing world, groups welcome, air-con, elevator, pay Wi-Fi, on Rio Terà A. Foscarini, Dorsoduro 909a, tel. 041-522-4077, fax 041-528-6214, www.donorione-venezia.it, info@donorione -venezia.it). From the Zattere vaporetto stop, turn right, then turn left. It's just after the church at #909a.

$ Ca' San Trovaso rents seven simple rooms split between the main building and a nearby annex. The location is peaceful, on a small canal (Sb-€90, Db-€115, Db with bigger canal view and air-con-€130, Tb-€145, these prices with cash—includes breakfast in your room, air-con in most rooms, free cable Internet, no common space except small roof terrace, off Fondamenta de le Romite at Dorsoduro 1350/51, tel. 041-277-1146, mobile 339-445-8821, fax 041-277-7190, www.casantrovaso.com, info@casantrovaso.com, Mark and his son Alessandro). From the Zattere vaporetto stop, exit left, and cross a bridge. Turn right at tiny Calle Trevisan, cross another bridge, cross the adjacent bridge, take an immediate right, and then the first left. Nearby, Mark's wife Cristina runs **Casa di Sara,** a brightly colored B&B with four quiet rooms, a tiny roof terrace, and the same prices (mobile 345-070-8547, www.casadi sara.com, info@casadisara.com).

North of the Accademia Bridge

$$$ Foresteria Levi, run by a foundation that promotes research on Venetian music, offers 35 quiet, institutional yet comfortable and spacious rooms (Sb-€100, Db-€190, Tb-€210, Qb-€240, ask for Rick Steves discount—10-20 percent in high season, 20-50 percent in low season; fans, elevator, free Wi-Fi, laundry, on Calle Giustinian at San Marco 2893, tel. 041-786-711, fax 041-786-766, www.foresterialevi.it, info@foresterialevi.it). It's 80 yards from the Accademia Bridge on the St. Mark's side. Leaving the bridge (opposite the Accademia vaporetto stop), take an immediate left, cross the Ponte Giustinian bridge, and go down Calle Giustinian

VENICE

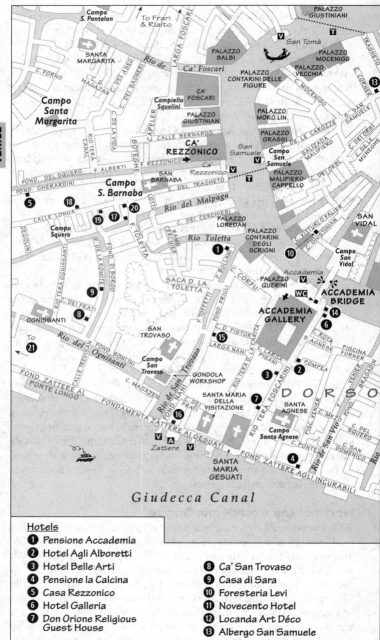

Hotels

1. Pensione Accademia
2. Hotel Agli Alboretti
3. Hotel Belle Arti
4. Pensione la Calcina
5. Casa Rezzonico
6. Hotel Galleria
7. Don Orione Religious Guest House
8. Ca' San Trovaso
9. Casa di Sara
10. Foresteria Levi
11. Novecento Hotel
12. Locanda Art Déco
13. Albergo San Samuele

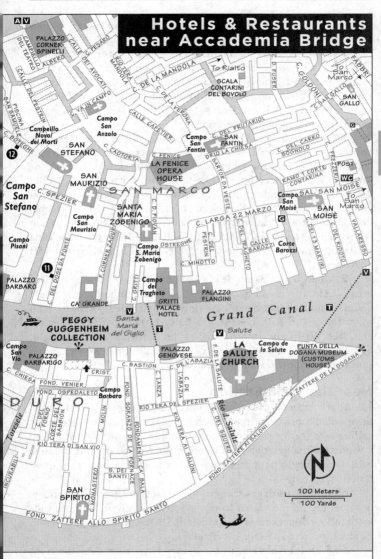

Hotels & Restaurants near Accademia Bridge

VENICE

Eateries

14 Ristorante/Pizzeria Accademia Foscarini

15 Enoteca Cantine del Vino Già Schiavi

16 Terrazza del Casin dei Nobili

17 Casin dei Nobili

18 Pane Vino e San Daniele

19 Enoteca e Trattoria la Bitta

20 Grom Gelateria

21 To Billa Supermarket

straight to the Fondazione Levi building. Buzz the *Foresteria* door to the right.

$$$ Novecento Hotel rents nine plush rooms on three floors. This boutique hotel is decorated circa-1900 throughout, with a big lounge and an elegant living room (Db-€240-260, air-con, lots of stairs, free Wi-Fi; on Calle del Dose, off Campo San Maurizio at San Marco 2683; tel. 041-241-3765, fax 041-521-2145, www .novecento.biz, info@novecento.biz).

$$ Locanda Art Déco is a charming little place, though there's not much Art Deco to be seen. A wrought-iron staircase leads from the inviting lobby to six small but thoughtfully deco-rated rooms on three floors (Db-€140-160, nicer Db-€170-200, Tb-€200-230, 3-night minimum on weekends, 5 percent cash dis-count, air-con, free Wi-Fi, lots of stairs; on Calle de le Botteghe, just north of the Accademia Bridge off Campo San Stefano, at San Marco 2966; tel. 041-277-0558, fax 041-270-2891, www.locanda artdeco.com, info@locandaartdeco.com). They also rent loft apartments.

$ Albergo San Samuele is a backpacker place: dumpy but in a great locale. It rents 12 basic rooms in a crumbling old palace near Campo San Stefano. Sleep here only if their price is far less than other listings (S-€70, D-€90, Db-€110, extra bed-€30, no break-fast, free Wi-Fi and Internet access, on Salizada San Samuele at San Marco 3358, tel. 041-520-5165, fax 041-522-8045, www.albergo sansamuele.it, info@albergosansamuele.it).

Near the Train Station

I don't recommend the train station area. It's crawling with noisy, disoriented tourists with too much baggage and people whose life's calling is to scam visitors out of their money. It's so easy just to hop a vaporetto upon arrival and sleep in the Venice of your dreams. Still, some like to park their bags near the station, and if so, these hotels stand out.

Nearby Laundry: Orange, the nearest self-service laundry, is across the Grand Canal from the station (daily 7:30-22:30, €14/load, follow directions to recommended Albergo Marin, on Ramo de le Chioverete at Santa Croce 665b).

$$$ Hotel Abbazia, in the dreary hotel zone near the train station, fills a former abbey with both history and class. The refec-tory makes a grand living room for guests, a garden fills the old courtyard, and the halls leading to 50 rooms are monkishly wide (Db-€180, larger Db-€210—choose Venetian or modern style, ask for 10 percent Rick Steves discount when you book direct, air-con, free Wi-Fi, no elevator but plenty of stairs, fun-loving staff, 2 blocks from the station on the very quiet Calle Priuli dei Cavaletti, Cannaregio 68, tel. 041-717-333, fax 041-717-949, www.abbazia

hotel.com, info@abbaziahotel.com).

$ Locanda Herion rents 17 basic rooms for a decent price (Db-€120, 10 percent discount with cash, air-con, pay Wi-Fi, on Campiello Augusto Picutti at Cannaregio 1697a, tel. 041-275-9426, fax 041-275-6647, www.locandaherion.com, info@locandaherion .com). Exiting the train station, turn left to follow Rio Terà Lista de Spagna. Cross the Ponte de Guglie bridge and turn right at the yellow *San Marcuola traghetto* sign to find the hotel.

$ Albergo Marin and its staff offer 19 good-value, quiet rooms handy to the train station (Sb-€110, D-€90, Db-€120, Tb-€150, 5 percent cash discount, fans on request, free Wi-Fi in public spaces, on Ramo de le Chioverete at Santa Croce 670b, tel. 041-718-022, fax 041-721-485, www.albergomarin.it, info@albergomarin.it, Giacomo). From the station, cross the stone bridge over the Grand Canal and go right along the embankment. Take the first left, then the first right, then right again to #670b.

$ The Chef's Wife B&B is run by American Stacy Gibboni. The "chef" is her Italian husband, who runs the La Colombina restaurant next door. Together they rent one sprawling and very cozy 2-bedroom apartment (with electric kettle and fridge but no kitchen) for two to four people (Db-€100, Tb/Qb-€150, ask for Rick Steves rate, 2-night minimum, simple breakfast; huge living room has piano, board games, and DVD player; no air-con, free Wi-Fi, adjacent to Stacy's art studio, on Campiello del Pegoloto at Cannaregio 1801, no phone calls, www.thechefswife.eu, stacys guesthouse@hotmail.it). It's near the San Marcuola vaporetto stop—see Stacy's website for directions.

$ Hotel S. Lucia, 150 yards from the train station, is oddly modern and sterile, with bright and spacious rooms and tight showers. Its 15 rooms are simple and clean. Guests enjoy their sunny garden area out front (S-€60, D-€80, Db-€105, Tb-€130, 5 percent cash discount, breakfast-€5, air-con, pay Wi-Fi, on Calle de la Misericordia at Cannaregio 358, tel. 041-715-180, fax 041-710-610, www.hotelslucia.com, info@hotelslucia.com, Gianni and Alessandra). Exit the station, head left, then take the second left onto Calle de la Misericordia. The hotel is 100 yards ahead on the right.

$ Alloggi Henry, a family-owned hotel, rents 15 simple and flowery rooms in a quiet residential neighborhood near the Jewish Ghetto. It's a 10-minute walk from the train station (D-€80, Db-€100, Tb-€130, Qb-€160, prices good with cash and this book through 2012, 10 percent discount if you stay at least 3 nights, no breakfast, air-con, free Wi-Fi, on Calle Ormesini at Cannaregio 1506e, tel. 041-523-6675, fax 041-715-680, www.alloggihenry.com, info@alloggihenry.com, Manola and Henry). From the station, follow Lista de Spagna, San Leonardo, and Farsetti. Turn left on

VENICE

Hotels near the Train Station

1. Hotel Abbazia
2. Locanda Herion
3. Albergo Marin & Launderette
4. The Chef's Wife B&B
5. Hotel S. Lucia
6. Alloggi Henry
7. Brek Cafeteria

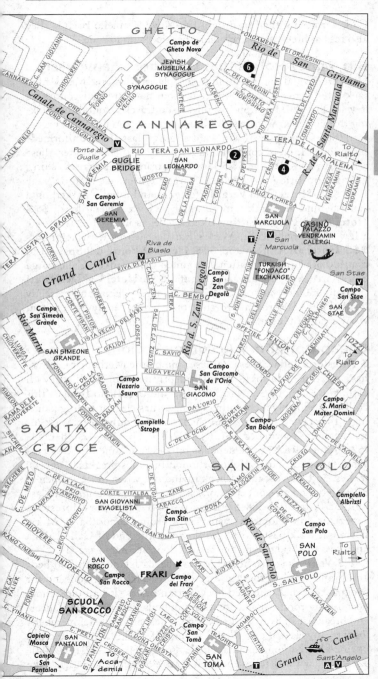

VENICE

Calle Ormesini, then turn right into tiny Campiello Briani. They also rent a three-room apartment that sleeps up to nine.

Big, Fancy Hotels that Discount Shamelessly

Here are several big, plush, four-star places with greedy, sky-high rack rates (around Db-€300) that often have great discounts (as low as Db-€120) for drop-ins, off-season travelers, or online booking through their websites. All are on the map on page 108, except for Hotel Giorgione. If you want sliding-glass-door, uniformed-receptionist kind of comfort and formality in the old center, these are worth considering: **$$$ Hotel Giorgione** (big, garish, shiny, near Rialto Bridge, www.hotelgiorgione.com, see map on page 114); **$$$ Hotel Casa Verardo** (elegant and quietly parked on a canal behind St. Mark's, more stately, www.casaverardo.it); **$$$ Hotel Donà Palace** (sitting like Las Vegas in the touristy zone a few blocks behind St. Mark's Basilica, works with neighbors **$$$ Hotel all'Angelo** and **$$$ Hotel al Ponte dei Sosperi** to rent 100 overpriced but often discounted rooms, all on Calle Larga San Marco, www.donapalace.it); and **$$$ Hotel Ca' Dei Conti** (five minutes northeast of St. Mark's Square, palatial and perfectly located but €500 rooms worth it only when deeply discounted, www.cadeiconti.com).

Cheap Dormitory Accommodations

$ Foresteria della Chiesa Valdese, run by the Methodist Church, has a mixture of dorms (6-9 beds) and private rooms (2-5 beds) with bath, close to both St. Mark's Square and the Rialto Bridge. This chilly, run-down yet charming old place has elegant ceiling paintings. They take reservations for the rooms, but only accept walk-ins for the dorms (dorm bed-€31, Db-€92-102, Tb-€111-117, Qb-€144-152, Quint/b-€170, price depends on view and amenities, €5/person less for stays of 2 nights or more; includes breakfast, sheets, towels, and lockers; must check in and out when office is open—8:30-20:00, no air-con, elevator, on Fondamenta Cavagnis at Castello 5170, tel. 041-528-6797, fax 041-241-6238, www.foresteria venezia.it, info@foresteriavenezia.it). From Campo Santa Maria Formosa, walk past Bar all'Orologio to the end of Calle Longa and cross the bridge—it's the second door, see map page 114.

$ Venice's youth hostel, on Giudecca Island with 260 beds and grand views across the Bay of San Marco, is a godsend for backpackers shell-shocked by Venetian prices. It's an old-school hostel—big rooms stacked with bunk beds (€25 beds with sheets and breakfast in 8- to 20-bed dorms, cheaper for hostel members, lockers, towels-€5, pay Wi-Fi, room lock-out 10:30-13:30, office open 24 hours, Fondamenta Zitelle 86, tel. 041-523-8211, fax 041-523-5689, www.ostellovenezia.it, info@ostellovenezia.it). Take vaporetto #41 from the bus or train stations (from the Tronchetto parking lot, take vaporetto #2) to the Zitelle stop, then walk right along the embankment to #86.

On the Mainland

While I prefer to stay in the heart of the action, these two places combine fine prices with easy bus links into Venice and are particularly good options for those who need to park a car.

$ **Villa Dolcetti** is a 1635 building with six comfortable rooms in a suburb of Venice. Art lovers Diego and Tatiana provide a buffet breakfast, free parking, and lots of sightseeing advice (Db-€75, superior Db-€85, Tb-€90-110, these prices for Rick Steves readers booking direct, air-con, free Internet access and Wi-Fi, tel. 041-563-1077, fax 041-563-1139, www.villadolcetti.com, info @villadolcetti.com). It's in the town of Oriago di Mira, at Via Venezia 85. Steps away is a bus stop on the Venice-Padua line that connects you to Venice's Piazzale Roma (2/hour, 25 minutes).

$ **Villa Mocenigo Agriturismo,** about 10 miles from Marco Polo Airport, is a working, family-run farm in a peaceful rural location between Venice and Padua. Its 10 rooms are furnished with antiques, and regional specialties are served for dinner (Sb-€40-55, Db-€60-74, extra bed-€20-25, dinner with wine-about €20 per person, air-con, free parking, Via Viasana 59 in Mirano-Venezia, tel. & fax 041-433-246, mobile 335-547-4728, www .villamocenigo.com, info@villamocenigo.com). Email them for directions by car or bus. Buses to Venice leave directly from the villa (3/hour, 45 minutes).

Eating in Venice

While touristy restaurants are the scourge of Venice, the following places are still popular with actual Venetians and respect the tourists who happen in. First trick: Walk away from triple-language menus. Second trick: For freshness, eat fish. Most seafood dishes are the catch-of-the-day. (But remember that seafood can be sold by weight—per 100 grams or *etto*—rather than a set price.) Third trick: Eat later. A place may feel really touristy at 19:00, but if you come back at 21:00 it can be filled with locals. Tourists eat barbarically early, which is fine with the restaurants because they fill tables that would otherwise be used only once in an evening.

Near the Rialto Bridge
North of the Bridge

These restaurants are located beyond Campo Santi Apostoli, along the Strada Nova, the main drag going toward the train station.

Trattoria da Bepi, bright and alpine-paneled, feels like a classic. Ask for the seasonal specialties—the crab dishes are excellent. There's good seating inside and out (€8-10 pastas, €14-18 *secondi*, €1.50 cover, Fri-Wed 12:00-14:30 & 19:00-22:00, closed Thu, half a block off Campo Santi Apostoli on Salizada Pistor at #4550, tel. 041-528-5031, Loris).

Little **Vini da Gigio** has a passion for good food and a traditional Venetian menu (€12-16 pastas, €18-22 *secondi*, no cover, Wed-Sun 12:00-14:30 & 19:00-22:30, closed Mon-Tue, 4 blocks from Ca' d'Oro vaporetto stop on Fondamenta San Felice at #3628a—it's behind the church on Campo San Felice, tel. 041-528-5140).

Trattoria Ca' d'Oro, while a little less accessible and inviting to the tourist, is a venerable favorite with a small, appealing menu and an enthusiastic following. Just to sip wine and enjoy *cicchetti* at the bar is a treat—their *polpette* (tuna and potato meatballs) are famous, and the house wine will set you back just €0.50. It's also fine for a meal (€9-10 pastas, €10-11 *secondi*, €1.50 cover, cash only, Fri-Sat and Mon-Wed 11:30-14:30 & 18:30-22:30, Sun 18:30-22:30, closed Thu, reservations recommended; from the Ca' d'Oro vaporetto dock, walk 100 yards directly away from the canal, cross Strada Nova into an alley called Ramo Ca' d'Oro, and it's straight ahead at #3912; tel. 041-528-5324).

Osteria al Bomba is a *cicchetti* bar with a female touch, thanks to Giovanna. It's unusual (clean, no toothpicks, no cursing) and quite good, with lots of veggies. You can stand and eat at the bar—try a little €3 *crostino* with polenta and cod—or oversee the construction of the house *"antipasto misto di cicchetti"* plate (€15, enough fish and vegetables for two) and choose your wine by the glass from the posted list. A seat at the long table comes with a €2 *coperto* (daily 12:00-15:00 & 18:00-23:00; on Calle de l'Oca; from Campo Santi Apostoli, walk toward the train station, find #4294 on your right and turn down the small alley to #4297 ahead of you; tel. 041-520-5175).

East of the Rialto Bridge

The first four listings are relatively close to the bridge. The rest are near Campo Santa Maria Formosa, one of my favorite community scenes. While the restaurants fronting the square aren't much, several good options for dining lie a short walk away.

Osteria "Alla Botte," despite being located a minute from the Rialto Bridge, is packed with a casual neighborhood clientele in two simple, woody rooms. For a classic Venetian taste, try the €18 all-seafood *antipasto misto* (daily 12:00-15:00 & 19:00-23:00, two short blocks off Campo San Bartolomeo in the corner behind the statue—down Calle de la Bissa at #5482, notice the "day after" photo showing a debris-covered Venice after the notorious 1989 Pink Floyd open-air concert, tel. 041-520-9775, Cristiano).

Osteria di Santa Marina, on the wonderful Campo Marina, serves pricey, near-gourmet cuisine in a dressy dining room. The presentation is impressive, but you feel there's more pretense than love of food. Cheap-eating tricks are frowned on in this elegant, borderline stuffy restaurant (enticing menu with €15 pastas and €25 *secondi*, €3 cover, €75-80 fixed-price meals, Tue-Sat 12:30-14:30 & 19:30-22:00, Mon 19:30-22:00, closed Sun, reserve for dinner, eat indoors or outdoors on pleasant little square, between Rialto Bridge and Campo Santa Maria Formosa on Campo Marina at #5911, tel. 041-528-5239).

Rosticceria San Bartolomeo is a cheap—if confusing—self-service diner, a throwback budget eatery with a likeably surly staff. Take it out, grab one of the few tiny tables, or munch at the bar—I'd skip the uninviting upper floor, where you pay higher prices and a €2 cover for table service (good €6-7 pasta, great fried *mozzarella al prosciutto* for €1.50, delightful fruit salad, €1 glasses of wine, prices listed on wall behind counter, no cover or service charge downstairs, daily 9:00-21:30, tel. 041-522-3569). To find it, imagine the statue on Campo San Bartolomeo walking backward 20 yards, turning left, and going under a passageway—now, follow him.

Osteria al Portego is a friendly neighborhood eatery—one of the best in town. Carlo serves good meals and excellent *cicchetti*—best enjoyed early, around 18:00 (from 19:00 to 21:00, tables are reserved for those ordering from the menu; the *cicchetti* are picked over by 21:00). Prices for food and wine are posted clearly on the wall. The *cicchetti* here can make a great meal, but you should also consider sitting down for a dinner from their fine menu. This place can get very busy, so reserve ahead if you want a table (€13 pastas, €0.80 glass of house wine, daily 10:30-15:00 & 18:00-21:30, near Campo Marina at #6015 on Calle Malvasia, tel. 041-522-9038). To find the Osteria, first find Rosticceria San Bartolomeo (listed above), then continue over a bridge to Campo San Lio, turn left, and follow Calle Carminati straight about 50 yards over another bridge; it's straight ahead.

Near Campo Santa Maria Formosa: **Osteria alle Testiere** is my top dining recommendation in Venice. Hugely respected, they are dedicated to quality, serving up creative, artfully presented market-fresh seafood (there's no meat on the menu), homemade pastas, and fine wine in what the chef calls a "Venetian Nouvelle" style. With only 22 seats, it's tight and homey, yet elegant. They have daily specials, 10 wines by the glass, and one agenda: a great dining experience. Luca, the owner/host, is gracious and passionate about his food. This is one place to let loose and trust your host.

VENICE

The Stand-Up Progressive Venetian Pub-Crawl Dinner

My favorite Venetian dinner is a pub crawl *(giro d'ombra)*—a tradition unique to Venice, where no cars means easy crawling. *(Giro* means stroll, and *ombra*—slang for a glass of wine—means shade, from the old days when a portable wine bar scooted with the shadow of the Campanile bell tower across St. Mark's Square.)

Venice's residential back streets hide plenty of characteristic bars *(bacari)* with countless trays of interesting toothpick munchies *(cicchetti)* and blackboards listing the wines that are uncorked and served by the glass. This is a great way to mingle and have fun with the Venetians. Bars don't stay open very late, and the *cicchetti* selection is best early, so start your evening by 18:00. Most bars are closed on Sunday. For a stress-free pub crawl, consider taking a tour with the charming Alessandro Schezzini (see page 58).

***Cicchetti* bars** have a social stand-up zone and a cozy gaggle of tables where you can generally sit down with your *cicchetti* or order from a simple menu. In some of the more popular places, the crowds happily spill out into the street. Food generally costs the same price whether you stand or sit.

I've listed plenty of pubs in walking order for a quick or extended crawl. If you've crawled enough, most

Reservations are almost always necessary for their three seatings: 12:30, 19:00, and 21:30 (€19 pastas, €25 *secondi*, plan on spending €50 for dinner, no cover or service charge, closed Sun-Mon; on Calle del Mondo Novo, just off Campo Santa Maria Formosa, at #5801; tel. 041-522-7220).

Osteria al Mascaron is where I've gone for years to watch Gigi, Momi, and their food-loving band of ruffians dish up rustic-yet-sumptuous pastas with steamy seafood to salivating foodies. The pastas seem pricey at €24-32, but they're meant for two (it's OK to ask for single portions). The €16 *antipasto misto* plate—have fun pointing—and two glasses of wine make a terrific light meal, and their seafood pastas make beautiful memories (€2 cover, Mon-Sat 12:00-15:00 & 19:00-23:00, closed Sun, reservations smart Fri-Sat; on Calle Longa Santa Maria Formosa, a block past Campo Santa Maria Formosa, at #5225; tel. 041-522-5995).

Fast and Cheap Eats: The veggie stand on Campo Santa Maria Formosa is a fixture. For *döner kebabs* (€3.50) and pizza to go (€2/

of these bars make a fine one-stop, sit-down dinner.

While you can order a plate, Venetians prefer going one-by-one...sipping their wine and trying this...then give me one of those...and so on. Try deep-fried mozzarella cheese, gorgonzola, calamari, artichoke hearts, and anything ugly on a toothpick. *Crostini* (small toasted bread with something on it) are popular, as are marinated seafood, olives, and prosciutto with melon. Meat and fish (*pesce;* PESH-ay) munchies can be expensive; veggies (*verdure*) are cheap, at about €3 for a meal-sized plate. In many places, there's a set price per food item (e.g., €1.50). To get a plate of assorted appetizers for €8 (or more, depending on how hungry you are), ask for *"Un piatto classico di cicchetti misti da €8"* (oon pee-AH-toh KLAH-see-koh dee cheh-KET-tee MEE-stee dah OH-toh ay-OO-roh). Bread sticks (*grissini*) are free for the asking.

Bar-hopping Venetians enjoy an *aperitivo,* a before-dinner drink. Boldly order a Bellini, a *spritz con Aperol,* or a Prosecco, and draw approving looks from the natives.

Drink the house wines. A small glass of house red or white wine (*ombra rosso* or *ombra bianco*) or a small beer (*birrino*) costs about €1. The house keg wine is cheap—€1 per glass, about €4 per liter. *Vin bon,* Venetian for fine wine, may run you from €2 to €6 per little glass. There are usually several fine wines uncorked and available by the glass. A good last drink is *fragolino,* the local sweet wine—*bianco* or *rosso.* It often comes with a little cookie (*biscotti*) for dipping.

slice), head down Calle Longa to **Peter Pan** at #6249 (daily 11:00-24:00). For classier pizza to go, visit **Cip Ciap** (next to Osteria alle Testiere near the bridge, at #5799a).

West of the Rialto Bridge

Most of these places are informal, serving *cicchetti* and/or light meals. The first bars listed are within 200 yards of each other, a few steps behind the Rialto fish market; the rest are farther away from this hive of eateries (see map on page 114). This area is very crowded by day, nearly empty early in the evening, and crowded with young Venetians later.

Most bars are closed 15:00-18:00 (though Cantina Do Mori and Ostaria ai Storti stay open all day), and offer glasses of house wine for under €1, better wine for around €2.50, and *cicchetti* for €1-2. At each place, look for the list of snacks and wine by the glass at the bar or on the wall. If you're ready for dessert, try dipping a Burano biscuit in a glass of strawberry-flavored *fragolino* or another sweet dessert wine.

A strip of five places between Campo San Giacomo and the Grand Canal (such as the recommended Bancogiro Bar and Al Mercà) make a thriving youth *spritz* scene that's worth a look even if you don't eat or drink there.

Cantina Do Mori has been famous with locals (since 1462) and savvy travelers (since 1982) as a convivial place for fine wine. You'll choose from a forest of little edibles on toothpicks and *francobolli* (a spicy selection of 20 tiny, mayo-soaked sandwiches nicknamed "stamps"). Go here to be abused in a fine atmosphere—the frowns are part of the shtick (Mon-Sat 8:30-20:00, closed Sun, stand-up only, arrive early before the *cicchetti* are gone, tel. 041-522-5401). From the Rialto Bridge, walk 200 yards down Ruga dei Orefici, away from St. Mark's Square—then turn left on Ruga Vechia San Giovanni, then right at Sotoportego Do Mori to #429.

Bar all'Arco, a bustling one-room joint that's almost across from Cantina Do Mori at #436, is particularly enjoyable for its tiny open-face sandwiches (closed Sun, tel. 041-520-5666).

Ostaria ai Storti, which has a homey feel, is a fun place to congregate. Check out the photo of the market in 1909, below the bar. Alessandro speaks English and enjoys helping educate travelers while serving *fragolino* (€8 pastas, €12 *secondi*, €1.50 cover, daily 9:00-22:30, Nov-March closes 15:00-18:00, 20 yards from Cantina Do Mori and around the corner on Calle San Matio at #819, tel. 041-523-6861).

Cantina Do Spade is run by Sebastiano, who clearly lists the *cicchetti* and wines of the day (daily 11:00-15:00 & 18:00-21:00, 30 yards down Calle de le Do Spade from Ostaria ai Storti at #860, tel. 041-521-0583).

At **Pesce Pronto,** you can sample fish while watching the market action. Bruno and Umberto serve artful fish hors d'oeuvres, *sfornato con pesce* (a savory, baked pastry), and many other fresh fish tidbits—all at a fair price. This fancy hole-in-the-wall is fun for a quick bite—eat standing up or take it to go. From 12:45 to 14:15, they serve €10-12 "express plates" of pasta and other choices (Tue and Sat 9:00-15:00 & 18:00-20:00, Wed-Fri 9:00-15:00 & 19:00-23:30, closed Sun-Mon, facing the fish market on Calle de le Becarie o Panataria at #319, tel. 041-822-0298).

The **Bancogiro Bar** is expensive but good if you like strong cheese and canalside tables (€3.50 cover, €2.50 *cicchetti* at bar, €15 cheese plate, Tue-Sun 12:00-23:00, closed Mon, on Campo San Giacomo at #122, tel. 041-523-2061).

Al Mercà, a few steps away and off the canal, is an even livelier little nook with a happy crowd, where young locals gather to grab drinks and little snacks. The price list is clear, and I've found the crowd to be welcoming to tourists interested in connecting (stand at the bar only—no tables, Mon-Sat 9:30-14:30 & 18:00-21:00, closed Sun, on Campo Cesare Battisti at #213).

Antica Ostaria Ruga Rialto, a.k.a. "the Ruga," is a neighborhood fixture where Giorgio and Marco serve great bar snacks and wine to a devoted clientele. Treats here are their polenta, sardine with onions, and veggies. Bar or table, no problem—they're happy to make you a €3, €6, or €10 mixed plate (daily 11:00-14:30 & 19:00-24:00, easy to find—just past the Chinese restaurant on Ruga Vechia San Giovanni at #695a, tel. 041-521-1243).

Osteria al Diavolo e l'Acquasanta, three blocks west of the Rialto Bridge, serves good—if pricey—Venetian dishes, and makes a handy lunch stop for sightseers. Though they list *cicchetti* and wine by the glass on the wall, I'd come here for a light meal rather than for appetizers (€8-11 pastas, €12-17 *secondi,* 12 percent service charge, Wed-Mon 12:00-14:30 & 19:00-21:30, closed Tue, hiding at #561 on Calle de la Madona—a quiet street just off Ruga Vechia San Giovanni, tel. 041-277-0307).

Antica Birraria la Corte is an everyday eatery on the delightful Campo San Polo, between the Rialto Bridge and the Frari Church. Popular for its €7-10 pizza, calzones, and salads, it fills the far side of this cozy, family-filled square. While the interior is a sprawling beer hall, it's a joy to eat on the square, where metal tables teeter on the cobbles, the wind plays with the paper mats, and children run free (€11-12 pastas, €14-19 *secondi,* €2 cover, daily 12:00-14:30 & 19:00-22:30, Campo San Polo 2168, tel. 041-275-0570).

Trattoria Pizzeria al Nono Risorto is unpretentious, inexpensive, youthful, and famous for serving good pizza in a nice setting. You'll sit in a gravelly garden under a leafy canopy, surrounded by Italians enjoying huge €8 salads, pastas, and pizzas, and €12-17 grilled meat or fish dishes (Fri-Tue 12:00-14:30 & 19:00-22:30, Thu 19:00-22:30, closed Wed, reservations smart on weekends; from Rialto fish market, get out your map and walk 3 minutes away from the Rialto to Campo San Cassiano—it's just over the bridge on Sotoportego de Siora Bettina at #2338; tel. 041-524-1169).

Near St. Mark's Square

For locations, see the map on page 108.

Dining near St. Mark's Square

The following three places are a few blocks east of St. Mark's Square and offer classy dining experiences. The first two listings are the best canalside dining values I've found in Venice. Both specialize in fish, and have a reasonable-for-the-romantic-setting menu. If you want a canalside seat for dinner, call to reserve it, and

Romantic Canalside Settings

Of course, if you want a meal with a canal view, it generally comes with lower quality or a higher price. But if you're aiming for a canalside memory, these places can be great. I've listed the better-value places below, along with advice for coping with the tourist traps.

Near the Rialto Bridge: Several *cicchetti* bars line the Grand Canal, with front tables just off **Campo San Giacomo** (a.k.a. "Giacometto"), between the market and the Rialto Bridge (described on page 130). You can get good light meals in this area, but these bars don't offer romantic dining per se.

Rialto Bridge Tourist Traps: Venetians are embarrassed by the lousy food and aggressive "service" at the string of joints dominating the best romantic, Grand Canal-fringing real estate in town. Still, if you want to linger over dinner with a view of the most famous bridge and the songs of gondoliers oaring by (and don't mind eating with other tourists), this can be enjoyable. Don't trust the waiter's recommendations for special meals. The budget ideal would be to get a simple pizza or pasta and a drink for €15, and savor the ambience without getting ripped off. But few restaurants will allow you to get off that easy. To avoid a dispute over the bill, ask if there's a minimum charge—before you sit down (most places have one).

Near the Accademia: Ristorante/Pizzeria Accademia **Foscarini,** next to the Accademia Bridge, offers decent pizzas overlooking the canal with no cover or service charge (see page 134).

East of St. Mark's Square: **Ristorante alla Conchiglia** and **Trattoria da Giorgio ai Greci,** a few blocks behind St. Mark's; both have a few tables next to one of the smaller canals frequented by gondoliers (see page 133).

Overlooking the Giudecca Canal: Terrazza del Casin dei **Nobili,** located in Zattere—on the Venice side of the wide Giudecca Canal—gets the warm, romantic evening sun (page 134).

On Fondamente Nove with a View of the Open Lagoon: **Ristorante Algiubagio** is a good opportunity to eat well while overlooking the lagoon (page 135).

On Burano: **Trattoria al Gatto Nero** sits on a tranquil canal under a tilting bell tower in the pastel townscape of Burano. If you're touring the lagoon and want to enjoy Burano without the crowds, go late and consider a dinner here (see page 96).

honor your reservation; don't go to another restaurant. To reach these from St. Mark's Square, head behind the basilica to Campo San Provolo, then follow Calle Osmarin to the Ponte dei Greci bridge and Fondamenta San Lorenzo. To get to the third, head up Chiesa from Campo San Provolo.

Ristorante alla Conchiglia has a few lovely tables that line the sleepy canal and a fresh, bright interior. They specialize in turbot, a flatfish similar to flounder. There's a €1.50 cover and 12 percent service charge, which is waived if you order the fixed-price meal (€7-10 pizzas lunch only, big €14 salads, basic €15 fixed-price meal, daily 12:00-22:30, closed Dec and Jan, on Fondamenta San Lorenzo at #4990, tel. 041-528-9095, Franco and son Alessandro).

Trattoria da Giorgio ai Greci, right next door, also has a half-dozen canalside tables. They offer €17 and €21 fixed-price meals with no cover or service charge—the €21 version has more interesting and authentic choices (€1.50 cover and 12 percent service charge for à la carte orders, daily 12:00-22:30, on Fondamenta San Lorenzo at #4988, tel. 041-528-9780, enthusiastically run by Giorgio and sons Davide and chatty Roberto).

Ristorante Antica Sacrestia is a classic restaurant where the owner, Pino, takes a hands-on approach to greeting guests. His staff serve creative €33-50 fixed-price meals and a humdrum €20 *turistico* one. You can also order à la carte; try the delightful €21 antipasto spread. There's no cover or service charge, and my readers are welcome to a free *sgroppino* (lemon vodka after-dinner drink) upon request (€12-16 pastas and pizzas, €17-30 *secondi*, Tue-Sun 11:30-15:00 & 18:00-22:30, closed Mon, immediately behind San Zaninovo/Giovanni Novo Church on Calle de la Sacrestia at #4442, tel. 041-523-0749).

Budget Eateries near St. Mark's Square

Picnicking isn't allowed on St. Mark's Square, but you can legally take your snacks to the nearby Giardinetti Reali, the small park along the waterfront west of the Piazzetta.

"Sandwich Row": On Calle de le Rasse, just steps away from the tourist intensity at St. Mark's Square, is a handy strip I call "Sandwich Row." Lined with sandwich bars, it's the closest place to St. Mark's to get a decent sandwich at an affordable price with a place to sit down (most places open daily 7:00-24:00, €1 extra to sit; from the Bridge of Sighs, head down the Riva and take the second lane on the left). I particularly like **Birreria Forst,** a café which serves a selection of meaty €2.80 sandwiches with tasty sauce on wheat bread, or made-to-order sandwiches for around €3.80 (Sun-Fri 10:00-21:00, closed Sat, air-con, rustic wood tables, Calle de le Rasse at #4540, tel. 041-523-0557) and **Bar Verde,** a more modern sandwich bar with fun people-watching views from

its corner tables (big €4 sandwiches, splittable €8 salads, fresh pastries, at the end of Calle de le Rasse at #4526, facing Campo Santi Filippo e Giacomo).

Ristorante alla Basilica, just one street behind St. Mark's Basilica, is a church-run, indoor, institutional-feeling place that serves a solid €13 fixed-price lunch (including water) daily from 11:45 to 15:00. It's not self-serve—you'll be seated and can choose a pasta, a *secondi,* and a vegetable side dish off the menu (sometimes a wait, air-con, great bathrooms, on Calle dei Albanesi at #4255, tel. 041-522-0524).

Rizzo, like most Venetian "bars," is an eat-at-the-counter café with sandwiches, pizza, pastries, and other reasonably priced snacks. It stands out for its handy location, north of St. Mark's Square on the main drag of Calle dei Fabbri, and its tiny grocery shelf with yogurt and other quick bites (Mon-Sat 8:00-20:00, closed Sun, on Calle dei Fabbri at #933a, tel. 041-522-3388).

In Dorsoduro
Near the Accademia Bridge

Ristorante/Pizzeria Accademia Foscarini, next to the Accademia Bridge and Galleria, offers decent €10-11 pizzas in a great canalside setting. Their toasted *farciti* sandwich is a local favorite (€6.50 at the table). Though the pizzas may be forgettable, this place is both scenic and practical—on each visit to Venice, I grab a pizza lunch here while I ponder the Grand Canal bustle (no cover or service charge, May-Oct Wed-Mon 7:00-22:30, Nov-April until 21:00, closed Tue, on Rio Terà A. Foscarini at #878c, tel. 041-522-7281).

Enoteca Cantine del Vino Già Schiavi is much-loved for its €1 *cicchetti* and €3.50-4 sandwiches (order from list on board). It's also a good place for a €1-2 glass of wine and appetizers (Mon-Sat 8:00-20:30, closed Sun, 100 yards from Accademia art museum on San Trovaso canal; facing Accademia, take a right and then a forced left at the canal to the second bridge—it's at #992, tel. 041-523-0034). You're welcome to enjoy your wine and finger food hanging out at the bar, sitting on the bridge out front, or in the nearby square—which actually has grass. This is primarily a wine shop with great prices for bottles to go—and plastic glasses for picnickers.

Terrazza del Casin dei Nobili, located on Zattere (the Venice side of the Giudecca Canal), takes full advantage of the warm, romantic evening sun. They serve finely crafted, regional specialties with creativity at tolerable prices. The canalside seating is breezy and beautiful, but comes with the rumble of *vaporetti* from the nearby stop. The interior is bright and hip (good €9-10 pizzas, €10-13 pastas, €15-25 *secondi,* €2 cover, Fri-Wed 12:00-23:00, closed Thu; from Zattere vaporetto stop, turn left to #924; tel. 041-

520-6895, Ruggiero and Eleonora). On Wednesday and Sunday evenings in summer, there's live music nearby on the Zattere promenade.

Near Campo San Barnaba

A number of restaurants are near this small square, a short walk from the Accademia. As these are each within a few steps of each other and the energy and atmosphere can vary, I like to survey the options before choosing (although reservations may be necessary later in the evening).

Casin dei Nobili ("Pleasure Palace of Nobles")—related to the Terrazza del Casin dei Nobili, listed above—has a high-energy, informal, modern setting with outdoor seating on a patio. The creative, €18 fixed-price lunch specials are worth it (€13 pastas, €13-25 *secondi*, good pizzas, €10 "fantasy salads," Tue-Sun 12:00-15:00 & 19:00-23:00, closed Mon; on Calle de le Casin, a half-block south of Campo San Barnaba, at #2765; tel. 041-241-1841, Damiano).

Pane Vino e San Daniele is a busy little place that feels real, with the TV on, an enticing blackboard listing the day's specials, and the kitchen action filling its dining room (€7.50 pastas, €10-12 salads and *secondi*, €1 cover, on Calle Longa San Barnaba at #2861, tel. 041-243-9865).

Enoteca e Trattoria la Bitta is dark and woody, with a soft-jazz bistro feel and a small, forgettable back patio. They serve beautifully presented, traditional Venetian food with—proudly—no fish. Their helpful waitstaff and small menu are clearly focused on quality. Reservations are required (€10 pastas, €16-25 *secondi*, €2 cover, dinner only, Mon-Sat 18:30-23:00, closed Sun, cash only, between previous two listings on Calle Longa San Barnaba at #2753a, tel. 041-523-0531).

Elsewhere in Venice

On Fondamente Nove: **Ristorante Algiubagio,** though not cheap, is a good place to eat well overlooking the northern lagoon. The name is a combination of the owners' four names—Alberto, Giulio, Barbara, and Giovanna—who strive to impress visitors with quality, creative Venetian cuisine made using the best ingredients. Reserve a table on the lagoon facing the island of San Michele or in their classy cantina dining room (€16-18 pastas, €24-25 *secondi*, €3.50 cover, €29-42 fixed-price meals, Wed-Mon 12:00-15:00 & 19:00-22:30, closed Tue; on Fondamente Nove, to the left of the vaporetto dock as you face the water, at #5039; tel. 041-523-6084). This is a convenient place to eat if you're taking the vaporetto out to the islands in the lagoon (see map on page 98).

Near Campo Santa Maria Nova: **Osteria da Alberto,** with excellent daily specials, €13 seafood dishes, €9-11 pastas, a good house wine, and a woody and characteristic interior, is one of my standbys. It's smart to reserve at night—I'd request a table in the front (€1.80 cover, Mon-Sat 12:00-14:30 & 18:30-22:30, closed Sun; on Calle Larga Giacinto Gallina, midway between Campo Santi Apostoli and Campo Santi Giovanni e Paolo, next to Ponte de la Panada bridge at #5401—see map on page 114; tel. 041-523-8153, run by Graziano and Giovanni).

Near the Train Station: There are piles of eateries near the station. The **food circus** in the station itself is quite good, with peaceful garden seating out back in summer, big €3-4 sandwiches, and slices of pizza for €2.90. A block away is a small branch of the efficient and economic **Brek,** a popular self-service cafeteria chain (€4-5 pastas, €6-9 *secondi*, daily 11:30-22:00, head left as you leave the station and walk about 50 yards past the bridge along Rio Terà Lista di Spagna to #124—see map on page 122).

Cheap Meals

The keys to eating affordably in Venice are pizza, bars/cafés, cafeterias, and picnics. *Panini* and *tramezzini* (sandwiches, described on page 34) are sold fast and cheap at bars everywhere and can stave off midmorning hunger. There's a great "sandwich row" of cheap cafés near St. Mark's Square (see page 133). For speed, value, and ambience, you can get a filling plate of typically Venetian appetizers at nearly any bar. For quick, fun eating, I like small, stand-up mini-meals at *cicchetti* **bars** best (see page 128).

Picnics

The **fruit and vegetable market** that sprawls for a few blocks just past the Rialto Bridge is a fun place to assemble a picnic (best Mon-Sat 8:00-13:00, closed Sun). The adjacent **fish market** is wonderfully slimy (closed Sun-Mon). Side lanes in this area are speckled with fine little hole-in-the-wall munchie bars, bakeries, and cheese shops.

A handy (but often mobbed) **Coop** supermarket is between St. Mark's and Campo Santa Maria Formosa, on the corner of Salizada San Lio and Calle del Mondo Novo at #5817. It has a great selection of picnic supplies, including packaged salads for less than €2 (daily 8:30-20:00). The largest supermarket in town is the **Coop** at Piazzale Roma, next to the vaporetto stop at #504-507 (daily 8:30-20:00). It's an easy walk from the train station, as is the **Billa** supermarket on Campo San Felice (at #3660, along the Strada Nova between the train station and Rialto area, Mon-Sat 8:30-20:00, Sun 9:00-20:00). Another **Billa** supermarket is convenient for those staying in Dorsoduro: It's at #1492, at the far west of the Zattere embankment, by the San Basilio vaporetto stop and the cruise-ship docks (Mon-Sat 8:00-20:00, Sun 9:00-19:00).

The only legal place to picnic in public in Venice is Giardinetti Reali, the waterfront park near St. Mark's Square. Eating anywhere outdoors, you may be besieged by pigeons. A picnic in your room can be a better bet.

Gelato

You'll find good *gelaterie* in every Venetian neighborhood, offering one-scoop cones for about €1.50. Look for the words *artigianale* or

produzione propria, which indicates that a shop makes its own gelato. The popular, inventive, upscale **Grom** ice-cream chain has two branches in Venice, one on Campo San Barnaba at #2761 (beyond the Accademia bridge), and another one at the Strada Nova at #3844, not far from the Rialto (cheapest cone-€2.50, both open Sun-Thu 12:00-22:30, Fri-Sat 12:00-23:30).

On St. Mark's Square, two venerable cafés have *gelato* counters in summer: **Gran Caffè Lavena** (April-Oct daily until 24:00, no gelato Nov-March, first café to left of the Clock Tower, behind the first orchestra, at #134) and **Todaro** (on the corner of the Piazzetta at #5, near the water and just under the column topped by St. Theodore slaying a crocodile).

Venice Connections

By Train

From Venice by Train to: Padua (2/hour, 30-50 minutes), **Vicenza** (2/hour, 45-75 minutes), **Verona** (2/hour, 1.25-2.25 hours), **Ravenna** (roughly hourly, 3-3.5 hours, transfer in Ferrara or Bologna), **Florence** (hourly, 2-3 hours, often crowded so make reservations), **Bolzano/Dolomites** (to Bolzano about hourly, 3-3.5 hours, transfer in Verona; catch bus from Bolzano into mountains), **Milan** (hourly, 2.5-3.5 hours), **Cinque Terre/Monterosso** (about hourly, 6-7 hours, 1-3 changes), **Rome** (hourly, 3.75 hours, also 1 direct night train from Mestre, 6 hours), **Naples** (almost hourly, 5.5-7 hours, change in Rome), **Brindisi** (5/day, 9 hours, change in Rome or Bologna; 1 direct night train from Mestre, 10 hours), **Interlaken** (7/day, 6-7.5 hours, 2-5 changes, no pleasant overnight option), **Luzern** (7/day, 6.5-7 hours, 1 direct, others change in Milan and Arth-Goldau), **Bern** (3/day, 6 hours, change in Milan or Brig), **Munich** (4-6/day, 7 hours, change in Verona; 1 direct night train, 8 hours; most trains reservable only via www.bahn.de), **Salzburg** (4/day, 6-7 hours, 1-2 changes, 1 direct night train, 7 hours), **Paris** (3/day, 10-12 hours with change in Milan, may also transfer in Basel or Zürich; 1 direct night train, 13.5 hours, important to reserve ahead, 2 more night trains with changes), **Ljubljana** (3/day, 7.5 hours—buy ticket at train station, take bus from Tronchetto to Villach in Austria, then transfer to train; 1 direct night train, 4 hours, but arrives at 2:00 in the morning), and **Vienna** (3/day, 8 hours—same system as Ljubljana; 1 direct night train, 11 hours).

From Venice by Bus to: Padua (2/hour, 30-50 minutes, easier by train). For buses to **Austria** run by Italian Railways, you have to buy tickets at the train station. For buses to Venice's airports, see below.

By Plane

Marco Polo is Venice's main airport. Some budget flights, including Ryanair, use the smaller airport in the nearby city of Treviso. (For more on budget carriers, see page 1030.)

Marco Polo Airport

Venice's small, modern airport is on the mainland shore of the lagoon, six miles north of the city. There's one sleek terminal, with a TI (daily 9:00-21:00), car-rental agencies, ATMs, a bank, and a few shops and eateries. For flight information, call tel. 041-260-9260, visit www.veniceairport.com, or ask your hotel.

Transportation between Marco Polo Airport and Venice

Here are three ways to get between the airport and downtown Venice:

- Alilaguna boats—Slowest trip, medium cost
- Water taxis—Fastest trip, most expensive
- Airport shuttle buses to Piazzale Roma—Faster than Alilaguna, slower than water taxi, least expensive

Each of these options is explained in detail below. An advantage of the Alilaguna boats is that you can reach most of this chapter's recommended hotels very simply, with no changes—except hotels near the train station, which are better served by the bus to Piazzale Roma.

Both Alilaguna boats and water taxis leave from the airport's boat dock, an eight-minute walk from the terminal. Exit the arrivals hall and turn left, following signs along a paved, level, covered sidewalk (easy for wheeled bags).

When flying out of Venice, allow yourself plenty of time to get to the airport. Water transport is slow. Plan to arrive at the airport least two hours before your flight, and remember that getting there can easily take another two hours. Consider alternatives ahead of time, especially if you're planning to take one of the Alilaguna boats (which are small and can fill up).

Alilaguna Airport Boats

These boats make the scenic (if slow) journey across the lagoon, each shuttling passengers between the airport and a number of different stops on the island of Venice (€15, €25 round-trip, 1-1.5-hour trip depending on your destination; boats leave every 30-60 minutes). Note that the Alilaguna boats are not part of the ACTV vaporetto system, so they aren't covered by city transit passes. But they do use the same docks and ticket windows as the regular *vaporetti*.

There are three Alilaguna lines (blue, red, orange), and it can get confusing. But if you know what stop you want, it's easy to find the line that goes there. Here are some key stops in Venice:

San Marco—Hotels west of St. Mark's Square
San Zaccaria—Hotels east of St. Mark's Square
Zattere—Dorsoduro hotels
Guglie—Hotels near Santa Lucia train station
Rialto—Hotels near the Rialto Bridge
Fondamente Nove—Hotels on the north side of the city, on the "fish's" back

For a full schedule, visit the TI, see the website (www.alilaguna.it), call 041-240-1701, ask your hotelier, or scan the schedules posted at the docks.

From the Airport to Venice: You can buy Alilaguna tickets at the airport's TI, the ticket desk in the terminal, vending machines inside the airport terminal (cash only), or simply at the ticket booth at the dock. Any ticket-seller can tell you which line to catch to get to your destination. Boats from the airport run from roughly 7:00 to midnight.

From Venice to the Airport: Ask your hotelier which dock and which line is best. Boats start leaving Venice as early as 3:40 so that passengers can catch early flights. Scope out the dock and buy your ticket in advance to avoid last-minute stress.

Water Taxis

Luxury taxi speedboats zip directly between the airport and your hotel, getting you within steps of your final destination in about 30 minutes. The official price is €100 for up to five people; add €10 for every extra person (10-passenger limit). There's a €10 surcharge between 22:00 and 7:00. You may get a higher quote—politely talk it down. A taxi can be a smart investment for small groups and those with an early departure.

From the airport, arrange your ride at the airport's water-taxi desk or with the boat captains lounging at the dock. From Venice, book your taxi trip the day before you leave. Your hotel will help (since they get a commission), or you can book directly with the Consorzio Motoscafi water taxi association (tel. 041-522-2303, www.motoscafivenezia.it/eng).

VENICE

Airport Shuttle Buses

Buses take you across the bridge from the mainland to the island, dropping you at Venice's bus station, at the "mouth of the fish" on a square called Piazzale Roma. From there, you can catch a vaporetto down the Grand Canal—convenient for hotels near the Rialto Bridge and St. Mark's Square. If you're staying near the train station, you can walk from Piazzale Roma to your hotel.

Two bus companies run between Piazzale Roma and the airport: ACTV (the local city bus company) and ATVO. Most of the day, both have departures twice an hour and cost the same (€3), although only ATVO offers a round-trip for €5.50. ATVO buses take 20 minutes and go nonstop. ACTV buses (route #5) make a few stops en route and take slightly longer (30 minutes), but are covered by Venice vaporetto passes (see page 55). Buses run from about 5:00 to 24:00; early and late, each company has just one bus an hour. Check schedules at www.atvo.it or www.actv.it.

From the Airport to Venice: Both buses leave from just outside the arrivals terminal. Buy tickets at the TI, or from ticket machines in the terminal or outside next to the buses; in a pinch at odd hours, ask the driver. Check which ticket you are buying—ATVO tickets are not valid on ACTV buses and vice versa. Double-check the destination; if taking ACTV, you want bus #5. See "By Bus," later, for directions into town from Piazzale Roma.

From Venice to the Airport: At Piazzale Roma, buy your ticket from the ACTV windows or ATVO office before heading out to the platforms. (If closed, politely ask the driver to sell you a ticket.) ACTV buses leave from platform A1; ATVO buses from platform D2. The first buses leave at around 5:00.

Private Shuttle Bus

Treviso Car Service offers a private minivan service between Marco Polo Airport and Piazzale Roma or the cruise port (minivan-€55, seats up to 8; car-€50, seats up to 3; mobile 348-900-0700 or 333-411-2840, www.tourleadervenice.com, info@tourleadervenice.com; they also offer tours—see page 60).

Treviso Airport

Several budget airlines, such as Ryanair, Wizz Air, and Germanwings, use Treviso Airport, 12 miles northwest of Venice (www.trevisoairport.it). Regular ATVO buses take you from the airport to Piazzale Roma (€6, about 2/hour, 1.25 hours, www.atvo.it). Buy your tickets at the ATVO desk in the airport and stamp them on the bus. The buses also stop at Mestre's train station. Treviso Car Service offers minivan service to Piazzale Roma (minivan-€75, seats up to 8; car-€65, seats up to 3; see private shuttle bus listing above).

By Cruise Ship

Most cruise ships visiting Venice dock at Stazione Marittima, which is roughly between the Tronchetto parking garage and Santa Lucia train station. The terminal forms "the fish's mouth" of Venice. Ships also tie up at the Santa Marta and San Basilio docks, which are south of the main port. The Venice port website has a map of the different docks (www.port.venice.it/en/terminals .html).

Check with your cruise line to find out where your ship will moor, and give yourself plenty of time if connecting between a flight and a cruise in Venice.

Getting into Town

Venice's public transportation is convenient and affordable; for a rundown of your travel options, see page 54. The handy Alilaguna express boat #M conveniently connects Stazione Marittima directly to St. Mark's Square (San Marco-Giardinetti dock) in just 20 minutes (€6.50 one-way, €12 round-trip, €3 per big bag, 2/hour in each direction, from cruise port 8:10-16:10, from St. Mark's Square 9:10-16:10; before boarding at the cruise terminal, buy ticket at kiosk in front of building #103 at the top of the harbor; www.alilaguna.it). Because this service is understandably popular, the boats can fill up; if you're arriving on a cruise ship, get to this dock as quickly as possible.

To reach the Grand Canal (and the start of my self-guided Grand Canal Cruise) from Stazione Marittima, hop on the People Mover monorail (€1) to Piazzale Roma. Or, if money is no object, you can spring for a water taxi to anywhere in town (€80). If all of these options are jammed up (as can happen when multiple cruise ships arrive all at once), you can walk to the Grand Canal in about 15 minutes, or all the way to St. Mark's Square in about 45 minutes.

If your ship is docked outside the main port, take vaporetto #2 from San Basilio to get into Venice.

Getting to Marco Polo Airport

The shuttle buses between Piazzale Roma and the airport are quick and inexpensive (described earlier). Buses leave between 5:00 and 24:00; from Stazione Marittima, take the People Mover monorail to Piazzale Roma (€1). You can also take a land taxi directly to the airport (€40). Keep in mind that the Alilaguna boats connecting directly to the airport have stops at Tronchetto or Piazzale Roma—but not at Stazione Marittima. From the Santa Marta or San Basilio docks, you can take a land taxi to the airport (€40).

NEAR VENICE

Padua • Verona • Ravenna

Venice is just one of many towns in the Italian region of Veneto (VEN-eh-toh), but few visitors venture off the lagoon. Several important towns and possible side-trips make zipping directly from Venice to Milan (or Florence) a route strewn with temptation.

Planning Your Time

The towns of Padua, Verona, and Ravenna are great stops. Each gives visitors a low-key slice of Italy that complements the urbanity of Venice, Florence, and Rome. If you can't make it to all three, pick the one that most interests you. Art-lovers will want to head to Padua to see Giotto's celebrated Scrovegni Chapel, or to Ravenna for its sumptuous Byzantine mosaics. History buffs should see Verona's impressive Roman ruins. Verona is also the pick for star-crossed lovers retracing Romeo and Juliet's steps. Architecture fans could consider a quick trip to Palladio-designed Vicenza, located about halfway between Padua and Verona.

Visiting Padua and Verona couldn't be easier:

Towns near Venice

They are roughly 30-45 minutes apart on the Venice-Milan line. Spending a day town-hopping between Venice and Milan—with stops at Padua and Verona—is exciting and efficient. Trains run frequently enough to allow flexibility and little wasted time. Of the towns included in this chapter, only Ravenna (2.5 hours from Padua and 3-3.5 hours from Venice) is not on the main Venice-Milan train line.

If you're Padua-bound, remember that you need to reserve ahead to see the Scrovegni Chapel. Mondays are not ideal for a trip to Verona, where most sights are closed (at least in the morning), or Vicenza, where the major sights are closed.

Padua *(Padova)*

Living under Venetian rule for four centuries seemed only to sharpen Padua's independent spirit. Nicknamed "the brain of Veneto," Padua (Padova in Italian) has a prestigious university (founded in 1222) that hosted Galileo, Copernicus, Dante, and Petrarch. Padua's old town center is elegantly arcaded, filled with students, and sprinkled with surprises. Padua's museums and churches hold their own in Italy's artistic big league—yet its hotels are reasonably priced and the city doesn't feel touristy.

Planning Your Time: Padua in Six Hours

Day-trippers can do a quick but enjoyable blitz of Padua—including a visit to the Scrovegni Chapel—in six hours. Buses and trains from Venice are cheap, take 30 to 50 minutes, and run frequently. Once in Padua, everything is a 10-minute walk or quick tram ride apart.

Your Scrovegni Chapel reservation will dictate the order of your sightseeing (see "Reservations" on page 153). When planning your day, also consider these factors: The station has a reliable baggage check desk; the open-air markets are vibrant in the morning, dead in the evening; student life is best at the university late in the day; and the Basilica of St. Anthony is open all day, but the reliquary chapel closes from 12:45 to 14:30.

Ideally, I'd do it this way: 9:00—market action and sightseeing in town center, 11:00—Basilica of St. Anthony, 14:00—Scrovegni Chapel tour.

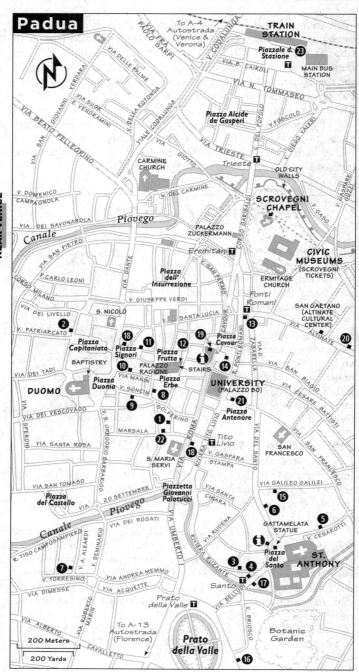

Padua

Padua Key

1. Hotel Majestic Toscanelli
2. Albergo Verdi
3. Hotel Al Fagiano
4. Hotel Belludi 37
5. Hotel/Rist. Casa del Pellegrino
6. Hotel Al Santo
7. Ostello Città di Padova
8. Osteria dei Fabbri
9. Osteria L'Anfora
10. Ristorante alle Piazze da Giorgio
11. La Lanterna Ristorante
12. Bar dei Osei
13. Brek Cafeteria
14. PAM Supermarket & Brek
15. Pizzeria Pago Pago
16. Zairo Rist./Pizzeria
17. Pollodoro la Gastronomica
18. Gelateria Grom (2)
19. Caffè Pedrocchi
20. Internet Café
21. Feltrinelli's Intl. Bookstore
22. Launderette
23. Buses to Venice & Marco Polo Airport

NEAR VENICE

Orientation to Padua

Padua's main tourist sights lie on a north-south axis through the heart of the city, from the train station to Scrovegni Chapel to the market squares (the center of town) to the Basilica of St. Anthony. It's roughly a 10-minute walk between each of these sights, or about 30 minutes from end to end. Padua's wonderful single tram line makes lacing things together quick and easy (see "Getting Around Padua," later).

Tourist Information

Padua has three TIs: in the **center** (in the alley behind Caffè Pedrocchi at Vicolo Cappellatto Pedrocchi 9, Mon-Sat 9:00-13:30 & 15:00-19:00, closed Sun, tel. 049-876-7927), at the **train station** (Mon-Sat 9:15-19:00, Sun 9:00-12:30, tel. 049-875-2077), and near the **Basilica of St. Anthony,** across the street on Piazza del Santo (April-Oct Mon-Sat 9:00-13:30 & 15:00-18:00, Sun 10:00-13:30 & 15:00-18:00, closed Nov-March, tel. 049-875-3087). Be aware the TIs may have shorter hours in 2012 due to budget cuts.

At any TI, pick up a map, a list of sights, and the seasonal *Padova Today* entertainment listing. The TI's free I-PADova audio tour is creative and works really well. You can download it for free from their website (www.turismopadova.it), or just borrow one of their MP3 players (leave your passport) and follow any of the five routes in town.

The **Padova Card** gives you (and one child under 14) unlimited tram travel, free parking at Piazza Rabin, various discounts, and entry to all the recommended sights in Padua, except the university's Anatomy Theater and the Basilica of St. Anthony's Oratory of St. George. While the card includes the Scrovegni Chapel, you still need to make a reservation to enter (which costs an extra €1). Padova Cards are also sold at all TIs, at included sights, and online at www.padovacard.it (€16/48 hours, €21/72 hours) and on the Scrovegni Chapel website (www.cappelladegli scrovegni.it). If you buy the card online, bring your confirmation number and pick it up at any TI or at the Scrovegni Chapel. If you reserve a Scrovegni Chapel ticket at the same time, pick up the ticket at the chapel.

Arrival in Padua

By Train: The efficient station is a user-friendly shopping mall with whatever you might need (Despar **supermarket** open Mon-Sat 7:00-21:00, Sun 10:00-21:00). **WCs** (€0.60) and **baggage deposit** (exactly €3.87, daily 6:30-18:00, bring photo ID) are along track 1.

If you need to speak to a real person about tickets but the lines are long, go to Leonardi Viaggi-Turismo, which offers ticketing services for a small fee a block away (Mon-Fri 9:00-13:00 & 14:30-19:00, Sat 9:00-13:00, closed Sun, up the main drag in front of the station, Corso del Popolo 14, tel. 049-650-455).

The easiest way to get downtown is to simply hop on Padua's handy **tram** (see "Getting Around Padua," later). Leaving the station, the tram stop is 30 yards to the right at the foot of the bridge (avoid the shady characters around here at night). A **taxi** into town (a good option after dark) costs about €8.

By Bus: The bus station is a few steps east of the train station, beyond the bicycle parking lot. Buses arrive here from Venice's Piazzale Roma and Marco Polo Airport.

Helpful Hints

Pronunciation: You say Padua (PAD-joo-wah), they say Padova (PAH-doh-vah).

Internet Access: Befitting a college town where every student has a laptop, Padua has few Internet cafés. The **central TI** offers free access for 15 minutes (if you fill out a form and show your passport). You can also walk to **Internet Point** (€2/hour, Mon-Sat 10:00-24:00, Sun 16:00-24:00, 10-minute walk east of the Ponte Romani tram stop at Via Altinate 145, tel. 049-659-292).

Bookstore: Feltrinelli's International Bookstore, with books in English, is a block from the main university building (Mon-Sat 9:00-19:30, Sun 10:00-13:00 & 15:30-19:30, Via San Francesco 7, tel. 049-875-4630).

Launderette: Lavami has only three washers and two dryers but it's the sole option in the city center (daily 7:00-22:00, Via Marsala 22 near intersection with Via dell'Arco, tel. 049-876-4532).

Local Guide: Charming and helpful **Cristina Pernechele** is a great teacher (€110/half-day, mobile 338-495-5453, cristina @pernechele.eu).

Best Gelato: Though **Grom** is expensive (one-scoop cones-€2.20), students line up for its unusual flavors and exotic ingredients (two locations at Via Roma 101 and Piazza dei Signori 33).

Getting Around Padua

While a tangle of buses serves the city, visitors should pretend there is only the **tram** and rely on it. There's just one line, which connects everything you care about efficiently and stress-free (€1.10 ticket good for 1.25 hours, buy tickets from machines at stops, departs every 8 minutes during the day Mon-Sat, every 20 minutes evenings and Sun, www.trampadova.it). The rubber-wheeled trams run on a single rail.

Before boarding, note the tram direction on posted schedules and above the front window (Pontevigodarzere is northbound, Capolinia Sud is southbound). Stops that matter include the following: Stazione FS (train and bus stations), Eremitani (Scrovegni Chapel), Ponti Romani (old town center, market squares, university), Tito Livio (ghetto, old town center, Hotel Majestic Toscanelli), Santo (Basilica of St. Anthony and neighborhood hotels), and Prato della Valle (hostel).

You'll see **hop-on, hop-off buses** at the station and around town. While these ubiquitous tourist transporters make sense in some places, they're not worth the time or money in Padua.

Sights in Padua

▲▲▲Basilica of St. Anthony

Friar Anthony of Padua, "Christ's perfect follower and a tireless preacher of the Gospel," is buried here. Construction of this

impressive Romanesque/Gothic church (with its Byzantine-style domes) started immediately after St. Anthony's death in 1231. And for nearly 800 years, his remains and this glorious church have attracted pilgrims to Padua.

Cost and Hours: The basilica is free and open April-late Oct daily 6:20-19:45; late Oct-March Mon-Fri 6:20-18:45, Sat-Sun 6:20-19:45. Note that the following sights within the basilica close around lunchtime: Chapel of the Reliquaries (daily April-late Oct 8:00-12:45 & 14:30-19:30, late Oct-March until 18:30), museum (€2.50, April-late Oct daily 9:00-13:00 & 14:00-18:00, late Oct-March closed Mon), and the Oratory of St. George (€2.50, daily

St. Anthony of Padua
(1195-1231)

One of Christendom's most popular saints, Anthony is known as a powerful speaker, a miracle worker, and the finder of lost articles.

Born in Lisbon to a rich, well-educated family, his life changed at age 25, when he saw the mutilated bodies of some Franciscan martyrs. Their sacrifice inspired him to join the poor Franciscans and dedicate his life to Christ. He moved to Italy and lived in a cave, studying, meditating, and barely speaking to anyone.

One day, he joined his fellow monks for a service. The appointed speaker failed to show up, so Anthony was asked to say a few off-the-cuff words to the crowd. He started slowly, but, filled with the Spirit, he became more confident and amazed the audience with his eloquence. Up in Assisi, St. Francis heard about Anthony and sent him on a whirlwind speaking tour.

Anthony had a strong voice, knew several languages, had an encyclopedic knowledge of theology, and could speak spontaneously as the Spirit moved him. It's said he even stood on the shores of the Adriatic Sea in Rimini and enticed a school of fish to listen. Anthony also was known as a prolific miracle worker.

In 1230, Anthony retired to Padua, where he founded a monastery and initiated reforms for the poor. An illness cut his life short at age 36. Anthony said, "Happy is the man whose words issue from the Spirit and not from himself!"

April-late Oct 9:00-12:30 & 14:30-19:00, late Oct-March until 17:00).

Information: A modest dress code is enforced inside the basilica. A helpful information desk with Anthony-related pamphlets is in the cloisters, on the right side of the church (daily 9:00-13:00 & 14:00-18:00, public WC nearby, Santo tram stop, tel. 049-822-5652, www.basilicadelsanto.org). The information desk has free English pamphlets on the saint's life and the basilica; make a donation in the Chapel of the Reliquaries to get a more-detailed booklet. A TI is on the square facing the church.

Basilica Exterior

St. Anthony looks down from the red-brick facade and blesses all. He holds a book, a symbol of all the knowledge he accumulated as a quiet monk before starting his preaching career.

Guarding the church is Donatello's life-size equestrian statue of the Venetian mercenary general, Gattamelata. Though it looks like a thousand other man-on-a-horse statues, it was a landmark in Italy's budding Renaissance—the first life-size, secular, equestrian statue cast from bronze in a thousand years.

The church is technically outside of Italy. When you pass the banisters that mark its property line, you're passing into Vatican territory.

Interior

Entering the basilica, grab a pew in the center of the nave. Sit and appreciate the space. Gaze past the crowds and through the incense haze to Donatello's glorious crucifix rising from the altar, and realize that this is one of the most important pilgrimage sites in Christendom.

Along with the crucifix, Donatello's bronze statues—Mary with Padua's six favorite saints—grace the high altar. Late in his career, the great Florentine sculptor spent more than a decade in Padua (1444-1455), creating the altar and Gattamelata.

St. Anthony's Tomb

Head to the left side of the nave to find the gleaming marble masterpiece that is the focus of the visiting pilgrims—the tomb of St. Anthony. Pilgrims file slowly through this side chapel around the tomb, so focused on the saint that they hardly notice the nine fine marble reliefs. These Renaissance masterpieces were carved during the 16th century, and show scenes and miracles from the life of the saint. As you enjoy each scene, notice the Renaissance mastery of realism and 3-D perspective and the intricate frames, which celebrate life with a burst of exuberance.

First Relief: This depicts St. Anthony receiving the Franciscan tunic. The open door illustrates the new ability to show depth by using mathematics. The cityscape above is Padua in about 1500.

Second Relief: A jealous husband has angrily stabbed his wife. Notice the musculature, the emotion, and the determination in the faces of loved ones. Above, Anthony intercedes with God to bring the woman back to life. Notice the etchings of familiar Paduan architecture at the top of the sculptures.

Third Relief: Above this panel, which shows Anthony bringing a young man back to life, is the Palazzo della Ragione looking as it still does today.

Fourth Relief: This scene, by the famous Florentine sculptor Jacopo Sansovino, shows three generations: a dead girl, her distraught mom, and a grandmother who's seen it all. Of course, Anthony will eventually change the mood, but right now it's pretty dire. Above is a relief of this basilica.

Fifth Relief: A fisherman holds a net, sadly having retrieved a drowned boy. The mother looks at Anthony, who blesses and revives the boy. Across from here is the saint's actual tomb. Under thoughtful lighting, it reads *Corpus S. Antonii.* Prayer letters are dropped behind the iron grill.

Sixth Relief: This shows "the miracle of the miser's heart." Anthony's helper dips his hand into a moneylender's side to demonstrate the absence of his heart. At his foot, the square tray with coins and a heart illustrates the scriptural verse "for where your treasure is, there your heart will be also."

Seventh Relief: Anthony holds the foot of a young man who confessed to kicking his mother. Taking a lesson from the saint about respecting your mother a little too literally, the man has cut off his own foot. The hysterical mother implores Anthony's help, and the saint's prayers to God enable him to reattach the foot.

Stand in the corner for a moment, observing the passionate devotion that pilgrims and Paduans alike have for Anthony. Touching his tomb or kneeling in prayer, the faithful believe Anthony is their protector—a confidant and intercessor for the poor. And they believe he works miracles. Believers leave offerings, votives, and written prayers to ask for help or to give thanks for miracles they believe Anthony has performed. By putting their hands on his tomb while saying silent prayers, pilgrims show devotion to Anthony and feel the saint's presence.

Popular Anthony is the patron saint of dozens of things: travelers, amputees, donkeys, pregnant women, infertile women, flight attendants, and pig farmers. Most pilgrims ask for his help in his role as the "finder of things"—from lost car keys to a life companion. You'll see dozens of photos posted on his tomb in prayer or as thanks, including many of fervently wished-for newborns.

Eighth Relief: This scene makes the point that—unlike St. Francis, who was a rowdy youth—Anthony was holy even as a child. He tosses the glass (representing his faith), which, rather than shattering, breaks the marble floor.

Ninth Relief: An angry husband accuses his wife of cheating. The wife asks Anthony to identify her baby's father. Anthony asks the child, who speaks and says that the husband is his real dad and his mother was not messing around. Everyone is reassured—whew!

Between scenes eight and nine, go into the next room, where you'll enter the oldest part of the church—the original chapel, where Anthony was first buried in 1231. To the left of the altar, note the fine (and impressively realistic for the 14th century) view of medieval Padua, with this church outside the wall (finished by 1300 and looking just like it does today).

Below the cityscape, in a circa-1380 fresco, Anthony on his cloud promises he'll watch over his town. Because people wanted to be buried near a saint, graves lie all around. If you could afford it, this was about the best piece of real estate a dead person could want. (The practice was ended with Napoleonic reforms in 1806.)

Chapel of the Reliquaries

Continue your circuit of the church by going behind the altar into the apse, to the Chapel of the Reliquaries. The most prized relic is in the glass case at center stage—Anthony's tongue. When Anthony's remains were exhumed 32 years after his death (1263), his body had decayed to dust, but his tongue was found miraculously unspoiled and red in color. How appropriate for the great preacher who, full of the Spirit, couldn't stop talking about God.

Work clockwise around the chapel, starting under the dome in front of the staircase at St. Anthony's holy, and holey, tunic *(tonaca)*. His rough-hewn wood coffin is on the left wall. His pillow—a comfy rock—is up the stairs (chest level in first glass case). The center display case contains (top to bottom) the saint's lower jaw *(il mento)*, his uncorrupted tongue *(lingua)*, and, finally, his vocal chords *(apparato vocale)* discovered intact when his remains were examined in 1981. In the last display case, a fragment of the True Cross *(la croce)* is held in a precious crucifix reliquary.

Above the relics is the *Glorification of St. Anthony*. In this Baroque fantasy, a cloud of angels and giddy *putti* tumble to the left and right in jubilation as they celebrate his presence in heaven.

Cloisters

From the right side of the nave as you face the altar, follow signs

to *chiostro;* from outside, find signs on the right side of the church. The main cloister is dominated by an exceptionally bushy magnolia tree, planted in 1810, and by the graves of the most illustrious Padovans, such as Gabriel Fallopius, the scientist who gave his name to his discovery, the Fallopian tube.

Wander around the various cloisters. Picnic tables invite pilgrims and tourists to enjoy meals within the solitude of one of the cloisters (it's covered and suitable even when rainy, also has WCs). The **multimedia exhibit** on the life of St. Anthony is a bit kitschy, as pilgrimage multimedia exhibits tend to be (30 minutes, you move three times as you use headphones to listen to the story of each tableau).

At the far end, a fascinating little **museum** is filled with votives and folk art that recounts miracles attributed to Anthony. The abbreviation *PGR* you'll see on many votives stands for *per grazia ricevuta*—for answered prayers.

NEAR VENICE

Oratory of St. George

The small but sumptuous Oratory of St. George faces the little square in front of the basilica. The oratory ("ora" means prayer) is not actually a church, though it's certainly a fine place to pray—it's filled with vivid, circa-1370 frescoes showing scenes not of Anthony, but from the life of St. Catherine. Because many lovers credit St. Anthony with finding them their partners—and this is the closest place to St. Anthony where you can be married—it's popular for weddings. While you can see it all from the door, paying the entry fee lets you sit and enjoy this peaceful spot.

Near the Basilica

Prato della Valle—The square is 150 yards southwest of the basilica (down Via Luca Belludi). Once a Roman theater and later Anthony's preaching grounds, this square claims to be the largest in Italy. It's a pleasant, 400-yard-long, oval-shaped piazza with fountains, walkways, dozens of statues of Padua's eminent citizens, and grass. It's also a lively **market** scene: fruit and vegetables

(Mon-Fri 8:00-13:00), clothing, shoes, and household goods (Sat 8:00-19:00), and antiques (third Sun 8:00-19:00).

Botanical Garden (Orto Botanico)—Green thumbs appreciate this nearly five-acre botanical garden, which contains the university's vast collection of rare plants. Founded in 1545 to cultivate medicinal plants, it's the world's oldest academic botanical garden still in its original location. A visitors center—in a little cottage to the right of the garden's entrance—contains models of the garden's layout and computer programs that describe the history and composition of the garden in English.

Cost and Hours: Garden—€4; April-Oct daily 9:00-13:00 & 15:00-19:00; Nov-March Mon-Sat 9:00-13:00, closed Sun; entrance 150 yards south of Basilica of St. Anthony—with your back to the facade, take a hard left, Santo tram stop, tel. 049-827-2119, www.ortobotanico.unipd.it.

▲▲▲Scrovegni Chapel (Cappella degli Scrovegni)

You must make reservations in advance to see this glorious, recently renovated chapel (see "Reservations," later). Wallpapered with Giotto's beautifully preserved cycle of nearly 40 frescoes, the chapel holds scenes depicting the lives of Jesus and Mary.

Painted by Giotto and his assistants from 1303 to 1305 and

considered by many to be the first piece of modern art, this work makes it clear: Europe was breaking out of the Middle Ages. A sign of the Renaissance to come, Giotto placed real people in real scenes, expressing real human emotions. These frescoes were radical for their 3-D nature, lively colors, light sources, emotion, and humanism.

The chapel was built out of guilt for white-collar crimes. Reginaldo degli Scrovegni (skroh-VEHN-yee) charged sky-high interest rates at a time when the Church forbade the practice. He even caught the attention of Dante, who placed him in one of the levels of hell in his *Inferno*. When Reginaldo died, the Church denied him a Christian burial. His son Enrico tried to buy forgiveness for his father's sins by building this superb chapel. After seeing Giotto's frescoes for the Franciscan monks of St. Anthony, Enrico knew he'd found the right artist to decorate the interior (and, he hoped, to save his father's soul). The Scrovegni residence once stood next to the chapel, but was torn down in 1824.

Cost and Hours: €13 combo-ticket with the Civic Museums (includes the worthwhile Pinacoteca and Multimedia Room). The chapel is open March-Oct Mon 9:00-19:00, Tue-Sun 9:00-22:00; Nov-Feb daily 9:00-19:00. When the Civic Museums are closed— after 19:00 and on Monday—tickets are €8.

Entry Times: Every 15 minutes (on the quarter-hour), visitors are admitted for a 15-minute video presentation in an anteroom, followed by 15 minutes in the chapel itself. After 19:00, visitors can enter every 20 minutes and get 20 minutes inside (last entry at 21:40). Daytime 20-minute visits are sometimes possible during the slowest midwinter months.

Reservations: To protect the paintings from excess humidity, only 25 people are allowed in the chapel at a time. Prepaid reservations are required. It's easiest to reserve online at www .cappelladegliscrovegni.it (also sells Padova Cards—described on page 145). If you reserve by phone, you may need to be persistent and call several times (tel. 049-201-0020; booking office open Mon-Fri 9:00-19:00, Sat 9:00-13:00, closed Sun, provide your credit-card number and hotel telephone number where you can be reached if necessary the day before your visit).

Helpful Hint: If you packed binoculars, bring them along for a better—and more comfortable—view of the uppermost frescoes.

Ideally, book your visit at least 72 hours in advance. It's sometimes possible to buy a ticket for the same day at the ticket office

NEAR VENICE

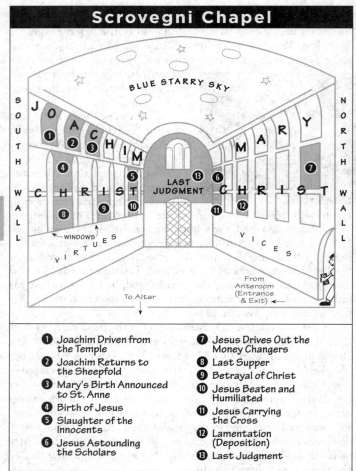

Scrovegni Chapel

BLUE STARRY SKY

SOUTH WALL

NORTH WALL

JOACHIM

MARY

CHRIST

LAST JUDGMENT

CHRIST

① ② ③ ④ ⑤ ⑧ ⑨ ⑩

⑬ ⑥ ⑦ ⑪ ⑫

← WINDOWS

VIRTUES

VICES

From Anteroom (Entrance & Exit) ←

To Altar ↓

① Joachim Driven from the Temple
② Joachim Returns to the Sheepfold
③ Mary's Birth Announced to St. Anne
④ Birth of Jesus
⑤ Slaughter of the Innocents
⑥ Jesus Astounding the Scholars
⑦ Jesus Drives Out the Money Changers
⑧ Last Supper
⑨ Betrayal of Christ
⑩ Jesus Beaten and Humiliated
⑪ Jesus Carrying the Cross
⑫ Lamentation (Deposition)
⑬ Last Judgment

(especially for single visitors), but don't count on it.

Getting There: From the train station, it's a 10- to 15-minute walk, or a quick, two-stop tram ride to the Eremitani stop. You'll enter through the Civic Museums building, where you'll find the ticket counter and mandatory bag check.

Getting In: You'll be instructed to pick up your tickets at the ticket office at least an hour before your visit. In practice, I've found that you can arrive later, but give yourself a minimum of 30 minutes to weather any commotion at the desk. Present your confirmation number, verify your time, pick up your ticket, and check any bags or purses.

While waiting for your reserved time, blitz the Pinacoteca

and Multimedia Room (described later). Read the chapel description (below) before you enter, since you'll only have a short time in the chapel itself.

The chapel is well-signed: From the ticket counter, go outside and walk 100 yards down the path. Be at the chapel doors at least five minutes before your scheduled visit. The doors are automatic, and if you're even a minute late, you'll forfeit your visit and have to rebook and repay to enter.

At your appointed time, you first enter an anteroom to watch a very instructive 15-minute video (with English subtitles) and to establish humidity levels before continuing into the chapel. No photos are allowed. Although you have only a short visit inside the chapel, it is divine. You're inside a Giotto time capsule, looking back at an artist who was ahead of his time.

Giotto's Frescoes in the Scrovegni Chapel

Giotto painted the entire chapel in 200 working days over two years, but you'll get only 15 minutes to see it.

As you enter the long, narrow chapel, look straight to the far end—the rear wall is covered with Giotto's big *Last Judgment.* Christ in a bubble is flanked by crowds of saints and by scenes of heaven and hell. This is the final, climactic scene of the story told in the chapel's 38 panels—the three-generation history of Jesus, his mother Mary, and Mary's parents.

The story begins with Jesus' grandparents, on the long south wall (with the windows) in the upper-left corner. ❶ In the first frame, a priest scolds the man who will be Mary's father (Joachim, with the halo) and kicks him out of the temple for the sin of being childless. ❷ In the next panel to the right, Joachim returns dejectedly to his sheep farm. ❸ Meanwhile (next panel), his wife is in the bedroom, hearing the miraculous news that their prayers have been answered—she'll give birth to Mary, the mother of Jesus.

From this humble start, the story of Mary and Jesus spirals clockwise around the chapel, from top to bottom. The top row (both south and north walls) covers Mary's birth and life.

Jesus enters the picture in the middle row of the south (windowed) wall. ❹ The first frame shows his birth in a shed-like manger. In the next frame, the Magi arrive and kneel to kiss his little toes. Then the child is presented in the tiny temple. Fearing danger, the family gets on a horse and flees to Egypt. ❺ Meanwhile, back home, all the baby boys are

Giotto di Bondone
(c. 1267-1337)

Though details of his life are extremely sketchy, we know that as a 12-year-old shepherd boy, Giotto was discovered painting pictures of his father's sheep on rock slabs. He became the wealthiest and most famous painter of his day. His achievements are especially remarkable because painters at that time weren't considered anything more than craftsmen and weren't expected to be innovators.

After making a name for himself by painting the life of St. Francis frescoes in Assisi, the Florentine tackled the Scrovegni Chapel (c. 1303-1305). At age 35, he was at the height of his powers. His scenes were more realistic and human than anything done for a thousand years. Giotto didn't learn technique by dissecting corpses or studying the mathematics of 3-D perspective; he had innate talent. And his personality shines through in the humanity of his art.

The Scrovegni frescoes break ground by introducing nature—rocks, trees, animals—as a backdrop for religious scenes. Giotto's people, with their voluminous, deeply creased robes, are as sturdy and massive as Greek statues, throwbacks to the Byzantine icon art of the Middle Ages. But these figures exude stage presence. Their gestures are simple but expressive: A head tilted down says dejection, an arm flung out indicates grief, clasped hands indicate hope. Giotto created his figures not just by drawing outlines and filling them in with single colors; he filled the outlines in with subtle patchworks of lighter and darker shades, and in doing so pioneered modern modeling techniques. Giotto's storytelling style is straightforward, and anyone with knowledge of the episodes of Jesus' life can read the chapel like a comic book.

The Scrovegni represents a turning point in European art and culture—away from scenes of heaven and toward a more down-to-earth, human-centered view.

slaughtered in an attempt to prevent the coming of the Messiah (*Slaughter of the Innocents*).

Spinning clockwise to the opposite (north) wall, you see (in a badly damaged fresco) ❻ the child Jesus astounding scholars with his wisdom. Next, Jesus is baptized by John the Baptist. His first miracle, at a wedding, is turning jars of water into wine. Next, he raises a mummy-like Lazarus from the dead. Riding a donkey, he enters Jerusalem triumphantly. ❼ In the temple, he drives out the wicked money changers.

Turning again to the south wall (bottom row), we see scenes from Jesus' final days. ❽ In the first frame, he and his followers gather at a table for a Last Supper. Next, Jesus kneels humbly to wash their feet. ❾ He is betrayed with a kiss and arrested. Jesus is tried. ❿ Then he is beaten and humiliated.

⓫ Finally (north wall, bottom row), he is forced to carry his own cross, is crucified, and prepared for burial, while his followers mourn (⓬ *Lamentation*). Then he is resurrected and ascends to heaven, leaving his disciples to carry on.

⓭ The whole story concludes on the rear wall, where Jesus reigns at the Last Judgment. The long south wall (ground level) features the Virtues that lead to heaven, while the north wall has the (always more interesting) Vices. And all this unfolds beneath the blue, starry sky overhead on the ceiling.

Some panels deserve a closer look:

Joachim Returns to the Sheepfold (south wall, upper left, second panel): Though difficult to appreciate from ground level, this oft-reproduced scene is groundbreaking. Giotto—a former shepherd himself—uses nature as a stage, setting the scene in front of a backdrop of real-life mountains, and adding down-home details like Joachim's jumping dog, frozen in midair.

Betrayal of Christ, a.k.a. *Il Bacio,* "The Kiss" (south wall, bottom row, center panel): Amid the crowded chaos of Jesus' arrest, Giotto focuses our eyes on the central action, where Judas ensnares Jesus in his yellow robe (the color symbolizing envy), establishes meaningful eye contact, and kisses him.

Lamentation, a.k.a. *Deposition* (north wall, bottom row, middle): Jesus has been crucified, and his followers weep and wail over the lifeless body. John the Evangelist spreads his arms wide and shrieks, his cries echoed by anguished angels above. Each face is a study in grief. Giotto emphasizes these saints' human vulnerability.

Last Judgment (big west wall): Christ in the center is a glorious vision, but the real action is in hell (lower right). Satan is a Minotaur-headed ogre munching on sinners. Around him, demons give sinners their just desserts in a scene right out of Dante...who was Giotto's friend and fellow Florentine. Front and center is Enrico Scrovegni, in a violet robe (the color symbolizing penitence), donating the chapel to the Church in exchange for forgiveness of his father's sins.

Before the guard scoots you out, take a look at the actual

altar. Though Enrico's father's tomb is lost, Enrico Scrovegni himself is in the tomb at the altar. The three statues are by Giovanni Pisano—Mary (in the center) supports baby Jesus on her hip with a perfectly natural, maternal, S-shape. She's flanked by anonymous deacons.

Civic Museums (Musei Civici Agli Eremitani)

The Eremitani, the building next to the Scrovegni Chapel that houses these three museums, was once an Augustinian hermit's monastery. While you can skip the ground-floor Archaeological Museum (with Roman and Etruscan artifacts and no English descriptions), the Pinacoteca and the Multimedia Room are worth visiting. Another part of the museum, Palazzo Zuckermann, is across the street.

Cost and Hours: €13 combo-ticket with Scrovegni Chapel, €10 without the chapel. The Pinacoteca, Archaeological Museum, and Palazzo Zuckermann are open Tue-Sun 9:00-19:00, closed Mon. The Multimedia Room is open daily 9:00-19:00. No photos are allowed, and there's a mandatory and free bag check. The museums are on Piazza Eremitani (Eremitani tram stop). Tel. 049-820-4551.

Pinacoteca

The museum's highlight is upstairs, in the Pinacoteca (picture gallery). The collection has 13th- to 18th-century paintings by Titian, Tintoretto, Giorgione, Tiepolo, Veronese, Bellini, Canova, Guariento, and other Veneto artists. But I'd make a beeline for the room with the Giotto crucifix. Ask for it: *"La Croce di Giotto?"*

Originally hung in the Scrovegni Chapel between the Scrovegni family's private zone and the public's worshipping zone, this crucifix is painted on wood by Giotto. If you actually sit on the floor and look up, the body really pops. The adjacent "God as Jesus" piece was the only painting in the otherwise frescoed chapel. (This is hung here because of preservation concerns. Its copy is the only non-original art in the chapel.) Studying these two masterpieces affirms Giotto's greatness.

Behind the crucifix room is a collection of 14th- and 15th-century art. While the works here are exquisite—and came well after Giotto—they're clearly not as modern.

Multimedia Room

The Multimedia Room, dedicated to taking a closer look at the Scrovegni Chapel, is adjacent to the Civic Museum (in the same building). To head straight from the museum entrance to the Multimedia Room, use the entrance to the right of the main entry, step into the courtyard, make a sharp right, and head down the stairs.

Rows of computer screens offer a virtual Scrovegni Chapel visit and provide cultural insights into daily life in the Middle Ages. There are explanations of the individual panels, Giotto's fresco technique, close-ups of the art, and a description of the restoration. They show a 12-minute video (English headphones available) that is similar—but not identical—to the one that precedes your chapel visit. For me, it's worth taking some time to enjoy a second video that features a mesmerizing, slow montage of close-ups of the Giotto frescoes.

Between the museum and the chapel are the scant remains of Roman Padua. The remnants are from the wall of an arena and nicely fitting pipes that once channeled water so that the arena could be flooded for special events.

Palazzo Zuckermann

This little-visited wing of the Civic Museum, just across a busy street, is included in the same ticket. Its first two floors offer a commotion of applied and decorative arts—such as clothes, furniture, and ceramics—from the Venetian Republic (1600s-1700s). On the top floor, the Bottacin collection takes you to the 19th century with coins and delightful (but no-name) pre-Impressionist paintings.

More Sights in the Center

Palazzo della Ragione—This grand 13th-century palazzo, commonly called *il Salone* (great hall), once held the medieval law

courts. The first floor consists of a huge hall—265 feet by 90 feet—that was at one time adorned with frescoes by Giotto. A fire in 1312 destroyed those paintings, and the palazzo was redecorated with the 15th-century art you see today: a series of 333 frescoes depicting the signs of the zodiac, labors of the month, symbols representing characteristics of people born under each sign, and, finally, figures of saints to legitimize the power of the courts in the eyes of the Church.

The hall is topped with a hull-shaped roof, which helps to support the structure without the use of columns—quite an architectural feat in its day, considering the building's dimensions. The curious black stone in the corner opposite the big wooden horse is the "Stone of Shame," which was the seat of debtors being punished during the Middle Ages. It was introduced as a compassionate alternative to prison by St. Anthony in 1230. Instead of being executed or doing prison time, debtors sat upon this stone, surrendered their possessions, and denounced themselves publicly before being exiled from the city. The computer kiosks (choose "English") provide excellent information with entertaining videos.

Cost and Hours: €4, March-Oct Tue-Sun 9:00-19:00, closed Mon; Nov-Feb Tue-Sun 9:00-18:00, closed Mon. Enter through the east end of Piazza delle Erbe, and go up the long staircase. Tel. 049-820-5006, Ponti Romani tram stop. The WCs are through the glass doors at the opposite end of the hall from the wooden horse.

▲▲Market Squares: Piazza delle Erbe, Piazza della Frutta, and Piazza dei Signori—The stately Palazzo della Ragione (described above) provides a dramatic backdrop for Padua's almost exotic-feeling market that fills the surrounding squares— **Piazza delle Erbe** and **Piazza della Frutta**—each morning and all day Saturday (Mon-Fri roughly 8:00-13:00, Sat 8:00-19:00, closed Sun). Second only

to the produce market in Italy's gastronomic capital of Bologna, this market has been renowned for centuries as having the freshest and greatest selection of herbs, fruits, and vegetables. As you wander, appreciate the local passion for good food: Residents can tell the month by the seasonal selections. Merchants share recipe tips with shoppers. The presentation is an art in itself. And don't miss the ground floor of the Palazzo della Ragione. Wandering through this H-shaped arcade—where you'll find various butchers, *salumerie* (delicatessens), cheese shops, bakeries, and fishmongers at work—is a sensuous experience.

Students gather in the squares after the markets have closed, spilling out of colorful bars and cafés—drinks in hand. Pizza by the slice is dirt cheap. A typical snack stand selling all kinds of fresh, hot, and ready-to-eat seafood appetizers sets up in Piazza della Frutta between 17:00 and 20:30 (daily except Sun). Belly up to the bar with your drink and try whatever's being served.

Piazza dei Signori, just a block away, is a busy clothing market in the morning and the most popular gathering place in the evening for students out for a drink. The circa-1400 clock deco-

rates the former palace of the ruling family. The aggressive lion with unfurled wings on the column was a reminder of the Venetian determination to assert its control. Today that lion can be seen as representing the Veneto region's independence from Rome: Italy's north (Veneto and Lombardy) is tired of subsidizing the south. Grumbling about this issue continues to stir talk of splitting the country.

Drinking a *Spritz* with the Student Crowd—Each early evening, before dinner, students enliven Padua by enjoying a convivial drink in their favorite places. Piazza dei Signori (described above) is the favorite square. Or you could sit in front of the university, nurse your drink, and watch the graduates get roasted with their gangs of crazy friends (see "Graduation Antics in Padua" sidebar, later). The drink of choice is a *spritz*, an aperitif generally made with Campari (liquor infused with bitter herbs), white wine, and sparkling water, and garnished with a blood-orange wedge. Most Paduan women seem to prefer a lighter *spritz* made with Aperol (orange-flavored liquor, less alcohol content).

Grab a table to be part of the scene, or get your *spritz* to take away *(da portar via)*, and join the young people out on the piazza. Either way, this is a classic opportunity to enjoy a real discussion with smart, English-speaking students who see tourists not as pests, but as interesting people from far away. For an instant conversation starter, ask about the current political situation in Italy, the right-wing party's policy on immigrants, or the cultural differences between Italy's north and south.

Caffè Pedrocchi—The white-columned, Neoclassical Pedrocchi building is much more than just a café on the ground floor. A

complex of meeting rooms and entertainment venues, it stirs the Italian soul (at least, patriotic Italian souls). Built in 1831 during the period of Austrian rule, Caffè Pedrocchi was inaugurated for the fourth Italian Congress of Scientists, which convened during the mid-19th century to stir up nationalistic fervor as Italy struggled to become a united nation. As a symbol of patriotic hope, it was the target (no surprise) of a student uprising plot in 1848. You can still see a bullet hole (framed in silver) in the wall of the Sala Bianca, where one of the insurgents was killed. Nowadays, you get more foam than fervor.

Each of the café's three dining rooms is decorated and furnished in a different color: red, white, or green—representing the colors of the Italian flag. In the outer, unheated Sala Verde (Green Room), people are welcome to sit and relax without ordering anything or having to pay. This is where older Italian gentlemen read their newspapers and gather with friends to chat about the old days. In the red room, the clock over the bar is flanked by marble reliefs of morning and night, signaling that it was once open 24 hours a day (in the 19th century). The maps of the hemispheres with south up top reflect the anti-conventional spirit of the place. The menu offers teahouse fare, including salads, sandwiches, and the writer Stendhal's beloved *zabaglione*, a creamy custard made with *marsala* wine (Sun-Thu 9:00-21:00, Fri-Sat 9:00-23:00, two entrances across from Via VIII Febbraio 14 and 20 near Ponti Romani tram stop, tel. 049-878-1231).

Piano Nobile: This upper, "noble floor" of the Pedrocchi building is more elaborate. The rooms are all in different styles, such as Greek, Etruscan, or Egyptian, with good English descriptions throughout. These rooms were intended to evoke memories of the glory of past epochs, which a united Italy had hopes of reliving.

Museum of the Risorgimento: The Piano Nobile hosts a small museum that traces Padua's role in Italian history, from the downfall of the Venetian Republic (1797) to the founding of the Republic of Italy (1948). Exhibits, a few with English descriptions, include uniforms, medals, weaponry, old artillery, Fascist propaganda posters, and a 30-minute propagandistic video (in Italian, but mostly fascinating footage without narration). The video, played on demand, is a "Luce" production (meaning a Mussolini production) and features great scenes of the town in the 1930s, including clips of Il Duce's visit and later WWII bombardments. The war and propaganda posters in the last room are haunting. An old woman pleads to those who might question the Fascist-driven war effort: "Don't betray my son." Another declares, "The Germans are truly our friends." And another asks, "And you...what are you doing?" (€4, Tue-Sun 9:30-12:30 & 15:30-18:00, closed Mon, tel. 049-820-5007.) To reach the Piano Nobile, find the stairway in the far wing of the café building.

▲**Baptistery**—This richly frescoed little building was originally the private chapel of Padua's ruling family. Then, in 1405, Venice took over, killing the family, and making the building a baptistery. Located next to Padua's skippable Duomo, the Baptistery was frescoed (c. 1370) by Giusto de' Menabuoi.

While it was created 70 years after Giotto, the Baptistery feels older. Because the artist was working for a private family, he needed to be politically correct and not threaten or offend the family's allies, especially the Church. While still mind-blowing, the Baptistery's art seems relatively conservative compared to Giotto's Scrovegni Chapel. Giotto, supported by the powerful Scrovegni family and the Franciscans, could get away with being more progressive and bold.

The Baptistery's complex design must have made perfect and cohesive sense to the faithful in centuries past. Almighty Christ is in majesty on top, while approachable Mary and the multitude of saints provide the devout with access to God. Find the world as it was known in the 14th century (the disk below Mary's feet). It kicks off a cycle of scenes illustrating creation (clockwise from the creation of Adam). The four evangelists (Matthew, Mark, Luke, and John) with their books and symbols fill the corners. A vivid crucifixion scene faces a gorgeous annunciation. And the altar niche features a dim, blue-toned, literal Apocalypse from the book of Revelation (€2.80, daily 10:00-18:00).

University of Padua—The main building of this prestigious university, known as Palazzo Bò, is adjacent to Caffè Pedrocchi. Founded in 1222, it's one of the first, greatest, and most progressive universities in Europe. Back when the Church controlled university curricula, a group of professors and students broke free from the University of Bologna to create this liberal school, which would be independent of Catholic constraints and accessible to people of alternative faiths.

NEAR VENICE

A haven for free thought, the university attracted intellectuals from all over Europe, including the great astronomer Copernicus, who realized here that the universe didn't revolve around him. And Galileo—notorious for disagreeing with the Church's views on science—called his 18 years on the faculty here the best of his life.

The gawking public is not really welcomed in the university, but you can poke into two courtyards (weekdays and Saturday mornings only; when closed, just peer through the gate). Find the entrance at Via VIII Febbraio 7, under the "Gymnasium" inscription (facing city hall, 30 yards from Caffè Pedrocchi). You'll pop into a 16th-century courtyard, the school's historic core. It's littered with the coats of arms of important faculty and leaders of the university over the ages. Classrooms, which open onto the square, are still used. Today, students gather here, surrounded by memories of illustrious alumni, including the first woman ever to receive a university degree (in 1678).

A passageway leads from here to an adjacent second courtyard from the Fascist era (c. 1938). The relief celebrates heroic students in World War I. Off of this courtyard, notice the richly decorated stairway, frescoed in the 1930s with themes celebrating art, science, and the pursuit of knowledge.

The big attraction among tourists is Europe's first great **Anatomy Theater** (from 1594), which you can visit only on a

Graduation Antics in Padua

With 60,000 students, Padua's university always seems to be hosting graduation ceremonies. There's a constant trickle of happy grads and their friends and families celebrating the big event.

During the school year, every 20 minutes or so, a student steps into a formal room (upstairs, above the university courtyard) to officially meet with the leading professors of his or her faculty. When they're finished, the students are given a green laurel wreath. They pose for ceremonial group photos and family snapshots. It's a sweet scene. Then, craziness takes over.

The new graduates replace their somber clothing with raunchy outfits, as gangs of friends gather around them on Via VIII Febbraio, the street in front of the university. The roast begins. The gang rolls out a giant butcher-paper poster with a generally obscene caricature of the student and a litany of *This Is Your Life* photos and stories. The new grad, subject to various embarrassing pranks, reads the funny statements out loud. The poster is then taped to the university wall for all to see. (Find the plastic panels to the right of the main entry, facing Via VIII Febbraio. Graduation posters are allowed to stay there for 24 hours. The panels are emptied each morning, but by nighttime a new set of posters is affixed to the plastic shields.)

During the roast, the friends sing the catchy but obscene local university anthem, reminding their newly esteemed friend not to get too huffy: *Dottore, dottore, dottore del buso del cul. Vaffancul, vaffancul* (loosely translated: "Doctor, doctor. You're just a doctor of the a-hole...go f-off, go f-off"). After you've heard this song (with its fanfare and oom-pah-pah catchiness) and have seen all the good-natured fun, you can't stop singing it.

The crazy show is usually staged late in the afternoon. Outdoor café tables afford great seats to enjoy the spectacle.

guided tour (explained below). Try to get a ticket, but keep in mind that it's not worth any heroics to see. The first two rooms of the tour are underwhelming: One features the supposed "pulpit of Galileo" (c. 1550) and portraits of 40 famous alums. The second is the Aula Magna, a ceremonial room for festivities. The historic Anatomy Theater itself is more impressive. Despite the Church's strict ban on autopsies, more than 300 students would pack this theater to watch professors dissect human cadavers (the bodies

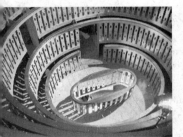

of criminals from another town). This had to be done in a "don't ask, don't tell" kind of way, because the Roman Catholic Church only started allowing the teaching of anatomy through dissection in the late 1800s.

Cost and Hours: While it's free to visit the university, you must sign up for a 30-minute tour (€5) to see the Anatomy Theater. Only 30 people may enter at a time. Tours run three times a day (March-Oct Mon, Wed, and Fri at 15:15, 16:15, and 17:15; Tue, Thu, and Sat at 9:15, 10:15, and 11:15; no tours on Sun, reduced schedule Nov-Feb—call number below, Ponti Romani tram stop, www.unipd.it). School groups often book the entire visit, and many of the guides speak no English.

Confirm tour times and availability by calling 049-827-3047 or stopping by the ticket window (opens 15 minutes before each tour, located just inside the palace, in the hall reached from the Fascist-era courtyard described earlier). The bar there is fun for a cheap drink and to see photos of university life.

Sleeping in Padua

Rooms in Padua's hotels are more spacious and a better value than those in Venice. Keep in mind that when large conventions take over the town—several times a year—all hotels raise prices. I've listed two hotels in the center and a group of accommodations near the basilica. All are reachable from the station by the tram; only Albergo Verdi is more than a five-minute walk from the nearest tram stop.

In the Center
$$$ Hotel Majestic Toscanelli is a central, fancy hotel with 34 pleasant, air-conditioned rooms and a touch of charm, buried in a characteristic ghetto with wonderful cobbled ambience. This area is popular with students at night, and it can be noisy until about 1:00 in the morning; as the hotel's windows are single-paned, request a quiet room on the back side (Sb-€95-110, Db-€150-160, ask for 10 percent Rick Steves discount, superior rooms and suites available at extra cost, check website for special discounts, includes a wonderful breakfast, free Wi-Fi, parking-€19/day, Via dell'Arco 2, Tito Livio tram stop, tel. 049-663-244, fax 049-876-0025, www.toscanelli.com, majestic@toscanelli.com). From the tram stop, follow the passageway next to #26 (locked after 20:30), then jog left down Via Marsala and turn right on Via dell'Arco.

Sleep Code

(€1 = about $1.40, country code: 39)
S = Single, **D** = Double/Twin, **T** = Triple, **Q** = Quad, **b** = bathroom, **s** = shower only. Unless otherwise noted, credit cards are accepted, breakfast is included, and English is spoken.

To help you easily sort through these listings, I've divided the accommodations into three categories based on the price for a standard double room with bath:

$$$ **Higher Priced**—Most rooms €130 or more.
$$ **Moderately Priced**—Most rooms between €90-130.
$ **Lower Priced**—Most rooms €90 or less.

Prices can change without notice; verify the hotel's current rates online or by email. For other updates, see www.ricksteves.com/update.

$$ Albergo Verdi, a modern little place, is crammed into an old building on a small back street beyond Piazza dei Signori. While public spaces are very tight, the 14 rooms are comfortable (Sb-€70, Db-€90-100, extra person-€30, air-con, elevator—could be Padua's smallest, pay Wi-Fi, Via Dondi dall'Orologio 7, Ponti Romani tram stop, tel. 049-836-4163, fax 049-878-0175, www.albergoverdipadova.it, info@albergoverdipadova.it). From Piazza dei Signori, walk through the arch under the clock tower and go to the far end of Piazza del Capitaniato; the hotel is on the side street to your right.

Near the Basilica of St. Anthony

Santo is the nearest tram stop for the following hotels. Use the Prato della Valle tram stop for the hostel.

$$ Hotel Al Fagiano feels like an art gallery with crazy, sexy modern art everywhere. The hotel is all about the union of a man and a woman (quite romantic). They rent 40 bright and cheery air-conditioned rooms, each uniquely decorated with Rossella Fagiano's canvases (Sb-€64, Db-€100, Tb-€115, ask for 5 percent Rick Steves discount, €7 per person less without breakfast, free Wi-Fi, parking-€10/day, 50 yards from the Santo tram stop at Via Locatelli 45, tel. & fax 049-875-3396, www.alfagiano.com, info@alfagiano.com).

$$ Hotel Belludi 37 is a slick, borderline-pretentious place renting 15 modern rooms shoehorned into an old building. The decor is dark, woody, fresh, and stylish (S-€80, Sb-€100, Db-€120, bigger Db-€135, ask for 10 percent Rick Steves discount, €7 less per person without breakfast, air-con, Wi-Fi, a block from the Santo tram stop at Via Luca Belludi 37, tel. 049-665-633, fax 049-658-685, www.belludi37.it, info@belludi37.it).

$ Hotel Casa del Pellegrino, with 150 spotless, cheap, institutional rooms and straight pricing, is home to the pilgrims who come to pay homage to St. Anthony in the basilica next door. But any visitor to Padua is welcome (S-€51, Sb-€69, D-€72, Db-€89, Tb-€106, Qb-€128, family rooms-€145, ask for a room off the street, €7 less per person without breakfast, air-con, elevator, free Wi-Fi, parking-€5/day, Via Cesarotti 21, tel. 049-823-9711, fax 049-823-9780, www.casadelpellegrino.com, info@casadelpellegrino.com). For better accommodations, request one of the 24 "superior" rooms in the *dipendenza,* the hotel's modern wing (€5 extra/night).

$ Hotel Al Santo, run with charm by Valentina and Antonio, offers 15 spacious rooms with all the comforts on two floors above their restaurant, a few steps from the basilica (Sb-€65-70, Db-€90, Tb-€120, Qb-€135, double-paned windows, quieter rooms off street, some rooms have views of basilica, air-con, elevator, free Wi-Fi, parking-€14/day, Via del Santo 147, tel. 049-875-2131, fax 049-878-8076, www.alsanto.it, alsanto@alsanto.it).

Hostel: **$ Ostello Città di Padova,** near Prato della Valle, is well-run and has 80 beds in 4-, 6-, and 9-bed rooms (beds with sheets and breakfast-€19; family rooms-€90; free Wi-Fi, laundry-€5.50/load, lockers, reception open 7:00-9:30 & 15:30-23:30, rooms locked during afternoon but reception staffed if you need to leave bags, 23:30 curfew; Via Aleardi 30, Prato de Valle tram stop, tel. 049-875-2219, fax 049-654-210, www.ostellopadova.it, ostellopadova@ctgveneto.it). From the tram stop, exit the square ahead of you to the right and make an immediate left down Via Memmo; after the church, continue straight one block on Via Torresini and turn right on Via Aleardi.

Eating in Padua

The university population means cheap, good food abounds. For picnic shopping, see "Market Squares," on page 160. My recommended restaurants are all centrally located in the historic core. You'd think there would be fine dining on the charming market squares, but on the piazzas it's a take-out-pizza-and-casual-bar scene (dominated by students after dark). La Lanterna, at the neighboring Piazza dei Signori, is the best on-square option I've found—but it's still basically pizza. The dreamily atmospheric ghetto neighborhood (just two blocks off the market squares) thrives after dark with trendy bars and a lively student *spritz* scene.

Fine Dining near the Center

Osteria dei Fabbri, with shared rustic tables, offers a good mix of class and accessibility, quality, and price. The dining room is spacious, and the dishes are traditional Venetian (€9 pastas, €14 *secondi*, €2.50 cover, Mon-Sat 12:30-14:30 & 19:30-22:30, closed Sun, Via dei Fabbri 13, on a side street on south side of Piazza Erbe, tel. 049-650-336).

Osteria L'Anfora is a classic place serving classic dishes in an informal, fun-loving space. Don't be put off by the woody, raffish decor and the fact that it's a popular hangout for a pre-meal drink. They take food seriously and serve it at good prices, and the energy and commotion add to a great dining experience (€9 pastas, €14-16 *secondi*, €2 cover, meals served Mon-Sat 12:30-15:00 & 19:30-22:30, closed Sun, Via dei Soncin 13, tel. 049-656-629, no reservations taken).

Ristorante alle Piazze da Giorgio is a respected fixture in town for its dressy white-tablecloth dining. They are passionate about their vegetarian dishes and proud of their bean soup, fish soup, cod, and squid. Reservations are smart at night (€9-11 pastas, €18-24 *secondi*, €3 cover, save with €14-18 single-plate specials and €20-28 three-course lunches, meals served 12:00-15:00 & 19:00-24:00, closed Sun, Via Daniele Manin 8, tel. 049-836-0973).

Cheap Eats near the Center

La Lanterna has a forgettable interior, but a pizza here on Piazza dei Signori includes a rare-in-Padua chance to sit in a grand square under the stars, surrounded by great architecture. Its pizzas are a local favorite—takeaway available—and reservations are recommended (€6.50-8.50 pizzas, €8 pastas, €14 *secondi*, €1.60 cover, Fri-Wed 12:00-14:30 & 18:00-24:00, closed Thu, Piazza dei Signori 39, tel. 049-660-770).

Bar dei Osei, on Piazza della Frutta, is a very simple sandwich bar with some of the best outdoor seats in town. While Paduans love their delicate *tremazzini* (white bread sandwiches with crusts cut off; €1.30/€1.80 with table service), I'd choose their grilled *porchetta*—pulled-pork sandwiches (€3.50/€3.80). The two-foot-long mother lode awaits on the counter for you to say how big a slice you'd like. Wines are listed on the board (Mon-Sat 7:00-21:00, closed Sun, Piazza della Frutta 1, tel. 049-875-9606). With a fast, cheap meal and drink in hand, grab a seat and enjoy the market scene.

Brek, with one entrance next to the Ponti Romani tram stop and another tucked into a corner of Piazza Cavour at #20, is an easy self-service chain *ristorante* with healthy and affordable choices. It's big, bright, practical, and family-friendly (pastas €4-5, no cover, daily 11:30-15:00 & 18:30-22:00, tel. 049-875-3788).

Brek Foccacceria (part of the same chain), across from Caffè Pedrocchi and next door to the PAM supermarket, is a café selling big sandwiches and slices of pizza that you can eat at outdoor tables (daily 8:00-22:00, Piazzetta della Garzeria 6, tel. 049-876-1651).

Stock up on picnic items at the outdoor markets, or visit the **PAM supermarket,** in the tiny *piazzetta* east of Caffè Pedrocchi (Mon-Sat 8:00-21:00, closed Wed after 14:00 and all day Sun, Piazzetta Garzeria 3).

Near the Basilica of St. Anthony

Pizzeria Pago Pago dishes up wood-fired Neapolitan pizzas (a local favorite) and daily specials depending on what's in season. Get there early for dinner or wait (€5.50-7.50 pizzas, €2.50 cover, Wed-Mon 12:00-14:00 & 19:00-24:00, closed Tue; 2 blocks from Basilica of St. Anthony, up Via del Santo and right onto Via Galileo Galilei to #59; tel. 049-665-558, Gaetano and Modesto).

Casa del Pellegrino Ristorante caters to St. Anthony pilgrims with simple, basic, and hearty meals, served in a cheery dining room just north of the basilica. *Baccalà* (cod) is a favorite here (€4-6 pastas, €7.50-9.50 *secondi*, €14 fixed-price meal includes water and coffee, €1.70 cover, daily 12:00-14:00 & 19:30-21:30, Via Cesarotti 21, tel. 049-876-0715).

Zairo is a huge indoor/outdoor *ristorante*/pizzeria with reasonable prices, delicious homemade pastas, Veneto specialties, snappy service, and a local clientele (€6-8 pastas, Tue-Sun 12:00-14:30 & 19:00-24:00, closed Mon, east side of the vast Prato della Valle square at #51, tel. 049-663-803).

Pollodoro la Gastronomica, my pick of the take-out delis near the basilica, sells roast chicken, pastas, pizza, and veggies, and will make sandwiches (Wed-Sat and Mon 9:00-14:00 & 17:00-20:00, Sun 9:00-14:00 only, closed Tue, 100 yards from basilica at Via Belludi 34, tel. 049-663-718). You can picnic at the nearby cloisters of the basilica.

Padua Connections

From Padua by Train to: Venice (2/hour, 30-50 minutes), **Vicenza** (2/hour, fewer on weekends, 15-30 minutes), **Milan** (1-2/hour, 2-3 hours), **Verona** (2/hour, 40-60 minutes), **Ravenna** (roughly hourly, 2.5-3 hours, change in Bologna or Ferrara).

By Bus to: Venice (45 min, €3.70, hourly at :25 past the hour from 5:25-22:25, also at :55 past the hour from 5:55-8:55 and 13:55-18:55) and Venice's **Marco Polo Airport** (65 min, €4.30 plus €1.10 per piece of luggage, same departure times). Buses depart from platform 11 at Padua's bus station, next to the train station; recheck times at www.sitabus.it. If flying into the airport, take this bus to get directly to Padua (buy tickets at windows in arrivals hall or at airport TI).

By Minibus to Airports: A minibus service runs from Padua to **Marco Polo Airport** (€28/person) or **Treviso Airport** (€39/person, reservations required, tel. 049-870-4425, www.airservice padova.it).

Near Padua: Vicenza

To many architects, Vicenza (vih-CHEHN-zah) is a pilgrimage site. Entire streets look like the back of a nickel. This is the city of Andrea Palladio (1508-1580), the 16th-century Renaissance architect who gave us the Palladian style that is so influential in countless British country homes. But as grandiose as Vicenza's Palladian facades may feel, there is little marble here. The city lacked the wealth to build with much more than painted wood and plaster.

If you're an architecture buff, Vicenza merits a quick day trip on any day but Monday, when major sights are closed. If you're packing light, it's an easy stop, located on the same train line as Padua, Verona, and Venice. But because you can't store bags at the train station, it's not worth stopping if you have lots of luggage.

Tourist Information: Vicenza has two TIs. The larger one is next to the Olympic Theater at Piazza Matteotti 12 (daily 9:00-13:00 & 14:00-18:00, tel. 0444-320-854, www.vicenzae.org) and the other is at Piazza dei Signori 8 (daily 9:00-14:00 & 14:30-18:30). Ask for the free brochure on Palladio's buildings. Architecture fans appreciate the €2.50 *Vicenza and the Villas of Andrea Palladio*.

Arrival in Vicenza: From the **train station,** I'd head straight for the most distant sight, the Olympic Theater (with a TI next door), and then see other sights on the way back. Go straight out the train station's front door, and use the crosswalk on the right side of the roundabout. From here, it's a five-minute walk straight ahead up wide Viale Roma to the PAM supermarket at the bottom of Corso Palladio; turn right through the gate and then it's a good 10 minutes more down the Corso to the Olympic Theater (a taxi costs €8). **Drivers** can park in one of the cheap parking lots (Parcheggio Bassano and Parcheggio Cricoli), and catch a free shuttle bus to the center.

Helpful Hints: All of the sights mentioned (except the villas outside of town) are covered by the **Card Musei** combo-ticket (€8.50/3 days, sold at Olympic Theater and Palazzo Leoni Montanari). In a pinch, the TIs may be willing to store bags for you while you walk around town.

Sights in Vicenza

Helpful bilingual signs in front of Palladio's buildings explain their history. Arrows around town point you to his major works, and you can also pick up a map from the TI.

▲▲Olympic Theater (Teatro Olimpico)—Palladio's last work, one of his greatest, shouldn't be missed. This indoor theater is

bursting with tricks of perspective, a wood-and-stucco festival of classical columns, statues, and an oh-wow stage.

Cost and Hours: Entry only with €8.50 Card Musei, which covers other Vicenza sights; audioguide available, Tue-Sun 9:00-17:00, closed Mon, last entry 30 minutes before closing, very occasionally closed when theater is in use, entrance to left of TI at Piazza Matteotti 11, tel. 0444-222-800, www.comune.vicenza .it. When you step back outside, look up the town's main drag—named after Palladio. It's the same main street you saw on the stage of his theater.

▲Church of Santa Corona—A block away from the Olympic Theater and currently being restored, this "Church of the Holy

Crown" was built in the 13th century to house a thorn from the Crown of Thorns, given to the Bishop of Vicenza by the French King Louis IX. The church has two artistic highlights: the art embellishing its high altar and Giovanni Bellini's fine painting, *Baptism of Christ*. During restoration, its paintings are on display at the Diocesan Museum.

Cost and Hours: €5, Tue-Sun 10:00-13:00 & 14:00-18:00, closed Mon, Piazza Duomo 12, tel. 0444-226-400, www.museo diocesanovicenza.it.

Archaeological and Natural History Museum—Located next door to the Church of Santa Corona, this museum has a ground floor featuring Roman antiquities (mosaics, statues, and artifacts excavated from Rome's Baths of Caracalla, plus swords) and a barbarian warrior skeleton complete with sword and helmet. Prehistoric scraps are upstairs. Look for English description sheets near exhibit entryways throughout.

Cost and Hours: Covered by Card Musei, Tue-Sun 9:00-17:00, closed Mon, Contrà Santa Corona 4, tel. 0444-222-811, www.museicivicivicenza.it.

Palazzo Leoni Montanari—Across the street from the Church of Santa Corona, this small museum is a palatial riot of Baroque, with cherub-cluttered ceilings jumbled like in some heavenly pre-school. A quick stroll shows off Venetian paintings and a floor of Russian icons.

Cost and Hours: €5, Tue-Sun 10:00-18:00, closed Mon, last entry 30 minutes before closing, Contrà Santa Corona 25, tel. 800-578-875, www.palazzomontanari.com.

Piazza dei Signori—Vicenza's main square has been the center of town ever since it was the site of the ancient Roman forum. The commanding **Basilica Palladiana,** with its 270-foot-tall, 13th-century tower, dominates the square (may be under renovation during your visit). It was a meeting place for local big shots. It was young Palladio's proposal—to redo Vicenza's dilapidated Gothic palace of justice in the Neo-Greek style—that established him as the city's favorite architect. The rest of Palladio's career was a one-man construction boom. When the basilica reopens sometime in 2012, it'll host special

exhibitions that sometimes involve a fee, but you can often pop in for a free look.

Villas on the Outskirts of Vicenza—Vicenza is surrounded by dreamy Venetian villas. Venice's commercial empire receded in the 1500s when trade began to pick up along the Atlantic seaboard and dwindle in the Mediterranean. Venice redirected its economic agenda to agribusiness, which led to the construction of lavish country villas, such as **Villa la Rotonda** (the inspiration for Thomas Jefferson's Monticello) and **Villa Valmarana ai Nani** (www.villavalmarana.com). Located southeast of the town center, both houses are furnished with period pieces and come with good English descriptions (closed Mon). Pick up the free English brochure on Palladio's villas from the TI if you plan to visit.

Vicenza Connections

From Vicenza by Train to: Venice (2/hour, 45-75 minutes), **Padua** (2/hour, fewer on weekends, 15-30 minutes), **Verona** (2/hour, 30-60 minutes), **Milan** (1-2/hour, 1.75-2.5 hours). Unless you crave speed or need to burn a railpass day, you'll save a lot of money by taking the slow *R* trains to Vicenza instead of the fast *ES* trains.

Verona

Romeo and Juliet made Verona a household word. Alas, a visit here has nothing to do with those two star-crossed lovers. You

can pay to visit the house that falsely claims to be Juliet's (with an almost believable balcony and a courtyard swarming with tour groups), join in the tradition of rubbing the breast of Juliet's statue to help find a lover (or to pick up the sweat of someone who can't), and even make a pilgrimage to what isn't "La Tomba di Giulietta."

Fiction aside, Verona—Italy's fourth-most-visited city—has been an important crossroads for 2,000 years and is therefore packed with genuine history. R and J fans will take some solace in the fact that two real feuding families, the Montecchi and the Cappellos, were the models for Shakespeare's Montagues and Capulets. And, if R and J had existed and were alive today, they would still recognize much of their "hometown."

Verona's main attractions are its wealth of Roman ruins; the remnants of its 13th- and 14th-century political and cultural boom; its 21st-century, quiet, pedestrian-only ambience; and its world-class opera festival, held each summer (www.arena.it). After Venice's festival of tourism, Veneto's second city (in population and in artistic importance) is a cool and welcome sip of pure Italy, where dumpsters are painted by schoolchildren as class projects and public spaces are the domain of locals, not tourists. If you like Italy but don't need blockbuster sights, this town is a joy.

Orientation to Verona

Verona's old town fills an easy-to-defend bend in the River Adige. The vibrant and enjoyable core of Verona is along Via Mazzini between Piazza Brà (pronounced "bra") and Piazza Erbe, Verona's market square since Roman times. Via Mazzini attracts mob scenes during the *passeggiata* (evening stroll), so don't neglect the parallel Corso Porta Borsari. Across the river, to the east of the old town, the quieter neighborhood of Veronetta offers a few sights and accommodations. For a good day trip to Verona, visit the Roman Arena and then take my self-guided walk.

Tourist Information

Verona's TI is just off **Piazza Brà**—from the square, head behind the big yellow building with columns and cross the street to Via degli Alpini 9 (Mon-Sat Feb-Nov 9:00-19:00, Dec-Jan 9:00-18:00; Sun 10:00-16:00 year-round, tel. 045-806-8680, www.tourism .verona.it). Pick up the free city map for a list of sights and opening hours, and confirm the walking-tour schedule. If you're staying the night, ask about concerts or pick up the monthly entertainment guide, *Carnet Verona* (free at TI, €1 at newsstands).

Verona Card: This tourist card covers bus transportation and entrance to all the recommended Verona sights, except the manicured Giusti Garden (€15/2 days or €20/5 days, sold at TIs and at participating sights). If you visit the Roman Arena (€6), climb Torre dei Lamberti (€6), explore Castelvecchio (€6), tour two churches (€5), and take a bus ride (€1.10), you'll pay €24.10. At €15, the card saves a day-tripper intent on blitzing the city almost 40 percent.

The €6 **Church Card,** sold at four churches (San Zeno, Duomo, Sant'Anastasia, and San Fermo) that require admission, pays off if you visit at least three (www.chieseverona.it). There's no need to get both tourist cards.

Arrival in Verona

By Train: Get off at the Verona Porta Nuova Station. You'll emerge into the station from one of two passages. In the main hall, you'll find WCs (€0.80) and a baggage check office (€4/5 hours, €11/24 hours, daily 7:00-23:00, 44 pounds max). Buses and taxis are immediately outside.

Avoid the boring 15-minute walk from the station to Piazza Brà by catching a **city bus.** Before boarding, buy an individual ticket from the tobacco shop inside the station (€1.10/1 hour, €3.50 day pass valid until midnight). Now find platform A in front of the station and hop on bus #11, #12, or #13. After 20:00 and all day Sunday though, you'll want bus #90, #92, or #98. If in doubt, confirm that your bus is headed to the city center by asking, *"Per il centro?"* (pehr eel CHEN-troh). Validate your ticket by stamping it in the machine on the bus. (For public transport information, visit www.atv.verona.it.)

Drivers don't announce stops, but you'll know Piazza Brà because of the can't-miss-it Roman Arena. The TI is just a few steps beyond the bus stop (keep walking along the medieval walls). You can catch return buses to the station (same numbers) from the stop on the piazza side of the street, or from another bus stop just outside the city wall on Corso Porta Nuova (on the right).

Taxis pick up only at taxi stands (at Piazza Brà and train station) and cost about €8 for the quick ride between the train station and the center of town.

By Car: The town center is closed to traffic, but if you're staying here, your hotel can get you permission to drive in—ask when you book. Otherwise your license plate could be photographed, and a €100 ticket might be waiting in the mail when you get home.

Drivers will find reasonably priced parking in well-marked lots and garages just outside the center. The underground **Cittadella garage,** at Piazza Cittadella (a block off Piazza Brà, behind the TI), is huge, convenient, and easy to find (€1.90/hour, €12/24 hours). The lot in front of the train station costs less (€9.40/24 hours), but you'll spend your savings on the bus to the center. Street parking costs €1.50 per hour (buy ticket at a tobacco shop to put on dashboard, spaces marked with blue lines, maximum two hours).

By Plane: Efficient buses connect Verona's airport (known as Catullo or Verona-Villafranca, 12 miles southwest of the city) with its train station (€5, buy tickets on board or at tobacco shop, daily about 5:40-23:00, 3/hour, 15 minutes, bus stop is by front door of train station, www.aeroportoverona.it).

From Brescia Airport, 40 miles west of Verona, a bus meets Ryanair flights and takes passengers to the train station (€11, buy tickets on board, bus schedule is coordinated with Ryanair arrivals and departures).

Helpful Hints

Sightseeing Schedules: Many sights are closed on Mondays, at least in the morning.

Opera: From mid-June through early September, Verona's opera festival brings the city to life, with 15,000 music fans filling the Roman Arena for almost nightly performances. The city is packed and festive—restaurants have prescheduled seatings for dinner and hotels jack up their prices (cheap upper-level seats about €27, book tickets either online at www.arena.it or by calling 045-800-5151; box office open Mon-Fri 9:00-12:00 & 15:15-17:45, Sat-Sun 9:00-12:00; during opera season, open daily 10:00-17:45, or until 21:00 on performance days; Via Dietro Anfiteatro 6B).

Internet Access: Try **Verona Web** (Mon-Fri 10:00-20:00, Sat-Sun 14:00-20:00, a couple of blocks off Piazza Brà toward Castelvecchio at Via Roma 17A, tel. 045-801-3394) or **Internet Etc.** (€5.50/hour, Tue-Sat 10:00-19:45, Sun-Mon 15:30-19:45, off Via Mazzini on Via Quattro Spade 3B, tel. 045-800-0222).

Tours in Verona

Walking Tours—The TI organizes 1.5-hour tours in English (March-Oct Fri-Sun 11:30, no tours off-season, €10 per person). Tours meet inside the Piazza Brà TI and stroll all the way through the old town (call to confirm schedule, no reservation necessary, tel. 045-806-8680).

Private Guides—Two excellent and enthusiastic Verona guides enjoy giving private tours of the town and region to readers of this book (€105/2 hours and €210/5 hours per group, tours tailored to your interests—villas, wine tasting, and so on). They are **Marina Menegoi** (tel. 045-801-2174, mobile 328-958-1108, mmenegoi @gmail.com) and **Valeria Biasi** (€65/hour, ask for Rick Steves discount, mobile 348-903-4238, www.aguideinverona.com, valeria @aguideinverona.com). For families with children, Valeria offers an interactive game in the city called Safari (€130/2.5 hours).

Self-Guided Walk

Welcome to Verona Town Walk

This walk covers the essential sights in the town core, starting at Piazza Brà and ending at the cathedral. Allow 1.5 hours (including the tower climb and dawdling, more with the optional detours).

❶ Piazza Brà

If you're wondering about the name, it comes from the local dialect and means "open space." A generation ago this piazza was noisy with cars. Now it's open and people friendly—the community family room and natural festival grounds.

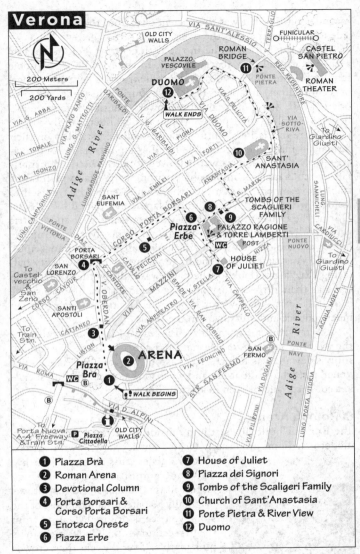

Verona

200 Meters

200 Yards

1. Piazza Brà
2. Roman Arena
3. Devotional Column
4. Porta Borsari & Corso Porta Borsari
5. Enoteca Oreste
6. Piazza Erbe
7. House of Juliet
8. Piazza dei Signori
9. Tombs of the Scaligeri Family
10. Church of Sant'Anastasia
11. Ponte Pietra & River View
12. Duomo

Grab a bench near the central fountain called "The Alps." This was a gift from Verona's sister city Munich, which is just over the mountains to the north. You'll see in the middle of the fountain the symbols of the two cities, with the peaks carved out of pink marble from this region.

The ancient Arena looming over the piazza is a reminder that the city's history goes back to Roman times. On this walk, we'll meander across what was the ancient city, from the Arena on this side to the theater across the river.

With the fall of Rome in the fifth century, Verona became a favored capital of barbarian kings. In the Middle Ages, noble families had to choose sides in the civil struggles between emperors (Ghibellines) and popes (Guelphs). During this time, the town bristled with San Gimignano-type towers, built by different families to symbolize their power. When the Scaligeri family rose to power here in the 14th century, they established stability on their terms and made the other noble families lop off their proud towers—only the Scaligeris were allowed to keep theirs. But interfamily feuds made it impossible for the Scaligeris to maintain a stable government, and in 1405 the town essentially gave itself to Venice, which ruled Verona until Napoleon stopped by in 1796. During the 19th century, a tug-of-war between France and Austria actually divided the city for a time, with the river marking the border of each country's domain. Eventually Verona, like Venice, fell into Austrian hands. The huge yellow Neoclassical city hall facing Piazza Brà (look for the flags) was built by the Austrians to serve as their 19th-century military headquarters. The big statue is of Italy's first king, Victor Emmanuel II, and celebrates Italian independence and unity, won in the 1860s.

Apart from all its history, Piazza Brà is about strolling... the evening *passeggiata* is a national sport in Italy. The broad, shiny sidewalk was named the "Liston" (ribbon) by 17th-century Venetians, who made it big and wide so that promenading socialites could see and be seen in all their finery.

❷ Roman Arena

The Romans built this stadium outside their town walls, just as modern stadiums are usually located outside downtown districts.

With 72 aisles, this elliptical 466-by-400-foot amphitheater is the third largest in the Roman world (and it was originally 50 percent taller). Most of the stone you see is original. Dating from the first century A.D., it looks great in its pink marble. Over the centuries, crowds of up to 25,000 spectators have cheered Roman gladiator battles, medieval executions, and modern plays—including the popular opera festival (held every summer), which takes advantage of the Arena's famous acoustics. While there's little to see inside except for the impressive stonework, it is memorable to visit a Roman arena that is still a thriving concert venue. If you climb to the top, you'll enjoy great city views.

Cost and Hours: €6, don't bother with the combo-ticket that includes the unimpressive Maffei Museum, Tue-Sun 8:30-19:30, Mon 13:30-19:30, closes at 14:00 during opera season from mid-June through early September, last entry one hour before closing, WC near entry, tel. 045-800-3204.

• *As you exit the Arena, look to your right. Where the street splits you'll see a column.*

❸ Devotional Column

In the Middle Ages, this column blessed a marketplace held here. Ten yards in front of it, a bronze plaque in the sidewalk shows the Roman city plan—a town of 20,000 placed strategically in the bend of the river, which provided protection on three sides. A wall enclosed the peninsula. The center of the grid was the forum, today's Piazza Erbe. (If you look down Via Mazzini, the busy main pedestrian drag, the bell tower in the distance marks Piazza Erbe.)

• *After viewing the bronze plaque, turn around so your back is to the Arena. Head straight down Via Oberdan and continue a couple of blocks until you see an ancient gate, the Porta Borsari. Walk up to it.*

❹ Porta Borsari and Corso Porta Borsari

You're standing before the main entrance to Roman Verona; back in the day, this gate functioned as a toll booth (*borsari* means purse,

referring to the collection of tolls here). Below the spiral, fluted columns (which parents nickname *"tortiglioni"*—a pasta kids can relate to), you'll see the names of patrons ("this arch was brought to you by the generous support of..."). Outside the adjacent Caffè Rialto, the stone on the curb is from a tomb—in Roman times, the roads outside the walls were lined with tombstones, because burials were not allowed within the town itself. Step into the café. A glass panel in the floor shows the original Roman foundations and pavement stones.

Now head into the ancient city and walk down Corso Porta Borsari, the Roman main drag, toward what was the forum. Make it a scavenger hunt. As you walk, discover bits of the town's illustrious past—chips of Roman columns, medieval reliefs, fine old facades, fossils in marble—as well as its elegant present of fancy shops, in a setting that prioritizes pedestrians over cars.

• *Between Corso Porta Borsari 13 and 15, detour right down Vicolo San*

Marco in Foro, following the Pozzo dell'Amore *sign. Twenty yards ahead on your right, you'll find...*

❺ Enoteca Oreste

This funky wine and grappa bar is still run by Oreste (with his Chicagoan wife, Beverly) like a 1970s, old-style *enoteca*. Browse and sample. This historic *enoteca* was once the private chapel of the archbishop of Verona. Traces of the past hide between the bottles—ask Beverly to tell you the story (Tue-Sun 8:00-20:00, closed Mon, Vicolo San Marco in Foro 7, tel. 045-803-4369).

• *Return to Corso Porta Borsari and continue one block until you hit a big square.*

❻ Piazza Erbe

This bustling market square is a photographer's delight. Its pastel buildings corral the fountains, pigeons, and people who have con-

gregated here since Roman times, when this was a forum. Notice the Venetian lion hovering above the square atop a column, reminding locals of the conquest of 1405. During medieval times, the stone canopy in the center of the square held the scales where mer-

chants measured the weight of goods they bought and sold, such as silk, wool, and wood. A fountain has bubbled here for 2,000 years. The original Roman statue lost its head and arms. After a sculptor added a new head and arms, the statue became Verona's Madonna. She holds a small banner that reads, "I want justice and I bring peace."

If you were standing here in the Middle Ages, you would have been surrounded by proud noble family towers. Medieval nobles showed off with towers. Renaissance nobles showed off with finely painted facades on their palaces. If you look carefully, you can see remnants of the 16th-century days when Verona was nicknamed "the painted city."

Locals like to start their evening with an *aperitivo* here. It's a trendy scene, as young Veronans fill the bars to enjoy their refreshing *spritz* drinks, olives, and chips.

• *At the far end of Piazza Erbe is a market column featuring St. Zeno, the patron of Verona, who looks at the crazy crowds flushing into the city's silly claim to touristic fame: the House of Juliet (100 yards down*

Via Cappello to #23—just follow the crowds). Side-trip there now (but watch your wallet—it's a pickpocket's haven).

❼ House of Juliet

The tiny, admittedly romantic courtyard is a spectacle in itself, with tourists from all over the world posing on the balcony, taking turns polishing Juliet's bronze breast, and amorous graffiti everywhere. Residents marvel that each year, about 1,600 Japanese tour groups break their Venice-Milan ride for an hour-long stop in Verona just to see this courtyard. Hang out and savor the scene. The information boxes (€1 for two people) offer a good story: "While no documentation has been discovered to prove the truth of the legend, no documentation has disproved it either." The "museum," which displays art inspired by the love story, plus costumes and the bed from Franco Zeffirelli's film *Romeo and Juliet,* is certainly not worth the €6 entry fee (Tue-Sun 8:30-19:30, Mon 13:30-19:30, tel. 045-803-4303).

Was there a Juliet Capulet? You just walked down Via Cappello, the street of the cap makers. Above the courtyard entry (looking out) is a coat of arms featuring a hat—representing a family that made hats and which would be named, logically, Capulet.

The world does love Juliet. Upstairs (through the embroidery store on the left as you enter the courtyard) is the home of Verona's Juliet Club (www.julietclub.com). Every day, volunteers respond to countless letters addressed simply to Juliet, Verona, Italy. You can see them at work and read a smattering of love letters (9:00-20:00). There's also a fine view of the courtyard from here.

• *Return to Piazza Erbe. From the middle of the piazza, head right on Via della Costa—look for the whale's rib suspended under an arch. It was likely a souvenir brought home by a traveling merchant, reminding the townspeople that there was a big world out there. Walk down Via della Costa, into the big square.*

❽ Piazza dei Signori

Literally the "Lords' Square," this is Verona's sitting room, quieter and more harmonious than Piazza Erbe. The buildings—which span five centuries—define the square and are all linked by arches. The long portico on the left is inspired by Brunelleschi's Hospital of the Innocents (considered the first Renaissance building) in Florence.

Locals call the square Piazza Dante for the statue of the Italian poet Dante Alighieri that dominates it. Dante—always pensive, never smiling—seems to wonder why the tourists choose Juliet over him. Dante was expelled from Florence for political reasons and was granted asylum in Verona by the Scaligeri family. With the whale's rib behind you, you're facing the brick, crenellated, 14th-century Scaligeri residence. Behind Dante is the yellowish, 15th-century Venetian Renaissance-style Portico of the Counsel. In front of Dante to his right is the 12th-century Romanesque **Palazzo della Ragione.**

Follow the white *WC* signs into the courtyard of the Palazzo della Ragione. The impressive stairway is the only surviving Renaissance staircase in Verona. For a grand city view, you can climb to the top of the palazzo's 13th-century **Torre dei Lamberti** (€6 for stairs or elevator, daily June-Sept 8:30-20:30, Oct-May 8:30-19:30, ticket office next to staircase). The elevator saves you 245 steps—but you'll still need to climb about 45 more to get to the first viewing platform. It's not worth continuing up the endless spiral stairs to the second viewing platform.

• *Exit the courtyard the way you entered and turn right, continuing downhill. Within a block, you'll find the...*

❾ Tombs of the Scaligeri Family

These exotic and very Gothic 14th-century tombs, with their fine, original, wrought-iron protective cages, evoke the age when one family ruled Verona. The Scaligeri were to Verona what the Medici family was to Florence. These were powerful people. They changed the law so that they could be buried within the town. They forbade the presence of any towers but their own. And, by building tombs atop pillars, they arranged to be looked up to even in death.

• *Continue 15 yards to the next corner and take a left on Vicolo Cavalletto. At the first* *corner, turn right along Corso Sant'Anastasia toward the big, unfinished brick facade of Verona's largest church. For a fragrant and potentially tasty diversion, pop into the recommended **Albertini** and **Gastronomia**, two classic, family-run* alimentari, *both located on your left in the next block. Either can rustle up tasty sandwiches (about €3-4), and Albertini sells cold beers and juices.*

❿ Church of Sant'Anastasia

This church was built from the late 13th century through the 15th century. Although the facade was never finished (the builders ran out of steam), the interior was—and still is—brilliant. Step inside to see the delightful way this region's medieval churches were painted. Note the grimacing hunchbacks holding basins of holy water on their backs (near main entrance at base of columns). And don't miss Pisanello's fresco of *St. George and the Princess of*

Trebizond (1438; at the tip of the arch, high above chapel to right of altar). Once colorful, it has oxidized over time to its current monochrome state. For a closer look at its wonderful detail, check out the images on the computer terminal below. Ask for the English brochure, which describes the story of the church.

Cost and Hours: €2.50, March-Oct Mon-Sat 9:00-18:00, Sun 13:00-18:00; Nov-Feb closes daily at 17:00, www.chieseverona.it.

• *Leaving the church, make two lefts, and walk along the right side of the church to Via Sottoriva. To the right, the Sottoriva arcade was once busy with colorful wine bars and* osterie, *some of which still exist (see "Eating in Verona," later). But for now, head to the left on Via Sottoriva. In a block, you'll reach a small riverfront area with stone benches that usually have a few modern-day Romeos and Juliets gazing at each other rather than the view. Belly up to the river view.*

⓫ Ponte Pietra and a River View

The white stones of the Ponte Pietra footbridge are from the original Roman bridge that stood here. After the bridge was bombed in World War II, the Veronese fished the marble chunks out of the river to rebuild it. From here, you can see across the river to the Roman Theater, built into the hillside behind the green hedge (see page 186). Way above the theater (behind the cypress trees) is the fortress, Castello San Pietro.

Continue up the river toward the bridge. You'll pass Gelateria Ponte Pietra (at #23, no sign because of city codes), where Mirko and Stefano dish out fine gelato—try the *riso* flavor (daily 14:30-20:00, until 23:00 in summer). Walk to the high point

on the bridge and enjoy the view. For some exercise, break away, cross the bridge to the Veronetta neighborhood: Visit the Roman Theater or head up to the Castello for an expansive city view (at the end of the bridge, go up the little road called Scalone Castello San Pietro, or climb the stairs to the left of the theater).

• *From the bridge, look back 200 yards at the tall spire...that's where you're heading.*

⓬ Duomo

Started in the 12th century, this church was built over a period of several hundred years. Before entering, note the fine Romanesque

carvings on its facade. Also notice the elevated tomb (high above on the left)—a donor was buried this way at his request. Step inside, and pick up the leaflet that explains the church's highlights.

Directly ahead is Titian's 16th-century *Assumption of the Virgin* (Mary calmly rides a cloud—direction up—to the shock and bewilderment of the crowd below). To the right of the Titian (through the last wooden door, left of high altar) are the ruins of an older church. These are the 10th-century foundations of the Church of St. Elena, turned intriguingly into a modern-day chapel featuring exposed fourth-century mosaic floors from the Roman church that originally stood here. Don't miss the adjacent baptistery, with its clean Romanesque lines, hanging 14th-century crucifix, and fine marble font. Try to identify the eight biblical scenes carved on its panels before referring to my answers. (Answers: Annunciation; first Christmas, with animals nuzzling baby Jesus and giving him a barnyard welcome; announcement to shepherds of Jesus' birth; Epiphany, with the Three Kings giving their gifts to Baby Jesus; Herod commanding to have firstborn sons killed; Slaughter of the Innocents; flight to Egypt; and finally, facing the entry door, John the Baptist baptizing Christ.) The peaceful Romanesque cloister is to the right as you leave the church, with mosaics from a fifth-century Christian church exposed below the walk.

Cost and Hours: €2.50; March-Oct Mon-Fri 10:00-17:30, Sat 10:00-16:00, Sun 13:30-17:30; off-season Tue-Sun closes half-hour earlier and also 13:00-13:30, closed Mon; www.chiese verona.it.

Sights in Verona

▲▲**Evening *Passeggiata***—For me, the highlight of Verona is the *passeggiata* (stroll)—especially in the evening. Make a big circle from Piazza Brà through the old town on Via Mazzini (one of Europe's many "first" pedestrian-only streets) to the colorful Piazza Erbe, and then back down Corso Porta Borsari to Piazza Brà. This is a small town, where people know each other, and they're all out on parade. Like peacocks, the young and nubile spread their wings. The classy shop windows are integral to the *passeggiata* as, for the ladies, shopping is a sport. Their never-finished wardrobes are considered a work in progress, and this is when they gather ideas. If you're going to complement your stroll with a sit in a café or bar, the best plan is to enjoy a *spritz* drink on Piazza Erbe (the oldest and most elegant bars are on the end farthest from Juliet's balcony).

▲**Castelvecchio**—Verona's powerful Scaligeri family built this castle (1343-1356) as both a residence and a fortress. Today, it's

a museum showing off Verona's glory days. The extensive collection of Verona's finest art is well displayed throughout the huge building. The religious statues, once brightly painted, were the city's medieval forte. The paintings were the city's Renaissance forte. You'll also find armor and have a chance to roam the

ramparts with fine views of the city and river. Info sheets with good English descriptions are available throughout, but the audioguide (€4, or €6/2 people) is worthwhile.

Cost and Hours: €6, Tue-Sun 8:30-19:30, Mon 13:30-19:30, Corso Castelvecchio 3, see map on page 189 for location.

Nearby: Next to Castelvecchio, the **Fortress Bridge** (Ponte Scaligero) is free, open to the public, and fun to stroll across. Destroyed by the Germans in World War II, it was rebuilt in the 1950s. Today it's understandably a favorite for wedding-day photos.

▲**Basilica of San Zeno Maggiore**—This church, outside the old center, is dedicated to the patron saint of Verona, whose remains are buried in the crypt under the main altar. In addition to being a fine example of Italian Romanesque, the basilica features Mantegna's *San Zeno Triptych* (1456-1459) with its marvelous perspective, peaceful double-columned cloisters, and a set of 48 paneled 11th-century bronze doors nicknamed "the poor man's Bible." Pretend you're an illiterate medieval peasant and do some reading. Facing the altar, on the walls of the right-side aisle, you can see frescoes painted on top of other frescoes and graffiti dating from the 1300s. These were done by people who fled into the church in times of war or flooding and scratched prayers into the walls. Druidic-looking runes are actually decorated letters typical of the Gothic period, like those in illuminated manuscripts.

Cost and Hours: €2.50, March-Oct Mon-Sat 8:30-18:00, Sun 12:30-18:00; Nov-Feb Tue-Sat 10:00-13:00 & 13:30-17:00, Sun 12:30-17:00, closed Mon; located on Piazza San Zeno, a good 15-minute walk upriver beyond Castelvecchio; www.chiese verona.it.

Roman Theater (Teatro Romano)—Dating from the first century A.D., this ancient theater was discovered in the 19th century

and restored. Admission includes the Roman Museum, located high in the building above the theater (reach it via elevator—start at the stage and walk up the middle set of stairs, then continue straight on the path through the bushes).

The museum displays a model of the theater, a small Jesuit chapel, and Roman artifacts, including mosaic floors, busts and other statuary, clay and bronze votive figures, and architectural fragments. You'll find helpful English information sheets throughout.

Cost and Hours: €4.50, Tue-Sun 8:30-19:30, Mon 13:30-19:30, last entry 45 minutes before closing, theater located across the river near Ponte Pietra footbridge, tel. 045-800-0360. From mid-June through August, the theater stages Shakespeare plays—only a little more difficult to understand in Italian than in Elizabethan English.

Giusti Garden (Giardino Giusti)—If you'd enjoy a Renaissance garden with manicured box hedges and towering cypress trees, you might find this worth the walk and fee.

Cost and Hours: €6, daily April-Sept

9:00-20:00, Oct-March 9:00-17:00; cross river at Ponte Nuovo, continue up Via Carducci, and turn left on Via Giardino Giusti, or take bus #72 from Piazza Brà and get off at Via Carducci.

Sleeping in Verona

I've listed rates you'll pay in regular season—most of April through May, and September through October. Prices soar (at least €20-30 more per night) from mid-June through early September (opera season), in early April (during the Vinitaly wine festival—see "The Wines of Verona" sidebar, later), and during big trade fairs or major holidays. Unless your goal is opera, consider coming before mid-June or after early September. Prices are lower from November to March. Hotel websites clearly explain their rates.

Near Piazza Erbe

$$$ Hotel Aurora, at the corner of Piazza Erbe and Via Pelliciai, has friendly family management, a terrace overlooking the piazza, and 19 fresh, air-conditioned rooms (S-€70, Sb-€125, Db-€140, Tb-€160, Qb-€200, elevator, free Wi-Fi, Piazzetta XIV Novembre 2, tel. 045-594-717, fax 045-801-0860, www.hotelaurora.biz, info @hotelaurora.biz, Rita). Coming from the train station, stay on the bus until the San Fermo stop (two stops past Piazza Brà) to get within an easy walk of the hotel.

$ Casa della Giovane, run by an association that houses poor women, also rents rooms and dorm beds to female tourists (and their children up to age 10). Buried deep in the old town and up several flights of stairs, the place offers 55 cheap beds in a clean,

---

Sleep Code

(€1 = about $1.40, country code: 39)

S = Single, **D** = Double/Twin, **T** = Triple, **Q** = Quad, **b** = bathroom, **s** = shower only. Hotels accept credit cards and provide breakfast unless otherwise noted. Everyone speaks English.

To help you easily sort through these listings, I've divided the accommodations into three categories, based on the price for a standard double room with bath:

  $$$ **Higher Priced**—Most rooms €120 or more.
    $$ **Moderately Priced**—Most rooms between €90-120.
     $ **Lower Priced**—Most rooms €90 or less.

Prices can change without notice; verify the hotel's current rates online or by email. For other updates, see www.ricksteves.com/update.

institutional, and peaceful setting (women only, €22/bed in 11-bed dorm, Sb-€35, Db-€60, Tb-€90, no breakfast, free Wi-Fi, reception open 9:00-23:00, Via Pigna 7, tel. 045-596-880, fax 045-088-5449).

Near Piazza Brà

You'll find several options in the quiet streets just off Piazza Brà, within 200 yards of the bus stop. From the square, yellow signs point you to the hotels. The first three are big, business-class places with the service and formality you'd expect. The Torcolo is more homey and friendly.

$$$ Hotel Giulietta e Romeo is on a quiet side street just 50 yards behind the Roman Arena. Nine of its 40 well-designed rooms have balconies (Sb-€110, Db-€120, bigger Db-€150, prices shoot up to €200/€230 during opera season, non-smoking, air-con, elevator, free Wi-Fi, free loaner bikes, fitness room, garage €19/day, Vicolo Tre Marchetti 3, tel. 045-800-3554, fax 045-801-0862, www.giuliettaeromeo.com, info@giuliettaeromeo.com).

$$$ Hotel Milano, a few doors from Hotel Giulietta e Romeo, is an arty hotel with 52 rooms. The lobby and fancier rooms are tricked out in black and chrome (rates vary wildly—see website—generally about Sb-€75-100, Db-€120-150, air-con, elevator, free Wi-Fi, garage €20/day, Vicolo Tre Marchetti 11, tel. 045-591-692, fax 045-801-1299, www.hotelmilano-vr.it, info@hotel milano-vr.it).

$$$ Hotel Europa offers sleek, modern comfort in springtime colors. Most of its 46 rooms are non-smoking, and a few rooms have little balconies overlooking the *piazzetta* below (Db-€120-180, 10 percent discount if you mention this book when reserving direct, air-con, elevator, free Wi-Fi, a couple of blocks off Piazza Brà at Via Roma 8, tel. 045-594-744, fax 045-800-1852, www.veronahoteleuropa.com, info@veronahoteleuropa.com).

$$ Hotel Torcolo offers 19 comfortable, lovingly maintained, non-smoking rooms with Grandma's furnishings (Sb-€65, Db-around €100, €8-14 for breakfast—optional except during opera season, air-con, fridge in room, elevator, pay Wi-Fi, garage €20/day; from Piazza Brà promenade, head down the alley to the right of #16 and walk to Vicolo Listone 3; tel. 045-800-7512, fax 045-800-4058, www.hoteltorcolo.it, hoteltorcolo@virgilio.it, well-run by Silvia, Diana, and helpful Caterina).

Near Castelvecchio

$ Albergo Arena, while borderline dreary, is a good value for those on a budget. Located in a peaceful courtyard off a busy street a few blocks from Piazza Brà, it offers 17 very basic, institutional, quiet rooms (S-€45, Sb-€60, D-€75, Db-€85, no air-con, free

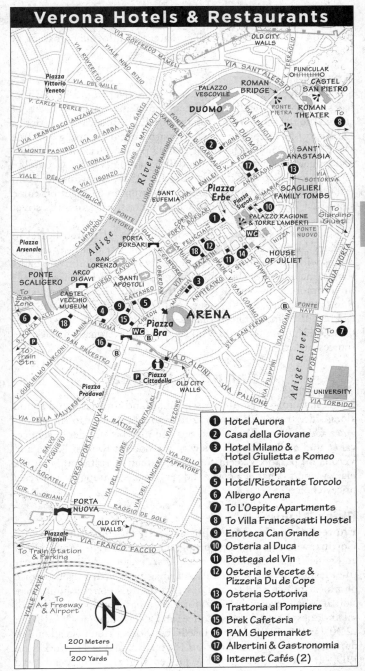

Verona Hotels & Restaurants

1. Hotel Aurora
2. Casa della Giovane
3. Hotel Milano & Hotel Giulietta e Romeo
4. Hotel Europa
5. Hotel/Ristorante Torcolo
6. Albergo Arena
7. To L'Ospite Apartments
8. To Villa Francescatti Hostel
9. Enoteca Can Grande
10. Osteria al Duca
11. Bottega del Vin
12. Osteria le Vecete & Pizzeria Du de Cope
13. Osteria Sottoriva
14. Trattoria al Pompiere
15. Brek Cafeteria
16. PAM Supermarket
17. Albertini & Gastronomia
18. Internet Cafés (2)

NEAR VENICE

Wi-Fi, just west of Castelvecchio at Stradone Porta Palio 2, tel. & fax 045-803-2440, www.albergoarena.it, info@albergoarena.it, Beatrice).

Across the River

$$ L'Ospite, a 10-minute walk across the river from Piazza Erbe, has six cozy, immaculate, fully equipped apartments and lots of stairs. The rooms, warmly managed by English-speaking Federica De Rossi, sleep from two to four, with air-conditioning and free Wi-Fi (Db-€95, Tb/Qb-about €40-55/person, discounts for cash and longer stays, no reception or daily cleaning; Via XX Settembre 3; tel. 045-803-6994, mobile 329-426-2524, www.lospite.com, info@lospite.com). Coming from the station by bus, get off three stops past Piazza Brà at the XX Settembre stop (across the street from the apartments).

   $ Villa Francescatti is a good, church-affiliated hostel in a pretty hillside setting (€18/bed in 6- or 8-bed sex-segregated rooms with hall bath, €20/bed in family rooms with private bathrooms, includes breakfast, €8 dinners, laundry €5/load, free Wi-Fi in common areas, rooms closed from 9:00 to 17:00 but reception open all day, 24:00 curfew; Salita Fontana del Ferro 15, bus #73 or #91 from station to Piazza Isolo plus short steep walk, tel. 045-590-360, fax 045-800-9127, www.ostelloverona.it, info@villa francescatti.it).

Eating in Verona

The restaurants I list are mostly small and intimate, and found along side streets. It's tempting to grab a table next to the *passeggiata* action along Piazza Brà, but you may be sacrificing service, value, and quality for your view of the floodlit Roman Arena and Verona on parade. Except for Brek Cafeteria, restaurants on the piazza tend to charge a cover and service fee, making even pizza a pricey choice.

Finer Dining

Enoteca Can Grande enthusiastically run by Giuliano and Corrina, who enjoy turning people on to great, well-matched food and wine. Their star offering is a €40 set menu including an aperitif, a festival of *antipasti* treats, an imaginative pasta, your choice of a meat or fish course, and dessert. They also offer a junior version at lunch (except Sunday) for €20: a pasta and your choice of salad or dessert, plus water, coffee, and a glass of wine (Wed-Mon 12:00-15:30 & 18:00-24:00, closed Tue, closed Mon instead of Tue during opera season; a block off Piazza Brà at Via Dietro Liston 19D—if the equestrian statue jogged slightly right, he'd head

The Wines of Verona

Wine connoisseurs love the high-quality wines of the Verona area. The hills to the east are covered with grapes to make Soave; to the north is Valpolicella country; and Bardolino comes from vineyards to the west.

Valpolicella grapes, which are used to make the fruity, red Valpolicella table wine (found everywhere), are also the basis for full-bodied red Amarone and the sweet dessert wine Recioto. To produce Amarone, grapes are partially dried (*passito*) before fermentation, then aged for a minimum of four years in oak casks, resulting in a rich, velvety, full-bodied red. Recioto, which in local dialect means "ears," uses only the grapes from the top of the cluster (so they sort of look like the "ears" of the cluster's "head"). Because these grapes get the most sun, they mature the fastest and have the highest concentration of sugar. Before pressing, the grapes are dried for months until all moisture has gone out; the wine is then aged for one to three years.

Bardolino, from the vineyards near Lake Garda, is a light, fruity wine, like a French Beaujolais. It's a perfect picnic wine.

Soave, which might be Italy's best-known white wine, goes well with seafood and risotto dishes. While Soave can vary widely in quality, the best are called "Soave Classico" and come from the heart of the region, near the Soave Castle. Soave is sometimes aged in oak casks, giving it a mellow, rounded flavor.

Sample these and many others at the numerous *enoteche* (wine-tasting bars) or at any restaurant around town. In early April, Verona hosts Vinitaly, the most important international convention of domestic and international wines. Vintners vie for prestigious awards for the past year's vintage. Tourists are welcome to attend at the end of the week, and are shuttled to the convention hall from Piazza Brà. Hotels book up months in advance. Check with the TI and www.vinitaly.com for details.

If you're visiting the area in the fall, consider a day trip to nearby Monteforte d'Alpone, east of Verona. The town hosts a fun, raucous wine festival in September—ask at the TI for more information on this and other regional wine festivals.

straight here; tel. 045-595-022).

Osteria al Duca is a fun, family-run place with a lively atmosphere and good traditional dishes. Locals line up for its affordable, two-course, €16 fixed-price meal. I much prefer their ground floor (*piano terra*—worth requesting). Reservations are advised (Mon-Sat 10:00-15:00 & 18:30-24:00, closed Sun, half-block east of Scaligeri family tombs at Via Arche Scaligere 2, tel. 045-594-474, Alessandro or Daniele).

Ristorante Torcolo is a warm family restaurant, with mom

(Paola) running the kitchen, and father and son (Roberto and Luca) serving. It's dressy but without pretense, and the service is professional yet fun-loving. There's a happy energy, stoked by carts of tempting boiled meat and desserts rolling through the dining room. They serve all the classic dishes, with an accessible menu and an extensive wine list (€9 pastas, €15 *secondi*, €3 cover, closed Mon, just behind the Piazza Brà scene on a quiet street, Via Carlo Cattaneo 11, tel. 045-803-3730).

Bottega del Vin is pricey, venerable, and proud to have a sister establishment in New York City. Under a high ceiling and walls of wine bottles, brisk black-vested waiters match traditional dishes (polenta, duck, game) with glasses of fine wine. Choose from 100 open bottles—glasses range from €1 to €15. The waitstaff, ambience, and food have deep roots in local culture. I like their front room best (€13 pastas, €18-22 *secondi,* good daily specials, daily 12:00-24:00; take third left off Via Mazzini as you're coming from Piazza Erbe, Via Scudo di Francia 3; tel. 045-800-4535, reservations smart for dinner).

Osteria le Vecete, just one room under open beams with walls of wine, has an enjoyable, intimate pub ambience. Slide up to the bar for wine and *tartine* (elaborate little open-faced sandwiches), or sit down and order a meal. Choose from daily specials of home-made pastas and Veronese dishes—as well as €10 salad plates. The blackboard lists plenty of wines by the glass (€9-12 pastas, €16-20 *secondi,* daily 12:30-15:30 & 18:30-23:00, drinks and snacks served between mealtimes and until late; from Piazza Erbe, put your back to the whalebone arch and walk down Via Pelliciai to #32A; tel. 045-594-748, Karen).

Pizzeria Du de Cope is a high-energy, informal place (with paper placemats) that buzzes with smartly attired young waiters and locals who consider the pizza here to be the best in town (big €11 salads, €9-13 pizzas, daily 12:00-14:00 & 19:00-23:00, flam-boyant desserts, family friendly, no reservations, a few doors past Osteria le Vecete at Galleria Pelliciai 10, tel. 045-595-562).

Osterie *on Via Sottoriva*: Historically, Verona's river served as the thoroughfare through town. Business deals could be made over a glass of wine at places along the river, set in a fine old covered arcade (the portico of Via Sottoriva). Several of these survive as rustic, characteristic eateries serving finger food. Browse around and consider the wonderful **Osteria Sottoriva,** with simple soups and pastas, and both indoor and outdoor seating (open from 18:30, behind the Church of Sant'Anastasia in the covered arcade, Via Sottoriva 9, tel. 045-801-4323).

Trattoria al Pompiere, which has a commitment to regional traditions, is a favorite of foodies and has earned its huge local following. Amid the bustle (contained by walls plastered with photos of local big shots), Stefano and his gang serve gourmet meats and cheeses as *antipasti*, ideal for a mixed plate to complement the huge selection of fine wines. Reservations are wise (€12-13 pastas, €16-17 *secondi*, lunch from 12:30, dinner from 19:30, closed Sun and at lunch on Mon, chivalry lives—ladies' menus come without prices; find Via Cappello 8, across from Juliet statue, and head down side street to Vicolo Regina d'Ungheria 5; tel. 045-803-0537).

Cheaper Eats

Brek Cafeteria, a well-run and modern chain, has a location at Piazza Brà with self-service prices (€5 pastas, €6 *secondi*, cheap salad plates, daily 9:30-15:00 & 18:30-22:00, full menu from 11:30, indoor/outdoor seating, facing equestrian statue at Piazza Brà 20, tel. 045-800-4561).

    Supermarket near Piazza Brà: **PAM supermarket** is just outside the historic gate on Piazza Brà (Mon-Sat 8:00-21:00, Sun 9:00-20:00, exit Piazza Brà through the gate and take the first right to Via dei Mutilati 3).

    The *döner kebab* place by Hotel Europa is cheap, fast, and not Italian (great €4 meals, daily 11:30-late; from Piazza Brà, walk down Via Roma and turn right before Hotel Europa toward Via Teatro Filharmonico 6).

    Delicatessens near Piazza Erbe: You'll find two family-run *alimentari* on Corso Sant'Anastasia, between the end of Vicolo Cavoletto and the Church of Sant'Anastasia. One is under the **Gastronomia** sign at Corso Sant'Anastasia 33 (Mon-Sat 8:00-20:00, Sun 9:00-13:30). A few doors down at #41 is **Albertini** (Mon-Sat 8:00-20:00, closed Sun). Either can sell you a €3-4 sandwich. Bakeries also sell sandwiches and pizza by the slice.

    A list of "official" picnicking spots can be picked up at the TI—freelance picnicking in Verona is strongly discouraged. One good spot is along the river by Ponte Pietra.

Verona Connections

From Verona by Train to: Venice (2/hour, 1.25-2.25 hours), **Padua** (2/hour, 40-60 minutes), **Vicenza** (2/hour, 30-60 minutes), **Florence** (listed as *Firenze* on train schedules, about hourly, 1.5 hours direct or 2.5 hours with transfer in Bologna), **Bologna** (hourly, 1.5 hours, a few faster trains), **Milan** (2/hour, 1.5-2 hours, a few faster trains), **Rome** (at least hourly, 4-5 hours, often with transfer in Bologna), **Bolzano** (2/hour, 1.75-2.25 hours, avoid "fast" trains that take the same amount of time but cost much more). For more information, visit www.trenitalia.com.

Ravenna

Ravenna is on the tourist map for one reason: its 1,500-year-old churches, decorated with best-in-the-West Byzantine mosaics.

The city's churches and mosaics date from the time (c. A.D. 400-600) when it was the center of Western civilization—a civilization in transition, from Roman to barbarian to Byzantine to medieval. You'll see all these layers in Ravenna.

In 402, barbarian tribes were zeroing in on the city of Rome. The Roman emperor moved his capital to Ravenna, a city well-known as a home port for the imperial navy (today's Classe). Because of its location, Ravenna kept close ties with the other Roman capital at Constantinople (called Byzantium).

Ravenna was conquered by the Goths from Hungary in 476, and the 1,000 years of the Roman Empire came to an end. But Ravenna continued on as the Goths' capital. They kept much of the Roman infrastructure and legitimized their rule by building sophisticated palaces and churches in the Roman style.

In 540, the Byzantine emperor Justinian conquered the Goths. This reunited Italy with the still-thriving Empire to the east. Justinian turned Ravenna into a pinnacle of civilization. It remained a flickering light in Europe's Dark Ages for another 200 years, until the Lombard tribe of Germany booted out the Byzantines (in 751). Ravenna melted into the backwaters of medieval Italy, staying out of historical sight for a thousand years.

In your sightseeing, you'll see art from each of these periods: Roman (Mausoleum of Galla Placidia, Neonian Baptistery), Gothic (Arian Baptistery, Basilica di Sant'Apollinare in Nuovo, Archiepiscopal Museum), Byzantine (Basilica di San Vitale, House of Stone Carpets, Church of Sant'Apollinare in Classe), and medieval (Tomb of Dante, Basilica di San Francesco).

Today, Ravenna's economy booms with a big chemical industry, the discovery of offshore gas deposits, and the construction of a new ship canal. The bustling town center is Italy's best for bicyclists. Residents go about their business, while busloads of tourists slip quietly in and out of town for the best look at the glories of Byzantium this side of Istanbul—specifically, the richest collection anywhere of mosaics from the fifth and sixth centuries. Many are pleasantly surprised by the peaceful charm of this untouristy town.

NEAR VENICE

Planning Your Time

Ravenna is a worthwhile four-hour stop, or even an overnight, particularly for mosaic lovers. Its inexpensive lodgings offer good value for your money. The town is also a doable, though long, day trip from Florence, Venice, or Padua. You could stop here on your way between Venice (or Padua) and Florence, but be aware that Ravenna provides no official place for visitors to check their bags (although the Strada Facendo café has offered to watch bags for my readers—see "Helpful Hints," below).

Orientation to Ravenna

Central Ravenna is quiet, with a pedestrian-friendly core and more bikes than cars. Keep to the sides of the streets; bikes take the center lane (subtly indicated by white brick paving) down the brick "pedestrian" streets. Listen for the outta-my-way bells.

On a quick visit to Ravenna, follow my self-guided walk and visit the Basilica di San Vitale, its adjacent Mausoleum of Galla Placidia, and the Basilica di Sant'Apollinare Nuovo. While the main sights are easily walkable from the station, it's also fun to do the city by bike. A handy bike-rental place is at the train station. If arriving by car, park near the station and pretend you arrived by train.

Tourist Information

The TI is a 15-minute walk (or a 5-minute pedal) from the train station (Mon-Sat 8:30-19:00, until 18:00 Oct-March, Sun 10:00-16:00 year-round, Via Salara 8, tel. 0544-35404, www.turismo.ra.it).

Combo-Ticket: Five of Ravenna's best mosaic sights are covered by a single combo-ticket; just pay €11.50 at the first sight you visit (€9.50 July-Feb). Included are the Basilica di San Vitale, Mausoleum of Galla Placidia, Basilica di Sant'Apollinare Nuovo, Archiepiscopal Museum (with its Chapel of Sant'Andrea), and Neonian Baptistery. All five sights are church-run and have virtually the same hours (daily April-Sept 9:00-19:00, Oct-March 9:00 or 9:30-17:00).

Helpful Hints

Baggage Storage: Remarkably, Ravenna has no place to deposit a bag. Friendly Mauro at the Strada Facendo café (across the street on the right-hand corner as you're leaving the station, closed Sun) has said he'd be happy to let travelers with this book drop bags there. Show this book at the café counter when you ask, as they normally say "no" to such requests.

Laundry: A self-service launderette is a five-minute walk from the train station (€3.50 wash, €3.50 dry, daily 7:00-22:00, go left

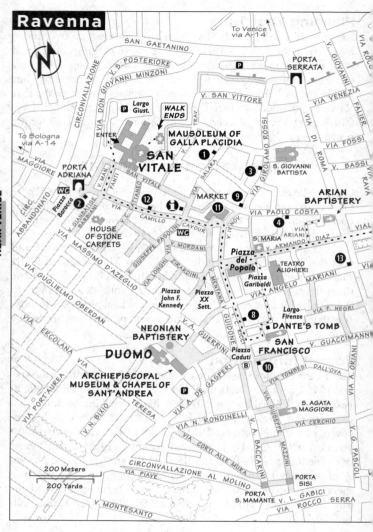

NEAR VENICE

as you exit the station, then take your first left over the grade crossing to Via Candiano 16, mobile 331-130-2072).

Bike Rental: Coop San Vitale, in front of the train station, rents bikes (€1.10/hour, €8.50/day, Mon-Fri 7:00-19:00, closed Sat-Sun, photo ID required, tel. 0544-37031). Many hotels have loaner bikes. The **TI** loans 20 one-speed bikes on a first-come, first-served basis (bring your passport). Ask the TI for the free "Cycler" bike-trail map, which includes rides to the sea, parks, and historical sights.

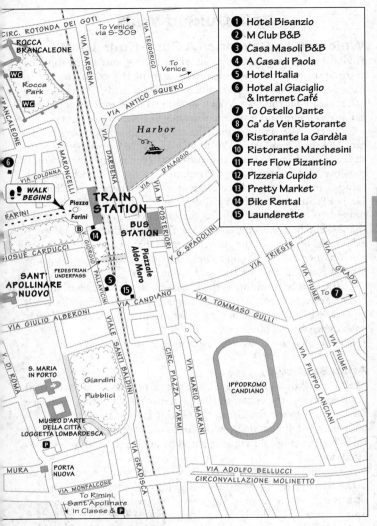

1. Hotel Bisanzio
2. M Club B&B
3. Casa Masoli B&B
4. A Casa di Paola
5. Hotel Italia
6. Hotel al Giaciglio & Internet Café
7. To Ostello Dante
8. Ca' de Ven Ristorante
9. Ristorante la Gardèla
10. Ristorante Marchesini
11. Free Flow Bizantino
12. Pizzeria Cupido
13. Pretty Market
14. Bike Rental
15. Launderette

NEAR VENICE

Parking: Don't drive into the center, or you'll be fined. Two inexpensive lots are near the historic core: one accessible from the west side of Via Roma, at Via Mura di Porta Serrata (€1.50/day), and another at Largo Giustiniano just north of the Basilica di San Vitale (€2.80/day). Or find a free lot near the station. Many lots are free overnight (20:00-8:00).

Local Guide: Private guide Claudia Frassineti is excellent (€95/half-day, mobile 335-613-2996, www.abacoguide.it, claudia.frassinetti@gmail.com).

Self-Guided Walk

Welcome to Ravenna (A Four-Hour Tour)

A visit to Ravenna can be as short as a four-hour loop from the train station. This walk brings you from the train station to Ravenna's top draw (Basilica di San Vitale), quickly taking in a few other sights on the way. When done, you'll be well-oriented and can use any remaining time to visit more of Ravenna's sights.

Start at the train station. The station and surrounding neighborhood were bombed in World War II. Walk (or pedal) the main drag, Viale Farini, from the station directly into town. You'll pass the St. John the Evangelist church on the left, with a rebuilt facade. This was the palace church of the fifth-century Empress Galla Placidia. She and her children were caught at sea in a storm, prayed to St. John (the protector of sailors), and survived. In thanks, she had this church built at the site of their first safe step ashore. At least that's the story. It is true that in ancient times, the town harbor came right up to here. Historic churches are so common in Ravenna that we'll skip this one.

The next big building is the high school, with students' motorbikes parked in front. After that, the boulevard becomes Via Diaz, an arcaded pedestrian shopping street. Remember that the lighter cobbles are for the bikes.

• At Via degli Ariani, side-trip to the right 50 yards to find the...

Arian Baptistery

Built during the reign of the Goths (c. 526), this small octagonal building marks the center of their Arian-style Christian faith (see sidebar). Theodoric the Great, the Gothic king of Italy (r. 493-526), built the church next door, with this as his baptistery. Imagine the small baptismal pool that once stood beneath this gloriously decorated dome.

The mosaic-covered dome shows Christ standing waist-deep in the River Jordan, being baptized by John the Baptist (in leopard-skin robe), as the dove of the Holy Spirit descends. The body builder on the left is the personified River Jordan, next to a vase from which the river springs. Notice the realism in John's stance. The 12 apostles, dynamic, with feet in motion, proceed around the dome. The empty throne between Paul (with scroll) and Peter (with keys) is a reminder that Judgment Day will come.

The mosaic is Arian, stressing Jesus' human rather than divine nature. Jesus is naked, with his genitals only partly obscured by the water. This emphasizes his mortal body, not his divine spirit. He's a beardless youth, suggesting his recent creation by God. The descending dove spews water to purify Jesus, marking the exact moment when Arians believed Jesus' divine nature emerged. Besides heretical Arian elements, there's also the pagan river god, shown in (pagan) Roman fashion as a bearded old man with a vase and river plant.

To modern eyes, these subtle details mean little. But to Emperor Justinian and the Nicenes, these were red flags announcing heresy. While most Arian art was destroyed when Justinian took control, this ceiling is one of the rare survivors.

The adjacent church is closed to the public. It was the cathedral of the Goths, with a simple main structure surviving from the sixth century and a Renaissance portico.

Cost and Hours: Free, daily 8:30-19:30, off-season until 16:00, tel. 0544-543-711, www.turismo.ravenna.it.

• *Now, return to the pedestrian boulevard, turn right, and continue to...*

Piazza del Popolo

Marking the town center, this square was created by Ravenna's Venetian rulers in the 15th century. The river once flowed to about where the two columns stand. But it got mucky and full of mosquitoes. (Dante died here...of malaria.) One column was topped by a Venetian lion until 1509 when, with the support of Rome, Ravenna won its independence from Venice. Ravenna's citizens pulled down that symbol of Venetian rule and did the local equivalent of tarring and feathering it. The lion was replaced by St. Vitale (a first-century Christian martyr). The column on the left is topped by Ravenna's first bishop, St. Apollinare. This square is a fine place to join the old guys on benches, watching the community parade by.

• *At the end of Piazza del Popolo, turn left down Via Cairoli two blocks and find the...*

Basilica di San Francesco

Pop into this basilica to see its flooded mosaic-covered crypt below the main altar. Today's water table is one yard above the Roman crypt's floor level— so there's a pond with goldfish over the fifth-century mosaics (spend a coin to turn on the light). The interior is simple and Franciscan; the altar

The Arian Heresy

Ravenna's art reflects a centuries-long battle of ideas among Europe's Christians that came to a violent head right here. As you wonder at the beauty of Ravenna's mosaics, you're also witnessing an epic clash between two different interpretations of Christianity.

Around 320 A.D. in Alexandria, a devout Christian priest named Arius (c. 256-336) began preaching a seemingly simple idea: Jesus, being the Son of God, was therefore created by God the Father. This idea touched off a firestorm of debate and division unmatched in Christianity until the Protestant Reformation. Arius had raised questions about the very nature of the Christian God: Is God a single entity (as the head of a monotheistic religion should be); three different persons (God the Father, Jesus Christ, and the Holy Spirit); or something in between?

To keep the peace, Roman Emperor Constantine convened a Council at Nicea (in 325 A.D., near modern Istanbul). Arius was accused of doubting the divinity of Christ, by making him separate from and inferior to God the Father. The Council branded Arius a heretic and burned his books. After splitting many theological hairs, they issued the Nicene Creed, which defined God as a Trinity: There was one God, existing in three persons "of the same substance." (Don't make me try to explain it further, or this book may end up getting burned by some sect somewhere.) The three-in-one Trinity became the standard throughout the Empire, and Arian sects were brutally suppressed.

features a fourth-century Christian sarcophagus with Jesus in the center and the 12 apostles.

Cost and Hours: Free, daily 7:00-12:00 & 15:00-18:00, Piazza San Francesco, tel. 0544-33256.

• *With your back to the church, cut right through the small wooded park. On your right, next to the double archway, is the...*

Tomb of Dante

After he was exiled from Florence for his political beliefs, Dante lived out the rest of his life in Ravenna. The Florentines forgave Dante posthumously and wanted to bring their famous poet's bones home to rest. To protect Dante's relics from theft by the Florentines, in 1519 Ravenna hid his bones in the Monastery of San Francesco. There they lay forgotten for three centuries, until they were rediscovered and eventually placed here in 1865. In the gar-

But that did not settle the matter. Constantine's own son, a fervent Arian, sent missionaries north across the Danube to convert the barbarian Goths to Arian-style Christianity. A century later, as Rome was falling, those same Goths came knocking on Italy's doorstep. They overran Ravenna (476) and made Arian Christianity the official religion of state, though they tolerated the Nicene Christianity of their Italian subjects.

The churches the Goths built—the Arian Baptistery, Basilica di Sant'Apollinare Nuovo, and Chapel of Sant'Andrea (at the Archiepiscopal Museum)—reflected their Arian faith. Arian mosaics of Jesus emphasized his humanness rather than his divinity. (Don't confuse the Arian sect with Nazi Germany's idea of an Aryan race.)

In 540, the Byzantine Emperor Justinian drove out the Goths. To unite his empire, he demanded both political and theological conformity. Anything with the slightest whiff of Arianism was wiped out. Mosaics were stripped from the walls, statues defaced, and churches were renamed for saints famous for fighting heretics. In their place came art that reflected Byzantine tastes and Trinitarian theology. You'll see evidence of this shift at many of Ravenna's top sights.

Ravenna was Arianism's Waterloo. Sects were snuffed out, Trinitarians triumphed, and the Nicene Creed (in some form) is still said in many Christian churches today.

den next door, find the mound *(tumulo)* where Dante's bones were hidden during World War II. The Dante memorial—often mistaken for a tomb—in Florence's Santa Croce Church is empty.

Cost and Hours: Free, daily April-Sept 9:30-18:30, Oct-March 9:00-12:00 & 14:00-17:00, Via D. Alighieri 9, tel. 0544-33662.

• *Turn your back to Dante's tomb and walk straight until you reach Piazza del Popolo again. Cross to the far right side of the piazza, where Via IV Novembre leads a block to the colorful...*

Covered Market

The Mercato Coperto, built in 1921, is good for picnic fixings (Mon-Sat 7:00-14:00, closed Sun) and has a busy self-serve cafeteria (closed Sat, more seating and WC upstairs).

• *With your back to the market's front door, jog right around the building onto Via Cavour, Ravenna's favored street for evening strolling and shopping. The Porta Adriana city gate will come into view ahead of you. Three blocks down, at #117, turn right on Via M. Fanti. As the street ends, continue straight through the squared-off archway. Now follow*

Basilica di San Vitale *signs around the left of the building and inside to the ticket office for the...*

▲▲▲Basilica di San Vitale

Imagine: It's A.D. 540. The city of Rome has been looted, the land is crawling with barbarians, and the infrastructure of Rome's thousand-year empire is crumbling fast. Into this chaotic world comes the emperor of the East (Justinian), bringing order and stability, briefly reassembling the empire, and making Ravenna a beacon of civilization.

After buying your ticket, you'll descend to the basilica's floor level, which is lower than today's ground level. First you'll see the basilica itself with its dazzling mosaics and then, across the yard, the small Mausoleum of Galla Placidia.

Cost and Hours: €11.50 combo-ticket (€9.50 July-Feb) also covers Mausoleum of Galla Placidia, Basilica di Sant'Apollinare Nuovo, Archiepiscopal Museum, and Neonian Baptistery; open daily April-Sept 9:00-19:00, Oct-March 9:00 or 9:30-17:00, tel. 0544-541-688, www.ravennamosaici.it.

Information: There's no audioguide, but the gift shop, behind the basilica altar, sells a DVD which also plays continually on a screen at the entrance.

❍ Self-Guided Tour: Step inside the church. The basilica—standing as a sanctuary of order in the midst of the madness after the fall of Rome—is covered with lavish mosaics: gold and glass chips the size of your fingernail. It's impressive enough to see a 1,400-year-old church. But it's rare to see one decorated in brilliant mosaics, still managing to convey the intended feeling that "This peace and stability was brought to you by your emperor and God." The art is an intricate ensemble of images that, with the help of a medieval priest, would teach volumes.

Stand before the altar. The centerpiece, high above, is God in

heaven, portrayed as Christ sitting on a celestial orb. He oversees his glorious creation, symbolized by the four rivers.

Running the show on earth is Justinian (left side), sporting both a halo and a crown to indicate that he's both leader of the Church and the state. Here, Justinian brings together the military leaders and the church leaders, all united by the straight line of eyes. The bald bishop of Ravenna—the only person who was actually here—is portrayed most realistically (with a name tag above reading *Maximanus*).

Facing the emperor (from the right side) are his wife, Theodora, and her entourage. Decked out in jewels and pearls, the former

 dancer who became Justinian's mistress (and then empress) carries a chalice with which to consecrate the new church.

The border inside the apse is decorated with horns of plenty (cornucopia), promising prosperity in return for the people's obedience to the Church and State (Justinian and Theodora).

NEAR VENICE

Sit in a wooden pew, front and center. Get in a medieval frame of mind and study the scene: On the floor a 16th-century inlaid marble labyrinth leads to the center, evocative of the belief that the pilgrimage of life on earth leads to salvation through Christ. The inlaid shell is the scallop shell of St. James—symbol of pilgrims.

While the decor behind you is Baroque and of no particular artistic importance, the walls and ceilings above and in front sparkle with colorful biblical scenes told with a sixth-century exuberance. (The Viennese artist Gustav Klimt sat right here around 1900 and was inspired by the glint of the light on the gold leaf.)

Okay. Now take a longitudinal, ground-up tour from your seat: The inlaid floor maze leads to the sixth-century marble altar (busy with iconography). Above that is Christ on the globe. Appreciate the symmetry. Two angels hold rays of sun (Christ is the origin of light). The scene is flanked by two cities: Bethlehem and Jerusalem (where Jesus was born and died). Above each city are potted grape vines producing wine, symbols of the blood of Christ. The circle with the monogram of Christ (I for Jesus and X for Christ) symbolizes perfection and eternity.

The ceiling above is a festive celebration of God's creation, with 80 different birds from the sixth century—most still flying around Ravenna today. (Bird-watchers—who visit with binoculars—can easily identify these by their exquisitely detailed and accurate feathers.) All creation swirls around Christ as the sacrificial lamb, supported by four angels.

Leading to the apse, arcing high above, is a triumphal arch. Its 15 medallions depict 12 apostles, two sons of St. Vitale, and a medieval bearded Christ.

The mid-sixth century was a time of transition, and many consider Ravenna's mosaics to be both the last ancient Roman and the first medieval European works of art. The beardless Christ (as he was depicted by ancient Romans) above the altar and the standard medieval portrayal atop the arch (with a beard) were created within the same generation.

The church's octagonal design—clearly Eastern in origin—inspired at least two churches, including Hagia Sofia, the church-turned-mosque-turned-museum built 10 years later in Constantinople (today's Istanbul). Emperor Charlemagne, the greatest ruler in Europe in A.D. 800, traveled to Ravenna, and was so impressed that when he returned to his capital, Aix-la-Chapelle (present-day Aachen in Germany), he built a church that many consider to be the first great stone building in northern Europe, modeled after this one.

The pilasters surrounding you are brick, covered by sliced marble veneers. Similar marble sheets once covered all the walls. Many were scavenged by Charlemagne to provide flooring for his great church.

• *From the basilica, head across the grounds to the Mausoleum of Galla Placidia. Look to the right to see a bit of contemporary mosaic art—a glassy round of hay (described on the adjacent plaque). Left over from a recent international festival of mosaics, it reminds visitors that the art form survives today.*

▲▲Mausoleum of Galla Placidia

Just across the courtyard from the Basilica di San Vitale is a tiny, humble-looking mausoleum, with the oldest—and, to many, the

most precious—mosaics in Ravenna. Ninety-five percent of the mosaics here are originals, dating from the late Roman period, when Ravenna was capital of a declining West.

Cost and Hours: Covered by Basilica di San Vitale combo-ticket, same hours and contact info as listed earlier for basilica.

Touring the Mausoleum: The Mausoleum of Galla Placidia (plah-CHEE-dee-ah) was likely designed to be the burial place of this daughter, sister, and mother of emperors, who died around A.D. 450. But Galla Placidia died in Rome, and wasn't buried here. The three sarcophagi, built for the imperial family but likely only used by later Christian leaders, stand empty today. The original floor was about four feet lower, explaining the stunted feel of the interior. The art's realistic portrayal of tunics and sandals gives us a peek at the fashions of fifth-century Romans.

The little light that sneaks through the thin alabaster panels brings a glow and a twinkle to the early Christian symbolism that fills the small room. Opposite the door is St. Lawrence being martyred on a fiery grill. He's legendary for mocking his executors, reportedly saying something like "I'm done on this side, you can turn me over now." He was famous as an example of the strength of the feisty early Christians. Note the four Gospels clearly labeled on the bookshelf, another inspiration for these first believers as they were persecuted by the Romans.

The dome is filled with stars. Along with Mark's lion, Luke's ox, Matthew's Archangel, and John's eagle, the golden cross rises from the east, bringing life to all. Doves drink from fountains, symbolic of souls finding nourishment in the Word of God. In both transepts are deer, reminding worshippers of Psalms 42: "Like the thirsty deer longs for spring water, so my soul longs for you, my God."

Look toward the back of the mausoleum. Cover the light from the door with your hand (or close the curtain) to see the standard Roman portrayal of Christ—beardless and as the Good Shepherd. Jesus, dressed in gold and purple like a Roman emperor, is the

King of Paradise—receiving the faithful (represented by lambs). The Eastern influence (perhaps inspired by the designs on fine Persian carpets or silks) is apparent in the vault's decorative patterns.

• *Our walk is done. Got a train to catch? Head straight back to the station. If you have more time, visit the other sights included on your basilica ticket on your way: the Neonian Baptistery, the Archiepiscopal Museum, and the Basilica di Sant'Apollinare Nuovo.*

More Sights in Ravenna

▲▲**Basilica di Sant'Apollinare Nuovo**—This austere sixth-century church, with a typical early-Christian-basilica floor plan, has two huge and wonderfully preserved side panels. One is a procession of haloed virgins, each bringing gifts to the Madonna and the Christ Child. Opposite, Christ is on his throne with four angels, awaiting a solemn procession of 26 martyrs. Ignoring the Baroque altar from a thousand years later, you can clearly see the rectangular Roman hall of justice  (basilica) floor plan—which was adopted by Christian churches and used throughout the Middle Ages.

This basilica started (c. 500) as an Arian church—the palace church of King Theodoric of the Goths. Theodoric decorated it with scenes of himself and his royal palace amid Christ and the saints. Look for original, surviving Arian art in the front (on the left, Mary and baby Jesus; on the right, Jesus and four angels) and in the rear (two cityscapes: Classe and Ravenna).

When Justinian arrived, he transformed the church in the Byzantine (and Nicene) style. If you study the arcades in the cityscapes you can see where Arian figures were erased, leaving only bits of hands and fingers on the columns, and blotted-out haloes behind the curtains. The brilliant white-robed figures parading on both sides were remade in the mid-500s with a Byzantine rather than Arian message. But the uppermost panels (hard to see without binoculars) are original Theodoric Arian: prophets (between windows), miracles of Christ (on the left), and scenes from the last week of Jesus' life and his Resurrection (on the right).

Cost and Hours: Covered by Basilica di San Vitale combo-ticket, daily April-Sept 9:00-19:00, Oct-March 9:30-17:00, on Via di Roma, tel. 0544-541-688, www.ravennamosaici.it.

Nearby: You can have a quick lunch at the air-conditioned, efficient Sant'Apollinare Self-Serve cafeteria on the church grounds (Mon-Fri 12:00-14:30, closed Sat-Sun). To see contemporary mosaic artists at work, follow the signs up to the second-floor mosaic laboratory in the church's courtyard (Mon-Fri 10:00-17:00, closed Sat-Sun).

▲**Archiepiscopal Museum**—This museum, in Ravenna's Duomo, contains the sixth-century Chapel of Sant'Andrea. Built as the private prayer chapel for Theodoric's bishop (c. 500), today it anchors a fine collection of Roman, Byzantine-Christian, and pagan statues, reliefs, and mosaics.

You'll enter the chapel under a sixth-century mosaic showing Christ as a religious warrior, stepping triumphantly on a lion and snake (ancient symbols of evil) and carrying the cross as if it were a weapon. The book he holds reads in Latin, "I am the way, the truth, and the life." This is a strong pro-Trinity statement (Jesus,

God, and the Holy Spirit are one) against the Arian heresy. The main chamber of the charming chapel is covered in rich mosaics, with lots of sixth-century symbolism and realistic portrait medallions.

In the next room is the museum's other highlight, an exquisite sixth-century Byzantine ivory throne, decorated with scenes from the life of Christ. It was carved for Bishop Maximian, Justinian's Trinitarian appointee, the man who oversaw construction of the Basilica di San Vitale, and whose bald head appears in its mosaics. In another room is an interesting circular calendar designed to keep track of the dates for Easter in the 500s and 600s.

Cost and Hours: Covered by Basilica di San Vitale combo-ticket, daily April-Sept 9:00-19:00, Oct-March 9:30-17:00, on Piazza Arcivescovado, tel. 0544-541-688, www.ravennamosaici.it.

▲**Neonian Baptistery**—Also known as the Baptistery of the Orthodox, this octagonal space dates from about the year 400.

Imagine pagan adults immersed in the pool under glorious ceiling mosaics as they convert to Christianity. The mosaic portrays the common baptistery theme: John the Baptist baptizing Christ, with the personification of the River Jordan looking on. The scene is ringed by empty chairs waiting to welcome you into the eternal heavenly banquet. Twelve apostles with dancing feet—their tunics and cloaks alternating between gold and white—give the room a joyful visual sense of rhythm. The acanthus flowers dividing the apostles were the botanic inspiration for the Corinthian capital, the Roman capital of choice. Decoration on the lower walls features green disks made of precious porphyry stone and a gold leafy arcade creating almond frames for the prophets.

Cost and Hours: Covered by Basilica di San Vitale combo-ticket, daily April-Sept 9:00-19:00, Oct-March 9:30-17:00, next to Ravenna's Duomo, tel. 0544-541-688, www.ravennamosaici.it.

House of Stone Carpets (Domus dei Tappeti di Pietra)—Discovered in 1993, the stone mosaic floors of this sixth-century Byzantine house show both pictorial images and abstract designs. Excavations revealed many layers, dating back to the second century B.C. All were peeled away and preserved elsewhere. Only the sixth-century floor (12 rooms on one level) was put back and exhibited here, very close to its original location. Because this was a private home, its art could break from the conservative norms for public art of the age. The highlight is the wonderfully realistic Dance of the Four Seasons. Don't miss the fourth-century Christ as a Shepherd, which some consider the earliest portrayal of Jesus (it's hung on a wall; part of the face was lost to modern excavations). A visit here is almost meaningless without the €1 audioguide.

Cost and Hours: €4; March-Oct daily 10:00-18:30, July-Aug Tue and Fri until 22:30; Nov-Feb Tue-Sun 10:00-17:00, closed Mon; ask for the 10-minute English-language video—the computer-generated images help visitors envision the place in action; entrance through Church of Sant'Eufemia, on Via Barbiani just off Via Cavour near Piazza Baracca, tel. 0544-32512, www .ravennantica.it.

Near Ravenna

▲▲**Church of Sant'Apollinare in Classe**—The final major sight for Byzantine mosaic fans is a sixth-century church standing a couple of miles outside of Ravenna in the suburb of Classe. It's impressive, but comes in fourth place after the Basilica di San Vitale, Mausoleum of Galla Placidia, and Basilica di Sant'Apollinare Nuovo. On a quick day trip, it's skippable.

The statue of Emperor Augustus, standing in front of the church, is a reminder that Classe was a strategic navy base in Roman times. In early Christian days, Classe was a big pilgrimage destination and home to a large Christian community. Today, little remains other than its church, and even that was nearly bombed-out in World War II when the Germans used its medieval tower as a lookout.

The artistic treasure here is the mosaic work in the apse, 90 percent of which is original from the sixth century. The scene is an abstract portrayal of the Transfiguration of Jesus. The cross with a tiny portrait of Christ in its center beams light. God's hand above affirms that "This is the Truth." The three lambs represent James, John, and Peter. The landscape is of pine trees, which once forested the region. And St. Apollinare, the first local bishop, is celebrated because it was he who brought Christianity to the area.

The rest of the church—its mosaics lost to time—is pretty plain. While many churches this old have settled and the bases of their columns are no longer visible, here the floor level remains unchanged and you can admire the columns' original bases. Near the entrance, a bilingual display panel gives detailed information on the church.

Cost and Hours: €3, Mon-Sat 8:30-19:30, Sun 13:00-19:30, Via Romea Sud, tel. 0544-473-569, www.turismo.ravenna.it.

Getting There: The church is two miles out of town—an easy bike ride. To go by bus, buy two local bus tickets (€1 each) at any tobacco shop, then catch bus #4 or #44 across the street from the train station (on the corner by the park; 3/hour Mon-Sat, 2/hour on Sun, 15 minutes). The bus also leaves from Piazza Caduti (stop is on the corner). To return to Ravenna from the church, walk back toward town along the main road about 100 yards to find the bus shelter on the right.

Overrated Sight—The nearby beach town of Rimini is a crowded mess.

Sleeping in Ravenna

In the Pedestrian Zone, near Piazza del Popolo

$$$ Hotel Bisanzio is a business-class splurge renting 38 rooms in the city center (Sb-€86, small Db-€108, mid-size Db-€124, large Db-€136, air-con, free Wi-Fi, usually free on-street parking with hotel permits; Via Salara 30, tel. 0544-217-111, fax 0544-32539, www.bisanziohotel.com, info@bizanziohotel.com). From Piazza del Popolo, take Via IV Novembre to the market, turn left onto Via Cavour, then take the first right.

$$ M Club B&B is a creative, comfortable, and stylish five-room place with generous public spaces, an elegant breakfast room, spacious bedrooms, and thoughtful touches. Each unique room is described on their website (straight pricing: Db-€70-120 depending on size, big Qb suite-€130, cheap cable Internet access, free Wi-Fi, loaner bikes, Piazza Baracca 26, tel. 333-955-6466, fax 0544-215-250, www.m-club.it, info@m-club.it, Michael). The M Club faces the Porta Adriana gate at the far end of the old town from the train station (a 15-minute walk).

$$ Casa Masoli B&B's six elegantly outfitted rooms include giant bathrooms in a wood-paneled Art Deco style. You're in a family home here; grandmotherly Signora Masoli works

---

Sleep Code

(€1 = about $1.40, country code: 39)
S = Single, **D** = Double/Twin, **T** = Triple, **Q** = Quad, **b** = bathroom, **s** = shower only. Unless otherwise noted, credit cards are accepted, English is spoken, and prices include breakfast.

To help you easily sort through these listings, I've divided the accommodations into three categories, based on the price for a standard double room with bath:

$$$ **Higher Priced**—Most rooms €100 or more.
$$ **Moderately Priced**—Most rooms between €60-100.
$ **Lower Priced**—Most rooms €60 or less.

Prices can change without notice; verify the hotel's current rates online or by email. For other updates, see www.ricksteves.com/update.

quietly alongside daughter Anna and grandchildren Chiara and Alessandro (Sb-€50, Db-€70, Tb-€90, 4th and 5th person-€20 each, peaceful garden, air-con, free Wi-Fi, library, Via G. Rossi 22, mobile tel. 335-609-9471 or 339-544-8405, www.casamasoli .it, anna@casamasoli.it). From Piazza del Popolo, walk up Via S. Ferruzzi, jogging left onto Via G. Rossi after a couple of blocks.

$$ A Casa di Paola is a converted private home (Paola's mother has an apartment on the ground floor) with eight nicely decorated rooms and comfy common spaces (Sb-€50, Db-€70, Tb-€90, Qb-€120, Quint/b-€140, air-con, free Internet access and Wi-Fi, Via P. Costa 26, tel. 0544-39425, mobile tel. 347-730-6386, www.acasadipaola.it, info@acasadipaola.it).

Near the Train Station

These places are convenient, but have less atmosphere.

$$ Hotel Italia, just 100 yards from the train station, feels like a chain hotel but is actually family-owned. Its 45 rooms lack character but provide comfort and lots of space (Sb-€60, Db-€90, Tb-€110, Qb-€130, ask about weekend deals, air-con, free Wi-Fi, free loaner bikes, free parking on first-come, first-served basis, turn left out of station, Viale Pallavicini 4, tel. 0544-212-363, fax 0544-217-004, www.hitalia.it, info@hotelitaliaravenna.com, Lucia and Mauro).

$ Hotel al Giaciglio, near the train station, has 16 very basic budget rooms, bordering on dreary. They offer loaner bikes in the summer (S-€35, D-€50, Db-€60, Tb-€80, Qb-€90, fans, Internet café down street, Via R. Brancaleone 42, tel. & fax 0544-39403, www.albergoalgiaciglio.com, info@albergoalgiaciglio.com, Barbara and Moanely).

Hostel: **$ Ostello Dante,** a 15-minute walk from the station, has Wi-Fi, loaner bikes, and a game room (140 beds, €16/bed in 4-bed rooms, Db-€44, family rooms with bath-€19/person, €3/night extra for non-hostel members, includes breakfast and sheets, towels-€1, laundry-€5/load, 11:00-14:30 lockout, 23:30 curfew or pay €1 for magnetic entrance key, closed Nov-Feb, Via Nicolodi 12, bus #70 from train station, tel. & fax 0544-421-164, www.hostel ravenna.com, hostelravenna@hotmail.com).

Eating in Ravenna

Ca' de Ven ("House of Wine"), the most famous restaurant in town, is affordable. It fills a 16th-century warehouse with communal seating and residents enjoying quality wine and traditional regional cuisine, including *piadina* (peeah-DEE-nah; unleavened bread served plain or with pizza-type stuffing). Their dessert specialty, *torta di marzapane*—a decadent almond-and-cocoa brownie—is good with sweet red wine. Reserve ahead for dinner (€4-6 *piadina*, €8-9 pastas, €12-13 *secondi*, no cover, Tue-Sun 11:00-14:15 & 18:00-22:00, closed Mon, 2-minute walk from Piazza del Popolo on Via Cairoli, which turns into Via C. Ricci, Via C. Ricci 24, tel. 0544-30163).

Ristorante la Gardèla is a favorite. Their *cappelletti*, a cheese-stuffed pasta, is served *in brodo* (soup) or *in ragu* (meat sauce). If Ravenna had a town dining room, this would be it. The fun-loving waitstaff has been here for years and the restaurant has all the nice touches without the pretense. While there are a few tables outside and upstairs, I like the jolly main floor (€5-6 pastas, €7-10 *secondi*, €15 and €25 set menus, €1.50 cover, Fri-Wed 12:00-14:30 & 19:00-22:00, closed Thu, from Piazza del Popolo follow Via IV Novembre past Piazza della Costa to corner of Via Ponte Marino 3, tel. 0544-217-147).

Ristorante Marchesini is an upscale self-serve restaurant (over a delicatessen) offering delicious salads and homemade pastas (€7 pastas, €10 *secondi*, €1.50 cover, Mon-Sat 12:00-14:30, closed Sun, 5-minute walk from Piazza del Popolo, on corner of Piazza Caduti at Via Mazzini 6—ride elevator to first floor, tel. 0544-212-309).

Free Flow Bizantino, inside the covered market, is a self-serve cafeteria serving lunch only (€4 pastas, €5 *secondi*, €8 three-course lunch, Mon-Fri 11:45-14:45, closed Sat-Sun, tel. 0544-32073).

Pizzeria Cupido is good for a cheap and traditional lunch or snack. Try their *piadina* or *crescione* (calzone-like) sandwich. These tasty sandwiches (€3.50-5) come stuffed with a variety of meats, cheeses, and vegetables. Consider one filled with *squacquerone*, a soft regional cream cheese (no cover, Tue-Sun 11:00-20:00, closed Mon, just up Via Cavour from the market at Via Cavour 43, mobile tel. 393-670-8225).

Supermarkets: For lunch, assemble a picnic at the **covered market** (Mon-Sat 7:00-14:00, closed Sun) and enjoy your feast in the shady gardens of the Rocca Brancaleone fortress (daily until 18:00; 5-minute walk from station, follow Via Maroncelli until you see the walls). If the covered market is closed, visit **Pretty Market,** on Via di Roma at the corner of Via A. Moriani (Mon-Sat 7:30-20:30, Sun 9:00-13:30 & 16:30-20:30).

Ravenna Connections

All of the following require a change in either Ferrara or Bologna.

From Ravenna by Train to: Venice (roughly hourly, 3-3.5 hours), **Padua** (roughly hourly, 2.5-3), **Florence** (about hourly, 2.5 hours by fast train, no slow train option).

THE DOLOMITES

Dolomiti

Italy's dramatic rocky rooftop, the Dolomites, offers some of the best mountain thrills in Europe. Bolzano is the gateway to the Dolomites, and Castelrotto is a good home base for your exploration of Alpe di Siusi, Europe's largest alpine meadow.

The sunny Dolomites are well-developed, and the region's famous valleys and towns suffer from après-ski fever. The cost for the comfort of reliably good weather is a drained-reservoir feeling. Lovers of other parts of the Alps may miss the lushness that comes with the unpredictable weather farther north. But the bold, light-gray cliffs and spires flecked with snow, above green meadows and beneath a blue sky, offer a powerful, unique, and memorable mountain experience. Dolomite, a sedimentary rock similar to limestone, gives these mountains their distinctive shape and color.

A hard-fought history has left the region bicultural, with an emphasis on the German. Most locals speak German first, and some wish they were still part of Austria. In the Middle Ages, as part of the Holy Roman Empire, the region faced north. Later, it was firmly in the Austrian Habsburg realm. By losing World War I, Austria's South Tirol became Italy's Alto Adige. Mussolini did what he could to Italianize the region, including giving each town an Italian name. But even as recently as the 1990s, local secessionist groups agitated violently for more autonomy—with some success (see sidebar).

The government has wooed locals with economic breaks, which have made this one of Italy's richest areas (as local prices attest), and today all signs and literature in the province of Alto Adige/Südtirol are in both languages. Many include a third lan-

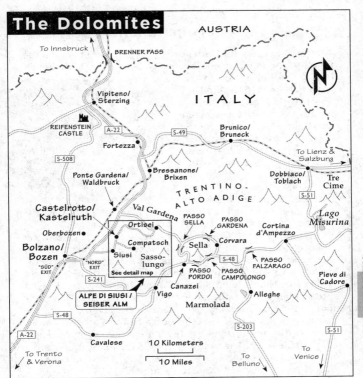

guage, Ladin—an ancient Romance language still spoken in a few traditional areas. (I have listed both the Italian and German, so the confusion caused by this guidebook will match that experienced in your travels.)

In spite of all the glamorous ski resorts and busy construction cranes, the local color survives in a warm blue-aproned, ruddy-faced, felt-hat-with-feathers way. There's yogurt and yodeling for breakfast. Culturally as much as geographically, the area is reminiscent of Austria. In fact, the Austrian region of Tirol is named for a village that is now part of Italy.

Planning Your Time

Train travelers can side-trip into the mountains from Bolzano (1.5 hours north of Verona). To get a feel for the alpine culture, spend at least one night in Castelrotto. But with two nights there, you can actually get out and hike. Tenderfeet ride the bus, catch a cable car, and stroll. For serious mountain thrills, do a six-hour hike. And for a memory that won't soon fade away, spend a night in a mountain hut. Always remember to check the latest transportation

Ich bin ein Italiener

With the exception of Bolzano, where Italian has become the primary language, you'll hear mostly German in Dolomite villages. Overall, seven in ten Italians living in the South Tirol speak German as their mother tongue. Many are fair-skinned and blue-eyed, prefer dumplings and strudel to pasta and gelato, and feel a closer bond with their ancestors in Austria than with their swarthy countrymen to the south. Most have a working knowledge of  Italian, but they watch German-language TV, read newspapers *auf Deutsch,* and live in Tirolean-looking villages.

At the end of World War I, the region was ceded by Austria (loser) to Italy (winner). Mussolini suppressed the Germanic cultural elements as part of his propaganda campaign to praise all things Italian. Many German-speakers hoped that Hitler would "liberate" them from Italy, but Hitler's close alliance with Mussolini prevented that from happening. Instead, in June 1939, residents were given six months to make a hard choice—move north to the Fatherland and become German citizens, or stay in their homeland *(Heimat)* under Italian rule. The vast majority (212,000, or 85 percent) made the decision to leave, but because of the outbreak of World War II, only 75,000 actually moved.

At the war's end, German-speakers were again disappointed when the Allied powers refused to grant them autonomy or the chance to become Austrian citizens. Instead, the victors decided to stick with the prewar arrangement.

The region rebuilt and the two linguistic groups patched things up, but for the remainder of the 20th century, there was always an underlying problem: German-speakers were continually outvoted by the Italian-speaking majority in the regional government (comprising two provinces, Italian-speaking Trentino and German-speaking Alto Adige/Südtirol). German-speakers lobbied the national government for more control on the provincial (not regional) level, even turning to demonstrations and violence. Over the years, Rome has slowly and grudgingly granted increased local control.

Today, Alto Adige/Südtirol has a large measure of autonomy written into the country's 2001 constitution, though it's still officially tied to Trentino. Roads, water, electricity, communications, and schools are all under local control, including the Free University of Bozen-Bolzano, founded in 1998.

THE DOLOMITES

timetables before you embark on an outing.

If you have a car, you can drive the three-hour loop from Bolzano or Castelrotto (Val Gardena-Sella Pass-Val di Fassa) and ride one of the lifts to the top for a ridge walk. Connecting Bolzano and Venice by the Great Dolomite Road takes two hours longer than by the autostrada, but is far more scenic (see "More Sights in the Dolomites" at the end of this chapter).

Hiking season is mid-June through mid-October. The region is particularly crowded, booming, and blooming from mid-July through mid-September (but once you're out on the trails, you'll leave the crowds behind). It's packed with Italian vacationers in August. Spring is usually dead, with lifts shut down, huts closed, and the most exciting trails still under snow. Many hotels and restaurants close in April and November. Ski season (Dec-Easter) is busiest of all. For more information, visit www.visitdolomites.com.

Bolzano (Bozen)

Willkommen to the Italian Tirol! If it weren't so sunny, you could be in Innsbruck. This enjoyable old town of 100,000 is the most convenient gateway to the Dolomites, especially if you're relying on public transportation. It's just the place to take a Tirolean stroll.

Orientation to Bolzano

Tourist Information

Bolzano's TI is helpful (Mon-Fri 9:00-19:00, Sat 9:30-18:00, closed Sun, Piazza Walther/Waltherplatz 8, tel. 0471-307-000, www.bolzano-bozen.it). Pick up the city map and the *Historic and Cultural Route* brochure (also downloadable from website).

Consider buying the **museummobil Card** (€20 from TIs and some hotels), which covers all trains and buses and most museums in the South Tirol (including the archaeology museum, with its famous Ice Man) as well as the Funivia del Renon/Rittner Seilbahn cable car for three days (www.mobilcard.info). This card pays for itself if you visit the Ice Man, ride the Ritten cable car, take the train round-trip from Bolzano to Klobenstein, and take the bus round-trip from Bolzano to Castelrotto. Don't bother with the Bolzano City Card (which offers discounts at five Bolzano museums and the skippable Runkelstein Castle), because the only sight that merits your time is the archaeology museum.

If you're not interested in museums but are taking public transportation, the *carta di valore* (value card) gives you discounts

Bolzano

1. Hotel Figl
2. Hotel Greif
3. Stadt Hotel Città
4. Parkhotel Laurin
5. Hotel Feichter
6. Kolpinghaus Bozen
7. Youth Hostel Bolzano
8. Weisses Rössl Restaurant
9. Ca' de Bezzi/Gasthaus Batzenhäusl
10. Hopfen & Co. Restaurant
11. Paulaner Stuben
12. Enoteca Il Baccaro
13. Gasthaus Fink
14. DeSpar Supermarkets (3)
15. Internet Café
16. Alpine Info Center
17. Launderette
18. Bike Rental

of up to 30 percent off regional train and bus fares. Cards come loaded with €5, €10, or €20 (valid on SAD and Silbernagl buses, regional trains as far as Trento, and some lifts—such as the lift to Oberbozen—but not those in Alpe di Siusi). If you're traveling with others, one card can cover multiple fares. Buy it at train and bus stations and on buses (tel. 840-000-471, www.sii.bz.it).

Serious hikers can visit the **Alpine Information Center** (Alpine Auskunft) run by the Alpenverein Südtirol, a local hiking club. It offers a map library (also available at http://trekking.suedtirol.info) and advice on trails and mountain huts. It's deep in the old town in an arcade that you enter at Via Dr. Streiter/Dr.-Streiter-Gasse 16; ring the bell and go upstairs (Mon-Tue and Thu 10:30-12:00 & 14:00-16:00, Fri 10:30-12:00, closed Wed and Sat-Sun, tel. 0471-999-955, www.alpine-auskunft.it).

Arrival in Bolzano

There are two train stations for Bolzano—you want just *Bolzano*, not *Bolzano Süd*. To get to the TI and downtown from the train station, veer left up the tree-lined Viale della Stazione/Bahnhofsallee, and walk past the bus station (on your left) two blocks to **Piazza**

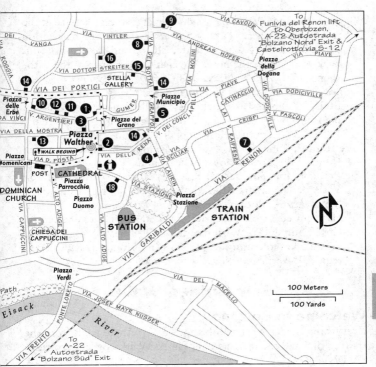

Walther/Waltherplatz. You'll see the TI on the right side of the square. The medieval heart of town is on the far side of the square: The arcaded Via dei Portici/Laubengasse is Bolzano's old main street. It leads to Piazza Erbe/Obstplatz, which has an open-air produce market (see "Markets," below); the Ice Man is a couple of blocks farther beyond.

Helpful Hints

Sleepy Sundays: The city is really dead on Sunday (young locals add "and during the rest of the week, too").

Markets: Piazza Erbe/Obstplatz hosts an ancient and still-thriving open-air produce market (Mon-Fri all day, Sat morning only, closed Sun). Wash your produce in the handy drinking fountain in the middle of the market. Another market (offering more variety, not just food) is held Saturday mornings on Piazza della Vittoria.

Internet Access: Multi Kulti Internet Point is a short walk from Piazza Walther/Waltherplatz at Via Dr. Streiter/Dr.-Streiter-Gasse 9 (€3/hour, Mon-Sat 10:00-22:00, closed Sun, tel. 0471-056-056).

Baggage Storage: While there's no baggage-storage service at the train station, there is a tiny *deposito bagagli* at the bus station just a block away (€3/24 hours, €10 refundable deposit, out back from where the buses leave, at the entrance to the bathrooms, daily 7:00-13:00 & 14:00-19:30).

Laundry: Lava e Asciuga launderette is at Via Rosmini/Rosmini Strasse 81, about two blocks west of the South Tirol Museum of Archaeology (€3 wash, €3 dry, English instructions, daily 7:30-22:30, last wash 21:00, mobile 340-220-2323).

Bike Rental: The city has a well-developed bike-trail system. Rental bikes are curiously cheap here. Plenty of bikes are available for rent just off Piazza Walther/Waltherplatz on Viale della Stazione/Bahnhofsallee on the right side (€1/6 hours, €2/6-24 hours, €5/24 hours, €10 refundable deposit, ID required, April-Sept Mon-Sat 7:30-19:50, Oct until 18:50, closed Sun and Nov-March, tel. 0471-997-578). The TI also has 10 bikes to rent for €5 per day (€10 refundable deposit, ID required, April-mid-Nov, ask for a map).

Self-Guided Walk

Welcome to Bolzano

Everything mentioned in Bolzano is a 10-minute walk from the train station and the main square, Piazza Walther/Waltherplatz.

• *Start in...*

Piazza Walther/Waltherplatz: The square's namesake, Walther von der Vogelweide, honored by the statue in the center, was a 12th-century politically incorrect German poet who courageously stood up to the Holy Roman Emperor. Walther's spunk against a far bigger power represents the Germanic pride of this region. The statue is made of marble quarried in the village of Laas, north of Bolzano. The US chose this same marble for the 86,000  crosses and Stars of David needed to mark the WWII dead buried at Normandy and other battlefields across Europe.

When not hosting Bolzano's Christmas market, flower market (May Day), or Speck Fest (a spring ham festival), Piazza Walther/Waltherplatz is simply the town's living room. And locals care about it. It was the site of Italy's first McDonald's, which—in the early 1990s—became the first McDonald's to be shut down by locals protesting American fast food. Today, the square is home to trendy cafés such as Café Walther, where (outside of meal times) you're welcome to nurse a "Venetian" *spritz* or a pricier cocktail as long as you like.

• *Cross the street to the big church.*

The Cathedral: The cathedral's glazed-tile roof is typical of the Germanic world, a reminder that from the sixth century until 1919, German was the region's official language. Then, suddenly: *Buon giorno!* Walk around to the right to the Romanesque Lion's Gate. The church was flattened in World War II (a distinct downside of being located near a train station in 20th-century Europe). Stepping inside, you get a Teutonic—not Italian—feel. The mostly Gothic interior is broken by an impressive Baroque tabernacle. Most of the art here is by Bavarian artists. There's a stiff, pre-Michelangelo, 15th-century *pietà* to the left of the altar. The sandstone pulpit (c. 1500), with its reliefs of the four Church fathers (whose presence gave credibility to sermons preached here) is reminiscent of Vienna's St. Stephen's Cathedral.

• *Leaving the church, walk diagonally across Piazza Walther/ Waltherplatz and find the street to the right of the big Sparkasse bank building. Go down it for one block, to...*

Piazza del Grano/Kornplatz: Nine hundred years ago, this was Bolzano's main square. The building to your right was the bishop's castle. The traditional food stand selling *Vollkornbrot* (dense, whole-grain bread) and pretzels is another reminder of German heritage. Find the flower beds at the top of the square; a bronze relief on a large stone shows Bolzano's street plan in the 12th century—a one-street arcaded town huddled within a fortified wall.

• *Continue uphill into the original medieval town, passing the "Wurstel Boutique" on your left (yet another reminder of this region's Germanic orientation).*

Via dei Portici/Laubengasse: This was the only street in 12th-century Bolzano. Step into the center (dodging bikes).

Looking east and west, you see the width of the original town. Thirty yards to the left is the old city hall—the street's only Gothic building (with frescoed pointed arches). The other buildings are all basically the same: Each had a storm cellar, cows out back, a ground-level shop, and living quarters upstairs. Bay windows were designed for maximum light—just right for clerks keeping track of accounts and for women doing their weaving. The arcades *(Lauben),* typical of Tirol, sheltered merchants and their goods from both snow and sun. Narrow side passages lead to neighboring streets. The only balcony marks the one Baroque building—once the mercantile center (with a fine worth-a-look courtyard), now a skippable museum.

• *Turn left on Via dei Portici/Laubengasse and continue to the end, where you'll find a bustling market.*

Piazza Erbe/Obstplatz: This square hosts an open-air produce market, liveliest in the morning (Mon-Fri all day, Sat mornings, closed Sun). The historic market fountain gives Bolzano its only hint of the sea—a 17th-century statue of Neptune. Stroll around and see what's in season. All of the breads, strudel, and hams *schmecken sehr gut.*

• *From the market, Via Museo/Museumstrasse (called Butcher Street until the 19th century, when a museum opened) leads straight to Frozen Fritz.*

Sights in Bolzano

▲▲South Tirol Museum of Archaeology (Museo Archeologico dell'Alto Adige/Südtiroler Archäologiemuseum)—

This excellent museum features the actual corpse of Ötzi the Ice Man. His frozen body was discovered high in the mountains on the Italian/Austrian border by a German couple in 1991. Police initially believed the corpse was a lost hiker, and Ötzi was chopped roughly out of the glacier, damaging his left side. But upon discovering his pre-Bronze Age hatchet, officials realized what they had found: a 5,300-year-old, nearly perfectly preserved man with clothing and gear in excellent condition for his age. Later, researchers pinned down the cause of death—an arrowhead buried in Ötzi's left shoulder.

As the body was found right on the border, Austria and Italy squabbled briefly over who would get him. Tooth enamel studies have now shown that he did grow up on the Italian side. An Austrian journalist dubbed him Ötzi, after the Ötztal valley, where he was discovered.

With Ötzi as the centerpiece, the museum takes you on an intriguing journey through time, recounting the evolution of humanity—from the Paleolithic era to the Roman period and finally to the Middle Ages—in vivid detail. The exhibit offers informative displays and models, video demonstrations of Ötzi's extraction and his personal effects, a great audioguide, and interactive computers.

You'll see Ötzi himself—still frozen—as well as an artist's reconstruction of what he looked like when alive. In his mid-40s at the time of his death, Ötzi was 5 feet, 3 inches tall, with brown hair and brown eyes. He weighed about 110 pounds and likely had trouble with his knees.

Glass cases display his incredibly well-preserved and fascinating clothing and gear, including a finely stitched two-color coat, his goathide loincloth, a fancy hat, shoes, a well-crafted hatchet, 14 arrows, a bow, and fire-making gadgets.

Cost and Hours: €9, essential audioguide-€2; Tue-Sun 10:00-18:00, closed Mon except July-Aug and Dec; last entry 30 minutes before closing, no photos, near the river at Via Museo/Museumstrasse 43, tel. 0471-320-100, www.iceman.it, museum @iceman.it.

Dominican Church (Chiesa dei Domenicani/Dominikanerkirche)—
Drop by this 13th-century church to see its Chapel of St. John (San Giovanni/St. Johannes; chapel is through the archway and on the right), frescoed in the 14th century by the Giotto School.

THE DOLOMITES

Cost and Hours: Free, €0.50 coin lights dim interior, Mon-Sat 9:30-17:00, Sun 12:00-18:00.

Lift to Oberbozen and the Ritten—
The **Funivia del Renon/Rittner Seilbahn** cable car whisks you over the hills from Bolzano to the touristy resort village of Oberbozen, where Sigmund Freud and wife once celebrated their wedding anniversary. The reasonably priced, 12-minute ride is the main attraction, offering views of the town, surrounding mountains, made-for-yodeling-farmsteads and 18-wheelers downshifting along the expressway from Austria. The cable car's valley station is a five-block walk east from the Bolzano train station along Via Renon/Rittner Strasse or from Piazza Municipio/Rathausplatz in the old center (€3.50 round-trip, departures year-round Mon-Sat 6:30-22:38, Sun 7:10-22:38; leaves every 4 minutes, every 12 minutes after 21:00; closes for maintenance for a week in March and Nov; for info call regional transport hotline at tel. 840-000-471 or visit www.sii.bz.it). While the cable car is fun, it is no replacement for a trip to Castelrotto and Alpe di Siusi.

At the end of the ride, **Oberbozen** (elevation 4,000 feet) is mostly a collection of resort hotels. From Oberbozen, a narrow-gauge train makes the 16-minute trip to **Klobenstein,** a larger and slightly less touristy village at 3,800 feet (€2.50 one-way, €3.50 round-trip, leaves daily at least hourly). The local TI has branches in both villages (www.ritten.com). In Oberbozen, the TI is in the train station building, just steps from the lift station (Mon-Fri 9:00-12:30 & 15:00-18:00, Sat 9:00-12:30, closed Sun in summer, tel. 0471-345-245). The Klobenstein TI is a five-minute walk from the train station (Mon-Fri 8:30-18:00, Sat 8:30-12:00, closed Sun, tel. 0471-356-100).

The lift station and TIs have brochures suggesting short walks. More interesting than Oberbozen itself (though not a must-

see) are the nearby **"earth pyramids,"** which are a 30-minute walk downhill from the cable-car station and can be glimpsed from the cable car itself. The pyramids, created by eroding glacial debris dumped at the end of the last ice age, are Bryce Canyon-like pinnacles that rise out of the ridge. Klobenstein has its own earth pyramids a 45-minute walk from town. Another walk is the Freudpromenade, a fairly level, 1.5-hour stroll between Oberbozen and Kloben-stein (you can take the train back).

Sleeping in Bolzano

All of the listed hotels are in the city center, within walking distance of the train and bus stations.

$$$ Hotel Figl, warmly run by Anton and Helga Mayr, has 23 comfy, bright, modern rooms and an attached café on a pedestrian square located a block from Piazza Walther/Waltherplatz. With rooms better than its humble public spaces and exterior, it's a fine value (Sb-€87-95, Db-€120-125, junior suite-€130-135; discount with this book for longer stays—ask when you reserve; breakfast-€4-12, air-con, elevator, non-smoking, free Internet access and Wi-Fi, Piazza del Grano/Kornplatz 9, tel. 0471-978-412, fax 0471-978-413, www.figl.net, info@figl.net, include a backup fax number if you email).

$$$ Hotel Greif, a luxury boutique hotel, is right on Piazza Walther/Waltherplatz. Each of the 33 individually designed rooms makes you feel like you're in a modern-art installation (its fine website gives a room-by-room tour). It's not cozy, but it is striking, and a stay here comes with one of the best breakfasts in Italy (comfort Sb-€148, comfort Db-€192, superior Db-€233, discounted Sat-Sun by request, ask for the 10 percent Rick Steves discount when you book online—availability limited, includes buffet breakfast, most rooms non-smoking, air-con, pay Internet access and Wi-Fi, Piazza Walther/Waltherplatz, entrance on Via della

---

Sleep Code

(€1 = about $1.40, country code: 39)
S = Single, **D** = Double/Twin, **T** = Triple, **Q** = Quad, **b** = bathroom, **s** = shower only. Unless otherwise noted, credit cards are accepted, English is spoken, and breakfast is included.

To help you sort easily through these listings, I've divided the accommodations into three categories based on the price for a standard double room with bath:

$$$ Higher Priced—Most rooms €100 or more.
 $$ Moderately Priced—Most rooms between €60-100.
  $ Lower Priced—Most rooms €60 or less.

Prices can change without notice; verify the hotel's current rates online or by email. For other updates, see www .ricksteves.com/update.

Rena/Raingasse, tel. 0471-318-000, fax 0471-318-148, www.greif .it, info@greif.it). Drivers follow signs to *Parking Walther* (€17/day) and enter the hotel from level -1 of the garage.

$$$ Stadt Hotel Città, a venerable old hotel with 99 modern if basic rooms, is ideally situated on Piazza Walther/Waltherplatz. The hotel's café spills out onto the piazza, offering a prime spot for people-watching (Sb-€98, Db-€140, bigger view Db-€180, Tb-€195, air-con, elevator, free Internet access and Wi-Fi, parking-€16/day, Piazza Walther/Waltherplatz 21, tel. 0471-975-221, fax 0471-976-688, www.hotelcitta.info, info@hotelcitta.info, Francesco and Alessandra). This place is an especially good value if you plan to spend an afternoon in their free-for-guests Wellness Center (mid-Sept-mid-June Mon-Sat 16:30-22:00, likely closed Sun; closed mid-June-mid-Sept; Turkish bath, whirlpool, Finnish sauna, biosauna, massage by appointment)—a fine way to unwind after a day of hiking in the Dolomites.

$$$ Parkhotel Laurin is an Old World luxury hotel located very close to the train station, with 100 tastefully decorated rooms, marble bathrooms, a chic dining room and terrace, a swimming pool, an extensive garden, attentive staff, and frescoes throughout the grand lobby depicting the legend of King Laurin (small Sb-€98, standard Sb-€111, standard Db-€142, comfort Db-€176, discounted Sat-Sun by request, pay Internet access and Wi-Fi, parking-€14/day, Via Laurin/Laurinstrasse 4, tel. 0471-311-000, fax 0471-311-148, www.laurin.it, info@laurin.it).

$$ Hotel Feichter is an inexpensive, well-kept, family-run place with simple but sufficient amenities in a great location. Some of the 30 rooms share a communal terrace overlooking the rooftops of Bolzano. Papà Walter, Mamma Hedwig, Hannes, Irene, and Wolfi Feichter have run this homey hotel since 1969 (Sb-€60, Db-€90, Tb-€110, parking-€5/day, ground-floor café serves lunches; from station, walk up Via Laurin/Laurinstrasse, which becomes Via Grappoli/Weintraubengasse—hotel is on the right at #15; tel. 0471-978-768, fax 0471-974-803, www.hotelfeichter.it, info@hotelfeichter.it).

$$ Kolpinghaus Bozen, modern, clean, and church-run, has 34 rooms with two twin beds (placed head to toe) and 71 new air-conditioned single rooms with all the comforts. Though institutional, it's a great deal...and makes me feel thankful (Sb-€60, Db-€90, Tb-€135, elevator, free cable Internet or Wi-Fi—varies by floor, Internet access, laundry-€6/big load, parking-€12/day, 4 blocks from Piazza Walther/Waltherplatz near Piazza Domenicani at Largo A. Kolping/Adolph-Kolping-Strasse 3, tel. 0471-308-400, fax 0471-973-917, www.kolpingbozen.it, info@kolpingbozen.it). The line of people in front of the building at lunchtime consists mainly of office workers waiting for the cafeteria to open (€10.50 three-course lunch, Mon-Fri 11:45-14:00, Sat 12:00-13:30, closed Sun).

$ Youth Hostel Bolzano is the most comfortable and inviting hostel that I've seen in Italy. It has 18 four-bed rooms (each with two bunk beds and a full bathroom) and 10 delightful singles with bath. The bright, clean, modern rooms make it feel like a dorm in a fancy university. With no age limit, no need for membership, easy reservations by email, great lockers, and cheap Internet access, it is the utopian hostel (bed in quad-€21, Sb-€24, €2 extra for 1-night stays, includes linens and buffet breakfast, towels-€1, laundry-€4/load, kitchen, free luggage storage, 9:00 checkout; 100 yards to the right as you leave the train station at Via Renon/Rittner Strasse 23; tel. 0471-300-865, fax 0471-300-858, http://bozen.jugendher berge.it, bozen@jugendherberge.it).

Eating in Bolzano

All of these recommendations are in the center of the old town. Prices are consistent (you can generally get a good plate of meat and veggies for €10). While nearly every local-style place serves a mix of Germanic/Tirolean and Italian fare, I favor eating Tirolean here in Bozen.

Weisses Rössl offers affordable, mostly Tirolean food with meat, fish, and fine vegetarian options. Located in a traditional woody setting, it's good for dining indoors among savvy locals (€11-14 main courses, €7-12 lunch specials, Mon-Fri 11:00-15:00 & 17:30-23:30—light meals only available between 15:00-17:30, Sat 11:00-15:00 only, closed Sun, 2 blocks north of Piazza Municipio

Tirolean Cuisine

During your visit to the Dolomites, take a break from Italian-style pizzas and pastas to sample some of the region's tra-

ditional cuisine...with a distinctly Austrian flavor. For simplicity, I've generally listed Italian names here, though local menus are in both Italian and German (and usually also English).

Wurst and sauerkraut are the Tirolean clichés. More adventurous eaters seek out *speck,* a raw (prosciutto-style) ham smoked for five months then thinly sliced and served as an antipasto or in sandwiches. *Canederli*—large dumplings with bits of *speck,* liver, spinach, or cheese—are often served in broth, or with butter and cheese. (Never cut a dumpling with a knife—it'll destroy the chef.)

The stars of Tirolean cuisine are the hearty meat dishes—which, unlike traditional Italian main courses, are nearly always served with side dishes of doughy dumplings or vegetables and potatoes. Try *stinco di maiale* (roasted pork shank, usually garnished with potatoes) and *crauti rossi* (a sweetish sauerkraut made from red cabbage). *Carrè affumicato* is pork shank that is first smoked, then boiled. *Selvaggine,* or wild game, comes in the form of *capriolo* (fawn), *cervo* (venison), or *camoscio* (chamois/antelope). Game is eaten smoked and thinly sliced in *antipasti;* in meat sauce *(ragù)* with fresh pasta or as ravioli stuffing; or in entrées, as tender chunks grilled or roasted in a rich sauce *(spezzatino).*

For dessert, strudel is everywhere, filled with the harvest from this region's renowned apple orchards. Cakes and pies are loaded with other locally grown fruits, raisins, and nuts. *Kaiserschmarrn* is an interesting alternative: a tall, eggy crêpe prepared with raisins and topped with powdered sugar and red currant jam.

Bier (birra) is king in the Alto Adige (the best-known brand, Forst, is brewed in nearby Merano), but the wines of the area are well-matched to the local fare. *Magdalaner* is a light, dry red made from Schiava grapes. *Lagrein scuro* is a full-bodied red, dry and fruity, similar to a cabernet sauvignon or merlot. *Gewürztraminer* is a dry white wine with a spicy fruit flavor. For something stronger, try grappa made from Williams pears (and served with a wedge of fresh pear), or *grappa Nocino*—a darker, sweeter brew similar to Jägermeister. *Guten Appetit und Prost!*

at Via Bottai/Bindergasse 6, tel. 0471-973-267).

Ca' de Bezzi/Gasthaus Batzenhäusl is historic. It's Bolzano's oldest inn, with two Teutonic-feeling upper floors; by contrast, the patio and back room are refreshingly modern and untouristy. They make their own breads and pastas, and serve traditional Tirolean fare (€12-14 main courses, daily 10:00-24:00, limited menu outside mealtimes, one of the rare places open on Sun, Via Andreas Hofer/Andreas-Hofer-Strasse 30, tel. 0471-050-950).

Hopfen and Company fills an 800-year-old house with happy eaters, drinkers, and the beer-lover's favorite aroma: hops... or *Hopfen*. A tavern since the 1600s, it's a stylish, fresh microbrewery today. This high-energy, boisterous place is packed with locals who come for its homemade beer, delicious Tirolean food, and reasonable prices. You'll enjoy the friendly English-speaking waitstaff (€10-15 main courses, €7-9 heavy traditional beer dumplings with salad, great €8 salads, daily 9:30-24:00, Piazza Erbe/Obstplatz 17, tel. 0471-300-788).

Paulaner Stuben is a restaurant-pizzeria-*Bierstube* serving good food and a favorite Bavarian beer. It has good outside seating and a take-me-to-Germany *Stube* (€6-7 pizzas and pastas, €7-8 salads, €10-14 main courses, Mon-Sat 11:30-24:00, limited menu from 15:00-18:00, closed Sun, Via Argentieri/Silbergasse 16—or use back entrance at Via dei Portici/Laubengasse 51, tel. 0471-980-407).

Enoteca Il Baccaro, a nondescript hole-in-the-wall wine bar, is an intriguing spot for a glass of wine (€1-4) and bar snacks amid locals. Wines available by the glass are listed on the blackboard (Mon-Fri 9:00-14:00 & 15:30-20:30, Sat 9:00-15:30, closed Sun, located a half-block east of Hopfen and Company on a hidden alley off Via Argentieri/Silbergasse 17, look for *vino* or *wein* sign next to fountain on south side of street and enter courtyard, tel. 0471-971-421).

Gasthaus Fink, a busy diner, serves typical Tirolean and Italian dishes. It has both indoor and outdoor seating on a quiet pedestrian street a few doors off Piazza Walther/Waltherplatz (€8 pastas, €10 antipasto plates, €14 *secondi*, Fri-Tue 9:00-22:00, Wed 9:00-15:00 only, closed Thu, Via della Mostra/Mustergasse 9, tel. 0471-975-047).

Picnic: Assemble the ingredients at the **Piazza Erbe/Obstplatz** market and dine in the park along the Talvera River (the green area with benches past the museum). Or visit one of the three **DeSpar supermarkets:** The largest, with longest hours, is at the end of the Galleria Greif arcade (enter arcade from Piazza Walther/Waltherplatz by Hotel Greif and walk to far end—the supermarket is downstairs; Mon-Fri 8:30-19:30, Sat 8:30-19:00, closed Sun). Smaller branches are on Piazza Erbe/Obstplatz and at Via Bottai/Bindergasse 29 (both open Mon-Fri 8:30-19:15, Sat 8:30-18:00, closed Sun).

Bolzano Connections

From Bolzano by Train to: Milan (about hourly, 3.5-4 hours, change in Verona), **Verona** (about hourly, 1.75-2.25 hours, take €8.70 "R" trains, avoid "fast" trains that take same time for €15-25), **Venice** (about hourly, 3-3.5 hours, change in Verona), **Florence** (every 1-2 hours, 3.5-5 hours, change in Verona and/or Bologna), **Innsbruck** (1-2/hour, 2-2.5 hours, some change in Brennero), **Munich** (called "Monaco" in Italy, 5/day direct, 3.75 hours).

By Bus to: Castelrotto (2/hour, 1/hour on weekends, 50 minutes, generally leaves Bolzano daily at :10, Mon-Fri also at :40; last departure Mon-Fri at 20:10, Sat-Sun at 19:10; pick up free schedule at bus station, €3.50 one-way, €5 round-trip, cheaper with *carta di valore*—see "Tourist Information" on page 215, toll-free tel. 800-846-047 or toll tel. 840-000-471, www.sii.bz.it). The bus leaves from Bolzano's bus station (one block west of train station), stops at the train station, and then winds high into the mountains, dropping you in the center of Castelrotto.

If you're heading directly to **Alpe di Siusi,** take the same bus, get off just past the Seiseralm Bergbahn cable-car station, and ascend on the cable car. For more on Alpe di Siusi, see page 237.

Castelrotto (Kastelruth)

The ideal home base for exploring Alpe di Siusi, Castelrotto (town population: 2,000; district population: 6,000; altitude: 3,475 feet) has more village character than any other town I know in the region. With a traffic-free center, a thousand years of history, an oversized and hyperactive bell tower, and traditionally clad locals, it seems lost in another world. Against a backdrop of mountains, Castelrotto conveys the powerful message that simple pleasures are enough. Stay two nights!

Orientation to Castelrotto

Tourist Information

The helpful TI is on the main square at Piazza Kraus 2 (Mon-Sat 8:30-12:00 & 14:30-18:00, closed Sun except July-Aug 9:00-12:00, shorter hours off-season, tel. 0471-706-333, www.seiseralm.it). If you plan to do any hiking, pick up the TI's list of suggested hikes, including estimated walking times and trail numbers.

For a longer stay, consider the **Combi-Card** (€35/any 3 days out of a 7-day validity period, €44/unlimited usage for 7 days, expires 1 week after time stamp, sold at TI). This card covers the Alpe di Siusi Express bus, Seiseralm Bergbahn cable car, Compatsch-Saltria shuttle bus (Almbus #11), other shuttle buses, regional orange SAD buses—such as the one to Bolzano from Castelrotto, and all trains in the Südtirol/Alto Adige region. For €72, the **Seiser Alm Card Gold** gets you all of the above-listed transport options plus free rides on all Alpe di Siusi lifts.

Helpful Hints

Annual Events: The Oswald-von-Wolkenstein Riding Tournament, held on the first weekend of June, features equestrian medieval-style tournament games, followed by a feast. The town also holds religious processions with locals dressed in traditional costumes, usually on Corpus Christi (June 7 in 2012); the feast day of the village protectors, Sts. Peter and Paul (June 26); and on the local Thanksgiving (first weekend in Oct).

Internet Access: You can get online at the recommended **Alla Torre** hotel, which has an Internet café (Thu-Tue 8:00-23:00, closed Wed, closed April and Nov, behind TI at Kofelgasse 8, tel. 0471-706-349), or the recommended **Residence Garni Trocker** (daily 8:00-20:00, on Fostlweg 3). Or visit the public library (Mon 14:00-18:00, Tue 9:00-12:00, Thu 15:00-19:00, Fri 9:00-12:00, tel. 0471-708-023).

Recreation: A heated outdoor swimming pool with alpine views and nearby tennis courts is near town (€6, mid-May-mid-Sept 9:00-20:00, tel. 0471-705-090, ask at your hotel for details). You can rent a horse at **Ober-Lanzinerhof Tezfen** (tel. 339-868-6868, www.suedtirol.info, Karin speaks some English).

For more excitement, tandem paragliding flights—you and the pilot—depart from Alpe di Siusi and land either where you started or in Castelrotto (tel. 335-603-6400, www.tandem-pilot.com, Marco, Ruben, and Kurt). You can rent skis and snowboards at **RC Sports and Rent** (Via Panider/Paniderstrasse 10, tel. 0471-711-079, Robert—mobile 339-293-9725, Christian—mobile 328-303-8045).

The Dramatic Dolomites

Located in northeastern Italy, the Dolomites have been called the most beautiful mountains on earth, and certainly they  are among the most dramatic. They differ from the rest of the Alps because of their dominant rock type, dolomite, which forms sheer vertical walls of white, gray, and pink that rise abruptly from green valleys and meadows. There is one national park (Dolomiti Bellunesi National Park) in this region, and many regional parks, such as Alpe di Siusi. Rail lines, roads, and a huge system of lifts make this group of mountains very accessible.

Once dubbed the "Pale Mountains" or the "Venetian Alps," this mountain range was named after French mineralogist Dolomieu, who in the late 1700s first described the rock type responsible for the region's light-colored bluffs and peaks. These sedimentary rocks (similar to limestone) were formed in warm tropical seas during the Triassic Period (about 250 million years ago). The marine sediments, along with the fossilized remains of coral reefs and other animals, were buried, hardened, and later scooped upward along with the rest of the Alps by the tectonic-plate action of Africa slowly smashing into Europe. Today, marine fossils are found atop the region's highest peaks, including the skyscraping, nearly 11,000-feet-high Marmolada (east of Bolzano).

During World War I, the front line between the Italian and Austro-Hungarian forces ran through these mountains, and many paths were cut into the range for military use. Today mountaineers follow a network of metal rungs, cables, and ladders called the *Via Ferrata*. One famous wartime trail is the "Road of Tunnels," which passes through 52 tunnels. Along with being a paradise for hikers and climbers, the Dolomites are a popular skiing destination. The 1956 Olympics in Cortina di Ampezzo put the region on the map. A popular winter activity for intrepid skiers is the "Sella Ronda"—circling the Sella massif using a system of lifts and 28 miles of ski runs.

Whether you experience the Dolomites with your hand on a walking stick, a ski pole, or an *aperitivo* while mountain-gazing from a café, it's easy to enjoy this spectacular region.

THE DOLOMITES

Castelrotto

1. Alla Torre (Gasthof zum Turm) Hotel, Rest. & Internet Café
2. Hotel Cavallino d'Oro (Goldenes Rössl) & Rest.
3. Hotel Wolf (Hotel al Lupo)
4. Residence Garni Trocker & Internet Cafe
5. Haus Trocker
6. To Tirler Hof B&B
7. To Villa Pircher, Residence Burghof & Sasso's Wine Bar
8. Saalstuben Restaurant
9. Zur alten Schmiede Pizzeria
10. Stern Café
11. Rubin's Wine Bar
12. Supermarkets (3)
13. Library (Internet)
14. RC Sports & Rent
15. ATM, WC & Phones
16. Mendel Haus
17. Kastelruther Spatzen-Laden Shop

Arrival in Castelrotto

The **bus station** *(Bushof)* is a few steps below the town's main square. The bus parking lot has a shelter with timetables. An ATM, WC, and phones are located in a building to the right. Take the stairs or elevator to get to the main square and TI.

Drivers can park in one of the two underground parking lots—one is near the bus station; the other is on Wolkensteinstrasse just past the recommended Saalstuben Restaurant (first hour free). Each of the recommended hotels also has free parking: For Alla

Torre and Hotel al Lupo, email for directions. For Hotel Cavallino d'Oro, drive through the traffic-free town center, drop off your luggage in front of the hotel, and then park in their garage. The recommended private homes will advise you of your options (see "Sleeping in Castelrotto," later).

Self-Guided Walk

Welcome to Castelrotto

Castelrotto has little to distract you other than the surrounding mountains and hikes. This quick walk will trace the town's history, from the ruling Krauses to yodelers who rule. Note that shops in Castelrotto close for siesta from 12:00-15:00—a good time for a long lunch, a hike in the hills...or a siesta of your own.

• Start in the...

Main Square: Piazza Kraus is named for the family who ruled the town 1550-1800. Their palace, now the City Hall and TI, overlooks the square and sports the Kraus family coat of arms.

Castelrotto uses its square well. The farmers market takes place here Friday mornings in the summer (June-Oct), and a clothing market fills the square most Thursday mornings. While touristy, Castelrotto is not a full-blown resort; if you're on the square weekdays at 14:45, you'll see local moms gather their preschoolers, chat, then stop by the playground on Plattenstrasse. Before and after Sunday Mass, the square is crowded with villagers and farmers (who fill the church) dressed in traditional clothing. The main Mass (at 20:00 on Sat—19:30 in winter—or 10:00 on Sun) is in German. Another Mass takes place in Italian throughout the tourist season (at 11:00) for visitors.

• A landmark in the square is the...

Bell Tower: At 250 feet, the freestanding bell tower dominates the town. It was once attached to a church, which burned in 1753. While the bell tower was quickly rebuilt, the present-day

church was constructed a century later next to the gutted church (which was then torn down to make space for the square). The wire between the church and tower connects the noisy bells. The sacristan can easily ring them using an electric switch.

When you feel the pride that the locals have in their tower—which symbolizes their town—you'll better understand why Italy is called "the land of a thousand bell towers." The bells of Castelrotto—a big part of the town experience—ring on the hour from 6:00 until 22:00. While sleepy tourists wonder why they clang so very early in the morning, locals—who grew up with the chimes—find them comforting. The bells mark the hours, summon people to work and to Mass, announce festivals, and warn when storms threaten. In the days when people used to believe that thunder was the devil approaching, the bells called everyone to pray. (Townspeople thought the bells' sound cleared the clouds.) Bells ring big at 7:00, noon, and 19:00. The biggest of the eight bells (7,500 pounds) peals only on special days. On Fridays, the bells ring at 15:00, commemorating Christ's sacrifice at the supposed hour of his death. The colorful poles in front of the church (yellow-and-white for the Vatican, red-and-white for Tirol) fly flags on festival days.

• *Also on the square is the...*

Church: Before entering, notice the plaque on the exterior. This commemorative inscription honors the tiny community's WWI dead—*Dorf* means from the village itself, and *Fraktion* is from an outlying district. Stepping into the church, you're surrounded by harmonious art from about 1850. The church is dedicated to Sts. Peter and Paul, and the paintings that flank the high altar show how each was martyred (crucifixion and beheading). The pews (and smart matching confessionals) are carved of walnut wood.

• *Back outside, belly up to the...*

Fountain: Opposite the bell tower, Castelrotto's fountain dates from 1884. St. Florian, the protector against fires, keeps an eye on it today as he did when villagers (and their horses) first came here for a drink of water.

• *With your back to the bell tower, look a half-block down the lane to see the finely frescoed...*

Mendel Haus: This house has a traditional facade and a wood-carvers' shop. Its frescoes (from 1886) include many symbolic figures, as well as an emblem of a carpenter above the door— a relic from the days when images, rather than address numbers, identified the house. Notice St. Florian again; this time, he's pouring water on a small painting of this very house engulfed in flames.

Inside Mendel Haus are fine carvings, a reminder that this region— especially nearby Val Gardena—is famous for its woodwork. You'll also see many witches, folk figures that date back to when this area was the Salem of this corner of Europe. Women who didn't fit society's  mold—including midwives, healers, redheads, and so on—were burned as witches.

• *Walk downhill to the left of Mendel Haus, then turn right and climb the stairs. At the top of the stairs, turn left on Dolomitenstrasse. In 20 yards, on the left at the end of the street, is a shop dedicated to Castelrotto's hometown heroes...*

Kastelruther Spatzen-Laden: The ABBA of the Alps, the folk-singing group Kastelruther Spatzen is a gang of local boys who put Castelrotto on the map. They have a huge following here and throughout the German-speaking world. At the big Castelrotto festival on the second weekend in October, they put on hometown concerts—filling this place with fans from as far away as the Alsace, Switzerland, and the Netherlands. They also have an open-air concert in June and a Christmas concert.

Inside this shop—where you'll undoubtedly hear their inimitable music—is a yodelers' Carnaby Street. Downstairs is a folksy little museum slathered with gifts, awards, and gold records. The group has won 13 Echo Awards..."more than Robbie Williams." Watch the continuously playing video (€2 museum downstairs, refunded if you spend €5 in the shop, Mon-Fri 9:00-12:00 & 14:00-18:00, Sat 9:00-12:00, closed Sun, Via Dolomitenstrasse 21, tel. 0471-707-439, www.spatzenladen.it, info@spatzenladen.it).

Sights in Castelrotto

Calvario Stroll—For a scenic stroll, take a short walk around the town's hill, originally the site of the ancient Roman fortress and later the fortified home of the medieval lord. One lane circles the hill while another spirals to the top past seven little chapels, each depicting a scene from Christ's Passion and culminating in the Crucifixion. Facing the TI, take the road under the arch to the right, and then follow signs to *Kofel* (to go around the hill) or *Kalvarienberg* (to get directly to the top). This 15-minute stroll is great after dark—romantically lit and under the stars. (The lead singer of Kastelruther Spatzen enjoyed his first kiss right here.) On a warm day, take the Friedensweg (Peace Trail) from the top of the hill to go back to the town square or below the village. This 30-minute forest walk is decorated with peace-themed artwork by local elementary students.

Marinzen Lift—The little Marinzen chairlift zips you up the

mountain to the Marinzenhütte café, which has an animal park for kids (open when the cable car runs). You can come back on the lift, or it's a one-hour hike down (€7 one-way, €9 round-trip, runs daily late May-mid-Oct 9:00-17:00, July-Aug Wed until 22:00, closed off-season

THE DOLOMITES

and rainy mornings, tel. 0471-707-160, www.seiseralm.it). From the town square, head downhill toward Wolkensteinstrasse, turn left and go another 50 yards down the road toward San Michele, and find the chairlift a few steps off the road on the right, behind the Co-op supermarket.

Nightlife in and near Castelrotto

If you're here on the weekend, the "Nightliner" shuttle bus connects you with local hot spots (Fri-Sat hourly 20:40-4:00 in the morning, schedules at TI and hotels; €2.50/ride, €4/all-night pass). **Rubin's,** next door to the Hotel Schgaguler in Castelrotto (tel. 0471-712-100), and **Sasso's,** on Schlernstrasse in the nearby town of Siusi/Seis (tel. 0471-708-068), are trendy wine bars. Two popular hangouts for the younger crowd in Siusi/Seis are **Santners,** at the Seiseralm Bergbahn cable-car station (tel. 0471-727-913), and the **Diskothek Salegg,** on the left off Schlernstrasse (tel. 0471-704-305).

Sleeping in Castelrotto

(€1 = about $1.40, country code: 39)

$$$ Alla Torre (in German, **Gasthof zum Turm**) is comfortable, clean, and alpine-traditional, with great beds and modern bathrooms (small Db-€82-130, big Db-€98-146, Tb-€140-187, one-night stay-€4 extra, price depends on season—highest in Aug, elevator, free Wi-Fi, free parking, closed April and Nov, behind TI at Kofelgasse 8, tel. 0471-706-349, fax 0471-707-268, www.zumturm.com, info@zumturm.com, Gabi and Günther).

$$$ Hotel Cavallino d'Oro (in German, **Goldenes Rössl**), on the main square, has plenty of Tirolean character and plush, welcoming public rooms. Run by friendly and helpful Stefan and Susanne, the entire place is dappled with artistic, woodsy touches and historic photos. If you love antiques by candlelight, this 650-year-old hotel is the best in town (Sb-€55-70, Db-€95-120, Db suite-€125-190 depending on season, 2 percent discount with cash, discount for 4-night stay, elevator, free Internet access and Wi-Fi, laundry, free parking, Piazza Kraus 1, tel. 0471-706-337, fax 0471-707-172, www.cavallino.it, cavallino@cavallino.it). Stefan converted his wine cellar into a Roman steam bath and Finnish sauna (free for guests, great after a hike, can book an hour for exclusive use)—complete with heated tile seats, massage rooms, a solarium for tanning, and tropical plants.

$$$ Hotel Wolf (in Italian, **al Lupo**) is pure Tirolean, with all the comforts in 23 neat-as-a-pin rooms, most with balconies (Sb-€55-70, Db-€95-120, prices vary with season and view, elevator, pay Wi-Fi, coin-op laundry, free parking, closed April-mid-May and Nov-mid-Dec, a block below main square at Wolkensteinstrasse 5, tel. 0471-706-332, fax 0471-707-030, www .hotelwolf.it, info@hotelwolf.it, Arno).

$$ Residence Garni Trocker is run by the Moser family, who rent 13 great rooms in a place that's bomb-shelter solid yet warm-wood cozy. Their compound is beautifully laid out with a café-bar, garden, and top-notch plumbing (Sb-€34-48, Db-€65-97 depending on season, apartments available, pay Internet access in lobby, Fostlweg 3, tel. 0471-705-200, fax 0471-707-427, www.residence trocker.com, garni@residencetrocker.com, Stefan). Nonsmokers should request a room far from the smoking rooms. Sunday is the family's day of rest; if you're coming on a Sunday, be sure to let them know in advance what time you'll arrive.

$ Haus Trocker, on the edge of town, is a modern home where the delightful Frau Trocker rents two lovely rooms that share one WC. Frau Trocker doesn't speak English, but after you meet her you won't care. Her son Roland can translate for you (D-€50; from the bus station, walk away from the church spire, past Hotel Kastel Seiseralm to Fostlweg 6, then look for yellow *Zimmer* sign at top of steps; tel. 0471-707-087).

$ Tirler Hof, the storybook Jaider family farm, has 40 cows, four Old World-comfy guest rooms, and a great mountain view. The ground-floor double has a private bath. The top-floor rooms share a bathroom and a great balcony. Take a stroll before breakfast (D/Db-€56, discount for stays longer than one night, cash only, open year-round, definitely most practical for drivers; it's the first farm outside of town on the right on road to San Michele, Via Panider/Paniderstrasse 44; tel. 0471-706-017, info@tirlerhof.it).

Near Castelrotto, in Siusi/Seis

These two accommodations are in the hamlet of Siusi/Seis, just five minutes from Castelrotto by bus (see "By Bus from Castelrotto" on page 240). Siusi/Seis has shops, restaurants, a TI, and other services—and the cable car to Alpe di Siusi. Both places listed below will pick you up from the Siusi/Seis bus station.

$$ At Villa Pircher, the friendly Pircher family rents out two view apartments just a short walk or bus ride from the cable-car station. Numerous trails begin nearby (Db-€48-70, price varies by season and number of people, no minimum stay, laundry service, parking, one stop past the Siusi/Seis bus station at Laranzweg 13, tel. 0471-707-440, mobile 339-191-3063, www.villapircher.com, info@villapircher.com, Thomas speaks some English).

$$ Residence Burghof offers fully equipped apartments in a rural setting with beautiful views only 10 minutes from the village. When he's not teaching skiing, English-speaking Patrick Fill

THE DOLOMITES

and his family run this Tirolean retreat (Sb-€48-64, Db-€65-80, Tb-€95-108, price depends on season, discounts for 3-night stay, family rates, sauna, Wi-Fi, free parking, rental bikes available, Burgfriedenstrasse 20, tel. 0471-706-243, fax 0471-706-056, www .residence-burghof.com, info@residence-burghof.com).

Eating in Castelrotto

Note that the first two options are also listed earlier under "Sleeping in Castelrotto."

Cavallino d'Oro Restaurant offers a variety of beautifully presented, homemade Tirolean cuisine—including wild game, *canederli* dumplings, and strudel—in a dressy but relaxed and woodsy ambience. The waiters, Marco and Monica, are very helpful; quiz them before you order. Reservations are smart (€30 meals, daily 18:00-21:00, tel. 0471-706-337).

Alla Torre Restaurant, homier and with the best terrace in town, is another fine option for traditional and international dishes. Try their *risotto ai funghi* (Thu-Tue 12:00-14:00 & 18:00-20:45, closed Wed, closed April and Nov, tel. 0471-706-349).

Saalstuben Restaurant dishes up a selection of reasonably priced Austrian-Italian dishes indoors or on their terrace. If you believe in dessert first, try the Kaiserschmarrn (€8.50), a favorite of Austrian Emperor Franz Josef. You won't need anything else (summer daily 11:30-14:00 & 17:30-21:00, closed Thu in winter, Wolkensteinstrasse 12, tel. 0471-707-394).

Zur alten Schmiede Pizzeria is a great place to enjoy an evening drinking Forst, the local beer, and playing darts (€6-9 pizzas and pastas, Tue-Sun 11:30-14:00 & 17:30-24:00 but kitchen closes at 23:00, closed Mon, outdoor seating, near bus station entrance at Paniderstrasse 7, tel. 0471-707-390).

Dessert: For strudel, locals like the no-nonsense **Stern** café, with its terrace seating (Tue-Sun 7:30-19:00, closed Mon; on Plattenstrasse—facing TI, go left through arch; tel. 0471-706-382).

Picnics: You can put together a picnic at **Euro Spar** (Mon-Sat 8:00-19:00, closed Sun, on Wolkensteinstrasse, tel. 0471-706-222), **M-Preis** (Mon-Sat 8:00-19:00, closed Sun, Paniderstrasse 21, tel. 0471-710-014), or **Co-op/Konsum-Market** (sells locally produced food, Mon-Sat 7:30-12:30 & 15:00-19:00, closed Sun and off-season Sat afternoons, Paniderstrasse 24, tel. 0471-706-330).

Castelrotto Connections

From Castelrotto by Bus to: Bolzano (2/hour on weekdays, 1/hour on weekends, 50 minutes, runs 6:15-19:00; €3.50 one-way, €5 round-trip, cheaper with *carta di valore*—see "Tourist

Information" on page 215; in Bolzano, the bus stops at the more central Bahnhofplatz, or train station—get off here to avoid the 200-yard walk from the bus station, where the bus terminates), **Canazei** (late June-mid-Sept only, 3-4/day, 2-2.25 hours), and **Ortisei/St. Ulrich** and **St. Cristina** (8/day, 30 minutes to Ortisei, then another 10 minutes to St. Cristina). Get bus schedules at the TI, call toll-free tel. 800-846-047, toll tel. 840-000-471, or check www.sii.bz.it or www.silbernagl.it. For **Alpe di Siusi** connections, see the next page.

To Munich: On Saturdays only late May-September, a bus departs Alpe di Siusi at 6:00 and Castelrotto at 6:25, and heads for Munich's main train station (arrives 11:00, €38) and airport (arrives 12:00, €46). You can be picked up at your hotel for an extra €5. For information and booking, contact the Castelrotto TI.

Alpe di Siusi (Seiser Alm)

Europe's largest high-alpine meadow, Alpe di Siusi separates two of the most famous Dolomite ski-resort valleys. Eight miles wide,

20 miles long, and soaring up to 6,500 feet high, Alpe di Siusi is dotted by farm huts and wildflowers (mid-June-July), surrounded by dramatic—if distant—Dolomite peaks and cliffs, and much appreciated by hordes of walkers.

Compatsch, the modern little tourist town at the entrance of the meadow, has a TI, food, two small shopping strips, and services (described later). Don't confuse the village of Siusi/Seis at the bottom of the cable car with Alpe di Siusi—the alpine meadow at the top.

The Sasso Lungo Mountains (Langkofel in German, Long Stone in English) at the head of the meadow provide a storybook Dolomite backdrop, while the spooky Schlern peak stands boldly staring into the haze of the peninsula. The Schlern, looking like a devilish *Winged Victory,* gave ancient peoples enough willies to spawn legends of supernatural forces. The Schlern witch, today's tourist-brochure mascot, was the cause of many a broom-riding medieval townswoman's fiery death.

Alpe di Siusi is my recommended one-stop look at the Dolomites because of Castelrotto's charm as a home base, its quintessential Dolomite mountain views, its easy accessibility for those with and without cars, and its variety of walks, hikes,

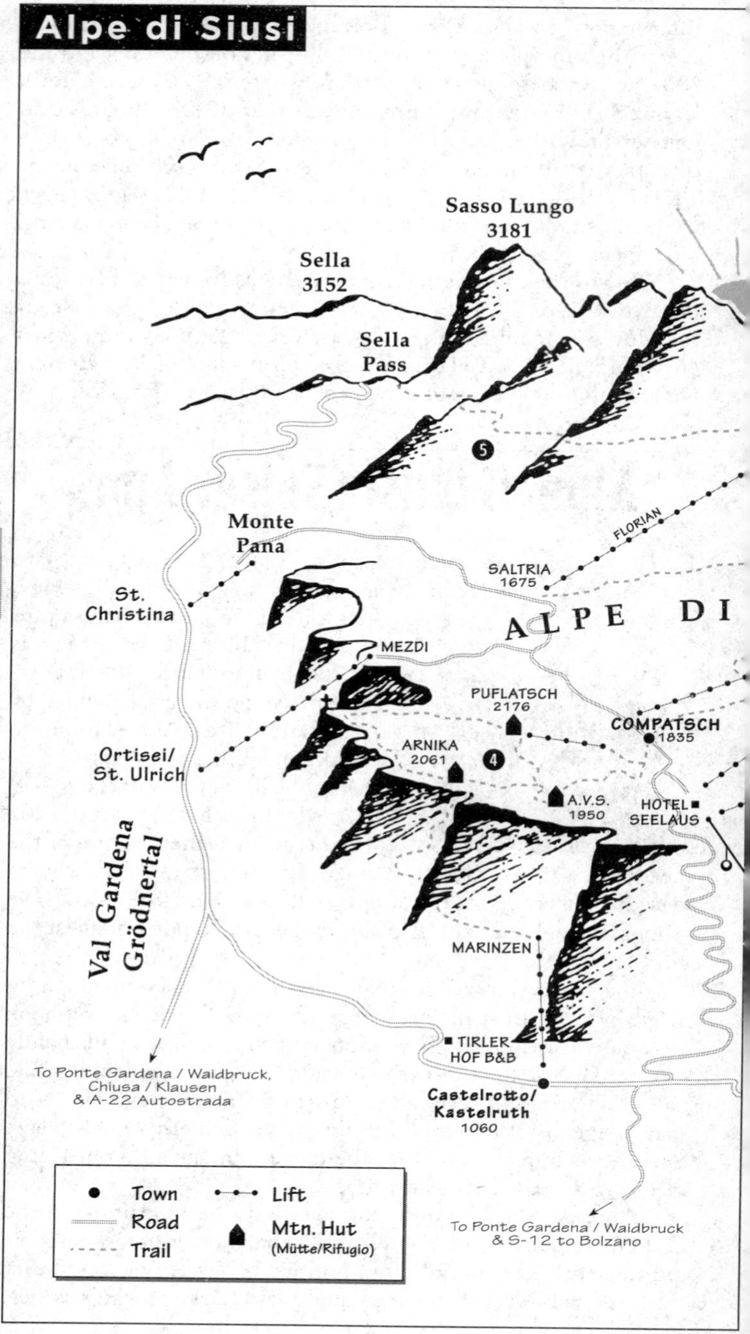

THE DOLOMITES

Alpe di Siusi

Sasso Lungo
3181

Sella
3152

Sella
Pass

5

Monte
Pana

FLORIAN

SALTRIA
1675

St.
Christina

ALPE   DI

MEZDI

PUFLATSCH
2176

COMPATSCH
1835

Ortisei/
St. Ulrich

ARNIKA
2061

4

A.V.S.
1950

HOTEL
SEELAUS

Val Gardena
Grödnertal

MARINZEN

TIRLER
HOF B&B

To Ponte Gardena / Waidbruck,
Chiusa / Klausen
& A-22 Autostrada

Castelrotto/
Kastelruth
1060

Symbol	Legend	Symbol	Legend
●	Town	•–•–•	Lift
	Road	▲	Mtn. Hut
-----	Trail		(Mütte/Rifugio)

To Ponte Gardena / Waidbruck
& S-12 to Bolzano

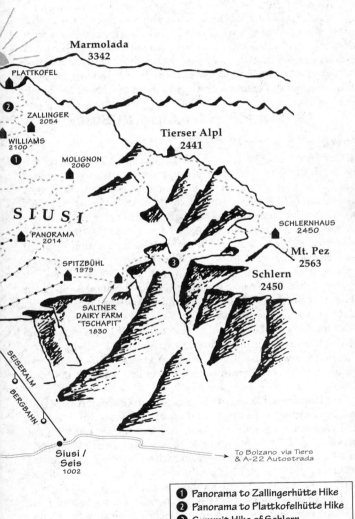

Note: This 3-D view looks southeast & is not to scale. elevations in meters

Marmolada 3342

PLATTKOFEL

ZALLINGER 2054

WILLIAMS 2100

MOLIGNON 2060

Tierser Alpl 2441

S I U S I

PANORAMA 2014

SCHLERNHAUS 2450

SPITZBÜHL 1979

Mt. Pez 2563

Schlern 2450

SALTNER DAIRY FARM "TSCHAPIT" 1830

SEISERALM

BERGBAHN

Siusi / Seis 1002

To Bolzano via Tiers & A-22 Autostrada

❶ Panorama to Zallingerhütte Hike
❷ Panorama to Plattkofelhütte Hike
❸ Summit Hike of Schlern
❹ "Trail of the Witches"
❺ Loop Around Sasso Lungo

THE DOLOMITES

and mountain-bike routes. While most hikers will enjoy the easy meadow strolls, the nearby Schlern tempts and rewards those with more energy and an adventurous spirit.

The meadow is famous for its wildflowers—a fragrant festival (best in June) blooming with flowers that grow only 5,900-7,800 feet above sea level. The cows munching away in this vast meadow produce 2.5 million gallons of milk annually, much of which is sent to Bolzano to make cheese. After tourism, dairy is the leading industry here. While cows winter in Castelrotto, they summer in Alpe di Siusi. The meadow is also dotted with small, idyllic hotels and chalet restaurants. It's extremely family-friendly, with playgrounds at each stop and plenty of animals to pet. Being here on a sunny summer day comes with the ambience of a day at the beach.

Orientation to Alpe di Siusi

Getting to Alpe di Siusi

By Car: A nature preserve, Alpe di Siusi is closed to cars during the day (9:00-17:00), unless you're staying in one of the area hotels. (Show your reservation confirmation as proof.) Parking at Compatsch (€14.50/day) requires that you arrive before the road closes at 9:00 in the morning, though you can drive back down at any time. Park officials encourage visitors to use the free parking lot located at the Seiseralm Bergbahn cable-car station in Siusi/Seis (see below); park your car and take the cable car *(cabinovia)* up to Compatsch.

By Cable Car from Siusi up to Alpe di Siusi: A cable car (Seiseralm Bergbahn) runs hikers and skiers from the village of Siusi/Seis to Compatsch, the gateway to the meadow (late May-mid-Sept daily 8:00-19:00, off-season 8:00-18:00, closed Nov and April-late May, 15-minute ride to the top, €10 one-way, €14.50 round-trip, www.seiseralmbahn.it). From Compatsch, you can take a shuttle bus farther into Alpe di Siusi to Saltria (€1.50/ride, €3/day).

By Bus from Castelrotto: Bus #3 links Castelrotto with Siusi/Seis and stops at the front door of the Seiseralm Bergbahn cable-car station (4/hour mid-June-mid-Oct during morning and afternoon peak times, otherwise 2/hour, 5 minutes). Less-frequent bus #4 connects the cable-car station with Siusi/Seis, Castelrotto, and Ortisei/St. Ulrich (2/hour, June-Oct only). Buses cost €1-4 per ride; one ride is free with a cable-car ticket.

Regional buses (such as the orange SAD bus to and from Bolzano) stop at Siusi/Seis and just below the cable-car station (frequent in summer, 4/day in each direction off-season, €2 one-way).

The Alpe di Siusi Express is a shuttle bus that runs from

Castelrotto all the way to Compatsch—denying you the fun experience of approaching the high meadow by cable car (6/day, 20 minutes, €10 one-way, €14.50 round-trip, see www.silbernagl.it for schedules).

Getting Around Alpe di Siusi

Shuttle Buses: As the meadow is essentially car-free, the park's buses shuttle visitors to and from key points along the tiny road all the way from Compatsch—at the entry to the meadow—to the end of the line at Saltria, at the foot of the postcard-dramatic Sasso peaks (every 20 minutes 9:00-18:30, 15 minutes from Compatsch to Saltria, €1.50, buy from driver). At the end of the day, buses can be jam-packed.

Cable Cars and Chair Lifts: The entire meadow is served by various lifts (marked on maps). These are worth the roughly €5-8 per ride to get you into the higher and more scenic hiking areas (or back to the shuttle buses quickly). Keep in mind that lifts and shuttle buses stop running fairly early (typically at about 17:00)—which can be a major disappointment if you're running out of steam and time, and are still high up after a long day's hike.

Compatsch

This tourist village (6,048 feet) at the entrance to the meadow is served by the Seiseralm Bergbahn cable car from the town of Siusi/Seis. You can drive to Compatsch if you are staying at a hotel in Alpe di Siusi (or if you arrive very early or leave very late, outside of park opening hours). Parking costs €14.50 per day.

Compatsch has a **TI** (Mon-Fri 8:15-12:30, Sat 8:15-12:00, closed Sun, tel. 0471-727-904, www.seiseralm.it/en). The cable-car station has WCs, sporting-goods stores, and restaurants. In the center of Compatsch, you'll also find a grocery store (open early-June–mid-Oct), ATMs, hotels, restaurants, and shops.

Sleeping near the Park Entrance: There are many chalets and huts with rooms for rent in Alpe di Siusi (which generally cost as much as a normal hotel; ask TI for details).

$$$ Hotel Seelaus, a 10-minute walk downhill from Compatsch, is a cozy, friendly, family-run place with an Austrian feel and down comforters (Sb-€65-130, Db-€120-240, Tb-€165-330, suite-€140-265; prices vary with season and type of room; family rates and week-stay discounts; includes buffet breakfast and hearty dinner, free and easy parking, and use of Wellness Center with sauna, hydro-massage, and mini-pool; free Wi-Fi, Via Compatsch 8, tel. 0471-727-954, fax 0471-727-835, www.hotelseelaus.it, info@hotelseelaus.it, Roberto). If you arrive in Siusi/Seis by bus, Roberto can pick you up—arrange in advance.

Helpful Hints

Bike Rental: You can rent mountain bikes at **Sporthaus Trocker** (€8/1 hour, €25/day, mid-May-mid-Oct, between Plaza Hotel and the local bank, tel. 0471-727-824, www.sporthaustrocker .it). There's a world of tiny paved and gravel lanes to pedal on. Pick up their suggested routes and consider those I've described later. Rentable baby buggies are popular for those hiking with toddlers.

Horse Rides: Trocker rents horses and provides guides (about €28/1 hour, €38/2 hours, €54/3 hours, mid-June-Sept, near cable-car station, follow gravel road between Pensione Animone and station to end, tel. 0471-727-807, no English spoken).

Horse-drawn carriage rides are available to the left of the TI (May-Oct 9:00-16:00). Prices vary widely; check the sign near the road for details.

Local Guide: American transplant **Kat Reno** loves sharing her knowledge of South Tirol history and folklore. She offers private walks, hikes, and other alpine adventures (half-day walking tour-€140, mobile 346-663-8340, dolomitefun@live.com).

Hiking in Alpe di Siusi

Easy meadow walks abound in Alpe di Siusi, giving novice hikers classic Dolomite views from baby-stroller trails. Experienced hikers should consider the tougher and more exciting treks. Before attempting a hike, call or stop by the local TI to confirm your understanding of the time and skills required. As always, when hiking in the mountains, assume weather can change quickly, and pack accordingly. Many lifts operate only mid-June through mid-October—check with the TI for specifics on open lifts. Meadow walks, for flower-lovers and strollers, are pretty—for advanced hikers, they're pretty boring. Chairlifts are springboards for more dramatic and demanding hikes. Trails are very well-marked, and the brightly painted numbers are keyed into local maps. Signs also display the next mountain hut along the trail. When asking for directions, most locals will know the trail by the huts it connects rather than its number. For simple hikes, you can basically string together three or four hut names. For anything more serious, invest in a good map, about €6 at the TI. The Kompass Bolzano map #54 covers everything in this chapter (scale 1:50,000). The Wanderkarte map of Alpe di Siusi (produced by Tabacco) offers more detail and focuses on just Alpe di Siusi (scale 1:25,000).

Walks and Hikes from Compatsch

Panorama to Zallingerhütte: The "Easy" Route—This is a basic four-hour walk that is moderately strenuous. It promises fine vistas from both ends of the meadow, fun stops along the way, and lifts up and down on each end. Start by riding the €5 lift to Panorama (6,600 feet), then hike 1.25 hours to Molignonhütte (6,725 feet)—from the chairlift, follow trail #2 across the meadow to the paved road and then join trail #7. Continue hiking two hours to Zallingerhütte (6,725 feet). From here it's a 10-minute walk to Williamshütte (6,888 feet), where you catch the €8 Florian lift back to Saltria and the shuttle-bus stop (for Compatsch). Both Molignonhütte and Zallingerhütte have great restaurants for a drink or meal. For shorter or cheaper versions, you can ride the lift up and stroll back down.

Panorama to Plattkofelhütte: The High Route—For a more thrilling two-hour extension of the previous hike, climb from Molignonhütte (6,725 feet) up to Plattkofelhütte (7,544 feet), follow the high trail #4 along the ridge for an hour, with commanding views both left and right, and then hike steeply back down to Williamshütte (6,888 feet).

Summit Hike of Schlern (Sciliar)—For a challenging 12-mile (six-hour) hike—with a possible overnight in a traditional moun-

tain refuge (generally open mid-June–mid-Oct)—consider hiking to the summit of Schlern and spending a night in Rifugio Bolzano/Schlernhaus. This route is popular with serious hikers as the best hike in the region.

Start at the Spitzbühl chairlift (€5 one-way, €7 round-trip, 5,659 feet, free parking lot, first bus stop in park, www.seiseralm.it), which drops you at Spitzbühl (6,348 feet). Trail #5 takes you through a high meadow, down to the Saltner dairy farm (6,004 feet—you want the Saltner dairy farm at Tschapit, not the one near Zallingerhütte), across a stream, and steeply up the Schlern mountain. About three hours into your hike, you'll meet trail #1 and walk across the rocky tabletop plateau of Schlern to the mountain hotel **Rifugio Bolzano/Schlernhaus** (7,544 feet, €24-30 bunks, some double rooms available, breakfast-€8, open early June-Sept, cold water only, summer only tel. 0471-612-024, off-season tel. 0471-724-094, can reserve by email before hut opens in June, www.schlernhaus.it, info@schlernhaus .it). From this dramatic setting, you can enjoy a meal and get a great view of the Rosengarten range. Hike 20 more minutes up the nearby peak (Monte Pez, 8,400 feet) where you'll find a lofty meadow, cows in the summer, and the region's ultimate 360-degree alpine panorama. From Rifugio Bolzano/Schlernhaus, you can hike back the way you came or walk farther along the Schlern (7 miles, 2 hours; past **Rifugio Alpe di Tires/Tierser Alpl**, 8,005 feet, €21-31 bunks, half-board available for €39-€49, open June-mid-Oct, showers-€3, tel. 0471-727-958 or 0471-707-460, mobile 333-654-6865, www.tierseralpl.com, info@tierseralpl.com) and descend back into Alpe di Siusi, to the road where the bus or cable car will return you to your starting point or hotel.

The "Trail of the Witches"—Take the new cable car from Compatsch to Puflatsch (€5 one-way, €7 round-trip) for the two-hour loop north to Arnikahütte (with a café) and back (elevation gain about 660 feet). An engraved map at the Engelrast (Angel's Rest) observation point near the top of the lift gives the names of the surrounding mountains. Walking among the legendary stone seats of witches, you'll enjoy fine views of the valley all the way down to Castelrotto.

Loop Around Sasso Lungo—Another dramatic but medium-difficulty hike is the eight-hour walk around the Sasso Lungo (Langkofel) mountains, called the Federico Augusto/Friederich August trail. The trail has sections of loose rocks; good shoes are essential. Ride the bus to Saltria (end of the line), take the chair-lift to Williamshütte, walk past the **Zallingerhütte** (overnight possible, €47/person in dorm room, Db-€63, includes breakfast and dinner, open late-May-mid-Oct, tel. 0471-727-947), and circle the Sasso Lungo group (get details and advice from the TI). On the opposite side, at Sella Pass, you ride a lift up Sasso Lungo to the Leo Demetz hut (8,790 feet), cross the saddle between Sasso Lungo and Sasso Piatto, and zigzag back into Alpe di Siusi with breathtaking views of rock climbers.

Trail Running—The new Running Park Seiser Alm includes 46 miles of signed running trails in the meadow. Year after year, the clean air and high mountain altitude attract many international runners, including the Kenyan marathon team (during a one-day event usually held in July, they invite the public to run with them... or at least try). Contact the Compatsch TI for trail info and maps.

Biking in Alpe di Siusi

Mountain bikes are easy to rent, welcome on many lifts, and permitted on Alpe di Siusi lanes. The Compatsch TI has a good information flier that lists the best routes (I've listed three here). Get local advice to confirm difficulty levels and your plan before starting any ride.

Mountain-Bike Rides from Compatsch

Easy High Alp Ride (2.5 Hours, Medium)—This ride stays in Alpe di Siusi and gives you the best basic look at this high meadow, with little altitude gain and easy lanes throughout.

Start from Compatsch (6,048 feet), bike or ride the lift to Panorama (6,600 feet), and take road #7, which runs generally uphill to Punta d'Oro/Goldknopf, and then follows a series of hills and dips to Mahlknechthütte/Molignonhütte (6,725 feet). Then take road #8 downhill to Saltria (5,575 feet) and back to Compatsch (6,048 feet).

Alpe di Siusi Meadow and Val Gardena (4 Hours, Medium to Difficult)—This route covers the great views of the Alpe di Siusi meadow, gets you into Val Gardena (a classic Südtirol valley) to see two resort towns, and then a lift gets you easily back to your starting point.

Start at Compatsch (6,048 feet), and take the road to Saltria (5,575 feet); from the bus stop, ride the unpaved road down to Monte Pana (5,366 feet). From here, an asphalt road zigzags steeply to St. Cristina (4,592 feet on valley floor far below), then heads down the valley to Ortisei/St. Ulrich (4,264 feet), where you take the cable car to Mezdi (6,560 feet, runs late May-Oct, €10.50 one-way, €15.20 round-trip). Complete your loop by rolling back down on a good road to Compatsch (6,048 feet).

Dramatic High Ridge Ride (4 Hours, Difficult)—This ride takes you into the dramatic rocks so characteristic of the Dolomites, with grand views and only the sound of your hardworking body and the rocks under your tires. If you get an early start, you can leave the bike at the Alpe di Tires/ Tierser Alpl hut (8,006 feet) while you hike to Rifugio Bolzano/Schlernhausern near the summit of the mighty Schlern—Monte Pez (2 hours, 8,400 feet).

Start at Compatsch (6,048 feet), ride the paved road downhill for 3.5 miles to Saltria (5,575 feet), then take road #8 for a huge uphill slog to the Tierser Alpl hut (8,006 feet; or you can ride the lift to Williamshütte to avoid half the altitude gain). From the Tierser Alpl hut, return the way you came until just below Hotel Floralpina/Seiser Alm Haus, where you'll take the left fork and follow road #7 to Mahlknechthütte/Molignonhütte (6,725 feet) and on through Punta d'Oro/Goldknopf (6,560 feet), and back down to Compatsch (6,048 feet).

More Sights in the Dolomites

▲▲Great Dolomite Road—This is the definitive Dolomite drive: Belluno-Cortina-Pordoi Pass-Val di Fassa-Bolzano. Connecting Venice with Bolzano this way (the Belluno-Venice autostrada is slick) takes three hours longer than the direct Bolzano-Verona-Venice autostrada. No public transit does this trip. In spring and early summer, passes labeled "closed" are often bare, dry, and, as far as local drivers are concerned, wide-open. Call 0471-200-198 for road conditions (in Italian or German only).

▲▲Abbreviated Dolomite Loop Drive—See the biggies in half the miles (allow four hours, Bolzano-Castelrotto-Val Gardena-Sella Pass-Val di Fassa-Bolzano). Val Gardena (Grodner Tal) is famous for its skiing and hiking resorts, traditional Ladin culture, and wood-carvers (the wood-carving company ANRI is from the Val Gardena town of St. Cristina). It's a bit overrated, but even if its culture has been suffocated by the big bucks of hedonistic European fun-seekers, it remains a good jumping-off point for trips into the mountains. Within an hour, you'll reach Sella Pass (7,349 feet). After a series of tight hairpin turns a half-mile or so over the pass, you'll see some benches and cars. Pull over and watch the rock climbers.

The town of Canazei, at the head of the valley and the end of the bus line, has the most ambience and altitude (4,642 feet). From there, a lift (€5 one-way, €8.50 round-trip) and a gondola (€6.50 one-way, €11 round-trip; or both lifts for €10 one-way, €17 round-trip; late April-late Oct daily 8:30-12:30 & 14:00-17:30, both closed late Oct-late April) take you to Col dei Rossi Belvedere, where you can hike the Bindelweg trail past Rifugio Belvedere along an easy but breathtaking ridge to Rifugio Viel del Pan (Canazei TI for lift info: tel. 0462-609-600, www.fassa.com, infocanazei@fassa.com). This three-hour round-trip hike has views of the highest mountain in the Dolomites—the Marmolada—and the Dolo-mighty Sella range.

▲▲Reifenstein Castle—For one of Europe's most intimate looks at medieval castle life, let the friendly lady of Reifenstein (Frau Steiner) show you around her wonderfully preserved castle. She leads a one-hour tour in German and Italian, squeezing in whatever English she can (€6, open May-Oct; tours Sun-Fri at 10:30, 14:00, and 15:00; mid-July-mid-Sept also at 16:00, always closed Sat, best to call ahead to reserve tour, minimum of 4 people needed for tour to run, picnic spot at drawbridge, tel. 339-264-3752, or TI tel. 0472-765-325, www.sterzing.com).

To drive to the castle, follow the A-22 autostrada toward Brenner Pass, exit at Vipiteno (Sterzing), and follow signs toward *Bolzano*, taking three rights. The castle is just west of the freeway; park at the base of the castle's rock. Of the two castles here, Reifenstein is the one to the west. While this is easy by car, it's probably not worth the trouble by train (6/day from Bolzano, one-hour train ride followed by a one-hour hike).

▲**Glurns**—Drivers connecting the Dolomites and Lake Como by the high road via Meran and Bormio can spend the night in the amazing little town of Glurns (45 minutes west of touristy Meran, between Schluderns and Taufers). Glurns still lives within its square wall on the Adige River, with a church bell tower that has a thing about ringing, and real farms rather than boutiques. The town's short archways seem to cause the locals, whose families go back eons, to take on a Quasimodo-like posture. There are several small hotels in the town, but I'd stay in a private home (such as **Family Hofer,** 4 rooms, €27/person with breakfast, less for 3 nights, cash only, 100 yards from town square, near church, just outside wall on river, Via Adige 1, tel. 0473-831-597, fax 0473-835-864, www.hofer.bz.it, privatzimmer.hofer@rolmail.net).

THE LAKES

Commune with nature where Italy is joined to the Alps, in the lovely Italian lakes district. In this land of lakes, the million-euro question is: Which one? For the best mix of accessibility, scenery, and offbeatness, Varenna on Lake Como is my top choice, followed by Stresa on Lake Maggiore. You'll get a complete dose of Italian-lakes wonder and aristocratic-old-days romance. Bustling Milan, just an hour away from either lake, doesn't even exist. Now it's your turn to be *chiuso per restauro* (closed for restoration). If relaxation's not on your agenda, the lakes shouldn't be either. If you must choose between Lake Como and Lake Maggiore, the former is a better place to linger, while the latter makes a good day trip from Milan.

Lake Como

Lake Como (Lago di Como)—lined with elegant 19th-century villas, crowned by snowcapped mountains, and busy with ferries, hydrofoils, and slow, passenger-only boats—is a good place to take a break from the intensity and obligatory-turnstile culture of central Italy. It seems like half the travelers you'll meet have tossed their itineraries into the lake and are actually relaxing.

Lake Como is Milan's quick getaway, and the sleepy mid-lake village of Varenna is the gateway to the lake and the handiest base of operations. With good connections to Milan, Malpensa Airport, and mid-lake destinations, Varenna is my favorite home base for the lakes. Today, the hazy, lazy lake's only serious indus-

try is tourism. Thousands of lakeside residents travel daily to nearby Lugano, in Switzerland, to find work. The lake's isolation and flat economy have left it pretty much the way the 19th-century Romantic poets described it: heaven on earth.

Planning Your Time
Even though there are no essential activities, plan for at least two nights so you'll have an uninterrupted day to see how slow you can get your pulse.

Getting Around Lake Como
By Boat: Lake Como is well-served by boats and hydrofoils. The lake service is divided into three parts: south-north from Como to Colico; mid-lake between Varenna, Bellagio, Menaggio, and Cadenabbia (Villa Carlotta); and

the southeastern arm to Lecco (Villa Balbianello). Unless you're going through Como, you'll probably limit your cruising to the mid-lake service (boat info: toll-free tel. 800-551-801 or tel. 031-579-211, www.navigazione laghi.it). Boats go about every 30

Boat Schedule Literacy Tips

Feriali	Monday-Saturday
Festivi	Sundays and holidays
Partenze da...	Departing from
Traghetto or *autotraghetto*	Car ferry (walk-on passengers, too)
Aliscafo or *servizio rapido*	Hydrofoil
Battello ship	Slow passenger-only boat going to Como
Battello navetta	Shuttle serving mid-lake only

minutes between Varenna, Menaggio, and Bellagio (€3.70 per hop, 15-20 minutes, daily approximately 7:00-22:30, confirm return trip when you disembark). Overnight stopovers aren't allowed, so buy individual tickets for each ride if you aren't planning to return the same day. The one-day €12 mid-lake pass saves you a little over the cost of three rides. It can be used to make unlimited trips between seven different villages bordering the lake, either on the *autotraghetto* (car ferry) or the passenger-only *battello* (but note that many travelers take only two rides in a day—a round-trip between Varenna and Bellagio).

The free schedule (available at TIs, hotels, and boat docks) lists boat times. Rates are displayed on posters at ticket windows. Confusingly, the schedule requires you to scan four different time-tables to know all the departures:

- car and passenger ferry (mid-lake ferryboat, or *autotraghetto*)
- hydrofoil (*servizio rapido,* costs a third more, enclosed, stuffy, speedy, less scenic)
- all-lake slow boat *(battello ship)*
- mid-lake shuttle ferry *(battello navetta)*

If you find the schedule impossible to decipher, simply ask at each dock when the next boat is leaving and which slip it's leaving from (Bellagio has several docks). Be sure to note whether you are traveling on a weekday (*feriali,* Mon-Sat) or a Sunday or holiday *(festivi).* Review your possible connections (ask your hotelier for help) before you set out so you can pace your day smartly. It's a shame to miss a boat and lose out on a hike or an eagerly antici-pated meal because of confusing timetables.

By Car: With parking problems, traffic jams, and expensive car ferries, this is no place to drive if you don't have to. While you can drive around the lake, the road is narrow, congested, and lined with privacy-seeking walls, hedges, and tall fences. Parking in Bellagio is more difficult than in Varenna. If you have a car in

Varenna, leave it there and use the boat.

While you can rent cars in Bellagio, for most travelers, it's best to take the train to Milan and pick up a car there, either at the central train station or at one of Milan's three airports.

Varenna

This town of 800 people offers the best of all lake worlds. Easily accessible by train, on the less-driven side of the lake, Varenna

has a romantic promenade, a tiny harbor, narrow lanes, and its own villa. It's just the right place to savor a lakeside cappuccino or *aperitivo*. There's wonderfully little to do here, and it's very quiet at night, unless you're here during one of the hundred or so annual American wedding parties. The *passerella* (lakeside promenade, lit at foot level and safe after dark) is adorned with caryatid lovers pressing silently against each other in the shadows. Varenna is a popular destination with my readers and European vacationers—book well in advance for visits in summer (May-Oct). Between November and mid-March, Varenna practically shuts down; hotels close for the winter, and restaurants and shops reduce their hours.

Orientation to Varenna

Tourist Information

Don't count on any tourist information. You may find a small office with sporadic hours at the train station, on the main square, or at the boat dock. Proloco Varenna, on the main square, may be open weekends during high season only (April-July and Sept Sat-Sun 10:00-12:30 & 15:30-18:30, same hours daily in Aug but not Sun afternoon, just past the tobacco shop, tel. 0341-830-367, www.varennaitaly.com, prolocovarenna@tin.it). Your hotel may have the latest edition of the *Varenna Tourist Info* booklet, with updated info on sights around Varenna and a list of restaurants, bars, and services in town.

Arrival in Varenna

By Train: From any destination covered in this book, you'll get to Lake Como via Milan. The quickest, easiest, and cheapest Milan connection to any point mid-lake (Varenna, Bellagio, or Menaggio) is via the train to Varenna. On arrival, set up and limit your activities to the scenic mid-lake area (Varenna and Bellagio).

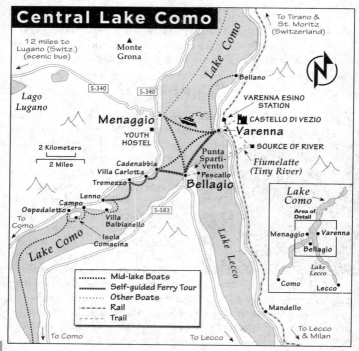

Central Lake Como

To Tirano &
St. Moritz
(Switzerland)

12 miles to
Lugano (Switz.)
(scenic bus)

Monte
Grona

Lago
Lugano

Bellano

VARENNA ESINO
STATION

CASTELLO DI VEZIO

Menaggio

Varenna

YOUTH
HOSTEL

SOURCE OF RIVER

Punta
Sparti-
vento

Fiumelatte
(Tiny River)

Cadenabbia
Villa Carlotta

Pescallo

Tremezzo

Bellagio

Lenno

Campo

Ospedaletto

Lake
Como

To
Como

Villa
Balbianello

Menaggio   Varenna

Area of
Detail

Isola
Comacina

Bellagio

Lake
Como

Lake
Lecco

Lake
Lecco

Como   Lecco

Mandello

.... Mid-lake Boats
━━━━ Self-guided Ferry Tour
━━ Other Boats
╌╌╌ Rail
╌ ╌ Trail

To Como   To Lecco

To Lecco
& Milan

THE LAKES

Here are the specifics: Leaving from Milan's central train station, catch a train heading for Sondrio or Tirano—sometimes the departure board also says "Lecco/Tirano." (Tirano is often confused with Torino...wrong city.) And, if you're heading for Varenna, be sure you don't accidentally catch a train to Verona. All Sondrio trains stop in Varenna, as noted in the fine print on the *Partenze* (departures) schedule posted at Milan's train station. Trains leave Milan about every two hours (€5.75, 1 hour, likely schedule—but confirm these times: 6:20, 8:20, 10:20, 12:20, 14:20, 16:20, 17:20, 19:20, 20:20, and 21:25). Get a second-class ticket, since first-class train cars are rare on the Sondrio-Tirano route. Stamp the ticket in the yellow box at the front of the tracks or risk a €50 fine. Sit on the left for maximum lake-view beauty. Get off at Varenna-Esino. Even though train schedules simply list Varenna, Varenna-Esino is what you'll see at the train station—same place.

Long trains serve Varenna's tiny station and stop for only about a minute. Know what time you're supposed to arrive in Varenna, so you can be ready to disembark with luggage in hand. Otherwise you'll be carried on to the next town and have to backtrack. You may have to open the train door yourself, and because trains can be longer than the station, your car may actually stop before or after the platform (causing you to mistakenly think that you're not there yet). Look out the window. If part of the train's at the station, you'll need to get out and walk to the platform. Tips: Board mid-train to land next to a platform. Leave from the door by which you entered, since you know it's working. If necessary, pull hard on the red handle to open the door.

By Train from Malpensa Airport (Milan): You can take the Malpensa Express train from Malpensa Airport to Milan's central train station (see page 332), then transfer to a Varenna-bound train (see above).

By Boat via Como: For a less convenient but more scenic trip, you can also get to Varenna from Milan via the town of Como (or vice versa). Trains take you from Milan to Como (hourly, 30- to 90-minute ride). It's a 10-minute walk to the dock, where you catch either the speedy hydrofoil or the leisurely *battello* (slow boat—great for enjoying the scenery) for the ride up the lake to Varenna (slow boat: 3/day, €9.30, 2 hours, last departure about 15:00; hydrofoil: 5/day Mon-Sat, 2/day Sun, €13, 1 hour, last departure about 19:00).

By Taxi: A taxi costs roughly €130-165 between Varenna and downtown Milan or Milan's airports. For a reputable taxi service, see "Taxi," page 255.

By Car: In Varenna, look for the color-coded lines to decipher the parking options: white is free anytime; yellow is for residents only; and blue means you pay (look for signs, €1.50/hour, payment times vary—often 8:00-19:00, otherwise free). Buy tickets from the newsstand on the main square, the tobacco shop just south of the square, or Bar Cambusa near the ferry dock, or put coins in the parking meter. Leave the ticket on your dashboard; overnight until 8:00 is OK.

Parking is free Monday-Friday at the train station, but you'll have to pay on Saturdays and Sundays during the high season (8:00-19:00, feed coins into meter at center of the lot and put the printed ticket on the dashboard). If you park elsewhere in town and aren't sure if your spot is legal, check with your hotelier.

Varenna's tight parking will soon be eased by a new parking lot that's scheduled to open at the south end of town, beyond Piazza San Giorgio.

Getting Around Varenna

Varenna is small, and everything is within a 15-minute walk (except for Hotel Eremo Gaudio). From the dock, walk up to the main road to avoid carting your luggage across the cobblestones.

If you'd prefer a taxi, you'll find them waiting at the train station and dock. From either arrival point, a taxi should charge about €9 for a ride to your hotel (see "Taxi," page 255).

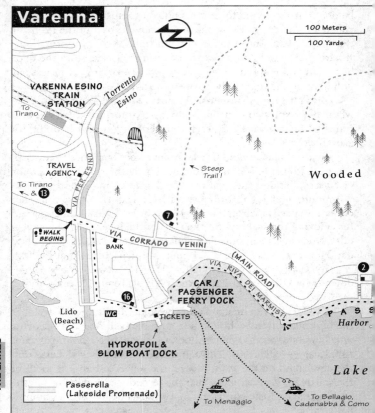

Helpful Hints

Money: One bank is near Varenna's main square; another is located inland from the boat dock. Both have cash machines (see town map).

Internet Access: Try **Barilott,** which also sells some train and local bus tickets, fresh *panini,* and wines by the glass (Internet access €5/hour, Mon-Sat 7:00-20:00, closed Sun, Via IV Novembre 6, tel. 0341-815-045, Claudia and Fabrizio).

Post Office: It's just off the main square (Mon-Fri 8:30-14:00, Sat 8:30-12:30, closed Sun).

Laundry: Lavanderia Pensa Barbara can wash and dry your laundry within 24 hours (€3.50/kilo—about 2 pounds, no self-service, no underwear but socks are OK, Mon-Fri 9:00-12:30 & 15:00-19:30, Sat 9:00-12:30, closed Sun, Via Venini 31, tel. 0341-830-478, mobile 340-466-2977).

1. Hotel du Lac
2. Albergo Milano & Ristorante la Vista
3. Villa Cipressi & Ristorante la Contrada
4. To Eremo Gaudio
5. Albergo/Rist. del Sole
6. Villa Elena
7. Hotel/Rist. Montecodeno
8. Albergo Beretta
9. Rist. il Cavatappi & Osteria Quatro Pass
10. Varennamonamour
11. Nilus Bar, Bar il Molo & La Frulleria
12. Gelateria Riva
13. To Ristorante il Caminetto & Cooking Course
14. Ristorante Isola Nuova
15. Vecchia Varenna
16. Hotel/Ristorante Olivedo
17. Grocery Stores (2)
18. Ornith. & Nat. Science Museum; Internet Café
19. Laundry
20. Villa Monastero Entrance

THE LAKES

Taxi: Reliable **Marco Barili** (or his wife Nelly) will meet you at the train station if you know your exact arrival time in Varenna. He can also get you to Milan and its airports and, unlike other drivers, he doesn't add surcharges for baggage or early/late departures (€130 to central Milan or Linate Airport, €140 to Malpensa Airport for up to 4 people—or €210 for 5-8 passengers in a minibus—€120 to Bergamo's Orio al Serio Airport, tel. 0341-815-061, taxi.varenna@tiscali.it).

Travel Agency: For bus and boat tours, consider Varenna's travel agency, **I Viaggi del Tivano,** next to Albergo Beretta, a block below the train station. They book planes, trains, and automobiles, and can offer half-day and daylong tours of the region and into Switzerland from April through October; book tours by noon the day before (office open Mon-Fri 8:30-12:30 & 15:00-19:00, Sat 9:00-12:00, closed Sun, can book rental cars here but pick up in Lecco, Via Esino 3, tel. 0341-814-009, www.tivanotours.com, info@tivanotours.com, helpful Cristina and Eleonora).

Self-Guided Walk

Welcome to Varenna

Since you came here to relax, this short walk gives you just the town basics.

Bridge Just Below Train Station: This main bridge spans the tiny Esino River. The river divides two communities: Perledo (which sprawls up the hill—notice the church spire high above) and the old fishing town of Varenna (huddled around its harbor). The train station, called Varenna-Esino, is named for a third community situated eight miles higher in the hills. Cross the bridge and follow the river down to the lakeside promenade by the ferry dock. The town's public beach (or *lido*) is just over the cute pedestrian bridge (obligatory lounge chairs for rent, €3/half-day). The inn facing the ferry dock, Hotel Olivedo, has greeted ferry travelers since the 19th century and is named for the olive groves you can see growing halfway up the hill. Natives claim this is the farthest north that olives grow in Europe.

• *Across from Hotel Olivedo is Varenna's...*

Ferry Landing: Since the coming of the train in 1892, Varenna has been *the* convenient access point from "mid-lake" (the communities of Bellagio, Menaggio, and Varenna) to Milan. From this viewpoint, you can almost see how Lake Como is shaped like a man. The head is the north end (to the right, up by the Swiss Alps). Varenna is the man's left hip (to the east). Menaggio, across the lake, is the right hip (to the west). And Bellagio (hiding behind the smaller wooded hill to your left) is where the legs come together, at the point called Punta Spartivento—literally, "point that divides the wind." In a more colorful description, a traditional poem says, "Lake Como is a man, with Colico the head, Lecco and Como the feet, and Bellagio the testicles." (In the regional dialect, this rhymes—ask a native to say it for you.)

The farthest ridges high above the right hip mark the border of Switzerland. The region's longtime poverty shaped the local character (much like the Great Depression shaped the outlook of a generation of Americans). Many still remember that this side of the lake was the poorest, because those on the Menaggio side controlled the lucrative cigarette-smuggling business over the Swiss border. Today, the entire region is thriving—thanks to tourism.

• *Walk past the ferry dock to Varenna's elevated shoreline walk, called the...*

Passerella: A generation ago, Varenna built this elegant lake-

side promenade, which connects the ferry dock with the old town center. Strolling this lane, you'll come to the tiny, two-dinghy, concrete breakwater of a villa. Lake Como is lined with swanky 19th-century villas; their front doors face the lake to welcome visitors arriving by boat. At this point, the modern *passerella* cuts between this villa's water gate and its private harbor. From here, enjoy a good Varenna town view. These buildings are stringently protected by preservation laws; you can't even change the color of your villa's paint.

Just over the hump (which allows boats into a covered moorage), look up at another typical old villa—with a private *passerella*, a lovely veil of wisteria, and a prime lakeview terrace. Many of these villas are owned by the region's "impoverished nobility." They were bred and raised not to work and, therefore, are now unable to pay for the upkeep of their sprawling houses. Lately, these villas are being bought by the region's nouveau riche.

• *At the community harbor, walk to the end of the pier for a town overview, then continue under the old-time arcades toward the multihued homes facing the harbor.*

Varenna Harborfront: There are no streets in the old town—just the characteristic stepped lanes called *contrade*. Varenna was originally a fishing commu-

nity. Even today, old-timers enjoy Lake Como's counterpart to the Norwegian lutefisk: *missoltino*, air-dried and salted lake "sardines." They're served with the region's polenta (different from Venice's because buckwheat is mixed in with the corn).

Imagine the harbor 200 years ago—busy with coopers expertly fitting chestnut and oak staves into barrels, stoneworkers carving the black marble that was quarried just above town, and fishing boats dragged onto the sloping beach. The little stone harbor dates from about 1600. Today, the fishing boats are just for recreation, and residents gather here with their kids to relax by the lake.

At the south end of the harbor (across from La Frulleria), belly up to the banister of the terrace for another colorful town view. Another traditional ditty goes, "If you love Lake Como, you know Bellagio is the pearl...but Varenna is the diamond."

• *Continue straight, leaving the harbor. A lane leads around Hotel du Lac (its fine lakeside terrace welcomes even non–guests for a drink) to the tiny pebbly town beach. From here, climb uphill to the town square, called...*

Piazza San Giorgio: Several churches face Varenna's town square. The main church (Chiesa di San Giorgio) dates from the 13th century. Romantic Varenna is an understandably popular spot for weddings—rice often litters the church's front yard. Stepping inside, you'll find a few humble but centuries-old bits of carving and frescoes. The black floor and chapels are made from the local marble. Outside, past the WWI monument, is the TI and the Ornithology and Natural Science Museum, with its small collection of stuffed birds and other wildlife (both typically open Sat-Sun only).

The Hotel Royal Victoria, also on the main square, recalls the 1839 visit of Queen Victoria, who registered herself as the Countess of Clare in an attempt to remain anonymous. The trees are planted to make a V for Varenna. The street plan survives from Roman times, when gutters flowed down to the lake. The little church on the lake side of the square is the baptistery. Dating from the ninth century, it's one of the oldest churches on the lake, but is rarely open for visits.

As you wander the lanes of Varenna, you'll notice plastic water bottles left out by the doors. Residents believe that these keep cats from peeing on their doorstep. Something about seeing their reflection causes the cats to get self-conscious...

Your walk is over. From this square, you can head south to visit the gardens (described below, under "Sights in Varenna"), north to go to the train station or ferry dock, or east to hike up to the castle.

Sights in Varenna

Castle—A steep and stony trail leads to Varenna's ruined hilltop castle, Castello di Vezio, located in a peaceful, traffic-free, one-chapel town. Start at the stairs to the left of Hotel Montecodeno, and figure on a 20-minute walk one-way. The castle is barren, but livened up by occasional art exhibits and a falconry-training center.

Cost and Hours: €4, daily May-Aug 10:00-19:00, March-April and Sept-Oct 10:00-18:00, Nov-Feb open Sun only 10:00-17:00, closed in bad weather, falconry shows usually around 15:30 but check website or call in morning for times, bar and restaurant at entrance, dinner by reservation only, mobile 333-448-5975, www.castellodivezio.it, info@castllodivezio.it, Nicola.

Gardens—Two manicured lakeside gardens—the terraces of Villa Cipressi and the adjacent, more open grounds of the Villa Monastero—are open to the public. Formerly a noble residence, the Villa Monastero, filled with overly ornate furnishings from the late 1800s, is also open to the public as a museum.

Cost and Hours: Villa Cipressi—€3; May-Nov; Villa Monastero—gardens-€3, gardens and museum-€6, April-Oct daily 9:00-19:00, closed Nov-March, villa closed for lunch 13:00-14:00, bar in garden serves snacks 9:00-18:00, tel. 0341-295-450, www.villamonastero.eu.

Swimming—There are three spots to swim in Varenna: the free little beach behind the Hotel Royal Victoria off Piazza San Giorgio, the central lakefront area by Nilus Bar, and the *lido*. The *lido* is by far the best-equipped for swimmers. Just north of the boat dock, it's essentially a wide concrete slab with sand and a swimming area off an old boat ramp. It has showers, bathrooms, a restaurant, a bar, and the obligatory lounge chairs for rent (€3/half-day, sunshades-€4, tel. 0341-815-3700). Swimming by the boat dock is strictly forbidden for safety reasons.

Speedboat Tours—**Taxiboat** organizes "villa-viewing trips" around the lake, gives personalized tours on the water, and provides a water-taxi service. Their 40-minute "Varenna seen from the water" tour (€10/person, €50 minimum, up to 10 people) is fun, and chartering the boat for 1.25 hours (€140, up to 5 people) gets you a mid-lake tour (May-Sept, mobile 349-229-0953, www.taxiboatlecco.com, info@taxiboatlecco.com, Luca). A similar company works out of Bellagio.

Near Varenna

▲▲Self-Guided Ferry Tour: Lake Como—The best simple day out is to take the *battello navetta* (mid-lake ferry) on its

entire 50-minute Varenna-Bellagio-Cadenabbia-Villa Carlotta-Tremezzo-Lenno route. On the return trip, stop at any sights that interest you (Lenno to see Villa del Balbianello, Cadenabbia for Villa Carlotta, and/or Bellagio). This commentary describes what you'll see along the way.

Leaving Varenna: Looking back at Varenna from the lake,

you'll see the castle rising above the town, with new Varenna on the left (bigger buildings and modern ferry dock), and old Varenna on the right (tighter buildings). The big development high on the hillside is an ugly example of cronyism (without the mayor involved, this would never have happened). Under the castle is a grove of olives (reputedly the most northern ones grown in Italy). Because the lake is protected from the north wind, exotic flowers grow well in the lake's many fine gardens. To the right of Varenna's castle are the town cemetery, a lift up to the recommended Eremo Gaudio hotel (a former hermitage), and a spurt of water gushing out of the mountain just above lake level. This is the tiny Fiumelatte, Italy's shortest river.

Mid-Lake: The Swiss Alps rise to the north. Across the lake is Menaggio, and just over the ridge from that is Lugano and the "Swiss Riviera." The winds alternate between north and south. In pre-industrial times, traders harnessed the wind to sail up and down the lake. Notice the V-shaped, fjord-like terrain. Lake Como is glacier-cut. And at more than 1,200 feet deep, it's Europe's deepest lake. You'll cruise past the Punta Spartivento, the point that literally splits the wind, and where the two "legs" of the lake join (Lake Lecco is on the left, to the east, and Lake Como on the right).

Approaching Bellagio: Survey the park to the left of Punta Spartivento—it's a pleasant walk from town. Bellagio has 10 times

the number of hotel rooms as Varenna, as you can see upon approach. The town, with its strip of three-star hotels, is bookended by Villa Serbelloni (5 stars) on the left, dominating the lakefront, and the sprawling Grand Hotel Bretagne (4 stars) on the right. In the 19th century, aristocratic Russians hung out in the Serbelloni, and well-heeled English chose the Bretagne. These days, the Serbelloni is the second-most luxurious hotel on the lake after Villa Este, while Bretagne is mired in a long renovation project.

Approaching Cadenabbia: From Bellagio, you cross the lake to Cadenabbia. Above Cadenabbia, the Church of St. Martin seems stranded halfway up the mountain. This side of the lake has nearly all the area's traffic, thanks to a big road that ended up separating many fine lakefront gardens from their villas. Farther north is the village of Dongo, where Mussolini and his girlfriend were captured in the last months of World War II as they tried to escape into Switzerland. They were shot here on the lake, and their bodies were hung ingloriously in Milan for public viewing.

Villa Carlotta: Because of lake taxes and high maintenance costs, owners of once-elite villas have been forced to turn them into hotels or to open their doors to the paying public. This is an example of the latter. One of the finest properties on the lake, Villa Carlotta is most visited for its Canova statue and lush garden (see listing on page 275).

Tremezzo: Notice the Grand Hotel Tremezzo, with its striking Liberty-style (Art Nouveau) facade and swimming pool floating on the lake. Above the town is a villa built in the 19th-century Romantic Age to resemble a medieval castle. After the Tremezzo stop (just before the Tremezzo church), you'll see a fine public park with a fountain. When the road separated this land from its villa, its owners gave it to the community. Here the lake is dotted by a string of fine old villas with elegant landings and gated boathouses. Built in the days before motors, they are now too small for most modern lake boats. Tullio Abbate is famous in this area for building speedy, high-end lake boats.

Lenno: This is your last stop. About 400 yards farther along the shore is a tiny dock for shuttle boats headed for Villa del Balbianello (of *Star Wars: Episode II* and *Casino Royale* fame—see page 276).

Sailing Home: From here you return to Bellagio or Varenna, stopping along the way as you like.

Hiking—The town of Fiumelatte, about a half-mile south of Varenna, was named for its milky river. It's the shortest river in Italy (at 800 feet) and runs—like most of the area tourist industry—only from April through September. The *La Sorgente del Fiumelatte* brochure, available at Varenna's TI or at the travel agency, lays out a walk from Varenna to the Fiumelatte, then to the castle, and back. It's a 30-minute hike to the source *(sorgente)* of the river (at Varenna's monastery, take the high road, drop into the tranquil and evocative cemetery, and climb steps to the wooded trail leading to the peaceful and refreshing cave from which the river spouts).

For a longer hike in the opposite direction with lake views, ask the TI about the Wayfarers' Path (hike one-way up the lake, about 1.5 hours, not quite as steep as Fiumelatte hike). You can return by train from Bellano (€1.20, Bellano not included on mid-lake pass, check schedule before you go), or take the ferry to Menaggio and catch a connecting boat back to Varenna.

▲**Cooking Course**—Chef Moreno of the recommended Ristorante il Caminetto picks you up in Varenna, zips you up the mountain to his restaurant (experience Italian driving!), and then teaches you some basics of Italian cooking. Learn how to handcraft fresh pasta or prep regional specialties. Classes last about three hours, plus add time to *mangiare* (€40 includes trip, lesson, and lunch complete with wine, cookies, and coffee; Mon, Tue, Thu, and Fri; 10:00 pick-up from Varenna landing, return by 16:00, reservations mandatory, tel. 0341-815-225, www.ilcaminettoonline .com, info@ilcaminettoonline.com). People love the experience and find Moreno a charming teacher and host.

Sleeping in Varenna

Reservations are tight in August, snug May through October, and wide open most of the rest of the year. Many places close in winter. High-season prices are listed here; prices get soft off-season (Nov-April).

$$$ Hotel du Lac, filling a refined and modernized 19th-century villa, is the finest hotel in town. From its exclusive private perch on the point, it offers a quiet lakefront breakfast terrace, generous public spaces, a friendly, professional staff, and 16 delightful rooms—all but three with lake views (standard Db-€190, bigger Db-€245, these high-season prices are for May-mid-Oct, €20 less in shoulder season, closed off-season, air-con, Wi-Fi, parking-€15, Via del Prestino 11, tel. 0341-830-238, fax 0341-831-081, www .albergodulac.com, albergodulac@tin.it).

$$$ Albergo Milano, located right in the old town, is graciously run by Egidio and his Swiss wife, Bettina. Fusing the best of Italy with the best of Switzerland, this well-run, romantic hotel has eight comfortable rooms with extravagant views, balconies, or big terraces (Sb-€125, Db-€160, €10 extra for view terrace, €5/day cash discount, no elevator, closed Dec-Feb; from the station, take main road to town and turn right at steep alley where sidewalk and guardrail break; Via XX Settembre 35, tel. 0341-830-298, fax 0341-830-061, www.varenna.net, hotelmilano@varenna.net). This place whispers *luna di miele*—honeymoon (see website for 3-night honeymoon deal). Nearby is **$$ Casa Rossa,** an annex with five

Sleep Code

(€1 = about $1.40, country code: 39)

S = Single, **D** = Double/Twin, **T** = Triple, **Q** = Quad, **b** = bathroom, **s** = shower only. Unless otherwise noted, you can assume the price includes breakfast, credit cards are accepted, and English is spoken.

To help you sort easily through these listings, I've divided the accommodations into three categories based on the price for a standard double room with bath:

$$$ Higher Priced—Most rooms €150 or more.
  $$ Moderately Priced—Most rooms between €100-150.
    $ Lower Priced—Most rooms €100 or less.

Prices can change without notice; verify the hotel's current rates online or by email. For other updates, see www.ricksteves.com/update.

comfortable rooms and two apartments that work well for families (Db-€130-160, proportionately more for third or fourth person, breakfast served at main hotel). Their Ristorante la Vista is worth considering for dinner.

$$ Villa Cipressi is a sprawling, centuries-old lakeside mansion with 33 warmly outfitted, modern rooms. Its public spaces are often busy with wedding parties. Rooms without views face the street and can be noisy. The villa sits in a huge, quiet terraced garden that non-guests pay to see (Sb-€130, non-view Db-€160, view Db-€180-190, extra cot-€40, extra bed-€60, prices promised with this book, elevator, Internet access, Wi-Fi, garden access, free mountain bike use for guests, Via IV Novembre 22, tel. 0341-830-113, fax 0341-830-401, www.hotelvillacipressi.it, info@hotelvilla cipressi.it, Davide).

$$ Eremo Gaudio stands out with a commanding lake view high above Varenna. Once an orphanage, it became a hermitage run by the Catholic Church, and then—since 2000—a modern hotel accessed by a private funicular. Perfect for monks with champagne tastes, it's peaceful, with awe-inspiring view balconies and a breakfast terrace. Thirteen bright, plain-but-comfy rooms climb up the main building, and 15 less dramatic but equally comfortable rooms huddle below at the foot of the funicular (upper rooms: Sb-€100, Db-€120, Db with balcony-€135; lower rooms: Db-€110-135; 5 percent discount with cash and 2-night stay, closed Nov-Feb, all rooms have lake views, air-con May-Oct, taxi from station recommended, quarter-mile south of Varenna's main square at Via Roma 25, tel. 0341-815-301, fax 0341-815-314,

THE LAKES

www.eremogaudio.it, eremogaudio@yahoo.it). Suppers are served on the terrace, weather permitting.

$$ Albergo del Sole is a no-frills hotel over a basic restaurant right on the town square. Run by a straight-faced family, the hotel has seven comfy rooms and no hint of a lake view (Sb-€70-85; Db-€120, €105 off-season; fans, hardwood floors, shiny bathrooms, Wi-Fi, no elevator, Piazza San Giorgio 17, tel. & fax 0341-815-218, www.albergodelsole.lc.it, albergo.sole@virgilio.it).

$ Villa Elena, a grandmotherly, low-energy place on the main square, offers a tranquil rest and the best budget beds in town. English-speaking Signora Seta ("Silk") Vitali, who lives downstairs, rents her three characteristic, antique-filled rooms at the same price—room #1 has a shabby bathroom and view terrace (first come, first served); room #3 also has a private bathroom, but room #2 does not. With only twin beds, it's not for romantics, but it is a great value (D-€50 with or without bath, cash only, no breakfast, it's the house with the vine-covered pergola at Piazza San Giorgio 7 near Via San Giovanni, tel. 0341-830-575, www.villaelenavarenna.it, info@villaelenavarenna.it).

$ Hotel Montecodeno, with 11 decent rooms and no views, is a functional concrete box just off the main road between the train station and lake (Sb-€70, Db-€90, extra bed-€10, air-con, Internet access, pay Wi-Fi, attached restaurant serves fresh fish and a €23 "Rick Steves" fixed-price meal if you show this book; if you stay 3 nights and pay cash, you get one meal included per guest or a 15 percent cash discount—take your pick; Via della Croce 2, tel. 0341-830-123, fax 0341-815-227, www.hotelmontecodeno.com, hmcodeno@tin.it, kind Marina Castelli and Lucia). Their nearby apartment sleeps up to five for €35-40 per person.

$ Albergo Beretta, on the main road a block below the station, has 10 pleasant rooms, several with balconies (and street noise). Second-floor rooms are quietest. This place, above a coffee shop that doubles as the reception, feels homey but lacks any lakeside glamour (D-€60, Db-€70, larger room-€80, extra bed-€12, breakfast-€6 but free with this book, no elevator, Via per Esino 1, tel. & fax 0341-830-132, www.hotelberetta.it, hotelberetta@iol.it, Signora Tosca doesn't speak English, but Giulia and Ariana do).

Eating in Varenna

Dining with a Lake View

Ristorante la Vista, at Albergo Milano, feels like a private hotel restaurant but also welcomes non-guests. On a balmy evening, their terrace overlooking the town and the lake is hard to beat. Egidio (or Egi—pronounced "edgy") and his staff give traditional cuisine a creative twist, and his selection is great for foodies with discerning tastes. I'd go with his €38 three-course fixed-price dinner (Mon and Wed-Sat 19:00-22:00, closed Sun and Tue, reservations required, Via XX Settembre 35, tel. 0341-830-298).

Ristorante la Contrada, with its terrace-side location, is run by the Villa Cipressi and takes advantage of the villa's elegant garden, trickling fountain, and lake view. Indoor seating glows with a warm and romantic air, and the garden is a delight on warm summer evenings. Fresh daily specialties and professional service make this a worthwhile splurge. However, weddings and conference groups can crowd the place and distract from the service (€35 meals plus wine, daily 12:30-14:00 & 19:15-21:30, may close for weddings, Via IV Novembre 22, tel. 0341-830-113).

Dining Without a Lake View

Ristorante il Cavatappi, a tiny place on a quiet lane just off the town square, serves old-time specialties, such as the antipasto *missoltino,* the air-dried lake fish that natives like more than tourists do. Helpful owner-chef Mario is happy to be considered a lunatic gourmet. With just five tables, he can connect personally with diners. Talk with him, make a plan, then let him loose. Plan on spending €28-38 plus wine (Thu-Tue 12:30-14:30 & 19:30-21:45, closed Wed, reservations recommended for dinner, tel. 0341-815-349).

Varennamonamour, a new upscale eatery hiding just up from the water, is sure to become popular with fashionable Italians. Its original menu (mainly fish) has a nouvelle cuisine flair, with some unlikely pairings such as guinea fowl and pumpkin dumplings. The cream-and-brown modern decor harmonizes well with the original exposed stone walls to create a classy, welcoming space (€13 pastas, €16 *secondi,* Wed-Sat 12:00-15:00 & 19:00-22:00, Sun 12:00-15:00, closed Tue, Contrada Scoscesa 7, tel. 033-181-4016, Constantino family).

Osteria Quatro Pass is a welcoming bistro known for its homemade pasta and fish. It offers 10 candlelit tables under picturesque vaults, plus sidewalk seating (Thu-Tue 12:00-14:00 & 19:00-22:00, closed Wed, Via XX Settembre 20, tel. 0341-815-091, Lollo).

Eating Simply on the Harbor

The harborfront is lined with several simple eateries, all with great lakefront seating.

Nilus Bar, with a young waitstaff, serves dinner crêpes, pizzas, big mixed salads, hot sandwiches, soup of the day, and cocktails with a smile. Pricing includes cover and service (March-Nov Wed-Mon 12:00-22:30, hours can vary and bar open longer, closed Tue and Dec-Feb, cash only, tel. 0341-815-228, Fulvia and Giovanni).

Bar il Molo, next door, is good for a casual meal on the harbor (€9 pizzas and pastas, salads, toasted sandwiches, daily 11:00-24:00, tel. 0341-830-070). They also have a room full of gifty edibles for sale.

La Frulleria is a sweet stop for drinks and desserts. It's a youthful place serving cold, sugary, and fruity treats from a fun menu. If you're eating dinner elsewhere without a lake view, consider skipping dessert and coming here for your finale. To sit at a lakeside table, you must order from the menu (€4-6 menu items, April-Oct Tue-Sun 12:00-24:00, closed Mon and Nov-March, two doors down from Nilus Bar, Samantha).

At **Gelateria Riva,** you can get a cup or cone to go, then grab a pillowy seat on the bulkhead. Duillo is the only guy in town who prepares his gelato fresh every day. Try his *nocciola* (hazelnut) before making your choice. Ask the day before if you want to watch the gelato being made (daily 13:00-21:00, open later June-Aug, closed off-season).

Eating Simply Without a Lake View

Ristorante del Sole, facing the town square, serves edible meals and Neapolitan-style pizzas (€5-9). Making few concessions to the tourist crowds, this family-friendly restaurant caters to residents, providing a fun atmosphere, a cozy, walled-in garden in back, and tables on the square (daily 12:00-15:00 & 19:00-22:00, pizza until 24:00, Piazza San Giorgio 21, tel. 0341-815-218).

Ristorante il Caminetto is a homey, backwoods mountain trattoria in Gittana, a tiny town high above Varenna. Getting there entails a curvy 10-minute drive—they'll pick you up for free in Piazza San Giorgio at 19:30, deliver you to the restaurant, and then dish up classic fare at small-town prices. Specialties such as grilled meats and risotto with porcini mushrooms and berries are made with pride by husband and wife Moreno and Rossella. This is a good place to set a price and trust your host to bring whatever's best (€16-20 *dégustation* menu, wine extra, Thu-Tue 12:30-14:30 & 19:30-21:30, closed Wed, reservations mandatory to confirm pickup from Varenna at 19:30, Viale Progresso 6, tel. 0341-815-225 or 0341-815-127, mobile 347-331-2238).

Other Eateries

Ristorante Montecodeno, a cozy little place on the big road in the new part of town, serves a plate of eight different tasty lake fish specialities (including *missoltino*) prepared by chef Ferruccio. **Ristorante Isola Nuova** is a newish restaurant with a fresh atmosphere, buried in the old town with no sea view. The venerable **Vecchia Varenna** is the only classy restaurant actually on the harbor (old place with new management). And at **Hotel Olivedo,** a grand old hotel facing the ferry dock, you can eat in a classic dining hall.

Picnics: Varenna's two little grocery stores have all you need for a tasty balcony or breakwater picnic-dinner. The *salumeria* on the square is best for meats, cheese, and bread; try their homemade salami (Tue-Sat 7:30-12:30 & 15:30-19:30, Sun-Mon 7:30-12:30 only). The store just north of the main square by the pharmacy stocks fresh fruits and veggies (daily 7:30-12:30, Tue-Sat also 16:00-19:30).

Varenna Connections

If leaving Varenna by train, you can't purchase tickets at the station. Instead, you'll have to buy them from the Barilott tobacco shop just off the main square, or from the travel agency, I Viaggi del Tivano, next door to the recommended Albergo Beretta hotel (see "Helpful Hints," earlier). Stamp your ticket in the yellow machine at the station before boarding. If both places are closed, win the sympathy of the conductor and buy your ticket on board for an additional fee. (Seek him out. If he finds you, you'll likely be charged a stiff penalty.)

Varenna to Milan by Train: Trains leave Varenna for Milano Centrale (€5.75, 1 hour, likely schedule for daily and direct trains: 5:36, 6:23, 6:39, 7:37, 8:37, 10:37, 12:37, 14:37, 16:37, 18:37, 20:37, 21:37, and 22:21; if you board a train at a time not listed here, it's likely a local milk-run train that will take twice as long).

Varenna to Stresa by Train: Trains run about every two hours (2.75-4 hours, transfer in Milan).

Varenna to St. Moritz in Switzerland by Train: From Varenna, you have easy access to the Bernina Express scenic train to St. Moritz. Note that this is only realistic from April through October. First, take the train to Tirano, and then transfer to the Bernina Express train to St. Moritz (4/day, allow 4-5 hours with transfer; for details see www.rhb.ch—click "E" for English). For information and a timetable for this route, stop by the I Viaggi del Tivano travel agency (see "Helpful Hints," earlier), or ask your hotelier for the handy tourist information book produced by local travel agencies. Don't forget your passport for trips into Switzerland.

Bellagio

The self-proclaimed "Pearl of the Lake" is a classy combination of tidiness and Old World elegance. If you don't mind that "tramp in a palace" feeling, it's a fine place to shop for ties and umbrellas while surrounding yourself with the more adventurous posh travelers.

THE LAKES

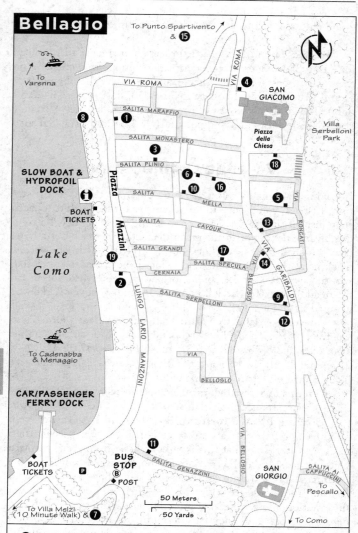

Bellagio

1. Hotel Florence
2. Hotel/Rist./Snack Bar Metropole
3. Hotel Centrale
4. Albergo Europa
5. Bellagio B&B Apartments
6. Il Borgo Apartments
7. To Giardini di Villa Melzi Apartments
8. The Florence Ristorante
9. Trattoria San Giacomo
10. Rist. Terrazza Barchetta
11. Enoteca Cava Turacciolo
12. Aperitivo Et Al
13. Gelateria del Borgo
14. Gilardoni Alimentari
15. To La Punta Ristorante
16. Internet Café
17. Launderette
18. Villa Serbelloni Park Tickets
19. Bellaggio Water-Taxi Lake Tours

Heavy curtains between the harborfront arcades create welcome shade and keep visitors and their poodles from sweating. Thriving yet still cute, Bellagio is a much more substantial town than Varenna (which has one-tenth the number of hotel beds and almost no shops).

Orientation to Bellagio

Tourist Information

The TI is right downtown, at the passenger boat dock (April-Oct Mon-Sat 9:00-12:30 & 13:00-18:00, Sun 10:00-14:00; Nov-March shorter hours and closed Sun and Tue; tel. 031-950-204, www .bellagiolakecomo.com). The TI offers a guided tour of nearby hamlets (Mon only at 9:15, €10, 2.5 hours, meet in office inside bell tower on church square).

Arrival in Bellagio

Bellagio is best reached via ferry from Varenna (€3.60); or by ferry, hydrofoil, or slow boat from Como. (For ferries, see pages 249; for hydrofoils and slow boats, see page 252.)

By Boat: Bellagio has two docks a few minutes' walk apart. The northern docks are for the passenger-only slow boat (*battello* or *battello navetta*) and the hydrofoil *(servizio rapido)*. The southern dock is for all "ferry boats" *(traghetti):* both the car ferry (cars and foot passengers) and the passenger-only ferry. Ask around to make sure you're waiting at the correct dock. Remember that if you want to know all your departure options beyond Varenna, Cadenabbia, and Menaggio, you need to study four different timetables (see "Getting Around Lake Como," page 249). Confirm your intentions at the kiosk near either dock.

By Car: Parking is difficult, but you can try for a spot near the lakeside or in the parking lot at the ferry dock (white lines are always free, yellow lines are for residents only, blue lines cost €1.50/hour—pay with coins in gray or blue machines and stick ticket in car window).

Helpful Hints

Internet Access: Bellagio Point has a slick Internet café, complete with great sandwiches, wine-tasting options, and free Wi-Fi if you buy a drink (€2/15 minutes, daily 10:00-22:00, Salita Plinio 8, tel. 032-950-437, www.bellagiopoint.com). Julio also rents apartments (listed later, under "Sleeping in Bellagio").

THE LAKES

Post Office: It's on the south end of Lungo Lago Mazzini (Mon-Fri 8:30-14:00, Sat 8:30-12:30, closed Sun).

Laundry: La Lavandera is bright and new. Don't be discouraged if it looks closed; the lights come on automatically when you enter (€7.50 wash/dry, open daily 24 hours, Salita Carlo Grandi 21—this street is also marked as Via Specula, tel. 339-410-6852).

Sights in Bellagio

Villa Serbelloni Park—If you need a destination, you can take a guided tour of this park, which overlooks the town. The villa itself, owned by the Rockefeller Foundation, is not open to the public.

  Cost and Hours: €8.50, April-Oct, tours Tue-Sun at 11:00 and 15:30, no tours Mon and when rainy, 1.5 hours, first two-thirds of walk is uphill, show up at the little tour office in the medieval tower on Piazza della Chiesa 15 minutes before tour time to buy tickets, confirm time at office, tel. 031-951-555.

Strolling—Explore the steep-stepped lanes rising from the harborfront. While Johnnie Walker and jewelry sell best at lake level, the natives shop up the hill. Piazza della Chiesa, near the top of town, has a worth-a-look church (with its art described in an English-language handout).

  The administrative capital of the mid-lake region, Bellagio is located where the two southern legs of the lake split off. For an easy break in a park with a great view, wander right on out to the crotch. Meander past the rich and famous Hotel Villa Serbelloni, and walk five minutes to Punta Spartivento ("point that divides the wind"). You'll find a Renoir atmosphere complete with an inviting bar-restaurant, a tiny harbor, and a chance to sit on a park bench and gaze north past Menaggio, Varenna, and the end of the lake to the Swiss Alps.

  For another stroll, head south from the car-ferry dock down the tree-shaded promenade. Ten minutes later, you'll pass the town's concrete swimming area (currently under restoration). The grassy, pebbly public San Giovanni beach (no showers) is another 20 minutes farther south from there.

Villa Melzi Gardens—A 10-minute walk south from the ferry dock, this picture-perfect lakeside expanse of exotic plants, flowers, trees, and Neoclassical sculpture was assembled by the vice president of Napoleon's Italian Republic in the early 19th century.

  Cost and Hours: €6, March-Oct daily 9:30-18:30, last entry at 17:30, mobile 339-457-3838, www.giardinidivillamelzi.it.

Hikes and Walks—The TI has free brochures for three well-crafted walking tours, varying from one to three hours, that explore the city and environs. Sites include villas, gardens, churches, an old-fashioned dairy shop, medieval towers, and a nautical instruments museum. The TI also sells a hiking map for €3 that shows four different hikes ranging in difficulty and duration.

Bellagio Water-Taxi Lake Tours—With a small stand at the boat docks, Jennine and Luca offer tours and private service in their luxurious and powerful boat. Their basic 2.5-hour tour, guided by Luca, includes a fun hour on mid-lake, with a float-by of Richard Branson's villa, as well as a stop at Villa del Balbianello (see listing on page 276), where you'll take an English tour.

Cost and Hours: €45 with a 10 percent discount for readers of this book, price includes entry and tour of villa—worth €12, generally at 14:00 but check blackboard for day's offerings or call, mobile 338-524-4914, www.bellagiowatertaxis.com, bellagiowater taxis@tin.it.

Sleeping in Bellagio

(€1 = about $1.40, country code: 39)
This is a "boom or bust" lake resort, with high-season prices (those listed here) straight through from May to September, plus a brief shoulder season (with discounted prices) in April and from October to November. Off-season (Dec-March), nearly everything is closed down.

$$$ Hotel Florence has a prime lakefront setting in the center of town. The 150-year-old, family-run place features 30 rooms, hardwood floors, bold earth tones, and a rich touch of Old World elegance (Sb-€125, Db-€145-200, Db suite-€230-260, prices depend on view and balcony, closed Nov-March, handheld showers, fans on request, Wi-Fi, tel. 031-950-342, fax 031-951-722, www.hotelflorencebellagio.it, info@hotelflorencebellagio.it, run by Austrian Ketzlar family).

$$$ Hotel Metropole, dominating Bellagio's waterfront between the ferry docks, is a grand old place with plush public spaces. Its modern rooms have all the comforts, but also an institutional feel. Many of its 42 rooms have lake views (Db-€160, €180 with balcony, €210 with terrace, air-con, Wi-Fi, stunning roof terrace, tel. 031-950-409, fax 031-951-534, www.albergometropole.it, info@albergometropole.it).

$$ Hotel Centrale, managed with pride and care by Giacomo Borelli, warmly welcomes its guests into a true-blue family operation: Signore Borelli's wife and two sons help out, his mama painted the art, and grandpa crafted much of the Art Deco-era furniture. This place has generous public spaces and many thoughtful touches—and its 17 comfortable rooms are a great value, even without lake views (Sb-€90-110, Db-€110-130, €10/night discount with this book, air-con, elevator, free Wi-Fi, Salita Plinio 7, tel. 031-951-940, fax 031-952-682, www.hc-bellagio.com, info@hc-bellagio.com).

$ Albergo Europa, run with low energy, is in a concrete annex behind a restaurant, away from the waterfront. Its 10 rooms have no charm but are comfortable (Db-€60-90, breakfast-€8, no elevator, free parking, Via Roma 21, tel. & fax 031-950-471, www.hoteleuropabellagio.it, info@hoteleuropabellagio.it, Marchesi family).

$ Bellagio B&B Apartments, with five units for rent, are located behind the *gelateria* at the top of town. Julio also runs the Bellagio Point Internet café, which serves as the reception (Db-€60, more for 3 or 4 people, two-night minimum, no breakfast, Wi-Fi, reception located at Salita Plinio 8, apartments located at Salita Cavour 37, tel. 031-951-680, fax 031-953-0025, www.bellagio bedandbreakfast.com, info@bellagiobedandbreakfast.com). Julio also has three large apartments a 15-minute walk from Bellagio (toward Como); email him for rates.

$ Il Borgo Apartments rents six modern *Better Homes and Gardens*-quality apartments with kitchenettes in the old center at great prices. Easygoing Flavio is available for check-in daily 9:00-12:00, or by appointment (Db-€90, 2 bigger apartments for up to 6 people-€110, cash discount, no breakfast, 2-night minimum required, air-con, Wi-Fi, Salita Plinio 4, tel. 031-952-497, mobile 338-193-5559, fax 031-951-585, www.borgoresidence.it, info@borgo residence.it).

$ Giardini di Villa Melzi Apartments provides modern accommodations in three double bedrooms and three studios with kitchenettes in the little harbor of Loppia, about a 15-minute walk south of Bellagio. A free pass allows guests to take a shortcut to Bellagio through the Villa Melzi Gardens (Db-€630 per week, 30 percent advance deposit required, one-week minimum but shorter stays sometimes possible, cash only, free parking, Via Melzi d'Eril 23, tel. 339-221-4394, www.bellagiowelcome.com, info@bellagio welcome.com, Ornella).

Eating in Bellagio

On the Lakefront

These places offer wonderful lakeside tables and, considering the setting, reasonable prices.

Hotel Metropole Ristorante, while a mediocre food value, has a full menu and is a relaxing delight for a meal with good service (€14 pastas, €16 *secondi*, April-Oct daily 12:00-14:30 & 19:00-21:30, closed Nov-March, tel. 031-950-409).

Hotel Metropole Snack Bar, next to the hotel's restaurant, is quite good, with simple pastas (€9), fine salads, and sandwiches (no cover charge, daily 12:00-21:30, good service, great locale).

The Florence is nicely situated under a trellis of flowers across from the Florence Hotel and away from the ferry fumes. This is a lovely perch for a drink or meal (€16 pastas, €20 *secondi*, no cover charge, simpler lunch menu of salads and such, bar open all day).

In the Old Town Without Lake Views

Trattoria San Giacomo is a high-energy place that's respected for its traditional cuisine, such as *riso e filetto di pesce* (rice and perch fillet in butter and sage). It has daily seasonal specials and an inviting €20-25 fixed-price meal based on regional specialties. Choose between fun seating on a steep, cobbled lane or tight seating inside (Mon and Wed-Thu 12:00-14:30 & 19:00-21:30, Fri-Sun open later midday and evenings, closed Tue, Salita Serbelloni 45, tel. 031-950-329, run by Aurelio).

Ristorante Terrazza Barchetta, set on a terrace with no lake view and bedecked with summery colors, puts a creative twist on regional favorites such as lake fish. Don't confuse it with the street-level bar-trattoria—head up the stairs to the second floor. Reservations are recommended (€15 pastas, €20 *secondi*, Wed-Mon 12:00-14:30 & 19:00-22:30, closed Tue, Salita Mella 13, tel. 031-951-389).

Other Options

Wine-Tasting: Step into the vaulted stone cellar rooms of the funky **Enoteca Cava Turacciolo** to taste three regional wines with a sampling of cheeses, meats, and breads (€18/person with this book, Thu-Tue 10:30-24:00, closed Wed, Salita Genazzini 3, tel. 031-950-975, Norberto and Rosy). **Aperitivo Et Al,** slick and jazzy, is a trendier wine bar, offering mixed *salumi* and *formaggi* plates (€12), big fresh salads (€10), and light lunches, along with a great selection of wines by the glass (€12.50 three-glass tasting—totaling a half-bottle of wine per person, add antipasto plate for €24, also Super Tuscan wine-tastings, Wed-Mon 11:30-24:00, closed Tue, free Wi-Fi, Salita Serbelloni 34, tel. 031-951-523, run by English expat Sarah).

Gelato: Residents agree that you won't find the best *gelateria* in town among the sundaes served on the waterfront. Instead, climb to the top of town to **Gelateria del Borgo** (daily April-Oct 10:00-22:30, closed Nov-March, Via Garibaldi 46, tel. 031-950-755, Stefania and Gianfranco).

Picnics: You'll find benches at the park, along the waterfront in town, and lining the promenade south of town. Pick up your picnic supplies at **Gilardoni Alimentari.** They have roast chicken, ribs, and focaccia, and are happy to make fresh sandwiches to your order (Mon-Sat 7:30-13:00 & 16:00-19:30, Sun 7:30-13:00 only, shorter hours off-season, on corner of Via Garibaldi and Via Carlo Bellosio, tel. 031-951-815).

Punto Spartivento: This dramatic natural park, a 10-minute walk north of town (see "Strolling," page 270), is a great place for either a picnic or a meal at **La Punta Ristorante** (€9 pastas, €13 fish, €22 meat courses, March-Oct daily 12:00-14:30 & 19:00-22:00, bar open through the afternoon for snacks only, closed Nov-Feb, tel. 031-951-888).

Menaggio

Menaggio has more urban bulk than its neighbors. Since many visitors find Lake Como too dirty for swimming, consider spending ing time in Menaggio's fine public pool (look for the "Lido"). This is the starting point for a few hikes. Only a few decades ago, cigarette smugglers used these trails at night to sneak back into Italy from Switzerland with their tax-free booty. The TI has information about mountain biking and  catching the bus to trailheads on nearby Mount Grona (TI in Piazza Garibaldi open daily 9:00-12:30 & 14:30-18:00, closed Sun and Wed Nov-March, tel. 0344-32-924, www.menaggio.com).

Getting to Menaggio: Buses may be making the trip (€13, 1 hour) between Milan's Malpensa Airport and Como—ask at the Airport 2000 ticket desk in the arrivals hall; at Como, change to public bus #C10 to get to Menaggio (€3, about hourly, 1-1.25 hours). Alternatively, take the Malpensa Express from the airport as far as Saronno, where you change for a train to Como (station: Como Lago), then catch the local bus #C10 for Menaggio as above.

Sleeping in Menaggio

(€1 = about $1.40, country code: 39)
$ La Marianna B&B has eight rooms and a fine restaurant in Cadenabbia, about a mile south of Menaggio on a busy road (Db with view-€95, optional €30 dinner, lakeside terrace at restaurant, air-con, free Wi-Fi, tel. 0344-43095, www.la-marianna.com, inn @la-marianna.com, Ty and Paola). The hourly Como-Menaggio bus #C10 stops here, and the ferry dock for mid-lake towns via Bellagio is 300 yards away.

$ La Primula Youth Hostel has a great location on the lake, a two-minute walk from the ferry dock (€17/person in dorm room, Db-€52, family room with bathroom and 4 beds-€74, €3 extra/night for nonmembers, pizzas from €5, Internet access and Wi-Fi, sailing school, kayak and mountain bike rentals, rock-climbing nearby, tel. & fax 0344-32356, www.lakecomohostel.com, info @lakecomohostel.com). The bus from Como (55 minutes) stops right by the hostel.

Menaggio Connections

From Menaggio to Milan: It's a 20-minute ferry to Varenna (boats hourly), where trains connect to Milan (every 1-2 hours, 1 hour, see "Varenna Connections," page 267). More fast trains depart from Como than Varenna. From Menaggio, take hourly local bus #C10 (€3.30, 1-2/hour, 1 hour) to Como, where you can catch the train (hourly, 30-60 minutes).

From Menaggio to Switzerland: Public bus #C12 departs about every hour or two from Piazza Roma for Lugano (€10 round-trip, 1 hour, buy tickets at newspaper shop in Piazza Garibaldi). In summer, the yellow Palm Express bus runs once daily to **Lugano** (1 hour) and **St. Moritz** (3 hours). Off-season (mid-Oct-mid-June), the bus runs only on weekends. Advance reservations are required (www.postbus.ch)—and remember to bring your passport.

More Sights on Lake Como

Villa Carlotta
If you plan to tour one of Lake Como's famed villas, this is the best for gardens and flowers (its forte). I see the lakes as a break from Italy's art, but if you're in need of a place that charges admission, Villa Carlotta offers an elegant Neoclassical interior, Antonio Canova's famous *Maddalena Penitente* statue, and a garden (the highlight—at its best in spring).

Cost and Hours: €8.50, daily April-mid-Oct 9:00-19:00, until 17:00 last 2 weeks of March and mid-Oct-mid-Nov, closed mid-Nov-mid-March, no photos inside the villa, tel. 034-440-405, www.villacarlotta.it.

Nearby: Tremezzo and **Cadenabbia** are pleasant lakeside resorts, each one an easy walk away. Boats serve both places (5-minute walk from either dock to the villa) and are reached by *traghetto* (ferry, dock in Cadenabbia) or the *battello* (slow boat, dock in Tremezzo).

To visit **Villa del Balbianello** (see below) after you see Villa Carlotta, catch the blue #C10 bus (turn right when exiting the villa and walk to the trash cans; bus departs at 11:10, 11:58, 13:05, 13:57,

14:36, 15:06, and 15:36; €1.20, pay on bus). Get off at the second stop in Lenno, walk 30 yards, turn left, and follow the signs.

Villa del Balbianello

On a romantic promontory overlooking Lake Como and facing Bellagio is the dreamiest villa on the lake. Built for a cardinal at the end of the 18th century on the remains of an old Franciscan church, the villa was the cardinal's palace of delights, where he could study and brainstorm with his friends. Today it reflects the exotic vision of its last owner, explorer Guido Monzino, who died in 1988—leaving the villa, his rich art collection, and mementos of his expeditions to the state. The upper floor serves as a museum of his expeditions, with memorabilia from his North Pole and Mount Everest adventures. The real masterpiece here is the terraced garden and elegant loggia, where the land fits the architecture and landscaping in a lovely way. This is a favorite choice for movie directors when they need a far-out villa to feature; scenes from *Casino Royale* and *Star Wars: Episode II* were filmed here.

Cost and Hours: Garden only-€6, garden with villa tour-€12, Thu-Sun and Tue 10:00-18:00, closed Mon and Wed, tel. 034-456-110, www.fondoambiente.it.

Getting There: You can reach it on **foot** (on Tue and Sat-Sun only) by walking six-tenths of a mile from Lenno through the park. Otherwise, catch the more glamorous **speedboat shuttle** from Lido di Lenno (€5 one-way, €6 round-trip, Igor can also be hired for private tours, mobile 333-410-3854).

Isola Comacina

This remote little island, just south of Bellagio, offers peace, ancient church foundations, a small archaeological museum, goats, sheep, nice swimming, and a lovely view of Lake Como. It takes 30-45 minutes to walk around the island, but longer to savor it. Bring a picnic or try the snack bar at the dock. The island is accessible every day in summer, but only during certain times (daily July-Aug 10:00-18:30, March-June and Sept-Oct 10:00-17:00; information at TI in mainland town of Ossuccio, tel. 034-456-369, www.isola -comacina.it, info@isola-comacina.it).

Getting There: The *isola* can be reached from Varenna (1 hour), Menaggio (50 minutes), or Bellagio (35 minutes). Look for trips to Isola Comacina (€5) on the Colico-Como *battello* schedule (listed in Lago di Como boat timetable, free at ticket booths at ferry docks, see page 249). Check return times carefully (Como-Colico direction) and don't miss your boat. Usually only one trip a day each way works out for a visit. Allow about six hours, including travel time. Or ask about organized excursions on Sundays (€18.50 including transport, tel. 034-456-369).

Como

On the southwest tip of the lake, Como has a good, traffic-free old town, an interesting Gothic/Renaissance cathedral, and a pleasant lakefront with a promenade (**TI** open June-Sept Mon-Sat 9:00-13:00 & 14:30-18:00, closed Sun, shorter hours off-season, tel. 031-330-0128, www.lakecomo.it). It's an easy 10-minute walk from the boat dock to the train station (trains to Milan depart at least hourly, 30-60 minutes). Boats leave Como about hourly for mid-lake (ferries-€8-10, 2 hours, departures 7:35-16:45; hydrofoils-€11-13, 1 hour, departures 8:45-19:10; tel. 031-579-211, www.navigazionelaghi.it).

Sleeping in Como: For a cheap overnight, try the **$ Villa Olmo Hostel** (€17, includes breakfast and sheets, €3/night extra for nonmembers, dinners-€6.50-10.50, free Wi-Fi and pay Internet access, laundry service available, baggage storage, free parking, bike rental, reception open 7:00-10:00 & 16:00-24:00, lockout 10:00-16:00, 24:00 curfew, closed mid-Nov-Feb, 20-minute walk from train station or dock, Via Bellinzona 2, tel. & fax 031-573-800, www.aighostels.com, ostellocomo@tin.it).

All-Day Lugano Side-Trip

From Varenna or Bellagio, you can make a loop that lets you nip into Switzerland to see the elegant lake resort of Lugano, pass through the town of Como, and cruise a good part of Lake Como. Here's a good day plan: 9:00—ferry to Menaggio; 10:00—bus to Lugano (45 minutes, bring your passport); 11:30—explore Lugano, train to Como (2/hour); 16:00—fast boat from Como to Varenna (departures also at about 17:00, 18:00, and 19:00). For information on Lugano, see www.ricksteves.com/lugano.

THE LAKES

Lake Maggiore

Lake Maggiore is ringed by mountains, snowcapped in spring and fall, and lined with resort towns such as Stresa. While crassly touristic, Stresa is a handy base from which to explore the exotic garden

islands of Lake Maggiore. And many consider it a pleasant last stop before flying home from nearby Malpensa Airport.

A visit to this region is worth the trouble for two islands, both with exotic gardens and lovely villas built by the Borromeo family. The

Borromeos—through many generations since 1630—lovingly turned their islands into magical retreats, with elaborate villas and fragrant gardens. Isola Bella has a palace and terraced garden; Isola Madre has a villa and sprawling English-style (more casual) garden. A third island, Isola Pescatori (a.k.a. Superiore), is simply small, serene, and residential. The Borromeos, who made their money from trade and banking, enjoyed the arts—from paintings (hung in lavish abundance throughout the palace and villa) to plays (performed in an open-air theater on Isola Bella) and marionette shows (you'll see the puppets that once performed here).

Tourists flock to the lakes in May and June, when flowers are in bloom, and in September. Concerts held in scenic settings draw music lovers, particularly during the Musical Weeks in August (get details from Stresa TI). For fewer crowds, visit in April, July, August (when Italians prefer the Mediterranean beaches), or October. In winter, the snow-covered mountains (with resorts a 1.5-hour drive away) attract skiers.

Planning Your Time

This region is best visited on a sunny day, when the mountains are clear, the lake is calm, and the heat of the sun brings out the scent of the blossoms. The two top islands for sightseeing are Isola Bella and Isola Madre. Isola Pescatori has no sights, but is a peaceful place for lunch.

Day Trip from Milan: Catch an early train from Milan to Stresa (take a one-hour fast train, check times as fast trains run less frequently mornings after 8:28). Upon arrival in Stresa, walk 10 minutes downhill to the boat dock, and catch a boat to Isola Madre. Then work your way back to Isola Pescatori for a lazy lunch, and on to Isola Bella for the afternoon, before returning to the town of Stresa and back to Milan.

Overnight: Small, touristy Stresa makes a fine first or last stop in Italy—its connections with Milan's airport, which is located about halfway between Stresa and Milan, don't involve a transfer in big Milan (see "Stresa Connections," page 288).

Getting Around Lake Maggiore

Boats link the islands and Stresa, running about twice hourly. Allow roughly 10 minutes between stops. Since short round-trip hops add up fast (€7 each for Isola Bella and Isola Pescatori, €9 for Isola Madre), it's best to simply buy the **all-day pass:** €10 for two islands (Bella and Pescatori), or €15 for all the islands plus Pallanza (a town on the opposite shore) and Villa Taranto. A **combo-ticket** combining the villas on Isola Bella and Isola Madre with the all-day boat pass is available in summer for €29.50 (credit cards accepted).

Boats run daily April through September. The map on page 280 shows the route: Stresa, Carciano/Lido, Isola Bella, Isola Pescatori, Baveno (lakeside town), Isola Madre, Pallanza, and Villa Taranto. This route is part of a longer one. To follow the boat schedule (free, available at boat docks, TI, and maybe your hotel), look at the Arona-Locarno timetable for trips from Stresa to the islands, and the Locarno-Arona timetable for the return trip to Stresa. Off-season, the boats cover a shorter route; check the time-table (public boat info: tel. 800-551-801 or 0322-233-200, www.navigazionelaghi.it, infomaggiore@navigazionelaghi.it).

Buy boat tickets directly from the dock ticket booth under the gallery to the left of the TI. Don't be fooled by the private taxi-boat drivers, most dressed in navy-blue uniforms and white hats (they look like Italian traffic cops); with their little sales booth on the sidewalk in front of the public boat launch, they'll try to talk you into paying way too much for private tours on their smaller boats.

Stresa

Stresa—which means "thin stretch"—was named for the origi-nal strip of fishermen's huts that lined the shore. Today, grand old hotels run along that same shore. The old town—basically a traffic-free touristy shopping mall—is just a few blocks deep, stretch-ing inland from the main boat dock. A fine waterfront promenade leads past the venerable old hotels to the Lido (with the Carciano boat dock and a mountain cable car). Stresa's stately 19th-century lakeside hotels date back to the days when this town was on the "Grand Tour" circuit. In any Romantic-age resort like Stresa, hotels had names designed to appeal to Victorian aristocrats...like Palace (rather than Palazzo), Astoria, Bristol, and Victoria.

Nineteen-year-old Ernest Hemingway first came to Stresa in 1918. Wounded in Slovenia as an ambulance driver for the Italian Red Cross, he was taken to the Grand Hotel des Iles Borromees. This was the first hotel on the shore (from 1862), and it served—like its regal neighbors—as an infirmary during World War I. Hemingway returned to the same hotel in 1948, stayed in the same room (#205, now called the "Hemingway suite"—you can stay there for a couple of thousand dollars a night), and signed the guest book as "an old client." Another "old client" was Winston Churchill, who honeymooned here.

Orientation to Stresa

Tourist Information

The helpful TI, located to the right of the ticket window at the boat dock, has free maps and boat schedules (March-Oct daily

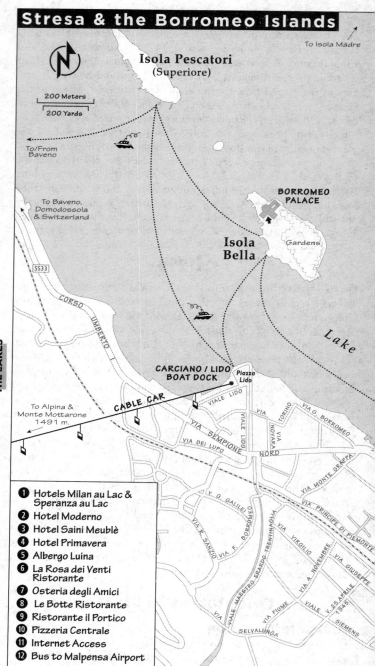

Stresa & the Borromeo Islands

THE LAKES

1 Hotels Milan au Lac & Speranza au Lac
2 Hotel Moderno
3 Hotel Saini Meublè
4 Hotel Primavera
5 Albergo Luina
6 La Rosa dei Venti Ristorante
7 Osteria degli Amici
8 Le Botte Ristorante
9 Ristorante il Portico
10 Pizzeria Centrale
11 Internet Access
12 Bus to Malpensa Airport

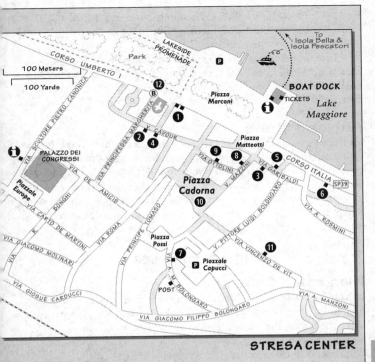

STRESA CENTER

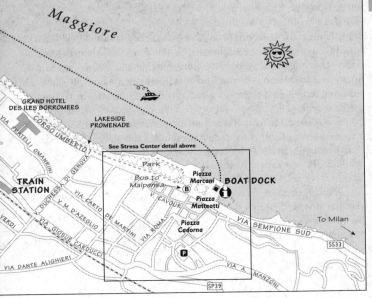

10:00-12:30 & 15:00-18:30; Nov-Feb Mon-Fri 10:00-12:30 & 15:00-18:30, Sat 10:00-12:30, closed Sun; Piazza Marconi 16, tel. 0323-30150, www.stresaturismo.it).

Internet Access: The **Newdata Internet Point** is a block off Piazza Cadorna in the old center (daily 9:30-12:30 & 15:00-22:00, until 19:30 in winter, Via de Vit 15A, tel. 0323-30323, www.newdata.too.it).

Arrival in Stresa

At the train station, ask for a free city map at the newsstand (to the far right of the tracks as you exit the train). To get downtown, exit right from the station and take your first left (on Viale Duchessa di Genova). This takes you straight down to the lake (the boat dock is about four blocks to your right; ask for boat schedule at ticket window). The TI is next door on the same dock. Taxis charge a fixed rate of €8 for even the shortest ride in town.

Sights in Stresa

Islands and Gardens

▲▲**Isola Bella**—This island, nearest Stresa, has a formal garden and a fancy Baroque palace. Looking like a stepped pyramid from the water, the island was named by Charles Borromeo (sponsor of Milan's Duomo) for his wife, Isabella. The island itself is touristy, with a gauntlet of souvenir stands and a corral of restaurants. A few back streets provide evidence that people actually live here. While the Borromeo family now lives in Milan, they spend a few weeks on Isola Bella each summer (when their blue-and-red family flag flies from the top of the garden).

Cost and Hours: Palace and garden-€12.50, picture gallery-€4 extra, €17.50 combo-ticket includes the villa at Isola Madre (but not Isola Bella's picture gallery), daily late-March-late-Oct 9:00-18:00, last entry 30 minutes before closing, closed late-Oct-late-March, tel. 0323-30556, www.borromeoturismo.it.

Audioguide: A fine €3 audioguide describes the palace, which also has posted English descriptions.

Services: A WC is at the garden entrance. Note that there are two docks on this island (one for each direction). Departure times are indicated by clocks at each dock. Picnicking is not allowed in the garden, but you can picnic at the point of the island (free and open to the public); take the mosaic sidewalk to the left of the palace entrance.

Visiting the Island: Your visit is a one-way tour, starting with the palace and finishing with the garden. (There's no way to see the garden without the palace.) From the dock, head left to the huge palace, passing the public WCs.

In the lavishly decorated Baroque **palace**, stairs lead to stucco crests of Italy's top families (balls signify the Medici, bees mean the Barberini, and a unicorn symbolizes the Borromeos' motto: Humility). Here, you can choose to pay for a supplementary ticket to walk through the picture gallery (containing 130 beautifully restored 16th-century paintings from the Borromeo family's private collection, followed by an ornate throne room). Otherwise, continue straight into the next room, where you'll see a portrait of the first Borromeo, and into a richly stuccoed grand hall, with an 80-foot-high dome and featuring an 18th-century model of the villa, including a grand entry that never materialized. The next room, with the musical instruments, was the site of the 1935 Stresa Conference, in which Mussolini met with British and French diplomats in a united attempt to scare Germany out of starting World War II. This "Stresa Front" soon fizzled when Mussolini attacked Ethiopia and joined forces with Hitler. A photocopy of the treaty with Mussolini's signature is on the wall next to the exit. Napoleon's bedroom comes with an engraving that depicts his 1797 visit (Napoleon is on a bench with his wife and sister enjoying festivities in his honor). The last rooms display souvenirs and gifts that the Borromeo family picked up over the generations.

Downstairs, many of the famous Borromeo marionettes are on display. (A larger collection is on Isola Madre.) The 18th-century grotto, decorated from ceiling to floor with shell motifs and black-and-white stones, still serves its original function of providing a cool refuge from Italy's heat. The dreamy marble statues are by Gaetano Monti, a student of Canova. Climbing out of the basement, look up at the unique cantilevered stairs; they're from a 16th-century fortress that predates this building.

The ornate hall of 16th-century Flemish tapestries leads to the finale of this island visit: the beautiful **garden**, complete with Chinese white peacocks, which give it an exotic splash. Baroque—which is exactly what you see here—is all about controlling nature. The terraced gardens are crowned by the Borromeo family unicorn. Circle around the garden to the left to visit the bookshop and café, or head to the right to go straight to the exit. Gardeners continue on to the second exit to pass through Elisa's Greenhouse, named for Napoleon's sister and home to tropical plants.

▲**Isola Pescatori**—This sleepy island—home to 35 families—is the smallest and most residential of the three. It has a couple of good seafood restaurants, picnic benches, views, and, blissfully, nothing much to do—all under arbors of wisteria. A delight for photographers and painters, the island is never really crowded, except at lunchtime.

▲▲**Isola Madre**—Don't come here unless you intend to tour the sight, because that's all there is: an interesting furnished villa and a lovely garden filled with exotic birds and plants.

Cost and Hours: Villa and garden-€10.50, €17.50 combo-ticket includes Isola Bella, late-March-late-Oct daily 9:00-18:00, last entry 30 minutes before closing, closed late-Oct-late-March, no photos in villa, WC next to chapel, tel. 0323-30556, www.borromeoturismo.it.

Visiting the Island: Visiting is a one-way affair, starting with

a long stroll through the garden and finishing with the villa. The sight-seeing route is clearly signed, taking you through the gardens and villa, and ending at the chapel. The €2.50 audioguide is devoted almost entirely to the garden—a good investment to properly appreciate the plantings.

Eight gardeners (with the help of water continually pumped from the lake) keep this English-style **garden** paradise lush. It's a joy, even for those bored by flowers and foliage. You'll see trees from around the world, and an exotic bird menagerie with golden and silver pheasants and Chinese peacocks. In front of the villa, a once-magnificent Himalayan cypress tree paints your world a streaky green. The 150-year-old tree, knocked down by a tornado in 2006 but successfully saved, is an attraction in its own right, with steel guy-wires now anchoring it firmly in place.

The 16th-century **villa** is the first of the Borromeo palaces. A century older than the Isola Bella villa, it's dark, somber, and dates from the Renaissance. The clever angled hinges keep the doors from flapping in the lake breeze. The family's huge collection of dolls, marionettes, and exquisite 17th-century marionette theater sets—painted by a famous La Scala opera set designer—fills several rooms. A corner room is painted to take you into an 18th-century Venetian Rococo sitting room under a floral greenhouse.

Some of the garden's best flowers are in view immediately after leaving the villa.

Eating: While eating is best on Isola Pescatori, Isola Madre has one eatery, **La Piratera Ristorante Bar** (€25 fixed-price tourist meal, daily 8:00-18:00, sit-down meals 12:00-15:00 and simple sandwiches to go anytime, picnic at rocky beach a minute's walk from restaurant, just to your right as you exit the gardens, tel. 0323-31171).

▲Villa Taranto Botanical Gardens—Garden-lovers will enjoy this large landscaped park, located on the mainland a 10-minute boat ride beyond Isola Madre (across the lake from Stresa). The gardens are a Scotsman's labor of love. Starting in the 1930s, Neil McEacharn created this garden of delights—bringing in thousands of plants from all over the world—and here he stays, in the small mausoleum. The park's highlight is a terraced garden with a series of cascading pools. Villa Taranto is directly across the street from the boat dock.

Cost and Hours: €9.50, daily April-Sept 8:30-19:30, Oct until 17:30, closed Nov-March, tel. 0323-404-555, www.villataranto.it.

Mountain Cable Car—From Stresa's Lido, a cable car takes you up—in two stages and a 20-minute ride—to the top of Mount Mottarone (about 5,000 feet). From here, you get great views of neighboring peaks and, by taking a short hike, a bird's-eye view of the small, neighboring Lake Orta.

Cost and Hours: €17.50 round-trip, €10.50 one-way, includes Alpine Gardens entry, daily 9:30-17:40 in summer, 8:30-17:00 in winter, closed Nov, 2-3/hour, bar midway up, tel. 0323-30295, www.stresa-mottarone.it.

Activities: To visit the **Alpine Gardens,** get off at the midway Alpina stop, where a 10-minute walk leads to the gardens (turn left

as you leave; included in round-trip cable-car ticket, April-Oct daily 9:30-18:00, closed Nov-March). The gardens come with great lake views and picnic spots, but can't compare to what you'll see on the islands.

If you plan to **hike** down, pick up the Trekking Map from the TI and allow 3.5 hours from the top of Mount Mottarone, or 1.5 hours from the Alpine Gardens.

You can rent a **bike** at the base of the cable-car lift (full-suspension mountain bike or road bike-€5/hour, €22/half-day, €27/day, €45/weekend, includes helmet, tel. 338-839-5692, Giorgio) and bring it on the cable car with you (€11 extra). It's a treacherous ride, enjoyable only for serious bikers. While the ride is nice on top, you'll fight traffic on congested, rough, and windy roads for the rest of the descent.

Day Trips from Stresa

▲Scenic Boat and Rail Trip to Locarno and Centovalli—This enjoyable all-day excursion from Stresa involves three segments. Before you embark on the trip, confirm all times, particularly the departure of the last boat from Locarno. Take the train from Stresa to Domodossola, then catch the "Centovalli" train for a 1.5-hour ride that links together remote mountain villages on your way to Locarno, in the Italian-speaking Swiss canton of Ticino (bring your passport). Spend an hour or so exploring this town, on the far end of Lake Maggiore. Then take the boat past loads of small lakeside hamlets back to Italy. As a relaxing finale, you'll cruise into your home port of Stresa. The trip can also be done in reverse (with the boat trip first). A special €32 "Lago Maggiore Express" ticket covers both the train and boat (you must reserve in advance; fax 0322-249-530 or email infomaggiore@navigazionelaghi.it—indicate the date you'll travel, number of passengers, and a return email address or fax number; call 800-551-801 or 0322-233-200, www.lagomaggioreexpress.com).

▲Lake Orta—Just on the other side of Mount Mottarone is the small lake of Orta. The lake's main town, Orta San Giulio, has a

beautiful lakeside piazza ringed by picturesque buildings. The piazza faces the lake with a view of Isola San Giulio. Taxi boats (€2.50 round-trip) make the five-minute trip throughout the day. The island is worth a look for the Church of San Giulio and the circular "path of silence," which takes about 10 minutes. In peak season, Orta is anything but silent, but off-season or early or late in the day, this place is full of peace and magic (**TI** open Mon 8:30-12:30, Tue-Sun 8:30-12:30 & 13:30-17:30, located on Via Panoramica next to the parking lot downhill from the train station, tel. 0322-905-163).

The train ride from Stresa to Orta-Miasino (a short walk from the lakeside piazza) takes 1.5-2 hours and requires a change or two (9/day). Public buses from Stresa's Piazza Marconi to Orta depart from near the TI (around €8 round-trip, 3/day mid-June-mid-Sept departing at 10:00, 14:00, and 17:00; return trip from Orta to Stresa departing at 11:00, 15:00, and 18:00; confirm schedule at TI).

Sleeping in Stresa

(€1 = about $1.40, country code: 39)

Because Stresa town is just a resort, I'd day-trip from Milan. But here are good options if you'd like to stay.

$$ Hotel Milan au Lac and its sister hotel next door, the yellow-brick **Speranza au Lac,** are impersonal four-star corporate-style hotels that cater mostly to tour groups, with 175 predictably comfortable rooms across from the boat dock (to the right as you leave the boat). Reception for both hotels is in Hotel Milan au Lac (Db-€100-170 depending on season and view, generally open April-Oct, air-con, elevator, tel. 0323-31178, fax 0323-32729, www.milansperanza.it, info@milansperanza.it).

$$ Hotel Moderno offers 54 peaceful and well-maintained pastel rooms on a pedestrian street a block from the main square (Db-€140, discount for Rick Steves readers depending on availability, closed Nov-mid-March, air-con, elevator, Internet access, pay Wi-Fi, Via Cavour 33; from the main square, with your back to the lake, find the church—hotel is behind the church on pedestrian street parallel to main road; tel. 0323-933-773, fax 0323-933-775, www.hms.it, moderno@hms.it).

$$ Hotel Saini Meublè is a cozy place with rustic stonework and warm hardwood floors, located in a pedestrian zone a couple of blocks from the boat dock in the old center. Its 14 rooms are big, modern, and quiet (Sb-€82, Db-€102, lower prices off-season, these rates promised to my readers through 2012, elevator, Internet access and Wi-Fi; from Piazza Matteotti head up Via Mazzini and turn left on Via Garibaldi, Via Garibaldi 10, tel. 0323-934-519, fax 0323-31169, www.hotelsaini.it, info@hotelsaini.it). Gianni (Johnny) greets you at reception.

$ Hotel Primavera, next door to Hotel Moderno, rents 37 cheaper, decent, air-conditioned rooms, most with little terraces that overlook the action in the streets below (Db-€75-100, pay Internet access and Wi-Fi, Via Cavour 39, tel. 0323-31286, fax 0323-33458, www.stresa.it, hotelprimavera@stresa.it).

$ Albergo Luina is a clean and homey family-run cheap sleep, with seven basic rooms above a restaurant (Sb-€35-52, Db-€50-80, some with little balconies for no extra charge, these prices for Rick Steves readers—mention this book when you reserve, breakfast-€4; 2 blocks off Piazza Matteotti—with back to lake, go left up small street; Via Garibaldi 21, tel. & fax 0323-30285, luinastresa@yahoo.it). Papa Marco cooks in the restaurant while Mamma Renata tends to the guests.

Eating in Stresa

La Rosa dei Venti, on the main drag, caters to locals with great €7 pizzas and lakefront dining. They proudly offer homemade pastas and creative risottos for €7 (big €7 salads, €13 *secondi*, Wed-Mon 12:00-15:00 & 19:00-23:00, closed Tue, everything made to order, 2 blocks south of the boat dock at Corso Italia 50, tel. 0323-31431).

Osteria degli Amici serves up tasty €10 risottos and pastas, with fast and friendly service under a canopy of grape and kiwi leaves (€7 wood-fired pizzas, daily 12:00-14:15 & 18:30-22:30, closed Wed Sept-June, deep in the old town past Piazza Cadorna at Via Bolongaro 33, tel. 0323-30453).

Le Botte offers a variety of Piedmont's regional specialties in a pub-grub casual atmosphere (€9 pastas, €13 *secondi*, daily 12:00-15:00 & 19:00-22:30 in summer, closed Thu Oct-March and all of Dec-Feb, Via Mazzini 6/8, tel. 0323-30462).

Ristorante il Portico is a cheerful, energetic place featuring several €16-26 multicourse tasting samplers and daily market specials on sidewalk tables or in their airy, fresh dining room. It's smart to reserve (piping-hot €6 pizzas, €7 pastas, €9 *secondi*, daily 12:00-16:00 & 19:00-24:00, closed off-season, Via Ottolini 9, tel. 0323-934-510).

The main square, **Piazza Cadorna,** is a carnival of residents selling things to tourists. Still, at night it has a certain charm. It seems anyone who claims to be a musician can get a gig singing for diners. The **Pizzeria Centrale** (on a platform in the center) is a good place to enjoy the ambience. Their pizzas are decent, but don't order any serious food here.

Stresa Connections

From Stresa by Train to: Milan (about hourly, 1-hour fast train—but there can be gaps in service so check timetable carefully, 90-minute slow train), **Varenna** (roughly every two hours, 2.75-4 hours, transfer in Milan), **Venice** (7/day, 4-4.5 hours, transfer in Milan), **Domodossola** (near the Swiss border, almost hourly, 30 minutes).

To Malpensa Airport: For a **train-bus combination,** take the train toward Milan (departs hourly) and get off at Gallarate (after about 40 minutes), where frequent, cheap shuttle buses run to Malpensa's Terminal 1 (€1.50, pay driver, about 1-2/hour, 25 minutes). From Gallarate, the bus departs from the train station and runs 5:55-20:15; from Malpensa's Terminal 1, the bus runs 5:34-19:50; tel. 0331-258-411, www.sea-aeroportimilano.it/en). For an early-morning flight, the first Stresa-Milan train departs at 5:23, connecting with Gallarate's first bus departure for Malpensa (confirm schedules locally).

Alibus Airport buses run between Stresa and Malpensa (€9, mid-April-Sept, 50 minutes; leaves Stresa from in front of the church next to Hotel Milan au Lac—near the ferry dock and TI—at 6:30, 9:30, 11:30, 13:30, 16:30, and 19:30; leaves airport from bus stop 22 outside Terminal 1 at 7:30, 10:30, 12:30, 14:30, 17:30, and 20:30; confirm schedule, must reserve by 11:00 the previous day or by 11:00 Sat if booking for Sun or Mon bus—call 0323-552-172, book online at www.safduemila.com, or email alibus @safduemila.com).

Taxis to the airport cost €90 (1-5 people, €100 if traveling between 22:00-7:00) and take about an hour; your hotel can arrange the taxi for you, but will charge extra for booking it. It's easy to arrange a taxi on your own at the train station's taxi stand. Salvo Taxi is reliable (mobile 335-707-8894).

MILAN

Milano

For every church in Rome, there's a bank in Milan. Italy's second city and the capital of Lombardy, Milan is a hardworking, fashion-conscious, time-is-money city of 1.3 million. It's a melting pot of people and history. Milan's industriousness may come from the Teutonic blood of its original inhabitants, the Lombards, or from the region's Austrian heritage. Milan is Italy's fashion, industrial, banking, TV, publishing, and convention capital. The economic success of post-war Italy can be blamed on this city of publicists and pasta power lunches.

As if to make up for its rough, noisy big-city-ness, its people are works of art. Milan is an international fashion capital with a refined taste. Window displays are gorgeous, cigarettes are chic, and even the cheese comes gift-wrapped. Yet thankfully, Milan is no more expensive for tourists than other Italian cities.

Three hundred years before Christ, the Romans called this place Mediolanum, or "the central place." By the fourth century A.D., it was the capital of the western half of the Roman Empire. Emperor Constantine issued the Edict of Milan from here, legalizing Christianity. After some barbarian darkness, medieval Milan rose to regional prominence under the Visconti and Sforza families. By the time of the Renaissance, it was nicknamed "the New Athens," and was enough of a cultural center for Leonardo da Vinci to call home. Then came 400 years of foreign domination (Spain, Austria, France, more Austria). Milan was a center of the 1848 revolution against Austria, and helped lead Italy to unification in 1870.

Mussolini left a heavy fascist touch on the architecture here (such as the central train station). His excesses also led to the

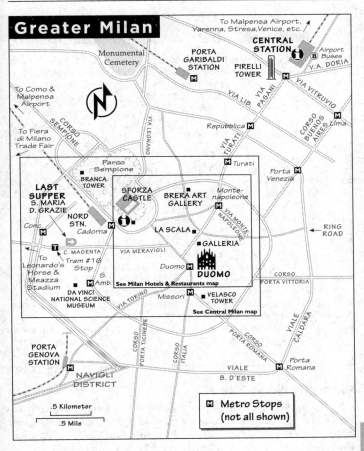

Greater Milan

To Malpensa Airport,
Varenna, Stresa, Venice, etc.

CENTRAL STATION
Airport Buses
V. A. DORIA

Monumental Cemetery

PORTA GARIBALDI STATION

PIRELLI TOWER

VIA LIB. VIA PISANI

VIA VITRUVIO

To Como & Malpensa Airport

CORSO SEMPIONE

VIA LEGNANO

VIA TIRATI

Repubblica

CORSO BUENOS AIRES

Lima

To Fiera di Milano Trade Fair

Parco Sempione

Turati

Porta Venezia

LAST SUPPER
S. MARIA D. GRAZIE

BRANCA TOWER

SFORZA CASTLE

BRERA ART GALLERY

Monte-napoleone

RING ROAD

Conc.

NORD STN.
Cadorna

LA SCALA

VIA MONTE NAPOLEONE

C. MAGENTA

GALLERIA

To Leonardo's Horse & Meazza Stadium

Tram #16 Stop

VIA MERAVIGLI

S. Amb.

Duomo

DUOMO

S.

See Milan Hotels & Restaurants map

CORSO PORTA VITTORIA

DA VINCI NATIONAL SCIENCE MUSEUM

VIA TORINO

Missori

VELASCO TOWER

See Central Milan map

PORTA GENOVA STATION

CORSO PORTA TICINESE

CORSO ITALIA

CORSO PORTA ROMANA

VIALE CALDARA

NAVIGLI DISTRICT

VIALE B. D'ESTE

Porta Romana

.5 Kilometer

.5 Mile

M Metro Stops
(not all shown)

MILAN

WWII bombing of Milan. But the city rose again. The 1959 Pirelli Tower (the skinny skyscraper in front of the station) was a trend-setter in its day. Today, Milan is people-friendly, with a great transit system and inviting pedestrian zones. And the city is busy with construction projects in an effort to beef up both its infrastructure and cultural offerings as it prepares to host the 2015 World's Fair.

Many tourists come to Italy for the past. But Milan is today's Italy, and no trip to this country is complete without visiting it. While it's not big on the tourist circuit, the city has plenty to see. And fortunately, seeing Milan—so manageable and well-organized—is not difficult.

For pleasant excursions from the city, consider visiting Lake Como or Lake Maggiore—both are about an hour from Milan by train (see The Lakes chapter).

Rome vs. Milan: A Classic Squabble

In Italy, the North and South bicker about each other, hurling barbs, quips, and generalizations. All the classic North/South traits can be applied to Milan (the business capital) and Rome (the government capital). Although the differences have become less pronounced lately, the sniping continues.

The Milanesi say the Romans are lazy. Roman government jobs come with short hours—cut even shorter by too many coffee breaks, three-hour lunches, chats with colleagues, and phone calls to friends and relatives. Milanesi contend that "Roma *ladrona*" (Rome, the big thief) is a parasite that lives off the taxes of people up North. There's still a strong Milan-based movement seriously promoting secession from the South.

Romans, meanwhile, dismiss the Milanesi as uptight workaholics with nothing else to live for—gray like their foggy city. Romans do admit that in Milan, job opportunities are better and based on merit. And the Milanesi grudgingly concede the Romans have a gift for enjoying life.

While Rome is more of a family city, Milan is the place for high-powered singles on the career fast track. Milanese yuppies

Planning Your Time

OK, it's a big city, so you probably won't linger. Compared to Rome and Florence, Milan's art is mediocre, but the city does have unique and noteworthy sights: the Duomo and Galleria Vittorio Emanuele, Pinacoteca Ambrosiana, La Scala Opera House, Brera Art Gallery, Michelangelo's last *Pietà* in the Sforza Castle, and Leonardo's *Last Supper*. It's best to reserve several months in advance to see *The Last Supper* (see page 317); if you haven't booked ahead, your best option is to take a bus-and-walking tour (see "Tours in Milan," later).

With two nights and a full day, you can gain an appreciation for the town and see the
major sights. On a short visit,
I'd focus on the center. Tour
the Duomo, hit what art you
like, browse through the elegant
shopping area and the Galleria
Vittorio Emanuele, and try to see
an opera. Technology buffs like
the Leonardo da Vinci National

mix with each other...not the city's longtime residents. Milan is seen as wary of foreigners and inward-looking, and Rome as fun-loving, tolerant, and friendly. In Milan, bureaucracy (like social services) works logically and efficiently, while in Rome, accomplishing even small chores can be exasperating. Everything in Rome—from finding a babysitter to buying a car—is done through friends. Meanwhile, people in Milan are more private.

Milanesi find Romans vulgar. The Roman dialect is considered one of the coarsest in the country. Much as they try, Milanesi

just can't say "Damn your dead relatives" quite as effectively as the Romans. Still, Milanesi enjoy Roman comedians and love to imitate the accent.

The Milanesi feel that Rome is dirty and Roman traffic nerve-wracking. But despite the craziness, Rome maintains a genuine village feel. People share family news with their neighborhood grocer. Milan lacks people-friendly piazzas, and entertainment comes at a high price. But in Rome, *la dolce vita* is as close as the nearest square, and a full moon is enjoyed by all.

Science and Technology Museum, while history and art buffs dig the city's early Christian churches, Brera Gallery, Pinacoteca Ambrosiana, and the Museum of Art and Science. People-watchers and pigeon-feeders could spend their entire visit never losing sight of the Duomo. And if you dig burial grounds, rattle through Milan's evocative Monumental Cemetery. To maximize your time in Milan, use the Metro and note which places stay open through the siesta.

Since Milan is a cold Italian plunge, and most flights to the US leave Milan early in the morning, you could save it for the end of your trip and start your journey softly by going directly by train from Milan to Lake Como (one-hour ride to Varenna), Lake Maggiore (about an hour to Stresa), or the Cinque Terre (4 hours to Vernazza). Then spend the last night or two of your trip in Milan before flying home.

Monday is a terrible sightseeing day, since many museums are closed (including Leonardo's *Last Supper*). August is oppressively hot and muggy, and locals who can vacate at this time, do, leaving the city pretty quiet. Those visiting in August find: the nightlife sleepy; many shops, restaurants, and some hotels closed; and many

MILAN

hotel rooms on the discounted push list.

A Three-Hour Tour: If you're just changing trains in Milan (as, sooner or later, you will), consider this blitz tour: Check your bag at the station, pick up a city map at the station TI, ride the subway to the Duomo (for specifics, see "Arrival in Milan," later), peruse the square, explore the cathedral's rooftop and interior, have a scenic coffee in the Galleria Vittorio Emanuele, spin on the floor mosaic of the bull for good luck, see a museum or two (most are within a 10-minute walk of the main square), and return by subway to the station. Art fans could make time for *The Last Supper* (if they've made reservations), the Michelangelo *Pietà* in the Sforza Castle (no reservations necessary), the Brera Art Gallery, or the Pinacoteca Ambrosiana (with its Leonardo exhibit).

Orientation to Milan

My coverage focuses on the old center. Most sights and hotels are within a 10-minute walk of the cathedral (Duomo), which is a straight eight-minute Metro ride from the train station.

Tourist Information

Milan has two TIs: The main TI is at Piazza Castello 1 (near Sforza Castle) and the other is at the train station, in front of track 13 (both share same hours: Mon-Fri 9:00-18:00, Sat 9:00-13:30 & 14:00-18:00, Sun 9:00-13:30 & 14:00-17:00, main TI tel. 02-7740-4343, train TI tel. 02-7740-4318, www.visitamilano.it, iat.info @provincia.milano.it). You can book Autostradale and Zani Viaggi city tours (see "Tours in Milan," later) at the companies' offices on Piazza Castello, near the main TI.

At either TI, confirm your sightseeing plans and pick up a free map. Also ask for the two free booklets listing Milan's sights (including hours, prices, and directions), events, concerts, films in English, expatriate groups, and cultural insights. *Hello Milano* is a monthly newspaper in English (www.hellomilano.it); *Milano Mese* is less helpful (scant event descriptions in English, events listed by category rather than date).

I've listed enough sights to keep you very busy for two days, but there's much more to see in Milan. Its many thousand-year-old churches make it clear that Milan was an important beacon in the Dark Ages. The TI, local guidebooks, and newspapers can point you in the right direction if you have more time.

Arrival in Milan

By Train: The huge, sternly decorated, fascist-built (in 1931) central train station, called Milano Centrale, is a sight in itself. Recently cleaned, the halls feel more monumental than ever. Notice how the art makes you feel that a powerful state is a good thing. In the front lobby, heroic people celebrate "modern" transportation (circa-1930 ships, trains, and cars) opposite reliefs depicting old-fashioned sailboats and horse carts.

The station has three levels of **shops and services.** On the ground level to the left (with your back to the tracks), you'll find taxis, travel agencies, shuttle buses to the airports, and a baggage check (marked *deposito bagagli*, €4/5 hours, €10/24 hours, 5-day maximum, daily 6:00-23:50, passport required, 45-pound bag limit). A supermarket is outside on the right (daily 8:00-22:00). ATMs are in front of the station, outside and to the right. Also in front of the station are the Metro and car-rental offices (clearly marked). The 24-hour pharmacy has a big green neon cross. The WCs are by track 22.

From the track level, down the moving walkways, you'll find the **Trenitalia ticket office** (daily 5:45-22:45) and user-friendly ticket sales machines (gray-and-blue for local train services only, red-white-and-green for all Italian trains, credit cards and cash accepted, you can't buy international tickets from machines).

The **365 Travel Agency**—which sells train tickets, supplements, and night-train berth reservations—has three offices at the station. One is across from the baggage-check *deposito* desk (has longest hours, daily 6:40-21:00, agency tel. 02-6738-2603, www.agenzie365.it); another is outside facing the airport shuttle buses on Piazza Luigi di Savoia; and a third is on the opposite side of the station near the Sisley fashion store (with your back to the tracks, exit to the right). Their 7 percent commission can be a reasonable price to pay to skip the Trenitalia ticket lines.

Taking the Metro to the Duomo and Back: For a quick visit, it's a straight shot on the underground from the station to the Duomo (buy €1 ticket at kiosk or from machines, validate in orange machine). Follow signs for yellow line 3 (direction: San Donato); after an eight-minute ride (four stops), you'll be facing the cathedral. To return, ride the same yellow line 3 back the other way (direction: Comasina).

By Car: Driving is bad enough in Milan to make the €20/day fee for a downtown garage a blessing. If you're driving, do Milan (and Lake Como) before or after you rent your car, not while you've got it. If you have a car, use the well-marked suburban *parcheggi* (parking lots), which offer affordable (€6/day) and safe parking at city-edge subway stations, with extremely easy access to the center by Metro.

By Plane: Frequent shuttle trains and buses connect the airports and train station. See "Milan Connections" at the end of this chapter.

Helpful Hints

Theft Alert: Be on guard. Milan's thieves target tourists, especially at the central train station, getting in and out of the subway, and around the Duomo. They can be dressed as tourists, businessmen, or beggars, or they can be gangs of too-young-to-arrest children. Watch out for ragged people carrying newspaper and cardboard—they'll thrust this item at you as a distraction while they pick your pocket. If you're ripped off and plan to file an insurance claim, fill out a report with the police (Police Station, "Questura," Via Fatebenefratelli 11, Metro: Turati, open daily 24 hours, tel. 02-62261). For police emergencies, call 113. For lost or stolen credit cards, see page 15.

US Consulate: It's at Via Principe Amedeo 2/10 (Metro: Turati, tel. 02-290-351 for recorded info and phone tree, http://milan.usconsulate.gov).

Medical Help: Dial 118 for medical emergencies. There are two medical clinics with emergency care facilities: the International Health Center in Galleria Strasburgo 3 (Mon-Thu 9:00-19:00, Fri 9:00-18:00, closed Sat-Sun, between Via Durini and Corso Europa, third floor, Metro: San Babila, tel. 02-7634-0720) and the American International Medical Center at Via Mercalli 11 (Mon-Fri 9:00-17:30, closed Sat-Sun, Metro: Missori or Crocetta, call for appointment, tel. 02-5831-9808, mobile 335-570-1055). A 24-hour pharmacy is in the central train station; look for the neon-green cross.

Street Markets: Milan has two very popular flea markets. **Fiera di Sinigallia** spills into a lot at Porta Genova every Saturday (8:30-17:00, later in summer, Metro: Porta Genova). If you continue along Viale d'Annunzio to Viale Papiniano, you'll run into the **Papiniano** market (Tue morning and Sat all day). Small street markets are held every morning except Sunday in various neighborhoods; *Hello Milano* has a complete listing (free at TI).

Internet Access: A **Mondadori Mediacenter** shop is near the Duomo on Piazza del Duomo at the corner of Via Marconi (daily 9:00-23:00, see map on page 300). Purchase an Internet card (*tessera*, €3/hour) on the ground floor, then go up two flights of stairs to the second floor to register. The shop also sells a wide selection of international newspapers.

Bookstores: The handiest major bookstore is **Libreria Feltrinelli,** under the Galleria Vittorio Emanuele. Books in English—fiction and guidebooks—are at opposite ends of the store (Mon-Sat 10:00-23:00, Sun 10:00-20:00; enter at Ricordi Mediastore next to McDonald's in center of Galleria and go downstairs, or through Autogrill restaurant on Piazza

MILAN

del Duomo, store is in basement level; also sells maps; tel. 02-8699-6903). The **American Bookstore** is at Via Camperio 16, near the Sforza Castle (Mon 13:30-19:00, Tue-Sat 10:30-19:00, closed Sun, tel. 02-878-920).

Travel Agencies: You can buy train tickets and reserve an overnight berth *(cuccetta)* at the **365 Travel Agency**'s train station locations (7 percent commission but faster than ticket windows; listed earlier, under "Arrival in Milan") or at a downtown travel agency such as **American Express,** near the Duomo (Mon-Fri 9:00-17:30, closed Sat-Sun, Italian train tickets only, Via Larga 4, two blocks southeast of the Duomo, tel. 02-721-041).

Getting Around Milan

By Public Transit: Use Milan's great subway system. The clean, spacious, fast, and easy three-line Metro zips you nearly anywhere you may want to go, and trams and city buses fill in the gaps. The handiest Metro line for a quick visit is the yellow line 3, which connects the train station to the Duomo. The other lines are red (1) and green (2). "ATM" is the acronym for the Milan public transit system.

A **ticket,** valid for 1.25 hours, can be used for one subway, tram, or bus ride, including a transfer either within the same or another system, but not a round-trip on the same system (€1, sold at newsstands, tobacco shops, shops with *ATM* sticker in window, and at machines in subway stations).

Validate tickets in the yellow or orange machines at the turnstiles, and keep them until you exit the Metro system. If you're caught riding on an unvalidated ticket, the fine is €33.

Other ticket options include: a *carnet* (€9.20 for 10 rides; one magnetic ticket that can be validated 10 times); a **24-hour pass** (€3, worthwhile if you take four rides); and a **48-hour pass** (€5.50). Passes use the same validation machines as standard tickets.

For transit information, visit the ATM Point (at Duomo stop, near Arengario exit, to right of Duomo as you face it, opposite La Scala ticket office, Mon-Sat 7:45-19:15, closed Sun, tel. 800-808-181, www.atm-mi.it).

I've keyed sightseeing to the subway system. Though most sights are within a few blocks of each other, Milan is an exhausting city for walking. With the Metro, you'll rarely wait more than five minutes for a train. The well-marked trams can also be useful, especially to get to *The Last Supper* (tram #16) and the Monumental Cemetery (#12 or #14).

By Taxi: Small groups go cheap and fast by taxi (drop charge-€3.10, €0.70/kilometer; drop charge doubles on Sun, holidays, and from 21:00 to 6:00 in the morning). It can be easier to

MILAN

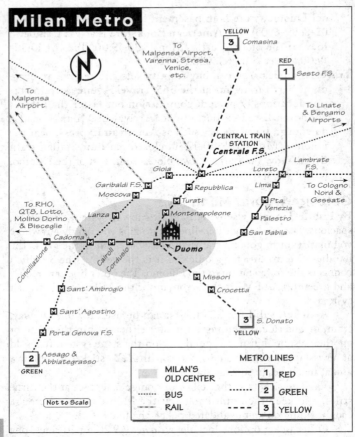

Milan Metro

YELLOW
3 Comasina

To Malpensa Airport, Varenna, Stresa, Venice, etc.

RED
1 Sesto F.S.

To Malpensa Airport

To Linate & Bergamo Airports

CENTRAL TRAIN STATION
Centrale F.S.

Lambrate F.S.

Gioia

Loreto

To Cologno Nord & Gessate

Garibaldi F.S.

Repubblica

Lima

Moscova

Turati

Pta. Venezia

To RHO, QT8, Lotto, Molino Dorino & Bisceglie

Lanza

Montenapoleone

Palestro

Cadorna

San Babila

Conciliazione

Cairoli

Corduslo

Duomo

Sant' Ambrogio

Missori

Crocetta

Sant' Agostino

Porta Genova F.S.

3 S. Donato
YELLOW

2 Assago & Abbiategrasso
GREEN

METRO LINES

MILAN'S OLD CENTER — 1 RED

BUS ...... 2 GREEN

RAIL --·-- 3 YELLOW

Not to Scale

walk to a taxi stand than to flag down a cab. Handy stands are at Piazza del Duomo and in front of the Sforza Castle.

Tours in Milan

Bus Tours—The three-hour **Autostradale** bus-and-walking tour is a good value, has a live guide describing the city's monuments in English, and guarantees you'll see Leonardo's *Last Supper*—useful if you haven't booked ahead for this important sight. The jam-packed itinerary also includes visits to the Duomo, Galleria Vittorio Emanuele, Sforza Castle, and La Scala Opera House (€55, departs Tue-Sun at 9:30, also Wed at 13:00 and Fri-Sat at 14:15). Tours leave from Piazza del Duomo, next to the taxi stand at the far end of the square from the church. There are four ways to reserve this tour: Book in advance online at www.autostradale.it;

ask your hotelier to book it for you; call the main TI at 02-7740-4343; or drop into the Autostradale office next to the TI at Piazza Castello 1 (Mon-Fri 8:30-18:00, Sat-Sun 9:00-16:00). Tickets may be available for the same-morning departure. To confirm details, call 02-3391-0794 or 02-7200-1304.

Zani Viaggi does a similar tour that includes *The Last Supper*. Guides lead two-language tours (one of which is always English), departing Tuesday through Sunday at 9:30 and 14:30 from their office at Foro Bonaparte 76, near the Sforza Castle (€60, 3.5 hours, no Mon tours; ticket office open Mon-Fri 9:00-19:00, Sat 9:00-17:00, closed Sun; tel. 02-867-131, www.zaniviaggi.it, excursions @zaniviaggi.it).

CitySightseeing Milano has hop-on, hop-off buses that do a circuit of the major sights accompanied by a recorded commentary; you can get off at a stop, tour the sight, and hop back on the bus to resume your tour (€20/24 hours, buy ticket on board, daily April-Oct 9:30-19:00, 2/hour; Nov-March 9:30-17:30, almost hourly; tel. 02-867-131. www.city-sightseeing.it). While you can hop on anywhere, it's easy at the Duomo (next to the taxi stand) and La Scala.

Local Guide—Lorenza Scorti is a hardworking young woman who knows her city's history and how to teach it. She can be booked well in advance (necessary in May and Sept) or on short notice (€125/3-hour tour, €250/day, same price for individuals or groups, evenings OK, tel. 02-4801-7042, mobile 347-735-1346, lorenza.scorti@libero.it).

Sights in Milan

The Cathedral and Nearby

▲▲**Duomo (Cathedral)**—The city's centerpiece is the fourth-largest church in Europe, after the Vatican's, London's, and

Seville's. Back when Europe was fragmented into countless tiny kingdoms and dukedoms, the dukes of Milan wanted to impress their counterparts in Germany and France. Their goal was to earn Milan recognition and respect from both the Vatican and the kings and princes of northern Europe by building a massive, richly ornamented cathedral. Even after Renaissance-style domes were in vogue elsewhere in Italy, conservative Milan's cathedral stayed on Gothic target. The dukes—thinking northerners would relate better to Gothic—loaded it with pointed arches and spires.

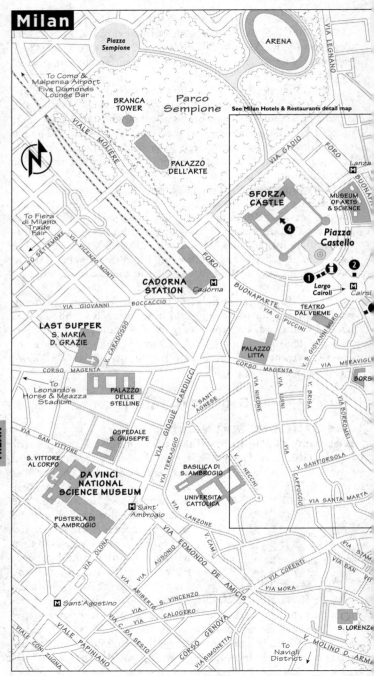

Milan

Piazza Sempione

ARENA

VIA LEGNANO

To Como &
Malpensa Airport
Five Diamonds
Lounge Bar

BRANCA
TOWER

Parco
Sempione

See Milan Hotels & Restaurants detail map

VIALE MOLIERE

PALAZZO
DELL'ARTE

VIA GADIO

FORO

Lanza
Ⓜ

BUONAP

SFORZA
CASTLE

MUSEUM
OF ARTS
& SCIENCE

To Fiera
di Milano
Trade
Fair

V. 20 SETTEMBRE

VIA VICENZO MONTI

FORO

Piazza
Castello

❹

CADORNA
STATION

Ⓜ
Cadorna

BUONAPARTE

Largo
Cairoli

ⓘ

❶

❷

Ⓜ
Cairol

VIA GIOVANNI   BOCCACCIO

TEATRO
DAL VERME

VIA G. PUCCINI

VIA GIOVANNI MURO

LAST SUPPER
S. MARIA
D. GRAZIE

V. CARADOSSO

PALAZZO
LITTA

CORSO MAGENTA

V. S. GIOVANNI

VIA MERAVIGLI

CORSO MAGENTA

To
Leonardo's
Horse & Meazza
Stadium

PALAZZO
DELLE
STELLINE

VIA GIOSUE CARDUCCI

V. SANT'
AGNESE

VIA NIRONE

VIA LUINI

V. BRISA

VIA BORROMEI

BORS

VIA SAN VITTORE

OSPEDALE
S. GIUSEPPE

VIA TERRAGGIO

VIA

V. L. NECCHI

V. SANT'ORSOLA

S. VITTORE
AL CORPO

BASILICA DI
S. AMBROGIO

LAPPUCCIO

VIA SANTA MARTA

DA VINCI
NATIONAL
SCIENCE MUSEUM

Ⓜ Sant'
Ambrogio

UNIVERSITA
CATTOLICA

VIA LANZONE

PUSTERLA DI
S. AMBROGIO

VIA EDMONDO   DE   AMICIS

V. CAMI

VIA COREMTI

VIA STAM

VIA BAN

VI

Ⓜ Sant'Agostino

VIA OLONA

VIA

VIA

AUSONIO

S. VINCENZO

VIA MORA

VIA ARIBERTO

VIA

VIA C. DA SESTO

CALOGERO

CORSO GENOVA

S. LORENZ

VIALE PAPINIANO

VIALE

VIALE COI ZUGNA

VIA SIMONETTA

To
Navigli
District ↓

V. MOLINO D. ARM

N

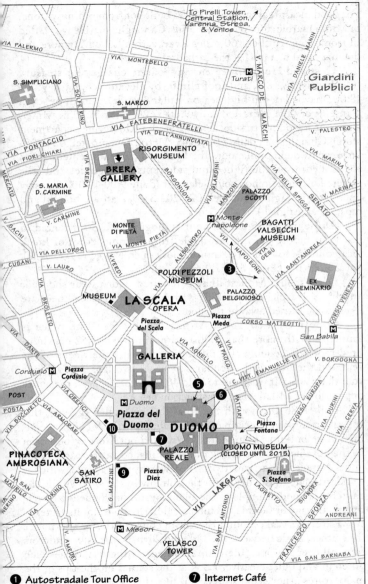

① Autostradale Tour Office
② Zani Viaggi Tours
③ Via Montenapoleone (High-Fashion Shops)
④ Museum of Ancient Art Entrance
⑤ Stairs to Duomo Roof
⑥ Elevators to Duomo Roof (2)
⑦ Internet Café
⑧ American Bookstore
⑨ Tram #16 to Last Supper, Leo's Horse & Meazza Stadium
⑩ Trams #12, #14 to Monumental Cemetery

MILAN

For good measure, the cathedral was built not from ordinary stone, but from marble, top to bottom. Pink Candoglia marble was rafted in from a quarry about 60 miles away, across Lake Maggiore and down a canal to a port at the cathedral.

Cost and Hours: Free entry; separate charges for treasury (€1), baptistery (€4), and roof climb (by elevator-€8, daily 9:00-18:00, maybe later in high season, enter outside at north or south transept; or take stairs-€5, daily 9:00-17:20, until 16:20 in winter, enter outside on north side, across from La Rinascente department store). Church open daily 7:00-18:45, Metro: Duomo, tel. 02-7202-2656, www.duomomilano.it. The Duomo Point info center behind the cathedral on the right-hand side rents audioguides and sells tickets for the Duomo's south elevator (daily 9:00-18:00, may stay open later in high season, tel. 02-7202-3375, staff are helpful and most speak English).

Audioguide: €5 for 1.5-hour audioguide, €2.50 if rented in last hour before closing (available from Duomo Point or kiosk located inside to right of entrance, kiosk open Mon-Fri 9:30-17:30, Sat 9:30-16:00, closed Sun, ID required).

Dress Code: Modest dress is required. Don't wear shorts or anything sleeveless. Even kids with bare shoulders or knees are likely to be turned away at the door.

◐ Self-Guided Tour: At 525 by 300 feet, the place is immense, with more than 2,000 statues inside and 52 one-hundred-foot-tall, sequoia-size pillars representing the weeks of the year and the liturgical calendar. If you do two laps, you've done your daily walk. It was built to hold 40,000 worshippers, the entire population of Milan when construction began.

Built 1386-1810, with the final touches added in 1965, this construction project originated the Italian phrase for "never-ending": "like building a cathedral." It started out Gothic (best seen in the apse behind the altar) and was finished in the early 1800s under Napoleon (particularly the noteworthy west facade, which is wonderful late in the day, with the sun low in the sky). While the church is a good example of the Flamboyant, or "flamelike," over-ripe final stage of Gothic, architectural harmony is not its forte.

Exterior: Walk around the entire church exterior and notice the statues, made between the 14th and 20th centuries by sculptors from all over Europe. There are hundreds of these statues—each different and quite creative. Look at the statues on the tips of the many spires...they seem so relaxed, like they're just hanging out, waiting for their big day. Functioning as drain spouts, the 96 fanciful gargoyle monsters are especially imaginative.

As you stand outside at the back, behind the altar, imagine the glory of this first wall. These were the earliest stones, laid in 1390. The sun-in-rose window was the proud symbol of the city's leading Visconti family; it's flanked by the angel telling Mary she's going to bear the Messiah. And behind you is a shrine to the leading religion of the 21st century: soccer. The Football Team store is filled with colorful vestments and relics of local soccer saints (go upstairs, daily 10:00-19:00).

Return to the front and enjoy the statues enlivening the facade. The lower ones—full of energy and movement—are early Baroque, from about 1600. Of the five doors, the center one is biggest. Made in 1907 in the Liberty style, it features the Joy and Sorrow of the Virgin Mary. Sad scenes are on the left, joyful ones on the right, and on top is the coronation of Mary in heaven by Jesus with all the saints and angels looking on.

Interior: Enter the church. Stand at the back of the fourth-longest nave in Christendom. The apse at the far end was started in 1386. The wall behind you wasn't finished until 1520. Even though the Renaissance had begun, builders stuck with the Gothic style. The two single stone-marble pillars behind you are the most precious ones in the church.

Notice two tiny lights: The little red one above the altar marks where a nail from the cross of Jesus is kept. This relic was brought to Milan by St. Helen (Emperor Constantine's mother) in the fourth century, when Milan was the capital of the Western Roman Empire. It's on display for three days a year (in mid-Sept). Now look high to the right and find a tiny pinhole of white light. This is designed to shine a 10-inch sunbeam at noon onto the bronze line that runs across the floor, indicating where we are on the zodiac (but local guides claim they've never seen it work).

Stained-Glass Windows: Wander deeper into the church up the right aisle. Check out the windows—15th-century mosaics of brilliant and expensive colored glass (stained, not painted). Bought by wealthy families seeking the Church's favor, they face the south and get the most light. The altars below generally honor the patron who made that window possible. Pick out familiar scenes in the windows. The purpose was to teach the illiterate masses the way to salvation through stories of the Old Testament and the life of Jesus. On the opposite wall (left side), many of the windows date from the time of Napoleon and are either made of dimmer, cheaper painted glass or are replacements for ones bombed out in World War II.

One window is clearly more modern, dating from the 1980s and celebrating the three top local cardinals, two of whom became saints (St. Ambrose, St. Charles Borromeo, and Cardinal Ferrari).

Altar: Belly up to the bar facing the high altar. While the church is Gothic, the area around the altar was made Baroque— the style of the Vatican in the 1570s (a Roman Catholic statement to counter the Protestant churches of the north, which were mostly

Milan at a Glance

▲▲**Duomo** Milan's showpiece cathedral, with an amazing roof you can walk on, amid a forest of spires. **Hours:** Church—daily 7:00-18:45, rooftop stairs—daily 9:00-17:20, until 16:20 in winter; rooftop elevator—daily 9:00-18:00, may close later in high season. See page 299.

▲▲**Galleria Vittorio Emanuele** Glass-domed arcade on the main square, perfect for window-shopping and people-watching. **Hours:** Always open. See page 307.

▲▲**La Scala Opera House and Museum** The world's most prestigious opera house. **Hours:** Museum daily 9:00-12:30 & 13:30-17:30. See page 308.

▲▲**Pinacoteca Ambrosiana** Oldest museum in Milan, with works by Raphael, Leonardo, Botticelli, Titian, and Caravaggio, and a special exhibit of Leonardo sketches (until 2015). **Hours:** Tue-Sun 10:00-18:00, closed Mon. See page 310.

▲**Piazza del Duomo** Milan's main square, full of energy, history, and pickpockets. **Hours:** Always open. See page 306.

▲**Brera Art Gallery** World-class collection of Italian paintings (13th-20th centuries), including Raphael, Caravaggio, Gentile da Fabriano, Piero della Francesca, Mantegna, and the Bellini brothers. **Hours:** Tue-Sun 8:30-19:00, closed Mon. See page 312.

▲**Risorgimento Museum** History of Italian unification. **Hours:** Tue-Sun 9:00-13:00 & 14:00-17:30, closed Mon. See page 313.

▲**Sforza Castle** Milan's castle containing a museum whose highlight is an unfinished Michelangelo *Pietà*. **Hours:** Tue-Sun 9:00-17:30, closed Mon. See page 313.

▲**Via Dante** Human traffic frolics to lilting accordions on one of Europe's longest pedestrian-only boulevards. **Hours:** Always open. See page 315.

MILAN

Gothic). Napoleon crowned himself King of Italy under this dome in 1805. Now look to the rear up at the ceiling and see the fancy "carving" (between the ribs)—nope, that's painted. It looks expensive, but paint is more affordable than carved stone.

Statue: Find the bald statue lit by the open door, by the wall in the south transept. This is a grotesque 16th-century statue of St. Bartolomeo, an apostle and first-century martyr skinned alive

▲**The Last Supper** Leonardo da Vinci's masterpiece, viewable only with a reservation—book several months in advance. **Hours:** Tue-Sun 8:15-18:45 (last visit), closed Mon. See page 316.

▲**Leonardo da Vinci National Science and Technology Museum** Leonardo's designs illustrated in wooden models, plus a vast collection of historical, scientific, and technological bric-a-brac and machines. **Hours:** Tue-Fri 9:30-17:00, Sat-Sun 9:30-18:30, closed Mon. See page 318.

▲**Monumental Cemetery** Evocative outdoor art gallery with tombs showcasing expressive art styles from 1870-1930. **Hours:** Tue-Sun 8:00-18:00, closed Mon. See page 320.

Church of Santa Maria presso San Satiro Pilgrim church with impressive 3-D paintings. **Hours:** Mon-Fri 7:30-11:30 & 15:30-18:30, Sat 15:30-19:00, Sun 10:00-12:00 & 15:30-19:00. See page 310.

Poldi Pezzoli Museum Italian paintings (15th-18th centuries), weaponry, and decorative arts. **Hours:** Wed-Mon 10:00-18:00, closed Tue. See page 313.

Bagatti Valsecchi Museum 19th-century Italian Renaissance furnishings. **Hours:** Tue-Sun 13:00-17:45, closed Mon. See page 313.

Branca Tower Great 360-degree views over the city. **Hours:** Erratic—call or confirm at TI before heading there, closed Mon and in bad weather. See page 315.

Museum of Art and Science Leonardo da Vinci's art and inventions, with hands-on exhibits on authenticating and dating various forms of art. **Hours:** Mon-Fri 10:00-18:00, closed Sat-Sun. See page 315.

Leonardo's Horse Gargantuan equestrian monument built according to Leonardo's designs. **Hours:** Tue-Sun 9:00-17:30, closed Mon. See page 319.

MILAN

by the Romans. Walk behind the poor guy wearing his skin like a robe to see his face, hands, and feet. Carved by a student of Leonardo da Vinci, this is a study in human anatomy learned by dissection, forbidden by the Church at the time.

Floor: Walk toward the altar and around the corner 30 steps, to a gate blocking entry to the apse. Look down at the fine 16th-century inlaid-marble floor. The pieces around the altar are original. You can tell that the black marble (quarried from Lake Como) is harder because it looks and feels less worn than the other colors (the white is from Lake Maggiore, the pink from Verona).

The apse is lit by three huge windows, all 19th-century painted copies. The originals, destroyed in Napoleonic times, were made of precious stained glass.

Treasury: Steps lead under the altar to the treasury and to the tombs of St. Charles Borromeo (1538-1584) and his family. Charles was bishop of Milan, and the second most important hometown saint after St. Ambrose. Silver reliefs around the ceiling show scenes from Charles' life. The treasury, or *tesoro*, features empty reliquaries and carved ivories (€1).

Paleo-Christian Baptistery: In the rear of the church (buy €4 ticket at bookshop kiosk, same hours as the Duomo), you can climb down into the church that stood here long before the present one. Milan was an important center of early Christianity. In Roman times, Mediolanum's street level was 10 feet below today's level. You'll see the scant remains of an eight-sided baptistery (where saints Augustine and Ambrose were baptized) and a little church. Back then, since you couldn't enter the church until you were baptized (which didn't happen until age 18), churches had a little "holy zone" just outside for the unbaptized. This included a baptistery like this one.

Cathedral Rooftop: This is the most memorable part of a Duomo visit. You'll wander through a fancy forest of spires with great views of the city, the square, and—on clear days—the crisp and jagged Italian Alps. And, 330 feet above everything, La Madonnina overlooks it all. This 15-foot-tall gilded Virgin Mary is a symbol of the city.

Climb the stairs or take the elevator; the entrances to both are outside the church (for specifics, see "Cost and Hours," earlier).

▲▲**Duomo Museum (Museo del Duomo)**—This fine museum, currently closed for extensive renovation, offers an excellent opportunity to understand Milan's cathedral and see its original art close up. It's likely to reopen in 2015.

▲**Piazza del Duomo**—Milan's main square is a classic European scene and a popular local gathering point. Professionals scurry, fashion-conscious kids loiter, young thieves peruse. Teens hang out near the Galleria entrance in the afternoons, waving at the balcony above in hopes of being filmed by MTV cameras located in an upper-floor studio.

Standing in the square (midway between the statue and the Galleria), you're surrounded by history. The statue is Victor Emmanuel II, first king of Italy. He's looking at the grand Galleria named for him. The words above the triumphal arch entrance read: "To Victor Emmanuel II, from the people of Milan."

Behind the statue (opposite the cathedral) is the center of medieval Milan: Piazza Mercanti. Dating from 1220, the medieval City Hall (look for its red-brick arches) marked the center of town back when the entire city stood within its immense fortified walls. The merchant's square is a strangely peaceful place today, with a fine smattering of old-time Milano architecture that escaped the bombs of World War II.

Opposite the Galleria are twin fascist buildings. Mussolini made grandiose speeches from their balconies. Study the buildings' relief panels, which tell—with fascist melodrama—the history of Milan. Between these buildings and the cathedral (set back a bit) is the historic ducal palace, Palazzo Reale. This building, now a venue for temporary art exhibits, was redone in the Neoclassical style by Maria Theresa in the late 1700s, when Milan was ruled by the Austrian Habsburgs. For a fine view of the Duomo and the piazza, climb the steps to the balcony of the skinny fascist-style building closest to the cathedral (can be closed for frequent *manifestazioni*—demonstrations—or any other perceived security threat). Behind the Duomo is a vibrant pedestrian shopping zone along Corso Vittorio Emanuele.

▲▲**Galleria Vittorio Emanuele**—A symbol of Milan is its great four-story glass-domed arcade on the cathedral square. Built dur-

ing the heady days of Italian unification (c. 1870), it was the first building in town to have electric lighting. Here you can turn an expensive cup of coffee into a good value by enjoying Europe's best people-watching (or get the same view for peanuts from the strategically placed McDonald's).

The venerable **Bar Zucca** (at the entry), with a friendly staff and an Art Deco interior typical of the 1920s, is the former haunt of famous opera composer Giuseppe Verdi and conductor Arturo

Toscanini, who used to stop by after their performances at La Scala. It's a fine place to enjoy a drink and people-watch (€3 for an espresso is a great deal if you relax and enjoy the view, or €1 at the bar just to enjoy the sumptuous interior). Once called the Campari café, this is considered the birthplace of the famous Campari bitter. Now a bitter aperitif, Zucca, is their signature drink (€3.70 standing or €9 seated, Tue-Sun 7:30-20:00, closed Mon and Aug, tel. 02-8646-4435).

Wander around the gallery. Its art celebrates the establishment of Italy as an independent country. Around the central dome, patriotic mosaics symbolize the four major continents. The mosaic floor is also patriotic. The white cross in the center represents the king. The she-wolf with Romulus and Remus (on the south side—facing Rome) honors the city that, since 1870, has been the national capital. On the west side (facing Torino, the provisional capital of Italy from 1861-1865), you'll find that city's symbol: a *torino* (little bull). For good luck, locals step on his irresistible little testicles. Two local girls explained to me that it works better if you spin. Find the poor little bull and observe for a few minutes...it's a cute scene. With so much spinning, the mosaic is replaced every few years.

Piazza della Scala—This smart little traffic-free square, out the back between the Galleria and the opera house, is dominated by a statue of Leonardo da Vinci. The statue (from 1870) is a reminder that Leonardo spent many years in Milan working for the Sforza family (who dominated Milan as the Medici family dominated Florence). Under the great Renaissance genius stand four of his greatest "Leonardeschi." (He apprenticed a sizable group of followers.) The reliefs show his various contributions as painter, architect, and engineer. Leonardo, wearing his hydro-engineer hat, re-engineered Milan's canal system, complete with locks. (Until the 1920s, Milan was one of Italy's major ports, with canals connecting the city to the Po River and Lake Maggiore.)

▲▲**La Scala Opera House and Museum**—The statue of Leonardo behind the Galleria is looking at a plain but famous Neoclassical building, arguably the world's most prestigious opera house: Milan's Teatrale alla Scala. La Scala opened in 1778 with an opera by Antonio Salieri (of *Amadeus* fame).

At Milan's famous opera house and its adjacent museum, opera buffs can see the museum's extensive collection and get a glimpse of the theater.

Museum: Well-described in English, the collection features things that mean absolutely nothing to the hip-hop crowd: Verdi's top hat, Rossini's eyeglasses, Toscanini's baton, Fettuccini's pesto, original scores, diorama stage sets, costumes, busts, portraits, and death masks of great composers and musicians. The museum allows you to peek into the actual theater. The stage is as big as the seating area on the ground floor. (You can see the towering stage box from Piazza della Scala across the street.) A recent five-year renovation corrected acoustical problems caused by WWII bombing and subsequent reconstruction. The royal box is just below your vantage point, in the center rear. Notice the massive chandelier made of Bohemian crystal (€5, daily 9:00-12:30 & 13:30-17:30, last entry 30 minutes before closing, Piazza della Scala, tel. 02-8879-7473, www.teatroallascala.org).

Opera: The show goes on at the world-famous La Scala Opera House. Schedules vary, but the opera season is nearly year-round (show time 20:00), and ballet and classical concerts are held from October through June. No performances are held in August (for information, call Scala Infotel Service, daily 9:00-18:00, tel. 02-7200-3744; for automated booking, call 02-860-775 and press 2 for English; or book online at www.teatroallascala.org). On the opening night of an opera, a dress code is enforced for men (suit and tie).

Tickets generally go on sale one month before a performance. Seats sell out quickly. On performance days, 140 sky-high gallery tickets are sold at a discount only at the box office (located down the left side of the theater toward the back on Via Filodrammatici, and marked with *Biglietteria Serale* sign). If you want a same-day discounted (but still not cheap) ticket, show up at 13:00 to get your name on the list. Return at 17:30 for the roll call. You must be present when your name is called in order to receive a voucher, which you'll then show at the ticket window to purchase a discounted ticket. One hour before show time, the box office sells any remaining tickets at a 25 percent discount. You can also buy tickets—but not the discounted ones—at a handy ticket office in the Duomo Metro station (daily 12:00-18:00, entrance is to right of the Duomo as you face it, underground, follow signs to *ATM Point*), as well as on the Internet (Web sales end one hour before show time).

Via Speronari—A block off Piazza del Duomo, this is one of Milan's oldest streets, and the most charming drag in the old center. Via Speronari—named for the spurs once made and sold here—is worth a wander. Street names around here recall their medieval crafts: *speronari*—spurs, *spadari*—swords, *armorari*—armor. The weaponry made on these streets was high fashion among Europe's warrior class...like having an Armani dagger. While right in the city center, the neighborhood feels vital because it's also a residential street. Banks of doorbells indicate that families live above the shops. Start at the corner of Via Mazzini and Via Speronari, one block southwest of the Duomo. A shop on your right—*L'Ortolan Pusae Vecc de Milan*—brags in the old Milanese language that this is the oldest fruit-and-veggie store in the city. The neighboring Princi bakery is understandably popular. Its brioches are rarely more than a few minutes old. The *tavola calda*—hot table—across the street sells fresh, hearty take-out to hungry businesspeople.

Where Via Speronari hits Via Torino, go 20 yards to the left to find the...

Church of Santa Maria presso San Satiro (Church of St. Mary at St. Satiro)—Hiding behind its Baroque facade, this church was the scene of a temper tantrum in 1242, when a losing gambler vented his anger by hitting the baby Jesus in the Madonna-and-Child altarpiece. Blood "miraculously" spurted out, and the beautiful little church has been on the pilgrimage trail ever since. While I've never seen any blood, I'd swear I've seen a 3-D background behind the basically flat altar (a *trompe l'oeil* illusion—only about a foot deep). This church—squeezed between the earlier church of San Satiro and a street—had no room for a real apse, so the Renaissance architect Donato Bramante created the illusion of an apse.

In the north transept, you'll find that original ninth-century church of San Satiro (brother of St. Ambrose, patron saint of Milan). This tiny church—with surviving bits of Byzantine fresco—predated the rest. From this chapel, look back at the main altar to see Bramante's 3-D work collapsed. On the opposite side (near entry)—with dimensions mirroring this old chapel—an eight-sided baptistery by Bramante from the 1480s shows the mathematically based values of the Renaissance. If you have a prayer in need of an extra boost, pop a coin into the box and "light" an electric candle.

Cost and Hours: Free entry, Mon-Fri 7:30-11:30 & 15:30-18:30, Sat 15:30-19:00, Sun 10:00-12:00 & 15:30-19:00, Via Torino at Via Speronari, tel. 02-874-683.

▲▲Pinacoteca Ambrosiana (with Leonardo exhibit)—This oldest museum in Milan was inaugurated in 1618 to house Cardinal Federico Borromeo's painting collection. And until 2015, the museum is both more expensive and more important, thanks to a long-running special exhibit displaying 22 pages from Leonardo's notebook. Think of your visit in two parts: the permanent collection of paintings (including the Leonardo Hall), and the last room, which has the notebook pages. While it's exciting to see the pages, the permanent material is still the highlight. Pick up the English-language map locating major works, and rent the €1 audioguide, which explains highlights of both the permanent and special exhibits.

Cost and Hours: €15, Tue-Sun 10:00-18:00, closed Mon, near Piazza del Duomo at Piazza Pio XI 2, tel. 02-8069-2221, www .ambrosiana.it.

Touring the Museum: Pinacoteca Ambrosiana began as a teaching academy, which explains its many replicas of famous works of art. Highlights include original paintings by Botticelli, Caravaggio, and Titian. As Cardinal Borromeo was a friend of Jan Brueghel, you'll find an entire room (#7) filled with delightful works by Brueghel and other Flemish masters. Study the wonderful detail in Brueghel's *Allegory of Fire* and *Allegory of Water*. The Flemish paintings are extremely detailed—many painted on copper to heighten the effect—and offer an insight into the psyche of the age. If the cardinal were asked why he enjoyed paintings that celebrated the secular life, he'd likely say, "Secular themes are God's book of nature."

Filling an entire wall, Raphael's charcoal-on-canvas cartoon served as an outline for the famous *School of Athens* fresco at the Vatican Museum. (A cartoon—*cartone* in Italian—is a large sketch that functions as a model for the making of a fresco.) While the Vatican's much-adored fresco is attributed entirely to Raphael, it was painted mostly by his students. But this *cartone* was wholly sketched by the hand of Raphael. To make the fresco, his assistants riddled this cartoon with pinpricks along the outlines of the characters, stuck it to the wall of the pope's study, and then applied a colored powder. When they removed the *cartone,* the characters' shapes were marked on the wall, and completing the fresco was a lot like filling in a coloring book. If you've seen the original fresco at the Vatican, you'll notice that the figure of Michelangelo (as a brooding stonecutter lounging on the steps in the foreground) is missing from the cartoon. Raphael added him to the fresco as a tribute after seeing his awe-inspiring work on the ceiling of the Sistine Chapel.

As Leonardo da Vinci spent many of his most productive years working in Milan, the city has an affinity for the Renaissance genius. The **Leonardo Hall,** with more of the gallery's permanent collection, features da Vinci's *Portrait of a Musician*, a copy of *The Last Supper*, and several fine Leonardo-type paintings by Luini and other disciples. During his Milan years, Leonardo created *The Last Supper* and painted several other famous canvases. Of these other paintings, only the *Portrait of a Musician*—as delicate, mysterious, and thought-provoking as the *Mona Lisa*—remains in Milan. The large fresco filling the far wall—with Christ receiving the crown of thorns—is by Luini. I find the painting of *The Last Supper* most interesting. When the cardinal realized that Leonardo's marvelous frescoed original was fading, he commissioned a careful copy to be created here for posterity. Today, this copy gives a rare chance to appreciate the original colorful richness of the now-faded masterpiece.

The Leonardo Hall leads into the somber library called Federiciana Hall, where you'll find the special Leonardo exhibit. The gallery, which owns da Vinci's *Codex Atlanticus,* is showing 22 of its 1,100 pages in themed exhibits changing quarterly until 2015. Soft period music accompanies your time with the 22 glass cases, each displaying a well-lit page from the notebook (the audioguide, which explains each page of the current exhibit, is essential to fully enjoy your visit). Don't enter the special exhibit until you are done with the permanent collection, as it's a one-way system and re-entry isn't allowed.

In the Brera Neighborhood

▲Brera Art Gallery—Milan's top collection of Italian paintings (13th-20th centuries) is world-class, but it can't top Rome's or Florence's. Established in 1809 to house Napoleon's looted art, it fills the first floor above a prestigious art college.

Enter the grand courtyard of a former monastery, where you'll be greeted by the nude *Napoleon with Tinkerbell* (by Antonio Canova). Climb the stairway (following signs to *Pinacoteca,* past all the art students), buy your ticket, and pick up an English map of the museum's masterpieces.

The gallery's highlights include works by Gentile da Fabriano, hinting at the realism of the coming Renaissance (check out the lifelike flowers and realistic, bright gold paint—he used real gold powder, Room IV). Andrea Mantegna's *The Dead Christ* is a text-book example of feet-first foreshortening (Room VI). Room XVIII hosts a permanent glass-enclosed restoration lab, allowing you to see various restoration works in progress.

In Room XXI, notice how Crivelli employs Renaissance technique (he was a contemporary of Leonardo), yet clings to the mystique of the Gothic Age (that's why I like him so much). Find eight Crivellis. Also, don't miss Raphael's *Wedding of the Madonna,* Piero della Francesca's *Madonna and Child with Four Angels* (Room XXIV), and the gritty-yet-intimate realism of Caravaggio's *Supper at Emmaus* (Room XXIX). Room XXXV features several of Canaletto's picture-postcards of Venetian cityscapes. This is Impressionism—not a single line in the works, just strategically placed daubs of paint that render palazzos and canals bathed in Venetian light with photographic precision. To spice things up, look for Francesco Hayez's hot and heavy *The Kiss (Il Bacio)* in Room XXXVII.

Java junkies will seek out the great, cheap cappuccino

MILAN

machine: Go through Napoleon's courtyard and straight through the art school to the end of the long hall; the machine's on your left. It's fun to explore the art school on the ground floor, mill about among the many young students, and wonder if there's a 21st-century Leonardo in your midst.

Cost and Hours: €5, more during special exhibits, Tue-Sun 8:30-19:00, closed Mon, last entry 45 minutes before closing, free lockers just before the ticket counter, no photos, Via Brera 28, Metro: Lanza or Montenapoleone, tel. 02-722-631, www.brera .beniculturali.it. Since there are no English descriptions, consider renting the audioguide (€5, ID required).

▲**Risorgimento Museum**—With a quick 30-minute swing through this quiet one-floor museum, you'll get an idea of the interesting story of Italy's rocky road to unity: from Napoleon (1796) to the victory in Rome (1870). However, there isn't much information in English. It's just around the block from the Brera Art Gallery at Via Borgonuovo 23.

Cost and Hours: €2, Tue-Sun 9:00-13:00 & 14:00-17:30, closed Mon, Metro: Montenapoleone, tel. 02-8846-4176, www .museodelrisorgimento.mi.it.

Near Montenapoleone

Poldi Pezzoli Museum—This classy house of art features top Italian paintings of the 15th through 18th centuries, old weaponry, and lots of interesting decorative arts, such as a roomful of old sundials and compasses.

Cost and Hours: €9, Wed-Mon 10:00-18:00, last entry one hour before closing, closed Tue, ask for English brochure and map at ticket desk, free English audioguides, Via Manzoni 12, Metro: Montenapoleone, tel. 02-796-334, www.museopoldipezzoli.it.

Bagatti Valsecchi Museum—This unique 19th-century collection of Italian Renaissance furnishings was assembled by two aristocratic brothers who spent a wad turning their home into a Renaissance mansion. Museum guards pack flashlights for closer examination of fine wood carvings.

Cost and Hours: €8, half-price on Wed, open Tue-Sun 13:00-17:45, closed Mon, free English audioguides and good English descriptions throughout, Via Gesù 5, Metro: Montenapoleone, tel. 02-7600-6132, www.museobagattivalsecchi.org.

Sforza Castle and Nearby

▲**Sforza Castle (Castello Sforzesco)**—The castle of Milan tells the story of the city in brick. Built in the late 1300s as a military fortress, it guarded the gate to the city wall and defended Milan from enemies "within and without." It was beefed up by the Sforza duke in 1450 in anticipation of a Venetian attack. Later, it was the Renaissance palace of the Sforza family and was even home to their in-house genius, Leonardo. During the many years of foreign rule (16th-19th centuries), it was a barracks for occupying Spanish, French, and Austrian soldiers. Today, it houses several museums.

Cost and Hours: €3, €6 during special exhibits, free entry 16:30-17:00 and Fri 14:00-17:00; open Tue-Sun 9:00-17:30, closed Mon, WCs and limited free lockers are downstairs from the ticket counter—get key and give ID at ticket desk, English info fliers throughout and at information office beside the Porta Umberto entrance, Metro: Cairoli, tel. 02-8846-3700, www.milanocastello.it.

Touring the Castle: The **gate** stands above a ditch that was once filled with water. A relief celebrates Umberto I, the second king of Italy. Above that, a statue of St. Ambrose, the patron of Milan (and a local bishop in the fourth century), oversees the action. Notice the chart, just outside the gate, showing how the city was encircled first by a crude medieval wall, and then by a state-of-the-art 16th-century wall—of which this castle was a key element. It's apparent from the enormity of these walls that Milan was a strategic prize. Today, the walls are gone, giving the city two circular boulevards.

This immense, often-bombed-and-rebuilt brick fortress—exhausting at first sight—can only be described as heavy. But its courtyard has a great lawn for picnics and siestas. Some parts of the roof and facade may be under renovation, but this shouldn't affect your visit. Its main museum, the **Museum of Ancient Art,** is fascinating, unlike the other museums in the castle. Enter the museum just past the ticket counter. It fills the old Sforza family palace with interesting medieval armor, furniture, early Lombard art, an Egyptian collection, and—for your finale—Michelangelo's unfinished *Pietà Rondanini* in Room XV.

This is a rare opportunity to enjoy a Michelangelo with no crowds. Michelangelo died while still working on this piece—his fourth *Pietà*. A *pietà*, by definition, is a representation of a dead Christ with a sorrowful Virgin Mary. This unfinished statue is surrounded by a fortress-like concrete wall to limit its viewing to a few tourists at a time, and is unique in that it shows the genius of Michelangelo midway through a major rework—Christ's head is cut out of Mary's right shoulder, and an earlier arm is still just hanging there. But there's a certain power to this rawness. Walk around the back to see the strain in Mary's back (and Michelangelo's rough chisel work) as she struggles to support her son. The sculpture's elongated form hints at the Mannerist style that would follow. Notice the ancient Roman altar underneath the *Pietà*. This sculpture was owned by the Rondanini family until just after World War II.

At the far end of the castle's grounds is the monumental **Arco della Pace**, a triumphal arch. They built the arch facing Paris to welcome Napoleon's rule, because locals believed he would bring with him the ideals of the French Revolution. When they learned he was just another megalomaniac, they turned the horses around, their tails facing France. The neighborhood near the arch is becoming a trendy nighttime district; see "Nightlife in Milan," later.

Branca Tower—This tower, a five-minute walk from the Sforza Castle through Milan's equivalent of Central Park, offers a commanding city view. You'll ride an elevator that takes you as high as the Mary that crowns the cathedral.

Cost and Hours: €4, hours are erratic, call or confirm at TI before heading out, closed Mon and in bad weather, tel. 02-331-4120.

Museum of Art and Science (Museo d'Arte e Scienza)—This hands-on museum offers an interesting look at Leonardo's works during the 20 years he spent in Milan. It includes his paintings and sketches, and inventions such as a clever drum machine and war machines in miniature. Another part of the museum describes how to tell the difference between genuine art and copies or fakes, with 10 demonstration stations. Oddly, a third collection features African and Buddhist art.

Cost and Hours: €8, Mon-Fri 10:00-18:00, closed Sat-Sun, English descriptions throughout, Via Q. Sella 4; tel. 02-720-2488, www.museoartescienza.com.

▲**Via Dante**—This grand pedestrian boulevard and popular shopping street leads from the Sforza Castle toward the town center and the Duomo. Since Via Dante was carved out of a medieval tangle of streets to celebrate Italian unification (c. 1870), all the facades lining it are relatively new. Over the vigorous complaints of merchants, the street became traffic-free in 1995. Today, they'd have it no other way. Enjoy strolling this beautiful people zone, where you'll hear the whir of bikes and the lilting melodies of accordion players instead of traffic noise. Photo exhibits are frequently displayed up and down the street. In front of the Sforza Castle, a commanding statue of Giuseppe Garibaldi, one of the heroes of the unification movement, looks down one of Europe's longest pedestrian zones. From here you can walk to the Duomo and beyond (about 1.5 miles) down streets that are all nearly traffic-free. Stroll and appreciate Italian design both in people and in windows (ignore the Foot Locker).

The Last Supper and Nearby

▲**Leonardo da Vinci's *The Last Supper* (Cenacolo)**—
Housed in the Church of Santa Maria delle Grazie, this is one
of the ultimate masterpieces of the Renaissance. Milan's leading
family, the Sforza, hired da Vinci to decorate the dining hall of
the Dominican monastery that adjoins the church. This gift was
essentially a bribe to the monks so that the Sforzas could locate
their family tomb in the church. Ultimately, the French drove
the Sforzas out of Milan, they were never buried here, and the
Dominicans got a great fresco for nothing. Note that this is a rare
sight, and entry must be booked months in advance (explained
later).

Because of Leonardo's experimental fresco technique, deterioration began within six years of its completion. The church was
bombed in World War II, but—miraculously, it seems—the wall
holding *The Last Supper* remained standing. A 21-year restoration
project (completed in 1999) peeled away 500 years of touch-ups,
leaving Leonardo's masterpiece faint but vibrant.

In a big, vacant whitewashed room, you'll see faded pastels
and not a crisp edge. The feet under the table look like negatives.
But the composition is dreamy—Leonardo captures the psycho-
logical drama as the Lord says, "One of you will betray me," and
the apostles huddle in stressed-out groups of three, wondering,
"Lord, is it I?" Some are scandalized. Others want more information. Simon (on the far right) gestures as if to ask a question
that has no answer. In this agitated atmosphere, only Judas (fourth
from left and the only one with his face in shadow)—clutching his
30 pieces of silver and looking pretty guilty—is not shocked.

The circle meant life and harmony to Leonardo. Deep into a
study of how life emanates in circles—like ripples on a pool hit by
a pebble—Leonardo positioned the 13 characters in a semicircle.

Jesus is in the center, from whence the spiritual force of God emanates, or ripples out.

The room depicted in the painting seems like an architectural extension of the church. The disciples form an apse, with Jesus as the altar—in keeping with the Eucharist. Jesus anticipates his sacrifice, his face sad, all-knowing, and accepting. His feet even foreshadowed his death by crucifixion. Had the door, which was cut out in 1652, not been added, you'd see how Leonardo placed Jesus' feet atop each other, ready for the nail.

The room was a refectory or dining room for the Dominican friars. Traditionally, they'd gather here to eat, with a Last Supper scene on one wall facing a Crucifixion scene on the opposite wall.

The perspective is mathematically correct. In fact, restorers found a tiny nail hole in Jesus' left eye, which anchored the strings Leonardo used to establish these lines. The table is cheated out to show the meal. Notice the exquisite lighting. The walls are lined with tapestries (as they would have been), and the one on the right is brighter in order to fit the actual lighting in the refectory (which has windows on the left). With the extremely natural effect of the light and the drama of the faces, Leonardo created an effective masterpiece.

Cost and Hours: €8, includes €1.50 reservation fee (9:30 and 15:30 visits require €3.25 extra for provided guided English tour). Open Tue-Sun 8:15-18:45 (last visit), closed Mon. Show up 20 minutes before your scheduled time. When an attendant calls your time, get up and move into the next room.

Reservations: Reservations are mandatory. Even though the hype surrounding the blockbuster novel and movie *The Da Vinci Code* has died down, spots are still booked more than a month in advance—so plan ahead. To minimize the humidity problem—even though the damage has already been done—only 900 visitors a day are allowed in. That's 25 tourists popping in every 15 minutes for exactly 15 minutes. Prior to your appointment time, you wait in several rooms to dehumidify, while doors close behind you and open up slowly in front of you. The posted information about Leonardo is mainly in Italian.

If you book by **phone,** you'll have a greater selection of days and time slots to choose from, since the website doesn't reflect cancellations, but you won't be able to reserve same-day tickets (tel. 02-9280-0360, or from the US dial 011-39-02-9280-0360, office open Mon-Sat 8:00-18:30, closed Sun; the number is often busy—once you get through, dial 2 for an English-speaking operator; the process takes about two minutes and you'll hang up with an appointed entry time and a number; pay with credit card upon booking).

MILAN

If you book **online** using the official website, www.cenacolo vinciano.net, choose "Cenacolo Vinciano." You'll see a calendar that shows available time slots for the current month. If the days are blank, it means that all the slots for those days have been filled. Be careful when you select the date—on this calendar the first day of the week is Monday. If you can't find a spot when you need it, try calling instead, because cancellations show up on the website as booked slots.

Last-Minute Tickets: While "reservations are required," if spots are available (more likely on weekdays and first thing in the morning) you can sometimes book one at the desk (even if *Sold Out* sign is posted). If fewer than 25 people show up for a particular time slot, you can get lucky. But those who show up without a reservation generally kill lots of time waiting around. Note that the Autostradale and Zani Viaggi bus tours (see "Tours in Milan," earlier) include entry to *The Last Supper*.

Audioguide: Consider the fine €2.50 audioguide. Its spiel fills every second of the time you're in the room—so try to start listening to it just before you enter (ideally in the waiting room while studying the reproduction of *The Last Supper*).

Photography: No photos are allowed.

Getting There: Take the Metro to Cadorna or Conciliazione (plus a 5-minute walk), or hop on tram #16 (catch it just off Piazza del Duomo on corner of Via Mazzini and Via Dogana), which drops you off in front of the Church of Santa Maria delle Grazie. The Science Museum (next listing) is two blocks away.

▲**Leonardo da Vinci National Science and Technology Museum (Museo Nazionale della Scienza e Tecnica "Leonardo da Vinci")**—The spirit of Leonardo lives here. Most tourists visit for the hall of Leonardo designs illustrated in wooden models, but Leonardo's mind is just as easy to appreciate by paging through a coffee-table edition of his notebooks in any bookstore. The rest of this immense collection of industrial cleverness is fascinating, with planes, trains, automobiles, ships, radios, old musical instruments, computers, batteries, telephones, chunks of the first transatlantic cable, interactive science workshops, and a 1960s "pocket-sized" submarine. Many exhibits include English descriptions. Some of the best exhibits (such as the Marconi radios) branch off the Leonardo hall. Ask for an English museum map from the ticket desk—you'll need it. Allow at least 1.5 hours here.

Cost and Hours: €10, guided tour of submarine-€8; Tue-Fri 9:30-17:00, Sat-Sun 9:30-18:30, closed Mon, Via San Vittore 21; bus #50 or #58 from the Sforza Castle; tram #16—catch it just off Piazza del Duomo, direction: San Siro; or Metro: Sant'Ambrogio; tel. 02-485-551, www.museoscienza.org.

Away from the Center

Leonardo's Horse—The largest equestrian monument in the world is a modern reconstruction of a model created in 1482 by

Leonardo da Vinci for the Sforza family. The clay prototype was destroyed in 1499 by invading French forces, who used it for target practice. In 1982, American Renaissance-art collector Charles Dent decided to build the 15-ton, 24-foot-long statue from Leonardo's design, planning to present it to the Italians in appreciation for their role in the Renaissance and in homage to Leonardo's genius.

Unfortunately, Dent died before the project could be completed. In 1997, American sculptor Nina Akamu created a new clay model that became the template for the final statue; it was unveiled in 1999. The exhibit, described in English, includes statue casts and photos of the construction.

Cost and Hours: Free, Tue-Sun 9:00-17:30, closed Mon, located on outskirts near Meazza soccer stadium and San Siro racetrack; from corner of Via Mazzini and Via Dogana, take tram #16, direction: San Siro, to Stratico Palatino stop—ask conductor when to get off, then head right on Via Palatino, and left on Piazzale dello Sport to #9; or you can walk a half-mile from Metro: Lotto.

Soccer—The Milanesi claim that their soccer (football, or *calcio*, in Italian) teams are the best in Europe. For a dose of Europe's soccer mania (which many believe provides a necessary testosterone vent to keep Europe out of a third big war), catch a match while you're here. A.C. Milan and Inter Milan are the ferociously competitive home teams (tickets-€10-350).

A.C. Milan tickets are sold at Intesa Sanpaolo banks (one's at Via Verdi 8, Mon-Fri 8:45-13:45 & 14:45-15:45, closed Sat-Sun), online at www.acmilan.com, or at the Milan Point Shop (Tue-Sat 10:00-19:00, closed Sun-Mon, Piazza XXVI Maggio next to Via San Gottardo). Inter Milan tickets are sold at Banca Popolare di Milano banks (one's at Piazza Meda 4, Metro: San Babila; Mon-Fri 8:45-13:45 & 14:45-15:45, closed Sat-Sun) or online at www .inter.it.

Games are held in the 85,000-seat Meazza stadium most Sunday afternoons from September to June (Metro: Lotto, or tram #16—catch it just off Piazza del Duomo, on corner of Via Mazzini and Via Dogana, direction: San Siro; take it to last stop, where you'll find the stadium). You'll need to have your passport when you buy your ticket and bring it with you to the stadium for security reasons. For more on the Italian passion for soccer, see page 820.

MILAN

▲**Monumental Cemetery (Il Cimitero Monumentale)**—
Europe's most artistic and dreamy cemetery experience, this grand
place was built just after unifica-
tion to provide a suitable final
resting spot for the city's "famous
and well-deserving men." Any
cemetery is evocative, but this
one—with its super-emotional
portrayals of the deceased and
their heavenly escorts (in art styles
c. 1870-1930)—is in a class by
itself. It's a vast garden art gallery

of proud busts and grim reapers, heartbroken angels and weeping
widows, too-young soldiers and countless old smiles, frozen on
yellowed black-and-white photos.

Cost and Hours: Free, Tue-Sun 8:00-18:00, closed Mon, pick
up map at the entrance gate, a long walk from Metro: Garibaldi
FS, or catch tram #12 or #14 from the corner of Via Orefici and Via
Cantu' near the Duomo, tel. 02-8846-5600, www.monumentale
.net.

Shopping in Milan

For world-class window-shopping, visit the "**Quadrilateral**," an
elegant high-fashion shopping area around Via Montenapoleone.
This was the original Beverly Hills of Milan. In the 1920s, the top
fashion shops moved in, and today it remains *the* place for designer
labels. Most places close Sunday and for much of August. On
Mondays, stores open only after 16:00. In this land where fur is
still prized, the people-watching is as entertaining as the window-
shopping. Notice also the exclusive penthouse apartments with
roof gardens high above the scene. Via Montenapoleone and the
pedestrianized Via della Spiga are the best streets.

Whether you're gawking or shopping, here's the best route:
From La Scala, walk up Via Manzoni to the Metro stop at
Montenapoleone, browse down Via Montenapoleone, cut left on
Via Santo Spirito (lined with grand aristocratic palazzos—peek
into the courtyard at #7), turn right to window-shop down Via
della Spiga, turn right on Via Sant'Andrea and then left, back
onto Montenapoleone, which leads you through a final gauntlet of
temptations to Piazza San Babila. Then (for less-expensive shopping thrills), walk back to the Duomo down the pedestrian-only
Corso Vittorio Emanuele. From the Duomo, go down Via Dante
to the Sforza Castle.

La Rinascente, next to the Duomo, is a Nordstrom-type
department store with something for everyone and an especially

good toy selection. Each floor has a fine collection of designer names sold out of independent shops, all functioning within the walls of this vast and venerable store. Simply riding the escalator up and up gives a fun overview of Italian design and marketing. The seventh floor is a top-end food circus, with terrace views of the Duomo and a public WC. Its name, meaning "the place reborn," fits its history. In an earlier life, it was a fine Liberty-style building until it burned down in 1918. It was rebuilt, only to be bombed in World War II and rebuilt once again (Mon-Thu 9:30-21:00, Fri-Sat 9:30-22:00, Sun 10:00-21:00, has a VAT refund office and recommended restaurants, faces north side of the Duomo on Piazza del Duomo).

Nightlife in Milan

For evening action, check out the artsy Brera area in the old center, with several swanky sidewalk cafés to choose from and lots of bars that stay open late. Home to Brera's Art University, this district has a sophisticated, lively people-watching scene. Another great neighborhood for nightlife, especially for a younger scene, is Navigli, Milan's formerly bohemian, now gentrified "Little Venice" (Metro: Porta Genova).

An up-and-coming area—which is expected to become the "in" place for evenings out during the 2015 World's Fair—is the neighborhood near Arco della Pace along Corso Sempione. Locals believe this street will become the Champs-Elysées of Milan. It's at the far end of the Sforza Castle grounds; just head for the triumphal arch. Find out what the fuss is about over an *aperitivo* during happy hour (18:00-21:00) at **Five Diamonds Lounge Bar,** an upmarket venue run by the owners of the recommended Ristorante Bruno (closed Mon; from Piazza Cordusio or La Scala, take tram #1, direction: Piazza Castelli; Corso Sempione 11, tel. 02-3459-3668).

There are always concerts and live music playing in the city at various clubs and concert halls. Specifics change quickly, so it's best to rely on the entertainment information in periodicals from the TI.

Sleeping in Milan

All recommended hotels are within a few minutes' walk of Milan's subway system. With Milan's fine Metro, you can get anywhere in town in a flash. Anytime in March, April, September, and October, the city can be completely jammed by conventions, and hotel prices jump way up. I've listed high-season prices, but not convention-gouging prices. (For the convention schedule, see

MILAN

Sleep Code

(€1 = about $1.40, country code: 39)
S = Single, **D** = Double/Twin, **T** = Triple, **Q** = Quad, **b** = bathroom, **s** = shower only. Unless otherwise noted, credit cards are accepted, English is spoken, and breakfast is included.

To help you sort easily through these listings, I've divided the accommodations into three categories based on the price for a standard double room with bath:

$$$ Higher Priced—Most rooms €150 or more.
 $$ Moderately Priced—Most rooms between €110-150.
  $ Lower Priced—Most rooms €110 or less.

Prices can change without notice; verify the hotel's current rates online or by email. For other updates, see www .ricksteves.com/update.

www.fieramilano.it.) Summer is usually wide-open and prices are discounted, though many hotels close in August for vacation. Hotels cater more to business travelers than to tourists, so Fridays and Saturdays are generally cheaper and available.

Lately I've noticed a trend in which small family-style hotels in the center are being neglected, and the big, modern business-class hotels around the train station are proliferating. I've tried to collect central places, where travelers feel appreciated and the staff feels like part of the family. If the following places are booked up, go online—there are lots of hotels near the train station.

Near the Duomo

The Duomo area is thick with people-watching, reasonably priced eateries, and the major sightseeing attractions. From the central train station to the Duomo, it's just four stops on a direct Metro line (yellow line 3, direction: San Donato) to Metro: Duomo.

$$$ Hotel Grand Duca di York is stuck oddly in the middle of banks and big-city starkness three blocks southwest of Piazza del Duomo. It's got lavish public spaces and 33 modern, bright rooms that are thoughtfully designed and decorated (Sb-€98-128, Db-€168-188, €30 more for terraces, air-con, elevator, free Wi-Fi, free minibar, near Metro stops: Cordusio or Duomo, Via Moneta 1, tel. 02-874-863, fax 02-869-0344, www.ducadiyork.com, info @ducadiyork.com).

$$$ Hotel Spadari boasts an Art Deco interior designed by the Milanese artist Giò Pomodoro ("Joe Tomato" in English). The 40 rooms have billowing drapes, big paintings, and designer doors. It's next door to the recommended Peck deli, and two blocks from the Duomo (standard Db-€198-248, deluxe Db-€268-328, no need for the pricier suites, Via Spadari 11, tel. 02-7200-2371, fax 02-861-184, www.spadarihotel.com, reservation@spadarihotel.com).

$ Hotel Vecchia Milano is a humble, clean, well-run place buried deep in the old town on a narrow lane. It rents 27 comfortable rooms at a great price for the location (Sb-€65, Db-€80-85, air-con, pay Wi-Fi, next to recommended Hostaria Borromei at Via Borromei 4, tel. 02-875-042, fax 02-8645-4292, www.hotel vecchiamilan.com, hotelvecchiamilano@tiscalinet.it).

Between La Scala and the Sforza Castle

$$$ Hotel Star, comfortable and modern, rents 30 sparkling, fresh, and spacious rooms (Sb-€165, Db-€215, prices drop about €40 outside convention times, check website for deals, interior rooms are quieter, air-con, fridge, Wi-Fi, usually closed Aug, Via dei Bossi 5, tel. 02-801-501, fax 02-861-787, www.hotelstar.it, info@hotelstar.it).

$$$ Antica Locanda dei Mercanti rents 15 rooms, some with terraces or kitchen facilities (Db-€175-250, more during conventions, breakfast extra, air-con, free Internet access and Wi-Fi, Via San Tomaso 6, Metro: Duomo or Cordusio; tel. 02-805-4080, fax 02-805-4090, www.locanda.it, locanda@locanda.it, Eri).

$$ London Hotel, a simple 30-room hotel with overstuffed little living rooms, an inviting breakfast room, and all the amenities, is tucked away on a quiet side street just off vibrant Via Dante. It's warmly run by the friendly Gambino family: mom and pop Elda and Franco don't speak English, but daughters Tanya and Licia do (S-€70, Sb-€90, D-€120, Db-€150, Tb-€180, prices much higher during conventions, skip their €8 breakfast and grab something on Via Dante, cheaper in July and Aug, book direct for these rates and get an additional 10 percent off with cash, air-con, elevator, near Metro: Cairoli at Via Rovello 3, tel. 02-7202-0166, fax 02-805-7037, www.hotellondonmilano.com, info@hotel londonmilano.com).

Near the Central Train Station

The train station neighborhood is more practical than characteristic. Its hotels are utilitarian business-class hotels with prices that bounce all over depending upon the convention schedule. You'll find more shady characters than shady trees in the parks, and lots of massage parlors. But you can't beat the convenience (near station, Metro to the center, shuttles to airports), and if you hit it outside of convention times, the prices are hard to beat. Here are two decent options:

$$ Hotel Florida is a comfortable, well-maintained business-class hotel with 55 rooms on a quiet street one block from the

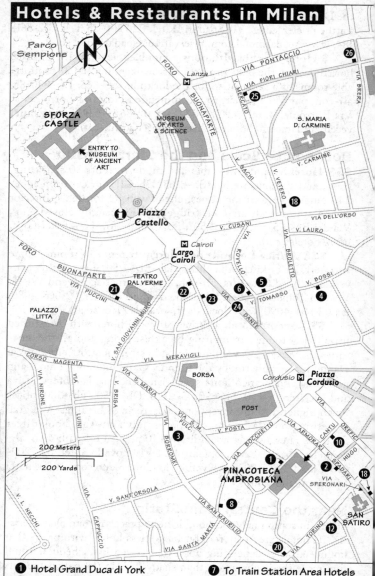

Hotels & Restaurants in Milan

Parco Sempione

VIA PONTACCIO
26

Lanza
V. Via FIORI CHIARI
25

FORO BUONAPARTE

MUSEUM OF ARTS & SCIENCE

S. MARIA D. CARMINE

SFORZA CASTLE

V. SACHI

V. CARMINE

ENTRY TO MUSEUM OF ANCIENT ART

V. VETERO
18

VIA DELL'ORSO

Piazza Castello

V. CUSANI

V. LAURO

FORO BUONAPARTE

Largo Cairoli

Cairoli

ROVELLO

V. BROLETTO

V. BOSSI

TEATRO DAL VERME

VIA PUCCINI

21

22

23

V. TOMASSO

6 5

4

24

VIA DANTE

PALAZZO LITTA

V. SAN GIOVANNI SUL MURO

CORSO MAGENTA

VIA MERAVIGLI

VIA NIRONE

VIA

V. BRISA

VIA S. MARIA

BORSA

Cordusio

Piazza Cordusio

LUINI

V. S. M. FULC.

POST

VIA ARMORARI

CANTU

VIA OREFICI

200 Meters

200 Yards

V. POSTA

VIA BOCCHETTO

V. SPADARI

HUGO

10

V. L. NECCHI

VIA BORROMEI

3

PINACOTECA AMBROSIANA

1

2

VIA SPERONARI

18

V. SANT'ORSOLA

VIA CAPPUCCIO

8

VIA SAN MAURILIO

SAN SATIRO

12

VIA SANTA MARTA

V. TORINO

20

MILAN

❶ Hotel Grand Duca di York	❼ To Train Station Area Hotels
❷ Hotel Spadari & Peck Gourmet Deli	❽ Trattoria Milanese
❸ Hotel Vecchia Milano & Hostaria Borromei	❾ Ristorante Bruno
❹ Hotel Star	❿ Peck Italian Bar
❺ Antica Locanda dei Mercanti	⓫ Elevator to La Rinascente Dept. Store Eateries
❻ London Hotel	⓬ Latteria Cucina Vegetariana

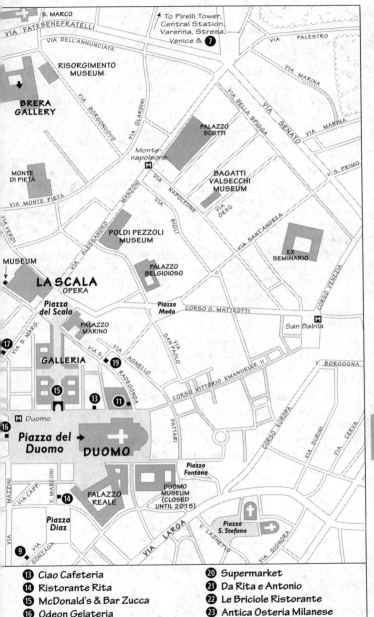

MILAN

⑬ Ciao Cafeteria
⑭ Ristorante Rita
⑮ McDonald's & Bar Zucca
⑯ Odeon Gelateria
⑰ Gelateria Grom
⑱ Princi Bakeries (2)
⑲ Luini Panzerotti

⑳ Supermarket
㉑ Da Rita e Antonio
㉒ Le Briciole Ristorante
㉓ Antica Osteria Milanese
㉔ Via Dante Eateries
㉕ Obikà Mozzarella Bar
㉖ Bar Brera

station. Prices plummet if you book direct and are not visiting during a convention (normally Db-€240 but often more like Sb-€70-100 and Db-€90-130, free Wi-Fi, Via Lepetit 33, tel. 02-670-5921, fax 02-669-2867, www.hotelfloridamilan.com, reception@hotel floridamilan.com). With the tracks to your back, leave the station's upper hall to the left, cross the taxi stand, and then cross the road. The hotel is on Via Lepetit, around the corner from Ristorante Giglio Rosso.

$$ Hotel Garda has 55 tidy, spotless rooms two and a half blocks from the station (Sb-€40-140, Db-€60-170; email first to get a promo code for a 10 percent discount when booking on their website; air-con, elevator, Via N. Torriani 21, tel. 02-6698-2626, fax 02-6698-2576, www.hotelgardamilan.com, info@hotelgarda milan.com). Exit the train station and head straight across the square, veering left onto Via N. Torriani. It's ahead on your right.

Hostels

For beds costing about €20-25, consider Milan's hostels. Most are away from the center, but the first one I've listed is closer to town.

$ Ostello la Cordata, a good choice, has 83 beds in both private rooms and in shared dorm rooms (€21-25 for beds in 6-, 8-, and 16-bed dorms; hotel-type rooms on the third floor—Sb-€40-60, Db-€70-80, Tb-€90-105; reserve ahead, 14:30-24:00 check-in but can leave bags earlier, no curfew, elevator, free Internet access and Wi-Fi, self-serve laundry, Via Burigozzo 11, Metro: Missori—on yellow line 3, tel. 02-5831-4675, fax 02-5830-3598, www.ostellola cordata.com, ostello@lacordata.it).

$ AIG Piero Rotta is larger and offers cheap, basic accommodation with a simple breakfast (€20 beds in 4-to 6-bed dorms, hostel membership required, non-members pay €3/night more, near Metro: QT8—on red line 1, at Viale Salmoiraghi 1, tel. 02-3926-7095, fax 02-3300-0191, www.ostellomilano.it, milano@aighostels .com).

Eating in Milan

This is a fast-food city, but fast food in a fashion capital isn't a burger and fries. Milan's bars, delis, *rosticcerie,* and self-service cafeterias cater to people with plenty of taste and more money than time. You'll find delightful eateries all over town (note that they take Aug off).

I find the price difference between basic and classy restaurants to be negligible (for example, pastas-€7-12, *secondi*-€12-20, cover-€1-3), so it's worth springing for the places that give the best experience. To eat mediocre food on a famous street with great

Milanese Specialties

Milan's signature dishes (often served together as a *piatto unico*, or "single dish") are *risotto alla milanese* and *ossobuco*. The risotto is flavored with saffron, which gives it its intense yellow color. It's said that a 16th-century Belgian glassworker first stumbled on the use of saffron as a spice. Initially, he used saffron to tint the glass mixture for completing the stained-glass windows of the Duomo in 1574. His master joked that he'd end up adding the precious spice to his food as well. On the day of his master's daughter's wedding, the glassworker persuaded the chef to add saffron to the rice cooked for the reception. After the guests got over their initial surprise, the dish was a great success, and has been a staple on Milan's menus ever since. The subtle flavor of the saffron pairs nicely with the *ossobuco* (meaning "marrow," or literally "hole in the bone," of the veal shank). The prized marrow is extracted with special little forks and is considered the best part of the meal.

people-watching, choose an eatery on the pedestrian-only Via Mercanti or Via Dante. To eat with students in trendy little trattorias, explore the Brera neighborhood. To eat well near the Duomo, consider the recommended places below.

Locals like to precede a lunch or dinner with an *aperitivo* (while Campari made its debut in Milan, a simple glass of *vino bianco* or prosecco, the Italian champagne, is just as popular). Bars fill their counters with inviting baskets of munchies, which are served free with these drinks, at about 17:00. A cheap drink (if you're either likable or discreet) can become a light meal. For example, check out the wonderful buffet spread at the recommended Bar Brera.

Breakfast is a bad value in hotels and fun on Via Dante or in bars. It's OK to quasi-picnic. Bring in a banana (or whatever) and order a toasted ham-and-cheese sandwich (called *toast*) or brioche with your cappuccino.

Near the Duomo
Dining with Class
Trattoria Milanese, sophisticated and family-run, is a splurge. It has an enthusiastic and local clientele—the restaurant didn't even bother to get a phone until 1988. Expect a Milanese ambience and quality traditional cuisine (Mon-Fri 12:00-14:45 & 19:00-22:45, closed Sat-Sun and mid-July-Aug, air-con, Via Santa Marta 11, 5-minute walk from the Duomo, near Pinacoteca Ambrosiana, tel. 02-8645-1991).

MILAN

Ristorante Bruno serves Tuscan cuisine with a passion for fresh fish. This place impresses with its dressy waiters, hearty food, inexpensive desserts, and a fine self-serve antipasto buffet (a plate full of Tuscan specialties for €9). You can eat inside or on the sidewalk under fascist columns (Sun-Fri 12:00-15:00 & 19:00-23:00, closed Sat and Aug, moderate prices, air-con, Via M. Gonzaga 6, reservations wise, tel. 02-804-364). Giuseppe (from Volterra) and Graziella take good care of their clientele.

Hostaria Borromei is where Milanese yuppies go for power lunches to impress clients with market-fresh traditional Italian dishes. Dine under an awning of vines in an elegant mellow-yellow interior courtyard or in their cantina-chic dining rooms. Reservations are recommended (€15 pastas, €20 *secondi*, €3 cover and service charge, Mon-Fri 12:30-14:45 & 19:30-22:45, Sat-Sun 19:30-22:45, Via Borromei 4, tel. 02-8645-3760).

Peck Italian Bar is a hit with the sophisticated office crowd, which mobs the place at lunch for its fast, excellent meals. It's owned by the same people who run the recommended high-end Peck deli (listed later), so be prepared to spend—this place's classiness alone makes it worth the money. Any time you find yourself among such a quality-conscious group of Milanesi, you know you're getting good food (€12 pastas, €18 *secondi*, Mon-Fri 7:30-20:30, Sat 9:00-20:30, closed Sun, Via Cantù 3, tel. 02-869-3017).

Dining at the Top of a Top-End Department Store with a Duomo View

The seventh floor of the La Rinascente department store, alongside the Duomo, has a Milanese-style food court, including a sunny outdoor terrace. You'll dine accompanied by views of the cathedral's rooftop (though anyone can pop up for a look at the cathedral). All three of the terrace-seating establishments recommended below are open 10:00-24:00, include cover charge with service, and can be accessed after store hours from elevators on Via S. Radegonda. (During open hours, you can go through the department store to take escalators to the top, but it's faster to take the elevators.)

Obikà is a swanky mozzarella bar offering this heavenly cheese in all its various forms—cow's milk, buffalo, and smoked—in salads or on splittable €10-19 antipasto sampler plates, accompanied by *salumi,* tapenades, and vegetables (another Obikà is north of the Duomo, see "In the Brera Neighborhood," later).

At the opposite end of the terrace, **Ristorante Maio** has pricey full-meal service (€13 pastas and pizzas, €22 *secondi*). In between is **Il Bar,** living-room cozy with cushy divans and low coffee tables, and serving light meals (salads, pasta), coffee, desserts, and cocktails.

Eating Simply

Latteria Cucina Vegetariana, with a 50-year history, is a bright hole-in-the-wall that serves a good vegetarian Italian lunch. This busy joint is overrun with tables where neighborhood workers enjoy soup, salads, pastas, and imaginative veggie entrées at affordable prices. Try the €13 *piatto misto al forno* for a delicious assortment of soufflés, quiches, and roasted and sautéed veggies (€10-15 meals, Mon-Sat 12:00-16:00, closed Sun, just off Via Torino at Via dell'Unione 6, 2 blocks southwest of the Duomo, tel. 02-874-401). Giorgio is a hit with camera-toting eaters.

Ciao, a self-service cafeteria, offers a low-stress, affordable meal above a fast-food arcade on Piazza del Duomo (daily 11:30-23:00, sometimes closes 22:30, inexpensive pasta and good salad bar, easy public WC). It's to the right of the Galleria entrance—enter through the ground floor Autogrill and go up to the second floor.

Ristorante Rita, a block behind Ciao, is a smart budget option (€4-5 pastas and *secondi*) without the Italian fast-food feel. While the downstairs has a take-out place, there's a sleek, modern restaurant upstairs with good food and cafeteria prices (Mon-Sat 12:00-15:00, closed Sun, on Via Marconi between Piazza del Duomo and Piazza Diaz, tel. 02-8699-7387).

Fast-food cheapskates enjoy the best people-watching in Milan inside the Galleria at **McDonald's** (long hours daily, salad/pasta plate and tall orange juice for around €5).

Gelato: Floodlit Mary gazes down on the **Odeon Gelateria** from the top of the Duomo for good reason (next to a McDonald's on Piazza del Duomo, on far side of square opposite Duomo facade, open nightly until 24:00, off-season until 19:30 if it's raining). While Odeon is convenient, **Gelateria Grom** (two blocks toward La Scala on Via Santa Margherita) is the connoisseurs' choice.

Picnics Milan-style

For a fun adventure, assemble an elegant dinner picnic by hitting the colorful deli, cheese, and produce shops on Via Speronari. The **Princi bakery** is mobbed with locals vying for focaccia, olive breadsticks, and luscious pastries. Notice the stacked-wood-oven action in the back. For most pastry items (like the brioche), pay the cashier first; for items sold by weight (such as pizza and cake), get it weighed before you pay. Consider a piping-hot pasta lunch (12:00-15:00 only) for €6 per plate (Mon-Sat 7:00-20:00, Sun 10:00-19:30, on Via Speronari, off Via Torino, a block southwest of Piazza del Duomo; a larger Princi bakery, more like a café, is near the Sforza Castle and is listed later).

Peck Gourmet Deli is an aristocratic deli with a fancy café/lunchroom/pastry and gelato shop upstairs, a gourmet grocery and *rosticceria* on the main level, and an expensive *enoteca* wine cellar in the basement. Even if all you can afford is the aroma, peek in. Check out the classic circa-1930 salami slicers and the gourmet assembly line in the kitchen in the back (Mon 15:30-19:30, Tue-Sat 9:15-19:30, closed Sun, Via Spadari 9, tel. 02-802-3161). The *rosticceria* serves fancy food to go for a superb picnic dinner in your hotel. It's delectable, beautiful, sold by weight (order by the *etto*—100-gram unit, 250 grams equals about a half-pound), and pricey. Try the risotto.

Luini Panzerotti serves up piping-hot mini-calzones *(panzerotti)* stuffed with mozzarella, tomatoes, ham, or whatever you like for €3-5 (Mon 10:00-15:00, Tue-Sat 10:00-20:00, closed Sun and Aug, Via S. Radegonda 16, tel. 02-8646-1917). From the back of the Duomo, head north and look for the lines of hungry locals out front. Order from the small menus posted behind the cash registers. Traditionally, Milanesi munch their hot little meals on nearby Piazza San Fedele. Don't overlook the *dolce* half of their menu—Panzerotti is popular for its sweets all day long.

Billa Superfresco Supermarket is within a few blocks of the Duomo (Mon-Sat 8:00-21:00, Sun 9:00-20:00, small deli on ground level, big supermarket in basement, on Via Torino at intersection with San Maurilio).

Near the Sforza Castle

Da Rita e Antonio is a favorite neighborhood restaurant, serving up well-prepared, reasonably priced Milanese specialties such as *costoletta* (breaded veal chop) and *ossobuco* (veal shank and risotto), as well as delicious €9 Neapolitan-style pizzas. It's a high-energy, brightly lit, dressy place, complete with waiters in bow ties and vests (€10 pastas, €20 *secondi*, great tiramisu, Tue-Fri and Sun 12:00-14:30 & 19:00-23:00, Sat 19:00-23:00, closed Mon, Via G. Puccini 2a, tel. 02-875-579). Facing the Sforza Castle from the end of Via Dante, it's about 100 yards to your left, built into the far side of the pink-and-white theater.

Le Briciole, run by the Campenella family, is small and folksy, drawing a local crowd for its quality Ligurian cuisine (pesto, seafood) and friendly family feel (€11 homemade pastas, Mon-Sat 12:15-14:30 & 19:15-22:30, closed Sun; Via Camperio 17, a block in front of castle, on small street at end of Via Dante, tel. 02-804-114; Anamaria and Sara).

Antica Osteria Milanese is a hardworking family place with a smart local following and spacious, stylish seating. They serve good-quality typical Milanese favorites (€8 pastas, €13 *secondi*, €2 cover, Mon-Sat 12:15-14:45 & 19:30-22:15, closed Sun, Via Camperio 12, tel. 02-861-367, Alessandro).

Fancy Via Dante Bars and Cafés: Thriving and central, Via

Dante is lined with hardworking eateries where you can join locals for a lively lunch. Or, for about the price of your forgettable hotel breakfast, you can start your day watching the parade of Milanesi heading to work.

Princi bakery, near the castle, works the same as the one on Via Speronari (listed earlier), only it's more of a restaurant, with seating both inside and on the street. While the bakery and café are open all day, they serve hot cafeteria-style lunches only 12:00-15:30 (Mon-Sat 7:00-20:00, Sun 10:00-19:30, Via Ponte Vetero 10, tel. 02-7201-6067).

In the Brera Neighborhood

The Brera neighborhood surrounding the Church of St. Carmine is laced with narrow, inviting pedestrian streets. Make an evening of your visit by having an *aperitivo* (pre-dinner drink) with snacks at recommended Bar Brera or any bar—most serve munchies with pre-dinner drinks 17:00-21:00. Afterwards, stroll along restaurant row (Via Fiori Chiari) to survey the sidewalk cafés. To locate these eateries, see the map on page 324.

Obikà is a trendy mozzarella eatery with a sleek, minimalist sushi-bar feel. It features fresh cow, buffalo, and smoked mozzarella; big organic gourmet salads; and top-quality *salumi*. Show up at happy hour (daily 18:30-21:00) to enjoy a generous buffet and select from a long list of €10 drinks (€9 pastas, Mon-Fri 12:00-15:30 & 18:30-24:00, Sat-Sun 12:00-24:00, on corner of Via Mercato and Via Fiori Chiari, at Via Mercato 28, tel. 02-8645-0568).

Bar Brera, across the street from the Brera Art Gallery, serves salads, sandwiches, and pastas to throngs of art students. During happy hour (daily 17:00-21:00), have a seat, order a drink, and then help yourself to the buffet (17:00-19:00), which has a generous variety of *antipasti*, from marinated veggies to prosciutto (buffet is free if you buy drinks; bar open daily 7:00-2:00 in the morning, great streetside seating, Via Brera 23, tel. 02-877-091).

MILAN

Milan Connections

By Train

From Milan by Train to: Venice (at least hourly, most departures at :05 or :35 past the hour, most are direct on high-speed ES trains, 2.5-3.5 hours), **Florence** (hourly, 1.75 hours), **Genoa** (about hourly, 1.5-2 hours, also look for trains to La Spezia or Livorno that stop at Genoa), **Rome** (hourly, 3-8 hours, overnight possible), **Brindisi** (4 direct/day, 2 are night trains, 9-15 hours, more with changes), **Cinque Terre/La Spezia** (about hourly, 3 hours direct or with change in Genoa; trains from La Spezia to the villages go nearly hourly), **Cinque Terre/Monterosso al Mare** (8/day direct, otherwise hourly, 3-4 hours, more with change in Genoa), **Varenna** on Lake Como (small line direct to Lecco/Sondrio/Tirano leaves at 6:20, 8:20, 10:20, 12:20, 14:20, 16:20, 17:20, 19:20, 20:20, and 21:20; 1 hour; confirm these times—if you take a train at a time not listed here, it will require a change in Lecco and an extra 30 minutes), **Stresa** on Lake Maggiore (about hourly, 1-hour fast train, 90-minute slow train; also look for trains to Domodossola and some international destinations that stop at Stresa), **Como** (at least hourly, 30-90 minutes, boats go from Como to Varenna until about 19:00), **Naples** (direct trains hourly, 5 hours, more with change in Rome, overnight possible).

International Destinations: Amsterdam (hourly with several changes, fastest via Basel or Zurich, 15 hours), **Barcelona** (14-20 hours, several with 1-5 changes), **Bern** (change required in Brig, at least 3.5 hours), **Frankfurt** (change in Basel or Zurich, at least 9-10 hours), **London** (3/day, 12-18 hours with changes), **Munich** (7/day, 8-12 hours with changes), **Nice** (5/day with change in Ventimiglia, night train possible, 5-6.5 hours), **Paris** (2/day direct, 7-8 hours, night train possible), **Lyon** (8/day, 6-8.5 hours with changes), **Vienna** (1/day direct, more with 1-3 changes, 11-14 hours). With dozens of budget airlines serving Europe's hub cities, flying to your international destination is often the most efficient and economical option (see "Cheap Flights," on page 1030).

By Plane

To get flight information for Malpensa or Linate airports or the current phone number of your airline, call 02-74851 or 02-232-323 and wait for English options, or check www.sea-aeroporti milano.it.

Malpensa Airport

Most international flights land at the manageable Malpensa Airport, 28 miles northwest of Milan. Customs guards fan you through, and even the security dog seems friendly. You'll most likely land at Terminal 1 (international flights), rather than Terminal 2 (charter flights); buses connect the two. Both have ATMs (at Terminal 1, between exit 4 and 5 at Banca Nazionale del Lavoro), banks, and exchange offices. Terminal 1 has a pharmacy, eateries, and a hotel reservation service disguised as a TI (daily 7:00-20:00; when you exit the baggage-carousel area, go right to reach services and exit; tel. 02-5858-0080). The tobacco shop sells phone cards—handy for confirming your hotel reservation.

You have three easy ways to get to downtown Milan: by train, shuttle bus, or taxi.

By Train: The Malpensa Express has two different lines serv-

Train Connections from Milan

ing downtown Milan. One line serves Milan's central train station—Milano Centrale—with rail links across Italy and beyond (€11, may have limited €7 special, 1-2/hour, 40-50 minutes). The other line zips between the airport and Milan's Cadorna station, which is both a Metro stop and a small train station; it's relatively close to the Duomo and Sforza Castle (€11, credit cards accepted, not covered by railpasses, 2/hour, 40 minutes; usually departs airport at :26 and :56 past the hour, generally departs Cadorna at :28 and :58 past the hour, tel. 800-500-005, www.malpensa express.it).

At the airport, as you pop out through customs, you'll see a *Treno per Malpensa* kiosk selling tickets and a big electric board on the wall indicating how many minutes until the next departure. Follow signs (*Treni* and *Malpensa Express*) down the stairs to the tracks. Check to make sure your train is going to the right destination—*Milano Centrale* or *Milano Cadorna*.

If you're leaving Milan to go to the airport, either go to Milan's central station or take the Metro to the Cadorna stop, surface, and buy a ticket at the Malpensa Express office in the station. Purchase your ticket before you board, or you'll pay €2.50 extra to buy it on the train. At Milano Centrale, check the departure board for the track number. Trains depart Cadorna from track 1; note that there

MILAN

are a few late-night departures to and from Cadorna by bus after midnight—ask when you buy your ticket. If your departure is by bus, the stop is outside the station; after you exit, find the stop 50 yards to the left on Via Paleocapa.

Malpensa Airport also has direct, high-speed rail links to **Florence** (2/day, 2.75 hours), **Rome** (1/day, 4.5 hours), and **Naples** (1/day, 6 hours). Check www.trenitalia.com for details.

By Shuttle Bus: Two bus companies offer virtually identical, competing services between Malpensa Airport and Milan's central train station. They each charge about €7.50 for the one-hour trip (buy ticket from driver) and depart from the same places: in front of the airport (outside exit 5, at stops 2 and 3) and from Piazza Luigi di Savoia (on the east side of Milan's train station—with your back to the tracks, exit to the left). You'll generally find a bus leaving about every 15 minutes, every day, nearly all day (from downtown roughly 3:45-0:30 in the morning and from the airport roughly 5:30-00:15 in the morning; Malpensa Shuttle tel. 02-5858-3185, www.malpensashuttle.it; Autostradale tel. 02-3391-0794, www.autostradale.it). They're almost comically competitive, with one offering three rides for the price of two. Play around a bit and you may save some money.

By Taxi: Taxis into Milan cost a fixed rate of €85; avoid hustlers in airport halls (catch taxis outside exit 6). Considering how far the city is from the airport and how good the train and bus services are, Milan is the last place I'd take an airport taxi. To get from Milan to the airport, I'd take the Metro to the central train station (or a taxi to the Cadorna station) and then catch the Malpensa Express train.

Getting Between Malpensa and Linate: The Malpensa Shuttle company runs a bus between the airports about hourly (€13, from Malpensa to Linate runs 7:50-00:25 in the morning, 1.25 hours, catch bus outside Malpensa's exit 3, stop 20, buy tickets from Airport 2000 offices; from Linate to Malpensa buses depart 4:30-21:30, bus stops at Malpensa's Terminal 1—you must request stop if you need Terminal 2; tel. 02-5858-3185, www.malpensa shuttle.it).

Linate Airport

Most European flights land at Linate, five miles east of Milan. The airport has a bank (just past customs; ATM, decent rates) and a hotel-finding service disguised as a TI (daily 7:30-23:30, tel. 02-7020-0443).

You can get to downtown Milan by bus or taxi (or to Malpensa Airport by bus; see above).

By Bus: Two different buses—Starfly and ATM—take you from Linate Airport to downtown. The Starfly bus zips you to the central train station (€4, buy ticket from driver, 3/hour, 30 minutes, bus runs from airport 6:00-22:00, from station 6:00-21:30, leaves from east side of train station at Piazza Luigi di Savoia, tel. 02-587-237, www.autostradale.it). The cheaper ATM city bus gets you to the San Babila Metro stop (specifically to Corso Europa, just around the corner from Piazza San Babila and its Metro station; from here it's one stop to the Duomo on red line 1, direction: Molino Dorino or Bisceglie, or a 7-minute walk). The bus costs €1, departs every 10 minutes, and takes 20 minutes (departures leave city center 5:35-00:35, from airport 6:00-01:05, www.atm-mi.it). Either bus company works fine: Wait for the one that's handier to your hotel, or hop on the first one that shows up. From where it drops you off, take the Metro or a taxi to your hotel. Both buses leave the airport from outside the arrivals hall.

By Taxi: Taxis from Linate to the Duomo cost about €25.

Bergamo (Orio Al Serio) Airport

Some budget airlines, such as Ryanair and Wizzair, use Bergamo Airport as their Milan hub (about 30 miles from Milan, tel. 035-326-323, www.sacbo.it).

An express bus, Orioshuttle, connects the airport to Milan's central train station (€10, daily 4:00-23:15, 2/hour, 1 hour, buy tickets from driver or online at http://ticketonline.orioshuttle.com, tel. 035-330-706). A different company, Oriobus Express, covers the same route (€9.90, €15 round-trip, daily 4:30-1:00 in the morning, 2/hour, 1 hour, tel. 02-3391-0794, www.autostradale.it).

MILAN

THE CINQUE TERRE

The Cinque Terre (CHINK-weh TAY-reh), a remote chunk of the Italian Riviera, is the traffic-free, lowbrow, underappreciated alternative to the French Riviera. There's not a museum in sight—just sun, sea, sand (well, pebbles), wine, and pure, unadulterated Italy. Enjoy the villages, swimming, hiking, and evening romance of one of God's great gifts to tourism. For a home base, choose among five *(cinque)* villages, each of which fills a ravine with a lazy hive of human activity—callused locals, sun-burned travelers, and no Vespas. While the Cinque Terre is now discovered (and can be quite crowded midday, when tourist boats and cruise-ship excursions drop by), I've never seen happier, more relaxed tourists.

The chunk of coast was first described in medieval times as "the five lands." In the feudal era, this land was watched over by castles. Tiny communities grew up in their protective shadows, ready to run inside at the first hint of a Turkish Saracen pirate raid. Marauding pirates from North Africa were a persistent problem until about 1400. Many locals were kidnapped and ransomed or sold into slavery, and those who remained built fires on flat-roofed watchtowers to relay warnings—alerting the entire coast to imminent attacks. The last major raid was in 1545.

As the threat of pirates faded, the villages prospered, catching fish and cultivating grapes. Churches were enlarged with a growing population. But until the advent of tourism in this generation, the towns remained isolated. Even today, traditions survive, and each of the five villages comes with a distinct dialect and its own proud heritage.

Sadly, a few ugly, noisy Americans give tourism a bad name

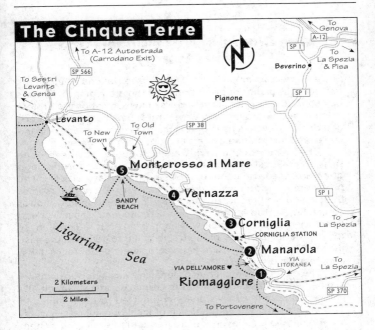

The Cinque Terre

To Genova
A-12
SP 1
To La Spezia & Pisa
Beverino
To A-12 Autostrada (Carrodano Exit)
SP 566
To Sestri Levante & Genoa
Pignone
SP 1
Levanto
To New Town
To Old Town
SP 38
5 Monterosso al Mare
SANDY BEACH
4 Vernazza
3 Corniglia
CORNIGLIA STATION
Ligurian Sea
2 Manarola
VIA LITORANEA
To La Spezia
VIA DELL'AMORE ♥
Riomaggiore
2 Kilometers
2 Miles
To Portovenere
SP 370
SP 1
To La Spezia

here. Even hip, young residents are put off by loud, drunken tourists. They say—and I agree—that the Cinque Terre is an exceptional place. It deserves a special dignity. Party in Viareggio or Portofino, but be mellow in the Cinque Terre. Talk softly. Help keep it clean. In spite of the tourist crowds, it's still a real community, and we are its guests.

In this chapter, I cover the five towns in order from south to north, from Riomaggiore to Monterosso. Since I still get the names of the towns mixed up, I think of them by number: #1 Riomaggiore (a workaday town), #2 Manarola (picturesque), #3 Corniglia (on a hilltop), #4 Vernazza (the region's cover girl, the most touristy and dramatic), and #5 Monterosso al Mare (the closest thing to a beach resort of the five towns).

Arrival in the Cinque Terre

By Train: Big, fast trains from elsewhere in Italy speed past the Cinque Terre (though some stop in Monterosso and Riomaggiore). Unless you're coming from a nearby town, you'll have to change trains at least once to reach Manarola, Corniglia, or Vernazza.

The Cinque Terre National Park—in Disarray

Since its creation in 1999, the Cinque Terre National Marine Park has brought plenty of good things to the area: money (visitors pay about €5 a day to hike the trails), new regulations to protect wildlife, and improved walkways, trails, beaches, breakwaters, and docks. Travelers have been able to take advantage of park-sponsored information centers and tiny folk museums.

The vision for the park was exciting—to have everyone thinking creatively about how to improve the area for the good of nature, the local communities, and their many visitors. The park administrators were well on their way to creating something unique in Europe. But, as so often happens in Italy, power and money corrupted the men entrusted to lead. Those working under them could see what was happening—but rather than try to stop the sleaze, many of them scrambled to get in on the easy money. The result is a vision gone completely out of focus and a park that's in disarray.

The park president, Franco Bonanini, was a powerful man—nicknamed "The Pharaoh" for his grandiose ideas. He initially impressed people as a visionary committed to the region and its precious land. But with a group of local bureaucrats—including Riomaggiore's mayor—he created a medieval-style system of favorites and enemies. This cabal was focused more on preserving their power than improving the park. As they started and stopped construction projects, funneling money here and there,

Generally, if you're coming from the north, you'll change trains in Sestri Levante or Genoa (specifically, Genoa's Piazza Principe station). If you're coming from the south or east, you'll most likely have to switch trains in La Spezia (change at La Spezia Centrale station—don't make the mistake of getting off at La Spezia Migliarina). No matter where you're coming from, it's best to check in the station before you leave to see your full schedule and route options (use the computerized kiosks or ask at a ticket window). Don't forget to validate your ticket by stamping it—ka-CHUNK!—in the yellow machines located on train platforms and elsewhere in the station. Conductors here are notorious for levying stiff fines on forgetful tourists. For more information on riding the train between Cinque Terre towns, see "Getting Around the Cinque Terre," later.

By Plane: If the Cinque Terre is your first, last, or only stop on this trip, consider flying into Pisa or Genoa, rather than Milan. These airports are less confusing than Milan's, and closer to the Cinque Terre. For more on Pisa's airport, see page 539.

By Car: If you're driving in the Cinque Terre (but, given the they derailed the park vision. In 2011, they were at last removed from power, but the damage had been done. Plans for future projects have been scuttled, and improvements already in place or underway—information offices, baggage deposits, mountain-biking opportunities, little museums, elevators for people with limited mobility, and even maintenance of the trails—have been abandoned.

Today, the park is run by a man from the central government whose plan, it seems, is to run the park as a business. But a park is a park, not a business. Ironically—and sadly, for the residents—using the park to wring money out of visitors while giving little back is not good for the livelihoods of the region's hardworking residents.

What does all this mean to the visitor? For 2012, no one knows exactly how the park will be functioning (for the latest, see www.parconazionale5terre.it). Otherwise, not much. The Cinque Terre is still my favorite chunk of Mediterranean coastline. Thankfully, the villages and dramatic stretches of land between them transcend any corrupt modern-day pharaohs. The people are endearing. The food, culture, and natural setting are uniquely enjoyable. But what's happened is disheartening. I thrill at the thought of people working together for a grand and noble vision that helps a community's economy by wisely treating a park as a park, rather than a moneymaker. And so far, the Cinque Terre has failed in that regard.

narrow roads and lack of parking, I wouldn't), see "Cinque Terre Connections" at the end of this chapter for directions.

Planning Your Time

The ideal stay is two or three full days; my recommended mini-mum stay is two nights and a completely uninterrupted day. The Cinque Terre is served by the local train from Genoa and La Spezia. Speed demons arrive in the morning, check their bags in La Spezia, take the five-hour hike through all five towns, laze away the afternoon on the beach or rock of their choice, and zoom away on the overnight train to somewhere back in the real world. But be warned: The Cinque Terre has a strange way of messing up your momentum. (The evidence is the number of Americans who have fallen in love with the region and/or one of its residents...and are still here.) Frankly, staying fewer than two nights is a mistake that you'll likely regret.

The towns are just a few minutes apart by hourly train or boat. There's no checklist of sights or experiences—just a hike, the towns themselves, and your fondest vacation desires. Study this chapter in advance and piece together your best day, mixing hiking, swimming, trains, and a boat ride. For the best light and coolest temperatures, start your hike early.

Market days perk up the towns from 8:00 to 13:00 on Tuesday in Vernazza, Wednesday in Levanto, Thursday in Monterosso and Sestri Levante, and Friday in La Spezia. (Levanto, Sestri Levante, and La Spezia are covered in the next chapter.)

The winter is really dead—most hotels and some restaurants close in December and January. The long Easter weekend (April 6-9 in 2012) and June and July are the peak of peak periods, the toughest times to find rooms. In spring, the towns can feel inundated with Italian school groups day-tripping on spring excursions (they can't afford to sleep in this expensive region).

For more information on the region, see www.cinqueterre.it.

Cinque Terre Park Cards

Visitors hiking between the towns need to pay a park entrance fee. This fee keeps the trails safe and open, and pays for viewpoints, picnic spots, WCs, and more. (Until recently, the fee also enriched corrupt local park managers—see the sidebar.) The popular coastal trail generates enough revenue to subsidize the development of trails and outdoor activities higher in the hills.

You have two options for covering the park fee: the Cinque Terre Park Card or the Cinque Terre Treno Park Card. Both are valid until midnight on the expiration date. Write your name on your card or risk a big fine.

The **Cinque Terre Park Card** costs €5 for one day of hiking or €9 for two (covers trails and shuttle buses but not trains, buy at trailheads and at most train stations, no validation required).

The **Cinque Terre Treno Park Card** covers what the Cinque Terre Park Card does, plus the use of the local trains (from Levanto to La Spezia, including all Cinque Terre towns). It's sold at TIs inside train stations, but not at trailheads (€10/1 day, €19/2 days, validate card at train station by punching it in the yellow machine). With this card, you have to hike and take three train trips every day just to break even.

Cards cost a bit more on weekends. Those under 18 or over 70 get a discount, as do families of four or more (see www.parco nazionale5terre.it).

Getting Around the Cinque Terre

Within the Cinque Terre, you can connect towns in three ways: by train, boat, or foot. Trains are cheaper, boats are more scenic, and hiking lets you enjoy more pasta. From a practical point of view, you should consider supplementing the often frustrating train with the sometimes more convenient boat. The trail between Riomaggiore and Manarola is a delight and takes just a few minutes, making the train not worth waiting for. The trail from Manarola to Corniglia is likely closed through much of 2012 (after a huge 2011 landslide).

By Train

Along the coast here, trains go in only two directions: *"per* [to] *Genova"* (the Italian spelling of Genoa), northbound; or *"per La Spezia,"* southbound. Assuming

you're on vacation, accept the unpredictability of Cinque Terre trains (they're often late...unless you are, too—in which case they're on time). Relax while you wait—buy a cup of coffee at a station bar. When the train comes (know which direction to look for: La Spezia or Genova), casually walk over and hop on. This is especially easy in Monterosso, with its fine café-with-a-view on track #1 (direction: Milano/Genova), and in Vernazza, where you can hang out at the Blue Marlin Bar with a prepaid drink and dash when the train pulls in.

Use the handy TV monitors in the station, which display upcoming departures for the next hour or so (as well as notes about which track they're on and whether they're late). Most of the northbound trains that stop at all Cinque Terre towns and are headed toward Genova will list Sestri Levante as the *destinazione*.

By train, the five towns are just a few minutes apart. Know your stop. Once the train leaves the town just before your destination, go to the door and get ready to slip out before the mobs flood in, making it impossible to get off. Words to the wise for novice tourists, who often miss their stop: The stations are small and the trains are long, so (especially in Vernazza) you might have to get off deep in a tunnel. Also, the doors don't open automatically—you may have to flip open the handle of the door yourself. If a door isn't working, go quickly to the next car to leave. (When leaving a town by train, if you find the platform jammed with people, walk down the platform into the tunnel, where things quiet down.)

It costs about €1.80 per ride within the region. Tickets are good for 75 minutes in one direction, so you could conceivably use one for a brief stopover. To make the ticket good for six hours (in one direction only), you need to buy a ticket good for 40 kilometers (€3.50). Stamp the ticket at the station machine before you board. Machines are often broken or out of ink (good luck explaining that to conductors), but riding without a validated ticket can be expensive ("minimum €25 fine" means they charge what they want—usually €50). If you have a Eurailpass, don't spend one of your valuable flexi-days on the cheap Cinque Terre.

Events in the Cinque Terre in 2012

For more festival information, check www.cinqueterre.it and www.turismoinliguria.it. The food festivals in particular are subject to change.

April 8-9	All towns: Easter Sunday and Monday
April 25	All towns: Liberation Day (stay away from the Cinque Terre this day, as locals literally shut down the trails)
May 1	All towns: Labor Day (another local holiday that packs the place)
Mid-May	Monterosso: Lemon Festival (usually the third Sunday)
May 17	All towns: Ascension Day
June 7	Monterosso: Feast of Corpus Domini (procession on carpet of flowers at 18:00)
Mid-June	Monterosso: Anchovy Festival
June 24	Riomaggiore and Monterosso: Feast day of St. John the Baptist (procession and fireworks; big fire on Monterosso's old town beach the day before)
June 29	Corniglia: Feast day of Sts. Peter and Paul
July 20	Vernazza: Feast day of patron saint, St. Margaret, with fireworks
Aug 10	Manarola: Feast day of patron saint, St. Lawrence
Aug 14	Monterosso: Fireworks on eve of feast of the Assumption
Aug 15	All towns: Feast of the Assumption (*Ferragosto*)
Mid-Sept	Monterosso: Anchovies and Olive Oil Festival (usually the second weekend)

Cinque Terre Train Schedule: Since the train is the Cinque Terre's lifeline, many shops and restaurants post the current schedule, and most hotels offer copies of it (one also comes with the Cinque Terre Park Card). But beware: The printed schedules can be misleading (half the listed departures don't go every day); the monitors in the stations are your best source of actual, current departure information. Note that fast trains leaving La Spezia zip right through the Cinque Terre; some stop only in Monterosso (town #5) and Riomaggiore (town #1). But any train that stops in Manarola, Corniglia, and Vernazza (towns #2, #3, and #4) will stop in all five towns (including the trains on the schedule below).

The times below are accurate as of this printing, but confirm schedules locally. These are the daily train times (a few do not run on Sunday; more trains are added in the busiest season, June-Sept):

Trains leave La Spezia Centrale for all or most of the Cinque Terre villages at 7:12, 8:12, 10:07, 11:10, 12:00, 13:17, 14:06, 15:10, 16:01, 17:05, 17:27, 18:06, 19:29, 20:18, 21:23, 23:07, and 00:50.

Going back to La Spezia, trains leave Monterosso at 6:20, 8:15, 9:29, 11:00, 11:58 12:19, 13:26, 14:20, 15:22, 16:15, 17:30, 18:18, 19:22, 20:15, 20:30, 21:32, 22:22, and 23:45 (these same trains depart Vernazza about four minutes later).

Again, convenient TV monitors posted at several places in each station clearly show exactly what times the next trains are leaving in each direction (and, if they're late, how late they are expected to be). I trust these monitors much more than my ability to read any printed schedule.

By Boat

From Easter through October, a daily boat service connects Monterosso, Vernazza, Manarola, Riomaggiore, and Portovenere.

Boats provide a scenic way to get from town to town and survey what you just hiked. And boats offer the only efficient way to visit the nearby resort of Portovenere (see next chapter; the alternative is a tedious train-bus connection via La Spezia). In peaceful weather, the boats can be more reliable than the trains, but if seas are rough, they don't run at all. Because the boats nose in and tourists have to gingerly disembark onto little more than a plank, even a small chop can cancel some or all of the stops.

I see the tour boats as a syringe, injecting each town with a boost of euros. The towns are addicted, and they shoot up hourly through the summer. (Between 10:00-15:00—especially on weekends—masses of gawkers unload from boats, tour buses, and cruise ships, inundating the villages and changing the feel of the region.)

Boats depart Monterosso about hourly (10:30-17:00), stopping at the Cinque Terre towns (except at Corniglia) and ending up an hour later in Portovenere. (Portovenere-Monterosso boats run 9:00-17:00.) The ticket price depends on the length of the boat ride (short hops-€4, longer hops-€8, five-town all-day pass-€16). Round-trip tickets are slightly cheaper than two one-way trips. You can buy tickets at little stands at each town's harbor (tel. 0187-732-987 and 0187-818-440). Another all-day boat pass for

€23 extends to Portovenere and includes a 40-minute scenic ride around three small islands (2/day). Boats are not covered by the Cinque Terre Park Card. Boat schedules are posted at docks, harbor bars, Cinque Terre park offices, and hotels (www.navigazione golfodeipoeti.it).

By Shuttle Bus

Shuttle buses connect each Cinque Terre town with its distant parking lot and various points in the hills (for example, a shuttle runs from Corniglia's train station to its hilltop town center). Note that these shuttle buses do not connect the towns with each other. Most rides cost €1.50 (and are covered by the Cinque Terre Park Card)—pick up bus schedules from TIs or note the times posted on bus doors and at bus stops. Some (but not all) departures from Vernazza, Manarola, and Riomaggiore go beyond the parking lots and high into the hills. Pay for a round-trip ride and just cruise both ways to soak in the scenery (round-trip 30-45 minutes).

Hiking the Cinque Terre

All five towns are connected by good trails, marked with red-and-white paint, white arrows, and some signs. You'll experience the area's best by hiking all the way from one end to the other (although, unfortunately, the Manarola-Corniglia stretch is likely closed in 2012). While you can detour to dramatic hilltop sanctuaries, I'd keep it simple by following trail #2—the low route between the villages. The entire seven-mile hike can be  done in about four hours, but allow five for dawdling. Germans (with their task-oriented *Alpenstock* walking sticks) are notorious for marching too fast through the region. Take it slow...smell the cactus flowers and herbs, notice the lizards, listen to birds singing in the olive groves, and enjoy vistas on all sides.

Trails can be closed in bad weather or because of landslides. Remember that hikers need to pay a fee to enter the trails (see "Cinque Terre Park Cards," earlier). If you're hiking the entire five-town route, consider that the trail between Riomaggiore (#1) and Manarola (#2) is easiest. The hike between Manarola and Corniglia (#3) has minor hills (and is likely closed in 2012). The trail from Corniglia to Vernazza (#4) is demanding, and the path from Vernazza to Monterosso (#5) is the most challenging. For that hike, you might want to start in Monterosso in order to tackle the toughest section while you're fresh—and to enjoy the region's most dramatic scenery as you approach Vernazza.

Other than the wide, easy Riomaggiore-Manarola segment, the trail is generally narrow, steep, rocky, and comes with lots of steps. Be warned that I get many emails from readers who say the trail was tougher than they expected. The rocks and metal grates can be slippery in the rain. While the trail is a bit of a challenge, it's perfectly doable for any fit hiker...and worth the sweat.

Maps aren't necessary for the basic coastal hikes described here. But for the expanded version of this hike (12 hours, from Portovenere to Levanto) and more serious hikes in the high country, pick up a good hiking map (about €5, sold everywhere). To leave the park cleaner than you found it, bring a plastic bag *(sacchetto di plastica)* and pick up a little trail trash along the way. It would be great if American visitors—who get so much joy out of this region—were known for this good deed.

Riomaggiore-Manarola (20 minutes): Facing the front of the train station in Riomaggiore (#1), go up the stairs to the

right, following signs for *Via dell'Amore.* The photo-worthy promenade—wide enough for baby strollers—winds along the coast to Manarola (#2). It's primarily flat, and it's even wheelchair-accessible since there are elevators at each end (elevators at Riomaggiore included in pass, elevator at Manarola for disabled use only). While there's no beach along the trail, stairs lead down to sunbathing rocks. A long tunnel and mega-nets protect hikers from mean-spirited falling rocks. A wine bar—Bar & Vini A Piè de Mà—is located at the Riomaggiore trailhead and offers light meals, awesome town views, and clever boat storage under the train tracks (for more info, see page 358). There's a picnic zone with a water fountain, shade, and a seagull that must have been human in a previous life hanging out just above the Manarola station (WC at Manarola station).

Manarola-Corniglia (45 minutes, likely closed in 2012): The walk from Manarola (#2) to Corniglia (#3) is a little longer, more rugged, and steeper than the Via dell'Amore. It's also less romantic. To avoid the last stretch (switchback stairs leading up to the hill-capping town of Corniglia), end your hike at Corniglia's train station and catch the shuttle bus to the town center (2/hour, €1.50, free with Cinque Terre Park Card, usually timed to meet the trains).

Corniglia-Vernazza (1.5 hours): The hike from Corniglia (#3) to Vernazza (#4)—the wildest and greenest section of the coast—is very rewarding but very hilly (going the other direction, from

Via dell'Amore

The Cinque Terre towns were extremely isolated until the last century. Villagers rarely married anyone from outside their town. After the blasting of a second train line in the 1920s, a trail was made between the first two towns: Riomaggiore and Manarola. The gunpowder warehouses built on each end, safely away from the townspeople, house cute little bars today.

Happy with the trail, the villagers asked that it be improved as a permanent connection between neighbors. But persistent landslides kept the trail closed more often than it was open. After World War II, the trail was reopened, and became established as a lovers' meeting point for boys and girls from the two towns. (After one extended closure in 1949, the trail was reopened for a Christmas marriage.) A journalist, who noticed all the amorous graffiti along the path, coined the trail's now-established name, Via dell'Amore: "Pathway of Love."

This new lane changed the social dynamics between the two villages, and made life much more fun and interesting for courting couples. Today, many tourists are put off by the cluttered graffiti that lines the trail. But it's all part of the history of the Cinque Terre's little lovers' lane.

You'll see padlocks locked to wires, cables, and fences. Closing a padlock with your lover at a lovey-dovey spot—often a bridge—is a common ritual in Italy (it was re-popularized by a teen novel a few years ago). In case you're so inclined, the hardware store next to Bar Centrale in Riomaggiore sells these locks. (You'll notice many of the locks come with the park logo.)

Major construction work—including the addition in 1994 of tunnels—has made the trail safer and keeps it open permanently. Notice how the brick-lined arcades match the train tunnel below. Rock-climbers from the north ("Dolomite spiders") were imported to help with the treacherous construction work. As you hike, look up and notice the massive steel netting bolted to the cliffside. Look down at the boulders that fell before the nets were added, and up at the boulders that have been caught...and be thankful for those Dolomite spiders.

Continuing the romance theme, benches along the way are named for lovers from Greek mythology. The many agave plants sport carved love notes—etched by amorous couples who likely don't know that the plant, which flowers once and then dies, is named for a tragic Greek story.

Vernazza to Corniglia, is steeper). From the Corniglia station and beach, zigzag up to the town (via the steep stairs, the longer road, or the shuttle bus). Ten minutes past Corniglia, toward Vernazza, you'll see Guvano beach far beneath you (once the region's nude beach). The scenic trail leads past a bar and picnic tables, through lots of fragrant and flowery vegetation, into Vernazza. If you need a break before reaching Vernazza, stop by Franco's Ristorante and Bar la Torre; it has a small menu but big views.

Vernazza-Monterosso (1.5 hours): The trail from Vernazza (#4) to Monterosso (#5) is a scenic up-and-down-a-lot trek and the most challenging of the bunch. Trails are narrow, steep, and crumbly, with a lot of steps (some readers report "very dangerous"), but easy to follow. Locals frown on camping at the picnic tables located midway. The views just out of Vernazza, looking back at the town, are spectacular.

Longer Hikes: Above the trails that run between the towns, higher-elevation hikes crisscross the region. Shuttle buses make the going easier, connecting coastal villages and trailheads in the hills. Ask locally about the more difficult six-mile inland hike to Volastra. This tiny village, perched between Manarola and Corniglia, hosts lots of Germans and Italians in the summertime. Just below its town center, in the hamlet of Groppo, is the Cinque Terre Cooperative Winery (open daily). For the whole trip on the high road between Manarola and Corniglia, allow two hours one-way. In return, you'll get sweeping views and a closer look at the vineyards. Shuttle buses run from Manarola to Volastra (€2.50 or free with Cinque Terre Park Card, pick up schedule from park office, 8/day, more departures in summer, 15 minutes); consider taking the bus up and hiking down.

Swimming, Kayaking, and Biking

Every town in the Cinque Terre has a beach or a rocky place to swim. Monterosso has the biggest and sandiest beach, with umbrellas and beach-use fees (but it's free where there are no umbrellas). Vernazza's is tiny—better for sunning than swimming. Manarola and Riomaggiore have the worst beaches (no sand), but Manarola offers the best deep-water swimming.

Wear your walking shoes and pack your swim gear. Several of the beaches have showers (no shampoo, please). Underwater sight-seeing is full of fish—goggles are sold in local shops. Sea urchins can be a problem if you walk on the rocks, and sometimes jellyfish wash up on the pebbles.

You can rent kayaks or boats in Riomaggiore, Vernazza, and Monterosso. (For details, see individual town listings in this chapter.) Some readers say kayaking can be dangerous—the kayaks tip easily, training is not provided, and lifejackets are not required.

THE CINQUE TERRE

Sleeping in the Cinque Terre

If you think too many people have my book, avoid Vernazza. You get fewer crowds and better value for your money in other towns. Monterosso is a good choice for sun-worshipping softies, those who prefer the ease of a real hotel, and the younger crowd (more nightlife). Hermits, anarchists, wine-lovers, and mountain goats like Corniglia. Sophisticated Italians and Germans choose Manarola. Riomaggiore is bigger than Vernazza and less resorty than Monterosso.

While the Cinque Terre is too rugged for the mobs that ravage the Spanish and French coasts, it's popular with Italians, Germans, and in-the-know Americans. Hotels charge more and are packed on holidays (including Easter); in June, July, and September; and on Fridays and Saturdays all summer. (With global warming, sweltering August is no longer considered peak season on this stretch of the Riviera.) While you can find doubles for €65 or €70 most of the season, you'll pay extra (around €80) in June and July. The prices I've listed are the maximum for April through October. For a terrace or view, you might pay an extra €20 or more. Apartments for four can be economical for families—figure around €120.

It's smart to reserve your room in advance in May, June, July, and September, and on weekends and holidays. At other times, you can land a double room on any day by just arriving in town (ideally by noon) and asking around at bars and restaurants, or simply by approaching locals on the street. Many travelers enjoy the opportunity to shop around a bit and get the best price by bargaining. Private rooms—called *affitta camere*—are no longer an intimate

stay with a family. They are generally comfortable apartments (often with small kitchens) where you get the key and come and go as you like, rarely seeing your landlord. Many landowners rent the buildings by the year to local managers, who then attempt to make a profit by filling them night after night with tourists.

For the best value, visit several private rooms and snare the best. Going direct cuts out the middleman and softens prices. Staying more than one night gives you bargaining leverage. Plan on paying cash. Private rooms are generally bigger and more comfortable than those offered by pensions and have the same privacy as a hotel room.

If you want the security of a reservation, make it at a hotel long in advance (smaller places generally don't take reservations very far ahead). Query by email, not fax. If you do reserve, honor your reservation (or, if you must cancel, do it as early as possible). Since people renting rooms usually don't take deposits, they lose money if you don't show up.

Eating in the Cinque Terre

Hanging out at a sea-view restaurant while sampling local specialties could become one of your favorite memories.

Tegame alla Vernazza is the most typical main course in Vernazza: anchovies, potatoes, tomatoes, white wine, oil, and herbs. Anchovies (*acciughe*; ah-CHOO-gay) are ideally served the day they're caught. There's nothing cool about being an anchovy virgin. If you've always hated anchovies (the harsh, cured-in-salt American kind), try them fresh here. *Pansotti* are ravioli with ricotta and a mixture of greens, often served with a walnut sauce... delightful and filling.

While antipasto means cheese and salami in Tuscany, here you'll get *antipasti frutti di mare*, a plate of mixed "fruits of the sea" and a fine way to start a meal. Many restaurants are particularly proud of their *antipasti frutti di mare*. For two diners, splitting one of these and a pasta dish can be plenty.

This region is the birthplace of pesto. Basil, which loves the temperate Ligurian climate, is ground with cheese (half parmigiano cow cheese and half pecorino sheep cheese), garlic, olive oil, and pine nuts, and then poured over pasta. Try it on spaghetti, *trenette* (the long, flat Ligurian noodle), or *trofie* (made of flour with a bit of potato, designed specifically for pesto to cling to). Many also like pesto lasagna, always made with white sauce, never red. If you become addicted, small jars of pesto are sold in the local grocery stores and gift shops. If it's refrigerated, it's fresh; this is what you want if you're eating it today. For taking home, get the jar-on-a-shelf pesto.

Focaccia, the tasty pillowy bread, also originates here in Liguria. Locals say the best focaccia is made between the Cinque Terre and Genoa. It's simply flatbread with olive oil and salt. The baker roughs up the dough with finger holes, then bakes it. Focaccia comes plain or with onions, sage, or olive bits, and is a local favorite for a snack on the beach. Bakeries sell it in rounds or slices by the weight (a portion is about 100 grams, or *un etto*).

Farinata, a humble fried bread snack, is made from chickpea meal, water, oil, and pepper, and baked on a copper tray in a wood-burning stove. *Farinata* is sold at pizza and focaccia places.

The *vino delle Cinque Terre*, while not one of Italy's top wines, flows cheap and easy throughout the region. It's white—great with seafood. For a sweet dessert wine, the *sciacchetrà* wine is worth the splurge (€4 per small glass, often served with a cookie). You could order the fun dessert *torta della nonna* (grandmother's cake) and dunk chunks of it into your glass. Aged *sciacchetrà* is dry and costly (up to €12/glass). While 10 kilos of grapes yield seven liters of local wine, *sciacchetrà* is made from near-raisins, and 10 kilos of grapes make only 1.5 liters of *sciacchetrà*. The word means "push and pull"—push in lots of grapes, pull out the best wine. If your room is up a lot of steps, be warned: *Sciacchetrà* is 18 percent alcohol, while regular wine is only 11 percent.

In the cool, calm evening, sit on Vernazza's breakwater with a glass of wine and watch the phosphorescence in the waves.

Nightlife in the Cinque Terre

While the Cinque Terre is certainly not noted for bumping beach-town nightlife like nearby Viareggio, you'll find some sort of travel-tale-telling hub in Monterosso, Vernazza, and Riomaggiore (Manarola and Corniglia are sleepy). Monterosso has a lively scene, especially in the summertime—but no *discoteca* yet. In Vernazza, the nightlife centers in the bars on the waterfront piazza, which is the small-town-style place to "see and be seen." A town law requires all bars to shut by midnight. Bar Centrale in Riomaggiore is, well, the central place for cocktails and meeting fellow travelers. (For details, see the "Nightlife" sections for these three villages.) Wherever your night adventures take you, have fun, but please remember that residents live upstairs.

Helpful Hints for the Cinque Terre

Tourist and Park Information: Each town (except Corniglia) has a well-staffed TI and park office (listed throughout this chapter).

Money: Banks and ATMs are plentiful throughout the region.

Baggage Storage: You can store bags at La Spezia's train station (€3/12 hours, 8:00-22:00, see page 433) and at Lucia's Lavarapido in Monterosso (€5/day).

Services: Every train station has a handy public WC. Otherwise, pop into a bar or restaurant.

Taxi: Cinqueterre Taxi covers all five towns (mobile 328-583-4969, www.cinqueterretaxi.com, info@cinqueterretaxi.com).

Local Guides: Andrea Bordigoni is both knowledgeable and a delight (€110/half-day, €175/day, mobile 347-972-3317, bordigo @inwind.it). Other local guides are **Marco Brizzi** (mobile 328-694-2847, marco_brizzi@yahoo.it) and **Paola Tommarchi** (paolatomma@alice.it).

Booking Agency: Miriana and Filippo at **Cinque Terre Riviera** book rooms in the Cinque Terre towns, Portovenere, and La Spezia for a 10 percent markup over the list price (can also arrange transportation, cooking classes, and weddings; Via Picedi 18 in La Spezia; tel. 0187-520-702, Miriana—mobile

340-794-7358, Filippo—mobile 393-939-1901, www.cinque
terreriviera.com, info@cinqueterreriviera.com, English
spoken).

Riomaggiore (Town #1)

The most substantial non-resort town of the group, Riomaggiore
is a disappointment from the train station. But once you leave that
neighborhood, you'll discover a fascinating tangle of pastel homes
leaning on each other like drunken sailors. Just walk through the
tunnel next to the train tracks, and you'll discover a more real,
laid-back, and workaday town than its touristy neighbors.

Orientation to Riomaggiore

Tourist Information

The TI is in the train station at the ticket desk (daily 8:00-18:00,
tel. 0187-920-633). If the TI in the station is crowded, buy your
hiking pass at the Cinque Terre park shop/information office next
door by the mural (daily 8:00-19:30, tel. 0187-760-515, netpoint
riomaggiore@parconazionale5terre.it).
For an informal information source, try
Ivo and Alberto, who run Bar Centrale
(see "Nightlife in Riomaggiore," later).

Arrival in Riomaggiore

The bus shuttles locals and tourists up and down Riomaggiore's steep
main street and continues to the parking lot outside town (€1.50 one-way,
€2.50 round-trip, free with Cinque
Terre Park Card, 2/hour but almost
comically erratic, main stop at the fork of Via Colombo and Via
Malborghetto, or flag it down as it passes).

Helpful Hints

Internet Access: The **park shop/information office** has eight
Internet terminals upstairs and Wi-Fi (€0.08/minute, daily
May-Sept 8:00-22:00, Oct-April until 19:30). **Hotel la Zorza**
has several terminals in town and charges about the same
(daily 11:00-21:30, under the archway just past the Co-op grocery store). **Bar Centrale** offers free Wi-Fi with the purchase
of a drink (see "Nightlife in Riomaggiore," later).

Laundry: A self-service launderette is on the main street (€3.50/

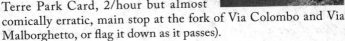

THE CINQUE TERRE

To Manarola

VIA DELL'AMORE

Cliffs

TRAIN STATION

MURALS

CINQUE TERRE INFO

ELEVATOR TO HIGH ROAD

VIA PECUNI

VIA SIGNORINI

PEDESTRIAN TUNNEL

VIA SANT'ANTONIO

PUNTA

Cliffs

VIA SANGIACOMO

BOAT DOCK

Harbor

BREAKWATER

BOAT TICKETS

Ligurian Sea

1. Locanda del Sole
2. Locanda Ca' dei Duxi
3. Hotel la Zorza
4. Locanda dalla Compagnia
5. Riomaggiore Reservations
6. La Dolce Vita Rooms
7. Edi's Rooms & Launderette
8. Camere Patrizia
9. Trattoria la Grotta
10. La Lanterna Ristorante
11. Te la Do Io la Merenda Snack Bar
12. Enoteca & Ristorante Dau Cila
13. Bar & Vini A Piè de Mà
14. Bar Centrale & Gelateria
15. Madonna di Montenero Trail
16. Park Office Kiosk

wash, €3.50/dry, daily 8:30-20:00, run by Edi's Rooms next door, Via Colombo 111).

Self-Guided Walk

Welcome to Riomaggiore

Here's an easy loop trip that maximizes views and minimizes uphill walking.

• *Start at the train station. (If you arrive by boat, cross beneath the tracks and take a left, then hike through the tunnel along the tracks to reach the station.) You'll come to some...*

Colorful Murals: These murals, with subjects modeled after real-life Riomaggiorians, glorify the nameless workers who constructed the nearly 300 million cubic feet of dry-stone walls (without cement) that run

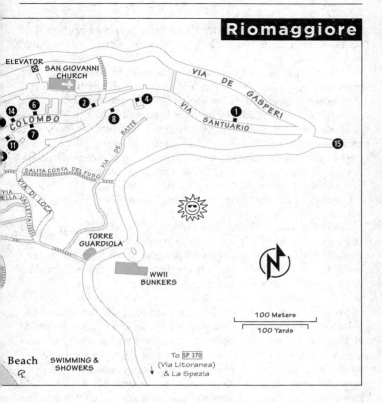

Riomaggiore

throughout the Cinque Terre. These walls give the region its characteristic *muri a secco* terracing for vineyards and olive groves. The murals, done by Argentinean artist Silvio Benedetto, are well-explained in English.

• *Head to the railway tunnel entrance, and ride the elevator to the top of town (€0.50 or €1 family ticket, free with Cinque Terre Park Card, daily 8:00–19:45). If the elevator is closed (likely), hike around to the left, following the road up and then right to the...*

Top o' the Town: Here you're treated to spectacular sea views. To continue the viewfest, go right and follow the walkway (ignore the steps marked *Marina Seacoast* that lead to the harbor). It's a five-minute level stroll to the church. You'll pass under the offices of the disgraced national park president and the city hall (flying two flags), with murals celebrating the heroic grape-pickers and fishermen of the region (also by Silvio Benedetto).

• *Before reaching the church, pause to enjoy the...*

Town View: The major river of this region once ran through this valley, as implied by the name Riomaggiore (local dialect for "river" and "major"). As in the other Cinque Terre towns, the river

THE CINQUE TERRE

ravine is now paved over, and the romantic arched bridges that once connected the two sides have been replaced by a practical modern road.

Notice the lack of ugly aerial antennae. In the 1980s, every residence got cable. Now, the TV tower on the hilltop behind the church steeple brings the modern world into each home. The church was rebuilt in 1870, but was first established in 1340. It's dedicated to St. John the Baptist, the patron saint of Genoa, the maritime republic that once dominated the region. The elevator next to the church may be completed by the time you get here. It's designed to help seniors get around the steep town, and also to link to the elevator near the Via dell'Amore trailhead.

• *Continue past the church down to Riomaggiore's main street, named...*

Via Colombo: Walk about 30 feet beyond the WC, go down the stairs, and—if it's open—pop into the tiny Cinque Terre Antiche museum (€0.50, free with Cinque Terre Park Card, generally closed). Sit down for a few minutes to watch a circa-1950 video of the Cinque Terre.

Continuing down Via Colombo, you'll pass a bakery, a couple of grocery shops, and the self-service laundry. There's homemade gelato next to the Bar Centrale. Above where Via Colombo dead-ends, a park-like square built over the train tracks gives the children of the town a level bit of land upon which to kick their soccer balls. The murals above celebrate the great-grandparents of these very children—the salt-of-the-earth locals who earned a humble living before the age of tourism. To the left, stairs lead down to the Marina neighborhood, with the harbor, the boat dock, a 200-yard trail to the beach *(spiaggia),* and an inviting little art gallery. To the right of the stairs is the pedestrian tunnel, running alongside the tracks, which takes you directly back to the station and the trail to the other towns. From here, you can take a train, hop a boat, or hike to your next destination.

Sights in Riomaggiore

Beach—Riomaggiore's rugged and tiny "beach" is rocky, but it's clean and peaceful. Take a two-minute walk from the harbor: Face the harbor, then follow the path to your left. Passing the rugged boat landing, stay on the path to the pebbly beach. There's a shower there in the summer, and another closer to town by the boat landing—where many enjoying sunning on and jumping from the rocks.

Kayaks and Water Sports—The town has a diving center (scuba, snorkeling, kayaks; office down the stairs and under the tracks on Via San Giacomo, daily May-Sept 9:00-18:00, tel. 0187-920-011, www.5terrediving.it).

Hikes—The cliff-hanging Torre Guardiola trail, a steep 20-minute climb from the beach up to old WWII bunkers and a hilltop botanical pathway, has been closed because of a rock slide. Another trail rises from Riomaggiore scenically to the 14th-century Madonna di Montenero sanctuary, high above the town (45 minutes, take the main road inland until you see signs, or ride the green shuttle bus 12 minutes from the town center to the sanctuary trail, then walk uphill 10 minutes).

Nightlife in Riomaggiore

Bar Centrale, run by sociable Ivo, Alberto, and the gang, offers "nightlife" any time of day—making it a good stop for Italian breakfast and music. Ivo, who lived in San Francisco, fills his bar with San Franciscan rock and a fun-loving vibe. During the day, this is a shaded place to relax with other travelers. At night, it offers the younger set the liveliest action (and best mojitos) in town. They also serve €5 fast-food pastas and microwaved pizzas (daily 7:30-24:00 or later, closed Mon in winter, free Wi-Fi with drink, in the town center at Via Colombo 144, tel. 0187-920-208). There's a good *gelateria* next door.

 Enoteca & Ristorante Dau Cila, a cool little hideaway with a mellow jazz-and-Brazilian-lounge ambience down at the miniscule harbor, is a counterpoint to wild Bar Centrale. It's cool for cocktails and open nightly until 24:00 (snacks and meals, fine wine by the glass; see "Eating in Riomaggiore," later).

 Bar & Vini A Piè de Mà, at the beginning of Via dell'Amore, has piles of charm, €6 cocktails, often music, and stays open until midnight June through September (see "Eating in Riomaggiore," later).

 The marvelous **Via dell'Amore** trail (described earlier), lit only with subtle ground lighting so that you can see the stars, welcomes romantics after dark. The trail is free after 19:30.

Sleeping in Riomaggiore

Riomaggiore has arranged its private-room rental system better than its neighbors. Several agencies—with regular office hours, English-speaking staff, and email addresses—line up within a few yards of each other on the main drag. Each manages a corral of local rooms for rent. These offices keep erratic hours, so it's smart to settle up the day before you leave in case they're closed when you need to depart. Expect lots of stairs. If you don't mind the hike, the street above town has safe overnight parking (free 20:00-8:00).

Sleep Code

(€1 = about $1.40, country code: 39)
S = Single, **D** = Double/Twin, **T** = Triple, **Q** = Quad, **b** = bathroom, **s** = shower only. Unless otherwise noted, credit cards are accepted, English is spoken, and breakfast is included (except in Vernazza).

To help you sort easily through these listings, I've divided the accommodations into three categories based on the price for a standard double room with bath:

$$$ Higher Priced—Most rooms €100 or more.
$$ Moderately Priced—Most rooms between €50-100.
$ Lower Priced—Most rooms €50 or less.

Prices can change without notice; verify the hotel's current rates online or by email. For other updates, see www.ricksteves.com/update.

Hotels

$$$ Locanda del Sole has seven modern, basic, and overpriced rooms with a shared and peaceful terrace. Located at the utilitarian top end of town, it's a five-minute walk downhill to the center. Easy (and free with this book) parking makes it especially appealing to drivers (Db-€110-120, air-con, Wi-Fi, Via Santuario 114, tel. & fax 0187-920-773, mobile 340-983-0090, www.locandadelsole.net, info@locandadelsole.net, Enrico).

$$$ Locanda Ca' dei Duxi rents 10 good rooms from an efficient little office on the main drag (Db-€100-130 depending on view and season, extra person-€20, air-con, Wi-Fi, parking-€10/day—book when you reserve, open year-round, Via Colombo 36, tel. & fax 0187-920-036, mobile 329-825-7836, www.duxi.it, info@duxi.it, Samuele and Anna). They also manage **Ca' dei Lisci**, with simpler and cheaper rooms (D-€60, Db-€70-80, www.cadeilisci.com).

$$$ Hotel la Zorza rents nine decent but overpriced rooms in the tangled lanes in the center of town (Db-€100-130, Qb apartment-€150, air-con, Wi-Fi, Via Colombo 36, tel. & fax 0187-920-036, mobile 329-825-7836, www.hotelzorza.com, info@duxi.it).

$$ Locanda dalla Compagnia rents five modern rooms at the top of town, just 300 yards below the parking lot and the little church. All rooms—nice but rather dim—are on the same tranquil ground floor, and share an inviting lounge. Franca runs it with the help of son Allessandro (Db-€80, cash only, air-con, mini-fridge, no view, Via del Santuario 232, tel. 0187-760-050, fax 0187-920-586, www.dallacompagnia.it, lacomp@libero.it).

Room-Booking Services

$$ Riomaggiore Reservations offers 12 rooms and 15 apartments, with American expats Amy and Maddy smoothing communications (Db-€60-90 depending on view, Db suite with top view-€120, cash only, reception open 9:00-17:00 in season, Via Colombo 181, tel. & fax 0187-760-575, www.riomaggiorereservations.com, info@riomaggiorereservations.com).

$$ La Dolce Vita offers three fine rooms on the main drag and two apartments around town (Db-€60-80, open daily 9:30-19:30; if they're closed, they're full; Via Colombo 120, tel. 0187-760-044, mobile 329-099-2741, agonatal@interfree.it, helpful Giacomo and Simone).

$$ Edi's Rooms rents 20 rooms and apartments. You pay extra for views (Db-€70-90 depending on room, apartment Qb-€100-160, reserve with credit card, office open daily in summer 8:30-20:00, in winter 10:30-12:30 & 14:30-19:00, some rooms involve climbing a lot of steps—ask before viewing or reserving, reception at Via Colombo 111, tel. 0187-760-842, tel. & fax 0187-920-325, www.lancoracinqueterre.com, edi-vesigna@iol.it).

Backpacker Dorms

$ Riomaggiore Reservations (listed above) runs a mini-hostel in a fine communal apartment with nine beds in three rooms, a cool living room, terrace, and kitchen in a good, quiet location. Take care of this little treasure so it survives (€22/bed, reception open 9:00-17:00 in season, Via Colombo 181, tel. & fax 0187-760-575, www.riomaggiorereservations.com, info@riomaggiorereservations.com).

$ Camere Patrizia rents cheap doubles and dorm bunk beds at €25 per person from its reception at Via Colombo 25, but books only through www.hostelworld.com or to drop-ins (mobile 333-165-6362).

Eating in Riomaggiore

Trattoria La Grotta, right in the town center (no view), serves reliably good food with a passion for anchovies and mussels. You'll enjoy friendly service surrounded by historic photos and wonderful stonework in a dramatic, dressy, cave-like setting. Venessa is warm and helpful while her mother, Isa, is busy cooking (€12 pastas, €15 *secondi*, 5 percent cash discount, Thu-Tue 12:00-14:30 & 17:30-22:30, closed Wed, Via Colombo 247, tel. 0187-920-187).

La Lanterna, with the ambience of an old fisherman's home inside and a few appealing harborside tables outside, is wedged into a niche in the Marina, overlooking the harbor under the tracks. Chef Massimo serves traditional plates, loves anchovies, and bakes fresh bread daily (€10 pastas, €18 *secondi*, no cover, daily 12:00-22:00, Via San Giacomo 10, tel. 0187-920-589).

Te La Do Io La Merenda ("I'll Give You a Snack") is good for a snack, pizza, or takeout. Their counter is piled with an assortment of munchies, and they have pastas, roasted chicken, and focaccia sandwiches to go (daily 9:00-21:00, Via Colombo 161, tel. 0187-920-148).

Enoteca & Ristorante Dau Cila is decked out like a black-and-white movie set in a centuries-old boat shed with extra tables outside on a rustic deck over dinghies. Try their antipasto specialty of several seafood appetizers, and listen to jazz with the waves lapping at the harbor below (€12 pastas, €18 *secondi*, March-Oct daily until 24:00, Via San Giacomo 65, tel. 0187-760-032, Luca).

Bar & Vini A Piè de Mà, at the trailhead on the Manarola end of town, is good for a scenic light bite or quiet drink at night. Enjoying a meal at a table on its dramatically situated terrace provides an indelible Cinque Terre memory (daily 10:00-20:00, June-Sept until 24:00, tel. 0187-921-037).

Picnics: Groceries and delis lining Via Colombo sell food to go, including pizza slices, for a picnic at the harbor or beach.

Manarola (Town #2)

Like Riomaggiore, Manarola is attached to its station by a 200-yard-long tunnel (lined with interesting photos). During WWII air raids, these tunnels provided refuge and a safe place for rattled villagers to sleep. The town itself fills a ravine, bookended by its wild little harbor to the west and a diminutive church square inland to the east. A delightful and gentle stroll from the church down to the harborside park provides the region's easiest vineyard walk (described in my "Self-Guided Walk," next page).

Orientation to Manarola

The **TI** at the train station is open daily 7:00-20:00.

A **shuttle bus** runs between the low end of Manarola's main street (at the tobacco shop and newsstand) and the parking lot (€1.50 one-way, €2.50 round-trip, free with Cinque Terre Park Card, 2/hour, just flag it down). Shuttle buses also run about hourly from Manarola to Volastra, near the Cinque Terre Cooperative Winery.

To get to the **dock** and the boats that connect Manarola with the other Cinque Terre towns, find the steps to the left of the harbor view—they lead down to the ticket kiosk. Continue around the left side of the cliff (as you're facing the water) to catch the boats.

Self-Guided Walk

Welcome to Manarola

From the harbor, this 30-minute circular walk shows you the town and surrounding vineyards, and ends at a fantastic viewpoint, perfect for a picnic.

• *Start down at the waterfront.*

The Harbor: Manarola is tiny and picturesque, a tumble of buildings bunny-hopping down its ravine to the fun-loving waterfront. Notice how the I-beam crane launches the boats. Facing the water, look to the right, at the hillside Punta Bonfiglio cemetery and park (where this walk ends).

The town's swimming hole is just below. Manarola has no sand, but offers the best deep-water swimming in the area. The first "beach" has a shower, ladder, and wonderful rocks. The second has tougher access and no shower, but feels more remote and pristine (follow the paved path toward Corniglia, just around the point). For many, the tricky access makes this beach dangerous.

• *Hiking inland up the town's main drag, you'll come to the train tracks covered by Manarola's new square, called...*

Piazza Capellini: Built in 2004, this square is an all-around great idea, giving the town a safe, fun zone for kids. Locals living near the tracks also enjoy a little less noise. Check out the mosaic that displays the varieties of local fish in colorful enamel.

• *Fifty yards uphill, you'll find the...*

Sciacchetrà Museum: Run by the national park, it's hardly a museum. But if it's open, pop in to its inviting room to see a tiny exhibit on the local wine industry (€0.50, free with Cinque Terre Park Card, generally closed, 15-minute video in English by request, 100 yards uphill from train tracks, across from the post office).

• *Hiking farther uphill, you can still hear...*

Manarola's Stream: As in Riomaggiore, Monterosso, and

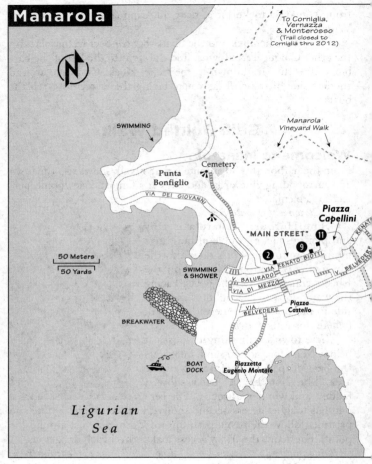

Manarola

To Corniglia, Vernazza & Monterosso (Trail closed to Corniglia thru 2012)

SWIMMING

Manarola Vineyard Walk

Punta Bonfiglio

Cemetery

VIA DEI GIOVANNI

Piazza Capellini

"MAIN STREET"

V. RENATO

2 9

VIA RENATO BIOTTI

V. BELVEDERE

50 Meters

50 Yards

SWIMMING & SHOWER

BALURADO

VIA DI MEZZO

VIA BELVEDERE

Piazza Castello

BREAKWATER

BOAT DOCK

Piazzetta Eugenio Montale

Ligurian Sea

Vernazza, Manarola's stream was covered over by a modern sewage system after World War II. Before that time, romantic bridges arched over its ravine. A modern waterwheel recalls the origin of the town's name—local dialect for "big wheel" (one of many possible derivations). Mills like this once powered the local olive oil industry.

• *Keep climbing until you come to the square at the...*

   Top of Manarola: The square is faced by a church, an oratory—now a religious and community meeting place—and a bell tower, which served as a watchtower when pirates raided the town (the cupola was added once the attacks ceased). Behind the church is Manarola's well-run youth hostel, originally the church's schoolhouse. To the right of the oratory, a stepped lane leads to

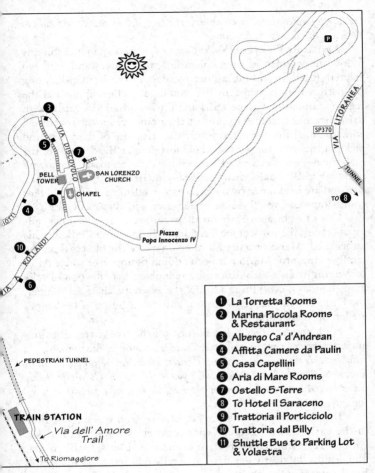

❶	La Torretta Rooms
❷	Marina Piccola Rooms & Restaurant
❸	Albergo Ca' d'Andrean
❹	Affitta Camere da Paulin
❺	Casa Capellini
❻	Aria di Mare Rooms
❼	Ostello 5-Terre
❽	To Hotel il Saraceno
❾	Trattoria il Porticciolo
❿	Trattoria dal Billy
⓫	Shuttle Bus to Parking Lot & Volastra

Manarola's sizable tourist-free zone.

While you're here, check out the church. According to the white marble plaque in its facade, the Parish Church of St. Lawrence (San Lorenzo) dates from "MCCCXXXVIII" (1338). Step inside to see two paintings from the unnamed Master of the Cinque Terre, the only painter of any note from this region (left wall and above main altar). While the style is Gothic, the work dates from the late 15th century, long after Florence had entered the Renaissance. Note the humble painted stone ceiling, which replaced the wooden original in the 1800s. It features Lawrence, patron saint of the Cinque Terre, with his grill, the symbol of his martyrdom (he was roasted on it).

• *Walk 20 yards below the church and find a wooden railing. It marks the start of a delightful stroll around the high side of town, and back to the seafront. This is the beginning of the...*

Manarola Vineyard Walk: Don't miss this experience. Simply follow the wooden railing, enjoying lemon groves and wild red valerian (used for insomnia since the days of the Romans). Along the path, which is primarily flat, you'll get a close-up look at the region's famous dry-stone walls and finely crafted vineyards (with dried-heather thatches to protect the grapes from the southwest winds). Smell the rosemary. Study the structure of the town, and pick out the scant remains of an old fort. Notice the S-shape of the main road—once a riverbed—that flows through town. The town's roofs are traditionally made of locally quarried slate, rather than tile, and are held down by rocks during windstorms. As the harbor comes into view, you'll see the breakwater, added just a decade ago.

Out of sight above you on the right are simple wooden religious scenes, the work of local resident Mario Andreoli. Before his father died, Mario promised him he'd replace the old cross on the family's vineyard. Mario has been adding figures ever since. After recovering from a rare illness, he redoubled his efforts. On religious holidays, everything's lit up: the Nativity, the Last Supper, the Crucifixion, the Resurrection, and more. Some of the scenes are left up year-round.

High above, a recent fire burned off the tree cover, revealing ancient terraces that line the terrain like a topographic map.

• *Follow this trail all the way to a T-intersection, where it hits the main coastal trail. Turn left. (A right takes you to the trail to Corniglia, likely closed in 2012.) Before descending back into town, take a right, detouring into...*

The Cemetery: Ever since Napoleon—who was king of Italy in the early 1800s—decreed that cemeteries were health risks, Cinque Terre's burial spots have been located outside the towns. The result: The dearly departed generally get first-class sea views. Each cemetery—with its evocative yellowed photos and finely carved Carrara marble memorial reliefs—is worth a visit. (The basic structure for all of them is the same, but Manarola's is the most easily accessible.)

In cemeteries like these, there's a hierarchy of four places to park your mortal remains: a graveyard, a spacious death condo *(loculo)*, a mini bone-niche *(ossario)*, or the communal ossuary. Because of the tight space, a time limit is assigned to the first three options (although many older tombs are grandfathered in). Bones go into the ossuary in the middle of the chapel floor after about a generation. Traditionally, locals make weekly visits to loved ones here, often bringing flowers. The rolling stepladder makes access to top-floor *loculi* easy.

• *The Manarola cemetery is on Punta Bonfiglio. Walk just below it, far-*

*ther out through a park (playground, drinking water, WC, and picnic
benches). Your Manarola finale: the bench at the tip of the point, offering
one of the most commanding views of the entire region. The easiest way
back to town is to take the stairs at the end of the point.*

Sleeping in Manarola

(€1 = about $1.40, country code: 39)

Manarola has plenty of private rooms. Ask in bars and restaurants.
There's a modern three-star place halfway up the main drag, a
sea-view hotel on the harbor, a big modern hostel, and a cluster
of options around the church at the peaceful top of the town (a
5-minute hike from the train tracks).

$$$ La Torretta is a trendy, upscale 13-room place that caters
to a demanding clientele. Probably the most elegant retreat in the
region, it's a peaceful refuge with all the comforts for those happy
to pay, including a communal hot tub with a view. Enjoy a com-
plimentary snack and glass of prosecco on arrival, free wine-tast-
ings during your stay, breakfast in your room, and a free minibar.
Each chic room is distinct and described on their website (smaller
Db-€145, regular Db-€190, Db suite-€250-400, 10 percent dis-
count with cash, book several months in advance as it's justifiably
popular, closed mid-Nov-mid-March, Wi-Fi, on Piazza della
Chiesa beside the bell tower at Vico Volto 20, tel. 0187-920-327,
fax 0187-760-024, www.torrettas.com, torretta@cdh.it).

$$$ Marina Piccola offers 13 bright, slick rooms on the
water—so they figure a warm welcome is unnecessary (Db-€120,
air-con, Wi-Fi, Via Birolli 120, tel. 0187-920-103, fax 0187-920-
966, www.hotelmarinapiccola.com, info@hotelmarinapiccola
.com).

$$$ Albergo Ca' d'Andrean, run by Simone, is quiet, com-
fortable, and modern—except for its antiquated reservation sys-
tem. While the welcome is formal at best, it has 10 big, sunny,
air-conditioned rooms and a cool garden oasis complete with
lemon trees (Sb-€72, Db-€100, breakfast-€6, cash only, send per-
sonal check to reserve from US—or call if you're reserving from
the road, closed Nov-Christmas, up the hill at Via A. Discovolo
101, tel. 0187-920-040, fax 0187-920-452, www.cadandrean.it,
cadandrean@libero.it).

$$ At Affitta Camere da Paulin, charming Donatella and
Eraldo (the town's retired policeman) rent very nice, well-equipped
rooms with a large and inviting common living room. It's in a
modern setting a few minutes' walk uphill from the train tracks
(Db-€70-80, view apartment Db-€105-130, Wi-Fi, Via Discovolo
126, tel. & fax 0187-920-706, mobile 334-389-4764, www.da
paulin.it, prenotazioni@dapaulin.it).

$$ Casa Capellini rents four rooms: One has a view balcony, another a 360-degree terrace—book long in advance (Sb-€45, Db-€65; €85 for the *alta camera* on the top, with a kitchen, private terrace, and knockout view; two doors down the hill from the church—with your back to the church, it's at 2 o'clock; Via Ettore Cozzani 12, tel. 0187-920-823, mobile 349-306-1046, www.casacapellini-5terre.it, casa.capellini@tin.it, Gianni and Franca don't speak English).

$$ Aria di Mare Rooms rents four sunny rooms and an apartment 20 yards beyond Trattoria dal Billy at the very top of town. Three rooms have spacious terraces with knockout views and lounge chairs. Maurizio speaks a little English, while Mamma Franca communicates with lots of Italian and toothy smiles (Db-€80, 2 adults and 1 child-€80, Db apartment-€90, these prices promised through 2012, no breakfast, Wi-Fi, up stairs on the left at Via Aldo Rollandi 137, tel. 0187-920-367, mobile 349-058-4155, www.ariadimare.info, ask at Billy's if no one's home).

$ Ostello 5-Terre, Manarola's modern and pleasant hostel, occupies the former parochial school above the church square and offers 48 beds in four- to six-bed rooms. Nicola and Riccardo run a calm and peaceful place—it's not a party hostel—and quiet is greatly appreciated. They rent dorm rooms as doubles. Reserve well in advance. Full means full—they don't accommodate the desperate on the floor (Easter-mid-Oct: dorm beds-€24, Db-€65-70, Qb-€100-110; 20 percent less off-season, closed Nov-Feb, not co-ed except for couples and families, no membership necessary, open to all ages, optional €5 breakfast and €6 pasta, office closed 13:00-16:00, rooms closed 10:00-16:00, strict midnight curfew, laundry, safes, phone cards, Internet access, book exchange, elevator, Via B. Riccobaldi 21, tel. 0187-920-215, fax 0187-920-218, www.hostel5terre.com, info@hostel5terre.com).

For Drivers: **$$$ Hotel il Saraceno,** with seven spacious, modern rooms, is a deal for drivers. Located above Manarola in the tiny town of Volastra (chock-full of vacationing Germans and Italians in summer), it's serene, clean, and right by the shuttle bus to Manarola (Db-€100, buffet breakfast, Wi-Fi, free parking, Via Volastra 8, tel. 0187-760-081, fax 0187-760-791, www.thesaraceno.com, hotel@thesaraceno.com, friendly Antonella).

Eating in Manarola

Many hardworking places line the main drag. The Scorza family works hard at **Trattoria il Porticciolo** (free glass of *sciacchetrà* dessert wine with this book, closed Wed, below train tracks at Via R. Birolli 92, tel. 0187-920-083). The harborside **Marina Piccola** is famous for great views, lousy service, and gouging naive tourists.

Trattoria dal Billy, hiding out high on the hill, is a hit, with good food and impressive views over the valley. With Edoardo and Dario's black pasta with seafood and squid ink, green pasta with artichokes, mixed seafood starters, and homemade desserts, many find it worth the climb. Dinner reservations are a must (€11 pastas, €14 *secondi*, generally daily 8:00-10:00 & 12:00-15:00 & 19:00-23:30, sometimes closed Thu, Via Aldo Rollandi 122, tel. 0187-920-628).

Corniglia (Town #3)

This is the quiet town—the only one of the five not on the water—with a mellow main square. According to a (likely fanciful) local

legend, the town was originally settled by a Roman farmer who named it for his mother, Cornelia (how Corniglia is pronounced). The town and its ancient residents produced a wine so famous that—some say—vases found at Pompeii touted its virtues. Regardless of the veracity of the legends, wine remains Corniglia's lifeblood today. Follow the pungent smell of ripe grapes into an alley cellar and get a local to let you dip a straw into a keg. Remote and less visited than the other Cinque Terre towns, Corniglia has fewer tourists, cooler temperatures, a few restaurants, a windy overlook on its promontory, and plenty of private rooms for rent (ask at any bar or shop, no cheaper than other towns). If you think of the Cinque Terre as the Beatles, Corniglia is Ringo.

Orientation to Corniglia

Arrival in Corniglia

From the station, a footpath zigzags up nearly 400 steps to the town. Or take the green shuttle bus, generally timed to meet arriving trains (€1.50 one-way, €2.50 round-trip, free with Cinque Terre Park Card, 2/hour). Before leaving for the bus, confirm departure times on the schedule posted at the stop. If you're driving, be aware that only residents can park on the main road between the recommended Villa Cecio and the point where the steep switchback staircase meets the road. Beyond that area, parking is €1.50 per hour.

Corniglia

200 Meters
200 Yards

To Vernazza →

HUNDREDS
OF STEPS

Harbor

SANTA MARIA
BELVEDERE

"CIAPPÀ"
SQUARE &
BUS STOP

LARGO
TARAGIO,
ORATORY & ❹

To
Manarola

TRAIN
STATION

Ligurian Sea

SWIMMING

❶ Pan e Vin Bar
   (Ricci Rooms Check-In)
❷ Villa Cecio Rooms
❸ Corniglia Hostel
❹ La Lanterna Restaurant
❺ Osteria Mananan
❻ Enoteca il Pirun
❼ La Posada Ristorante
❽ Gelateria
❾ Butiega Shop

Self-Guided Walk

Welcome to Corniglia

We'll explore this tiny town—population 240—and end at a scenic viewpoint.

• *Begin near the bus stop, located at a...*

Town Square: The gateway to this community is "Ciappà" square, with an ATM, phone booth, old wine press, and bus stop. The Cinque Terre's designation as a national park sparked a revitalization of the town. Corniglia's young generation is more likely now to stay put, rather than migrate into big cities the way locals did in the past.

• *Stroll the spine of Corniglia, Via Fieschi. In the fall, the smell of grapes (on their way to becoming wine) wafts from busy cellars. Along this main street, you'll see...*

Corniglia's Enticing Shops: Alberto's Gelateria dishes up the best homemade gelato in town. Before ordering, get a free taste of Alberto's *miele di Corniglia*, made from local honey. His local lemon slush takes pucker to new heights. **Enoteca il Pirun**—named for a type of oddly shaped old-fashioned wine pitcher designed to aerate the wine and give the alcohol more kick—is located in a cool cantina at Via Fieschi 115. Sample some local wines (generally free for small tastes). If you buy something, they may gift you with a souvenir bib. In the **Butiega** shop at Via Fieschi 142, Vincenzo and

Diego sell organic local specialties (daily 8:00-19:30). For picnickers, they offer €2.50 made-to-order ham-and-cheese sandwiches and a fun €3.50 *antipasto misto* to go. (There are good places to picnic farther along on this walk.)

• *Following Via Fieschi, you'll end up at the...*

Main Square: On Largo Taragio, tables from two bars and a trattoria spill around a WWI memorial and the town's old well. It once piped in natural spring water from the hillside to locals living without plumbing. What looks like a church is the Oratory of Santa Caterina. (An oratory is a kind of a spiritual clubhouse for a service group doing social work in the name of the Catholic Church. For more information, see "Oratory of the Dead" on page 392.) Behind the oratory, you'll find a clearing that local children have made into a soccer field. The stone benches and viewpoint make this a peaceful place for a picnic (less crowded than the end-of-town viewpoint, described below).

• *Opposite the oratory, notice how steps lead steeply down on Via alla Marina to Corniglia's non-beach. It's a five-minute paved climb to sunning rocks, a shower, and a small deck (with a treacherous entry into the water). From the square, continue up Via Fieschi to the...*

End-of-Town Viewpoint: The Santa Maria Belvedere, named for a church that once stood here, marks the scenic end of Corniglia. This is a super picnic spot. From here, look high to the west, where the village and sanctuary of San Bernardino straddle a ridge (a good starting point for a hike; accessible by shuttle bus from Monterosso or a long uphill hike from Vernazza). Below is the tortuous harbor, where locals hoist their boats onto the cruel rocks.

Sights in Corniglia

Beaches—This hilltop town has rocky sea access below its train station (toward Manarola). Once a beach, it's all been washed away and offers no services. Look for signs that say *al mare* or *Marina*. A trail leads from the town center steeply down to sunning rocks on the closest thing Corniglia has to a beach (with a shower).

The infamous **Guvano beach** (a bit along the coast toward Vernazza) is now essentially closed down. Guvano was created by an 1893 landslide that cost the village a third of its farmland. Notorious throughout Italy as a nude beach, Guvano was accessed via an unused train tunnel and attracted visitors with an appetite for drug use. Now the tunnel is closed, and the national park wants people to keep their clothes on and forget about Guvano.

Sleeping in Corniglia

(€1 = about $1.40, country code: 39)

Perched high above the sea on a hilltop, Corniglia has plenty of private rooms. To get to the town from the station, catch the shuttle bus or make the 15-minute uphill hike. The town is riddled with humble places that charge too much (generally Db-€65) and have meager business skills and a limited ability to converse with tourists—so it's almost never full.

$$ Cristiana Ricci is an exception to the rule. She communicates well and is reliable, renting four small, clean, and peaceful rooms—two with kitchens and one with a terrace and sweeping view—just inland from the bus stop (Db-€60-70, Qb-€90, €10/day less when you stay 2 or more nights, free Internet access, check in at the Pan e Vin bar at Via Fieschi 123, mobile 338-937-6547, cri_affittacamere@virgilio.it, Stefano). Her mom rents a big, modern apartment (€90 for 2-4 people).

$$ Villa Cecio (pronounced "chay-choe") feels like an abandoned hotel. They offer eight well-worn rooms on the outskirts of town, with saggy beds and little character or warmth (Db-€65 promised in 2012, breakfast-€5, cash preferred, great views, on main road 200 yards toward Vernazza at Via Serra 58, tel. 0187-812-043, fax 0187-812-138, mobile 334-350-6637, www.cecio5terre.com, info@cecio5terre.com, Giacinto). They also rent eight similar rooms (Db-€60) in an annex on the square where the bus stops.

$ Corniglia Hostel was formerly the town's schoolhouse. It rents 24 beds in a pastel-yellow building up some steps from the main square where the bus stops. The playground in front is often busy with happy kids. Despite its institutional atmosphere, the hostel's prices, central location, and bright and clean rooms ensure its popularity. Its hotelesque double rooms are open to anyone (€24/bed in two 8-bed dorms, €27 with minimal breakfast; four Db-€55, €60 with breakfast; air-con, lockers, Internet access, Wi-Fi, self-serve laundry, mountain bikes for rent, no public spaces except lobby, office open 7:00-13:00 & 15:00-24:00, rooms closed 13:00-15:00, 1:30 curfew, Via alla Stazione 3, tel. 0187-812-559, fax 0187-763-984, www.ostellocorniglia.com but reserve at www.hostelworld.com, ostellocorniglia@gmail.com, helpful Andrea).

Eating in Corniglia

Corniglia has few restaurants.

The trattoria **La Lanterna,** on the main square, is the most atmospheric (but without particularly charming service).

Osteria Mananan—between the Ciappà bus stop and the main square on Via Fieschi—serves what many consider the best food in town in its small, stony, elegant interior (Fri-Wed 12:15-14:30 & 19:45-21:15, closed Tue, no outdoor seating, tel. 0187-821-166).

Enoteca il Pirun, also on Via Fieschi, has a small restaurant above the wine bar, where Mario serves typical local dishes (€28 fixed-price meal includes homemade wine, daily 12:00-16:00 & 19:30-23:30, tel. 0187-812-315).

La Posada Ristorante offers dinner in a garden under trees, overlooking the Ligurian Sea. To get here, stroll out of town to the top of the stairs from the station (€10 pastas, €10 *secondi*, €15 tourist *menu*, nightly from 19:00, tel. 0187-821-174).

Vernazza (Town #4)

With the closest thing to a natural harbor—overseen by a ruined castle and a stout stone church—Vernazza is the jewel of the Cinque Terre. Only the occasional noisy slurping up of the train by the mountain reminds you of the modern world.

The action is at the harbor, where you'll find outdoor restaurants, a bar hanging on the edge of the castle, and a breakwater with a promenade, corralled by a natural amphitheater of terraced hills. In the summer, the beach becomes a soccer field, where teams fielded by local bars and restaurants provide late-night entertainment. In the dark, locals fish off the promontory, using glowing bobbers that shine in the waves.

Proud of their Vernazzan heritage, the town's 500 residents like to brag: "Vernazza is locally owned. Portofino has sold out." Fearing the change it would bring, keep-Vernazza-small proponents stopped the construction of a major road into the town and region. Families are tight and go back centuries; several generations stay together. In the winter, the population shrinks, as many people return to their more comfortable big-city apartments to spend the money they reaped during the tourist season.

Leisure time is devoted to taking part in the *passeggiata*—strolling lazily together up and down the main street. Sit on a bench and study the passersby doing their *vasche* (laps). Explore the characteristic alleys, called *carugi*. Learn—and live—the phrase "*la vita pigra di Vernazza*" (the lazy life of Vernazza).

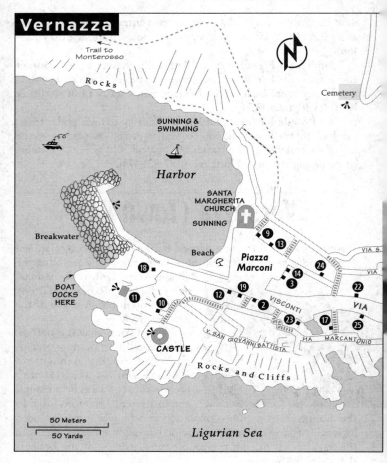

Orientation to Vernazza

Tourist Information

The TI/park information/train ticket office is one desk buried in a gift shop between the two tracks at the train station (daily 8:00-19:30, tel. 0187-812-524). Some of the staff may ring the owner of the room you have reserved as a courtesy, but they cannot make reservations. Public WCs are nearby in the station.

Arrival in Vernazza

By Train: Vernazza's train station is only about three cars long, but the trains are much longer, so most of the cars come to a stop in a long, dark tunnel. Get out anyway, and walk through the tunnel to the station.

1. Pensione Sorriso
2. Trattoria Gianni Rooms/Ristorante
3. Albergo Barbara
4. Tonino Basso Rooms & Il Pirata della Cinque Terre
5. Camere Fontana Vecchia
6. Giuliano Basso Rooms
7. Vernazza Rooms
8. Blue Marlin Bar & Café
9. Ananasso Bar
10. Ristorante al Castello
11. Ristorante Belforte
12. Gambero Rosso Ristorante
13. Trattoria del Capitano
14. Ristorante Pizzeria Vulnetia
15. Trattoria da Sandro
16. Antica Osteria il Baretto
17. Ristorante Incadase da Piva
18. Bar Baia Saracena
19. Burgus Wine Bar
20. Enoteca Sotto l'Arco
21. Franco's Ristorante & Bar la Torre
22. Forno (Bakery)
23. Gelateria
24. Launderette
25. Internet Point

By Car: There's a nonresident parking lot, but be aware that parking can be tough from May through September (€2/hour, €12/24 hours, cash only, about 500 yards above town, pay first at the parking stand before getting your spot). A hardworking shuttle service, generally with friendly English-speaking Beppe, Simone, or Pietro behind the wheel, connects the lot to the top of town (€1.50, free with Cinque Terre Park Card, 3-4/hour, runs 7:00-19:00). Yellow lines mark parking spots for residents. The highest lot (a side-trip uphill) is for overnight stays.

Helpful Hints

Internet Access: The **Blue Marlin Bar,** run by Massimo and Carmen, has the lowest prices and longest hours (€0.10/minute, Internet available Thu-Tue 10:00-22:30—but opens earlier for breakfast, closed Wed, see listing on page 383). The slick, six-terminal **Internet Point,** run by Alberto and Isabella, is in the village center (€0.15/minute, €0.10/minute after 30 minutes, daily June-Oct 9:30-23:00, until 20:00 Nov-May, Wi-Fi, will burn your digital photos to a CD or DVD for €5). The recommended **Il Pirata delle Cinque Terre** bar, at the top of the town, offers free Wi-Fi.

Laundry: Lavanderia il Carugetto is completely self-serve and hides out on a narrow lane a block off the main drag (coin-op, €6/wash, €5/dry, daily 8:00-22:00, opposite the pharmacy—go ten steps up and turn left, operated by Domenico and Barbara at the fish shop).

Massage: Stephanie, an American expat, gives a good, strong therapeutic massage in a neat little studio at the top of town. Famous among locals as the physical therapist who massaged an old woman back to health, Stephanie can counsel you on tuning up your body while giving insights into the social intricacies of the village (€50/hour, mobile 338-9429-494, stephsette@gmail.com). **Kate** offers a softer and more aromatic style: reflexology, holistic, and hot stone massage (mobile 333-568-4653, www.vernazzamassage5terre.com).

Best Views: A steep 10-minute hike in either direction from Vernazza gives you a classic village photo op (for the best light, head toward Corniglia in the morning, and toward Monterosso in the evening).

Self-Guided Walks

Welcome to Vernazza

This tour includes Vernazza's characteristic town squares and ends on its scenic breakwater.

• *From the train station, walk uphill until you hit the parking lot, with a bank, a post office, and a barrier that keeps out all but service vehicles. Vernazza's shuttle buses run from here to the parking lot and into the hills. Walk to the tidy, modern square called...*

Fontana Vecchia: Named after a long-gone fountain, this is where older locals remember the river filled with townswomen doing their washing. Now they enjoy checking on the baby ducks. A lane leads from here up to the cemetery. Imagine the entire village sadly trudging up here during funerals. (The cemetery is peaceful and evocative at sunset, when the fading light touches each crypt.)

• *Glad to be here in happier times, begin your saunter downhill to the harbor. Just before the* Pensione Sorriso *sign, on your right (big brown wood doors), you'll see the...*

Ambulance Barn: A group of volunteers is always on call for a dash to the hospital, 40 minutes away in La Spezia. Opposite the barn is a big empty lot. Like many landowners, the owner of Pensione Sorriso had plans to expand, but since the 1980s, the government has said "No." While some landowners are frustrated, the old character of these towns survives. A few steps farther down is the town clinic. The *guarda medica* (emergency doctor—see buzzer) sleeps upstairs.

• *At the corner across from the playground, you'll see a...*

World Wars Monument: Look for a marble plaque in the wall to your left, dedicated to those killed in the World Wars. Not a family in Vernazza was spared. Listed on the left are soldiers *morti in combattimento,* who died in World War I; on the right is the World War II section. Some were deported to *Germania;* others—labeled *Part* (stands for *partigiani,* or partisans, generally communists)—were killed while fighting against Mussolini. Cynics considered partisans less than heroes. After 1943, Hitler called up Italian boys over 15. Rather than die on the front for Hitler, they escaped to the hills. They became "resistance fighters" in order to remain free.

The path to Corniglia leaves from here (behind and above the plaque). Behind you is a small square and playground, decorated with three millstones, once used to grind local olives into oil. There's a good chance you'll see an expat mom here at the village playground with her kids. I've met many American women who fell in love with a local guy, stayed, and are now happily raising families here. (But I've rarely met an American guy who moved in with a local girl.)

From here, Vernazza's tiny river goes underground. Until the 1950s, the river ran openly through the center of town. Old-timers recall the days before the breakwater, when the river cascaded down and the surf sent waves rolling up Vernazza's main drag. Back then, this place was nicknamed "Little Venice" for the series of romantic bridges that arched over the stream, connecting the two sides of the town before the main road was built.

Before the tracks (on the left), the wall has 10 spaces, one reserved for each political party's ads during elections—a kind of campaign pollution control. On the wall under the tracks (right side), a big photo shows the old road into town before there were cars, back when vineyards entirely covered the hills. A map shows the region's hiking trails—trail #2 is the basic favorite. The green box on the wall (on the right) lists which days volunteer ambulance drivers are on call. You'll notice that family names repeat a lot. A few big families dominate the town, and in the local dialect, everyone in your village is called "cousin." Finally, a community event board says what's happening in town. The second set of tracks (nearer the harbor) was recently renovated to lessen the disruptive noise, but locals say it made no difference.

• *Follow the road downhill to...*

Vernazza's "Business Center": Here, you'll pass many locals doing their *vasche* (laps). At Enoteca Sotto l'Arco, Gerry and Paola sell wine—they can uncork it and throw in plastic glasses—and delightful jars of local pesto, which goes great on bread (Via Roma 70). Next, you'll pass the Blue Marlin Bar (Vernazza's top night-spot) and the tiny Chapel of Santa Marta (the small stone chapel with iron grillwork over the window), where Mass is celebrated only on special Sundays. Farther down, you'll walk by a grocery, *gelateria*, bakery, pharmacy, another grocery, and another *gelateria*. There are plenty of fun and cheap food-to-go options here.

• *On the left, in front of the second* gelateria, *an arch (with a peaceful little sitting perch atop it) leads to what was a beach, where the town's stream used to hit the sea back in the 1970s. Continue down to the...*

Harbor Square and Breakwater: Vernazza, with the only natural harbor of the Cinque Terre, was established as the sole place boats could pick up the fine local wine. The two-foot-high square stone at the foot of the stairs by the Burgus Wine Bar is marked *Sasso del Sego* (stone of tallow). Workers crushed animal flesh and fat in its basin to make tallow, which drained out of the tiny hole below. The tallow was then used to waterproof boats or wine barrels. For more town history, step into the Burgus to see fascinating old photos of Vernazza on the wall. Stonework is the soul of the region. Take some time to appreciate the impressive stonework of the restaurant interiors facing the harbor.

On the far side (behind Ristorante Pizzeria Vulnetia), peek into the tiny street with its commotion of arches. Vernazza's most characteristic side streets, called *carugi*, lead up from here. The trail (above the church, toward Monterosso) leads to the quintessential view of Vernazza.

Located in front of the harborside church, the tiny piazza—decorated with a river-rock mosaic—is a popular hangout spot. It's where Vernazza's old ladies soak up the last bit of sun, and kids enjoy a patch of level ball field.

Vernazza's harborfront church is unusual for its strange entry-way, which faces east (altar side). With relative peace and pros-perity in the 16th century, the townspeople doubled the church in size, causing it to overtake a little piazza that once faced the west facade. From the square, use the "new" entry and climb the steps, keeping an eye out for the level necessary to keep the church high and dry. Inside, the lighter pillars in the back mark the 16th-century extension. Three historic portable crosses hanging on the walls are carried through town during Easter processions. They are replicas of crosses that Vernazza ships once carried on crusades to the Holy Land.

• *Finish your town tour seated out on the breakwater (perhaps with a glass of local white wine or something more interesting from a nearby bar—borrow the glass, they don't mind). Face the town, and see...*

The Harbor: In a moderate storm, you'd be soaked, as waves routinely crash over the *molo* (breakwater, built in 1972). Waves can even wash away tourists squinting excitedly into their cameras. (I've seen it happen.) In 2007, an American woman was swept away and killed by a rogue wave. Enjoy the new waterfront piazza—carefully.

The train line (to your left) was constructed in 1874 to tie together a newly united Italy, and linked Turin and Genoa with Rome. A second line (hidden in a tunnel at this point) was built in the 1920s. The yellow building alongside the tracks was Vernazza's first train station. You can see the four bricked-up alcoves where people once waited for trains. Notice the wonderful new concrete sunbathing strip (and place for late-night privacy) laid below the tracks along the rocks.

Vernazza's fishing fleet is down to just a couple of boats (with the net spools). Vernazzans are still more likely to own a boat than a car, and it's said that you stand a better chance of surviving if you mess with a local man's wife than with his boat. Boats are on buoys, except in winter or when the red storm flag (see pole at start of breakwater) indicates bad seas. At these times, the boats are pulled up onto the square—which is usually reserved for restaurant tables. In the 1970s, tiny Vernazza had one of Italy's top water polo teams, and the harbor was their "pool." Later, when the league required a real pool, Vernazza dropped out.

The Castle: On the far right, the castle, which is now a grassy park with great views (and nothing but stones), still guards the town (€1.50 donation supports the local emergency doctor and volunteer ambulance group, daily 10:00-19:00; from harbor, take stairs by Trattoria Gianni and follow *Ristorante al Castello* signs, tower is a few steps beyond). This was the town's watchtower back in pirate days, and a Nazi lookout in World War II. The castle tower looks new because it was rebuilt after the British bombed it, chasing out the Germans. The highest umbrellas mark the recommended Ristorante Al Castello. The squat tower on the water is great for a glass of wine or a meal. From the

breakwater, you could follow the rope to the Ristorante Belforte and pop inside, past the actual submarine door. A photo of a major storm showing the entire tower under a wave (not uncommon in the winter) hangs near the bar.

The Town: Vernazza has two halves. *Sciuiu* (Vernazzan dialect for "flowery") is the sunny side on the left, and *luvegu* (dank) is the shady side on the right. Houses below the castle were connected by an interior arcade—ideal for fleeing attacks. The "Ligurian pastel" colors are regulated by a commissioner of good taste in the regional government. The square before you is locally famous for some of the area's finest restaurants. The big red central house—on the site where Genoan warships were built in the 12th century—used to be a guardhouse.

In the Middle Ages, there was no beach or square. The water went right up to the buildings, where boats would tie up, Venetian-style. Imagine what Vernazza looked like in those days, when it was the biggest and richest of the Cinque Terre towns. Buildings had a water gate (facing today's square) and a front door on the higher inland side. There was no pastel plaster, just fine stonework (traces of which survive above the Trattoria del Capitano). Apart from the added plaster, the general shape and size of the town has changed little in five centuries. Survey the windows and notice inhabitants quietly gazing back.

Above the Town: The small, round tower above the red guardhouse—another part of the city fortifications—reminds us of Vernazza's importance in the Middle Ages, when it was a key ally of Genoa (whose archenemies were the other maritime republics, especially Pisa). Franco's Ristorante and Bar la Torre, just behind the tower, welcomes hikers who are finishing, starting, or simply contemplating the Corniglia-Vernazza hike, with great town views. That tower recalls a time when the entire town was fortified by a stone wall. Vineyards fill the mountainside beyond the town. Notice the many terraces. Someone—probably after too much of that local wine—calculated that the roughly 3,000 miles of dry-stone walls built to terrace the region's vineyards have the same amount of stonework as the Great Wall of China.

Wine production is down nowadays, as the younger residents choose less physical work. But locals still maintain their tiny plots and proudly serve their family wines. The patchwork of local vineyards is atomized and complex because of inheritance traditions. Historically, families divided their land between their children. Parents wanted each child to get some good land. Because some lots were "kissed by the sun" while others were shady, the lots were split into increasingly tiny and eventually unviable pieces.

A single steel train line winds up the gully behind the tower. It is for the vintner's *trenino*, the tiny service train. Play "Where's *trenino?*" and see if you can find two trains. The vineyards once stretched as high as you can see, but since fewer people sweat in the fields these days, the most distant terraces have gone wild again.

The Church, School, and City Hall: Vernazza's Ligurian Gothic church, built with black stones quarried from Punta Mesco (the distant point behind you), dates from 1318. Note the gray stone that marks the church's 16th-century expansion. The gray-and-red house above the spire is the local elementary school (about 25 children attend; education through age 14 is obligatory). High-schoolers go to the "big city": La Spezia. The red building to the right of the schoolhouse, a former monastery, is the City Hall. Vernazza and Corniglia function as one community. Through most of the 1990s, the local government was Communist. In 1999, residents elected a coalition of many parties working to rise above ideologies and simply make Vernazza a better place. That practical notion of government continues here today. Finally, on the top of the hill, with the best view of all, is the town cemetery.

Sights in Vernazza

Tuesday-Morning Market—Vernazza's skimpy business community is augmented Tuesday mornings (8:00-13:00) when a meager gang of cars and trucks pulls into town for a tailgate market.

Beach—The harbor's sandy cove has sunning rocks and showers by the breakwater. There's also a ladder on the breakwater for deep-water access. The new sunbathing lane directly under the church also has a shower.

Boat Rental—Vincenzo of Nord Est rents canoes and small motorboats from his stand on the harbor, and also takes people out for mini-cruises. With a rental boat, you can reach a tiny *acqua pendente* (waterfall) cove between Vernazza and Monterosso; locals call it their *laguna blu* (motorboats-€60/2 hours, €80/4 hours, plus gas—usually about €15, includes snorkeling gear, May-Oct only, mobile 338-700-0436, info@manuela-vernazza.com).

Shuttle Bus Joyride—For a cheap and scenic joyride, with a chance to chat about the region with friendly Beppe, Simone, or Pietro, ride the shuttle bus from the top of town for the entire route for the cost of a round-trip ticket. Some buses also head to two sanctuaries in the hills above town (5/day—usually at 7:00, 9:45, 12:00, 15:00, and 17:30; schedule posted at park office, train station, and bus stop in front of post office; €2.50 one-way, free with Cinque Terre Park Card, churches at sanctuaries usually closed). The high-country 40-minute loop—buses are marked *Drignana*—gives you lots of scenery without having to hike (don't take buses marked *No panoramic*, as these won't take scenic routes).

Nightlife in Vernazza

Vernazza's younger generation of restaurant workers lets loose after-hours. They work hard through the tourist season, travel in the winter, speak English, and enjoy connecting with international visitors. After the restaurants close down, the town is quiet except for a couple of nightspots. For more information on the Blue Marlin, Ananasso, Il Pirata, and Ristorante Incadase, see their listings under "Eating in Vernazza," later. All bars must close by 24:00.

Blue Marlin Bar dominates the late-night scene with a mix of locals and tourists, home-cooked food until 22:00, good drinks, and piano jam sessions. If you're young and hip, this is *the* place to hang out. If you play the piano, you're welcome to contribute to the scene.

Ananasso Bar offers early-evening happy-hour fun and cocktails (called *"aperitivi"*) that both locals and visitors enjoy. Its harborfront tables get the last sunshine of the day.

Burgus Wine Bar, chic and cool with a jazzy ambience, is a popular early-evening and after-dinner harborside hangout. Sip local wine or a cocktail. Valerio and Lorenza specialize in Ligurian wines and can explain the historic town photos and museum cases of artifacts (closed Tue, free Wi-Fi with a drink, Piazza Marconi 4).

Il Pirata delle Cinque Terre, at the top of the town, features the entertaining Cannoli brothers, who fill a happy crowd of tourists with wonderful Sicilian pastries and drinks each evening. Many come for dinner and end up staying because of these two wild and crazy guys and the camaraderie they create among their diners (erratic hours driven by demand, free Wi-Fi).

Ristorante Incadase da Piva (tucked up the lane behind the pharmacy) is the haunt of Piva, Vernazza's troubadour. Piva often gets out his guitar and sings traditional local songs as well as his own compositions. If you're looking for a local Hemingway, check here.

Top of the Town: A couple of bars with light meals have great perches high above the town (on the trail to Corniglia).

Really Late: There's a little cave on the beach just under the church that lends itself to fun in the wee hours, when everything else is closed.

Sleeping in Vernazza

(€1 = about $1.40, country code: 39)

Vernazza, the spindly and salty essence of the Cinque Terre, is my top choice for a home base. Off-season (Oct-March), you

THE CINQUE TERRE

can generally arrive without a reservation and find a place, but at other times, it's smart to book ahead (especially June-July and weekends).

People recommended here are listed for their communication skills (they speak English, have email, and are reliable with bookings) and because they rent several rooms. Consequently, my recommendations cost more than comparable rooms you'll find if you shop around. Comparison-shopping will likely save you €10-20 per double per night—and often get you a better place and view to boot. The real Vernazza gems are stray single rooms with owners who have no interest in booking in advance or messing with email. Arrive by early afternoon and drop by any shop or bar and ask; most locals know someone who rents rooms.

Anywhere you stay here requires some climbing, but keep in mind that more climbing means better views. Most do not include breakfast (for suggestions, see "Eating in Vernazza," later). Cash is preferred or required almost everywhere. Night noise can be a problem if you're near the station. Rooms on the harbor come with church bells (but only between 7:00 and 22:00).

Pensions

These pensions are located on the Vernazza map, earlier in this chapter.

$$$ Pensione Sorriso, the oldest pension in town (where I stayed on my first visit in 1975), rents 19 overpriced rooms above the train station. While the main building has the charm, it comes with train noise and saggy beds; the annex, up the street, is in a quieter apartment that feels forgotten (S-€65, Sb-€80, D-€100, Db-€140-150, Tb-€130, includes breakfast, some with air-con, Wi-Fi, Via Gavino 4, tel. 0187-812-224, fax 0187-821-198, www.pensionesorriso.com, info@pensionesorriso.com, Francesca and Aldo).

$$$ Trattoria Gianni rents 27 small rooms and three apartments just under the castle. The rooms are in three buildings—one funky, two modern—up a hundred tight, winding spiral stairs. The funky ones, which may or may not have private baths, are artfully decorated à la shipwreck, with tiny balconies and grand sea views *(con vista sul mare)*. The comfy new *(nuovo)* rooms lack views. Both have modern bathrooms and access to a super-scenic cliff-hanging guests' garden. Steely Marisa requires check-in before 16:00

or a phone call to explain when you're coming. Emanuele (Gianni's son, who now runs the restaurant), Simona, and the staff speak a little English (S-€45, D-€80, Db-€100-120, Tb-€120-140, 10 percent discount with cash and this book—request when you reserve, cancellations less than a week in advance are charged one night's deposit, closed Jan-Feb, Piazza Marconi 5, tel. & fax 0187-812-228, tel. 0187-821-003, on Wed call mobile 393-9008-155 instead, www.giannifranzi.it, info@giannifranzi.it). Pick up your keys at Trattoria Gianni's restaurant on the harbor square.

$$ Albergo Barbara rents nine simple, clean, and modern rooms overlooking the harbor square—most with small windows and small views. It's run by English-speaking Giuseppe and his no-nonsense Swiss wife, Patricia (D-€55, Db-€65-70, big Db with nice harbor view-€110, extra bed-€10, 2-night stay preferred, closed Dec-Feb, reserve online with credit card but pay cash, free Wi-Fi, Piazza Marconi 30, tel. & fax 0187-812-398, mobile 338-793-3261, www.albergobarbara.it, info@albergobarbara.it).

Private Rooms (Affitta Camere)

Vernazza is honeycombed with private rooms year-round, offering the best values in town. Owners may be reluctant to reserve rooms far in advance. It's easiest to call a day or two ahead or simply show up in the morning and look around. Doubles cost €55-100, depending on the view, season, and plumbing—you get what you pay for. Most places accept only cash. Some have killer views, come with lots of stairs, and cost the same as a small, dark place on a back lane over the train tracks. Little English is spoken at many of these places. If you call to let them know your arrival time (or call when you arrive, using your mobile phone or the pay phone just below the station), they'll meet you at the train station.

Well-Managed and Well-Appointed Rooms in the Inland Part of Town

$$$ Tonino Basso rents four sparkling-clean, modern rooms—at a steep price. Each room has its own computer for free Internet access. He's in the only building in Vernazza with an elevator. You get tranquility and air-conditioning, but no views (Sb-€65, Db-€120, Tb-€150, Qb-€180, prices go down Nov-March, call Tonino's mobile number upon arrival and he'll meet you, tel. 0187-821-264, mobile 335-269-436, fax 0187-812-807, toninobasso @libero.it). If you can't locate Tonino, ask his friends at Enoteca Sotto l'Arco at Via Roma 70.

$$ Camere Fontana Vecchia is a delightful place, with four bright, spacious, quiet rooms and an apartment near the post office (no view). As the only place in Vernazza with almost no stairs to climb and the sound of a babbling brook outside your window, it's one of the best values in town (D-€70, Db-€80, T-€95, Tb-€110, super-trendy 2-person apartment-€100, fans and heat, open all year, Via Gavino 15, tel. 0187-821-130, mobile 333-454-9371, fax 0187-812-261, m.annamaria@libero.it, youthful and efficient Anna speaks English). If no one answers, ask at Enoteca Sotto l'Arco on the main drag.

$$ Giuliano Basso rents four pleasant rooms, crafted with care, just above town in the terraced wilds (sea views from terraces). Straddling a ravine among orange trees, it's an artfully decorated Robinson Crusoe-chic wonderland, proudly built out of stone by Giuliano himself—the town's last stone-layer, who "has stone in his blood" (Db-€80, Db suite with air-con-€100, Db suite with private rooftop balcony-€100, extra bed-€25, fridge access, free Internet access, more train noise than others, above train station, take the ramp just before Pensione Sorriso, mobile 333-341-4792, or have Enoteca Sotto l'Arco contact him, www.cdh.it/giuliano, giuliano@cdh.it).

Other Reliable Places Scattered Through Town and the Harborside

These places are not located on this book's map; ask for directions when you reserve.

$$$ La Malà is Vernazza's jetsetter pad. Four pristine white rooms boast four-star-hotel-type extras and a common terrace looking out over the rocky shore (Db-€155, Db suite-€220, includes breakfast at a bar, air-con, Wi-Fi, tel. 334-287-5718, fax 0187-812-218, www.lamala.it, info@lamala.it, Giamba and Armanda). It's a climb—way, way up to the top of town—but they'll gladly carry your bags to and from the station. They also rent the simpler "Armanda's Room" nearby (no view, Db-€75, ring bell at Piazza Marconi 15).

$$$ Martina Callo's four air-conditioned rooms overlook the square; they're up plenty of steps near the silent-at-night church tower (room #1: Tb-€110 or Qb-€120 with harbor view; room #2: huge Qb family room with no view-€110; room #3: Db with grand view terrace-€100; room #4: roomy Db with no view-€60; free Wi-Fi, ring bell at Piazza Marconi 26, tel. & fax 0187-812-365, mobile 329-435-5344, www.roomartina.com, roomartina @roomartina.com).

$$ Monica Lercari rents several classy rooms with modern comforts, perched at the top of town. Guests are welcome to borrow the family rowboat or mountain bike (Db-€80, sea-view D-€100, grand sea-view terrace D-€120, "honeymoon suite" Db-€180, includes breakfast, air-con, Wi-Fi, next to recommended Ristorante al Castello, tel. 0187-812-296, alcastello vernazza@yahoo.it).

$$ Memo Rooms has three clean and spacious rooms that offer good value. They overlook the main street, in what feels like a miniature hotel. Enrica will meet you if you call upon arrival (Db-€70, Via Roma 15, tel. 0187-812-360, mobile 338-285-2385, www.memorooms.com, info@memorooms.com).

$$ Nicolina rents five recently renovated units with double-paned windows. Two rooms are in the center over the pharmacy, up a few steep steps—one has only sleeper sofas (Db-€80); two others are in a different building beyond the church with great views (Db-€100, Tb-€120, Qb-€150); and the last unit is a two-bedroom quadruple with even better views (€200). Inquire at Pizzeria Vulnetia on the harbor square (Piazza Marconi 29, tel. & fax 0187-821-193, www.camerenicolina.it, camerenicolina.info @cdh.it).

$$ Rosa Vitali rents two four-person apartments across from the pharmacy overlooking the main street (and beyond the train noise). One has a terrace and fridge (top floor); the other has windows and a full kitchen (Db-€95, Tb-€115, Qb-€125, reception at Via Visconti 10 between the grotto and Piazza Marconi, tel. 0187-821-181, mobile 340-267-5009, www.rosacamere.it, rosa.vitali @libero.it).

$$ Francamaria and her kind husband Andrea rent eight sharp, comfortable, and creatively renovated but expensive rooms—all described in detail on her website. While their reception desk is on the harbor square (on the ground floor facing the harbor at Piazza Marconi 30—don't confuse it with Albergo Barbara at same address), the rooms they manage are all over town (Db-€80-120 depending on size and view, Qb-€125-160, extra person-€20, tel. & fax 0187-812-002, mobile 328-711-9728, www.francamaria.com, francamaria@francamaria.com).

More Private Rooms in Vernazza

$$ Maria Capellini rents a couple of simple, clean rooms, including one on the ground floor right on the harbor (Db with kitchen-€85, Tb-€110, cash only, fans, mobile 338-436-3411, www.mariacapellini.com, mariacapellini@hotmail.it, Maria and Giacomo).

$$ Il Pirata delle Cinque Terre rents two basic rooms with the sounds of the river below. Managed by Noelia and Leyla, wives of the Cannoli brothers (see listing under "Eating in Vernazza"), the rooms are at the top of the town, 100 yards beyond their bar (Db-€90, Tb-€130, Qb-€160, includes breakfast with this book at Il Pirata bar—which also functions as the reception, 2-night minimum, cash only, tel. 0187-812-047, mobile 338-596-2503, www.ilpiratarooms.com, ilpiratarooms@libero.it).

$$ Ivo's Camere rents two simple no-terrace rooms high above the main street, as well as a studio apartment (Db-€75, studio-€100, free Wi-Fi, Via Roma 6, reception at Pizzeria Fratelli Basso—Via Roma 1, tel. 0187-821-042, mobile 333-477-5521, www.ivocamere.com, post@ivocamere.com).

$$ Vernazza Rooms, run by Daria Bianchi, Chiara, and Davide, rents 12 decent rooms from their office near the station. Four rooms are above the Blue Marlin Bar looking down on the main street, and eight are below the City Hall (Db-€60-95, Qb-€100-120, fans, reception next to Blue Marlin Bar at Via del Santo 9, tel. 0187-812-151, mobile 338-581-4688 or 338-418-8696, www.vernazzarooms.com, info@vernazzarooms.com).

$$ Emanuela Colombo has two rooms—one spacious and basic on the harbor square, the other *molto* chic and located on a quiet side street (Db-€90, Tb-€110, tel. 339-834-2486, www.vacanzemanuela.it, manucap64@libero.it).

More Options: **$$ Affitta Camere Alberto Basso** (a clean, modern room with a noisy harbor/piazza view, Db-€75, check in at Internet Point, albertobasso@hotmail.com); **$$ Capitano Rooms** (3 recently remodeled rooms above the main drag, Db-€90, ask for Paolo or Barbara at the Trattoria del Capitano restaurant, tel. 0187-812-201); **$$ Eva's Rooms** (3 rooms overlooking main street with train noise, Db-€60-80, ring at Via Roma 56, tel. 0187-821-134, www.evasrooms.it, massimoeva@libero.it); **$$ Manuela Moggia** (3 rooms, Db-€80, Tb-€95, Qb with kitchen-€125, top of the town at Via Gavino 22, tel. 0187-812-397, mobile 333-413-6374, www.manuela-vernazza.com, info@manuela-vernazza.com); and **$$ Elisabetta Rooms** (3 tired rooms at the tip-top of town with Vernazza's ultimate 360-degree roof terrace, Db-€65, Tb-€90, Qb-€100, fans, Via Carattino 62, mobile 347-451-1834, www.elisabettacarro.it, carroelisabetta@hotmail.com, Elisabetta and Pino).

Eating in Vernazza

Breakfast

Locals take breakfast about as seriously as flossing. A cappuccino and a pastry or a piece of focaccia from a bar or bakery does it. Most of my recommended accommodations don't come with breakfast (when they do, I've noted so in my listings). Assuming you're on your own, you have four basic options: Blue Marlin Bar for its extensive menu, including bacon and eggs; Il Pirata delle Cinque Terre for sugary stuff and a lively welcome; Ananasso Bar for coffee and a sweet roll on the harborfront; or any bakery for picnic goodies.

Blue Marlin Bar (mid-town, just below the train station) serves a good array of clearly priced à la carte items including eggs and bacon (only after 8:45), adding up to the priciest breakfast in town (likely to total €10). It's run by Massimo and Carmen (Thu-Tue 7:00-24:00, closed Wed, tel. 0187-821-149). If you're awaiting a train any time of day, the Blue Marlin's outdoor seating beats the platform.

Il Pirata delle Cinque Terre is located at the top of the town, where the dynamic Sicilian duo Gianluca and Massimo (hard-working twins, a.k.a. the Cannoli brothers) enthusiastically offer a great assortment of handcrafted authentic Sicilian pastries. Their fun and playful service makes up for the lack of a view. Gianluca is a pastry artist, hand-painting fanciful sculptured marzipan. Their sweet pastry breakfasts are a hit, with a stunning array of hot-out-of-the-oven treats like *panzerotto* (made of ricotta, cinnamon, and vanilla, €2.50) and hot cheese and pesto bruschetta (€3). Other favorites include their *granite* (slushees made from fresh fruit), but they proudly serve no bacon and eggs (since "this is Italy"). While the atmosphere of the place seems like suburban Milan, it has a curious charisma among its customers—bringing Vernazza a welcome bit of Sicily (daily 6:30-24:00, also simple lunches and tasty dinners, Via Gavino 36, tel. 0187-812-047).

Ananasso Bar feels Old World, with youthful energy and a great location with little tables right on the harbor. They offer toasted *panini,* pastries, and designer cappuccino. You can eat a bit cheaper at the bar (you're welcome to picnic on the nearby bench or seawall rocks with a Mediterranean view) or enjoy the best-situated tables in town (Fri-Wed 8:00-late, closed Thu).

Picnic Breakfast: Drop by one of Vernazza's several little bakeries, focaccia shops, or grocery stores to assemble a breakfast to eat on the breakwater. Top it off with a coffee in a nearby bar.

Lunch and Dinner

If you enjoy Italian cuisine and seafood, Vernazza's restaurants are worth the splurge. All take pride in their cooking. Wander around at about 20:00 and compare the ambience, but don't wait too late to eat—many kitchens close at 22:00. To get an outdoor table on summer weekends, reserve ahead. Expect to spend €10 for pastas, €12-16 for *secondi,* and €2-3 for a cover charge. Harborside restaurants and bars are easygoing. You're welcome to grab a cup of coffee or glass of wine and disappear somewhere on the breakwater, returning your glass when you're done. If you dine in Vernazza but are staying in another town, be sure to check train schedules before sitting down to eat, as trains run less frequently in the evening.

Above the Harbor, by the Castle

Ristorante al Castello is run by gracious and English-speaking Monica, her husband Massimo, kind Mario, and the rest of her family (you won't see mamma—she's busy personally cooking each home-style *secondo*). Hike high above town to just below the castle for commanding views. Their *lasagne al pesto*, "spaghetti on the rocks" (noodles with shellfish), and scampi crêpes are time-honored family specialties. For simple fare and a special evening, reserve one of the dozen romantic cliff-side sea-view tables for two. Some of these tables snake around the castle, where you'll feel like you're eating all alone with the Mediterranean. Monica offers a free *sciacchetrà* or *limoncello* with biscotti if you have this book (€10 pastas, €12 *secondi*, Thu-Tue 12:00-15:00 for lunch, 19:00-22:00 for dinner, closed Wed and Nov-April, tel. 0187-812-296).

Ristorante Belforte's experimental, beautifully presented, creative cuisine includes a hearty *zuppa Michela* (€23 for a boatload of seafood), fishy *spaghetti Bruno* (€13), and *trofie al pesto* (hand-rolled noodles with pesto). Their classic *antipasto del nostro chef* (€36 for six plates) is plenty for two people. From the breakwater, follow either the stairs or the rope that leads up and around to the restaurant. You'll find a tangle of tables embedded in four levels of the lower part of the old castle. For the ultimate seaside perch, call and reserve one of four tables on the *terrazza con vista* (view terrace). Most of Belforte's seating is outdoors—if the weather's bad, the interior can get crowded (€15 pastas, €23 *secondi*, €3 cover, Wed-Mon 12:00-15:00 & 19:00-22:00, closed Tue and Nov-March, tel. 0187-812-222, Michela).

Harborside
Gambero Rosso ("Red Prawn," the same name as Italy's top restaurant guide) is considered Vernazza's most venerable restaurant. It feels dressy and costs more than the others. Try Chef Claudio's namesake risotto (€15 pastas, €20 *secondi*, €3 cover, Tue-Sun 12:00-15:00 & 19:00-22:00, closed Mon and Dec-Feb, Piazza Marconi 7, tel. 0187-812-265).

Trattoria del Capitano serves *spaghetti con frutti di mare* (pasta entangled with various types of seafood) and *grigliata mista* (a mix of seasonal Mediterranean fish) among their offerings (€10 pastas, €16 *secondi*, €2 cover, Wed-Mon 12:00-15:00 & 19:00-22:00, closed Tue except in Aug, closed Nov-Dec, tel. 0187-812-201, while Paolo and Eduardo speak English, grandpa Giacomo doesn't need to).

Trattoria Gianni is an old standby for locals and tourists who appreciate the best prices on the harbor. You'll enjoy well-prepared seafood and receive steady, reliable, and friendly service from Emanuele and Alessandro. Ask about "off-menu specials." While the outdoor seating is basic, the indoor setting is classy (€15 pastas, €15 *secondi*, €3 cover, check their *menù cucina tipica Vernazza*, Thu-Tue 12:00-15:00 & 19:00-22:00, closed Wed except July-Aug, tel. 0187-812-228).

Ristorante Pizzeria Vulnetia is simpler, serving regional specialties such as prizewinning *tegame alla Vernazza*—anchovies, tomatoes, and potatoes baked in the oven (€8 pizzas, €12 pastas, €16 *secondi*, €2 cover, Tue-Sun 12:00-15:30 & 18:30-22:00, closed Thu, Piazza Marconi 29, tel. 0187-821-193, Giuliano).

Inland, on or near the Main Street

Several of Vernazza's inland eateries manage to compete without the harbor ambience, but with slightly cheaper prices.

Trattoria da Sandro, on the main drag, mixes Genovese and Ligurian cuisine with friendly service. It can be a peaceful alternative to the harborside scene, plus they dish up award-winning stuffed mussels (€13 pastas, €15 *secondi*, Wed-Mon 12:00-15:00 & 18:30-22:00, closed Tue, Via Roma 62, tel. 0187-812-223, Gabriella and Alessandro).

Antica Osteria il Baretto is another solid bet for homey, reasonably priced traditional cuisine, run by Simone and Jenny. As it's off the harbor and a little less glitzy than the others, it's favored by locals who prefer less noisy English while they eat great homemade fish ravioli. Sitting deep in their interior can be a peaceful escape (€12 pasta, €14 *secondi*, Tue-Sat 12:00-15:00 & 19:00-22:00, closed Mon, indoor and outdoor seating, Via Roma 31).

Ristorante Incadase da Piva is a rare bit of old Vernazza. For 25 years, charismatic Piva has been known for his *tegame alla Vernazza,* his *risotto con frutti di mare* (seafood risotto), and his love of music. The town troubadour, he often serenades his guests when the cooking's done (€13 pastas, €16 *secondi*, Fri-Wed 10:30-15:00 & 18:00-22:30, closed Thu, tucked away 20 yards off the main drag, up a lane behind the pharmacy).

Other Eating Options

Il Pirata delle Cinque Terre, popular for breakfast, is also a favorite for lunch and dinner (€9 pastas, great salads, Sicilian specialties), and its homemade desserts and drinks. The Cannoli twins entertain while they serve, as diners enjoy delicious meals while laughing out loud in this simple café/pastry shop. The menu offers a break from the predictable Ligurian fare, and the bread is literally hot out of the oven (at the top of town; for complete description, see listing under "Breakfast," earlier).

Bar Baia Saracena ("Saracen Bay") serves decent pizza and microwaved pastas out on the breakwater. Eat here for the economy and the view (€5-7 salads, €9 pizza, tel. 0187-812-113, Luca).

Pizzerias, Sandwiches, and Groceries: Vernazza's main street creatively fills tourists' needs. Two pizzerias stay busy, and while they mostly do take-out, each will let you sit and eat for the same cheap price. One has tables on the street, and the other **(Ercole)** hides a tiny terrace and a few tables out back (it's the only pizzeria in town with a wood-fired oven). **Forno Bakery** has good focaccia and veggie tarts, and several bars sell sandwiches and pizza by the slice. **Grocery stores** also make inexpensive sandwiches to order (generally Mon-Sat 8:00-13:00 & 17:00-19:30, closed Sun). Tiny jars of pesto spread give elegance to picnics.

Gelato: The town's three *gelaterias* are good. What looks like **Gelateria Amore Mio** (near the grotto, mid-town), is actually Gelateria Stalin—founded in 1968 by a pastry chef with that unfortunate name. His niece Sonia, who speaks "ice cream," and nephew Francesco now run the place, and are generous with free tastes. They have a neat little licking zone with tiny benches hidden above the crowds; look for it on the little bridge a few steps past their door. They also have good coffee (daily 8:00-24:00, closes at 19:00 off-season, 24 flavors, sit there or take it to go).

Monterosso al Mare (Town #5)

This is a resort with a few cars and lots of hotels, rentable beach umbrellas, crowds, and a little more late-night action than the

neighboring towns. Monterosso al Mare—the only Cinque Terre town built on flat land—has two parts: A new town (called Fegina) with a parking lot, train station, and TI; and an old town (Centro Storico), which cradles Old World charm in its small, crooked lanes. In the old town, you'll find hole-in-the-wall shops, pastel townscapes, and a new generation of creative small-businesspeople eager to keep their visitors happy.

A pedestrian tunnel connects the old with the new—but take a small detour around the point for a nicer walk. It offers a close-up view of two sights: a 16th-century lookout tower, built after the last serious pirate raid in 1545; and a Nazi "pillbox," a small, low concrete bunker where gunners hid. (During World War II, nearby La Spezia was an important Axis naval base, and Monterosso was bombed while the Germans were here.)

Strolling the waterfront promenade, you can pick out each of the Cinque Terre towns decorating the coast. After dark, they sparkle. Monterosso is the most enjoyable of the five for young travelers wanting to connect with others looking for a little evening action. Even so, Monterosso is not a full-blown Portofino-style resort—and locals appreciate quiet, sensitive guests.

THE CINQUE TERRE

Orientation to Monterosso

Tourist Information

The TI Proloco is next to the train station (April-Oct daily 9:00-19:00, closed Nov-March, exit station and go left a few doors, tel. 0187-817-506, www.prolocomonterosso.it, Annamaria). If you arrive late on a summer day, head to the Internet café for tourist information (see next page).

Arrival in Monterosso

By Train: Train travelers arrive in the new town, from which it's a scenic, flat 10-minute stroll to all the old-town action (leave station to the left; to reach hotels in the new town, turn right out of station). The bar at track 1, which overlooks the beach, is a handy place to wait while waiting for your train to pull in.

Shuttle buses run roughly hourly along the waterfront between the old town (Piazza Garibaldi, just beyond the tunnel), the train station, and the parking lot at the end of Via Fegina (*Campo Sportivo* stop). While the buses can be convenient—saving you a 10-minute schlep with your bags—they only go once an hour, and are likely not worth the trouble (€1.50, free with Cinque Terre Park Card).

The other alternative is to take a **taxi** (certain vehicles have permission to drive in the old city center). They usually wait outside the train station, but you may have to call (€7 from station to the old town, mobile 335-616-5842 or 335-628-0933).

By Car: Monterosso is 30 minutes off the freeway (exit: Levanto-Carrodano). Note that about three miles above Monterosso, a fork directs you to either *Centro Storico* (old part of town—Via Roma parking lot with a few spots, and possibly the new Loreto garage) or *Fegina* (the new town and beachfront parking, most likely where you want to go). At this point you must choose which area, because you can't drive directly from the new town to the old center (which is closed to cars without special permits).

Parking is easy (except July-Aug and summer weekends) in the huge beachfront guarded lot in the new town (€14/24 hours). If you're heading to the old town, you'll find the lot on Via Roma, a 10-minute downhill walk to the main square (€1.70/hour, €18/24 hours in the parking structure). The big, new Loreto parking garage at the top of the old town should be open in 2012.

For the cheapest Monterosso rates, park along the blue lines (5 minutes farther uphill from Via Roma parking structure) for €8 per day. See "Cinque Terre Connections" at the end of this chapter for directions from Milan and tips on driving in the Cinque Terre.

Helpful Hints

Medical Help: The town's bike-riding, leather bag-toting, English-speaking physician is **Dr. Vitone,** who charges €50-80 for a simple visit (less for poor students, mobile 338-853-0949).

Internet Access: The Net, a few steps off the main drag (Via Roma), has 10 high-speed computers (€1.50/10 minutes) and Wi-Fi. Enzo happily provides information on the Cinque Terre, has a line on local accommodations, and can burn your photos onto a DVD for €6 (daily 9:30-23:00, off-season closes for lunch and dinner breaks, Via Vittorio Emanuele 55, tel. 0187-817-288, mobile 335-778-5085, www.monterossonet .com).

Baggage Storage: Lucia's Lavarapido, two blocks from the station, provides a wonderful bag-check service—just drop off your bag for €5 (see details in next listing).

Laundry: For full-service laundry in the new town, **Lucia's Lavarapido** will return your laundry to your hotel (€12/13 pounds, daily 8:30-22:00, Via Molinelli 17, mobile 339-484-0940, Lucia and Ivano). For self-service in the old town, **Wash and Dry Lavanderia** is new and modern (€6/wash and dry, daily 7:30-23:30, Via Roma 43).

Massage: Giorgio Moggia, the local physiotherapist, gives good massages at your hotel or in his studio (€60/hour, tel. 339-314-6127, giomogg@tin.it).

Self-Guided Walk

Welcome to Monterosso

• *Hike out from the dock in the old town and climb five rough steps to the very top of the concrete...*

Breakwater: If you're visiting by boat, you'll start here anyway. From this point, you can survey Monterosso's old town and new town (stretching to the left, with train station and parking lot), and actually see all *cinque* of the *terre* from one spot: Vernazza, Corniglia (above the shore), Manarola, and a few buildings of Riomaggiore beyond that. The little fort above, which dates from 1550, is now a private home.

These days, the harbor hosts more paddleboats than fishing boats. Sand erosion is a major problem. The partial breakwater is designed to save the beach from washing away. While old-timers remember a vast beach, their grandchildren truck in sand each spring to give tourists something to lie on. (The Nazis liked the Cinque Terre, too—find two of their bomb-hardened bunkers, near left and far right.)

The fancy €300-a-night, four-star Hotel Porto Roca (on the far right) marks the trail to Vernazza. High above, you see an example

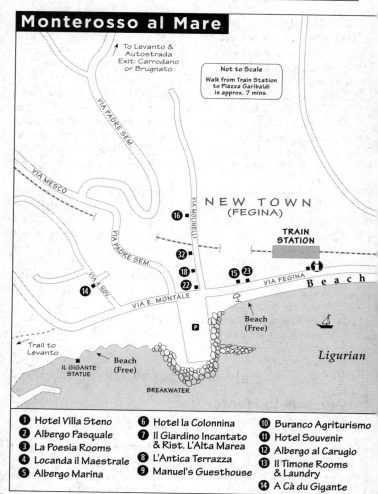

Monterosso al Mare

To Levanto & Autostrada
Exit: Carrodano or Brugnato

Not to Scale

Walk from Train Station to Piazza Garibaldi is approx. 7 mins.

VIA PADRE SEM.

VIA MESCO

VIA PADRE SEM.

VIA A NOV.

VIA MOLINELLI

N E W   T O W N
(FEGINA)

TRAIN STATION

16

32

18

22

15 **23**

14

VIA E. MONTALE

VIA FEGINA

i

B e a c h

Beach (Free)

P

Trail to Levanto

IL GIGANTE STATUE

Beach (Free)

BREAKWATER

Ligurian

- **1** Hotel Villa Steno
- **2** Albergo Pasquale
- **3** La Poesia Rooms
- **4** Locanda il Maestrale
- **5** Albergo Marina
- **6** Hotel la Colonnina
- **7** Il Giardino Incantato & Rist. L'Alta Marea
- **8** L'Antica Terrazza
- **9** Manuel's Guesthouse
- **10** Buranco Agriturismo
- **11** Hotel Souvenir
- **12** Albergo al Carugio
- **13** Il Timone Rooms & Laundry
- **14** A Cà du Gigante

of the costly roads built in the 1980s to connect the Cinque Terre towns with the freeway over the hills. The two capes (Punta di Montenero and Punta Mesco) define the Cinque Terre region. The closer cape, Punta Mesco, marks an important sea-life sanctuary, home to a rare sea grass that provides an ideal home for fish eggs. Buoys keep fishing boats away. The cape was once a quarry, providing employment to locals who chipped out the stones used to build the local towns (the green stones making up part of the breakwater below you are from there).

On the far end of the new town, marking the best free beach around, you can just see the statue named *Il Gigante*. It's 45 feet tall

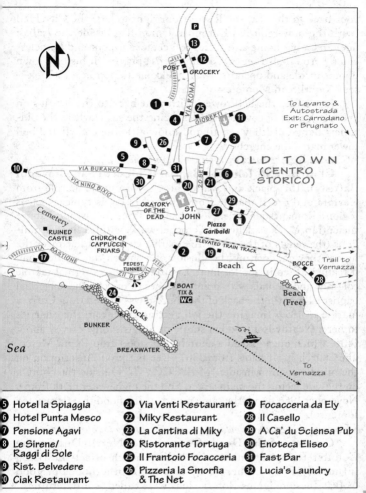

5 Hotel la Spiaggia	**21** Via Venti Restaurant
6 Hotel Punta Mesco	**22** Miky Restaurant
7 Pensione Agavi	**23** La Cantina di Miky
8 Le Sirene/ Raggi di Sole	**24** Ristorante Tortuga
9 Rist. Belvedere	**25** Il Frantoio Focacceria
10 Ciak Restaurant	**26** Pizzeria la Smorfia & The Net

27 Focacceria da Ely
28 Il Casello
29 A Ca' du Sciensa Pub
30 Enoteca Eliseo
31 Fast Bar
32 Lucia's Laundry

and once held a trident. While it looks as if it were hewn from the rocky cliff, it's actually made of reinforced concrete and dates from the beginning of the 20th century, when it supported a dancing terrace for a *fin de siècle* villa. A violent storm left the giant holding nothing but memories of Monterosso's glamorous age.

• *From the breakwater, walk into the old-town square (just under the train tracks and to the right). Find the statue of a dandy holding what looks like a box cutter in...*

Piazza Garibaldi: The statue honors Giuseppe Garibaldi, the dashing firebrand revolutionary who, in the 1860s, helped unite the people of Italy into a modern nation. Facing Garibaldi, with your back to the sea, you'll see (from right to left) the City Hall (with the now-required European Union flag beside the Italian one) and a big home and recreation center for poor and homeless elderly. You'll also see A Ca' du Sciensa pub (with historic town photos inside and upstairs; you're welcome to pop in for a look—see "Nightlife in Monterosso," later).

Just under the bell tower (with your back to the sea, it's on your left), a set of covered arcades facing the sea is where the old-timers hang out (they see all and know all). The crenellated bell tower marks the church.

• Go to church (the entrance is on the inland side).

Church of St. John the Baptist (Chiesa di San Giovanni Battista): This black-and-white church, with white marble from Carrara and green marble from Punte Mesco, is typical of this region's Romanesque style. Note the lacy, stone rose window above the entrance. It's as delicate as crochet work, with 18 slender mullions (the petals of the rose). The marble stripes get narrower the higher they go, creating the illusion of a church that's taller than it really is. Step inside for more Ligurian Gothic: original marble columns and capitals with pointed arches to match. The octagonal baptismal font (in the back of the church) was carved from Carrara marble in 1359. Imagine the job getting that from the quarries to here. Nearby is a wooden statue of St. Anthony, carved about 1400, which once graced a church that stood atop Punta Mesco. The church itself dates from 1307—see the proud inscription on the middle column inside: "MilleCCCVII." Outside the church, on the side facing the main street, find the high-water mark from a November 1966 flood (the same month as the flood that devastated Florence).

• Leaving the church, immediately turn left and go to church again.

Oratory of the Dead (Oratorio dei Neri): During the Counter-Reformation, the Catholic Church offset the rising influence of the Lutherans by creating brotherhoods of good works. These religious Rotary clubs were called "confraternities." Monterosso had two, nicknamed White and Black. This building is the oratory of the Black group, whose mission—as the macabre decor filling the interior indicates—was to arrange for funerals and take care of widows, orphans, the shipwrecked, and the souls of those who ignore the request for a €1 donation. It dates from the 16th century, and membership has passed from father to son for generations. Notice the fine carved choir stalls (c. 1700) just inside the door, and the haunted-house chandeliers. Look up at the ceiling to find the symbol of the confraternity: a skull-and-crossbones and an hourglass...death awaits us all.

• Return to the beach and find the brick steps that lead up to the hill-capping convent (starting between the train tracks and the pedestrian *tunnel). Stop above the castle at a statue of St. Francis and a wolf taking in a grand view. Enjoy another opportunity to see all five of the Cinque Terre towns. From here, backtrack 20 yards and continue uphill.*

The Switchbacks of the Friars: Follow the yellow brick road (OK, it's orange...but I couldn't help singing as I skipped skyward). Climb uphill until you reach a convent church, then a cemetery, in a ruined castle at the summit. The lane *(Salita dei Cappuccini)* is nicknamed *Zii di Frati* ("switchbacks of the friars").
• *When you reach a gate marked* Convento e Chiesa Cappuccini, *you have arrived.*

Church of the Capuchin Friars: The former convent is now manned by a single caretaker friar. Before stepping inside, notice the church's striped Romanesque facade. It's all fake. Tap it—no marble, just cheap 18th-century stucco. Sit in the rear pew. The high altarpiece painting of St. Francis can be rolled up on special days to reveal a statue of Mary standing behind it. Look at the statue of St. Anthony to the right and smile (you're on convent camera). Wave at the security camera—they're nervous about the precious painting to your left.

This fine painting of the Crucifixion is attributed to Anthony van Dyck, the 17th-century Flemish master who lived and worked for years in nearby Genoa (though art historians suspect that, at best, it was painted by someone in the artist's workshop). When Jesus died, the earth went dark. Notice the eclipsed sun in the painting, just to the right of the cross. Do the electric candles work? Pick one up, pray for peace, and plug it in. (Leave €0.50, or unplug it and put it back.)
• *Leave and turn left to hike 100 yards uphill to the cemetery that fills the remains of the castle, capping the hill. Look out from the gate and enjoy the view.*

Cemetery in the Ruined Castle: In the Dark Ages, the village huddled within this castle. Slowly it expanded. Notice the town view from here—no sea. You're looking at the oldest part of Monterosso, huddled behind the hill, out of view of 13th-century pirates. Explore the cemetery, but remember that cemeteries are sacred and treasured places (as is clear by the abundance of fresh flowers). Ponder the black-and-white photos of grandparents past. *Q.R.P.* is *Qui Riposa in Pace* (a.k.a. R.I.P.). Rich families had their own little tomb buildings. Climb to the very summit—the castle's keep, or place of last refuge. Priests are buried in a line of graves closest to the sea, but facing inland, toward the town's holy sanctuary high on the hillside (above the road, with its triangular steeple peeking above the trees). Each Cinque Terre town has a lofty sanctuary, dedicated to Mary and dear to the village hearts.
• *From here, your tour is over—any trail leads you back into town.*

Sights in Monterosso

Beaches—Monterosso's beaches, immediately in front of the train station, are easily the Cinque Terre's best and most crowded. This town is a sandy resort with rentable beach extras: Figure €20 to rent two chairs and an umbrella for the day. Light lunches are served by beach cafés to sunbathers at their lounge chairs. It's often worth the euros to enjoy a private beach. If you see umbrellas on a beach, it means you'll have to pay a rental fee; otherwise the sand is free (all the beaches are marked on this book's Monterosso al Mare map). Don't use your white hotel towels; most hotels will give you beach towels—sometimes for a fee. The local hidden beach, which is free, gravelly, and generally less crowded, is tucked away under Il Casello restaurant at the east end of town, near the trailhead to Vernazza. The bocce ball court (next to Il Casello) is busy with the old boys enjoying their favorite pastime.

Kayaks—**Samba** rents kayaks on the beach (€7/hour for 1-person kayak, €12/hour for 2-person kayak, to the right of train station as you exit, mobile 339-681-2265, Domenico). The paddle to Vernazza is a favorite.

Shuttle Buses for High-Country Hikes—Monterosso's bus service (described earlier, under "Arrival in Monterosso") continues beyond the town limits, but check the schedules—only one or two departures a day head into the high country. Some buses go to the Sanctuary of Our Lady of Soviore, from where you can hike back down to Monterosso (1.5 hours, moderately steep). Rides cost €1.50 (free with Cinque Terre Park Card, pick up schedule from park office). Or you can hike to Levanto (no Cinque Terre Park card necessary, not as stunning as the rest of the coastal trail, 2.5 hours, straight uphill and then easy decline, follow signs at west end of the new town). For hiking details, ask at the train station TI.

Wine-Tasting—Buranco Agriturismo offers visits to their vineyard and cantina daily at 12:00. You'll taste two of their wines plus a grappa and a *limoncino*, along with home-cooked food (€25/person with snacks, €40/person for full lunch, reservations advised at least three days in advance, English may be limited, follow Via Buranco uphill to path, 10 minutes above town, tel. 0187-817-677, www.burancocinqueterre.it). They also rent apartments; see "Sleeping in Monterosso," later.

Boat Rides—From the old-town harbor, boats run nearly hourly (10:30-17:00) to Vernazza, Manarola, Riomaggiore, and Portovenere. Schedules are posted in Cinque Terre park offices (for details, see "Getting Around the Cinque Terre—By Boat," on page 343).

Nightlife in Monterosso

A Ca' du Sciensa has nothing to do with science—it's the last name of the town moneybags who owned this old mansion. The antique dumbwaiter is still in use—a remnant from the days when servants toiled downstairs while the big shots wined and dined up top. This classy yet laid-back pub offers breezy square seating, bar action on the ground level, an intimate lounge upstairs, and discreet balconies overlooking the square to share with your best travel buddy. It's a good place for light meals from a fun and accessible menu: €5-6 sandwiches, salads, and microwaved pastas. They offer €6 cocktails and mojitos with free *aperitivo* snacks from 17:30 to 20:30. Luca welcomes you to wander around the place and view the old Cinque Terre photo collection (daily 10:00-24:00, closed Nov-March, Piazza Garibaldi 17, tel. 0187-818-233).

Enoteca Eliseo, the first (and I'd say best) wine bar in town, comes with operatic ambience. Eliseo and his wife, Mary, love music and wine. You can select a fine bottle from their shop shelf, and for €7 extra, enjoy it and the village action from their cozy tables. If you've ever wanted an education in grappa, talk to Eliseo—he stocks 96 varieties. Wines sold by the glass *(bicchiere)* are posted (Wed-Mon 9:00-24:00, closed Tue, Piazza Matteotti 3, a block inland behind church, tel. 0187-817-308).

Fast Bar, the best bar in town for young travelers and night owls, is located on Via Roma in the old town. Customers mix travel tales with big, cold beers, and the crowd (and the rock 'n' roll) gets noisier as the night rolls on. Come here to watch Italian or American sporting events on TV any time of day (sandwiches and snacks usually served until midnight, open nightly until 2:00, closed Nov-March, Alex, Francisco, and Stefano).

La Cantina di Miky, in the new town just beyond the train station, is a trendy bar-restaurant with an extensive cocktail and grappa menu. The seating is in three zones: overlooking the beach, in the garden, or in the cellar. Run by Manuel, son of well-known local restaurateur Miky, it sometimes hosts live music. Manuel offers a fun "five villages" wine-tasting with local meats and cheeses (daily until well after 24:00, Via Fegina 90, tel. 0187-802-525).

Sleeping in Monterosso

(€1 = about $1.40, country code: 39)

Monterosso, the most beach-resorty of the five Cinque Terre towns, offers maximum comfort and ease. The TI Proloco just outside the train station can give you a list of €70-80 double rooms. Rooms in Monterosso are a better value for your money than similar rooms in crowded Vernazza, and the proprietors seem more

THE CINQUE TERRE

genuine and welcoming. To locate the hotels, see the Monterosso al Mare map.

In the Old Town

$$$ Hotel Villa Steno is lovingly managed and features great view balconies, panoramic gardens with sun beds, air-conditioning, and the friendly help of English-speaking Matteo and his wife, Carla. Of their 16 rooms, 12 have view balconies (Sb-€110, Db-€170, Tb-€195, Qb-€225, includes hearty buffet breakfast, €10 per night discount with cash and this book in 2012, Internet access and Wi-Fi, laundry, parking-€8—reserve in advance, Via Roma 109, tel. 0187-817-028 or 0187-818-336, fax 0187-817-354, www.villa steno.com, steno@pasini.com). It's a 15-minute hike (or €8 taxi ride) from the train station to the top of the old town. Readers get a free Cinque Terre info packet and a glass of the local sweet wine, *sciacchetrà*, when they check in—ask for it.

$$$ Albergo Pasquale is a modern, comfortable place with 15 rooms, run by the same family as the Hotel Villa Steno (above). It's conveniently located just a few steps from the beach, boat dock, tunnel entrance to the new town, and train tracks. While there is some traffic and train noise, it's mostly a lullaby of waves. Located right on the harbor, it has an elevator and offers easier access than most (same prices and welcome drink as Villa Steno; air-con, all rooms with sea view, Via Fegina 8, tel. 0187-817-550 or 0187-817-477, fax 0187-817-056, www.hotelpasquale.com, pasquale@pasini .com, Felicita and Marco).

$$$ La Poesia has four warmly colored rooms that share a peaceful garden terrace, where you'll enjoy a complimentary *aperitivo* upon arrival (Db-€150, suite-€40 extra, small discount for multi-night stays, air-con, Via Genova 4, tel. 0187-817-283, www .lapoesia-cinqueterre.com, info@lapoesia-cinqueterre.com, mamma Nicoletta speaks little English, daughter Veronica speaks more).

$$$ Locanda il Maestrale rents six small, stylish rooms in a sophisticated and peaceful little inn. Although renovated with all the modern comforts, it retains centuries-old character under frescoed ceilings. Its peaceful sun terrace overlooking the old town and Via Roma action is a delight (small Db-€115, Db-€145, suite-€170, less off-season, 10 percent discount with cash and this book, air-con, Wi-Fi, Via Roma 37, tel. 0187-817-013, mobile 338-4530-531, fax 0187-817-084, www.locandamaestrale.net, maestrale @monterossonet.com, Stefania).

$$$ Albergo Marina, creatively run by enthusiastic husband-and-wife team Marina and Eraldo, has 23 thoughtfully appointed rooms and a garden with lemon trees. With a free and filling buffet featuring local specialties from 14:00 to 17:00 daily, they offer a fine value (standard Db-€130, 10 percent discount with cash and this book in 2012, elevator, air-con, Wi-Fi, free use of kayak and snorkel equipment, Via Buranco 40, tel. 0187-817-613, fax 0187-817-242, www.hotelmarina5terre.com, marina@hotelmarina5terre.com).

$$$ Hotel la Colonnina, a comfy, modern place with 21 big and pretty rooms, is buried in the town's fragrant and sleepy back streets with no sea views (Db-€142, Tb-€200, Qb-€225, €15 more for bigger rooms with viewless terrace, cash only, air-con, Internet access and Wi-Fi, fridges, elevator, inviting rooftop terrace with sun beds, garden, Via Zuecca 6, tel. 0187-817-439, fax 0187-817-788, www.lacolonninacinqueterre.it, info@lacolonninacinqueterre.it, Christina). The hotel is in the old town behind the statue of Garibaldi (take street to left of A Ca' du Sciensa one block up).

$$$ Il Giardino Incantato ("The Enchanted Garden") is a charming four-room B&B in a tastefully renovated 16th-century Ligurian home in the heart of the old town. Breakfast is served in a hidden garden, which is illuminated with candles in the evening (Db-€170, Db suite-€200, air-con, free minibar and tea and coffee service, Via Mazzini 18, tel. 0187-818-315, mobile 333-264-9252, www.ilgiardinoincantato.net, giardino_incantato@libero.it, kind and eager-to-please Fausto and Mariapia).

$$$ L'Antica Terrazza rents four classy rooms right in town. With a pretty terrace overlooking the pedestrian street and minimal stairs, Raffaella and John offer a good deal (Db-€110, 5 percent discount with cash, air-con, Internet access and Wi-Fi, Vicolo San Martino 1, tel. 0187-817-499, mobile 347-132-6213, www.antica terrazza.com, post@anticaterrazza.com).

$$$ Manuel's Guesthouse, perched among terraces, is a garden getaway ruled by disheveled artist Manuel and run by his nephew Lorenzo. They have seven big, bright rooms and a grand view. Their killer terrace is hard to leave—especially after a few drinks (Db-€100, big Db with grand-view balcony-€120, prices good with this book, cash only, air-con, Internet access and Wi-Fi, in old town, up about 100 steps behind church at top of town, Via San Martino 39, mobile 333-439-0809 or 329-547-3775, www.manuelsguesthouse.com, info@manuelsguesthouse.com).

$$$ Buranco Agriturismo, a 10-minute walk from the old town, has wonderful gardens and views over the vine-covered valley. Its primary business is wine and olive-oil production, but they offer three apartments at a good price. It's a rare opportunity to stay in a farmhouse but still be able to get to town on foot (2-6 people-€60/person including breakfast, €30/child under 12, dinner on request, air-con, free shuttle from station, open year-round, tel. 0187-817-677, mobile 349-434-8046, fax 0187-802-084, www.burancocinqueterre.it, info@buranco.it, informally run by Loredana, Mary, and Giulietta).

$$ Hotel Souvenir is Monterosso's cash-only backpacker hotel. It has 30 rooms in two buildings, each utilitarian but comfortable (one more stark than the other). Both share a lounge and pleasant leafy courtyard. The basic one is popular with students (S-€30, Sb-€35, D-€55, Db-€70, T-€105, breakfast-€5); the other is nicer and pricier (Sb-€45, Db-€80, Tb-€120, includes breakfast; walk three blocks inland from the main old-town square to Via Gioberti 24, tel. 0187-817-822, tel. & fax 0187-817-595, hotel _souvenir@yahoo.com, Beppe).

$$ Albergo al Carugio is a simple, practical nine-room place in a big apartment-style building at the top of the old town. It's quiet, comfy, and functional (Db-€75-80, air-con, Wi-Fi, Via Roma 100, tel. 0187-817-453, www.alcarugio.it, info@alcarugio.it, Andrea and Simona).

$$ Il Timone Rooms, a little B&B by the post office, has three tidy, modern rooms. Francesco also rents a few rooms near the cemetery, but they aren't worth the hike (Db-€90, breakfast at a bar, air-con, Wi-Fi, Via Roma 75, tel. 349-870-8666, www .iltimonedimonterosso.it).

In the New Town

$$$ A Cà du Gigante, despite its name, is a tiny yet stylish refuge with nine rooms. About 100 yards from the beach (and surrounded by blocky apartments on a modern street), the interior is tastefully done with modern comfort in mind (Db-€160, Db sea-view suite-€180, 10 percent discount with 3-night stay and this book in 2012, occasional last-minute deals, air-con, free parking, Via IV Novembre 11, tel. 0187-817-401, fax 0187-817-375, www.ilgigante cinqueterre.it, gigante@ilgigantecinqueterre.it, Claudia).

$$$ Hotel la Spiaggia is a venerable old 19-room place facing the beach and run with attitude by Poggi Andrea and his gentle daughter Maria. Half of the rooms come with air-con and half with sea views, but all are the same price—request what you like when you reserve (Db-€160, €10 discount for 2-night stays, includes breakfast and parking, elevator, Via Lungomare 98, tel. 0187-817-567, fax 0187-817-075, www.laspiaggiahotel.com, hotel laspiaggia@libero.it).

$$$ Hotel Punta Mesco is a tidy, well-run little haven renting 17 quiet, modern rooms. While none have views, 10 rooms have small terraces. For the price, it may offer the best comfort in town (Db-€132, Tb-€170, 5 percent discount with cash, air-con, Wi-Fi, free loaner bikes, free parking, Via Molinelli 35, tel. & fax 0187-817-495, www.hotelpuntamesco.it, info@hotelpuntamesco.it, Diego and Anna).

$$$ Pensione Agavi has 10 spartan, hostel-like, overpriced rooms, about half overlooking the beach near the big rock. This is not a place to party—it feels like an old hospital with narrow hallways (D-€80, Db-€110, Tb-€140, same price with or without view, 10 percent discount for 2 nights or more, no breakfast, cash only, refrigerators, turn left out of station to Fegina 30, tel. 0187-817-171, mobile 333-697-4071, fax 0187-818-264, hotel.agavi@libero.it, Hillary).

$ Le Sirene/Raggi di Sole, with nine simple rooms in two humble buildings, is about the cheapest place in town. It's run from a hole-in-the-wall reception desk a block from the station, just off the water. I'd request the Le Sirene building, which doesn't have train noise and is a bit nicer than Raggi di Sole (Db-€80, third person-€40, fans, Via Molinelli 10, mobile 393-935-7683, www.sirenerooms.com, sirenerooms@gmail.com, Ermanna).

Eating in Monterosso

Restaurants

Ristorante Belvedere, big and sprawling, is *the* place for a good-value meal indoors or outdoors on the harborfront. Their *amfora belvedere*—mixed seafood stew—is huge, and can easily be split among up to four diners (€45). Share with your group and add pasta for a fine meal. Mussel fans will enjoy the *tagliolini della casa* (€8). It's energetically run by Federico and Roberto (€9 pastas, €12 *secondi,* €2 cover, Wed-Mon 12:00-14:30 & 19:00-22:00, usually closed Tue, on the harbor in the old town, tel. 0187-817-033).

L'Alta Marea offers special fish ravioli, the catch of the day, and huge crocks of fresh, steamed mussels. Young chef Marco cooks with charisma, while his wife, Anna, takes good care of the guests. This place is quieter, buried in the old town two blocks off the beach, and has covered tables out front for people-watching. This is a good opportunity to try rabbit (€9 pastas and pizza, €12-15 *secondi,* €2 cover, 10 percent discount with cash and this book in 2012, Thu-Tue 12:00-15:00 & 18:00-22:00, closed Wed, Via Roma 54, tel. 0187-817-170).

Ciak—high-energy and tightly packed—is a local institution with reliably good food and higher prices. It's known for its huge, sizzling terra-cotta crock for two crammed with the day's catch and accompanied by risotto or spaghetti, or served swimming in a soup *(zuppa).* Another popular choice is the seafood *antipasto Lampara.* Stroll a couple of paces past the outdoor tables up Via Roma to see what Ciak has on the stove (Thu-Tue 12:00-15:00 & 19:00-22:30, closed Wed, tel. 0187-817-014).

Via Venti is a quiet little trattoria, hidden in an alley deep in the heart of the old town, where Papa Ettore creates imaginative seafood dishes using the day's catch and freshly made pasta. Ilaria and her partner Michele serve up delicate and savory gnocchi (tiny potato dumplings) with crab sauce, tender ravioli stuffed with fresh fish, and pear-and-cheese pasta. There's nothing pretentious here... just good cooking, service, and prices (€11 pastas, €16 *secondi*, Fri-Wed 12:00-15:00 & 18:30-22:30, closed Thu, tel. 0187-818-347). From the bottom of Via Roma, with your back to the sea and the church to your left, head to the right down Via XX Settembre and follow it to the end, to #32.

Miky is packed with well-dressed locals who know their seafood and want to eat it in a classy environment without spending a fortune. For elegantly presented, top-quality food, this is my Cinque Terre favorite. It's clearly a proud family operation: Miky (dad), Simonetta (mom), and charming Sara (daughter, who greets guests) all work hard. All their pasta is "pizza pasta"—cooked normally but finished in a bowl that's encased in a thin pizza crust. They cook the concoction in a wood-fired oven to keep in the aroma. Miky's has a fine wine list with many available by the glass if you ask. If I were ever to require a dessert, it would be their mixed sampler plate, *dolce mista*—€10 and plenty for two (€15 pastas, €22 *secondi*, €8 sweets, Wed-Mon 12:00-15:00 & 19:00-23:00, closed Tue, reservations wise in summer, diners tend to dress up a bit, in the new town 100 yards north of train station at Via Fegina 104, tel. 0187-817-608).

La Cantina di Miky, a few doors down toward the station, serves Ligurian specialties (chef Boris loves anchovies) that follow in Miky's family tradition of quality (it's run by son Manuel). It's more trendy and informal than Miky's, and you can sit downstairs, in the garden, or overlooking the sea (€16 anchovy tasting plate, €13 pastas, €15 *secondi*, creative desserts, daily 12:00-24:00 or later, Via Fegina 90, tel. 0187-802-525). This place doubles as a cocktail bar in the evenings—see "Nightlife in Monterosso," earlier.

Ristorante Tortuga is the top option in Monterosso for seaview elegance, with gorgeous outdoor seating on a bluff and an elegant white-tablecloth-and-candles interior. If you're out and about, drop by to consider which table you'd like to reserve for later (€15 pastas, €20 *secondi*, Tue-Sun 12:00-14:30 & 18:00-22:00, closed Mon, just outside the tunnel that connects the old and new town, tel. 0187-800-065, mobile 333-240-7956, Silvia and Giamba).

Il Casello is the only place for a fun meal on a terrace overlooking the old-town beach. With outdoor tables on a rocky outcrop, it's a pleasant spot for a salad or a sandwich, or well-prepared pasta or *secondi* (lunch only, daily April-Oct, closed Nov-March, mobile 333-492-7629, Bacco).

Light Meals, Take-Out Food, and Breakfast

Lots of shops and bakeries sell pizza and focaccia for an easy picnic at the beach or on the trail. At **Il Frantoio,** Simone makes tasty pizza to go or to munch perched on a stool (Fri-Wed 9:00-14:00 & 16:00-19:30, closed Thu, just off Via Roma at Via Gioberti 1, tel. 0187-818-333). **Pizzeria la Smorfia** also cooks up good pizza to eat in or take out. Pizzas come in two sizes—the large can feed three (Fri-Wed 11:30-15:00 & 18:00-23:00, closed Thu, Via Vittorio Emanuele 73, tel. 0187-818-395). **Focacceria da Ely** makes airy focaccia and thick-crust pizzas for casual seating or take-out (daily 10:30-20:00, until 24:00 in summer, Emigliano).

For a quick bite right at the train station, consider **Il Massimo della Focaccia**. Massimo and Daniella serve local quiche-like tortes, sandwiches, focaccia pizzas, and desserts. With benches just in front, this is a good bet for a €4 light meal with a sea view (daily, Via Fegina 50 at the entry to the station).

Cinque Terre Connections

By Train

The five towns of the Cinque Terre are on a pokey milk-run train line (described in "Getting Around the Cinque Terre—By Train," on page 341). Erratically timed but roughly hourly trains connect each town with the others, plus La Spezia, Genoa, and Riviera towns to the north. While a few of these local trains go to more distant points (Milan or Pisa), it's much faster to change in La Spezia, Monterosso, or Sestri Levante to a bigger train (local train info tel. 0187-817-458, www.trenitalia.com).

From La Spezia Centrale by Train to: Rome (7/day, 3-4.5 hours, more with changes, €45; an evening train—departing around 20:00—gives you a complete day in the region while still getting you to Rome that night), **Pisa** (about hourly, 1-1.5 hours, €5), **Florence** (5/day direct, otherwise nearly hourly, 2.5 hours, €9.30), **Milan** (about hourly, 3 hours direct or with change in Genoa, €22), **Venice** (about hourly, 5-6 hours, 1-3 changes, €50).

From Monterosso by Train to: Venice (about hourly, 6-7 hours, 1-3 changes, €52), **Milan** (8/day direct, otherwise hourly with change in Genoa, 3-4 hours, €22), **Genoa** (hourly, 1.2-2 hours, €8), **Turin** (8/day, 3-4 hours, €20), **Pisa** (hourly, 1-2 hours, €6-10), **Sestri Levante** (hourly, 20-40 minutes, most trains to Genoa stop here, €3), **La Spezia** (hourly, 20-30 minutes), **Levanto** (2-3/hour, 4 minutes), **Santa Margherita Ligure** (at least hourly, 45 minutes, €2), **Rome** (hourly, 4.5 hours, change in La Spezia, €50). For destinations in **France,** change trains in Genoa.

By Car

Because these towns are close together and have frequent transportation connections, bringing a car to the Cinque Terre is not the best idea. If your plans require it, however, here are some basic

THE CINQUE TERRE

tips: stay in a hotel that includes parking, use public transportation or hike between towns, and for day-trip parking, go to Monterosso (€14-18/day), Riomaggiore (€22/day), or Manarola (€15/day). Don't drive to Vernazza, as finding a spot is tough. Parking anywhere on the Cinque Terre is truly a mess in July and August.

Milan to the Cinque Terre (130 miles): Drivers speed south on autostrada A-7 from Milan, skirt Genoa, and drive a little bit of Italy's curviest and narrowest freeways, passing the Cinque Terre toward the port of La Spezia (A-12). Another option is to take the slightly straighter A-1 via the city of Parma, followed by A-15 to La Spezia. This route takes the same amount of time (about 2.5 hours), even though it covers more miles.

Coming from either direction, and for either Monterosso or Vernazza, exit autostrada A-12 at *uscita Carrodano*, northwest of La Spezia. Don't take Cinque Terre exits before Carrodano to reach these towns.

Monterosso is 30 minutes from the autostrada. Remember that the highway divides as you approach Monterosso—you must choose between the road to Centro Storico (the old town) or the one to Fegina (the new town and beachfront parking).

Vernazza is 45 minutes from the autostrada. The drive down to Vernazza is scenic, narrow, and scary, and you'll probably lose time looking for parking.

To drive to **Riomaggiore, Corniglia,** or **Manarola,** leave the freeway at La Spezia.

Within the Cinque Terre: On busy weekends, holidays, and in July and August, both Vernazza and Monterosso fill up, and police at the top of town will deny entry to anyone without a hotel reservation. It's smart to have a confirmation in hand. If you don't, insist (politely) that they allow you to enter—but only if you actually have a room reserved (the police might call your hotel to check your story).

Parking Tips: Each Cinque Terre town has a parking lot and a once-an-hour shuttle bus to get you into town (except Corniglia), though all parking areas are no more than a 10-minute walk uphill from the center.

White signs post valid hours for pay parking, which usually don't charge 24:00-8:00. Anyone can park where there are blue lines. Parking is cash only in all towns (except Riomaggiore, where some readers have been overcharged on their credit cards—best to pay in cash).

If you plan to find parking in any of the Cinque Terre towns, try to arrive between 10:00-11:00, when overnight visitors are usually departing. Or you can park your car in Levanto (see next chapter), then take the train into the town of your choice. In these bigger towns, confirm that your parking spot is OK, and leave nothing inside to steal.

A few hotels offer parking for free or a daily charge. In **Monterosso,** consider Hotel Villa Steno, A Cà du Gigante, or Hotel Punta Mesco. For **Riomaggiore,** try Locanda del Sole, Locanda Ca' dei Duxi, or Villa Argentina. In Volastra (a shuttle ride above **Manarola**), try Hotel il Saraceno. Rooms listed in this book for Corniglia and Vernazza do not offer parking.

RIVIERA TOWNS NEAR THE CINQUE TERRE

Levanto • Sestri Levante • Santa Margherita Ligure • Portofino • La Spezia • Carrara • Portovenere

The Cinque Terre is tops, but several towns to the north have a breezy beauty and more beaches. Towns to the south offer a mix of marble, trains, and yachts.

Levanto, the northern gateway to the Cinque Terre, has a long beach and a scenic, strenuous trail to Monterosso al Mare. Sestri Levante, on a narrow peninsula flanked by two beaches, is for sun-seekers. Santa Margherita Ligure is more of a real town, with actual sights, beaches, and easy connections with Portofino by trail, bus, or boat. All three towns are a straight shot to the Cinque Terre by train.

South of the Cinque Terre, you'll likely pass through the workaday town of La Spezia (don't stay here unless you're desperate), the southern gateway to the Cinque Terre. Carrara is a quickie for marble-lovers who are driving between Pisa and La Spezia. The picturesque village of Portovenere, near La Spezia, has scenic boat connections with Cinque Terre towns.

Public transportation is the best way to get around this region. All of the places in this chapter are well connected by train and/or boat.

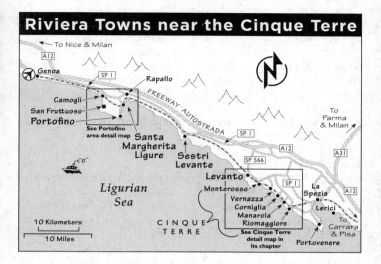

North of the Cinque Terre

Levanto

Graced with a long, sandy beach, Levanto is packed in summer and popular with surfers. The rest of the year, it's just a small, sleepy town, with less charm and fewer tourists than the Cinque Terre. With quick connections to Monterosso (4 minutes by train), Levanto makes a decent home base if you can't snare a room in the Cinque Terre.

Levanto has a new section (with a regular grid street plan) and a twisty old town (bisected by a modern street), plus a few pedestrian streets and a castle (not tourable). From Levanto, you can take a no-wimps-allowed hike to Monterosso (2.5 hours) or hop a boat to the Cinque Terre towns and beyond.

Orientation to Levanto

Tourist Information

The helpful TI is on Piazza Mazzini (daily 9:00-13:00 & 15:00-18:00, tel. 0187-808-125, www.comune.levanto.sp.it).

Arrival in Levanto

By Train: It's a 10-minute walk from the Levanto train station to the TI in town (head down stairs in front of station, turn right, cross bridge, then follow Corso Roma to Piazza Mazzini).

By Car: Drivers can use the cheap short-term parking in the lots in front of and on either side of the train station (€6/8 hours, €9/24 hours, note that you have to pay at the machines each day—so long-term parking is difficult). Another option is the lot across the river from the hospital on the way into town (first left after the hospital, cross bridge and immediately turn left), or north of the church on Via del Mercato (free during high season, except Wed before 14:00). For long-term parking, try the lots at Piazza Mazzini or behind the TI (€15/day).

Helpful Hints

Markets: Levanto's modern covered *mercato,* which sells produce and fish, is on Via del Mercato, between the TI and train station (Mon-Sat 8:00-13:00, closed Sun). On Wednesday morning, an **open-air market** with clothes, shoes, and housewares fills the street in front of the *mercato.*

Internet Access: Try **Viaggi Beraldi** at Via Garibaldi 102 (€2/30 minutes, Mon-Sat 9:00-12:30 & 15:30-19:15, closed Sun, tel. 0187-800-818).

Baggage Storage: None is available at the station. Baggage storage is available in La Spezia (see page 433), Monterosso (page 389), and possibly Santa Margherita Ligure (page 417).

Laundry: A self-service launderette stuffed with snack and drink vending machines is at Piazza Staglieno 38 (wash-€5 including soap, dry-€5, open 24 hours daily, mobile 338-701-6341).

Bike Rental: Cicli Raso North Shore rents bikes (€8-20/day depending on type of bike, daily 9:30-12:30 & 15:30-19:30, closed Sun Nov-April, Via Garibaldi 63, tel. 0187-802-511, www.cicliraso.com).

Sports Rentals: Rosa dei Venti rents kayaks, canoes, surfboards, and windsurfing equipment right on the beach (Marco mobile 349-520-7538, Nicola mobile 349-520-7538, www.levantorosa deiventi.it).

Sights in Levanto

Beach—The beach is just two blocks away from the TI. As you face the harbor, the boat dock is to your far left, and the diving center is to your far right (rental boats available at either place in summer). You can also rent a kayak or canoe on the beach, just below the east end of the Piazza Mazzini parking lot.

During the summer, three parts of the beach are free: both sides of the boat dock, and behind the TI. The rest of the beach is broken up into private sections that charge admission. You can always stroll along the beach, even through the private sections—just don't sit down. Off-season, roughly October through May, the

Levanto

1. Albergo Primavera
2. Villa Margherita
3. A Durmì Guesthouse
4. Rist. la Loggia Rooms/Rist.
5. Villa Clelia B&B
6. La Rosa dei Venti Rooms
7. Garden Hotel
8. To Erba Persa Agriturismo
9. Ostello Ospitalia del Mare
10. Osteria Tumelin
11. Da Rino Trattoria
12. Ristorante Moresco
13. Taverna Garibaldi & Bike Rental
14. La Picea Pizzeria
15. Focacceria il Falcone
16. Il Laboratorio del Pesto
17. Dimarket Supermarket
18. Crai Supermarkets (2)
19. Il Pinguino Gelateria
20. Il Porticciolo Gelateria
21. Internet Café
22. Launderette
23. Canoe & Kayak Rental

To 8 & P

To Monterosso & Autostrada A-12 (Carrodano exit)

TRAIN STATION

MARKET

TOWN HALL

Piazza Cavour

SCALINATA DELL' OROLOGIO

NEW TOWN

POST

Piazza Staglieno

Piazza del Popolo

OLD TOWN SANTA ANDREA

CASTLE

Piazza Mazzini

BEACH

POOL (PRIVATE)

FREE BEACH

PEDESTRIAN UNDERPASS

FREE BEACH

Ligurian Sea

Trail to Monterosso

FREE BEACH

To Bonassola via Waterfront Path

100 Meters
100 Yards

Boate to Cinque Terre

Ghiararo River

entire beach is free, and you can lay your towel anywhere you like.

Old Town and Trailhead—The old town, several blocks from the TI and beach, clusters around Piazza del Popolo. Until a few decades ago, the town's open-air market was held at the 13th-century loggia (covered set of archways) in the square. Explore the back streets.

To reach the trailhead to Monterosso: From Piazza del Popolo, head uphill to the striped church, Chiesa di Sant'Andrea (with your back to the loggia, go straight ahead—across the square and up Via Don Emanuele Toso to the church). From the church courtyard, follow the sign to the *castello* (a private residence), go under the stone arch, and continue uphill. Or, if you're coming from the seaside promenade (Via Gaetano Semenza), head under the arches and up the stairs, and follow the signs to the *castello*. Either route leads you to a sign that points you toward Punta Mesco, the rugged tip of the peninsula. From here, you can hike up to Monterosso (2.5 hours).

Hike or Bike to Bonassola—Cross the river bridge located by the TI to wander along this waterfront path, good for walking or cycling. You'll encounter shaded tunnels and two sunny beaches on the way to the small but modern town of Bonassola with its sandy beach (25 minutes by foot, 10 minutes by bike, public beaches located a minute's walk down from trail).

Sleeping in Levanto

In this popular beach town, many hotels want you to take half-pension (lunch or dinner) in summer, especially in July and August. Prices listed here are the maximum for high season (July-Aug); smaller rooms or those without views may have a lower maximum. Expect to pay €10-30 less per night for April-June and September-October, and even less for the rest of the year. The longer your stay, the greater your bargaining power. The high number of four-person rooms in Levanto makes it particularly welcoming to families who want to explore the Cinque Terre. Many hotels rent out large apartments with kitchenettes (without a half-pension requirement), and parking is free or very reasonable.

$$$ Albergo Primavera is family-run, with 17 recently redecorated, tasteful rooms—10 with balconies but no views—just a half-block from the beach. Owner Carlo is a great cook. Try dining here once during your visit (€25 fixed-price meal); let him know a couple of hours in advance if you'd like dinner (Db-€130, request a quiet room off the street, includes hearty breakfast buffet with local hams and cheeses, air-con, Internet access and Wi-Fi; parking-€8/day June-Sept, free off-season; Via Cairoli 5, tel. 0187-808-023, fax 0187-801-588, www.primaverahotel.com, info@primaverahotel.com). Friendly Carlo, cheerful Daniela, and older daughter Giuditta speak some English, and younger daughter Gloria does her homework in the dining room.

$$$ Villa Margherita is 300 yards out of town, but the shady gardens, 11 characteristic colorfully tiled rooms (some with little view terraces), and tranquility are worth the walk (Db-€160, Tb-€175, 5 percent discount with cash and this book, elevator one flight up from street level, Internet access and Wi-Fi, free parking,

Sleep Code

(€1 = about $1.40, country code: 39)

S = Single, **D** = Double/Twin, **T** = Triple, **Q** = Quad, **b** = bathroom, **s** = shower only. Unless otherwise noted, credit cards are accepted, English is spoken, and breakfast is included.

To help you sort easily through these listings, I've divided the accommodations into three categories based on the price for a standard double room with bath:

$$$ **Higher Priced**—Most rooms €110 or more.

$$ **Moderately Priced**—Most rooms between €50-110.

$ **Lower Priced**—Most rooms €50 or less.

Prices can change without notice; verify the hotel's current rates online or by email. For other updates, see www.ricksteves.com/update.

10-minute walk to town with stairs, 5-minute walk to train station, free shuttle service from station if you tell them when you'll arrive, Via Trento e Trieste 31, tel. 0187-807-212, fax 0187-803-717, mobile 328-842-6934, www.villamargherita.net, info@villamargherita.net).

$$ A Durmì is a happy little *affitta camere* (guesthouse) owned by Graziella, Gianni, and their two daughters, Elisa and Chiara. Their sunny patios, green leafy gardens, six immaculate modern new rooms, and five sunlit apartments make a welcoming place to stay (Db-€100, extra bed-€20; apartments-€150—no minimum stay required; rooms cleaned daily, breakfast-€7, air-con, power showers, Internet access and Wi-Fi, bar, parking-€5/day, Via D. Viviani 12, tel. 0187-800-823, mobile 349-105-6016, www.adurmi.it, info@adurmi.it).

$$ Ristorante la Loggia has four pleasant, cozy, summery rooms perched above the old loggia on Piazza del Popolo (Db-€70, cash only, request balcony, quieter rooms in back, two basic side-by-side apartments great for families of 4-8, air-con, free parking, Piazza del Popolo 7, tel. & fax 0187-808-107, mobile 335-641-7701, www.tigulliovino.it, Nerina).

$$ Villa Clelia B&B has six peaceful, dark, air-conditioned rooms (named for the winds—*scirocco, maestrale,* and so on) with mini-fridges and terraces in a garden courtyard just 50 yards from the sea (Db-€70-90, minimal in-room breakfast, free parking, with loggia on your left it's straight ahead at Piazza da Passano 1, tel. 0187-808-195, mobile 328-797-6403, www.villaclelia.it, info@villaclelia.it). They also have seven central apartments that economically sleep up to five (€700/week, 3-night minimum stay). B&B

rooms are cleaned daily; you're on your own at the apartments.

$$ La Rosa dei Venti is an *affitta camere* just a couple of blocks from the beach. Enthusiastic Rosanna and her son Marco rent five super-clean rooms with dark hardwood floors, comfy rugs, and a hodgepodge of seashore decor (Db-€100, Tb-€135, includes homemade breakfast and free parking, behind Enoteca Tumelin across from Piazza del Popolo, Via della Compera, tel. 0187-808-165, mobile 333-701-3213, www.larosadeiventilevanto.com, larosa deiventi1983@libero.it).

$$ Garden Hotel offers 17 simple, bright, and modern rooms, all with balconies (but most lack views due to the elevated street), a block from the beach on busy Corso Italia (Db-€115, new fifth-floor rooms with views and terraces go for Db-€140, 5 percent discount with cash and this book, lower floors closed mid-Nov–mid-March, air-con, elevator for some floors, free Internet access and Wi-Fi, free parking but not on-site—can unload bags and then park near the station, Corso Italia 6, tel. 0187-808-173, fax 0187-803-652, www.nuovogarden.com, info@nuovogarden.com, Davide and Damiano).

$$ Erba Persa Agriturismo, a rustic farmhouse run by sunny Grazia Lizza and her gardener husband Claudio, hosts cats, dogs, pet rabbits, and donkeys among their plots of organic fruits and vegetables. It's a 10-minute walk from the train station and about a 20-minute walk from town (D-€50, Db with balcony and view-€70, Tb-€80, free Internet access, free parking, free mosquitoes, Via N. S. della Guardia 21, mobile 339-400-8587 or 348-344-7695, fax 0187-801-376, www.erbapersa.it, erbapersa@alice.it).

Hostel: **$ Ostello Ospitalia del Mare** has 70 beds, airy rooms, an elevator, and a terrace in a well-renovated medieval palazzo a few steps from the old town (beds-€19-27 in 4-, 6-, and 8-bed rooms with private bath, Db-€70; includes breakfast, towels, and sheets; Internet access and Wi-Fi, self-service laundry-€7.50, microwave, fridge, non-members welcome, co-ed unless you strenuously object, no curfew, no lockout; office open daily April-Oct 8:00-13:00 & 16:00-20:00, until 23:00 weekend nights, slightly shorter hours off-season; may close Nov-March, Via San Nicolò 1, tel. 0187-802-562, fax 0187-803-696, www.ospitaliadelmare.it, info@ospitaliadelmare.it).

Eating in Levanto

Osteria Tumelin, a local favorite, is more expensive than other options, but has a dressy, sophisticated ambience and a wide selection of fresh seafood. Reservations are smart on weekends or if you want to dine outside (daily 12:00-14:30 & 19:00-22:00, closed

Thu Oct-May, aquarium containing giant lobster and moray eels in first dining room on the right, Via D. Grillo 32, across street from loggia, tel. 0187-808-379).

Da Rino, a small trattoria on a quiet pedestrian lane, dishes up reasonably priced fresh seafood and homemade Ligurian specialties prepared with care. Consider the grilled *totani* (squid), *pansotti con salsa di noci* (cheese ravioli with walnut sauce), and *trofie al pesto* (local pasta with pesto sauce). Dine indoors, or at one of the few outdoor tables. On busy nights, they open up a second dining room across the street (€8 pastas, €13 *secondi,* cash only, daily 19:00-22:00, closed Tue Nov-mid-March, Via Garibaldi 10, tel. 0187-813-475).

Ristorante la Loggia, next to the old loggia, makes fine gnocchi with scampi and saffron sauce. Their daily fish specials are served in a homey wood-paneled dining room or on a little terrace overlooking the square (€10 pastas, €15 *secondi,* Thu-Tue 12:30-14:00 & 19:00-22:00, closed Wed, closed Nov-Feb, Piazza del Popolo 7, tel. 0187-808-107).

Ristorante Moresco serves large portions of pasta and seafood at reasonable prices in a vaulted, candlelit room decorated with Moorish-style frescoes. The best value is their €25 four-course tasting *menu* (doesn't include drinks, 2-person minimum). Skip the house white wine and order something more drinkable from their wine list (daily 12:00-14:00 & 19:00-21:00, until 23:00 in summer, may close Sun evenings in winter, reservations appreciated, Via Jacopo 24, tel. 0187-807-253, busy Roberto and Francesca).

Taverna Garibaldi is a good-value, cozy place on the most characteristic street in Levanto, serving focaccia with various toppings, made-to-order *farinata* (savory chickpea crêpe), 34 types of pizza, and salads (€8 light meals, daily in summer 19:30-22:00, closed Tue Sept-June, Via Garibaldi 57, tel. 0187-808-098).

La Picea serves up wood-fired pizzas to go, or dine at one of their few small tables (Tue-Sun 16:30-21:45, closed Mon, just off the corner near Via Varego at Via della Concia 18, tel. 0187-802-063).

A Picnic or Bite on the Go: Focaccerie, rosticcerie, and delis with take-out pasta abound on Via Dante Alighieri. **Focacceria il Falcone** has a great selection of focaccia with different toppings (daily 9:30-22:00, until 20:00 Oct-May, Via Cairoli 19, tel. 0187-807-370). For more picnic options, try the *mercato* (mornings except Sun; see "Helpful Hints," page 406). It's fun to grab a crusty loaf of bread, then pair it with a pot of freshly made Genovese *pesto* from **Il Laboratorio del Pesto** (sometimes closed Wed afternoons, Via Dante 14, tel. 0187-807-441). The **Dimarket supermarket** just below the train station has a good deli counter and opens at

7:00—handy for those taking an early train. There are two **Crai supermarkets:** One is just off Via Jacopo da Levanto at Via del Municipio 5 (Mon-Sat 8:00-13:00 & 17:00-20:00, Sun 8:00-13:00 & 16:30-19:30); the other is nearby on Piazza Staglieno (for a shaded setting, lay out your spread on a bench in the grassy park at this piazza). Another excellent picnic spot is Piazza Cristoforo Colombo, located east of the swimming pool, with benches and sea views.

And for Dessert: Compare **Il Pinguino Gelateria** at Piazza Staglieno 2 (daily until late) with **Il Porticciolo Gelateria,** at the end of Via Cairoli at Piazzetta Marina (daily in summer, closed Mon Sept-June, mobile 393-228-1570).

Levanto Connections

From Levanto: To get to the Cinque Terre, take the **train** (2-3/hour, 4 minutes to Monterosso) or the **boat,** which stops at every Cinque Terre town—except Corniglia—before heading to Portovenere (2/day Easter-Oct, none Nov-Easter; €6 one-way to Monterosso, €11 round-trip, or €18 for half-day pass to Portovenere and scenic ride—departing Levanto at about 10:10 and 14:30, with 1-hour stop before return to Levanto; as much as €25 for all-day pass on a weekend to Portovenere; 1 return boat each day from Portovenere departs at about 17:00; pick up boat schedule and price sheet from TI or boat dock, or call 0187-732-987, or—on weekends—0187-777-727).

Sestri Levante

This peninsular town is squeezed as skinny as a hot dog between its two beaches. The pedestrian-friendly Corso Colombo, which runs down the middle of the peninsula, is lined with shops that sell take-away pizza, pastries, and beach paraphernalia.

Hans Christian Andersen enjoyed his visit here in the mid-1800s, writing, "What a fabulous evening I spent in Sestri Levante!" One of the bays—Baia delle Favole—is named in his honor (*favole* means "fairy tale"). The small mermaid curled on the edge of the fountain behind the TI is another nod to the beloved Danish storyteller.

During the last week of May, the town holds a street festival, culminating in a ceremony for locals who write the best fairy tales (four prizes for four age groups, from pre-kindergarten to adult). The "Oscar" awards are little mermaids.

Orientation to Sestri Levante

Tourist Information
From the train station, it's a five-minute walk to the TI, where you can pick up a map (Tue-Sun 9:30-13:00 & 14:00-17:30, closed Mon; go straight out of station on Via Roma, turn left at fountain in park, TI in next square—Piazza Sant'Antonio 10; tel. 0185-457-011).

Helpful Hints
Market Day: It's on Saturday at Piazza Aldo Moro (8:00-13:00).
Baggage Storage: None is available at the station.

Sights in Sestri Levante

Stroll the Town—From the TI, take Corso Colombo (to the left of Bermuda Bar, eventually turns into Via XXV Aprile), which runs up the peninsula. Follow this street—lively with shops, eateries, and delightful pastel facades—for about five minutes. Just before you get to the large white church at the end, turn off for either beach (free Silenzio beach is on your left). Or take the street on the left of the church to head uphill. You'll pass the evocative arches of a ruined chapel (bombed during World War II, and left as a memorial). Continue a few minutes farther, past a stony Romanesque church, to the Hotel Castelli and consider a drink at their view café (so-so view, reasonably priced drinks, daily 10:00-24:00, café entrance is at end of parking lot). The rocky, forested bluff at the end of the town's peninsula is actually the huge private backyard of this fancy hotel.

Beaches—These are named after the bays *(baie)* that they border. The bigger beach, Baia delle Favole, is divided up much of the year (May-Sept) into sections that you must pay to enter. The fees, which can soar up to €30 per day in August (no hourly rate), generally include chairs, umbrellas, and fewer crowds. There are several small free sections: at the ends and in the middle (look for *libere* signs, and ask *"Gratis?"* to make sure that it's free). For less-expensive sections of beach (where you can rent less than the works), ask for *spiaggia libera attrezzata* (spee-AH-jah LEE-behr-ah ah-treh-ZAHT-tah). The usual beach-town activities are clustered along this *baia:* boat rentals, sailing lessons, and bocce courts—ask if you can get in on a game.

The town's other beach, Baia del Silenzio, is narrow, virtually all free, and packed, providing a good chance to see Italian families at play. There isn't much more to do here than unroll a beach towel and join in. At the far end of Baia del Silenzio (under Hotel Helvetia) is Citto Beach bar, which offers front-row seats of bay views (drinks daily June-Aug 10:00-24:00, May and Sept-Oct until 20:00, sandwiches and salads at lunchtime only, closed Nov-April, Gilberto).

Sleeping in Sestri Levante

(€1 = about $1.40, country code: 39)
Prices listed here are the maximum during the high season (July-Aug). Prices will be €10-20 less April-June and September-October, and soft the rest of the year. Some hotels are closed off-season, so call ahead.

$$$ Hotel Due Mari, located in an old Genoese palazzo with sprawling public spaces, has three stars, 65 fine rooms, and a rooftop terrace with a super view of both beaches. Ideally, reserve well in advance. The extra services and grand communal spaces are the draw (small Db-€110, bigger Db-€140-190 depending on view and type of room, half-pension in aristocratic restaurant required July-Aug-€35/person, closed mid-Oct-Dec, air-con, Wi-Fi, elevator, garden, outdoor and heated indoor seawater swimming pools, wet sauna, small gym, parking-€15/day, take Corso Colombo to the end, hotel is behind church in Piazza Matteotti—take either alleyway flanking church, Vico del Coro 18, tel. 0185-42695, fax 0185-42698, www.duemarihotel.it, info@duemarihotel.it).

$$$ Hotel Helvetia, overlooking Baia del Silenzio, is another three-star bet, with 21 bright rooms, a large sun terrace, and a peaceful garden atmosphere—but apathetic management (viewless Db-€170, Db with view/balcony-€220, closed Nov-March, air-con, elevator, swimming pool, off-site parking-€5-15/day with free shuttle, from Corso Colombo turn left on Via Palestro and angle left at the small square to Via Cappuccini 43, tel. 0185-41175, fax 0185-457-216, www.hotelhelvetia.it, helvetia@hotelhelvetia.it).

$$$ Hotel Celeste, a dream for beach-lovers, rests along the waterfront. Its 41 rooms are modern and plainly outfitted—you pay for the sea breeze (Db-€165, with view and balcony €15-25 more, optional half-pension, air-con, elevator, Internet access, deals on beach chairs, attached beachside bar, Lungomare G. Descalzo 14, tel. 0185-485-005, fax 0185-411-166, www.hotelceleste.com, info@hotelceleste.com, Franco).

$$$ Hotel Genova, run by the Bertoni family, is a ship-shape hotel with 27 shiny-clean, modern, and cheery rooms, sunny lounge, rooftop sundeck, free loaner bikes, and a good location just two blocks from Baia delle Favole (Sb-€75, Db-€125, superior Db-€140, Tb-€169, ask for quieter room in back, air-con, elevator, Internet access and Wi-Fi, parking-€4/day; from the train station, walk straight ahead, turn right at the T-intersection, and find the cream building ahead on the right, Viale Mazzini 126; tel. 0185-41057, fax 0185-455-739, www.hotelgenovasestrilevante.com, info@hotelgenovasestrilevante.com).

$$ Albergo Marina's friendly Magda and her brother Santo rent 23 bright, peaceful, and clean rooms done in sea-foam green. Though the hotel is located on a busy boulevard, all rooms are at the back facing a quiet courtyard and parking lots...and priced right (Db-€65-80, half-pension optional, air-con, elevator, self-service laundry, pool table; exit the train station and angle left down Via Eraldo, at Piazza Repubblica take an easy left onto Via Fasce and find the hotel ahead on the right, Via Fasce 100; tel. & fax 0185-487-332, www.marinahotel.it, marinahotel@marinahotel.it).

$$ Villa Jolanda is a homey, kid-friendly, basic *pensione* with 17 simple rooms, five with little balconies but no views, new bathrooms, and a garden courtyard/sun terrace—perfect for families on a budget...and the owner's cats (Db-€75-90, Qb-€100-120, 3-night minimum stay required with advance reservation, €6.50 breakfast isn't worth it but owner Mario's €23 home-cooked dinners are, free parking, located near Baia del Silenzio—take alley just to the right of the church on Piazza Matteotti, Via Pozzetto 15, tel. & fax 0185-41354, www.villaiolanda.com, info@villaiolanda.com).

Eating in Sestri Levante

Everything I've listed is on classic Via XXV Aprile, which also abounds with *focaccerie,* take-out pizza by the slice, and little grocery shops. Assemble a picnic or try one of the places below.

At **L'Osteria Mattana,** where everyone shares long tables in two dining rooms (the second one is in the back, past the wood oven and brazier), you can mix with locals while enjoying traditional cuisine, listed on the chalkboard menus (Tue-Fri 19:30-22:00, Sat-Sun 12:30-14:30 & 19:30-22:30, closed Mon except in Aug, cash only; follow Corso Colombo from TI as it turns into Via XXV Aprile, restaurant on right at #36; tel. 0185-457-633, Marco).

Polpo Mario is classier but affordable, with a fun people-watching location on the main drag (€40 fixed-price tasting menu, Tue-Sun 12:15-15:00 & 19:30-23:00, closed Mon, Via XXV Aprile 163, tel. 0185-480-203).

Ristorante Mainolla offers pizzas, big salads, focaccia sandwiches, and reasonably priced pastas near Baia del Silenzio (daily in summer 12:00-16:00 & 19:00-22:00, closed Tue off-season, Via XXV Aprile 187, mobile 338-157-0877).

Gelato: Locals flock to **Ice Cream's Angels** at the intersection of Via XXV Aprile and Via della Chiusa. Riccardo and Elena artfully load up your cone with intermingling flavors, and top it with a dollop of Nutella chocolate-hazelnut cream (open daily until late in summer, closed Tue off-season, mobile 348-402-1604). **Bacciolo** enjoys a similar popularity among residents (closed Thu, Via XXV Aprile 51, on the right just before the church).

Supermarket: You can stock up on picnic supplies at two locations of **Carrefour Express** on Piazza della Repubblica, at #1 and #28 (daily 8:00-13:30 & 15:30-20:00).

Deli: For a take-out meal, head to **Rosticceria Bertolone** for roasted anything—beef, pork, chicken, or vegetables. Assemble an entire meal from their deli and ask them to heat it for you (Mon-Sat 7:30-13:00 & 16:00-19:30, closed Wed afternoon and all day Sun, Via Fasce 12, tel. 0185-487-098).

Sestri Levante Connections

Sestri Levante is just 20-40 minutes away from Monterosso by **train** (hourly connections with Monterosso, nearly hourly with other Cinque Terre towns).

Boats depart to the Cinque Terre, Santa Margherita Ligure, Portofino, and San Fruttuoso from the dock *(molo)* on the peninsula (boats run Easter-Oct, see "Santa Margherita Ligure Connections," page 426, for details; to get to the dock: facing the church in Piazza Matteotti, take the road on the right with the sea on your right, about halfway down Via P. Queirolo; tel. 0185-284-670, mobile 336-253-336, www.traghettiportofino.it).

Santa Margherita Ligure

If you need the movie stars' Riviera, park your yacht at Portofino. Or you can settle down in the nearby and more personable Santa Margherita Ligure (15 minutes by bus from Portofino and one hour by train from the Cinque Terre). While Portofino's velour allure is tarnished by snobby residents and a nonstop traffic jam in peak season, Santa Margherita tumbles easily downhill from its train station. The town has a fun resort character and a breezy harborfront.

On a quick day trip from Milan or the Cinque Terre, walk the beach promenade and see the small old town of Santa Margherita Ligure before catching the bus (or boat) to Portofino to see what all the fuss is about. With more time, Santa Margherita makes a fine overnight stop.

Orientation to
Santa Margherita Ligure

Tourist Information

Pick up a map at the harborside TI on Piazza Veneto (daily April-Sept 9:30-12:30 & 14:30-19:00, Oct-March closes at 17:30 and all day Sun, tel. 0185-287-485, www.turismoinliguria.it).

Arrival by Train

To get from the station to the city center, take the stairs marked *Mare* (sea) down to the harbor. The harborfront promenade is as wide as the skimpy beach. (The real beaches, which are pebbly, are a 10-minute walk further on, past the port.)

To reach the pedestrian-friendly old town and the TI, take a right at Piazza Veneto (with the roundabout, flags, and park) onto Largo Antonio Giusti. For the TI, angle left on Via XXV Aprile. For the old town (a block off Piazza Veneto), head toward the TI, but turn left on Via Torino, which opens almost immediately onto Piazza Caprera, a square with a church and morning fruit vendors in the midst of pedestrian streets.

Helpful Hints

Internet Access: There are two terminals at **Papiluc Bar** (€3/30 minutes, daily 6:30 until late, Via del Arco 20, tel. 0185-282-580).

Post Office: It's just down the road from the train station on Via Roma (Mon-Fri 8:00-18:30, Sat 8:00-13:00, closed Sun, Via Roma 36).

Baggage Storage: There's no official left-luggage office, but day-trippers arriving by train may be able to stash their bags at the station's café-bar (outside the station on the left).

Bike Rental: GM Rent is at Via XXV Aprile 11 (€10/5 hours, €20/24 hours, also rents scooters and Smart Cars, daily 10:00-13:00 & 16:30-20:00, mobile 329-406-6274, www.gmrent.it, Francesco).

Taxi: Taxis wait outside the train station, and charge a minimum of €13 for a ride from the train station to anywhere in town (they justify the high price by the short tourist season).

Driver: Helpful taxi driver **Alessandro** is also available for airport transfers and local excursions (mobile 338-860-2349, www.alessandrotaxi.com, alessandrotaxi@yahoo.it).

Parking: The recommended **Hotel Mediterraneo** and **Villa Anita** offer free parking to their guests, and a few hotels have limited

Santa Margherita Ligure

100 Meters
100 Yards

TRAIN STATION

CORSO E. RAINUSSO

To ⑩

CORSO MATTEOTTI

③ ②①

VIA XXV APRILE

VIA GIMELLI

POST

VIA ZARA

LARGO ROMA

VIA ROMA

⑱

⑭

Largo Giusti

⑰

Piazza Veneto

VIA TRIESTE

VIA PAGANA

VIA GRAMSCI

VIA A. DORIA

FREE BEACH

To Rapallo & Freeway

T.I. KIOSK

BUS STOP TO PORTOFINO

Ⓑ

VIA BELVEDERE

⑥ ⑦

VIA

Piazza Mazz.

⑪

VIA PALESTRO

VIA CAIROLI

⑮

VIA CAVOUR

Piazza Caprera

VIA FARÀ

VIA PESCINO

Piazza della Libertà

VIRGIN MARTYR STATUE

⑯

VIA SOLIMANO

VIA GIUNCHETO

VIA DOGALI

VIA GORIZIA

④

SANTA MARGHERITA

VILLA DURAZZO

Durazzo Park

VIA F. P. CENTURIONE

⑫

SANT' ERASMO

⑬

BOAT DOCK

CASTLE

Ligurian Sea

SAN GIACOMO

VIA G. GIACOMO

VIA TRE NOV. MANARA

⑨

⑤

Ⓟ

FISH MARKET

S. GIACOMO

CORSO G. MARCONI

Marina

VIA FAVALE

To Portofino, Paraggi Beach & ⑧

---

① La Locanda di Colombo
② Hotel Jolanda
③ Hotel Tigullio et de Milan
④ Hotel Mediterraneo
⑤ Hotel Laurin
⑥ Hotel Fasce
⑦ Hotel Nuova Riviera
⑧ To Villa Anita, Rist. A' Lampara & Via Tomaso Bottaro Eateries

⑨ La Cambusa Ristorante
⑩ To Dal Baffo Ristorante
⑪ Da Pezzi Ristorante
⑫ Da Gennaro Pizzeria
⑬ Simonetti Gelateria
⑭ Gelateria Centrale
⑮ Seghezzo Grocery
⑯ D'Oro Centry Supermarket
⑰ Bike Rental
⑱ Internet Café

---

spots for a fee. When you reserve your room, mention that you'll have a car. Otherwise, try a private lot (about €10-15/half-day, €15-20/24 hours) such as **Autorimessa Europa,** next to the post office (Via Roma 38, tel. 0185-287-818). There's an hourly parking lot by the harbor, in front of the fish market (pay at blue machine in front of Laurin Hotel, Mon-Sat 8:00-20:00, Sun 8:00-23:00, first hour-€2, successive hours-€2.50). The TI has a list of parking spots (generally free where there are white lines) and paid parking lots.

Local Guide: Roberta De Beni knows the Ligurian Coast, its history, and its art very well (€100/half-day, €165/day, mobile 349-530-4778, www.xeniaguide.it, diodebe@inwind.it).

Self-Guided Walk

Welcome to Santa Margherita Ligure

Explore Santa Margherita Ligure on the following stroll.

• *Begin at Piazza della Libertà. Walk out to the tip of the boat dock and turn around to survey the...*

Town View: From here you can take in all of Santa Margherita Ligure, from the villas dotting the hills and the castle built in the 16th century (closed except for special exhibitions) to the exclusive hotels. Sharing the dock with you is a statue of "Santa Margherita Virgin Martyr."

• *Wander along the harborfront (down Corso Marconi) past the castle and to the...*

Marina: What's left of the town's fishing fleet ties up here. The fishing industry survives, drag-netting octopus, shrimp, and miscellaneous "blue fish"—plus mountains of anchovies attracted to midnight lamps. The fish market (inside the rust-colored building with arches and columns) wiggles weekdays at about, oh, maybe 16:00-20:00 or so. Residents complain that it's easier to buy their locally caught fresh fish in Milan than here.

• *Behind the fish market, up a flight of stairs by the war memorial, stands the...*

Oratory of Sant'Erasmo: This small church is named for St. Erasmus (a.k.a. "St. Elmo"), the protector of sailors. Notice the fine and typically local black-and-white pebble mosaic *(riseu)* in front of the church (with maritime themes). The church is actually an "oratory," where a brotherhood of faithful men who did anonymous good deeds congregated and worshipped. It's decorated with ships and paintings of storms that—thanks to St. Erasmus—the local seafarers survived. The huge crosses are carried through town on special religious holidays (the church is supposedly open only during Mass, but often open at other times, too).

• *Next, double back to climb the looooong stairway (Via Tre Novembre) overlooking the bay to reach the...*

Church of San Giacomo: Even though this is a secondary church in a secondary town, it's impressively lavish (daily 7:30-19:00, may close earlier in winter, avoid visiting during Mass—usually 7:45-9:00). The region's aristocrats amassed wealth from trade in the 11th to the 15th centuries. When Constantinople fell to the Turks, free trade in the Mediterranean stopped and Genovese traders became bankers—making even more money. A popular saying of the day was, "Silver is born in America, lives in Spain, and dies in Genoa." Bankers here served Spain's 17th-century

Rise of a Resort: The History of Santa Margherita Ligure

This town, like the entire region (from the border of France to La Spezia), was once ruled by the Republic of Genoa. In the 16th century, when Arab pirates from North Africa plagued the entire coastal area, Genoa built castles in the towns and lookout towers in the neighboring hills.

At the time, Santa Margherita was actually two bickering towns—each with its own bay. In 1800, Napoleon came along, took over the Republic of Genoa, and turned the rival towns into one city—naming it Porto Napoleone. When Napoleon fell in 1815, the town stayed united and took the name of the patron saint of its leading church, Santa Margherita.

In 1850, residents set to work creating a Riviera resort. They imported palm trees from North Africa and paved a fine beach promenade. Santa Margherita (and the surrounding area) was studded with fancy villas built by the aristocracy of Genoa (which was controlled by just 35 families). English, Russian, and German aristocrats also discovered the town in the 19th century. Mass tourism only hit in the last generation. Even with the increased crowds, the town decided to stay chic and kept huge developments out. Its neighbor, Rapallo, chose the extreme opposite—giving the Italian language a new word for uncontrolled growth ruining a once-cute town: *rapallizzazione*.

royalty and aristocracy, and the accrued wealth paid for a Golden Age of art. Wander the church, noticing the inlaid-marble floors and chapels.

• *Step out of the church and enjoy the sea view. Then turn left and step into...*

Durazzo Park (Parco Comunale Villa Durazzo): This park was an abandoned shambles until 1973, when the city took it over (free, daily May-Sept 9:00-19:00, maybe until 20:00 July-Aug, Oct-April 9:00-17:00). Today it's a delight, with a breezy café enjoyed mostly by locals (generally daily from 10:30 except closed Tue May-Aug) and free Wi-Fi (ask at the cafe for the password). The garden has two distinct parts: the carefully coiffed Italian garden (designed to complement the villa's architecture) and the calculatedly wild "English garden" below. The Italian garden is famous for its varied collection of palm trees, and an extensive collection of camellias. It's OK to feed the large turtles in the central pond (they like bits of fish or meat).

• *In the building next to the café, you'll see...*

Villa Durazzo: This was the home of a local journalist and writer, Vittorio G. Rossi (1898-1978), whose office has been preserved as he left it. Typical of the region, this palazzo has some period furniture, several grand pianos, chandeliers, and paintings strewn with cupids on the walls and ceilings. Look for King Umberto's letter offering condolences on Rossi's death. For most people, it's probably not worth the entry fee (€5.50, more for special exhibits; daily 9:00-13:00 & 14:00-18:00, Oct-March until 17:00, last entry 30 minutes before closing, WC opposite entry on left, tel. 0185-293-135, www.villadurazzo.it, villa.durazzo @comunesml.it). Classical music concerts are held here in July and August (ask at TI or villa ticket desk, or call for the schedule).

• *Your self-guided walk is over. Enjoy the park.*

Sights in Santa Margherita Ligure

Church of Santa Margherita (Basilica di Nostra Signora della Rosa)—The town's main church is textbook Italian Baroque. Its 18th-century facade hides a 17th-century interior. The chapels to the right of the high altar contain religious "floats" used in local festival parades. The wooden groups in the niches higher up used to be part of the processions, too. The altar is typical of 17th-century Ligurian altars—shaped like a boat, with lots of shelf space for candles, flowers, and relics. Remember, Baroque is like theater. After the Vatican II decrees of the 1960s, priests began to face their flocks instead of the old altars. For this reason, all over the Catholic world, modern tables serving as post-Vatican II altars stand in front of earlier altars that are no longer the center of attention during the Mass.

Cost and Hours: Free, daily 7:30-12:00 & 15:00-18:30, tel. 0185-286-555.

Via Palestro—This promenade (a.k.a. *caruggio*—"the big street" in local dialect) is *the* strolling street for window-shopping, people-watching, and studying the characteristic Art Nouveau house painting from about 1900. Before 1900, people distinguished their buildings with pastel paint and distinctive door and window frames. Then they decided to get fancy and paint entire exteriors with false balconies, weapons, saints, beautiful women, and 3-D Gothic concentrate.

As you wander from the Church of Santa Margherita inland, pop into the fanciest grocer-deli in town—the recommended

Seghezzo (immediately to the right of the church on Via Cavour). Locals know that this venerable institution has whatever odd ingredient the most obscure recipe calls for.

Farther up Via Palestro, you might drop into the traditional old **Panificio** bakery for a slice of fresh focaccia. Saying *"Vorrei un etto di focaccia"* will get you a Ligurian olive-oily, 100-gram, €1.50 hunk of every kid's favorite beach munchie. Locals claim the best focaccia in Italy is made along this coast.

Markets—On weekday afternoons, fishing boats unload their catch, which is then sold to waiting customers at **Mercato del Pesce** (roughly Mon-Fri 17:00-20:00, opens an hour earlier for wholesalers, Oct-April might open at 15:30). Find it in the rust-colored building with arches and columns on Corso Marconi, on the harbor, just past the castle. The open-air market, a commotion of clothes and produce, is held every Friday morning along Corso Matteotti, inland from Piazza Mazzini (8:00-13:00). Piazza Caprera (facing the main church) daily hosts a few farmers selling their produce from stalls.

Beaches—The handiest free Santa Margherita beaches are just below the train station toward the boat dock. But the best beaches are on the south side of town. Among these, I like "Gio and Rino beach" (just before Covo di Nord Est)—not too expensive, with fun, creative management and a young crowd. Also nice is the beach on the south side of Hotel Miramare, which offers a more relaxing sun-worshipping experience. Both beaches have free entry and rentable chairs and umbrellas. They're a 20-minute walk from downtown, or take the bus from either the train station or Piazza Veneto (€1.50 each way if bought in advance from kiosk, news-stands, tobacco shops, or the green ATP ticket office next to the TI; €3 if bought on board).

Paraggi beach, which is halfway to Portofino (with an easy bus connection—see "Portofino," later in this chapter), is better than any Santa Margherita beach, but it's *very* expensive. One Paraggi beach operator, Bosetti, offers a reasonable rate (€25/day, no hourly rates, includes umbrella, lounge chair, and towel), while rates at other beaches may soar up to €50 per day in July and August. In high season, the Paraggi beach may be all booked up by big shots from Portofino, which has no beach—only rocks. Off-season, the entire Paraggi beach is all yours and free of charge. A skinny patch of sand smack-dab in the middle of Paraggi beach is free year-round.

Sleeping in Santa Margherita Ligure

(**€1 = about $1.40, country code: 39**)
All of these are in the center; for specific locations, see the map on page 418. La Locanda di Colombo, Hotel Jolanda, and Hotel

Tigullio et de Milan are closest to the station. Prices listed here are the maximum price for the high season of July-August. Expect April-June and September-October to be €10-15 cheaper, and the rest of the year to be cheaper still.

$$$ La Locanda di Colombo has six stylish and contemporary rooms and two small, relaxing patios (Db-€150, tell them "Rick sent me" to get a 5 percent discount on stays of 1-3 days, 10 percent discount on longer stays; air-con, disabled access, Via XXV Aprile 12, tel. 0185-293-129, fax 0185-291-937, www.la locandadicolombo.it, sml@lalocandadicolumbo.it, welcoming hosts Massimiliano and Raffaella).

$$$ Hotel Jolanda, just around the corner from La Locanda di Colombo, is a solid, professionally run hotel with 50 rooms, a revolving door, a good breakfast buffet, and a friendly staff. With lavish public spaces and regal colors, this place makes you feel like nobility (Db-€150, superior Db-€170, 10 percent discount with this book if you mention it when you reserve, Internet access and Wi-Fi, air-con, elevator, free one-hour use of small weight room, wet and dry saunas, Jacuzzi, 10 free loaner bikes on request, Via Luisito Costa 6, tel. 0185-287-512, fax 0185-284-763, www.hotel jolanda.it, info@hoteljolanda.it).

$$$ Hotel Tigullio et de Milan, run by Giuseppe of Hotel Jolanda, has equally fine rooms with creamy hues and lower prices. You don't get all the luxurious extras, but the breezy sun terrace on top—with a bar in summertime—makes for a relaxing retreat (Db-€140, bigger Db with terrace-€150, 10 percent discount with this book if you mention it when you reserve, air-con, elevator but lots of stairs down to reception, parking-€20-25, Via Rainusso 6, tel. 0185-287-455, fax 0185-281-860, www.hoteltigullio.eu, info @hoteltigullio.eu).

$$$ Hotel Mediterraneo, run by the Melegatti family, offers 30 spacious rooms (a few with balconies or sun terraces) in a family-friendly, comfy 18th-century palazzo a five-minute walk from Piazza Veneto. They have a park-like sun garden with lounge chairs and lots of semi-private space. Pia Pauli makes great Ligurian specialties for dinner (Sb-€100, Db-€150, Tb-€160, great breakfast, five-course dinner-€30/person, free laundry service with 3-day stay or longer, free parking, free loaner bikes, closed Jan-March, take street immediately to the right of Church of Santa Margherita and find hotel straight ahead at Via della Vittoria 18A, tel. 0185-286-881, fax 0185-286-882, www.sml-mediterraneo.it, info@sml-mediterraneo.it).

$$$ Hotel Laurin offers slick, modern, air-conditioned, American-style lodgings fixated on harborfront views. All of its 43 rooms face the sea, most have terraces, and there's a small pool on the sundeck, as well as a gym and wet sauna. As it's a Best

Western, it feels corporate (Sb-€157, Db-€222, 10 percent discount if you book direct—mention this book when you reserve and show book on arrival, double-paned windows, elevator, 15-yard walk past the castle or €15 taxi ride from station, Corso Marconi 3, tel. 0185-289-971, fax 0185-285-709, www.laurinhotel.it, info@laurin hotel.it).

$$$ **Hotel Fasce,** a 16-room hotel surrounded by flowers and greenery, is run enthusiastically by intense Englishwoman Jane Fasce, her husband Aristide, and son Alessandro. Jane gets mixed reviews from my readers—some find her helpful, while others find her rules too strict...my advice is to toe the line (Sb-€100, Db-€124, Tb-€145, Qb-€190, see website for deals, no-nonsense 21-day cancellation policy, two rooms have private bathroom located across the hall, no elevator, free loaner bikes, rooftop garden, laundry service-€18, parking-€20, free round-trip train tickets to Cinque Terre with 3-night stay if you book room direct or through their website, 10-minute walk or €15 cab ride from station at Via Bozzo 3, tel. 0185-286-435, fax 0185-283-580, www.hotelfasce.it, hotel fasce@hotelfasce.it).

$$$ **Villa Anita** is an elegant-yet-homey family hotel run by hospitable Daniela and her friendly son, Sandro. They rent 12 tidy rooms—nearly all with terraces, and several with new, high-tech bathrooms—overlooking a peaceful residential neighborhood just a five-minute walk from the seaside boulevard. Daniela makes great cakes, and the in-house chef offers a varying menu of Ligurian specialties (Db-€140, optional half-pension-€90, air-con, free Wi-Fi, free parking, €15 cab ride from station, Via Tigullio 10, tel. 0185-286-543, fax 0185-283-005, www.hotelvillaanita.com, info@hotelvillaanita.com).

$$$ **Hotel Nuova Riviera** is an old villa surrounded by a garden, with nine institutional-feeling rooms (Db-€115, Tb-€138, Qb-€165, these prices good in 2012 if you book direct and mention this book when you reserve, additional 5 percent discount with cash, fans, some balconies, no elevator, 15-minute walk from station or easy cab ride; if you're driving, follow signs to hospital, then watch for hotel signs on Piazza Mazzini; if you're walking, enter Piazza Mazzini and see signs from there; Via Belvedere 10, tel. & fax 0185-287-403, www.nuovariviera.com, info@nuova riviera.com). They also run a nearby annex with six renovated rooms and one apartment with a tiny corner kitchen (Db-€100, Tb-€110, Qb-€125, cash only, breakfast at Hotel Nuova Riviera is optional and extra, tel. 0185-287-403, www.sabinirentals.com, sabinirentals@gmail.com).

Eating in Santa Margherita Ligure

For information on some of the regional specialties, see page 349.

Ristorante "A' Lampara" is the locals' favorite for *casalinga* (home-style) Genovese cuisine, prepared by the endearing Barbieri family: Mamma Maria Luisa oversees the dining room, son Mario cooks, and daughter Natalina serves. Try their specialties, such as *ravioli di pesce* (homemade fish ravioli with red mullet sauce) or *pansotti con salsa di noci*—cheese ravioli with walnut sauce (Fri-Wed 12:30-14:00 & 19:30-22:00, closed Thu, veggie options; follow Corso Marconi 4 blocks past the fish market, turn right onto Via Maragliano, and find #33 a block and a half ahead on left; tel. 0185-288-926).

La Cambusa is perched above the culinary heart of Santa Margherita Ligure—the fish market. Popular with tourists and resident romantics, its terrace has an unbeatable view over the harbor. In cooler weather, the terrace is covered and heated. Pick your favorite yacht while tucking into their seafood dishes with a Ligurian twist (€13 pasta, €20 main dishes, July-Sept daily 9:00-15:00 & 19:00-24:00 except closed Thu morning, Oct-June closed all day Thu, Via T. Bottaro, tel. 0185-287-410; Luciano, wife Antonella, and serious but efficient Vittorio).

Dal Baffo is a bustling mom-and-pop eatery popular for its traditional Ligurian specialties, including homemade pasta, wood-fired pizzas (folks queue up to watch the *pizzaioli* make their €7 pies to go), fresh fish, and grilled steaks at reasonable prices (Wed-Mon 12:00-15:00 & 19:00-23:30, closed Tue; from Piazza Caprera, head inland—both pedestrian streets eventually turn into busy Corso Matteotti; Corso Matteotti 56, tel. 0185-288-987).

Da Pezzi, with a cheap cafeteria-style atmosphere, is packed with locals at midday and at night. They're munching *farinata* (crêpes made from chickpeas, available Oct-May) standing at the bar, or enjoying pesto and fresh fish in the dining room. Consider the deli counter with its Genovese picnic ingredients (Sun-Fri 12:00-14:00 & 18:15-21:00, closed Sat, Via Cavour 21, tel. 0185-285-303, Giancarlo and Giobatta).

Waterfront Dining: All along Via Tomaso Bottaro, you'll find restaurants, pizzerias, and bars serving food with a harbor view. **Da Gennaro Pizzeria,** at Piazza della Libertà 30 by the boat dock, makes popular Neapolitan-style pizzas. **Bar Giuli,** the only place actually on the harbor, serves forgettable salads and sandwiches for a reasonable price (about 150 yards south of the fish market).

Gelato: The best *gelateria* I found in town—with chocolate-truffle *tartufato*—is **Simonetti** (daily 8:30 until late, closed Mon off-season, under the castle, closest to the water at Piazza della Libertà 48). **Gelateria Centrale,** just off Piazza Veneto near the cinema, serves up their specialty—*pinguino* (penguin), a cone with your choice of gelato dipped in chocolate (daily 7:00-late, closed Wed Sept-May).

Groceries: **Seghezzo** is classiest and great for a meal to go—ask them to *riscaldare* (heat up) their white *lasagne al pesto* or grilled veggies (daily June-Aug 7:30-13:00 & 15:30-20:00, closed Wed Sept-May, right of the church on Via Cavour). The **D'Oro Centry** supermarket, just off Piazza Mazzini at #38, has better prices (Mon-Sat 8:00-13:30 & 15:30-19:30, Sun 8:00-13:00, during summer Sat open all day long, tel. 0185-286-470).

Santa Margherita Ligure Connections

From Santa Margherita Ligure by Train to: Sestri Levante (2/hour, 30 minutes, €2.40), **Monterosso** (at least hourly, 45 minutes, €4.10), **La Spezia** (hourly, 1-1.5 hours, €5.50), **Pisa** (1-2/hour, 2-2.5 hours, InterCity/IC goes direct, other connections may require transfer in La Spezia, €14.50), **Milan** (8/day, 2-2.5 hours, more with transfer in Genoa, €19), **Ventimiglia**/French border (4/day, 4 hours; or hourly with change in Genoa, €13), **Venice** (8/day, 6-7 hours with 1-3 changes, €41-50). For **Florence,** transfer in Pisa (8/day, 3.5-4 hours, €20-26). See "Getting Around the Cinque Terre —By Train" on page 341 for details.

By Boat to the Cinque Terre: For the latest, pick up a schedule of departures and excursion options from the TI, ask at your hotel, call 0185-284-670 or 335-709-0870, or check online at www.traghettiportofino.it. The routes mentioned below run at least twice weekly from May through September or October, increasing in frequency in July and August.

The "Linea 3" boat does an all-day trip that includes two stop-overs: one hour in Vernazza and three hours in Portovenere, plus a scenic trip around an island (May-mid-Oct depart Sun at 9:00, plus Tue and Thu late July-mid-Sept, €21 one-way, €32 round-trip).

The half-day "Linea 4" boat sails to the Cinque Terre with a one-hour stopover in Vernazza (May-Oct depart Mon and Fri at 13:30, €17 one-way, €24.50 round-trip).

The "Super Cinque Terre, Linea 5" boat offers day-trip cruises from Santa Margherita Ligure to the Cinque Terre, departing at 8:45 and stopping in three Cinque Terre towns: three hours in Monterosso, and an hour each in Vernazza and Riomaggiore (May-Sept Wed and Sat only, €21 one-way, €32 round-trip).

Portofino

Santa Margherita Ligure, with its aristocratic architecture, hints at old money, whereas nearby Portofino, with its sleek shops, reeks

of new money. Fortunately, a few pizzerias, *focaccerie,* bars, and grocery shops are mixed in with Portofino's jewelry shops, art galleries, and haute couture boutiques, making the town affordable. The *piccolo* harbor, classic Italian architecture, and wooded peninsula can even turn glitzy Portofino into an appealing package. It makes a fun day trip from Santa Margherita Ligure.

Ever since the Romans founded Portofino for its safe harbor, it has had a strategic value (appreciated by everyone from Napoleon to the Nazis). In the 1950s, *National Geographic* did a beautiful exposé on the idyllic port, and locals claim that's when the Hollywood elite took note. Liz Taylor and Richard Burton came here annually (as did Liz Taylor and Eddie Fisher). During one famous party, Rex Harrison dropped his Oscar into the bay (it was recovered). Ava Gardner came down from her villa each evening for a drink—sporting her famous fur coat. Greta Garbo loved to swim naked in the harbor, not knowing that half the town was watching. Truman Capote also called Portofino home. But VIPs were also here a century earlier. In one of his books, Friedrich Nietzsche wrote about philosophizing with the mythical prophet Zarathustra on the path between Portofino and Santa Margherita.

My favorite Portofino plan: Visit for the evening. Leave Santa Margherita on the bus at about 16:30 and hike the last 20 minutes from Paraggi beach. Explore Portofino. Splurge for a drink on the harborfront, or get a take-out fruity sundae (*paciugo*; pah-CHOO-goh) and sit by the water. Then return by bus to Santa Margherita for dinner (confirm late departures). Portofino does offer fancy harborside dining, but the quality doesn't match the high prices.

Getting to Portofino

Portofino makes an easy day trip from Santa Margherita by bus, boat, bike, or foot.

By Bus: Catch bus #82 from Santa Margherita's train station or at bus stops along the harbor (main stop in front of TI, €1, 2-3/hour, 15 minutes, goes to Paraggi or Portofino). Buy tickets at the bar next to the station, at Piazza Veneto's green bus kiosk (next door to the TI; daily 7:15-19:45), from the green machine on

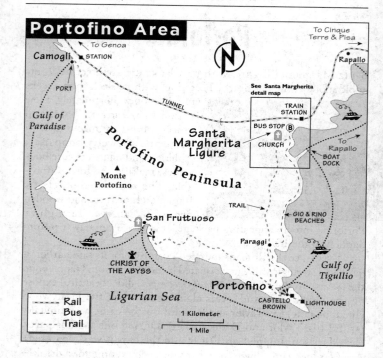

Portofino Area

To Genoa

To Cinque Terre & Pisa

Camogli ■ STATION

Rapallo

PORT

Gulf of Paradise

TUNNEL

See Santa Margherita detail map

TRAIN STATION

BUS STOP Ⓑ

Santa Margherita Ligure

CHURCH

To Rapallo

BOAT DOCK

Portofino Peninsula

Monte Portofino

TRAIL

GIO & RINO BEACHES

San Fruttuoso

Paraggi

CHRIST OF THE ABYSS

Gulf of Tigullio

Portofino

Ligurian Sea

CASTELLO BROWN

LIGHTHOUSE

----- Rail
---- Bus
---- Trail

1 Kilometer

1 Mile

the side of the kiosk, or at any newsstand, tobacco shop, or shop that displays a *Biglietti Bus* sign. You can usually buy tickets on the bus—for double the cost. If you're at the Piazza Veneto kiosk, grab a bus schedule, which will come in handy if you travel in the evening (last bus around 23:00, #882).

In Portofino, get tickets at the newsstand or from the machine next to the bus stop (go uphill and you'll come to Piazza Martiri della Libertà, machine and bus stop on right side, directions in English).

By Boat: The boat makes the 15-minute trip with more class and without the traffic jams (€5.50 one-way, €8.50 round-trip, €0.50 more on Sun and holidays; daily May-Sept nearly hourly departures 10:15-16:15, Oct-April at 10:15 and 14:15 only; dock is a 2-minute walk from Piazza Veneto off Piazza Martiri della Libertà, call to confirm or pick up schedule from TI or your hotel, tel. 0185-284-670, mobile 336-253-336, check at www.traghetti portofino.it). This company also runs boats from Santa Margherita to the Cinque Terre (see page 426). The boat from Portofino back to Santa Margherita departs nearly hourly in summer (May-Sept daily 12:00-18:00; Oct-April at 12:00 and 16:00 only).

The boats run between Rapallo and the San Fruttuoso Abbey, stopping en route at Santa Margherita Ligure and Portofino.

(Another boat line runs from Recco, Camogli, and Punta Chiappa to the abbey.)

By Bike: The 25-minute bike ride from Santa Margherita to Portofino is doable for cautious cyclists. While there are no steep hills to struggle up, the road is narrow, with many blind corners. Many of my recommended hotels provide free loaner bikes (though they may not be in the best condition); you can also rent your own wheels (see page 417).

On Foot: To hike the entire distance from Santa Margherita Ligure to Portofino, you have two options: You can follow the sidewalk along (and sometimes hanging over) the sea (1 hour, 2.5 miles)—although traffic can be noisy. Or, if you're hardy and ambitious, you can take a quieter two-hour hike by leaving Santa Margherita at Via Maragliano, then follow the Ligurian-symbol trail markers (look for red-and-white stripes—they're not always obvious, sometimes numbered according to the path you're on, usually painted on rocks or walls, especially at junctions). This hike takes you high into the hills. Keep left after Cappelletta delle Gave. Several blocks past a castle, you'll drop down into the Paraggi beach, where you'll take the Portofino trail the rest of the way.

Bus and Hike Option: For a shorter hike (20 minutes) into Portofino, ride bus #82 from Santa Margherita only as far as the small but ritzy Paraggi beach. (Ask on board where to get off, as the Paraggi stop is not labeled—watch for an inland bay with green water and a sandy beach.) At the far end of the beach, cross the street, climb the steps, and follow the hilly, paved trail marked *Pedonali per Portofino* high above the road. Twenty minutes later, you'll enter Portofino at a yellow-and-gray-striped church labeled *Divo Martino*—which I figure means "the divine Martin" and has something to do with Dean Martin giving us all "Volare" (which I couldn't get out of my head for the rest of the day).

Orientation to Portofino

Tourist Information

Portofino's TI is downhill from the bus stop, on your right under the portico. Pick up a free town map and a rudimentary hiking map (Easter-Sept daily 10:00-13:00 & 14:00-18:00; Oct-Easter Tue-Sat 9:30-13:30 & 14:00-17:00, closed Sun-Mon; Via Roma 35, tel. 0185-269-024).

Sights in Portofino

Museo del Parco—For an artsy break, walk around the harbor to the right, where you can stroll around a park littered with 148 contemporary sculptures by top artists (€5, May-Oct Wed-Mon

10:00-13:00 & 15:00-19:00, closed Tue, closed Nov-April and in bad weather, mobile 337-333-737).

Hikes—One option is the paved stone path that winds up and down to the **lighthouse** *(faro)* at a scenic point with a bar (bar open May-Sept, hedges block views until the end, 25-minute walk). Consider popping into **Castello Brown,** a medieval castle, on the way. It features lush gardens and a black-and-white portrait gallery of stars and famous personages who once frequented Portofino, including Clark Gable, Sophia Loren, Kim Novak, Grace Kelly, John Wayne, Ernest Hemingway, Humphrey Bogart, and Lauren Bacall. Original decorations and photos are explained in English (€4, daily 10:00-19:00, until 17:00 in winter, tel. 0185-267-101, www.castellobrown.it).

Or you could stroll the hilly pedestrian promenade through the trees from Portofino to **Paraggi beach**, and, if you're lucky, see a wild boar en route (20 minutes, path starts to the right of yellow-and-gray-striped Divo Martino church—look for clock tower, parallels main road, ends at ritzy Paraggi beach, where it's easy to catch bus back to Santa Margherita Ligure).

Another option is to hike out to **San Fruttuoso Abbey** and the nearby underwater Christ statue (described next; the hike there is steep at beginning and end, takes about 2.5 hours from Portofino—pick up the trailhead at the inland-most point of town, past Piazza della Libertà and the *carabinieri* station; you can also hike all the way there from Santa Margherita in about 4.5 hours via Portofino).

Near Portofino

San Fruttuoso Abbey—This 11th-century abbey is accessible only by foot (a 2.5-hour hike from Portofino, 4.5 hours from Santa Margherita) or boat (from either Portofino or Santa Margherita; abbey entry-€5, more for special exhibits; June-Sept daily 10:00-17:45; Oct-May daily 10:00-15:45 except closed Mon in winter; last entry 45 minutes before closing, tel. 0185-772-703). But the abbey itself isn't the main attraction. The more intriguing draw is 60 feet underwater, offshore from the abbey: the statue *Christ of the Abyss (Cristo degli Abissi)*. A rowboat will take you from the dock below the Portofino boat dock to the statue, where you can look down through a lens to just barely see the arms of Jesus—outstretched,

reaching upward. Some people bring goggles and dive in for a better view. The statue was placed there in 1954 for the divine protection of the region's divers. As the rowboats don't run in rough seas, call the abbey to confirm before making the trip (about €4, 20-minute round-trip, rowboats run only during boat arrival hours from Portofino—generally daily May-Sept 9:00-17:00).

From Easter through September, boats continue north from San Fruttuoso Abbey to Punta Chiappa and Camogli (€5 one-way, can return to Santa Margherita by train or buy round-trip boat tickets, call 0185-772-091 or inquire at Portofino or Santa Margherita TI for information).

Eating in Portofino

Food and drink are expensive in Portofino. **Bar Moreno da Ucio,** on the first outdoor terrace along the harbor to the left of the TI, has somewhat reasonable drink prices...by Portofino standards (€8 sparkling wine, €3 cappuccino, Fri-Wed 7:30-late, closed Thu).

South of the Cinque Terre

La Spezia

While just a quick train ride away from the fanciful Cinque Terre (20-30 minutes), the working town of La Spezia feels like "reality Italy." Primarily a jumping-off point for travelers, the town is slim on sights, and has no beaches.

The pedestrian zone on Via del Prione to the gardens along the harbor makes a pleasant stroll. The nearly deserted **Museo Amedeo Lia** displays Italian paintings from the 13th to 18th centuries, including minor works by Venetian masters Titian, Tintoretto, and Canaletto (€6.50, Tue-Sun 10:00-18:00, closed Mon, last entry 30 minutes before closing, English descriptions on laminated sheets in most rooms, audioguide-€3, WCs down the hall from ticket desk, no photos allowed, 10-minute walk from station at Via del Prione 234, tel. 0187-731-100, http://mal.spezia.net.it).

Stay in the Cinque Terre if you can. But if you're in a bind, I've listed several La Spezia accommodations. I've also listed (under "Eating in La Spezia") some places to grab a meal while you wait for a train.

Orientation to La Spezia

Tourist Information

The TI is in a separate building in front of the north end of the train station, by the pine trees (daily April-Sept 9:00-19:00,

La Spezia

Oct-March 9:00-17:00, tel. 0187-770-900, www.turismoprovincia
.laspezia.it). The Cinque Terre National Park office is inside the
train station (daily 7:00-13:00 & 13:30-20:00, until 17:00 off-
season, www.parconazionale5terre.it). A second TI is near the
waterfront (with same phone and hours as the train station TI,
Viale Italia 5).

Arrival in La Spezia

By Train: Get off at the La Spezia Centrale stop. You can check
your bags at the train station (see "Helpful Hints," below). Exit
the station down the road to the left, where several recommended hotels and eateries are located. From beside the TI, a less-
convenient set of stairs descends to Via Fiume. A new train station
exit may be added when work on the underground parking lot is
complete.

By Car: A parking lot is being built underneath the train station, but may not be finished by your visit. You'll find free parking
at Piazza d'Armi; from there, it's a 20-minute walk to the train
station, or take the €1 shuttle service to Piazza Brin, a five-min-

400 Meters
400 Yards

To Pisa

SPALLANZANI TUNNEL

To A12 Autostrada

VIA CRISPI

VIA VENETO

VIALE ITALIA

CRISTO RE CATHEDRAL

Piazza Europa

To Santa Maria del Mare Monastery

POST

V. CHIODO

AZIO

V. MAZZINI

VIALE ITALIA

WATERFRONT PROMENADE

BOATS TO CORSICA & SARDINIA

MOLO ITALIA

Harbor

Boats to Lerici, Portovenere & Cinque Terre (April-Oct)

1. Hotel Firenze e Continentale
2. Hotel Astoria
3. Hotel Venezia
4. Albergo Parma
5. La Stazione del Golfo dei Poeti Rooms
6. La Stazione del Golfo dei Poeti Reception
7. Casa da Nè/ Tre Frè Rooms
8. L'Arca di Noè B&B
9. Ristorante Roma da Marcellin
10. Il Pomodoro Pizzeria
11. Covered Market
12. Supermarket & Launderette
13. Piazza d'Armi (Free Parking)
14. Piazza d'Armi Shuttle Drop-Off
15. AciPark Garage
16. Portovenere Bus Stop

ute walk from the station (3/hour). To reach Piazza d'Armi from the highway, follow the La Spezia autostrada as it becomes Viale Carducci and ends at Viale Italia, then turn left and follow the road as it bends right, following signs for parking.

A guarded parking garage is on Via Crispi, just after the Galleria (tunnel) Spallanzani on the right. Look for the *AciPark* sign (€20/day for 1-3 days, €16/day for longer stays, Mon-Fri 7:00-20:15, Sat 7:00-13:30, closed Sun, reserve in advance only if you'll be arriving when they're closed, tel. 0187-510-545, aci park@libero.it).

Helpful Hints

Market Days: A colorful covered market sets up in Piazza Cavour (Mon-Sat 8:00-13:00). On Fridays, a huge all-day open-air market sprawls along Viale Garibaldi, about six blocks from the station.

Baggage Storage: A left-luggage service is at the train station along track 1 (facing the tracks on platform 1, go left; it's next to the WC). It's secure, though it isn't always staffed—ring the bell to the left of the doorway to call the attendant. Since you may have to wait, allow plenty of time to pick up your baggage before departing (€3/12 hours, daily 8:00-22:00, they'll photocopy your passport).

Laundry: A handy self-service launderette is just below the train station. Head down toward town, and immediately at the first piazza take a sharp right on Via Fiume—it's on your left at #95 (€8.50 one-hour wash and dry, Mon-Sat 8:00-22:00, Sun 9:00-22:00, mobile 348-543-7924, Edoardo).

Supermarket: DiMeglio is at Via Fiume 125, near the recommended launderette (daily 8:00-20:00, tel. 0187-704-059).

Booking Agency: Cinque Terre Riviera books rooms and apartments in La Spezia, the Cinque Terre, and Portovenere for a 10 percent markup (Mon-Fri 9:30-13:00 & 15:00-19:30, closed Sat-Sun, check website for day trips and cooking lessons, Via Picedi 18, tel. 0187-520-702, www.cinqueterreriviera.com, info@cinqueterreriviera.com).

Getting to the Cinque Terre: Trains leave at least twice hourly for the Cinque Terre, though not all trains stop at all towns. The Cinque Terre Treno Park Card (covers train ride to Cinque Terre as well as hiking fee—see page 340) is sold at the train-station ticket window and at the national park office in the station (see "Tourist Information," at the beginning of this section). For more details, see "Getting Around the Cinque Terre" on page 340.

Sleeping in La Spezia

(€1 = about $1.40, country code: 39)
Remember, sleep in La Spezia only as a last resort. These hotels and rooms are within a five-minute walk of La Spezia's station—except the last two listings, which are for drivers only.

Hotels
$$$ Hotel Firenze e Continentale is grand and Old World, but newly restored with a mountain-view breakfast room to boot. Just to the left of the station, its 67 rooms have all the usual comforts. Maria Gabriella will throw in a Cinque Terre food specialty for my readers (Sb-€85, Db-€125, large superior Db-€150, these special prices when you book direct with this book, cheaper during slow times, non-smoking rooms, double-paned windows, air-con, elevator, outdoor parking-€8/day, indoor parking-€18/day, Via Paleocapa 7, tel. 0187-713-200, fax 0187-714-930, www.hotel firenzecontinentale.it, info@hotelfirenzecontinentale.it).

$$ Hotel Astoria, with 48 decent rooms, has a combination lobby and breakfast room as large as a school cafeteria. It's a fine backup if the hotels nearer the train station are full (Db without air-con-€80; Db-€130 for the 10 summery, modern rooms with air-con and double-paned windows; elevator, free parking garage; take Via Milano left of Albergo Parma, go 3 blocks, and turn left to reach Via Roma 139; tel. 0187-714-655, fax 0187-714-425, www .albergoastoria.com, info@albergoastoria.com).

$$ Hotel Venezia, across the street from Hotel Firenze e Continentale, is run with low energy but its 19 rooms are pleasantly modern and recently remodeled (Sb-€55, Db-€90, air-con, elevator, free parking out front but must request when you reserve, Via Paleocapa 10, tel. & fax 0187-733-465, www.hotelveneziala spezia.it, hotelvenezia@telematicaitalia.it).

$$ Albergo Parma, with 36 rooms, is a little worn around the edges but inexpensive (D-€50, Db-€60, breakfast-€4, no fans, double-paned windows, just below train station and down the stairs at Via Fiume 143, tel. 0187-743-010, fax 0187-743-240, albergo parma@libero.it, some English spoken, Aurelio).

Private Rooms

Affitta camere, meaning rented rooms with no official reception, abound near the station. Expect good deals, modest English skills, and no breakfast (buy yourself a coffee and pastry at a nearby bar).

$$ La Stazione del Golfo dei Poeti rents four cute, clean, and contemporary rooms on the busy Via Fiume. Arrange to meet welcoming Rita outside the building or at the reception desk at Via Bixio 66—see map (Db-€80, cash only, air-con, Via Fiume 52, tel. 0187-714-416, mobile 345-352-6567, www.lastazionedelgolfodei poeti.it, info@lastazionedelgolfodeipoeti.it).

$$ Casa da Nè/Tre Frè, next door to the recommended Hotel Venezia, has 11 chic rooms with comfy linens and orange trees outside the door. It's located so close to the station that some rooms look out at the tracks; luckily, the windows are double-paned (Db-€80, air-con, Wi-Fi, Via Paleocapa 4, mobile 347-351-3239, www .trefre.it, info@trefre.it, Giovanna).

$$ L'Arca di Noè B&B is homey, with three bright and artsy rooms that share two bathrooms for one of the best deals on the Cinque Terre. A group could take the entire massive apartment (D-€50, Q-€80, includes breakfast, air-con, communal kitchen, 5-minute walk from station at Via Fiume 39, mobile 320-485-2434 or 348-916-9378, g.brunella@email.it, Brunella and Alessandra).

Near La Spezia

$$ Il Gelsomino, for drivers only, is a homey B&B in the hills above La Spezia overlooking the Gulf of Poets. It has three tranquil rooms: one with a bay-view terrace, one with hillside views, and a third that lacks views or a terrace. Don't confuse it with another

B&B called Il Gelsomino d'Oro (Db-€60, Tb-€90/Qb-€110, reconfirm a day in advance with your arrival time, large breakfast, Via dei Viseggi 9, tel. & fax 0187-704-201, www.ilgelsomino.biz, ilgelsomino@inwind.it, gracious Carla and Walter Massi).

$ **Santa Maria del Mare Monastery,** a last resort for drivers, rents 15 comfortable rooms to spiritual travelers high above La Spezia in a scenic but institutional setting (donation only, recommended offerings: dorm bed-€35, Db-€60, includes breakfast, additional €15/person for a meal, Via Montalbano 135B, tel. 0187-711-382, fax 0187-708-490, mobile 347-848-3993, www.santamaria delmare.it, madre@santamariadelmare.191.it).

Eating in La Spezia

Ristorante Roma da Marcellin, a one-minute walk from the station, has a cool, leafy terrace that's ideal for relaxing while you await your train. Grandpa Ottorino cooks up the freshest catch and a homemade filled pasta called *cappelletti* (daily 12:15-15:00 & 19:30-23:00; as you exit the station, turn left—it's across from Hotel Firenze e Continentale at Via Paleocapa 18; tel. 0187-715-921).

Il Pomodoro Pizzeria, just a few doors farther down on the corner of Via Zampino, offers more reasonable prices and an extensive selection of pizzas from €5. Practice your Italian with the chalkboard display of pastas of the day (Mon-Fri 12:00-14:00 & 19:00-23:00, Sat 19:00-23:00, closed Sun, Piazza S. Bon 5, tel. 0187-739-911).

La Spezia Connections

From La Spezia by Train to: Monterosso (2/hour, 25 minutes, €2.40), **Carrara** (2/hour, 25 minutes, €2.40), **Viareggio** (2/hour, 30-60 minutes, €4), **Pisa** (hourly, 1-1.5 hours, €5-9), **Florence** (4/day direct, otherwise nearly hourly, 2.5 hours, change in Pisa, €9), **Rome** (every 2 hours, 3.5-5 hours, €35-45), **Milan** (about hourly, 3 hours direct or with change in Genoa, €22-29), **Venice** (nearly hourly, 5 hours, 1-3 changes, €50-55).

By Bus to Portovenere: City buses generally depart from Viale Garibaldi (2/hour, 30 minutes, €1.90 each way, buy tickets at tobacco shops or newsstands, bus stop 11P—just past Corso Cavour; but note that Friday buses depart from Corso Cavour). From the La Spezia train station, exit left and head downhill, following the street to the first square (Piazza S. Bon). Continue down the pedestrian stretch of Via Fiume to Piazza Garibaldi, then turn right at the fountain in the square onto Viale Garibaldi; the bus stop for Portovenere-bound buses is after the first stoplight on the right side of the street. A timetable is posted by the bus stop.

Carrara

Perhaps the world's most famous marble quarries are just east of La Spezia in Carrara. Michelangelo himself traveled to these val-

leys to pick out the marble that he would work into his masterpieces. The towns of the region are dominated by marble. The quarries higher up are vast digs that dwarf the hardworking trucks and machinery coming and going. The **Marble Museum** traces the story of marble-cutting here from pre-Roman times until today (€4.50, May-Sept Mon-Sat 9:30-13:00 & 15:30-18:00, Oct-April Mon-Sat 9:00-12:30 & 14:30-17:00, closed Sun year-round, Viale XX Settembre 85, tel. 0585-845-746, http://urano.isti.cnr.it:8880/museo/home.php).

For a guided visit, **Sara Paolini** is excellent (€80/half-day tour, mobile 373-711-6695, sarapaolini@hotmail.com). She is accustomed to meeting drivers at the Carrara freeway exit, or she can pick you up at the train station.

Portovenere

While the gritty port of La Spezia offers little in the way of redeeming touristic value, the nearby resort of Portovenere is enchanting. This Cinque Terre-esque village clings to a rocky promontory that juts into the sea and protects the harbor from the crashing waves. On the harbor, next to colorful bobbing boats, a row of restaurants—perfect for al fresco dining—feature local specialties such as *trenette* pasta with pesto and *spaghetti con frutti di mare*.

Local boats take you on a 40-minute excursion around three nearby islands or over to Lerici, the town across the bay. Lord Byron swam to Lerici (not recommended). Hardy hikers enjoy the five-hour (or more) hike to Riomaggiore, the nearest Cinque Terre town.

Getting There: Portovenere—not to be confused with Portofino—is an easy day trip from the Cinque Terre by **boat**

(Easter–Oct, 4–6/day 9:00–15:00, 1 hour, €12 one-way, €23 day pass includes hopping on and off and either Lerici or a jaunt around three small islands near Portovenere, www.navigazionegolfo deipoeti.it). You can also cruise between Portovenere and Santa Margherita Ligure, with stops in Vernazza and Sestri Levante, using another boat line (www.traghettiportofino.it)—see "Santa Margherita Ligure Connections" on page 426. Pick up a schedule of departures and excursion options from the TI, or ask at your hotel. Or you can take the **bus** from La Spezia (2/hour, 30 minutes, €1.90, in La Spezia buy tickets at tobacco shops or newsstands; in Portovenere get tickets at TI; for directions to the bus stop in La Spezia, see page 436). **Parking** is a nightmare here from May through September, but Albergo Il Genio offers free parking. In peak season, buses shuttle drivers from the parking lot just outside Portovenere to the harborside square. Otherwise, test your luck with the spots on the seaside (€1.50/hour).

Tourist Information: The TI is easy to find in the main square (June–Sept Thu–Tue 10:00–12:00 & 16:00–19:00, closed Wed; Oct–May Thu–Tue 10:00–12:00 & 15:00–18:00, closed Wed; Piazza Bastreri 7, tel. 0187-790-691).

Sleeping in Portovenere: If you've forgotten your yacht, try **$$$ Albergo Il Genio,** in the building where the main street hits the piazza (Db-€125, some rooms with views, no elevator, Internet access, free parking but request when you reserve, Piazza Bastreri 8, tel. & fax 0187-790-611, www.hotelgenioportovenere.com, info@hotelgenioportovenere.com). If your *vita* is feeling *dolce,* consider **$$$ Grand Hotel Portovenere,** which has striking sea views (from €121 for a viewless Db off-season to €280 for a view suite in summer, optional half-pension-€30–39/person, Internet access, tel. 0187-792-610, fax 0187-790-661, Via Garibaldi 5, www.portovenerehotel.it, ghp@village.it).

FLORENCE

Firenze

Florence, the home of the Renaissance and the birthplace of our modern world, has the best Renaissance art in Europe. In a single day, you can look Michelangelo's *David* in the eyes, fall under the seductive sway of Botticelli's *Birth of Venus,* and climb the modern world's first dome, which still dominates the skyline.

Get your bearings with a Renaissance walk. Florentine art goes beyond paintings and statues—enjoy the food, fashion, and street markets. Lick Italy's best gelato while enjoying some of Europe's best people-watching.

Planning Your Time

If you're in Italy for three weeks, Florence deserves at least one well-organized day: see the Accademia *(David)*, tour the Uffizi Gallery (Renaissance art), visit the underrated Bargello (best statues), and do the Renaissance Walk (explained on page 463; to avoid heat and crowds, do this walk in the morning or late afternoon). Art-lovers will want to chisel out another day of their itinerary for the many other Florentine cultural treasures. Shoppers and ice cream-lovers may need to do the same.

Plan your sightseeing carefully; follow the tips and tricks in this chapter to save time and avoid lines. This is particularly important if you'll be in town for only a day or two during the crowded summer months.

The Uffizi Gallery and Accademia nearly always have long ticket-buying lines, especially in peak season (April-Oct) and on holiday weekends. Crowds thin out weekdays in the off-season. Whatever time of year you visit, you can easily avoid the wait by making reservations (see page 452) or buying a Florence Card

FLORENCE

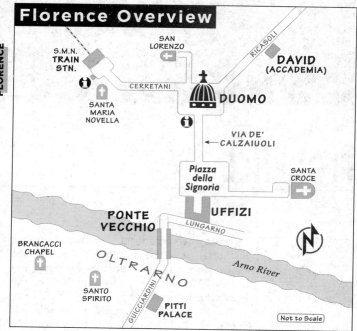

Florence Overview

S.M.N. TRAIN STN.

SAN LORENZO

RICASOLI

DAVID (ACCADEMIA)

CERRETANI

SANTA MARIA NOVELLA

DUOMO

VIA DE' CALZAIUOLI

Piazza della Signoria

SANTA CROCE

PONTE VECCHIO

LUNGARNO

UFFIZI

BRANCACCI CHAPEL

OLTRARNO

SANTO SPIRITO

GUICCIARDINI

Arno River

PITTI PALACE

Not to Scale

(see page 457). Note that both of these major sights are closed on Monday.

Some sights close early; see the early-closing warning in the "Daily Reminder" on page 446. Other museums close early only on certain days (e.g., the first Sunday of the month, second and fourth Monday, etc.). In general, Sundays and Mondays are bad, with many museums either closed or with shorter hours.

Connoisseurs of smaller towns should consider taking the bus to Siena for a day or evening trip (75 minutes one-way, confirm when last bus returns). Siena is magic after dark. For more information, see the Siena chapter.

Orientation to Florence

The best of Florence lies on the north bank of the Arno River. The main historical sights cluster around the red-brick dome of the cathedral (Duomo). Everything is within a 20-minute walk of the train station, cathedral, or Ponte Vecchio (Old Bridge). The less impressive but more characteristic Oltrarno area (south bank) is just over the bridge. Though small, Florence is intense. Prepare for scorching summer heat, slick pickpockets, few WCs, steep prices, and long lines. The big news for visitors to Florence is the energetic young mayor's passion for traffic-free zones. Once brutal for pedestrians, the city is now a delight on foot.

Tourist Information

The main Florence TI is across the square from the train station (Mon-Sat 8:30-19:00, Sun 8:30-14:00; with your back to tracks, exit the station—it's 100 yards away, across the square in wall near corner of church at Piazza Stazione 4; tel. 055-212-245, www.firenzeturismo.it). In the train station, avoid the Hotel Reservations "Tourist Information" window (marked *Informazioni Turistiche Alberghiere*) near the McDonald's; it's not a real TI but a hotel-reservation business.

A small but very central TI is on Piazza del Duomo, at the west corner of Via Calzaiuoli; it's inside the Bigalla Museum/ Loggia (Mon-Sat 9:00-17:00, Sun 9:00-14:00). Another TI is a couple of blocks north of the Duomo (Mon-Sat 8:30-18:30, Sun 8:30-13:30, Via Cavour 1 red, tel. 055-290-832, international bookstore across street).

The TIs sell the €50 Florence Card, an expensive but handy pass for busy sightseers (see page 457).

At any TI, pick up these free, handy resources in English:

- a city map (ask for the transit map, which has bus routes of interest to tourists on the back; your hotel likely has freebie maps, too)
- a current museum-hours listing (extremely important, since no guidebook—including this one—has ever been able to accurately predict the hours of Florence's sights for the coming year)
- a list of current exhibitions
- a printout of what's happening that day
- information on entertainment, including the TI's monthly Florence and Tuscany News (good for events and entertainment listings)
- the ad-driven monthly *Florence Concierge Information* magazine (which lists museums, plus concerts, markets, sporting events, church services, shopping ideas, some bus and train connections, and an entire similar section on Siena)
- *The Florentine* newspaper (published every other Thu in English, for expats and tourists, with great articles giving cultural insights; download latest issue at www.theflorentine.net)

The magazine and newspaper listed above are also often available at hotels throughout town.

Arrival in Florence

By Train

Florence's main train station is called **Santa Maria Novella**

FLORENCE

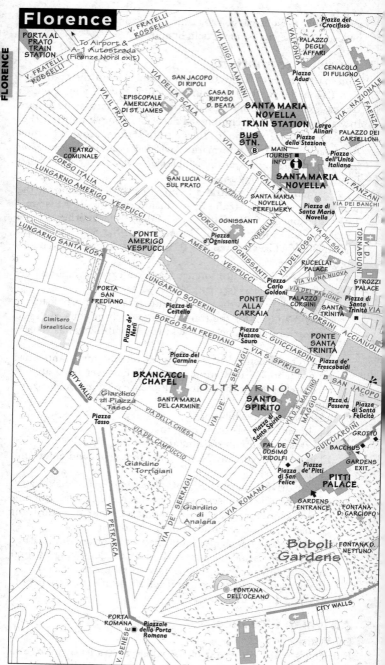

FLORENCE

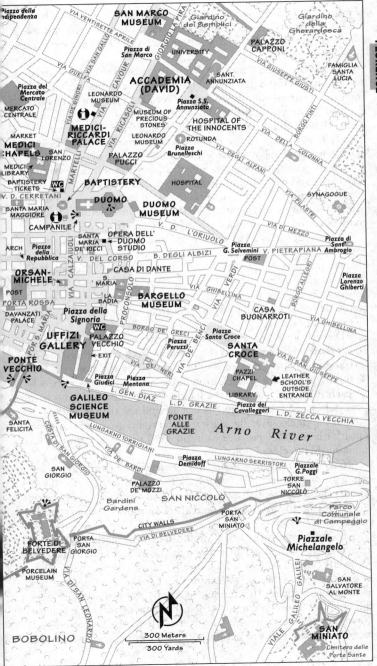

(*Firenze S.M.N.* on schedules and signs). Built in Mussolini's "Rationalism" style back between the wars, in some ways the station seems to have changed little—notice the 1930s-era lettering and architecture.

Florence also has two suburban train stations: **Firenze Rifredi** and **Firenze Campo di Marte.** Note that some trains don't stop at the main station—before boarding, confirm that you're heading for S.M.N., or you may overshoot the city. (If this happens, don't panic; the other stations are a short taxi ride from the center.)

Take advantage of the user-friendly, automated "Fast Ticket" machines that display schedules, issue tickets, and even make reservations for railpass-holders. Some take only credit cards; others take cards and cash. Using them is easy, and can actually be fun; just tap "English." If you need tickets within Italy, there's no reason to stand in line at a ticket window. But to get international tickets, you'll need to either go to a ticket window or a travel agency.

To orient yourself to the station and nearby services, stand with your back to the tracks. Look left to see a 24-hour pharmacy (*Farmacia,* near McDonald's), the fake "Tourist Information" office (funded by hotels), and baggage storage near track 16 (€4/5 hours, then €0.60/hour for 6-12 hours and €0.20/hour for over 12 hours, daily 6:00-23:50, passport required, maximum 40 pounds, no explosives—sorry).

Directly ahead of you is the way to the real TI (see page 441). To get there, walk away from the tracks and exit the station; the TI is straight across the square, 100 yards away, by the stone church. (If there's construction, circle around the torn-up square to the left to reach it.) For cheap eats, the handy Conad supermarket—with sandwiches and salads to go—is just around the corner (with your back to the tracks leave the station to the right, go down the steps, and it's immediately on your right on Via Luigi Alamanni, Mon-Sat 8:00-20:00, closed Sun).

Getting to the Duomo and City Center: The Duomo and town center are to your left (with your back to the tracks). Out the doorway to the left, you'll find city buses and the taxi stand. Taxis cost about €8 to the Duomo, and the line moves fast, except on holidays.

To walk into town (10-12 minutes), exit the station to the left and find the stairs/escalators down to the underground passageway/mall called Galleria S.M. Novella. Head toward the Church of Santa Maria Novella. (Warning: Pickpockets—often dressed as tourists—frequent this tunnel, especially the surface point near the church.) You come out on the other side of the square; head down Via dei Panzani which leads directly to the Duomo. Most recommended hotels are within a 10- or 15-minute walk from the station.

By Bus

The bus station is next to the train station, with the TI across the square. For more information on buses, see page 450.

By Car

The autostrada has several exits for Florence. Get off at the *Nord*, *Sud*, or *Certosa* exits and follow signs toward—but not into—the *Centro*.

Don't even attempt driving into the city center. Florence has a traffic-reduction system that's complicated and confusing even to locals. Every car passing into the *Zona Traffico Limitato (ZTL)* is photographed; those who haven't jumped through bureaucratic hoops to get a permit can expect to receive a €100 ticket in the mail. If you get lost and cross the line several times...you get several fines. The no-go zone (defined basically by the old medieval wall, now a boulevard circling the historic center of town—watch for *Zona Traffico Limitato* signs) is roughly the area between the river, main train station, Piazza della Libertà, Piazza Donatello, and Piazza Beccaria.

Fortunately, the city center is ringed with big, efficient parking lots (signposted with the standard big *P*), each with taxi and bus service into the center. Check www.firenzeparcheggi.it for details on all their parking lots, availability, and prices. From the freeway, follow the signs to *Centro*, then *Stadio*, then *P*. I usually head for "Parcheggio del Parterre," just beyond Piazza della Libertà (€1.50/ hour, €18/day, €65/week, open 24 hours daily, tel. 055-500-1994, 600 spots, automated, pay with cash or credit card, never fills up completely). To get into town, find the taxi stand at the elevator exit, or ride one of the *elettrico* minibuses that connect all of the major parking lots with the city center (see www.ataf.net for routes).

You can park for free along any suburban curb near a bus stop that feels safe, and take the bus into the city center from there. Check for signs that indicate parking restrictions—for example, a circle with a slash through it and "*dispari giovedi, 0,00-06,00*" means "don't park on Thursdays between midnight and six in the morning."

Free parking is easy up at Piazzale Michelangelo (see page 483), but don't park where the buses drop off passengers; park on the side of the piazza farthest from the view. To get from Piazzale Michelangelo to the center of town, take bus #12 or #13.

If you're picking up a rental car upon departure, don't struggle with driving into the center. Taxi with your luggage to the car-rental office, and head out from there.

By Plane

Amerigo Vespucci Airport, also called Peretola Airport, is about

Daily Reminder

Sunday: The Duomo's dome, Museum of Precious Stones, and Mercato Centrale are closed. At the Church of Santa Maria Novella, the Museum and Cloisters are closed, but the church itself is open (13:00–17:00). These sights close early: Duomo Museum (at 13:40) and the Baptistery's interior (at 14:00). A few sights are open only in the afternoon: Duomo (12:00–17:00), Santa Croce Church (13:00–17:30), Church of San Lorenzo (13:30–17:00), Brancacci Chapel and Church of Santa Maria Novella (both 13:00–17:00), and Santo Spirito Church (16:00–17:30). The Museum of San Marco and the Bargello are closed on the first, third, and fifth Sundays of the month. Palazzo Davanzati and the Medici Chapels close on the second and fourth Sundays. Need a calendar? Look in the appendix.

It's not possible to reserve tickets by phone on Sunday for the major sights (Accademia and Uffizi Gallery) because the telephone-reservation office for both is closed; try other options instead (see page 452 for details).

Monday: The biggies are closed, including the Accademia (David) and the Uffizi Gallery, as well as the Orsanmichele Church, and the Pitti Palace's Palatine Gallery, Royal Apartments, and Modern Art Gallery.

The Museum of San Marco and the Bargello close on the second and fourth Mondays. At the Pitti Palace, the Argenti Museum and the Boboli and Bardini Gardens close on the first and last Mondays. Palazzo Davanzati is closed on the first, third, and fifth Mondays. The San Lorenzo Market is closed Monday in winter.

Target these sights on Mondays: the Duomo and its dome, Duomo Museum, Campanile, Baptistery, Medici-Riccardi Palace, Brancacci Chapel, Mercato Nuovo, Mercato Centrale, Casa Buonarroti, Galileo Science Museum, Palazzo Vecchio, and churches (including Santa Croce and Santa Maria Novella). Or take a walking tour.

five miles northwest of Florence (open 5:10–24:00, no overnighting allowed, TI, cash machines, car-rental agencies, airport info tel. 055-306-1630, flight info tel. 055-306-1700—domestic only, www.aeroporto.firenze.it). Shuttle buses (far right of airport as you exit arrivals hall) connect the airport with Florence's SITA bus station, 100 yards west of the train station on Via Santa Caterina da Siena (2/hour, 30 minutes, daily 6:00–23:30, €5, first bus leaves for airport from Florence at 5:30). Allow about €22 and 30 minutes for a taxi.

By Cruise Ship

For detailed instructions for arriving at Florence's port, Livorno, see page 515.

Tuesday: All sights are open, except Casa Buonarroti and the Brancacci Chapel. The Galileo Science Museum closes early (13:00).

Wednesday: All sights are open, except the Medici-Riccardi Palace and Santo Spirito Church.

Thursday: All sights are open. These sights close early: the Palazzo Vecchio (14:00) and off-season, the Duomo (16:00 in May and Oct, 16:30 in winter).

Friday: All sights are open except the Museum and Cloisters at the Church of Santa Maria Novella (church open 11:00-17:30).

Saturday: All sights are open, but the Duomo's dome closes earlier than usual, at 17:40.

Early-Closing Warning: Some of Florence's sights close surprisingly early most days. Palazzo Davanzati closes at 13:50 and the Museum of San Marco closes at 13:50 on weekdays (open later on Sat and when open on Sun). In winter, the Medici Chapels and Bargello close at 13:50. The Museum of Precious Stones closes at 14:00, as does the Mercato Centrale (except in winter, when it stays open until 17:00 on Sat).

Late-Hours Relief: The Accademia, Uffizi Gallery, and the Pitti Palace's Palatine Gallery and Royal Apartments are open until 18:50 daily except Monday.

Many sights are open until 19:00 on a single day or more: San Lorenzo Market (daily, but closed Mon in winter), Medici-Riccardi Palace (Thu-Tue), the Duomo's dome (Mon-Fri), Baptistery (Mon-Sat, except first Sat of month until 14:00), and the Palazzo Vecchio (Fri-Wed).

These sights are open until 19:30: Campanile (daily), Duomo Museum (Mon-Sat), San Miniato Church (daily but closes at 13:00 in winter), and the Boboli and Bardini Gardens at the Pitti Palace (daily except some Mon, June-Aug only). The Mercato Nuovo is open daily until 20:00.

Helpful Hints

Theft Alert: Florence has particularly hardworking gangs of thieves who hang out where you do: near the train station, the station's underpass (especially where the tunnel surfaces), and at major sights. American tourists—especially older ones—are considered easy targets. Some thieves even dress like tourists to fool you. Also be on guard at two squares frequented by drug pushers (Santa Maria Novella and Santo Spirito). Bus #7 (to the nearby town of Fiesole, with great Florence views) is a favorite with tourists and, therefore, with thieves.

Medical Help: There's no shortage of English-speaking medical help in Florence. To reach a doctor who speaks English, call **Medical Service Firenze** at 055-475-411; the phone is answered 24/7. Rates are reasonable. For a doctor to come to your hotel within an hour of your call, you'd pay €100-200 (higher rates apply on Sun, holidays, or for late visits). You pay only €50 if you go to the clinic when the doctor's in (Mon-Fri 11:00-12:00 & 17:00-18:00, Sat 11:00-12:00, closed Sun, no appointment necessary, Via L. Magnifico 59, near Piazza della Libertà). A second clinic is available at Via Porta Rossa 1 (Mon-Sat 13:00-15:00, closed Sun).

Dr. Stephen Kerr is an English doctor specializing in helping sick tourists (clinic open for drop-ins Mon-Fri 15:00-17:00, other times by appointment, €50 per visit, Piazza Mercato Nuovo 1, between Piazza della Repubblica and Ponte Vecchio, tel. 055-288-055, mobile 335-836-1682, www.dr-kerr .com). The TI has a list of other English-speaking doctors.

There are 24-hour **pharmacies** at the train station and on Borgo San Lorenzo (near the Baptistery).

Museum Strategies: If you want to see a lot of museums, the pricey Florence Card—which saves you from having to wait in line or make reservations for the Uffizi and Accademia—can be a good value (see page 457).

Churches: Some churches now operate like museums, charging an admission fee to see their art treasures. Modest dress for men, women, and even children is required in some churches (including the Duomo, Santa Maria Novella, Santa Croce, and the Medici Chapels), and recommended for all of them—no bare shoulders, short shorts, or short skirts. Be respectful of worshippers and the paintings; don't use a flash. Churches usually close from 12:00 or 12:30 to 15:00 or 16:00.

Addresses: Street addresses list businesses in red and residences in black (color-coded on the actual street number and indicated by a letter following the number in printed addresses: "r" = red; no indication or "n" = black, for *nero*). *Pensioni* are usually black but can be either. The red and black numbers each appear in roughly consecutive order on streets but bear no apparent connection with each other. I'm lazy and don't concern myself with the distinction (if one number's wrong, I look for the other) and can easily find my way around.

Chill Out: Schedule several cool breaks into your sightseeing where you can sit, pause, and refresh yourself with a sandwich, gelato, or coffee. Carry a water bottle to refill at Florence's twist-the-handle public fountains. Try the *fontanello* (dispenser of free cold water) on Piazza della Signoria, behind the statue of Neptune (to the left of the Palazzo Vecchio).

Internet Access: In bustling, tourist-filled Florence, you'll see small Internet cafés on virtually every street. **V.I.P. Internet**

has cheap rates, numerous terminals, and long hours (€1.50/ hour, daily 9:00-24:00, near recommended hotel Katti House at Via Faenza 49 red, tel. 055-264-5552). **Internet Train,** the dominant chain, is pricier, with bright and cheery rooms, speedy computers, and decent hours (€4.30/hour, cheaper for students, reusable card good for any other Internet Train location, open daily roughly 9:00-20:00, www.internettrain .it). Find branches near Piazza della Repubblica (Via Porta Rossa 38 red), behind the Duomo (Via dell'Oriolo 40), and on Piazza Santa Croce (Via de Benci 36 red). Internet Train also offers Wi-Fi, phone cards, compact-disc burning, and other related services.

If you have a smartphone, you can access free Wi-Fi for two hours at the **TI** near the train station. At the Hotspot machine, enter your mobile phone number (include the international access code if it's a US phone) to receive a text message with a user name and password.

Bookstores: Local guidebooks (sold at kiosks) are cheap, and give you a map and a decent commentary on the sights. For brand-name guidebooks in English, try **Feltrinelli International** (Mon-Sat 9:00-19:30, closed Sun, a few blocks north of the Duomo and across the street from TI and Medici-Riccardi Palace at Via Cavour 12 red, tel. 055-219-524); **Edison Bookstore** (also has CDs, plus novels on the Renaissance and much more on its four floors; Mon-Sat 9:00-24:00, Sun 10:00-24:00, facing Piazza della Repubblica, tel. 055-213-110); **Paperback Exchange** (cheaper, all books in English, bring in your used book for a discount on a new one, Mon-Fri 9:00-19:30, Sat 10:30-19:30, closed Sun, just south of the Duomo on Via delle Oche 4 red, tel. 055-293-460); or **BM Bookshop** (with perhaps the city's largest collection of English books and guidebooks—including mine; Mon-Sat 9:30-19:30, closed Sun, near Ponte alla Carraia at Borgognissanti 4 red, tel. 055-294-575).

Services: WCs are scarce. Use them when you can, in any café or museum you patronize.

Laundry: The **Wash & Dry Lavarapido** chain offers long hours and efficient, self-service launderettes at several locations (about €7 for wash and dry, bring plenty of coins, daily 8:00-22:00, tel. 055-580-480 or toll-free 800-231-172). These are close to recommended hotels: Via dei Servi 102 red (and a rival launderette at Via Guelfa 55, off Via San Zanobi; both near *David*), Via del Sole 29 red and Via della Scala 52 red (between train station and river), Via Ghibellina 143 red (Palazzo Vecchio), Via Faenza 26 (near station), and Via dei Serragli 87 red (across the river in Oltrarno neighborhood).

Bike Rental: The **city of Florence** rents bikes cheaply at several locations: the train station, Piazza Santa Croce, and Piazza Ghiberti (€1.50/1 hour, €4/5 hours, €8/24 hours, tel. 055-650-5295; for more information, ask at any TI). **Florence by Bike** rents two-wheelers of all sizes (€3/hour, €8/5 hours, includes bike lock and helmet, €3 extra for child seat, April-Nov daily 9:00-19:30, Via San Zanobi 120 red, tel. 055-488-992, www.florencebybike.it, info@florencebybike.it).

Travel Agency: While it's easy to buy train tickets to destinations within Italy at handy machines at the station, travel agencies can be more convenient and helpful for getting international tickets, reservations, and supplements. The cost is either the same or the charge is minimal. Ask your hotel for the nearest travel agency.

Getting Around Florence

I organize my sightseeing geographically and do it all on foot. I think of Florence as a Renaissance treadmill—it requires a lot of walking.

Buses: The city's full-size buses don't cover the old center well, especially now that the whole area around the Duomo has been declared off-limits to motorized traffic. Of the many bus lines, I find these to be of most value for seeing outlying sights: Lines #12 and #13 go from the train station to Porta Romana, up to San Miniato Church and Piazzale Michelangelo, and on to Santa Croce. Most other lines leave from Piazza San Marco (near the Accademia and Museum of San Marco), including bus #7, which goes to Fiesole, a small town with big views of Florence. To get from the train station to Piazza San Marco, either walk or take bus #1, #6, #14, or #23.

Fun little *elettrico* **minibuses** wind through the tangled old center of town and up and down the river—just €1.20 gets you a 90-minute joyride. These buses, which run every 10 minutes, are popular with sore-footed sightseers and eccentric local seniors. *Elettrico* #C2 twists through the congested old center from the train station to Piazza Beccaria. *Elettrico* #C3 goes up and down the Arno River from Ognissanti to Santa Croce Church and beyond; #C1 winds around Piazza Repubblica, then heads north up to Piazza Libertà. *Elettrico* #D goes from the train station to Ponte Vecchio, cruising through Oltrarno, and finishing at Ponte San Niccolò. The minibuses connect many major parking lots with the historical center (tickets sold at machines at lots). Routes are shown on the free TI map (see the handy inset) and the "La Rete dei Bussini Potenziata" leaflet, free at the ATAF bus office, located just east of the train station, on Piazza della Stazione.

Buy bus tickets at tobacco shops, newsstands, or the ATAF

bus office (€1.20/1.5 hours, €4.50/4 tickets, €5/24 hours, €12/3 days, 1-day and 3-day passes aren't always available in tobacco shops, validate in machine on the bus, tel. 800-424-500, www .ataf.net). You can buy tickets on board, but you'll pay more (€2) and you'll need exact change. Follow general bus etiquette: Board at front or rear doors, exit out the center.

Taxi: The minimum cost for a taxi ride is €5, or €6 after 22:00 and on Sundays (rides in the center of town should be charged as tariff #1). A taxi ride from the train station to Ponte Vecchio costs about €9. Taxi fares and supplements (e.g., €2 extra if you call a cab rather than hail one) are clearly explained on signs in each taxi.

Tours in Florence

Tour companies big and small offer plenty of tours that go out to smaller towns in the Tuscan countryside (the most popular day trips: Siena, San Gimignano, Pisa, and into Chianti country for wine tasting). They also do Florence city tours, but for most people, the city is really best on foot (and the book you're holding provides at least as much information as you'll get with a generic bus tour).

I've produced a series of free audio tours that illuminate Florence's top sights and historic core: the Accademia, Uffizi Gallery, and Renaissance Walk. You can download the tours to your mobile device and sightsee on your own (see sidebar on page 19).

For insight with a personal touch, consider the tour companies and individual Florentine guides listed here. Hardworking and creative, they offer a worthwhile array of organized sightseeing activities. Study their websites for details. If you're taking a city tour, remember that individuals save money with a scheduled public tour (such as those offered daily by Florencetown or Artviva). If you're traveling as a family or small group, however, you're likely to save money by booking a private guide (since rates are based on roughly €55/hour for any size of group).

Walking (and Biking) Tours

Artviva Walking Tours—This company offers a variety of tours (up to 12/day year-round) featuring downtown Florence, museum highlights, and Tuscany day trips. Their guides are native English-speakers. The three-hour "Original Florence" walk hits the main sights but gets offbeat to weave a picture of Florentine life in medieval and Renaissance times. Tours go rain or shine with as few as four participants (€25, daily at 9:15). Museum tours include the Uffizi Gallery (€39, includes admission, 2 hours), Accademia (called "Original David" tour, €35, includes admission, 1 hour), and "Original Florence in One Day" (€94, includes admission to Uffizi and Accademia, 6 hours). Their brochure and website list

Make Reservations to Avoid Lines

Florence has an optional reservation system for its state-run sights, which include the Accademia, Uffizi Gallery, Bargello, Medici Chapels, and the Pitti Palace. Many travelers skip the reservation process by getting a Florence Card instead (see page 457).

If you make reservations, I'd recommend getting them only for the Accademia (Michelangelo's *David*) and the Uffizi (Renaissance paintings), but not the others.

The Brancacci Chapel is the only sight in Florence that requires reservations (even with the Florence Card). These are free and simple to make a day in advance. For details, see page 482.

The Uffizi and Accademia

If you're not planning to get a Florence Card, your best strategy is to get reservations for these two top sights as soon as you know when you'll be in town. Although you can generally get an entry time for the Accademia within a few days, the Uffizi can be booked well in advance.

There are several ways to make a reservation: Have your hotelier arrange it, call the reservation number directly, book online, take a tour, or go in person in advance to the museums or the Orsanmichele Church ticket window. Here are details on these options:

• When you make your **hotel** reservation, ask if they can book your museum reservations for you (some hoteliers will do this for free; others charge a €3-5 fee). This is your easiest option.

• Reserve by **phone** before you leave the States (from the US, dial 011-39-055-294-883, or within Italy call 055-294-883; €4/ticket reservation fee; booking office open Mon-Fri 8:30-18:30,

more activities and events, including talks by artists, writers, and experts on wine and cuisine (Mon-Sat 8:00-18:00, Sun 8:30-13:30, near Piazza della Repubblica at Via dei Sassetti 1, second floor, above Odeon Cinema, tel. 055-264-5033 during day or mobile 329-613-2730 from 18:00-20:00, www.italy.artviva.com).

Florencetown Tours on Foot or by Bike—This well-organized company runs a variety of English-language tours. The boss, Luca Perfetto, offers student rates (10 percent discount) to anyone with this book, with an additional 10 percent off for second tours. Three tours—their basic town walk, bike tour, and cook-

Sat 8:30-12:30, closed Sun). The reservation line is often busy, and even if you get through, you may be disconnected while on hold. Be persistent and try again. When you do get through, an English-speaking operator walks you through the process, and a few minutes later you say *grazie*, with an appointment and a six-digit confirmation number. Bring the confirmation(s) with you and pay cash at the sight(s). The advantage to phoning versus booking online is that you pay nothing upfront when you phone.

• Using a credit card, you can reserve your visit **online.** Pricey middleman sites—such as www.uffizi.com and www.tick italy.com—are reliable, but their booking fees are exorbitant, running about €10 per ticket. Or you could take your chances with the city's troublesome official site (www.firenzemusei.it) in the hopes that its glitches have been fixed. It's the cheapest place to make reservations online (€4/ticket reservation fee), but even when it's working, the site often reverts to Italian-only (*"Annulia operazione"* means "cancel!"), you can't book a time before noon, and some readers report not receiving vouchers they've paid for.

• Take a **tour** that includes your museum admission. Artviva Walking Tours offers tours of the Uffizi (€39/person, 2 hours), Accademia (€35/person, 1 hour), and both museums (€94/person, 6 hours; see listing on page 451, or visit www.italy.artviva .com).

• To **reserve in Florence**, here are your choices: call the reservation number (see above); ask your hotelier for help; or head to the booking window at Orsanmichele Church (€4 reservation fee, daily 10:00-17:00, along Via de' Calzaiuoli—see location on map on page 462). For another Uffizi option, go to its ticket office and pay cash (Tue-Sun 8:15-18:50, use the main entrance— door #2, enter to the left of the ticket-buying line).

Off-Season: If you're in Florence off-season (Nov-March), you can probably get into the Uffizi or Accademia without a reservation in the late afternoon (after 16:00). But why not make a reservation? After seeing hundreds of bored tourists waiting in lines, it's hard not to be amazed at their cluelessness.

ing class—are worth considering: The "Walk and Talk Florence" tour, which takes 2.5 hours, hits all the basic spots, including the Oltrarno neighborhood (€19, daily at 10:00). The "I Bike Florence" tour gives you two hours on a vintage one-speed bike following a fast-talking guide on a two-hour blitz of the town's top sights (€29, daily at 10:00 and 15:00, helmets optional, 15 stops on both sides of the river; in bad weather, the bike tours go as a €19 walking tour). The cooking class costs €79 and includes a market tour; see the "Cooking Class" listing, below. Their office is two blocks from the Palazzo Vecchio at Via de Lamberti 1—find steps off Via de'

Florence at a Glance

▲▲▲**Accademia** Michelangelo's *David* and powerful (unfinished) *Prisoners*. Reserve ahead or get a Florence Card. **Hours:** Tue-Sun 8:15-18:50, closed Mon. See page 458.

▲▲▲**Duomo Museum** Underrated cathedral museum with sculptures. **Hours:** Mon-Sat 9:00-19:30, Sun 9:00-13:40. See page 469.

▲▲▲**Bargello** Underappreciated sculpture museum (Michelangelo, Donatello, Medici treasures). **Hours:** Tue-Sat 8:15-13:50, until 16:50 during special exhibits (typically April-Oct); also open first, third, and fifth Mon and second and fourth Sun of each month. See page 470.

▲▲▲**Uffizi Gallery** Greatest collection of Italian paintings anywhere. Reserve well in advance or get a Florence Card. **Hours:** Tue-Sun 8:15-18:50, closed Mon. See page 473.

▲▲**Museum of San Marco** Best collection anywhere of artwork by the early Renaissance master Fra Angelico. **Hours:** Tue-Fri 8:15-13:50, Sat 8:15-16:50; also open 8:15-16:50 on second and fourth Sun and 8:15-13:50 on first, third, and fifth Mon of each month. See page 460.

▲▲**Medici Chapels** Tombs of Florence's great ruling family, designed and carved by Michelangelo. **Hours:** Tue-Sat April-Oct 8:15-16:50, Nov-March 8:15-13:50; also open first, third, and fifth Sun and second and fourth Mon of each month. See page 463.

▲▲**Duomo** Gothic cathedral with colorful facade and the first dome built since ancient Roman times. **Hours:** Mon-Fri 10:00-17:00, Thu until 16:00 Oct-May, Sat 10:00-16:45, Sun 12:00-17:00. See page 465.

▲▲**Palazzo Vecchio** Fortified palace, once the home of the Medici family, wallpapered with history and Renaissance themes. **Hours:** Fri-Wed 9:00-19:00, often until 24:00 in summer, Thu 9:00-14:00. See page 475.

▲▲**Galileo Science Museum** Fascinating old clocks, telescopes, maps, and three of Galileo's fingers. **Hours:** Wed-Mon 9:30-18:00, Tue 9:30-13:00. See page 477.

▲▲**Santa Croce Church** Precious art, tombs of famous Florentines, and Brunelleschi's Pazzi Chapel in 14th-century church. **Hours:** Mon-Sat 9:30-17:30, Sun 13:00-17:30. See page 477.

▲▲**Church of Santa Maria Novella** Thirteenth-century Dominican church with Masaccio's famous 3-D painting. **Hours:** Church—Mon-Thu 9:00-17:30, Fri 11:00-17:30, Sat 9:00-17:00, Sun 13:00-17:00; museum—Mon-Thu and Sat 9:00-17:00, closed Fri and Sun. See page 478.

▲▲**Pitti Palace** Several museums in lavish palace plus sprawling Boboli and Bardini Gardens. **Hours:** Palatine Gallery, Royal Apartments, and Modern Art Gallery: Tue-Sun 8:15-18:50, closed Mon; Argenti Museum, Costume Gallery, Porcelain Museum, and Boboli and Bardini Gardens: Daily 8:15-18:30, until 19:30 June-Aug, closed first and last Mon of each month, shorter hours in winter. See page 479.

▲▲**Brancacci Chapel** Works of Masaccio, early Renaissance master who reinvented perspective. **Hours:** Mon and Wed-Sat 10:00-17:00, Sun 13:00-17:00, closed Tue. Reservations required. See page 482.

▲▲**San Miniato Church** Sumptuous Renaissance chapel and sacristy showing scenes of St. Benedict. **Hours:** Daily April-Oct 8:30-19:30, Nov-March 8:30-13:00. See page 484.

▲**Medici-Riccardi Palace** Lorenzo the Magnificent's home, with fine art, frescoed ceilings, and Gozzoli's lovely Chapel of the Magi. **Hours:** Thu-Tue 9:00-19:00, closed Wed. See page 464.

▲**Climbing the Duomo's Dome** Grand view into the cathedral, close-up of dome architecture, and 463 steps to a glorious Florence vista. **Hours:** Mon-Fri 8:30-19:00, Sat 8:30-17:40, closed Sun. Long and slow lines, go early, no reservations. See page 468.

▲**Campanile** Views similar to Duomo's, 50 fewer steps, and fewer lines. **Hours:** Daily 8:30-19:30. See page 468.

▲**Baptistery** Bronze doors fit to be the gates of paradise. **Hours:** Doors always viewable; interior open Mon-Sat 12:15-19:00 except first Sat of each month 8:30-14:00, Sun 8:30-14:00. See page 469.

▲**Ponte Vecchio** Famous bridge lined with gold and silver shops. **Hours:** Bridge always open (shops closed at night). See page 476.

▲**Casa Buonarroti** Early, lesser-known works by Michelangelo. **Hours:** Wed-Mon 10:00-17:00, closed Tue. See page 478.

▲**Piazzale Michelangelo** Hilltop square with stunning view of Duomo and Florence. **Hours:** Always open. See page 483.

Calzaiuoli on the river side of Orsanmichele Church, tel. 055-012-3944, www.florencetown.com).

Walks Inside Florence—Three art historians—Paola Barubiani and her partners Emma Molignoni and Marzia Valbonesi—provide quality guiding. Their company offers a daily three-hour introductory tour (€60/person or €180 for groups up to 8 people, outside except for a visit inside to see *David*) and three-hour private tours as well (€60/hour for up to 4 people, ask about Rick Steves discount, mobile 335-526-6496, www.walksinsideflorence.com, paola@walksinsideflorence.it).

Florentia—Top-notch, private walking tours—geared for thoughtful, well-heeled travelers with longer-than-average attention spans—are led by Florentine scholars. The tours range from introductory city walks and museum visits to in-depth thematic walks, such as the Oltrarno neighborhood, "Unusual Florence," and side-trips into Tuscany (tours-€175/half-day, €350/day, reserve in advance, tel. 338-890-8625, www.florentia.org, info@florentia.org).

Context Florence—This scholarly group of graduate students and professors leads "walking seminars," such as a three-hour study of Michelangelo's work and influence (€85/person, includes Accademia admission) and a two-hour evening orientation stroll (€35/person). I enjoyed the fascinating three-hour fresco workshop (€75/person, you take home a fresco you make yourself). See their website for other innovative offerings: Medici walk, lecture series, food walks, kids' tours, and programs in Venice, Rome, Naples, London, and Paris (tel. 069-762-5204, US tel. 888-467-1986, www.contexttravel.com, info@contexttravel.com).

Florencetown Cooking Class and Market Tour

For something special, consider this five-hour experience. You'll start with a trip to the Mercato Centrale for shopping and tasting, then settle into their kitchen for a cooking lesson, and finish with a big feast eating everything you've just cooked. You'll meet butchers and bakers, and make bruschetta, pasta, a main course, and dessert (likely tiramisu). Groups are intimate and small (from 1-14 people, €79/person, 10 percent Rick Steves discount, Mon-Sat 10:00-15:00, runs rain or shine, chef Giovanni, Via de Lamberti 1, tel. 055-012-3944, www.florencetown.com).

Local Guides for Private Tours

Alessandra Marchetti, a Florentine who has lived in the US, gives private walking tours of Florence and driving tours of Tuscany (€60-75/hour, mobile 347-386-9839, aleoberm@tin.it). **Paola Migliorini** and her partners at Tuscany Tours offer museum tours, city walking tours, private cooking classes, wine tours, and Tuscan excursions by van—you can tailor tours as you like (€55/hour without car, €65/hour in an 8-seat van, tel. 055-472-448, mobile 347-657-2611, www.florencetour.com, info@florencetour.com); they also do private tours from the cruise-ship port of Livorno. **Karin Kibby**, an Oregonian living in Livorno who leads Rick Steves tours, also offers day tours throughout Tuscany, including excursions for cruise-ship passengers docking at Livorno. She'll work with you to find the best solution for your budget and interests (2-10 people, mobile 333-108-6348, karinkintuscany@yahoo.it).

Hop-on, Hop-off Bus Tours

Around town, you'll see big double-decker sightseeing buses double-parking near major sights. Tourists on the top deck can listen to brief recorded descriptions of the sights, snap photos, and enjoy an effortless drive-by look at the major landmarks (€22, valid for two days, pay as you board, www.firenze.city-sightseeing.it). As the name implies, you can hop off when you want and catch the next bus (usually every 30 minutes). As most sights are buried in the old center where big buses can't go, Florence doesn't really lend itself to this kind of tour bus. Look at the route map before committing.

Sights in Florence

You have two good options for bypassing the long lines at Florence's top two sights, the Accademia and Uffizi Gallery. Either buy a Florence Card (see below) or make reservations to visit both sights (see page 452 for details).

Florence Card

The pricey Florence Card (€50) gives you admission to many top sights (including the Uffizi Gallery and Accademia), plus many lesser ones. It also gives you free use of Florence city buses.

Though the card is unlikely to save you much money, it can certainly save time. With the card, you don't need reservations and don't need to wait in ticket-buying lines. You simply go to the entrance, show the card, and walk in (though there may be delays at top sights if they're reached maximum capacity). For people seeing five or six major sights in a short time, the card is probably worth it. (But if you only want to see the Uffizi and Accademia, you'll save at least €20 by making reservations instead; see page 452.)

The Florence Card is valid for 72 hours from when you validate it at your first museum (e.g., Tue at 15:00 until Fri at 15:00). It includes the regular admission price as well as any temporary exhibits (which are commonly tacked on at major sights such as the Uffizi). The card is good for one visit per sight and is not shareable.

Non-EU citizens are not eligible for discounts.

To figure out if the Florence Card is a good deal for you, tally up the entry fees of what you want to see. For example, here's a list of popular sights and their admission fees:

Uffizi Gallery (€6.50 base price, usually €11 with temporary exhibits, as much as €15 with €4 reservation fee)

Accademia (same fees as Uffizi, above)

Palazzo Vecchio (€6)

Bargello (€4 base, €7 with exhibits)

Medici Chapels (€7 base, €9 with exhibits)

Museum of San Marco (€4)

Medici-Riccardi Palace (€5 base, €7 with exhibits)

If you saw these sights without the card, you'd pay about €60, including the exhibit and reservation fees. Other covered sights featured in this book are the: Pitti Palace (both Palatine Gallery and Boboli Gardens), Brancacci Chapel (though you still must make a free reservation), Museum of Precious Stones, Palazzo Davanzati, and Museum of Santa Maria Novella. The card is great for popping into lesser sights you otherwise wouldn't pay for. For a complete list of included sights, see www.firenzecard.it.

Notable exceptions are: the Duomo dome climb, Campanile, Duomo Museum, Baptistery, Church of Santa Maria Novella, Santa Croce Church, Galileo Science Museum, Casa Buonarroti, Casa di Dante, and the two Leonardo museums.

Getting the card makes the most sense in peak season, from April through October, when crowds are worst. Off-season travelers could do without it and probably save a few euros.

You can buy the card at many participating outlets. The best places to buy (with no lines) are: the TI at Via Cavour 1 red (a couple of blocks north of the Duomo), the Uffizi Gallery's door #2 (enter to the left of the ticket-buying line), or the never-crowded Museum of Santa Maria Novella (near the train station). You can also buy the card online (www.firenzecard.it), obtain a voucher, and then pick up the card at TI or some participating sights.

Think ahead to make the most of your card. Validate it only when you're ready to tackle the covered sights on three consecutive days. Make sure the sights you want to visit will be open (many sights are closed Sundays or Mondays). For details, see the "Daily Reminder" on page 446.

North of the Arno River
North of the Duomo (Cathedral)
▲▲▲**Accademia (Galleria dell'Accademia)**—When you look into the eyes of Michelangelo's magnificent sculpture of *David*, you're looking into the eyes of Renaissance Man.

In 1501, Michelangelo Buonarroti, a 26-year-old Florentine, was commissioned to carve a large-scale work. The figure comes from a Bible story. The Israelites are surrounded by barbarian warriors, who are led by a brutish giant named Goliath. When

the giant challenges the Israelites to send out someone to fight him, a young shepherd boy steps forward. Armed only with a sling, David defeats the giant. This 17-foot-tall symbol of divine victory over evil represents a new century and a whole new Renaissance outlook.

Originally, *David* was meant to stand on the roofline of the Duomo, but was placed more prominently at the entrance of Palazzo Vecchio (where a copy stands today). In the 19th century, *David* was moved indoors for his own protection, and stands under a wonderful Renaissance-style dome designed just for him.

Nearby are some of the master's other works, including his powerful (unfinished) *Prisoners, St. Matthew,* and a *Pietà* (possibly by one of his disciples). Florentine Michelangelo Buonarroti, who would work tirelessly through the night, believed that the sculptor was a tool of God, responsible only for chipping away at the stone until the intended sculpture emerged. Beyond the magic marble are some mildly interesting pre-Renaissance and Renaissance paintings, including a couple of lighter-than-air Botticellis, the plaster model of Giambologna's *Rape of the Sabines,* and a musical instrument collection with an early piano.

Cost and Hours: €6.50, up to €11 with mandatory temporary exhibits, plus €4 fee for reservation (see page 452 for details), Tue-Sun 8:15-18:50, closed Mon, last entry 45 minutes before closing, Via Ricasoli 60, tel. 055-238-8609 or 055-294-883, www.polo museale.firenze.it).

Avoiding Lines: In peak season (April-Oct), the museum is most crowded on Sun, Tue, and right when it opens. It's smart to reserve ahead (see page 452) or buy the Florence Card (see page 457). Those with reservations or the Florence Card line up at the entrance labeled *With Reservations.* On off-season weekdays (Nov-March) before 8:30 or after 16:00, you can sometimes get in with no reservation and no lines.

Audioguides: The museum rents a €5.50 audioguide (€8/2 people; rent from souvenir counter in ticket lobby). You can download a free Rick Steves audio tour of the Accademia to your mobile device; see page 19.

Nearby: Piazza S.S. Annunziata, behind the Accademia, displays lovely Renaissance harmony. Facing the square are two fine buildings: the 15th-century Santissima Annunziata church (worth

a peek) and Filippo Brunelleschi's Hospital of the Innocents (Spedale degli Innocenti, not worth going inside), with terra-cotta medallions by Luca della Robbia. Built in the 1420s, the hospital is considered the first Renaissance building. I love sleeping on this square (at the recommended Hotel Loggiato dei Serviti) and picnicking here during the day (with the riff-raff, who remind me of the persistent gap—today as in Medici times—between those who appreciate fine art and those just looking for some cheap wine).

▲▲Museum of San Marco (Museo di San Marco)—Located one block north of the Accademia, this 15th-century monastery houses the greatest collection anywhere of frescoes and paintings by the early Renaissance master Fra Angelico.

The ground floor features the monk's paintings, along with some works by Fra Bartolomeo. Upstairs are 43 cells decorated

by Fra Angelico and his assistants. While the monk/painter was trained in the medieval religious style, he also learned and adopted Renaissance techniques and sensibilities, producing works that blended Christian symbols and Renaissance realism. Don't miss the cell of Savonarola, the charismatic monk who rode in from the Christian right, threw out the Medici, turned Florence into a theocracy, sponsored "bonfires of the vanities" (burning books, paintings, and so on), and was finally burned himself when Florence decided to change channels.

Cost and Hours: €4, Tue-Fri 8:15-13:50, Sat 8:15-16:50; also open 8:15-16:50 on second and fourth Sun and 8:15-13:50 on first, third, and fifth Mon of each month; last entry 30 minutes before closing, reservations possible but unnecessary, on Piazza San Marco, tel. 055-238-8608, www.polomuseale.firenze.it.

Museum of Precious Stones (Museo dell'Opificio delle Pietre Dure)—This unusual gem of a museum features room after room of exquisite mosaics of inlaid marble and other stones. The Medici loved colorful stone table tops and floors; you'll even find landscapes and portraits (find Cosimo I in Room I). Upstairs, you'll see wooden work benches from the Medici workshop (1588), complete with foot-powered power tools. Rockhounds can browse 500 different stones (lapis lazuli, quartz, agate, marble, and so on) and the tools used to cut and inlay them. There's English info in each room.

Cost and Hours: €4, Mon-Sat 8:15-14:00, closed Sun, around corner from Accademia at Via degli Alfani 78, tel. 055-265-1357.

Church of San Lorenzo—This red-brick dome—which looks like the Duomo's little sister—is the Medici church and the burial

place of the family's founder, Giovanni di Bicci de' Medici (1360-1429). The facade is big, ugly, and unfinished, because Pope Leo X (also a Medici) pulled the plug on the project due to dwindling funds—after Michelangelo had labored on it for four years (1516-1520). Inside, though, is the spirit of Florence in the 1420s, with gray-and-white columns and arches in perfect Renaissance symmetry and simplicity. The Brunelleschi-designed church is lit by an even, diffused light. The Medici coat of arms (with the round pills of these "medics") decorates the ceiling, and everywhere are images of St. Lawrence, the Medici patron saint who was martyred on a grill.

Highlights of the church include two finely sculpted Donatello pulpits (in the nave). In the Martelli Chapel (left wall of the left transept), Filippo Lippi's *Annunciation* features a smiling angel greeting Mary in a sharply 3-D courtyard. Light shines through the vase in the foreground, like the Holy Spirit entering Mary's womb. The Old Sacristy (far left corner), designed by Brunelleschi, was the burial chapel for the Medici. Bronze doors by Donatello flank the sacristy's small altar. Overhead, the dome above the altar shows the exact arrangement of the heavens on July 4, 1442, leaving scholars to hypothesize about why that particular date was used. Back in the nave, the round inlaid marble in the floor before the main altar marks where Cosimo the Elder—Lorenzo the Magnificent's grandfather—is buried. Assistants in the church provide information on request, and the information brochure is free and in English.

Cost and Hours: €3.50, Feb-Oct Mon-Sat 10:00-17:00, Sun 13:30-17:00, closed Nov-Jan.

Nearby: Outside the church, along the left side, is a **cloister** with peek-a-boo Duomo views and the **San Lorenzo Museum**. This collection of fancy reliquaries is included in your church admission, but is hardly worth the walk, except to see Donatello's grave. Also in the cloister is the **Laurentian Library** (not included in church entry and only open during special exhibits). The library, largely designed by Michelangelo, stars his impressive staircase, which widens imperceptibly as it descends. Michelangelo also did

FLORENCE

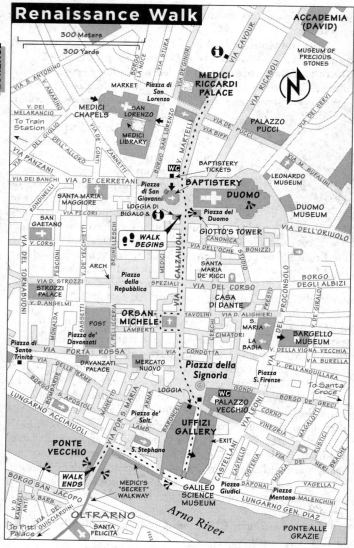

Renaissance Walk

300 Meters

300 Yards

ACCADEMIA (DAVID)

MUSEUM OF PRECIOUS STONES

MEDICI-RICCARDI PALACE

MARKET

Piazza di San Lorenzo

MEDICI CHAPELS

SAN LORENZO

MEDICI LIBRARY

To Train Station

PALAZZO PUCCI

LEONARDO MUSEUM

BAPTISTERY TICKETS

WC

BAPTISTERY

Piazza di San Giovanni

LOGGIA DI BIGALO &

DUOMO

Piazza del Duomo

DUOMO MUSEUM

WALK BEGINS

GIOTTO'S TOWER

SANTA MARIA MAGGIORE

SAN GAETANO

CANONICA

SANTA MARIA DE' RICCI

ARCH

Piazza della Repubblica

STROZZI PALACE

CASA DI DANTE

ORSAN-MICHELE

POST

Piazza de' Davanzati

BARGELLO MUSEUM

S. MARIA LA BADIA

Piazza di Santa Trinita

DAVANZATI PALACE

MERCATO NUOVO

Piazza della Signoria

Piazza S. Firenze

To Santa Croce

LOGGIA

WC

PALAZZO VECCHIO

PONTE VECCHIO

Piazza de' Salt.

UFFIZI GALLERY

EXIT

WALK ENDS

S. Stephano

MEDICI'S "SECRET" WALKWAY

GALILEO SCIENCE MUSEUM

Piazza Giudici

Piazza Mentana

OLTRARNO

Arno River

PONTE ALLE GRAZIE

To Pitti Palace

SANTA FELICITA

the walls in the vestibule (entrance) that feature empty niches, scrolls, and oddly tapering pilasters. Climb the stairs and enter the Reading Room—a long, rectangular hall with a coffered-wood ceiling—designed by Michelangelo to host scholars enjoying the Medici's collection of manuscripts. The library is well-worthwhile if it's open (€3, includes special exhibits, generally 9:30-13:00).

A **street market** bustles outside the church (listed after the

A Renaissance Walk Through Florence

During the Dark Ages, it was especially obvious to the people of Italy—sitting on the rubble of Rome—that there had to be a brighter age on the horizon. The long-awaited rebirth, or Renaissance, began in Florence for good reason. Wealthy because of its cloth industry, trade, and banking; powered by a fierce city-state pride (locals would pee into the Arno with gusto, knowing rival city-state Pisa was downstream); and fertile with more than its share of artistic genius (imagine guys like Michelangelo and Leonardo attending the same high school)—Florence was a natural home for this cultural explosion.

Take a two-hour walk through the core of Renaissance Florence from the Duomo (cathedral) to Ponte Vecchio on the Arno River. You can download a free Rick Steves audio tour of this walk (see page 19).

Begin at the Duomo to marvel at the dome that kicked off the architectural Renaissance. Step inside the Baptistery to view a ceiling covered with preachy, flat, 2-D, medieval mosaic art. Then, to learn what happened when art met math, check out the realistic 3-D reliefs on the doors; the man who painted them, Giotto, also designed the bell tower—an early example of a Renaissance genius who excelled in many areas.

Continue toward the river on Florence's great pedestrian mall, Via de' Calzaiuoli—part of the original grid plan given to the city by the ancient Romans. Stop by any gelato shop for some cool refreshment. Down a few blocks, compare medieval and Renaissance statues on the exterior of the Orsanmichele Church. Via de' Calzaiuoli connects the cathedral with the central square (Piazza della Signoria), the city palace (Palazzo Vecchio), and the Uffizi Gallery, which contains the greatest collection of Italian Renaissance paintings in captivity. Finally, walk through the Uffizi courtyard—a statuary thinktank of Renaissance greats—to the Arno River and Ponte Vecchio.

Medici Chapels, next). Around the back end of the church is the entrance to the Medici Chapels and the New Sacristy, designed by Michelangelo for a later generation of dead Medici.

▲▲Medici Chapels (Cappelle Medicee)—The burial site of the ruling Medici family in the Church of San Lorenzo includes the dusky Crypt; the big, domed Chapel of Princes; and the magnificent, all-Michelangelo New Sacristy, featuring the master's architecture, tombs, and statues. The Medici made their money in

textiles and banking, and patronized a dream team of Renaissance artists that put Florence on the cultural map. Michelangelo, who spent his teen years living with the Medici, was commissioned for the family's final tribute.

Cost and Hours: €7, €9 with mandatory exhibits, audioguide-€5.50 (€8/2 people), Tue-Sat April-Oct 8:15-16:50, Nov-March 8:15-13:50; also open first, third, and fifth Sun and second and fourth Mon of each month; last entry 30 minutes before closing; modest dress required, tel. 055-238-8602, www.polomuseale .firenze.it.

▲**San Lorenzo Market**—Florence's vast open-air market sprawls around the Church of San Lorenzo. Most of the leather stalls are run by Iranians selling South American leather that was tailored in Italy. Prices are soft (daily 9:00-19:00, closed Mon in winter, between the Duomo and train station).

▲**Mercato Centrale (Central Market)**—Florence's giant iron-and-glass-covered central market, a wonderland of picturesque produce, is fun to explore. While the nearby San Lorenzo Market—with its garment stalls in the streets—feels like a step up from a haphazard flea market, the Mercato Centrale retains a Florentine elegance. Wander around. You'll see parts of the cow you'd never dream of eating (no, that's not a turkey neck), enjoy generous free samples, watch pasta making, and have your pick of plenty of fun eateries sloshing out cheap and tasty pasta to locals (Mon-Sat 7:00-14:00, in winter open Sat until 17:00, closed Sun). For eating ideas in and around the market, see "Eating in Florence," later.

▲**Medici-Riccardi Palace (Palazzo Medici-Riccardi)**— Lorenzo the Magnificent's home is worth a look for its art. The tiny Chapel of the Magi contains color-ful Renaissance gems like the *Procession of the Magi* frescoes by Benozzo Gozzoli. The former library has a Baroque ceiling fresco by Luca Giordano, a prolific artist from Naples known as "Fast Luke" *(Luca fa presto)* for his speedy workmanship. While the Medici originally occupied this 1444 house, in the 1700s it became home to the Riccardi family, who added the Baroque flourishes.

Cost and Hours: €5, €7 with mandatory special exhibits, Thu-Tue 9:00-19:00, closed Wed, last entry 30 minutes before closing; ticket entrance is north of the main gated entrance, Via Cavour 3, tel. 055-276-0340, www.palazzo-medici.it.

Leonardo Museums—Two different-but-similar entrepreneurial establishments several blocks apart show off reproductions of

Leonardo's ingenious inventions. Either one is fun for anyone who wants to crank the shaft and spin the ball bearings of Leonardo's fertile imagination. While there are no actual historic artifacts, each museum shows several dozen of Leonardo's inventions and experiments made into working models. You might see a full-size armored tank, walk into a chamber of mirrors, operate a rotating crane, or watch experiments in flying. The exhibits are described in English, and what makes these places special is that you're encouraged to touch and play with the models—it's great for kids. The museum on Via dei Servi is a bit larger.

Cost and Hours: Admission to each museum is €7. Museo Leonardo da Vinci—daily 10:00-19:00, closes at 18:00 in winter, Via dei Servi 66 red, tel. 055-282-966, www.mostredileonardo .com. Le Macchine di Leonardo da Vinci—April-Oct daily 9:30-19:30; Nov-March Mon-Fri 11:00-17:00, Sat-Sun 9:30-19:30; in Galleria Michelangelo at Via Cavour 21, tel. 055-899-9471, www .macchinedileonardo.com.

Duomo and Nearby

▲▲**Duomo (Cattedrale di Santa Maria del Fiore)**—Florence's Gothic cathedral has the third-longest nave in Christendom. The church's noisy neo-Gothic facade from the 1870s is covered with pink, green, and white Tuscan marble. In the interior, you'll see a huge *Last Judgment* by Giorgio Vasari and Federico Zuccari (inside the dome). Much of the church's great art is stored in the Duomo Museum behind the church.

The cathedral's claim to artistic fame is Brunelleschi's magnificent dome—the first Renaissance dome and the model for domes to follow. Think of the confidence of the age: The Duomo was built with a big hole in its roof, awaiting a dome...but it was built before the technology to span the hole with a dome even existed. No *problema.* They knew that someone soon could rise to the challenge... and the local architect Filippo Brunelleschi did. First, he built the grand white skeletal ribs, which you can see, then filled them in with interlocking bricks in a herringbone pattern. The dome grew upward like an igloo, supporting itself as it proceeded from the

FLORENCE

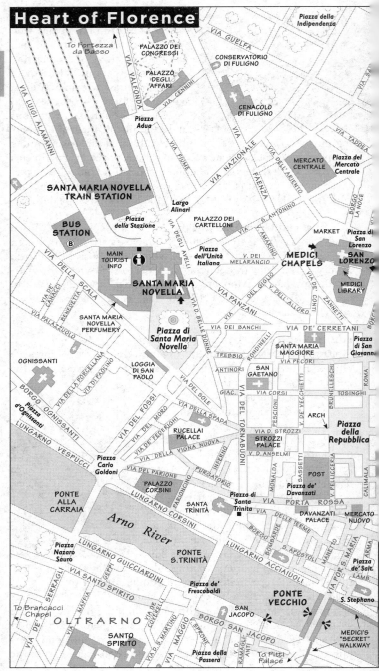

base. When the ribs reached the top, Brunelleschi arched them in and fixed them in place with the cupola at the top. His dome, built in only 14 years, was the largest since Rome's Pantheon.

Massive crowds line up to see the huge church, which is a major sight but not worth a long wait. Either go late (the crowds subside by late afternoon), or take the Terraces tour mentioned below.

Cost and Hours: Free entry, Mon-Fri 10:00-17:00, Thu until 16:00 Oct-May, Sat 10:00-16:45, Sun 12:00-17:00, modest dress code enforced, tel. 055-230-2885, www.operaduomo.firenze.it.

Crowd-Beating Tip: Taking the "**Terraces of the Cathedral and Dome**" tour allows you to skip the long lines to enter the cathedral and to climb the dome. After a short guided tour of the interior, you'll climb up onto the exterior terrace, where great views reward the hike up the stairs (see "Climbing the Duomo's Dome," next). When the tour is finished on the terrace, you can continue on your own up to the top of the dome (€15, 45 minutes; offered Mon-Fri at 10:30, 12:00, and 15:00; Sat at 10:30 and 12:00, no tours on Sun, buy tickets at nearby Duomo Museum and they'll tell you where to meet your guide). If you're planning to climb the dome anyway (€8), the tour is a fine value.

▲**Climbing the Duomo's Dome**—For a grand view into the cathedral from the base of the dome, a peek at some of the tools

used in the dome's construction, a chance to see Brunelleschi's "dome-within-a-dome" construction, a glorious Florence view from the top, and the equivalent of 463 plunges on a Renaissance StairMaster, climb the dome. Michelangelo, setting out to construct the dome of St. Peter's in Rome, drew inspiration from the dome of Florence. He said, "I'll make its sister...bigger, but not more beautiful." To avoid the long, dreadfully slow-moving line, arrive by 8:30 or drop by very late. Those taking the "Terraces" tour of the Duomo (see earlier) can skip the line.

Cost and Hours: €8, cash only, Mon-Fri 8:30-19:00, Sat 8:30-17:40, closed Sun, last entry 40 minutes before closing, enter from outside church on north side, tel. 055-230-2885.

▲**Campanile (Giotto's Tower)**—The 270-foot bell tower has 50 fewer steps than the Duomo's dome (but that's still 413 steps—no elevator); offers a faster, less-crowded climb; and has a view of the Duomo to boot, but the cage-like top makes taking good photographs difficult.

Cost and Hours: €6, daily 8:30-19:30, last entry 40 minutes before closing.

▲**Baptistery**—Michelangelo said its bronze doors were fit to be the gates of paradise. Check out the gleaming copies of Lorenzo Ghiberti's bronze doors facing the Duomo (the original panels are in the Duomo Museum). Making a breakthrough in perspective, Ghiberti used mathematical laws to create the illusion of receding distance on a basically flat surface.

The doors on the north side of the building were designed by Ghiberti when he was young; he'd won the honor and opportunity by beating Brunelleschi in a competition (the rivals' original entries are in the Bargello).

Inside, sit and savor the medieval mosaic ceiling, where it's always Judgment Day and Jesus is giving the ultimate thumbs-up and thumbs-down. The rest of the ceiling mosaics tell the history of the world, from Adam and Eve (over the north/entrance doors, top row), to Noah and the Flood (over south doors, top row), to the life of Christ (second row), to the beheading of John the Baptist (bottom row)—all bathed in the golden glow of pre-Renaissance heaven.

Cost and Hours: €4, €7 with mandatory exhibits, interior open Mon-Sat 12:15-19:00 except first Sat of month 8:30-14:00, Sun 8:30-14:00, last entry 30 minutes before closing, tel. 055-230-2885. The bronze doors are on the outside, so they are always "open" and viewable.

▲▲▲**Duomo Museum (Museo dell'Opera del Duomo)**—The

underrated cathedral museum, behind the church (at Via del Proconsolo 9), is great if you like sculpture. On the ground floor, look for a late Michelangelo *Pietà* and statues from the original Baptistery facade. Upstairs, you'll find Brunelleschi's models for his dome, as well as Donatello's anorexic *Mary Magdalene* and playful choir loft. The museum features Ghiberti's original bronze "Gates of Paradise" panels (the ones on the Baptistery's doors today are copies); throughout years of restoration, only some of the panels have been on display, but as of late

June 2012, all are slated to be shown.

Cost and Hours: €6, Mon-Sat 9:00-19:30, Sun 9:00-13:40, last entry 40 minutes before closing, one of the few museums in Florence always open on Mon, Via del Proconsolo 9, tel. 055-230-2885, www.operaduomo.firenze.it. At this museum, you can purchase tickets for the "Terraces of the Cathedral and Dome" tour mentioned earlier (page 468), which allows you to bypass the long cathedral-entry and dome-climbing lines. The audioguide costs €5. Guided English tours are generally offered on Mon, Thu, Sun at 10:30 (€9).

Nearby: If you find this church art intriguing, head to the left around the back of the Duomo to find Via dello Studio (near the south transept), then walk a block toward the river to #23a. You can look through the open doorway of the Opera del Duomo art studio and see workers sculpting new statues, restoring old ones, or making exact copies. They're carrying on an artistic tradition that dates back to the days of Brunelleschi.

Between the Duomo and Piazza della Signoria

▲▲▲Bargello (Museo Nazionale)—This underappreciated sculpture museum is in a former police station-turned-prison that looks like a mini-Palazzo Vecchio. It has Donatello's very influential, painfully beautiful *David* (the first male nude to be sculpted in a thousand years), works by Michelangelo, and rooms of Medici treasures explained only in Italian (politely suggest to the staff that English descriptions would be wonderful).

Moody Donatello, who embraced realism with his lifelike statues, set the personal and artistic style for many Renaissance artists to follow. The best works are in the ground-floor room at the foot of the outdoor staircase and in the room directly above.

Cost and Hours: €4, €7 with mandatory exhibits, Tue-Sat 8:15-13:50, until 16:50 during exhibits (generally April-Oct); also open first, third, and fifth Mon and the second and fourth Sun of each month; last entry 40 minutes before closing, Via del Proconsolo 4, reservation tel. 055-238-8606, www.polomuseale.firenze.it.

Casa di Dante (Dante's House)—Dante Alighieri (1265-1321), the poet who gave us *The Divine Comedy,* is the Shakespeare of Italy, the father of the modern Italian language, and the face on the country's €2 coin. However, most Americans know little of him, and this museum is not the ideal place to start. Even though it has English information, this small museum (in a building near

where he likely lived) assumes visitors have prior knowledge of the poet. It's not a medieval-flavored house with period furniture—it's just a small, low-tech museum about Dante. Still, Dante lovers can trace his interesting life and works through pictures, models, and artifacts. And because the exhibits are as much about medieval Florence as they are about the man, novices can learn a little about Dante and the city he lived in.

Cost and Hours: €4, summer daily 10:00-18:00; winter Tue-Sun 10:00-17:00, closed Mon; last entry 30 minutes before closing, near the Bargello at Via Santa Margherita 1, tel. 055-219-416, www.museocasadidante.it.

▲**Orsanmichele Church**—In the ninth century, this loggia (covered courtyard) was a market used for selling grain (stored upstairs). Later, it was enclosed to make a church.

Outside are dynamic, statue-filled niches, some with accompanying symbols from the guilds that sponsored the art. Donatello's *St. Mark* and *St. George* (on the northeast and northwest corners) step out boldly in the new Renaissance style.

The interior has a glorious Gothic tabernacle (1359) housing the painted wooden panel that depicts *Madonna delle Grazie* (1346). The iron bars spanning the vaults were the Italian Gothic answer to the French Gothic external buttresses. Look for the rectangular holes in the piers—these were once wheat chutes that connected to the upper floors.

Cost and Hours: Free, Tue-Sun 10:00-17:00, closed Mon, niche sculptures always viewable from the outside. You can give the *Madonna della Grazie* a special thanks if you're in town when an evening concert is held inside the Orsanmichele (tickets sold on day of concert from door facing Via de' Calzaiuoli; also books Uffizi and Accademia tickets, ticket window open daily 10:00-17:00).

▲**Mercato Nuovo (a.k.a. the Straw Market)**—Just a block away, this market loggia is how Orsanmichele looked before it became a church. Originally a silk and straw market, Mercato Nuovo still functions as a rustic yet touristy market (at the intersection of Via Calimala and Via Porta Rossa). Prices are soft, but the San Lorenzo Market (listed earlier) is much better for haggling. Notice the circled X in the center, marking the spot where people hit after being hoisted up to the top and dropped as punishment for bankruptcy. You'll also find *Porcellino* (a statue of a wild boar nicknamed "little pig"), which people rub and give coins to in order to ensure their return to Florence. This new copy, while only a few years old, already has a polished snout. At the back corner, a wagon sells tripe (cow innards) sandwiches—a local favorite (daily 9:00-20:00).

▲**Piazza della Repubblica and Nearby**—This large square sits on the site of the original Roman Forum. Florence was a river-side garrison town set below the older town of Fiesole—essentially a rectangular fort with the square marking the intersection of the two main roads (Via Corso and Via Roma). The square's lone col-umn—nicknamed "the belly but-ton of Florence"—once marked the intersection (the Roman streets were about nine feet below

the present street level). All that survives of Roman Florence is this column and the city's street plan. Look at any map of Florence today (there's one by the benches—where the old boys hang out to talk sports and politics), and you'll see the ghost of Rome in its streets: a grid-plan city center surrounded by what was the Roman wall. The Braille model of the city makes the design clear.

Venerable cafés and stores line the square. During the 19th century, intellectuals met in cafés on the square. The La Rinascente department store, facing Piazza della Repubblica, is one of the city's mainstays (WC on fourth floor, continue up the stairs from there to the bar with a rooftop terrace with great Duomo and city views).

▲**Palazzo Davanzati**—This five-story, late-medieval tower house offers a rare look at a noble dwelling built in the 14th cen-

tury. Currently only the ground and first floors are open to visitors, though the remaining floors can be vis-ited by appointment. Like other buildings of the age, the exterior is festooned with 14th-century horse-tethering rings made out of iron, torch holders, and poles upon which to hang laundry and fly flags. Inside, though the furnishings are pretty sparse, you'll see richly painted walls, a long chute that functioned as a well, plenty of fireplaces, a lace display, and even a modern toilet.

Cost and Hours: €2, Tue-Sat 8:15-13:50; also open second and fourth Mon and first, third, and fifth Sun of each month; Via Porta Rossa 13, tel. 055-238-8610.

On and near Piazza della Signoria

The main civic center of Florence is dominated by the Palazzo Vecchio, Uffizi Gallery, and marble greatness of old Florence littering the cobbles. The Piazza della Signoria still vibrates with the echoes of Florence's past—executions, riots, and great celebrations. Today, it's a tourist's world with pigeons, postcards, horse buggies, and tired hubbies. And, if it would make your tired companion happy, stop in at the recommended but expensive **Rivoire** café to enjoy its fine desserts, pudding-thick hot chocolate, and the best view seats in town. It's expensive—but if you linger, it can be a great value.

▲▲▲**Uffizi Gallery**—This greatest collection of Italian paintings anywhere features works by Giotto, Leonardo, Raphael, Caravaggio, Rubens, Titian, and Michelangelo, and a roomful of Botticellis, including his *Birth of Venus*.

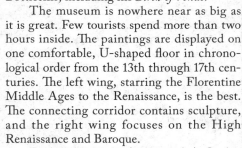

The museum is nowhere near as big as it is great. Few tourists spend more than two hours inside. The paintings are displayed on one comfortable, U-shaped floor in chronological order from the 13th through 17th centuries. The left wing, starring the Florentine Middle Ages to the Renaissance, is the best. The connecting corridor contains sculpture, and the right wing focuses on the High Renaissance and Baroque.

Essential stops are (in this order): Gothic altarpieces (narrative, pre-Realism, no real concern for believable depth) including Giotto's altarpiece, which progressed beyond "totem-pole angels"; Paolo Uccello's *Battle of San Romano,* an early study in perspective with a few obvious flubs (under restoration but hopefully back on display in 2012); and Fra Filippo Lippi's cuddly Madonnas. The Botticelli room is filled with masterpieces and classical fleshiness (the famous *Birth of Venus* and the *Allegory of Spring*), plus two minor works by Leonardo da Vinci. The octagonal classical sculpture room has a copy of Praxiteles' *Venus de' Medici,* considered the epitome of beauty in Elizabethan Europe. Next comes the view of Ponte Vecchio through the window, dreamy at sunset. Rounding it off are Michelangelo's only surviving easel painting, the round *Holy Family;* Raphael's noble *Madonna of the Goldfinch;* and Titian's voluptuous *Venus of Urbino.* Enjoy Duomo views from the café terrace.

Cost and Hours: €6.50, €11 with mandatory exhibits, extra €4 for recommended reservation, cash required to pick up reserved tickets; Tue-Sun 8:15-18:50, closed Mon, last entry 45 minutes before closing, museum info tel. 055-238-8651, www.polomuseale .firenze.it.

Uffizi Gallery Overview

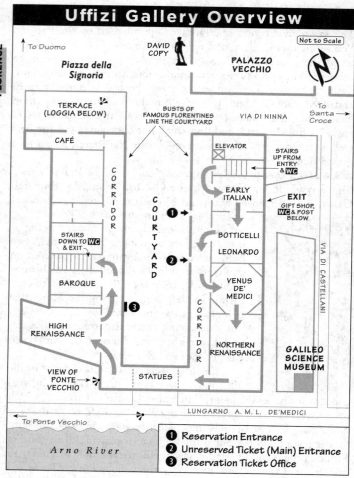

↑ To Duomo

Piazza della Signoria

DAVID COPY

PALAZZO VECCHIO

Not to Scale

TERRACE (LOGGIA BELOW)

CAFÉ

BUSTS OF FAMOUS FLORENTINES LINE THE COURTYARD

VIA DI NINNA

To Santa Croce

CORRIDOR

ELEVATOR

STAIRS UP FROM ENTRY & WC

EARLY ITALIAN

EXIT
GIFT SHOP, WC & POST BELOW

STAIRS DOWN TO WC & EXIT

COURTYARD

BOTTICELLI

LEONARDO

VIA DI CASTELLANI

BAROQUE

❸

VENUS DE' MEDICI

HIGH RENAISSANCE

CORRIDOR

NORTHERN RENAISSANCE

GALILEO SCIENCE MUSEUM

VIEW OF PONTE VECCHIO

STATUES

LUNGARNO A. M. L. DE'MEDICI

← To Ponte Vecchio

Arno River

❶ Reservation Entrance
❷ Unreserved Ticket (Main) Entrance
❸ Reservation Ticket Office

Avoiding Lines: To avoid the notoriously long ticket-buying lines, either book ahead (for details, see page 452) or get a Florence Card (see page 457). During summer and on weekends, the Uffizi can be booked up a month or more in advance. Sometimes, by the end of the day (an hour before closing), you can just walk right in, but generally you'll encounter lines even off-season (and waits of up to three hours in peak season, April-Oct). The busiest days are Tuesday, Saturday, and Sunday.

Getting In: There are several entrances (see map). Which one you use depends on whether you have a Florence Card, a reservation, or neither. Florence Card-holders enter at door #1 (labeled *Reservation Entrance*), close to the Palazzo Vecchio. There are two lines at this entrance: Get in the line for individuals, not groups. If you're buying a ticket, line up with everyone else at door #2. If you've made a reservation and need to pick up your ticket, go to door #3 (labeled *Reservation Ticket Office*); hand over your reservation number or voucher, pay in cash (if you didn't already pay when you made the reservation), and get your ticket. Then walk briskly past the 200-yard-long ticket-buying line—pondering the IQ of this gang—to door #1. Show your ticket and walk in. (You can check baggage, but can't bring bottled liquids inside the museum.)

Audioguides: A 1.5-hour audioguide costs €5.50 (€8/2 people; must leave ID). You can download a free Rick Steves audio tour of the Uffizi on your mobile device; see page 19.

In the Uffizi's Courtyard: Enjoy the courtyard (free), full of artists and souvenir stalls. (Swing by after dinner when it's completely empty.) The surrounding statues honor earthshaking Florentines: artists (Michelangelo), philosophers (Niccolò Machiavelli), scientists (Galileo), writers (Dante), explorers (Amerigo Vespucci), and the great patron of so much Renaissance thinking, Lorenzo "the Magnificent" de' Medici.

▲▲**Palazzo Vecchio**—With its distinctive castle turret and rustic stonework, Cosimo I de' Medici's fortified "Old Palace"—the City Hall—is a Florentine landmark.

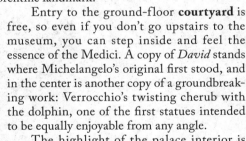

Entry to the ground-floor **courtyard** is free, so even if you don't go upstairs to the museum, you can step inside and feel the essence of the Medici. A copy of *David* stands where Michelangelo's original first stood, and in the center is another copy of a groundbreaking work: Verrocchio's twisting cherub with the dolphin, one of the first statues intended to be equally enjoyable from any angle.

The highlight of the palace interior is the **Grand Hall,** also called the Hall of Five Hundred, as it was designed to accommodate—and impress—that many guests. In the center of the ceiling is Cosimo I, the first Medici with a royal title, dressed as if he were Holy Roman Emperor. In a niche at the front is Leo X, the first of three Medici popes, and the walls show off Florence's victories over Pisa and Siena. Underneath Siena is Michelangelo's *Victory,* the prototype of the hall's other spiral-shaped statues (all of which came after Verrocchio's cherub in the courtyard).

After the Grand Hall, climb the stairs to visit a series of richly decorated rooms, including the Room of the Elements (where we see Cosimo I controlling the air, earth, fire, and water) and the private apartments of Grand Duchess Eleonora di Toledo (Cosimo's high-maintenance wife), which include a chapel decorated by Bronzino. The Room of the Lilies has two standout highlights: views of the Duomo, and Donatello's bronze *Judith and Holofernes*. The nearby Hall of Geographical Maps is full of maps made in a fit of post-1492 fascination with the wider world.

Cost and Hours: €6, €8 combo-ticket with Brancacci Chapel, Fri-Wed 9:00-19:00, often open until 24:00 in high season, Thu 9:00-14:00, ticket office closes one hour earlier (Piazza della Signoria, tel. 055-276-8224). The Palazzo Vecchio offers many kids' activities (call or ask at the reception by the ticket office). Skip the €4 audioguide (ID required) unless you want to know the fine details of Florentine political leaders. Free tours in English are offered daily, but the schedule varies and you must reserve (call to arrange).

Nearby: In the **loggia** on Piazza della Signoria, look for Benvenuto Cellini's bronze statue of Perseus holding the head of Medusa. The **plaque** on the pavement in front of the fountain marks the spot where the monk Savonarola was burned in MCDXCVIII, or 1498.

▲**Ponte Vecchio**—Florence's most famous bridge has long been lined with shops. Originally these were butcher shops that used the river as a handy disposal system. Then, when the powerful and princely Medici built the Vasari Corridor (described next) over the bridge, the stinky meat market was replaced by the more elegant gold and silver shops that remain there to this

day. A statue of Benvenuto Cellini, the master goldsmith of the Renaissance, stands in the center, ignored by the flood of tacky tourism. This is a romantic spot late at night, when lovers gather and a top-notch street musician performs.

Vasari Corridor—This elevated and enclosed passageway, constructed in 1565, gave the Medici a safe, private commute over Ponte Vecchio from their Pitti Palace home to their Palazzo Vecchio offices. It's open only by special appointment, and while enticing to lovers of Florence, the actual tour experience isn't much. Entering from inside the Uffizi Gallery, you walk along a modern-feeling hall (wide enough to carry a Medici on a sedan chair) across Ponte Vecchio, and end in the Pitti Palace. Half the corridor is lined with Europe's best collection of self-portraits, along with other paintings (mostly 17th- and 18th-century) that seem like they didn't make the cut to be hung on the walls of the Uffizi.

The best way to get inside the corridor is to go with a tour company such as Florencetown (€89; Tue, Fri, and Sun at 15:30; 2 hours, tel. 055-012-3944, www.florencetown.com) or Artviva (€84, Tue and Sat at 13:30, 3 hours, tel. 055-264-5033, www.italy.artviva .com). The tours, which include a tour of the Uffizi, are expensive because of steep city entrance fees and the requirement that groups be accompanied by attendants and a guide.

▲▲**Galileo Science Museum (Museo Galilei e Istituto di Storia della Scienza)**—When we think of the Florentine Renaissance, we think of visual arts: painting, mosaics, architec-

ture, and sculpture. But when the visual arts declined in the 1600s (abused and co-opted by political powers), music and science flourished in Florence. The first opera was written here. And Florence hosted many scientific breakthroughs, as you'll see in this fascinating collection of Renaissance and later clocks, telescopes, maps, and ingenious gadgets. Trace the technical innovations as modern science emerges from 1000 to 1900. One of the most talked-about bottles in Florence is the one here that contains Galileo's finger. Exhibits include various tools for gauging the world, from a compass and thermometer to Galileo's telescopes. Other displays delve into clocks, pumps, medicine, and chemistry. It's friendly, comfortably cool, never crowded, and just a block east of the Uffizi on the Arno River.

Cost and Hours: €8, €20 family ticket, Wed-Mon 9:30-18:00, Tue 9:30-13:00, last entry 30 minutes before closing, Piazza dei Giudici 1, tel. 055-265-311, recorded info tel. 055-293-493, www .museogalileo.it.

Tours: The €5 audioguide is well-produced, and offers both a highlights tour as well as dial-up info (with video) on each exhibit. The 1.5-hour English-language guided tour covers the collection plus behind-the-scenes areas, and includes hands-on demonstrations of some of the devices (€50 flat fee for 2-14 people, doesn't include museum entry, book at least a week in advance, great for kids, tel. 055-2653-1160, groups@museogalileo.it).

East of Piazza della Signoria

▲▲**Santa Croce Church**—This 14th-century Franciscan church, decorated with centuries of precious art, holds the tombs of great Florentines. The loud 19th-century Victorian Gothic facade faces a huge square ringed with tempting shops and littered with tired tourists. Escape into the church and admire its sheer height and spaciousness. On the left wall (as you face the altar) is the **tomb**

FLORENCE

of **Galileo Galilei** (1564-1642), the Pisan who lived his last years under house arrest near Florence. Having defied the Church by saying that the earth revolved around the sun, his heretical remains were only allowed in the church long after his death. Directly opposite (on the right wall) is the **tomb of Michelangelo Buonarroti** (1475-1564).

The first chapel to the right of the main altar features the famous fresco by Giotto of the *Death of St. Francis*. With simple but eloquent gestures, Francis' brothers bid him a sad farewell.

In the hallway near the bookstore, notice the photos of the devastating flood of 1966. Beyond that is the leather school (free entry).

Exit between the Rossini and Machiavelli tombs into the cloister (open-air courtyard). On the left, enter Brunelleschi's Pazzi Chapel, which captures the Renaissance in miniature.

Cost and Hours: €5, audioguide-€5, Mon-Sat 9:30-17:30, Sun 13:00-17:30, last entry 30 minutes before closing, modest dress code is enforced, 10-minute walk east of the Palazzo Vecchio along Borgo de' Greci, tel. 055-246-6105, www.santacroce.firenze .it. The leather school is free and sells tickets to the church. If the church has a long line, come here to avoid it (daily 10:00-18:00, has own entry behind church plus an entry within the church, www .leatherschool.com).

▲**Casa Buonarroti (Michelangelo's House)**—Fans enjoy a house standing on property once owned by Michelangelo. The house was built after Michelangelo's death by the artist's grand-nephew, who turned it into a little museum honoring his famous relative. You'll see some of Michelangelo's early, less-than-monumental statues and a few sketches. Be warned: Michelangelo's descendants attributed everything they could to their famous relative, but very little here (beyond two marble relief panels and a couple of sketches) is actually by Michelangelo.

Cost and Hours: €6.50, Wed-Mon 10:00-17:00, closed Tue, English descriptions, Via Ghibellina 70, tel. 055-241-752.

Santa Maria Novella Sights near the Train Station

▲▲**Church of Santa Maria Novella**—This 13th-century Dominican church is rich in art. Along with crucifixes by Giotto and Brunelleschi, it contains every textbook's example of the early Renaissance mastery of perspective: *The Holy Trinity* by Masaccio. The exquisite chapels trace art in Florence from medieval times

to the early Baroque period. The outside of the church features a dash of Romanesque (horizontal stripes), Gothic (pointed arches), Renaissance (geometric shapes), and Baroque (scrolls). Step in and look down the 330-foot nave for a 14th-century optical illusion. Next to the church are the cloisters and the museum, located in the old Dominican convent of Santa Maria Novella. The museum's highlight is the breathtaking Spanish Chapel, with walls covered by a series of frescoes by Andrea di Bonaiuto.

Cost and Hours: Church—€3.50, audioguide-€3, Mon-Thu 9:00-17:30, Fri 11:00-17:30, Sat 9:00-17:00, Sun 13:00-17:00, last entry 30 minutes before closing, modest dress required, tel. 055-219-257, www.museicivicifiorentini.it; museum—€2.70, Mon-Thu and Sat 9:00-17:00, closed Fri and Sun, tel. 055-282-187.

Farmacia di Santa Maria Novella—This palatial perfumery has long been run by the Dominicans of Santa Maria Novella. Thick with the lingering aroma of centuries of spritzes, it started as the herb garden of the Santa Maria Novella monks. Well-known even today for its top-quality products, it is extremely Florentine. Pick up the history sheet at the desk, and wander deep into the shop. The first room features perfumes, the middle (green) room offers items for the home, and the third room, which sells herbal products and dates from 1612, is the most historic. From here, you can peek at the dreamy frescoes of one of Santa Maria Novella's cloisters and imagine a time before Vespas and tourists.

Cost and Hours: Free but shopping encouraged, inconsistent hours but likely daily 9:30-19:30, a block from Piazza Santa Maria Novella, 100 yards down Via della Scala at #16—located on map on page 442, tel. 055-216-276, www.smnovella.com.

South of the Arno River
To locate these sights, see the map on page 480.

▲▲**Pitti Palace**—The imposing Pitti Palace, several blocks southwest of Ponte Vecchio, is not only home to the second-best collection of paintings in town, the **Palatine Gallery,** but also happens to be the most sumptuous palace you can tour in Florence. The

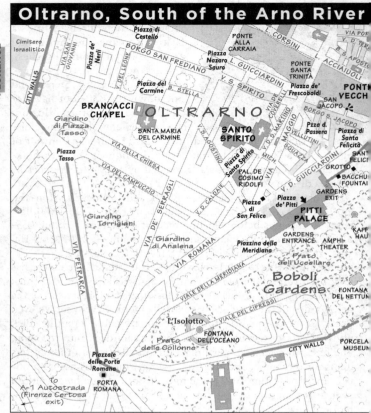

Oltrarno, South of the Arno River

building itself is mammoth, holding several different museums and anchoring two gardens. Stick primarily to the gallery, forget about everything else, and the palace becomes a little less exhausting.

You'll walk through one palatial room after another, walls sagging with masterpieces by 16th- and 17th-century masters, including Rubens, Titian, and Rembrandt. Its Raphael collection is the second-biggest anywhere—the Vatican beats it by one. Each room has some descriptions in English, though the paintings themselves have limited English labels.

The collection is all on one floor. To see the highlights, walk straight down the spine through a dozen or so rooms. Before you exit, consider a visit to the Royal Apartments. These 14 rooms (of which only a few are open at any one time) are where the Pitti's rulers lived in the 18th and 19th centuries. Each room features a different color and time period. Here, you get a real feel for the splendor of the dukes' world.

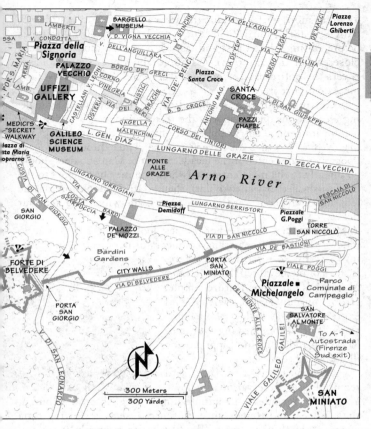

The rest of the Pitti Palace is skippable, unless the various sights match your interests: the **Modern Art Gallery** (second floor, features Romantic, Neoclassical, and Impressionist works by 19th- and 20th-century Tuscan painters), **Argenti Museum** (on the ground and mezzanine floors; displays Medici treasures from jeweled crucifixes to gilded ostrich eggs), **Costume Gallery**, **Porcelain Museum**, and **Boboli and Bardini Gardens** (behind the palace; enter from Pitti Palace courtyard).

The main reason to visit the Pitti Palace is to see the Palatine Gallery, but you can't buy a ticket for the gallery alone; to see it you'll need to buy ticket #1, which includes the Palatine Gallery, Royal Apartments, and Modern Art Gallery. Ticket #2 covers the Boboli and Bardini Gardens, Argenti Museum, Costume Gallery, and Porcelain Museum.

Cost and Hours: Ticket #1—€8.50 but often €12 with mandatory exhibits, cash only, Tue-Sun 8:15-18:50, closed Mon. Ticket

#2—€6, more with special exhibits, cash only, audioguide-€5, daily 8:15-18:30, until 19:30 June-Aug, last entry 30-60 minutes before closing, closed first and last Mon of each month, gardens close earlier in winter. An €11.50 combo-ticket (valid 3 days) covers the entire palace complex. Tel. 055-238-8614, www.polo museale.firenze.it.

Getting In: If there's a long line, you can bypass it by making reservations on the spot at the ticket window (€3 reservation fee) for immediate entry. The ticket office is at the far right of the massive facade. Once you have your ticket, enter through the main doorway in the center of the facade. Florence Card-holders should go directly to the main entrance (where you may be ushered to the head of the security checkpoint); then go to the bookstore on the left side of the courtyard to have your card swiped and get your tickets.

▲▲**Brancacci Chapel**—For the best look at works by Masaccio (one of the early Renaissance pioneers of perspective in painting), see his restored frescoes here.  Instead of medieval religious symbols, Masaccio's paintings feature simple, strong human figures with facial expressions that reflect their emotions. The accompanying works of Masolino and Filippino Lippi provide illuminating contrasts.

Reservations are free and required (see "Reservations," below). Your ticket includes a 40-minute film in English on the church, the frescoes, and Renaissance Florence (reserve a viewing time when you book your entry). The film starts promptly at the top of the hour. Computer animation brings the paintings to life—making them appear to move and giving them 3-D depth—while narration describes the events depicted in the panels. Yes, it's a long time commitment, and the film takes liberties with the art. But it's visually interesting and it's your best way to see the frescoes close up. The film works great either before or after you visit the frescoes.

Cost and Hours: €4, €8 combo-ticket with Palazzo Vecchio, includes worthwhile 40-minute film in English—reserve viewing time when you book entry, Mon and Wed-Sat 10:00-17:00, Sun 13:00-17:00, closed Tue, last entry 30 minutes before closing; in Church of Santa Maria del Carmine, reservations tel. 055-276-8224 or 055-276-8558, chapel tel. 055-284-361, www.museicivici fiorentini.it.

Reservations: Reservations are mandatory and free; call the chapel at least a day ahead. No same-day reservations can be made, even if there are openings (tel. 055-276-8224 or 055-276-8558, English spoken, call center open Mon-Sat 9:30-17:00, Sun 9:30-12:30). If the line is busy, keep trying—it's best to call around 14:00-15:00 or just before the ticket office closes at 16:30. Reservation times begin every 15 minutes, with a maximum of 30 visitors per time slot (you have 15 minutes inside the chapel). Remember when you call to reserve to book a time to see the film.

Walk-ins are welcome to stop by the chapel to see if there are any openings. You can also try calling ahead to the Brancacci chapel's direct line (tel. 055-284-361). They can't make a reservation for you, but they can tell you how crowded it is. The least crowded time tends to be 13:00-14:00.

Dress Code: Shorts and bare shoulders are OK in the chapel, but modest dress is requested when visiting the rest of the church.

Santo Spirito Church—This church has a classic Brunelleschi interior—enjoy its pure Renaissance lines (and ignore the later Baroque altar that replaced the original).

Notice Brunelleschi's "dice"—the cubes of marble added above the column capitals that contribute to the nave's playful lightness. The church's art treasure is a painted, carved wooden crucifix attributed to 17-year-old Michelangelo. The sculptor donated this early work to the monastery in appreciation for allowing him to dissect and learn about bodies. The Michelangelo *Crocifisso* is displayed in the sacristy, through a door midway down the left side of the nave (if it's closed, ask someone to let you in). Copies of Michelangelo's *Pietà* and *Risen Christ* flank the nave (near the door). Beer-drinking, guitar-playing rowdies decorate the church steps.

Cost and Hours: Free, Mon-Tue and Thu-Sat 10:00-12:30 & 16:00-17:30, Sun 16:00-17:30 only, closed Wed, Piazza di Santo Spirito, tel. 055-211-716.

▲Piazzale Michelangelo—Overlooking the city from across the river (look for the huge statue of *David*), this square has a superb

view of Florence and the stunning dome of the Duomo (see photo on page 439).

It's worth the 30-minute hike, drive (free parking), or bus ride (either #12 or #13 from the train station—takes a long time). It makes sense to take a taxi or ride the bus up, and then enjoy the easy downhill walk back into town. An inviting café with great views is just below the overlook. The best photos are taken from the street immediately below the overlook (go around to the right and down a few steps). Off the west side of the piazza is a somewhat hidden terrace, an excellent place to retreat from the mobs. After dark, the square is packed with schoolkids licking ice cream and each other. About 200 yards beyond all the tour groups and teenagers is the stark, beautiful, crowd-free, Romanesque San Miniato Church (next listing).

The hike down is quick and enjoyable. Take the steps between the two bars on the San Miniato Church side of the parking lot (Via San Salvatore al Monte), and in a couple of minutes you walk through the old wall (Porta San Miniato) and emerge in the delightful little Oltrarno neighborhood of San Niccolò.

▲▲**San Miniato Church**—According to legend, the martyred St. Minias—this church's namesake—was beheaded on the banks of the Arno in A.D. 250. He picked up his head and walked here (this was before the #12 bus), where he died and was buried in what became the first Christian cemetery in Florence. In the 11th century, this church was built to house Minias' remains. The church's green-and-white marble facade (12th century) is classic Florentine Romanesque. The church has wonderful 3-D paintings, a plush ceiling  of glazed terra-cotta panels by Luca della Robbia, and a sumptuous Renaissance chapel (located front and center). The highlight for me is the brilliantly preserved art in the sacristy (behind altar in the room on right) showing scenes from the life of St. Benedict (circa 1350, done by a follower of Giotto). Drop a euro in the box to light the room for five minutes. The daily 17:30 Mass with the monks chanting in Latin offers a meditative worship experience—a peaceful way to end your visit.

Cost and Hours: Free, daily April-Oct 8:30-19:30, Nov-March 8:30-13:00, Gregorian chants April-Sept daily at the 17:30 Mass (17:00 in winter), 200 yards above Piazzale Michelangelo, bus #12 or #13 from train station—get off at Piazzale Michelangelo and walk, tel. 055-234-2731.

Shopping in Florence

Florence is a great shopping town—known for its sense of style since the Medici days. Many people spend entire days shopping. Smaller stores are generally open 9:00-13:00 and 15:30-19:30,

usually closed on Sunday, often closed on Monday, and sometimes closed for a couple of weeks around August 15. Many stores have promotional stalls in the market squares.

Busy street scenes and markets abound, especially near San Lorenzo, near Santa Croce, on Ponte Vecchio, and at Mercato Nuovo (the covered market square 3 blocks north of Ponte Vecchio, described on page 471). Prices are soft in the markets—go ahead and bargain. Leather, gold, silver, art prints, and tacky plaster mini-*David*s are most popular.

For shopping ideas, ads, and a list of markets, see *The Florentine* newspaper or *Florence Concierge Information* magazine (free from TI and many hotels). For a list of bookstores, see page 449.

For ritzy Italian fashions, browse along Via de' Tornabuoni, Via della Vigna Nuova, Via del Parione, and Via Strozzi. The main **Ferragamo** store fills a classy 800-year-old building with a fine selection of shoes and bags (daily 10:00-19:30, Via de' Tornabuoni 2).

Typical chain department stores are **Coin,** the Italian equivalent of Macy's (Mon-Sat 10:00-19:30, Sun 10:30-19:30, on Via de' Calzaiuoli, near Orsanmichele Church); the similar, upscale **La Rinascente** (Mon-Sat 9:00-21:00, Sun 10:30-20:00, on Piazza della Repubblica); and **Oviesse,** a discount clothing chain, the local JCPenney (Mon-Sat 9:00-19:30, Sun 9:00-13:00 & 15:00-17:30, near train station at intersection of Via Panzani and Via del Giglio).

Sleeping in Florence

Competition among hotels is stiff. When things slow down, fancy hotels drop their prices and become a much better value for travelers than the cheap, low-end places.

Nearly all of my recommended accommodations are located in the center of Florence, within minutes of the great sights. If arriving by train, you can either walk (usually around 10 minutes) or take a taxi (roughly €8) to reach most of my recommended accommodations, as buses don't cover the center very well.

Florence is notorious for its mosquitoes. If your hotel lacks air-conditioning, request a fan and don't open your windows, especially at night. Many hotels furnish a small plug-in bulb *(zanzariere)*—usually set in the ashtray—that helps keep the blood-suckers at bay. If not, you can purchase one cheaply at any pharmacy *(farmacia)*.

Sleep Code

(€1 = about $1.40, country code: 39)
S = Single, **D** = Double/Twin, **T** = Triple, **Q** = Quad, **b** = bathroom, **s** = shower only.

You can assume a hotel takes credit cards unless you see "cash only" in the listing. Unless otherwise noted, hotel staff speak basic English and breakfast is included.

To help you easily sort through these listings, I've divided the accommodations into three categories based on the price for a standard double room with bath during high season:

$$$ Higher Priced—Most rooms €160 or more.
$$ Moderately Priced—Most rooms between €100-160.
$ Lower Priced—Most rooms €100 or less.

Prices can change without notice; verify the hotel's current rates online or by email. For other updates, see www .ricksteves.com/update.

Museumgoers take note: If you don't plan to get a Florence Card (see page 457), ask if your hotelier will reserve entry times for you to visit the popular Uffizi Gallery and the Accademia (Michelangelo's *David*). Request this service when you book your room; it's fast, easy, and offered free or for a small fee by most hotels—the only requirement is advance notice. Ask them to reserve your visits for any time the day after your arrival. If you'd rather make the reservations yourself, see page 452 for details.

North of the Arno River
Between the Duomo and the Train Station

$$ Hotel Accademia, which comes with marble stairs, parquet floors, and attractive public areas, has 21 pleasant rooms and a floor plan that defies logic (Db-€145, Tb-€170, 10 percent cash discount with this book, air-con, Internet access and Wi-Fi, Via Faenza 7, tel. 055-293-451, fax 055-219-771, www.hotelaccademiafirenze .com, info@hotelaccademiafirenze.com, Tea and Edward).

$$ Hotel Centrale, with 31 spacious rooms, is indeed central (Db-€150, superior Db-€176, Tb-€182, suites available, 10 percent discount with this book, ask for Rick Steves rate when you reserve, 20 percent discount if booked 3 months in advance, air-con, elevator, Internet access and free Wi-Fi, Via dei Conti 3, tel. 055-215-761, fax 055-215-216, www.hotelcentralefirenze.it, info @hotelcentralefirenze.it, Margherita and Roberto).

$ Katti House and the nearby **Soggiorno Annamaria** are run by house-proud mama-and-daughter team Maria and Katti, who keep their 15 rooms spotless, inviting, and well-maintained. While both offer equal comfort, Soggiorno Annamaria has a more historic setting, with frescoed ceilings, unique tiles, timbered beams, and quieter rooms. Katti House serves as reception for both places (Db-€70-100, air-con, Internet access and Wi-Fi, Via Faenza 21, tel. & fax 055-213-410, www.kattihouse.com, info@kattihouse .com).

$ **Hotel Lorena,** just across from the Medici Chapels, has 19 rooms (six of which share a bathroom) and a tiny lobby. Though it's a bit like a youth hostel, it's cheap and conveniently located. Chatty Roberto speaks little English, but is eager to please (Sb-€50, D-€60, Db-€75, Tb-€95, breakfast-€5, air-con, Wi-Fi, Via Faenza 1, tel. 055-282-785, fax 055-288-300, www.hotellorena .com, info@hotellorena.com).

North of the Duomo
North of the Mercato Centrale

After dark, this neighborhood can feel a little sketchy, but I've never heard of anyone running into harm here. It's a short walk from the train station and an easy stroll to all the sightseeing action. While workaday, it's practical, with plenty of good budget restaurants and markets nearby.

$$ **Galileo Hotel,** a classy business hotel of 31 rooms, is run with familial warmth (Db-€130, Tb-€150, ask for 10 percent Rick Steves discount when you book direct and pay cash, quadruple-pane windows effectively shut out street noise, Wi-Fi, Via Nazionale 22a, tel. 055-496-645, fax 055-496-447, www .galileohotel.it, info@galileohotel.it, Rhuna).

$$ **Grand Tour Firenze** has seven charming rooms on a mundane street between the train station and the Accademia. This cozy B&B will make you feel right at home; it's thoughtfully appointed and the owners, Cristina and Giuseppe, live here. The delightful and spacious suites come with a garden ambience on the ground floor (Db-€110, suite-€130, 10 percent discount when you book direct and pay cash, includes breakfast voucher for the corner bar, air-con, Wi-Fi, Via Santa Reparata 21, tel. 055-283-955, www .florencegrandtour.com, info@abacusreservations.com). They run a more romantic, pricier place a couple of blocks away.

$ **Hotel Il Bargellino,** run by Bostonian Carmel and her Italian husband Pino, feels like it's in a residential neighborhood. They rent 10 summery rooms decorated with funky antique furniture and Pino's modern paintings. Guests enjoy relaxing with Carmel and Leopoldo the parrot on the big, breezy, momentum-slowing terrace adorned with lemon shrubs (S-€45, D-€80, Db-€90, 10 percent discount if you book direct and pay cash, extra bed-€25, no breakfast, Wi-Fi, north of the train station at

FLORENCE

Florence Hotels

1. Hotel Accademia
2. Hotel Centrale
3. Katti House & Soggiorno Annamaria
4. Hotel Lorena
5. Galileo Hotel
6. Grand Tour Firenze
7. Hotel Il Bargellino
8. Hotel Enza
9. Casa Rabatti
10. Soggiorno Magliani
11. Hotel Loggiato dei Serviti
12. Hotel Dei Macchiaioli
13. Hotel Europa
14. Hotel Morandi alla Crocetta
15. Arti e Hotel
16. Palazzo Niccolini al Duomo
17. Residenza dei Pucci
18. Hotel Duomo
19. Soggiorno Battistero
20. La Residenza del Proconsolo B&B
21. Panella's Residence
22. Residenza il Villino
23. B&B Il Bargello
24. Hotel Cardinal of Florence
25. Hotel Dalí
26. Oblate Sisters of the Assumption
27. Locanda de' Ciompi
28. Hotel Il Duca
29. In Piazza della Signoria B&B
30. Hotel Pendini
31. Hotel Olimpia
32. B&B Dei Mori
33. Residenza Giotto B&B
34. Hotel Torre Guelfa
35. Relais Uffizi
36. Hotel Davanzati
37. Hotel Alessandra
38. Bellevue House & Albergo Margaret
39. To Villa Camerata & Hostel 7 Santi

FLORENCE

Via Guelfa 87, tel. 055-238-2658, www.ilbargellino.com, carmel @ilbargellino.com).

$ Hotel Enza rents 19 dark, relaxing rooms (Sb-€55, Db-€80, prices promised through 2012 with this book, extra bed-€20, optional breakfast-€5, air-con, Internet access and Wi-Fi, Via San Zanobi 45 black, tel. 055-490-990, fax 055-473-672, www .hotelenza.it, info@hotelenza.it, Diana).

$ Casa Rabatti is the ultimate if you always wanted to have a Florentine mama. Its four simple, clean rooms are run with warmth by Marcella. This is a great place to practice your Italian, since Marcella loves to chat and speaks minimal English. Seeing nearly two decades of my family Christmas cards on their walls, I'm reminded of how long she has been keeping budget travelers happy (D-€50, Db-€60, €25 extra per bed in shared quad or quint, prices good with this book, cash only but secure reservation with credit card, no breakfast, fans available, Wi-Fi, 5 blocks from station at Via San Zanobi 48 black, tel. 055-212-393, casarabatti@inwind.it).

If Marcella's booked, she'll put you up in her daughter's place nearby, at Via Nazionale 20 (five big, airy, family-friendly rooms; €25/person, fans, no breakfast, closer to the station). While daughter Patrizia works, her mom runs the place. Getting bumped to Patrizia's gives you slightly more comfort and slightly less personality...certainly not a net negative.

$ Soggiorno Magliani is central and humble, with six bright, no-frills rooms (sharing two baths) that feel and smell like a great-grandmother's home. It's run by the friendly duo Vincenza and her English-speaking daughter Cristina, and the price is right (S-€36, D-€46, T-€63, cash only but secure reservation with credit card, no breakfast, near Via Guelfa at Via Santa Reparata 1, tel. 055-287-378, hotel-magliani@libero.it).

Near the Accademia

$$$ Hotel Loggiato dei Serviti, at the most prestigious address in Florence on the most evocative Renaissance square in town, gives you Old World romance with hair dryers. Stone stairways lead you under open-beam ceilings through this 16th-century monastery's monumental public rooms—it's so artful, you'll be snapping photos everywhere. The 33 cells—with air-conditioning, TVs, mini-bars, and telephones—would be unrecognizable to their original inhabitants. The hotel staff is both professional and warm (Sb-€120, Db-€160-170, superior Db-€190, family suites from €263, ask for their Rick Steves rate when you book, elevator, valet parking-€20/day, Piazza S.S. Annunziata 3, tel. 055-289-592, fax 055-289-595, www.loggiatodeiservitihotel.it, info@loggiato deiservitihotel.it; Fabio, Chiara, and Simonetta). When full, they rent five spacious and sophisticated rooms in a 17th-century annex a block away. While it lacks the monastic mystique, the annex rooms are bigger, gorgeous, and cost the same.

$$$ Hotel Dei Macchiaioli offers 15 fresh and spacious rooms on one high-ceilinged, noble floor in a restored *palazzo* owned for generations by a well-to-do Florentine family. You'll eat breakfast under original frescoed ceilings while enjoying modern comforts (Sb-€100, Db-€180, Tb-€220, 10 percent Rick Steves discount if you book direct, air-con, Wi-Fi, Via Cavour 21, tel. 055-213-154, www.hoteldeimacchiaioli.com, info@hoteldei macchiaioli.com, helpful Francesca and Paolo).

$$ Hotel Morandi alla Crocetta, a former convent, envelops you in a 16th-century cocoon. Located on a quiet street with 12 rooms, period furnishings, parquet floors, and wood-beamed ceilings, it takes you back a few centuries and up a few social classes (Sb-€100, Db-€140, low-season discounts online, air-con, Wi-Fi, a block off Piazza S.S. Annunziata at Via Laura 50, tel. 055-234-4747, fax 055-248-0954, www.hotelmorandi.it, welcome@hotel morandi.it, well-run by Maurizio, Rolando, and Frank).

$$ Hotel Europa, run by cheery Miriam, Roberto, and daughter Priscilla since 1970, has a welcoming atmosphere. The breakfast room is spacious, and some of the 20 rooms have views of the Duomo (Sb-€89, Db-€150, Tb-€180, 10 percent cash discount, air-con, elevator, Wi-Fi, Via Cavour 14, tel. 055-239-6715, fax 055-268-984, www.webhoteleuropa.com, firenze@webhotel europa.com).

$$ Arti e Hotel rents 11 large, new, and tastefully furnished rooms well-located on a quiet street just far enough away from the tourist scene. As there's no real public space, the emphasis is on classy rooms and a helpful reception desk (Db-€135, 10 percent discount if you book direct and pay cash—ask for their Rick Steves price, third bed-€30, air-con, elevator, Wi-Fi, Via dei Servi 38, tel. 055-264-5307, fax 055-290-140, www.artiehotel.it, info@artie hotel.it, Mario).

Near the Duomo

All of these places are within a block of Florence's biggest church and main landmark.

$$$ Palazzo Niccolini al Duomo, one of five elite Historic Residence Hotels in Florence, is run by Niccolini da Camugliano. The lounge (where free chamomile tea served in the evenings) is palatial, but the 12 rooms, while splendid, vary wildly in size. If you have the money and want a Florentine palace to call home, this can be a good bet (Db-€150 and up, fancier and pricier suites with DVD players, ask for 10 percent Rick Steves discount when you book, check online to choose a room and consider last-minute deals, Wi-Fi, Via dei Servi 2, tel. 055-282-412, fax 055-290-979, www.niccolinidomepalace.com, info@niccolinidomepalace.com).

$$ Residenza dei Pucci rents 12 pleasant rooms (each one different) spread over three floors. The decor is a mix of soothing earth tones and aristocratic furniture (Sb-€135, Db-€150, Tb-€170, Qb-€238, 10 percent discount with cash and this book, air-con, no elevator, reception open 9:00-20:00—let them know if you'll arrive late, Via dei Pucci 9, tel. 055-281-886, fax 055-264-314, www.residenzadeipucci.com, residenzadeipucci@residenza deipucci.com, Mirella).

$$ Hotel Duomo, big and venerable, rents 24 rooms four floors up. The Duomo looms like a monster outside the hotel's windows. The rooms, while pretty forgettable, are comfortable enough, and the location can't be beat (Db-€100-170, 10 percent cash discount with this book, Internet access and Wi-Fi, Piazza del Duomo 1, tel. 055-219-922, www.hotelduomofirenze.it, info @hotelduomofirenze.it, Alberto and Sonia).

$$ Soggiorno Battistero rents seven simple, airy rooms, most with great views, overlooking the Baptistery and the Duomo square. Choose a view or a quieter room in the back when you book by email. It's a pristine, fresh, and minimalist place run by Italian Luca and his American wife Kelly, who makes the hotel particularly welcoming (Sb-€78, Db-€103, Tb-€140, Qb-€150, prices good with this book, 5 percent cash discount if you book direct, breakfast served in room, air-con, Wi-Fi, Piazza San Giovanni 1, third floor—no elevator, tel. 055-295-143, fax 055-268-189, www .soggiornobattistero.it, info@soggiornobattistero.it).

$$ La Residenza del Proconsolo B&B, run by helpful Mariano, has five pleasantly appointed rooms a minute from the Duomo (three rooms have Duomo views). The place lacks public spaces, but the rooms are quite large and nice—perfect for eating breakfast, which is served in your room (Sb-€90, Db-€140, Tb-€150, Wi-Fi, Via del Proconsolo 18n, tel. 055-264-5657, mobile 335-657-4840, www.proconsolo.com, info@proconsolo.com).

East of the Duomo
$$ Panella's Residence, once a convent and today part of owner Graziella's extensive home, is a classy B&B, with six chic, romantic, and ample rooms, antique furnishings, and historic architectural touches (Db-€140, superior Db-€165, these prices are with cash, discounts for 3 or more nights, air-con, Wi-Fi, Via della Pergola 42, tel. 055-234-7202, fax 055-247-9669, www.panella residence.com, panella_residence@yahoo.it).

$$ Residenza il Villino, popular and friendly, aspires to offer a Florentine home away from home. It has 10 rooms and a picturesque, peaceful little courtyard (small Db-€110, Db-€130, family suite that sleeps up to six—price upon request, 5 percent discount with cash and this book, air-con, Internet access and Wi-Fi, just north of Via degli Alfani at Via della Pergola 53, tel. 055-200-1116, fax 055-200-1101, www.ilvillino.it, info@ilvillino.it; Sergio, Elisabetta, and son Lorenzo).

$ B&B Il Bargello is a home away from home, run by friendly and helpful Canadian expat Gabriella. Hike up three long flights to reach six smart, relaxing rooms. Gabriella offers a cozy communal living room, kitchen access, and an inviting rooftop terrace with close-up views of Florence's towers (Db-€100, ask for Rick Steves rate when you book direct and pay cash, air-con, Internet access and Wi-Fi, 20 yards off Via Proconsolo at Via de' Pandolfini 33 black, tel. 055-215-330, mobile 339-175-3110, www.firenze-bedandbreakfast.it, info@firenze-bedandbreakfast.it).

$ Hotel Cardinal of Florence is a third-floor walk-up with 17 new, tidy, and sun-splashed rooms overlooking either a silent court-yard (many with views of Brunelleschi's dome) or a quiet street. Relax and enjoy Florence's rooftops from the sun terrace (Sb-€60, Db-€95, these prices for Rick Steves readers, additional €5 cash discount, €15/day limited parking—request when you reserve, Borgo Pinti 5, tel. 055-234-0780, fax 055-234-3389, www.hotelcardinalofflorence.com, info@hotelcardinalofflorence.com, Mauro and Ida).

$ Hotel Dalí has 10 decent, basic rooms with new baths in a nice location for a great price. Samanta and Marco, who run this guesthouse with a charming passion and idealism, are a delight to know (S-€40, D-€70, Db-€85, extra bed-€25, no breakfast, fans but no air-con, request quiet room when you book, Wi-Fi, free parking, 2 blocks behind the Duomo at Via dell'Oriuolo 17, tel. & fax 055-234-0706, www.hoteldali.com, hoteldali@tin.it).

$ Oblate Sisters of the Assumption run an institutional 30-room hotel in a Renaissance building with a dreamy garden, great public spaces, appropriately simple rooms, and a quiet, prayerful ambience (€45/person in single, double, triple, or quad rooms with bathrooms, cash only, single beds only, air-con, elevator, €10/day limited parking—request when you book, Borgo Pinti 15, tel. 055-248-0582, fax 055-234-6291, sroblateborgopinti@virgilio.it, sisters are likely to speak French but not English, Sister Theresa is very helpful).

$ Locanda de' Ciompi, overlooking the inviting Piazza dei Ciompi antiques market in a young and lively neighborhood, is just right for travelers who want to feel like a part of the town. Riccardo runs a minimalist place—just five quiet, clean, tasteful rooms along a thin hallway (Db-€100, Tb-€115, 10 percent discount with this book if you book direct and pay cash, includes breakfast at nearby bar, air-con, Wi-Fi, 8 blocks behind the Duomo at Via Pietrapiana 28, tel. 055-263-8034, www.locandadeciompi.it, li.ga@locandadeciompi.it).

$ Hotel Il Duca—a big, bright, old place—seems like a basic building wearing a fancy coat. Located on a quiet street a few blocks behind the Duomo, it rents 13 rooms at a good price (Db-€90, third bed-€25, air-con, Wi-Fi, Via della Pergola 34, tel. 055-906-2167, www.hotelilduca.it, info@hotelilduca.it).

South of the Duomo
Between the Duomo and Piazza della Signoria

These are the most central of my accommodations recommendations (and therefore a little overpriced). While worth the extra cost for many, given Florence's walkable, essentially traffic-free core, nearly every hotel I recommend here can be considered central.

$$$ In Piazza della Signoria B&B, overlooking Piazza della Signoria, is peaceful, refined, and homey at the same time. Fit for a honeymoon, the 10 rooms come with all the special touches and little extras you'd expect in a top-end American B&B (viewless Db-€220, view Db-€250, Tb-€280, ask for 10 percent discount when you book direct with this book, family apartments, lavish bathrooms, air-con, tiny elevator, Internet access and Wi-Fi, Via dei Magazzini 2, tel. 055-239-9546, mobile 348-321-0565, fax 055-267-6616, www.inpiazzadellasignoria.com, info@inpiazzadella signoria.com, Sonia and Alessandro).

$$ Hotel Pendini, with three tarnished stars, fills the top floor of a grand building constructed to celebrate Italian unification in the late 19th century. It overlooks Piazza della Repubblica, and as you walk into the lobby, you feel as if you are walking back in time. The 40-room place is memorable—and can be a good value (Db-€80-190, Internet access and Wi-Fi, Via Strozzi 2, tel. 055-211-170, www.hotelpendini.it, info@hotelpendini.it).

$$ Hotel Olimpia is a friendly, well-worn, established place renting 24 utilitarian rooms on the fourth floor overlooking Piazza della Repubblica. But you pay for the location (Db-€140-160, air-con, Wi-Fi, Piazza della Repubblica 2, tel. 055-219-781, fax 055-267-0383, www.hotel-olimpia.it, info@hotel-olimpia.it, Marziano).

$$ B&B Dei Mori, a peaceful haven with a convivial and welcoming living room, rents five tastefully appointed rooms ideally located on a quiet pedestrian street near Casa di Dante. Accommodating Suzanne and Danny offer lots of tips on dining and sightseeing in Florence (D-€100, Db-€120, 10 percent discount for my readers—ask when you book, air-con-€5 extra, Wi-Fi, reception open 8:00-19:00, Via Dante Alighieri 12, tel. 055-211-438, www.deimori.com, deimori@bnb.it).

$$ Residenza Giotto B&B offers you the chance to stay on Florence's upscale shopping drag, Via Roma. Occupying the top floor of a 19th-century building, this place has six bright rooms and a terrace with knockout views of the Duomo's tower (Sb-€90, Db-€140, extra bed-€25, 10 percent discount if you book direct and pay cash, elevator, Wi-Fi, Via Roma 6, tel. 055-214-593, fax 055-264-8568, www.residenzagiotto.it, info@residenzagiotto .it, Giorgio speaks English). Let them know your arrival time in advance.

Near Ponte Vecchio

$$$ Hotel Torre Guelfa is topped by a fun medieval tower with a panoramic rooftop terrace and a huge living room. Its 24 pricey rooms vary wildly in size. Room 315, with a private terrace (€245), is worth reserving several months in advance (Db-€170- 190, Db junior suite-€230, family deals, check their website for discounts, air-con, elevator, Wi-Fi, a couple blocks northwest of Ponte Vecchio, Borgo S.S. Apostoli 8, tel. 055-239-6338, fax 055- 239-8577, www.hoteltorreguelfa.com, info@hoteltorreguelfa.com, Sandro and Barbara).

$$$ Relais Ufizzi is a peaceful little gem, with 15 classy rooms tucked away down a tiny alleyway off Piazza della Signoria. The lounge has a huge window overlooking the action in the square below (Sb-€140, Db-€180, Tb-€220, buffet breakfast, elevator, Wi-Fi, Chiasso de Baroncelli/Chiasso del Buco 16, tel. 055-267- 6239, fax 055-265-7909, www.relaisuffizi.it, info@relaisuffizzi.it, charming Alessandro and Elizabetta).

$$$ Hotel Davanzati, bright and shiny with artistic touches, has 19 cheerful rooms with all the comforts. The place is a family affair, thoughtfully run by friendly Tommaso and father Fabrizio, who offer drinks and snacks each evening at their candlelit happy hour (Sb-€122, Db-€189, Tb-€259, these rates good with this book though prices soft off-season, 10 percent cash discount; PlayStation, DVD player, and laptop with free Wi-Fi in every room; air-con, next to Piazza Davanzati at Via Porta Rossa 5, tel. 055-286-666, fax 055-265-8252, www.hoteldavanzati.it, info @hoteldavanzati.it).

$$ Hotel Alessandra is 16th-century, tranquil, and sprawl- ing, with 27 big, tasteful rooms (S-€67, Sb-€110, D-€110, Db-€150, Tb-€195, Qb-€215, 5 percent cash discount, air-con, Internet access and Wi-Fi, Borgo S.S. Apostoli 17, tel. 055-283-438, fax 055-210- 619, www.hotelalessandra.com, info@hotelalessandra.com, Anna and son Andrea).

Near the Train Station

$ Bellevue House is a third-floor (no elevator) oasis of tranquility, with six spacious rooms flanking a long, mellow-yellow lobby. It's a peaceful time warp thoughtfully run by Rosanna and Antonio di Grazia (Db-€70-95, family deals; 10 percent discount if you

Oltrarno Hotels & Restaurants

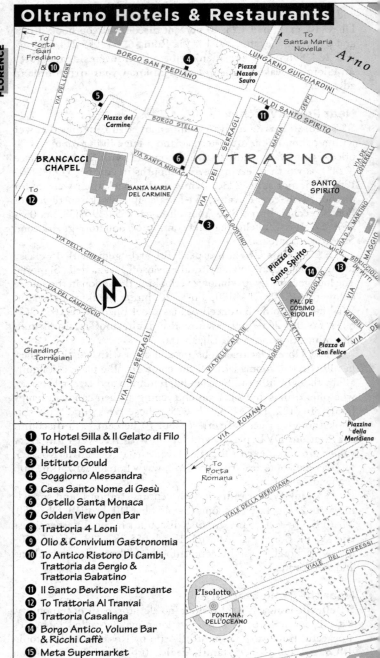

1 To Hotel Silla & Il Gelato di Filo
2 Hotel la Scaletta
3 Istituto Gould
4 Soggiorno Alessandra
5 Casa Santo Nome di Gesù
6 Ostello Santa Monaca
7 Golden View Open Bar
8 Trattoria 4 Leoni
9 Olio & Convivium Gastronomia
10 To Antico Ristoro Di Cambi, Trattoria da Sergio & Trattoria Sabatino
11 Il Santo Bevitore Ristorante
12 To Trattoria Al Tranvai
13 Trattoria Casalinga
14 Borgo Antico, Volume Bar & Ricchi Caffè
15 Meta Supermarket

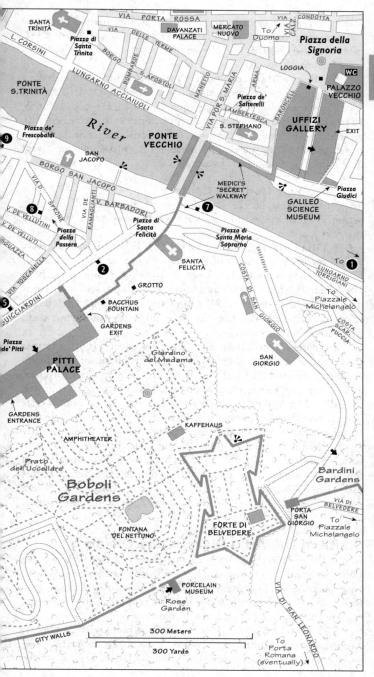

stay two nights, pay cash, and book direct; optional €3 breakfast in street-level bar, air-con, Via della Scala 21, tel. 055-260-8932, mobile 333-612-5973, fax 055-265-5315, www.bellevuehouse.it, info@bellevuehouse.it).

$ Albergo Margaret, homey yet minimalist, doesn't have a public lounge or offer breakfast. Run by the Cristantielli family, it has seven peaceful and simple rooms (D-€40, Ds-€60, Db-€75, 10 percent discount if you book direct and pay cash, extra bed-€10, air-con, Wi-Fi, near Santa Maria Novella at Via della Scala 25, tel. & fax 055-210-138, www.hotel-margaret.it, info@hotel-margaret .it; Francesco, Anna, and Graziano).

Hostels Away from the Center

These two hostels, northeast of downtown, are a bus ride from the action. A far more central hostel is in Oltrarno (listed at the end of the next section).

$ Villa Camerata, classy for an IYHF hostel, is in a pretty villa three miles northeast of the train station, on the outskirts of Florence (€20/bed with breakfast, 4- to 6-bed rooms, must have hostel membership card or pay additional €3/night, self-serve laundry, Via Righi 2—take bus #11 from the train station to Salviatino stop, tel. 055-601-451, fax 055-610-300, www.aighostels.com, firenze@aighostels.com).

$ Hostel 7 Santi calls itself a "travelers' haven." It fills a former convent, but you'll feel like you're in an old school. Still, it offers some of the best cheap beds in town, is friendly to older travelers, and comes with the services you'd expect in a big, modern hostel, including free Wi-Fi and self-serve laundry. It's in a more residential neighborhood near the Campo di Marte stadium, about a 10-minute bus ride from the center (200 beds in 60 rooms, mostly 4- or 6-bed dorms with a floor of doubles and triples, €20/dorm bed, Sb-€40, Ds-€60, Db-€70; includes breakfast, sheets, and towels; no curfew; Viale dei Mille 11—from train station, take bus #10, #17, or #20, direction: Campo di Marte, to bus stop Chiesa dei Sette Santi; tel. 055-504-8452, www.7santi.com, info@7santi .com).

South of the Arno River, in the Oltrarno

Across the river in the Oltrarno area, between the Pitti Palace and Ponte Vecchio, you'll find small, traditional crafts shops, neighborly piazzas, and family eateries. The following places are an easy walk from Ponte Vecchio. Only the first two are real hotels—the rest are a ragtag gang of budget alternatives.

$$$ Hotel Silla is a classic three-star hotel with 35 cheery, spacious, pastel, and modern rooms. It faces the river and overlooks a park opposite Santa Croce Church (Db-€140-180, ask for

Rick Steves rate when you book, third person-€50 extra, air-con, elevator, Wi-Fi, Via dei Renai 5, tel. 055-234-2888, fax 055-234-1437, www.hotelsilla.it, hotelsilla@hotelsilla.it; Laura, Chiara, Massimo, and Stefano).

$$ Hotel la Scaletta rattles with musty charm. This old-school place, with 15 functional rooms hiding in a tortured floor plan, has a fabulous rooftop terrace overlooking Boboli Gardens (Db-€125, third bed-€20, breakfast-€6, air-con, Wi-Fi, Via de' Guicciardini 13, tel. 055-283-028, fax 055-283-013, www.hotel lascaletta.it, info@hotellascaletta.it).

$ Istituto Gould is a Protestant Church-run place with 40 clean and spartan rooms that have twin beds and modern facilities (Sb-€45, Db-€56-68, Tb-€75, Qb-€92, breakfast-€6, quieter rooms in back, no air-con but rooms have fans, Via dei Serragli 49, tel. 055-212-576, fax 055-280-274, www.istitutogould.it, foresteria firenze@diaconiavaldese.org). You must arrive when the office is open (Mon-Fri 8:45-13:00 & 15:00-19:30, Sat 9:00-13:30 & 14:30-18:00, no live check-in on Sundays but they'll email you a code).

$ Soggiorno Alessandra has five bright, comfy, and smallish rooms. Because of its double-paned windows, you'll hardly notice the traffic noise (D-€58-73, Db-€78, Tb-€98, Qb-€128, 5 percent discount with 2-night stay, air-con-€8, just past the Carraia Bridge at Via Borgo San Frediano 6, tel. 055-290-424, fax 055-218-464, www.soggiornoalessandra.it, info@soggiornoalessandra .it, Alessandra).

$ Casa Santo Nome di Gesù is a grand, 29-room convent whose sisters—Franciscan Missionaries of Mary—are thankful to rent rooms to tourists. Staying in this 15th-century palace, you'll be immersed in the tranquil atmosphere created by a huge, peaceful garden, generous and prayerful public spaces, and smiling nuns (D-€70, Db-€85, twin beds only, no air-con but rooms have fans, memorable convent-like breakfast room, elevator, strict 23:29 curfew, Piazza del Carmine 21, tel. 055-213-856, fax 055-281-835, www.fmmfirenze.it, info@fmmfirenze.it).

Hostel: **$ Ostello Santa Monaca,** a well-run hostel a long block south of the Brancacci Chapel, attracts a young backpacking crowd (€15-24/bed with sheets, 2- to 20-bed dorms, 10:00-14:00 lock-out, 2:00 in the morning curfew, free Internet access and Wi-Fi, self-serve laundry, kitchen, Via Santa Monaca 6, tel. 055-268-338, fax 055-280-185, www.ostello.it, info@ostello.it).

Eating in Florence

Remember, restaurants like to serve what's fresh. If you're into flavor, go for the seasonal best bets—featured in the *piatti del giorno* ("special of the day") section on menus. For dessert, it's gelato (see

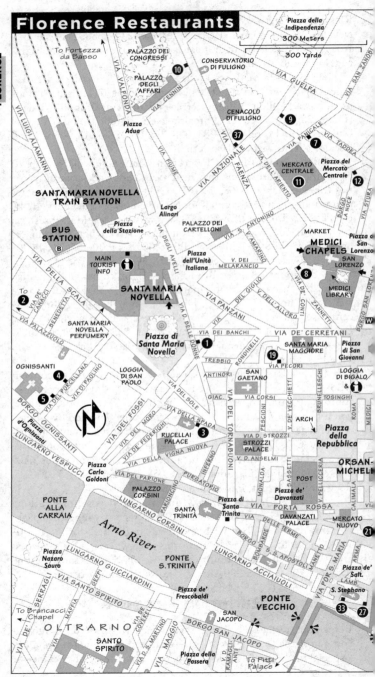

Florence Restaurants

Piazza della Indipendenza

300 Meters
300 Yards

To Fortezza da Basso

PALAZZO DEI CONGRESSI
PALAZZO DEGLI AFFARI

VIA VALFONDA
VIA CENNINI

CONSERVATORIO DI FULIGNO

VIA GUELFA

10

CENACOLO DI FULIGNO

Piazza Adua

VIA FIUME

VIA NAZIONALE

VIA FAENZA

37

9

VIA PANZALE

VIA TADDEA

7

MERCATO CENTRALE

Piazza del Mercato Centrale

11

12

SANTA MARIA NOVELLA TRAIN STATION

Largo Alinari

PALAZZO DEI CARTELLONI

VIA S. ANTONINO

BORGO LA NOCE

VIA STURA

BUS STATION

Piazza della Stazione

VIA DEGLI AVELLI

Piazza dell'Unità Italiana

V. DEI MELARANCIO

MARKET

MEDICI CHAPELS

Piazza o San Lorenzo

SAN LORENZO

MAIN TOURIST INFO

SANTA MARIA NOVELLA

VIA PANZANI

V. DEL GIGLIO

V. DELL'ALLORO

8

VIA DE' CONTI

MEDICI LIBRARY

BORGO SAN LORENZO

To
2

VIA DE' CANACCI

VIA DELLA SCALA

BENEDETTA

VIA PALAZZUOLO

SANTA MARIA NOVELLA PERFUMERY

VIA D. BELLE DONNE

Piazza di Santa Maria Novella

VIA DEI BANCHI

1

TREBBIO

RONDINELLI

VIA DE' CERRETANI

SANTA MARIA MAGGIORE

Piazza di San Giovanni

19

W

OGNISSANTI

4

VIA DEL PORCELLANA

5

BORGO OGNISSANTI

Piazza d'Ognissanti

LUNGARNO VESPUCCI

VIA DEL PAOLINO

LOGGIA DI SAN PAOLO

VIA DEL FOSSI

VIA DEL MORO

VIA DEL SOLE

ANTINORI

SAN GAETANO

VIA PECORI

VIA CORSI

GIAC.

VIA D. VECCHIETTI

PESCIONI

LOGGIA DI BIGALO & i

TOSINGHI

BRUNELLESCHI

KOMA

MEDIC

ARCH

Piazza della Repubblica

ORSAN-MICHELL

VIA DELLA SPADA

RUCELLAI PALACE

3

VIA DI FEDERIGH

VIA DELLA VIGNA NUOVA

INFERNO

VIA D. STROZZI

STROZZI PALACE

V. D. ANSELMI

MONALDA

SASSETTI

VIA PELLICCERIA

CALIMALA

VI

Piazza Carlo Goldoni

PALAZZO CORSINI

VIA DEL PARIONE

PURGATORIO

PARIONINO

SANTA TRINITÀ

Piazza di Santa Trinita

POST

Piazza de' Davanzati

DAVANZATI PALACE

VIA PORTA ROSSA

MERCATO NUOVO

21

PONTE ALLA CARRAIA

LUNGARNO CORSINI

Arno River

LUNGARNO ACCIAIUOLI

BORGO S. S. APOSTOLI

VIA POR S. MARIA

ARMA

LAMB.

VIA DELLE TERME

Piazza Nazaro Sauro

LUNGARNO GUICCIARDINI

PONTE S. TRINITÀ

Piazza de' Frescobaldi

PONTE VECCHIO

Piazza de' Salt.

S. Stephano

33

27

To Brancacci Chapel

OLTRARNO

VIA DE' SERRAGLI

VIA SANTO SPIRITO

VIA DE COVERELLI

SAN JACOPO

BORGO SAN JACOPO

SANTO SPIRITO

VIA MAGGIO

VIA D. S. MARTINO

Piazza della Passera

V. D. RAMAGLI ANTI

To Pitti Palace

N

1. Trattoria al Trebbio
2. Trattoria "da Giorgio"
3. Trattoria Marione
4. Trattoria Sostanza-Troia
5. Trattoria 13 Gobbi
6. Trattoria Zà-Zà & Trattoria Mario's
7. Trattoria la Burrasca
8. Trattoria Lo Stracotto
9. Osteria Vineria i'Brincello
10. Trattoria Nerone Pizzeria
11. Mercato Centrale & Nerbone in the Market
12. Casa del Vino
13. Pugi Pizza
14. Barbecue
15. Pasticceria Robiglio
16. La Mescita Fiaschetteria
17. Il Centro Supermercati
18. To Antica Trattoria da Tito
19. Self-Service Rist. Leonardo
20. Turkuaz Döner Kebab
21. Rivoire Café
22. Frescobaldi Ristorante & Wine Bar
23. Ristorante Paoli, Cantinetta dei Verrazzano & Perchè No! Gelateria
24. Osteria Vini e Vecchi Sapori
25. I Fratellini
26. L'Antico Trippaio
27. 'Ino Bottega di Alimentari e Vini
28. Trattoria Icche C'è C'è
29. Ristorante del Fagioli
30. Boccadama Enoteca Rist.
31. Trattoria Anita
32. Gelateria Grom
33. Gelateria Carrozze
34. Gelateria Carabè
35. Vivoli's Gelateria
36. Gelateria de' Neri
37. The Bermuda Triangle

sidebar, later).

To save money and time for sights, keep lunches fast and simple, eating in one of the countless pizzerias and self-service cafeterias. Picnicking is easy—there's no shortage of corner *supermercatos*, or you can picnic your way through the Mercato Centrale.

North of the Arno River
Near the Church of Santa Maria Novella

Trattoria al Trebbio serves traditional food, especially rabbit and steak, with simple Florentine elegance in its candlelit interior. Tables spill out onto a romantic little square—an oasis of Roman Trastevere-like charm (€8 pastas, €13 *secondi*, daily 12:00-15:00 & 19:15-23:00, reserve for outdoor seating, half a block off of Piazza Santa Maria Novella at Via delle Belle Donne 47, tel. 055-287-089, Antonio).

Trattoria "da Giorgio" is a family-style diner serving up piping-hot, delicious home cooking to happy locals and tourists alike. Their three-course, fixed-price meal, including water and a drink, is a great value for €12. Choose from among the daily specials or the regular menu (Mon-Sat 12:00-14:30 & 18:00-22:00, closed Sun, Via Palazzuolo 100 red, tel. 055-284-302, Silvano).

Trattoria Marione serves sincerely home-cooked-style meals to a mixed group of tourists and Florentines in a happy, crowded, food-loving, and steamy ambience (€9 pastas, €10 *secondi*, daily 12:00-17:30 & 19:00-23:00, Via della Spada 27 red, tel. 055-214-756, Fabio).

Trattoria Sostanza-Troia, characteristic and well established, is famous for its beef. Hearty steaks and pastas are splittable. Whirling ceiling fans and walls strewn with old photos evoke earlier times, while the artichoke pies remind locals of Grandma's cooking. Crowded, shared tables with paper tablecloths give this place a bistro feel. They offer two dinner seatings, at 19:30 and 21:00, which require reservations (dinners for about €30 plus wine, cash only, lunch Mon-Sat 12:30-14:00, closed Sun, closed Sat in off-season, Via del Porcellana 25 red, tel. 055-212-691).

Trattoria 13 Gobbi ("13 Hunchbacks") is a trendy favorite, glowing with candles around a tiny garden. Romantic in front and kid-friendly in back, it serves beautifully presented Tuscan food (they're enthusiastic about their steak) on big, fancy plates to a mostly tourist crowd (€10 pastas, €15 *secondi*, daily 12:00-15:00 & 19:30-23:00, Via del Porcellana 9 red, tel. 055-284-015, Enrico).

Near the Mercato Centrale

The following market-neighborhood eateries all have a distinct vibe. They're within a few blocks of each other: Scout around and choose your favorite.

Trattoria Zà-Zà is a fun, characteristic, high-energy place facing the Mercato Centrale. It offers a family-friendly festival of standard Tuscan dishes such as *ribollita* and *bistecca alla fiorentina*, plus a variety of big, splittable €8 salads. Though it's more touristy than ever, the food is still great, and everyone's happy. Arrive early or make a reservation. Choose between the folkloric interior or the fine outdoor piazza. Understand your itemized bill, and don't mistake their outside seating with the neighboring restaurant's (€9 pastas, €16 *secondi*, daily 11:00-23:00, Piazza del Mercato Centrale 26 red, tel. 055-215-411).

Trattoria la Burrasca is Flintstone-chic. Friendly duo Elio and Simone offer a limited menu of Tuscan home cooking with seasonal specials. It's small—10 tables—and often filled with my readers. If Archie Bunker were Italian, he'd eat at this trattoria for special nights out (€6 pastas, €8 *secondi*, no cover or service charge, Tue-Sun 12:00-15:00 & 19:00-22:30, closed Mon, Via Panicale 6, north corner of Mercato Centrale, tel. 055-215-827).

Trattoria Lo Stracotto is a stylish, truffle-colored eatery just steps away from the Medici Chapels. It's run with enthusiasm and flair by two cousins, who serve up tasty, traditional dishes such as *bistecca alla fiorentina* and *ribollita* (based on grandfather's recipe), and good chocolate soufflé. Enjoy the candlelit ambience and soft music as you sit either in the dining room or out on the terrace (€7 pastas, €10 *secondi*, daily 11:00-23:00, Piazza Madonna degli Aldobrandi 16/17, tel. 055-230-2062, Francesco and Tomasso).

Osteria Vineria i'Brincello is a bright, happy, no-frills diner with tasty food, lots of spirit, friendly service, and no hint of snobbishness. It features a list of Tuscan daily specials hanging from the ceiling and great prices on good bottled wine (€7 pastas, daily 12:00-15:00 & 19:00-23:00, corner of Via Nazionale and Via Chiara at Via Nazionale 110 red, tel. 055-282-645, Fredi cooks while Claudia serves).

Trattoria Nerone Pizzeria, serving up cheap, hearty Tuscan dishes and decent pizzas, is a tourist-friendly, practical standby in the hotel district. The lively, flamboyantly outfitted space (once the garden courtyard of a convent) feels like a good but kitschy American-Italian chain restaurant (€7 pizzas, €7 pastas, €10 *secondi*, daily 12:00-15:00 & 18:30-23:00, just north of Via Nazionale at Via Faenza 95 red, tel. 055-291-217, Tulio).

Eating Cheaply in or near the Mercato Centrale

Note that none of these eateries is open for dinner.

Mercato Centrale (Central Market) is great for an ad-lib lunch. It offers colorful piles of picnic produce, people-watching, and rustic sandwiches (Mon-Sat 7:00-14:00, Sat in winter until 17:00, closed Sun, a block north of San Lorenzo street market).

Meat, fish, and cheese are sold on the ground level, with fruit and veggies mostly upstairs. The thriving ground-level eateries within the market (such as Nerbone, described next) serve some of the cheapest hot meals in town. The fancy deli, Perini, is famous for its quality products and generous free samples. Buy a picnic of fresh mozzarella cheese, olives, fruit, and crunchy bread to munch on the steps of the nearby Church of San Lorenzo, overlooking the bustling street market.

Nerbone in the Market is a venerable café and the best place for a sit-down meal within the Mercato Centrale. Join the shoppers and workers who crowd up to the bar to grab their €5 plates. Of the several cheap market diners, this feels the most authentic (lunch menu served 12:00-14:00, sandwiches available all day, cash only, inside the Mercato Centrale on the side closest to the Church of San Lorenzo, mobile 339-648-0251). As intestines are close to Florentines' hearts, tripe is very big here.

Trattoria Mario's, around the corner from Trattoria Zà-Zà (listed earlier), has been serving hearty lunches to marketgoers since 1953 (Fabio and Romeo are the latest generation). Their simple formula: bustling service, old-fashioned good value, a lunch-only fixed-price meal, and shared tables. It's *cucina casalinga*—home cooking *con brio*. This place is high-energy and jam-packed. Their best dishes often sell out first, so go early. If there's a line, put your name on the list (€5 pastas, €8 *secondi,* cash only, Mon-Sat 12:00-15:30, closed Sun and Aug, no reservations, Via Rosina 2, tel. 055-218-550).

Casa del Vino, Florence's oldest operating wine shop, offers glasses of wine from among 25 open bottles (see the list tacked to the bar). Owner Gianni, whose family has owned the Casa for more than 70 years, is a class act. Gianni's *carta dei panini* lists delightful €3.50 sandwiches and €1 crostini; the *I Nostri Panini* (classic sandwiches) richly reward adventurous eaters. During busy times, it's a mob scene. You'll eat standing outside alongside workers on a quick lunch break (Mon-Sat 9:30-17:00, closed Sat in summer and Sun year-round, hidden behind stalls of San Lorenzo Market at Via dell'Ariento 16 red, tel. 055-215-609).

Near the Accademia
Budget-Lunch Places Surrounding the Accademia

For pizza by the slice, try **Pugi**, at Piazza San Marco 10. For a break from pasta and pizza, grab a quick kebab lunch from **Barbecue: The Taste of Istanbul** (Via Cavour 41).

Pasticceria Robiglio, a smart little café, opens up its stately dining area and sets out a few tables on the sidewalk for lunch. They have a small menu of daily pasta and *secondi* specials, and seem determined to do things like they did in the elegant, pre-tourism days (generous €9 plates, a great €8 *niçoise*-like "fantasy salad," pretty pastries, smiling service, daily 12:00-15:00, longer hours as a café, a block toward the Duomo off Piazza S.S. Annunziata at Via dei Servi 112 red, tel. 055-212-784). Before you leave, be tempted by their pastries—famous among Florentines.

La Mescita Fiaschetteria is a characteristic hole-in-the-wall just around the corner from *David*—but a world away from all the tourism. It's where locals and students enjoy daily pasta specials and hearty sandwiches with good €1 house wine. You can trust Mirco and Alessio (as far as you can throw them)—just point to what looks good (such as their €5 pasta plate), and you'll soon be eating well and inexpensively. The place can either be mobbed by students or in a peaceful time warp, depending on when you stop by (Mon-Sat 12:00-16:00, closed Sun, Via degli Alfani 70 red, mobile 347-795-1604).

Picnic on the Ultimate Renaissance Square: **Il Centro Supermercati**, a handy supermarket a half-block north of the Accademia, has a curbside sandwich bar (Panineria) with an easy English menu that includes salads to go (Mon-Sat 10:00-16:00, Sun 11:00-19:00, supermarket open longer hours, Via Ricasoli 109). With your picnic in hand, hike around the block and join the bums on Piazza S.S. Annunziata, the first Renaissance square in Florence. There's a fountain for washing fruit on the square. Grab a stony seat anywhere you like, and savor one of my favorite cheap Florence eating experiences. Or, drop by any of the places listed earlier for an easy lunch (pizza, kebab, or sandwich plus juice) to go.

Dining with Bobo Away from the Center

Antica Trattoria da Tito, a 10-minute hike from the Accademia along Via San Gallo, is a long, drawn-out event of a meal. The boss, Bobo, is a fire hose of restaurateur energy who has clearly found his niche—making people happy with quality traditional food and lots of wine. His staff is as loyal as his clientele. While the food is great, there's no pretense. It's just a playground of Tuscan cuisine with "no romance allowed." As for the music he plays, Bobo says, "We are slaves of '80s." I'd come late and plan to party. To gorge on a feast of *antipasti* (meats, cheeses, fava beans, and bruschetta), consider ordering *fermami* (literally "stop me")—for €14, Bobo brings you food until you say, "*Fermami!*" A couple can get *fermami*, desserts, and a nice bottle of wine for €60 total. Ask for *vino* recommendations to experience that perfect pairing of food and wine. If you go with the flow here, you'll walk back to your hotel fat and filled with memories (€10 pastas, €12 *secondi*, €14 *gran tagliere*—big plate of cheese and meat, travelers with this book get a free after-dinner drink, Mon-Sat

12:30-15:00 & 19:00-23:00, closed Sun, reservations generally necessary, Via San Gallo 112 red, tel. 055-472-475).

Fast and Cheap near the Duomo

Self-Service Ristorante Leonardo is inexpensive, air-conditioned, quick, and handy. Eating here, you'll get the sense that they're passionate about the quality of their food. Stefano and Luciano (like Pavarotti) run the place with enthusiasm and put out free pitchers of tap water. It's just a block from the Duomo, southwest of the Baptistery (tasty €4 pastas, €5 main courses, Sun-Fri 11:45-14:45 & 18:45-21:45, closed Sat, upstairs at Via Pecori 11, tel. 055-284-446).

Döner Kebab: A good place to try this cheap Middle Eastern specialty is Turkuaz, a couple of blocks northeast of the Duomo (Via dei Servi 65).

Near Piazza della Signoria

Piazza della Signoria, the scenic square facing Palazzo Vecchio, is ringed by beautifully situated yet touristy eateries serving overpriced, bad-value, and probably microwaved food. If you're determined to eat on the square, have pizza at Ristorante il Cavallino or bar food from the Irish pub next door. Piazza della Signoria's saving grace is **Rivoire** café, famous for its fancy desserts and thick hot chocolate. While obscenely expensive, it has the best view tables on the square (Tue-Sun 7:30-24:00, closed Mon, tel. 055-214-412).

Fine Dining near Piazza della Signoria

Frescobaldi Ristorante and Wine Bar, the showcase of Italy's aristocratic wine family, is a good choice for a formal dinner in Florence. Candlelight reflects off glasses of wine, and high-vaulted ceilings complement the sophisticated dishes. They offer the same menu in three different dining areas: cozy interior, woody wine bar, and breezy terrace. If coming for dinner, make a reservation, dress up, and hit an ATM (€12 appetizers and pastas, €20 *secondi*, lunch salads, Tue-Sat 12:00-14:30 & 19:00-22:30, Mon 19:00-22:30, closed Sun and Aug, air-con, half a block north of Palazzo Vecchio at Via dei Magazzini 2-4 red, tel. 055-284-724, Francesco is the lead waiter).

Ristorante Paoli dishes up wonderful, traditional cuisine to loads of cheerful eaters being served by jolly little old men under a richly frescoed Gothic vault. Because of its fame and central location, it's filled mostly with tourists, but for a sophisticated, traditional Tuscan splurge meal, this is a fine choice. Salads are dramatically cut and mixed from a trolley right at your table. The walls are sweaty with memories that go back to 1824, and the service is flamboyant and fun-loving (but don't get taken—confirm prices). Woodrow Wilson slurped spaghetti here—his bust looks down on you as you eat (€11 pastas, €15 *secondi,* €25 tourist fixed-price meal, daily 12:00-15:00 & 19:00-23:00, reserve for dinner, between Piazza della Signoria and the Duomo at Via dei Tavolini 12 red, tel. 055-216-215).

Eating Cheaply and Simply near Piazza della Signoria

Cantinetta dei Verrazzano, a long-established bakery/café/wine bar, serves delightful sandwich plates in an old-time setting. Their *selection Verrazzano* is a fine plate of four little crostini (like mini-bruschetta) proudly featuring different breads, cheeses, and meats from the Chianti region (€7.50). The *tagliere di focacce,* a sampler plate of mini-focaccia sandwiches, is also fun (€14 for big plate for two). Add a €5 glass of Chianti to either of these dishes to make a fine, light meal. Office workers pop in for a quick lunch, and it's traditional to share tables. Be warned: Prices can add up here in a hurry. Jonathan, the high-powered and helpful manager, explains each dish and offers those with this book a free cup of coffee to cap your meal (Mon-Sat 8:00-21:00, closed Sun, just off Via de' Calzaiuoli, across from Orsanmichele Church at Via dei Tavolini 18, tel. 055-268-590). They also have benches and tiny tables for eating at take-out prices. Simply step to the back and point to a hot *focacce* sandwich (€3), order a drink at the bar, and take away your food or sit with Florentines and watch the action while you munch.

Osteria Vini e Vecchi Sapori, half a block north of the Palazzo Vecchio, is a colorful 16-seat hole-in-the-wall restaurant serving Tuscan food with a fun, accessible menu of delicious €8 pastas and €10 *secondi* (Tue-Sat 12:30-15:00 & 19:30-22:00, Sun 12:30-15:00, closed Mon, reserve for dinner; facing the bronze equestrian statue in Piazza della Signoria, go behind its tail into the corner and to your left; Via dei Magazzini 3 red, tel. 055-293-045, run by Mario while wife Rosanna cooks and son Thomas serves).

I Fratellini is an informal eatery where the "little brothers" have served peasants 29 different kinds of sandwiches and cheap glasses of Chianti wine (see list on wall) since 1875. Join the local crowd to order, then sit on a nearby curb or windowsill to eat, placing your glass on the wall rack before you leave (€4 for sandwich and wine, daily 9:00-20:00 or until the bread runs out, closed Sun in winter, 20 yards in front of Orsanmichele Church on Via dei Cimatori, tel. 055-239-6096). Be adventurous with the menu (easy-order by number). Consider *finocchiona* (#15, a special Tuscan salami), *lardo di Colonnata* (#22, lard aged in Carrara marble), and *cinghiale* (#19, spicy wild boar) sandwiches. Order the most expensive wine they're selling by the glass (Brunello for €5; bottles are labeled).

Gelato

Gelato is an edible art form. Italy's best ice cream is in Florence—one souvenir that can't break and won't clutter your luggage.

But beware of scams at touristy joints on busy streets that turn a simple request for a cone into a €10 "tourist special" rip-off. To avoid this, survey the size options and be very clear in your order (for example, "a €3 cone").

A key to gelato appreciation is sampling liberally and choosing flavors that go well together. Ask, as Italians do, for *"Un assaggio, per favore?"* (A taste, please?; oon ah-SAH-joh pehr fah-VOH-ray) and *"Che si sposano bene?"* (What marries well?; kay see spoh-ZAH-noh BEN-ay).

Artiginale, nostra produzione, and *produzione propia* mean gelato is made on the premises; also, gelato displayed in covered metal tins (rather than white plastic) is more likely to be homemade. Gelato aficionados avoid colors that don't appear in nature—for fewer chemicals and real flavor, go for mellow hues (bright colors attract children). These places are open daily for long hours.

Near the Duomo: The recent favorite in town, **Grom** uses organic ingredients and seasonal fresh fruit, along with biodegradable spoons and tubs. This clever chain markets its traditional approach with a staff quick to tell customers, "This gelato reminds me of my childhood." But there's no question that the quality is great—because the menu goes with what's in season (daily 10:30-24:00, Via delle Oche 24 red). Their *liquirizia* (licorice) flavor is worth a sample.

L'Antico Trippaio, an antique tripe stand, is a fixture in the town center (daily 9:00-20:00, on Via Dante Alighieri, mobile 339-742-5692). Cheap and authentic as can be, this is where Florentines come daily for €3.50 sandwiches *(panino),* featuring specialties like *trippa alla fiorentina* (tripe), *lampredotto* (cow's stomach), and a list of more appetizing options. Roberto and Maurizio offer a free plastic glass of rotgut Chianti with each sandwich for travelers with this book. The best people-watching place to enjoy your sandwich is three blocks away, on Piazza della Signoria.

Near Ponte Vecchio

'Ino Bottega di Alimentari e Vini is a mod little shop filled with gifty edibles. Alessandro and his staff serve sandwiches and wine—you'll get your €5-8 sandwich on a napkin with an included

Near Ponte Vecchio: **Gelateria Carrozze** is a longtime favorite (daily 11:00-20:00, until 1:00 in the morning in summer, on riverfront 30 yards from Ponte Vecchio toward the Uffizi at Piazza del Pesce 3).

Near the Accademia: A Sicilian choice on a tourist thoroughfare, **Gelateria Carabè** is particularly famous for its luscious *granite*—Italian ices made with fresh fruit (daily 11:00-20:00; from the Accademia, it's a block toward the Duomo at Via Ricasoli 60 red).

Near Orsanmichele Church: **Perchè No!** is located just off the busy main pedestrian drag, Via de' Calzaiuoli, and serves a stunning array of flavors (Via dei Tavolini 19).

Near the Church of Santa Croce: The venerable favorite, **Vivoli's** still has great gelato—but it's more expensive and stingy in its servings. Before ordering, try a free sample of their rice flavor—*riso* (closed Mon, Aug, and Jan; opposite the Church of Santa Croce, go down Via Torta a block and turn right on Via Stinche). Locals flock to **Gelateria de' Neri** (Via de' Neri 26 red), also owned by Vivoli's.

Near the Mercato Centrale: **The Bermuda Triangle** (a.k.a., I Gelati Del Bondi) is a hit both for its fresh ingredients and for the big-hearted energy of its owner, Vetulio (Via Nazionale 61 red, where it crosses Via Faenza, tel. 055-287-490).

Across the River: If you want an excuse to check out the little village-like neighborhood across the river from Santa Croce, enjoy a gelato at the tiny **Il Gelato di Filo** (named for Filippo and Lorenzo) at Via San Miniato 5 red, a few steps toward the river from Porta San Miniato. Gelato chef Edmir is proud of his fruity sorbet as well.

glass of their wine of the day as you perch on a tiny stool. They can also make a fine €12 *piatto misto* of cheeses and meats with bread (daily 11:00-17:00, immediately behind Uffizi Gallery on Ponte Vecchio side, Via dei Georgofili 3 red, tel. 055-219-208).

Between Palazzo Vecchio and Santa Croce Church

Trattoria Icche C'è C'è (EE-kay chay chay; dialect for "whatever there is, there is") is a small, family-style restaurant where fun-loving Gino and his wife Mara serve quality, local food, including a €13 three-course, fixed-price meal. While filled with tourists, the place exudes a charming mom-and-pop warmth (€8 pastas, €12 *secondi*, Tue-Sun 12:30-14:30 & 19:30-22:30, closed Mon and two weeks in Aug, midway between Bargello and river at Via Magalotti 11 red, tel. 055-216-589).

Ristorante del Fagioli is an enthusiastically run eatery where you feel the heritage. The dad, Gigi, commands the kitchen while family members Antonio, Maurizio, and Simone keep the throngs of loyal customers returning. The cuisine: home-style bread-soups, hearty steaks, and Florentine classics. Don't worry—while *fagioli* means "beans," that's the family name, not the extent of the menu (€9 pastas, €9 *secondi*, cash only, closed Sat-Sun, reserve for dinner, between Santa Croce Church and the Alle Grazie bridge at Corso dei Tintori 47, tel. 055-244-285).

Boccadama Enoteca Ristorante is a stylish, shabby-chic wine bistro serving traditional Tuscan fare based on seasonal produce. Eat in the intimate dining room with candles reflecting off bottle-lined walls or at one of the few tables on the dramatic Piazza Santa Croce. Reservations are smart (€9 *primi*, €14 *secondi*, daily 11:00-16:00 & 18:30-24:00, on south side of Piazza Santa Croce at 25-26 red, tel. 055-243-640, Marco).

Trattoria Anita, midway between the Uffizi and Santa Croce, offers a good lunch special: two hearty Tuscan courses for €8 (Mon-Sat 12:00-14:30 & 19:00-22:15, closed Sun, on the corner of Via Vinegia and Via del Parlagio at #2 red, tel. 055-218-698, run by three brothers: Nicola, Gianni, and Maurizio).

South of the River, in the Oltrarno
Dining with a Ponte Vecchio View

Golden View Open Bar is a lively, trendy bistro, good for a romantic meal or just a salad, pizza, or pasta with fine wine and a fine view of Ponte Vecchio and the Arno River. Reservations for window tables are essential unless you drop in early for dinner (reasonable prices, €10 pizzas and big salads, daily 11:30-24:00, impressive wine bar, 50 yards upstream from Ponte Vecchio at Via dei Bardi 58, tel. 055-214-502, run by Antonio, Marco, and Tomaso). They have four seating areas (with the same menu and prices) for whatever mood you're in: a riverside pizza place, a classier restaurant, a jazzy lounge, and a wine bar (they also serve a buffet of appetizers free with your drink from 19:00 to 21:00). Mixing their fine wine, river views, and live jazz makes for a wonderful evening (jazz nightly at 20:30 except Tue and Thu off-season).

Dining Well in the Oltrarno

Of the many good and colorful restaurants in the Oltrarno, these are my favorites. Reservations are a good idea in the evening.

Trattoria 4 Leoni creates the quintessential Oltrarno dinner scene. The Tuscan-style food is made with an innovative twist and an appreciation for vegetables. You'll enjoy the fun energy and characteristic seating, both inside and on the colorful square, Canto ai Quattro Pagoni. While the wines by the glass are pricey, the house wine is very good (€10 pastas, €15 *secondi,* daily 12:00-24:00, dinner reservations smart; from Ponte Vecchio walk four blocks up Via de' Guicciardini, turn right on Via dello Sprone, then slightly left to Via de' Vellutini 1; tel. 055-218-562).

Olio & Convivium Gastronomia is primarily a catering company for top-end events, and this is where they showcase their cooking. It started as an elegant deli whose refined oil-tasting room morphed into a romantic, aristocratic restaurant. Their three intimate rooms are surrounded by fine *prosciutti,* cheeses, and wine shelves. It can seem intimidating and a little pretentious, but well-dressed foodies will appreciate this place for its quiet atmosphere. Their list of €13-20 *gastronomia* plates offers an array of taste treats and fine wines by the glass (€14 pastas, €18 *secondi,* stylish €18 lunches with wine, €3 cover, Tue-Sat 12:00-14:30 & 19:00-22:30, Mon lunch only, closed Sun, strong air-con, Via di Santo Spirito 4, tel. 055-265-8198, Monica).

Antico Ristoro Di' Cambi is a meat-lover's dream—thick with Tuscan traditions, rustic touches, and T-bone steaks. The bustling scene has a memorable, beer-hall energy. As you walk in, you'll pass a glass case filled with red chunks of Chianina beef that's priced by weight (€40/kilo, standard serving is half a kilo per person). Before you OK your investment, they'll show you the cut and tell you the weight. While the steak comes nearly uncooked, it's air dried for 21 days so it's not really raw, just very tasty and tender—making you so happy you're sitting at the top of the food chain. This is also a good chance to enjoy the famous *bistecca alla fiorentina,* sitting inside the convivial woody interior or outside on a square (€8 pastas, €12 *secondi,* closed Sun, reserve on weekends and to sit outside, Via Sant'Onofrio 1 red, one block south of Ponte Amerigo Vespucci, tel. 055-217-134, run by Stefano and Fabio, the Cambi cousins).

Trattoria da Sergio is a tiny eatery about a block before Porta San Frediano, one of Florence's medieval gates. It has charm and a strong following, so reservations are a must. The food is on the gourmet side of home-cooking—mama's favorites with a modern twist—and therefore a bit more expensive (€9 pastas, €15 *secondi,* Tue-Sun 12:00-15:00 & 19:15-23:00, closed Mon, Borgo San Frediano 145 red, tel. 055-223-449, Sergio and Marco).

Il Santo Bevitore Ristorante, lit like a Rembrandt painting and filled with dressy tables, serves creative Tuscan cuisine. They're enthusiastic about matching quality produce from the area with the right wine (€10 pastas, €8-15 meat-and-cheese plates or *tagliere,* good wine list by the glass or bottle, come early or make reservations, no outside seating, Via di Santo Spirito 64, tel. 055-211-264).

Trattoria Al Tranvai, with tight seating and small dark-wood tables, looks like an old-time tram filled with the neighborhood gang. A 10-minute walk from the river at the edge of the Oltrarno, it feels like a small town's favorite eatery (€8 pastas, €10 *secondi*, closed Sun, Piazza T. Tasso 14 red, tel. 055-225-197).

Eating Cheaply in the Oltrarno

Trattoria Sabatino, the farthest away and least touristy of my Oltrarno listings, is a spacious, brightly lit mess hall—disturbingly cheap—with family character and a simple menu. It's a super place to watch locals munch. You'll find it just outside Porta San Frediano, a 15-minute walk from Ponte Vecchio (€4 pastas, €5 *secondi*, Mon-Fri 12:00-15:00 & 19:15-22:00, closed Sat-Sun, Via Pisana 2 red, tel. 055-225-955, little English spoken).

Trattoria Casalinga, an inexpensive standby, comes with aproned women bustling around the kitchen. Florentines and tourists alike pack the place and leave full and happy, with euros to spare for gelato (€6 pastas, €8 *secondi*, Mon-Sat 12:00-14:30 & 19:00-21:45, after 20:00 reserve or wait, closed Sun and Aug, just off Piazza di Santo Spirito, near the church at Via de' Michelozzi 9 red, tel. 055-218-624, Andrea).

Borgo Antico is the hit of Piazza di Santo Spirito, with enticing pizzas, big deluxe plates of pasta, a delightful setting, and a trendy and boisterous young crowd (€9 pizza and pasta, €16 *secondi*, daily 12:00-24:00, best to reserve for a seat on the square, Piazza di Santo Spirito 6 red, tel. 055-210-437, Andrea and Michele—feel his forearm). **Volume**, the bar next door, is run by the same gang.

Ricchi Caffè, next to Borgo Antico, has fine gelato, homemade desserts, shaded outdoor tables, and pasta dishes at lunch (daily 7:00-24:00, tel. 055-215-864). After noting the plain facade of the Brunelleschi church facing the square, step inside the café and pick your favorite picture of the many ways the facade might be finished.

Supermarket: Facing the Pitti Palace, **Meta Supermarket** seems designed to rescue poor, hungry, and thirsty travelers (daily 9:00-21:00, Piazza de' Pitti 33 red).

Florence Connections

Florence is Tuscany's transportation hub, with fine train, bus, and plane connections to virtually anywhere in Italy. The city has several train stations, a bus station (next to the main train station), and an airport (plus Pisa's airport is nearby). Livorno, on the coast west of Florence, is a major cruise-ship port for passengers visiting Florence, Pisa, and other nearby destinations.

By Train

From Florence by Train to: Pisa (2-3/hour, 1.25 hours, €5.80), **Lucca** (2/hour, 1.5 hours, €5), **Siena** (direct trains hourly, 1.5 hours, €6.20; bus is better because Siena's train station is far from the center), **Livorno**—cruise ship port described later (hourly, 1.5 hours, some change in Pisa), **La Spezia** (for the Cinque Terre, 5/day direct, 2 hours, otherwise nearly hourly with change in Pisa, €9.30), **Milan** (hourly, 1.75 hours), **Milan's Malpensa Airport** (2/day direct, 2.75 hours), **Venice** (hourly, 2-3 hours, may transfer in Bologna; often crowded—reserve ahead), **Assisi** (8/day direct, 2-3 hours, €11), **Orvieto** (hourly, 2 hours, some with change in Campo di Marte or Rifredi station), **Rome** (at least hourly, 1.5 hours, most connections require seat reservations, €45), **Naples** (hourly, 3 hours), **Brindisi** (8/day, 8 hours with change in Bologna or Rome, €90), **Interlaken** (8/day, 6-7 hours, 2-3 changes), **Frankfurt** (1/day, 12 hours, 1-3 changes), **Paris** (3/day, 10-15 hours, 1-2 changes, important to reserve overnight train ahead), **Vienna** (1 direct overnight train, or 5/day with 1-3 changes, 10-16 hours).

By Bus

The SITA bus station (100 yards west of the Florence train station on Via Santa Caterina da Siena) is traveler-friendly—a big, old-school lot with numbered stalls and all the services you'd expect. Schedules for regional trips are posted everywhere, and TV monitors show imminent departures. Bus service drops dramatically on Sunday.

By Bus to: San Gimignano (hourly, 1.25-2 hours, change in Poggibonsi, less frequent on Sat-Sun, €6.25), **Siena** (2/hour, 1.25-hour *corse rapide* buses are fastest—even faster than the train, €7), **Volterra** (4/day, 1/day Sun, 2 hours, change in Colle Val d'Elsa where you catch a convenient CPT bus, €7.60), Florence's **Amerigo Vespucci Airport** (2/hour, 30 minutes, €5, just pay driver, always from platform 1). Try to buy bus tickets in the station, as you'll pay 30 percent more if you buy tickets on the bus. Bus info: www.sitabus.it or tel. 800-373-760 (Mon-Fri 8:30-18:30, Sat 8:30-12:30, closed Sun); some schedules are listed in the *Florence Concierge Information* magazine.

By Taxi

For small groups with more money than time, zipping to nearby towns by taxi can be a good value (e.g., €120 from your Florence hotel to your Siena hotel).

A more comfortable alternative is to hire a private car service. Florence-based **Transfer Chauffeur Service** has a fleet of modern vehicles with drivers who can whisk you between cities, to and from the cruise ship port, and through the Tuscan countryside

FLORENCE

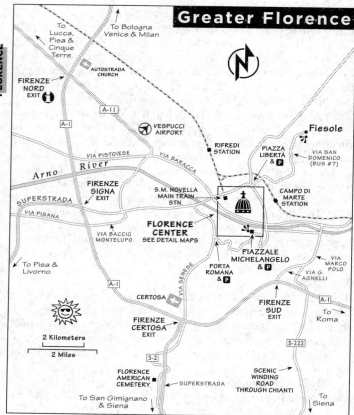

Greater Florence

for around the same price as a cab (€130 for Florence to Siena, tel. 055-614-2182, mobile 338-862-3129, www.transfercs.com, marco .masala@transfercs.com, Marco).

By Plane

For information on Florence's **Amerigo Vespucci Airport,** see page 445. For Pisa's **Galileo Galilei Airport,** see page 539.

By Cruise Ship

Florence's port is Livorno (sometimes called "Leghorn" in English), a coastal town located about 60 miles west of Florence.

Of the excursion options, **Florence** is the most time-consuming to reach (roughly two hours each way by public transit); it will take you the whole day.

Pisa is closer (about an hour each way), and—since Pisa is well-connected with **Lucca**—it's possible to combine those two cities into one long day. (If doing this, save Pisa until after lunch to avoid the cruise crowds in the morning, and be aware that most shops and restaurants in Lucca are closed Sun-Mon.)

No matter where you go, if you're taking the train, keep in mind that it takes 30 minutes just to get from Livorno's cruise port to the train station across town. Also, be sure to plan your day conservatively, as trains can be delayed.

Tourist Information: Livorno's TI kiosk is on Piazza del Municipio, right next to the stop for the shuttle bus to the port (May-Oct daily 8:00-18:00; Nov-April Mon-Sat 9:00-17:00, closed Sun; tel. 0586-204-611). Public **WCs** are in City Hall, across the street from the TI on Piazza del Municipio.

Livorno Arrival and Connections

Livorno's port (at the western edge of town) is vast and sprawling, but most arriving cruise ships dock in one of two places: Molo 75, at the **Porto Mediceo;** or the adjacent **Molo Capitaniera.** Livorno's city center clusters around two nearby squares: **Piazza Grande** (stop for bus #1 to train station) and **Piazza del Municipio** (TI, public WCs, stop for shuttle bus to the port). The squares are connected by the two-block-long Via Cogorano (ATMs).

Most cruise lines offer a **shuttle bus** to the center of Livorno, dropping you off at a bus stop near the TI kiosk in Piazza del Municipio (sometimes free, possibly about €5 round-trip).

Taxis to Florence, Pisa, and Lucca are very expensive (explained later); any budget-minded traveler with patience can use public transportation to go from Livorno to any of these places, and back again before your ship departs. The basic plan is this: Walk or ride the cruise line's shuttle bus from the port to downtown Livorno; then ride a public bus to Livorno's train station; then take the train to wherever you're going.

Public Transportation Between Livorno and Florence, Pisa, and Lucca

From Livorno Centrale Station, trains zip to Florence, Pisa, Lucca, and other points in Italy. Note that all train lines go first to Pisa, then split: north to Lucca or east to Florence.

To Florence: Hourly, usually departs at :10 after the hour, arrive in Florence at :32 past the following hour—1 hour and 22 minutes total, €6.70 on a regional train. (There are also some departures that are a few minutes shorter, but require you to change trains at Pisa Centrale.)

To Pisa: 2-3/hour, 20 minutes, €1.90 on a regional train.

To Lucca: About hourly, around 1 hour (up to 1.25 hours), transfer at Pisa Centrale, €3.70 on a regional train.

To Lucca and Pisa: If you want to visit Lucca and Pisa in one

FLORENCE

day, take the train to Lucca first. A handy bus connects Lucca's Piazzale Giuseppe Verdi to Pisa's Field of Miracles (hourly, 30 minutes, €3.50).

Taxi Excursions

Taxis meet arriving cruise ships and offer various day trips around the area (the cabbie drops you off for a designated amount of time in one or two cities). Here are some ballpark round-trip fares: **Pisa**—€120, **Pisa and Lucca**—€220, **Florence**—€320. The fare can vary, depending on the number of people and the season. Some cabs fit up to eight people, bringing the cost down to about €40 per person.

Taxis both at the port and in the city offer the same rates. Clarify the fare beforehand, even though by law the driver must have the meter on (the quoted price will usually be less than the meter).

Near Florence: Fiesole

Perched on a hill overlooking the Arno valley, Fiesole gives weary travelers a break in the action and—during the heat of summer—

a breezy location from which to admire the city below. It's a small town with a main square, a few restaurants and shops, a few minor sights, and a great view. The ancient Etruscans knew a good spot when they saw one, and chose to settle here, establishing Fiesole about 400 years before the Romans founded Florence. Wealthy Renaissance families in pre-air-conditioning days also chose Fiesole (fee-AY-zoh-lay) as a preferred vacation spot, building villas in the hillsides surrounding the town. Later, 19th-century Romantics spent part of the Grand Tour admiring the vistas, much like the hordes of tourists do today. Most come here for the view—the actual sights pale in comparison to those in Florence. Shutterbugs visit in the morning for the best light.

Getting to Fiesole: From Florence's Piazza San Marco, take bus #7—enjoying a peek at gardens, vineyards, orchards, and villas—to the last stop, Piazza Mino (4/hour, fewer after 20:00, 30 minutes, €1.20 or €2 if bought on bus; departs Florence from Piazza San Marco; wear your money belt—thieves frequent this bus). Taxis from Florence cost about €20 (ride to highest point you want to visit—La Reggia Ristorante for view terrace or Church of San Francesco—then explore downhill).

Tourist Information: The TI, immediately to the right of the Roman Archaeological Park, is a two-minute walk from the bus stop—head behind the church (daily 10:30-17:00, Via Portigiani 3, tel. 055-598-720).

Market Day: A modest selection of food and household items fills Via Portigiani, just off Piazza Mino, on Saturday mornings until 13:00.

Sights in Fiesole

Fiesole's main sights are either free or covered under one €10 combo-ticket, available at the Roman Theater.

▲▲**Terrace and Garden with a View**—Catch the sunset (and your breath) from the view terrace just below La Reggia Ristorante. It's a steep seven-minute hike from the Fiesole bus stop: Face the bell tower and take Via San Francesco, on the left. (For similar views and a peek at residential Fiesole, climb up the opposite side of the square, along the road hugging the ridgeline.)

Church of San Francesco—For even more hill-climbing, continue up from the view terrace to this charming little church. The small scale and several colorful altar paintings make this church more enjoyable than Fiesole's Duomo (free, Mon-Sat 8:00-12:00 & 15:00-19:00, Sun 7:00-11:00 & 15:00-19:00, Via San Francesco 13, tel. 055-59175).

Ethnographic Missionary Museum—This eclectic little collection, hidden beneath the church of San Francesco, includes an Egyptian mummy, ancient coins, Chinese Buddhas, and the *in situ* ruins of a third-century Etruscan wall (donation suggested, Tue-Sun 9:30-12:00 & 15:00-19:00, closed Mon, unmarked door inside church leads to cloisters and museum).

Duomo—While this church has a drab, 19th-century exterior, the interior is worth a look, if only for the blue-and-white glazed Giovanni della Robbia statue of St. Romulus over the entry door (free, daily 10:00-17:00, across Piazza Mino from the bus stop).

Roman Theater and Archaeological Park—Occasionally used today for plays, this well-preserved theater held up to 2,000 people. The site's other ruins are, well, ruined, and lacking in explanation. But the valley view and peaceful setting are lovely (€10 combo-ticket also covers Civic and Bandini museums, daily 10:00-18:00; from the bus stop cross Piazza Mino, heading toward the back of the Duomo).

Civic Museum—Located within the Archaeological Park, the museum imparts insight into Fiesole's Etruscan and Roman roots with well-displayed artifacts and with a few English description sheets in the corners (covered by €10 combo-ticket, daily 10:00-18:00).

Bandini Museum—This petite museum displays the wooden panels of lesser-known Gothic and Renaissance painters as well as the glazed terra-cotta figures of Andrea della Robbia (covered by €10 combo-ticket, daily 10:00-18:00, behind Duomo at Via Dupre 1).

Eating in Fiesole

These two restaurants are on Piazza Mino, where the bus from Florence stops.

Ristorante Perseus, a local favorite, lacks views but serves authentic Tuscan dishes at a fair price in a rambling interior, at a few sidewalk tables, or on a shady garden terrace in fair weather (Fri-Wed 12:30-14:30 & 19:30-23:30, closed Thu, tel. 055-59-143, Leonardo).

Ristorante Aurora is an upscale alternative with a view terrace overlooking the city of Florence (daily 12:00-14:30 & 19:00-22:30, tel. 055-59-363).

Picnics: Fiesole is made-to-order for a scenic and breezy picnic. Grab a pastry at Fiesole's best *pasticceria*, **Alcedo** (head up the main drag from the bus stop to Via Gramsci 27). Round out your goodies at the **Co-op** supermarket on Via Gramsci before walking up to the panoramic terrace. Or, for more convenience and less view, picnic at the shaded park on the way to the view terrace (walk up Via San Francesco about halfway to the terrace, and climb the stairs to the right).

PISA AND LUCCA

Florence is within easy striking distance of a number of great cities—as their fortifications attest. Along with Siena (see the Siena chapter), Pisa and Lucca show that Florence wasn't the only power and cultural star of the late Middle Ages and Renaissance.

Pisa's famous Field of Miracles (Leaning Tower, Duomo, and Baptistery) is touristy but worth a visit. Lucca, contained within its fine Renaissance wall, has a charm that causes many connoisseurs of Italy to claim it as a favorite stop.

The two towns are 30 minutes from each other by hourly bus. Each is about 1.5 hours (or less) by train from Florence and well-served by excellent highways. Using public transportation, you could day-trip from Florence to both cities. But with more time, stay overnight in Lucca. Take the train to Pisa in the morning, do your sightseeing, catch the bus to Lucca late in the afternoon, enjoy the evening scene, and stay the night. Sightsee Lucca the next day, then move on to your next destination by train.

Pisa

In A.D. 1200, Pisa's power peaked. For nearly three centuries (1000-1300), Pisa rivaled Venice and Genoa as a sea-trading power, exchanging European goods for luxury items in Muslim lands. As a port near the mouth of the Arno River (six miles from the coast), the city enjoyed easy access to the Mediterranean, plus the protection of sitting a bit upstream. The Romans had made it a navy base, and by medieval times it was a major player in the region.

Pisa's 150-foot galleys cruised the Mediterranean, gaining control of the islands of Corsica, Sardinia, and Sicily, and trading with other Europeans, Muslims, and Byzantine Christians as far south as North Africa and as far east as Syria. European Crusaders hired Pisan boats to carry them and their supplies as they headed off to conquer the Muslim-held Holy Land. The Pisan "Republic" prided itself on its independence from both popes and emperors. The city used its sea-trading wealth to build the grand monuments of the Field of Miracles, including the now-famous Leaning Tower.

But the Pisan fleet was routed in battle by Genoa (1284, at Meloria, off Livorno), their overseas outposts were taken away, the port silted up, and Pisa was left high and dry, with only its Field of Miracles and its university to keep it on the map.

Pisa's three important sights—the Duomo, Baptistery, and the Tower—float regally on the best lawn in Italy. The architectural style throughout is Pisa's very own "Pisan Romanesque." Even as the church was being built, Piazza del Duomo was nicknamed the "Campo dei Miracoli," or Field of Miracles, for the grandness of the undertaking.

The Tower has reopened after a decade of restoration and top-ple-prevention. To ascend, you'll have to get your ticket and book a time at least a few hours in advance (for details, see page 529).

Planning Your Time

For most visitors, Pisa is a touristy quickie—seeing the Tower, visiting the square, and wandering through the church are 90 percent of their Pisan thrills. But it's a shame to skip the rest of the city; considering its historic importance and the wonderful ambience created by its rich architectural heritage and vibrant student population, Pisa deserves a half-day visit. For many, the lack of tourists outside the Field of Miracles is both a surprise and a relief.

If you want to climb the Tower, upon arrival in the city go straight to the ticket office to snag an appointment—usually for a couple of hours later (for directions to the Field of Miracles, see "Arrival in Pisa," later). For an extra €2, you can book a time online (at least 15 days in advance) at www.opapisa.it. If you'll be seeing both the town and the Field of Miracles, plan on a six-hour stop. If you're just blitzing the Field of Miracles, three hours is the minimum. Spending the night lets you savor a great Italian city scene.

If you're day-tripping to Pisa from Lucca, or doing a Lucca/Pisa day trip from Florence, note that a handy bus runs hourly between the Field of Miracles and Lucca, saving time and hassle (see page 539 for details).

Orientation to Pisa

The city of Pisa is framed on the north by the Field of Miracles (Leaning Tower) and on the south by the Pisa Centrale train station.

tion. The Arno River flows east to west, bisecting the city. Walking from Pisa Centrale directly to the Tower takes about 30 minutes (but allow up to an hour if you take my self-guided walk). The two main streets for tourists and shoppers are Via Santa Maria (running south from the Tower) and Corso Italia/Borgo Stretto (running north from the station).

Tourist Information

One TI is about 200 yards from Pisa Centrale train station—exit and walk straight up the left side of the street to the big, circular Piazza Vittorio Emanuele II. The TI is on the left, around the corner from #16 (Mon-Sat 9:00-19:00, Sun 9:00-16:00, tel. 050-42291). Another TI is east of the Tower, in the Duomo Museum, although it may close or move in 2012 (if open, daily April-Sept

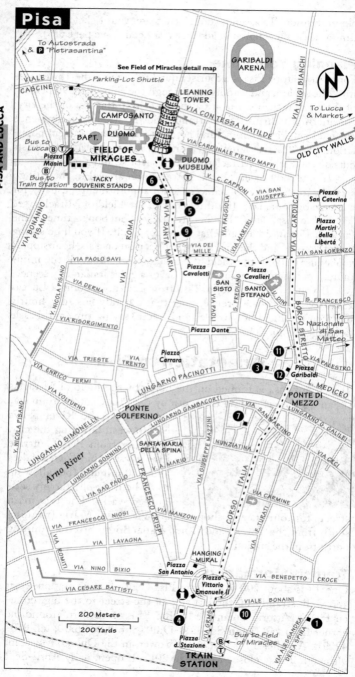

Pisa

To Autostrada & P "Pietrasantina"

GARIBALDI ARENA

See Field of Miracles detail map

VIALE CASCINE

Parking-Lot Shuttle

VIA LUIGI BIANCHI

To Lucca & Market

LEANING TOWER

VIA CONTESSA MATILDE

CAMPOSANTO

DUOMO

VIA CARDINALE PIETRO MAFFI

OLD CITY WALLS

Bus to Lucca

BAPT.

Piazza Manin

FIELD OF MIRACLES

DUOMO MUSEUM

V. C. CAPPONI

Bus to Train Station

TACKY SOUVENIR STANDS

6

VIA SAN GIUSEPPE

Piazza San Caterina

VIA BONANNO PISANO

ROMA

8

2

5

VIA FAGGIOLA

VIA MARTIRI

Piazza Martiri della Libertà

VIA G. CARDUCCI

9

VIA SANTA MARIA

VIA DEI MILLE

VIA SAN LORENZO

VIA PAOLO SAVI

VIA NICOLA PISANO

VIA

VIA DERNA

Piazza Cavalotti

SAN SISTO

S. FREDIANO

Piazza Cavalieri

SANTO STEFANO

U. DINI

S. FRANCESCO

VIA RISORGIMENTO

To Nazionale di San Matteo

BORGO STRETTO

VIA TRIESTE

VIA TRENTO

Piazza Dante

Piazza Carrara

VIA PALESTRO

VIA ENRICO FERMI

LUNGARNO PACINOTTI

11

VIA VOLTURNO

3

Piazza Garibaldi

12

L. MEDICEO

V. NICOLA PISANO

LUNGARNO SIMONELLI

PONTE SOLFERINO

Lungarno Gambacorti

PONTE DI MEZZO

LUNGARNO G. GALILEI

Arno River

LUNGARNO SONNINO

SANTA MARIA DELLA SPINA

V. A. MARIO

NUNZIATINA

7

VIA SAN MARTINO

VIA CEGI

LUNGARNO PAOLO

V. FRANCESCO CRISPI

VIA GIUSEPPE MAZZINI

VIA FRANCESCO NIOSI

VIA MANZONI

CORSO ITALIA

VIA CARMINE

VIA LAVAGNA

VIA ROMITI

VIA NINO BIXIO

HANGING MURAL

Piazza San Antonio

VIA BENEDETTO CROCE

VIA CESARE BATTISTI

Piazza Vittorio Emanuele II

VIALE BONAINI

200 Meters

4

VIA GRAMSCI

10

1

200 Yards

Piazza d. Stazione

Bus to Field of Miracles

VIA ALESSANDRA DELLA SPINA

TRAIN STATION

Pisa Key

1. Hotel Alessandro della Spina
2. Hotel Villa Kinzica
3. Hotel Royal Victoria & Caffè dell'Ussero
4. Hotel Milano
5. Pensione Helvetia
6. La Buca Pizzeria/Trattoria
7. Ristorante Bagus
8. Paninoteca il Canguro
9. Panetteria Antiche Tradizioni
10. La Lupa Ghiotta Tavola Calda
11. Via delle Colonne Produce Market & Restaurants
12. La Bottega del Gelato

9:30-19:30, Oct-March 10:00-17:00). There's also a TI at the airport (daily 9:30-23:30).

Arrival in Pisa

By Train

Most trains (and visitors) arrive at Pisa Centrale Station, about a mile south of the Tower and Field of Miracles. A few trains also stop at the smaller Pisa S. Rossore Station, which is just four blocks from the Tower (not all trains stop here, but if yours does, hop off).

Pisa Centrale: This station has a baggage-check desk—look for *deposito bagagli* (€3/bag for 12 hours, daily 6:00-21:00, they photocopy your passport to check ID). As you get off the train, it's to the right at the far end of platform 1, just after the police station.

To get from this station to the Field of Miracles, you can **walk** (get free map from TI, 30 minutes direct, one hour if you follow my self-guided walk), take a **taxi** (€7-10, tel. 050-541-600, taxi stand at station), or go by **bus.** Take bus LAM Rossa (4-6/hour, after 20:00 3/hour, 15 minutes), which stops across the street from the train station, in front of the NH Cavalieri Hoteles. Buy a €1.10 bus ticket from the tobacco/magazine kiosk in the train station's main hall or at any tobacco shop (€1.50 if you buy it on board, smart to have exact change, good for 1 hour, round-trip permitted). Before getting on the bus, confirm that it is indeed going to "Campo dei Miracoli" (ask driver, a local, or TI) or risk taking a long tour of Pisa's suburbs. The correct buses let you off at Piazza Manin, in front of the gate to the Field of Miracles; drivers make sure tourists don't miss the stop.

To return to the train station from the Tower, catch the bus in front of the BNL bank, across the street from where you got off (again, confirm the destination—"Stazione Centrale," staht-see-OHN-ay chen-TRAHL-ay). You'll also find a taxi stand 30 yards from the Tower (at Bar Duomo).

Pisa S. Rossore: To get from this station to the Field of

Miracles, it's just a four-block walk. Follow Viale delle Cascine east, continuing as it turns into Via Contessa Matilde, and follow signs to *La Torre*—or just head toward the dome of the Baptistery. From this station, the nearest TI is the one at the Duomo Museum.

By Car

It's best to leave your car at the big Pietrasantina parking lot, designed for tour buses (which pay €110 to park) and tourists with cars (who park for free). From there, a regular city bus shuttles you to the Field of Miracles (driving in the city center will likely net you a steep fine—cameras catch you and the city sends you a ticket by mail).

To reach the parking lot, exit the autostrada at *Pisa Nord* and follow signs to *Pisa* (on the left). Pass the second traffic light and turn left toward the city center. Go straight, following the *Bus Parking* signs, until you see the gas station. The parking lot is on the left. Here you'll find a cafeteria, WC, lots of big buses, and a bus stop for the Line C shuttle that goes back and forth between the lot and the Largo Cocco Griffi bus stop, just behind the walls of the Field of Miracles (6/hour, daily 8:30-19:20, €1.50, buy round-trip ticket on board). Or, if you have more time and want to follow my self-guided walk through Pisa to the Field of Miracles, take bus LAM Rossa to Pisa Centrale train station (4-6/hour, after 20:00 3/hour, €1.10 if you buy ticket at parking-lot cafeteria, €1.50 if purchased on board, en route also stops near the Tower).

By Plane

For details on Pisa's Galileo Galilei Airport, see page 539.

Helpful Hints

Markets: An open-air produce market attracts picnickers to Piazza della Vettovaglie, one block north of the Arno River near Ponte di Mezzo, and nearby Piazza Sant'Uomobuono (Mon-Sat 7:00-18:00, main section closes at 13:00, closed Sun). A street market—with more practical goods than food—bustles on Wednesday and Saturday mornings between Via del Brennero and Via Paparrelle (8:00-13:00, just outside of wall, about 6 blocks east of the Tower).

Festivals: The first half of June has many events, culminating in a celebration for Pisa's patron saint (June 16-17).

Local Guide: Dottore Vincenzo Riolo is a great guide for Pisa and the surrounding area (€130/3 hours, mobile 338-211-2939, www.pisatour.it, info@pisatour.it).

Tours: To get beyond the tourist mobs and understand the cultural powerhouse that Pisa once was, consider the "Walking in Pisa" tour. Local guides lead a two- to three-hour walking tour in English (and Italian) that covers the city rather than the famous Tower sights (€12, ask at hotel or check website for times, tel. 050-830-253, mobile 328-144-6855 after hours, www.pisatour.it, Vincenzo).

Self-Guided Walk

Welcome to Pisa: From Pisa Centrale Train Station to the Tower

A leisurely one-hour stroll from the station to the Tower is a great way to get acquainted with the more subtle virtues of this Renaissance city. Because the hordes who descend daily on the Tower rarely bother with the rest of the town, you'll find most of Pisa to be delightfully untouristy—a student-filled, classy, Old World town with an Arno-scape much like its upstream rival, Florence. Pisa is pretty small, with just 100,000 people. But its 45,000 students keep it lively, especially at night.

• *From Pisa Centrale train station, walk north up Viale Gramsci to the circular square called...*

Piazza Vittorio Emanuele II

As Pisa was considered to be of strategic importance in World War II, both the train station and its main bridge were targeted. For that reason, 40 percent of this district was destroyed. Looking at the makeshift walls that surround the square, you may think it's still a bombed-out zone. The piazza is being rebuilt to include an underground parking lot, but the project was delayed after workers

accidentally damaged an ancient structure while digging. The entire wall of a building just to the left of the piazza was painted by American artist Keith Haring in 1989 to create *Tuttomondo (Whole Wide World)*. Haring (who died of AIDS in 1990) brought New York City graffiti into the mainstream. This painting is a celebration of diversity, chaos, and the liveliness of our world, vibrating with energy. On the piazza, you'll also find a TI.

• *Walk up Corso Italia to the river.*

Corso Italia

Cutting through the center of town, this is Pisa's main drag. As it leaves Piazza Vittorio Emanuele II, look to the right to see the circa-1960 wall map of Pisa with a steam train (on the wall of the bar on the corner). You'll also see plenty of youthful fashions, as kids are out making the scene here. Be on guard for pickpockets—too young to arrest, they can only be kicked out of town. Pushed out of their former happy hunting grounds, the Field of Miracles, they now work the crowds here, often dressed as tourists.

• *Follow the pedestrianized Corso Italia straight north to the Arno River and Ponte di Mezzo. Stop in the center of the bridge.*

PISA AND LUCCA

Ponte di Mezzo

This modern bridge, constructed on the same site where the Romans built one, marks the center of Pisa. In the Middle Ages, this bridge (like Florence's Ponte Vecchio) was lined with shops. It's been destroyed several times by floods and in 1943 by British and American bombers. Enjoy the view from the center of the bridge, with its long lines of elegant mansions recalling days of trading glory—the cityscape feels a bit like Venice's Grand Canal. Pisa sits on shifting delta sand, making construction tricky. The entire town leans. With innovative arches above ground and below, architects didn't stop the leaning—but they have made buildings that wobble without being threatened.

• *Cross the bridge to...*

Piazza Garibaldi

This square is named for the charismatic leader of the Risorgimento, the unification movement that led to Italian independence in 1870. Knowing Pisa was strongly nationalist, Garibaldi came here when wounded to be nursed back to health. Many Pisans died in the national struggle. **La Bottega del Gelato,** Pisa's favorite gelato place, is on Piazza Garibaldi (daily 11:30-24:00). You can side-trip about 100 yards downstream to **Caffè dell'Ussero** (famous for its fine 14th-century red terra-cotta original facade, at #28, Sun-Fri 7:00-21:00, closed Sat) and browse its time-warp interior, lined with portraits and documents from the struggle for Italian independence.

• *Continue north up the elegantly arcaded...*

Borgo Stretto

Welcome to Pisa's main shopping street. On the right, the Church of St. Michael, with its fine Pisan Romanesque facade, still sports some 16th-century graffiti. I'll bet you can see some modern graffiti across the street. Students have been pushing their causes here—or simply defacing things—for five centuries.

From here, look farther up the street and notice how it undulates like a flowing river. In the sixth century B.C., Pisa was born when two parallel rivers were connected by canals. This street echoes the flow of one of those canals. An 11th-century landslide rerouted the second river, destroying ancient Pisa, and the entire city had to regenerate.

• *After a few steps, detour left onto Via delle Colonne, and walk one block down to...*

Piazza delle Vettovaglie

Pisa's historic market square, Piazza delle Vettovaglie, is lively day and night. Its Renaissance loggia has hosted the fish and vegetable market for generations. The stalls are set up in this piazza during the morning (Mon-Sat 7:00-13:00, closed Sun), and stay open later in the neighboring piazza to the west (Piazza Sant'Uomobuono, Mon-Sat 7:00-18:00, closed Sun). You could cobble together a picnic from the sandwich shops and fruit-and-veggie stalls ringing these squares.

• *Continue north on Borgo Stretto another 100 yards, passing an ugly bomb site on the right, with its horrible 1960s reconstruction. Take the second left on nondescript Via Ulisse Dini (it's not obvious—turn left immediately at the arcade's end, just before the pharmacy). This leads to Pisa's historic core, Piazza dei Cavalieri.*

Piazza dei Cavalieri

With its old clock and colorfully decorated palace, this piazza was once the seat of the independent Republic of Pisa's government. In

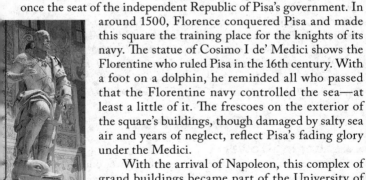

around 1500, Florence conquered Pisa and made this square the training place for the knights of its navy. The statue of Cosimo I de' Medici shows the Florentine who ruled Pisa in the 16th century. With a foot on a dolphin, he reminded all who passed that the Florentine navy controlled the sea—at least a little of it. The frescoes on the exterior of the square's buildings, though damaged by salty sea air and years of neglect, reflect Pisa's fading glory under the Medici.

With the arrival of Napoleon, this complex of grand buildings became part of the University of Pisa. The university is one of Europe's oldest, with roots in a law school that dates back as far as the 11th century. In the mid-16th century, the city was a hotbed of controversy, as spacey professors like Galileo Galilei studied the solar system—with results that challenged the church's powerful doctrine. More recently, the blind tenor Andrea Bocelli attended law school in Pisa before embarking on his well-known musical career.

• *From here, take Via Corsica (to the left of the clock).*

The humble **Church of San Sisto,** ahead on the left (side entrance on Via Corsica), is worth a quick look. With simple bricks, assorted reused columns, heavy walls, and few windows,

Field of Miracles Tickets

Pisa has a combo-ticket scheme designed to get you into its neglected secondary sights: the Baptistery, Camposanto Cemetery, Duomo Museum, and Museum of the Sinopias (fresco pattern museum). For €5, you get your choice of one of these sights; for two of these sights or one plus the Duomo, the cost is €6; for three of the above you pay €8; and for the works, you'll pay €10 (credit cards accepted). By comparison, the Duomo alone is a bargain (€2).

You can buy any of these tickets either behind the Leaning Tower or at the Museum of the Sinopias (near Baptistery, almost suffocated by souvenir stands). Both ticket offices have big, yellow, triangle-shaped signs.

No matter what ticket you get, you'll have to pay an additional €15 to climb the Tower. Tickets for the Tower are sold at the ticket offices or online at least 15 days in advance at www .opapisa.it (€2 fee).

this was the typical Romanesque style that predated the more lavish Pisan Romanesque style of the Field of Miracles structures.
• Follow Via Corsica as it turns into Via dei Mille (and grab a quick bite at the recommended **Panetteria Antiche Tradizioni**), then turn right on Via Santa Maria, which leads north, through increasingly touristy claptrap, directly to the Field of Miracles and the Tower.

Sights in Pisa

▲▲▲Leaning Tower

A 15-foot lean from the vertical makes the Tower one of Europe's most recognizable images. You can see it for free; it's always viewable. And, after years of cleaning and stabilization efforts, it has shed its scaffolding and reopened for climbing.

Cost and Hours: €15 to climb Tower (restrictions apply to youth; see "Reservations to Climb the Tower," below); daily June-Aug 8:30-23:00, April-May and Sept 8:30-20:30, Oct 9:00-19:30, Nov-Feb 10:00-16:30, March

9:00-18:00; ticket office opens 30 minutes early, last entry 30 minutes before closing. For details on how to get to the Tower from the train station, see page 523.

Reservations to Climb the Tower: Every 30 minutes, 40 people can clamber up the 294 tilting stairs to the top. Children under age 6 are not allowed to go up. Children ages 6-12 must be accompanied by—and hold hands at all times with—an adult. Teenagers (up to and including 18-year-olds) must also be accompanied by an adult.

You can reserve a time in person, or for an extra €2, book at www.opapisa.it. Online bookings are accepted no more than 45 days—and no fewer than 15 days—in advance. You must pick up your ticket(s) at least 30 minutes before your time slot.

To reserve in person, go to the ticket office behind the Tower, on the left in the yellow building, or to the Museum of the Sinopias ticket office hidden behind the souvenir stalls. You choose a 30-minute time slot for your visit. If you visit in summer, it will likely be a couple of hours before you're able to go up (see the rest of the monuments and grab lunch while waiting). The wait is usually much shorter at the beginning or end of the day.

Baggage Check: You can't take any bags up the Tower, but day-bag-size lockers are available at the ticket office—show your Tower ticket to check your bag. You may check your bag 10 minutes before your reservation time and must pick it up immediately after your Tower visit.

❍ Self-Guided Tour: Rising up alongside the cathedral, the Tower is nearly 200 feet tall and 55 feet wide, weighing 14,000 tons and currently leaning at a five-degree angle (15 feet off the vertical axis). It started to lean almost immediately after construction began. Count the eight stories—a simple base, six stories of columns (forming arcades), and a belfry on top. The inner structural core is a hollow cylinder built of limestone bricks, faced with white marble barged here from San Giuliano, northeast of the city. The thin columns of the open-air arcades make the heavy Tower seem light and graceful.

The Tower was built over two centuries by at least three different architects. You can see how each successive architect tried to correct the leaning problem—once halfway up (after the fourth story), once at the belfry on the top.

The first stones were laid in 1173, probably under the direction of the architect Bonanno Pisano (who also designed the Duomo's bronze back door). Five years later, just as they'd finished the base and the first arcade, someone said, "Is it just me, or does that look crooked?" The heavy Tower—resting on a very shallow 13-foot foundation—was obviously sinking on the south side into the marshy, multilayered, unstable soil. (Actually, all of the Campo's

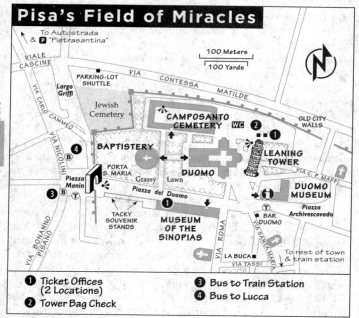

Pisa's Field of Miracles

To Autostrada
& P "Pietrasantina"

VIALE CASCINE

VIA CARLO CAMMEO

VIA CONTESSA MATILDE

PARKING-LOT SHUTTLE

Largo Griffi

Jewish Cemetery

VIA NICOLINI

CAMPOSANTO CEMETERY   WC   ❷   ❶

OLD CITY WALLS

❹   BAPTISTERY

PISA AND LUCCA

PORTA S. MARIA

Grassy   Lawn

DUOMO

LEANING TOWER

VIA C. P. MAFFI

Piazza Manin

❸ Ⓑ Ⓣ

Piazza del Duomo

DUOMO MUSEUM

Piazza Archivescovado

Ⓣ   BAR DUOMO

VIA BONANNO PISANO

TACKY SOUVENIR STANDS

MUSEUM OF THE SINOPIAS

VIA ROMA

VIA SANTA MARIA

LA BUCA

VIA TASSI

To rest of town & train station

100 Meters
100 Yards

N

❶ Ticket Offices (2 Locations)
❷ Tower Bag Check
❸ Bus to Train Station
❹ Bus to Lucca

buildings tilt somewhat.) The builders carried on anyway, until they'd finished four stories (the base, plus three arcade floors). Then, construction suddenly halted—no one knows why—and for a century the Tower sat half-finished and visibly leaning.

Around 1272, the next architect continued, trying to correct the problem by angling the next three stories backward, in the opposite direction of the lean. The project then again sat mysteriously idle for nearly another century. Finally, Tommaso Pisano put the belfry on the top (c. 1350-1372), also kinking it backward.

After the Tower's completion, several attempts were made to stop its slow-motion fall. The architect/artist/writer Giorgio Vasari reinforced the base (1550), and it actually worked. But in 1838, well-intentioned engineers pumped out groundwater, destabilizing the Tower and causing it to increase its lean at a rate of a millimeter per year.

It got so bad that in 1990 the Tower was closed for repairs, and $30 million was spent trying to stabilize it. Engineers dried the soil with steam pipes, anchored the Tower to the ground with steel cables, and buried 600 tons of lead on the north side as a counterweight (not visible)—all with little success. The breakthrough came when they drilled 15-foot holes in the ground on the north side and sucked out sixty tons of soil, allowing the Tower to sink on the north side and straighten out its lean by about six inches.

In addition to gravity, erosion threatens the Tower. Since its construction, 135 of the Tower's 180 marble columns have had to be replaced. Stone decay, deposits of lime and calcium phosphate, accumulations of dirt and moss, cracking from the stress of the lean—all of these are factors in its decline.

Thanks to the Tower's lean, there are special trouble spots. The lower south side (which is protected from cleansing rain and wind) is black from dirty airborne particles, while the stone on the upper areas, though clean, has more decay (from eroding rain and wind).

The Tower, now stabilized, has recently been cleaned. Cracks were filled, and accumulations of dirt removed with carefully for-mulated atomized water sprays and poultices of various solvents.

All the work to shore up, straighten, and clean the Tower has probably turned the clock back a few centuries. In fact, art histori-ans figure it leans today as much as it did for Galileo, who, accord-ing to legend, threw objects off the Tower to time their falls and study gravity.

Climbing the Tower: Show up 10 minutes before your appointment at the meeting point outside the ticket office. You wind your way up the outside of the Tower along a spiraling ramp. For your 30-minute time slot, figure about 10 minutes to climb and 10 to descend, leaving about 10 minutes for vertigo at the top. Even though it's technically a "guided" visit, that only means you're accompanied by a museum guard who makes sure you don't stay up past your scheduled appointment time.

Caution: The railings are skinny, the steps are slanted, and rain makes the marble slippery. Anyone with balance issues of any sort should think twice before ascending.

▲▲Duomo (Cathedral)

The gargantuan Pisan Romanesque cathedral, with its carved pulpit by Giovanni Pisano, is artistically more important than its more famous bell tower.

Cost and Hours: €2, cov-ered by various combo-tickets (see sidebar on page 528); daily April-Sept 10:00-20:00, Oct 10:00-19:00, Nov-Feb 10:00-12:45 & 14:00-17:00, March 10:00-18:00; last entry 30 min-utes before closing.

Information: Shorts are OK as long as they're not too short, and shoulders should be covered (although it's not really enforced). Big backpacks are not allowed, nor is storage provided—if you have a day bag, carry it. The €2 coin-operated "phone guides" are a waste, as they use narration from a bygone era.

○ Self-Guided Tour: Begun in 1063, the Duomo is the centerpiece of the Field of Miracles' complex of religious buildings. Start by admiring its facade.

Exterior: The architect Buschetto created the style of Pisan Romanesque that set the tone for the Baptistery and Tower. Five decades later (1118), the architect Rainaldo added the impressive main-entrance facade (which also leans out about a foot).

The **bronze back doors** (Porta San Ranieri, at the Tower end) were designed by Bonanno Pisano (c. 1186). The doors have 24 different panels that show Christ's story using the same simple, skinny figures found in Byzantine icons. (The doors are actually copies; the originals are housed—but not always on display—in the Duomo Museum.) Cast using the lost-wax technique, these doors were an inspiration for Lorenzo Ghiberti's bronze doors in Florence.

Nave: Inside, the 320-foot nave was the longest in Christendom when it was built. The striped marble and arches-on-columns give it an exotic, almost mosque-like feel.

Dim light filters in from the small upper windows of the galleries, where the women worshipped. The gilded coffered ceiling has shields of Florence's ruling Medici family, including the round symbols (pills). This powerful family—who began as doctors, later became cloth merchants, and finally bankers—took over Pisa after its glory days had passed.

In the apse (behind the altar) is a **mosaic** (c. 1300, partly done by Cimabue) showing Christ as the Ruler of All (Pantocrator), between Mary and John the Evangelist. The Pantocrator image of Christ is standard fare among Eastern Orthodox Christians—that is, the "Byzantine" people who were Pisa's partners in trade.

Giovanni's Pulpit: The 15-foot-tall, octagonal pulpit is by Giovanni Pisano (c. 1250-1319), who left no stone uncarved in his pursuit of beauty. Four hundred intricately sculpted figures smother the pulpit, blurring the architectural outlines. In addition, the relief panels are actually curved, making it look less like an octagon than a circle. The creamy-white Carrara marble has the look and feel of carved French ivories, which the Pisanos loved. At

the base, lions roar and crouch over their
prey, symbolizing how Christ (the lion)
triumphs over Satan (the horse, as in
the Four Horsemen of the Apocalypse).
Four of the pulpit's support "columns"
are statues. The central "column" features three graceful ladies representing
Faith, Hope, and Charity, the three
pillars of Christianity. Around the top
of the pulpit, Christ's life unfolds in a
series of panels saturated with carvings.

Galileo's Lamp: The bronze
incense burner that hangs from the
ceiling of the north transept (to the left of the altar) is a replica of
the one that supposedly caught teenage Galileo's attention when
a gust of wind set the lamp swinging. He timed the swings and
realized that the burner swung back and forth in the same amount
of time regardless of how wide the arc. (This pendulum motion
was a constant that allowed Galileo to measure our ever-changing
universe.)

Tomb of Holy Roman Emperor Henry VII: Pause at the
tomb of this German king (c. 1275-1313), who invaded Italy
and was welcomed by the Pisans as a leader of unity and peace.
Unfortunately, Henry took ill and died young, leaving Ghibelline
Pisa at the mercy of its Guelph rivals, such as rising Florence. Pisa
never recovered.

St. Ranieri's Body: In a glass-lined casket on the altar, Pisa's
patron saint lies mummified, encased in silver at his head and feet,
with his hair shirt covering his body. The silver, mask-like face
dates from 2000 and is as realistic as possible—derived from an
FBI-style computer scan of Ranieri's skull. The son of a rich sea-
trader, Ranieri (1117-1161) was a hard-partying, touring musician
who one night was inspired to set fire to his musical instrument,
open his arms to the heavens (à la Jimi Hendrix), and return to his
father's shipping business, where he amassed a fortune. He later
gave away his money, joined a monastery, and delivered spirited
sermons from the Duomo pulpit.

▲▲▲Field of Miracles (Campo dei Miracoli)

Scattered across a golf-course-green lawn are the five grand buildings of the Field of Miracles: the cathedral (or Duomo), its bell
tower (the Leaning Tower), the Baptistery, the hospital (today's
Museum of the Sinopias), and the Camposanto Cemetery. The
buildings are constructed from similar material—bright white
marble—and have comparable decoration. Each has a simple
ground floor and rows of delicate columns and arches that form

open-air arcades, giving the Campo a pleasant visual unity.

The style is called Pisan Romanesque. Unlike traditional Romanesque, with its heavy, fortress-like feel—thick walls, barrel arches, few windows— Pisan Romanesque is light and elegant. At ground level, most of the structures have simple half-columns and arches. On the upper levels, you'll see a little of everything: tight rows of thin columns; pointed Gothic gables and prickly spires; Byzantine mosaics and horseshoe arches; and geometric designs (such as diamonds) and striped, colored marbles inspired by mosques in Muslim lands.

Architecturally, the Campo is unique and exotic. Theologically, the Campo's buildings mark the main events of every Pisan's life: christened in the Baptistery, married in the Duomo, honored in ceremonies at the Tower, healed in the hospital, and buried in the Camposanto Cemetery.

Lining this field of artistic pearls is a gauntlet of Europe's tackiest souvenir stands, as well as dozens of amateur mimes "propping up" the Leaning Tower while tourists take photos. There's a TI inside the Duomo Museum (may close or move in 2012).

Secondary Sights on the Field of Miracles

The next four sights—the Baptistery, Camposanto Cemetery, Museum of the Sinopias, and Duomo Museum—share the same pricing and schedule.

Cost and Hours: It's €5 for one sight, but most visitors buy one of the various combo-tickets to save money (see sidebar on page 528). Open daily April-Sept 8:00-19:30, Oct 8:30-19:00, Nov-Feb 9:30-16:30, March 8:30-17:30, last entry 30 minutes before closing.

Locations: The Baptistery is in front of the Duomo's facade. The Camposanto Cemetery is behind the church on the north side of the Field of Miracles. The Museum of the Sinopias is hidden behind souvenir stands, across the street from the Baptistery entrance. The Duomo Museum is housed behind the Tower.

▲**Baptistery**—The round Baptistery is the biggest in Italy. It's interesting for its pulpit and interior ambience, and especially great for its acoustics.

○ **Self-Guided Tour:** The building is 180 feet tall—John the Baptist, on top, looks eye-to-eye with the tourists atop the nearly 200-foot-tall Leaning Tower. Notice that the Baptistery leans nearly six feet to the north (the Tower leans 15 feet to the south). The building (begun in 1153) is modeled on the circular domed Church of the Holy Sepulchre in Jerusalem, seen by Pisan Crusaders who occupied Jerusalem in 1099.

Inside, it's simple, spacious, and baptized with light. Tall arches encircle just a few pieces of religious furniture. In the center sits the **octagonal font** (1246). A statue of the first Baptist, John the Baptist, stretches out his hand and says, "Welcome to my Baptistery." The font contains plenty of space for baptizing adults by immersion (the medieval custom), plus four wells for dunking babies.

The **pulpit** by Nicola Pisano, Giovanni's father, is arguably the world's first Renaissance sculpture. It's the first authenticated (signed) work by the "Giotto of sculpture," working in what came to be called the Renaissance style. The freestanding sculpture has classical columns, realistic people and animals, and 3-D effects in the carved panels. The speaker's platform stands on columns that rest on the backs of animals, representing Christianity's triumph over paganism. The relief panels, with scenes from the life of Christ, are more readable than the Duomo pulpit. Read left to right, starting from the back: Nativity, Adoration of the Magi, Presentation in the Temple, Crucifixion, Last Judgment.

The **acoustics** are impressive. Make a sound in here and it echoes for a good 10 seconds. A priest standing at the baptismal font (or a security guard today) can sing three tones within the 10 seconds—"Ave Maria"—and make a chord, singing haunting harmonies with himself. This medieval form of digital delay is due to the 250-foot-wide dome. Recent computer analysis suggests that the 15th-century architects who built the dome intended this building to function not just as a Baptistery, but also as a musical instrument. A security guard sings every half-hour, starting when the doors open in the morning. Climb 75 steps to the interior gallery (midway up) for an impressive view back down on the baptismal font.

Camposanto Cemetery—This site has been a cemetery since ancient times. The building's cloistered open-air courtyard, lined with traces of fresco on the bare-brick walls, is surrounded by an arcade with intricately carved tracery in the arches and dozens of ancient Roman sarcophagi. The courtyard's grass grows on special "Holy Land" dirt (said to turn a body into bones in a single day), shipped here by returning Crusaders from Jerusalem's Mount Calvary, where Christ was crucified. The 1,000-square-foot fresco, *The Triumph of Death* (c. 1340), captures Pisa's mood in the wake of the bubonic plague (1348), which killed one in three Pisans. Grim stuff, but appropriate for the Camposanto's permanent residents.

In 1944, the Camposanto took a direct hit from an Allied incendiary grenade (the rest of the Field of Miracles was miraculously unscathed). It melted the lead-covered arcade roof and peeled historic frescoes from the walls—one of the many tragic artistic losses of World War II (look for photos of the bombed-out Camposanto at the back). The Americans liberated the city on September 2 and later rebuilt the Camposanto.

Museum of the Sinopias (Museo delle Sinopie)—Housed in a 13th-century hospital, this museum features the preparatory sketches (sinopias) for the Camposanto's WWII-damaged frescoes (including *The Triumph of Death*, described earlier). Sinopias are sketches in red paint painted directly on the wall, designed to guide the making of the final colored fresco. The master always did the sinopia himself; if he liked the results, his assistants made a "cartoon" by tracing the sinopia onto large sheets of paper *(cartone)*. Then the sinopia was plastered over, and the assistants redrew the outlines, using the cartoon as a guide. While the plaster was still wet, the master and his team quickly filled in the color and details, producing the final frescoes (now on display at the Camposanto). These sinopias—never meant to be seen—were uncovered by the bombing and restoration of the Camposanto and brought here.

Whether you pay to go in or not, you can watch two free videos in the entry lobby that serve to orient you to the square: a 10-minute, 3-D computer tour of the complex, and a 15-minute story of the Tower, its tilt, and its fix.

Duomo Museum (Museo dell'Opera del Duomo)—This museum behind the Leaning Tower is big on Pisan art, displaying treasures of the cathedral, paintings, silverware, and sculptures (from the 12th to 14th centuries, particularly by the Pisano dynasty), as well as ancient Egyptian, Etruscan, and Roman artifacts. It houses many of the original statues and much of the artwork that once adorned the Campo's buildings (where copies stand today), notably the statues by Nicola and Giovanni Pisano. You can stand face-to-face with the Pisanos' very human busts, which once ringed the outside of the Baptistery.

Also on display are the Duomo's original 12th-century bronze doors of St. Ranieri, done by Bonanno Pisano, which feature scenes from the life of Jesus. You'll also see a mythical sculpted hippogriff (a medieval jackalope) and other oddities brought back from the Holy Land by Pisan Crusaders, along with several large-scale wooden models of the Duomo, Baptistery, and Tower. The museum's grassy interior courtyard has a two-story, tourist-free view of the Tower, Duomo, and Baptistery.

More Sights in Pisa

Museo Nazionale di San Matteo—On the river and in a former convent, this art museum displays 12th- to 15th-century sculptures, illuminated manuscripts, and paintings on wood by Martini, Masaccio, and others. It's a fine collection—especially its painted wood crucifixes—and gives you a chance to see Pisan innovation in 11th- to 13th-century art, before Florence took the lead.

Cost and Hours: €5, Tue-Sat 8:30-19:00, Sun 8:30-13:00, closed Mon, near Piazza San Paolo at Lungarno Mediceo, a 5-minute walk upriver from the main bridge, tel. 050-541-865.

Sleeping in Pisa

To locate these hotels, see the map on page 522.

$$$ Hotel Alessandro della Spina, in a nondescript neighborhood near Pisa Centrale train station, has 16 elegant and colorful rooms, each named after a flower (Sb-€120, Db-€140, discounts off-season and for drop-ins, air-con, parking-€10/day; head straight out of train station, turn right on Viale F. Bonaini, and take the third right on Via Alessandro della Spina to find the hotel on your left at #5; tel. 050-502-777, fax 050-20583, www.hotel dellaspina.it, info@hoteldellaspina.it).

$$ Hotel Villa Kinzica has 30 tired but decent rooms with high ceilings, indifferent management, and a prime location just steps away from the Field of Miracles—ask for a room with a view of the Tower (Sb-€80, Db-€110, Tb-€126, Qb-€137, air-con, elevator, attached restaurant, Piazza Arcivescovado 2, tel. 050-560-419, fax 050-551-204, www.hotelvillakinzica.it, info@hotelvilla kinzica.it).

$$ Hotel Royal Victoria, a classy place on the Arno River, has been run by the Piegaja family since 1837. It's conveniently located dead-center between the Tower and Pisa Centrale train station (D-€80, standard Db-€100, better Db-€130, suite-€190, family room-€200, 10 percent discount with this book if you pay cash and book direct, check website for special deals, lush communal terrace, Lungarno Pacinotti 12, tel. 050-940-111, fax 050-940-180, www.royalvictoria.it, mail@royalvictoria.it).

$ Hotel Milano, near Pisa Centrale train station, offers 10 spacious, recently remodeled rooms. Ask for an upstairs room, which should be a bit quieter, when you book (D-€55, Db-€78, 10 percent discount for Rick Steves readers if you pay cash and book direct, breakfast extra, air-con, Via Mascagni 14, tel. 050-23-162, fax 050-44-237, www.hotelmilano.pisa.it, info@hotelmilano .pisa.it).

$ Pensione Helvetia is a no-frills, homey, clean, and quiet inn just 100 yards from the Tower. Its 29 economical rooms are

Sleep Code

(€1 = about $1.40, country code: 39)

S = Single, **D** = Double/Twin, **T** = Triple, **Q** = Quad, **b** = bathroom, **s** = shower only. Unless otherwise noted, credit cards are accepted, breakfast is included (but sometimes optional), and English is generally spoken.

To help you sort easily through these listings, I've divided the accommodations into three categories based on the price for a standard double room with bath:

$$$ Higher Priced—Most rooms €120 or more.

  $$ Moderately Priced—Most rooms between €80-120.

    $ Lower Priced—Most rooms €80 or less.

Prices can change without notice; verify the hotel's current rates online or by email. For other updates, see www.ricksteves.com/update.

spread over four floors (no elevator); the lower your room number, the lower your altitude (S-€62, Sb-€72, D-€69, Db-€79, lower prices off-season, vending-machine breakfast, ceiling fans, free Wi-Fi, Via Don G. Boschi 31, tel. 050-553-084, www.pensionehelvetiapisa.com, info@pensionehelvetiapisa.com). Take advantage of the free walking tour they offer all guests.

Eating in Pisa

La Buca, a pizzeria/trattoria just a block from the Tower, is adequate and convenient for a quick lunch or dinner (Sat-Thu 12:00-15:00 & 18:00-22:30, closed Fri, at Via Santa Maria 171 and Via A. G. Tassi 6b, tel. 050-560-660).

Ristorante Bagus boasts trendy twists on Tuscan fare—their specialty is an extra-rare burger made with the famous Chianina beef. For a change from the basic Italian trattorias and tourist traps, this place promises an upscale lunch or dinner (€25 fixed-price meal, Mon-Fri 12:30-14:30 & 19:30-22:00, Sat 19:30-22:00 only, closed Sun; heading south on Corso Italia, turn right on Via Nunziata and take your first right after Piazza Griletti to Piazza dei Facchini 13; tel. 050-26196).

At **Paninoteca il Canguro,** Gaetano and Mario make warm, hearty sandwiches to order. Try the popular primavera sandwich (daily 10:00-24:00, Via Santa Maria 151, tel. 050-561-942).

Panetteria Antiche Tradizioni—not to be confused with another Panetteria across the street—is a sandwich/bread shop with complete fixings for a picnic on the lawn at the Field of

Miracles or a sit-down lunch ordered from their menu (limited pastas, soups, and salads). Build your own sandwich with home-made bread or focaccia, then choose fruit from the counter, fresh pastries from the window, and cold drinks or wine to round out your meal (daily 8:00-20:00, Via Santa Maria 66, mobile 327-570-5210).

Drop by cheery **La Lupa Ghiotta Tavola Calda** for a cheap, fast, and tasty meal a few steps from Pisa Centrale train station. It's got everything you'd want from a *ristorante* at half the price and with faster service (build your own salad—five ingredients for €4.50; Mon and Wed-Sat 12:15-15:00 & 19:15-23:30, Tue 12:15-15:00 only, closed Sun, Viale F. Bonaini 113, tel. 050-21018).

The street that houses the daily market, **Via delle Colonne** (a block north of the Arno, west of Borgo Stretto), has a few atmospheric, mid-priced restaurants and several fun, greasy take-out options.

Pisa Connections

Pisa is well-connected by trains, buses (particularly with Lucca), and highways, with a busy airport nearby.

From Pisa Centrale Station by Train to: Florence (2-3/hour, 1.25 hours), **Rome** (2/hour, many change in Florence, 3-4 hours), **La Spezia,** gateway to Cinque Terre (about hourly, 1-1.5 hours), **Siena** (2/hour, 1.75 hours, change at Empoli, €7), **Lucca** (1-2/hour, 30 minutes, bus is better, €3). Even the fastest trains stop in Pisa, so you might change trains here whether you plan to stop or not.

By Bus to Lucca: A handy bus connects the Field of Miracles with Lucca's Piazzale Giuseppe Verdi in 30 minutes, with hourly departures (in Pisa, wait at the Vai Bus signpost, immediately outside the wall behind the Baptistery; buy €3.50 ticket on bus, toll-free tel. 800-602-947). This makes a half-day side-trip to Pisa from Lucca particularly easy.

By Car: The drive between Pisa and Florence is that rare case where the non-autostrada highway is a better deal than the autostrada—it's free, more direct, and at least as fast.

By Plane: Pisa's **Galileo Galilei Airport** handles more and more international and domestic flights (TI open daily 9:30-23:30, ATM, car-rental agencies; baggage storage from 8:00-20:00 only, €7/bag; self-service cafeteria, tel. 050-849-300, www.pisa-airport.com).

To get into **Pisa,** you can take bus LAM Rossa (4-6/hour, after 20:00 3/hour, 15 minutes, €1.10, departs from in front of the arrivals hall); a train (departs from the far left of the arrivals hall as you face the exits); or a taxi (€10-12).

You can connect to **Florence** easily by train (2-3/hour, 1.25

hours, €5.80, most transfer at Pisa Centrale) or by Terravision bus (about hourly, 1.25 hours, €10 one-way, ticket kiosk is at the right end of the arrivals hall as you're facing the exits, catch bus outside and to the far right of the bus parking lot, www.terravision.eu).

Lucca

Surrounded by well-preserved ramparts, layered with history, alternately quaint and urbane, Lucca charms its visitors. The city is a paradox. Though it hasn't been involved in a war since 1430, it is Italy's most impressive fortress city, encircled by a perfectly intact wall. Most cities tear down their wall to make way for modern traffic. But Lucca's wall effectively keeps out both traffic and, it seems, the stress of the modern world. Locals are very protective of their wall, which they enjoy like a community rooftop garden.

Lucca, known for being Europe's leading producer of toilet paper and tissue (with a monopoly on the special machinery that makes it), is nothing to sneeze at. However, the town has no single monumental sight to attract tourists—it's simply a uniquely human and undamaged, never-bombed city. Romanesque churches seem to be around every corner, as do fun-loving and shady piazzas filled with soccer-playing children.

Locals say Lucca is like a cake with a cherry filling in the middle...every slice is equally good. Despite Lucca's charm, few tourists seem to put it on their maps, and it remains a city for the Lucchesi (loo-KAY-zee).

Orientation to Lucca

Tourist Information

The main TI is just inside the Porta Santa Maria gate, on Piazza Santa Maria (daily May-Oct 9:00-20:00, Nov-April 9:00-12:30 & 15:00-18:30, pricey Internet access, WCs, no-fee room booking, Piazza Santa Maria 35, tel. 0583-919-931, www.luccatourist .it, info@luccaturismo.it).

Another TI, on Piazzale Giuseppe Verdi, offers information, a no-fee room-booking service, and baggage check (daily 9:00-18:30, futuristic WC, bike rental, 80-minute city-walk audioguide-€9, additional audio-guide-€3 more; bag storage-€1.50/

hour per bag, they need to photocopy your passport; tel. 0583-583-150). A third TI, just inside Porta Elisa, also has a no-fee reservations service (daily 9:00-13:30 & 14:30-18:00, WC-€0.60, baggage check, tel. 0583-495730).

Arrival in Lucca

By Train: There is no baggage check at the train station, but you may be able to leave bags at nearby Hotel Rex (see "Baggage Storage," page 544). If not, you can lug them to the bag check at the TI on Piazzale Giuseppe Verdi or near Porta Elisa (TIs described above).

To reach the city center from the train station, walk toward the walls and head left, to the entry at Porta San Pietro. Taxis are sparse, but try calling 025-353 (ignore any recorded message—just wait for a live operator); a ride from the station to Piazza dell'Anfiteatro costs about €6.

By Car: The key for drivers—don't try to drive within the walls. The old town is ringed by lots (with two just inside the walls, both usually full). Parking is always free in Piazzale Don Franco, a five-minute walk north of the city walls. Otherwise, try lots just outside Porta San Donato, on Viale Europa between Porta San Pietro and Porta Sant'Anna (a.k.a. Vittorio Emanuele), or just inside Porta Santa Maria (€1/hour). Or consider parking outside the gates near the train station or on the boulevard surrounding the city (meter rates vary; also about €1/hour). Lucca's TIs have maps showing the location of free parking lots just outside the walls. Overnight parking (20:00-8:00) is free in the lots at Porta Santa Maria and on Viale Europa, and €1.50/night at Ex-Caserma Mazzini, right by Villa Guinigi, just inside Porta Elisa.

Helpful Hints

Combo-Tickets: A €6 combo-ticket includes visits to the Ilaria del Carretto tomb in San Martino Cathedral (€2), Cathedral Museum (€4), and San Giovanni Church (€2.50). A €5 combo-ticket combines the Guinigi Tower (€3.50) and the Clock Tower (€3.50). Yet another combo-ticket covers Palazzo Mansi and Villa Guinigi for €6.50 and is valid for three days (€4 each if purchased separately).

Shops and Museums Alert: Shops close most of Sunday and Monday mornings. Many museums are closed on Monday as well.

Markets: Lucca's atmospheric markets are worth visiting. Every third weekend of the month (wherever the third Sun falls), one of the largest **antiques markets** in Italy unfurls in the blocks between Piazza Antelminelli and Piazza San Giovanni (8:00-19:00). The last weekend of the month, local artisans

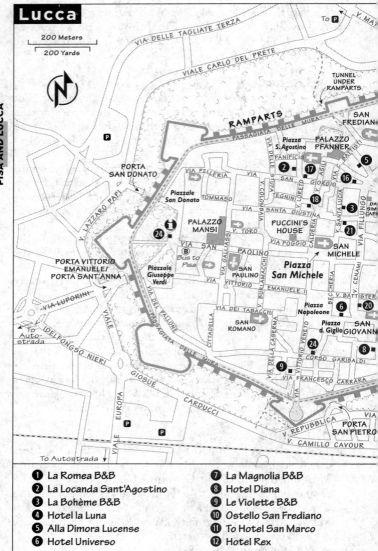

Lucca

200 Meters
200 Yards

To P

V. MAT

VIA DELLE TAGLIATE TERZA

VIALE CARLO DEL PRETE

RAMPARTS

TUNNEL UNDER RAMPARTS

SAN FREDIAN

PASSAGGIATA DELLE MURA

Piazza S. Agostino

PALAZZO PFANNER

PORTA SAN DONATO

VIA PELLERIA

Piazzale San Donato

TOMMASO

PALAZZO MANSI

PUCCINI'S HOUSE

SAN MICHELE

PORTA VITTORIO EMANUELE/ PORTA SANT'ANNA

Bus to Pisa

Piazzale Giuseppe Verdi

SAN PAULINO

Piazza San Michele

VIA LUPORINI

VIA IDELFONGSO NIERI

VITTORIO EMANUELE II

Piazza Napoleone

SAN GIOVANNI

To Autostrada

SAN ROMANO

Piazza d. Giglio

CORSO GARIBALDI

VIA FRANCESCO CARRARA

GIOSUE CARDUCCI

PORTA SAN PIETRO

V. REPUBBLICA

V. CAMILLO CAVOUR

To Autostrada

① La Romea B&B
② La Locanda Sant'Agostino
③ La Bohème B&B
④ Hotel la Luna
⑤ Alla Dimora Lucense
⑥ Hotel Universo
⑦ La Magnolia B&B
⑧ Hotel Diana
⑨ Le Violette B&B
⑩ Ostello San Frediano
⑪ To Hotel San Marco
⑫ Hotel Rex

PISA AND LUCCA

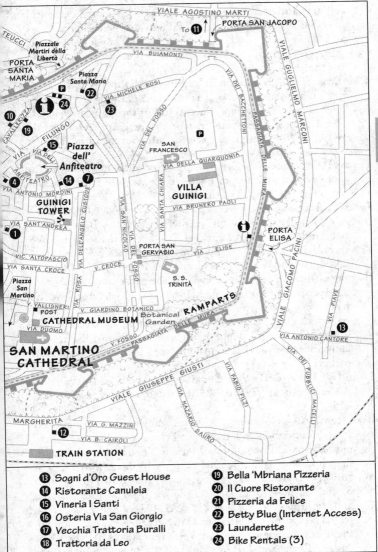

- ⑬ Sogni d'Oro Guest House
- ⑭ Ristorante Canuleia
- ⑮ Vineria I Santi
- ⑯ Osteria Via San Giorgio
- ⑰ Vecchia Trattoria Buralli
- ⑱ Trattoria da Leo
- ⑲ Bella 'Mbriana Pizzeria
- ⑳ Il Cuore Ristorante
- ㉑ Pizzeria da Felice
- ㉒ Betty Blue (Internet Access)
- ㉓ Launderette
- ㉔ Bike Rentals (3)

sell **arts and crafts** around town, mainly near the cathedral (also 8:00–19:00). At the **general market,** held Wednesdays and Saturdays, you'll find produce and household goods (8:30–13:00, from Porta Elisa to Porta San Jacopo on Via dei Bacchettoni).

Concerts: San Giovanni Church hosts one-hour concerts featuring a pianist and singers performing highlights from hometown composer Giacomo Puccini (€17 at the door, some hotels offer tickets for the same price or cheaper, April–Oct nightly at 19:00, Nov–March check schedule and location at www.puccinielasualucca.com).

Festival: On September 13 and 14, the city celebrates Volto Santo ("Holy Face"), with a procession of the treasured local crucifix and a fair in Piazza Antelminelli.

Internet Access: You can get online (expensively) at the main **TI** (see "Tourist Information," earlier) or at **Betty Blue,** a wine bar handy to the recommended launderette (€4.50/hour, two terminals and cables to plug in your laptop, Thu–Tue 11:00–24:00, closed Wed, Via del Gonfalone 16, tel. 0583-492-166).

Baggage Storage: For train travelers, the most convenient storage spot is the recommended **Hotel Rex.** However, they don't have much space, so it's best to email or call in advance (€4/bag all day, tel. 0583-955-443, info@hotelrexlucca.com). The **TIs** on Piazzale Giuseppe Verdi and near Porta Elisa are less convenient but workable options (see "Tourist Information," earlier).

Laundry: Lavanderia Self-Service Niagara is just off Piazza Santa Maria at Via Rosi 26 (€9 wash and dry, daily 7:00–23:00).

Bike Rental: A one-hour rental gives you time for two leisurely loops around the ramparts. Several places with identical prices cluster around Piazza Santa Maria (€3/hour, €12.50/day, tandem bikes available, free helmets, daily about 9:00–19:30 or sunset). Try these easygoing shops: **Antonio Poli** (Piazza Santa Maria 42, tel. 0583-493-787, enthusiastic Cristiana) and, right next to it, **Cicli Bizzarri** (Piazza Santa Maria 32, tel. 0583-496-682, Australian Dely). At the west end of town, the **TI** on Piazzale Giuseppe Verdi rents bikes. At the south end, at Porta San Pietro, you'll find **Chrono,** which rents bikes and offers guided bike tours (same rates and hours as the competition, Corso Garibaldi 93, tel. 0583-490-591, www.chronobikes.com).

Local Magazine: For insights into American and British expat life and listings of concerts, markets, festivals, and other special events, pick up a copy of *The Grapevine* (€2), available at newsstands.

Cooking Class: Gianluca invites you to the hills above Lucca to learn to make Tuscan fare. You prepare and then eat a three-course meal. Depending on how many others attend, the price ranges from €50 (a steal) to a whopping €125 per person. This is great for groups of four or more (€14 cab ride from town, 3-hour lesson plus time to dine, includes wine, reserve at least 2 days in advance, Via di San Viticchio 414, mobile 347-678-7447, www.italiancuisine.it, info@italiancuisine.it).

Local Guide: Gabriele Calabrese knows and shares his hometown well (€120/3 hours, by foot or bike, mobile 347-788-0667, www.turislucca.com, turislucca@turislucca.com).

Sights in Lucca

▲▲**Bike the Ramparts**—Lucca's most remarkable feature, its Renaissance wall, is also its most enjoyable attraction—espe-

cially when circled on a rental bike. Stretching for 2.5 miles, this is an ideal place to come for an overview of the city by foot or bike.

Lucca has had a protective wall for 2,000 years. You can read three walls into today's map: the first rectangular Roman wall, the later medieval wall (nearly the size of today's), and the 16th-century Renaissance wall, which still survives.

With the advent of cannons, thin medieval walls were suddenly vulnerable. A new design—the same one that stands today—was state-of-the-art when it was built (1550-1650). Much of the old medieval wall (look for the old stones) was incorporated into the Renaissance wall (with uniform bricks). The new wall was squat: a 100-foot-wide mound of dirt faced with bricks, engineered to absorb a cannonball pummeling. The townspeople cleared a wide no-man's-land around the town, exposing any attackers from a distance. Eleven heart-shaped bastions (now inviting picnic areas) were designed to minimize exposure to cannonballs and to maximize defense capabilities. The ramparts were armed with 130 cannons.

The town invested a third of its income for more than a century to construct the wall, and—since it kept away the Florentines and nasty Pisans—it was considered a fine investment. In fact, nobody ever bothered to try to attack the wall. Locals say that the only time it actually defended the city was during an 1812 flood of the Serchio River, when the gates were sandbagged and the ramparts kept out the high water.

Today, the ramparts seem made-to-order for a leisurely bike ride (20-minute pedal, wonderfully smooth). You can rent bikes cheaply and easily from one of several bike-rental places in town (listed earlier, under "Helpful Hints").

Piazza dell'Anfiteatro—Just off the main shopping street, the architectural ghost of a Roman amphitheater can be felt in the delightful Piazza dell'Anfiteatro. With the fall of Rome, the theater (which seated 10,000) was gradually cannibalized for its stones and inhabited by people living in a mishmash of huts. The huts were cleared away at the end of the 19th century to better appreciate the town's illustrious past. Today, the square is a circle of touristy shops and mediocre restaurants that becomes a lively bar-and-café scene after dark. The modern street level is nine feet above the original arena floor. The

only bits of surviving Roman stonework are a few arches on the northern exterior (at Via Fillungo 42 and on Via dell'Anfiteatro).

Via Fillungo—This main pedestrian drag stretches southwest from Piazza dell'Anfiteatro. *The* street to stroll, Via Fillungo takes you from the amphitheater almost all the way to the cathedral. Along the way, you'll get a taste of Lucca's rich past, including several elegant, century-old storefronts. Many of the original storefront paintings, reliefs, and mosaics survive—even if today's shopkeeper sells something entirely different.

At #97 is a classic old **jewelry store** with a rare storefront that has kept its T-shaped arrangement (when closed, you see a wooden T, and during open hours it unfolds with a fine old-time display). This design dates from a time when the merchant sold his goods in front, did his work in the back, and lived upstairs.

Di Simo Caffè, at #58, has long been the hangout of Lucca's artistic and intellectual elite. Composer and hometown boy Giacomo Puccini tapped his foot while sipping coffee here. Pop in to check out the 1880s ambience (handy €10 buffet lunch served daily 12:30-14:30, café open 9:00-24:00).

A surviving five-story **tower house** is at #67. There was a time when nearly every corner sported its own tower (see sidebar on page 548). The stubby stones that still stick out once supported wooden staircases (there were no interior connections between floors). So many towers cast shadows over this part of town that the street just before it is called Via Buia (Dark Street). Look away from this tower and down Via San Andrea for a peek at the town's tallest tower, Guinigi, in the distance—with its characteristic oak trees sprouting from the top.

At #45 and #43, you'll see two more good examples of tower houses. Across the street, the **Clock Tower** (Torre delle Ore) has a hand-wound Swiss clock that has clanged four times an hour since 1754 (€3.50 to climb up and see the mechanism flip into action on the quarter-hour—if it's actually working, €5 combo-ticket includes Guinigi Tower, daily April-Oct 9:30-18:30, Nov-March 9:30-16:30, corner of Via Fillungo and Via del'Arancio).

The intersection of Via Fillungo and Via Roma/Via Santa Croce marks the center of town (where the two original Roman roads crossed). As you go right down Via Roma, you'll pass the fine Edison Bookstore on your left before reaching Piazza San Michele.

Piazza San Michele—This square has been the center of town since Roman times, when it was the forum. It's dominated by the Church of San Michele. Towering above the church's fancy Pisan Romanesque facade, the archangel Michael stands ready to flap his wings—which he was known to do on special occasions.

The square is surrounded by an architectural hodgepodge. The loggia, which dates from 1495, is the first Renaissance building in town. There's a late-19th-century interior in Buccellato Taddeucci, a 130-year old pastry shop (#34). The left section of the BNL bank (#5; in front of the church) sports an Art Nouveau facade that celebrates both Amerigo Vespucci and Cristoforo Colombo.

Perhaps you've noticed that the statues of big shots that decorate many an Italian piazza are mostly absent from Lucca's squares. That's because unlike Venice, Florence, and Milan—which were dominated by a few powerful dynasties—Lucca was traditionally run by an oligarchy of a hundred leading families, with no one central figure to commemorate in stone. But after Italian unification, when leaders were fond of saying, "We have created Italy... now we need to create Italians," stirring statues of national heroes popped up everywhere—even in Lucca. The statue on Piazza San Michele is a two-bit local guy, dredged up centuries after his death because he favored strong central government.

Look back at the church facade, which also has an element of patriotism—designed to give roots and legitimacy to Italian statehood. Perched above many of the columns are the faces of heroes in the Italian independence and unification movement: Victor Emmanuel II (above the short red column on the right), the Count of Cavour (next to Victor, above the column with black zigzags), and Giuseppe Mazzini.

The History of Lucca

Lucca began as a Roman settlement. In fact, the grid layout of the streets (and the shadow of an amphitheater) survives from Roman times. Trace the rectangular Roman wall—indicated by today's streets—on the map. As in typical Roman towns, two main roads quartered the fortified town, crossing at what was the forum (main market and religious/political center)—today's Piazza San Michele.

Christianity came here early; it's said that the first bishop of Lucca was a disciple of St. Peter. While churches were built here as early as the fourth century, the majority of Lucca's elegant Romanesque churches date from about the 12th century.

Feisty Lucca, though never a real power, enjoyed a long period of independence (maintained by clever diplomacy). Aside from 30 years of being ruled from Pisa in the 14th century, Lucca was basically an independent city-state until Napoleon came to town.

In the Middle Ages, wealthy Lucca's economy was built on the silk industry, dominated by the Guinigi (gwee-NEE-gee) family. Without silk, Lucca would have been just another sleepy Italian town. In 1500, the town had 3,000 silk looms employing 25,000 workers. Banking was also big. Many pilgrims stopped here on their way to the Holy Land, deposited their money for safety...and never returned to pick it up.

In its heyday, Lucca packed 160 towers—one on nearly every corner—and 70 churches within its walls. Each tower was the home of a wealthy merchant family. Towers were many stories tall, with single rooms stacked atop each other: ground-floor shop, upstairs living room, and top-floor fire-safe kitchen, all connected by exterior wooden staircases. The rooftop was generally a vegetable garden, with trees providing shade. Later, the wealthy city folk moved into the countryside, trading away life in their city palazzos to establish farm estates complete with fancy villas. (You can visit some of these villas today—the TI has a brochure—but they're convenient only for drivers and are generally not worth the cost of admission.)

In 1799, Napoleon stormed into Italy and took a liking to Lucca. He liked it so much that he gave it to his sister as a gift. It was later passed on to Napoleon's widow, Marie Louise. With a feminine sensitivity, Marie Louise was partially responsible for turning the city's imposing (but no longer particularly useful) fortified wall into a fine city park that is much enjoyed today.

▲**San Martino Cathedral**—This cathedral, begun in the 11th century, is an entertaining mix of architectural and artistic styles. It's also home to the exquisite 15th-century tomb of Ilaria del Carretto, who married into the wealthy Guinigi family.

Cost and Hours: Cathedral-free, Ilaria tomb-€2, €6 combo-ticket includes Cathedral Museum and San Giovanni Church; Mon-Fri 9:30-17:45, Sat 9:30-18:45; Sun open sporadically between Masses: 9:30-10:45 & 12:00-17:45; Piazza San Martino.

⊘ **Self-Guided Tour:** Dominating the piazza is the cathedral's elaborate Pisan Romanesque **facade,** featuring Christian teaching scenes, animals, and candy-cane-striped columns.

The central figure is St. Martin, a Roman military officer from Hungary who, by offering his cloak to a beggar, more fully understood the beauty of Christian compassion. (The impressive original, a fine example of Romanesque sculpture, hides from pollution just inside, to the right of the main entrance.) Each of the columns on the facade is unique. Notice how the facade is asymmetrical: The 11th-century bell tower was already in place when the rest of the cathedral was built, so the builders cheated on the

right side to make it fit the space. Over the right portal (as if leaning against the older tower), the architect Guideo of Como holds a document declaring that he finished the facade in 1204. On the right (at eye level on the pilaster), a labyrinth is set into the wall. The maze relates the struggle and challenge our souls face in finding salvation. (French pilgrims on their way to Rome could relate to this, as it's the same pattern they knew from the floor of the church at Chartres.) The Latin plaque just left of the main door is where moneychangers and spice traders met to seal deals (on the doorstep of the church—to underscore the reliability of their promises). Notice the date: *An Dni MCXI* (A.D. 1111).

The **interior** features Gothic arches, Renaissance paintings, and stained glass from the 19th century. On the left side of the nave, a small, elaborate, birdcage-like temple contains the wooden crucifix—beloved by locals—called Volto Santo. It's said to have been sculpted by Nicodemus in Jerusalem and set afloat in an unmanned boat that landed on the coast of Tuscany, from where wild oxen miraculously carried it to Lucca in 782. The sculpture (which is actually 12th-century Byzantine-style) has quite a jewelry collection, which you can see in the Cathedral Museum (described next).

On the right side of the nave, the sacristy houses the enchantingly beautiful **memorial tomb of Ilaria del Carretto** by Jacopo della Quercia (1407). Pick up a handy English description to the right of the door as you enter the sacristy. This young bride of silk baron Paolo Guinigi is decked out in the latest, most expensive fashions, with the requisite little dog (symbolizing her loyalty) curled up at her feet in eternal sleep. She's so realistic that the statue was nicknamed "Sleeping Beauty." Her nose is partially worn off because of a long-standing tradition of lonely young ladies rubbing it for luck in finding a boyfriend.

Cathedral Museum (Museo della Cattedrale)—This beautifully presented museum houses original paintings, sculptures, and vestments from the cathedral and other Lucca churches. The first room displays jewelry made to dress up the Volto Santo crucifix, including gigantic gilded silver shoes. Upstairs, notice the fine red brocaded silk—a reminder that this precious fabric is what brought riches and power to the city. The exhibits in this museum have very brief descriptions and are meaningful only with the slow-talking €1 audioguide—if you're not in the mood to listen, skip the place altogether.

Cost and Hours: €4, €6 combo-ticket includes Ilaria tomb and San Giovanni Church; April-Oct daily 10:00-18:00; Nov-March Mon-Fri 10:00-14:00, Sat-Sun 10:00-17:00; to the left of the cathedral as you're facing it, Piazza Antelminelli, tel. 0583-490-530, www.museocattedralelucca.it.

San Giovanni Church—This first cathedral of Lucca is interesting only for its archaeological finds. The entire floor of the 12th-century church has been excavated in recent decades, revealing layers of Roman houses, ancient hot tubs that date back to the time of Christ, early churches, and theological graffiti. Sporadic English translations help you understand what you're looking at. As you climb under the church's present-day floor and wander the lanes of Roman Lucca, remember that the entire city sits on similar ruins.

Cost and Hours: €2.50, €6 combo-ticket includes Ilaria tomb and Cathedral Museum, audioguide-€1; mid-March-Oct daily 10:00-18:00; Nov-mid-March Sat-Sun 10:00-17:00, closed Mon-Fri; see concert info on page 544; kitty-corner from cathedral at Piazza San Giovanni.

Church of San Frediano—This impressive church was built in 1112 by the pope to counter Lucca's bishop and his spiffy cathedral. Lucca was the first Mediterranean stop on the pilgrim route from northern Europe, and the pope wanted to remind pilgrims that the action, the glory, and the papacy awaited them in Rome. Therefore, he had the church made "Roman-esque." The pure marble facade frames an early Christian Roman-style mosaic of Christ with his 12 apostles. Step inside and you're struck by the sight of 40 powerful (if recycled) ancient Roman columns. The message: Lucca may be impressive, but the finale of your pilgrimage—in

Rome—is worth the hike.

Inside, there's a notable piece of art in each corner: At rear left is the 12th-century baptistery, with some interesting Church propaganda showing the story of Moses (the evil Egyptians are played by Holy Roman Empire troops). At rear right is St. Zita's actual body, put there in 1278. At front left is a particularly elegant Virgin Mary, depicted at the moment she gets the news that she'll bring the Messiah into the world (carved and painted by Lucchesi artist Matteo Civitali, c. 1460). And at front right is a painting on wood of the *Assumption of the Virgin* (c. 1510), with Doubting Thomas receiving Mary's red belt as she ascends so he'll doubt no more. The pinball-machine composition serves as a virtual catalog of the fine silk material produced in Lucca—a major industry in the 16th century.

Cost and Hours: Free, Mon-Sat 8:30-12:00 & 15:00-17:30, Sun 9:00-11:30 & 15:00-17:30, Piazza San Frediano, tel. 0583-493-627.

Palazzo Mansi—Minor paintings by Tintoretto, Pontormo, Veronese, and others vie for attention, but the palace itself—a sumptuously furnished and decorated 17th-century confection—steals the show. This is your chance to appreciate the wealth of Lucca's silk merchants. Since all visitors must be accompanied by a museum employee, during high season you may have to wait a bit for your chance to enter.

Cost and Hours: €4, €6.50 combo-ticket includes Villa Guinigi, hours prone to change but generally Tue-Sat 8:30-19:30, Sun 8:30-13:30, closed Mon, no photos, request English booklet at ticket desk, Via Galli Tassi 43, tel. 0583-55-570.

Guinigi Tower (Torre Guinigi)— Many Tuscan towns have towers, but none is quite like the Guinigi family's. Up 227 steps is a small garden with fragrant trees, surrounded by fantastic views.

Cost and Hours: €3.50, €5 combo-ticket includes Clock Tower, likely open daily April-Sept 9:00-19:30, Oct 10:00-18:00, Nov-March 9:30-16:30, Via Sant'Andrea 41.

Puccini's House—Opera enthusiasts (but nobody else) will want to visit the home where Giacomo Puccini (1858-1924) grew up, but—tragedy—it's been closed for several years. However, it was recently sold by Puccini's grandniece, and according to local scuttlebutt, it may reopen in 2012. The museum has the great composer's piano and a small collection of his personal belongings.

Cost and Hours: If open, likely €3, daily 10:00-18:00 though may be closed Mon, Corte San Lorenzo 9, tel. 0583-584-028.

Palazzo Pfanner—Garden enthusiasts (and anyone needing a break from churches) will enjoy this 18th-century palace built for a rich Swiss expat who came to Lucca to open a brewery. His sudsy legacy includes Baroque furniture, elaborate frescoes, a centuries-old kitchen, and a lavish garden.

Cost and Hours: Garden or residence-€4 apiece, €5.50 for both, April-Oct daily 10:00-18:00, closed Nov-March, Via degli Asili 33, tel. 0583-954-029, www.palazzopfanner.it.

Villa Guinigi—Built by Paolo Guinigi in 1418, the family villa is now a stark, abandoned-feeling museum displaying a hodgepodge of Etruscan artifacts, religious sculptures, paintings, inlaid wood-work, and ceramics. Monumental paintings by the multitalented Giorgio Vasari are the best reason to visit.

Cost and Hours: €4, €6.50 combo-ticket includes Palazzo Mansi, Tue-Sat 8:30-19:30, Sun 8:30-13:30, closed Mon, may have to wait in high season for a museum employee to accompany you, Via della Quarquonia, tel. 0583-496-033.

Sleeping in Lucca

(€1 = about $1.40, country code: 39)

Fancy Little Boutique B&Bs Within the Walls

$$$ La Romea B&B, in an air-conditioned, restored, 14th-century palazzo near Guinigi Tower, feels like a royal splurge. Its four posh rooms and one suite are lavishly decorated in handsome colors and surround a big, plush lounge with stately Venetian-style floors (Db-€100-135 depending on season, big suite-€160, extra bed-€20-25; 10 percent discount when you book direct, show this book, and pay cash; Wi-Fi; from the train station, take Via Fillungo, turn right on Via Sant'Andrea, then take the second right to Vicolo delle Ventaglie 2; tel. 0583-464-175, www.laromea.com, info@laromea.com, Giulio and wife Gaia).

$$$ La Locanda Sant'Agostino has three romantic, bright, and spacious rooms. The vine-draped terrace, beautiful breakfast spread, and quaint views invite you to relax (Db-€160, extra bed-€25, 5 percent discount with cash and this book, air-con, Internet access and Wi-Fi, from Via Fillungo take Via San Giorgio to Piazza Sant'Agostino 3, best to reserve by email, tel. 0583-443-100, mobile 347-989-9069, www.locandasantagostino.it, info @locandasantagostino.it).

$$$ La Bohème B&B has a cozy yet elegant ambience, offering six large, charming, chandeliered rooms, each painted with a different rich color scheme (Db-€120, less off-season, 10 percent discount with this book if you pay cash and book direct, air-con, free Wi-Fi, Via del Moro 2, tel. & fax 0583-462-404, www .boheme.it, info@boheme.it, Sara).

Sleeping More Forgettably Within the Walls

$$ Hotel la Luna, run by the Barbieri family, has 29 rooms in a great location, right in the heart of the city. Updated rooms are split between two adjacent buildings just off of the main shopping street. The annex may have an elevator, but I prefer the rooms in the main building, which are larger and classier (Sb-€83, Db-€113, suite-€175, these prices for Rick Steves readers who book direct, air-con, pay Internet access, parking-€15/day, Via Fillungo at Corte Compagni 12, tel. 0583-493-634, fax 0583-490-021, www .hotellaluna.com, info@hotellaluna.com, Sara).

$$ Alla Dimora Lucense's seven newer rooms are bright, modern, clean, and peaceful, with all the comforts. Enjoy their relaxing, sunny interior courtyard (Db-€115, suite for 2-4 people-€150-200; 10 percent discount if you pay cash, book direct, and show this book; optional breakfast-€5, air-con, Wi-Fi, half a block from Via Fillungo at Via Fontana 17, tel. 0583-495-722, fax 0583-441-210, www.dimoralucense.it, info@dimoralucense.it).

$$ Hotel Universo, renting 56 rooms right on Piazza Napoleone and facing the theater and Palazzo Ducale, is a 19th-century town fixture. While it clearly was once elegant, now it's old and tired, with a big Old World lounge and soft prices ("comfort" Db-€100, "superior" Db with updated bath-€130, Wi-Fi, Piazza del Giglio 1, tel. 0583-493-678, www.universolucca.com, info@universolucca.com).

$$ La Magnolia B&B offers five basic rooms and one apartment with an intimate atmosphere and relaxing garden. It's buried in a ramshackle old palace in a central location (Sb-€65, Db-€85, Qb-€90, includes breakfast at nearby bar, 5 percent discount with this book if you pay cash and book direct, a block behind amphitheater at Via Mordini 63, tel. 0583-467-111, www.lamagnolia .com, info@lamagnolia.com, Andrea and Laura).

$ Hotel Diana is a dreary little family-run hotel, with nine rooms in the main building and another six slightly nicer, sound-proofed, and air-conditioned rooms in the annex just around the corner (D-€50, Db-€65, annex Db-€85, south of the cathedral at Via del Molinetto 11, tel. 0583-492-202, fax 0583-467-795, www .albergodiana.com, info@albergodiana.com).

$ At Le Violette B&B, friendly Anna (who's still learning English; her granddaughter Sara speaks English) will settle you into one of her six homey rooms near the train station inside Porta San Pietro (D-€60, Db-€75, extra bed-€15, Wi-Fi, communal kitchen, €5 to use washer and dryer, Via della Polveriera 6,

tel. 0583-493-594, mobile 349-823-4645, fax 0583-429-305, www
.leviolette.it, leviolette@virgilio.it).

$ Ostello San Frediano, in a central, sprawling ex-convent
with a peaceful garden, is a cut above the average hostel, though
it's still filled mainly with a young crowd. Its 29 rooms are bright
and modern, and some have fun lofts (€20 beds in 6- to 8-person
dorms, 140 beds, Db-€60, Tb-€78, Qb-€100, includes sheets, €3
extra/night for non-members, cash only, breakfast extra, no curfew, lockers, Internet access, cheap restaurant, free parking, Via
della Cavallerizza 12, tel. 0583-469-957, fax 0583-461-007, www
.ostellolucca.it, info@ostellolucca.it).

Outside the Walls

$$$ Hotel San Marco, a seven-minute walk outside the Porta
Santa Maria, is a postmodern place decorated à la Stanley Kubrick.
Its 42 recently remodeled rooms are sleek, with all the comforts
(Sb-€87, Db-€126, extra bed-€10, includes nice breakfast spread,
air-con, Wi-Fi, elevator, pool, bikes-€5/half-day, free parking,
taxi from station-€6, Via San Marco 368, tel. 0583-495-010, fax
0583-490-513, www.hotelsanmarcolucca.com, info@hotelsan
marcolucca.com).

$$ Hotel Rex rents 25 rooms in a practical modern building
on the train station square. While in the modern world, you're just
200 yards away from the old town and get more space for a better price (Db-€80-100, 10 percent discount with this book if you
pay cash and book direct, air-con, Wi-Fi, free bike rental, a few
steps from the train station at Piazza Ricasoli 19, tel. 0583-955-
443, www.hotelrexlucca.com, info@hotelrexlucca.com).

$ Sogni d'Oro Guest House ("Sleep like Gold"), run by
Davide, is a handy budget option for drivers, with five basic rooms
and a cheery communal kitchen (grocery store next door). It's a
10-minute walk from the train station and a five-minute walk from
the city walls (D-€50, Db-€65, Q-€70, 10 percent discount with
cash; free ride to and from station with advance notice—then call
when your train arrives in Lucca; from the station, head straight
out to Viale Regina Margherita and turn right, follow the main
boulevard as it turns into Viale Giuseppe Giusti, at the curve turn
right onto Via Antonio Cantore to #169; tel. 0583-467-768, mobile
329-582-5062, fax 0583-957-612, www.bbsognidoro.com, info
@bbsognidoro.com).

Eating in Lucca

Ristorante Canuleia makes everything fresh in their small
kitchen. While the portions aren't huge, the food is tasty. You
can eat in their dressy little dining room or outside on the garden

---

Specialties in Lucca

Lucca has some tasty specialties worth seeking out. *Ceci* (CHEH-chee), also called *cecina* (cheh-CHEE-nah), makes an ideal cheap snack any time of day. This garbanzo-bean crepe is sold in pizza shops and is best accompanied by a nip of red wine.

Farro, a grain (spelt) dating back to ancient Roman cuisine, shows up in restaurants in soups or as a creamy rice-like dish *(risotto di farro).*

Tordelli, the Lucchesi version of *tortelli,* is homemade ravioli. It's traditionally stuffed with meat and served with more meat sauce, but chefs creatively pair cheeses and vegetables, too.

Meat, not fish, is the star at most restaurants, especially steak, which is listed on menus as *filetto di manzo* (filet), *tagliata di manzo* (thin slices of grilled tenderloin), or the king of steaks, *bistecca alla fiorentina*. Order *al sangue* (rare), *medio* (medium rare), *cotto* (medium), or *ben cotto* (well). Anything more than *al sangue* is considered a travesty for steak connoisseurs.

Note that steaks (as well as fish) are often sold by weight, noted on menus as *s.q.* (according to quantity ordered) or *l'etto* (cost per 100 grams—250 grams is about an 8-ounce steak).

For something sweet, bakeries sell *buccellato,* bread dotted with raisins, lightly flavored with anise, and often shaped like a wreath. It's only sold in large sizes, but luckily it stays good for a few days (and it also pairs well with *vin santo*— fortified Tuscan dessert wine). An old proverb says, "Coming to Lucca without eating the *buccellato* is like not having come at all." *Buon appetito!*

---

courtyard (€10 pastas, €17 *secondi*, Mon-Sat 12:30-14:00 & 19:30-21:30, closed Sun, Via Canuleia 14, tel. 0583-467-470, reserve for dinner).

Vineria I Santi is pricey but good if you appreciate quality food and fine wine, and just want to lie back and be pampered. Leonardo serves food with a sexy jazz ambience that would work well in a bordello. Relax in the peaceful indoors among wine bottles, or on a quiet square outside (€11 pastas, €18 *secondi*, Thu-Tue 12:30-14:30 & 19:30-22:00, closed Wed, Via dell'Anfiteatro 29, tel. 0583-496-124).

Osteria Via San Giorgio, owned by Daniela and her brother Piero, is a cheery family eatery that satisfies both fish-lovers and meat-lovers. Sample the splittable *antipasto fantasia*—five small courses such as *ceviche* (seafood salad), scallops au gratin, squid sautéed with potatoes, or whatever else was caught that day in

Viareggio; they also offer a meatier version. Dinner-size salads are bright and fresh, pasta is homemade, and Daniela's desserts tempt (daily 12:00-16:00 & 19:00-23:00, Via San Giorgio 26, tel. 0583-953-233).

Vecchia Trattoria Buralli, on quiet Piazza Sant'Agostino, is a good bet for traditional cooking and juicy steaks, with fine indoor and piazza seating (€7 pastas, €10 *secondi*, €12-30 fixed-price meals, Thu-Tue 12:00-14:45 & 19:00-22:30, closed Wed, Piazza Sant'Agostino 10, tel. 0583-950-611).

Trattoria da Leo, a brother of Vecchia Trattoria Buralli, packs in chatty locals for typical, cheap home-cooking in a hash-slingin' Mel's-diner atmosphere. This place is a high-energy winner...you know it's going to be good as soon as you step in. Arrive early or reserve in advance (€6 pastas, €10 *secondi*, Mon-Sat 12:00-14:30 & 19:30-22:30, sometimes open Sun, cash only, leave Piazza San Salvatore on Via Asili and take the first left to Via Tegrimi 1, tel. 0583-492-236).

Bella 'Mbriana Pizzeria focuses on doing one thing very well: turning out piping-hot, wood-fired pizzas to happy locals in a welcoming wood-paneled dining room. Order and pay at the counter, take a number, and they'll call you when your pizza's ready. Consider take-out to munch on the nearby walls. Prices range from €5 for your basic *Napolitano* to €8 for their specialty, with buffalo mozzarella and other gourmet ingredients (Wed-Mon 12:30-14:30 & 18:30-23:00, closed Tue, to the right as you face the Church of San Frediano, Via della Cavallerizza 29, tel. 0583-495-565).

Il Cuore Enogastronomia includes a delicatessen and restaurant. For a fancy picnic, drop in the deli for ready-to-eat lasagna, saucy meatballs, grilled and roasted vegetables, vegetable soufflés, Tuscan bean soup, fruit salads, and more, sold by weight and dished up in disposable trays to go. Ask them to heat your order *(riscaldare),* then picnic on nearby Piazza Napoleone. For curious traveling foodies on a budget who want to eat right there, they can assemble a €10 "degustation plate"—just point to what you want from among the array of tasty treats under the glass (Tue-Sun 9:30-19:30, closed Mon, Via del Battistero 2, tel. 0583-493-196, Marianna and Cristina).

Il Cuore Ristorante, located across the way, is a trendy find for wine-tasting or a meal on a piazza. Try the €8 *aperitivo* (available 18:00-20:00), which includes a glass of wine and a plate of cheese, *salumi,* and snacks, or feast on fresh pastas and other high-quality dishes from their lunch and dinner menus (Wed-Sun 12:00-22:00 with limited menu 15:00-19:30, Tue 12:00-15:00, closed Mon, Via del Battistero, tel. 0583-493-196).

Pizzeria da Felice is a little mom-and-pop hole-in-the-wall serving *cecina* (chickpea crepes) and slices of freshly baked pizza to throngs of snackers. Grab a *cecina* and a short glass of wine for €2.50 (Mon-Sat 10:00-20:30, closed Sun and 3 weeks in Aug, Via Buia 12, tel. 0583-494-986).

Lucca Connections

From Lucca by Train to: Florence (2/hour, 1.5 hours), **Pisa** (roughly 1-2/hour Mon-Sat, 30 minutes, bus is better), **Milan** (2/hour except Sun, 4-5 hours, transfer in Florence), **Rome** (1/hour except Sun, 3-4 hours, change in Florence).

From Lucca by Bus to Pisa: Direct buses from Lucca's Piazzale Giuseppe Verdi drop you right at the Leaning Tower, making Pisa an easy day trip (hourly, 30 minutes, €3.50). Even with a car, I'd opt for this much faster and cheaper option.

SIENA

Siena was medieval Florence's archrival. And while Florence ultimately won the battle for political and economic superiority, Siena still competes for the tourists. Sure, Florence has the heavyweight sights. But Siena seems to be every Italy connoisseur's favorite pet town. In my office, whenever Siena is mentioned, someone moans, "Siena? I looove Siena!"

Once upon a time (about 1260-1348), Siena was a major banking and trade center, and a military power in a class with Florence, Venice, and Genoa. With a population of 60,000, it was even bigger than Paris. Situated on the north-south road to Rome (Via Francigena), Siena traded with all of Europe. Then, in 1348, the Black Death (bubonic plague) that swept through Europe hit Siena and cut the population by more than a third. Siena never recovered. In the 1550s, Florence, with the help of Philip II's Spanish army, conquered the flailing city-state, forever rendering Siena a non-threatening backwater. Siena's loss became our sightseeing gain, as its political and economic irrelevance pickled the city in a purely medieval brine. Today, Siena's population is still 60,000, compared with Florence's 420,000.

Siena's thriving historic center, with red-brick lanes cascading every which way, offers Italy's best medieval city experience. Most people do Siena, just 35 miles south of Florence, as a day trip, but it's best experienced at twilight. While Florence has the blockbuster museums, Siena has an easy-to-enjoy soul: Courtyards sport flower-decked wells, alleys dead-end at rooftop views, and the sky is a rich blue dome.

For those who dream of a Fiat-free Italy, Siena is a haven.

Pedestrians rule in the old center of Siena. Sit at a café on the main square. Wander narrow streets lined with colorful flags and iron rings to tether horses. Take time to savor the first European city to eliminate automobile traffic from its main square (1966) and then, just to be silly, wonder what would happen if they did it in your hometown.

Planning Your Time

On a quick trip, consider spending two nights in Siena (or three nights with a whole-day side-trip into Florence). Whatever you do, enjoy a sleepy medieval evening in Siena. The next morning, you can see the city's major sights in half a day.

Orientation to Siena

SIENA

Siena lounges atop a hill, stretching its three legs out from Il Campo. This main square, the historic meeting point of Siena's

neighborhoods, is pedestrian-only—and most of those pedestrians are students from the university.

Just about everything mentioned in this chapter is within a 15-minute walk of the square. Navigate by three major landmarks (Il Campo,

Duomo, and Church of San Domenico), following the excellent system of street-corner signs. The typical visitor sticks to the Il Campo-San Domenico axis. Make it a point to stray from this main artery.

Siena itself is one big sight. Its individual sights come in two little clusters: the square (Civic Museum and City Tower) and the cathedral (Baptistery and Duomo Museum, with its surprise viewpoint). Check these sights off, and then you're free to wander.

Tourist Information

The TI on Il Campo can be an exasperating place. Think about the importance of tourism in this town—and yet this office charges €0.50 for a map and lets tour commissions color its advice (daily 9:00-19:00, on Il Campo at #56, tel. 0577-280-551, www.terre siena.it, incoming@terresiena.it). The helpful booklet *Siena* from their *Terre di Siena* series lists current hours and prices for sights in Siena and outlying towns. The TI organizes **walking tours** of the old town (€20, daily April-Sept at 11:00, 2.5 hours, no interiors, usually only in English).

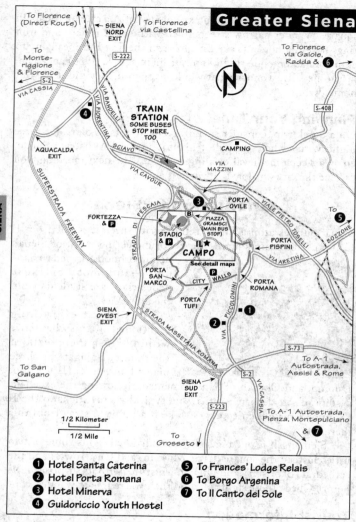

Greater Siena

To Florence
(Direct Route)

SIENA
NORD
EXIT

To Florence
via Castellina

To
Monte-
riggione
& Florence

VIA CASSIA

S-2

S-222

VIA BANDELLI

VIA FIORENTINA

To Florence
via Gaiole,
Radda & ❻

S-408

AQUACALDA
EXIT

SCIAVO

TRAIN
STATION
SOME BUSES
STOP HERE,
TOO

VIA CAVOUR

CAMPING

VIA
MAZZINI

VIALE PIETRO TOSELLI

To
❺
BOZZONE

SUPERSTRADA FREEWAY

STRADA DI PESCAIA

FORTEZZA
& 🅿

STADIO
& 🅿

Ⓑ

PIAZZA
GRAMSCI
(MAIN BUS
STOP)

PORTA
OVILE

❸

IL ★
CAMPO

See detail maps

PORTA
PISPINI

VIA ARETINA

PORTA
ROMANA

SIENA
OVEST
EXIT

PORTA
SAN
MARCO

CITY
WALLS

🅿

PORTA
TUFI

❷

❶

VIA PICCOLOMINI

STRADA MASSETANA ROMANA

S-73

To A-1
Autostrada,
Assisi & Rome

To San
Galgano

SIENA
SUD
EXIT

S-2

VIA CASSIA

To A-1 Autostrada,
Pienza, Montepulciano
& ❼

S-223

To
Grosseto

1/2 Kilometer

1/2 Mile

❶ Hotel Santa Caterina
❷ Hotel Porta Romana
❸ Hotel Minerva
❹ Guidoriccio Youth Hostel

❺ To Frances' Lodge Relais
❻ To Borgo Argenina
❼ To Il Canto del Sole

SIENA

Arrival in Siena
By Train

The small train station, located on the edge of town, has a bar, a TI (daily 9:30-13:30), a bus office (Mon-Sat 7:15-19:30, Sun 7:15-17:45), and a newsstand (which sells bus tickets—buy one now if you're taking the city bus into town), but no baggage check or lockers (stow bags at Piazza Gramsci—see "By Intercity Bus," later). A shopping mall is right in front of the station.

To get from the station to the city center by **city bus**, you'll have to walk about 100 yards to the bus stop (even though buses from the center drop off at the station's curb): Exit the station, cross the plaza while veering left, and follow bus-stop signs to the shopping mall's glass doors. Enter the right-hand door and use the elevator to go down. If you didn't buy bus tickets in the train station, you can get them from the blue machine (touch the screen for English and select "urban" for type of ticket). Buses leave frequently (6/hour, fewer on Sun and after 22:00, €1); double-check the destination with the driver by asking *"Centro?"* Punch your ticket in the machine onboard to validate it. Ride to Piazza Gramsci.

If you're leaving Siena and you need to get to the train station, catch an orange or red-and-silver city bus from Piazza Gramsci. Confirm with the driver that the bus is going to the *stazione* (stat-zee-OH-nay); remember to purchase your ticket in advance from a tobacco shop, then validate it on board.

The **taxi stand** is to your right as you exit the train station, but as the city is chronically short on cabs, getting one here can take awhile (about €9 to Il Campo, taxi tel. 0577-49222).

By Intercity Bus

Most buses arrive in Siena at Piazza Gramsci, a few blocks from the city center. (Some buses only go to the train station; others go first to the train station, then continue to Piazza Gramsci.) The main bus companies are Sena and the confusingly named Tra-In (pronounced TRAH-in; not connected at all to the railway). Day-trippers can store baggage underneath Piazza Gramsci in Sottopassaggio la Lizza (€5.50/day, open daily 7:00-19:00, carry-on-sized luggage no more than 33 pounds, no overnight storage). For more on buses, see page 594.

By Car

Siena is not a good place to drive. Plan on parking in a big lot or garage, and walking into town.

Drivers coming from the autostrada take the *Siena Ovest* exit and follow signs for *Centro,* then *Stadio* (stadium). The soccer-ball signs take you to the stadium lot (Parcheggio Stadio, €1.60/hour, pay when you leave) near the huge, bare-brick Church of San Domenico. The Fortezza lot nearby charges the same amount. Another good option is the underground Santa Caterina garage (you'll see signs on the way to the stadium lot, same price). From the garage, hike 150 yards uphill through a gate to an escalator on the right, which carries you up into the city. If you're staying in the south end of town, try the Il Campo lot, near Porta Tufi.

On parking spots, blue stripes mean "pay and display"; white stripes mean free parking. You can park for free in the lot west of the Fortezza; in white-striped spots behind the Hotel Villa Liberty (behind the Fortezza); and overnight in most city lots from 20:00 to 8:00. Watch for signs showing a street cleaner and a day of the week—that's when the street is closed to cars for cleaning.

Driving within Siena's city center is restricted to local cars and policed by automatic cameras. If you drive or park anywhere marked *Zona Traffico Limitato (ZTL)*, you'll likely have a hefty ticket waiting for you in the mail back home.

Technically, hotel customers are allowed to drop off bags at their hotel before finding a place to park overnight, but getting permission to do so isn't worth the trouble.

Helpful Hints

Combo-Tickets: A deranged person cobbled together a pile of illogically paired combo-tickets for the sights in Siena—nothing covers everything, and the savings are often meager. If you're planning on seeing all the sights, survey your ticket options at the first one you visit. Of the various combo-tickets available, the two worth considering are the €10 combo-ticket that includes the Duomo, Duomo Museum, Crypt, and Baptistery (a savings of €8 if you plan on seeing all of those sights) and the €13 combo-ticket covering the Civic Museum and City Tower (a €3 savings).

Wednesday Morning Market: The weekly market (clothes, knick-knacks, and food) sprawls between the Fortezza and Piazza Gramsci along Viale Cesare Maccari and the adjacent Viale XXV Aprile.

Internet Access: In this university town, there are lots of places to get plugged in. **Cheap Phone Center** is hidden in a small shopping mall near Il Campo (€2/hour to use terminals, €1/hour for Wi-Fi, daily 10:00-22:00; coming from Il Campo, go uphill past recommended Albergo Tre Donzelle, turn left at Via Cecco Angiolieri, after 20 yards look for #16). **Internet Point** is located upstairs at Via di Città 80, with the entrance around the corner on Via delle Campane (€3/hour, daily 9:00-21:00).

Post Office: It's on Piazza Matteotti (Mon-Fri 8:15-19:00, Sat 8:15-13:30, closed Sun).

Books: Libreria Senese sells books (including my guidebooks), newspapers, and magazines in English, with an emphasis on Italian-related topics (daily 9:00-20:00, Via di Città 62, tel. 0577-280-845). The **Feltrinelli** bookstore at Banchi di Sopra 52 also sells books and magazines in English (Mon-Sat 9:00-19:30, closed Sun, tel. 0577-271-104).

Laundry: Two modern, self-service launderettes are **Express Wash** (near Logge del Papa at Via di Pantaneto 38) and **Onda Blu** (50 yards from Il Campo at Via del Casato di Sotto 17). Both launderettes are open daily 8:00-22:00 with last loads at 21:00.

Travel Agency: Palio Viaggi, on Piazza Gramsci, sells train tickets downstairs (under the arch) and plane tickets upstairs (Mon-Fri 9:00-12:15 & 15:00-19:00, Sat 9:00-12:30, closed Sun, opposite the columns of NH Excelsior Hotel at La Lizza 12, tel. 0577-280-828, info@palioviaggi.it).

Wine Classes: The **Tuscan Wine School** gives two-hour classes in English on Italian wines, including samples of five vintages. Morning classes cover wines from all over Italy (11:00), and afternoon classes focus on Tuscany (16:00). They also offer a one-hour "crash course" at 14:00. Rebecca and her fellow sommeliers keep things entertaining and offer tastings for as few as two people (€40/person, 20 percent student discount to anyone with this book, €25 for one-hour course, classes offered daily, Via di Stalloreggi 26, 30 yards from recommended Hotel Duomo, tel. 0577-221-704, mobile 333-722-9716, www.tuscanwineschool.com, info@tuscanwineschool.com). Their outlet store sells wine from local producers at cost.

Tours in Siena

Local Guides—Roberto Bechi, a hardworking Sienese guide, specializes in off-the-beaten-path tours of the surrounding countryside by minibus (up to eight passengers, convenient pickup at hotel). Married to an American (Patti) and having run restaurants in Siena and the US, Roberto communicates well with Americans. His passions are Sienese culture, Tuscan history, and local cuisine. It's ideal to book well in advance, but you might be able to schedule a tour if you call the day before (seven different tours—explained on his website, €90/person for full-day tours, €60/person for off-season four-hour tours, entry fees extra, assistant Anna can schedule city tours as well as other guides if Roberto is booked, Anna's mobile 320-147-6590, Roberto's mobile 328-425-5648, www.toursbyroberto.com, toursbyroberto@gmail.com).

Federica Olla is a smart, youthful guide with a knack for creative teaching (€55/hour, mobile 338-133-9525, info@ollaeventi.com).

SGO Guides Co-op is a group of 10 young guides who offer good tours covering all of Tuscany and Umbria (€130/half-day, €260/full day, mobile 331-949-3869, www.guidesienaeoltre.com). Among them, charming Stefania Fabrizi specializes in Siena (mobile 338-640-7796).

Bus Tours—Somehow a company called My Tour has a lock on all hotel tour-promotion space. Every hotel has a rack of their brochures, which advertise a variety of five-hour big-bus tours into the countryside (€38, depart from Piazza Gramsci).

Siena at a Glance

▲▲▲**Il Campo** Best square in Italy. **Hours:** Always open. See page 565.

▲▲▲**Duomo** Art-packed cathedral with mosaic floors and statues by Michelangelo and Bernini. **Hours:** March-Sept Mon-Sat 10:30-20:00, Sun 13:30-18:00; Oct-Feb Mon-Sat 10:30-18:00, Sun 13:30-17:30. See page 572.

▲▲**Duomo Museum** Museum displaying cathedral art (including Duccio's *Maestà*) and offering sweeping Tuscan view. **Hours:** Daily March-Sept 9:30-19:30, Oct-Feb 10:00-17:00. See page 576.

▲**Civic Museum** City museum in City Hall with Sienese frescoes of Good and Bad Government. **Hours:** Daily March-Oct 10:00-19:00, Nov-Feb 10:00-17:15. See page 570.

▲**City Tower** 330-foot tower climb. **Hours:** Daily March-Oct 10:00-19:00, Nov-Feb 10:00-16:00. See page 570.

▲**Pinacoteca** Fine Sienese paintings. **Hours:** Tue-Sat 8:15-19:15, Sun-Mon 9:00-13:00. See page 571.

▲**Baptistery** Cave-like building with baptismal font decorated by Ghiberti and Donatello. **Hours:** Daily 9:30-19:30. See page 578.

▲**Santa Maria della Scala** Museum with vibrant ceiling and wall frescoes depicting day-to-day life in a medieval hospital, much of the original Fountain of Joy, and an Etruscan artifact exhibit. **Hours:** Daily 10:30-18:00, until 16:00 in winter. See page 578.

Crypt Site of 12th-century church, housing some of Siena's oldest frescoes. **Hours:** Daily 9:30-19:30. See page 578.

Church of San Domenico Huge brick church with St. Catherine's head and thumb. **Hours:** Daily 9:00-18:30. See page 579.

Sanctuary of St. Catherine Home of St. Catherine. **Hours:** Daily 8:00-18:00. See page 579.

Sights in Siena

▲▲▲ Il Campo: Siena's Main Square

Il Campo is the heart—geographically and metaphorically—of Siena. The square fans out from City Hall (Palazzo Pubblico) to create an amphitheater. It's the only town square I've ever seen where people stretch out as if at the beach. Il Campo's shining moment is the famous Palio horse races, which take place in summer (see sidebar on page 568).

Originally, this area was just a field *(campo)* located outside the former city walls. Bits of those original walls, which circled the Duomo (and curved against today's square), can be seen above the pharmacy (the black-and-white stones, to the left as you face City Hall). In the 1200s, with the advent of the Sienese Republic, the city expanded—once a small medieval town circling its cathedral, it became a larger, humanistic city gathered around its towering City Hall. In this newer and relatively secular age, the focus of power shifted from the bishop to the city council.

As the city expanded, Il Campo eventually became the historic junction of Siena's various competing *contrade* (neighborhood districts) and the old marketplace. The brick surface is divided into nine sections, representing the council of nine merchants and city bigwigs who ruled medieval Siena. The square and its buildings are the color of the soil upon which they stand...a color known to artists and Crayola-users as "Burnt Sienna."

City Hall: This secular building, with its 330-foot tower, dominates the square. In medieval Siena, this was the center of the city, and the whole focus of Il Campo still flows down to it.

The **City Tower** (Torre del Mangia), Italy's tallest secular tower, was named after a hedonistic watchman who consumed his earnings like a glutton consumes food—his chewed-up statue is in the courtyard, to the left as you enter. (For details on climbing the tower, see "City Tower" listing, later.)

The open **chapel** located at the base of the tower was built in 1348 as thanks to God for ending the Black Death (after it killed more than a third of the population). It should also be used

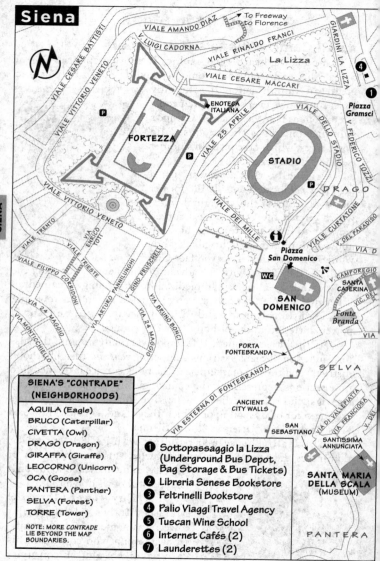

Siena

To Freeway to Florence

VIALE AMANDO DIAZ

V. LUIGI CADORNA

VIALE RINALDO FRANCI

La Lizza

VIALE CESARE MACCARI

GIARDINI LA LIZZA

Piazza Gramsci

V. FEDERICO TOZZI

VIALE DELLO STADIO

VIALE CESARE BATTISTI

VIALE VITTORIO VENETO

ENOTECA ITALIANA

FORTEZZA

VIALE 25 APRILE

STADIO

DRAGO

VIALE CURTATONE

VIALE VITTORIO VENETO

VIALE TRENTO

VIA ENRICO TOTI

VIALE TRIESTE

VIA GIRO FRUSCHELLI

VIA ARTURO PANNILUNGHI

VIALE DEI MILLE

V. DEL PARADISO

VIA D

Piazza San Domenico

V. CAMPOREGIO

SANTA CATERINA

VIALE FILIPPO CORRIDONI

VIA 24 MAGGIO

VIA MONTICCHIELLO

VIA BRUNO BONCI

VIA 24 MAGGIO

WC

SAN DOMENICO

VIC. DEL

Fonte Branda

VIA

PORTA FONTEBRANDA

SELVA

ANCIENT CITY WALLS

VIA ESTERNA DI FONTEBRANDA

SAN SEBASTIANO

SANTISSIMA ANNUNZIATA

VIA DI VALLEPIATTA

VIA FRANCIOSA

V. DEL

SANTA MARIA DELLA SCALA (MUSEUM)

PANTERA

SIENA'S "CONTRADE" (NEIGHBORHOODS)

AQUILA (Eagle)
BRUCO (Caterpillar)
CIVETTA (Owl)
DRAGO (Dragon)
GIRAFFA (Giraffe)
LEOCORNO (Unicorn)
OCA (Goose)
PANTERA (Panther)
SELVA (Forest)
TORRE (Tower)

NOTE: MORE CONTRADE LIE BEYOND THE MAP BOUNDARIES.

❶ Sottopassaggio la Lizza (Underground Bus Depot, Bag Storage & Bus Tickets)
❷ Libreria Senese Bookstore
❸ Feltrinelli Bookstore
❹ Palio Viaggi Travel Agency
❺ Tuscan Wine School
❻ Internet Cafés (2)
❼ Launderettes (2)

SIENA

SIENA

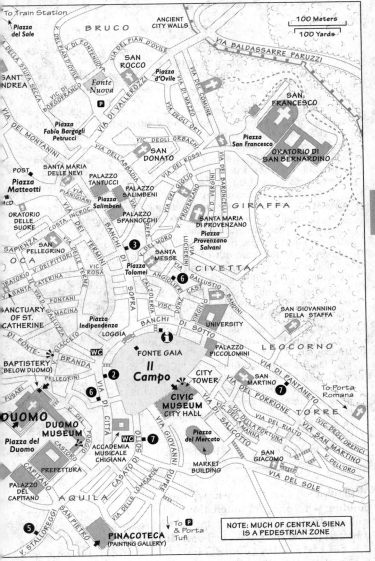

Siena's Palio

In the Palio, the feisty spirit of Siena's 17 neighborhoods lives on. Each *contrada* has a parish church, well or fountain, and sometimes even a historical museum. Each is represented by a mascot (porcupine, unicorn, wolf, etc.) and unique colors worn proudly by residents.

Contrada pride is evident year-round in Siena's parades and colorful banners, lamps, and wall plaques. (If you hear the thunder of distant drumming, run to it for some medieval action—there's a good chance it'll feature flag throwers.) You are welcome to participate in these lively neighborhood festivals. Buy a scarf in *contrada* colors, grab a glass of Chianti, munch on some *panforte*, and join the merriment.

Contrada passion is most visible twice a year—on July 2 and August 16—when the city erupts during its world-famous horse race, the Palio di Siena. Ten of the 17 neighborhoods compete (chosen by rotation and lot), hurling themselves with medieval abandon into several days of trial races and traditional revelry. Jockeys—usually from out of town—are considered hired guns, no better than paid mercenaries. Bets are placed on which *contrada* will win...and lose. Despite the shady behind-the-scenes dealing, on the big day the horses are taken into their *contrada*'s church to be blessed. ("Go and return victorious," says the priest.) It's considered a sign of luck if a horse leaves droppings in the church.

On the evening of the race, Il Campo is stuffed to the brim with locals and tourists. Dirt is brought in and packed down over the gray pavement of the perimeter to create the track's surface, while mattresses pad the walls of surrounding buildings. The most treacherous spots are the sharp corners, where many a rider has bitten the dust.

---

to thank God that the top-heavy tower—just plunked onto the building with no extra foundation and no iron reinforcement—still stands. These days, the chapel is used solely to bless the Palio contestants, and the tower's bell only rings for the race.

Fountain of Joy (Fonte Gaia): This 15th-century work by Jacopo della Quercia marks the square's high point. The joy is all about how the Sienese Republic blessed its people with water. Notice Lady Justice with her scales, overseeing the free distribution of water to all. Imagine residents gathering here in the 1400s to fill their jugs. The Fountain of Joy still reminds locals that life in Siena is good. Notice the pigeons politely waiting their turn to

Picture the scene: Ten snorting horses and their nervous riders line up near the pharmacy (on the right side of the square) to await the starting signal. Then they race like crazy while spectators wave the scarves of their neighborhoods. Every possible vantage point and perch is packed with people straining to see the action. One lap around the course is about a third of a mile (350 meters); three laps make a full circuit. In this literally no-holds-barred race—which lasts just over a minute—

a horse can win even without its rider (jockeys perch precariously, without saddles, on the sweaty horses' backs, and often fall off).

When the winner crosses the line, 1/17th of Siena—the victorious neighborhood—goes berserk. Winners receive a *palio* (banner), typically painted by a local artist and always featuring the Virgin Mary. But the true prize is proving that your *contrada* is *numero uno,* and mocking your losing rivals.

All over town, sketches and posters depict the Palio. This is not some folkloric event—it's a real medieval moment. If you're packed onto the square with 60,000 people, all hungry for victory, you won't see much, but you'll feel it. Bleacher and balcony seats are expensive, but it's free to join the masses in the square. Be sure to go with an empty bladder as there are no WCs, and be prepared to surrender any sense of personal space.

While the actual Palio packs the city, you could side-trip in from Florence to see the horse-race trials—called *prove* (proh-vay)—on any of the three days before the main event (usually at 9:00 and after 19:00, free seats in bleachers). For more information, visit www.ilpalio.org.

tightrope gingerly down slippery spouts to slurp a drink from wolves' snouts. The relief panel on the left (as you face the fountain) shows God creating Adam by helping him to his feet. It's said that this reclining Adam influenced Michelangelo when he painted his Sistine Chapel ceiling. This fountain is a copy—you can see most of the original fountain in an interesting exhibit at Siena's Santa Maria della Scala (described later).

SIENA

▲Civic Museum (Museo Civico)—At the base of the tower is Siena's City Hall, the spot where secular government got its start in early Renaissance Europe. There you'll find city government still at work, along with a sampling of local art, including Siena's first fresco (with a groundbreaking down-to-earth depiction of the Madonna).

Cost and Hours: €8, daily March-Oct 10:00-19:00, Nov-Feb 10:00-17:15, last entry 45 minutes before closing, tel. 0577-292-615.

Touring the Museum: Start in the Sala del Risorgimento, with dramatic scenes of Victor Emmanuel II's unification of Italy (surrounded by statues that don't seem to care).

Passing through the chapel, where the city's governors and bureaucrats prayed, enter the Sala del Mappamondo. On opposite walls are two large frescoes by Siena's great Simone Martini. His *Maestà* (*Enthroned Virgin*, 1315) is groundbreaking as Siena's first fresco showing a Madonna not in a faraway, gold-leaf heaven, but under the blue sky of the real world that we inhabit. Facing the *Maestà* is Martini's faded *Guidoriccio da Fogliano,* which depicts a mercenary general surveying the imposing castle that his armies have just conquered.

Next is the Sala della Pace—where the city's fat cats met.

Looking down on the oligarchy during their meetings were two fascinating frescoes showing the *Effects of Good and Bad Government,* by Sienese painter Ambrogio Lorenzetti. Compare the whistle-while-you-work happiness of the utopian community ruled by the utopian government (in the better-preserved fresco) against the crime, devastation, and societal mayhem of a community ruled by politicians with more typical values. The message: Without justice, there can be no prosperity.

On your way out, climb up to the loggia (using the stairs just before the Sala del Risorgimento) for a sweeping view of the city and its surroundings. (For a less impressive version of this view, you could skip the stairs and simply peek behind the curtains in the Sala della Pace.)

▲City Tower (Torre del Mangia)—Siena gathers around its City Hall more than its church. Medieval Siena was a proud republic, and this tall tower is the exclamation point of its "declaration of independence." Its 300

steps get pretty skinny at the top, but the reward is one of Italy's best views.

Cost and Hours: €8, daily March-Oct 10:00-19:00, Nov-Feb 10:00-16:00, last entry 45 minutes before closing, closed in rain, free and mandatory bag check. Admission is limited to 50 people at a time, so be prepared for long lines and try to avoid midday crowds—it's often sold out.

Near Il Campo

▲**Pinacoteca**—If you're into medieval art, you'll likely find this quiet, uncrowded, colorful museum delightful. The museum walks you through Siena's art chronologically, from the 12th through the 16th century, when a revolution in realism was percolating in Tuscany.

Cost and Hours: €4, Tue-Sat 8:15-19:15, Sun-Mon 9:00-13:00, last entry 30 minutes before closing, free and mandatory bag check; from Il Campo, walk out Via di Città and go left on Via San Pietro; tel. 0577-281-161 or 0577-286-143.

Touring the Museum: In general, the collection lets you follow the evolution of painting styles from Byzantine to Gothic, then to International Gothic, and finally to Renaissance. Long after Florentine art went realistic, the Sienese embraced a timeless, otherworldly style glittering with lots of gold.

As you walk through the museum, note that Sienese art features more than just paintings. In this city of proud craftsmen, the gilding and carpentry of the frames almost competes with the actual paintings. The exquisite attention to detail gives a glimpse into the wealth of the 14th and 15th centuries, Siena's Golden Age. Take time to trace the delicate features with your eyes. The woven silk and gold clothing you'll see was worn by the very people who once walked these halls, when this was a private mansion (appreciate the colonnaded courtyard).

The core of the collection is on the second floor, in Rooms 1-19. Works by Duccio (artist of the *Maestà* in the Duomo Museum) feature groundbreaking innovations that are subtle to the layman's eyes: less gold-leaf background, fewer gold creases in robes, transparent garments, inlaid-marble thrones, and a more human Mary and Jesus.

St. Augustine of Siena, by Duccio's assistant, Simone Martini (who did the *Maestà* in the Civic Museum), sets the saint's life in pretty realistic Sienese streets, buildings, and landscapes. The saint occasionally pops out at the oddest (difficult to draw) angles to save the day.

Also look for two famous small wooden panels by Ambrogio Lorenzetti (who created the *Effects of Good and Bad Government* in the Civic Museum). *La Città sul Mare (City by the Sea)* and

Castello in Riva al Lago (Castle on the Lakeshore) feature the strange, medieval Cubism seen in the work of his contemporary, Martini's *Guidoriccio da Fogliano* (in the Civic Museum). Notice the weird, melancholy light that captures the sense of the Dark Ages. These images are replicated on postcards found throughout the city.

Several colorful rooms on the first floor are dedicated to Domenico Beccafumi (1486-1551), who designed many of the Duomo's inlaid pavement panels (including *Slaughter of the Innocents*). With strong bodies, twisting poses, and dramatic gestures, Beccafumi's works epitomize the Mannerist style.

Cathedral Area

▲▲▲Duomo

If the Campo is the heart of Siena, the Duomo (or cathedral) is its soul. The white and dark-green striped church, sitting on an

artificial platform atop Siena's highest point, is visible for miles around. This ornate but surprisingly secular shrine to the Virgin Mary is stacked with colorful art inside and out, from the inlaid-marble floors to the stained-glass windows. The interior is a Renaissance riot of striped columns, intricate marble inlays, Michelangelo statues, and Bernini sculptures. In the Piccolomini Library, a series of captivating frescoes by the Umbrian painter Pinturicchio tells the story of Aeneas Piccolomini, Siena's consummate Renaissance Man, who became Pope Pius II.

Cost and Hours: €3 includes cathedral and Piccolomini Library, buy ticket at Duomo Museum entrance (facing the cathedral entry, the museum is 100 yards to the right, near the south transept); open March-Sept Mon-Sat 10:30-20:00, Sun 13:30-18:00; Oct-Feb Mon-Sat 10:30-18:00, Sun 13:30-17:30; last entry 30 minutes before closing.

Dress Code: Modest dress is required, but stylish paper ponchos are provided for the inappropriately attired.

Information: Inside the Duomo are €1 video terminals that give a history of the cathedral floor. The €5 audioguide provides a good, basic commentary covering the church and library (€7/2 people). Other audioguide tours of various lengths and prices, and covering sights all over town are also available in the church (but you have to return your player here).

◑ Self-Guided Tour: Grab a spot on a stone bench opposite the entry to take in this architectural festival of green, white, pink, and gold.

Exterior: Like a medieval altarpiece, the facade is divided into sections, each frame filled with patriarchs and prophets, studded with roaring gargoyles, and topped with prickly pinnacles. Imagine pilgrims arriving at this church, its facade trumpeting the coming of Christ and the correct path to salvation.

The current structure dates back to 1215, with the major decoration done during Siena's heyday (1250 to 1350). The lower story, by Giovanni Pisano (who worked from 1284 to 1297), features remnants of the fading Romanesque style (round arches over the doors), topped with the pointed arches of the new Gothic style that was seeping in from France. The upper half, in full-blown Gothic, was designed and built a century later.

• *Step inside, once again putting yourself in the mindset of a pilgrim as you take in this trove of religious art. (With a maximum capacity of 700 visitors, you may have to wait—the current number is indicated on a computer screen at the turnstile.)*

Nave: The heads of 172 popes—who reigned from Peter's time to the 12th century—peer down from above, looking over the fine inlaid art on the floor. With a forest of striped columns, a coffered dome, a large stained-glass window at the far end (described later), and an art gallery's worth of early Renaissance art, this is one busy interior. If you look closely at the popes, you'll see the same four faces repeated over and over.

For almost two centuries (1373-1547), 40 artists paved the marble floor with scenes from the Old Testament, allegories, and intricate patterns. The series starts near the entrance with historical allegories; the larger, more elaborate scenes surrounding the altar are mostly stories from the Old Testament. Many of the floor panels are roped off to prevent further wear and tear.

• *Look for the marble altarpiece decorated with statues.*

Piccolomini Altar: This was designed for the tomb of the Sienese-born Pope Pius III. It was commissioned when he was the cardinal of Siena, but because he later became a pope (see the fresco of his coronation with Pius wearing the golden robe—above and to the right of the Michelangelo statue), he was buried in the Vatican and this fancy tomb was never used. It's most interesting for its statues—one by Michelangelo, three by his students. Michelangelo was originally contracted to do 15 statues, but the marble blocks had been started by another sculptor, and his heart was never in the project. He personally finished only one—St. Paul (lower right, who is clearly more interesting than the bland, bored popes above him).

• *Now grab a seat under the...*

Dome: The dome sits on a 12-sided base, but its "coffered" ceiling is actually a painted illusion. Get oriented to the array of sights by thinking of the church floor as a big 12-hour clock. You're the middle, and the altar is high noon: You'll find the *Slaughter of the Innocents* roped off on the floor at 10 o'clock, Pisano's pulpit between two pillars at 11 o'clock, a copy of Duccio's round stained-glass window at high noon, Bernini's chapel at 3 o'clock, the Piccolomini Altar with the Michelangelo statue (next to doorway leading to a shop, snacks, and WC) at 7 o'clock, the Piccolomini Library at 8 o'clock, and a Donatello statue at 9 o'clock.

Pisano's Pulpit: The octagonal Carrara marble pulpit (1268) rests on the backs of lions, symbols of Christianity triumphant.

Like the lions, the Church eats its catch (devouring paganism) and nurses its cubs. The seven relief panels tell the life of Christ in rich detail. (Buy light from the coin-op machine.) The pulpit is the work of Nicola Pisano (c. 1220-1278), the "Giotto of sculpture," whose revival of classical forms (columns, sarcophagus-like relief panels) signaled the coming Renaissance. His son Giovanni (c. 1240-1319) carved many of the panels, mixing his dad's classicism and realism with the decorative detail and curvy lines of French Gothic—a style that would influence Donatello and the other Florentines.

Duccio's Stained-Glass Rose Window: This is a copy of the original window, which was moved to the Duomo Museum a couple of years ago. The famous rose window was created in 1288 and dedicated to the Virgin Mary (for more details, see page 577).

Slaughter of the Innocents: This inlaid pavement panel shows Herod (left), sitting enthroned amid Renaissance arches, as he orders the massacre of all babies to prevent the coming of the promised Messiah. It's a chaotic scene of angry soldiers, grieving mothers, and dead babies, reminding locals that a republic ruled by a tyrant will experience misery.

• *Step into the chapel to the right of the library to see...*

St. John the Baptist Statue: The statue of the rugged saint in his famous rags was created by Donatello. The aging Florentine sculptor, whose style was now considered passé in Florence, came here to build bronze doors for the church (similar to Ghiberti's in Florence). He didn't complete the door project, but he did finish this bronze statue (1457). Notice the cherubs high above it, playfully dangling their feet.

• *Cross beneath the dome to find the...*

Bernini Chapel: To understand why Gian Lorenzo Bernini (1598-1680) is considered the greatest Baroque sculptor, step into his sumptuous chapel. This last work in the cathedral (1659) is enough to make even a Lutheran light a candle. Move up to the altar and look back at the two Bernini statues: Mary Magdalene in a state of spiritual ecstasy and St. Jerome playing the crucifix like a violinist lost in beautiful music.

Over the altar is the *Madonna del Voto,* a Madonna and Child painted by Duccio and adorned with a real crown of gold and jewels. In typical medieval fashion, the scene is set in the golden light of heaven. Mary has the almond eyes, long fingers, and golden folds in her robe that are found in orthodox icons of the time. Still, this Mary tilts her head and looks out sympathetically, ready to listen to the prayers of the faithful. This is the Mary to whom the Palio is dedicated, dear to the hearts of the Sienese.

The faithful's prayers to Mary are accompanied by offerings, found outside the chapel, hanging on the wall to the left as you exit.

• *Cross back to the other side of the church to find the...*

Piccolomini Library: Brilliantly frescoed, the library captures the exuberant, optimistic spirit of the 1400s, when humanism and the Renaissance were born. The never-restored frescoes look nearly as vivid now as the day they were finished 550 years ago. (With the bright window light, candles were unnecessary in this room—and didn't sully the art with soot.) The painter Pinturicchio (c. 1454-1513) was hired to celebrate the life of one of Siena's hometown boys—a man many call "the first humanist," Aeneas Piccolomini (1405-1464), who became Pope Pius II. Each of the 10 scenes is framed with an arch, as if Pinturicchio were opening a window onto the spacious 3-D world we inhabit.

The library also contains intricately decorated, illuminated music scores, and a statue (a Roman copy of a Greek original) of the Three Graces, who almost seem to dance to the beat. The oddly huge sheep-skin sheets of music are from the days before individual hymnals—they had to be big so that many singers could read the music at the same time from a distance. Appreciate the fine painted decorations on the music—the gold-leaf highlights, the newly discovered (and quite expensive) cobalt for blue tones, and the miniature figures. All of this exquisite detail was lovingly crafted by Benedictine monks for the glory of God. Find your favorite—I like the blue, totally wild god of wind with the big hair (in the fourth case).

• *Exit the Duomo and make a U-turn to the left, walking alongside the church to Piazza Jacopo della Quercia.*

Unfinished Church: After rival republic Florence began its grand cathedral (1296), proud Siena planned to build one even bigger, the biggest church in all Christendom.

Construction began in the 1330s on an extension off the right side of the existing Duomo (today's cathedral would have been used as a transept). The nave of the Duomo was supposed to be where the piazza is today. Worshippers would have entered the church from the far end of the piazza through the unfinished wall. (Look way up at the highest part of the wall. That's the view-point accessible from inside the Duomo Museum.) Some of the nave's green-and-white striped columns were built, and are now filled in with a brick wall. White stones in the pavement mark where a row of pillars would have been.

The vision was grand, but it underestimated the complexity of constructing such a building without enough land for it to sit upon. That, coupled with the devastating effects of a plague, killed the city's ability and will to finish the project. Look through the unfinished entrance facade, note blue sky where the stained-glass windows would have been, and ponder the struggles, triumphs, and failures of the human spirit.

▲▲Duomo Museum (Museo dell'Opera e Panorama)

Located at the back of the Duomo on the right, Siena's most enjoyable museum was built to house the cathedral's art. Stand eye-to-

eye with the saints and angels who once languished unknown in the church's upper reaches (where copies are found today).

Cost and Hours: €6, daily March-Sept 9:30-19:30, Oct-Feb 10:00-17:00; next to the Duomo, in the skeleton of the unfinished part of the church on the Il Campo side—look for the yellow signs.

Information: There's a good 40-minute audioguide for €3. An €8 combo-audioguide available only at the Duomo includes the museum, the Duomo, and its library (€12/2 people, ID required for deposit). Tel. 0577-283-048, www.operaduomo.siena.it.

❍ **Self-Guided Tour:** Start your tour at the bottom and work your way up.

Ground Floor: This floor is filled with the cathedral's original Gothic sculptures by Giovanni Pisano, who spent 10 years in the late 1200s carving and orchestrating the decoration of the cathedral with saints, prophets, sibyls, animals, and the original she-wolf with Romulus and Remus.

On the ground floor you'll also find Donatello's fine, round *Madonna and Child* carved relief. A slender, tender Mary gazes down at her chubby-cheeked baby, as her sad eyes say that she knows the eventual fate of her son.

On the opposite side of the room is Duccio's original stained-glass rose window, which until recently was located above and behind the Duomo's altar. Now the church has a copy, and art lovers can enjoy a close-up look at this masterpiece. The rose window—20 feet across, made in 1288—is dedicated (like the church and the city itself) to the Virgin Mary. The work was designed by Siena's most famous artist, Duccio di Buoninsegna (c. 1255-1319), and combines elements from rigid Byzantine icons (Mary's almond-shaped bubble, called a *mandorla*, and the full-frontal saints that flank her) with a budding sense of 3-D realism (the throne turned at a three-quarter angle to simulate depth, with angels behind).

Duccio's *Maestà*: Upstairs awaits a private audience with the *Maestà* (*Enthroned Virgin*, 1311), whose panels were once part of the Duomo's main altarpiece. Although the former altarpiece was disassembled (and the frame was lost), most of the pieces are displayed here, with the front side (*Maestà*, with Mary and saints) at one end of the room, and the back side (Passion panels) at the other.

The *Maestà* was revolutionary for the time in its sheer size and opulence, and in Duccio's budding realism, which broke standard conventions. Duccio, at the height of his powers, used every innovative arrow in his quiver. He replaced the standard gold-leaf background (symbolizing heaven) with a gold, intricately patterned curtain draped over the throne. Mary's blue robe opens to reveal her body, and the curve of her knee suggests real anatomy beneath the robe. Baby Jesus wears a delicately transparent garment. Their faces are modeled with light—a patchwork of bright flesh and shadowy valleys, as if lit from the left (a technique he likely learned from his contemporary Giotto during a visit to Florence).

The flip side of the *Maestà* features 26 smaller panels—the medieval equivalent of pages—showing colorful scenes from the Passion of Christ.

Panorama del Facciatone: About 60 claustrophobic spiral stairs take you to the first viewpoint. You can continue up another similar spiral staircase to reach the very top. Standing on the wall from this high point in the city, you're rewarded with a stunning view of Siena...and an interesting perspective. Look toward the Duomo and consider this: If Siena's grandiose plans to expand the cathedral had come to fruition, you'd be looking straight down the nave toward the altar.

▲**Baptistery**—Siena is so hilly that there wasn't enough flat ground on which to build a big church. What to do? Build a big church anyway and prop up the overhanging edge with the Baptistery. This dark and quietly tucked-away cave of art is worth a look for its cool, tranquil bronze panels and angels by Ghiberti, Donatello, and others that adorn the pedestal of the baptismal font.

Cost and Hours: €3, daily 9:30-19:30, last entry 30 minutes before closing.

Crypt—The cathedral "crypt" is archaeologically important. The site of a small 12th-century Romanesque church, it was filled in with dirt a century after its creation in order to provide a foundation for the huge church that sits atop it today. Recently excavated, the several rediscovered frescoed rooms show off what are likely the oldest frescoes in town.

Cost and Hours: €6, daily 9:30-19:30, entrance is halfway up the stairs between the Baptistery and Duomo Museum.

▲**Santa Maria della Scala**—This museum (opposite the Duomo entrance) was used as a hospital until the 1980s. Its labyrinthine 12th-century cellars—carved out of volcanic tuff and finished with brick—go down several floors, and during medieval times were used to store supplies for the hospital upstairs. Today, the hospital and its cellars are filled with exhibits (well-described in English) and can be a welcome refuge from the hot streets. Stop in for a cool and quiet break in the air-conditioned lobby, which offers a fine bookshop and big, comfy couches, all under great 15th-century timbers.

Cost and Hours: €6, daily 10:30-18:00, until 16:00 in winter, last entry 30 minutes before closing, bookstore, café, tel. 0577-534-511, www.santamariadellascala.com.

Touring the Museum: The main attractions include the fancily frescoed Pellegrinaio Hall (ground floor), most of the original Fountain of Joy, St. Catherine's Oratory chapel (first basement), and the Etruscan collection in the Archaeological Museum (second basement). Just inside the complex is the Church of the Santissima Annunziata.

Sumptuously frescoed, **Pellegrinaio Hall** shows medieval Siena's innovative health care and social welfare system in action (c. 1442, wonderfully described in English). Starting in the 11th century, the hospital nursed the sick and cared for abandoned children, as is vividly portrayed in these frescoes. The good works paid off, as bequests and donations poured in, creating the wealth that's evident throughout this building.

Downstairs you'll find an engaging exhibit on Jacopo della Quercia's early 15th-century **Fountain of Joy** (Fonte Gaia)—and the disassembled pieces of the original fountain itself. In the 19th century, after serious deterioration, the ornate fountain was dismantled and plaster casts were made. (From these casts, they formed the replica that graces Il Campo today.) Here you'll see the eroded original panels paired with their restored casts, along with the original statues that once stood on the edges of the fountain.

Descend into the cavernous second basement under groin vaults to the **Archaeological Museum,** where you can be alone with piles of ancient Etruscan stuff excavated from tombs dating centuries before Christ (displayed in a labyrinthine exhibit). Remember, the Etruscans dominated this part of Italy before the Roman Empire swept through—some historians think even Rome originated as an Etruscan town.

Siena's San Domenico Area

Church of San Domenico—This huge brick church is worth a quick look. The spacious, plain interior (except for the colorful

flags of the city's 17 *contrade*, or neighborhoods) fits the austere philosophy of the Dominicans and invites meditation on the thoughts and deeds of St. Catherine. Walk up the steps in the rear to see paintings from the life of St. Catherine. Halfway up the church on the right, find a metal bust of St. Catherine, a small case housing her thumb (on the left), and a glass box on the lowest shelf containing the chain she used to scourge herself. In the chapel (15 feet to the left) surrounded with candles, you'll see Catherine's actual head atop the altar. Through the door just beyond are the sacristy and the bookstore.

Cost and Hours: Free, daily 9:00-18:30, gift shop tel. 0577-286-848, www.basilicacateriniana.com. A WC (€0.50) is at the far end of the parking lot, to the right as you face the church entrance.

Sanctuary of St. Catherine—Step into the cool and peaceful site of Catherine's home. Siena remembers its favorite home-town gal, a simple, unschooled, but mystically devout soul who, in the mid-1300s, helped convince the pope to return from France to Rome. Pilgrims have visited this place since 1464, and architects and artists have greatly embellished what was probably once a humble home (her family worked as wool dyers). You'll see paintings throughout showing scenes from her life.

SIENA

St. Catherine of Siena
(1347-1380)

The youngest of 25 children born to a Sienese cloth dyer, Catherine began experiencing heavenly visions as a child. At 16 she became a Dominican nun, locking herself away for three years in a room in her family's house. She lived the life of an ascetic, which culminated in a vision wherein she married Christ. Catherine emerged from solitude to join her Dominican sisters, sharing her experiences, caring for the sick, and gathering both disciples and enemies. At age 23, she lapsed into a spiritual coma, waking with the heavenly command to spread her message to the world. She wrote essays and letters to kings, dukes, bishops, and popes, imploring them to find peace for a war-ravaged Italy. While visiting Pisa during Lent of 1375, she had a vision in which she received the stigmata, the wounds of Christ.

Still in her twenties, Catherine was invited to Avignon, France, where the pope had taken up residence. With her charm, sincerity, and reputation for holiness, she helped convince Pope Gregory XI to return the papacy to the city of Rome. Catherine also went to Rome, where she died young. She was canonized in the next generation (by a Sienese pope), and her relics were distributed to churches around Italy.

Because of her intervention in the papal schism, today Catherine is revered (along with St. Benedict) as the patron saint of Europe, and remembered as a rare outspoken medieval woman still appreciated for her universal message: that this world is not a gift from our fathers, but a loan from our children.

Enter through the courtyard, and walk down the stairs at the far end. The church on your right contains the wooden crucifix upon which Catherine was meditating when she received the stigmata. Take a pew, gaze at it, and try to imagine the scene. The chapel on your left stands where the kitchen once was. Go down the stairs (left of the gift shop) to reach the saint's room. Catherine's bare cell is behind wrought-iron doors.

Cost and Hours: Free, daily 8:00-18:00, a few downhill blocks toward the center from San Domenico—follow signs to *Santuario di Santa Caterina*—at Costa di Sant'Antonio 6, tel. 0577-288-175.

Shopping in Siena

The main drag, Via Banchi di Sopra, is a cancan of fancy shops. Here are some things to look for:

Flags: For easy-to-pack souvenirs, get some of the colorful scarves/flags that depict the symbols of Siena's 17 different neighborhoods (such as the wolf, the turtle, and the snail). They're good for gifts or to decorate your home (sold in varying sizes at souvenir stands).

Sweets: All over town, **Prodotti Tipici** shops sell Sienese specialties. Siena's claim to caloric fame is its *panforte,* a rich, chewy concoction of nuts, honey, and candied fruits that impresses even fruitcake-haters. There are a few varieties: *Margherita,* dusted in powdered sugar, is more fruity, while *panpepato* has a spicy, peppery crust. Locals prefer a chewy, white macaroon-and-almond cookie called *ricciarelli.*

Sleeping in Siena

Finding a room in Siena is tough during Easter or the Palio (July 2 and Aug 16). Many hotels won't take reservations until the end of May for the Palio, and even then they might require a four-night stay. While day-tripping tour groups turn the town into a Gothic amusement park in midsummer, Siena is basically yours in the evenings and off-season.

Part of Siena's charm is its lively, festive character—this means that all hotels can be plagued with noise, even (and sometimes especially) the hotels in the pedestrian-only zone. If tranquility is important for your sanity, ask for a room that's off the street, or consider staying at one of the recommended places outside the center.

Fancy Sleeps, Southwest of Il Campo

These classy and well-run places are a 10-minute walk from Il Campo.

$$$ Hotel Duomo has 20 spacious rooms, a picnic-friendly roof terrace, and a bizarre floor plan (Sb-€105, Db-€130, Db suite-€180, Tb-€180, Qb-€230, includes breakfast, air-con, Internet access, discounted parking; follow Via di Città, which becomes Via di Stalloreggi, to #38; tel. 0577-289-088, fax 0577-43-043, www.hotelduomo.it, booking@hotelduomo.it, Alessandro). If you're arriving by train, take a taxi (€10) or ride bus #3 to the Porta Tufi stop, just a few minutes' walk from the hotel; you can also arrange to have Alessandro take you to/from the train station or airport (with this book: train station-€10, Florence's Vespucci Airport-€105, Pisa's Galilei Airport-€165; he'll also take you to

Sleep Code

(€1 = about $1.40, country code: 39)
S = Single, **D** = Double/Twin, **T** = Triple, **Q** = Quad, **b** = bathroom,
s = shower only.

Breakfast is not included unless noted. If your hotel doesn't provide breakfast, eat at a bar on Il Campo or near your hotel. Credit cards are generally accepted, but I note in the listings if they aren't. (If not, there are ATMs all over town.) Hotel staff generally speak English unless noted otherwise.

To help you easily sort through these listings, I've divided the accommodations into three categories based on the price for a standard double room with bath or for a bunk at a hostel:

$$$ Higher Priced—Most rooms €130 or more.
  $$ Moderately Priced—Most rooms between €90-130.
    $ Lower Priced—Most rooms €90 or less.

Prices can change without notice; verify the hotel's current rates online or by email. For other updates, see www.ricksteves.com/update.

nearby hill towns, e.g. Florence-€105 and Pisa-€165). If you're driving, go to Porta San Marco, turn right, and follow signs to the hotel—drop your bags, then park in the nearby Il Campo lot near Porta Tufi.

$$$ Pensione Palazzo Ravizza is elegant and friendly, with an aristocratic feel, which is fitting since it was once the luxurious residence of a noble. Guests enjoy a peaceful garden set on a dramatic bluff, along with a Steinway in the upper lounge (Sb-€150, small loft Db-€130, standard Db-€170, superior Db-€200, Tb-€240, family suites-€300, see website for room differences, rooms in back overlook countryside, includes breakfast, air-con, elevator, Wi-Fi, Via Piano dei Mantellini 34, tel. 0577-280-462, fax 0577-221-597, www.palazzoravizza.com, bureau@palazzoravizza .it, Ariol). As parking is free, this is a particularly good value for drivers.

Simple Places near Il Campo

Most of these listings are forgettable but inexpensive, and just a horse wreck away from one of Italy's most wonderful civic spaces.

$$ Piccolo Hotel Etruria has 20 basic, air-conditioned rooms. The hotel is overpriced for what it is, though well-located and restful (S-€50, Sb-€55, Db-€110, Tb-€138, Qb-€170, optional breakfast-€6, next to recommended Albergo Tre Donzelle at Via delle Donzelle 1-3, tel. 0577-288-088, fax 0577-288-461, www

.hoteletruria.com, info@hoteletruria.com, Fattorini family).

$ Albergo Tre Donzelle is a fine budget value with 20 plain, institutional, well-worn rooms. Although the showers have seen better days, these may be the cheapest rooms in the center. Don't hang out here...think of Il Campo, a block away, as your terrace (S-€38, D-€49, Db-€60, T-€70, Tb-€85, no rooms available for Palio, breakfast-€5, Wi-Fi; with your back to the tower, head away from Il Campo toward 2 o'clock to Via delle Donzelle 5; tel. 0577-280-358, www.tredonzelle.com, info@tredonzelle.com, Maurizio).

$ Hotel Cannon d'Oro, a few blocks up Via Banchi di Sopra, is a labyrinthine slumber mill renting 30 no-frills rooms (Sb-€71, Db-€90, Tb-€115, Qb-€136, these discounted prices good with this book through 2012, family deals, includes breakfast, fans, Wi-Fi, a couple of blocks from the bus hub at Via dei Montanini 28, tel. 0577-44-321, fax 0577-280-868, www.cannondoro.com, info@cannondoro.com; Maurizio, Tommaso, and Rodrigo).

B&Bs in the Old Center

$$ Palazzo Masi B&B, run by Alizzardo and Daniela, is just below Il Campo. They rent six pleasant, spacious rooms with shared common areas on the second and third floors of an old building (D-€80, Db-€120 if you book direct, discounts for 4 or more nights, cash only, Wi-Fi; from City Hall, walk 50 yards down Via del Casato di Sotto to #29; mobile 349-600-9155, www.palazzo masi.com, info@palazzomasi.it). The place is generally unstaffed, so phone upon arrival.

$ B&B Siena in Centro is a clearinghouse managing five good and centrally located private apartments. Their handy office functions as a reception renting out a total of about 20 rooms; stop by here to pick up your key and be escorted to your apartment. The rooms are generally spacious, quiet, and comfortable, but with no air-conditioning or Wi-Fi. Their website lets you visualize your options (Sb-€45-60, Db-€70-90, Tb-€90-120, includes breakfast, reception open 9:00-10:30 & 15:00-19:00, other times by phone request, OK to leave bags at reception, Via di Stalloreggi 14, tel. 0577-43041, mobile 331-281-4137 or 347-465-9753, www.bbsiena incentro.com, info@bbsienaincentro.com; Patrizia, Paolo, Gioia, and Michela).

$ B&B Alle Due Porte is a charming little establishment renting four big rooms with sweet furniture under big medieval beams. The shared breakfast room is delightful. The manager, Egisto, is a phone call and five-minute scooter ride away (Db-€85, windowless Db-€65, Tb-€110, Wi-Fi, Via di Stalloreggi 51, tel. 0577-287-670, mobile 368-352-3530, www.sienatur.it, soldatini @interfree.it).

Siena Hotels & Restaurants

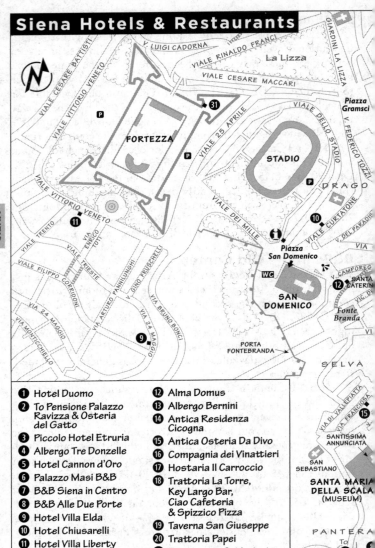

SIENA

1 Hotel Duomo
2 To Pensione Palazzo Ravizza & Osteria del Gatto
3 Piccolo Hotel Etruria
4 Albergo Tre Donzelle
5 Hotel Cannon d'Oro
6 Palazzo Masi B&B
7 B&B Siena in Centro
8 B&B Alle Due Porte
9 Hotel Villa Elda
10 Hotel Chiusarelli
11 Hotel Villa Liberty

12 Alma Domus
13 Albergo Bernini
14 Antica Residenza Cicogna
15 Antica Osteria Da Divo
16 Compagnia dei Vinattieri
17 Hostaria Il Carroccio
18 Trattoria La Torre, Key Largo Bar, Ciao Cafeteria & Spizzico Pizza
19 Taverna San Giuseppe
20 Trattoria Papei
21 Ristorante Guidoriccio

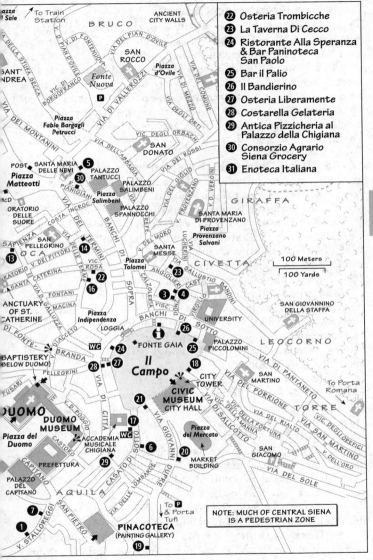

22 Osteria Trombicche
23 La Taverna Di Cecco
24 Ristorante Alla Speranza & Bar Paninoteca San Paolo
25 Bar il Palio
26 Il Bandierino
27 Osteria Liberamente
28 Costarella Gelateria
29 Antica Pizzicheria al Palazzo della Chigiana
30 Consorzio Agrario Siena Grocery
31 Enoteca Italiana

SIENA

NOTE: MUCH OF CENTRAL SIENA IS A PEDESTRIAN ZONE

Near San Domenico Church

These hotels are within a 10-minute walk northwest of Il Campo. Albergo Bernini and Alma Domus, which offer views of the old town and cathedral, are about the best values in town.

$$$ Hotel Villa Elda rents 11 bright and light rooms in a recently renovated villa. Classy, stately, and pricey, it's in a fine neighborhood just a few minutes' walk past the Church of San Domenico (Db-€140-170, more with view, extra person-€30, includes breakfast, air-con, Wi-Fi, garden and view terrace, Viale Ventiquattro Maggio 10, tel. 0577-247-927, www.villaeldasiena.it, info@villaeldasiena.it).

$$$ Hotel Chiusarelli, with 48 recently renovated rooms in a beautiful Neoclassical villa, has a handy location but is on a very busy street. Expect traffic noise at night—ask for a quieter room in the back (can be guaranteed with reservation). The bells of San Domenico are your 7:00 wake-up call (Sb-€98, Db-€138, Tb-€175, ask for Rick Steves discount when you book, air-con, Wi-Fi free with this book, rental bikes-€4/half-day, across from San Domenico at Viale Curtatone 15, tel. 0577-280-562, fax 0577-271-177, www.chiusarelli.com, info@chiusarelli.com).

$$$ Hotel Villa Liberty, a bit farther out, is a former private mansion. It has 16 big, bright, comfortable rooms and lots of street noise (Sb-€80, Db-€140, Tb-€170, air-con, elevator, Wi-Fi, bar, courtyard, free and easy street parking, facing fortress at Viale Vittorio Veneto 11, tel. 0577-44-966, fax 0577-44-770, www.villaliberty.it, info@villaliberty.it).

$ Alma Domus is a church-run hotel renting 43 clean, quiet little rooms for a steal. Bright lamps, quaint balconies, fine views, grand public rooms, and a pleasant atmosphere make this a great value. The 10:00 checkout time is strict, but they will store your luggage in their secure courtyard (Sb-€45, Db-€75, Tb-€95, Qb-€110, includes breakfast, ask for view room—*con vista*, central air-con, elevator, Internet access; from San Domenico, walk downhill toward the view with the church on your right, turn left down Via Camporegio, make a U-turn down the brick steps to Via Camporegio 37; tel. 0577-44-177, fax 0577-47-601, www.hotelalmadomus.it, info@hotelalmadomus.it, Louis).

$ Albergo Bernini makes you part of a Sienese family in a modest, clean home with 10 traditional rooms. Giovanni, charming wife Daniela, and their three daughters welcome you to their spectacular view terrace for breakfast and picnic lunches and dinners (Sb-€78, D-€65, Db-€85, less in winter, optional breakfast-€7.50, cash only, Wi-Fi, on the main Il Campo-San Domenico drag at Via della Sapienza 15, tel. & fax 0577-289-047, www.albergobernini.com, hbernin@tin.it).

$ Antica Residenza Cicogna is a seven-room guesthouse with a homey elegance and an ideal location. It's warmly run by the young and charming Elisa, who has biscotti, *vin santo*, and tea out all day for her guests (Db-€90, suite Db-€120, third bed-€15; 10 percent discount if you book direct, show this book, stay two nights, and pay cash; air-con, Wi-Fi, Via dei Termini 67, tel. 0577-285-613, mobile 347-007-2888, www.anticaresidenzacicogna .it, info@anticaresidenzacicogna.it).

Farther from the Center

These places, about a 10-minute walk from the center, are great for drivers (see locations on the map on page 560). The first two are about 200 yards outside the Porta Romana city gate. To get to downtown Siena from here, catch any small shuttle bus uphill. To reach the bus and train stations, take bus #2 (which becomes #17 at Piazza del Sale; when arriving in Siena, catch #17 from the station). If driving, from the freeway, take the Siena Sud exit, continue in direction Romana, then at the first light turn left, following *Pta Romana/Centro* signs for about half a mile until you see the big city gate.

$$$ Hotel Santa Caterina is a three-star, 18th-century place renting 22 comfy rooms. It's professionally run with real attention to quality. While it's on a big city street, it has a delightful garden (Sb-€115, four small Db-€115, Db-€155, Tb or Qb-€195, prices promised with this book through 2012, garden side is quieter, air-con, fridge in room, elevator, Wi-Fi, parking-€15/day—request when you reserve, Via E.S. Piccolomini 7, tel. 0577-221-105, fax 0577-271-087, www.hscsiena.it, info@hscsiena.it, Lorenza and Andrea).

$$ Hotel Porta Romana is at the edge of town, off a busy road. Fifteen rooms face the open countryside, and breakfast is served in the garden (Sb-€90, Db-€110, extra person-€20, 10 percent Rick Steves discount if you book direct, cash preferred, Internet access, free Wi-Fi with this book, free parking, Via E.S. Piccolomini 35, tel. 0577-42299, fax 0577-232-905, www.hotel portaromana.com, info@hotelportaromana.com; Marco, Evelia, and Stefania).

$$ Hotel Minerva is your big, professional, plain, efficient option. While its 56 rooms are boring, with institutional furniture and no character, they don't hide any unpleasant surprises. It's ideal for those with cars—parking is reasonable (€10/day), it's just inside Porta Ovile, and it's only a 10-minute walk from the action (Sb-€74, Db-€118, Tb-€160, bigger suites available for more, air-con, Internet access, Via Garibaldi 72, tel. 0577-284-474, fax 0577-43343, www.albergominerva.it, info@albergominerva.it).

$ Guidoriccio Youth Hostel, which has 90 cheap beds and an institutional ambience, welcomes anyone who's down with its student/backpacker vibe (€20/bed in doubles, triples, and dorms with sheets; co-ed rooms, includes breakfast, Internet access, self-service laundry-€6, lock-out 10:00-14:00; take bus #10 or #77 from train station or bus #10 or #15 from Piazza Gramsci—about 20 minutes to Via Fiorentina 89 in Stellino neighborhood; tel. 0577-52212, fax 0577-50277, www.ostellosiena.it, info@ostellosiena.it).

Outside of Siena

The following accommodations are set in the lush, peaceful countryside surrounding Siena, and are best for those traveling by car (see locations on the map on page 560).

$$$ Frances' Lodge Relais is a tranquil and delightfully managed farmhouse B&B a mile out of Siena. Each of its seven rooms is bursting with character (all well-described on their website). Franca and Franco run this rustic-yet-elegant old place, which features a 19th-century orangery that's been made into a "better homes and palaces" living room, as well as a peaceful garden, eight acres of olive trees and vineyards, and great views of Siena and its countryside—even from the swimming pool (small Db-€170, Db-€190, Db suite-€200, Tb-€210-220, Tb suite-€250, Qb suite-€300, these prices promised to Rick Steves readers through 2012, air-con-€10, Internet access and Wi-Fi, free parking, Strada di Valdipugna 2, tel. & fax 0577-42379, mobile 337-671-608, www.franceslodge.it). To the center, it's a five-minute bus ride plus a five-minute walk, or €10 by taxi. Consider having an al fresco dinner in the gazebo, complete with view (make your own picnic, or have them assemble one for €20).

$$$ Borgo Argenina has seven rooms in a well-maintained, pricey splurge of a B&B. Run by helpful Elena Nappa, it's 20 minutes north of Siena by car in the Chianti region (Db-€170, beautiful gardens, tel. 0577-747-117, www.borgoargenina.it, info@borgoargenina.it).

$$ Il Canto del Sole is a restored 18th-century farmhouse turned family-friendly B&B located about six miles outside of the Porta Romana city gate. Run by Laura, Luciano, and their son Marco, it features 10 bright and airy rooms and two apartments with original antique furnishings, a saltwater swimming pool, a game room, and bike rentals (Db-€100, Tb-€130, extra bed-€20, apartment-€180-220, air-con in swimming-pool-facing rooms and apartment only, Wi-Fi, dinner cooked on request, Val di Villa Canina 1292, 53014 Loc. Cuna, tel. 0577-375-127, fax 0577-373-378, www.ilcantodelsole.com, info@ilcantodelsole.com).

Eating in Siena

Sienese restaurants are reasonable by Florentine and Venetian standards. You can enjoy ordering high on the menu here without going broke. For me, the best €5 you can spend in Siena is on a cocktail at **Bar Il Palio**, overlooking Il Campo.

For a special dessert or a sweet treat any time of day, stop by **Nannini**—considered the top-end pastry shop and *the* place to go for quality local specialties (Banchi di Sopra 24). Across the street is the wonderful **Gelateria Grom** (see "Nightlife in Siena" sidebar, later)—but you have my permission to sample every gelateria in town to pick your own favorite.

Fine Dining in the Old Town

Antica Osteria Da Divo is *the* place for a dressy and atmospheric €45 meal. The kitchen is creative, the ambience is candlelit, and the food is fresh, delicate, and top-notch. While the cuisine is flamboyant and almost over-the-top, Chef Pino and his wife Susanna serve up my favorite splurge dinner in town. Pino is a fanatic for fresh ingredients, enjoys giving traditional dishes his creative spin, and is understandably proud of his desserts. The wine is good, too—you can order it by the glass (€4-7) if you ask (€10 pastas, €20 *secondi*, €3 cover, Wed-Mon 12:00-14:30 & 19:00-22:30, closed Tue, reservations smart; facing Baptistery door, take the far right street and walk one long curving block to Via Franciosa 29; tel. 0577-284-381). Those dining here with this book can finish with a complimentary biscotti and *vin santo* or coffee (upon request).

Compagnia dei Vinattieri serves modern Tuscan dishes with a creative twist. In this elegantly unpretentious space, you can enjoy a quiet and romantic meal under graceful brick arches. The menu is small and accessible, and the young staff will help you match your meal with the right wine. Marco, the owner, is happy to take you down to their marvelous wine cellar (€10 pastas, €16 *secondi*, leave this book on the table for a complimentary *aperitivo* or dessert drink, daily 12:30-15:00 & 19:30-23:00, near Via dei Pittori at Via delle Terme 79, tel. 0577-236-568).

Hostaria Il Carroccio seats guests in an artsy, sea-foam-green dining room and serves elegantly presented, traditional "slow food" recipes with innovative flair at affordable prices (€7 pastas, €15 *secondi*, €30 tasting *menu*—minimum two people, cash only, reservations wise, Thu-Tue 12:30-15:00 & 19:30-22:00, closed Wed, Via del Casato di Sotto 32, tel. 0577-41-165, sweet Renata and Mauro).

Traditional and Rustic Places in the Old Town

Trattoria La Torre is a thriving *casalinga* (home-cooking) eatery, popular for its homemade pasta, plates of which entice customers as they enter. The sound of its busy open kitchen adds to the conviviality. Ten tables are packed under one medieval brick arch. Study the menu in the window before entering; otherwise, the owner likes to just recite his long list of dishes (€7 pastas, €9 *secondi*, €2 cover, Fri-Wed 12:00-15:00 & 19:00-22:00, closed Thu, just steps below Il Campo at Via Salicotto 7, tel. 0577-287-548, Alberto Boccini).

Taverna San Giuseppe, a local favorite, offers modern Tuscan cuisine in a chic grotto atmosphere. Check the posters tacked around the entry for daily specials. Reserve or arrive early to get a table (€8 pastas, €18 *secondi*, Mon-Sat 12:00-14:30 & 19:00-22:00, closed Sun, reservations wise, air-con, 7-minute climb up street to the right of City Hall at Via Giovanni Dupre 132, tel. 0577-42-286, Matteo).

Osteria del Gatto is a classic little hole-in-the-wall, thriving with townspeople and powered by a passion for serving good Sienese cuisine. Marco Coradeschi and his engaged staff cook and serve daily specials with attitude. As it's so small and popular, it can get loud (€7 pastas, €8 *secondi*, 5-minute walk away from the center at Via di San Marco 8, tel. 0577-287-133).

Trattoria Papei is a Sienese favorite, featuring a rollicking family atmosphere and friendly servers dishing out generous portions of rib-stickin' Tuscan specialties and grilled meats. This big, sprawling place under tents in a parking lot is often jammed—so call to reserve (€7 pastas, €10 *secondi*, daily 12:00-15:00 & 19:00-22:30, closed Mon off-season, Piazza del Mercato 6, tel. 0577-280-894; for 50 years Signora Giuliana has ruled her kitchen, Amadeo speaks English).

Ristorante Guidoriccio, just a few steps below Il Campo, feels warm and welcoming. You'll get smiling service from Ercole and Elisabetta. While mostly filled with tourists, the place has a charm—especially if you follow gentle Ercole's suggestions as you explore the menu together (€8 pastas, €13 *secondi*, Mon-Sat 12:30-14:30 & 19:00-22:30, closed Sun, air-con, Via Giovanni Dupre 2, tel. 0577-44-350).

Osteria Trombicche takes you back to another age—cheap and small, with tight indoor seating and two tiny outdoor tables from which to watch the street scene. Bobby and Davide serve fast, hearty food to a local crowd (€5 *ribollita*—bean-and-vegetable soup—in spring and summer, €6 mixed-vegetable antipasto plates, hand-cut prosciutto, Mon-Sat 11:00-15:00 & 17:30-22:00, closed Sun, Via delle Terme 66, tel. 0577-288-089).

La Taverna Di Cecco is a simple, comfortable little eatery where earnest Luca serves tasty salads and Sienese specialties made from fresh ingredients for a fair price (€10 pastas, €14 *secondi,* daily 12:00-16:00 & 19:00-24:00, Via Cecco Angiolieri 19, tel. 0577-288-518).

Places on Il Campo

If you choose to eat on perhaps the finest town square in Italy, you'll pay a premium, meet waiters who don't need to hustle, and get mediocre food. And yet I recommend it. The clamshell-shaped square is lined with venerable cafés, bars, restaurants, and pizzerias.

To experience Il Campo without paying for a full meal, consider having drinks or breakfast on the square. Some bars serve food. And if your hotel doesn't include breakfast or if you'd like something more memorable, Il Campo has plenty of options. A cappuccino and a *cornetto* (croissant) run about €5-6.

Dining and Drinks on the Square

Ristorante Alla Speranza has perhaps the best view in all of Italy. If you're looking to eat reasonably on Il Campo, this is your place (€10 pastas and pizzas, €20 *secondi,* no cover charge, daily 9:00-late, tel. 0577-280-190). It's smart to reserve the view table of your choice—either by phone, or simply stop by while you're sightseeing in the square earlier in the day.

Il Bandierino serves *pici* (PEE-chee), a fat Sienese spaghetti (€9 salads, €11 pizzas, €11 pastas; no cover but a 20 percent service fee, daily 11:00-23:00, tel. 0577-282-217).

Bar Il Palio is the best bar on Il Campo for a pre- or post-dinner drink: It has straightforward prices, no cover, decent waiters, and a fantastic perspective out over the square.

Dynamic little **Osteria Liberamente** (on the square, not above it) has a trendy vibe and is popular with young people (fine wine by the glass, cocktails with good tapas, Pino).

Drinks or Snacks from Balconies Overlooking Il Campo

Three places have skinny balconies with benches overlooking the main square for their customers. Sipping a coffee or nibbling a pastry here while marveling at the Il Campo scene is one of my favorite things to do in Europe. And it's very cheap. Survey these three places from Il Campo (from the base of the tower, imagine a 12-hour clock—they are at 10 o'clock, high noon, and 3 o'clock, respectively).

The little **Costarella Gelateria,** on the corner of Via di Città and Costa dei Barbieri, has good ice cream, drinks, and light snacks such as cute little €2.50 sandwiches (daily 8:00-late, Via di

Nightlife in Siena

Evenings are a wonderful time to be out and about in Siena, after the tour groups have left for the day.

Join the evening *passeggiata* (peak strolling time is 19:00) along Via Banchi di Sopra with gelato in hand. I like **Gelateria Grom,** which serves "Gelato like it used to be." Its seasonal flavors and all-natural ingredients make it a popular stop for any Sienese in need of something cool and sweet to lick while strolling (a little pricier than the competition, Banchi di Sopra 13).

A fun trend in Siena is the *aperitivo*. All over town, you'll find bars attracting an early evening crowd by serving a free buffet of food with the purchase of a drink. For many, this can be a light dinner for the cost of a drink. Or consider starting or ending a meal with a drink or dessert on Il Campo. For suggestions, see "Places on Il Campo."

Enoteca Italiana is a good wine bar in a cellar in the Fortezza, funded in part by the government to promote Italian wine production. They have 30 different bottles open on any given day, and offer tastings at three different prices: €3, €4, and €6.50. To get there, enter the Fortezza via the bridge, cross the running track, and—after passing a tree—go left down a ramp (Mon-Sat 12:00-24:00, closed Sun, snacks served when the bar's pricey restaurant is between mealtimes, outside terrace, tel. 0577-228-832).

Città 33). While the restaurant is for regular service, you're welcome to take anything from the bar out to the simple benches and eat there.

Bar Paninoteca San Paolo has a youthful pub ambience and a row of stools lining a skinny balcony overlooking the square. It serves big €7 salads and 50 kinds of sandwiches, hot and cold (€4 each, order and pay at the counter, food served daily 12:00-2:00 in the morning, on Vicolo di San Paolo).

Key Largo Bar has two benches in the corner offering a wonderful secret perch. Buy your drink or snack at the bar (no cover and no extra charge to sit on balcony), climb upstairs, and slide the ancient bar to open the door. Enjoy stretching out, and try to imagine how, during the Palio, three layers of spectators cram into this space—note the iron railing used to plaster the top row of sardines up against the wall. Suddenly you're picturing Palio ponies zipping wildly around the corner (€4 cocktails, daily 7:00-24:00, on the corner of Via Rinaldini).

Eating Cheaply in the Center

Antica Pizzicheria al Palazzo della Chigiana may be the official name, but I bet locals just call it Antonio's. For most of his life, frenzied Antonio has carved salami and cheese for the neighborhood. A hungry line often spills onto the street as people wait for their sandwiches—meat and cheese sold by weight—with a good bottle of Chianti (Italian law dictates that he must sell you a bottle of wine—cheap and good—and lend you the glasses). Antonio and his boys offer a big cheese-and-meat plate (about €18 gets you 30 minutes of eating) and pull out a tiny tabletop in the corner so you can munch or sip while standing and watching the ham-hock-y scene. He's also got a small table outside (daily 8:00-20:00, Via di Città 95, tel. 0577-289-164). Even if you don't get a sandwich, pop in to inhale the commotion or peruse Antonio's gifty traditional edibles.

Ciao Cafeteria, at the bottom of Il Campo, offers good-value, self-service lunches, but no ambience or views (daily 12:00-15:00). The crowded **Spizzico,** a pizza counter in the front half of Ciao, serves huge, inexpensive quarter-pizzas; on sunny days, people take the pizza—trays and all—out on Il Campo for a picnic (daily 11:00-21:00, to left of City Tower as you face it).

Budget eaters look for *pizza al taglio* shops, scattered throughout Siena, which sell pizza by the slice. Of all the grocery shops, the biggest is **Consorzio Agrario Siena.** Ask them to make you up a *panino* (Mon-Sat 8:00-19:30, sometimes open Sun, a block off Piazza Matteotti, toward Il Campo at Via Pianigiani 5).

Siena Connections

Siena has sparse train connections but is a great hub for buses to the hill towns, though frequency drops on Sundays and holidays. For most, Florence is the gateway to Siena. Even if you are a railpass-user, connect these two cities by bus—it's faster than the train, and Siena's bus station is more convenient and central than its train station. (Note: Many travelers mistake signs for one of Siena's bus companies, Tra-In, as signs for trains or the train station. Tra-In buses have nothing to do with the railway.)

By Train

Siena's train station is at the edge of town. For details on getting between the town center and the station, see page 560.

From Siena by Train to: Florence (direct trains hourly, 1.5-2 hours, €6.20; bus is better), **Pisa** (2/hour, 1.75 hours, change at Empoli, €7), **Assisi** (8/day, 4-5 hours, most involve 2 changes, bus is faster), **Rome** (1-2/hour, 3.25-3.75 hours, transfer in Florence or Chiusi, €13-21 depending on type of train), **Orvieto** (12/day, 2-2.5

hours, change in Chiusi). For more information, visit www.tren italia.com.

By Bus

The main bus companies are Sena and Tra-In. On schedules, the fastest buses are marked *rapida*. I'd stick with these. Some buses depart Siena from Piazza Gramsci; others leave from the train station (confirm when you buy your ticket).

By Bus to: Florence (2/hour, 1.25-hour *corse rapide* buses are faster than the train, avoid the 2-hour *diretta* buses unless you have time to enjoy the beautiful scenery en route, €7, by Tra-In bus, tickets available at tobacco shops if bus-ticket office is closed, Florence-bound buses depart from in front of NH Excelsior Hotel on Piazza Gramsci), **San Gimignano** (8/day, 1.25 hours, €5.50, by Tra-In bus, tickets sometimes available at tobacco shops), **Volterra** (4/day Mon-Sat, no buses on Sun, 2 hours, change in Colle Val d'Elsa), **Assisi** (daily at 11:40 and 16:40, 2 hours, €12, by Sena bus, bus departs from the train station; terminates 3 miles below Assisi at Santa Maria degli Angeli, where a city bus finishes the ride), **Rome** (8/day, 3 hours, €21, by Sena bus from Piazza Gramsci, arrives at Rome's Tiburtina station on Metro line B with easy connections to the central Termini train station), **Naples** (1/day overnight bus, 6.5 hours, bus departs at 23:59), **Milan** (3/day, 4 hours, €31, by Sena bus, departs from Siena's train station, arrives at Milan's Cadorna Station with Metro access and direct trains to Malpensa Airport), **Pisa's Galileo Galilei Airport** (2/day, 1.75 hours, €14, by Tra-In bus, via Poggibonsi). To reach the town center of **Pisa,** the train is better (see "By Train," earlier).

Tickets and Information: You can get tickets for Tra-In buses and Sena buses at the train station's bus-ticket kiosk (cash only, Mon-Sat 6:15-20:15, Sun 7:30-12:30 & 14:30-18:30). You can also buy tickets at **Sottopassaggio la Lizza,** located under Piazza Gramsci—look for stairwells to the underground passageway in front of NH Excelsior Hotel (credit cards accepted; Tra-In bus office: Mon-Sat 7:00-19:30, Sun 7:30-19:30, tel. 0577-204-246, www.trainspa.it; Sena bus office: Mon-Sat 7:15-19:45, closed Sun, tel. 0577-208-282, www.sena.it; on Sundays, when the Sena bus ticket office is closed, buy tickets next door at Tra-In office). If necessary, you can buy tickets from the driver, but it costs €3 extra.

Services: Sottopassaggio la Lizza also has luggage storage (see "By Intercity Bus" on page 561 for details), posted bus schedules, TV monitors listing all imminent departures for several bus companies, and WCs (€0.50).

ASSISI

Assisi is famous for its hometown boy, St. Francis, who made very good. While Francis the saint is interesting, Francesco Bernardone the man is even more so, and mementos of his days in Assisi are everywhere—where he was baptized, a shirt he wore, a hill he prayed on, and a church where a vision changed his life.

About the year 1200, this simple friar from Assisi countered the decadence of Church government and society in general with a powerful message of non-materialism and a "slow down and smell God's roses" lifestyle. Like Jesus, Francis taught by example, living without worldly goods and aiming to love all creation. A huge monastic order grew out of his teachings, which were gradually embraced (some would say co-opted) by the Church. Christianity's most popular saint and purest example of simplicity is now glorified in beautiful churches, along with his female counterpart, St. Clare. In 1939, Italy made Francis one of its patron saints.

Francis' message of love, simplicity, and sensitivity to the environment has a broad and timeless appeal. But every pilgrimage site inevitably gets commercialized, and Francis' legacy is now Assisi's basic industry. In summer, this Umbrian town bursts with flash-in-the-pan Francis fans and Franciscan knickknacks. Those able to see past the glow-in-the-dark rosaries and bobblehead friars can actually have a "travel on purpose" experience.

Planning Your Time

Assisi is worth a day and a night. Its old town has a half-day of sightseeing and another half-day of wonder. The essential sight is the Basilica of St. Francis. For a good visit, take my self-guided "Welcome to Assisi" walk, ending at the Basilica of St. Francis.

Schedule time to wander the back streets and linger on the main square, Piazza del Comune.

Most visitors are day-trippers. While the town's a zoo by day, it's a delight at night. Assisi after dark is closer to a place Francis could call home.

Orientation to Assisi

Crowned by a ruined castle, Assisi spills downhill to its famous Basilica of St. Francis. The town is beautifully preserved and rich in history. A 5.5-magnitude earthquake in 1997 did more damage to the tourist industry than to the town's buildings. Fortunately, tourists—whether art-lovers, pilgrims, or both—have returned, drawn by Assisi's special allure.

The city sprawls across a ridge that rises from a flat plain. The Basilica of St. Francis sits at the low end of town; Piazza Matteotti (with bus station and parking lot) is at the high end; and the main square, Piazza del Comune, lies in between. Via San Francesco runs from Piazza del Comune to the basilica. Capping the hill above the town is a ruined castle called the Rocca Maggiore, and rising above that is Mount Subasio. The town is small, and slopes uphill from west to east. Walking uphill from the basilica to Piazza Matteotti takes 30 minutes, while the downhill journey takes about 15 minutes. Some Francis sights lie outside the city walls, in the valley beneath the ridge and in the hills above.

Tourist Information

The TI is in the center of town on Piazza del Comune (Mon-Sat 8:00-14:00 & 15:00-18:00, Sun 10:00-13:00 & 14:00-17:00, tel. 075-813-8680). Ask for one of their fine, free maps.

Arrival in Assisi

By Train and Bus: The train station is about two miles outside of Assisi, but orange city buses connect the station with the old town on the hilltop (2/hour, 15 minutes, €1), stopping at Piazza Giovanni Paolo II (near Basilica of St. Francis), then Largo Properzio (near Basilica of St. Clare), and finally Piazza Matteotti (top of old town). Buses usually leave from the train station at :15 and :45 past the hour (buy tickets at the newsstand inside the train station for €1, or on board the bus for €1.50—exact change only, valid one hour after being stamped, good for any bus within the old town). You can check bags at the newsstand (€3/12 hours, daily 6:30-13:00 & 14:30-19:00), but not in the old town.

Going from the old town to the train station, the orange buses usually run from Piazza Matteotti at :10 and :40 past the hour (stopping outside Porta Nuova at Largo Properzio a couple of

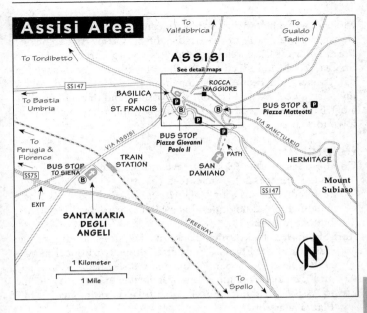

minutes later, and in Piazza Giovanni Paolo II a few minutes after that).

At Piazza Giovanni Paolo II (the big parking lot #A for cars and buses below the Basilica of St. Francis), there are two bus stops *(fermata bus):* one is for Linea C, which goes to the train station (the sign reads *per f.s. S.M. Angeli, Linea C*; the orange bus headed for Piazza Matteotti also stops here—check the front of the bus for its destination); and the other is for Linea B, a pale-yellow minibus that runs through the center of the old town to Piazza del Comune. Hop on a bus marked *Piazza Matteotti* if you're exhausted after your basilica visit and need a sweat-free five-minute return to the top of the old town (near many of my recommended hotels).

Taxis from the train station to the old town cost about €15. There are extra charges for luggage, night service, additional people (four is customary)...and sometimes just because you're a tourist. When departing the old town, you'll find taxi stands at Piazza Giovanni Paolo II, the Basilica of St. Francis, the Basilica of St. Clare, and Piazza del Comune (or have your hotel call for you, tel. 075-813-100). Expect to pay a minimum of €10 for any ride.

By Car: Drivers coming in for the day can follow the signs to several handy parking lots *(parcheggi).* Piazza Matteotti's wonderful underground parking garage (#C) is at the top of the town and comes with bits of ancient Rome in the walls (daily 7:00-21:00, until 23:00 in summer). Another big lot, Parcheggio Giovanni Paolo II (#A), is 200 yards below the Basilica of St. Francis. Parcheggio

Mojano, while below the town wall, comes with an escalator that transports you nearly to the Basilica of St. Clare. At Parcheggio Porta Nuova (#B), an elevator delivers you to Porta Nuova near St. Clare's. The lots all cost about the same (€1/hour, €15/day). For day-trippers, the best plan is to park at Piazza Matteotti, follow my self-guided town walk, tour the basilica, and then either catch a bus back to Piazza Matteotti or simply wander back up through town to your car.

Helpful Hints

Combo-Ticket: One €8 ticket covers three minor sights: Rocca Maggiore (castle), Pinacoteca (paintings), and the newly restored Roman Forum (*biglietto cumulativo*, valid for 1 day, may include audioguide). It's available at these three sights, but not from the TI.

Best Shopping: Tacky knickknacks line the streets leading to the Basilica of St. Francis. For better shops (with local handicrafts), head to Via San Rufino and Corso Mazzini (both just off Piazza del Comune, shops described later in the "Welcome to Assisi" self-guided walk). A Saturday-morning market fills Piazza Matteotti.

Festivals: Assisi annually hosts several interesting festivals commemorating St. Francis and life in the Middle Ages. **Festa di Calendimaggio** is a springtime medieval festival featuring costume parades, concerts, and competitions among Assisi's rival neighborhoods (www.calendimaggiodiassisi.it). Rustic medieval "taverns" pop up around the center offering *porchetta* (roasted pig) and *vino* (starts the first Thu-Sat in May; if one of these days is already a public holiday, it's held the following week). The **Settimana Francescana** commemorates the beginning of the end of Francis' life, when he made his way for the last time to the Porziuncola Chapel (Sept 28). This week-long celebration culminates in the **Festa di San Francesco,** which marks his death with religious processions, special services, and an arts, crafts, and folklore fair (Oct 3-4). The TI has a monthly *Assisi Informa* booklet with details on upcoming festivals and celebrations; see also the event listings at www.assisi.regioneumbria.eu.

Internet Access: Facing the Cathedral of San Rufino, the recommended **Caffè Duomo** offers Internet access (€3/hour, daily 7:30-23:00, snacks, Piazza San Rufino 5, tel. 075-813-023).

Laundry: Belleblu' Lavanderia has a few self-service machines (€5/wash, €4/dry, Mon-Fri 9:00-18:00, Sat 9:00-13:00, closed Sun, Via Borgo Aretino 6a, tel. 075-816-084).

Travel Agencies: You can purchase train and most bus tickets (except for Siena) at **Agenzia Viaggi Stoppini,** between

St. Francis of Assisi
(1181-1226)

In 1202, young Francesco Bernardone donned armor and rode out to battle the Perugians (residents of Umbria's capi-

tal city). The battle went badly, and Francis was captured and imprisoned for a year. He returned a changed man. He avoided friends and his father's lucrative business, and spent more and more time outside the city walls fasting, praying, and searching for something.

In 1206, a vision changed his life, culminating in a dramatic confrontation. He stripped naked before the town leaders, threw his clothes at his father—turning his back on the comfortable material life—and declared his loyalty to God alone.

Idealistic young men flocked to Francis, and they wandered Italy like troubadours, spreading the joy of the Gospel to rich and poor. Francis became a cult figure, attracting huge crowds. They'd never seen anything like it—sermons preached outdoors, in the local language (not Church Latin), making God accessible to all. Francis' new order of monks was also extremely unmaterialistic, extolling poverty and simplicity. Despite their radicalism, the order eventually gained the pope's approval and spread through the world. Francis, who died in Assisi at the age of 45, left a legacy of humanism, equality, and love of nature that would eventually flower in the Renaissance.

In Francis' Sandal-Steps

1. Baptized in Assisi's **Cathedral of San Rufino** (then called St. George's).
2. Raised in the family home just off Piazza del Comune (now the **Chiesa Nuova**).
3. Heard call to "rebuild church" in **San Damiano.** (The crucifix of the church is now in the **Basilica of St. Clare.**)
4. Settled and established his order of monks at the **Porziuncola Chapel** (inside today's St. Mary of the Angels Basilica).
5. Met Clare. (Her tomb and possessions are at the **Basilica of St. Clare.**)
6. Received the pope's blessing for his order (1223 document in the relic chapel at the **Basilica of St. Francis**).
7. Had many visions and was associated with miracles during his life (depicted in **Giotto's frescoes** in the Basilica of St. Francis' upper level).
8. Died at the **Porziuncola,** his body later interred beneath the **Basilica of St. Francis.**

Piazza del Comune and the Basilica of St. Clare (Mon-Fri 9:00-12:30 & 15:30-18:30, Sat 9:00-12:30, closed Sun, Corso Mazzini 31, tel. 075-812-597). Fabrizio, who runs the agency, is patient with tourists' needs and charges exactly what you'd pay at the train station for tickets.

Bus tickets for Siena and many other destinations are sold at **Agenzia Viaggi Mavitur** (Mon-Fri 8:30-13:00 & 15:00-18:30, Sat 9:00-13:00, closed Sun, Via Frate Elia 1b, just below the Basilica of St. Francis, tel. 075-812-377). This agency sells tickets for buses, boats, and planes, but not trains.

Some tickets can be bought on the bus, though it'll cost you an extra couple of euros (see "Assisi Connections," at the end of this chapter).

Local Guide: Giuseppe Karabotis is a good, licensed guide (€110/2 hours, mobile 328-867-0567, iokarabot@libero.it); if he's busy, he can recommend other guides.

Local Guide with Car: Daniela Moretti is a hardworking young guide from Perugia who knows Assisi well. Besides touring in Assisi, she'll take you anywhere in Umbria with her car, which comfortably fits three travelers and jams in four (on foot: €120/half-day, €200/full day; with car: €150/half-day, €250/full day; mobile 335-829-9984, www.danyguide.com, danyguide@hotmail.com).

Getting Around Assisi

Cute, pale-yellow electrical minibuses, labeled *Linea A* and *Linea B,* connect the top of the town with the bottom. While it's only a 15-minute stroll down the hill, the climb back up can have you looking for a lift. Before boarding, confirm the destination (catch the bus below the Basilica of St. Francis at the Porta San Francisco, Piazza del Comune, or Piazza Matteotti). You can buy a bus ticket (good on any city bus) at a newsstand or kiosk for €1, or get a ticket from the driver for €1.50 (exact change only). After you've stamped your ticket on board the bus, it's valid for an hour.

Self-Guided Walk

▲▲Welcome to Assisi

There's much more to Assisi than just St. Francis and what the blitz tour groups see. This walk covers the town from top (Piazza Matteotti) to bottom (Basilica of St. Francis). To get to Piazza Matteotti, ride the bus from the train station (or from Piazza Giovanni Paolo II) to the last stop; drive (underground parking); or hike five minutes uphill from Piazza del Comune.

• *Start 50 yards beyond Piazza Matteotti (away from city center—see map).*

❶ The Roman Amphitheater (Anfiteatro Romano)

A lane named Via Anfiteatro Romano skirts the cozy neighborhood built around a Roman amphitheater—a reminder that Assisi was once an important Roman town. Circle the amphitheater counterclockwise. Imagine how colorful the town laundry basin (on the right) must have been in previous generations, when the women of Assisi gathered here to do their wash. Adjacent to the basin is a small rectangular pool filled with water; above it are the coats of arms of Assisi's leading families. A few steps farther, leave the amphitheater, hiking up the stairs to the right to the top of the hill, for an aerial view of the ancient oval. The Roman stones have long been absorbed into the medieval architecture. It was Roman tradition to locate the amphitheater outside of town, which this used to be. While the amphitheater dates from the first century A.D., the buildings filling it today were built in the 13th and 14th centuries.

• *Continue on, enjoying the grand view of the fortress in the distance. The lane leads down to a city gate and an...*

❷ Umbrian View

Step outside of Assisi at the Porta Perlici for a commanding view. Umbria, called the "green heart of Italy," is the country's geographical center and only landlocked region. Enjoy the various shades of green: silver green on the valley floor (olives), emerald green (grapevines), and deep green on the hillsides (evergreen oak trees). Also notice Rocca Maggiore ("big fortress"), which provided townsfolk a refuge in times of attack, and, behind you atop the nearer hill, Rocca Minore ("little fortress"), which gives the town's young lovers a little privacy. The quarry (under the Rocca Maggiore) was a handy source for Assisi's characteristic pink limestone.

• *Go back through the gate and follow Via Porta Perlici downhill— it's immediately on your right—into town (toward Hotel La Rocca).*

Enjoy the higgledy-piggledy architecture (this neighborhood has some of the most photogenic back lanes in town). You'll pass a wall containing an aqueduct (on the left) that goes back to Roman times. It still brings water from a mountain spring into the city (push the brass tap for a taste). After another 50 yards, turn left through a medieval town gate (with Hotel La Rocca on your right). Just after the hotel, you'll pass a second gate dating from Roman times. Follow Via Porta Perlici downhill until you hit a fine square facing a big church.

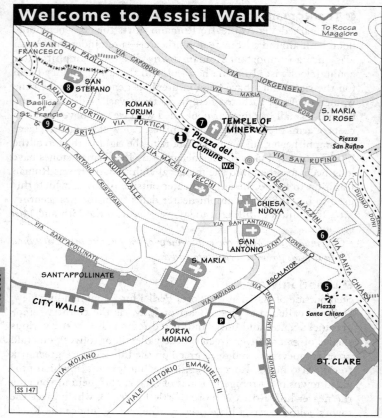

Welcome to Assisi Walk

(Map labels:)

VIA SAN PAOLO · VIA SAN FRANCESCO · VIA CAPOBOVE · VIA JORGENSEN · To Rocca Maggiore

VIA S. MARIA DELLE ROSA · S. MARIA D. ROSE

SAN STEFANO **8**

ROMAN FORUM

To Basilica of St. Francis **9** · VIA ARNALDO FORTINI · VIA BRIZI · VIA PORTICA

7 TEMPLE OF MINERVA

Piazza del Comune · WC

Piazza San Rufino

VIA SAN RUFINO · CORSO G. MAZZINI

VIA QUINTAVALLE · VIA ANTONIO CRISTOFANI · VIA MACELLI VECCHI

CHIESA NUOVA

VIA SANT'ANTONIO

SAN ANTONIO · SANT'AGNESE

VIA SANT'APOLLINATE · S. MARIA

SANT'APPOLLINATE

CITY WALLS

VIA ESCALATOR · VIA MOIANO · **6** · VIA SANTA CHIARA

5 Piazza Santa Chiara

VIA DELLE FONTI DEL MOIANO

PORTA MOIANO

ST. CLARE

VIA MOIANO · VIALE VITTORIO EMANUELE II

SS 147

ASSISI

❸ Cathedral of San Rufino (Cattedrale San Rufino)

Trick question: Who's Assisi's patron saint? While Francis is one of Italy's patron saints, Rufino (the town's first bishop, martyred and buried here in the third century) is Assisi's. The cathedral (seat of the local bishop) is 11th-century Romanesque with a Neoclassical interior. Although it has what is considered to be one of the best and purest Romanesque facades in all of Umbria, the big triangular top of it (just a decorative wall) was added in Gothic times. Study the lions at the base of the facade: One is eating a Christian martyr, reminding worshippers of the courage of early Christians.

Enter the church. While the front of the church is an unre-

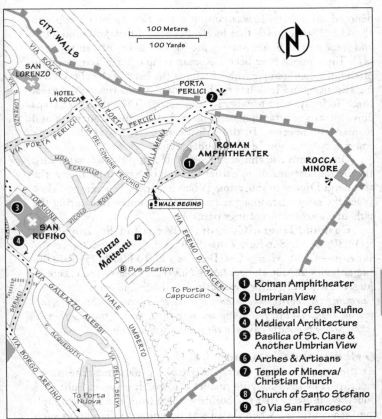

1 Roman Amphitheater
2 Umbrian View
3 Cathedral of San Rufino
4 Medieval Architecture
5 Basilica of St. Clare &
  Another Umbrian View
6 Arches & Artisans
7 Temple of Minerva/
  Christian Church
8 Church of Santo Stefano
9 To Via San Francesco

markable mix of 17th- and 18th-century Baroque and Neoclassical, the rear (near where you enter) has several points of interest. Notice first the two fine statues: St. Francis and St. Clare (by Giovanni Dupré, 1888). To your right is an old baptismal font (in the corner with the black iron grate). In about 1181, a baby boy was baptized in this font. His parents were upwardly mobile Francophiles who called him Francesco ("Frenchy"). In 1194, a nobleman baptized his daughter Clare here. Eighteen years later, their paths crossed in this same church, when Clare attended a class and became mesmerized by the teacher—Francis. Traditionally, the children of Assisi are still baptized here.

The striking glass panels in the floor reveal foundations preserved from the ninth-century church that once stood here. You're walking on history. After the 1997 earthquake, structural inspectors checked the church from ceiling to floor. When they looked under the paving stones, they discovered graves (until Napoleon decreed otherwise, it was common practice to bury people in churches). Underneath that level, they found Roman foundations and some animal bones (suggesting the possibility of animal sacrifice). There might have been a Roman temple here; churches were often built upon temple ruins. Stand at the back of the church facing the altar, and look left to the Roman cistern (inside the great stone archway, next to where you entered). Take the three steps down (to trigger the light) and marvel at the fine stonework and Roman engineering. In the Middle Ages, this was the town's emergency water source when under attack.

Underneath the church, incorporated into the Roman ruins, are the foundations of an earlier Church of San Rufino, now the crypt and **Diocesan museum**. When it's open, you can go below to see the saint's sarcophagus and the small museum featuring the cathedral's art from centuries past.

Cost and Hours: Cathedral—free, Mon-Fri 7:00-12:30 & 14:30-19:00, Sat-Sun 7:00-19:00, tel. 075-812-283; crypt/museum—€3.50, March-Oct Thu-Tue 10:00-13:00 & 15:00-18:00, longer hours in Aug, shorter hours Nov-Feb, closed Wed except in Aug, tel. 075-812-712, www.assisimuseodiocesano.com.

• *Leaving the church, take a sharp left (at the pizza-by-the-slice joint, on Via Dono Doni), following the sign for Santa Chiara. After 20 yards, take a right and go down the stairway to see some...*

❹ Medieval Architecture

At the bottom of the stairs, notice the pink limestone pavement, part of the surviving medieval town. The arches built over doorways indicate that the buildings date from the 12th through the 14th centuries, when Assisi was booming. Italian cities such as Assisi—thriving on the north-south trade between northern Europe and Rome—were in the process of inventing free-market capitalism, dabbling in democratic self-rule, and creating the modern urban lifestyle. The vaults you see that turn lanes into tunnels are reminders of medieval urban expansion (mostly 15th century). While the population grew, people wanted to live within the town's protective walls. Medieval Assisi had several times the population density of modern Assisi.

Notice the blooming balconies; Assisi holds a flower competition each June.

• Continue steeply downhill. When you arrive at a street, turn left, going slightly uphill for a block, then take the low road at the Y, and head down Via Sermei. Continue ahead, following the *S. Chiara* sign downhill to the big church. Cross the street and walk under the three massive buttresses to Piazza Santa Chiara and the front of the church.

St. Clare
(1194-1253)

The 18-year-old rich girl of Assisi fell in love with Francis' message, and made secret arrangements to meet him. The night of Palm Sunday, 1212, she slipped out of her father's mansion in town and escaped to the valley below. A procession of friars with torches met her and took her to (what is today) St. Mary of the Angels Basilica. There, Francis cut her hair, clothed her in a simple brown tunic, and welcomed her into a life of voluntary poverty. Clare's father begged, ordered, and physically threatened her to return, but she would not budge.

Clare was joined by other women who banded together as the Poor Clares. She spent the next 40 years of her life within the confines of the convent of San Damiano: barefoot, vegetarian, and largely silent. Her regimen of prayer, meditation, and simple manual labor—especially knitting—impressed commoners and popes, leading to her canonization almost immediately after her death. St. Clare is often depicted carrying a monstrance (a little temple holding the Eucharist wafer).

❺ Basilica of St. Clare (Basilica di Santa Chiara)

Dedicated to the founder of the Order of the Poor Clares, this Umbrian Gothic church is simple, in keeping with the nuns' dedication to a life of contemplation. In Clare's lifetime, the order was located in the humble Church of San Damiano, in the valley below, but after Clare's death, they needed a bigger and more glorious building. The church was built in 1265, and the huge buttresses were added in the next century.

The interior's fine frescoes were whitewashed in Baroque times. The battered remains of one on the left shows how the fresco surface was hacked up so whitewash would stick. Imagine all the pristine frescoes hiding behind the whitewash (here and all over Europe).

The Chapel of the Crucifix of San Damiano, on the right, has the wooden crucifix that changed Francis' life. In 1206, an emaciated, soul-searching, stark-raving Francis knelt before this crucifix (then located in the Church of San Damiano) and asked for guidance. The crucifix spoke: "Go and rebuild my Church, which you can see has fallen into ruin." Francis followed the call.

Stairs lead from the nave down to the tomb of St. Clare. Her tomb is at the far end (the image is wax; her bones lie underneath). As you circulate with the crowd of pilgrims, notice the paintings on the walls depicting spiritual lessons from Clare's life and death (see sidebar). At the opposite end of the crypt (back between the stairs, in a large glassed-in area) are important relics: the saint's robes, hair (in a silver box), and an enormous tunic she made—along with relics of St. Francis (including a blood-stained stocking he wore after receiving the stigmata). The attached cloistered community of the Poor Clares has flourished for 700 years.

Cost and Hours: Daily 6:30-12:00 & 14:00-19:00, until 18:00 in winter.

• *Leave the church and belly up to the viewpoint at the edge of the square for...*

Another Umbrian View: On the left is the convent of St. Clare (global headquarters of all the Poor Clares). Below you lies the olive grove of the Poor Clares, which has been there since the 13th century. In the distance is a grand Umbrian view. Assisi overlooks the richest and biggest valley in otherwise hilly and mountainous Umbria. The municipality of Assisi has a population of 25,000, but only 3,500 people live in the old town. The lower town grew up with the coming of the railway in the 19th century. In the haze, the blue-domed church is St. Mary of the Angels (Santa Maria degli Angeli, described later), the cradle of the Franciscan order. A popular pilgrimage site today, it marks the place where St. Francis lived and worked.

Spanish-speaking Franciscans settled in California. Three of their missions grew into major cities: Los Angeles (named after this church), San Francisco (named after St. Francis), and Santa Clara (named after St. Clare).

• *From the church square, step out into Via Santa Chiara.*

❻ Arches and Artisans

Notice the three medieval town gates (two behind the church, and one uphill toward the town center). The gate over the road beyond the church dates from 1265. (Farther on, you can just see the crenellations of the 1316 Porta Nuova, which marks the final expansion of Assisi.) Toward the city center (on Via Santa Chiara, the high road), an arch marks the site of the Roman wall. These three gates represent the town's three walls, illustrating how much the city has grown since ancient times.

Walk uphill along Via Santa Chiara (which becomes Corso Mazzini) to the city's main square. The street is lined with interesting shops selling traditional embroidery, religious souvenirs, and gifty local edibles. The shops on Corso Mazzini, on the stretch between the gate and the Piazza del Comune, show off many local crafts. As you browse, watch for the following shops: Galleria d'Arte Perna (on the left, #20) sells the medieval fantasy townscapes of Paolo Grimaldi, a local painter who runs this shop with his brother, Alessandro. A helpful travel agency is across the street (at #31, Agenzia Viaggi Stoppini; see "Helpful Hints," earlier). Next, the shop L'Ulivo Sculture (on the left at #14d) sells olive-wood carvings, as does Piesis, across the street at #23. It's said that St. Francis made the first nativity scene to help humanize and, therefore, teach the Christmas message. That's why you'll see so many crèches in Assisi. (Even today, nearby villages are enthusiastic about their "living" manger scenes, and Italians everywhere enjoy setting up elaborate crèches in churches for Christmas.) Adjacent to #14 is a bakery, Bar Sensi, selling the traditional raisin-and-apple strudel called *rocciata* (roh-CHAH-tah, €3.50 each). Farther along on the left (at #2) is Il Duomo, selling religious art, manger scenes, and crucifixion figurines. Across the street, on the right, is a respected embroidery shop. And on the square (at #34, opposite the flags), La Bottega dei Sapori is worth a visit for edible and drinkable souvenirs.

You've walked up what was, in ancient times, the main drag into town. Ahead of you, the six fluted Corinthian columns of the Temple of Minerva marked the forum (today's Piazza del Comune). Sit at the fountain on the piazza for a few minutes of people-watching—don't you love Italy? Within a few hundred yards of this square, on either side, were the medieval walls. Imagine the commotion of 5,000 people confined within these walls. No wonder St. Francis needed an escape for some peace and quiet.

• *Now, head over to the temple on the square.*

❼ Temple of Minerva/Christian Church

Assisi has always been a spiritual center. The Romans went to great lengths to make this first-century B.C. Temple of Minerva a center-

piece of their city. Notice the columns that cut into the stairway. It was a tight fit here on the hilltop. In ancient times, the stairs went down—about twice as far as they do now—to the main drag, which has gradually been filled in over time. The Church of Santa Maria sopra ("over") Minerva was added in the ninth century. The bell tower is from the 13th century.

Pop inside the temple/church. Today's interior is 17th-century Baroque. Walk to the front. Flanking the altar are the original Roman temple floor stones. You can even see the drains for the bloody sacrifices that took place here. Behind the statues of Peter and Paul, the original Roman embankment peeks through.

Cost and Hours: Free, Mon-Sat 7:15-19:30, Sun 8:00-19:30, in winter closes at sunset and midday.

• *Across the square at #11, step into the 16th-century frescoed vaults of the...*

Old Market: Notice the Italian flair for design. Even this smelly market was once finely decorated. The art style is called "grotesque"—literally from a cave (grotto-esque), named for the fanciful Roman paintings found on the walls of Italian caves. This scene was indisputably painted after 1492. How do art historians know? Because it features turkeys—first seen in Europe after Columbus returned from the Americas with his bag of exotic souvenirs. The turkeys painted here may have been that bird's European debut.

• *From the main square, hike past the temple up the high road, Via San Paolo. After 200 yards (across from #24), a sign directs you down a stepped lane to the...*

❽ Church of Santo Stefano (Chiesa di Santo Stefano)

Surrounded by cypress, fig, and walnut trees, Santo Stefano—which used to be outside the town walls in the days of St. Francis—is a delightful bit of offbeat Assisi. Legend has it that Santo Stefano's bells miraculously rang on October 3, 1226, the day St. Francis died. Step inside. This is the typical rural Italian Romanesque church—no architect, just built by simple stonemasons who put together the most basic design. And hundreds of years later, it still stands.

Cost and Hours: Free, daily 8:30-21:30, Sept-May until 18:30.

• *The lane zigzags down to Via San Francesco. Turn right and walk under the arch toward the Basilica of St. Francis.*

❾ Via San Francesco

This main drag leads from the town to the basilica holding the body of St. Francis. Francis was a big deal even in his own day. He was made a saint in 1228—the same year that the basilica's foundations were laid—and his body was moved here by 1230. Assisi was a big-time pilgrimage center, and this street was its booming hub. The arch marks the end of what was Assisi in St. Francis' day. Notice the fine medieval balcony immediately below the arch. A few yards farther down (on the left), cool yourself at the fountain, as medieval pilgrims might have. The hospice next door was built in 1237 to house pilgrims. Notice the three surviving faces of its fresco: Jesus, Francis, and Clare. Farther down, across from #12a (on the left), is the Oratorio dei Pellegrini, dating from the 1450s. A brotherhood ran a hostel here for travelers passing through to pay homage to St. Francis. The chapel offers a richly frescoed space in which to contemplate the saint's message.

• *Continuing on, you'll eventually reach Assisi's main sight, the Basilica of St. Francis.*

Self-Guided Tour

▲▲▲Basilica of St. Francis (Basilica di San Francesco)

The basilica is one of the artistic and religious highlights of Europe. It rises where, in 1226, St. Francis was buried (with the outcasts he

had stood by) outside of his town on the "Hill of the Damned"—now called the "Hill of Paradise." The basilica is frescoed from top to bottom with scenes by the leading artists of the day: Cimabue, Giotto, Simone Martini, and Pietro Lorenzetti. A 13th-century historian wrote, "No more exquisite monument to the Lord has been built."

From a distance, you see the huge arcades "supporting" the basilica. These were 15th-century quarters for the monks. The arcades that line the square and lead to the church housed medieval pilgrims.

Cost and Hours: Free entry; lower basilica daily 6:00-18:45, until 17:45 in winter; relic chapel in lower basilica open 9:00-18:00 but occasionally closed for religious services; upper basilica daily 8:30-18:45, until 18:00 in winter. Modest dress is required to enter the church—no sleeveless tops or shorts for men, women, or children.

Information: The church courtyard at the entrance of the lower basilica has an info office (Mon-Sat 9:15-12:00 & 14:15-17:30, closed Sun, tel. 075-819-001, www.sanfrancescoassisi.org). To find out about upcoming concerts at the basilica, try tel. 075-819-0084.

Tours: Audioguides (boring and old-school) are available at the kiosk located outside the entrance of the upper basilica (€5 donation requested, daily 9:00-17:00, 40 minutes). You can also take an English tour, offered daily except Sunday (€10 donation requested, call or email to reserve, tel. 075-819-0084, www.sanfrancescoassisi.org, assisisanfrancesco@libero.it).

Services: The church bookshop is behind the upper and lower basilica. It sells the excellent guidebook *The Basilica of Saint Francis: A Spiritual Pilgrimage* (€3, by Goulet, McInally, and Wood; I used this book, and a tour with Brother Michael, as sources for this self-guided tour). There are two different pay WCs within a half-block of the lower entrance—up the road in a squat building, and halfway down the big piazza on the left.

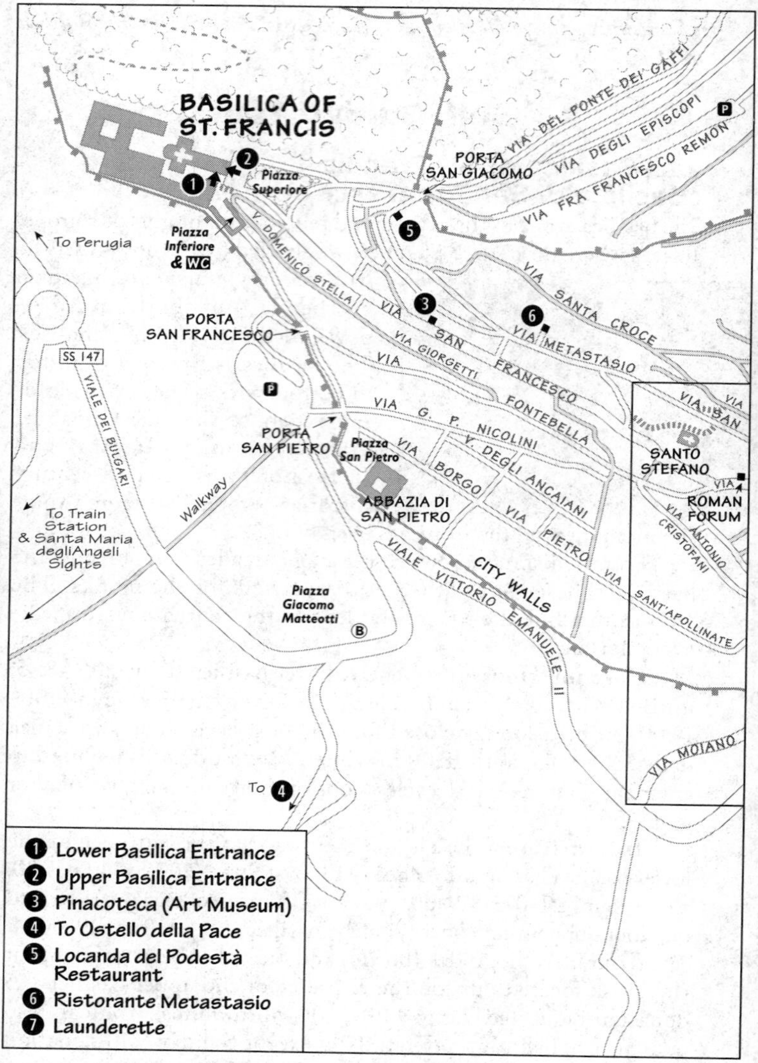

BASILICA OF ST. FRANCIS

1 Lower Basilica Entrance
2 Upper Basilica Entrance
3 Pinacoteca (Art Museum)
4 To Ostello della Pace
5 Locanda del Podestà Restaurant
6 Ristorante Metastasio
7 Launderette

Attending Mass: To worship in the basilica, consider joining the Franciscan brothers in the lower basilica in the morning at 7:15 or 11:00, or experience a Mass sung by the basilica choir many Sundays at 10:30. English and additional sung Mass services don't follow a set schedule. Call the basilica to find out when English-speaking pilgrimage groups or choirs have reserved Masses, and attend with them (tel. 075-819-0084).

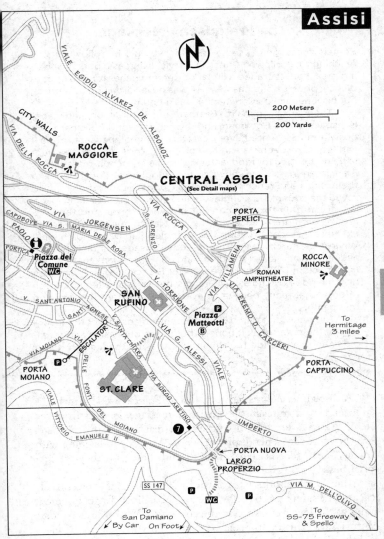

Overview

The Basilica of St. Francis, a theological work of genius, can be difficult for the 21st-century tourist/pilgrim to appreciate.

Since the basilica is the reason that most people visit Assisi, and the message of St. Francis has even the least devout sightseers blessing the town Vespas, I've designed this self-guided tour with an emphasis on the place's theology (rather than art history).

The Franciscan Message

Francis' message caused a stir. Not only did he follow Christ's teachings, he followed Christ's lifestyle, living as a poor, wandering preacher. He traded a life of power and riches for one of obedience, poverty, and chastity. He was never ordained as a priest, but his influence on Christianity was monumental.

The Franciscan realm (Brother Sun, Sister Moon, and so on) is a space where God, man, and the natural world frolic harmoniously. Francis treated every creature—animal, peasant, pope—with equal respect. He and his "brothers" (*fratelli*, or friars) slept in fields, begged for food, and exuded the joy of non-materialism. Franciscan friars were known as the "Jugglers of God," modeling themselves on French troubadours (*jongleurs*, or jugglers) who roved the countryside singing, telling stories, and cracking jokes.

In an Italy torn by conflict between towns and families, Francis promoted peace and the restoration of order. (He set an example by reconstructing the crumbled San Damiano chapel.) While the Church was waging bloody Crusades, Francis pushed ecumenism and understanding. And the Franciscan message had an impact. In 1288, just 62 years after Francis died, a Franciscan became pope (Nicholas IV). Francis' message also led to Church reforms that many believe delayed the Protestant Reformation by a century.

This richly decorated basilica seems to contradict the teachings of the poor monk it honors, but it was built as an act of religious and civic pride to remember the hometown saint. It was

ASSISI

A disclaimer before we start: Just as Francis used many biblical legends to help teach the Christian message, legends from the life of Francis were told in later ages to teach the same message. Are they true? In general, probably not. Are they in keeping with Francis' message? Yes. Do I share legends here as if they are historic? Sure.

The church has three parts: the upper basilica, the lower basilica, and the saint's tomb (below the lower basilica). To get oriented, stand at the lower entrance in the courtyard. While empty today, centuries ago this main plaza was cluttered with pilgrim services and the medieval equivalent of souvenir shops. Opposite the entry to the lower basilica is the information center.

Enter through the grand doorway of the lower basilica. Just inside, decorating the top of the first arch, look up and see St. Francis, who greets you with a Latin inscription. Sounding a bit like John Wayne, he says the equivalent of, "Slow down and be joyful, pilgrim. You've reached the Hill of Paradise. And, if you're observant and thoughtful, this church will knock your spiritual socks off."

also designed—and still functions—as a pilgrimage center and a splendid classroom. Though monks in robes may not give off an "easy-to-approach" vibe, the Franciscans of today are still God's jugglers (and many of them speak English).

Here is Francis' message, in his own words:

The Canticle of the Sun
Good Lord, all your creations bring praise to you!
Praise for Brother Sun, who brings the day. His radiance
reminds us of you!
Praise for Sister Moon and the stars, precious and beautiful.
Praise for Brother Wind, and for clouds and storms
and rain that sustain us.
Praise for Sister Water. She is useful and humble,
precious and pure.
Praise for Brother Fire who cheers us at night.
Praise for our sister, Mother Earth, who feeds us
and rules us.
Praise for all those who forgive because you have
forgiven them.
Praise for our sister, Bodily Death, from whose embrace
none can escape.
Praise and bless the Lord, and give thanks, and, with
humility, serve him.

• *Start with the tomb. To get there, turn left into the nave. Midway down, follow the signs and go right, to the tomb downstairs.*

The Tomb

The saint's remains are above the altar in the stone box with the iron ties. In medieval times, pilgrims came to Assisi because St. Francis was buried here. Holy relics were the "ruby slippers" of medieval Europe. Relics gave you power—they answered your prayers and won your wars—and ultimately helped you get back to your eternal Kansas. Assisi made no bones about promoting the saint's relics, but hid his tomb for obvious reasons of security. His body was buried secretly while the basilica was under construction, and over the next 600 years, the exact location was forgotten. When the tomb was to be opened to the public in 1818, it took more than a month to find his actual remains.

Francis' four closest friends and first followers are memorialized in the corners of the room. Opposite the altar, up four steps between the entrance and exit, notice the small copper box behind the metal grill. This contains the remains of Francis' rich Roman patron, Jacopa dei Settesoli. She traveled to see him on his death-bed, but was turned away because she was female. Francis waived the rule and welcomed "Brother Jacopa" to his side. These five tombs—in the Franciscan spirit of being with your friends—were added in the 19th century.

The candles you see are the only real candles in the church (others are electric). Pilgrims pay a coin, pick up a candle, and place it at the tomb. Franciscans will light it later.

• *Climb back up to the lower nave.*

Lower Basilica

Appropriately Franciscan—subdued and Romanesque—this nave is frescoed with parallel scenes from the lives of Christ (right) and Francis (left), connected by a ceiling of stars. The Passion of Christ and the Compassion of Francis lead to the altar built over Francis' tomb. After the church was built and decorated, side chapels were erected to provide mausoleums for the rich families that patron-ized the work of the order. Unfortunately, in the process, huge arches were cut out of some frescoed scenes, but others survive. In the fresco directly above the entry to the tomb, Christ is being taken down from the cross (just the bottom half of his body can be seen, to the left), and it looks like the story is over. Defeat. But in the opposite fresco (above the tomb's exit), we see Francis preach-ing to the birds, reminding the faithful that the message of the Gospel survives.

These stories directed the attention of the medieval pilgrim to the altar, where he could meet God through the sacraments. The church was thought of as a community of believers sailing toward God. The prayers coming out of the nave (*navis,* or ship) fill the triangular sections of the ceiling—called *vele,* or sails—with spiri-tual wind. With a priest for a navigator and the altar for a helm, faith propels the ship.

Stand behind the altar (toes to the bottom step, facing the entrance) and look up. The three scenes above you represent the creed of the Franciscans: Directly above the tomb of St. Francis, to the right, **Obedience** (Francis appears twice, wearing a rope har-ness and kneeling in front of Lady Obedience); to the left, ***Chastity*** (in her tower of purity held up by two angels); and straight ahead, ***Poverty.*** Here Jesus blesses the marriage as Francis slips a ring on Lady Poverty. In the foreground, two "self-sufficient" yet pint-size merchants (the new rich of a thriving northern Italy) are throwing sticks and stones at the bride. But Poverty, in her patched wedding dress, is fertile and strong, and even bare brambles blossom into a rosebush crown.

The three knots in the rope that ties the Franciscan robe sym-bolize the monks' vows of obedience, chastity, and poverty. St.

ASSISI

Basilica of St. Francis—Lower Level

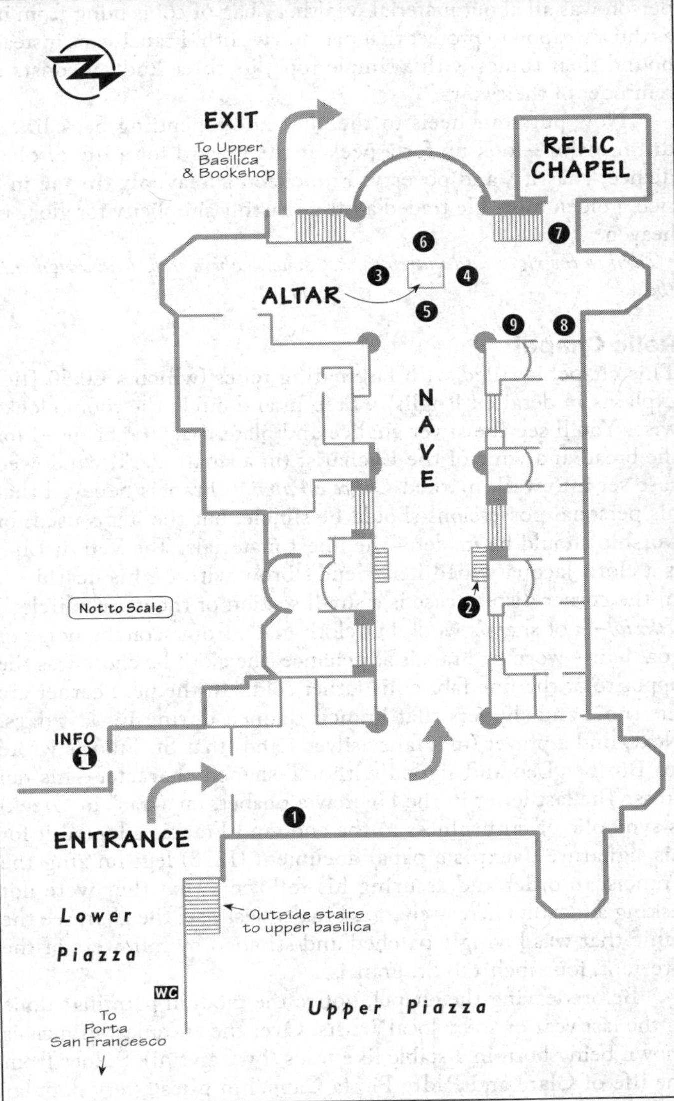

EXIT
To Upper
Basilica
& Bookshop

RELIC CHAPEL

ALTAR

NAVE

Not to Scale

INFO ⓘ

ENTRANCE

Lower Piazza

Outside stairs
to upper basilica

WC

To
Porta
San Francesco
↓

Upper Piazza

ASSISI

1 St. Francis
2 Stairs to Tomb Entrance
3 Obedience (on Ceiling)
4 Chastity (on Ceiling)
5 Poverty (on Ceiling)
6 Francis on a Heavenly Throne
7 Relic Chapel Entrance
8 GIOTTO–Crucifixion
9 CIMABUE–St. Francis

Francis called money the "devil's dung." The jeweled belt of a rich person was all about material wealth. A bag of coins hung from it, as did a weapon to protect that person's wealth. Franciscans instead bound their tunics with a simple rope, its three knots a constant reminder of their vows.

Now put your heels to the altar and—bending back like a drum major—look up for a peek at the reward for a life of obedience, chastity, and poverty: **Francis on a heavenly throne** in a rich, golden robe. He traded a life of earthly simplicity for glory in heaven.

• *Turn to the right and march to the corner, where steps lead down into the...*

Relic Chapel

This chapel is filled with fascinating relics (which a €0.50 flier explains in detailed English). Step in and circle the room clockwise. You'll see the silver chalice and plate that Francis used for the bread and wine of the Eucharist (in a small, dark, windowed case set into wall, marked *Calice e Patena*). Francis believed that his personal possessions should be simple, but the items used for worship should be made of the finest materials. The Veli di Lino is a cloth Jacopa wiped her friend's brow with on his deathbed. In the corner display case is a small section of the itchy haircloth *(cilizio)*—not sheep's wool, but cloth made from scratchy horse or goat hair—worn by Francis as penance (the cloth he chose was the opposite of the fine fabric his father sold.) In the next corner are the tunic and slippers that Francis donned during his last days. Next, find a prayer (in a fancy silver stand) that St. Francis wrote for Brother Leo and signed with a T-shaped character—his tau cross. The last letter in the Hebrew alphabet, tav ("tau" in Greek) is symbolic of faithfulness to the end, and Francis adopted it for his signature. Next is a papal document (1223) legitimizing the Franciscan order and assuring his followers that they were not risking a (deadly) heresy charge. Finally, just past the altar, see the tunic that was lovingly patched and stitched by followers of the five-foot, four-inch-tall St. Francis.

Before leaving the chapel, notice the modern paintings done in the last year or so by local artists. Over the entrance, Francis is shown being born in a stable like Jesus (by Capitini). Scenes from the life of Clare and Padre Pio (a Capuchin priest, very popular in Italy, who was sainted in 2002) were painted by Stefanelli and Antonio.

• *Return up the stairs, stepping into the...*

Transept of Lower Basilica

The decoration of this church brought together the greatest Sienese

(Lorenzetti and Simone Martini) and Florentine (Cimabue and Giotto) artists of the day. Look around at the painted scenes. In 1300, this was radical art—believable homespun scenes, landscapes, trees, real people. Study **Giotto's painting of the Crucifixion,** with the eight sparrow-like angels. For the first time, holy people are expressing emotion: One angel turns her head sadly at the sight of Jesus, and another scratches her hands down her cheeks, drawing blood. Mary (lower left), previously in control, has fainted in despair. The Franciscans, with their goal of bringing God to the people, found a natural partner in Europe's first modern (and therefore naturalist) painter, Giotto.

To grasp Giotto's artistic leap, compare his work with the painting to the right, by Cimabue. It's Gothic, without the 3-D architecture, natural backdrop, and slice-of-life reality of Giotto's work. **Cimabue's St. Francis** (far right) shows the saint with the stigmata—Christ's marks of the Crucifixion. Contemporaries described Francis as being short, with a graceful build, dark hair, and sparse beard. (This is considered the most accurate portrait of Francis—done according to the description of one who knew him.) The sunroof haircut (tonsure) was standard for monks of the day. According to legend, the brown robe and rope belt were inventions of necessity. When Francis stripped naked and ran away from Assisi, he grabbed the first clothes he could, a rough wool peasant's tunic and a piece of rope, which became the uniform of the Franciscan order. To the left, at eye level under the sparrow-like angels, are paintings of saints and their exquisite halos (by Simone Martini or his school). To the right of the door at the same level, see five of Francis' closest followers—clearly just simple folk.

Francis' friend, "Sister Bodily Death," was really not all that terrible. In fact, Francis would like to introduce you to her now (above and to the right of the door leading into the relic chapel). Go ahead, block the light from the door with this book and meet her. Before his death, Francis added a line to *The Canticle of the Sun*: "Praise for our sister, Bodily Death, from whose embrace none can escape."

• *Now cross the transept to the other side of the altar (enjoying some of the oldest surviving bits of the inlaid local-limestone flooring—c. 13th century), and find the staircase going up. Immediately above the stairs is Pietro Lorenzetti's* Francis Receiving the Stigmata. *(Francis is considered the first person ever to earn the marks of the cross through his great faith and love of the Church.) Make your way to the...*

Courtyard

The courtyard overlooks the 15th-century cloister, the heart of this monastic complex. Pope Sixtus IV (of Sistine Chapel fame) had it built as a secure retreat for himself. Balanced and peaceful by design, the courtyard also functioned as a cistern to collect rainwater, supplying enough for 200 monks (today, there are about 40). The Franciscan order emphasizes teaching. This place functioned as a kind of theological center of higher learning, which rotated monks in for a six-month stint, then sent them back home more prepared and better inspired to preach effectively. That explains the complex narrative of the frescoes wallpapering the walls and halls here. The treasury *(Museo del Tesoro)* to the left of the bookstore is free (donation requested) and features ornately decorated chalices, reliquaries, vestments, and altarpieces.

• *From the courtyard, climb the stairs (next to the bookshop) to the...*

Upper Basilica

Built later than its counterpart below, the brighter upper basilica is considered the first Gothic church in Italy (started in 1228). You've followed the intended pilgrims' route, entering the lower church and finishing here. Notice how the pulpit can be seen and heard from every spot in the packed church. The spirit of the order was to fill the church and preach. See also the design in the round window in the west end (high above the entry). The tiny center piece reads "IHS" (the first three letters of Jesus' name in Greek). And, as you can see, this trippy kaleidoscope seems to declare that all light radiates from Jesus. The windows here are treasures from the 13th and 14th centuries. Those behind the apse are among the oldest and most precious in Italy. Imagine illiterate medieval peasants entranced by these windows, so full of meaning that they were nicknamed "Bibles of the Poor." But for art-lovers, the basilica's draw is that Giotto and his assistants practically wallpapered it circa 1297-1300. Or perhaps the job was subcontracted to other artists—scholars debate it (for more on Giotto, see page 156). Whatever the case, the anatomy, architectural depth, and drama of these frescoes helped to kick off the Renaissance. The gallery of frescoes shows 28 scenes from the life of St. Francis. The events are a mix of documented history and folk legend.

• *Get oriented by facing the basilica's main altar. Working clockwise, start on the right-hand (north) wall, and follow along with the help of the numbered map key. The subtitles in the black strip below the frescoes describe each scene in clear Latin—and affirm my interpretation.*

❶ **A common man spreads his cape before Francis** in front of the Temple of Minerva on Piazza del Comune. Before his conversion, young Francis was the model of Assisian manhood—

Basilica of St. Francis—Upper Level

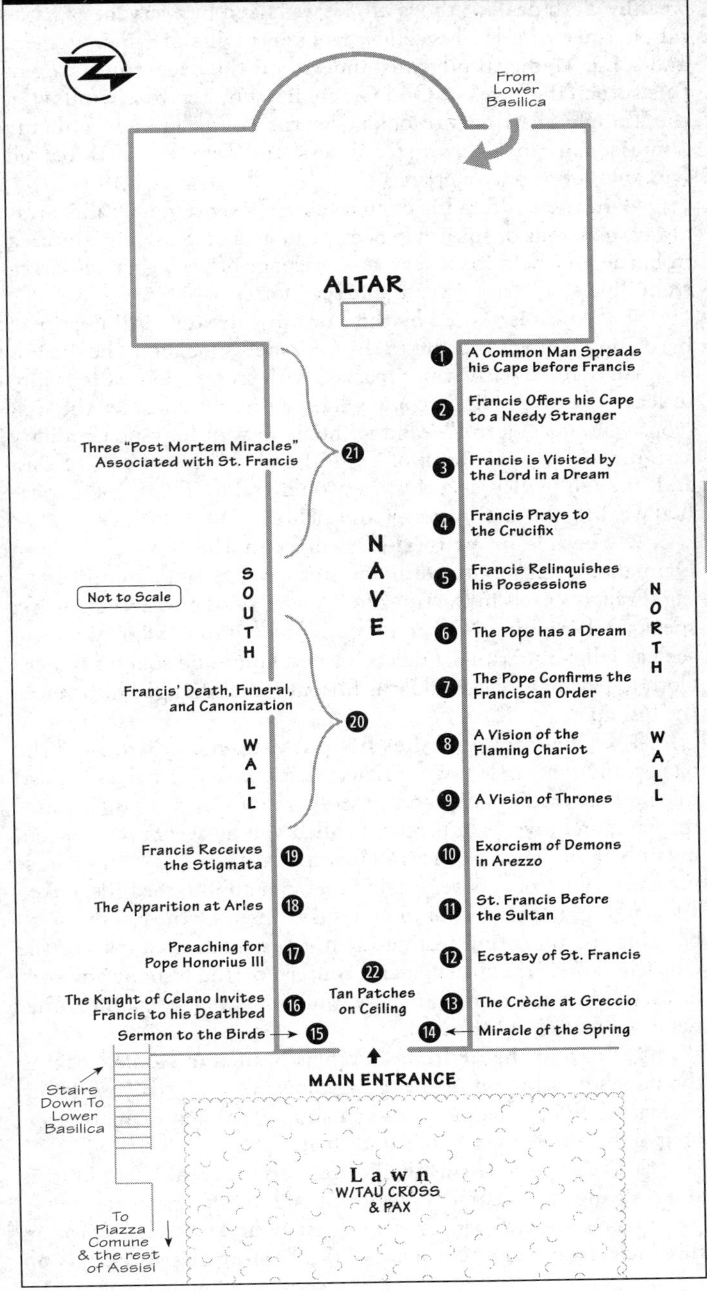

From Lower Basilica

ALTAR

NAVE

SOUTH WALL

NORTH WALL

Three "Post Mortem Miracles" Associated with St. Francis — **21**

Not to Scale

Francis' Death, Funeral, and Canonization — **20**

19 Francis Receives the Stigmata

18 The Apparition at Arles

17 Preaching for Pope Honorius III

16 The Knight of Celano Invites Francis to his Deathbed

15 Sermon to the Birds →

22 Tan Patches on Ceiling

1 A Common Man Spreads his Cape before Francis

2 Francis Offers his Cape to a Needy Stranger

3 Francis is Visited by the Lord in a Dream

4 Francis Prays to the Crucifix

5 Francis Relinquishes his Possessions

6 The Pope has a Dream

7 The Pope Confirms the Franciscan Order

8 A Vision of the Flaming Chariot

9 A Vision of Thrones

10 Exorcism of Demons in Arezzo

11 St. Francis Before the Sultan

12 Ecstasy of St. Francis

13 The Crèche at Greccio

14 → Miracle of the Spring

MAIN ENTRANCE ↑

Stairs Down To Lower Basilica

To Piazza Comune & the rest of Assisi ↓

L a w n
W/TAU CROSS & PAX

ASSISI

handsome, intelligent, and well dressed, befitting the son of a wealthy cloth dealer. Above all, he was liked by everyone, a natural charmer who led his fellow teens in nights of wine, women, and song. Medieval pilgrims understood the deeper meaning of this scene: The "eye" of God (symbolized by the rose window in the Temple of Minerva) looks over the young Francis, a dandy "imprisoned" in his own selfishness (the Temple—with barred windows—was once a prison).

❷ Francis offers his cape to a needy stranger. Francis was always generous of spirit. He became more so after being captured in battle and held for a year as a prisoner of war, then suffering from illness. Charity was a Franciscan forte.

❸ Francis is visited by the Lord in a dream. Still unsure of his calling, Francis rode off to the Crusades. One night, he dreams of a palace filled with armor marked with crosses. Christ tells him to leave the army—to become what you might consider the first "conscientious objector"—and go home to wait for a non-military assignment in a new kind of knighthood. He returned to Assisi and, though reviled as a coward, would end up fighting for spiritual wealth, not earthly power and riches.

❹ Francis prays to the crucifix in the Church of San Damiano. After months of living in a cave, fasting, and meditating, Francis kneels in the run-down church and prays. The crucifix speaks, telling him: "Go and rebuild my Church, which you can see has fallen into ruin." Francis hurried home and sold his father's cloth to pay for God's work. His furious father dragged him before the bishop.

❺ Francis relinquishes his possessions. In front of the bishop and the whole town, Francis strips naked and gives his dad his clothes, credit cards, and time-share on Capri. Francis raises his hand and says, "Until now, I called you father. From now on, my only father is my Father in Heaven." Notice God's hand blessing the action from above. Francis then ran off into the hills, naked and singing. In this version, Francis is covered by the bishop, symbolizing his transition from a man of the world to a man of the Church. Notice the disbelief and concern on the bishop's advisors' faces; subtle expressions like these wouldn't have made it into other medieval frescoes of the day.

❻ The pope has a dream. Francis headed to Rome, seeking the pope's blessing on his fledgling movement. Initially rebuffing Francis, the pope then dreams of a simple, barefooted man propping up his teetering Church, and then...

❼ The pope confirms the Franciscan order, handing Francis and his gang the document now displayed in the relic chapel.

Francis' life was peppered with visions and miracles, shown in three panels in a row: **❽ vision of the flaming chariot, ❾ vision** of thrones, and ❿ **exorcism of demons in Arezzo.**

• *Next see...*

⓫ **St. Francis before the sultan.** Francis' wandering ministry took him to Egypt during the Crusades (1219). He walked unarmed into the Muslim army camp. They captured him, but the sultan was impressed with Francis' manner and let him go, reportedly whispering, "I'd convert to your faith, but they'd kill us both." Here the sultan gestures from his throne.

⓬ **Ecstasy of St. Francis.** This oft-painted scene shows the mystic communing with Christ.

⓭ **The Crèche at Greccio.** A creative teacher, Francis invents the tradition of manger scenes.

• *Around the corner, see the...*

⓮ **Miracle of the spring.** Shown here getting water out of a rock to quench a stranger's thirst, Francis felt closest to God when in the hills around Assisi, seeing the Creator in the creation.

⓯ **Sermon to the birds.** In his best-known miracle, Francis is surrounded by birds as they listen to him teach. Francis embraces all levels of creation. One interpretation of this scene is that the birds, which are of different species, represent the diverse flock of humanity and nature, all created and beloved by God and worthy of one another's love.

This image of well-fed birds is an appropriate one to take with you. It's designed to remind pilgrims that, like the birds, God gave us life, plenty of food, feathers, wings, and a world to fly around in. Francis, patron saint of the environment and animals, taught his followers to count their blessings. A monk here reminded me that even a student backpacker today eats as well as the wealthiest nobleman in the days of Francis.

• *Continue to the south wall for the rest of the panels.*

Despite the hierarchical society of his day, Francis was welcomed by all classes, shown in these three panels: ⓰ **the knight of Celano invites Francis to his deathbed;** ⓱ **preaching for Pope Honorius III,** who listens carefully; and ⓲ **the apparition at Arles,** which illustrates how Francis could be in two places at once (something only Jesus and saints can pull off). The proponents of Francis, who believed he was destined for sainthood, show him performing the necessary miracles.

⓳ **Francis receives the stigmata.** It's September 17, 1224, and Francis is fasting and praying on nearby Mount Alverna when a six-winged angel (called a seraph)

appears with holy laser-like powers to burn in the marks of the Crucifixion, the stigmata. For the strength of his faith, Francis is given the marks of his master, the "battle scars of love." These five wounds suffered by Christ (nails in palms and feet, lance in side) marked Francis' body for the rest of his life.

The next panels deal with ❷⓿ **Francis' death, funeral, and canonization.** The last panels show ❷❶ **miracles** associated with the saint after his death, proving that he's in heaven and bolstering his eligibility for sainthood.

Francis died thanking God and singing his *Canticle of the Sun.* Just as he referred to the sun as his brother and the moon as his sister, Francis called his body "brother." On his deathbed he conceded, "Maybe I was a bit tough on brother ass." Ravaged by an aestheticism extreme enough to earn him the stigmata and tuberculosis, Francis died in 1226.

Before leaving through the front entrance, look up at the ceiling and the walls near the rose window to see ❷❷ **large tan patches.** In 1997, when a 5.5-magnitude quake hit Assisi, it shattered the upper basilica's frescoes into 300,000 fragments, which were meticulously picked up and pieced back together. Shortly after the quake, an aftershock shook the ceiling frescoes down, killing two monks and two art scholars standing here.

Outside, on the lawn, the Latin word *pax* (peace) and the Franciscan tau cross are "sculpted" from shrubbery. For a drink or snack, the Bar San Francisco (facing the upper basilica) is handy. For *pax*, take the high lane back to town, up to the castle, or into the countryside.

More Sights in Assisi

▲**Roman Forum (Foro Romano)**—For a look at Assisi's Roman roots, tour the Roman Forum, which is underneath Piazza del Comune. The floor plan is clearly explained in English, as are the surviving odd bits and obscure pieces. During your visit, you'll walk on an ancient Roman road.

Cost and Hours: €4, included in €8 combo-ticket that also covers next two sights, daily 10:00-13:00 & 14:30-18:00, until 19:00 in July-Aug, until 17:00 in winter; from Piazza del Comune, go a half-block down Via San Francesco—it's on your right; tel. 075-815-5077.

Pinacoteca—This small museum attractively displays its 13th- to 17th-century art (mainly frescoes), with general English information in nearly every room. There's a damaged Giotto Madonna and a rare secular fresco (to the right of the Giotto art), but it's mainly a peaceful walk through a pastel world—best for art-lovers.

Cost and Hours: €3, included in €8 combo-ticket, same hours as Roman Forum, Via San Francesco, across from #13C—look for banner above entryway, on main drag between Piazza del Comune and Basilica of St. Francis, tel. 075-815-5077.

▲**Rocca Maggiore**—The "big castle" offers a good look at a 14th-century fortification and a fine view of Assisi and the Umbrian countryside. If you're pinching your euros, the view is just as good from outside the castle. There's talk of restoring some rooms in their original medieval style, possibly in time for your visit.

Cost and Hours: €5, included in €8 combo-ticket, daily from 10:00 until an hour before sunset—about 19:15 in summer, tel. 075-815-5077.

Commune with Nature—For a picnic with the same birdsong and views that inspired St. Francis, leave the tourists behind and hike to the Rocca Minore (small private castle, not tourable) above Piazza Matteotti.

In Santa Maria degli Angeli

This modern part of Assisi sits in the flat valley below the hill town (see "Assisi Area" map, earlier). It has two sights: the basilica that marks the spot where Francis lived, worked, and died; and the church where the crucifix spoke to him.

▲▲**St. Mary of the Angels Basilica (Basilica Patriarcale di Santa Maria degli Angeli in Porziuncola)**—This huge basilica,

towering above the buildings below Assisi, was built in the 16th century around the tiny but historic Porziuncola Chapel (now directly under the dome). The last part of the church's Italian name ("in Porziuncola") means literally "over the Porziuncola Chapel." After Francis' conversion, some local monks gave him this *porziuncola,* or "small portion"—a little land with a fixer-upper chapel. Francis lived here after he founded the Franciscan Order, and this was where he consecrated St. Clare as a Bride of Christ. What would humble Francis think of the huge church—Christianity's 10th largest—built over his tiny chapel?

Behind the chapel on the right, find the Cappella del Transito, which marks the site of Francis' death on October 3, 1226. Francis died as he'd lived—simply, in a small hut located here. On his last night on earth, he invited some friars to join him in a Last Supper-style breaking of bread. Then he undressed, lay down on the bare ground, and began to recite Psalm 141, "Lord, I cry unto thee." He spoke the last line, "Let the wicked fall into their own traps, while I escape"...and he passed on.

Follow *Roseto* signs to the rose garden. Francis, fighting a temptation that he never named, once threw himself onto the roses. As the story goes, the thorns immediately dropped off. Thornless roses have grown here ever since.

When you reach the statue of Francis petting a sheep, look to the right, through the window, at the rose garden. The Rose Chapel (Cappella delle Rose) is built over the place where Francis lived.

In the autumn, a room in the next hallway displays a giant animated nativity scene (a reminder to pilgrims that Francis first established the tradition of manger scenes as a teaching aid). The bookshop has some works in English, while the Porziuncola Museum features a few monastic cells of interest to pilgrims, a model of Assisi during Francis' lifetime, and religious art and objects from the basilica (€2.50, museum open May-Oct Tue-Sun 9:30-12:30 & 15:30-19:00, Nov-April Tue-Sun 9:30-12:30 & 15:00-18:00, closed Mon, tel. 075-805-1419, www.porziuncola .org).

Cost and Hours: The basilica is free to enter and open Mon-Sat 6:15-12:50 & 14:30-19:30; it opens 30 minutes later on Sun (tel. 075-805-11). A little TI kiosk is across the street from the souvenir stands (generally daily 10:00-12:30 & 16:00-18:30 but hours a bit erratic, tel. 075-804-4554). As you face the church, the best WC is on your right.

Getting There: From Assisi's train station, it's a five-minute walk to the basilica (exit station left, after 20 yards take the new underground pedestrian walkway on your left, then look for the dome in the distance). When you leave the basilica, you can catch an orange bus that goes to the station and on to Assisi's old town (leaving the church, the stop is on your right, by the side of the church). These orange city buses run twice hourly (buses to the old town depart the basilica at :10 and :40 after the hour; tickets cost €1 if you buy at a tobacco shop or the newsstand near the TI, €1.50 if you buy from driver—have exact change ready, stamp your ticket on board; 20-minute ride up to old town). It's efficient to visit this basilica either on your way to the old town of Assisi or when you leave.

Museo Pericle Fazzini—This small museum, housed in the arcaded building opposite St. Mary of the Angels Basilica, features works by the contemporary Italian sculptor Pericle Fazzini. The collection includes bronzes, wooden sculptures (including one of St. Francis), and the original bronze casting of "The

Resurrection"—a miniature of Fazzini's famous bronze of Jesus rising from a nuclear-bomb crater, commissioned by the pope for the Sala Nervi audience hall of the Vatican. Biographical information on the sculptor is provided in English.

Cost and Hours: €5, Tue-Sun 10:00-13:00 & 16:00-19:00, closed Mon, tel. 075-804-4586, www.museo.periclefazzini.it.

Church of San Damiano (Chiesa di San Damiano)—Located in the valley beneath the Basilica of St. Clare, this church and convent was where Francis received his call and where Clare spent her days as mother superior of the Poor Clares. Today, there's not much to see, but it's a relatively peaceful escape from touristy Assisi. Drivers can zip right there, while walkers descend pleasantly from Assisi for 15 minutes through an olive grove.

In 1206, Francis was inside the church when he heard the wooden crucifix order him to rebuild the church. (The crucifix in San Damiano is a copy; the original is now displayed in the Basilica of St. Clare.) Francis initially interpreted these miraculous words as a call to rebuild crumbling San Damiano. He sold his father's cloth for money to fix the church. (The church we see today, however, was rebuilt later by others.) Eventually, Francis realized his charge was to revitalize the Christian Church at large.

As he approached the end of his life, Francis came to San Damiano to visit his old friend Clare. She set him up in a simple reed hut in the olive grove, where he was inspired to write his poem *The Canticle of the Sun* (see page 613).

Cost and Hours: Daily, convent open 10:00-12:00 & 14:00-18:30, closes at 16:30 in winter, church opens at 6:30, start walking from the Porta Nuova parking lot at the south end of Assisi and follow the signs, tel. 075-812-273, www.assisiofm.it.

Outside of Assisi

Hermitage (Eremo delle Carceri)—If you want to follow further in St. Francis' footsteps, take a trip up the rugged slopes of nearby Mount Subasio to the humble hermitage where Francis and his followers retreated for solitude. Today the spot is marked by a 14th-century convent. The highlight is a look at the tiny, dank cave where Francis would retire for private prayer.

Cost and Hours: Free, daily 6:30-19:00, until 17:30 off-season, last entry 30 minutes before closing, tel. 075-812-301, www.eremocarceri.it.

Getting There: There is no public transportation; either drive, take a taxi, or hike. Starting from Assisi's Porta Cappuccini gate, it's a stiff three-mile, 1.5-hour hike with an elevation gain of about 1,000 feet. You'll walk along a narrow, switchbacked, paved road enjoying brisk air and vast views. A souvenir kiosk at the entrance sells drinks and sandwiches.

Sleeping in Assisi

Assisi accommodates large numbers of pilgrims on religious holidays (see list on page 1037). Finding a room at any other time should be easy. Few hotels are air-conditioned. Locals suggest that you keep your windows closed in the middle of the day so that your room will be as cool as possible in the evening.

Hotels and Rooms

$$$ Hotel Umbra, a quiet villa in the middle of town, has 24 spacious rooms with great views and fine accommodations (Sb-€75, standard Db-€110, superior Db-€125, Tb-€155, 10 percent cash discount for 2 or more nights with this book, air-con, elevator, Wi-Fi, peaceful garden and view sun terrace, most rooms have views, closed Dec-March, just off Piazza del Comune under the arch at Via degli Archi 6, tel. 075-812-240, fax 075-813-653, www.hotelumbra.it, info@hotelumbra.it, family Laudenzi).

$$ Hotel Ideale, on a ridge overlooking the valley, offers 14 airy, modern rooms (all with views, 12 with balconies), a tranquil garden setting, and free parking (Sb-€50, Db-€90, prices good with this book through 2012, 10 percent discount for stays of 3 or more nights, may be cheaper off-season, air-con, confirm your arrival time especially if it's after 17:00, Piazza Matteotti 1, tel. 075-813-570, fax 075-813-020, www.hotelideale.it, info@hotelideale.it, friendly sisters Lara and Ilaria). The hotel is close to the bus stop (and parking lot) at Piazza Matteotti at the top end of town.

$$ Hotel Belvedere, a great value, is a modern building with 16 big, spacious rooms—nine come with sweeping views (Sb-€45, Db-€65, breakfast-€5, elevator, large communal view terrace, 2 blocks past Basilica of St. Clare at Via Borgo Aretino 13, tel. 075-812-460, fax 075-816-812, www.assisihotelbelvedere.it, info@assisihotelbelvedere.it, run by Enrico and Mary from New Jersey).

$$ La Pallotta offers seven clean, bright rooms and a communal view room on the top floor. They provide guests with a loaner Assisi guidebook, map, and audioguide, as well as a bus ticket and English helpline number (Sb-€35-45, Db-€58-75, free Internet access and Wi-Fi, free use of washer and clothesline, free hot drinks and cake at teatime; a block off Piazza del Comune at Via San Rufino 6—go up a short flight of stairs outside building, above the arch, to reach entrance; tel. & fax 075-812-307, www.pallottaassisi.it, pallotta@pallottaassisi.it, helpful Stefano, Serena, and family). If you're driving, head to Piazza San Rufino, where they'll meet you at their office. They also have a good restaurant (see "Eating in Assisi," later).

Sleep Code

(€1 = about $1.40, country code: 39)
S = Single, **D** = Double/Twin, **T** = Triple, **Q** = Quad, **b** = bathroom, **s** = shower only. Unless otherwise noted, credit cards are accepted, English is spoken, and breakfast is included.

To help you sort easily through these listings, I've divided the accommodations into three categories based on the price for a standard double room with bath:

$$$ Higher Priced—Most rooms €100 or more.
$$ Moderately Priced—Most rooms between €55-100.
$ Lower Priced—Most rooms €55 or less.

Prices can change without notice; verify the hotel's current rates online or by email. For other updates, see www .ricksteves.com/update.

$$ Hotel Sole, renting 38 rooms in a 15th-century building, is tired and forgettable, but the location is central. Half of its rooms are in a newer annex across the street (Sb-€50, Db-€70, Tb-€90, ask for a discount, breakfast-€5, air-con-€5 extra, easy parking, 100 yards before Basilica of St. Clare at Corso Mazzini 35, tel. 075-812-373, fax 075-813-706, www.assisihotelsole.com, info@assisihotelsole.com).

$$ Hotel San Rufino offers a great locale, solid stone quality, and 11 comfortable rooms (Sb-€47, Db-€58, Tb-€78, breakfast-€4; from Cathedral of San Rufino, follow sign to Via Porta Perlici 7; tel. & fax 075-812-803, www.hotelsanrufino.it, info @hotelsanrufino.it). Their nine-room annex, Albergo Il Duomo (listed later), saves you about €5 a night for a double with no loss in comfort.

$$ Hotel La Rocca, on the peaceful top end of town, has 32 solid and modern rooms in a medieval shell (Sb-€46, Db-€59, Tb-€80, breakfast-€4, parking-€6, sunny rooftop terrace, decent restaurant upstairs, 3-minute walk from Piazza Matteotti at Via Porta Perlici 27, tel. 075-812-284, fax 075-816-467, www.hotela rocca.it, info@hotelarocca.it).

$ Mariani Marini Camere, in a utilitarian building rebuilt after the earthquake, rents 10 basic, perfectly sleepable rooms. While there's a tiny sun deck and a little reception area, it's an extremely basic place (Db-€45 for two or more nights, €50 for one-night stay, extra bed-€10, cash only, Via A. Cristofani 5, tel. 075-812-508, mobile 348-733-2610, www.cameremarianimarini.com, info@cameremarianimarini.com, Antonio and Fabrizio).

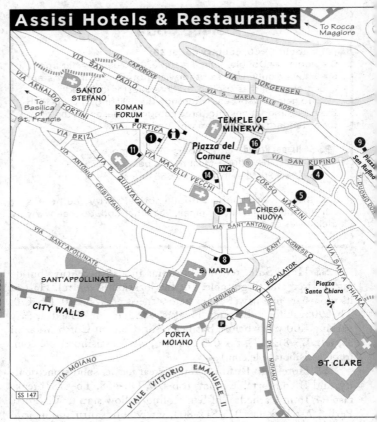

Assisi Hotels & Restaurants

$ Camere Carli has six shiny, spacious, new rooms in a solid, minimalist place above a shop (Sb-€37, Db-€48, Qb-€60, show this book to get these prices, family lofts, Wi-Fi, free parking nearby, facing the Duomo at Via Porta Perlici 1, tel. 075-812-490, mobile 339-531-1366, www.camerecarli.it, carliarte@live.it, Carli).

$ Albergo Il Duomo's nine rooms are tidy and *tranquillo*. Located on a stair-stepped lane one block up from Hotel San Rufino, it's more atmospheric and has nicer bathrooms than its parent hotel (Sb-€43, Db-€53, breakfast-€4, Vicolo San Lorenzo 2 but check in at Hotel San Rufino—see earlier, tel. & fax 075-812-742, www.hotelsanrufino.it, info@hotelsanrufino.it).

$ Camere Annalisa Martini is a cheery home in the town's medieval core that swims in vines and roses. Annalisa enthusiastically accommodates her guests with a picnic garden, a washing

1 Hotel Umbra
2 Hotel Ideale
3 Hotel Belvedere
4 La Pallotta Rooms
5 Hotel Sole & Agenzia Viaggi Stoppini
6 Hotel San Rufino
7 Hotel La Rocca
8 Mariani Marini Camere
9 Carli Rooms & Caffè Duomo
10 Albergo Il Duomo
11 Camere Annalisa Martini
12 St. Anthony's Guest House
13 Ristorante Medioevo
14 La Pallotta Restaurant
15 Trattoria da Erminio
16 La Bottega dei Sapori

machine (€7/small load, includes line drying), a communal refrigerator, and six homey rooms (S-€27, Sb-€30, D-€38, Db-€42, Tb-€58, Qb-€68, cash only but credit card required for deposit, 3 rooms share 2 bathrooms, no breakfast; 1 block from Piazza del Comune—go downhill toward basilica, turn left on Via San Gregorio to #6; tel. & fax 075-813-536, cameremartini@libero.it, Mamma Rosignoli—"roh-sin-YOH-lee"—doesn't speak English, but Annalisa does).

Hostel: Francis probably would have bunked with the peasants in Assisi's **$ Ostello della Pace** (€17 beds in 4- to 8-bed rooms, €19/person in private 2- to 4-person rooms with bath, dinner-€10.50, laundry service-€4, lockout 10:00-16:00, midnight curfew; get off bus at Piazza Giovanni Paolo II, then walk 15 minutes downhill to Via di Valecchie 177—see map on page 610; tel. & fax 075-816-767, www.assisihostel.com, assisi.hostel@tiscalinet.it).

Sweet Dreams in a Convent

Assisi is filled with convents, most of which rent rooms to pilgrims and travelers. While you don't need to be a pilgrim or even a Christian to be welcome, it's just common sense to stay in a convent *only* if you're approaching Assisi with a contemplative mindset. Convents feel institutional, house many groups, and are not particularly cheap—but they come with all the facilities you might need to enjoy a spirit-filled visit to Assisi.

$$ St. Anthony's Guest House is where the Franciscan Sisters of the Atonement (including several Americans and Canadians) offer a very warm and tranquil welcome. Their oasis of peace is just above the Basilica of St. Clare. With only 35 beds in 20 rooms at a reasonable price, they book up literally months in advance (Sb-€40-45, Db-€60-65, Tb-€80-85, 2-night minimum, cash only for short stays, no problem if couples want to share a bed, 23:00 curfew, closed mid-Nov-Feb, library, views, picnic garden, parking-€3 donation, just below Piazza Matteotti at Via Galeazzo Alessi 10, tel. 075-812-542, fax 075-813-723, atoneassisi@tiscali.it).

Eating in Assisi

I've listed decent, central, good-value restaurants. Assisi's food is heavy and rustic. Locals brag about their sausage and love to grate truffles on pasta. To bump up any meal, consider a glass or bottle of the favorite homegrown red wine, Sagrantino de Montefalco. Sagrantino is Umbria's answer to Brunello (although many wine-lovers around here would say that it's vice versa). Before or after dinner, enjoy a drink on the main square facing the Roman temple...or hang out with the local teens with a take-away beer under the temple's columns.

Fine Dining

Ristorante Medioevo is my vote for your best splurge. With heavy but spacious cellar vaults, William Ventura's restaurant is an elegant, accessible playground of gastronomy. Manager Massimo will guide you to the best of Umbrian cuisine. He features traditional cuisine with a modern twist, dictated by what's in season. While his first passion is cooking, his second is music—mellow jazz and bossa nova give a twinkle to the medieval atmosphere. Dishes are well-presented; beef and game dishes are the specialties, and the wonderful Sagrantino wine is served by the glass. As a special treat, when readers of this book order a glass of Sagrantino, they'll receive a small slice of just the right strong pecorino cheese—to better understand the Italian fascination with "a good marriage" between food and wine (€10 pastas, €14 *secondi,* Tue-Sun 12:30-15:00 & 19:30-22:45, closed Mon; from the fountain on Piazza del

Comune, hike downhill two blocks to Via Arco dei Priori 4; tel. 075-813-068).

La Pallotta, a local favorite run by a friendly and hardworking family—with Margarita in charge of the kitchen—offers delicious, well-presented regional specialties, such as *piccione* (squab, a.k.a. pigeon) and *coniglio* (rabbit). And they like to serve split courses *(bis)* featuring the two local pastas. Reservations are smart (€8 pastas, €15 *secondi*, good €27 fixed-price sampler of local specialties, Wed-Mon 12:15-14:30 & 19:15-23:00, last orders at 21:30, closed Tue, vegetarian options, a few steps off Piazza del Comune across from temple/church at Vicolo della Volta Pinta 2, tel. 075-812-649).

Casual Eateries

Trattoria da Erminio is charming, with peaceful tables on a tiny square, or indoor seating under a big, medieval (but air-conditioned) brick vault. Run by Federico and his family for three generations, it specializes in local meat cooked on an open-fire grill. They have good Umbrian wines—before you order, ask Federico or Giuliana for a taste of the Petranera wine (€9 pastas, €12 grilled meats, €16-20 tourist fixed-price meal featuring local recipes based on seasonal produce—changes weekly, Fri-Wed 12:00-14:30 & 19:00-21:00, closed Thu; from Piazza San Rufino, go a block up Via Porta Perlici and turn right to Via Montacavallo 19; tel. 075-812-506).

At **Locanda del Podestà,** chef Stelvio cooks up tasty grilled Umbrian sausages, *gnocchi alla locanda,* and all manner of truffles, while Romina graciously serves happy diners who know a good value. Try the tasty *scottaditto* ("scorch your fingers") lamb chops (€7 pastas, €12 *secondi*, Thu-Tue 12:00-14:30 & 19:00-21:30, closed Wed and Jan, 5-minute walk uphill along Via Cardinale Merry del Val from basilica, San Giacomo 6c—see map on page 610, tel. 075-816-553).

Ristorante Metastasio, just up the street from Podestà, offers a traditional menu. While not beloved for its cooking, it boasts Assisi's best view terrace for dining (€9 pastas, €12 *secondi*, closed Wed, terrace closed in colder weather, Via Metastasio 9, tel. 075-816-525).

Picnic on the Main Square

There are many little grocery stores *(alimentari)* nearby.

Try **La Bottega dei Sapori** for a picnic of Umbrian treats: good prosciutto sandwiches and specialty items, including truffle paste and olive oil. Friendly Fabrizio, who is a slow-food enthusiast, may give you a taste. He also stocks the best Umbrian wines at good-to-go prices—nice if you have an appointment with your terrace for sunset (daily 9:00-20:00, until 21:00 in summer, closed Jan-Feb, Piazza del Comune 34, tel. 075-812-294).

Assisi Connections

From Assisi by Train to: Rome (nearly hourly, 2-3.5 hours, 5 direct, most others change in Foligno), **Florence** (8/day direct, 2-3 hours), **Orvieto** (roughly hourly, 2-2.5 hours, with transfer in Terontola or Orte), **Siena** (8/day, 4-5 hours, most involve 2 transfers; bus is faster), **Cortona** (every 2 hours, 70 minutes to Camucia-Cortona station). The train station's ticket office is often open only 13:00-19:35; when the office is closed, use the ticket machine (may only accept credit cards). You can get train information and tickets from Agenzia Viaggi Stoppini in the middle of town (see "Helpful Hints" on page 598). Train station tel. 075-804-0272 (generally unresponsive; you're better off asking at Agenzia Viaggi Stoppini or checking online at www.trenitalia.com).

By Bus: Service to **Rome** is operated by Sulga bus company (2/day, 3 hours, €16, pay driver, departs from Piazza San Pietro, arrives at Rome's Tiburtina station where you can connect with the train to Fiumicino airport, tel. 800-099-661, www.sulga.it). A bus for **Siena** (1/day at 10:20, 2 hours, €12) usually departs from St. Mary of the Angels; you can't buy Siena tickets from the driver—you must buy them at Assisi's Agenzia Viaggi Mavitur at Via Frate Elia 1b (see "Helpful Hints" on page 600). A bus operated by Curreri leaves twice a week to **Sorrento** (Thu and Sun at 16:00, 6 hours, book online but pay driver, www.curreriviaggi.it).

Don't take the bus to **Florence;** the train is better. To see either **Gubbio** (described on page 725) or **Todi** as a side-trip from Assisi, you'll need a car—bus schedules don't accommodate daytrippers. Day trips to **Spello** (described on page 726) and **Lake Trasimeno** work by train, but not by bus. A day trip to **Perugia** is possible with buses operated by APM (www.apmperugia.it).

By Plane: Perugia/Assisi Airport, about 10 miles from Assisi, has daily connections to London Stansted airport (on Ryanair), Milan, and—seasonally—to Barcelona and Trapani in Sicily. No public transport runs between Assisi and the airport; a taxi costs about €30 (tel. 075-592-141, www.airport.umbria.it).

HILL TOWNS OF CENTRAL ITALY

San Gimignano • Volterra • Montalcino • Pienza •
Montepulciano • Cortona • Orvieto • Civita di Bagnoregio

The sun-soaked hill towns of central Italy offer what to many is the quintessential Italian experience: sun-dried tomatoes, homemade pasta, wispy cypress-lined driveways following desolate ridges to fortified 16th-century farmhouses, atmospheric *enoteche* serving Tuscany's famously tasty wines, and dusty old-timers warming the same bench day after day while soccer balls buzz around them like innocuous flies.

The hill towns of central Italy—in Tuscany, Le Marche, and Umbria—retain their medieval charm, and are best enjoyed by adapting to the pace of the countryside. So, slow...down...and savor the delights that these villages offer. Spend the night if you can, since many hill towns are mobbed by day-trippers.

Planning Your Time

How in Dante's name does a traveler choose from Italy's hundreds of hill towns? I've listed some of my favorites in this chapter. The one(s) you visit will depend on your interests, time, and mode of transportation.

Multi-towered San Gimignano is a classic, but because it's such an easy hill town to visit (about 1.25 hours by bus from Florence), peak-season crowds can overwhelm its charms. For rustic vitality not completely trampled by tourist crowds, out-of-the-way Volterra is the clear winner. Wine aficionados head for Montalcino and Montepulciano—each a happy gauntlet of wine shops and art galleries (Montepulciano being my favorite). Fans of architecture and urban design appreciate Pienza's well-planned streets and squares. Art-lovers and those enamored by Frances Mayes' memoir *(Under the Tuscan Sun)* make the pilgrimage to Cortona. Urbino, well off

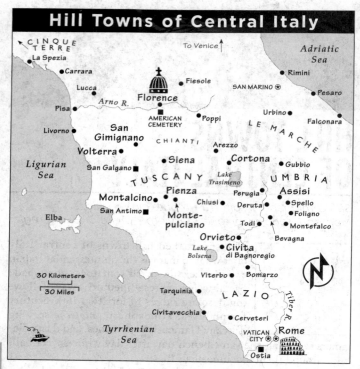

Hill Towns of Central Italy

the tourist track and quite remote, is known for its huge Ducal Palace. The grand, classic town of Orvieto is famous for its wine, ceramics, and colorful cathedral. But my longtime favorite is the tiny, obscure hill town of Civita di Bagnoregio (pictured on previous page). Assisi and Siena, while technically hill towns, are in a category by themselves: Bigger and with more major artistic and historic sights, they each get their own chapter.

For a relaxing break from big-city Italy, settle down in an *agriturismo*—a farmhouse that rents out rooms to travelers (usually for a minimum of a week in high season). These rural B&Bs—almost by definition in the middle of nowhere—provide a good home base from which to find the magic of Italy's hill towns. I've listed several good options throughout this chapter (for more information, see "Agritourism" on page 28).

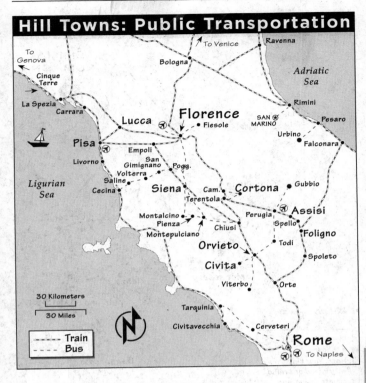

Hill Towns: Public Transportation

Getting Around the Hill Towns

Bigger destinations (such as Cortona and Orvieto) are doable by public transportation, but most hill towns are easier and more efficient to visit by car.

By Bus or Train

Traveling by public transportation is cheap and connects you with the locals. While trains link some of the towns, hill towns—being on hills—don't quite fit the railroad plan. Stations are likely to be in the valley a couple of miles from the town center, usually connected efficiently by a local bus.

Buses are often the only public-transportation choice to get between small hill towns. If you're pinched for time, it makes sense to narrow your focus to one or two hill towns, or rent a car to see more. For more on traveling by bus in Italy, see the appendix.

By Car

Exploring small-town Tuscany, Le Marche, and Umbria by car can be a great experience. But since a car is an expensive, worthless

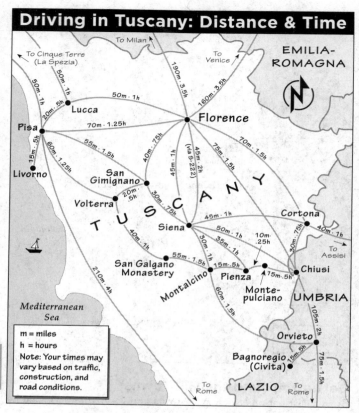

Driving in Tuscany: Distance & Time

To Milan

To Venice

EMILIA-ROMANGA

To Cinque Terre
(La Spezia)

50m · 1h
50m · 1h
50m · 1h
20m · .5h

Lucca

190m · 3.5h

160m · 3.5h

Pisa

50m · 1h

Florence

70m · 1.25h

15m · .5h
60m · 1.25h

Livorno

55m · 1.5h
40m · .75h

45m · 1h

45m · 2h
(via S-222)

75m · 1.5h

70m · 1.5h

San
Gimignano

Volterra

20m · .5h
30m · .75h

TUSCANY

45m · 1h

Cortona

Siena

50m · 1h

10m · .25h

30m · .75h

40m · 1h

To
Assisi

40m · 1h

35m · 1h

30m · 1h

Chiusi

San Galgano
Monastery

55m · 1.5h

15m · .5h

Pienza

75m · .5h

UMBRIA

Montalcino

Monte-
pulciano

210m · 4h

60m · 1.5h

Mediterranean
Sea

105m · 2h

m = miles
h = hours
Note: Your times may
vary based on traffic,
construction, and
road conditions.

Orvieto

Bagnoregio
(Civita)

15m · .5h

75m · 1.5h

To
Rome

LAZIO

To
Rome

headache in Florence and Siena, wait to pick up your car until the last big city you visit (or pick it up at the nearest airport to avoid big-city traffic). Then use the car for lacing together the hill towns and exploring the countryside. For more on car rentals and driving in Italy, see the appendix.

A big, detailed regional road map (buy one at a newsstand or gas station) and a semiskilled navigator are essential. Freeways (such as the toll autostrada and the non-toll *superstrada*) provide the fastest way to connect two points, but the smaller roads, including the super-scenic S-222, which runs through the heart of the Chianti region (connecting Florence and Siena), are more rewarding. For more joyrides—from Siena to Montalcino, and from Montalcino to Montepulciano—see "Crete Senese Drives" on page 691.

Parking throughout this region can be challenging. Some towns don't allow visitors to park in the city center, so you'll need to leave your car outside the walls and walk into town. Signs reading *Zona Traffico Limitato (ZTL)*—often above a red circle—mark areas where no driving or parking is allowed. Parking lots, indicated by big blue *P* signs, are usually free and plentiful outside city walls. In some towns, you can park on the street; nearby kiosks sell "pay and display" tickets. I'd advise parking in guarded lots whenever possible;, they are worth the expense to reduce the threat of theft (no guarantees, though).

San Gimignano

The epitome of a Tuscan hill town, with 14 medieval towers still standing (out of an original 72), San Gimignano (sahn jee-meen-YAH-noh) is a perfectly preserved tourist trap. There are no important interiors to sightsee, and the town is packed with crass commercialism. The locals seem corrupted by the easy money of tourism, and most of the  rustic is faux. The fact that this small town supports two torture museums is a comment on the caliber of the masses who choose to visit. But San Gimignano is so easy to reach and visually so beautiful that it remains a good stop. I find the place enchanting at night.

In the 13th century—back in the days of Romeo and Juliet—feuding noble families ran the hill towns. They'd periodically battle things out from the protection of their respective family towers. Pointy skylines, like San Gimignano's, were the norm in medieval Tuscany.

San Gimignano's cuisine is mostly what you might find in Siena—typical Tuscan home cooking. *Cinghiale* (cheeng-GAH-lay, wild boar) is served in almost every way: stews, soups, cutlets, and, my favorite, salami. Most shops will give you a sample before you commit to buying. The city is well known for having some of the best saffron in Italy; look for it on menus at finer restaurants (it's fairly expensive). Although Tuscany is normally a red-wine region, the most famous Tuscan white wine comes from here: the inexpensive, light, and fruity Vernaccia di San Gimignano. Look for the green "DOCG" label around the neck for the best quality (see "Wines Labels and Lingo" on page 32).

HILL TOWNS

San Gimignano

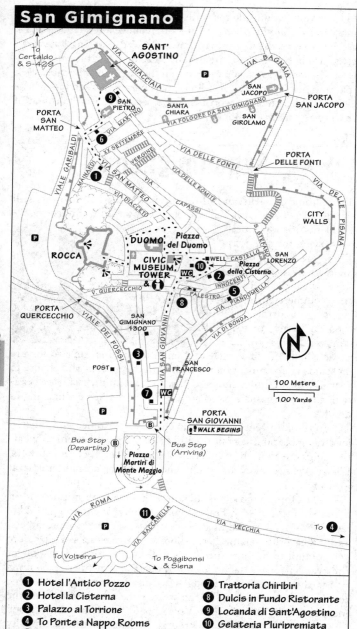

To Certaldo & S-429

SANT' AGOSTINO

VIA GHIACCIAIA

VIA BAGNAIA

SAN JACOPO

PORTA SAN JACOPO

SANTA CHIARA

VIA FOLGORE DA SAN GIMIGNANO

SAN GIROLAMO

PORTA SAN MATTEO

SAN PIETRO

VIA MARTINO

XX SETTEMBRE

VIA DELLE FONTI

PORTA DELLE FONTI

VIALE GARIBALDI

VIA MAINARDI

VIA SAN MATTEO

VIA DIACCETO

VERGINE

VIA CAPASSI

VIA DELLE FONTI

VIA DELLE ROMITE

VIA DELLE PISANA

CITY WALLS

ROCCA

DUOMO

Piazza del Duomo

CIVIC MUSEUM, TOWER & i

V. QUERCECCHIO

WELL

WC

CASTELLO

S. STEFANO

SAN LORENZO

Piazza della Cisterna

PORTA QUERCECCHIO

VIALE DEI FOSSI

SAN GIMIGNANO 1300

INNOCENTI

PALESTRO

VIA PIANDOMELLA

VIA DI BONDA

POST

VIA SAN GIOVANNI

SAN FRANCESCO

WC

PORTA SAN GIOVANNI

WALK BEGINS

Bus Stop (Departing)

Bus Stop (Arriving)

Piazza Martiri di Monte Maggio

VIA ROMA

VIA BAGNANELLA

VIA VECCHIA

To 4

To Volterra

To Poggibonsi & Siena

100 Meters

100 Yards

N

1 Hotel l'Antico Pozzo
2 Hotel la Cisterna
3 Palazzo al Torrione
4 To Ponte a Nappo Rooms
5 Le Vecchie Mura Camere & Ristorante
6 Locanda il Pino

7 Trattoria Chiribiri
8 Dulcis in Fundo Ristorante
9 Locanda di Sant'Agostino
10 Gelateria Pluripremiata "di Piazza"
11 Co-op Supermarket

Orientation to San Gimignano

While the basic ▲▲▲ sight here is the town of San Gimignano itself, there are a few worthwhile stops. From the town gate, head straight up the traffic-free town's cobbled main drag to Piazza della Cisterna (with its 13th-century well). The town sights cluster around the adjoining Piazza del Duomo.

Tourist Information: The helpful TI is in the old center on Piazza del Duomo (daily March-Oct 9:00-13:00 & 15:00-19:00, Nov-Feb 9:00-13:00 & 14:00-18:00, free maps, sells bus tickets, books rooms, tel. 0577-940-008, www.sangimignano.com).

The town offers a two-hour **guided walk** in English and Italian several days a week (April-Oct Sat-Sun at 11:00, €20; includes admission to Civic Museum and Tower; pay and meet at TI). They also give two-hour guided walks into the surrounding countryside for the same price (April-Oct Tue and Thu at 15:00).

Arrival in San Gimignano: The bus stops at the main town gate, Porta San Giovanni. There's no baggage storage anywhere in town, so you're better off leaving your bags in Siena or Florence. You can't drive within the walled town. There are three pay lots a short walk outside the walls; the handiest is Parcheggio Montemaggio, just outside Porta San Giovanni. The one below the roundabout and Co-op supermarket is least expensive (€1/hour, €6/day, Giubileo 1).

Helpful Hints: Thursday is **market** day on Piazza del Duomo (8:00-13:00), but for local merchants, every day is a sales frenzy. A public **WC** is just off Piazza della Cisterna (€0.75), and another is around the corner from Porta San Giovanni. A little electric **shuttle bus** does its laps all day from Porta San Giovanni to Piazza della Cisterna to Porta San Matteo (€0.50, 2/hour, buy ticket from TI, tobacco shop, or from coin-operated machine on bus).

Self-Guided Walk

Welcome to San Gimignano

This quick walking tour will take you across town, from the bus stop at Porta San Giovanni through the town's main squares to the Duomo, and on to the Sant'Agostino Church.

• *Start, as most tourists do, at the Porta San Giovanni gate at the bottom end of town.*

Porta San Giovanni: San Gimignano lies about 25 miles from both Siena and Florence, a good stop for pilgrims en route to those cities, and on a naturally fortified hilltop that encouraged settlement. The town's walls were built in the 13th century, and gates like this helped regulate who came and went. Today, modern posts keep out all but service and emergency vehicles. The small square just outside the gate features a memorial to the town's WWII dead. Follow the pilgrims' route (and flood of modern tourists) through the gate and up the main drag.

About 100 yards up, on the right, is a pilgrims' shelter (12th-century, Pisan Romanesque). The Maltese cross indicates that this was built by the Knights of Malta. It was one of 11 such shelters in town. Today, only the wall of this shelter remains.

• *Carry on, up to the town's central Piazza della Cisterna. Sit on the steps of the well.*

Piazza della Cisterna: The piazza is named for the cistern that served by the old well standing in the center of this square.

A clever system of pipes drained rainwater from the nearby roof-tops into the underground cistern. This square has been the center of the town since the ninth century. Turn in a slow circle and observe the commotion of rustic-yet-proud facades crowding in a tight huddle around the well. Imagine this square in pilgrimage times, lined by inns and taverns for the town's guests. Now finger the grooves in the lip of the well and imagine generations of maids and children fetching water. Each Thursday, the square fills with a market—as it has for more than a thousand years.

• *Notice San Gimignano's famous towers.*

The Towers: Of the original 72 towers, only 14 survive. Before effective city walls were developed, rich people fortified their own

homes with these towers: They provided a handy refuge when ruffians and rival city-states were sacking the town. These towers became a standard part of medi-eval skylines. Even after town walls were built, the towers continued to rise—now to fortify noble families feuding within a town (Montague and Capulet-style).

In the 14th century, San Gimig-nano's good times turned very bad. In the year 1300, about 13,000 people lived within the walls. Then in 1348, a six-month plague decimated the popula-tion, leaving the once-mighty town with barely 4,000 survivors. Once fiercely independent, now crushed and demoralized, San Gimignano came under Florence's control and was forced to tear down its towers. (The Banca Toscana building occupies the remains of one such toppled tower.) And, to add insult to injury, Florence redirected the vital trade route away from San Gimignano. The town never recovered, and poverty left it in a 14th-century architectural time warp. That well-preserved cityscape, ironically, is responsible for the town's prosperity today.

• *From the well, walk 30 yards uphill to the adjoining square with the cathedral.*

Piazza del Duomo: The square faces the former cathedral. The twin towers to the right are 10th-century, among the first in

town. The stubby tower opposite the church is typical of a merchant's tower: main door on ground floor, warehouse upstairs, holes to hold beams that once supported wooden balconies and exterior staircases, heavy stone on the first floor, cheaper and lighter brick for upper stories.

• *On the piazza are the Civic Museum and Tower, worth checking out (see "Sights in San Gimignano," later). You'll also see the...*

Duomo (or Collegiata): Walk inside San Gimignano's Romanesque cathedral. Sienese Gothic art (14th century) lines the nave with parallel themes, Old Testament on the left and New Testament on the right. (For example: the suffering of Job opposite the suffering of Jesus, Creation facing the Annunciation, and the birth of Adam facing the Nativity.) This is a classic use of art to teach. Study the fine Creation series (top left). Many scenes are portrayed with a local 14th-century "slice of life" setting, to help lay townspeople relate to Jesus—in the same way that many white Christians are more comfortable thinking of Jesus as Caucasian (€3.50, €5.50 combo-ticket includes mediocre Religious Art Museum, daily April-Oct 10:00-19:00, Nov-March 10:00-16:40).

• *From the church, hike uphill (passing the church on your left) following signs to* Rocca e Parco di Montestaffoli. *Keep walking until you enter a peaceful hilltop park and olive grove within the shell of a 14th-century fortress.*

Hilltop Views: On the far side, a few steps take you to the top of a little tower (free) for the best views of San Gimignano's skyline; the far end of town and the Sant'Agostino Church (where this walk ends); and a commanding 360-degree view of the Tuscan countryside. San Gimignano is surrounded by olives, grapes, cypress trees, and—in the Middle Ages—lots of wild dangers. Back then, farmers lived inside the walls and were thankful for the protection.

• *Return to the bottom of Piazza del Duomo, turn left, and continue your walk across town, cutting under the double arch (from the town's first wall). In around 1200, this defined the end of town. The Church*

HILL TOWNS

of San Bartolo stood just outside the wall. The Maltese cross indicates that it likely served as a hostel for pilgrims. Continuing on down Via San Matteo, you pass a fascinating array of stone facades from the 13th and 14th centuries—now a happy cancan of wine shops and galleries. Eventually you reach...

Sant'Agostino Church: This tranquil church, at the opposite end of town (built by the Augustinians who arrived in 1260), has fewer crowds and more soul. Behind the altar, a lovely fresco cycle by Benozzo Gozzoli (who painted the exquisite Chapel of the Magi in the Medici-Riccardi Palace in Florence) tells of the life of St. Augustine, a North African monk who preached simplicity. The kind, English-speaking friars (from Britain and the US) are happy to tell you about their church and way of life, and also have Mass in English on Sundays at 11:00. Pace the tranquil cloister before heading back into the tourist mobs (free, €0.50 lights the frescoes; April-Oct daily 7:00-12:00 & 15:00-19:00; Nov-March Tue-Sun 7:00-12:00 & 15:00-18:00, Mon 16:00-18:00). Their fine little shop, with books on the church and its art, is worth a look.

Sights in San Gimignano

Civic Museum and Tower (Museo Civico and Torre Grossa)—This small, fun museum, consisting of just three unfurnished rooms and a tower, is inside City Hall (Palazzo Comunale). The main room, called Sala di Consiglio (a.k.a. Danti Hall), is covered in festive frescoes, including the *Maestà* by Lippo Memmi. This virtual copy of Simone Martini's *Maestà* in Siena proves that Memmi didn't have quite the same talent as his famous brother-in-law. Upstairs, the Pinacoteca displays a classy little painting collection, with a 1422 altarpiece by Taddeo di Bartolo honoring St. Gimignano. You can see the saint, with the town—bristling with towers—in his hands, surrounded by events from his life.

As you exit, be sure to stop by the Mayor's Room (Camera del Podesta). Frescoed in 1310 by Memmo di Filippuccio, it offers an intimate and candid peek into the 14th century. The theme: profane love. As you enter, look to the left corner where a young man is ready to experience the world. He hits his parents up for a bag of money and is free. Almost immediately he's entrapped by two prostitutes, who lead him into a tent where he loses his money (above the window), is turned out, and is beaten. Above the door from left to right you see a parade of better choices: marriage, the cradle of love, the bride led to the groom's house, and newlyweds bathing together and retiring happily to their bed.

The highlight for most visitors is a chance to climb the **Tower** (Torre Grossa). The city's tallest tower, 200 feet and 218 steps up, rewards those who climb it with a commanding view. You leave via a delightful stony loggia and courtyard out back.

Cost and Hours: €5 includes museum and tower, daily March-Oct 9:30-19:00, Nov-Feb 10:00-17:30, Piazza del Duomo.

San Gimignano 1300—This modern attraction is a trip back in time. Located inside the Palazzo Ficarelli in the town center, it features a scale model of San Gimignano at the turn of the 14th century. You can see the 72 original "tower houses," peek into cross-sections of buildings, and view scenes of medieval life within the city walls. While fun for adults, it's even more so for kids.

Cost and Hours: €5, daily 9:00-19:00, June-Sept until 20:00, Via Berignano 23, tel. 0577-941-078, www.sangimignano1300 .com.

Sleeping in San Gimignano

Although the town is a zoo during the daytime, locals outnumber tourists when evening comes, and San Gimignano becomes peaceful and enjoyable. Drivers can unload near their hotels, then park outside the walls in recommended lots. Hotel websites provide instructions.

$$$ Hotel l'Antico Pozzo is an elegantly restored, 15th-century townhouse with 18 tranquil, comfortable rooms, a peaceful interior courtyard terrace, and an elite air (Db-€140 and higher depending on the room, air-con, elevator, Wi-Fi, near Porta San Matteo at Via San Matteo 87, tel. 0577-942-014, fax 0577-942-117, www.anticopozzo.com, info@anticopozzo.com, Emanuele). If arriving by bus, save a cross-town walk by asking for the Porta San Matteo stop (rather then getting off at the main stop near Porta San Giovanni).

$$$ Hotel la Cisterna, right on Piazza della Cisterna, offers 49 predictable rooms, some with panoramic view terraces (Sb-€78, Db-€100, Db with view-€120, Db with view terrace-€145, 10 percent discount with this book when you book direct, buffet breakfast, air-con, elevator, Wi-Fi, good restaurant with great view, closed Jan-Feb, Piazza della Cisterna 23, tel. 0577-940-328, fax 0577-942-080, www.hotelcisterna.it, info@hotelcisterna.it, Alessio).

Sleep Code

(€1 = about $1.40, country code: 39)

S = Single, **D** = Double/Twin, **T** = Triple, **Q** = Quad, **b** = bathroom, **s** = shower only. Unless otherwise noted, credit cards are accepted and breakfast is included (but usually optional). English is generally spoken, but I've noted exceptions.

To help you sort easily through these listings, I've divided the accommodations into three categories based on the price for a standard double room with bath:

$$$ **Higher Priced**—Most rooms €100 or more.
  $$ **Moderately Priced**—Most rooms between €70-100.
    $ **Lower Priced**—Most rooms €70 or less.

Prices can change without notice; verify the hotel's current rates online or by email. For other updates, see www.ricksteves.com/update.

$$$ Ponte a Nappo, run by enterprising Carla Rossi (who doesn't speak English) and her son Francesco (who does), has seven comfortable rooms and two apartments in a kid-friendly farmhouse. Located a long half-mile below town, this place has killer views (Db-€100-120, 2-6 person apartment-€130-220, air-con extra, free Wi-Fi, parking, pool, free loaner bikes, 15-minute walk or 5-minute drive from Porta San Giovanni, tel. 0577-907-282, mobile 349-882-1565, fax 0577-941-268, www.accommodation-sangimignano.it, info@rossicarla.it). A picnic dinner—lounging on their comfy garden furniture as the sun sets—is good Tuscan living. About 100 yards below the monument square at Porta San Giovanni, find Via Vecchia (not left or right, but down a tiny road) and follow it down a dirt road for five minutes by car. They also rent a dozen or so rooms and apartments in town (each described on their website).

$$ Palazzo al Torrione, just inside Porta San Giovanni, is quiet and handy, and generally better than most hotels, though they don't have a full-time reception. Their 10 modern rooms are spacious and tastefully appointed (Db-€80, terrace Db-€100, Tb-€98, terrace Tb-€113, Qb-€120-130, 10 percent discount with this book when you book direct, breakfast-€5, communal kitchen, parking-€6/day, inside and left of gate at Via Berignano 76; operated from tobacco shop 2 blocks away, on the main drag at Via San Giovanni 59; tel. 0577-940-480, mobile 338-938-1656, fax 0577-955-605, www.palazzoaltorrione.com, palazzoaltorrione@palazzoaltorrione.com, Vanna and Francesco).

$ Le Vecchie Mura Camere offers three good rooms above their restaurant in the old town (Db-€60, no breakfast, air-con, Via Piandornella 15, tel. 0577-940-270, www.vecchiemura.it, info @vecchiemura.it, Bagnai family).

$ Locanda il Pino has just seven rooms and a big living room. It's dank but super-clean and quiet. Run by English-speaking Elena and her family, it sits above their elegant restaurant just inside Porta San Matteo (Db-€55, no breakfast, easy parking just outside the gate, Via Cellolese 4, tel. 0577-940-415, locanda@risto ranteilpino.it). If you're arriving by bus, ask for the Porta San Matteo stop, rather than the main stop near Porta San Giovanni.

Eating in San Gimignano

Trattoria Chiribiri, just inside Porta San Giovanni, serves home-made pastas and desserts at remarkably fair prices. While its petite size and tight seating make it hot in the summer, it's a fine value (€7 pastas, €9 *secondi*, daily 11:00-23:00, Piazza della Madonna 1, tel. 0577-941-948, Maria and Maurizio).

Dulcis in Fundo Ristorante, small and family-run, proudly serves local cuisine with a modern twist, gourmet presentation, and slow food values in a jazz ambience (€12 pastas, €15 *secondi*, meals served 12:30-14:30 & 19:30-21:30, closed Wed, Vicolo degli Innocenti 21, tel. 0577-941-919).

Le Vecchie Mura Ristorante is my choice for good ser-vice, great prices, tasty home cooking, and the ultimate view. It's romantic indoors or out. They have a dressy, modern interior where you can dine with a view of the busy stainless-steel kitchen under rustic vaults, but I'd come for the incredible cliffside garden ter-race. Cliffside tables are worth reserving in advance by calling or dropping by: Ask for "front view" (€9 pastas, €13 *secondi*, open only for dinner from 18:00, last order at 22:00, closed Tue, Via Piandornella 15, tel. 0577-940-270, Bagnai family).

Locanda di Sant'Agostino spills out onto the peaceful square, facing Sant'Agostino Church. It's cheap and cheery, serving lunch and dinner daily—a great place for salads, pizza, or a rustic dish of pasta. Dripping with wheat stalks and atmosphere on the inside, there's shady on-the-square seating outside (€8 pastas, €12 *sec-ondi*, daily 11:00-22:00, closed Tue off-season, also closed Jan-Feb, Piazza Sant'Agostino 15, tel. 0577-943-141, Genziana and sons).

Picnics: The big, modern **Co-op supermarket** sells all you need for a nice spread (Mon-Sat 8:30-20:00, closed Sun, at parking lot below Porta San Giovanni). Or browse the little shops guarded by wild boar heads within the town walls; they sell boar meat *(cin-ghiale)*. Pick up 100 grams (about a quarter pound) of boar, cheese, bread, and wine and enjoy a picnic in the garden at the Rocca or the park outside Porta San Giovanni.

Gelato: To cap the evening and sweeten your late-night city stroll, stop by **Gelateria Pluripremiata "di Piazza"** on Piazza della Cisterna (at #4). Gelato-maker Sergio was a member of the Italian team that won the official Gelato World Cup (daily 8:00-24:00, tel. 0577-942-244, Dondoli family).

San Gimignano Connections

Bus tickets are sold at the bar just inside the town gate or at the TI.

From San Gimignano by Bus to: Florence (hourly, less on Sat-Sun, 1.25-2 hours, change in Poggibonsi, €6.25), **Siena** (8/day direct, 1.25 hours, €5.50), **Volterra** (4/day Mon-Sat; on Sun only 1/day—usually crowded—with no return to San Gimignano; 2 hours, change in Colle Val d'Elsa).

By Car: San Gimignano is an easy 45-minute drive from Florence (take the A-1 exit marked *Firenze Certosa*, then a right past tollbooth following *Siena per 4 corsie* sign; exit the freeway at Poggibonsi). From San Gimignano, it's a scenic and windy half-hour drive to Volterra.

Volterra

Encircled by impressive walls and topped with a grand fortress, Volterra sits high above the rich farmland surrounding it. More than 2,000 years ago, Volterra was one of the most important Etruscan cities, a city much larger than the one we see today. Greek-trained Etruscan artists worked here, leaving a significant stash of art, particularly funerary urns. Eventually Volterra was absorbed into the Roman Empire, and for centuries it was an independent city-state. Volterra fought bitterly against the Florentines, but like many Tuscan towns, it lost in the end

and was given a fortress atop the city to "protect" its citizens.

Unlike other famous towns in Tuscany, Volterra feels not cutesy or touristy...but real, vibrant, and almost oblivious to the allure of the tourist dollar. A refreshing break from its more commercial neighbors, it's my favorite small town in Tuscany.

Orientation to Volterra

Compact and walkable, the city stretches out from the pleasant Piazza dei Priori to the old city gates.

Tourist Information

The helpful TI is on the main square, at Piazza dei Priori 19 (daily 10:00-13:00 & 14:00-18:00, tel. 0588-87257, www.volterratur.it). The TI's excellent €5 audioguide narrates 20 stops (2-for-1 discount on audioguides with this book).

Arrival in Volterra

By Public Transport: Buses stop at Piazza Martiri della Libertà in the town center. Train travelers can reach the town with a short bus ride (see "Volterra Connections," later.)

By Car: Drivers will find the town ringed with easy numbered parking lots (#3 and #5 are free; #3 is most likely to have a place, but comes with a steeper hike into town). The most central lots are the pay lots at Porta Fiorentina and underground at Piazza Martiri della Libertà (€1.50/hour, €11/24 hours).

Helpful Hints

Market Day: The market is on Saturday morning near the Roman Theater (8:00-13:00, in Piazza dei Priori in winter).

Festivals: Volterra's Medieval Festival takes place the third and fourth Sundays of August (Aug 19 and 26 in 2012). Fall is a popular time for food festivals—check with the TI for dates and events planned.

Internet Access: Web & Wine has a few terminals, fine wine by the glass, and organic food (€3/hour, no minimum, summer daily 9:30-1:00 in the morning, off-season closed Thu, Via Porta all'Arco 11-15, tel. 0588-81531, www.webandwine.com, Lallo speaks English). **Enjoy Café Internet Point** has a couple of terminals in their basement (€3/hour, daily 6:30-1:00 in the morning, Piazza dei Martiri 3, tel. 0588-80530).

Local Guide: American **Annie Adair** is an excellent city guide. She and her husband Francesco, a sommelier, organize private food and wine tours and even Tuscan weddings for Americans (€50/hour, minimum 2 hours, tel. 0588-87774, mobile 347-143-5004, www.tuscantour.com, info@tuscantour.com).

Sights in Volterra

▲▲**Guided Volterra Walk**—Annie Adair and her colleagues offer a great one-hour, English-only introductory walking tour of Volterra for €10. The walk touches on Volterra's Etruscan, Roman,

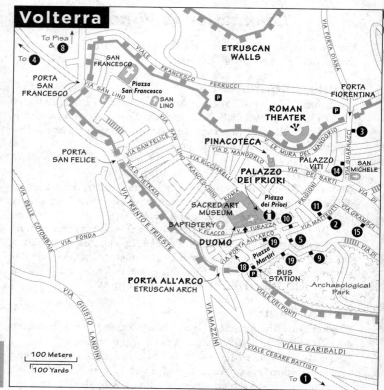

and medieval history, as well as the contemporary cultural scene (April-July and Sept-Oct daily, rain or shine, at 18:00; meet in front of alabaster shop on Piazza Martiri della Libertà, no need to reserve—just show up, they need a minimum of 3 people—or €30—to make the tour go, www.volterrawalkingtour.com or www.tuscantour.com, info@volterrawalkingtour.com). There's no better way to spend €10 and one hour in this city.

▲▲**Self-Guided Historic Town Walk**—You can easily lace the town's top sights and my descriptions together to make your own handy little town walk. Here's the spine of the walk (all described in this order below): Start with the Etruscan Arch, browse up what I call "Artisan Lane," follow my tour of Via Matteotti, side-trip to the main square and Duomo, detour (if you like) to the Pinacoteca and Roman Theater, head over to the Etruscan Museum and Alabaster Workshop, and finish with a drink under all the bras with Bruno and Lucio at La Vena di Vino. The town's other sights are easily grafted onto this route.

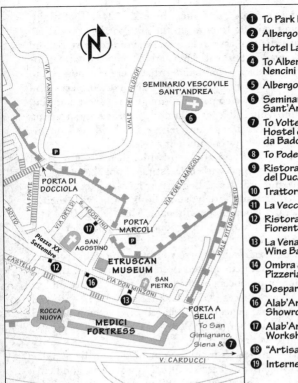

1	To Park Hotel Le Fonti
2	Albergo Etruria
3	Hotel La Locanda
4	To Albergo Villa Nencini
5	Albergo Nazionale
6	Seminario Vescovile Sant'Andrea
7	To Volterra Youth Hostel & Trattoria da Bado
8	To Podere Marcampo
9	Ristorante Enoteca del Duca
10	Trattoria Don Beta
11	La Vecchia Lira
12	Ristorante il Sacco Fiorentino
13	La Vena di Vino Wine Bar
14	Ombra della Sera & Pizzeria Tavernetta
15	Despar Market
16	Alab'Arte Alabaster Showroom
17	Alab'Arte Alabaster Workshop
18	"Artisan Lane"
19	Internet Cafés (2)

HILL TOWNS

▲**"Porta all'Arco" Etruscan Arch**—Volterra's most famous sight is its Etruscan arch, built of massive, volcanic tuff stones

in the fourth century B.C. (for more information on tuff, see the sidebar on page 714). Volterra's original wall was four miles around—twice the size of the wall that encircles it today. With 25,000 people, Volterra was a key Etruscan trade center—one of 12 leading towns that made up the Etruscan *Dodecapolis* (a league of Etruscan cities). The three seriously eroded heads, dating from the first century B.C., show what happens when you leave something outside for 2,000 years. The newer stones are part of the 13th-century city wall, which incorporated parts of the much older Etruscan wall.

A plaque just outside remembers June 30, 1944. That night, Nazi forces were planning to blow up the arch to slow the Allied advance. To save their treasured landmark, Volterrans ripped up the stones that pave Via Porta all'Arco and plugged the gate, managing to convince the Nazi commander that there was no need to blow up the arch. Today, all the stones are back in their places, and like silent heroes, they welcome you through the oldest standing Etruscan gate into Volterra. Locals claim this as the only surviving round arch of the Etruscan age and believe this is where Romans got the idea for using a keystone in their arches.

"Artisan Lane"—Via Porta all'Arco (which leads to and from the Etruscan arch) is lined with interesting shops featuring the work of artisans and producers. Because of its alabaster heritage, Volterra attracted artisans and artists, who brought with them a rich variety of crafts (shops generally open Mon-Sat 10:00-13:00 & 16:00-19:00, closed Sun; the TI produces a free booklet called *Handicraft in Volterra*).

From the Etruscan Arch, browse your way up the hill, checking out these shops and items (listed from bottom to top): La Mia Fattoria—a co-op of producers of cheese, salami, and olive oil lets you buy direct at farm prices (#52); alabaster shops (#57, #50, and #45); book bindery and papery (#26); jewelry (#25); etchings and silk screening (#23); leather (#16); Web & Wine (Internet access; #11-15); and bronze work (#6).

▲**Via Matteotti**—The town's main drag, named after the popular Socialist leader killed by the Fascists in 1924, provides a good cultural scavenger hunt. The street starts 30 yards from Palazzo dei Priori (City Hall and cathedral, described later).

At #1 is a typical Italian bank security door. (Step in and say, "Beam me up, Scotty.") Look up and all around. Find the medieval griffin torch holder—symbol of Volterra—and imagine it holding a lit torch. The pharmacy sports the symbol of its medieval guild. As you head down Via Matteotti, notice how the doors show centuries of refitting work.

At #2, look up and imagine heavy beams cantilevered out, supporting extra wooden rooms and balconies crowding out over the street. Throughout Tuscany, today's stark and stony old building fronts once supported a tangle of wooden extensions. Doors that once led to these extra rooms are now partially bricked up to make windows. Contemplate urban density in the 14th century, before the plague thinned out the population. Be careful: There's a wild boar (a local delicacy) at #10.

At #12, notice the line of doorbells: This typical palace, once the home of a single rich family, is now occupied by many middle-class families. After the social revolution in the 18th century and the rise of the middle class, former palaces were condominium-

Vampire Volterra

Sitting on its stony main square at midnight, watching bats dart about as if they own the place, I realize there really is something supernatural about Volterra. The cliffs of Volterra inspired Dante's "cliffs of hell." In the winter, the town's vibrancy is smothered under a deadening cloak of clouds. The name Volterra means "land that floats"—referring to the clouds that often seem to cut it off from the rest of the world below.

The people of Volterra live in a cloud of mystery, too. Their favorite cookie, crunchy with almonds, is called Ossi di Morta ("bones of the dead"). The town's first disco was named Catacombs. And in the 1970s, when Volterra was the set of a wildly popular TV horror series called *Ritratto di Donna Velata (Portrait of a Veiled Woman)*, all of Italy tuned in to Volterra every week for a good scare.

In recent years, the town has attracted international attention for its connection to the bestselling *Twilight* series of vampire romance novels and movies. Part of the second movie, *New Moon* (2009), is set in Volterra. Even though most of it was actually filmed in Montepulciano, the TI plays a video clip of *New Moon* continuously and is proud of Volterra's Hollywood connection.

As a result, the town is seeing lots of "Twihards," who come not for the Etruscan Museum, but to run across the sun-drenched square at noon and retrace the footsteps of Edward and Bella down dark alleyways. The enthusiasm may be past its peak, but the tourism board clings to the vampire vibe—it's in their blood.

ized. Even so, like in *Dr. Zhivago*, the original family still lives here. Apartment #1 is the home of Count Guidi.

At #16, pop in to an alabaster showroom. Alabaster, mined nearby, has long been a big industry here. Volterra alabaster—softer and more porous than marble—was sliced thin to serve as windows for Italy's medieval churches.

At #19, the recommended La Vecchia Lira is a lively cafeteria. The Bar L'Incontro across the street is a favorite for homemade gelato and pastries.

Across the way, up Vicolo delle Prigioni, is a fun bakery *(panificio)*. They're happy to sell small quantities if you want to try the local *cantuccini* (almond biscotti) or munch a cannoli.

At #51, a bit of Etruscan wall is artfully used to display more alabaster art. And #56A is the alabaster art gallery of Paolo Sabatini.

Locals gather early each evening at Osteria dei Poeti (at #57) for the best cocktails in town—served with free munchies. The cinema is across the street. Movies in Italy are rarely in *versione originale*; Italians are used to getting their movies dubbed into Italian.

At #66, another Tuscan tower marks the end of the street. This noble house has a ground floor with no interior access to the safe upper floors. Rope ladders were used to get upstairs. The tiny door was wide enough to let in your skinny friends...but definitely not anyone wearing armor and carrying big weapons.

Across the street stands the ancient Church of St. Michael. After long years of barbarian chaos, the Lombards moved in from the north and asserted law and order in places like Volterra. That generally included building a Christian church on the old Roman forum to symbolically claim and tame the center of town. The church standing here today is Romanesque, dating from the 12th century. Find the crude little guys under its eaves—they've been making faces at the passing crowds for 800 years.

Palazzo dei Priori—Volterra's City Hall (c. 1209) claims to be the oldest of any Tuscan city-state. It clearly inspired the more famous Palazzo Vecchio in Florence. Town halls like this are emblematic of an era when city-states were powerful. They were architectural exclamation points declaring that, around here, no pope or emperor called the shots. Towns such as Volterra were truly city-states—proudly independent and relatively democratic. They had their own armies, taxes, and even weights and measures. Notice the horizontal "cane" cut into the City Hall wall. For a thousand years, this square hosted a market, and the "cane" was the local yardstick. When not in use for meetings or weddings, the city council chambers—lavishly painted and lit with fun dragon lamps, as they have been for centuries of town meetings—are open to visitors.

Cost and Hours: €1.50, April-Oct daily 10:30-17:30, Nov-March Sat-Sun only 10:00-17:00.

Duomo—A common arrangement in the Middle Ages was for the church to face the baptistery (you couldn't enter the church until you were baptized)...and for the hospital to face the cemetery. All of these overlooked the same square. That's how it is in Pisa, and that's how it is here. This 12th-century church is not as elaborate as its cousin in Pisa, but the simple facade and central nave, flanked by monolithic stone columns, are beautiful examples of the Pisan Romanesque style.

Cost and Hours: Free, daily 8:00-12:30 & 15:00-17:00.

Touring the Church: The chapel to the left of the entry has painted terra-cotta statue groups. The interior was decorated mostly in the late 16th century, during Florentine rule under the Medici family. You'll see a lot of the Medici coat of arms (with the six pills, representing the family's first trade—as doctors, or *medici*). The 12th-century marble pulpit is beautifully carved. All of the apostles are together except Judas, who's under the table with the evil dragon (his name is the only one not carved into the relief).

Just before the pulpit (in the Rosary Chapel, on the left), check out the *Annunciation* by Fra Bartolomeo (who was a student of Fra Angelico and painted this in 1497). Bartolomeo delicately gives worshippers a way to see Mary "conceived by the Holy Spirit." Note the vibrant colors, exaggerated perspective, and Mary's *contrapposto* pose—all attributes of the Renaissance.

To the right of the main altar is a dreamy painted-and-gilded-wood *Deposition* (Jesus being taken down from the cross), restored to its original form. Painted in 1228, a generation before Giotto, it shows emotion and motion way ahead of its time.

The glowing windows in the transept and behind the altar are sheets of alabaster. These, along with the recorded Gregorian chants, add to the church's wonderful ambience.

Sacred Art Museum—This humble four-room museum collects sacred art from deconsecrated churches and small, unguarded churches from nearby villages.

Cost and Hours: €10 combo-ticket includes Etruscan Museum and Pinacoteca, daily 9:00-13:00 & 15:00-18:00, morning only in winter, well-explained in English, next to the Duomo at Via Roma 1, tel. 0588-86290.

Pinacoteca—This museum fills a 14th-century palace with fine paintings that feel more Florentine than Sienese—a reminder of whose domain this town was in. Its highlights are Luca Signorelli's beautifully lit *Annunciation*, an example of classic High Renaissance (from the town cathedral), and (to the right) *Deposition from the Cross*, the groundbreaking Mannerist work by Rosso Fiorentino (note the elongated bodies and harsh emotional lighting and colors). Notice also Ghirlandaio's *Christ in Glory*. The two devout-looking kneeling women are actually pagan, pre-Christian Etruscan demigoddesses, Attinea and Greciniana, but the church identified them as obscure saints to make the painting acceptable.

Cost and Hours: €6, €10 combo-ticket includes Etruscan and Sacred Art museums, daily 9:30-19:00, Nov-mid-March until 13:45, Via dei Sarti 1, tel. 0588-87580.

Palazzo Viti—Go behind the rustic, heavy stone walls of the city and see how the nobility lived (in this case, rich from 19th-century alabaster wealth). One of the finest private residential buildings in Italy, with 12 rooms open to the public, Palazzo Viti feels remarkably lived in because it is. You'll also find Senora Viti herself selling admission tickets. It's no wonder this time warp is so popular with Italian movie directors. Remember, you're helping keep a noble family in leotards.

Cost and Hours: €5 includes a glass of wine, samples of cheese, and olive oil; pick up the loaner English description, April-Oct daily 10:00-13:00 & 14:30-18:30, closed Nov-March, Via dei Sarti 41, tel. 0588-84047, www.palazzoviti.it.

Roman Theater—Built in about 10 B.C., this well-preserved theater is considered to have some of the best acoustics of its kind. Because of the fine aerial view you get from the city wall promenade, you may find it unnecessary to pay admission to enter. Belly up to the 13th-century wall and look down. The wall that you're standing on divided the theater from the town center...so, naturally, the theater became the town dump. Over time, the theater was forgotten—covered in the garbage of Volterra. Luckily, it was rediscovered in the 1950s.

The stage wall was standard Roman design—with three levels from which actors would appear: one level for mortals, one for heroes, and the top one for gods. Parts of two levels still stand. Gods leaped out onto the third level for the last time in the fourth century A.D., when the town decided to abandon the theater and use its stones to build fancy baths instead. You can see the remains of the baths behind the theater, including the round sauna with brick supports that raise the heated floor.

From the vantage point on the city wall promenade, you can trace Volterra's vast Etruscan wall. Find the church in the distance, on the left, and notice the stones just below. They are from the Etruscan wall that followed the ridge into the valley and defined Volterra five centuries before Christ.

Cost and Hours: €3.50, but you can view the theater free from Via Lungo le Mure, April-Oct daily 10:30-17:30, Nov-March Sat-Sun only 10:00-16:00.

▲▲Etruscan Museum (Museo Etrusco Guarnacci)—Filled top to bottom with rare Etruscan artifacts, this museum—even with few English explanations and its dusty, almost neglectful, old-school style—makes it easy to appreciate how advanced this pre-Roman culture was.

Cost and Hours: €8, €10 combo-ticket includes—like it or not—the Pinacoteca and Sacred Art Museum; daily April-Oct 9:00-19:00, Nov-March 9:00-13:45; ask at the ticket window for mildly interesting English pamphlet, €3 audioguide fleshes out your visit well, Via Don Minzoni 15, tel. 0588-86347, www.comune.volterra.pi.it/english.

Touring the Museum: The collection starts with pre-Etruscan Villanovian artifacts (c. 1500 B.C.), but its highlight is a seemingly endless collection of Etruscan funerary urns (designed to contain the ashes of cremated loved ones).

Each urn is tenderly carved with a unique scene, offering a

peek into the still-mysterious Etruscan society. While contemporaries of the Greeks, the Etruscans were more libertine. Their religion was less demanding, and their women were a respected part of both the social and public spheres. Women and men alike are depicted lounging on Etruscan urns. While they seem to be just hanging out, the lounging dead were actually offering the gods a banquet—in order to gain their favor in the transition to the next life. The outcome of the banquet had eternal consequences.

On urns dating from the seventh to the first century B.C., the dearly departed are often depicted holding scrolls, blank wax tablets (symbolizing blank new lives in the next world), and libation cups—offering wine to the gods. Realistic scenes show the fabled horseback-and-carriage ride to the underworld, where the dead are greeted by Caron, with his hammer and pointy ears. While the finer urns are carved of alabaster, most are made of volcanic tuff. Most lids are mismatched—casualties of reckless 18th- and 19th-century archaeological digs. Look at the faces, and imagine the lives they lived and the loved ones they left behind.

On the top floor is a re-created grave site, with several urns and artifacts that would have been buried with the deceased. Some of these were funeral dowry (called *corredo*) that the dead would pack along. You'll see artifacts such as mirrors, coins, hardware for vases, votive statues, pots, pans, and jewelry.

Fans of Alberto Giacometti will be amazed at how the tall, skinny figure called *The Shadow of Night (L'Ombra della Sera)* looks just like the modern Swiss sculptor's work—but is 2,500 years older.

Nearby: After your visit, duck across the street to the alabaster showroom and the wine bar (both described next).

▲**Alabaster Workshop**—Alab'Arte offers a fun peek into the art of alabaster. Their showroom is across from the Etruscan Museum. A block downhill, in front of Porta Marcoli, is their powdery work-

shop, where you can watch Roberto Chiti and Giorgio Finazzo at work. They are delighted to share their art with visitors. Lighting shows off the translucent quality of the stone and the expertise of these artists. For more artisans in action,

Under the Etruscan Sun

Around 550 B.C.—just before the Golden Age of Greece—the Etruscan people of central Italy had their own Golden Age. Though their origins are mysterious, their mix of Greek-style art with Roman-style customs helped lay a civilized foundation for the rise of the Roman empire. As you travel through Italy—particularly in Tuscany (from "Etruscan"), Umbria, and North Latium—you'll find traces of the long-lost Etruscans.

The Etruscans first appeared in the ninth century B.C., when a number of cities sprouted up in sparsely populated Tuscany and Umbria. Possibly immigrants from Turkey, but more likely local farmers who moved to the city, they became traders and craftsmen, and welcomed new ideas from Greece.

More technologically advanced than their neighbors, the Etruscans mined metal, exporting it around the Mediterranean, both as crude ingots and as some of the finest-crafted jewelry in the known world. They drained and irrigated large tracts of land, creating the fertile farmland of central Italy's breadbasket. With their disciplined army, warships, merchant vessels, and (from the Greek perspective) pirate galleys, they ruled central Italy and the major ports along the Tyrrhenian Sea. For nearly two centuries (c. 700-500 B.C.), much of Italy lived a Golden Age of peace and prosperity under the Etruscan sun.

Judging from the frescoes and many luxury items that have survived, the Etruscans enjoyed the good life: They look healthy, vibrant, and well-dressed (including the slaves), as they play flutes, dance with birds, or play party games. Etruscan artists celebrated individual people, showing their wrinkles, crooked noses, silly smiles, and funny haircuts.

Thousands of surviving ceramic plates and cups attest to the importance of food. Men and women ate together, propped on their elbows on dining couches, surrounded by colorful decor. The banqueters were entertained with music and dancing, and served by elegant and well-treated slaves.

Scholars today have deciphered the Etruscans' Greek-style alphabet and some individual words, but they have yet to fully crack the code. Much of what we know of the Etruscans comes from their tombs. The tomb was a home in the hereafter, complete with all of the deceased's belongings. The sarcophagus might have a statue on the lid of the deceased at a banquet—lying across a dining couch, spooning with his wife, smiles on their faces, living the good life for all eternity.

Seven decades of wars with the Greeks (545-474 B.C.) disrupted their trade routes and drained the Etruscan League, just as a new Mediterranean power was emerging: Rome. In 509 B.C., the Romans overthrew their Etruscan king, and Rome expanded, capturing Etruscan cities one by one (the last in 264 B.C.). Etruscan resisters were killed, the survivors intermarried with Romans, and their kids grew up speaking Latin. By Julius Caesar's time, the only remnants of Etruscan culture were its priests, who became

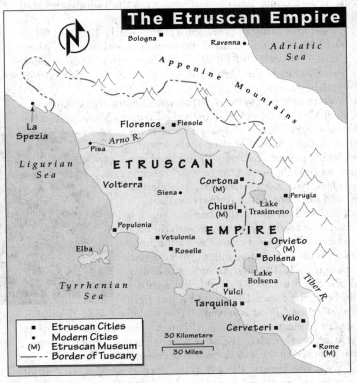

The Etruscan Empire

Rome's professional soothsayers. Interestingly, the Etruscan prophets had foreseen their own demise, having predicted that Etruscan civilization would last 10 centuries.

But Etruscan culture lived on in Roman religion (pantheon of gods, household gods, and divination rituals), art (realism), lifestyle (the banquet), and in a taste for Greek styles—the mix that became our "Western civilization."

Etruscan Sights in Italy

Here are some of the more important and more accessible Etruscan sights (all are mentioned in this book):

Rome: Traces of original Etruscan engineering projects (e.g., Circus Maximus), Vatican Museum artifacts, and Villa Giulia Museum, with the famous "husband and wife sarcophagus."

Orvieto: Archaeological Museum (coins, dinnerware, and a sarcophagus), necropolis, and underground tunnels and caves.

Volterra: Etruscan gate (Porta dell'Arco, from fourth century B.C.) and Etruscan Museum (funerary urns).

Chiusi: Museum, tombs, and tunnels.

Cortona: Museum and dome-shaped tombs.

visit "Artisan Lane," described earlier, or ask the TI for their list of the town's many workshops open to the public.

Cost and Hours: Free, showroom—daily 10:30-13:00 & 15:30-19:00, Via Don Minzoni 18; workshop—March-Oct Mon-Sat 9:30-13:00 & 15:00-19:00, closed Sun, usually closed Nov-Feb—call ahead, Via Orti Sant'Agostino 28; tel. 0588-87968, www.alabarte.com.

▲**La Vena di Vino (Wine-Tasting with Bruno and Lucio)**—La Vena di Vino, also just across from the Etruscan Museum, is a fun *enoteca* where two guys who have devoted them-

selves to the wonders of wine share it with a fun-loving passion. Each day Bruno and Lucio open six or eight bottles, serve your choice by the glass, pair it with characteristic munchies, and offer fine music (guitars available for patrons) and an unusual decor (the place is strewn with bras). Hang out here with the local characters. This is your chance to try the Super Tuscan wine—a creative mix of international grapes grown in Tuscany. According to Bruno, "While the Brunello (€7/glass) is just right for wild boar, the Super Tuscan (€6) is just right for meditation." Food is served all day, including some hot dishes or a plate of meats and cheeses. Although Volterra is famously quiet late at night, this place is full of action. There's a vintage dentist chair attached to the karaoke machine downstairs.

Cost and Hours: Pay per glass, open Wed-Mon 11:30-1:00 in the morning, closed Tue, 3- and 5-glass wine tastings, shipping options available, Via Don Minzoni 30, tel. 0588-81491, www.lavenadivino.com.

Medici Fortress and Archaeological Park—The Parco Archeologico marks what was the acropolis of Volterra from 1500 B.C. until A.D. 1472, when Florence conquered the pesky city and burned its political and historic center, turning it into a grassy commons and building the adjacent Medici Fortezza. The old fortress—a symbol of Florentine dominance—now keeps people in rather than out. It's a maximum-security prison housing only about 60 special prisoners. (When you're driving from San Gimignano to Volterra, you pass another big, modern prison—almost surreal in the midst of all the Tuscan wonder.) Authorities prefer to keep organized crime figures locked up far away from their family ties in Sicily. To the right of the meadows and playground is an archaeological dig, which costs €3 to enter, but can be viewed through a fence for free.

Cost and Hours: Park—free to enter, closes at 20:00 in summer, 17:00 in winter.

HILL TOWNS

Sleeping in Volterra

(€1 = about $1.40, country code: 39)

$$$ Park Hotel Le Fonti, a 10-minute walk downhill from Porta all'Arco, is a spacious, imposing building with 67 rooms, many with views. While overpriced at peak times, the hotel can be a good value if you manage to snag a deal. In addition to the swimming pool, guests can use a small spa with sauna, hot tub, and an intriguing "emotional shower" (Db-€89-165 but prices vary wildly depending on season, elevator, on-site restaurant, wine bar, free parking, Via di Fontecorrenti 5, tel. 0588-85219, fax 0588-92728, www.parkhotellefonti.com, info@parkhotellefonti.com).

$$$ Hotel La Locanda is well-located and rents 18 decent rooms (Db-€93-125, air-con, Wi-Fi, Via Guarnacci 24/28, tel. 0588-81547, www.hotel-lalocanda.com, staff@hotel-lalocanda .com, Jenny, Stefania, and Irina).

$$ Albergo Etruria, on Volterra's main drag, rents 21 fresh, modern, and spacious rooms within an ancient stone structure. They have a welcoming TV lounge and a peaceful garden out back (Sb-€75, Db-€95, Tb-€115, 10 percent discount with cash and this book when you book direct, fans, Wi-Fi, Via Matteotti 32, tel. 0588-87377, fax 0588-92784, www.albergoetruria.it, info @albergoetruria.it, Lisa and Giuseppina are fine hosts).

$$ Albergo Villa Nencini, just outside of town, is big, modern, and professional, with 36 fine rooms. A few rooms have terraces and many have views. Guests also enjoy the large pool and free parking (Sb-€67, Db-€88, Tb-€115, 10 percent discount with cash and this book, Borgo Santo Stefano 55, a 15-minute uphill walk to main square, tel. 0588-86386, fax 0588-80601, www .villanencini.it, info@villanencini.it, Nencini family).

$$ Albergo Nazionale, with 38 big rooms, is simple, a little musty, short on smiles, popular with school groups, and steps from the bus stop (Sb-€60-70, Db-€80-90, Tb-€105, 10 percent discount with cash and this book if you book direct, reception closes at midnight, Via dei Marchesi 11, tel. 0588-86284, fax 0588-84097, www.hotelnazionale-volterra.it, info@hotelnazionale-volterra.it).

$ Seminario Vescovile Sant'Andrea has been training priests for more than 500 years. Today, the remaining eight priests still train students, but when classes are over, their 16 rooms—separated by vast and holy halls in an echoing old mansion—are rented very cheaply. Look for the 15th-century Ascension ceramic by Andrea della Robbia, tucked away in a corner upstairs (S-€17, Sb-€22, D-€30, Db-€38, T-€44, Tb-€56, breakfast-€3, elevator, closes at 24:00, groups welcome, free parking, easy 7-minute walk from Etruscan Museum, Viale Vittorio Veneto 2, tel. 0588-86028, semvescovile@diocesivolterra.it; Alberto, Angela, and Sergio).

$ Volterra Youth Hostel fills a wing of the restored Convent of San Girolamo with 85 beds. It's spacious and has lots of services, but it's a 15-minute hike out of town, in a boring area, and no cheaper than the more memorable seminary option closer to town (bed in 6-bed dorm-€17, Db-€60, breakfast-€3, lockers, tel. 0588-86613, www.ostellovolterra.it, info@ostellovolterra.it).

Near Volterra

$$ Podere Marcampo is a newer *agriturismo* about four miles outside Volterra on the road to Pisa. Run by Genuino (owner of the recommended Ristorante Enoteca del Duca) and his wife, this peaceful spot has three well-appointed rooms and three apartments, plus a swimming pool with panoramic views. Genuino produces his award-winning Merlot on site and offers €15 wine-tastings with cheese and homemade salami. Cooking classes are also available (Db-€94, apartment-€125-160, includes breakfast, air-con, Wi-Fi, free parking, tel. 0588-85393, mobile 348-514-9782, www.agriturismo-marcampo.com, info@agriturismo-marcampo.com).

Eating in Volterra

Menus feature a Volterran take on regional dishes. *Zuppa alla Volterrana* is a fresh vegetable-and-bread soup, similar to *ribollita* (except that it isn't made from leftovers). *Torta di ceci*, also known as *cecina*, is a savory-pancake-like dish made with garbanzo beans. Those with more adventurous palates dive into *trippa* (tripe; comes in a bowl like stew), the traditional breakfast of the alabaster carvers.

Ristorante Enoteca del Duca, with a locally respected chef named Genuino, serves well-presented and creative Tuscan cuisine. You can dine under a medieval arch with walls lined with wine bottles, in a stark dining room (with an Etruscan statuette at each table), or on a nice little patio out back. It's a good place for truffles, and has a fine wine list (which includes Genuino's own merlot) and friendly staff. The spacious seating, dressy clientele, and calm atmosphere make this a good choice for a romantic meal (€42 food-sampler fixed-price meal, €10 pastas, €17 *secondi*, Wed-Mon 12:30-15:00 & 19:30-22:00, closed Tue, near City Hall at Via di Castello 2, tel. 0588-81510).

Trattoria da Bado, a 10-minute hike out of town, is every local's favorite for its *tipica cucina Volterrana*. Giacomo and family offer a rustic atmosphere and serve food with no pretense—"the way you wish your mamma cooks" (meals from 12:30 and 19:30, closed Wed, Borgo San Lazzero 9, tel. 0588-86477, reserve before you go as it's often full).

Don Beta is a family-run trattoria on the main drag, popular with travelers for its stylish home cooking. Mirko supervises the lively young team as they whisk out steaming plates of seafood pasta and homemade desserts (€7 pastas, €15 *secondi*, daily 12:00-14:30 & 18:45-22:00, reservations smart, Via Matteotti 39, tel. 0588-86730; Paolo, Azzura, and Mamica).

La Vecchia Lira, bright and cheery, is a classy self-serve eatery that's a hit with locals as a quick and cheap lunch spot by day, and a fancier restaurant at night (Fri-Wed 12:00-14:30 & 19:00-22:30, closed Thu, Via Matteotti 19, tel. 0588-86180, Lamberto and Massimo).

Ristorante il Sacco Fiorentino is a local favorite for traditional cuisine and seasonal seafood specials (€8 pastas, €15 *secondi*, Thu-Tue 12:00-15:00 & 19:00-22:00, closed Wed, Piazza XX Settembre 18, tel. 0588-88537).

La Vena di Vino is an *enoteca* serving up simple and traditional dishes and the best of Tuscan wine in a fun atmosphere (closed Tue, Via Don Minzoni 30, tel. 0588-81491). For more details, read the description on page 658.

Pizzerias: **Ombra della Sera** dishes out what local kids consider the best pizza in town. At €6 a pop, their pizzas make for a cheap date (Tue-Sun 12:00-15:00 & 19:00-22:00, closed Mon, Via Guarnacci 16, tel. 0588-85274). **Pizzeria Tavernetta**, next door, is more romantic, with delightful indoor and on-the-street seating. Its upstairs has a romantically frescoed dining room. Marco, who

looks like Billy Joel, serves €7 pizzas (closed Wed, Via Guarnacci 14, tel. 0588-87630).

Picnic: You can assemble a picnic at the few *alimentari* around town (try Despar Market at Via Gramsci 12, Thu-Tue 7:30-13:00 & 17:00-20:00, Wed only 7:30-13:00) and eat in the breezy Archaeological Park.

Volterra Connections

The nearest train station is in **Saline di Volterra,** a 15-minute bus ride away (7/day, 4/day Sun). In Volterra, buses come and go from Piazza Martiri della Libertà (buy tickets at any tobacco shop).

From Volterra by Bus to: Florence (4/day, 1/day Sun, 2 hours, change in Colle Val d'Elsa), **Siena** (4/day, none on Sun, 2 hours, change in Colle Val d'Elsa), **San Gimignano** (4/day, 1/day Sun, 2 hours, change in Colle Val d'Elsa), **Pisa** (9/day, 2 hours, change in Pontedera). For Siena, Florence, and San Gimignano, C.P.T. bus tickets get you only as far as Colle Val d'Elsa (4/day, 50 minutes, €2.75); you must then buy another ticket (from another bus company) at the newsstand near the bus stop.

Montalcino

On a hill overlooking vineyards and valleys, Montalcino—famous for its delicious and pricey Brunello di Montalcino red wines—is a must for wine-lovers. Everyone touring this area seems to be relaxed and in an easy groove...as if enjoying a little wine buzz.

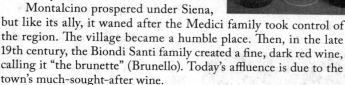

In the Middle Ages, Montalcino (mohn-tahl-CHEE-noh) was considered Siena's biggest ally. Originally aligned with Florence, the town switched sides after the Sienese beat up Florence in the Battle of Montaperti in 1260. The Sienese persuaded the Montalcini to join their side by forcing them to sleep one night in the bloody Florentine-strewn battlefield.

Montalcino prospered under Siena, but like its ally, it waned after the Medici family took control of the region. The village became a humble place. Then, in the late 19th century, the Biondi Santi family created a fine, dark red wine, calling it "the brunette" (Brunello). Today's affluence is due to the town's much-sought-after wine.

Non-wine-lovers may find Montalcino a bit too focused on *vino*, but one sip of Brunello makes even wine skeptics believe that Bacchus was onto something. Note that Rosso di Montalcino (a younger version of Brunello) is also very good, at half the price. Those with a sweet tooth will enjoy crunching the Ossi di Morta ("bones of the dead") cookies popular in Tuscany.

Orientation to Montalcino

Sitting atop a hill amidst a sea of vineyards, Montalcino is surrounded by walls and dominated by the Fortezza (a.k.a. "La Rocca"). From here, roads lead down into the two main squares: Piazza Garibaldi and Piazza del Popolo.

Tourist Information: The TI, just off Piazza Garibaldi in City Hall, can find you a room for no fee. They have information on taxi service to nearby towns, abbeys, and monasteries (daily 10:00-13:00 & 14:00-17:30, tel. & fax 0577-849-331, www.proloco montalcino.it).

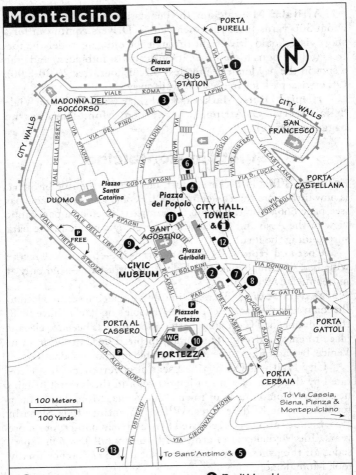

Montalcino

1 Hotel Dei Capitani

2 Palazzina Cesira B&B

3 Albergo Giardino

4 Affittacamere Mariuccia

5 To La Crociona Agriturismo

6 Taverna il Grappolo Blu

7 Ristorante-Pizzeria San Giorgio

8 Re di Macchia

9 Co-op Supermarket

10 Enoteca la Fortezza di Montalcino

11 Caffè Fiaschetteria Italiana

12 Enoteca di Piazza

13 To Banfi & Argiano Wineries

Arrival in Montalcino: The bus station is on Piazza Cavour, about 300 yards from the town center. Drivers coming in for a short visit should drive right through the old gate under the fortress (follow signs to *Fortezza;* it looks almost forbidden) and grab a spot in the pay lot at the fortress (€1.50/hour, free 20:00-8:00). Otherwise, park for free a short walk away.

Helpful Hints: Market day is Friday (7:00-13:00) on Viale della Libertà. Day-trippers be warned: Montalcino has **no baggage storage.**

Sights in Montalcino

Fortezza—This 14th-century fort, built under the rule of Siena, is now little more than an empty shell. People visit for its wine bar (see page 666). You can climb the ramparts to enjoy a panoramic view of the Asso and Orcia valleys, or enjoy a picnic in the park surrounding the fort.

Cost and Hours: €4 for rampart walk—buy ticket in the wine bar, €6 combo-ticket includes Civic Museum—sold only at museum, daily 9:00-20:00.

Piazza del Popolo—All roads in tiny Montalcino seem to lead to the main square, Piazza del Popolo ("People's Square"). Since 1888, the recommended Caffè Fiaschetteria Italiana has been *the* elegant place to enjoy a drink. Its founder, inspired by Caffè Florian in Venice, brought fine coffee to this humble town of woodcutters.

City Hall was the fortified seat of government. It's decorated by the coats of arms of judges who, in the interest of fairness, were from outside of town. Like Siena, Montalcino was a republic in the Middle Ages. When Florentines took Siena in 1555, Siena's ruling class retreated here and held out for four more years. The Medici coat of arms (with the six pills), which supersedes all the others, is a reminder that in 1559 Florence finally took Montalcino.

The one-handed clock was the norm until 200 years ago. For five centuries the arcaded loggia hosted the town market. And, of course, it's fun to simply observe the *passeggiata*—these days mostly a parade of tourists here for the wine.

Civic Museum (Museo Civico)—Gothic sacred art is the star of this museum, with works from Montalcino's heyday, the 13th to 16th centuries. Most of the art was created by local artists. Among the museum's highlights are a glazed terra-cotta altarpiece and statue of St. Sebastian by Andrea della Robbia. The ground floor is best, with an impressive collection of crucifixes. A recently opened archaeological section displays interesting artifacts from the area dating back as far as—gulp—200,000 B.C.

Cost and Hours: €4.50, €6 combo-ticket includes rampart

walk at Fortezza, Tue-Sun 10:00-13:00 & 14:00-17:50, closed Mon, Via Ricasoli 31, to the right of Sant'Agostino Church, tel. 0577-846-014.

Sleeping in Montalcino

(€1 = about $1.40, country code: 39)

$$$ Hotel Dei Capitani, at the end of town near the bus station, is well-run and rents 29 rooms. It has plush public spaces, an inviting pool, and a cliffside terrace offering plenty of reasons for lounging (Db-€138 with this book in 2012, extra bed-€40, air-con, half the rooms come with vast Tuscan views for the same price—request a view room when you reserve, Wi-Fi in lounge, free parking, Via Lapini 6, tel. 0577-847-227, www.deicapitani.it, info@deicapitani.it).

$$ Palazzina Cesira, right in the heart of the old town, rents five spacious and tastefully decorated rooms in a fine 13th-century residence with a palatial lounge. You'll enjoy a refined and tranquil ambience, a nice breakfast, and the chance to get to know Lucilla and her American husband Roberto (Db-€95, suites-€115, cash only, 2-night minimum, 3-night minimum on holiday weekends, air-con, Wi-Fi, Via Soccorso Saloni 2, tel. & fax 0577-846-055, www.montalcinoitaly.com, p.cesira@tin.it).

$ Albergo Giardino, old and basic, has nine big simple rooms, no public spaces, and a fine locale (Db-€55-60, 10 percent discount with this book outside May and Sept, no breakfast, Piazza Cavour 4, tel. & fax 0577-848-257, mobile 338-684-3163, albergoilgiardino@virgilio.it, Roberto and his dad, Mario).

$ Affittacamere Mariuccia has three basic, Ikea-chic rooms on the main drag over a heaven-scented bakery (Db-€50, no breakfast, check-in across the street at Enoteca Pierangioli before 20:00 or let them know arrival time, Piazza del Popolo 16, rooms at #28, tel. 0577-849-113, mobile 348-392-4780, www.affittacamere mariuccia.it, enotecapierangioli@hotmail.com, Alessandro speaks English).

Near Montalcino

$$ La Crociona, an *agriturismo* farm and working vineyard, rents seven fully equipped apartments. Fiorella Vannoni and Roberto and Barbara Nannetti offer cooking classes and tastes of the Brunello wine grown and bottled on the premises (Db-€95, or €65 in Oct-mid-May; Qb-€130, or €95 in Oct-mid-May; lower weekly rates, metered gas heating, laundry-€8/load, pool, La Croce 15, tel. 0577-847-133, fax 0577-846-994, www.lacrociona .com, crociona@tin.it). The farm is two miles south of Montalcino on the road to the Sant'Antimo Monastery (look for big yellow

HILL TOWNS

Piombaia La Crociona sign on left, then follow directions to Tenuta Crocedimezzo e Crociona). A good restaurant is next door.

Eating in Montalcino

Taverna il Grappolo Blu is unpretentious, friendly, and serious about its wine, serving local specialties and vegetarian options to an enthusiastic crowd (€8.50 pastas, €12.50 *secondi*, daily 12:00-15:00 & 19:00-22:00, reservations smart, near the main square, a few steps off Via Mazzini at Scale di Via Moglio 1, tel. 0577-847-150).

Ristorante-Pizzeria San Giorgio is a homely trattoria/pizzeria with kitschy decor and great prices (€4.50-7 pizza served evenings only, daily 12:00-15:00 & 19:00-22:30, near recommended hotel Palazzina Cesira at Via Soccorso Saloni 10-14, tel. 0577-848-507, Mara).

Re di Macchia is an invitingly intimate restaurant where Antonio serves up the Tuscan fare Roberta cooks. Look for their seasonal menu and Montalcino-only wine list. Try the €26 fixed-price meal, and for €16 more, have it paired with local wines carefully selected to accompany each dish (€9 pastas, €16 *secondi*, Fri-Wed 12:00-14:00 & 19:00-21:00, closed Thu, reservations strongly recommended, Via Soccorso Saloni 21, tel. 0577-846-116).

Picnic: Gather ingredients at the **Co-op supermarket** on Via Sant'Agostino (just off Via Ricasoli in front of Sant'Agostino Church, closed Sun), then enjoy your feast up at the Madonna del Soccorso Church, with vast territorial views.

Wine Tasting and Wineries

Enoteca la Fortezza di Montalcino offers a chance to taste top-end wines by the glass, each with an English explanation. While wine snobs turn up their noses, the medieval setting inside Montalcino's fort is a hit for most visitors. Spoil yourself with Brunello in the cozy *enoteca* or at an outdoor table (€13 for 3 tastings; €5-9 sampler plates of cheeses, *salumi*, honeys, and olive oil; daily 9:00-20:00, closes at 18:00 in off-season, inside the Fortezza, tel. 0577-849-211, www.enotecalafortezza.it).

Caffè Fiaschetteria Italiana was founded by Ferruccio Biondi Santi, who created the famous Brunello wine. The wine library in the back of the café boasts many local choices. A meeting place since 1888, this grand café also serves light lunches and espresso to tourists and locals alike (€6-15 for a glass of Brunello and a plate of snacks; same prices inside, outside, or in back room; Fri-Wed 7:30-23:00, closed Thu, Piazza del Popolo 6, tel. 0577-849-043). And if it's coffee you need, this place—with its classic 1961 espresso machine—is considered the best in town.

Enoteca di Piazza is one of a chain of wine shops with a system of mechanical dispensers. You get a card that keeps track of the samples you take, and you'll pay from €1 to €9 for each 50-mililiter taste of the 100 different wines kept fresh in the fancy machines. The only nibbles are saltine-type crackers. They hope you'll buy a bottle of the samples you like, and are happy to educate you in English. (Rule of thumb: A bottle costs about 10 times the cost of the sample. If you buy a bottle, the sample of that wine is free.) While the place feels a little formulaic and sterile, it can be fun—and the wine is great (daily 9:00-20:00, near Piazza del Popolo at Via Matteotti 43, tel. 0577-848-104, www.enotecadipiazza.com).

Wineries: While Montalcino has plenty of *enoteche,* there are no real wineries inside the city. The nearby countryside, however, is littered with them, and some offer tastings. A few require an appointment, but many are happy to serve a glass to potential buyers and show them around. **Banfi** is run by the Italian-American Mariani brothers. Huge and touristy, it produces well-respected wines (daily 10:00-18:00, tours daily at 16:00, reserve in advance, 10-minute drive south of Montalcino in Sant'Angelo Scalo, tel. 0577-877-500, www.castellobanfi.com, reservations@banfi.it). **Argiano** claims to be the oldest working winery in the region, dating back to 1580. Not far from Banfi at Sant'Angelo in Colle, their one-hour tour in English includes the vineyards, the exterior of a historic villa, and ancient moldy cellars full of wine casks. They also rent on-site apartments—handy for those who have oversampled (€20 tour includes six wine samples, reserve in advance, tel. 0577-844-037, www.argiano.net, argiano@argiano.net, coming by car the last two miles are along a rough-but-drivable track through vineyards). The Montalcino TI can give you a list of more than 150 regional wineries. Or check with the vintners' consortium (tel. 0577-848-246, www.consorziobrunellodimontalcino.it, info @consorziobrunellodimontalcino.it).

Montalcino Connections

The nearest train station is a 30-minute bus ride (running nearly hourly) away in Buonconvento. Montalcino's bus station is on Piazza Cavour, within the town walls. Bus tickets are sold at the bar on Piazza Cavour or at tobacco shops, but not on board. Check schedules at the TI, at the bus station, or at www.sienamobilita.it.

From Montalcino by Bus to: Siena (6/day, 1.5 hours, €3.50), **Pienza** (5/day, none on Sun, change to line #114 in Torrenieri, 1 hour plus changing time), **Sant'Antimo** (3/day, none on Sun, 15 minutes, €1.50, buy tickets on board). Anyone going to Florence changes in Siena—the most convenient route is by bus to Buonconvento, then by train to Florence.

Pienza

Set on a crest and surrounded by green, rolling hills, the small town of Pienza packs a lot of Renaissance punch. In the 1400s, locally born Pope Pius II of the Piccolomini family decided to remodel his birthplace in the style that was all the rage: Renaissance. Propelled by papal clout, the town of Corsignano was transformed—in only five years' time—into a jewel of Renaissance architecture. It was

renamed Pienza, after Pope Pius. The plan was to remodel the entire town, but work ended in 1464 when both the pope and his architect, Bernardo Rossellino, died. Their vision—what you see today—was completed a century later. The architectural focal point is the square, Piazza Pio II, surrounded by the Duomo and the pope's family residence, Palazzo Piccolomini. While Piazza Pio II is Pienza's pride and joy, the entire town—a mix of old stonework, potted plants, and grand views—is fun to explore, especially with a camera or sketchpad in hand. You can walk every lane in the tiny town in a few minutes.

Cute as the town is, it also feels a bit greedy, and is entirely given over to snaring the tourist dollar. Because of that, I'd recommend popping in to enjoy the setting, and perhaps touring the palace, but not lingering overnight.

Nearly every shop sells the town's specialty: Pecorino cheese. This pungent sheep's cheese is available fresh *(fresco)* or aged *(secco)*, and sometimes contains other ingredients, such as truffles or peppers. Look on menus for warm Pecorino *(al forno* or *alla griglia)*, often topped with honey or pears and served with bread. Along with a glass of local wine, this just might lead you to a new understanding of *la dolce vita*.

Orientation to Pienza

Tourist Information: The TI is 10 yards up the street from Piazza Pio II, inside the Diocesan Museum (daily 10:00-13:00 & 15:00-18:00, shorter hours Nov-March, tel. 0578-749-905). Ignore the kiosk just outside the gate, labeled *Informaturista*, which is a private travel agency.

Arrival in Pienza: Free street parking is available—if you can find it. Otherwise you can park at the large lot near Largo Roma outside of the old town (€1.50/hour, often completely full in the morning).

Helpful Hints: Market day is Friday morning. A public **WC**, marked *gabinetto,* is on the right just outside the town gate on Piazza Dante Alighieri.

Sights in Pienza

▲Piazza Pio II—One of Italy's classic piazzas, this square is famous for its elegance and artistic unity. The square and the surrounding buildings were all designed by Rossellino to form an "outdoor room." Spinning around clockwise, you'll see City Hall (13th-century bell tower with a Renaissance facade and a fine loggia), the Bishop's Palace (now an art museum), the Duomo, and the Piccolomini family palace. Just to the left of the church, a lane leads to the best viewpoint in town.

Duomo—Its classic, symmetrical Renaissance facade—dated 1462 with the Piccolomini family coat of arms immodestly front and center—dominates Piazza Pio II. The interior is charming, with several Gothic altarpieces and painted arches. Windows feature the crest of Pius II, with five half-moons advertising the number of crusades that his family funded. The interior art is Sienese Gothic, on the cusp of the Renaissance. As the local clay and *tufo* stone were not ideal building material for the foundation, the church is slouching. See the cracks in the apse walls, and get seasick behind the main altar.

Cost and Hours: Free, generally open daily 7:00-13:00 & 14:30-19:00.

▲▲Palazzo Piccolomini—The home of Pius II (see page 575) and the Piccolomini family (until 1962) can be visited with a guided tour. While the 30-minute tour (in English and Italian) visits only six rooms and the loggia, it offers a fascinating slice of 15th-century aristocratic life and is the sightseeing highlight of the town. In fact, it's the most impressive small-town palace experience I've found in Tuscany. You can check out the well-preserved, painted courtyard for free. In Renaissance times, most buildings were covered with elaborate paintings like these.

Cost and Hours: €7, Tue-Sun 10:00-13:00 & 14:00-18:30, closed Mon, tel. 0578-748-392, www.palazzopiccolominipienza.it.

Diocesan Museum (Museo Diocesano)—This collection of religious paintings from local churches fills the cardinal's Renaissance palace. The art is provincial Sienese, displayed—in chronological order from the 12th through 17th centuries—conveniently, all on one floor.

Cost and Hours: €4; mid-March-Dec Wed-Mon 10:00-13:00 & 15:00-18:00, closed Tue; Jan-mid-March Sat-Sun only 10:00-13:00 & 15:00-18:00; Corso il Rossellino 30.

View Terrace—As you face the church, the upper lane leading left brings you to the panoramic promenade. Views from the terrace include the Tuscan countryside and Monte Amiata, the largest mountain in southern Tuscany, in the distance.

Pienza Connections

Bus tickets are sold at the *edicola/libreria* just outside Pienza's town gate and at some tobacco shops (or pay a little extra and buy tickets from the driver). Montepulciano is the nearest transportation hub to other points.

From Pienza by Bus to: Siena (5/day, none on Sun, 1.5 hours), **Montepulciano** (8/day, 30 minutes).

Montepulciano

Curving its way along a ridge, Montepulciano (mohn-teh-pull-chee-AH-noh) delights visitors with *vino* and views. Alternately under Sienese and Florentine rule, the city still retains its medieval *contrade* (districts), each with a mascot and flag. The neighborhoods compete the last Sunday of August in the Bravio delle Botti, where teams of men push large wine casks uphill from Piazza Marzocco to Piazza Grande, all  hoping to win a banner and bragging rights. The entire last week of August is a festival: Each *contrada* arranges musical entertainment and prepares food at outdoor eateries that offer generous tastings of the local *vino*.

The city is a collage of architectural styles, but the elegant San Biagio Church, at the base of the hill, is its most impressive Renaissance building. Most visitors ignore the architecture and focus more on the city's other creative accomplishment, the tasty Vino Nobile di Montepulciano red wine.

HILL TOWNS

Orientation to Montepulciano

The commercial action in Montepulciano centers in the lower town, mostly along Via di Gracciano nel Corso (nicknamed "Corso"). Strolling here, you'll find cheap eateries, gift shops, and tourist traps. The back streets are worth exploring. The main square at the top of town is Piazza Grande. Standing proudly above all the touristy sales energy, it has a noble, Florentine feel.

Tourist Information: The TI is near the bus station, in Piazza Don Minzoni. It books hotels and rooms for no fee, sells train tickets, has an Internet terminal (€3.50/hour), and can book one of the town's two taxis (Mon-Sat 9:30-12:30 & 15:00-18:00, Sun 9:30-12:30, daily until 19:00 in summer except until 20:00 in Aug, tel. 0578-757-341, www.prolocomontepulciano.it).

Note that there's a more central office that looks like a TI, but is actually a privately run "Strada del Vino" (Wine Road) agency. They don't have city info, but they do provide wine-road maps, and organize **wine tours** in the city and minibus winery tours farther afield. They also offer other tours (olive oil, cheese, and slow food), cooking classes, and more, depending on season and demand (Mon-Fri 10:00-13:00 & 15:00-18:00, Sat 10:00-13:00, closed Sun, closed Sat off-season, Piazza Grande 7, tel. 0578-717-484, www .stradavinonobile.it).

Arrival in Montepulciano: Most visits begin at the fortified Porta al Prato gate, near the bus station. From the gate, it's a 15-minute walk uphill along the Corso, the bustling main drag (note the Etruscan reliefs on the foundation of Palazzo Bucelli—see photo on previous page) to the main square, Piazza Grande. If you arrive at the bus station, an orange shuttle bus can take you to Piazza Grande (2/hour); it's a good strategy to take the bus up and walk back down.

Drivers arriving by car should park outside the walls (don't try to tackle the tiny roads inside the city), either at the bus station or the numerous lots on the edge of town. For a free spot near the top of the hill, follow signs for lots #7 and #8. If you're sleeping in town, your hotelier will give you a permit to park within the walls.

Helpful Hints: Market day is Thursday. There's no official **baggage storage** in town, but the TI might let you leave bags with them if they have space. Public **WCs** are located at the TI, to the right of Palazzo Comunale, and at the Sant'Agostino Church. A self-service **laundry** is at Via del Paolino 2 (€4 wash, €4 dry, daily 8:00-22:00, tel. 0578-717-544). For a **taxi**, call 335-617-7126.

Sights in Montepulciano

Piazza Grande—This pleasant, lively piazza is surrounded by a grab bag of architectural sights. If the medieval Palazzo Comunale reminds you of Palazzo Vecchio in Florence, it's because Florence dominated this town in the 15th and 16th centuries. The crenellations along the roof were never intended to hide soldiers—they're just meant to symbolize power. A cistern system fed by rainwater draining from the roofs of surrounding palaces supplied the courtyard's fine well. Check out its

19th-century pulleys, the grills to keep animals from contaminating the water supply, and the Medici coat of arms (with lions symbolizing the political power of Florence).

Climbing the **tower** rewards you with a windy but commanding view from the terrace below the clock. Go into the Palazzo Comunale, head up the stairs to your left, and pay on the second floor (€3, daily 10:00-18:00, closed in winter). The Palazzo de' Nobili-Tarugi is a Renaissance-arcaded confection; meanwhile, the unfinished Duomo looks glumly on, wishing the city hadn't run out of money for its facade. The Contucci Palace (left of the church) is lucky enough to have a 16th-century Renaissance facade. The Contucci family still lives in their palace, producing and selling their own wine. The town is fortunate to be graced with so many bold and noble palazzos—Florentine nobility favored Montepulciano as a breezy and relaxed place for a secondary residence.

Duomo—This church's unfinished facade—rough stonework left waiting for the final marble veneer—is not that unusual. Many Tuscan churches were built just to the point where they had a functional interior, and then, for various practical reasons, the facades were left unfinished. But step inside and you'll be rewarded with some fine art. A beautiful Andrea della Robbia glazed-terracotta *Altar of the Lilies* is behind the baptismal font (on the left as you enter). The high altar features a luminous, early-Renaissance Assumption triptych by the Sienese artist Taddeo di Bartolo. Showing Mary in her dreamy eternal sleep as she ascends to be crowned by Jesus, it illustrates how Siena clung to the Gothic aesthetic—elaborate gold leaf and lacy pointed arches—to show heavenly grandeur at the expense of realism.

Cost and Hours: Free, daily 9:00-13:00 & 15:00-18:30.

▲▲**Contucci Cantina**—Montepulciano's most popular attraction isn't made of stone...it's the famous wine, Vino Nobile. This

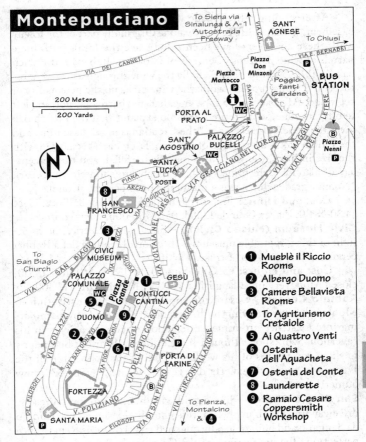

Montepulciano

To Siena via
Sinalunga & A-1
Autostrada
Freeway

To Chiusi

VIA CAI

SANT'
AGNESE

VIA F. BERNABEI

VIA DEI CANNETI

Piazza Don
Minzoni

Piazza
Marzocco

SANGALLO

Poggiofanti
Gardens

BUS
STATION

VIA DELLE LETERE

200 Meters

200 Yards

PORTA AL
PRATO

WC

Piazza
Nenni

SANT'
AGOSTINO

PALAZZO
BUCELLI

VIALE I MAGGIO

VIALE DELLE

SANTA
LUCIA

PIANA
ARCHI

VIA POGGIOLO

POST

WC

VIA GRACCIANO NEL CORSO

SAN
FRANCESCO

RICCI

VIA VOLTAIA NEL CORSO

CIVIC
MUSEUM

To
San Biagio
Church

PALAZZO
COMUNALE

WC

Piazza
Grande

GESÙ

CONTUCCI
CANTINA

VIA DI SAN BIAGIO

DUOMO

VIA D. ORIOLO

VIA COLLAZZI

VIA SAN DONATO

VIA FOR. VECCHIA

VIA DELL'OPIO NEL CORSO

TEATRO

PORTA DI
FARINE

VIA DI SAN PIETRO

FORTEZZA

V. POLIZIANO

VIA CIRCONVALLAZIONE

To Pienza,
Montalcino
& ❹

VIA DEI FILOSOFI

FILOSOFI

SANTA MARIA

1. Mueblè il Riccio Rooms
2. Albergo Duomo
3. Camere Bellavista Rooms
4. To Agriturismo Cretaiole
5. Ai Quattro Venti
6. Osteria dell'Aquacheta
7. Osteria del Conte
8. Launderette
9. Ramaio Cesare Coppersmith Workshop

robust red can be tasted in any of the cantinas lining Via Ricci and Via di Gracciano nel Corso, but the cantina in the basement of the Contucci Palace is both historic and fun. Skip the palace's formal wine-tasting showroom facing the square, and instead head down the lane on the right to the actual cellars, where you'll meet

lively Adamo, who has been making wine since 1953 and welcomes tourists into his cellar. While at the palace, you may meet Andrea Contucci, whose family has lived here since the 11th century. He loves to share his family's products with the public. Adamo and Signor Contucci usually have a dozen bottles open.

After sipping a little wine with Adamo, explore the palace basement, with its 13th-century vaults. Originally part of the town's wall, these chambers have been filled since the 1500s with huge barrels of wine. Dozens of barrels of Croatian, Italian, and French oak (1,000-2,500 liters each) cradle the wine through a two-year in-the-barrel aging process, while the wine picks up the personality of the wood. After about 35 years, an exhausted barrel has nothing left to offer its wine, so it's retired. Adamo explains that the French oak gives the wine "pure elegance," the Croatian is more masculine, and the Italian oak is a marriage of the two. Each barrel is labeled with the size in liters, the year the wine was barreled, and the percentage of alcohol (determined by how much sun shone in that year). "Nobile"-grade wine needs a minimum of 13 percent alcohol.

Cost and Hours: Free drop-in tasting, daily 8:30-12:30 & 14:30-18:30, Piazza Grande 13, tel. 0578-757-006, www.contucci.it.

Civic Museum (Museo Civico)—Small and eclectic, the highlight of this forgettable museum is its colorful Andrea della Robbia ceramic altarpieces and Etruscan artifacts.

Cost and Hours: €5, Tue-Sun 10:00-13:00 & 15:00-18:00, closed Mon, very little English, Via Ricci 10, tel. 0578-717-300.

Ramaio Cesare—Cesare the coppersmith is an institution in Montepulciano, carrying on his grandfather's trade by hammering into existence an immense selection of copper objects in his cavernous workshop. Though his English is limited, he's happy to show you photos of his work—including the copper top of the Duomo in Siena (Piazzetta del Teatro, tel. 0578-758-753, www.rameria.com).

San Biagio Church—Just outside of town, down a picturesque driveway lined with cypresses, this church—designed by Antonio da Sangallo and built of locally quarried travertine—is Renaissance perfection. The proportions of the Greek cross floor plan give the building a pleasing rhythmic quality. Bramante, who designed St. Peter's at the Vatican in 1516, was inspired by this dome. The lone tower was supposed to have a twin, but it was never built. The soaring interior, with a high dome and lantern, creates a fine Renaissance space. Walk around the building to study the free-standing towers, and consider a picnic or snooze on the grass in back. The street called Via di San Biagio, leading from the church up into town, makes for an enjoyable, if challenging, walk.

Cost and Hours: Free, normally open daily 8:30-18:30.

Sleeping in Montepulciano

(€1 = about $1.40, country code: 39)

$$$ Mueblè il Riccio ("Hedgehog") is medieval-elegant, with six modern and spotless rooms, an awesome roof terrace, and friendly owners (Sb-€80, Db-€100, Tb-€116, breakfast-€8, air-con, Internet access and Wi-Fi, limited free parking—request when you reserve, a block below the main square at Via Talosa 21, tel. & fax 0578-757-713, www.ilriccio.net, info@ilriccio.net, Gió and Ivana speak English). Gió and his son Iacopo give tours of the countryside (€30/hour) in one of their classic Italian cars; for details, see their website. Ivana makes wonderful breakfast tarts.

$$ Albergo Duomo, renting 13 rooms, is big, fairly modern, and recently redecorated, with a comfortable lounge downstairs and a decent breakfast (small Db-€75, standard Db-€95, Tb-€115, family deals, air-con in some rooms, Wi-Fi, free parking nearby, Via di San Donato 14, tel. 0578-757-473, www.albergoduomo.it, albergoduomo@libero.it, Elisa and Saverio).

$$ Camere Bellavista has 10 basic rooms, most of them freshly renovated, and some with better views than others. Room 6 has a view terrace worth reserving (Db-€75, terrace Db-€90, cash only, optional €3 breakfast at a bar in the piazza, no elevator, Via Ricci 25, no reception—call before arriving or ring bell, mobile 347-823-2314, fax 0578-716-341, bellavista@bccmp.com, Gabriella, little English spoken).

Between Montepulciano and Montalcino: A Green Acres *Agriturismo* Holiday

$$$ Agriturismo Cretaiole, in pristine farmland on the Montalcino-Pienza road, is warmly run by Isabella and her hus-

band, Carlo. This family-friendly farm, deeply rooted in the culture, welcomes visitors for weeklong stays (generally Sat-Sat) in six comfortable apartments. Eager to share their local traditions, they create a community of about 14-20 travelers who are looking for a rich cultural education. Carlo is a professional olive-oil taster. Carlo's father, Luciano, is in charge of the grappa and tends the vegetable garden (take your pick of the free veggies). Included in your stay are a pasta-making class hosted by Isabella, a Tuscan dinner, a visit to a local farm (with samples), an olive oil tasting, and a wine tasting. You may also have the chance to help with truffle hunting and/or grape and olive harvesting. While there's no swimming pool—for philosophical reasons—many thoughtful touches and extras, such as Wi-Fi, mountain bikes, and loaner mobile phones, are provided (Db-€825/week, small Db apartment-€990/week, large Db apartment-€1,290/week, same apartment for four-€1,595/week, prices soft mid-Nov-mid-March, non-included activities are fairly priced, tel. & fax 0578-748-083, Isabella's mobile 338-740-9245, www.cretaiole.it, info@cretaiole.it). It's on the Montalcino-Pienza road (S-146), about 11 miles out of Montalcino, and about three miles out of Pienza. While they prefer weeklong stays, when things are slow they may accept guests for as few as three nights (for this you must book less than a month in advance, Db-€110, 3-night minimum). They also rent rooms in an even posher (and significantly pricier) house, Casa Moriciani, which features dreamy views, plush interiors, loads of extras, and pure Tuscan luxury (well-described on their website).

Eating in Montepulciano

Ai Quattro Venti is fresh, flavorful, fun, and right on Piazza Grande, offering good indoor and outdoor seating. Try their very own organic olive oil and wine (€8.50 pastas, Fri-Wed 12:30-14:30 & 19:30-22:30, closed Thu, next to City Hall on Piazza Grande, tel. 0578-717-231, Chiara).

Osteria dell'Aquacheta is a carnivore's dream come true, famous among locals for its excellent beef steaks. Its long, narrow room is jammed with shared tables and tight seating, with an open fire in back and a big hunk of red beef lying on the counter like a corpse on a gurney. Giulio, with a pen tucked into his ponytail, whacks off slabs with a cleaver, confirms the weight and price with the diner, and tosses the meat on the grill—seven minutes per side. Steaks are sold by weight (€3/100 grams, or *etto*, one kilo is about the smallest they serve, two can split it for €30). They also serve hearty €6 pastas and salads and a fine house wine (Wed-

Mon 12:30-15:00 & 19:30-22:30, closed Tue, Via del Teatro 22, tel. 0578-758-443). In the tradition of old trattorias, they serve one glass, which you use alternately for wine and water.

Osteria del Conte, an attractive but humble family-run bistro, offers a €30 *menù del Conte*—a four-course dinner of local specialties including wine—as well as à la carte options and cooking like mom's (€7 pastas, €12 *secondi*, indoor and outdoor seating, Thu-Tue 12:30-14:30 & 19:30-21:30, closed Wed, Via San Donato 19, tel. 0578-756-062).

Montepulciano Connections

All buses leave from Piazza Pietro Nenni. Check www.siena mobilita.it for schedules.

From Montepulciano by Bus to: **Florence** (3/day with a change in Bettole), **Siena** (8/day, 1.25 hours, none on Sun), **Pienza** (8/day, 30 minutes). There are hourly bus connections to **Chiusi**, a town on the main Florence-Rome rail line; Chiusi is a much better bet than the distant Montepulciano station (5 miles away), which is served only by milk-run trains. Buses connect Montepulciano's bus station and its train station (8/day, none on Sun).

To Montalcino: This connection is problematic by public transportation—consider asking at the TI for a **taxi**. Although expensive (about €60), a taxi could make sense for two or more people. Otherwise you can take a bus to Buonconvento, then change to get to Montalcino (2 hours). **Drivers** find route S-146 to Montalcino particularly scenic (see "Crete Senese Drives" on page 691).

Cortona

Cortona blankets a 1,700-foot hill surrounded by dramatic Tuscan and Umbrian views. Frances Mayes' books, such as *Under the*

Tuscan Sun, placed this town in the touristic limelight, just as Peter Mayle's books popularized the Luberon region in France. But long before Mayes ever published a book, Cortona was popular with Romantics and considered one of the classic Tuscan hill towns. Unlike San Gimignano, Cortona maintains a rustic and gritty personality— even with its long history of foreigners who, enamored with its Tuscan charm, made this their adopted home.

The city began as one of the largest Etruscan settlements, the remains of which can be seen at the base of the city walls, as well as in the nearby tombs. It grew to its present size in the 13th to 16th centuries, when it was a colorful and crowded city, eventually allied with Florence. The farmland that fills almost every view from the city was marshy and uninhabitable until about 200 years ago, when it was drained and turned into some of Tuscany's most fertile land.

Art-lovers know Cortona as the home of Renaissance painter Luca Signorelli, Baroque master Pietro da Cortona (Berretini), and the 20th-century Futurist artist Gino Severini. The city's museums and churches reveal many of the works of these native sons.

Orientation to Cortona

Most of the main sights, shops, and restaurants cluster around the level streets on the Piazza Garibaldi-Piazza del Duomo axis, but Cortona will have you huffing and puffing up some steep hills. From Piazza Garibaldi, it's a level five-minute walk down bustling shop-lined Via Nazionale to Piazza della Repubblica, the heart of the town, which is dominated by City Hall (Palazzo del Comune). From this square, a two-minute stroll leads you past the TI, the interesting Etruscan Museum, and the theater to Piazza del Duomo, where you'll find the recommended Diocesan Museum. Steep streets, many of them stepped, go from Piazza della Repubblica up to the San Niccolò and Santa Margherita churches and the Medici Fortress (a 30-minute climb from Piazza della Repubblica).

Tourist Information

To reach the helpful TI, head to Piazza Signorelli, then walk through the courtyard of the Etruscan Museum and up a short flight of steps, at the back (Mon-Sat 9:00-13:00 & 15:00-19:00, Sun 9:00-13:00, closed Sun off-season, sells train and bus tickets, tel. 0575-637-223 or 0575-637-276, www.apt.arezzo.it).

Arrival in Cortona

By Train: Train travelers arrive at the desolate-feeling Camucia-Cortona station, which has an unstaffed ticket office. From here, Cortona is about four miles away—not reasonably walkable, especially given the hills and lack of sidewalks.

Blue local **buses** zip you right up to town in 10 minutes (generally 2/hour, €1.10, buy tickets at newsstand—*edicola*—200 yards from station or on board for €1 more, check that the bus is heading up to Cortona and not on to Terontola). Bus schedules are posted in front of the station, to the right. In town, buses stop at Piazza Garibaldi.

If you arrive during the occasional hourly gap between buses, consider taking a **taxi** into town (€10, call for Dejan and his seven-seater cab, mobile 348-402-3501—Dejan also arranges day trips, see "Local Guides," later; or you can ask your hotel to arrange a taxi).

By Car: You'll find several free lots right outside the walls; Viale Cesare Battisti may be your best bet. A free lot just after the big Santo Spirito Church has an escalator leading to Piazza Garibaldi. Piazza Garibaldi itself may have a handful of pay spots available (marked by blue lines, pay & display, free 20:00-8:00). The small town is actually very long, and it can be smart to drive to the top for sightseeing up there (free parking at Santa Margherita Basilica).

Helpful Hints

Market Day: The market is on Saturday on Piazza Signorelli (from early morning until 14:00).

Internet Access: Foto Lamentini Internet Point has several computer terminals (€3/hour, daily April-Oct 10:00-20:00, Nov-March 10:30-13:00 & 14:00-19:30, Via Nazionale 33, tel. 0575-62588).

Services: The town has **no baggage storage,** so try asking nicely at a hotel to leave your bag there. The best public **WC** is located in Piazza del Duomo, under Santa Margherita's statue.

Tuscan Cooking Classes: Husband-and-wife team **Romano and Agostina** hold morning hands-on cooking and cheese making classes, as well as wine-, cheese-, and oil-tasting courses three mornings a week in the kitchen of their recommended Ristorante La Bucaccia. In the three-hour class, you'll prepare two *antipasti,* two types of pasta, an entrée, and a dessert, which you then get to eat (roughly €90/person, price includes wine, 5 percent discount with this book, classes start at 9:30, book in advance, personalized classes available, Via Ghibellina 17, tel. 0575-606-039, www.labucaccia.it, info @labucaccia.it).

Local Guides: Giovanni Adreani exudes energy and a love of his city and Tuscan high culture. He is great at bringing the fine points of the city to life and can take visitors around in his car for no extra charge. As this region is speckled with underappreciated charms, having Giovanni for a day as your driver/guide promises to be a fascinating experience (€110/half-day, €200/day, tel. 0575-630-665, mobile 347-176-2830, www.adreanigiovanni.com, adreanigiovanni@libero.it). Reliable, English-speaking taxi driver **Dejan** (DAY-yan) can also take you on full-day tours to Pienza, Montalcino, Siena, Assisi, and Chianti—email him and devise your own itinerary (€220-250/day depending on number of passengers, mobile 348-402-3501, dejanprvi@yahoo.it).

Self-Guided Walk

Welcome to Cortona

This introductory walking tour will take you from Piazza Garibaldi and up the main strip to the town center, its piazzas, and the Duomo.

• *Start at the bus stop in...*

Piazza Garibaldi: Many visits start and finish in this square, thanks to its bus stop. While the piazza, bulging out from the town fortifications like a big turret, looks like part of an old rampart, it's really a souvenir of those early French and English Romantics—

HILL TOWNS

Cortona

To Etruscan Tombs & Arezzo

CITY WALLS

PORTA COLONIA

VIA MURA ETRUSCHI

VIALE MURA ETRUSCHI

VIA MURE D. DUOMO

DUOMO

VIA DARDANO

VIA DELLE SALVATORE

VICOLO RADI

PORTA SANTA MARIA

Piazza del Duomo

DIOCESAN MUSEUM

THEATER

VIA MAZZONI

VIA MAFFEI

Piazza Pescaia

VIA ROMA

CASALI

VIA BENEDETTI

POST

13

VIA BERRETTINI

VIA MONETI

VIA SAN MARCO

Piazza Signorelli

ETRUSCAN MUSEUM IN CASALI PALACE

CITY HALL

Piazza della Repubblica

SAN FRANCESCO

VIA MERCATO

VIA GHIBELLINA

12

4

10

VIA MAFFEI

7

ETRUSCAN GATE

11

Piazza della Repubblica

15

16

3

WALK BEGINS

VIA GUELFA

VIA MURA V. SAN BENEDETTO

9

14

VIA NAZIONALE

1

Piazza Garibaldi

P

SAN AGOSTINO

VIA BENEDETTO

VIA DEL GIARDINO

B

BUS STOP

VIA SAN SEBASTIANO

8

P

VIALE CESARE BATTISTI

PORTA SANT'AGOSTINO

SANTO SPIRITO

STRADA UMBRO CORTONESE

P

To Camucia & Terontola (nearest train stations)

HILL TOWNS

the ones who first created the notion of a dreamy, idyllic Tuscany. During the Napoleonic Age, the French built this balcony (and the scenic little park behind the adjacent San Domenico Church) simply to enjoy a commanding view of the Tuscan countryside.

With Umbria about a mile away, Cortona marks the end of Tuscany. This is a major cultural divide, as Cortona was the last town in Charlemagne's empire and the last under Medici rule. Umbria, just to the south, was papal territory for centuries. These deep-seated cultural disparities were a great challenge for the visionaries who unified the fractured region to create the modern nation of Italy during the 1860s. A statue in the center of this square honors one of the heroes of the struggle for Italian unification—the brilliant revolutionary general Giuseppe Garibaldi.

Enjoy the commanding view from here. Assisi is just over the ridge on the left. Lake Trasimeno peeks from behind the hill, looking quite normal today. But, according to legend, it was blood-red after Hannibal defeated the Romans here in 217 B.C., when 15,000 died in the battle. The only sizable town you can see, on the

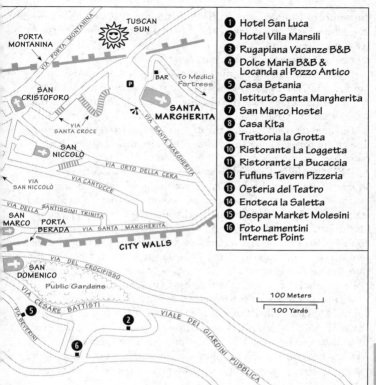

Map Legend:

1. Hotel San Luca
2. Hotel Villa Marsili
3. Rugapiana Vacanze B&B
4. Dolce Maria B&B & Locanda al Pozzo Antico
5. Casa Betania
6. Istituto Santa Margherita
7. San Marco Hostel
8. Casa Kita
9. Trattoria la Grotta
10. Ristorante La Loggetta
11. Ristorante La Bucaccia
12. Fufluns Tavern Pizzeria
13. Osteria del Teatro
14. Enoteca la Saletta
15. Despar Market Molesini
16. Foto Lamentini Internet Point

right, is Montepulciano. Cortona is still defined by its Etruscan walls—remnants of these walls, with stones laid 2,500 years ago, stretch from here in both directions.

Frances Mayes put Cortona on the map for many Americans with her book (and later movie) *Under the Tuscan Sun*. The book describes her real-life experience buying, fixing up, and living in a run-down villa in Cortona with her husband, Ed. The movie romanticized the story, turning Frances into a single, recently divorced writer who restores the villa and her peace of mind. Mayes' villa isn't "under the Tuscan sun" very often; it's named "Bramasole"—literally, "craving sun." On the wrong side of the hill, it's in the shade after 15:00. She and her husband still live there part of each year and are respected members of their adopted

community (outside the walls, behind the hill on the left—a 20-minute walk away; ask at the TI for directions if you'd like to see it up close).

• *From this square, head into town along...*

Via Nazionale: The only level road in town, locals have nick-named Via Nazionale the *ruga piana* (flat wrinkle). This is the main commercial street in this town of 2,500, and it's been that way for a long time. Every shop seems to have a medieval cellar or an Etruscan well. Notice the crumbling sandstone door frames. The entire town is constructed out of this grainy, eroding rock.

• *Via Nazionale leads to...*

Piazza della Repubblica: City Hall faces Cortona's main square. Note how City Hall is a clever hodgepodge of twin medi-eval towers, with a bell tower added to connect them, and a grand staircase to lend some gravitas. Notice also the fine wood balconies on the left. In the Middle Ages, wooden extensions like these were common features on the region's stone buildings. These balconies (not original, but rebuilt in the 19th century) would have fit right into the medieval cityscape. These days, you usually see only the holes that once supported the long-gone wooden beams.

This spot has been the town center since Etruscan times. Four centuries before Christ, an important street led from here up to the hill-capping temple. Later, the square became the Roman forum. Opposite City Hall is the handy, recommended Despar Market Molesini, good for cheap sandwiches. Above that is the loggia—once a fish market, now the recommended Ristorante La Loggetta.

• *The second half of the square, to the right of City Hall, is...*

Piazza Signorelli: Dominated by Casali Palace, this square was the headquarters of the Florentine captains who used to con-trol the city. Peek into the palace entrance for a look at the coats of arms. Every six months, Florence would send a new captain to Cortona, who would help establish his rule by inserting his family coat of arms into the palace's wall. These date from the 15th to the 17th century, and were once painted with bright colors. Cortona's fine Etruscan Museum (described later, under "Sights in Cortona") is in the Casali Palace courtyard, which is lined with many more of these family coats of arms. The inviting Caffè del Teatro fills the loggia of the theater that is named for the town's most famous art-ist, Luca Signorelli.

• *Head down the street just to the right of the museum to...*

Piazza del Duomo: Here you'll find the Diocesan Museum (listed later, under "Sights in Cortona"), cathedral, and a statue of Santa Margherita. The cathedral's facade, though recently renovated, still seems a little underwhelming and tucked away. Cortona so loves its hometown saint, Margherita, that it put the energy it would otherwise have invested in its cathedral into the Santa Margherita Basilica, at the top of the hill. Margherita was a 13th-century rich girl who took good care of the poor and was an early follower of St. Francis and St. Clare. Many locals believe that Margherita protected Cortona from WWII bombs.

The Piazza del Duomo terrace comes with a commanding view of the Tuscan countryside. Find the town cemetery in the distance. If you were standing here before the time of Napoleon, you'd be surrounded by tombstones. But Cortona's graveyards—like other urban graveyards throughout Napoleon's realm—were cleaned out in the early 1800s to reclaim land and improve hygiene.

• *Next, enter the...*

Duomo: The Cortona cathedral is not—strictly speaking—a cathedral, because it no longer has a bishop. The white-and-gray Florentine Renaissance-style interior is mucked up with lots of Baroque chapels filling once-spacious side niches. In the rear (on the right) is an altar cluttered with relics. Technically, any Catholic altar, in order to be consecrated, needs a relic embedded in it. Go ahead—gently lift up the tablecloth. The priest here doesn't mind. You'll see a little marble patch that holds a bit of a saint (daily 7:30-12:30 & 15:00-18:30, shorter hours in winter, closed during Mass).

• *From here, you can visit the nearby Diocesan Museum, or head back toward Piazza della Repubblica to visit the Etruscan Museum in Piazza Signorelli (both listed next) or to get a bite to eat (see "Eating in Cortona," later).*

Sights in Cortona

▲Etruscan Museum (Museo dell'Accademia Etrusca)— Located in the 13th-century Casali Palace, this fine gallery (established in 1727) is one of the first dedicated to artifacts from the Etruscan civilization. You'll see an exhibit on the Roman settlement and take a virtual tour of the Etruscan "Il Sodo" tombs. The Cortona Tablet (*Tabula Cortonensis*, second century B.C.), a 200-word contract inscribed in bronze, contains dozens of Etruscan words archaeologists had never seen before its discovery in 1992. Along with lots of gold and jewelry, you'll find a seventh-century B.C. grater (for some *very* aged Parmesan cheese) and a magnificent fourth-century B.C. bronze oil lamp with 16 spouts, set in a small four-pillared temple. The library of the Etruscan Academy, founded in 1727 to promote an understanding of the city through the study of archaeology, is upstairs. This eclectic museum also has an Egyptian section, fine Roman mosaics, and a room dedicated to modern abstract works by Severini, all lovingly described in English.

Cost and Hours: €8, €10 combo-ticket includes Diocesan

Museum; April-Oct daily 10:00-19:00; Nov-March Tue-Sun 10:00-17:00, closed Mon; Casali Palace on Piazza Signorelli, tel. 0575-637-235, www.cortonamaec.org.

▲**Diocesan Museum (Museo Diocesano)**—This collection of art from the town's many churches has works by Fra Angelico and Pietro Lorenzetti, and masterpieces by hometown hero and Renaissance master Luca Signorelli.

Don't miss Fra Angelico's sumptuous *Annunciation*. In this scene, Mary says "Yes," consenting to bear God's son. Notice how the house sits on a pillow of flowers...the new Eden. The old Eden, featuring the expulsion of Adam and Eve from Paradise, is in the upper left. The painting comes with comic strip-like narration of scenes from Mary's life: The angel's words are top and bottom, while Mary's answer is upside down (logically, since it's directed to God, who would be reading while looking down from heaven).

The crucifix (by Pietro Lorenzetti, c. 1325, just to the right of the Fra Angelico) is impressive in its severity. Notice the gripping realism—even the tendons in Jesus' arms are pulled tight. Another highlight is Luca Signorelli's *Mourning of the Dead Christ (Compianto sul Cristo Morto)*. Signorelli was a generation ahead of Michelangelo and, with his passion for painting ideas, was an inspiration for the younger artist (for more on Signorelli, see page 704). Everything in his painting has a meaning: The skull of Adam sits under the sacrifice of Jesus; the hammer represents the Passion (the Crucifixion leading to the Resurrection); the lake is blood; and so on. I don't understand all of the medieval symbolism, but it is intense.

Cost and Hours: €5, €10 combo-ticket includes Etruscan Museum, helpful audioguide-€3; April-Oct daily 10:00-19:00; Nov-March Tue-Sun 10:00-17:00, closed Mon; Piazza del Duomo 1, tel. 0575-62-830.

Church of St. Francis—Established by St. Francis' best friend, Brother Elias, this church dates from the 13th century. The wooden beams of the ceiling are original. While the place was redecorated in the Baroque age, some of the original frescoes that once wall-papered the church peek through the whitewash in a chapel on the left. Francis fans visit for its precious Franciscan relics. To the left of the altar, you'll find one of Francis' tunics, his pillow (inside a fancy cover), and his gospel book. Behind the altar is Elias' very simple tomb. It reads "Frate Elia da Cortona." Notice how the entire high altar seems designed to frame its precious relic—a piece of the cross Elias brought back from his visit to the patriarch in Constantinople. You're welcome to climb the altar for a close-up look.

Cost and Hours: Free, daily 9:00-17:30; Mass Mon-Sat at 17:00, Sun at 10:00.

San Niccolò Church—Signorelli enthusiasts will want to make the pilgrimage up to this tiny church, a steep 10-minute walk beyond the Church of St. Francis. Ring the bell on the left side of the church and the caretaker might give you a short tour in Italian. The highlight of this humble church is an altarpiece painted on both sides by Signorelli. The caretaker activates a tricky arm mechanism that moves the picture away from the wall to reveal the painting behind it.

Cost and Hours: €1 donation, daily in summer 9:00-12:00 & 15:00-19:00, off-season until 17:00, verify hours with TI, as the church may be between caretakers during your visit. Even if you can't get in, it's still worth the walk just to explore the picturesque neighborhood.

Santa Margherita Basilica—From San Niccolò Church, another steep path leads uphill 10 minutes to this basilica, which houses the remains of Margherita, the town's favorite saint. Santa Margherita, an unwed mother from Montepulciano, found her calling with the Franciscans in Cortona, tending to the sick and poor. The well-preserved and remarkably emotional 13th-century crucifix on the right is the cross that, according to legend, talked to Margherita.

Cost and Hours: Free, daily 9:00-12:00 & 15:00-19:00, tel. 0575-603-116.

Nearby: Still need more altitude? Head uphill five more minutes to the recently renovated **Medici Fortezza Girifalco** (€3, usually open daily April-Sept 9:00-12:00 & 15:00-18:00, July-Aug until 19:00, closed Oct-March, sometimes closed for rehearsals by Italian rock legend Jovanotti, who lives in a villa beyond San Niccolò Church—check with TI). The views are stunning, stretching all the way to distant Lago Trasimeno.

Etruscan Tombs near Cortona—Guided tours to nearby "Il Sodo" tombs (called *melone* for their melon-like shape) are complicated to arrange. But the excavation site and bits of the ruins are easy to visit and can be seen from outside the fence in the morning. It's just a couple of miles out of Cortona on the Arezzo road (R-71), at the edge of Camucia at the foot of the Cortona hill; ask anyone for "Il Sodo."

Sleeping in Cortona

(€1 = about $1.40, country code: 39)

$$$ Hotel San Luca, perched on the side of a cliff, has 57 modern, impersonal business-class rooms, half with stunning views of Lago Trasimeno. While tired and a bit run-down, it's friendly and conveniently located, right at the bus stop (Sb-€85, Db-€120, Tb-€155, request a view room when you reserve, popular with Americans and groups, Piazza Garibaldi 1, tel. 0575-630-460, fax

0575-630-105, www.sanlucacortona.com, info@sanlucacortona
.com). If driving, you might find a spot at the small public parking
lot at the hotel (cheap and easy meters).

$$$ Hotel Villa Marsili is a comfortable splurge just below
town. It was originally a 15th-century church, then an elegant 18th-
century home. Its 25 rooms and public areas have been recently
redecorated and restored. Guests can enjoy an evening aperitif on
the panoramic terrace (Db-€130-250, Db suite-€270-350, Jacuzzi
in some rooms, air-con, Wi-Fi and Internet access, Viale Cesare
Battisti 13, tel. 0575-605-252, fax 0575-605-618, www.villamarsili
.net, info@villamarsili.net, charming Stefano).

$$ Rugapiana Vacanze B&B rents four doubles and four
apartments, each described separately on their website. Located
on Cortona's main drag, it's beautifully furnished with plenty of
thoughtful touches (apartment-€100-115 or Db-€95 with breakfast
at a nearby bar, 10 percent discount with this book, family suites,
Wi-Fi, Via Nazionale 63, tel. & fax 0575-630-712, mobile 340-
808-6879, www.rugapianavacanze.com, info@rugapianavacanze
.com, Massimo).

$$ Dolce Maria B&B is located in a 16th-century building
with high-beamed ceilings. Though the breakfast area is small, the
six rooms themselves are good-value, luminous, and spacious, with
tasteful period furnishings and modern bathrooms. The B&B is
run by warm and efficient Paola, who also runs the Antico Pozzo
restaurant next door—the two businesses share a patio (Db-€80-
100, Via Ghini 12, tel. 057-563-0397, fax 057-560-4627, www
.cortonastorica.com, info@cortonastorica.com).

$ Casa Betania, a big, wistful convent with an inviting view
terrace, rents 30 fine rooms (mostly twin beds) for the best price
in town. While it's primarily for "thoughtful travelers," anyone
looking for a peaceful place to call home will feel welcome in this
pilgrims' resort (S-€32, D-€44, Db-€48, Tb-€66, extra bed-€20,
breakfast-€4, free parking, about a third of a mile out of town, a
few minutes' walk below Piazza Garibaldi and through iron gates
at Via Gino Severini 50, tel. & fax 0575-630-423, www.casaperferie
betania.com, info@casaperferiebetania.com).

$ Istituto Santa Margherita, run by the Serve di Maria
Riparatrici sisters, rents 22 cheap and simple rooms in a smaller
and more institutional-feeling convent across the street from Casa
Betania (Sb-€42, Db-€58, Tb-€75, Qb-€86, breakfast-€5, eleva-
tor, free parking, Viale Cesare Battisti 17, tel. 0575-178-7203 or
0575-630-336, fax 0575-630-549, www.santamargherita.smr.it,
comunitacortona@smr.it).

$ San Marco Hostel, at the top of town, is housed in a remod-
eled 13th-century palace (bed in dorm-€16, in 2-bed and 4-bed
rooms-€20, includes breakfast, dinner-€10.50, lockout 10:00-

13:00; from Piazza Garibaldi head up steep Via Santa Margherita, then turn left to find Via Maffei 57; tel. & fax 0575-601-392, www .cortonahostel.com, ostellocortona@libero.it).

$ Casa Kita, renting four fine rooms, is a homely place at the edge of town with breathtaking views from its terrace (Db-€40-60, 100 yards below Piazza Garibaldi at Vicolo degli Orti 7, tel. 389-557-9893, www.casakita.com, info@casakita.com, Lorenzini family).

Eating in Cortona

Trattoria la Grotta, just off Piazza della Repubblica, is a traditional place serving daily specials to an enthusiastic clientele under grotto-like vaults (€8 pastas, €8 meat dishes, good wine by the glass, Wed-Mon 12:00-14:30 & 19:00-22:00, closed Tue, Piazza Baldelli 3, tel. 0575-630-271).

Ristorante La Loggetta serves up big portions of well-presented Tuscan cuisine on the loggia overlooking Piazza della Repubblica. While they have fine indoor seating, I'd eat here for the chance to gaze at the square over a meal (€8 pastas, €7-15 meat dishes, Thu-Tue 12:30-15:00 & 19:30-23:00, closed Wed, Piazza Pescheria 3, tel. 0575-630-575).

Ristorante La Bucaccia is a family-run eatery set in a rustic medieval wine cellar. It's dressy and romantic. They take great pride in their Chianina beef entrées and homemade pastas. With an evangelical pride in their food, Romano hosts and his wife Agostina cooks (€9 pastas, €13, entrées, daily 12:00-15:30 & 19:00-24:00, show this book for a 5 percent discount and a small free appetizer, Via Ghibellina 17, tel. 0575-606-039).

Fufluns Tavern Pizzeria (that's the Etruscan name for Dionysus) is easy-going, friendly, and remarkably unpretentious for its location in the town center. It's popular with locals for its good, inexpensive Tuscan cooking and friendly staff (cheap, lots of €6 pizza and pasta plus big salads, good house wine, Wed-Mon 12:15-14:30 & 19:15-22:30, closed Tue, a block below Piazza della Repubblica at Via Ghibellina 3, tel. 0575-604-140).

Osteria del Teatro tries very hard to create a romantic Old World atmosphere, and does it well. Chef and owner Emiliano serves nicely presented and tasty international and local cuisine (taking creative liberties with traditions). There's good outdoor seating, too (Thu-Tue 12:30-14:30 & 19:30-21:30, closed Wed, 2 blocks uphill from the main square at Via Maffei 2—look for the gnomes on the steps, tel. 0575-630-556).

Locanda al Pozzo Antico offers an affordable menu of Tuscan fare, with a focus on fresh, quality produce, and using their own homemade olive oil. Eat in a classy, minimalist dining room or tucked away in a tranquil secret courtyard. Paola is a charming hostess (€8 pastas, €13 *secondi*, Fri-Wed 12:30-14:30 & 19:30-22:00, closed Thu, Via Ghini 12, tel. 057-562-091 or 057-563-0397; Paola, husband Franco, and son Gianni).

Enoteca la Saletta, dark and classy, is good for fine wine and a light meal. You can sit inside surrounded by wine bottles or outside to people-watch on the town's main drag (daily 7:30-24:00, meals served 12:00-24:00, free Wi-Fi, Via Nazionale 26, tel. 0575-603-366).

Picnic: On the main square, the chic little **Despar Market Molesini** makes tasty sandwiches, served with a smile (see list on counter and order by number, or invent your own), and sells whatever else you might want for a picnic (Mon-Sat 7:00-13:30 & 16:00-19:30, closed Sun, Piazza della Repubblica 23). Munch your picnic across the square on the steps of City Hall, or just past Piazza Garibaldi in the public gardens behind San Domenico Church.

Cortona Connections

Cortona has good train connections with the rest of Italy through its Camucia-Cortona station. Arrive with small bills and coins, as the station is usually unstaffed, and its very basic ticket machine takes only cash-and for change only gives vouchers (which you can use to pay for a future journey). To get to the train station at the foot of the hill, take a taxi or hop the blue bus (see "Arrival in Cortona," earlier; buy tickets at newsstand, TI, or tobacco shop, or buy from driver for €1 more). Some buses from Piazza Garibaldi only take you as far as the newsstand that's 200 yards in front of the station, while some continue on to Terontola.

From Cortona by Train to: Rome (9/day, 2.5 hours), **Florence** (hourly, 1.5 hours), **Assisi** (every 2 hours, 70 minutes, change in Terontola), **Montepulciano** (10/day, 1-2 hours, change in Chiusi—because few buses serve Montepulciano's town center from its distant train station, it's better to go by train to Chiusi, then by hourly bus to Montepulciano), **Chiusi** (hourly, 30 minutes). Most trains stop at the Camucia-Cortona train station, but some trains to/from Rome, Florence, and Assisi stop at Terontola, 10 miles away (about 10 buses/day to Terontola, leaves from Piazza Garibaldi, €2, check the schedule at the bus stop by the tree in the square or pick up printed bus schedule from the TI).

More Tuscan Sights

▲San Galgano Monastery

Of southern Tuscany's several evocative monasteries, San Galgano is the best. Set in a forested area called the Montagnolo (medium-size mountains), the isolated abbey and chapel are postcard-perfect, though you'll need a car to get here. Other, more accessible Tuscan monasteries worth visiting include Sant'Antimo (6 miles south of Montalcino) and Monte Oliveto Maggiore (15 miles south of Siena, mentioned in "Crete Senese Drives," later).

Cost and Hours: Free, summer daily 9:00-20:00, shoulder season until 18:30, erratic hours Nov-Dec, closed Jan-Feb, tel. 0577-756-738, www.prolocochiusdino.it; concerts sometimes held here in summer—ticket info tel. 0555-978-308. For a quick snack, a small, touristy bar at the end of the driveway is your only option.

Getting There: Although a bus reportedly comes here from Siena, this sight is realistically accessible only for drivers. It's just outside of Monticiano (not Montalcino), about an hour south of Siena. A warning to the queasy: These roads are curvy.

Touring the Monastery: St. Galgano was a 12th-century saint who renounced his past as a knight to become a hermit. Lacking a cross to display, he created his own by miraculously burying his sword up to its hilt in a stone, à la King Arthur, but in reverse. After his death, a large Cistercian monastery complex grew. Today, all you'll see is the roofless, ruined abbey and, on a nearby hill, the Chapel of San Galgano with its fascinating dome and sword in the stone.

This picturesque Cistercian **abbey** was once a powerful institution in Tuscany. Known for their skill as builders, the Cistercians oversaw the construction of Siena's cathedral. But after losing most of its population in the plague of 1348, the abbey never really recovered and was eventually deconsecrated.

The Cistercian order was centered in France, and the architecture of the abbey shows a heavy French influence. Notice the large, high windows and the pointy, delicate arches. This is pure French Gothic, a style that never fully caught on in Italy (compare it with the chunky, elaborately decorated cathedral in Siena, built about the same time).

As you enter the church, notice the small section of the cloister wall to the left. This used to surround the garden and was the only place where the monks were allowed to talk, for one hour each day. From inside the church, the empty windows frame the view of the chapel up on the hill.

A path from the abbey leads up the hill to the **Chapel of San Galgano.** The unique, beehive-like interior houses St. Galgano's sword and stone, recently confirmed to date back to the 12th century. Don't try and pull the sword from the stone—the small chapel to the left displays the severed arms of the last guy who tried. The chapel also contains some deteriorated frescoes and more interesting *sinopie* (fresco sketches). The adjacent gift shop sells a little bit of everything, from wine to postcards to herbs, some of it monk-made.

▲Chiusi

This small hill town (rated ▲▲ for Etruscan fans) was once one of the most important Etruscan cities. Today, it's a key train junction and a pleasant, workaday Italian village with an enjoyable historic center and few tourists.

Tourist Information: The TI is on the main square (May-Sept Tue-Sun 10:00-13:00 & 15:00-17:00, closed Mon; Oct-April Tue-Sun 9:30-12:30, closed Mon; tel. 0578-227-667).

Arrival in Chiusi: The region's trains (to Florence, Siena, Orvieto, and Assisi) go through or change at this hub, making Chiusi an easy day trip. Buses link the train station with the town center two miles away (every 40 minutes, buy tickets at tobacco shop). Easy and free parking lots are a five-minute walk from the center. To rent a car, find the Hertz office near the train station (Via M. Buonarroti 21, tel. 057-822-3000).

Sights in Chiusi: The **Archaeological Museum**, just off the main square, thoughtfully presents a high-quality collection with plenty of explanations in English. The collection of funerary urns, some in painted terra-cotta and some in *pietra fetida* ("stinky stone"), are remarkably intact (€4, July-Sept daily 9:00-20:00, Via Porsenna 93, tel. 0578-20177, www.archeotoscana.beniculturali.it). The museum also arranges tours to visit **tombs** outside of town. One of the tombs is multichambered, with several sarcophagi. Another, the Tomba della Scimmia (Tomb of the Monkey), has some well-preserved frescoes. Visiting the tombs requires a guide, a car, and an advance reservation (€2; Tue, Thu, and Sat only; March-Oct at 11:00 and 16:00, Nov-Feb at 11:00 and 14:30; 25 visitors per tour).

Troglodyte alert! The **Cathedral Museum** on the main square has a dark, underground labyrinth of Etruscan tunnels. The mandatory guided tour of the tunnels ends in a large Roman cistern, from which you can climb the church bell tower for an expansive view of the countryside (museum-€2, labyrinth-€3, combo-ticket-€4, daily June-Oct 9:30-12:30 & 16:00-19:00, Nov-May

9:30-12:30 only, 30-minute tunnel tours run every 40 minutes during museum hours, Piazza Duomo 1, tel. 0578-226-490).

Craving more underground fun? The **Museo Civico** provides hourly tours of the Etruscan water system, which includes an underground lake (€3; May-Oct Tue-Sun at 10:15, 11:30, 12:45, 15:15, 16:30, and 17:45; closed Mon, fewer tours off-season, call to confirm times, Via II Ciminia 1, tel. 0578-227-667, mobile 334-626-6851).

▲Florence American Cemetery and Memorial

The compelling sight of endless rows of white marble crosses and Stars of David recalls the heroism of the young Americans who fought so valiantly to free Italy (and ultimately Europe) from the grip of fascism. This particular cemetery is the final resting place of more than 4,000 Americans who died in the liberation of Italy during World War II. Climb the hill past the perfectly manicured lawn lined with grave markers, to the memorial, where maps and a history of the Italian campaign detail the Allied advance.

Cost and Hours: Free, daily 9:00-17:00; 7.5 miles south of Florence, off Via Cassia, which parallels the *superstrada* between Florence and Siena, 2 miles south of Florence Certosa exit on A-1 autostrada; buses from Florence stop just outside the cemetery; tel. 055-202-0020, www.abmc.gov.

▲▲Crete Senese Drives

South of Siena, the hilly area known as the "Sienese Crests" is full of colorful fields and curvy, scenic roads. You'll see an endless parade of classic Tuscan scenes, rolling hills topped with medieval towns, olive groves, rustic stone farmhouses, and a skyline punctuated with cypress trees. You won't find many wineries here, since the clay soil is better for wheat and sunflowers, but you will find the pristine, panoramic Tuscan countryside that you see on calendars and postcards.

During the spring, the fields are painted in yellow and green with fava beans and broom, dotted by red poppies on the fringes. Sunflowers decorate the area during June and July, and expanses of windblown grass fill the landscape almost all year.

Most roads to the southeast of Siena will give you a taste of this area, but one of the most scenic stretches is the Lauretan road (Siena-Asciano-San Giovanni d'Asso, #438 on road maps; you can also take S-2—Via Cassia—toward Rome and turn off at *Asciano* sign, either way allows you to easily continue to Montalcino). You'll come across plenty of turnouts for panoramic photo opportunities on this road, as well as a few roadside picnic areas.

For a break from the winding road, about 15 miles from Siena, you'll find the quaint and non-touristy village of **Asciano.** With a medieval town center and several interesting churches and museums, this town offers a rare look at everyday Tuscan living—and is a great place for lunch (TI open Tue-Fri 10:30-13:00 & 15:00-18:00, Sat-Sun 10:30-13:00, closed Mon, at Corso Matteotti 18, tel. 0577-719-510). If you're in town on Saturday, gather a picnic at the outdoor market (Via Amendola, 8:00-13:00).

Five miles south of Asciano, the **Abbey of Monte Oliveto Maggiore** houses a famous fresco cycle of the life of St. Benedict, painted by Renaissance masters Il Sodoma and Luca Signorelli (free, daily 9:15-12:00 & 15:15-18:00, Nov-March until 17:00, Gregorian chanting Sun at 11:00 and Mon-Sat at 18:15, call to confirm, tel. 0577-707-611, www.monteolivetomaggiore.it). Once you reach the town of **San Giovanni d'Asso,** it's only another 12 miles southwest to Montalcino.

Another scenic drive is the lovely stretch between Montalcino and Montepulciano. This route (S-146 on road maps) alternates between the grassy hills of the Crete Senese and sunbathed vineyards of the Orcia River valley. Stop by Pienza en route.

Sleeping in the Crete Senese: **$$ Agriturismo il Molinello** rents five apartments, two built over a medieval mill. Hardworking Alessandro and Elisa share their organic produce and offer weekly wine tastings for a minimum of four people. From May through October, they offer free guided tours of Siena on Tuesday afternoons. With children, friendly dogs, toys, and a swimming pool, this is ideal for families (Qb-€70-100, apartment for up to 8-€80-200 depending on season and number of people, optional organic breakfast-€9.50, one-week stay required in summer, discounts and no minimum stay off-season, free Internet access, mountain-bike rentals, biking maps and guided bike tours, near Asciano, 30 minutes southeast of Siena, tel. 0577-704-791, mobile 335-692-5720, fax 0577-705-605, www.molinello.com, info@molinello.com).

Urbino

If you're driving through central Italy, Urbino is worth a stop for its sprawling, fascinating Ducal Palace. Although Urbino is the hometown of the artist Raphael and the architect Donato Bramante, it's better known for the Duke of Montefeltro, a mercenary general who built the palace and turned Urbino into an important Renaissance center. For my expanded coverage of Urbino, see www.ricksteves.com/urbino.

A classic hill town, Urbino has a medieval wall with four gates, and two main roads that crisscross at the town's main square, Piazza della Repubblica. The tiny TI is just across from the Ducal Palace (March-Oct Mon-Sat 9:00-19:00, Nov-Feb Mon-Sat 9:00-13:30 & 14:30-18:00, closed Sun year-round, Piazza Duca Federico 35, tel. 0722-2613, www.urbinoculturaturismo.it).

The **Ducal Palace** (Palazzo Ducale), which has more than 300 rooms, was built in the mid-1400s. While the rooms are fairly bare, the palace holds a few very special paintings, as well as exquisite inlaid-wood decorations. It's a monument to how one man—the Duke of Montefeltro—brought the Renaissance to his small town (€5, but sometimes €9 for special exhibits, Mon 8:30-14:00, Tue-Sun 8:30-19:15, last entry one hour before closing, tel. 072-232-2625).

The highlights of the palace include great paintings such as Raphael's *Portrait of a Gentlewoman* (a.k.a. *La Muta*); the Renaissance **courtyard** patterned after the trendsetting Medici-Riccardi Palace in Florence; the richly paneled and inlaid-wood walls of the duke's **study;** and the vast **cellars** that include a giant stable with a clever horse-pie disposal system.

Stop by the **Oratory of St. John** to see its remarkable frescoed interior that tells the story of the life of St. John the Baptist (€2.50, Mon-Sat 10:00-12:30 & 15:00-17:30, Sun 10:00-12:30, 5-minute walk from main square—follow signs, Piazza Baricci 31; if no one's there, find attendant at the Oratory of San Giuseppe a few steps away; mobile 347-671-1181).

Finally, for the ultimate Urbino view, climb up to the grassy park surrounding the **fortress** (interior closed, but grounds open to the public). The Franciscan church spire, on the left, marks the main square.

Getting There: Urbino is easier for drivers, but public transportation is an option. Buses link Urbino with Pesaro, on the Ravenna-Pescara train line (buses run hourly, 1-hour trip). From Venice, Florence, or Rome, trains leave for Pesaro almost hourly (taking 3-5 hours). In Urbino, buses come and go from the Piazza

Mercatale parking lot below the town, where an elevator lifts you up to the base of the Ducal Palace (or take a 5-minute steep walk up Via Mazzini to Piazza della Repubblica).

Sleeping in Urbino: The hotel scene is limited to a few comfortable, expensive places, including **Albergo San Domenico** (www.viphotels.it), **Hotel Raffaello** (www.albergoraffaello.com), and **Albergo Italia** (www.albergo-italia-urbino.it). The TI has a line on lots of families renting rooms.

Eating in Urbino: Try **Taverna degli Artisti** (Via Donato Bramante 52) and **Il Coppiere** (Via Santa Margherita 1), or **Ristorante/Pizzeria Tre Piante** (Via Voltaccia della Vecchia 1).

Orvieto

Just off the freeway and the main train line, Umbria's grand hill town entices those heading to and from Rome. While no secret, it's well worth a visit. The town sits majestically a thousand feet above the valley floor on a big chunk of tuff *(tufa),* an easy-to-dig volcanic rock. A regional power in the Middle Ages, a few centuries before Christ it was also one of the dozen major Etruscan cities. Some historians believe Orvieto may have been a kind of Etruscan Mecca (locals are looking for archaeological proof—the town and surrounding countryside are dotted with Etruscan ruins).

Orvieto, which has three popular claims to fame (cathedral, Classico wine, and ceramics), is loaded with tourists by day and quiet by night. Drinking a shot of the local white wine in a ceramic cup as you gaze up at the cathedral lets you experience Orvieto's three C's all at once. (Is the cathedral best in the afternoon, when the facade basks in golden light, or early in the morning, when it rises above the hilltop mist? You decide.) And a visit to Orvieto comes with a wonderful bonus: an easy bus connection with my favorite hill town, Civita di Bagnoregio (covered later in this chapter).

Orientation to Orvieto

Orvieto has two distinct parts: the old-town hilltop and the new town below. Whether coming by train or car, you first arrive in the forgettable, modern lower part of town. From there you can drive or take the funicular, elevator, or escalator up to the medieval upper town, an atmospheric labyrinth of streets and squares where all the sightseeing action is.

Tourist Information

A **seasonal TI** is at the top of the funicular, to your right as you exit into Piazza Cahen, the start of the upper town (daily March-Sept 10:00-13:00 & 15:00-18:00, no mid-day break May-mid-Aug, closed Oct-Feb). The **main TI** is on the cathedral square at Piazza del Duomo 24 (Mon-Fri 8:15-13:50 & 16:00-19:00, Sat-Sun 10:00-13:00 & 15:00-18:00, tel. 076-334-1772). Pick up the free city map and their green city guide, and ask about train and bus schedules. The ticket office (next to the main TI) sells combo-tickets, and books reservations for the underground tours (tel. 0763-340-688).

Combo-Ticket: The €18 **Carta Unica** combo-ticket covers Orvieto's top sights (virtually every sight recommended here, including Underground Orvieto Tours) and includes either five hours of parking (at *parcheggio* Campo della Fiera) or one round-trip on the bus and/or funicular (www.cartaunica.it). To cover your funicular ride, you can buy the combo-ticket at the bar at the train station upon arrival (if they haven't run out), or at a seasonal ticket office in the train station parking lot (tel. 0763-302-378). It's also available at the ticket office on Piazza del Duomo, as well as at most of the sights it covers.

Arrival in Orvieto

By Train: From the train station at the foot of the hill town, a **funicular** carries you to the top. Buy your ticket at the entrance to the *funiculare;* look for the *biglietteria* sign (€1, €0.80 with same-day train ticket, good for 70 minutes, includes minibus from Piazza Cahen to Piazza del Duomo, Mon-Sat 7:20-20:30, Sun 8:00-20:30, every 10 minutes). Or buy a Carta Unica combo-ticket (described earlier) to cover your funicular ride. If you arrive outside the funicular's operating hours, you can take a taxi or bus to the upper town (buses run roughly 2/hour until midnight, buy €1.50 ticket from driver). There's no baggage storage at the train station (the nearest place for day-trippers to store bags is the recommended Hotel Picchio, €4/bag, see page 711).

As you exit the funicular at the top, you're in Piazza Cahen, located at the east end of the upper town. To your left is a ruined fortress with a garden and a commanding view. To your right is the seasonal TI (closed Oct-Feb) and, down a steep road, St. Patrick's Well. Farther to the right is a park with Etruscan ruins and another sweeping view. Just in front of you is the orange shuttle bus, waiting to take you to Piazza del Duomo. The bus fills up fast, but the views from the ruined fortress are worth pausing for—if you miss the bus, you can wait for the next one, or just walk to the cathedral

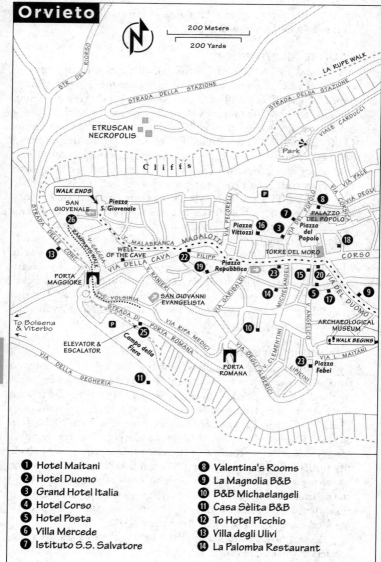

Orvieto

200 Meters
200 Yards

- ❶ Hotel Maitani
- ❷ Hotel Duomo
- ❸ Grand Hotel Italia
- ❹ Hotel Corso
- ❺ Hotel Posta
- ❻ Villa Mercede
- ❼ Istituto S.S. Salvatore
- ❽ Valentina's Rooms
- ❾ La Magnolia B&B
- ❿ B&B Michaelangeli
- ⓫ Casa Sèlita B&B
- ⓬ To Hotel Picchio
- ⓭ Villa degli Ulivi
- ⓮ La Palomba Restaurant

HILL TOWNS

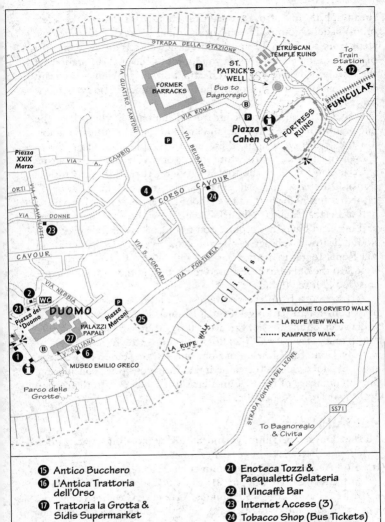

15 Antico Bucchero

16 L'Antica Trattoria dell'Orso

17 Trattoria la Grotta & Sidis Supermarket

18 Trattoria del Moro Aronne

19 Pizzeria & Restaurant Charlie

20 L'Oste del Re

21 Enoteca Tozzi & Pasqualetti Gelateria

22 Il Vincaffè Bar

23 Internet Access (3)

24 Tobacco Shop (Bus Tickets)

25 La Rupe View Walk Access

26 Romantic Ramparts Walk

27 MoDo Art Galleries & National Arch. Museum

(head uphill on Corso Cavour; after about 10 minutes take a left onto Via del Duomo). The bus drops you in Piazza del Duomo, just steps from the main TI and within easy walking distance of most of my recommended sights. If you forgot to check at the station for the train schedule to your next destination, no problem—the train schedule is posted at the top of the funicular and is also available at the TI.

By Car: You can park for free at the base of the hill at the huge lot behind the train station (5 minutes off the autostrada, follow the *P funiculare* signs, then see "By Train," above); in Piazza Cahen (north half, with white lines); or inside the Ex-Caserma (just as you arrive at the top of Orvieto, turn right and follow signs). Otherwise go to the small pay lot to the right of Orvieto's cathedral (€1.50 for first hour, €1/hour thereafter) or the blue-lined half of Piazza Cahen (€1/hour). Generally, white lines indicate free parking, and blue lines require you to buy a "pay and display" slip from a nearby machine. While you can drive up Via Postierla and Via Roma to get to central parking lots, Corso Cavour and other streets in the old center are closed to traffic and monitored by cameras (look for red lights).

If arriving from the southwest, Campo della Fiera is your most convenient parking lot (€0.80/hour). From its top level, it's still a steep climb up; you can avoid it by taking an escalator (7:00-21:00) or an elevator (7:00-24:00) to the upper town (both free).

By Taxi: Taxis line up in front of the train station and charge about €12 for a ride to the cathedral (a ridiculous price considering the fun and ease of the €1 funicular/shuttle-bus ride to the cathedral square, tel. 360-433-057).

Helpful Hints

Market Days: On Thursday and Saturday mornings, Piazza del Popolo becomes a busy farmers market.

Internet Access: Caffè Montanucci has four terminals (€2.50/30 minutes, Corso Cavour 21, daily 7:00-24:00), **Copisteria ESPA** has three (€3/30 minutes, Via Felice Cavallotti 9, Mon-Fri 9:00-13:00 & 16:00-19:40, Sat 9:00-13:00, closed Sun), and the **library** on Piazza Febei offers free Internet access during its limited hours (Mon-Fri 8:30-13:30; Sept-June also Mon, Wed, and Fri 15:30-18:30; closed Sat-Sun).

Driver: For a private car hire, consider Giuliotaxi, enthusiastically run by charming, English-speaking Giulio and his sister Maria Serena. They charge about €50 for a ride to Bagnoregio, and provide a good way to explore the region (mobile 360-433-057, www.argoweb.it/giuliotaxi, giuliotaxi@tiscali.it).

Local Guide: Manuela Del Turco is good (€100/2.5-hour tour, mobile 333-221-9879, manueladel@virgilio.it).

After Dark: In the evening, there's little going on other than strolling and eating. The big *passeggiata* scene is down Via del Duomo and Corso Cavour. **Il Vincaffè** is *the* place for the classy young crowd late at night, with lots of good wines by the glass (Via Filippeschi 39).

Self-Guided Walk

Welcome to Orvieto

A quickie L-shaped walk takes you through Orvieto's historic center. Each evening, this route is the scene of the local *passeggiata*. Facing the cathedral, head left. Stroll under the clock tower (first put here in 1347 for the workers building the cathedral), which marks the start of Via del Duomo, lined with shops selling ceramics. Via dei Magoni (first left) has several artisan shops and the crazy little Il Mago di Oz ("Wizard of Oz") shop, a wondrous toyland created by eccentric Giuseppe Rosella (Via dei Magoni 4, tel. 076-334-2063; he runs another store nearby at Via Pedota 9). Have Giuseppe push a few buttons, and you're far from Kansas (no photos allowed).

Via del Duomo continues to Orvieto's main intersection, where it meets Corso Cavour and a tall, stark tower—the Torre del Moro. The tower marks the center of town, serves as a handy orientation tool, and is decorated by the coats of arms of past governors. The elevator leaves you with 173 steps still to go to earn a commanding view (€2.80, daily March-Oct 10:00-19:00, May-Aug until 20:00, shorter hours off-season).

This crossroads divides the town into four quarters (notice the *Quartiere* signs on the corners). Residents of these four districts compete in a lively equestrian competition on Piazza del Popolo during the annual Corpus Christi celebration. Historically, the four streets led from here to the market and the fine palazzo on Piazza del Popolo, the well, the Duomo, and City Hall.

Before heading left down Corso Cavour, side-trip a block farther ahead, behind the tower, for a look at the striking Palazzo del Popolo. Built of local *tufa*, this is a textbook example of a fortified medieval public palace: a fortress designed to house the city's leadership and military, with a market at its base, fancy meeting rooms upstairs, and aristocratic living quarters on the top level.

Return to the tower and head down Corso Cavour (turning right) past classic storefronts to Piazza della Repubblica and City Hall. The original vision—though it never came to fruition—was for City Hall to have five arches flanking the main central arch (marked by the flags today). The Church of Sant'Andrea (left of City Hall) sits atop an Etruscan temple that was likely the birthplace of Orvieto centuries before Christ. Inside is an interesting architectural progression: Romanesque (with scant frescoes surviving), Gothic, and a Renaissance barrel vault in the apse (behind the altar)—all lit by fine alabaster windows.

From City Hall, you can continue to the far end of town to the Church of San Giovenale—where, if you have the MoDo ticket (see page 705), you can see the statues of the apostles that once stood in the Duomo (these statues may be moved back inside the Duomo in 2012). From here you can take a left and walk the cliffside ramparts (see "View Walks," later).

Sights in Orvieto

▲▲Duomo

The cathedral has Italy's liveliest facade (from 1330, by Lorenzo Maitani and others). This colorful, prickly Gothic facade, divided by four pillars, has been compared to a medieval altarpiece. Grab a gelato (buy it to the left of the church) and study this gleaming mass of mosaics, stained glass, and sculpture.

At the base of the cathedral, the four broad marble pillars carved with biblical scenes tell the story of the world from left to right in four acts: Genesis, Old Testament, New Testament, and Revelation. The relief on the far left shows the Creation (see God performing surgery as he extracts Adam's rib, and the snake tempting Eve). Next is the Tree of Jesse (Jesus' family tree—with Mary, then Jesus on top) flanked by Old Testament stories, then the New Testament (look for the unique manger scene and other famous scenes from the life of Christ). On the far right is the Last Judgment (Christ judging on top, with a commotion of sarcophagi popping open and all hell breaking loose at the bottom).

Each pillar is topped by a bronze symbol of one of the Evangelists: angel (Matthew), lion (Mark), eagle (John), and ox (Luke). The bronze doors are modern, by the Sicilian sculptor Emilio Greco. (A gallery devoted to Greco's work is to the immediate right of the church; see page 705.) In the mosaic below the rose window, Mary is transported to heaven. In the uppermost mosaic, Mary is crowned.

Step inside. The nave feels spacious and less cluttered than most Italian churches. Until 1877 it was much busier, with statues of the apostles at each column and fancy chapels. Then the people decided they wanted to "un-Baroque" their church. More recently, however, there's been talk of returning the apostles to their original locations—perhaps in time for your visit.

HILL TOWNS

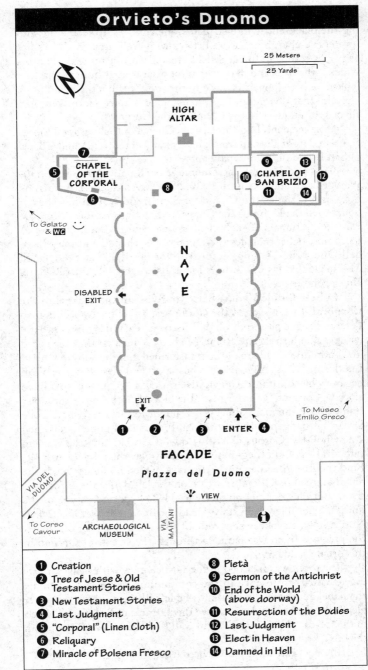

Orvieto's Duomo

25 Meters
25 Yards

HIGH ALTAR

7

5 **CHAPEL OF THE CORPORAL**

6

8

9 **13**

10 **CHAPEL OF SAN BRIZIO** **12**

11 **14**

To Gelato & WC :)

N A V E

DISABLED EXIT

To Museo Emilio Greco

EXIT

1 **2** **3** **ENTER** **4**

FACADE

Piazza del Duomo

VIA DEL DUOMO

To Corso Cavour

ARCHAEOLOGICAL MUSEUM

VIA MAITANI

VIEW

HILL TOWNS

1. Creation
2. Tree of Jesse & Old Testament Stories
3. New Testament Stories
4. Last Judgment
5. "Corporal" (Linen Cloth)
6. Reliquary
7. Miracle of Bolsena Fresco
8. Pietà
9. Sermon of the Antichrist
10. End of the World (above doorway)
11. Resurrection of the Bodies
12. Last Judgment
13. Elect in Heaven
14. Damned in Hell

The interior is warmly lit by alabaster windows, highlighting the black-and-white striped stonework. Why such a big and impressive church in such a little town? Well, first of all, it's not as big as it looks. The architect created an illusion—the nave is wider at the back and narrower at the altar so that from the back, it looks like it's a longer distance to the front. Still, it's a big and rich church. That's because of a famous blood-stained cloth, kept in a silver-gilt reliquary in the Chapel of the Corporal.

Visit the church in three parts: Chapel of the Corporal (north transept, left of altar, in front), high altar (center front), and Chapel of San Brizio (left front, paid entry).

Cost and Hours: The Duomo is open daily April-Sept 7:30-19:30, March and Oct until 18:30, Nov-Feb until 17:30. Admission is €3 and includes the Chapel of San Brizio, which has shorter hours than the Duomo. The Chapel of San Brizio is open Mon-Sat 9:30-19:00, Sun 13:30-18:30 (closes one hour earlier in winter). A €5 combo-ticket includes the Duomo, the chapel, and the Museo dell'Opera del Duomo—the "MoDo" (available at the chapel; MoDo alone costs €4). Admission is also covered by the €18 Carta Unica combo-ticket.

○ **Self-Guided Tour:** Start your visit in the **Chapel of the Corporal.** In 1263, or so the story goes, a skeptical priest named Peter of Prague passed through Bolsena (a few miles from Orvieto) while on a pilgrimage to Rome. He had doubts that the bread used in Communion could really be transformed into the body of Christ. But during Mass, as he held the host aloft and blessed it, the bread began to bleed, running down his arms and dripping onto a linen cloth (a "corporal") on the altar. The bloody cloth (in the turquoise frame above the main altar) was brought to Orvieto, where Pope Urban IV happened to be visiting. The amazed pope proclaimed a new holiday, Corpus Christi (Body of Christ), and the Orvieto cathedral was built (begun in 1290) to display the miraculous relic. Find the fine gilded enamel **reliquary** (which no longer holds the blood-stained relic) in a glass case on the left. Until the 1970s, this silver-and-blue enamel reliquary (c. 1358)—considered one of the finest medieval jewels in Italy—held the linen relic as if in a frame. Notice how it evokes the facade of this cathedral. For centuries, the precious linen was paraded through the streets of Orvieto in this ornate reliquary.

The room was frescoed in the 14th century with scenes attesting to Christ's presence in the communion wafer (for example, the panel above the glass case to the left illustrates how the wafer bleeds if you cook it). You can see the **Miracle of Bolsena** depicted in the fresco on the chapel's right wall (light it with a €0.50 coin in the box).

The new cathedral put Orvieto (then known as "Urbs Vetus")

on the map, and with lots of pilgrims came lots of wealth. Two future popes used the town as a refuge when their enemies forced them to flee Rome.

Now leave the Chapel of the Corporal and walk to the middle front of the church, where you'll see a patch in the marble floor, a fine marble statue, and the highly decorated **high altar.**

The brilliant stained glass from the 14th century is original and painstakingly restored. The fine organ has more than 5,000 pipes. The marble *pietà* (statue of Mary holding Jesus' just-crucified body) was carved in 1579 by local artist Ippolito Scalza. Clearly inspired by Michelangelo's *Pietà*, this exceptional piece with four figures was sculpted from one piece of marble. Notice the texture Scalza gave this wonderful work. Look at the alabaster rose window. Also note how the architect's trick, making the church look bigger from the rear, works in reverse from here. If you look to the back, the church feels stubbier than it actually is.

As the Roman Catholic church countered the Reformation, it made reforms of its own. For instance, altars were moved back to let people get closer to the religious action. The confused patching on the marble floor is evidence that, prior to the Counter-Reformation, the altar stood here.

The **Chapel of San Brizio,** to the right of the altar, is Orvieto's one must-see artistic sight. It features Luca Signorelli's brilliantly lit frescoes of the Apocalypse (painted 1499-1504). Step into the

chapel and you're surrounded by vivid scenes crammed with figures. The frescoes depict events at the end of the world, but they also reflect the turbulent political and religious atmosphere of late 15th-century Italy.

The chapel is decorated in one big and cohesive story. Follow the plot (counterclockwise): Antichrist, end of world (above the arch facing the nave), Resurrection, hell, Judgment Day (Fra Angelico's Jesus above the window), and finally heaven. Now the story: In the **Sermon of the Antichrist** (left wall), a crowd gathers around a man preaching from a pedestal. It's the Antichrist, who comes posing as Jesus to mislead the faithful. This befuddled Antichrist forgets his lines mid-speech, but the Devil is on hand to whisper what to say next. His words sow wickedness through the world, including executions (upper right). The worried woman in red and white (foreground, left of pedestal) gets money from a man for something she's not proud of (perhaps receiving funds from a Jewish moneylender—notice the Stars of David on his purse).

Most likely, the Antichrist himself is a veiled reference to Savonarola (1452-1498), the charismatic Florentine monk who defied the pope, drove the Medici family from power, and riled the populace with apocalyptic sermons. Many Italians—including the painter Signorelli—viewed Savonarola as a tyrant and heretic, the Antichrist who was ushering in the Last Days.

In the upper left, notice the hardworking angel. He looks as if he's at batting practice, hitting followers of the Antichrist back to earth as they try to get through the pearly gates. In the bottom left corner of the scene is a self-portrait of the artist, **Luca Signorelli** (c. 1450-1523), well-dressed in black with long golden hair. Signorelli, from nearby Cortona, was at the peak of his powers, and this chapel was his masterpiece. He looks out proudly as if to say, "I did all this in just five years, on time and on budget," confirming his reputation as a speedy, businesslike painter. Next to him is the artist Fra Angelico, who started the chapel decoration five decades earlier, but completed only a small part of it.

Around the arch, opposite the windows, are signs of the **end of the world:** eclipse, tsunami, falling stars, earthquakes, violence in the streets, and a laser-wielding gray angel.

On the right wall (opposite the Antichrist) is the **Resurrection of the Bodies.** Trumpeting angels blow a wake-up call, and the dead climb dreamily out of the earth to be clothed with new bodies. On the same wall (below the action, at eye level) is a gripping *pietà*. Also by Signorelli, this *pietà* gives an insight into the genius and personality of the artist. Look at the emotion in the faces of the two Marys and consider that Signorelli's son had just died. The Deposition scene (behind Jesus' leg) seems inspired by ancient Greek scenes of a pre-Christian hero's death. In the confident spirit of the Renaissance, the artist incorporates a pagan scene to support a Christian story. This 3-D realism in a 2-D sketch shows the work of a talented master.

The altar wall (with the windows) features the **Last Judgment.** To the left of the altar (and continuing on the left wall) are the **Elect in Heaven.** They spend eternity posing like bodybuilders while listening to celestial Muzak. To the right (and continuing on the right wall) are the **Damned in Hell,** in the scariest mosh pit ever. Devils torment sinners in graphic detail, while winged demons control the airspace overhead. In the center, one lusty demon turns to tell the frightened woman on his back exactly what he's got planned for their date. (According to legend, this was Signorelli's lover, who betrayed him...and ended up here. You'll see this couple all over town.) Signorelli's ability to tell a story through human actions and gestures, rather than symbols, inspired his younger contemporary, Michelangelo, who meticulously studied the elder artist's nudes.

In this chapel, Christian theology sits physically and figuratively upon a foundation of classical logic. Below everything are Greek and Latin philosophers, plus Dante, struggling to reconcile Classic truth with Church doctrine. You can see the intellectual challenge on their faces as they ponder this puzzle. They're immersed in fanciful Grotesque (i.e., grotto-esque) decor. Dating from 1499, this is one of the first uses of the frilly, nubile, and even sexy "wallpaper pattern" so popular in the Renaissance. (It was inspired by the decorations found in Nero's Golden House in Rome, which had been discovered under street level just a few years earlier and was mistaken for an underground grotto.)

During the Renaissance, nakedness symbolized purity. When attitudes changed during the Counter-Reformation, the male figures in Signorelli's frescoes were given penis-covering sashes. During a 1982 restoration, most—but not all—of the sashes were removed. A little of that prudishness survives to this day, as those in heaven were left with their sashes modestly in place.

After leaving the cathedral, if you want to visit a **viewpoint park,** exit left and pass the small parking lot and WC.

Near the Duomo: MoDo and Other Museums
▲▲MoDo City Museum (Museo dell'Opera del Duomo)— This museum is a confusing ensemble of several different sights, scattered around town: the cathedral art collections split between two small galleries behind the cathedral; the Emilio Greco collection (next to the cathedral, in Palazzo Soliano); and, at the far end of town, the Church of San Giovenale, which has statues of the 12 apostles that were added to the Duomo in the Baroque Age (c. 1700) and removed in the late 1800s.

Cost and Hours: €4 MoDo ticket covers all MoDo sights (or get the €5 combo-ticket that includes the Duomo and Chapel of San Brizio), open daily 9:30-19:00, off-season 9:30-13:00 & 14:00-17:00.

Cathedral Art Collections: Behind the Duomo in Palazzi Papali, a complex of medieval palaces shows off the city's best art. The highlight is just inside the door: the *Sala della Maestà*—a bronze Mary-and-child with exquisite angels, under a canopy that once filled the niche in the center of the cathedral's facade. This is proto-Renaissance, dating from around 1300.

Other highlights include fine inlaid woodwork from the original choir; a room full of sinopias (wall charts for frescoes, with a roughed-up surface so the wet plaster would stick); a *Madonna with Child* from 1322 by Sienese great Simone Martini, who worked in Orvieto; and paintings from the late 1500s that decorated the side chapels with a harsher Counter-Reformation message.

Museo Emilio Greco: Emilio Greco (1913-1995) was a

Sicilian artist who designed the modern doors of Orvieto's cathedral. His sketches and about 30 of his bronze statues are on display here, showing his absorption with gently twisting and turning nudes. Greco's sketchy outlines of women are simply beautiful. The artful installation of his work in this palazzo, with walkways and even a spiral staircase up to the ceiling, allows you to view his sculptures from different angles.

National Archaeological Museum of Orvieto—This small four-room collection, immediately behind the cathedral in the ground floor of Palazzi Papali (under MoDo), beautifully shows off a trove of well-preserved Etruscan bronze, terra-cotta, and ceramics—some with painted colors surviving from 500 B.C. The reconstructed Golini tombs (named after the man who discovered them in 1836) show scenes from an Etruscan banquet in the afterlife.

Cost and Hours: €3, daily 8:30-19:30. The overpriced audioguide gives a virtual visit to the excavation sites (€5, 30 minutes). For background on the Etruscans, see page 656.

Archaeological Museum (Museo Claudio Faina e Museo Civico)—A former palace, across from the entrance to the cathedral, holds an Etruscan collection. The highlights of the first floor are the Roman coins; push the brass buttons and they rotate so you can see both sides. The best of the Etruscan vases and bronzes are on the top floor.

Cost and Hours: €4.50; April-Sept daily 9:30-18:00; Oct-March Tue-Sun 10:00-17:00, closed Mon; English descriptions throughout, tel. 076-334-1511, www.museofaina.it.

Underground Orvieto

If you're short on time and have to choose one means of going underground in Orvieto, I'd recommend Well of the Cave or St. Patrick's Well over Underground Orvieto Tours.

▲**St. Patrick's Well (Pozzo di San Patrizio)**—Modern engineers are impressed by this deep well—175 feet deep and 45 feet wide—designed in the 16th century with a double-helix pattern. The two spiral stairways allow an efficient one-way traffic flow: intriguing now, but critical then. Imagine if donkeys and people, balancing jugs of water, had to go up and down the same stairway. At the bottom is a bridge that people could walk on to scoop up water.

The well was built because a pope got nervous. After Rome was sacked in 1527 by renegade troops of the Holy Roman Empire, the pope fled to Orvieto. He feared that even this little town (with no water source on top) would be besieged. He commissioned a well, which was started in 1527 and finished 10 years later. It was a huge project. (As it turns out, the town was never besieged, but supporters believe that the well was worth the cost and labor because of its deterrence value—attackers would think twice about besieging a town with a water source.) Even today, when a local is faced with a difficult task, people say, "It's like digging St. Patrick's Well." It's a total of 496 steps up and down—lots of exercise and not much to see other than some amazing 16th-century engineering.

Cost and Hours: €5; interesting €1 audioguide, ID required; daily April-Sept 9:00-20:00, shorter hours in winter, the well is to your right as you exit the funicular. Bring a sweater if you plan to descend to the chilly depths.

Well of the Cave (Pozzo della Cava)—While renovating its trattoria, an Orvieto family discovered a vast underground network of Etruscan-era caves, wells, and tunnels. The excavation started in 1984 and continues to this day. It's well-explained in English and makes for a fun subterranean wander.

Cost and Hours: €3, Tue-Sun 9:00-20:00, closed Mon, Via della Cava 28, tel. 076-334-2373.

Underground Orvieto Tours (Parco delle Grotte)—Guides weave archaeological history into a good, hour-long look at about 100 yards of Etruscan and medieval caves. You'll see the remains of an old olive press, an impressive 130-foot-deep Etruscan well shaft, what's left of a primitive cement quarry, and an extensive dovecote (pigeon coop) where the birds were reared for roasting (pigeon dishes are still featured on many Orvieto menus; look for—or avoid—*piccione*).

Cost and Hours: €6; 1-hour English tours depart from ticket office next to main TI at 11:15, 12:30, 16:15, and 17:15; more often with demand, book tour at ticket office, confirm times at TI or by calling 076-334-0688, www.orvietounderground.it.

Etruscan Necropolis—Below town, at the base of the cliff, is a remarkable "city of the dead" that dates back to about five centuries before Christ. The tombs, which are laid out in a kind of street

grid, are empty, and there's precious little to see here other than the basic stony construction. But it is both eerie and fascinating to wander the streets of an Etruscan cemetery.

Cost and Hours: €3, daily April-Sept 8:30-19:00, Oct-March 8:30-17:00.

View Walks

▲**Hike Around the City on the Rupe**—Orvieto's Rupe is a peaceful paved path that completely circles the town at the base of the cliff upon which it sits.

With the help of the TI brochure on "la Rupe," you'll see there are three access points from the town for the three-mile walk. Once on the trail, it's fairly level and easy to follow. On one side you have the cliff, with the town high above. On the other side you have Umbrian views stretching into the distance. I'd leave Orvieto at Piazza Marconi and walk left (counterclockwise) three-quarters of the way around the town (there's a fine view down onto the Etruscan Necropolis mid-way), and ride the escalator and elevator back up to the town from the big new Campo della Fiera parking lot. If you're ever confused about the path, follow the *la Rupe* and *Giro dell'Umbria* signs.

▲**Shorter Romantic Rampart Stroll**—Thanks to its dramatic hilltop setting, several fine little walks wind around the edges of Orvieto. My favorite after dark, when it's lamplit and romantic, is along the ramparts at the far west end of town. Start at the Church of San Giovenale. With your back to the church, go a block to the right to the end of town. Then head left along the ramparts, with cypress-dotted Umbria to your right, and follow Vicolo Volsinia to the Church of San Giovanni Evangelista.

Near Orvieto

Wine-Tasting—Orvieto Classico wine is justly famous. For a short tour of a winery with Etruscan cellars, visit **Tenuta Le Velette,** where English-speaking Corrado and Cecilia (cheh-CHEEL-yah) Bottai will welcome you—if you've called ahead to set up an appointment (€8-18 for tour and tasting, price varies depending on wines, Mon-Fri 8:30-12:00 & 14:00-17:00, Sat 8:30-12:00, closed Sun, also have accommodations—see listing on page 712, tel. 076-329-090, mobile 348-300-2002, www.levelette.it). From their sign (5-minute drive past Orvieto at top of switchbacks just before Canale, on road to Bagnoregio), cruise down a long tree-lined drive, then park at the striped gate (must call ahead; no drop-ins).

Custodi is another respected family-run winery that produces Orvieto Classico, grappa, and olive oil on their 140-acre estate. Stop by for a tour of their cantina, an explanation of the winemaking process, and a tasting of four of their wines. Reserve ahead for an assortment of *salumi* and local cheeses or lunch to go with your wine-tasting (€7/person for wines only, €16/person with light lunch, daily 8:30-12:30 & 15:30-18:30 except closed Sun afternoons, Viale Venere S.N.C. Loc. Canale; on the road from Orvieto to Civita, a half-mile after Le Velette, it's the first building before Canale; tel. 076-329-053, mobile 392-161-9334, www.cantinacustodi.com, info@cantinacustodi.com). Helpful Chiara and Laura Custodi speak English.

Sleeping in Orvieto

(€1 = about $1.40, country code: 39)

Most of my recommended hotels are in the old town. The exceptions: Casa Sèlita B&B and Villa degli Ulivi are near the Campo della Fiera elevator, and Hotel Picchio is in a more modern neighborhood near the station.

$$$ Hotel Maitani is an overpriced time warp with antiquated outlets and rotary phones. Still, its grand public spaces and 39 rooms—each elegant and individual—offer a memorable splurge in a venerable, centuries-old building half a block from the Duomo (Sb-€79, Db-€130, Db suite-€152 and €175, claim your 8 percent Rick Steves discount if you book direct, I'd skip their €10 breakfast, calls from the room are very expensive, air-con, elevator, pay Wi-Fi, 20 yards from the bus stop behind the TI at Via Lorenzo Maitani 5, tel. & fax 076-334-2011, www.hotelmaitani.com, direzione@hotelmaitani.com, Giuseppi and Norma).

$$$ Hotel Duomo is centrally located and modern, with splashy art and 17 sleek rooms. Double-paned windows keep the sound of the church bells well-muffled (Sb-€80, Db-€120, Db suite-€140, Tb-€150, extra bed-€10, 10 percent cash discount with this book, buffet breakfast, air-con, elevator, free Internet access, pay Wi-Fi, private parking-€10, sunny terrace, a block from Duomo behind *gelateria* at Vicolo di Maurizio 7, tel. 076-334-1887, fax 076-339-4973, www.orvietohotelduomo.com, hotelduomo@tiscalinet.it, Gianni and Maura Massaccesi don't speak English, daughter Elisa does). The Massaccesi family also owns a three-room B&B 50 yards from the hotel (Sb-€70, Db-€90, Tb-€110, breakfast at the main hotel).

$$$ Grand Hotel Italia, new and top-end, rents 46 modern and spacious rooms farther into the old town (Db-€140, extra bed-€20, air-con, elevator, stay-awhile lobby and terrace, Internet access and Wi-Fi, Via di Piazza del Popolo 13, tel. 0763-342-065, www.grandhotelitalia.it, hotelita@libero.it).

$$ Hotel Corso is friendly, with 18 comfy, contemporary rooms—some with balconies and views. Everyone can enjoy their sunlit little terrace (Sb-€70, Db-€95, Tb-€115, 10 percent discount with this book, buffet breakfast-€6.50, ask for quieter room off street, air-con, elevator, pay Wi-Fi, free parking nearby and on main street up from funicular toward Duomo at Corso Cavour 339, tel. 076-334-2020, fax 076-334-0648, www.hotelcorso.net, info@hotelcorso.net, Carla).

$$ Casa Sèlita B&B, a peaceful country house, offers easy access to Orvieto for drivers and train trippers. It's nestled in an orchard just below the town cliffs (under the big Campo della Fiera parking lot, with its handy escalator up into town). Its six rooms with terraces are airy and fresh, with dark hardwood floors, fluffy down comforters, and modern baths. Enjoy the views from the relaxing garden. Sèlita, her husband Ennio, and daughter Elena are gracious hosts (Sb-€55, Db-€80, Tb-€90, €5 less with stays of two or more nights, €5 more off-season for heat, these prices promised to my readers through 2012 if you book direct, cash only, fans, free Internet access and Wi-Fi, free parking, Strada di Porta Romana 8, tel. 076-334-4218, www.casaselita.com, info@casa selita.com).

$ Hotel Posta is a dumpy, long-ago-elegant palazzo renting 20 quirky rooms with vintage furniture—among the cheapest in town (S-€31, Sb-€37, D-€44, Db-€56, breakfast-€6, cash only, Via Luca Signorelli 18, tel. & fax 076-334-1909, www.orvietohotels.it, hotelposta@orvietohotels.it, little English spoken, Alessia).

$ Villa Mercede, a wonderful value, is a religious institution offering 23 cheap, simple twin-bedded rooms, each with a big modern bathroom and many with glorious Umbrian views (Sb-€50, Db-€70, Tb-€90, free parking, Wi-Fi, a half-block from Duomo at Via Soliana 2, tel. 076-334-1766, fax 076-334-0119, www.argoweb.it/casareligiosa_villamercede, villamercede @orvienet.it).

$ Istituto S.S. Salvatore rents nine spotless twin rooms and five singles in their convent, which comes with a peaceful terrace and garden, and a 22:30 curfew (Sb-€38, Db-€58 April-Sept, Db-€48 Oct-March, cash only, no breakfast, elevator, free parking, just off Piazza del Popolo at Via del Popolo 1, tel. & fax 076-334-2910, istitutosansalvatore@tiscali.it). Though the nuns don't speak English, tech-savvy Sister Maria Stella has mastered Google Translator, and will happily use it to answer your questions.

$ Valentina's Rooms include six clean, airy, well-appointed rooms and two apartments, all with big beds and antique furniture. Her place is located in the heart of Orvieto, behind the palace on Piazza del Popolo (Db-€58 for two or more nights, Db-€65 for one-night, Tb-€75, studio with kitchen-€80; bright, spacious family apartment for up to 5 people-€150 for two or more nights, €170 for one night; these special discounted cash-only prices with this book, breakfast-€4, air-con-€5, Wi-Fi, Via Vivaria 7, tel. 076-334-1607, mobile 393-970-5868, www.bandbvalentina.com, valentina.z@tiscalinet.it). Valentina also rents three rooms across the square that share a kitchen (Db-€50, no air-con).

$ La Magnolia B&B has lots of fancy terra-cotta tiles, a couple of rooms with frescoed ceilings, terraces, and other welcoming touches. Its seven unique rooms, some like mini-apartments with kitchens, are cheerfully decorated and *tranquillo* despite being on the town's main drag (Db-€65, plush Db apartment-€70-75, extra person-€15, family deals, book direct and stay at least two nights to get a 10 percent Rick Steves discount, cash only, no elevator, use of washer-€3.50, Via Duomo 29, tel. 076-334-2808, mobile 338-902-7400, www.bblamagnolia.it, info@bblamagnolia.it, Serena and Loredana).

$ B&B Michaelangeli, tucked round the corner from La Palomba restaurant, is run by eager-to-please Francesca, who provides homey touches and free tea, coffee, and breakfast supplies in her two comfortable and well-appointed apartments (Db-€70, kids-€10 extra, fully equipped kitchen, washing machine, free underground parking, Via Saracinelli 22, tel. 076-339-3862, mobile 347-089-0349, www.bbmichelangeli.com, f_michelangeli @alice.it).

$ Hotel Picchio is a hardworking little family-run place with 27 overpriced rooms stuck back in the modern world, in a forgettable zone 300 yards from the train station at the base of the hill. A trail leads from here up to the old town (Sb-€45, Db-€62, superior Db-€85, Tb-€80-95, higher rates are for newer and brighter rooms in annex across street, 10 percent discount with this book when you book direct, air-con-€6, Wi-Fi, free outdoor parking, Via G. Salvatori 17, tel. & fax 076-330-1144, mobile 339-819-1823, www .hotelpicchio.it, hotelpicchio@tin.it, Alessandra and Giovanna both speak English). Alessandra and Giovanna also run **Villa degli Ulivi,** a classier place on the opposite side of town (works well for drivers but otherwise inconvenient, Sb-€60, Db-€90, Tb-€100, air-con, Wi-Fi, double-paned windows keep out most traffic noise, free parking, small garden and breakfast terrace, near the base of the Campo della Fiera elevator at Strada delle Conce 23).

Near Orvieto

$$$ Agriturismo Fattoria di Vibio produces olive oil and honey, sells organic products, and offers classes and spa services. In August, its 14 rooms rent at peak prices (and for one week during the month they require a minimum seven-night stay, with arrivals and departures on Saturdays). The rest of the year, no minimum stay is required, although rates drop dramatically for longer visits (Db-€250-320, includes breakfast and dinner). Its three cottages sleep 4-7 people and rent only by the week (€1,120-1,680/week depending on amenities, see complicated rate table on website, farthest cottage is 20 miles northeast of Orvieto, tel. 075-874-9607, fax 075-878-0014, www.fattoriadivibio.com, info@fattoriadivibio.com).

$$$ Agriturismo La Rocca Orvieto, run by Emiliano and Sabrina, is a fancy spa-type place, located 15 minutes north of Orvieto by car. They produce their own olive oil and wine and have nine rooms and 10 apartments—all with air-conditioning and Wi-Fi (Db-€98-140, 10 percent discount with this book—mention when you reserve, pool, panoramic view restaurant, wellness center with Jacuzzi and steam room, gym, mountain bikes, bocce court, hiking paths, tel. 076-334-4210 or 076-339-3437, fax 076-339-5155, mobile 348-640-0845, www.laroccaorvieto.com, info@larocca orvieto.com).

At **$$$ Agriturismo Locanda Rosati,** you'll be greeted by gracious hosts Cristina and Giampiero Rosati, who rent 10 tastefully decorated rooms in a pleasant, homey atmosphere (Db-€110-140, Tb-€140-160, full traditional dinners for €35 on request with this book, air-con, swimming pool, 5 miles from Orvieto on the road to Viterbo, tel. 076-321-7314, www.locandarosati.it, info@locandarosati.it).

$$$ Borgo Fontanile is a vacation home with a swimming pool, terrace, and kids' play area. Its five new apartments with rustic wood beams and terra-cotta tile floors sleep 2-4 people (€50-60/night per person, discounts for longer stays, €400-800/apartment per week, air-con, Vocabolo Fornace 159, Loc. Baschi, tel. & fax 074-495-7342, www.borgofontanile.com, info@borgofontanile.com).

$$ Tenuta Le Velette is a sprawling, family-run farmhouse. Cecilia and Corrado Bottai rent six fully furnished apartments and villas, housing 2-14 people in perfect Umbrian rural peace and tranquility (Db apartment-€90-110, see website for details on various villas, 3-night minimum, 20 percent discount for weekly stay, cash only, pool, bocce court, 5 minutes from Orvieto—drive toward Bagnoregio-Canale and follow *Tenuta le Velette* signs, fax 076-329-114, mobile 348-300-2002, www.levelette.it, cecilia levelette@libero.it). They also offer wine-tastings (see listing on page 708).

$$ Agriturismo Cioccoleta has eight rooms named after the grapes that grow in its vineyards. It's cozy, family-run, and offers sweeping views (Db-€70, Tb-€90, Qb-€110, 10 percent discount with this book—mention when you reserve, includes breakfast, 3 miles north of Orvieto at Località Bardano 34 in Bardano, tel. 0763-316-011, mobile 349-860-9780, www.cioccoleta.it, info@cioccoleta.it, Angela Zucconi).

$ Agriturismo Pomonte Umbria, seven miles east of Orvieto, offers home-cooked meals, lovely vistas, and seven comfortable rooms in a recently built guest house (Db-€60, includes breakfast, €94-half-pension, €120-full pension, Loc. Canino di Orvieto 1, Corbara, tel. 076-330-4041, mobile 392-410-2115, fax 076-330-4080, www.pomonte.it, info@pomonte.it, Enrico).

Eating in Orvieto

La Palomba features game and truffle specialties in a wood-paneled dining room. Gianpiero, Enrica, and the Cinti family take care of their regulars and visiting travelers alike, offering both a fine value and a classy conviviality. Seating is comfortable and not too crowded. Truffles are ground right at your table—try the *ombricelli al tartufo* (homemade pasta with truffles), then follow that up with some *piccione* (pigeon). As firm believers in the slow-food movement, they use ingredients that are mostly organic and locally produced (€8 pastas, €12 *secondi,* daily 12:30-14:15 & 19:30-22:00 except closed Wed Oct-April, reservations smart, just off Piazza della Repubblica at Via Cipriano Manente 16, tel. 076-334-3395).

Antico Bucchero, a bit mod under a big white vault, makes a nice splurge with its candlelit ambience and delicious food (€8 pastas, €12 *secondi,* Thu-Tue 12:00-15:00 & 19:00-23:00, closed Wed, indoor/outdoor seating, a half-block south of Corso Cavour, between Torre del Moro and Piazza della Repubblica at Via de Cartari 4, tel. 076-334-1725, Piero and Silvana).

L'Antica Trattoria dell'Orso offers well-prepared Umbrian cuisine paired with fine wines in a homey and peaceful atmosphere. Ciro and chef Gabriele enjoy getting to know their diners, and will steer you toward the freshest seasonal plates of their famous pastas and passionately prepared vegetables. Or just trust Gabriele, and go for their €30 complete tasting meal, which includes wine (Wed-Sun 12:00-14:00 & 19:30-22:00, closed Mon-Tue, just off Piazza della Repubblica at Via della Misericordia 18/20, tel. 076-334-1642).

Trattoria la Grotta, pricey and chic, prides itself on serving only the freshest food and finest wine. The decor is Signorelli mod and the ambience is quiet, with courteous service. Owner-chef Franco has been at it for 50 years, and promises diners a free coffee, grappa, *limoncello,* or *vin santo* with this book (Wed-Mon opens at 12:00 for lunch and at 19:00 for dinner, closed Tue, Via Luca Signorelli 5, tel. 076-334-1348).

Trattoria del Moro Aronne is a long-established family bistro run by Cristian and his mother Rolanda, who lovingly prepare homemade pasta and market-fresh meats and produce for their typical Umbrian specialties. Be sure to sample the *nidi*—folds of fresh pasta enveloping warm, gooey Pecorino cheese sweetened

Italy Is Made of Tuff Stuff

Tuff (*tufa* in Italian) is a light-colored volcanic rock that is common in Italy. A part of Tuscany is even called the "Tuff Area." The seven hills of Rome are made of tuff, and quarried blocks of this stone can be seen in the Colosseum, Pantheon, and Castel Sant'Angelo. Just outside of Rome, the catacombs were carved from tuff. Sorrento rises above the sea on a tuff outcrop. Orvieto, Civita di Bagnoregio (pictured), and many other hill towns perch on bluffs of tuff.

Italy's early inhabitants, including the Etruscans and Romans, carved caves, tunnels, burial niches, and even roads out of tuff. Blocks of this rock were quarried to make houses and walls. Tuff is soft and easy to carve when it's first exposed to air, but hardens later, which makes it a good building stone.

Italy's tuff-producing volcanoes resulted from a lot of tectonic-plate bumping and grinding. This violent geologic history is reflected in Italy's volcanoes, like Vesuvius and Etna, and earthquakes such as the 2009 quake in the L'Aquila area northeast of Rome.

Tuff is actually just a big hardened pile of old volcanic ash. When volcanoes hold magma that contains a lot of water, they erupt explosively (think heat + water = steam = POW!). The exploded rock material gets blasted out as hot volcanic ash, which settles on the surrounding landscape, piles up, and over time welds together into the rock called tuff.

So when you're visiting an area in Italy of ancient caves or catacombs built out of this material, you'll know that at least once (and maybe more) upon a time, it was a site of a lot of volcanic activity.

with honey. The crème brûlée is a winner for dessert. Three small and separate dining areas make the interior feel intimate. This place is known locally as a good value (€12 pastas, €14 *secondi*, Wed-Mon 12:30-15:00 & 19:30-22:00, closed Tue, Via San Leonardo 7, tel. 076-334-2763).

Pizzeria & Restaurant Charlie is a local favorite. It's popular with families and students for casual dinners of wood-fired €8 pizzas, big salads, homemade pasta, or grilled meat. In a quiet courtyard guarded by a medieval tower, it's centrally located a block southwest of Piazza della Repubblica (Wed-Mon 12:00-14:30 & 19:00-23:30, closed Tue, Via Loggia dei Mercanti 14, tel. 076-334-4766).

L'Oste del Re, a simple trattoria on Corso Cavour, serves lunch with a focus on local cheeses and meats, and pizza in the evenings (Thu-Tue 11:00-15:30 & 19:00-22:30, closed Wed, Corso Cavour 58, tel. 0763-343-846).

Enoteca Tozzi, to the left of the Duomo, serves up rustic *panini*—try the roast suckling pig *(porchetta)* if it's available (daily 9:00-19:00, open sporadically in winter, Piazza del Duomo 13, tel. 076-334-4393).

Sidis supermarket, tucked away two minutes from the Duomo, has what you need to put together a functional picnic or stock your hotel room pantry (daily 8:00-13:30 & 16:30-19:30 except closed Wed evenings, just past recommended Trattoria la Grotta at Via Luca Signorelli 23).

Gelato: For dessert, try the deservedly popular *gelateria* **Pasqualetti** (daily 11:30-21:00, open later June-Aug, closed in winter, next to left transept of church, Piazza del Duomo 14; another branch is at Corso Cavour 56, open daily 11:00-23:00, closes at 19:00 in winter).

Orvieto Connections

From Orvieto by Train to: Rome (hourly, 1.25 hours), **Florence** (hourly, 2 hours, use Firenze S.M.N. train station—see page 441), **Siena** (12/day, 2.5 hours, change in Chiusi, all Florence-bound trains stop in Chiusi), **Assisi** (roughly hourly, 2.5 hours, 1 or 2 transfers). The train station's Buffet della Stazione is surprisingly good if you need a quick *focaccia* sandwich or pizza picnic for the train ride.

By Bus to Bagnoregio (30-minute walk from Civita di Bagnoregio, described next): It's a one-hour trip (€2 one-way or €4 round-trip if bought in advance from bar or tobacco shop, €7 one-way or €14 round-trip if purchased from driver). Here are likely departure times (but confirm) from Orvieto's Piazza Cahen on the blue Cotral bus, daily except Sunday (when this bus does not run at all): 6:20, 7:50, 12:45, 15:45, 17:40, and 18:20 (buses stop at Orvieto's train station 5 minutes later). During the school year (roughly Sept-June), there are additional departures at 7:20 and 13:55. Confirm the schedule and buy your round-trip ticket at the train-station bar or at the tobacco shop on Corso Cavour, a block up from the funicular (daily 8:00-13:00 & 16:00-20:00; remember, if you wait to buy your ticket from the driver, you'll pay much more). The schedule is also posted across the street from the bus parking lot (look for sign saying *A.Co.Tral Capolinea*). To find the bus stop, face the funicular. The bus stop is at the far left end of Piazza Cahen. Be sure to confirm departure and return times with the driver—the bus you want says *Bagnoregio* in the window. The

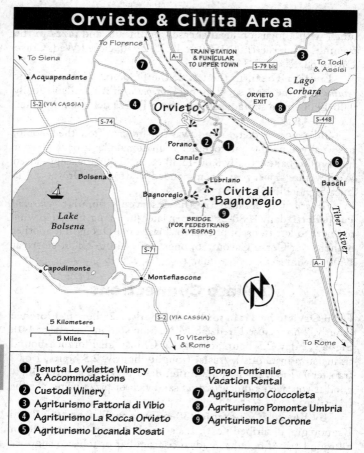

Orvieto & Civita Area

To Florence

To Siena

TRAIN STATION & FUNICULAR TO UPPER TOWN

A-1

S-79 bis

To Todi & Assisi

Acquapendente

Lago Corbara

S-2 (VIA CASSIA)

Orvieto

ORVIETO EXIT

S-74

Porano

Canale

S-448

Baschi

Bolsena

Lubriano

Civita di Bagnoregio

Bagnoregio

Tiber River

Lake Bolsena

BRIDGE (FOR PEDESTRIANS & VESPAS)

S-71

A-1

Capodimonte

Montefiascone

5 Kilometers

5 Miles

S-2 (VIA CASSIA)

To Viterbo & Rome

To Rome

① Tenuta Le Velette Winery & Accommodations
② Custodi Winery
③ Agriturismo Fattoria di Vibio
④ Agriturismo La Rocca Orvieto
⑤ Agriturismo Locanda Rosati
⑥ Borgo Fontanile Vacation Rental
⑦ Agriturismo Cioccoleta
⑧ Agriturismo Pomonte Umbria
⑨ Agriturismo Le Corone

last bus back from Bagnoregio usually leaves at 17:25. If you catch the bus down below at Orvieto's train station, wait to the left of the funicular station (as you're facing it). For schedule and tickets, visit the tobacco shop/bar in the train station, call 0761-760-049 (may be Italian-only), or see www.cotralspa.it (though this site's timetables are often out of date).

Tip for Drivers: If you're thinking of driving to Rome, consider stashing your car in Oriveto instead. You can easily park the car, safe and free, behind the Orvieto train station (for up to a week or more), and zip effortlessly into Rome by train (1.25 hours).

Civita di Bagnoregio

Perched on a pinnacle in a grand canyon, the traffic-free village of Civita di Bagnoregio is Italy's ultimate hill town. In the last decade, the real Civita (chee-VEE-tah) has died—the last of its lifelong residents have moved away. But relatives and newcomers are moving in and revitalizing the village, and it remains an amazing place to visit. (It's even become popular as a backdrop for movies, soap operas, and advertising campaigns.) Civita is connected to the world and the town of Bagnoregio by a long pedestrian bridge—and a website (www.civitadibagnoregio.it, run by B&B owner Franco).

Civita's history goes back to Etruscan and ancient Roman times. In the early Middle Ages, Bagnoregio was a suburb of Civita, which had a population of about 4,000. Later, Bagnoregio surpassed Civita in size—especially following a 1695 earthquake, after which many residents fled Civita to live in Bagnoregio, fearing their houses would be shaken off the edge into the valley below. You'll notice Bagnoregio is dominated by Renaissance-style buildings while, architecturally, Civita remains stuck in the Middle Ages.

While Bagnoregio lacks the pinnacle-town romance of Civita, it's actually a healthy, vibrant community (unlike Civita, the suburb now nicknamed "the dead city"). In Bagnoregio, get a haircut, sip a coffee on the square, and walk down to the old laundry (ask, *"Dov'è la lavanderia vecchia?"*). Off-season, when Civita and Bagnoregio are deadly quiet—and cold—I'd side-trip in quickly from Orvieto rather than spend the night.

Orientation to Civita

Arrival in Bagnoregio, near Civita

If you're taking the **bus** from Orvieto, you'll get off at the bus stop in Bagnoregio. Look at the posted bus schedule and write down the return times to Orvieto, or check with the driver.

From Bagnoregio to Civita: Civita sits at the opposite end of Bagnoregio, about a mile away. From Bagnoregio, you can walk (allow around 30 minutes) or take a little **shuttle bus**—orange or white—to the base of the bridge to Civita (hourly, 10-minute ride, €1 round-trip, pay driver, first bus runs Mon-Sat at about 7:30, Sun at 8:50, last at 18:45, no buses 13:00-15:30, fewer buses June-Aug). Catch the bus at the gas station by waving your book at the driver (Bagnoregio's new mayor, a Colin Firth lookalike, is eager to welcome my readers—though the shuttle doesn't usually stop here, the mayor has instructed drivers to stop for anyone waving a copy

Civita di Bagnoregio

NOTE: MAP NOT TO SCALE; A WALK ACROSS CIVITA TAKES APPROX. 5 MINUTES—BUT DON'T RUSH IT!

To Lubriano Town

Cliffs

Cliffs

OSTERIA AL FORNO DI AGNESE

ANTICO FORNO TRATTORIA & CIVITA B&B

LOCANDA DELLA BUONA VENTURA

CAMPANILE (BELL TOWER)

OLIVE PRESS & BRUSCHETTERIA

MARIA'S GARDEN

OLD LAUNDRY & WC

Piazza

CHURCH

FOOTBRIDGE

ARCH

MAIN STRADA

To Bagnoregio

PALACE

SNACK BAR

ETRUSCAN COLUMNS

WINE BAR PEPPONE

WINE CELLAR & BRUSCHETTE

ANTICA CIVITA MUSEUM

CAVES & CHAPEL CARVED IN ROCK

Cliffs

RUINS OF HOUSE OF ST. BONAVENTURE

Trail to Etruscan tunnel under Civita

of this book). From the base of the bridge, you have to walk the rest of the way (a 10-minute uphill hike across a pedestrian bridge). To return to Bagnoregio by bus, check the schedule posted near the bridge (at edge of parking lot, where bus let you off) before heading up to Civita, or ask at the recommended Trattoria Antico Forno.

To **walk** from the Bagnoregio bus stop to the base of Civita's bridge (at least 20 minutes, fairly level, leave heavy bags with Mauro—see "Helpful Hints," below), take the road going uphill, Via Garibaldi (overlooking the big parking lot). Once on the road, take the first right and an immediate left onto the main drag, Via Roma. Follow this straight out to the belvedere for a superb viewpoint. From the viewpoint, backtrack a few steps (staircase at end of viewpoint is a dead end) and take the stairs down to the road leading to the bridge.

A **taxi** from Orvieto to the base of the pedestrian bridge costs around €50 (see "Helpful Hints" on page 698).

Drivers coming from Orvieto or elsewhere can avoid a long walk by driving through Bagnoregio and parking under the bridge at the base of Civita (for more tips, see "Bagnoregio Connections" on page 724).

Helpful Hints

Market Day: A lively market fills the Bagnoregio bus-station parking lot each Monday.

Baggage Storage: While there's no official baggage-check service in Bagnoregio, I've arranged with Mauro Laurenti, who runs the **Bar/Enoteca/Caffè Gianfu** and **Cinema Alberto Sordi,** to let you leave your bags there (€1/bag, Fri-Wed 6:00-13:00 & 13:30-24:00, closed Thu). As you get off the bus, go back 50 yards or so in the direction that the Orvieto bus just came from, and go right around corner.

Food near Bagnoregio Bus Stop: About 100 yards from the bus stop, within a few steps of the Porta Albana (old gate to the town), you'll find both a small grocery store and a great little bakery (**L'Arte del Pane**—with fresh pizza by the slice, Via Matteotti 5, opposite the cinema).

Orvieto Bus Tickets: To save money on bus fare to Orvieto, buy a ticket before boarding from the newsstand near the Bagnoregio bus stop, across from the gas station (€2 one-way or €4 round-trip; otherwise €7 one-way or €14 round-trip if purchased from driver).

Self-Guided Walk

Welcome to Civita

Civita was once connected to Bagnoregio, before the saddle between the separate towns eroded away. Photographs around town show the old donkey path, the original bridge. It was bombed in World War II and replaced in 1966 with the new footbridge that you're climbing today. The town's hearty old folks hang on to the bridge's handrail when fierce winter weather rolls through.

• *Entering the town, you'll pass through a cut in the rock and a 12th-century Romanesque...*

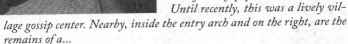

Arch: This was the main Etruscan road leading to the Tiber Valley and Rome. The stone passageway was cut by the Etruscans 2,500 years ago.

• *Inside the town gate, to the left, is an unmarked WC, behind the Bottega souvenir store. It faces the town's old laundry, which dates from just after World War II, when water was finally piped into the town. Until recently, this was a lively village gossip center. Nearby, inside the entry arch and on the right, are the remains of a...*

Renaissance Palace: The wooden door and windows (above the door) lead only to thin air. They were part of the facade of one of five palaces that once graced Civita. Much of the palace fell into the valley, riding a chunk of the ever-eroding rock pinnacle. Today, the door leads to a remaining section of the palace—complete with

Civita's first hot tub, as it was once owned by the "Marchesa," a countess who married into Italy's biggest industrialist family. Check out the canyon viewpoint a few steps to the left of the palace. Lean over the banister and listen to the sounds of the birds and the bees. Just beyond that is the site of the long-gone home of Civita's one famous son, St. Bonaventure, known as the "second founder of the Franciscans" (look for the small plaque on the wall to your right).

• *Now wander to the main square and Civita's church.*

Piazza: Here in the town square you'll find Wine Bar Peppone (if it's chilly, go inside for the inviting fire), two restaurants, and wild donkey races on the first Sunday of June and the second Sunday of September. At Christmastime, a living nativity scene is enacted in this square, and if you're visiting at the end of July or beginning of August, you might catch a play here. The pillars that stand like giants' bar

stools are ancient Etruscan. The church with its *campanile* (bell tower) marks the spot where an Etruscan temple, and then a Roman temple, once stood.

• *Go into the church.*

Church: A cathedral until 1699, the church houses records of about 60 bishops that date back to the seventh century (church open daily 9:30-13:00 & 15:00-18:00). Inside you'll see frescoes and statues from "the school of Donatello." The central altar is built upon the relics of the Roman martyr St. Victoria, who once was the patron saint of the town. St. Marlonbrando served as a bishop here in the ninth century; an altar dedicated to him is on the right.

The fine crucifix, carved out of pear wood in the 15th century, is from the school of Donatello. It's remarkably expressive and greatly venerated by locals. Jesus' gaze is almost haunting. Some say his appearance changes based on what angle you view him from: looking alive from the front, in agony from the left, and dead from the right. Regardless, his eyes follow you from side to side. On Good Friday, this crucifix goes out and is the focus of the midnight procession.

On the left side of the nave above an altar is an intimate fresco of the Madonna of the Earthquake, given this name because—in the shake of 1695—the whitewash fell off and revealed this tender fresco of Mary and her child. (During the Baroque era, a white-and-bright interior was in vogue, and churches such as these—

which were covered with precious and historic frescoes—were simply whitewashed over.) On the same wall—toward the front—find a faded portrait of Santa Apollonia, the patron saint of your teeth; notice the scary-looking pincers. Say hello to Annarita, the church attendant. Drop a coin into the offering box.

• *Just around the corner from the church, on the main street, are several...*

Eateries: At Rossana and Antonio's cool **Bruschette con Prodotti Locali,** pull up a chair and let them or their daughters, Arianna and Antonella, serve you *panini* (sandwiches), bruschetta (garlic toast with optional tomato topping), *salumi*, grilled sausages, wine, and a local cake called *ciambella*. After eating, wander down to see their cellar with its traditional winemaking gear and provisions for rolling huge kegs up the stairs. Tap on the kegs in the bottom level to see which are full (daily 11:00-17:00, in summer until 20:00, tel. 0761-793-270).

The rock below Civita is honeycombed with ancient cellars like this (for keeping wine at the same temperature all year) and cisterns (for collecting rainwater, since there was no well in town). Many date from Etruscan times.

Farther down on the left, you'll find **Antico Frantoio Bruschetteria,** a rustic, super-atmospheric place for a bite to eat. Vittoria's sons Sandro and Felice, and her grandsons Maurizio and Fabrizio, toast delicious bruschetta (roughly 10:00-20:00 in summer, off-season open weekends only 10:00-19:00, mobile 328-689-9375; Fabrizio also runs a recommended *agriturismo* outside of town). Peruse the menu, choose your topping (chopped tomato is super), and get a glass of wine for a fun, affordable snack.

While waiting for your bruschetta, take a look around to see Vittoria's mill *(mulino),* an interesting collection of old olive presses. The huge **olive press** in the entry is about 1,500 years old. Until the 1960s, blindfolded donkeys trudged in the circle here, crushing olives and creating paste that filled the circular filters and was put into a second press. Notice the 2,500-year-old sarcopha-

gus niche. The hole in the floor (with the glass top) was a garbage hole. In ancient times, residents would toss their jewels down when under attack; excavations uncovered a windfall of treasures (if you're not eating here, a €1 donation is requested).

• *Across the street and down a tiny lane, find...*

Antica Civita: This is the closest thing the town has to a museum. The humble collection is the brainchild of Felice, Vittoria's son, who has hung old black-and-white photos, farm tools, olive presses, and local artifacts in a series of old caves. Felice wants to give visitors a feeling for life in Civita when its traditional economy was strong (€1, daily 9:30-19:00, some English explanations).

• *On the left 20 yards farther down is...*

Maria's Garden (Maria's Giardino): Maria is too frail to live in Civita these days, but you may be able to peek into her garden and enjoy her view. She and her husband, Peppone (who passed away in 2009), used to carry goods on a donkey back and forth 40 times a day on the path between the old town and Bagnoregio. She's now the last native Civita resident still living. As you view the canyon in which Civita is stranded, imagine the work the two rivers did—in the same style as the Colorado River—to carve all this. Listen to the roosters and voices from distant farms.

• *At the end of town, the main drag winds downhill. On your right are small...*

Etruscan Caves: The first two caves were used as stables until a few years ago. The third cave is an unusual chapel, cut deep into the rock, with a barred door; this is the **Chapel of the Incarcerated** (Cappella del Carcere). In Etruscan times, the chapel—with a painted tile depicting the Madonna and child—may have originally been a tomb, and in medieval times, it was used as a jail. When Civita's few residents have a religious procession, they come here in honor of the Madonna of the Incarcerated.

• *After the chapel, the paving-stone path peters out into a dirt trail leading down and around to the right to an...*

Etruscan Tunnel: This tunnel dates from pre-Roman times. Tall enough for a woman with a jug on her head to pass through, it may have served as a shortcut to the river below. It was widened in the 1930s so that farmers could get between their scattered fields more easily. Think of the scared villagers who huddled here for refuge during WWII bombing raids.

• *Backtrack to return to the...*

Piazza: Evenings on Civita's town square are a bite of Italy. The same people sit on the same church steps under the same moon, night after night, year after year. I love my cool, late evenings in Civita. If you visit in the morning, have cappuccino and rolls at the small café/wine bar on the town square.

Whenever you visit, stop halfway up the donkey path and listen to the sounds of rural Italy. Reach out and touch one of the Monopoly houses. If you know how to turn the volume up on the crickets, do so.

Sleeping in Civita or Bagnoregio

(€1 = about $1.40, country code: 39)

In Civita and Bagnoregio, there are 15 B&B rooms up for grabs, and one newly remodeled hotel. Outside the town there are plenty of *agriturismi;* otherwise, there's always Orvieto.

In Civita

$$$ Locanda della Buona Ventura has four rooms decorated medieval-rustic-mod, filling the old mayor's house and overlooking Civita's piazza. The local-products shop just across the square functions as the reception, and has an old well down steep stairs worth checking out (Db-€100-120 depending on demand, breakfast at nearby café, mobile 347-627-5628, raffaele_rocchi@libero.it, Lara).

$ Civita B&B, run by Franco Sala (who also owns Trattoria Antico Forno), has three fine little rooms, each overlooking Civita's main square (S-€45, Sb-€50, D-€65, Db-€70, T-€90, continental breakfast, Wi-Fi, Piazza del Duomo Vecchio, tel. 076-176-0016, mobile 347-611-5426, www.civitadibagnoregio.it, fsala@pelagus.it).

In Bagnoregio

$$ Romantica Pucci B&B is a haven for city-weary travelers. Its eight spacious rooms are indeed romantic, with canopied beds and flowing veils. Both homey and elegant, it's like sleeping at Katharine Hepburn's place. Lamberto takes special care of his guests (Db-€80, air-con, free time-limited Internet access, free parking, "Pucci Speciality" €20 family-style dinner is popular with guests—non-guests are also welcome for dinner, Piazza Cavour 1, tel. 076-179-2121, www.hotelromanticapucci.it, hotelromantica pucci@libero.it). It's just above the parking lot you see when you arrive in Bagnoregio—look for a sign marking its private parking place. From the bus stop, take Via Garibaldi uphill above the parking lot, bear right at the tobacco shop onto Via Roma, then look for the hotel sign straight ahead.

$ Hotel Divino Amore has 23 bright, modern rooms, some with perfect views of a miniature Civita (Db-€70, Tb-€80, Via Fidanza 25-27, tel. & fax 076-178-0882, mobile 329-344-8950, www.hoteldivinoamore.com, info@hoteldivinoamore.com). From the bus stop, follow Via Garibaldi uphill above the parking lot, where it becomes Via Fidanza, and continue straight along for about 200 yards; #25 is on the left.

Outside of Town

$ Agriturismo Le Corone, in the valley below Civita, is an economical answer if you dream of a lazy few days relaxing among the olive trees. Flexible Fabrizio of Antico Frantoio Bruschetteria will pick you up from Bagnoregio, then drive you 10 minutes along a winding road to a simple but cozy home with a kitchen/living room, two bedrooms, and small garden. Civita is a steep- but- picturesque 45-minute uphill hike away (or persuade Fabrizio to give you a ride), and firewood is provided for romantic evenings (€35/night per person, maximum 6 people, no minimum occupancy, home-cooked pasta dinner—€10, Strade della Valle—see map on page 716, mobile 328-689-9375, www.corone-civita.com, info @corone-civita.com).

Eating in Civita or Bagnoregio

In Civita

Osteria Al Forno di Agnese is a delightful spot where Manuela and her friends serve visitors simple yet delicious meals on a covered patio just off Civita's main square (€8 pastas, €9 *secondi*, opens daily at 12:00 for lunch and at 19:00 for dinner, sometimes closed Tue, tel. 340-1259-721).

Trattoria Antico Forno cooks up rustic dishes, homemade pasta, and salads at affordable prices. Try their homemade pasta with truffles (€7 pastas, €8 *secondi*, daily for lunch 12:30-15:30 and dinner 19:00-22:00, on main square, also rents rooms—see Civita B&B listing on previous page, tel. 076-176-0016, Franco and his assistants Gina and Nina).

In Bagnoregio

Hostaria del Ponte is *the* place for serious cooking. It offers light, creative, and traditional cuisine with a great view terrace at the parking lot at the base of the bridge to Civita. Big space heaters make it comfortable to enjoy the wonderful view as you dine from their rooftop terrace, even in spring and fall (€8 pastas, €10 *secondi*, reservations often essential, Tue-Sun 12:30-14:30 & 19:30-21:30, closed Mon; Nov-April also closed Sun eve, tel. 076-179-3565, Lorena).

Bagnoregio Connections

From Bagnoregio to Orvieto: Public buses (6/day, 1 hour, €2 one-way or €4 round-trip if purchased in advance, €7 one-way or €14 round-trip from driver) connect Bagnoregio to the rest of the world via Orvieto. Departures from Bagnoregio—daily except Sunday and some holidays—are likely to be (but confirm): 5:30, 9:55, 10:25, 13:00, 14:25, and 17:25. During the school year (roughly Sept-June), buses also run at 6:30, and 13:35 (for info on coming from Orvieto, see "Orvieto Connections," page 715). Remember to save money by buying your ticket in Bagnoregio before boarding the bus—purchase one from the newsstand near the bus stop, across from the gas station.

From Bagnoregio to Points South: Public buses run to **Viterbo,** which has a good train connection to Rome (buses go weekdays at 5:10, 7:15, 7:40, 10:00, 13:00, 13:45, 14:20, 14:50, and 18:05; less frequent Sat-Sun, 35 minutes).

Driving from Orvieto to Bagnoregio: Orvieto overlooks the autostrada (and has its own exit). The shortest way to Civita from the freeway exit is to turn left (below Orvieto) and then simply follow the signs to *Lubriano* and *Bagnoregio.*

A more winding and scenic route takes 20 minutes longer: From the freeway, pass under hill-capping Orvieto (on your right, signs to *Lago di Bolsena,* on Viale I Maggio), then take the first left (direction: Bagnoregio), winding up past great Orvieto views through Canale, and through farms and fields of giant shredded wheat to Bagnoregio.

Either way, just before Bagnoregio, follow the signs left to *Lubriano* and pull into the first little square by the church on your right for a breathtaking view of Civita. You'll find an even better view farther inside the town, from the tiny square at the next church (San Giovanni Battista). Then return to the Bagnoregio road.

Drive through the town of Bagnoregio (following yellow *Civita* signs) to the lot at the base of the steep pedestrian bridge. Park for free in spaces with no blue lines (plenty under the bridge). The €1 fee for parking in the blue-lined spaces is loosely enforced. While you're supposed to pay at the restaurant or shop opposite (same family), if no one's there, just park and don't worry. The bridge at this parking lot leads up to the traffic-free 2,500-year-old canyon-swamped pinnacle town of Civita di Bagnoregio.

More Hill Towns

If you haven't gotten your fill of hill towns, here are more to check out.

▲Gubbio

This handsome town climbs Monte Ingino in northeast Umbria. Tuesday is market day, when Piazza 40 Martiri (named for 40 local martyrs shot by Nazis) bustles. Nearby are the ruins of the Roman amphitheater, and a park close by that's perfect for a picnic. Head up Via della Repubblica to the main square with the imposing Palazzo dei Consoli. Farther up, Via San Gerolamo leads to the

funky lift that will carry you up
the hill, in two-person "baskets,"
for a stunning view from the top,
where the Basilica of San Ubaldo
is worth a look. The **TI** is at Via
della Repubblica 15 (April-Sept
8:30-13:45 & 15:30-18:30, Oct-
March closes at 18:00 daily; tel.
075-922-0693, www.gubbio-alto

chiascio.umbria2000.it). Buses from Gubbio run directly to Rome
and Perugia (where you can transfer to Florence).

▲Bevagna

This sleeper of a town south of Assisi has Roman ruins, interesting churches, and more. Locals offer their guiding services for free
(usually Italian-speaking only) and are excited to show visitors
their town. Get a map at the **TI** at Piazza Silvestri 1 (daily 9:30-
12:30 & 15:30-19:30, tel. 074-236-1667) and wander. Highlights
are the Roman mosaics, remains of the arena, a paper-making
workshop, the Romanesque Church of San Silvestro, and a gem
of a 19th-century theater. Bevagna has all the elements of a hill
town except one: a hill. You can see the main sights easily in a cou-
ple of hours. For an overnight stay, consider the fancy **$$ Hotel
Palazzo Brunamonti** (Sb-€55, Db-€80-100, Tb-€110, air-con,
Corso Giacomo Matteotti 79, tel. 074-236-1932, fax 074-236-1948,
www.brunamonti.com, hotel@brunamonti.com). Buses connect
Bevagna with Foligno (except on Sun).

▲Spello

Umbrian hill town aficionados always include Spello on their list.
Just six miles south of Assisi, this town is much less touristy than
its neighbor to the north. Spello will give your legs a workout.
Via Consolare goes up, up, up to the top of town. Views from the
terrace of the **Il Trombone** restaurant (possibly closed for part of
2012) will have you singing a tune. The **TI** is on Piazza Giacomo
Matteotti 3 (daily 9:30-12:30 & 15:30-18:00, afternoons 15:00-
17:00 in winter, tel. 074-230-1009, www.prospello.it). Spello is on
the Perugia-Assisi-Foligno train line.

HILL TOWNS

ROME

Roma

Rome is magnificent and brutal at the same time. It's a showcase of Western civilization, with astonishingly ancient sights and a modern vibrancy. But if you're careless, you'll be run down or pickpocketed. And with the wrong attitude, you'll be frustrated by the kind of chaos that only an Italian can understand. On my last visit, a cabbie struggling with the traffic said, *"Roma chaos."* I responded, *"Bella chaos."* He agreed.

While Paris is an urban garden, Rome is a magnificent tangled forest. If your hotel provides a comfortable refuge; if you pace yourself; if you accept—and even partake in—the siesta plan; if you're well-organized for sightseeing; and if you protect yourself and your valuables with extra caution and discretion, you'll love it. (And Rome is much easier to live with if you can avoid the midsummer heat.)

For me, Rome is in a three-way tie with Paris and London as Europe's greatest city. Two thousand years ago, the word "Rome" meant civilization itself. Everything was either civilized (part of the Roman Empire, and Latin- or Greek-speaking) or barbarian. Today, Rome is Italy's political capital, the capital of Catholicism, and the center of the ancient world, littered with evocative remains. As you peel through its fascinating and jumbled layers, you'll find Rome's buildings, cats, laundry, traffic, and 2.7 million people endlessly entertaining. And then, of course, there are its stupendous sights.

Visit St. Peter's, the greatest church on earth, and scale Michelangelo's 448-foot-tall dome, the world's tallest. Learn something about eternity by touring the huge Vatican Museum. You'll find the story of creation—bright as the day it was painted—in the restored Sistine Chapel. Do the "Caesar Shuffle" through ancient Rome's Forum and Colosseum. Savor Europe's most sumptuous building, the Borghese Gallery, and take an early evening "Dolce Vita Stroll" down Via del Corso with Rome's beautiful people. Enjoy an after-dark walk from Campo de' Fiori to the Spanish Steps, lacing together Rome's Baroque and bubbly nightspots. Dine well at least once.

Planning Your Time

Rome is wonderful, but it's huge and exhausting. On a first-time visit, many travelers find that Rome is best done quickly—Italy is more charming elsewhere. But whether you're here for a day or a week, you won't be able to see all of these sights, so don't try—you'll keep coming back to Rome. After several dozen visits, I still have a healthy list of excuses to return.

Rome in a Day: Some people actually try to "do" Rome in a day. Crazy as that sounds, if all you have is a day, it's one of the most exciting days Europe has to offer. Start at 8:30 at the Colosseum. Then explore the Forum, hike over Capitol Hill, and cap your "Caesar Shuffle" with a visit to the Pantheon. After a quick lunch, taxi to the Vatican Museum (the lines usually die down mid-afternoon, or you can reserve a visit online in advance). See the Vatican Museum, then St. Peter's Basilica (open until 19:00 April-Sept). Taxi back to Campo de' Fiori to find dinner. Finish your day lacing together all the famous floodlit spots (follow my self-guided Heart of Rome Walk). If you only want a day in Rome, consider side-tripping in from Orvieto or Florence, or fit it in before taking the night train to Venice.

Rome in Two to Three Days: On the first day, do the "Caesar Shuffle" from the Colosseum to the Forum, then over Capitol Hill to the Pantheon. After a siesta, join the locals strolling from Piazza del Popolo to the Spanish Steps (follow my self-guided "Dolce Vita Stroll"). On the second day, see Vatican City (St. Peter's, climb the dome, tour the Vatican Museum). Have dinner on the atmospheric Campo de' Fiori, then walk to the Trevi Fountain and Spanish Steps (following my Heart of Rome Walk). With a third day, add the Borghese Gallery (reservations required) and the National Museum of Rome.

Orientation to Rome

Sprawling Rome actually feels manageable once you get to know it. The old core, with most of the tourist sights, sits in a diamond formed by Termini train station (in the east), the Vatican (west), Villa Borghese Gardens (north), and the Colosseum (south). The Tiber River runs through the diamond from north to south. In the

ROME

Rome's Neighborhoods

VATICAN MUSEUM

VATICAN CITY

ST. PETER'S

NORTH ROME

PIAZZA DEL POPOLO

VILLA BORGHESE

BORGHESE GALLERY

"SHOPPING TRIANGLE"

SPANISH STEPS

TERMINI

TRAIN STATION

NATIONAL MUSEUM

PANTHEON NEIGHBORHOOD

PIAZZA VENEZIA

Tiber River

CAPITOL HILL

ANCIENT ROME

FORUM

EAST ROME

PILGRIM'S ROME

SAN GIOVANNI IN LATERANO

COLOSSEUM

SANTA MARIA

TRASTEVERE

TESTACCIO

SOUTH ROME

SOUTH OF TESTACCIO

E.U.R.

APPIAN WAY

Not to Scale

center of the diamond sits Piazza Venezia, a busy square and traffic hub. It takes about an hour to walk from Termini train station to the Vatican.

Think of Rome as a series of neighborhoods, huddling around major landmarks.

Ancient Rome: In ancient times, this was home to the grandest buildings of a city of a million people. Today, the best of the classical sights stand in a line, from the Colosseum to the Forum to the Pantheon.

Pantheon Neighborhood: The Pantheon anchors the neighborhood I like to call the heart of Rome. It stretches eastward from the Tiber River through Campo de' Fiori and Piazza Navona, past the Pantheon to the Trevi Fountain.

Vatican City: Located west of the Tiber, it's a compact world of its own, with two great, huge sights: St. Peter's Basilica and the Vatican Museum.

North Rome: With the Spanish Steps, Villa Borghese Gardens, and trendy shopping streets (Via Veneto and the "shopping angle"), this is a more modern, classy area.

East Rome: This includes the area around the Termini station, with its many recommended hotels and public-transportation connections. Nearby is the neighborhood I call "Pilgrim's Rome," with several prominent churches dotting the area south of the station.

South Rome: South of Vatican City is Trastevere, the seedy, colorful, wrong-side-of-the-river neighborhood that provides a look at village Rome. It's the city at its crustiest—and perhaps most "Roman." Across the Tiber River, directly south of the city center, are the gritty/colorful Testaccio neighborhood, the 1930s suburb of E.U.R., and the Appian Way, home of the catacombs.

Within each of these neighborhoods, you'll find elements from the many layers of Rome's 2,000-year history: the marble ruins of ancient times; tangled streets of the medieval world; early Christian churches; grand Renaissance buildings and statues; Baroque fountains and church facades; 19th-century apartments; and 20th-century boulevards choked with traffic.

Since no one is allowed to build taller than St. Peter's dome, and virtually no buildings have been constructed in the city center since Mussolini got distracted in 1938, Rome has no modern skyline. The Tiber River is basically ignored—after the last floods (1870), the banks were built up very high, and Rome turned its back on its naughty river.

Tourist Information

Rome has two tourist information offices and numerous kiosks. The TI offices are at the airport (terminal 3) and Termini train station (daily 8:00-21:00, way down track 24, look for signs). Little kiosks (generally open daily 9:30-19:00) are near the Forum (on Piazza del Tempio della Pace), in Trastevere (on Piazza Sonnino), on Via Nazionale (at Palazzo delle Esposizioni), near Castel Sant'Angelo (at Piazza Pia), at the Church of Santa Maria Maggiore (on Via dell'Olmata), near Piazza Navona (at Piazza delle Cinque Lune), and near the Trevi Fountain (at Via del Corso and Via Minghetti). The TI's website is http://en.turismoroma.it.

At any TI, ask for a city map, a listing of sights and hours (in the free *Museums of Rome* booklet), and the free *Evento* booklet, with English-language pages listing the month's cultural events. The TIs don't offer room-booking services. If a commercial info-center offers to book you a room, just say no—you'll save money by booking direct.

If all you need is a **map,** skip the TI and pick up a freebie map at your hotel. The best map I found is published by Rough Guide (€8 in bookstores).

Rome's single best source of up-to-date tourist information

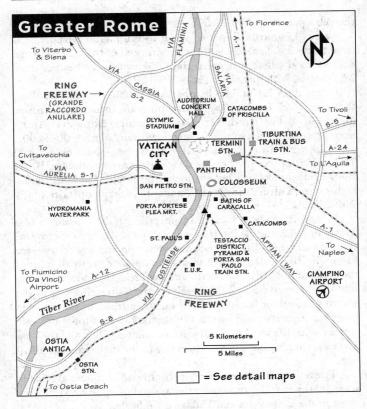

is its **call center,** with English-speakers on staff. Dial 06-0608 (answered daily 9:00-21:00, press 2 for English).

Several English-oriented **websites** provide insight into events and daily life in the city: www.inromenow.com (light tourist info on lots of topics), www.wantedinrome.com (events and accommodation rentals), and http://rome.angloinfo.com (on living in and moving to Rome).

Arrival in Rome

By Train at Termini Station

Termini, Rome's main train station, is a buffet of tourist services. While information desks are jammed with travelers, very handy red info kiosks at the head of the tracks can answer your simple questions.

Along track 24, about 100 yards down, you'll find the **TI** (daily 8:00-21:00), a **post office** (Mon-Fri 8:30-14:00, Sat 8:30-13:00, closed Sun), a **hotel booking** office, and **car rental** desks. The **baggage storage** (*deposito bagagli*) is downstairs (€4/5 hours, then cheaper, daily 6:00-24:00).

The **"Leonardo Express" train** to Fiumicino Airport runs from tracks 25-28; access is at the very far end of track 24 (see page 868). A good self-service **cafeteria,** Ciao, is near the head of track 24, upstairs, with fine views (daily 11:00-22:30).

Near track 1, you'll find a **pharmacy** (daily 7:30-22:00); along the same track is a **waiting room** and **train information office** (open 24/7). The handy **Drugstore Conad,** selling everything from groceries to electronics, is just downstairs (daily 6:00-24:00).

Elsewhere in the station are **ATMs,** late-hours banks, and 24-hour thievery. In the station's main entrance lobby, **Borri Books** sells books in English, including popular fiction, Italian history and culture, and kids' books, plus maps upstairs (daily 7:00-23:00).

Termini is also a local transportation hub. The city's two Metro lines (A and B) intersect downstairs at Termini Metro station. Buses (including Rome's hop-on, hop-off bus tours—see "Tours in Rome," later) leave across the square directly in front of the main station hall. The Metro and bus areas are under construction until sometime in 2012—look for signs directing you to the Metro platform or bus stop. Taxis queue in front; avoid con men hawking "express taxi" services in unmarked cars (only use cars marked with the word *taxi* and a phone number). To avoid the long taxi line, simply hike out past the buses to the main street and hail one.

From Termini, most of my recommended hotels are easily accessible by foot (for those near this train station) or by Metro (for those in the Colosseum and Vatican neighborhoods).

The station has some sleazy sharks with official-looking business cards; avoid anybody selling anything unless they're in a legitimate shop at the station.

By Train or Bus at Tiburtina Station

Tiburtina, Rome's second-largest train station, is located in the city's northeast corner. In general, slower trains (from Milan, Bolzano, Bologna, Udine, and Reggio di Calabria) and some night trains (from Munich, Milan, Venice, Innsbruck, and Udine) use Tiburtina, as does the night bus to Fiumicino Airport. Direct night trains from Paris and Vienna use Termini train station instead.

Tiburtina is better known as a hub for bus service to destinations all across Italy. Buses depart from the piazza in front of the station. Ticket offices are located in the piazza and around the corner on Circonvallazione Nomentana.

Within the train station are a currency-exchange office and a 24-hour grocery. The Tiburtina station is on Metro line B, with easy connections to Termini (a straight shot, four stops away) and the entire Metro system. Or take bus #492 from Tiburtina to various city-center stops (such as Piazza Barberini, Piazza Venezia, and Piazza Cavour) and the Vatican neighborhood.

By Car

The Grande Raccordo Anulare circles greater Rome. This ring road has spokes that lead you into the center. Entering from the north, leave the autostrada at the Settebagni exit. Following the ancient Via Salaria (and the black-and-white *Centro* signs), work your way doggedly into the Roman thick of things. This will take you along the Villa Borghese Gardens and dump you right on Via Veneto in downtown Rome. Avoid rush hour and drive defensively: Roman cars stay in their lanes like rocks in an avalanche.

Parking in Rome is dangerous. Park near a police station or get advice at your hotel. The Villa Borghese underground garage is handy (Metro: Spagna). Garages charge about €24 per day.

Consider this: Your car is a worthless headache in Rome. Avoid a pile of stress and save money by parking at the huge, easy, and relatively safe lot behind the train station in the hill town of Orvieto (follow *P* signs from autostrada) and catching the train to Rome (hourly, 1-1.5 hours).

If you absolutely must drive and park a car in Rome, try to avoid commuter traffic by arriving Friday evening, or anytime during the weekend, and by leaving town during the weekend. Park your car at Tiburtina station (€1/hour, www.atac.roma.it) and take a 10-minute ride on the Metro line B into the center.

By Plane or Cruise Ship

For information on Rome's airports and Civitavecchia's cruise ship terminal, see the end of this chapter.

Helpful Hints

Sightseeing Tips: Avid sightseers can save money by buying the Roma Pass (see "Tips on Sightseeing in Rome" sidebar, later), available at TIs and participating sights—buy one before visiting the Colosseum or Forum, and you can skip the long lines there. If you want to see the Borghese Gallery, remember to reserve ahead (see page 806). To bypass the long Vatican Museum line, reserve an entry time online (see page 796 for details).

Internet Access: If your hotel doesn't offer free or cheap Internet access, your hotelier can point you to the nearest Internet café.

Bookstores: These stores (all open daily except Anglo American and Open Door) sell travel guidebooks, including mine. The first two are chains, while the others have a more personal

Daily Reminder

Sunday: These sights are closed—the Vatican Museum (except for the last Sunday of the month, when it's free and even more crowded), Villa Farnesina, and the Catacombs of San Sebastiano. In the morning, the Porta Portese flea market hops, and the old center is delightfully quiet. In the evening, Via dei Fori Imperiali is closed to traffic and fun to stroll.

Monday: Many sights are closed, including the National Museum of Rome, Borghese Gallery, Capitoline Museums, Catacombs of Priscilla, Museum of the Imperial Forums (includes Trajan's Market and Trajan's Forum), Castel Sant'Angelo, Ara Pacis, Montemartini Museum, E.U.R.'s Museum of Roman Civilization, Etruscan Museum, Museum of the Liberation of Rome, some Appian Way sights (Tomb of Cecilia Metella; Circus and Villa of Maxentius; and the San Sebastiano Gate and Museum of the Walls), and Ostia Antica.

　　Major sights that are open include the Colosseum, Forum, and Vatican Museum, among others. Churches are open as usual. The Baths of Caracalla close early in the afternoon.

Tuesday: All sights are open in Rome. This isn't a good day to side-trip to Naples, because its Archaeological Museum is closed.

Wednesday: All sights are open, except for the Catacombs of San Callisto. St. Peter's Basilica may be closed in the morning for a papal audience.

Thursday/Friday: All sights are open.

Saturday: Most sights are open in Rome, except for the Synagogue and Jewish Museum.

ROME

touch. **Borri Books** is at Termini station, and **Feltrinelli International** has two branches (at Largo Argentina, and just off Piazza della Repubblica at Via Vittorio Emanuele Orlando 84, tel. 06-482-7878). **Anglo American Bookshop** has great art and history sections (closed all day Sun and Mon morning, a few blocks south of Spanish Steps at Via della Vite 102, tel. 06-679-5222). **Libreria Fanucci** is centrally located (a block toward the Pantheon from Piazza Navona at Piazza Madama 8, tel. 06-686-1141). In Trastevere, Irishman Dermot at the **Almost Corner Bookshop** stocks an Italian-interest section (Via del Moro 45, tel. 06-583-6942), and the **Open Door Bookshop** carries the only used books in English in town (closed Sun, Via della Lungaretta 23, tel. 06-589-6478).

Laundry: Your hotelier can direct you to the nearest launderette. The **ondablu** chain usually comes with Internet access; one of their more central locations is near Termini station (€2/hour, about €8 to wash and dry a 15-pound load, usually open daily 8:00-22:00, Via Principe Amedeo 70b, tel. 06-474-4647).

Travel Agencies: You can get train tickets and railpass-related reservations and supplements at travel agencies (at little or no additional cost), avoiding a trip to a train station. Your hotelier will know of a convenient agency nearby.

Dealing with (and Avoiding) Problems

Theft Alert: While violent crime is rare in the city center, petty theft is rampant. With sweet-talking con artists meeting you at the station, well-dressed pickpockets on buses, and thieving gangs of children at the ancient sites, Rome is a gauntlet of rip-offs. Although it's not as bad as it was a few years ago, and pickpockets don't want to hurt you—they usually just want your money—green or sloppy tourists will be scammed. Thieves strike when you're distracted. Don't trust kind strangers. Keep nothing important in your pockets. Be most on guard while boarding and leaving buses and subways. Thieves crowd the door, then stop and turn while others crowd and push from behind. You'll find less crowding and commotion—and less risk—waiting for the end cars of a subway rather than the middle cars. The sneakiest thieves pretend to be well-dressed businessmen (generally with something in their hands), or tourists wearing fanny packs and toting cameras and even Rick Steves guidebooks.

Scams abound: Don't give your wallet to self-proclaimed "police" who stop you on the street, warn you about counterfeit (or drug) money, and ask to see your cash. If a bank machine eats your ATM card, see if there's a thin plastic insert with a tongue hanging out that thieves use to extract it.

If you know what to look out for, fast-fingered moms with babies and gangs of children picking the pockets and handbags of naive tourists are not a threat, but an interesting, albeit sad, spectacle. Pickpockets troll through the tourist crowds around the Colosseum, Forum, Piazza della Repubblica, and train and Metro stations. Watch them target tourists who are overloaded with bags or distracted with a video camera. The kids look like beggars and hold up newspapers or cardboard signs to confuse their victims. They scram like stray cats if you're on to them.

Reporting Losses: To report lost or stolen items, file a police report (at Termini station, with *polizia* at track 11 or with Carabinieri at track 20; offices are also at Piazza Venezia). You'll need the report to file an insurance claim for lost gear, and it can help with replacing your passport—first file the police report, then

Tips on Sightseeing in Rome

These tips will help you use your time and money efficiently, making the Eternal City seem less eternal and more entertaining. For general advice on sightseeing, see page 18.

Passes

Roma Pass: Rome offers several sightseeing passes to help you save money. For most visitors, the Roma Pass (www.romapass .it) is the clear winner. The Roma Pass costs €25 and is valid for three days, covering public transportation and free or discounted entry to Roman sights. You get free admission to your first two sights (where you also get to skip the ticket line), and then a discount on the rest within the three-day window. Sights covered (or discounted) by the pass

include the following: Colosseum/Palatine Hill/Roman Forum, Borghese Gallery (though you still must make a reservation and pay the €2 booking fee), Capitoline Museums, Castel Sant'Angelo, Montemartini Museum, Ara Pacis, Museum of Roman Civilization, Etruscan Museum, Baths of Caracalla, Trajan's Market, and some of the Appian Way sights. The pass also covers four branches of the National Museum of Rome, considered as a single "sight": Palazzo Massimo (the most important of the lot), Crypta Balbi (medieval art), Palazzo Altemps (sculpture collection), and Museum of the Bath (ancient inscriptions).

If you'll be visiting any two of the major sights in a three-day period, get the pass. It's sold at participating sights, TIs, and even the tobacco shop in the Colosseo Metro station. Try to buy it at a less crowded TI or sight. Don't bother to order it online—you have to physically pick up the pass in Rome, which negates any time-saving advantage.

Validate your Roma Pass by writing your name and validation date on the card. Then insert it directly into the turnstile at your first two (free) sights. At other sights, show it at the ticket office to get your reduced *(ridotto)* price—about 30 percent off.

To get the most of your pass, visit the two most expensive sights first—for example, the Colosseum (€12) and the National Museum (€10). Definitely use it to bypass the long ticket line at the Colosseum. For sights that normally sell a combined ticket (such as the Colosseum/Palatine Hill/Roman Forum or the National Museum branches), visiting the combined sight counts as a single entry.

The Roma Pass comes with a three-day transit pass. Write your name and birth date on the transit pass, validate it on your first bus or Metro ride by passing it over a sensor at a turnstile or validation machine (look for a yellow circle), and you can take unlimited rides within Rome's city limits until midnight of the third day.

ROME

The TI's other passes—Roma & Più Pass ("Rome & More") and the Archeologia Card—are generally not worth the trouble for most tourists.

Combo-Ticket for Colosseum, Forum, and Palatine Hill: A €12 combo-ticket covers these three adjacent sights (no individual tickets are sold per sight). The combo-ticket allows one entry per sight, and is valid for two days. Note that these sights are also covered by the Roma Pass. To avoid ticket-buying lines at the Colosseum and Forum, purchase your combo-ticket or Roma Pass at the lesser-visited Palatine Hill. Between the combo-ticket or Roma Pass, the pass is the better deal, unless you're planning on seeing only the sights covered by the combo-ticket.

Top Tips

Museum Reservations: The marvelous Borghese Gallery requires reservations in advance (for specifics, see page 806). You can reserve online to avoid long lines at the Vatican Museum (see page 796).

Opening Hours: Rome's sights have notoriously variable hours from season to season. Get a current listing of opening times from one of Rome's TIs—ask for the free booklet *Museums of Rome*. Or check online at www.060608.it/en (find "Cultural Heritage" in the menu under "Culture and Leisure"; search by using the Italian names of sights). On holidays, expect shorter hours or closures.

Churches: Many churches, which have divine art and free entry, open early (around 7:00-7:30), close for lunch (roughly 12:00-15:00), and close late (about 19:00). Kamikaze tourists maximize their sightseeing hours by visiting churches before 9:00 or late in the day, and, during the siesta, seeing the major sights that stay open all day (St. Peter's, Colosseum, Forum, Pantheon, Capitoline Museums, and National Museum of Rome). Many churches have "modest dress" requirements, which means no bare shoulders, miniskirts, or shorts—for men, women, or children. However, this dress code is only strictly enforced in Vatican City (most stringently inside St. Peter's Basilica, but also the Vatican Museum and anywhere inside the Vatican walls) and St. Paul's Outside the Walls. Elsewhere, you'll see many tourists in

shorts (but not skimpy shorts) touring churches.

Picnic Discreetly: Public drinking and eating is not allowed at major sights, though the ban has proven difficult to enforce. To avoid the risk of being fined, choose an empty piazza for your picnic, or keep a low profile.

Miscellaneous Tips: I carry a plastic water bottle and refill it at Rome's many public drinking spouts. Because public restrooms are scarce, use toilets at museums, restaurants, and bars.

ROME

call your embassy to make an appointment (US embassy: tel. 06-46741, Via Vittorio Veneto 121, www.usembassy.it). For information on how to report lost or stolen credit cards, see page 15.

Emergency Numbers: Police—tel. 113. Ambulance—tel. 118.

Pedestrian Safety: Your main safety concern in Rome is crossing streets safely, using extreme caution. Scooters don't need to stop at red lights, and even cars exercise what drivers call the "logical option" of not stopping if they see no oncoming traffic. As noisy gasoline-powered scooters are replaced by electric ones, the streets get quieter (hooray), but more dangerous for pedestrians. Follow locals like a shadow when you cross a street (or you'll spend a good part of your visit stranded on curbs). When you do cross alone, don't be a deer in the headlights. Find a gap in the traffic and walk with confidence while making eye contact with approaching drivers—they won't hit you if they can tell where you intend to go.

Staying/Getting Healthy: The siesta is a key to survival in summertime Rome. Lie down and contemplate the extraordinary power of gravity in the Eternal City. I drink lots of cold, refreshing water from Rome's many drinking fountains (the Forum has three).

There's a pharmacy (marked by a green cross) in every neighborhood. Several pharmacies stay open late in Termini station (daily 7:30-22:00) and at Piazza dei Cinquecento 51 (open 24 hours daily, next to Termini station on the corner of Via Cavour, tel. 06-488-0019).

Embassies can recommend English-speaking doctors. Consider MEDline, a 24-hour home-medical service; doctors speak English and make calls at hotels for €150 (tel. 06-808-0995). Anyone is entitled to free emergency treatment at public hospitals. The hospital closest to Termini station is Policlinico Umberto 1 (entrance for emergency treatment on Via Lancisi, translators available, Metro: Policlinico). Readers also report that the staff at Santa Susanna Church, home of the American Catholic Church in Rome, offers useful advice and medical referrals (see page 816).

Getting Around Rome

Sightsee on foot, by city bus, by Metro, or by taxi. I've grouped your sightseeing into walkable neighborhoods. Make it a point to visit sights in a logical order. Needless backtracking wastes precious time.

The public transportation system, which is cheap and efficient, consists primarily of buses, a few trams, and the two underground subway (Metro) lines. Consider it part of your Roman experience.

ROME

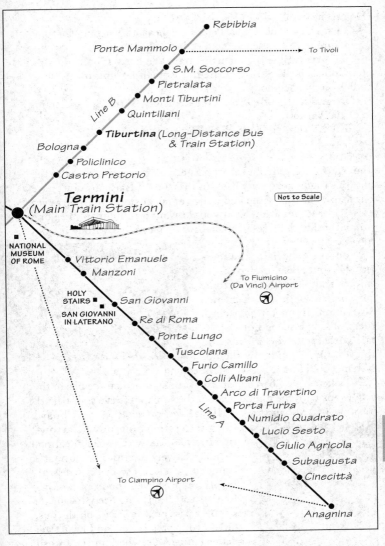

station, shuttle train to airport, National Museum of Rome, and recommended hotels

Repubblica (line A): Baths of Diocletian, Via Nazionale, and recommended hotels

Barberini (line A): Cappuccin Crypt, Trevi Fountain, and Villa Borghese

Spagna (line A): Spanish Steps and classy shopping area

Flaminio (line A): Piazza del Popolo, start of recommended

"Dolce Vita Stroll" down Via del Corso

> **Ottaviano** (line A): St. Peter's Basilica and Vatican Museum
>
> **Cipro** (line A): Recommended hotels
>
> **Tiburtina** (line B): Tiburtina train and bus station
>
> **Colosseo** (line B): Colosseum, Roman Forum, bike rental, and recommended hotels
>
> **Piramide** (line B): Protestant Cemetery, Testaccio, and trains to Ostia Antica
>
> **E.U.R.** (line B): Mussolini's futuristic suburb

By Bus

The Metro is handy, but it won't get you everywhere—take the bus. Bus routes are clearly listed at the stops. TIs usually don't have bus maps, but with some knowledge of major stops, you won't necessarily need one (though if you do want a route map, find one printed inside the free-at-hotels *Evento* magazine, or buy it from tobacco shops).

Buses—especially the touristy #40 and #64—are havens for thieves and pickpockets. Assume any commotion is a thief-created distraction. If one bus is packed, there's likely a second one on its tail with far fewer crowds and thieves. Once you know the bus system, you'll find it's easier than searching for a cab.

Tickets have a barcode and must be stamped on the bus in the yellow box with the digital readout (be sure to retrieve your ticket).

Validate your ticket as you board (magnetic-strip side down, arrow-side first)—otherwise you're cheating. While relatively safe, riding without a stamped ticket on the bus is stressful. Inspectors fine even innocent-looking tourists €50. There's no need to validate a transit pass or Roma Pass on the bus, unless your pass is new and hasn't yet been stamped elsewhere in the transit system. Bus etiquette (not always followed) is to board at the front or rear doors and exit out the middle.

Regular bus lines start running at about 5:30, and during the day they run every 5-10 minutes. After 23:30, and sometimes earlier (such as on Sundays), buses are less frequent but dependable. Night buses are also reliable, and are marked with an *N* and an owl symbol on the bus-stop signs.

These are the major bus routes:

Bus #64: This bus cuts across the city, linking Termini station with the Vatican, stopping at Piazza della Repubblica (sights), Via Nazionale (recommended hotels), Piazza Venezia (near Forum), Largo Argentina (near Pantheon), and St. Peter's Basilica (get off just past the tunnel). Ride it for a city overview and to watch pickpockets in action. The #64 can get horribly crowded.

Bus #40: This express bus following the #64 route is especially helpful—with fewer stops and crowds.

The following three routes conveniently connect Trastevere with other parts of Rome:

Bus #H: This express bus, linking Termini station and Trastevere, makes a few stops on Via Nazionale (for Trastevere, get off at Piazza Belli, just after crossing the Tiber River).

Bus #8: This tram connects Largo Argentina with Trastevere (get off at Piazza Belli).

Buses #23 and #280: These link the Vatican with Trastevere and Testaccio, stopping at the Vatican Museum (nearest stop is Via Leone IV), Castel Sant'Angelo, Trastevere (Piazza Belli), Porta Portese (Sunday flea market), and Piramide (Metro and gateway to Testaccio).

Here are other useful routes:

Bus #62: Largo Argentina to St. Peter's Square.

Bus #81: San Giovanni in Laterano, Largo Argentina, and Piazza Risorgimento (Vatican).

Buses #85 and #87: Piazza Venezia, Colosseum, San Clemente, and San Giovanni in Laterano.

Bus #492: Travels east-west across the city, connecting Tiburtina (train and bus stations), Piazza Barberini, Piazza Venezia, Piazza Cavour (Castel Sant'Angelo), and Piazza Risorgimento (Vatican).

Bus #714: Termini station, Santa Maria Maggiore, San Giovanni in Laterano, Terme di Caracalla (Baths of Caracalla), and on to E.U.R.

***Elettrico* Minibuses:** Two cute *elettrico* minibuses wind through the narrow streets of old and interesting neighborhoods, and are great for transport or simple joyriding. The ***elettrico* #116** runs through the medieval core of Rome: Ponte Vittorio Emanuele II (near Castel Sant'Angelo) to Campo de' Fiori, Pantheon, Piazza Barberini, and the southern edge of the scenic Villa Borghese Gardens. The ***elettrico* #117** connects San Giovanni in Laterano, Colosseo, Via dei Serpenti, Trevi Fountain, Piazza di Spagna, and Piazza del Popolo—and vice versa. Where Via del Corso hits Piazza del Popolo, a #117 is usually parked and ready to go. Riding it from here to the end of the line, San Giovanni in Laterano, makes for a fine joyride that leaves you, conveniently, at a great sight.

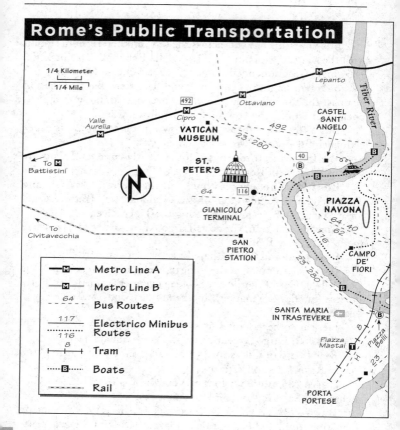

Rome's Public Transportation

1/4 Kilometer

1/4 Mile

Lepanto

Tiber River

492

Ottaviano

Cipro

Valle
Aurelia

CASTEL
SANT'
ANGELO

VATICAN
MUSEUM

492

23 280

To
Battistini

ST.
PETER'S

40

64

116

GIANICOLO
TERMINAL

PIAZZA
NAVONA

64 40
62

To
Civitavecchia

116

SAN
PIETRO
STATION

CAMPO
DE'
FIORI

23 280

Metro Line A

Metro Line B

64 **Bus Routes**

117 **Electtrico Minibus**
116 **Routes**

8 **Tram**

·B· Boats

Rail

SANTA MARIA
IN TRASTEVERE

8

Piazza
Mastai

T

Piazza
Belli

H

23

PORTA
PORTESE

By Taxi

I use taxis in Rome more often than in other cities. They're reasonable and useful for efficient sightseeing in this big, hot metropolis. Taxis start at €2.80, then charge about €1.30 per kilometer (surcharges: €1 on Sun, €3 for late-night hours of 22:00-7:00, one regular suitcase or bag rides free, tip by rounding up to the nearest euro). Sample fares: Termini station to Vatican-€10; Termini station to Colosseum-€6; Colosseum to Trastevere-€7 (or look up your

route at www.worldtaximeter.com). Three or four companions with more money than time should taxi almost everywhere.

It's tough to wave down a taxi in Rome, especially at night. Find the nearest taxi stand by asking a passerby or a clerk in a shop,

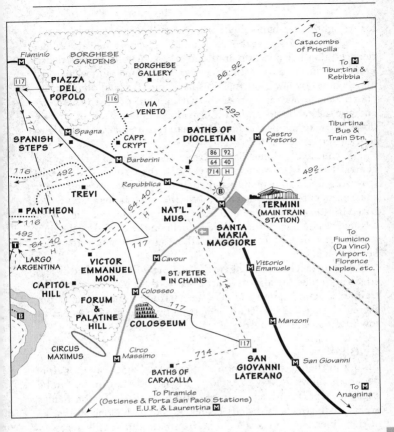

"Dov'è una fermata dei taxi?" (doh-VEH OO-nah fehr-MAH-tah
DEHee TAHK-see). Some taxi stands are listed on my maps. To
save time and energy, have your hotel or restaurant call a taxi for
you; the meter starts when the call is received (generally adding a
euro or two to the bill). To call a cab on your own, dial 06-4994 or
06-6645. It's routine for Romans to ask the waiter in a restaurant
to call a taxi when they ask for the bill. The waiter will tell you how
many minutes you have to enjoy your coffee.

Beware of corrupt taxis. A common cabbie scam is to take
your €20 note, drop it, and pick up a €5 note (similar color), claim-
ing that's what you gave him. To avoid this scam, pay in small bills;
if you only have a large bill, show it to the cabbie as you state its
face value.

If hailing a cab on the street, be sure the meter is restarted
when you get in (should be around €2.80, or around €5 if you or
your hotelier phoned for the taxi). Many meters show both the fare
and the time elapsed during the ride—and some tourists pay €10

for an eight-and-a-half-minute trip (more than the fair meter rate).

When you arrive at the train station or airport, beware of hustlers conning naive visitors into unmarked, rip-off "express taxis." Only use official taxis, with a *taxi* sign and phone number marked on the door. By law, they must display a multilingual official price chart. If you have any problems with a taxi, point to the chart and ask the cabbie to explain it to you. Making a show of writing down the taxi number (to file a complaint) can motivate a driver to quickly settle the matter.

If you take a Rome city cab from the airport to anywhere in central Rome within the old city walls, the cost should be €40 (covering up to four people and their bags); however, every year some readers report being ripped off. The catch is that cabbies *not* based in Rome can charge €60. At the airport, look specifically for a Rome city cab, with the "SPQR" shield on the door. By law, they can charge only €40 for the ride (still, be sure to establish the price before you get in).

Tired travelers arriving at the airport will likely find it less stressful to take the airport shuttle van to their hotel, or catch the train to Termini station and take the Metro or a cheaper taxi from there (see page 868 for details on getting from the airport to downtown Rome via taxi, shuttle, or train).

By Bike

Biking in the big city of Rome can speed up sightseeing or simply be an enjoyable way to explore. Though Roman traffic can be stressful, Roman drivers are respectful of cyclists. The best rides are on small streets in the city center. A bike path along the banks of the Tiber River makes a good 20-minute ride (easily accessed from the ramps at Porta Portese and Ponte Regina Margherita, near Piazza del Popolo). Get a bike with a well-padded seat—the little stones that pave Roman streets are unforgiving.

Top Bike Rental and Tours is professionally run by Roman bike enthusiasts who want to show off their city. Your rental comes with a handy map that suggests a route and indicates less-trafficked streets. Owner Ciro also offers four-hour-long English-only guided tours around the city and the Ancient Appian Way; check his website for days and times (rental: €8/half-day, €13/day, 10 percent discount with this book, best to reserve in advance via email; bike tours: start at €29, reservations required; daily 9:30-19:00, leave ID for deposit, from Santa Maria Maggiore TI kiosk take Via dell'Olmata and turn left one block down, Via dei Quattro Cantoni 40, tel. 06-488-2893, www.topbikerental.com, info@top bikerental.com).

Cool Rent, near the Colosseo Metro stop, is cheaper but less helpful (€3/hour, €10/day, 3-person bike cart-€10/hour, daily 9:30-

20:00, driver's license or other ID for deposit, 10 yards to the right as you exit the Metro). A second outlet is just off Via del Corso (on Largo di Lombardi, near corner of Via del Corso and Via della Croce, mobile 388-695-9303, Sasin).

Tours in Rome

Walking Tours

Finding the best guided tours in Rome is challenging. Local guides are good but pricey. Tour companies are cheaper, but quality and organization are unreliable. To help, I've produced a series of free audio tours that illuminate some of the major sights and neighborhoods, covered the way my readers appreciate (see sidebar on page 19 for details); you can download the tours and sightsee on your own.

If you hire a private Italian guide, consider organizing a group of four to six people from your hotel to split the cost (€180 for a half-day tour); this ends up costing about the same per person as going on a scheduled tour from one of the walking-tour companies listed below (about €25, generally expat guides).

Local Guides—I've worked with each of these licensed independent local guides. They're worth every euro. They speak excellent English, and enjoy tailoring tours to your interests. Their prices (roughly €50/hour, €180/half-day) flex with the day, season, and demand. Arrange your date and price by email.

Francesca Caruso loves to teach and share her appreciation of her city, and has contributed generously to this chapter (francesca inroma@gmail.com). Popular with my readers, Francesca understandably books up quickly; if she's busy, she'll recommend one of her colleagues. **Carla Zaia** is an engaging expert on all things Roman (mobile 349-759-0723, carlaromeguide@gmail.com). **Cristina Giannicchi** has an archaeology background (mobile 338-111-4573, www.crisacross.com, crisgiannicchi@gmail.com). **Sara Magister,** a Roman with a doctorate in art history, is an official Vatican guide and author of a book on Renaissance Rome (tel. 06-583-6783, mobile 339-379-3813, a.magister@iol.it). **Giovanna Terzulli** is a personable, knowledgeable art historian (terzulli @tiscali.it).

Walking-Tour Companies—Rome has many highly competitive tour companies, each offering a series of themed walks through various slices of Rome. Three-hour guided walks generally cost €25-30 per person. Guides are usually native English speakers, often American expats. Tours are limited to small groups, geared to American tourists, and given in English only. I've listed some here, but without a lot of details on their offerings. Before your trip, spend some time on these companies' websites to get to know your options, as each company has a particular teaching and guiding personality. Some are highbrow, and others are less scholarly. It's sometimes required, and always smart, to book a spot in advance (easy online). I must add that we get a lot of negative feedback on some of these tour companies. Readers report that their advertising can be misleading, and that scheduling mishaps are not uncommon.

Context Rome's walking tours are more intellectual than most, designed for travelers with longer-than-average attention spans. They are more expensive than others, and are led by "docents" rather than guides (tel. 06-9762-5204, US tel. 800-691-6036, www.contextrome.com). **Enjoy Rome** offers five different walks and a website filled with helpful information (Via Marghera 8a, tel. 06-445-1843, www.enjoyrome.com, info@enjoyrome.com). **Rome Walks** has put together several particularly creative itineraries (mobile 347-795-5175, www.romewalks.com, info@romewalks.com, Annie). **Roman Odyssey** gives readers of this book a 10 percent discount on their walks and private tours (tel. 06-580-9902, mobile 328-912-3720, www.romanodyssey.com, Rahul). **Through Eternity** offers travelers with this book a 10 percent discount on most tours and a 20 percent discount on its Underground Rome and Secret Rome tours; book through their website for the best discount (tel. 06-700-9336, mobile 347-336-5298, www.througheternity.com, info@througheternity.com, Rob). **Walks of Italy** has passionate, fun guides who lead a variety of good, reliable walks for groups no bigger than 12 people at a time (10 percent discount for readers of this book, US tel. 202/684-6916, Italian mobile 334-974-4274, www.walksofitaly.com, Jason Spiehler).

Hop-on, Hop-off Bus Tours

Several different agencies, including the ATAC public bus company, run hop-on, hop-off tours around Rome. These tours are constantly evolving and offer varying combinations of sights. You can grab one (and pay as you board) at any stop; Termini station and Piazza Venezia are handy hubs. Although the city is perfectly walkable and traffic jams can make the bus dreadfully slow, these open-top bus tours remain popular.

Trambus 110 seems to be the best. It's operated by the ATAC city-bus lines, and offers an orientation tour on big red double-decker buses with an open-air upper deck. In less than two hours, you'll have 80 sights pointed out to you (with a next-to-

worthless recorded narration). While you can hop on and off, the service can be erratic (mobbed midday, not ideal in bad weather) and it can be very slow in heavy traffic. It's best to think of this as a two-hour quickie orientation with scant information and lots of images. Stops include Ara Pacis, Piazza Cavour, St. Peter's Square, Corso Vittorio Emanuele (for Piazza Navona), Piazza Venezia, Colosseum, and Via Nazionale. Bus #110 departs every 20 minutes. You can catch it at any stop, including Termini station. Buy the €15 ticket as you board (runs daily 8:30-20:30, tel. 06-684-0901, www.trambusopen.com).

Archeobus is an open-top bus, also operated by ATAC, that runs twice hourly from Termini station out to the ancient Appian

Way (with stops at the Colosseum, Baths of Caracalla, San Callisto, San Sebastiano, and the Tomb of Cecilia Metella). This is a handy way to see the sights down this ancient Roman road, but it can be frustrating for various reasons— sparse narration, sporadic service, and difficult to hop on and off (€12, €30 combo-ticket with Trambus 110, ticket valid 24 hours, 1.5-hour loop, daily 8:30-16:30, from Termini station and Piazza Venezia, tel. 06-684-0901, www .trambusopen.com). A similar bus laces together all the Christian sights.

Car and Minibus Tours

You can hire your own private car or minibus with driver through **Autoservizi Monti Concezio,** run by gentle, capable, and English-speaking Ezio (car-€35/hour, minibus-€40/hour, 3-hour minimum for city sightseeing, long rides outside Rome are more expensive, mobile 335-636-5907 or 349-674-5643, www.monti tours.com, conceziomonti@gmail.com).

Miles & Miles Private Tours is a family-run company offering a number of tours (all explained on their website) in Mercedes minibuses and cars, all with good English-speaking driver/guides (€60/hour for up to 8 people, 5-hour minimum, Rick Steves readers booking direct get a 10 percent discount off any web prices they offer, tel. 06-6618-0403, mobile 331-466-4900, www.milesand miles.net, info@milesandmiles.net, Francesco answers the mobile phone, while Kimberly—an American—runs their office). They can also provide unguided long-distance transportation (cheaper per hour than a tour); if traveling with a small group or a family from Rome to Florence or Siena, consider paying extra to turn the trip into a memorable day tour with door-to-door service.

Weekend Tour Packages for Students in Rome

Andy Steves (my son) runs Weekend Student Adventures, offering experiential three-day weekend tours for €250, designed for American students studying abroad (www.wsaeurope.com for details on tours of Rome and other great cities).

Self-Guided Walks

Here are three walks that give you a moving picture of Rome, an ancient yet modern city. You'll walk through history (Roman Forum Walk), take a refreshing early-evening walk ("Dolce Vita Stroll"), and enjoy the thriving local scene, which is best at night (Heart of Rome Walk).

Roman Forum Walk

The Forum was the political, religious, and commercial center of the city. Rome's most important temples and halls of justice were here. This was the place for religious processions, political demonstrations, elections, important speeches, and parades by conquering generals. As Rome's empire expanded, these few acres of land became the center of the civilized world.

Cost: €12 combo-ticket (€9 base price plus frequent, mandatory exhibition fees), also includes Colosseum and Palatine Hill, valid two consecutive days, one entry per sight; also covered by Roma Pass. To avoid standing in a long ticket-buying line, see tips on "Avoiding Lines" on page 772.

Hours: The Roman Forum, Colosseum, and Palatine Hill are all open daily 8:30 until one hour before sunset: April-Sept until 19:15, Oct until 18:30, Nov-mid-Feb until 16:30, mid-Feb-mid-March until 17:00, mid-March-late March until 17:30; last entry one hour before closing.

Getting There: The closest Metro stop is Colosseo. The Forum has two entrances. The main entrance is on Via dei Fori Imperiali ("Road of the Imperial Forums"). From the Colosseo Metro stop, walk away from the Colosseum on Via dei Fori Imperiali to find the low-profile Forum ticket office (look closely), located where Via Cavour spills into Via dei Fori Imperiali.

The other entrance is at the Palatine Hill ticket office on Via di San Gregorio—after buying your ticket, take the path to the right (not up the hill), and wind around to enter the Forum at the Arch of Titus.

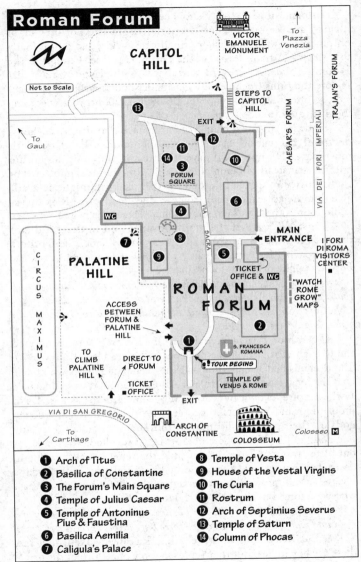

Roman Forum

Not to Scale

CAPITOL HILL

VICTOR EMANUELE MONUMENT

To Piazza Venezia

To Gaul

STEPS TO CAPITOL HILL

EXIT

CAESAR'S FORUM

TRAJAN'S FORUM

VIA DEI FORI IMPERIALI

⑬

⑪ ⑫

⑭ ③ FORUM SQUARE

⑩

⑥

WC

④

VIA SACRA

MAIN ENTRANCE

I FORI DI ROMA VISITORS CENTER

⑦

⑧

PALATINE HILL

⑨

⑤

TICKET OFFICE & WC

"WATCH ROME GROW" MAPS

C I R C U S M A X I M U S

R O M A N F O R U M

②

ACCESS BETWEEN FORUM & PALATINE HILL

S. FRANCESCA ROMANA

① TOUR BEGINS

TO CLIMB PALATINE HILL

DIRECT TO FORUM

TICKET OFFICE

TEMPLE OF VENUS & ROME

EXIT

VIA DI SAN GREGORIO

To Carthage

ARCH OF CONSTANTINE

COLOSSEUM

Colosseo Ⓜ

ROME

① Arch of Titus
② Basilica of Constantine
③ The Forum's Main Square
④ Temple of Julius Caesar
⑤ Temple of Antoninus Pius & Faustina
⑥ Basilica Aemilia
⑦ Caligula's Palace
⑧ Temple of Vesta
⑨ House of the Vestal Virgins
⑩ The Curia
⑪ Rostrum
⑫ Arch of Septimius Severus
⑬ Temple of Saturn
⑭ Column of Phocas

Information: A free visitors center (called I Fori di Roma), located across Via dei Fori Imperiali from the Forum's main entrance, has a TI, bookshop, small café, WCs, and a film (daily 9:30-18:30). A bookstore is at the Forum entrance. Vendors at the Forum sell *Rome: Past and Present* books with plastic overlays that restore the ruins (includes DVD, smaller book marked €15, prices soft, so offer €10). Info office tel. 06-3996-7700, http://archeoroma .beniculturali.it/en.

Tours: An unexciting yet informative **audioguide** helps decipher the rubble (€5, €7 version includes Palatine Hill, must leave ID), but you'll have to return it to one of the Forum entrances instead of being able to exit directly to Capitol Hill or the Colosseum. Official **guided tours** in English might be available (inquire at ticket office). You can download a free Rick Steves audio tour of the Forum to your mobile device; see page 19.

Tips: WCs are at the main entrance and in the middle of the Forum (near #8 on the map). Wear sturdy shoes; the Forum's ancient paving is uneven. I carry a water bottle and refill it at the Forum's public drinking fountains.

• *Start at the Arch of Titus (Arco di Tito). It's the white triumphal arch that rises above the rubble on the east end of the Forum (closest to the Colosseum). Stand at the viewpoint alongside the arch and gaze over the valley known as the Forum.*

❶ **Arch of Titus (Arco di Tito):** This arch commemorated the Roman victory over the province of Judaea (Israel) in A.D. 70. The Romans had a reputation as benevolent conquerors who tolerated the local customs and rulers. All they required was allegiance to the empire, shown by worshiping the emperor as a god. No problem for most conquered people, who already had half a dozen gods on their prayer lists anyway. But Israelites believed in only one god, and it wasn't the emperor. Israel revolted. After a short but bitter war, the Romans defeated the rebels, took Jerusalem, destroyed their temple (leaving only the foundation wall—today's revered "Wailing Wall"), and brought home 50,000 Jewish slaves... who were forced to build this arch (and the Colosseum).

• *Walk down Via Sacra into the Forum. After about 50 yards, turn right and follow a path uphill to the three huge arches of the...*

❷ **Basilica of Constantine (a.k.a. Basilica Maxentius):** Yes, these are big arches. But they represent only one-third of the original Basilica of Constantine, a mammoth hall of justice. The arches were matched by a similar set along the Via Sacra side (only a few squat brick piers remain). Between them ran the central hall, which was spanned by a roof 130 feet high—about 55 feet higher than the side arches you see. (The stub of brick you see sticking up began an arch that once spanned the central hall.) The hall itself was as long as a football field, lavishly furnished with colorful inlaid mar-

> ## Rome: Republic and Empire
> ### (500 B.C.-A.D. 500)
>
> Ancient Rome spanned a thousand years, from about 500 B.C. to A.D. 500. During that time, Rome expanded from a small tribe of barbarians to a vast empire, then dwindled slowly to city size again. For the first 500 years, when Rome's armies made her ruler of the Italian peninsula and beyond, Rome was a republic governed by elected senators. Over the next 500 years, a time of world conquest and eventual decline, Rome was an empire ruled by a military-backed dictator.
>
> Julius Caesar bridged the gap between republic and empire. This ambitious general and politician, popular with the people because of his military victories and charisma, suspended the Roman constitution and assumed dictatorial powers in about 50 B.C. A few years later, he was assassinated by a conspiracy of senators. His adopted son, Augustus, succeeded him, and soon "Caesar" was not just a name but a title.
>
> Emperor Augustus ushered in the Pax Romana, or Roman peace (A.D. 1-200), a time when Rome reached her peak and controlled an empire that stretched even beyond Eurail—from England to Egypt, Turkey to Morocco.

ble, a gilded bronze ceiling, and statues, and filled with strolling Romans. At the far (west) end was an enormous marble statue of Emperor Constantine on a throne. (Pieces of this statue, including a hand the size of a man, are on display in Rome's Capitoline Museums.)

The basilica was begun by the emperor Maxentius, but after he was trounced in battle (see page 775), the victor, Constantine, completed the massive building. No doubt about it, the Romans built monuments on a more epic scale than any previous Europeans, wowing their "barbarian" neighbors.

• *Now stroll deeper into the Forum, downhill along Via Sacra, through the trees. Many of the large basalt stones under your feet were walked on by Caesar Augustus 2,000 years ago. Pass by the only original bronze door still swinging on its ancient hinges (the green door at the Tempio di Romolo, on the right) and continue between ruined buildings until the Via Sacra opens up to a flat, grassy area.*

❸ **The Forum's Main Square:** The original Forum, or main square, was this flat patch about the size of a football field, stretching to the foot of Capitol Hill. Surrounding it were temples, law courts, government buildings, and triumphal arches.

Rome was born right here. According to legend, twin brothers Romulus (Rome) and Remus were orphaned in infancy and raised by a she-wolf on top of Palatine Hill. Growing up, they found it hard to get dates. So they and their cohorts attacked the nearby Sabine tribe and kidnapped their women. After they made peace, this marshy valley became the meeting place and then the trading center for the scattered tribes on the surrounding hillsides.

The square was the busiest and most crowded—and often the seediest—section of town. Besides the senators, politicians, and currency exchangers, there were even sleazier types—souvenir hawkers, pickpockets, fortune-tellers, gamblers, slave marketers, drunks, hookers, lawyers, and tour guides.

The Forum is now rubble, but imagine it in its prime: blindingly brilliant marble buildings with 40-foot-high columns and shining metal roofs; rows of statues painted in realistic colors; processional chariots rattling down Via Sacra. Mentally replace tourists in T-shirts with tribunes in togas. Imagine the buildings towering and the people buzzing around you while an orator gives a rabble-rousing speech from the Rostrum. If things still look like just a pile of rocks, at least tell yourself, "But Julius Caesar once leaned against these rocks."

• *At the near (east) end of the main square (the Colosseum is to the east) are the foundations of a temple now capped with a peaked wood-and-metal roof.*

❹ **Temple of Julius Caesar (Tempio del Divo Giulio, or Ara di Cesare):** Julius Caesar's body was burned on this spot (under the metal roof) after his assassination. Peek behind the wall into the small apse area, where a mound of dirt usually has fresh flowers—given to remember the man who, more than any other, personified the greatness of Rome.

Caesar (100-44 b.c.) changed Rome—and the Forum—dramatically. He cleared out many of the wooden market stalls and began to ring the square with even grander buildings. Caesar's house was located behind the temple, near that clump of trees. He walked right by here on the day he was assassinated ("Beware the Ides of March!" warned a street-corner Etruscan preacher).

Though he was popular with the masses, not everyone liked Caesar's urban design or his politics. When he assumed dictatorial powers, he was ambushed and stabbed to death by a conspiracy of senators, including his adopted son, Brutus *("Et tu, Brute?").*

The funeral was held here, facing the main square. The citizens gathered, and speeches were made. Mark Antony stood up to say (in Shakespeare's words), "Friends, Romans, countrymen, lend me your ears. I come to bury Caesar, not to praise him." When Caesar's body was burned, the citizens who still loved him threw anything at hand on the fire, requiring the fire department to come put it out. Later, Emperor Augustus dedicated this temple in his name, making Caesar the first Roman to become a god.

• *Behind and to the left of the Temple of Julius Caesar are 10 tall columns (which may be covered with restoration scaffolding). These belong to the...*

❺ **Temple of Antoninus Pius and Faustina:** The Senate built this temple to honor Emperor Antoninus Pius (A.D. 138-161) and his deified wife, Faustina. The 50-foot-tall Corinthian (leafy) columns must have been awe-inspiring to out-of-towners who grew up in thatched huts. Although the temple has been inhabited by a church, you can still see the basic layout—a staircase led to a shaded porch (the columns), which admitted you to the main building (now a church), where the statue of the god sat. Originally, these columns supported a triangular pediment decorated with sculptures.

Picture these columns, with gilded capitals, supporting brightly painted statues in the pediment, and the whole building capped with a gleaming bronze roof. The stately gray rubble of today's Forum is a faded black-and-white photograph of a 3-D Technicolor era.

The building is a microcosm of many of the changes that occurred after Rome fell. In medieval times, the temple was pillaged. Note the diagonal cuts high on the marble columns—a failed attempt by scavengers to cut through the pillars to pull them down for their precious stone. (They used vinegar and rope to cut the marble...but because vinegar also eats through rope, they abandoned the attempt.) In 1550, a church was housed inside the ancient temple. The door shows the street level at the time of Michelangelo. The long staircase was underground until excavated in the 1800s.

• *There's a ramp next to the Temple of A. and F. Walk halfway up it and look to the left to view the...*

❻ **Basilica Aemilia:** A basilica was a covered public forum, often serving as a Roman hall of justice. In a society that was as legal-minded as America is today, you needed a lot of lawyers—and a big place to put them. Citizens came here to work out matters such as inheritances and building permits, or to sue somebody.

Notice the layout. It was a long, rectangular building. The stubby columns all in a row form one long, central hall flanked by two side aisles. Medieval Christians required a larger meeting hall for their worship services than Roman temples provided, so they used the spacious Roman basilica as the model for their churches. Cathedrals from France to Spain to England, from Romanesque to Gothic to Renaissance, all have the same basic floor plan as a Roman basilica.

• *Return again to the Temple of Julius Caesar. To the right of the temple are the three tall Corinthian columns of the Temple of Castor and Pollux. Beyond that is Palatine Hill—the corner of which may have been...*

❼ Caligula's Palace (a.k.a. the Palace of Tiberius): Emperor Caligula (ruled A.D. 37-41) had a huge palace on Palatine Hill overlooking the Forum. It actually sprawled down the hill into the Forum (some supporting arches remain in the hillside).

Caligula was not a nice person. He tortured enemies, stole senators' wives, and parked his chariot in handicap spaces. But Rome's luxury-loving emperors only added to the glory of the Forum, with each one trying to make his mark on history.

• *To the left of the Temple of Castor and Pollux, find the remains of a small white circular temple.*

❽ Temple of Vesta: This is perhaps Rome's most sacred spot. Rome considered itself one big family, and this temple represented a circular hut, like the kind that Rome's first families lived in. Inside, a fire burned, just as in a Roman home. And back in the days before lighters and butane, you never wanted your fire to go out. As long as the sacred flame burned, Rome would stand. The flame was tended by priestesses known as Vestal Virgins.

• *Around the back of the Temple of Vesta, you'll find two rectangular brick pools. These stood in the courtyard of the...*

❾ House of the Vestal Virgins: The Vestal Virgins lived in a two-story building surrounding a long central courtyard with these two pools at one end. Rows of statues depicting leading Vestal Virgins flanked the courtyard. This place was the model—both architecturally and sexually—for medieval convents and monasteries.

Chosen from noble families before they reached the age of 10, the six Vestal Virgins served a 30-year term. Honored and revered by the Romans, the Vestals even had their own box opposite the emperor in the Colosseum. The statues that line the courtyard honor dutiful Vestals.

As the name implies, a Vestal took a vow of chastity. If she served her term faithfully—abstaining for 30 years—she was given a huge dowry and allowed to marry. But if they found any Virgin who wasn't, she was strapped to a funeral car, paraded through the streets of the Forum, taken to a crypt, given a loaf of bread and a lamp...and buried alive. Many women suffered the latter fate.

• *Return to the Temple of Julius Caesar and head to the Forum's west end (opposite from the Colosseum). As you pass alongside the big open space of the Forum's main square, consider how the piazza is still a standard part of any Italian town. It has reflected and accommodated the gregarious and outgoing nature of the Italian people since Roman times.*

Stop at the big, well-preserved brick building (on right) with the triangular roof. Look in at...

❿ The Curia (Senate House): The Curia was the most important political building in the Forum. While the present building dates from A.D. 283, this was the site of Rome's official center of government since the birth of the republic. (Note that ongoing archaeological work may restrict access to the Curia, as well as the Arch of Septimius Severus—described later—and the exit to Capitol Hill.) Three hundred senators, elected by the citizens of Rome, met here to debate and create the laws of the land. Their wooden seats once circled the building in three tiers; the Senate president's podium sat at the far end. The marble floor is from ancient times. Listen to the echoes in this vast room—the acoustics are great.

Rome prided itself on being a republic. Early in the city's history, its people threw out the king and established rule by elected representatives. Each Roman citizen was free to speak his mind and have a say in public policy. Even when emperors became the supreme authority, the Senate was a power to be reckoned with. The Curia building is well-preserved, having been used as a church since early Christian times. In the 1930s, it was restored and opened to the public as a historic site. (Note: Although Julius Caesar was assassinated in "the Senate," it wasn't here—at the time, the Senate was temporarily meeting across town.)

A statue and two reliefs inside the Curia help build our mental image of the Forum. The statue, made of porphyry marble in about A.D. 100 (with its head, arms, and feet now missing), was a tribute to an emperor, probably Hadrian or Trajan. The two relief panels may have decorated the Rostrum. Those on the left show people (with big stone tablets) standing in line to burn their debt records following a government amnesty. The other shows the distribution of grain (Rome's welfare system), some buildings in the background, and the latest fashion in togas.

• *Go back down the Senate steps and find the 10-foot–high wall just to the left of the big arch, marked...*

⓫ Rostrum (Rostri): Nowhere was Roman freedom more apparent than at this "Speaker's Corner." The Rostrum was a raised platform, 10 feet high and 80 feet long, decorated with statues, columns, and the prows of ships (rostra).

On a stage like this, Rome's orators, great and small, tried to draw a crowd and sway public opinion. Mark Antony rose to offer Caesar the laurel-leaf crown of kingship, which Caesar publicly (and hypocritically) refused while privately becoming a dictator. Men such as Cicero railed against the corruption and decadence that came with the city's newfound wealth. In later years, daring citizens even spoke out against the emperors, reminding them that Rome was once free. Picture the backdrop these speakers would have had—a mountain of marble buildings piling up on Capitol Hill.

In front of the Rostrum are trees bearing fruits that were

Rome Falls

Remember that Rome lasted 1,000 years—500 years of growth, 200 years of peak power, and 300 years of gradual decay. The fall had many causes, among them the barbarians who pecked away at Rome's borders. Christians blamed the fall on moral decay. Pagans blamed it on Christians. Socialists blamed it on a shallow economy based on the spoils of war. (Republicans blamed it

on Democrats.) Whatever the reasons, the far-flung empire could no longer keep its grip on conquered lands, and it pulled back. Barbarian tribes from Germany and Asia attacked the Italian peninsula and even looted Rome itself in a.d. 410, leveling many of the buildings in the Forum. In 476, when the last emperor checked out and switched off the lights, Europe plunged into centuries of ignorance, poverty, and weak government—the Dark Ages.

But Rome lived on in the Catholic Church. Christianity was the state religion of Rome's last generations. Emperors became popes (both called themselves "Pontifex Maximus"), senators became bishops, orators became priests, and basilicas became churches. The glory of Rome remains eternal.

sacred to the ancient Romans: olives (provided food, light, and preservatives), figs (tasty), and wine grapes (made a popular export product).

• *The big arch to the right of the Rostrum is the...*

⓬ Arch of Septimius Severus: In imperial times, the Rostrum's voices of democracy would have been dwarfed by images of the empire, such as the huge six-story-high Arch of Septimius Severus (A.D. 203). The reliefs commemorate the African-born emperor's battles in Mesopotamia. Near ground level, see soldiers marching captured barbarians back to Rome for the victory parade. Despite Severus' efficient rule, Rome's empire was crumbling under the weight of its own corruption, disease, decaying infrastructure, and the constant attacks by foreign "barbarians."

• *Pass underneath the Arch of Septimius Severus and turn left. On the slope of Capitol Hill are the eight remaining columns of the...*

⓭ Temple of Saturn: These columns framed the entrance to the Forum's oldest temple (497 B.C.). Inside was a humble, very old wooden statue of the god Saturn. But the statue's pedestal held the gold bars, coins, and jewels of Rome's state treasury, the booty collected by conquering generals.

• *Standing here, at one of the Forum's first buildings, look east at* *lone, tall...*

⑭ Column of Phocas—Rome's Fall: This is the Forum's last monument (A.D. 608), a gift from the powerful Byzantine Empire to a fallen empire—Rome. Given to commemorate the pagan Pantheon's becoming a Christian church, it's like a symbolic last nail in ancient Rome's coffin. After Rome's 1,000-year reign, the city was looted by Vandals, the population of a million-plus shrank to about 10,000, and the once-grand city center—the Forum—was abandoned, slowly covered up by centuries of silt and dirt. In the 1700s, an English historian named Edward Gibbon overlooked this spot from Capitol Hill. Hearing Christian monks singing at these pagan ruins, he looked out at the few columns poking up from the ground, pondered the "Decline and Fall of the Roman Empire," and thought, "Hmm, that's a catchy title...."

• *From here, you have several options:*

1. Exiting past the Arch of Titus lands you at the Colosseum (described on page 771).

2. Exiting past the Arch of Septimius Severus leads you to the stairs up to Capitol Hill (described on page 781).

3. The Forum's main entrance spills you back out onto Via dei Fori Imperiali (for Trajan's Column, Market, and Museum of the Imperial Forums, described on page 779).

4. From the Arch of Titus, you can climb Palatine Hill to the top—see page 778.

Dolce Vita Stroll

This is the city's chic stroll, from Piazza del Popolo (Metro: Flaminio) down a wonderfully traffic-free section of Via del Corso, and up Via Condotti to the Spanish Steps. It takes place from around 17:00 to 19:00 each evening (Fri and Sat are best), except on Sunday, when it occurs earlier in the afternoon. Leave before 18:00 if you plan to visit the Ara Pacis (Altar of Peace), which closes at 19:00 and is closed Monday.

As you stroll, you'll see shoppers, people-watchers, and flirts on the prowl, filling this neighborhood, which has some of Rome's most fashionable stores (some open after siesta 16:30-19:30). While both the crowds and the shops along Via del Corso have gone downhill recently, elegance survives in the grid of streets between here and the Spanish Steps. If you get hungry during your stroll,

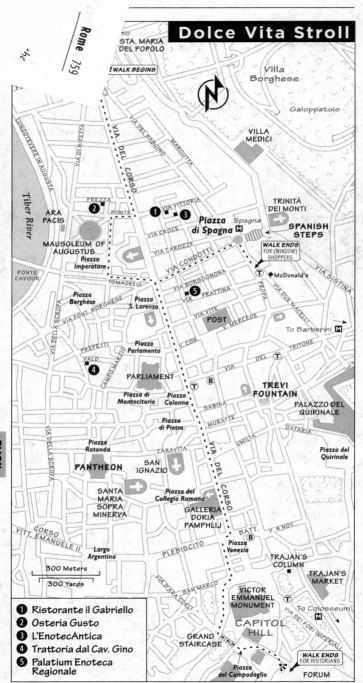

Dolce Vita Stroll

1 Ristorante il Gabriello
2 Osteria Gusto
3 L'EnotecAntica
4 Trattoria dal Cav. Gino
5 Palatium Enoteca Regionale

ROME

The *Passeggiata*

Throughout Italy, early evening is time to stroll. While elsewhere in Italy this is called the *passeggiata,* in Rome it's a cruder, big-city version called the *struscio* (meaning "to rub").

Unemployment among Italy's youth is very high; many stay with their parents even into their thirties. They spend a lot of time being trendy and hanging out. Like American kids gathering at the mall, working-class suburban youth *(coatto)* converge on the old center, as there's little to keep them occupied in Rome's dreary outskirts (which lack public spaces). The hot *vroom-vroom* motor scooter is their symbol; haircuts and fashion are follow-the-leader.

In a more genteel small town, the *passeggiata* comes with sweet whispers of *"bella"* and *"bello"* ("pretty" and "handsome"). In Rome, the admiration is stronger, oriented toward consumption—they say *"buona"* and *"buono"*—meaning roughly "tasty." But despite how lusty this all sounds, you'll see just as many chunky, middle-aged Italians out and about as hormone-charged youth.

see page 861 for descriptions of neighborhood wine bars and restaurants.

To reach **Piazza del Popolo,** where the stroll starts, take Metro line A to Flaminio and walk south to the square. Delightfully car-free, Piazza del Popolo is marked by an obelisk that was brought to Rome by Augustus after he conquered Egypt. (It used to stand in the Circus Maximus.) In medieval times, this area was just inside Rome's main entry (for more background on the square, see page 809).

If starting your stroll early enough, the Baroque church of **Santa Maria del Popolo** is worth popping into (Mon-Sat until 18:30, Sun until 19:30, next to gate in old wall on north side of square). Inside, look for Raphael's Chigi Chapel (KEE-gee, second chapel on left) and two paintings by Caravaggio (in the Cerasi Chapel, left of altar; see listing on page 810).

From Piazza del Popolo, shop your way down **Via del Corso.** With the proliferation of shopping malls, many chain stores lining Via del Corso are losing customers and facing hard times. Still, this remains a fine place to feel the pulse of Rome at twilight.

Historians side-trip right down Via Pontefici past the fascist architecture to see the massive, rotting, round-brick **Mausoleum of Augustus,** topped with overgrown cypress trees. Beyond it, next to the river, is Augustus' **Ara Pacis,** enclosed within a protective glass-walled museum (described on page 812). From the mausoleum, walk down Via Tomacelli to return to Via del Corso and the 21st century.

From Via del Corso, window-shoppers should take a left down **Via Condotti** to join the parade to the **Spanish Steps**. The streets that parallel Via Condotti to the south (Borgognona and Frattina) are more elegant and filled with high-end boutiques. A few streets to the north hides the narrow Via Margutta. This is where Gregory Peck's *Roman Holiday* character lived (at #51); today it's filled with pricey artisan shops.

Historians: Ignore Via Condotti and forget the Spanish Steps. Stay on Via del Corso, which has been straight since Roman times, for a half-mile down to the Victor Emmanuel Monument. Climb Michelangelo's stairway to his glorious (especially when flood-lit) square atop Capitol Hill. Stand on the balcony (just past the mayor's palace on the right), which overlooks the Forum. As the horizon reddens and cats prowl the unclaimed rubble of ancient Rome, it's one of the finest views in the city.

Heart of Rome Walk

Rome's most colorful neighborhood features narrow lanes, intimate piazzas, fanciful fountains, and some of Europe's best people-watching. During the day, this walk shows off the colorful Campo de' Fiori market and trendy fashion boutiques, as it meanders past major monuments such as the Pantheon and the Spanish Steps.

But, when the sun sets, unexpected magic happens. A stroll in the cool of the evening brings out all the romance of the Eternal City. Sit so close to a bubbling fountain that traffic noise evaporates. Jostle with kids to see the gelato flavors. Watch lovers straddling more than the bench. Jaywalk past polizia in flak-proof vests. And marvel at the ramshackle elegance that softens this brutal city for those who were born here and can't imagine living anywhere else. These are the flavors of Rome, best tasted after dark.

This walk is equally pleasant in reverse order. You could ride the Metro to the Spanish Steps and finish at Campo de' Fiori, near many recommended restaurants. To lengthen this walk, you could start in Trastevere; see directions on page 820.

• *Start this walk at Campo de' Fiori, my favorite outdoor dining room (especially after dark—see "Eating in Rome," page 854). It's a few blocks east of Largo Argentina, a major transportation hub. Buses #64 and 40 stop at both Largo Argentina and along Corso Vittorio Emanuele II, a long block north of Campo de' Fiori. A taxi from Termini train station costs about €8.*

Campo de' Fiori: One of Rome's most colorful spots, this bohemian

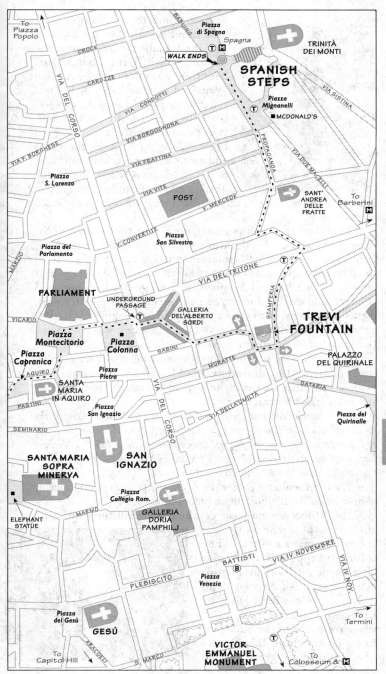

To
Piazza
Popolo

CROCE

VIA DEL CORSO

VIA CAROZZE

Babuino

Piazza
di Spagna

Spagna

WALK ENDS

TRINITÀ
DEI MONTI

SPANISH
STEPS

VIA SISTINA

VIA CONDOTTI

Piazza
Mignanelli

MCDONALD'S

VIA BORGOGNONA

PROPAGANDA

VIA DUE MACELLI

VIA F. BORGHESE

VIA FRATTINA

Piazza
S. Lorenzo

VIA VITE

POST

V. MERCEDE

SANT'
ANDREA
DELLE
FRATTE

To
Barberini

V. CONVERTITE

Piazza
San Silvestro

Piazza del
Parlamento

MARZIO

PARLIAMENT

VICARIO

UNDERGROUND
PASSAGE

GALLERIA
DEL'ALBERTO
SORDI

VIA DEL TRITONE

STAMPERIA

TREVI
FOUNTAIN

Piazza
Montecitorio

Piazza
Colonna

SABINI

MURATTE

PALAZZO
DEL QUIRINALE

Piazza
Capranica

AQUIRO

Piazza
Pietra

DATARIA

PASTINI

SANTA
MARIA
IN AQUIRO

VIA DEL CORSO

VIA DELL'UMILTA

Piazza del
Quirinale

SEMINARIO

Piazza
San Ignazio

ROME

SANTA MARIA
SOPRA
MINERVA

SAN
IGNAZIO

Piazza del
Quirinale

MARMO

Piazza
Collégio Rom.

ELEPHANT
STATUE

GALLERIA
DORIA
PAMPHILJ

BATTISTI

VIA IV NOVEMBRE

VIA IV NOV

PLEBISCITO

Piazza
Venezia

To
Termini

Piazza
del Gesú

GESÚ

ARACOELI

To
Capitol Hill

S. MARCO

VICTOR
EMMANUEL
MONUMENT

To
Colosseum &

covered, since the headwaters were unknown then. The Ganges holds an oar. The Danube turns to admire the obelisk, which Bernini had moved here from a stadium on the Appian Way. And Uruguay's Río de la Plata tumbles backward in shock, wondering how he ever made the top four. Bernini enlivens the fountain with horses plunging through the rocks and exotic flora and fauna from these newly discovered lands. Homesick Texans may want to find the armadillo. (It's the big, weird, armor-plated creature behind the Plata river statue.)

The Plata river god is gazing upward at the **Church of St. Agnes**, worked on by Bernini's former student-turned-rival, Francesco Borromini. Borromini's concave facade helps reveal the dome and epitomizes the curved symmetry of Baroque. Tour guides say that Bernini designed his river god to look horrified at Borromini's work. Or maybe he's shielding his eyes from St. Agnes' nakedness, as she was stripped before being martyred. But either explanation is unlikely, since the fountain was completed two years before Borromini even started work on the church.

Piazza Navona is Rome's most interesting night scene, with street music, artists, fire-eaters, local Casanovas, ice cream, and outdoor cafés that are worthy of a splurge if you've got time to sit and enjoy Italy's human river.

• *Leave Piazza Navona directly across from Tre Scalini (famous for its rich chocolate ice cream), and go east down Corsia Agonale, past rose peddlers and palm readers. Jog left around the guarded building (where Italy's senate meets), and follow the brown sign to the Pantheon, which is straight down Via del Salvatore.*

The Pantheon: Sit for a while under the portico of this ancient temple (romantically floodlit and moonlit at night).

The 40-foot, single-piece granite columns of the Pantheon's entrance show the scale the ancient Romans built on. The columns support a triangular Greek-style roof with an inscription that says "M. Agrippa" built it. In fact, it was built *(fecit)* by Emperor Hadrian (A.D. 120), who gave credit to the builder of an earlier structure. This impressive entranceway gives no clue

that the greatest wonder of the building is inside—a domed room that inspired later domes, including Michelangelo's St. Peter's and Brunelleschi's Duomo (in Florence).

If it's open, pop into the Pantheon for a look around (interior described on page 787). If you have extra time, consider detouring to several interesting churches near the Pantheon (listed on page 788).

• *With your back to the Pantheon, veer to the right, uphill toward the yellow sign that reads* Casa del Caffè *at the Tazza d'Oro coffee shop on Via Orfani.*

From the Pantheon to the Trevi Fountain: Tazza d'Oro Casa del Caffè, one of Rome's top coffee shops, dates back to the days when this area was licensed to roast coffee beans. Locals come here for its fine *granita di caffè con panna* (coffee slush with cream).

• *Continue up Via Orfani to...*

Piazza Capranica is home to the big, plain Florentine Renaissance-style Palazzo Capranica (directly opposite as you enter the square). Big shots, like the Capranica family, built towers on their palaces—not for any military use, but just to show off.

• *Leave the piazza to the right of the palace, heading down Via in Aquiro.*

The street Via in Aquiro leads to a sixth-century B.C. **Egyptian obelisk** taken as a trophy by Augustus after his victory in Egypt over Mark Antony and Cleopatra. The obelisk was set up as a sundial. Walk the zodiac markings to the well-guarded front door. This is Italy's **parliament building,** where the lower house meets; you may see politicians, political demonstrations, and TV cameras.

• *To your right is Piazza Colonna, where we're heading next—unless you like gelato...*

A two-block detour to the left (past Albergo Nazionale) brings you to Rome's most famous *gelateria.* **Giolitti's** is cheap for take-out or elegant and splurge-worthy for a sit among classy locals (open daily until past midnight, Via Uffici del Vicario 40); get your gelato in a cone *(cono)* or cup *(coppetta).*

Piazza Colonna features a huge second-century column. Its reliefs depict the victories of Emperor Marcus Aurelius over the barbarians. When Marcus died in A.D. 180, the barbarians began to get the upper hand, beginning Rome's long three-century fall. The big, important-looking palace houses the headquarters for the deputies (or cabinet) of the prime minister.

Noisy **Via del Corso** is Rome's main north-south boulevard. It's named for the Berber horse races—without riders—that took place here during Carnevale. This wild tradition continued until the late 1800s, when a series of fatal accidents (including, reportedly, one in front of Queen Margherita) led to its cancellation.

Rome at a Glance

▲▲▲**Colosseum** Huge stadium where gladiators fought. **Hours:** Daily 8:30 until one hour before sunset: April-Sept until 19:15, Oct until 18:30, off-season closes as early as 16:30. See page 771.

▲▲▲**Roman Forum** Ancient Rome's main square, with ruins and grand arches. **Hours:** Same hours as Colosseum. See page 777.

▲▲▲**Pantheon** The defining domed temple. **Hours:** Mon-Sat 8:30-19:30, Sun 9:00-18:00, holidays 9:00-13:00, closed for Mass Sat at 17:00 and Sun at 10:30. See page 787.

▲▲▲**St. Peter's Basilica** Most impressive church on earth, with Michelangelo's *Pietà* and dome. **Hours:** Church—daily April-Sept 7:00-19:00, Oct-March 7:00-18:00, often closed Wed mornings; dome—daily April-Sept 8:00-18:00, Oct-March 8:00-16:45. See page 791.

▲▲▲**Vatican Museum** Four miles of the finest art of Western civilization, culminating in Michelangelo's glorious Sistine Chapel. **Hours:** Mon-Sat 9:00-18:00. Closed on religious holidays and Sun, except last Sun of the month (open 9:00-14:00). May be open some Fri nights by online reservation only. Hours are subject to change. See page 796.

▲▲▲**Borghese Gallery** Bernini sculptures and paintings by Caravaggio, Raphael, and Titian in a Baroque palazzo. Reservations mandatory. **Hours:** Tue-Sun 9:00-19:00, closed Mon. See page 805.

▲▲▲**National Museum of Rome** Greatest collection of Roman sculpture anywhere. **Hours:** Tue-Sun 9:00-19:45, closed Mon. See page 814.

▲▲**Palatine Hill** Ruins of emperors' palaces, Circus Maximus view, and museum. **Hours:** Same as Colosseum. See page 778.

▲▲**Capitoline Museums** Ancient statues, mosaics, and expansive view of Forum. **Hours:** Tue-Sun 9:00-20:00, closed Mon. See page 783.

▲▲**Ara Pacis** Shrine marking the beginning of Rome's Golden Age. **Hours:** Tue-Sun 9:00-19:00, closed Mon. See page 812.

▲▲**Dolce Vita Stroll** Evening *passeggiata,* where Romans strut their stuff. **Hours:** Roughly Mon-Sat 17:00-19:00 and Sun afternoons. See page 759.

▲▲**Catacombs** Underground tombs, mainly Christian, some outside the city. **Hours:** Generally open 9:00-12:00 & 14:00-17:00. See page 811 and page 834.

▲**Arch of Constantine** Honors the emperor who legalized Christianity. **Hours:** Always viewable. See page 775.

▲**St. Peter-in-Chains** Church with Michelangelo's *Moses.* **Hours:** Daily 8:00-12:30 & 15:00-19:00, until 18:00 in winter. See page 775.

▲**Trajan's Column, Market, and Museum of the Imperial Forums** Tall column with narrative relief, and museum with entry to Trajan's Market. **Hours:** Column always viewable; museum open Tue-Sun 9:00-19:00, closed Mon. See page 779.

▲ **Piazza del Campidoglio** Square atop Capitol Hill, designed by Michelangelo, with a museum, grand stairway, and Forum overlooks. **Hours:** Always open. See page 781.

▲**Victor Emmanuel Monument** Gigantic edifice celebrating Italian unity, with Rome From the Sky elevator ride up to 360-degree city view. **Hours:** Monument open daily 9:30-18:30; elevator open Sun-Thu 9:30-19:30 (until 18:30 in winter), Fri-Sun 9:30-23:30 (until 19:30 in winter). See page 785.

▲**Trevi Fountain** Baroque hot spot into which tourists throw coins to ensure a return trip to Rome. **Hours:** Always flowing. See page 789.

▲**Castel Sant'Angelo** Hadrian's Tomb turned castle, prison, papal refuge, now museum. **Hours:** Tue-Sun 9:00-18:30, closed Mon. See page 803.

▲**Cappuccin Crypt** Decorated with the bones of 4,000 Franciscan friars. **Hours:** Daily 9:00-12:00 & 15:00-18:00. See page 808.

▲**Baths of Diocletian** Once ancient Rome's immense public baths, now a Michelangelo church. **Hours:** Mon-Sat 7:00-18:30, Sun 7:00-19:30, closed to sightseers during Mass. See page 815.

▲**Santa Maria della Vittoria** Church with Bernini's swooning *St. Teresa in Ecstasy.* **Hours:** Mon-Sat 8:30-12:00 & 15:30-18:00, Sun 15:30-18:00. See page 815.

Historically the street was filled with meat shops. When it became one of Rome's first gas-lit streets in 1854, these butcher shops were banned and replaced by classier boutiques, jewelers, and antiques dealers. Nowadays most of Via del Corso is closed to traffic for a few hours every evening and becomes a wonderful parade of Romans out for a stroll (see the "Dolce Vita Stroll," earlier).

• *Cross Via del Corso to enter a big palatial building with columns, which houses the Galleria Alberto Sordi shopping mall. Inside, take the fork to the right and exit out the back. (If you're here after 22:00, when the mall is closed, circle around the right side of the Galleria on Via dei Sabini.) Once out the back, head up Via de Crociferi, to the roar of the water, lights, and people of the...*

Trevi Fountain: The Trevi Fountain shows how Rome took full advantage of the abundance of water brought into the city by its great aqueducts. This watery Baroque avalanche by Nicola Salvi was completed in 1762. Salvi used the palace behind the fountain as a theatrical backdrop for the figure of "Ocean," who represents water in every form. The statue surfs through his wet kingdom—with water

gushing from 24 spouts and tumbling over 30 different kinds of plants—while Triton blows his conch shell.

The magic of the square is enhanced by the fact that no streets directly approach it. You can hear the excitement as you draw near, and then—*bam!*—you're there. The scene is always lively, with lucky Romeos clutching dates while unlucky ones clutch beers. Romantics toss a coin over their shoulder, thinking it will give them a wish and assure their return to Rome. That may sound silly, but every year I go through this tourist ritual...and it actually seems to work.

Take some time to people-watch (whisper a few breathy *bellos* or *bellas*) before leaving. There's a peaceful zone at water level on the far right.

• *From the Trevi Fountain, we're 10 minutes from our next stop, the Spanish Steps. Just use a map to get there, or follow these directions: Facing the Trevi Fountain, go forward, walking along the right side of the fountain on Via della Stamperia. Cross the busy Via del Tritone. Continue 100 yards and veer right at Via delle Fratte, a street that changes its name to Via Propaganda before ending at the...*

Spanish Steps: Piazza di Spagna, with the very popular Spanish Steps, is named for the Spanish Embassy to the Vatican, which has been here for 300 years. It's been the hangout of many

Romantics over the years (Keats, Wagner, and others). In the 1700s, British aristocrats of Europe came here to ponder Rome's de John Keats pondered his mortality, then age 25 in the pink building on the right side of the Romantic Lord Byron lived across the square at #66.

The **Sinking Boat Fountain** at the foot of the steps, built by Gian Lorenzo Bernini or his father, Pietro, is powered by an aqueduct. Actually, all of Rome's fountains are aqueduct-powered; their spurts are determined by the water pressure provided by the various aqueducts. This one, for instance, is much weaker than Trevi's gush.

The piazza is a thriving scene at night. It's clear that the main sight here is not the famous steps, but the people who sit on them. Window-shop along Via Condotti, which stretches away from the steps. This is where Gucci and other big names cater to the trendsetting jet set. Facing the Spanish Steps, you can walk right, about a block, to tour one of the world's biggest and most lavish McDonald's (salad bar, WC).

• *Our walk is finished. If you'd like to reach the top of the steps sweat-free, there's a free elevator just outside the Spagna Metro stop (elevator closes at 21:00; Metro stop is to the left of the Spanish Steps). Afterward, you can zip home on the Metro (usually open until 23:30, Fri–Sat until 1:30 in the morning) or grab a taxi at either the north or south side of the piazza.*

Sights in Rome

I've clustered Rome's sights into walkable neighborhoods, some quite close together (see the "Rome's Neighborhoods" map on page 729). Save transit time by grouping your sightseeing according to location. For example, the Colosseum and the Forum are a few minutes' walk from Capitol Hill; a 10-minute walk beyond that is the Pantheon. I like to tour these sights in one great day, starting at the Colosseum and ending at the Pantheon.

Ancient Rome

The core of ancient Rome, where the grandest monuments were built, is between the Colosseum and Capitol Hill. Among the ancient forums, a few more modern sights have popped up.

The Colosseum and Nearby

▲▲▲**Colosseum (Colosseo)**—This 2,000-year-old building is the classic example of Roman engineering. The Romans pioneered the use of concrete and the rounded arch, which enabled them to build on such a tremendous scale. While the essential structure

of the Colosseum is Roman, the four-story facade is decorated with mostly Greek columns—Doric-like Tuscan columns on the ground level, Ionic on the second story, Corinthian on the next level, and at the top, half-columns with a mix of all three. Built when the Roman Empire was at its peak in A.D. 80, the Colosseum represents Rome at its grandest. The Flavian Amphitheater (the Colosseum's real name) was an arena for gladiator contests and public spectacles. When killing became a spectator sport, the Romans wanted to share the fun with as many people as possible, so they stuck two semicircular theaters together to create a freestanding amphitheater. The outside (where slender cypress trees stand today) was decorated with a 100-foot-tall bronze statue of Nero that gleamed in the sunlight. In a later age, the colossal structure was nicknamed a "coloss-eum," the wonder of its age. It could accommodate 50,000 roaring fans (100,000 thumbs). This was where ancient Romans—whose taste for violence was the equal of modern America's—enjoyed their *Dirty Harry-* and *Terminator-*style spectacles. Gladiators, criminals, and wild animals fought to the death in every conceivable scenario. The bit of reconstructed Colosseum floor gives you an accurate sense of the original floor and the subterranean warren where animals were held, then lifted up in elevators. Released at floor level, animals would pop out from behind blinds into the arena—the gladiator didn't know where, when, or by what he'd be attacked.

Cost and Hours: €12 with temporary exhibits, this combo-ticket includes Roman Forum and Palatine Hill—see page 737, open daily 8:30 until one hour before sunset—for specifics, see "Hours" on page 750, last entry one hour before closing, Metro: Colosseo, tel. 06-3996-7700, http://archeoroma.beniculturali.it/en.

Avoiding Lines: You can save lots of time by buying your combo-ticket in advance, having the Roma Pass, or booking a guided tour. Here are some options:

1. Buy your combo-ticket (or Roma Pass) at the less-crowded Palatine Hill entrance, 150 yards away on Via di San Gregorio (facing the Forum, with Colosseum at your back, go left down the

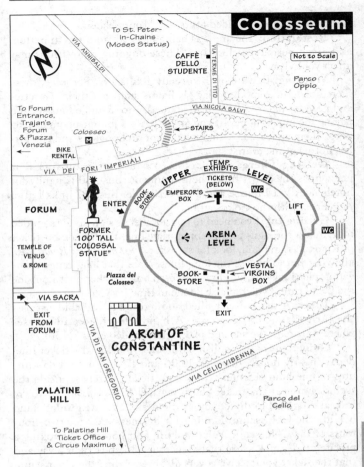

Colosseum

Not to Scale

To St. Peter-in-Chains (Moses Statue)

CAFFÈ DELLO STUDENTE

Parco Oppio

VIA ANNIBALDI

VIA TERME DI TITO

VIA NICOLA SALVI

To Forum Entrance, Trajan's Forum & Piazza Venezia

Colosseo M

STAIRS

BIKE RENTAL

VIA DEI FORI IMPERIALI

FORMER 100' TALL "COLOSSAL STATUE"

FORUM

ENTER

BOOK-STORE

UPPER LEVEL

TEMP EXHIBITS

TICKETS (BELOW)

EMPEROR'S BOX

WC

LIFT

ARENA LEVEL

WC

TEMPLE OF VENUS & ROME

Piazza del Colosseo

BOOK-STORE

VESTAL VIRGINS BOX

VIA SACRA

EXIT FROM FORUM

EXIT

VIA DI SAN GREGORIO

ARCH OF CONSTANTINE

VIA CELIO VIBENNA

PALATINE HILL

Parco del Celio

To Palatine Hill Ticket Office & Circus Maximus

ROME

street). You can also buy a Roma Pass at the tobacco shop in the Colosseo Metro station. (Avoid buying your ticket or Roma Pass at the Forum, which also tends to have lines.)

2. Buy a combo-ticket online at www.ticketclic.it (€1.50 booking fee, not changeable). Note that the "free tickets" you'll see listed are valid only for EU citizens with ID.

3. Pay to join an official guided tour (€5 plus Colosseum ticket). This lets you march right up to the Colosseum's guided visits *(Visite Guidate)* desk, thus bypassing the ticket lines. Alternatively, private walking-tour guides linger outside the Colosseum, offering tours that allow you to skip the line (€22, includes admission, tours also cover Palatine Hill and Forum). Be aware that these private guides may mislead you into thinking the Colosseum lines are longer than they really are—it's hard for a novice to judge. For more

on official or private guided tours, see "Tours," later.

Restoration: The arena is being cleaned from top to bottom and given permanent lighting. These ongoing renovations may affect your visit.

Warning: Beware of the **greedy gladiators.** For a fee, these incredibly crude, modern-day gladiators snuff out their cigarettes and pose for photos. They intimidate easy-to-swindle tourists into paying too much money. If you go for it, €4-5 for one photo usually keeps them appeased. Also, look out for **pickpockets** and con artists in this prime tourist spot.

Getting There: The Colosseo Metro stop on line B is just across the street from the monument. Bus #60 is handy for hotels near Via Firenze and Via Nazionale. Bus #87 links Largo Argentina with the Colosseum.

Getting In: If you need to buy a ticket or sign up for a guided tour, follow the signs for the appropriate line. With a combo-ticket or Roma Pass in hand, look for signs for *ticket holders* or *Roma Pass*, allowing you to bypass the long lines. Note that long-range renovation plans include building a free-standing ticket booth outside the Colosseum, which may be done in time for your visit.

Tours: A dry but fact-filled **audioguide** is available just past the turnstiles (€5.50/2 hours). A handheld **videoguide** senses where you are in the site and plays related video clips (€5.50).

Guided tours in English (which let you skip the ticket line) depart nearly hourly between 10:00 and 17:00, and last 45 minutes to one hour (€5 plus Colosseum ticket, purchase inside the Colosseum near the ticket booth marked *Visite Guidate;* if you're lost, ask a guard to direct you to the desk). **Private guides** stand outside the Colosseum, looking for business (€22 for two-hour tours of the Colosseum, Palatine Hill, and Forum). If booking a private guide, make sure that your tour will start right away and that the ticket you receive covers all three sights: the Colosseum, Forum, and Palatine Hill.

You can download a free Rick Steves **audio tour** of the Colosseum to your mobile device; see page 19.

A **behind-the-scenes tour** takes you through restricted areas, including underground passageways and the third floor, which are off-limits to regular Colosseum visitors. To do this, you'll need to book a 1.5-hour tour with Pierreci, a private company, at least a day in advance (€8 plus Colosseum ticket, call 06-3996-7700 during business hours, Mon-Fri 9:00-18:00, Sat 9:00-14:00, closed Sun, no same-day reservations). After dialing, wait for English instructions on how to reach a live operator, then reserve a time and pre-pay with a credit card. Without a reservation, you can go to the Colosseum and try to join the next available behind-the-scenes tour, even if it's in Italian. Once you have your Colosseum entrance ticket and are at the turnstiles, look for the tour meeting point just past the ticket desk; pay the guide directly.

▲**Arch of Constantine**—If you are a Christian, were raised a Christian, or simply belong to a so-called "Christian nation,"

ponder this arch. It marks one of the great turning points in history—the military coup that made Christianity mainstream. In A.D. 312, Emperor Constantine defeated his rival Maxentius in the crucial Battle of the Milvian Bridge. The night before, he had seen a vision of a cross in the sky. Constantine—whose mother and sister were Christians—became sole emperor and legalized Christianity. With this one battle, a once-obscure Jewish sect with a handful of followers was now the state religion of the entire Western world. In A.D. 300, you could be killed for being a Christian; a century later, you could be killed for not being one. Church enrollment boomed.

The restored arch is like an ancient museum. It's decorated entirely with recycled carvings originally made for other buildings. By covering it with exquisite carvings of high Roman art—works that glorified previous emperors—Constantine put himself in their league. Hadrian is featured in the round reliefs, with Marcus Aurelius in the square reliefs higher up. The big statues on top are of Trajan and Augustus. Originally, Augustus drove a chariot similar to the one topping the modern Victor Emmanuel II Monument. Fourth-century Rome may have been in decline, but Constantine clung to its glorious past.

▲**St. Peter-in-Chains Church (San Pietro in Vincoli)**—Built in the fifth century to house the chains that held St. Peter, this church is most famous for its Michelangelo statue. Check out the much-venerated chains under the high altar, then focus on mighty Moses. (Note that this isn't the famous St. Peter's Basilica, which is at Vatican City.)

Pope Julius II commissioned Michelangelo to build a massive tomb, with 48 huge statues, topped with a grand statue of this egomaniacal pope. The pope had planned to have his tomb placed in the center of St. Peter's Basilica. When Julius died, the work had barely been started, and no one had the money or necessary commitment to Julius to finish the project.

In 1542, some of the remnants of the tomb project were brought to St. Peter-in-Chains and pieced together by Michelangelo's assistants. Some of the best statues ended up elsewhere, such as

the *Prisoners* in Florence and the *Slaves* in the Louvre. *Moses* and the Louvre's *Slaves* are the only statues Michelangelo personally completed for the project. Flanking *Moses* are the Old Testament sister-wives of Jacob, Leah (to our right) and Rachel, both begun by Michelangelo but probably finished by pupils.

This powerful statue of Moses—one of Michelangelo's most artistically mature works—is worth studying. The artist worked on it in fits and starts for 30 years. Moses has received the Ten Commandments. As he holds the stone tablets, his eyes show a man determined to stop his tribe from worshipping the golden calf and idols...a man determined to win salvation for the people of Israel. Why the horns? Centuries ago, the Hebrew word for "rays" was mistranslated as "horns."

Cost and Hours: Free, daily April-Sept 8:00-12:30 & 15:00-19:00, Oct-March 8:00-12:30 & 15:00-18:00, modest dress required; the church is a 15-minute uphill, zigzag walk from the Colosseum, or a shorter, simpler walk from the Cavour Metro stop—from that station, go downhill on Via Cavour a half-block,

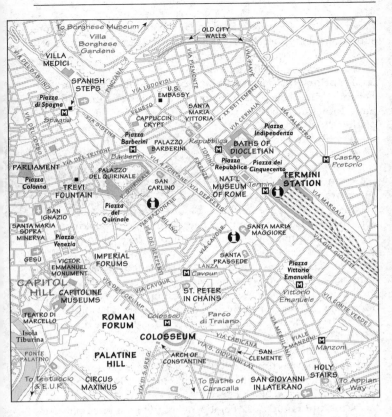

then climb the pedestrian staircase called Via di San Francesco di Paola, which leads right to the church.

The Roman Forum and Nearby

▲▲▲**Roman Forum (Foro Romano)**—This is ancient Rome's

birthplace and civic center, and the common ground between Rome's famous seven hills. As just about anything important that happened in ancient Rome happened here, it's arguably the most important piece of real estate in Western civilization. While only a few fragments of that glorious past remain, history-seekers find plenty to ignite their imaginations amid the half-broken columns and arches.

Cost and Hours: €12 combo-ticket includes Colosseum and

Palatine Hill—see page 737, open daily 8:30 until one hour before sunset, last entry one hour before closing, Metro: Colosseo, tel. 06-3996-7700, http://archeoroma.beniculturali.it/en.

See my self-guided walk on page 750.

▲▲**Palatine Hill (Monte Palatino)**—The hill overlooking the Forum is jam-packed with history—"the huts of Romulus," the huge Imperial Palace, a view  of the Circus Maximus—but there's only the barest skeleton of rubble left to tell the story.

We get our word "palace" from this hill, where the emperors chose to live. The Palatine Hill was once so filled with palaces that later emperors had to build out. (Looking up at it from the Forum, you see the substructure that supported these long-gone palaces.)

The Palatine museum contains statues and frescoes that help you imagine the luxury of the imperial Palatine. From the pleasant garden, you'll get an overview of the Forum. On the far side, look down into an emperor's private stadium and then beyond at the grassy Circus Maximus, once a chariot course. Imagine the cheers, jeers, and furious betting.

While many tourists consider the Palatine Hill just extra credit after the Forum, it offers an insight into the greatness of Rome. (And, if you're visiting the Colosseum or Forum, you've got a ticket whether you like it or not.)

Cost and Hours: €12 combo-ticket (€9 base price plus frequent, mandatory exhibition fees), also includes Roman Forum and Colosseum—see page 737; open same hours as Roman Forum and Colosseum.

The Palatine's entrance is on Via di San Gregorio (facing the Forum with the Colosseum at your back, it's down the street to your left). You can also enter the Palatine from within the Roman Forum—just climb the hill from the Arch of Titus.

Audioguides cost €5 (€7 version includes Roman Forum, must leave ID), and guided tours in English might be available (inquire at the ticket booth). WCs are at the ticket office when you enter, at the museum in the center of the site, and hiding among the orange trees in the Farnese Gardens.

Mamertine Prison—This 2,500-year-old cistern-like prison is where, according to Christian tradition, the Romans imprisoned Saints Peter and Paul. Though it was long a charming and historic sight, its artifacts have been removed, and today it's run by a commercial tour-bus company charging €10 for a cheesy "multimedia" walk-through. Don't go in. Instead, stand outside

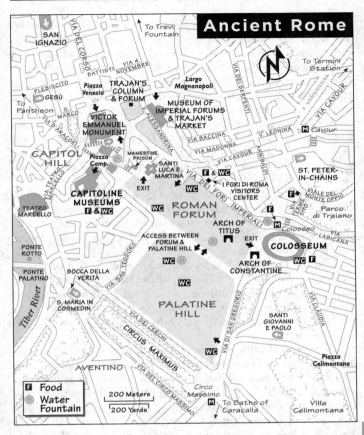

and imagine how this dank cistern once housed prisoners of the emperor. Amid fat rats and rotting corpses, unfortunate humans awaited slow deaths. It's said that a miraculous fountain sprang up inside so Peter could convert and baptize his jailers, who were also subsequently martyred. Before the commercial ruination of this sacred and ancient site, on the walls you could read lists of notable prisoners (Christian and non-Christian) and the ways they were executed: *strangolati, decapitato, morto per fame* (died of hunger). The sign by the Christian names read, "Here suffered, victorious for the triumph of Christ, these martyr saints." Today this sight itself has been martyred by a city apparently desperate to monetize its heritage.

▲**Trajan's Column, Market, and Museum of the Imperial Forums**—This grand column is the best example of "continuous narration" that we have from antiquity. More than 2,500 figures spiral around the 140-foot-high column, telling of

Trajan's victorious Dacian campaign (circa A.D. 103, in present-day Romania), from the assembling of the army at the bottom to the victory sacrifice at the top. At one point, the ashes of Trajan and his wife were held in the base, and the sun glinted off a polished bronze statue of Trajan at the top. (Today, St. Peter is on top.) Study the propaganda that winds up the column like a scroll, trumpeting Trajan's wonderful military exploits (for a rolled-out version of the column's story, visit the E.U.R.'s Museum of Roman Civilization). This column marked "Trajan's Forum," which was built to handle the shopping needs of a wealthy city of more than a million people. Commercial, political, religious, and social activities all mixed in the forum.

Nestled into the cutaway curve of Quirinal Hill is the semicircular brick complex of Trajan's Market. It was likely part shopping mall, part warehouse, and part administration building. Or, as some archaeologists have recently suggested, it may have contained mostly government offices.

Paying the admission fee gets you inside Trajan's Market, Trajan's Forum, and the **Museum of the Imperial Forums.** The museum features discoveries from the forums of emperors Julius Caesar, Augustus, Nerva, and Trajan, with fragments of statues and a slideshow that reconstructs how the forum looked in each emperor's time.

Cost and Hours: Museum—€7.50, includes entry to the market ruins—also viewable for free from Via dei Fori Imperiali, Tue-Sun 9:00-19:00, closed Mon, last entry 30 minutes before closing, entrance is uphill from the column on Via IV Novembre 94, tel. 06-0608, www.mercatiditraiano.it.

Getting There: Trajan's Column is just a few steps off Piazza Venezia (a hub for major bus routes #40, #64, and #87), on Via dei Fori Imperiali, across the street from the Victor Emmanuel Monument. Trajan's Market can be entered only through the Museum of the Imperial Forums at Via IV Novembre 94 (up the staircase from Trajan's Column). Trajan's Forum stretches southeast of the column toward the Colosseo Metro stop and the Colosseum itself.

Bocca della Verità—The legendary "Mouth of Truth" at the Church of Santa Maria in Cosmedin draws a playful crowd. Stick your hand in the mouth of the gaping stone face in the porch wall. As the legend goes (it was popularized by the 1953 film *Roman Holiday,* starring Gregory Peck and Audrey Hepburn), if you're a liar, your hand will be gobbled up. The mouth is only accessible when the church gate is open, but it's always (partially) visible through the gate even when closed.

Cost and Hours: €0.50, daily 9:30-17:50, closes earlier off-season, Piazza Bocca della Verità, near the north end of Circus Maximus.

Capitol Hill

Of Rome's famous seven hills, this is the smallest, tallest, and most famous—home of the ancient Temple of Jupiter and the

center of city government for 2,500 years. There are several ways to get to the top of Capitol Hill (a.k.a. Capitoline Hill). If you're coming from the north (from Piazza Venezia), take Michelangelo's impressive stairway to the right of the big, white Victor Emmanuel Monument. Coming from the southeast (the Forum), take the steep staircase near the Arch of Septimius Severus. From near Trajan's Forum along Via dei Fori Imperiali, take the winding road. All three converge at the top, in the square called Campidoglio (kahm-pee-DOHL-yoh).

▲**Piazza del Campidoglio (Capitol Hill Square)**—This square atop the hill, once the religious and political center of ancient Rome, is still the home of the city's government. In the 1530s, the pope called on Michelangelo to re-establish this square as a grand center. Michelangelo placed the ancient equestrian statue of Marcus Aurelius as the square's focal point. Effective. (The original statue is now in the adjacent museum.) The twin buildings on either side are the Capitoline Museums. Behind the replica of the statue is the mayoral palace (Palazzo Senatorio).

Michelangelo wanted people to approach the square from his grand stairway off Piazza Venezia. From the top of the stairway, you see the new Renaissance face of Rome, with its back to the Forum. Michelangelo gave the buildings the "giant order"—huge pilasters make the existing two-story buildings feel one-storied and more harmonious with the new square. Notice how the statues atop these buildings welcome you and then draw you in.

The terraces just downhill (past either side of the mayor's palace) offer grand views of the Forum. To the left of

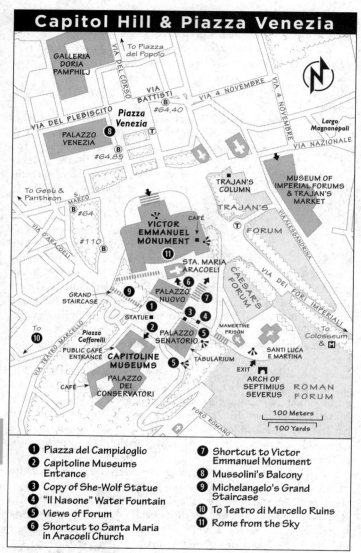

Capitol Hill & Piazza Venezia

1. Piazza del Campidoglio
2. Capitoline Museums Entrance
3. Copy of She-Wolf Statue
4. "Il Nasone" Water Fountain
5. Views of Forum
6. Shortcut to Santa Maria in Aracoeli Church
7. Shortcut to Victor Emmanuel Monument
8. Mussolini's Balcony
9. Michelangelo's Grand Staircase
10. To Teatro di Marcello Ruins
11. Rome from the Sky

the mayor's palace is a copy of the famous She-Wolf statue on a column. Farther down is *il nasone* ("the big nose"), a refreshing water fountain (see photo previous page). Block the spout with your fingers, and water spurts up for drinking. Romans joke that a cheap Roman boy takes his date out for a drink at *il nasone*. Near the She-Wolf statue is the staircase leading to a shortcut to the Victor Emmanuel Monument (see sidebar).

Shortcut to the Victor Emmanuel Monument and Aracoeli Church

A clever shortcut lets you go directly from Piazza del Campidoglio, the square atop Capitol Hill, to Santa Maria in Aracoeli Church and an upper level of the Victor Emmanuel Monument, avoiding long flights of stairs. Facing the square's equestrian statue, head to the left, climbing the wide set of stairs near the She-Wolf statue. Midway up the stairs (at the column), turn left to reach the back entrance to the Aracoeli Church. To reach the Victor Emmanuel Monument, pass by the column and continue to the top of the steps, pass through the iron gate, and enter the small unmarked door at #13 on the right. You'll soon emerge on a café terrace that leads to the monument and the Rome from the Sky elevator.

▲▲**Capitoline Museums (Musei Capitolini)**—Some of ancient Rome's most famous statues and art are housed in the two palaces (Palazzo dei Conservatori and Palazzo Nuovo) that flank the equestrian statue in Piazza del Campidoglio. They're connected by an underground passage that leads to the vacant Tabularium and panoramic views of the Roman Forum.

Cost and Hours: €7.50-11 depending on price of temporary exhibit, Tue-Sun 9:00-20:00, closed Mon, last entry one hour before closing, audioguide-€5 or €6.20/2 people, tel. 06-8205-9127 or 06-0608, www.museicapitolini.org.

◑ Self-Guided Tour: The museum's layout—with two different buildings connected by an underground passage—can be confusing. You'll enter at the Palazzo dei Conservatori (on your right as you face the equestrian statue), cross underneath the square (beneath the Palazzo Senatorio, or mayoral palace, not open to public), and exit from the Palazzo Nuovo (on your left).

The **Palazzo dei Conservatori** claims to be one of the world's oldest museums, founded in 1471 when a pope gave ancient statues to the citizens of Rome. In the courtyard, enjoy the massive chunks of Constantine: his head, hand, and foot. When intact, this giant held the place of honor in the Basilica of Constantine in the Forum. The museum is worthwhile, with lavish rooms and several great statues. You'll see the 13th-century *Capitoline*

She-Wolf (the little statues of Romulus and Remus were added in the Renaissance). Don't miss the *Boy Extracting a Thorn* and the enchanting *Commodus as Hercules.* Behind Commodus is a statue of his dad, Marcus Aurelius, on a horse. The greatest surviving equestrian statue of antiquity, this was the original centerpiece of the square (where a copy stands today). Christians in the Dark Ages thought that the statue's hand was raised in blessing, which probably led to their misidentifying him as Constantine, the first Christian emperor. While most pagan statues were destroyed by Christians, "Constantine" was spared.

The second-floor café, **Caffè Capitolino,** has a splendid patio offering city views. It's lovely at sunset (public entrance for non-museum-goers off Piazza Caffarelli and through door #4).

Go downstairs to the **Tabularium.** Built in the first century B.C., these sturdy vacant rooms once held the archives of ancient Rome. The word Tabularium comes from "tablet," on which Romans wrote their laws. You won't see any tablets, but you will see a stunning head-on view of the Forum from the windows.

Leave the Tabularium and enter the **Palazzo Nuovo,** which houses mostly portrait busts of forgotten emperors. But it also has two must-see statues: the *Dying Gaul* and the *Capitoline Venus* (both on the first floor up).

Santa Maria in Aracoeli Church—The church atop Capitol Hill is old, and dear to the hearts of Romans. It stands on the site where

Emperor Augustus (supposedly) had a premonition of the coming of Mary and Christ standing on an "altar in the sky" (*ara coeli*). The church is Rome in a nutshell, where you can time-travel across 2,000 years by standing in one spot.

Cost and Hours: Free, daily 9:00-12:30 & 15:00-18:30. While dedicated pilgrims climb up the long, steep staircase from street level (the right side of Victor Emmanuel Monument, as you face it), savvy sightseers prefer to enter through the shortcut atop Capitol Hill (see sidebar).

Piazza Venezia

This vast square, dominated by the big, white Victor Emmanuel Monument, is a major transportation hub and the focal point of modern Rome. (The square has been dug up for years—Metro line C is under construction, and when anything of archaeological importance is uncovered, progress is interrupted, hence the canopied site on the square today.) With your back to the monument (you'll get the best views from the terrace by the guards and eternal flame), look down Via del Corso, the city's axis, surrounded by Rome's classiest shopping district. In the 1930s, Benito Mussolini whipped up Italy's nationalistic fervor from a balcony above the square (it's the less-grand balcony on the left). Fascist masses filled the square screaming, "Four more years!"—or something like that. Mussolini created the boulevard Via dei Fori Imperiali (to your right) to open up views of the Colosseum in the distance to impress his visiting friend Adolf Hitler. Mussolini lied to his people, mixing fear and patriotism to push his country to the right and embroil the Italians in expensive and regrettable wars. In 1945, they shot and hung Mussolini from a meat hook in Milan. (Berlusconi's headquarters are located—thought-provokingly—just behind Mussolini's. That explains all the security on Via del Plebiscito.)

Circling around the right side of the Victor Emmanuel Monument, look down into the ditch on your left to see the ruins of an ancient apartment building from the first century A.D.; part of it was transformed into a tiny church (faded frescoes and bell tower). Rome was built in layers—almost everywhere you go, there's an earlier version beneath your feet. (The hop-on, hop-off Trambus 110 stops just across the busy intersection from here.)

Continuing on, you reach two staircases leading up Capitol Hill. One is Michelangelo's grand staircase up to the Campidoglio. The longer of the two leads to the Santa Maria in Aracoeli Church, a good example of the earliest style of Christian churches (described earlier). The contrast between this climb-on-your-knees ramp to God's house and Michelangelo's elegant stairs illustrates the changes Renaissance humanism brought civilization.

From the bottom of Michelangelo's stairs, look right several blocks down the street to see a condominium actually built upon the surviving ancient pillars and arches of Teatro di Marcello.

▲**Victor Emmanuel Monument**—This oversize monument to Italy's first king, built to celebrate the 50th anniversary of the country's unification in 1861, was part of Italy's push to overcome

the new country's strong regionalism and create a national identity. At the base of this statue, Italy's Tomb of the Unknown Soldier (flanked by Italian flags and armed guards) is watched over by the goddess Roma (with the gold mosaic background).

The scale of the monument is over-the-top—200 feet high, 500 feet wide. The 43-foot-long statue of the king on the horse is the biggest equestrian statue in the world. The king's moustache forms an arc five feet long, and a person could sit within the horse's hoof. With its gleaming white sheen (from a recent scrubbing) and enormous scale, the monument provides a vivid sense of what ancient Rome looked like at its peak—imagine the Forum filled with shiny, grandiose buildings like this one.

The "Vittoriano" (as locals call it) is open and free to the public. You can simply climb the front stairs, or go inside from one of several entrances: midway up the monument through doorways flanking the central statue, on either side at street level, and at the base of the colonnade (two-thirds of the way up, near the shortcut from Capitol Hill). The little-visited **Museum of the Risorgimento** (free) fills many floors with displays on the movement and war that led to the unification of Italy in 1870. A café is at the base of the top colonnade, on the monument's north side.

You can climb the stairs to the midway point for a decent view, keep climbing to the base of the colonnade for a better view, or, for the best view, ride the **Rome from the Sky** elevator, which zips you from the top of the stair climb (at the back of the monument) to the rooftop for the grandest, 360-degree view of the center of Rome—even better than from the top of St. Peter's dome. Helpful panoramic dia-

grams describe the skyline, with powerful binoculars available for zooming in on particular sights. It's best in late afternoon, when it's beginning to cool off and Rome glows.

Cost and Hours: Monument—Free, daily 9:30-18:30, a few WCs scattered throughout, tel. 06-679-3598. Elevator—€7, Sun-Thu 9:30-19:30 (until 18:30 in winter), Fri-Sun 9:30-23:30 (until 19:30 in winter), ticket office closes 45 minutes earlier, WC at entrance, tel. 06-6920-2049; follow *ascensori panoramici* signs inside the Victor Emmanuel Monument or take the shortcut from Capitol Hill (no elevator access from street level).

Pantheon Neighborhood

Besides being home to ancient sights and historic churches, this neighborhood gives Rome its urban-village feel. Wander narrow streets, sample the many shops and eateries, and gather with the locals in squares marked by bubbling fountains. Exploring is especially good in the evening, when the restaurants bustle and streets are jammed with foot traffic. For a self-guided walk of this neighborhood, from Campo de' Fiori to the Trevi Fountain, see my Heart of Rome Walk on page 762.

Getting There: To reach the Pantheon neighborhood, you

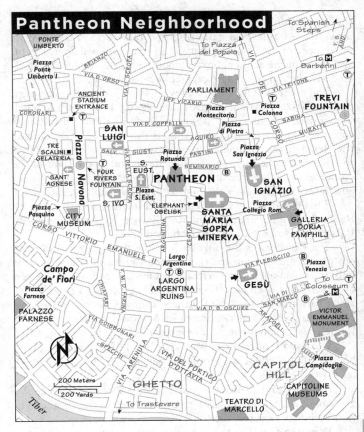

Pantheon Neighborhood

can walk (it's a 20-minute walk from Capitol Hill), take a taxi, or catch a bus. Buses #64 and #40 carry tourists and pickpockets frequently between the Termini train station and Vatican City, stopping at a chaotic square called Largo Argentina, located a few blocks south of the Pantheon. (Take either Via dei Cestari or Via di Torre Argentina north to the Pantheon.) The *elettrico* minibus #116 runs between Campo de' Fiori and Piazza Barberini via the Pantheon. The most dramatic approach is on foot, coming from Piazza Navona along Via Giustiniani, which spills directly into Piazza della Rotunda, offering the classic Pantheon view.

▲▲▲**Pantheon**—For the greatest look at the splendor of Rome, antiquity's best-preserved interior is a must. Built two millennia ago, this influential domed temple served as the model for Michelangelo's dome of St. Peter's and many others.

Because the Pantheon became a church dedicated to the martyrs just after the fall of Rome, the barbarians left it alone, and the locals didn't use it as a quarry. The portico is called "Rome's umbrella"—a fun local gathering in a rainstorm. Walk past its one-piece granite columns (biggest in Italy, shipped from Egypt) and through the original bronze doors. Sit inside under the glorious skylight and enjoy classical architecture at its best.

The dome, 142 feet high and wide, was Europe's biggest until the Renaissance. Michelangelo's dome at St. Peter's, while much higher, is about three feet narrower. The brilliance of this dome's construction has astounded architects through the ages. During the Renaissance, Brunelleschi was given permission to cut into the dome (see the little square hole above and to the right of the entrance) to analyze the material. The concrete dome gets thinner and lighter with height—the highest part is volcanic pumice.

This wonderfully harmonious architecture greatly inspired Raphael and other artists of the Renaissance. Raphael, along with Italy's first two kings, chose to be buried here.

The Pantheon is the only ancient building in Rome continuously used since its construction. When you leave, notice that the building is sunken below current street level, showing how the rest of the city has risen on 20 centuries of rubble. The nearest WCs are at bars and cafés on the Pantheon's square. Several reasonable eateries are a block or two north up Via del Pantheon. Some of Rome's best gelato is nearby. For recommendations, see page 859.

Cost and Hours: Free, Mon-Sat 8:30-19:30, Sun 9:00-18:00, holidays 9:00-13:00, closed for Mass Sat at 17:00 and Sun at 10:30, tel. 06-6830-0230.

Audioguide: 25-minute audioguide-€5 or €8.50/2 people. You can download a free Rick Steves audio tour of the Pantheon to your mobile device; see page 19.

When to Go: Try to get to the Pantheon first thing in the morning: While it's jammed with people midday, you'll have it all to yourself before 9:00.

▲▲Churches near the Pantheon—The **Church of San Luigi dei Francesi** has a magnificent chapel painted by Caravaggio (free, Fri-Wed 10:00-12:30 & 16:00-19:00, closed Thu, between the Pantheon and the north end of Piazza Navona). The only Gothic church in Rome is the **Church of Santa Maria sopra Minerva,** with a little-known Michelangelo statue, *Christ Bearing the Cross* (free, Mon-Fri 7:00-19:00, Sat-Sun 8:00-13:00 & 15:30-19:00, on a little square behind Pantheon, to the east). The **Church of San Ignazio,** several blocks east of the Pantheon, is a riot of Baroque illusions with a false dome (free, daily 7:30-19:00). A few blocks away, across Corso Vittorio Emanuele, is the rich and Baroque **Gesù Church,** headquarters of the Jesuits in Rome (free, daily 7:00-12:30 & 16:00-19:45, interesting daily service at 17:30).

▲**Galleria Doria Pamphilj**—This underappreciated gallery, in the heart of the old city, offers a rare chance to wander through a noble family's lavish rooms with the prince who calls this downtown mansion home. Well, almost. Through an audioguide, the prince lovingly narrates his family's story, as you tour the palace and its world-class art. Don't miss Velázquez's intense, majestic, ultra-realistic portrait of Pope Innocent X (1574-1655), patriarch of the Pamphilj (pahm-FEEL-yee) family. It stands alongside an equally impressive bust of the pope by Bernini. Stroll through a mini-Versailles-like hall of mirrors to more paintings, including works by Titian and Raphael. Finally, relax along with Mary, Joseph, and Jesus, and let the angel serenade you in Caravaggio's *Rest on the Flight to Egypt.*

Cost and Hours: €10, includes worthwhile 90-minute audioguide, daily 10:00-17:00, last entry 45 minutes before closing, elegant café, from Piazza Venezia walk 2 blocks up Via del Corso to #305, tel. 06-679-7323, www.dopart.it/roma.

Piazza di Pietra (Piazza of Stone)—The square was actually a quarry set up to chew away at the abandoned Roman building. You can still see the holes that hungry medieval scavengers chipped into the columns to steal the metal pins that held the slabs together (two blocks toward Via del Corso from Pantheon).

▲**Trevi Fountain**—The bubbly Baroque fountain, worth ▲▲ by night, is a minor sight to art scholars...but a major nighttime gathering spot for teens on the make and tourists tossing coins. The coins tourists deposit daily are collected to feed Rome's poor (for more on the fountain, see page 770).

Palazzo del Quirinale—This presidential palace, and former home of several popes, feels like a combination White House/Palace of Versailles (free, Sun 8:30-12:00 only—closed rest of the week, 200 yards east of Trevi Fountain on Piazza del Quirinale, tel. 06-46991).

Vatican City

Vatican City, the world's smallest country, contains St. Peter's Basilica (with Michelangelo's exquisite *Pietà*) and the Vatican Museum (with Michelangelo's Sistine Chapel). A helpful **TI** is just to the left of St. Peter's Basilica as you're facing it (Mon-Sat 8:30-19:00, closed Sun, tel. 06-6988-1662, Vatican switchboard tel. 06-6982, www.vatican.va). The entrances to St. Peter's and to the Vatican Museum are a 15-minute walk apart (follow the outside of

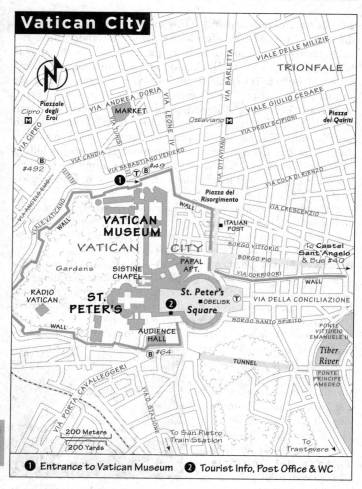

Vatican City

Piazzale degli Eroi
Cipro M

VIA ANDREA DORIA

MARKET

VIALE DELLE MILIZIE

TRIONFALE

VIA BARLETTA

VIALE GIULIO CESARE

Ottaviano M

Piazza del Quiriti

VIA DEGLI SCIPIONI

VIA CIPRO

VIA CANDIA

VIA TUNISI

VIA LEONE IV

VIA SEBASTIANO VENIERO

VIA OTTAVIANO

VIA COLA DI RIENZO

#492 B

#49 B T

①

Piazza del Risorgimento

VIA CRESCENZIO

VIA-ANGELO-EMO

VIALE VATICANO

WALL

VATICAN MUSEUM

VATICAN CITY

■ITALIAN POST

BORGO VITTORIO

To Castel Sant'Angelo & Bus #40

Gardens

SISTINE CHAPEL

PAPAL APT.

BORGO PIO

VIA CORRIDORI

WALL

RADIO VATICAN

ST. PETER'S

St. Peter's Square
■OBELISK ② T

VIA DELLA CONCILIAZIONE

WALL

BORGO SANTO SPIRITO

PONTE VITTORIO EMANUELE II

AUDIENCE HALL

#64 B

TUNNEL

Tiber River

PONTE PRINCIPE AMEDEO

VIA PORTA CAVALLEGGERI

VIA DI STAZIONE

200 Meters
200 Yards

To San Pietro Train Station

To Trastevere

① Entrance to Vatican Museum   ② Tourist Info, Post Office & WC

ROME

the Vatican wall, which links the two sights). The nearest Metro stops still involve a 10-minute walk to either sight: For St. Peter's,

the closest stop is Ottaviano; for the Vatican Museum, it's Cipro.

Modest dress is required of men, women, and children throughout the Vatican City, even outdoors. Otherwise the Swiss Guard can turn you away. Cover your shoulders; bring a light jacket or cover-up if you've got on a tank top. Wear long pants instead of shorts. Skirts or dresses should extend below your knee.

▲▲▲St. Peter's Basilica (Basilica San Pietro)

There is no doubt: This is the richest and grandest church on earth. To call it vast is like calling Einstein smart. Plaques on the floor show where other, smaller churches would end if they were placed inside. The ornamental cherubs would dwarf a large man. Birds roost inside, and thousands of people wander about, heads craned heavenward, hardly noticing each other. Don't miss Michelangelo's *Pietà* (behind bulletproof glass) to the right of the entrance. Bernini's altar work and twisting, towering canopy are brilliant.

Hours: The **church** is open daily April-Sept 7:00-19:00, Oct-March 7:00-18:00. It closes on Wednesday mornings during papal audiences. **Mass** is held daily in Italian—Mon-Sat at 8:30, 9:00, 10:00, 11:00, 12:00, and 17:00; Sun and holidays at 9:00, 10:30 (in Latin), 11:30, 12:15, 13:00, 16:00, and 17:45. Confirm the schedule (on-site, or go to www.saintpetersbasilica.org and click on the "Tourist Info" link) and location; it's generally in the south (left) transept.

The **Museum-Treasury** is open daily April-Sept 9:00-18:15, Oct-March 9:00-17:15. The **Crypt** closes one hour earlier than the church does. The **dome** is open to climbers daily April-Sept 8:00-18:00, Oct-March 8:00-16:45.

When to Go: The best time to visit the church is early or late; at 17:00, when the church is fairly empty, sunbeams can work their magic, and the late-afternoon Mass fills the place with spiritual music.

Avoiding Lines: To bypass the long security-checkpoint line, visit the Vatican Museum first (though it has its own long lines and checkpoint), then take the shortcut from the Sistine Chapel directly to St. Peter's. (Note, though, that this shortcut isn't always open—see page 802 for specifics.)

Dress Code: No shorts, above-the-knee skirts, or bare shoulders (this applies to everyone). Attendants strictly enforce this dress code, even in hot weather.

Getting There: Take the Metro to Ottaviano, then walk 10 minutes south on Via Ottaviano. There are two good bus options: The #40 express bus drops off at Piazza Pio, next to Castel Sant'Angelo—a 10-minute walk to St. Peter's. The more crowded bus #64 is convenient for pickpockets and stops just outside St. Peter's Square to the south (get off the bus after it crosses the Tiber, at the first stop past the tunnel; backtrack toward the tunnel and turn left when you see the rows of columns). A taxi from Termini train station to St. Peter's costs about €11.

Tours: The Vatican TI conducts free 1.5-hour tours of **St. Peter's** (depart from TI Mon-Fri 14:15, plus Tue and Thu 9:45, confirm schedule at TI, tel. 06-6988-1662). Audioguides can be rented near the checkroom (€5 plus ID, for church only, daily 9:00-17:00). You can download a free Rick Steves audio tour of St. Peter's Basilica to your mobile device; see page 19.

If you want to see the **Vatican Gardens,** you must book a tour online at least two days in advance at http://biglietteriamusei .vatican.va. No response means they're booked up (€31, 2 hours, usually daily except Wed and Sat, includes entry to Vatican Museum; tours start at 9:30 or 10:00 at Vatican Museum tour desk).

To see St. Peter's original grave, you can take a **Scavi "Excavations"** tour into the Necropolis (€12, 1.5 hours, ages 15 and older only, no photos). Book at least a month in advance by phone (tel. 06-6988-5318), email (scavi@fsp.va), or fax (06-6987-3017), following the detailed instructions at www.vatican.va (search on "Excavations Office"); no response means they're booked up.

Dome Climb (Cupola): You can take the elevator or stairs to the roof (231 steps), then climb another 323 steps to the top of the dome. The entry to the elevator is just outside the basilica on the north side of St. Peter's (near the secret exit from the Sistine Chapel). Look for signs to the cupola.

Baggage Check: The free bag check (mandatory for bags larger than a purse or daypack) is outside the basilica (to the right as you face the entrance), and just inside the security checkpoint.

Services: WCs are to the right and left on St. Peter's Square, near baggage storage past the security checkpoint, and on the roof.

◑ Self-Guided Tour: For a quick walk through the basilica, follow these points:

❶ The atrium is itself bigger than most churches. The huge white columns on the portico date from the first church (fourth century). Notice the historic doors (the Holy Door, on the right, won't be opened until the next Jubilee Year, in 2025).

❷ The purple, circular porphyry stone marks the site of Charlemagne's coronation in A.D. 800 (in the first St. Peter's church that stood on this site). From here, get a sense of the immensity of the church, which can accommodate 60,000 worshippers standing on its six acres.

❸ Michelangelo planned a Greek-cross floor plan, rather than the Latin-cross standard in medieval churches. A Greek cross, symbolizing the perfection of God, and by association the goodness of man, was important to the humanist Michelangelo. But accommodating—and impressing—large crowds was important to the Church in the fancy Baroque age, which followed Michelangelo, so the original nave length was doubled. Stand halfway up the nave

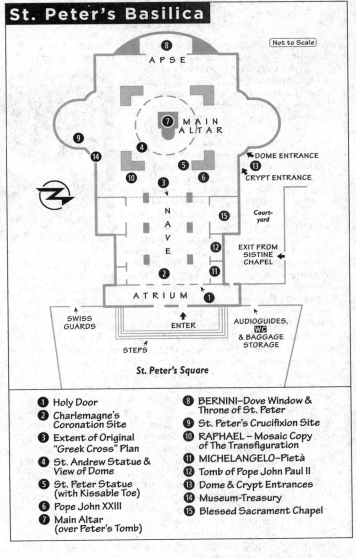

St. Peter's Basilica

Not to Scale

APSE

MAIN ALTAR

DOME ENTRANCE

CRYPT ENTRANCE

NAVE

Courtyard

EXIT FROM SISTINE CHAPEL

ATRIUM

SWISS GUARDS

ENTER

AUDIOGUIDES, WC & BAGGAGE STORAGE

STEPS

St. Peter's Square

1. Holy Door
2. Charlemagne's Coronation Site
3. Extent of Original "Greek Cross" Plan
4. St. Andrew Statue & View of Dome
5. St. Peter Statue (with Kissable Toe)
6. Pope John XXIII
7. Main Altar (over Peter's Tomb)
8. BERNINI–Dove Window & Throne of St. Peter
9. St. Peter's Crucifixion Site
10. RAPHAEL – Mosaic Copy of The Transfiguration
11. MICHELANGELO–Pietà
12. Tomb of Pope John Paul II
13. Dome & Crypt Entrances
14. Museum-Treasury
15. Blessed Sacrament Chapel

ROME

and imagine the stubbier design that Michelangelo had in mind.

❹ View the magnificent dome from the statue of St. Andrew. See the vision of heaven above the windows: Jesus, Mary, a ring of saints, rings of angels, and, on the very top, God the Father.

❺ The statue of St. Peter, with an irresistibly kissable toe, is one of the few pieces of art that predate this church. It adorned the first St. Peter's church.

Benedict XVI

When Josef Ratzinger became the 265th pope, he introduced himself as "a simple, humble worker in the vineyard of the Lord." But the man has a complex history, a reputation for intellectual brilliance, a flair for the piano, and a penchant for controversy for his unbending devotion to traditional Catholic doctrine.

Born in small-town Bavaria in 1927, he lived under Nazi rule as many Germans did—outwardly obeying leaders while inwardly conflicted. Like all 14-year-old boys, he joined the Hitler Youth and, like most German men, was drafted into the army. During World War II, he trained to spray flak from anti-aircraft guns, saw Jews transported to death camps, and, like many Germans in the final days of the war, deserted his post.

After the war, he completed his studies in theology and became a rising voice of liberal Catholicism, serving as an advisor at the Second Vatican Council (1962-1965). But after the May 1968 student revolts rocked Europe's Establishment, he became increasingly convinced that Church tradition was needed to offset the growing chaos of the world.

Pope John Paul II appointed him to several positions, and Ratzinger became the pope's closest advisor and good friend. Every Friday afternoon for two decades, they met for lunch, intellectual sparring, and friendly conversation.

Under John Paul II, Ratzinger served as the "enforcer" of Church doctrine, earning the nickname "God's Rottweiler." He spoke out against ordaining women, chastised Latin American priests for fomenting class warfare (Liberation theology), reassigned bishops who were soft on homosexuality, reaffirmed opposition to birth control, and wrote thoughtful papers challenging the secular world's moral relativism. He also punished pedophile priests, though critics charged him with being too focused on preserving the Church's image. (In 2010, he was criticized again, now as Pope, for not dealing forcefully enough with sex abusers.)

Ratzinger chose the name of "Benedict" to recall both Pope Benedict XV (who tried to bring Europeans together after World War I) and the original St. Benedict (c. 480-543), the monk who symbolizes Europe's Christian roots. A true pan-European who speaks many languages, Ratzinger heads a Church that thrives everywhere except Europe, which is becoming increasingly secular (with the notable exception of an increasing Muslim population). Benedict XVI has continued John Paul II's two priorities: defending Catholic doctrine in a changing world and building bridges with fellow Christians.

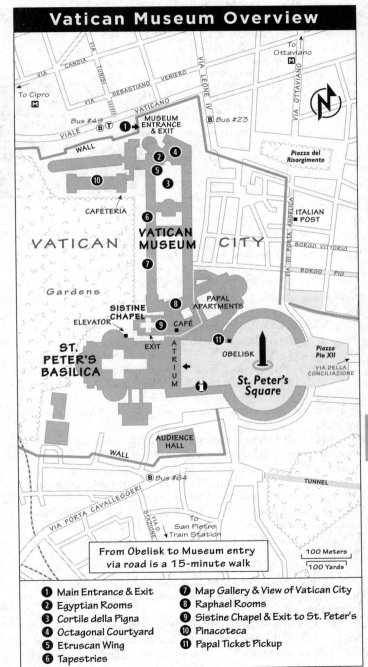

Vatican Museum Overview

1. Main Entrance & Exit
2. Egyptian Rooms
3. Cortile della Pigna
4. Octagonal Courtyard
5. Etruscan Wing
6. Tapestries
7. Map Gallery & View of Vatican City
8. Raphael Rooms
9. Sistine Chapel & Exit to St. Peter's
10. Pinacoteca
11. Papal Ticket Pickup

From Obelisk to Museum entry via road is a 15-minute walk

100 Meters
100 Yards

Is the Pope Catholic?

Rome's tour guides, who introduce tourists to the city's great art and Christian history, field a lot of interesting questions and comments from their groups. Here are a few of their favorites:

- Oh, to be here in Rome... where our Lord Jesus walked.
- Is this where Christ fought the lions?
- Who's the guy on the cross?
- This guy who made so many nice things, Rene Sance, who is he? (Say it fast, and you'll get the gist.)
- Was John Paul II the son of John Paul I?
- What's the Sistine Chapel worth in US dollars?
- How did Michelangelo get Moses to pose for him?
- What's Michelangelo doing now?
- (Upon seeing the arrow-pierced St. Sebastian) Oh, you Italians had problems with the Indians, too.

When to Go: The museum is generally hot and crowded, with waits of up to two hours to buy tickets (figure about a 10-minute wait for every 100 yards in line). The worst days are Saturdays, the last Sunday of the month (when it's free), Mondays, rainy days, and any day before or after a holiday closure. Mornings are most crowded. To see the Sistine Chapel with fewer crowds, visit at the end of the day (remember, the chapel closes 1.5 hours before the museum).

Avoiding Lines: The best way to skip the long lines is to **reserve tickets** in advance (described above). If you book a **guided tour** (see "Tours," next page), you can approach the guard with your voucher and go right in. If you book with a private tour company, you may still have a short wait at crowded times.

For a steep price, you can buy **same-day, skip-the-line tickets** through a tour company called Roma Cristiana, from their kiosk at St. Peter's Square (€15 ticket plus €11 booking fee, entrances almost hourly, tel. 06-6980-6380, www.operaromanapellegrinaggi.org).

If you don't have a reservation, **try arriving after 14:00,** when crowds subside somewhat. Another good time is during the papal audience, on Wednesday at 10:30, when many tourists are at St. Peter's Basilica.

Make sure you get in the right line. Generally, individuals without tickets line up against the Vatican City wall (to the left of the entrance as you face it), and reservation holders (both individuals and groups) enter on the right.

Dress Code: Remember, modest dress (no shorts, above-knee skirts, or bare shoulders) is required.

Getting There: Metro stop Cipro is a 10-minute walk from the entrance, including a climb up a big flight of stairs. The Ottaviano Metro stop is slightly farther from the entrance, but may be closer to the end of the ticket-buying line. Taxis are reasonable (hop in and say, "moo-ZAY-ee vah-tee-KAH-nee").

Tours: A €7 **audioguide** is available at the top of the spiral ramp/escalator (ID required). If you rent an audioguide, you lose the option of taking the shortcut from the Sistine Chapel to St. Peter's (described later, under "Museum Strategies"), since audioguides must be returned to the museum entrance/exit.

You can download a free Rick Steves **audio tour** of the Sistine Chapel to your mobile device; see page 19.

The Vatican offers **English tours** that are easy to book online (€31, includes admission, http://mv.vatican.va). As with individual ticket reservations, present your confirmation voucher to a guard to the right of the entrance, then, once inside, go to the Guided Tours desk (in the lobby, up a few stairs).

Both **private tour** companies and private guides offer English tours of the museum, usually allowing you to skip the long ticket-buying line. For a listing of several companies, see page 747.

Security and Baggage Check: To enter the museum, you pass through a metal detector (no pocket knives allowed). The baggage check (upstairs from the lobby) takes only big bags; you'll need to carry your day bag with you.

Museum Strategies: There are two exits from the museum, and you'll want to decide which you'll take before you enter. The main exit is right near the entrance. Use this one if you want to rent an audioguide (which you must return at the entrance) or if you plan on following this self-guided tour exactly as laid out, visiting the Pinacoteca (painting gallery) at the end.

The other exit is a shortcut that leads from the Sistine Chapel directly to St. Peter's Basilica (spilling out alongside the church; see map on page 793). This route saves you a 30-minute walk (15 minutes back to the Vatican Museum entry/exit, then 15 minutes to St. Peter's) and lets you avoid the often-long security line at the basilica's main entrance. If you take this route, you'll have to do the following: Forgo an audioguide, skip the Pinacoteca or tour it earlier, and be prepared for the odd chance that the shortcut is simply closed—which sometimes happens.

◐ Self-Guided Tour: Start, as civilization did, in **Egypt and Mesopotamia.** Decorating the museum's courtyard are some of the best **Greek and Roman statues** in captivity, including the *Laocoön* group (first century B.C., Hellenistic) and the *Apollo Belvedere* (a

ROME

Vatican City

This tiny independent country of little more than 100 acres, contained entirely within Rome, has its own postal system, armed guards, helipad, mini-train station, and radio station (KPOP). It also has two huge sights: St. Peter's Basilica (with Michelangelo's *Pietà*) and the Vatican Museum (with the Sistine Chapel). Politically powerful, the Vatican is the religious capital of 1.1 billion Roman Catholics. If you're not a Catholic, become one for your visit.

The pope is both the religious and secular leader of Vatican City. For centuries, locals referred to him as "King Pope." Italy and the Vatican didn't always have good relations. In fact, after unification (in 1870), when Rome's modern grid plan was built around the miniscule Vatican, it seemed as if the new buildings were designed to be just high enough so no one could see the dome of St. Peter's from street level. Modern Italy was created in 1870, but the Holy See didn't recognize it as a country until 1929, when the pope and Mussolini signed the Lateran Pact, giving sovereignty and a few nearby churches to the Vatican.

Like every European country, Vatican City has its own versions of the euro coin (with a portrait of Pope Benedict XVI, and before him, of Pope John Paul II). You're unlikely to find one in your pocket, though, as they are snatched up by collectors before they fall into circulation.

Post Office: The Vatican postal service is famous for its stamps, which you can get from offices on St. Peter's Square (next to TI) or in the Vatican Museum (Mon-Sat 8:30-18:30, closed Sun). Vatican stamps are good throughout Rome, but to use the Vatican's mail service, you need to mail your cards from the Vatican; write your postcards ahead of time. (Note that the Vatican won't mail cards with Italian stamps.)

Seeing the Pope: Your best chances for a sighting are on Sunday or Wednesday. The pope usually gives a blessing at noon on Sunday from his apartment on St. Peter's Square (except in July and August, when he speaks at his summer residence at

second-century Roman copy of a Greek original). The centerpiece of the next hall is the *Belvedere Torso* (just a 2,000-year-old torso, but one that had a great impact on the art of Michelangelo). Finishing off the classical statuary are two fine fourth-century porphyry sarcophagi. These royal purple tombs were made (though not used) for the Roman emperor Constantine's mother and daughter. They were Christians—and therefore outlaws—until Constantine made Christianity legal in A.D. 313, and they became saints. Both sarcophagi were quarried and worked in Egypt. The technique for working this extremely hard stone (a special tempering of metal was required) was lost after this, and porphyry marble was not

Castel Gandolfo, 25 miles from Rome, reachable by train from Rome's Termini train station). St. Peter's is easiest (just show up) and, for most, enough of a "visit." Those interested in a more formal appearance (though not more intimate) can get a ticket for the Wednesday general audience (at 10:30) when the pope, arriving in his bulletproof Popemobile, greets and blesses the crowds at St. Peter's from a balcony or canopied platform on the square (except in winter, when he speaks at 10:30 in the 7,000-seat Paolo VI Auditorium, next to St. Peter's Basilica). If you only want to see St. Peter's—but not the pope—avoid these times (the basilica closes during papal audiences and crowds are substantial).

For the Wednesday audience, while anyone can observe from a distance, you need a (free) ticket to actually get close to the papal action (and get a seat). To find out the pope's schedule and request a ticket, call 06-6988-3114 or fax 06-6988-5863.

The American Catholic Church in Rome, Santa Susanna, lets you order tickets online (free, with no booking charge) for the Wednesday general audience. Pick up your reserved tickets, or check for last-minute availability, at the church the Tuesday before the audience between 17:00 and 18:45 (consider staying for the 18:00 English Mass) or Wednesday morning between 7:30 and 8:30 (Via XX Settembre 15, near recommended Via Firenze hotels, Metro: Repubblica, tel. 06-4201-4554—charming Rosanna speaks English, get all the details at www.santasusanna.org).

Probably less convenient—because of the long line—is getting a ticket at St. Peter's Square from the Vatican guard at their station at the bronze doors (open Tue 12:00-19:30; last-minute tickets may be available Wed morning—just join the line). It's under the "elbow" of Bernini's colonnade, on the right side of the square as you face the basilica (see map on page 797).

While many visitors come hoping for a more intimate audience, private audiences ended with the death of Pope John Paul II. Pope Benedict doesn't do them.

ROME

chiseled again until Renaissance times in Florence.

Overachievers may first choose to pop into the Etruscan wing—labeled *Museo Etrusco*—located a few steps up from this level. Others have permission to save their aesthetic energy for the Sistine.

After long halls of tapestries, old maps, broken penises, and fig leaves, you'll come to what most people are looking for: the Raphael Rooms and Michelangelo's Sistine Chapel.

After fancy rooms illustrating the "Immaculate Conception of Mary" (in the 19th century, the Vatican codified this hard-to-sell doctrine, making it a formal part of the Catholic faith) and the triumph of Constantine (with divine guidance, which led to his conversion to Christianity), you enter rooms frescoed by **Raphael** and his assistants. The highlight is the restored *School of Athens*. This is remarkable for its blatant pre-Christian classical orientation, especially since it originally wallpapered the apartments of Pope Julius II. Raphael honors the great pre-Christian thinkers—Aristotle, Plato, and company—who are portrayed as the leading artists of Raphael's day. There's Leonardo da Vinci, whom Raphael worshipped, in the role of Plato. Michelangelo broods in the foreground, added later. When Raphael snuck a peek at the Sistine Chapel, he decided that his arch-competitor was so good that he had to put their personal differences aside and include him in this tribute to the artists of his generation. Today's St. Peter's was under construction as Raphael was working. In the *School of Athens*, he gives us a sneak preview of the unfinished church.

Next is the brilliantly restored **Sistine Chapel.** This is the pope's personal chapel and also the place where, upon the death of the ruling pope, a new pope is elected (as in April 2005).

The Sistine Chapel is famous for Michelangelo's pictorial culmination of the Renaissance, showing the story of creation, with a powerful God weaving in and out of each scene through that busy first week. This is an optimistic and positive expression of the High Renaissance and a stirring example of the artistic and theological maturity of the 33-year-old Michelangelo, who spent four years on this work.

Later, after the Reformation wars had begun and after the Catholic army of Spain had sacked the Vatican, the reeling Church began to fight back. As part of its Counter-Reformation, a much older Michelangelo was commissioned to paint the *Last Judgment* (behind the altar). After the chapel's recent and painstaking restoration, the message is as clear as the day Michelangelo finished it: Christ is returning, some will go to hell and some to heaven, and some will be saved by the power of the rosary.

In the controversial restoration project, no paint was added. Centuries of dust, soot (from candles used for lighting and Mass), and glue (added to make the art shine) were removed, revealing the bright original colors of Michelangelo. Photos are allowed (without a flash) elsewhere in the museum, but as part of the deal with the company who did the restoration, no photos are allowed in the Sistine Chapel.

For a **shortcut directly to St. Peter's Basilica** (see "Museum Strategies," earlier), exit out the far-right corner of the Sistine Chapel (with your back to the altar). This route saves you a 30-minute walk and the wait in the St. Peter's security line, but if you exit here, you're done with the museum—you can't get back to the main entrance/exit (where audioguides need to be returned) or the Pinacoteca (described next). Though this corner door is likely labeled "Exit for private tour groups only," you can usually just slide through with the crowds (or protest that your group has left you behind). If for some reason this exit is closed (which can happen without notice), hang out in the Sistine Chapel for a few more minutes—it'll likely reopen shortly.

If you skip the shortcut and take the long march back, you'll find the **Pinacoteca** (the Vatican's small but fine collection of paintings, with Raphael's *Transfiguration*, Leonardo's unfinished *St. Jerome*, and Caravaggio's *Deposition*), a cafeteria (long lines, uninspired food), and the underrated early-Christian art section, before you exit via the souvenir shop.

Near Vatican City

▲**Castel Sant'Angelo**—Built as a tomb for the emperor, this building was used through the Middle Ages as a castle, prison,

and place of last refuge for popes under attack. Today it's a museum, a giant pile of ancient bricks that is packed with history.

Ancient Rome allowed no tombs—not even the emperor's—within its walls. So Emperor Hadrian grabbed the most commanding position just outside the walls and across the river and built a towering tomb (c. A.D. 139) well within view of the city. His mausoleum was a huge cylinder (210 by 70 feet) topped by a cypress grove and crowned by a huge statue of Hadrian himself riding a chariot. For nearly a hundred years, Roman emperors (from Hadrian to Caracalla, in A.D. 217) were buried here.

In the year 590, the archangel Michael appeared above the mausoleum to Pope Gregory the Great. Sheathing his sword, the angel signaled the end of a plague. The fortress that was Hadrian's mausoleum eventually became a fortified palace, renamed for the "holy angel."

Castel Sant'Angelo spent centuries of the Dark Ages as a fortress and prison, but was eventually connected to the Vatican via an elevated corridor at the pope's request (1277). Since Rome was repeatedly plundered by invaders, Castel Sant'Angelo was a handy place of last refuge for threatened popes. In anticipation of long sieges, rooms were decorated with papal splendor (you'll see paintings by Carlo Crivelli, Luca Signorelli, and Andrea Mantegna). In

1527, during a sacking of Rome by troops of Charles V of Spain, the pope lived inside the castle for months with his entourage of hundreds (an unimaginable ordeal, considering the food service at the top-floor bar).

Touring the place is a stair-stepping workout. After you walk around the entire base of the castle, take the small staircase down to the original Roman floor (following the route of Hadrian's funeral procession). In the atrium, study the model of the mausoleum as it was in Roman times. Imagine being surrounded by a veneer of marble, and the niche in the wall filled with a towering "welcome to my tomb" statue of Hadrian. From here, a ramp leads to the right, spiraling 400 feet. While some of the fine original brickwork and bits of mosaic survive, the marble veneer is long gone (notice the holes in the wall that held it in place). At the end of the ramp, a bridge crosses over the room where the ashes of the emperors were kept. From here, the stairs continue out of the ancient section and into the medieval structure (built atop the mausoleum) that housed the papal apartments. Don't miss the Sala del Tesoro (Treasury), where the wealth of the Vatican was locked up in a huge chest. (*Do* miss the 58 rooms of the military museum.) From the pope's piggy bank, a narrow flight of stairs leads to the rooftop and perhaps the finest view of Rome anywhere (pick out landmarks as you stroll around). From the safety of this dramatic vantage point, the pope surveyed the city in times of siege. Look down at the bend of the Tiber, which for 2,700 years has cradled the Eternal City.

Cost and Hours: €8, more for special exhibits, Tue-Sun 9:00-18:30, closed Mon, last entry one hour before closing, near Vatican City, Metro: Lepanto or bus #64, tel. 06-681-9111.

Ponte Sant'Angelo—The bridge leading to Castel Sant'Angelo was built by Hadrian for quick and regal access from downtown to his tomb. The three middle arches are actually Roman originals, and a fine example of the empire's engineering expertise. The statues of angels (each bearing a symbol of the passion of Christ—nail, sponge, shroud, and so on)

are Bernini-designed and textbook Baroque. In the Middle Ages, this was the only bridge in the area that connected St. Peter's and the Vatican with downtown Rome. Nearly all pilgrims passed this bridge to and from the church. Its shoulder-high banisters recall a tragedy: During a Jubilee Year festival in 1450, the crowd got so huge that the mob pushed out the original banisters, causing nearly 200 to fall to their deaths.

ROME

North Rome
Borghese Gardens and Via Veneto

▲**Villa Borghese Gardens**—Rome's semi-scruffy three-square-mile "Central Park" is great for its shade and for people-watching all of the modern-day Romeos and Juliets. The best entrance is at the head of Via Veneto (Metro: Barberini, then 10-minute walk up Via Veneto and through the old Roman wall at Porta Pinciana, or catch a cab to Via Veneto—Porta Pinciana). There you'll find a cluster of buildings with a café, a kiddie arcade, and bike rental (€4/ hour). Rent a bike or, for roman-

tics, a pedaled rickshaw *(riscio)*. Bikes come with locks to allow you to make sightseeing stops. Follow signs to discover the park's cafés, fountains, statues, lake, great viewpoint over Piazza del Popolo, and prime picnic spots. Some sights require paid admission, including Rome's zoo, the National Gallery of Modern Art (which holds 19th-century art; not to be confused with MAXXI, described later), and the Etruscan Museum, described below.

▲▲▲**Borghese Gallery (Museo e Galleria Borghese)**—This plush museum, filling a cardinal's mansion in the park, offers one of Europe's most sumptuous art experiences. You'll enjoy a collection of world-class Baroque sculpture, including Bernini's *David* and his excited statue of Apollo chasing Daphne, as well as paintings by Caravaggio, Raphael, Titian, and Rubens. The museum's slick, mandatory reservation system keeps crowds to a manageable size.

The essence of the collection is the connection of the Renaissance with the classical world. As you enter, notice the second-century Roman reliefs with Michelangelo-designed panels above either end of the portico. The villa was built in the early 17th century by the great art collector Cardinal Scipione Borghese, who wanted to prove that the glories of ancient Rome were matched by the Renaissance.

In the main entry hall, high up on the wall, is a thrilling first-century Greek sculpture of a horse falling. The Renaissance-era rider was added by Pietro Bernini, father of the famous Gian Lorenzo Bernini.

Each room seems to feature a Baroque masterpiece. The best of all is in Room III: Bernini's ***Apollo and Daphne.*** It's the perfect Baroque subject—capturing a thrilling, action-filled moment. In the mythological story, Apollo—made stupid by Cupid's arrow of love—chases after Daphne, who has been turned off by the "arrow

Borghese Gallery—Ground Floor

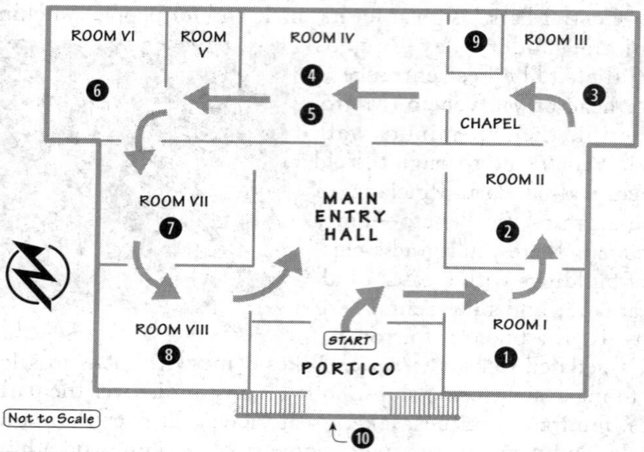

ROOM VI

ROOM V

ROOM IV

❾

ROOM III

❻

❹

❺

❸

CHAPEL

ROOM VII

MAIN ENTRY HALL

ROOM II

❼

❷

ROOM VIII

START

ROOM I

❽

PORTICO

❶

Not to Scale

❿

❶ CANOVA – Pauline Borghese as Venus

❷ BERNINI – David

❸ BERNINI – Apollo and Daphne

❹ BERNINI – The Rape of Proserpina

❺ UNKNOWN – Diana the Hunter; Other Marbles

❻ BERNINI – Aeneas, Anchises, and Ascanius

❼ "Theater of the Universe"

❽ CARAVAGGIO – Various

❾ Stairs up to Pinacoteca

❿ To Basement (Tickets, Info, Shop, WC)

of disgust." Just as he's about to catch her, she calls to her father to save her. Magically, her fingers begin to sprout leaves, her toes become roots, her skin turns to bark, and she transforms into a tree. Frustrated Apollo will end up with a handful of leaves. Walk slowly around the statue. It's more air than stone.

Cost and Hours: €8.50, or €12.50 during special exhibits; both prices include basic €2 reservation fee, credit cards accepted, Tue-Sun 9:00-19:00, closed Mon, ticket office closes one hour before museum does, no photos, all bags and cameras must be checked (free).

Reservations: Reservations are mandatory and simple to get. It's easiest by booking online (www.ticketeria.it, €1 extra booking fee, user-friendly website). You can also reserve by telephone (tel. 06-32810, all operators speak English, pay for tickets on arrival), but it's not always easy to reach a live operator. Call during Italian office hours: Mon-Fri 9:00-18:00, Sat 9:00-13:00, office closed Sat in Aug and Sun year-round. If you reach an Italian recording, wait for the English translation.

Every two hours, 360 people are allowed to enter the museum. Entry times are 9:00, 11:00, 13:00, 15:00, and 17:00. Reserve a *minimum* of several days in advance for a weekday visit, and at least a week ahead for weekends. Reservations are tightest at 11:00 and 15:00, on Tuesdays, and on weekends. For off-season weekdays (but not weekends), your chances of getting a same-day reservation are fairly high if you're flexible about the entry time.

After you reserve a day and time, you'll get a claim number. Be at the Borghese Gallery 30 minutes before your appointed time to pick up your ticket in the lobby on the lower level. You can skip the ticket pickup line by paying with a credit card at one of the computer kiosks.

You can use a Roma Pass for entry, but you still need to make a reservation (by phone only—not online) and pay the €2 fee.

If you don't have a reservation, you can try arriving near the top of the hour, when the museum sells unclaimed tickets to those standing by. Generally, out of 360 reservations, a few will fail to show (but more than a few may be waiting to grab them). You're most likely to land a stand-by ticket at 13:00 or 17:00.

Getting There: The museum is set idyllically but inconveniently in the vast Villa Borghese Gardens. To avoid missing your appointment, allow yourself plenty of time to find the place. A taxi drops you 100 yards from the museum. Your destination is the Galleria Borghese (gah-leh-REE-ah bor-GAY-zay). Be sure *not* to tell the cabbie "Villa Borghese"—which is the park, not the museum.

Bus #910 goes from Termini train station to the Via Pinciana stop (a few steps from the villa). Coming from Campo de' Fiori or Via del Corso (at Via Minghetti), bus #116 drops you off at the southern edge of the park. From Largo Argentina, bus #63 takes you to the US Embassy on Via Veneto; walk uphill on Via Veneto to the southern edge of the park.

By Metro, from the Barberini Metro stop, walk 10 minutes up Via Veneto, enter the park, and turn right, following signs.

Tours: €6 guided English tours are offered at 9:10 and 11:10 (may also be offered on busy weekends at 13:10 and 15:10). You can't book a tour when you make your museum reservation—sign up as soon as you arrive. Or consider the excellent 1.5-hour audioguide tour for €5.

Museum Strategy: Visits are strictly limited to two hours. Budget most of your time for the more interesting ground floor, but set aside 30 minutes for the paintings of the Pinacoteca upstairs (highlights are marked by the audioguide icons). Avoid the crowds by seeing the Pinacoteca first. The fine bookshop and cafeteria are best visited outside your two-hour entry window.

Etruscan Museum (Villa Giulia Museo Nazionale Etrusco)— The fascinating Etruscan civilization thrived in Italy around

600 B.C., when Rome was an Etruscan town. The Villa Giulia (a fine Renaissance palace in the Villa Borghese Gardens) hosts a museum that tells the story. The star of the museum is the famous "husband and wife sarcophagus"— a dead couple seeming to enjoy an everlasting banquet from atop their tomb (sixth century B.C., from Cerveteri). Historians also dig the gold sheets from Pyrgi, with inscriptions in two languages—the "Etruscan Rosetta Stone" that has helped scholars decipher their odd language, and the Apollo of Veio, which stood atop Apollo's temple. The smiling god welcomes Hercules, while his mother Latona stands nearby cradling baby Apollo. For more on the Etruscans, see the sidebar on page 656.

Cost and Hours: €8, Tue-Sun 8:30-19:30, closed Mon, last entry one hour before closing, scant English information, 20-minute walk from Borghese Gallery, Piazzale di Villa Giulia 9, tel. 06-322-6571.

Via Veneto—In the 1960s, movie stars from around the world paraded down curvy Via Veneto, one of Rome's glitziest nightspots. Today it's still lined with the city's poshest hotels and the US Embassy, but any hint of local color has faded to bland.

▲Cappuccin Crypt—If you want to see artistically arranged bones, this is the place. The crypt is below the Church of Santa Maria della Immacolata Conce-

zione on Via Veneto, just up from Piazza Barberini.

The bones of more than 4,000 friars who died between 1528 and 1870 are in the basement, all lined up in a series of six crypts for the delight—or disgust—of the always-wide-eyed visitor. The monastic message on the wall explains that this is more than just a macabre exercise: "We were what you are...you will become what we are now."

As you leave (humming "the foot bone's connected to the..."),

Chigi's great-grandson hired Bernini to make two of the four statues, and Bernini delivered a theatrical episode. In one corner, Daniel straddles a lion and raises his praying hands to God for help. Kitty-corner across the chapel, an angel grabs Habbakuk's hair and tells him to go take some food to poor Daniel.

In the Cerasi Chapel (left of altar), Caravaggio's *The Conversion on the Way to Damascus* shows Paul sprawled on his back beside his horse while his servant looks on. The startled future saint is blinded by the harsh light as Jesus' voice asks him, "Why do you persecute me?" In the style of the Counter-Reformation, Paul receives his new faith with open arms.

In the same chapel, Caravaggio's *Crucifixion of St. Peter* is shown as a banal chore; the workers toil like faceless animals. The light and dark are in high contrast. Caravaggio liked to say, "Where light falls, I will paint it."

Cost and Hours: Free, Mon-Sat 7:00-12:00 & 16:00-18:30, Sun 8:00-13:30 & 16:30-19:30, often partially closed to accommodate its busy schedule of Masses, on north side of Piazza del Popolo—as you face the gate in the old wall from the square, the church entrance is to your right.

▲▲**Catacombs of Priscilla (Catacombe di Priscilla)**—While most tourists and nearly all tour groups go out to the ancient

Appian Way to see the famous catacombs of San Sebastiano and San Callisto, the Catacombs of Priscilla (on the other side of town) are less commercialized and crowded, and just feel more intimate, as catacombs should.

You enter from a convent and explore the result of 250 years of tunneling that occurred from the second to the fifth centuries. Visits are by 30-minute guided tour only (English-language tours go whenever a small group gathers—generally every 20 minutes or so). You'll see a few thousand of the 40,000 niches carved here, along with some beautiful frescoes, including what is considered the first depiction of Mary nursing the baby Jesus.

Cost and Hours: €8, Tue-Sun 8:30-12:00 & 14:30-17:00, closed Mon, last entry 30 minutes before closing, closed one random month a year—check website or call first, tel. 06-8620-6272, www.catacombepriscilla.com.

Getting There: The catacombs are northeast of Termini train station (at Via Salaria 430), far from the center (a €15 taxi ride) but well-served by buses (20-30 minutes). From Termini, take bus #92 or #86 from Piazza Cinquecento. From Piazza Venezia and along Via del Corso, take bus #63 or #630. Tell the driver "Piazza Crati" and "kah-tah-KOHM-bay" and he'll let you off near Piazza Crati (at the Nemorense/Crati stop). From there, walk through the little market in Piazza Crati, then down Via di Priscilla (about 5 minutes). The entrance is in the orange building on the left at the top of the hill.

For more information, see "Catacombs" on page 834.

MAXXI—Rome's "National Museum of Art of the 21st Century" is the big news on the museum scene here—as you can imagine it would be, after the 10 years and €150 million it took to make it happen. To me, it comes off as a second-rate Pompidou Center. Judging by the lack of energy here, I'm not alone in my opinion.

Cost and Hours: €11, Tue-Sun 11:00-19:00, Thu and Sat until 22:00, closed Mon, two exhibits per year—preview on their site, tram #2 from Piazza del Popolo to Piazza Apollo Doro, Via Guido Reni 4a, tel. 06-322-5178, www.fondazionemaxxi.it.

From the Spanish Steps to the Ara Pacis

▲Spanish Steps—The wide, curving staircase, culminating with an obelisk between two Baroque church towers, makes for one of Rome's iconic sights. Beyond that, it's a people-gathering place. By day, the area hosts shoppers looking for high-end fashions; on warm evenings, it attracts young people in love with the city. For more, see my Heart of Rome Walk on page 762.

"Shopping Triangle"—The triangular-shaped area between the Spanish Steps, Piazza Venezia, and Piazza del Popolo (along Via del Corso; see map on page 809) contains Rome's highest concentration of upscale boutiques and fashion stores.

▲▲Ara Pacis (Altar of Peace)—On January 30, 9 B.C., soon-to-be-emperor Augustus led a procession of priests up the steps

and into this newly built "Altar of Peace." They sacrificed an animal on the altar and poured an offering of wine, thanking the gods for helping Augustus pacify barbarians abroad and rivals at home. This marked the dawn of the Pax Romana (c. A.D. 1-200), a Golden Age of good living, stability, dominance, and peace *(pax)*. The Ara Pacis (AH-rah PAH-chees) hosted annual sacrifices by the emperor until the area was flooded by the Tiber River. Buried under silt, it was abandoned and forgotten until the 16th century, when various parts were discovered and excavated. Mussolini gathered the altar's scattered parts and reconstructed them here in 1938. In 2006, the Altar of Peace reopened to the public in a striking modern building. As the first new building allowed to be built in the old center since 1938, it's been controversial, but its quiet, air-conditioned interior may signal the dawn of another new age in Rome.

The Altar of Peace was originally located east of here, along today's Via del Corso. The model shows where it stood in relation to the Mausoleum of Augustus (now next door) and the Pantheon. Approach the Ara Pacis and look through the doorway to see the raised altar. This simple structure has just the basics of a Roman temple: an altar for sacrifices surrounded by cubicle-like walls that enclose a consecrated space.

The reliefs on the north and south sides probably depict the parade of dignitaries who consecrated the altar, while the reliefs on the west side (near the altar's back door) celebrate the two things Augustus brought to Rome: peace (goddess Roma as a conquering Amazon, right side) and prosperity (fertility goddess surrounded by children, plants, and animals). Imagine the altar as it once was, standing in an open field, painted in bright colors—a mingling of myth, man, and nature.

Cost and Hours: €9, tightwads can look in through huge windows for free; Tue-Sun 9:00-19:00, closed Mon, last entry one hour before closing; €3.50 audioguide also available as free podcast at www.arapacis.it, good WC downstairs. The Ara Pacis is a long block west of Via del Corso on Via di Ara Pacis, on the east bank of the Tiber near Ponte Cavour, Metro: Spagna; a 10-minute walk down Via dei Condotti, tel. 06-0608.

▲**Fausto delle Chiaie (Fausto of the Beach)**—This eccentric fellow (who's likely more sane than the rest of us) is a self-appointed part of the Ara Pacis. Fausto's installation art, usually strewn along the curb that runs between the Ara Pacis and Mausoleum of Augustus, aims to take you to a different dimension. Though he sits next to the local art academy, he stresses that the proximity is merely a coincidence. Charming Fausto speaks English and reminds you that his "plastic secretary" (a tip box) is at the end of the curb. He may be mini compared to the nearby museum, but for me he's more entertaining than the MAXXI.

East Rome

Near Termini Train Station

These sights are within a 10-minute walk of the train station. By Metro, use the Termini stop for the National Museum and the Repubblica stop for the rest.

ROME

Near Termini Station

▲▲▲National Museum of Rome (Museo Nazionale Romano Palazzo Massimo alle Terme)—The National Museum's main branch, at Palazzo Massimo, houses the greatest collection of ancient Roman art anywhere. It's a historic yearbook of Roman marble statues with some rare Greek originals. On the ground floor alone, you can look eye-to-eye with Julius and Augustus Caesar, Alexander the Great, and Socrates.

On the first floor, along with statues and busts showing such emperors as Trajan and Hadrian, you'll see the best-preserved Roman copy of the Greek *Discus Thrower*. Statues of athletes like this commonly stood in the baths, where Romans cultivated healthy bodies, minds, and social skills, hoping to lead well-rounded lives. Other statues on this floor originally stood in the pleasure gardens of the Roman rich—surrounded by greenery with the splashing sound of fountains, all painted in bright, lifelike colors. Though executed by Romans, the themes are mostly Greek, with godlike humans and human-looking gods.

The second floor contains frescoes and mosaics that once decorated the walls and floors of Roman villas. They're remarkably realistic and unstuffy, featuring everyday people, animals, flowery patterns, and geometrical designs. The Villa Farnese frescoes—

in black, red, yellow, and blue—are mostly architectural designs, with fake columns, friezes, and garlands. The Villa di Livia frescoes immerse you in a leafy green garden full of birds and fruit trees, symbolizing the gods.

Finally, descend into the basement to see fine gold jewelry, dice, an abacus, and vault doors leading into the best coin collection in Europe, with fancy magnifying glasses maneuvering you through cases of coins from ancient Rome to modern times.

Cost and Hours: €10, this combo-ticket covers three other branches—all skippable, Tue-Sun 9:00-19:45, closed Mon, last entry 45 minutes before closing, audioguide-€5, about 100 yards from train station, Metro: Termini, tel. 06-3996-7700. The museum is about 100 yards from Termini train station—as you leave the station, it's the sandstone-brick building on your left. Enter at the far end, at Largo di Villa Peretti.

▲**Baths of Diocletian (Terme di Diocleziano)**—Around A.D. 300, Emperor Diocletian built the largest baths in Rome. This sprawling meeting place—with baths and schmoozing spaces to accommodate 3,000 bathers at a time—was a big deal in ancient times.

While much of it is still closed, the best part is open: the Church of Santa Maria degli Angeli. From noisy Piazza della Repubblica, step into the vast and cool church built upon the remains of a vast and steamy Roman bath complex. The church we see today was (at least partly) designed by Michelangelo (1561), who used the baths' main hall as the nave. Later, when Piazza della Repubblica became an important Roman intersection, another architect renovated the church. To allow people to enter from the grand new piazza, he spun it 90 degrees, turning Michelangelo's nave into a long transept. The eight red granite columns are original, from ancient Rome—stand next to one and feel its five-foot girth. (Only the eight in the transept proper are original. The others are made of plastered-over brick.) In Roman times, this hall was covered with mosaics, marble, and gold, and lined with statues.

Cost and Hours: Free, Mon-Sat 7:00-18:30, Sun 7:00-19:30, closed to sightseers during Mass, faces Piazza della Repubblica.

▲**Church of Santa Maria della Vittoria**—This church houses Bernini's statue, the swooning *St. Teresa in Ecstasy*. Inside the church, you'll find St. Teresa to the left of the altar. Teresa has just been stabbed with God's arrow of fire. Now, the angel pulls it out and watches her reaction. Teresa swoons, her eyes roll up, her hand goes limp, she parts her lips...and moans. The smiling, cherubic angel understands just how she feels. Teresa, a 16th-century Spanish nun, later talked of the "sweetness" of "this intense pain," describing her oneness with God in ecstatic, even erotic, terms.

Bernini, the master of multimedia, pulls out all the stops to

ROME

make this mystical vision real. Actual sunlight pours through the alabaster windows, bronze sunbeams shine on a marble angel holding a golden arrow. Teresa leans back on a cloud and her robe ripples from within, charged with her spiritual arousal. Bernini has created a little stage-setting of heaven. And watching from the "theater boxes" on either side are members of the family who commissioned the work.

Cost and Hours: Free, pay €0.50 for light, Mon-Sat 8:30-12:00 & 15:30-18:00, Sun 15:30-18:00, about 5 blocks northwest of Termini train station on Largo Susanna, Metro: Repubblica.

Santa Susanna Church—The home of the American Catholic Church in Rome, Santa Susanna holds Mass in English daily at 18:00 and on Sunday at 9:00 and 10:30. They arrange papal audience tickets (see page 800), and their excellent website contains tips for travelers and a list of convents that rent out rooms.

Cost and Hours: Free, daily 9:00-12:00 & 16:00-18:00, Via XX Settembre 15, near recommended Via Firenze hotels, Metro: Repubblica, tel. 06-4201-4554, www.santasusanna.org.

Pilgrim's Rome

East of the Colosseum (and south of Termini train station) are several venerable churches that Catholic pilgrims make a point of visiting. Near one of the churches is a small WWII museum.

Church of San Giovanni in Laterano—Built by Constantine, the first Christian emperor, this was Rome's most important church through medieval times. A building alongside the church houses the Holy Stairs (Scala Santa) said to have been walked up by Jesus, which today are ascended by pilgrims on their knees.

Cost and Hours: Free, church—daily 7:00-18:30, Holy Stairs—daily April-Sept 6:15-12:00 & 15:30-18:30, Oct-March 6:15-12:00 & 15:00-18:00; €5 audioguide available at info desk near statue of Constantine, €1 discount with this book (ID required); Piazza San Giovanni in Laterano, Metro: San Giovanni, or bus #85 or #87; tel. 06-6988-6409.

Museum of the Liberation of Rome (Museo Storico della Liberazione di Roma)—This small memorial museum, near the Church of San Giovanni in Laterano, is housed in the prison wing of the former Nazi police headquarters of occupied Rome. Other than a single printed sheet to help, there's little in English. Still, for those interested in resistance movements and the Nazi occupation, it's a stirring visit. You'll see a few artifacts, many photos of heroes, and a couple of cells preserved as they were found on

June 4, 1944, when the city was liberated.

Cost and Hours: Free, Tue-Sun 9:30-12:30; Tue and Thu-Fri also 15:30-19:30; closed Mon and Aug; just behind the Holy Stairs at Via Tasso 145; tel. 06-700-3866.

Church of Santa Maria Maggiore—Some of Rome's best-surviving mosaics line the nave of this church built as Rome was falling. The nearby Church of Santa Prassede has still more early mosaics.

Cost and Hours: Free, daily 8:30-18:00, Piazza Santa Maria Maggiore, Metro: Termini or Vittorio Emanuele, tel. 06-6988-6802.

▲**Church of San Clemente**—Besides visiting the church itself, with frescoes by Masolino, you can also descend into the ruins of an earlier church. Descend yet one more level and enter the eerie remains of a pagan temple to the god Mithras.

Cost and Hours: Upper church—free, lower church—€5,

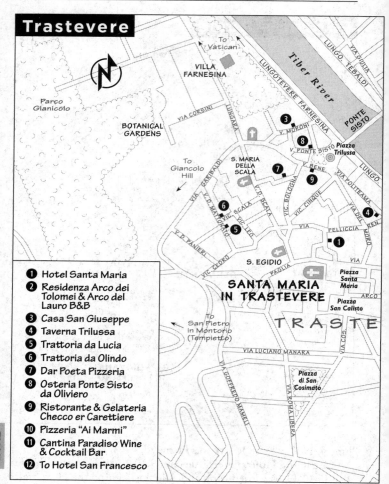

Trastevere

1. Hotel Santa Maria
2. Residenza Arco dei Tolomei & Arco del Lauro B&B
3. Casa San Giuseppe
4. Taverna Trilussa
5. Trattoria da Lucia
6. Trattoria da Olindo
7. Dar Poeta Pizzeria
8. Osteria Ponte Sisto da Oliviero
9. Ristorante & Gelateria Checco er Carettiere
10. Pizzeria "Ai Marmi"
11. Cantina Paradiso Wine & Cocktail Bar
12. To Hotel San Francesco

both open Mon-Sat 9:00-12:30 & 15:00-18:00, Sun 12:00-18:00, last entry for lower church 20 minutes before closing; Via di San Giovanni in Laterano, Metro: Colosseo, or bus #85 or #87; tel. 06-774-0021, www.basilicasanclemente.com.

South Rome

The area south of the center contains some interesting but widely scattered areas, from Trastevere to the Jewish Quarter to Testaccio to E.U.R.

Trastevere and Nearby

Trastevere is the colorful neighborhood across *(tras)* the Tiber

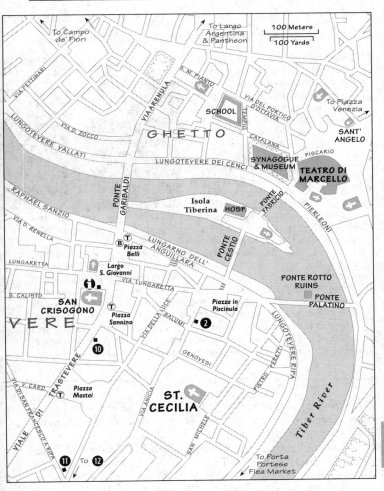

(Tevere) River. Trastevere (trahs-TAY-veh-ray) offers the best look at medieval-village Rome. The action unwinds to the chime of

the church bells. Go there and wander. Wonder. Be a poet. This is Rome's Left Bank. (You can download a free Rick Steves audio tour of this neighborhood to your mobile device; see page 19.)

This proud neighborhood was long a working-class area. Now that it's becoming trendy, high rents are driving out the source of

Soccer: The National Obsession

One of Rome's most local "sights" is a soccer match. Winston Churchill said that Italians lose wars like soccer matches and soccer matches like wars. Soccer

(*calcio*) is the national obsession: Everyone, regardless of age or social class, is an expert, quick with an opinion on a coach's lousy decision or a referee's unprofessional conduct. Fans love to insult officials: A favorite is *"arbitro cornuto!"*—the referee is a cuckold (i.e., his wife sleeps around). The country's obsession turned into jubilation on July 9, 2006, when Italy won the World Cup, and Rome—along with every other city, town, and village in Italy—went crazy with joy.

Rome has a special passion for soccer. It has two teams, Roma (representing the city) and Lazio (the region), and the rivalry is fanatic. When Romans are introduced, they ask each other, *"Laziale o romanista?"* The answer can compromise a relationship. Both Roma (jersey: yellow and red; symbol: she-wolf) and Lazio (jersey: light blue and white; symbol: imperial eagle) claim to be truly Roman. Lazio is older (founded in 1900), but Roma has more supporters. Lazio is supposed to be more upper-class, Roma more popular, but the social division is blurred.

so much of its original color. Still, it's a great people scene, especially at night. Stroll the back streets (for restaurant recommendations, see page 852).

To reach Trastevere by foot from Capitol Hill, cross the Tiber on Ponte Cestio (over Isola Tiberina). You can also take tram #8 from Largo Argentina, or bus #H from Termini and Via Nazionale (get off at Piazza Belli). From the Vatican (Piazza Risorgimento), it's bus #23 or #271.

Linking Trastevere with the Heart of Rome Walk: You can walk from Trastevere to Campo de' Fiori to link up with the beginning of my Heart of Rome Walk (see page 762): From Trastevere's church square (Piazza di Santa Maria), take Via del Moro to the river and cross at Ponte Sisto, a pedestrian bridge that has a good view of St. Peter's dome. Continue straight ahead for one block. Take the first left, which leads down Via di Capo di Ferro through the scary and narrow darkness to Piazza Farnese, with the imposing Palazzo Farnese. Michelangelo contributed to the facade of this palace, now the French Embassy. The fountains on the square feature huge one-piece granite hot tubs from the ancient Roman

The most eagerly awaited sporting event of the year is the derby, when the two teams fight it out at the Olympic Stadium. All of Italy acknowledges that team spirit is most fervent in Rome. Fans prepare months in advance, and on the day of the match they fill the entire stadium with team colors, flags, banners, and smoke candles.

Witty slogans on banners work like dialogues: A Roma banner proclaimed, "Roma: Only the sky is higher than you." The Lazio banner replied, "In fact, the sky is blue and white" (like its team colors). The exchange revealed that there had been a Lazio informer on the Roma side, which traumatized Roma fans for weeks. Tourists go to a match more for the action in the stands than the action on the field—it's one of the most Roman of all experiences.

Both teams call the Stadio Olimpico home, so you can catch a game most weekends from September to May (Metro line A to Flaminio, then catch tram #2 to the end of the line, Piazza Mancini, and cross the bridge to the stadium). If you're coming from Termini train station, take bus #910; from the Vatican, take bus #32 from Piazza Risorgimento.

Baths of Caracalla. One block from there (opposite the palace) is the atmospheric square, Campo de' Fiori.

▲**Church of Santa Maria in Trastevere**—One of Rome's oldest churches, this was made a basilica in the fourth century, when

Christianity was legalized. It was the first church dedicated to the Virgin Mary. Its portico (covered area just outside the door) is decorated with fascinating fragments of stone—many of them lids from catacomb burial niches—and filled with early Christian symbolism. The church is on Piazza di Santa Maria, the Trastevere neighborhood's most important meeting place. With its broad and inviting steps, the 17th-century fountain was actually designed to be the "sofa" of the neighborhood. During major soccer games, a large screen is set up here so that everybody can share in the tension and excitement. At other times, children gather here

with a ball and improvise matches of their own.

Cost and Hours: Free, daily 7:30-21:00.

▲**Villa Farnesina**—Here's a unique opportunity to see a sumptuous Renaissance villa in Rome decorated with Raphael paintings. It was built in the early 1500s for the richest man in Renaissance Europe, Siennese banker Agostino Chigi. Architect Baldassare Peruzzi's design—a U-shaped building with wings enfolding what used to be a vast garden—successfully blended architecture and nature in a way that both ancient and Renaissance

Romans loved. Orchards and flower beds flowed down in terraces from the palace to the riverbanks. Later construction of modern embankments and avenues robbed the garden of its grandeur, leaving it with a more melancholy charm.

In the Loggia of Galatea, find Raphael's painting of the nymph Galatea (on the wall by the entrance door). Galatea is considered Raphael's vision of female perfection—not a portrait of an individual woman, but a composite of his many lovers in an idealized vision. Raphael and his assistants also painted the subtly erotic Loggia of Psyche.

Cost and Hours: €5; Mon-Sat 9:00-13:00, closed Sun; across the river from Campo de' Fiori, a short walk from Ponte Sisto and a block behind the river at 230 Via della Lungara, tel. 06-680-271.

Gianicolo Hill Viewpoint—From this park atop a hill, the city views are superb, and the walk to the top holds a treat for architecture buffs. Start at Trastevere's Piazza di San Cosimato, and follow Via Luciano Manara to Via Garibaldi, at the base of the hill. Via Garibaldi winds its way up the side of the hill to the Church of San Pietro in Montorio. To the right of the church, in a small courtyard, is the Tempietto by Donato Bramante. This tiny church, built to commemorate the martyrdom of St. Peter, is considered a jewel of Italian Renaissance architecture.

Continuing up the hill, Via Garibaldi connects to Passeggiata del Gianicolo. From here, you'll find a pleasant park with panoramic city views. Ponder the many Victorian-era statues, including that of baby-carrying, gun-wielding, horse-riding Anita Garibaldi. She was the Brazilian wife of the revolutionary General Giuseppe Garibaldi, who helped forge a united Italy in the late 19th century.

Near Trastevere: Jewish Quarter

From the 16th through the 19th centuries, Rome's Jewish population was forced to live in a cramped ghetto at an often-flooded bend of the Tiber River. While the medieval Jewish ghetto is long gone, this area—just across the river and toward Capitol Hill from Trastevere—is still home to Rome's synagogue and fragments of its Jewish heritage.

You can download a free Rick Steves **audio tour** of this neighborhood to your mobile device; see page 19.

Synagogue (Sinagoga) and Jewish Museum (Museo Ebraico)—Rome's modern synagogue stands proudly on the spot where the medieval Jewish community lived in squalor for more than 300 years. The site of a historic 1986 visit by Pope John Paul II, this synagogue features a fine interior and a museum filled with artifacts of Rome's Jewish community. Modest dress is required. The only way to visit the synagogue—unless you're here for daily prayer service—is with a tour (€10 ticket includes museum and guided hourly tour of synagogue; June-Sept Sun-Thu 10:00-19:00, Fri 10:00-16:00, closed Sat; Oct-May Sun-Thu 10:00-17:00, Fri 9:00-14:00, closed Sat; last entry 45 minutes before closing, English tours usually at :15 past the hour, 30 minutes, check schedule at ticket counter; on Lungotevere dei Cenci, tel. 06-6840-0661, www.museoebraico.roma.it). Walking tours of the Jewish Ghetto are conducted at least once a day except Saturday (€8, usually at 13:15, sign up at museum 30 minutes before departure, minimum of 3 required).

Testaccio

In the gritty Testaccio neighborhood, several fascinating but lesser sights cluster at the Piramide Metro stop between the Colosseum and E.U.R. (This is a quick and easy stop as you return from E.U.R., or when changing trains en route to Ostia Antica.)

Working-class since ancient times, the Testaccio neighborhood has recently gone trendy-bohemian. Visitors wander through an awkward mix of yuppie and proletarian worlds, not noticing—but perhaps sensing—the "Keep Testaccio for the Testaccians" graffiti.

Pyramid of Gaius Cestius—An Egyptian-style pyramid from ancient Rome stands next to the Piramide Metro stop. The Mark Antony/ Cleopatra scandal (c. 30 B.C.) brought exotic Egyptian styles into vogue. A rich Roman magistrate, Gaius Cestius, had this pyramid built as his tomb, complete with a burial chamber inside. Made of brick covered in

ROME

marble, the 90-foot structure was completed in just 330 days (as stated in its Latin inscription). While smaller than actual Egyptian pyramids, its proportions are correct. It was later incorporated into the Aurelian Wall, and it now stands as a marker to the entrance of Testaccio.

Porta Ostiense and Museo della Via Ostiense—This formidable gate (also next to the Piramide Metro stop) is from the Aurelian Wall, begun in the third century under Emperor Aurelian. The wall, which encircled the city, was 12 miles long and averaged about 26 feet high, with 14 main gates and 380 72-foot-tall towers. Most of what you'll see today is circa A.D. 400, but the barbarians reconstructed the gate later, in the sixth century.

Inside the gate is a tiny free museum (find entrance near pyramid; open Tue-Sat and first and third Sun of month 9:00-13:30, closed Mon). The museum offers a free ramble along the ramparts, plus exhibits on Ostia Antica, Rome's ancient port (for more information, see page 835). You'll see models of the ancient city and its famed hexagonal harbor, and of the Ostian Way—the straight Roman road that paralleled the curvy Tiber for 15 miles from Rome to the sea. (For more on the Aurelian Wall, visit the San Sebastiano Gate and Museum of the Walls, described on page 832.)

ROME

Protestant Cemetery—The Cemetery for the Burial of Non-Catholic Foreigners (Cimitero Acattolico per gli Stranieri al

Testaccio) is a tomb-filled park, running along the wall just beyond the pyramid. The cemetery is also the only English-style landscape (rolling hills, calculated vistas) in Rome, and a favorite spot for quiet picnics and strolls. From the Piramide Metro stop, walk between the pyramid and the Roman gate on Via Persichetti/Via Marmorata.

Then go left on Caio Cestio to the gate of the cemetery. Originally, none of the Protestant epitaphs were allowed to make any mention of heaven. Signs direct visitors to the graves of notable non-Catholics who died in Rome since 1738. Many of the buried were diplomats. And many, such as the poets Percy Shelley (1792-1822) and John Keats (1795-1821), were from the Romantic Age. They came on the Grand Tour and—"captivated by the fatal charms of Rome," as Shelley wrote—never left.

Head 90 degrees left to find Keats' tomb, in the far corner. Keats died in his twenties, unrecognized. He wanted to be unnamed on a tomb that read, "Young English Poet, 1821. Here lies one whose name was writ in water." (To see Keats' tomb when the cemetery is closed, look through the tiny peephole on Via Caio Cestio, 10 yards off Via Marmarata.) Shelley's tomb is straight ahead from the entrance, up the hill, at the base of the stubby tower.

Cost and Hours: €2 suggested donation—leave in box by entrance, Mon-Sat 9:00-17:00, Sun 9:00-13:00, last entry 30 minutes before closing, staff at info office can help you find specific graves, www.cemeteryrome.it.

Monte Testaccio—This small hill is a popular nightlife spot near the Protestant Cemetery (as you leave the cemetery, turn left and continue two blocks down Caio Cestio). The hill, actually a 115-foot-tall ancient trash pile, is made of broken *testae*—earthenware jars mostly used to haul oil 2,000 years ago, when this was a gritty port warehouse district. For 500 years, rancid oil vessels were discarded here. Slowly, Rome's lowly eighth hill was built. Because the caves dug into the hill stay cool, trendy bars, clubs, and restaurants compete with gritty car-repair places for a spot. The neighborhood was once known for a huge slaughterhouse and a Roma (Gypsy) camp that squatted inside an old military base. Now it's home to the Testaccio Village (a site for concerts and techno raves—dead until late at night, when it thrives), a farmers' market (described below), and branch of the MACRO contemporary art gallery (Metro: Piramide).

Testaccio Market and Neighborhood—The covered Mercato di Testaccio (on Via Galvani, across from Monte Testaccio) dominates the center of the neighborhood. It'll likely be closed for renovation during your visit; when it reopens, it'll be more modern and hygienic, yet is sure to remain one of the best authentic food markets in Rome (Mon-Sat until 13:00). It's where Romans shop while tourists flock to Campo de' Fiori. High-end shoe and clothing boutiques have moved into the market and the neighborhood nearby, and this is now one of the best areas in Rome to have shoes custom-made. Testaccio has long been the neighborhood of slaughterhouses, and its restaurants are renowned for their ability to cook up the least palatable part of the animals...the "fifth quarter."

South of Testaccio

▲Montemartini Museum (Musei Capitolini Centrale Montemartini)—This museum houses a dreamy collection of 400 ancient statues, set evocatively in a classic 1932 electric power plant, among generators and *Metropolis*-type cast-iron machinery. While the art is not as famous as the collections you'll see downtown, the effect is fun and memorable—and you'll encounter absolutely no tourists. If you're tackling Rome with kids, this museum is ideal: It's uncrowded and cool, immersed in an old power plant, with art placed at kid-level.

Cost and Hours: €5.50, often €7.50 with special exhibits, €10.50-13 combo-ticket with Capitoline Museums, Tue-Sun 9:00-19:00, closed Mon, last entry 30 minutes before closing, look for red banner marking Via Ostiense 106, a short walk from Metro: Garbatella, tel. 06-574-8030, www.centralemontemartini.org.

▲St. Paul's Outside the Walls (Basilica San Paolo Fuori le Mura)—This was the last major construction project of Imperial Rome (c. A.D. 380) and the largest church in Christendom until St. Peter's.

After a tragic 19th-century fire, St. Paul's was rebuilt in the same general style and size as the original. The column-lined courtyard leading up to the church is typical of early Christian churches—the first version of St. Peter's Basilica also had this kind of welcoming zone.

Step inside and feel as close as you'll get in the 21st century to experiencing a monumental Roman basilica. Marvel at the ceiling, and imagine building it with those massive wood beams in A.D. 380.

South of Testaccio

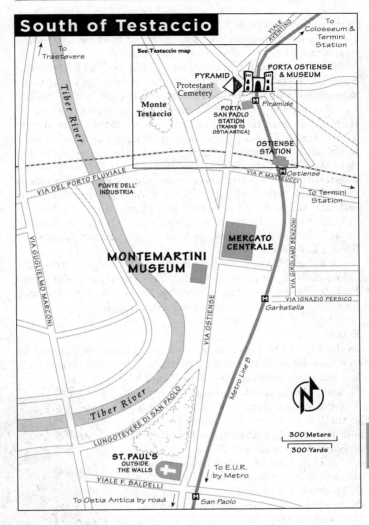

Alabaster windows light the vast interior. It feels sterile, but in a good way—like you're already in heaven. Along with St. Peter's Basilica, San Giovanni in Laterano, and Santa Maria Maggiore, this church is, legally speaking, part of the Vatican rather than Italy. The triumphal arch leading to the altar has a fifth-century mosaic of Christ raising his hand in blessing. The church is built upon the supposed grave of St. Paul. According to tradition, Paul was decapitated two miles from this spot. His head was preserved at San Giovanni in Laterano, and his body was buried here under the altar. In 2006, archaeologists unearthed a sarcophagus which had early inscriptions identifying it as Paul's.

Ringing the upper part of the church are round mosaic portraits of 265 popes, from St. Peter (the first one in the right transept) to the present. Find the recent popes to the right of the altar—not in the nave, but farther to the right, under the arches of the dim right aisle. You'll see globetrotting John Paul II *(Jo Paulus II)* and progressive John XXIII, who oversaw the Vatican II changes of the 1960s. A portrait of Pope #265—Benedict XVI—was recently installed, alongside blank medallions for future popes.

The peaceful 13th-century cloister (€4) has elegant Romanesque columns and arches, and fragments of early Christian/ Roman sarcophagi.

Cost and Hours: Free, daily 7:00-18:30, modest dress code enforced, dry audioguide €5 plus ID, Via Ostiense 186, Metro: San Paolo, exit the Metro station following *via Ostiense* sign, and look for the church's round tower, www.basilicasanpaolo.org.

E.U.R.

In the late 1930s, Italy's dictator, Benito Mussolini, planned an international exhibition to show off the wonders of his fascist society. But these wonders brought us World War II, and Il Duce's celebration never happened. The unfinished mega-project was completed in the 1950s, and today it houses government offices and big, obscure museums filled with important, rarely visited relics.

If Hitler and Mussolini had won the war, our world might look like E.U.R. (AY-oor). Hike down E.U.R.'s wide, pedestrian-mean boulevards. Patriotic murals, aren't-you-proud-to-be-an-extreme-right-winger pillars, and stern squares decorate the soulless planned grid and stark office blocks. Boulevards named for Astronomy, Electronics, Social Security, and Beethoven are more exhausting than inspirational.

Despite its grim past, E.U.R. is now an up-and-coming place of young people and trendy cafés. It's worth a trip for its Museum of Roman Civilization (described below). And because a few landmark buildings of Italian modernism are located here and there, E.U.R. has become an important destination for architecture buffs.

ROME